# EMPIRICAL RESEARCH
# IN CAPITAL MARKETS

**McGraw-Hill Series in Advanced Topics
in Finance and Accounting**

CONSULTING EDITORS
Clifford W. Smith, Jr.
Ray Ball


**Ball and Smith:** The Economics of Accounting Policy Choice
**Schwert and Smith:** Empirical Research in Capital Markets
**Smith:** The Modern Theory of Corporate Finance

# EMPIRICAL RESEARCH IN CAPITAL MARKETS

EDITED BY

## G. William Schwert
## Clifford W. Smith, Jr.

*William E. Simon Graduate School*
*Of Business Administration*
*University of Rochester*

**McGraw-Hill, Inc.**

New York   St. Louis   San Francisco   Auckland
Bogotá   Caracas   Lisbon   London   Madrid   Mexico
Milan   Montreal   New Delhi   Paris   San Juan
Singapore   Sydney   Tokyo   Toronto

EMPIRICAL RESEARCH IN CAPITAL MARKETS

1 2 3 4 5 6 7 8 9 0    DOC DOC    9 0 9 8 7 6 5 4 3 2 1

ISBN 0-07-056079-X

The editors were Kenneth A. MacLeod and Joseph F. Murphy;
the production supervisor was Leroy A. Young.
The cover was designed by Karen K. Quigley.
R. R. Donnelley & Sons Company was printer and binder.

Library of Congress Cataloging-in-Publication Data

Empirical research in capital markets / [edited by] G. William Schwert, Clifford W. Smith, Jr.
    p.      c.m.— (McGraw-Hill series in advanced topics in finance and accounting)
    Includes bibliographical references.
    ISBN 0-07-056079-X
    1. Capital market.     I. Schwert, G. William (George William),
(date).    II. Smith, Clifford W.    III. Series.
HG4523.E46       1992
332'.0414 — dc20                  91-35199

# CONTENTS

## III  PORTFOLIO THEORY AND ASSET PRICING

# INTRODUCTION

This book contains reprints of articles that have been previously published in the *Journal of Financial Economics*, the *Journal of Finance*, the *Journal of Business*, *Econometrica*, and the *Financial Analysts Journal*. These papers cover many topics that are frequently discussed in courses on capital markets or investments.

There are several high-quality textbooks on investments or capital markets that do a good job of summarizing the theory of efficient capital markets, portfolio choice, asset pricing models, and contingent claims pricing. These texts are usually limited, however, in the extent to which they can cover the important empirical evidence that relates to the theories.

Accordingly, the focus of this book is on papers that present *empirical evidence*. Some of these papers do not present new data or tests; rather, they clarify the results of others. Usually, however, the papers in this book present important new facts about the behavior of asset prices. We have used these papers ourselves in capital markets courses at the William E. Simon Graduate School of Business Administration at the University of Rochester. We thus believe that readings from this book can provide a valuable complement to a textbook in designing courses in capital markets or investments.

Finance is practically unique among the fields of economics because it has access to very large, high-quality datasets. Much of the expansion of academic and practical interest in this area has paralleled the development of these computer-readable datasets. Anyone comparing the content of an investments course taught 25 years ago with that taught today will see a high rate of technological progress that was largely driven by the well-documented set of facts reflected by the papers in this book.

We have organized the readings into seven sections. At the beginning of each is a brief introduction that describes the role this section might play in a capital markets course. We also provide a brief summary of the papers in this section, with references to related papers that are not in this book. We show the readings in this book in **bold**, while related readings are not highlighted. All references in these section introductions appear at the end of the book.

Often, papers could belong in more than one section. This is particularly true for the papers in the first section, "The Statistical Properties of Security Returns." Of course, instructors can choose to assign papers in any order they find useful.

We would like to acknowledge the assistance that all the authors and publishers gave us in producing this book of readings. We hope that it will help to extend the knowledge contained in these papers to a broader set of finance students.

G. William Schwert
Clifford W. Smith, Jr.

# ACKNOWLEDGMENTS

The editors wish to thank the following authors for permission to reprint their articles:

Yakov Amihud, Faculty of Management, Tel Aviv University
Fischer Black, Goldman Sachs Asset Management
Ted Bloomfield (deceased)
Michael Bradley, Graduate School of Business Administration, University of Michigan
D. T. Breeden, Fuqua School of Business, Duke University
Stephen J. Brown, Stern School of Business, New York University
Michael Canes, American Petroleum Institute
Richard C. Carr, Brinson Partners
George M. Constantinides, Graduate School of Business, University of Chicago
Peter Lloyd-Davies, Federal Home Loan Mortgage Corporation
Anand S. Desai, School of Business, University of Florida
Eugene F. Fama, Graduate School of Business, University of Chicago
Kenneth R. French, Graduate School of Business, University of Chicago
Michael R. Gibbons, Graduate School of Business, Stanford University
R. D. Henriksson, Kidder-Peabody & Company, Inc.
Roger G. Ibbotson, School of Organization and Management, Yale University
J. E. Ingersoll, School of Organization and Management, Yale University
Michael C. Jensen, School of Business, Harvard University
E. Han Kim, School of Business Administration, University of Michigan
Richard W. Leftwich, Graduate School of Business, University of Chicago
Robert H. Litzenberger, Wharton School, University of Pennsylvania
John Long, Simon Graduate School of Business Administration, University of Rochester
David Mayers, Academic Faculty of Finance, The Ohio State University
Haim Mendelson, Graduate School of Business, Stanford University
Wayne H. Mikkelson, College of Business Administration, University of Oregon
M. M. Partch, College of Business Administration, University of Oregon
J. M. Patell, Graduate School of Business, Stanford University
S. M. Phillips, Graduate School of Business, University of Iowa
Krishna Ramaswamy, Graduate School of Management, Columbia University
Edward M. Rice, School of Business Administration, University of Washington
H. Roberts, Graduate School of Business, University of Chicago
Anthony W. Robinson, Brinson Partners
Richard Roll, Graduate School of Management, UCLA
Stephen A. Ross, School of Organization and Management, Yale University
G. William Schwert, Simon Graduate School of Business Administration, University of Rochester
H. N. Seyhun, Graduate School of Business Administration, University of Michigan
Jay Shanken, Simon Graduate School of Business Administration, University of Rochester
Clifford W. Smith, Jr., Simon Graduate School of Business Administration, University of Rochester
Robert F. Stambaugh, Wharton School, University of Pennsylvania
Jerold B. Warner, Simon Graduate School of Business Administration, University of Rochester
Robert E. Whaley, Fuqua School of Business, Duke University
M. A. Wolfson, Graduate School of Business, Stanford University

The editors wish to acknowledge the sources of the articles in this volume as follows:

**American Finance Association:**

Douglas T. Breeden, Michael R. Gibbons, and Robert H. Litzenberger, "Empirical Tests of the Consumption-Oriented CAPM," *Journal of Finance*, 44 (June 1989), pp. 231–262.

Eugene F. Fama, "A Note on the Market Model and the Two-Parameter Model," *Journal of Finance*, 28 (December 1973), pp. 1181–1185.

Michael C. Jensen and George A. Bennington, "Random Walks and Technical Theories: Some Additional Evidence," *Journal of Finance*, 25 (May 1970), pp. 469–482.

Robert H. Litzenberger and Krishna Ramaswamy, "The Effects of Dividends on Common Stock Prices: Tax Effects or Information Effects?" *Journal of Finance*, 37 (May 1982), pp. 429–443.

Harry Roberts, "Stock Market 'Patterns' and Financial Analysis: Methodological Suggestions," *Journal of Finance*, 14 (March 1959), pp. 1–10.

G. William Schwert, "Why Does Stock Market Volatility Change over Time?" *Journal of Finance*, 44 (December 1989), pp. 1115–1153.

Jay Shanken, "The Arbitrage Pricing Theory: Is It Testable?" *Journal of Finance*, 37 (December 1982), pp. 1129–1140.

**Association for Investment Management and Research:**

Fischer Black, "The Investment Policy Spectrum: Individuals, Endowment Funds and Pension Funds," *Financial Analysts Journal*, 32 (January 1976), pp. 23–31.

Roger G. Ibbotson, Richard C. Carr, and Anthony W. Robinson, "International Equity and Bond Returns," *Financial Analysts Journal,* 38 (July 1982), pp. 61–83.

**Econometric Society:**

Michael R. Gibbons, Stephen A. Ross, and Jay Shanken, "A Test of the Efficiency of a Given Portfolio," *Econometrica*, 57 (September 1989), pp. 1121–1152.

**North-Holland Publishing Company:**

Yakov Amihud and Haim Mendelson, "Asset Pricing and the Bid-Ask Spread," *Journal of Financial Economics*, 17 (December 1986), pp 223–249.

Ted Bloomfield, Richard Leftwich, and John B. Long, "Portfolio Strategies and Performance," *Journal of Financial Economics,* 5 (November 1977), pp. 201–218.

Michael Bradley, Anand Desai, and E. Han Kim, "Synergistic Gains from Corporate Acquisitions and Their Division between the Stockholders of Target and Acquiring Firms," *Journal of Financial Economics*, 21 (May 1988), pp. 3–40.

Stephen J. Brown and Jerold B. Warner, "Measuring Security Price Performance," *Journal of Financial Economics*, 8 (September 1980), pp 205–258.

George M. Constantinides and Jonathan E. Ingersoll, "Optimal Bond Trading with Personal Taxes," *Journal of Financial Economics*, 10 (September 1984), pp. 299–336.

Eugene F. Fama and Kenneth R. French, "Business Conditions and Expected Returns on Stocks and Bonds," *Journal of Financial Economics*, 25 (November 1989), pp. 23–49.

Eugene F. Fama and G. William Schwert, "Asset Returns and Inflation," *Journal of Financial Economics*, 5 (November 1977), pp. 115–146.

Kenneth R. French, "A Comparison of Futures and Forward Prices," *Journal of Financial Economics,* 12 (November 1983), pp. 311–342.

Kenneth R. French and Richard Roll, "Stock Return Variances: The Arrival of Information and the Reaction of Traders," *Journal of Financial Economics,* 17 (September 1986), pp. 5–26.

David Mayers and Edward M. Rice, "Measuring Portfolio Performance and the Empirical Content of Asset Pricing Models," *Journal of Financial Economics*, 7 (March 1979), pp 3–28.

Wayne H. Mikkelson and M. Megan Partch, "Stock Price Effects and Costs of Secondary Distributions," *Journal of Financial Economics*, 14 (June 1985), pp. 165–194.

James M. Patell and Mark A. Wolfson, "The Intraday Speed of Adjustment of Stock Prices to Earnings and Dividend Announcements," *Journal of Financial Economics,* 13 (June 1984), pp. 223–252.

Susan M. Phillips and Clifford W. Smith, "Trading Costs for Listed Options: The Implications for Market Efficiency," *Journal of Financial Economics*, 8 (June 1980), pp. 179–201.

Richard Roll, "A Critique of the Asset Pricing Theory's Tests; Part I: On Past and Potential Testability of the Theory," *Journal of Financial Economics*, 4 (March 1977), pp. 129–176.

G. William Schwert, "Size and Stock Returns, and Other Empirical Regularities," *Journal of Financial Economics*, 12 (June 1983), pp. 3–12.

H. Nejat Seyhun, "Insiders' Profits, Cost of Trading and Market Efficiency," *Journal of Financial Economics*, 16 (June 1986), pp. 189–212.

Robert F. Stambaugh, "The Information in Forward Rates: Implications for Models of the Term Structure," *Journal of Financial Economics*, 21 (May 1988), pp. 41–70.

Robert E. Whaley, "Valuation of American Call Options on Dividend-Paying Stocks: Empirical Tests," *Journal of Financial Economics*, 10 (March 1982), pp. 29–59.

**University of Chicago Press:**

Roy D. Henrikkson, "Market Timing and Mutual Fund Performance: An Empirical Investigation," *Journal of Business*, 57 (January 1984), pp. 73–96.

Peter Lloyd-Davies and Michael Canes, "Stock Prices and the Publication of Second-Hand Information," *Journal of Business*, 51 (January 1978), pp. 43–56.

# EMPIRICAL RESEARCH IN CAPITAL MARKETS

# I

# THE STATISTICAL PROPERTIES OF SECURITY RETURNS

**1** Ibbotson, R. C., R. C. Carr, and A. W. Robinson, "International Equity and Bond Returns," *Financial Analysts Journal* (July 1982), pp. 61–83.
**2** Schwert, G. W., "Why Does Stock Market Volatility Change over Time?" *Journal of Finance*, 44 (December 1989), pp. 1115–1153.
**3** Brown, S. J., and J. B. Warner, "Measuring Security Price Performance," *Journal of Financial Economics*, 8 (September 1980), pp. 205–258.
**4** French, K. R., and R. Roll, "Stock Returns Variances: The Arrival of Information and the Reaction of Traders," *Journal of Financial Economics*, 17 (September 1986), pp. 5–26.

Finance, perhaps more than any other area of economics, has benefitted from the wealth of data available on the behavior of security returns. The accumulation of evidence on the behavior of stock and bond prices has stimulated much of the theoretical development. From this perspective, which Arnold Zellner (1971, Chapter 1) calls reductive reasoning, we must understand the stylized facts about stock and bond returns to know the types of theoretical models that are likely to be consistent with the facts. We feel this basic familiarity with facts is an important introduction to a course on capital markets or investments.

Because of the growing interest in international markets, we include **Ibbotson, Carr, and Robinson (1982),** which documents some important facts about the cross-sectional behavior of international asset returns. Most models of asset pricing involve cross-sectional differences in means and standard deviations of returns. **Ibbotson, Carr, and Robinson** analyze stock and bond returns for 18 countries from 1960 to 1980. First, stock returns have higher means and standard deviations than bond returns. Second, while stock and bond returns are positively correlated, they are not perfectly correlated, so international diversification can reduce the risk of a portfolio of these types of assets compared with a portfolio limited to either domestic stocks or bonds. Finally, inflation and exchange rate differences can have a large effect on the payoffs to investments in foreign securities. This paper extends the frequently cited Ibbotson Associates (1989) book that focuses on monthly stock and bond returns from 1926 to 1988 in the United States. In addition, readers interested in historical summaries of stock returns in the United States should read Wilson and Jones (1987) and Schwert (1990c).

Since the **Ibbotson, Carr, and Robinson** paper was published in 1982, its data are now somewhat outdated. Table 1 shows updated statistics for returns to foreign stocks and government bonds through 1989 and 1988, respectively. These statistics, from Ibbotson, Siegel, and Waring (1990) and Brown and Siegel (1990), are similar to those in **Ibbotson, Carr, and Robinson** for 1960 to 1980.

TABLE 1  MEANS AND STANDARD DEVIATIONS OF ANNUAL PERCENTAGE RETURNS TO FOREIGN STOCKS AND BONDS, IN BOTH LOCAL CURRENCIES AND U.S. DOLLARS, 1961–1989

| | Long-term government bonds, 1961–1989 | | | | | Equities, 1969–1988 | | | | |
| | Local currency | | U.S. dollars | | | Local currency | | U.S. dollars | | |
| | Mean | Std dev | Mean | Std dev | Corr w/ U.S. | Mean | Std dev | Mean | Std dev | Corr w/ U.S. |
|---|---|---|---|---|---|---|---|---|---|---|
| Australia | 7.69 | 11.19 | 6.56 | 12.72 | 0.07 | 13.98 | 29.37 | 12.59 | 28.64 | 0.61 |
| Canada | 7.94 | 8.58 | 7.42 | 8.99 | 0.81 | 12.17 | 17.13 | 11.58 | 17.11 | 0.66 |
| France | 8.39 | 9.33 | 8.41 | 15.51 | 0.46 | 21.70 | 44.11 | 22.91 | 53.57 | 0.35 |
| Germany | 7.31 | 7.01 | 11.34 | 14.25 | 0.36 | 10.56 | 25.05 | 15.65 | 31.48 | 0.39 |
| Italy | 9.88 | 15.95 | 8.04 | 21.59 | 0.35 | 17.19 | 40.06 | 14.67 | 47.23 | 0.34 |
| Japan | 7.76 | 6.37 | 13.33 | 17.80 | 0.05 | 20.99 | 29.35 | 28.68 | 35.69 | 0.39 |
| Netherlands | 7.46 | 7.21 | 10.92 | 14.97 | 0.50 | 13.31 | 23.85 | 16.08 | 21.59 | 0.76 |
| Switzerland | 4.51 | 6.28 | 9.93 | 16.85 | 0.15 | 6.42 | 22.28 | 12.47 | 27.09 | 0.51 |
| United Kingdom | 9.83 | 15.97 | 8.51 | 21.07 | 0.16 | 18.31 | 37.86 | 16.79 | 35.55 | 0.66 |
| United States | 6.70 | 11.17 | | | | 10.99 | 17.82 | | | |

Note: Equity return statistics from Ibbotson, Siegel, and Waring (1990) and long-term government bond return statistics from Brown and Siegel (1990).

Another fact that has received increasing attention is that the volatility (standard deviation) of stock and bond returns is not constant over time. **Schwert (1989a)** analyzes the volatility of U.S. stock and bond returns from 1857 to 1986 and tries to explain some factors that cause volatility to vary. For example, the Great Depression (1929–1939) was a period when stock and bond returns were very volatile, as were industrial production, the money supply, and other macroeconomic variables. Stock returns are more volatile during recessions, but they are not unusually volatile during wars. On the other hand, bond returns and consumer price inflation are usually more volatile during and after wars. Readers interested in additional material on stock and bond market volatility should read Officer (1973) and Schwert (1989b, 1990a,b).

Most studies of stock market efficiency involve the time series behavior of returns. **Brown and Warner (1980)** show how to use monthly stock returns to draw inferences about unusual events affecting a firm or set of firms. They compare several statistical methods for defining "normal" performance of stocks. These methods provide a benchmark to study the effects on stock prices of corporate events such as earnings or dividend announcements, stock splits, takeovers, or antitrust litigation. Their evidence shows that simple methods can be used reliably to measure "abnormal" returns to stocks. Readers interested in further information should read Fama (1970), Schwert (1981), and Brown and Warner (1985).

**French and Roll (1986)** show how the standard deviation of daily stock returns varies depending on whether weekends or holidays occur between trading days. Interestingly, the standard deviation does not increase much when several nontrading days occur between trading days. **French and Roll** consider several possible explanations for this curious result, including differences in the production of private information during trading periods (when information advantages can result in profitable trading). Other papers that address unusual aspects of the time series properties of stock returns include French (1980), Keim (1983) and Keim and Stambaugh (1984).

While many instructors may use the papers in this section as part of their discussion of asset pricing models or the efficient markets hypothesis, we feel that these papers are general enough that they also can be used at the start of a course to provide background for the more narrowly focused papers that deal with specific models or theories.

by Roger G. Ibbotson, Richard C. Carr and Anthony W. Robinson

# International Equity and Bond Returns

The opportunity set for U.S. investors will be affected by whether international bond and equity markets are segmented or integrated. Historical data allow one to examine this idea and, by including exchange rate and inflation data, capital market proportionality and parity theorems. Total equity and bond returns for 18 countries over the 1960-80 period are presented.

*Winner of 1982*
### Graham and Dodd
### Scroll Award for Excellence
*presented by*
*The Financial Analysts Federation*

An examination of the returns on equities, domestic bonds and crossborder bonds of the U.S. and 17 foreign countries over the 21-year period 1960-80 indicates that foreign stocks and bonds generally outperformed U.S. securities, although the U.S. was the outstanding performer in some periods. On a beta-adjusted basis, U.S. equities underperformed the market-value-weighted world equity market portfolio by $-0.69$ per cent per year, with a beta on the world market of 1.08. While bonds yields were high in the United States, non-U.S. bonds benefited from appreciation against the dollar in the 1970s, making them superior investments from a U.S. dollar investor's perspective.

International investors may expect gains from diversification. In addition, any imperfections in international capital markets may allow them additional profit opportunities. The data presented here suggest that the economic relationships often posited between international stock and bond expected returns, inflation and exchange rates hold only imperfectly. Deviations from the international parity theorems occur often, especially over short periods of time.

The relationships exhibited between stock, bond and inflation returns within each country and in the world framework are instructive for the one-country investor, as well as the international investor. They indicate that risk is generally rewarded (with stocks outperforming bonds in most countries), and that inflation hurts both the stock and long-term bond markets in most countries, while a country's short-term securities tend to track its inflation rate.

THE OPPORTUNITY set for United States investors includes equities and bonds in foreign countries as well as those in the United States. Non-U.S. equities and bonds make up a large and growing proportion of world wealth and have had high returns. We regard equities and bonds in all countries as part of a world market that is at least somewhat integrated, although the flow of capital between countries may be inhibited by taxes, regulations and political and exchange risk.

It is instructive to examine aggregate market values and returns in the world market because we want to know the dimensions of the market in which we invest and because we want to be able to compare the realized returns from a wide variety of alternative investments. Furthermore, the comparative behavior of securities in different countries tells us about the extent of integration in world capital markets—that is, the extent to which goods, capital and labor actually cross national boundaries in response to profit opportunities.

The development of a world market for equities and bonds raises some challenging issues in financial economics. If there are no barriers to in-

*Roger Ibbotson is Senior Lecturer in Finance and Executive Director of the Center for Research in Security Prices at the Graduate School of Business of the University of Chicago. Richard Carr is Vice President of The First National Bank of Chicago. Anthony Robinson is Assistant Vice President of The First National Bank of Chicago London Branch.*

ternational investment (i.e., if national and currency borders are irrelevant), then world capital market results should reflect the traditional proportionality and parity theorems expounded by Irving Fisher and others. The world market is integrated only to the extent that national and currency borders actually are irrelevant. The data on non-U.S. asset returns presented here, while not formally testing proportionality and parity theorems, will suggest conclusions as to the realism of the parity assumptions.

This article presents annual total returns on equities and bonds, along with correlations and regression results, exchange and inflation rates and some other macroeconomic data, for 18 countries for the period 1960 through 1980. It also compares long-term and short-term yields, exchange returns and inflation rates on a country-by-country basis, suggests interpretations of the data in the light of intranational and international parity theorems, and discusses the implications of international diversification and currency risk for

the United States investor. The appendix documents methodologies and sources of data.

## Equities: Returns and Aggregate Market Values

The composition of the world equity and bond market at the end of 1980 is depicted in Figure A. Bonds make up a slightly larger share than equities. The United States represents more than half of the equity market, but less than half of the bond market. It should be noted that, as U.S.-based researchers, we have access to more information on the United States than on foreign countries. Our estimate of U.S. equity aggregate market value includes the New York and American stock exchanges and nearly every stock of any size traded over-the-counter; the non-U.S. equity measures are not as broad. A further caveat is that some companies traded in both the United States and a foreign stock exchange may be double-counted.

Figure B shows the market values in U.S.

**Figure A:** Size of World Equity and Bond Markets at the End of 1980 in Billions of U.S. Dollars
(World Total = $5,289.9 Billion)

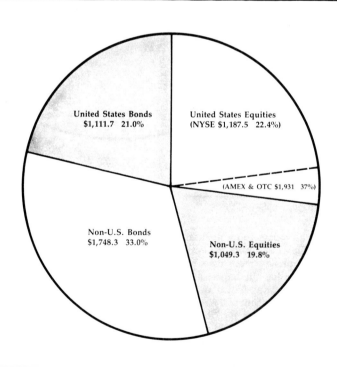

**Figure B:** Market Values of Non-U.S. Equities at the End of 1980 in Billions of U.S. Dollars (Non-U.S., Equity Total = $1,049.3 Billion)

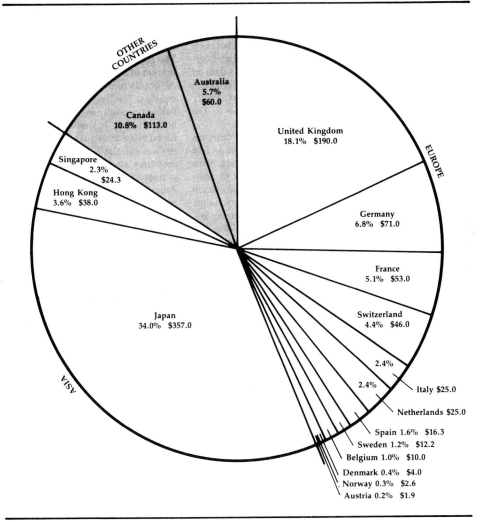

dollars of the various equity markets as of the end of 1980. The U.S. equity market is by far the largest, comprising more than half the world market. Japan has the largest non-U.S. equity market, representing 15 per cent of the world equities and 34 per cent of the non-U.S. market. The United Kingdom has the largest equity market in Europe. The world equity market had a value of approximately $2.4 trillion at the end of 1980. Year-by-year aggregate market values for

each country are presented in billions of U.S. dollars in Table I.

Table II presents summary statistics for country-by-country and portfolio returns on equities. We formed market-value-weighted portfolios of various regions (Europe, Asia, etc.) and of the world, using as the weight of a country for a given year its aggregate market value (as reported in Table I) at the end of the previous year. All returns are converted to U.S. dollars and

**Table I**  World Equities: Aggregate Market Values in Billions of U.S. Dollars

| | | | | | | | | | | | | |
|---|---|---|---|---|---|---|---|---|---|---|---|---|
| | | | | | | **World Equities** | | | | | | |
| | | | | | | Non-U.S. | | | | | | |
| | | | | | | Europe | | | | | | |
| End of Year | Austria | Belgium | Denmark | France | Germany | Italy | Nether-lands | Norway | Spain | Sweden | Switzer-land | United Kingdom |
| 1959 | 0.3 | 3.5 | 0.6 | 16.4 | 13.7 | 7.5 | 8.2 | 0.3 | 5.2 | 2.1 | 6.4 | 38.8 |
| 1960 | 0.5 | 3.4 | 0.6 | 18.7 | 22.6 | 13.4 | 9.6 | 0.4 | 5.0 | 2.5 | 9.1 | 49.3 |
| 1961 | 0.7 | 4.0 | 0.6 | 19.6 | 30.4 | 17.7 | 10.8 | 0.5 | 5.8 | 2.9 | 15.6 | 59.8 |
| 1962 | 0.6 | 3.7 | 0.7 | 21.7 | 20.7 | 14.6 | 9.2 | 0.4 | 7.2 | 2.9 | 14.0 | 50.9 |
| 1963 | 0.6 | 3.7 | 0.8 | 22.5 | 22.6 | 12.6 | 10.9 | 0.4 | 7.8 | 3.1 | 12.1 | 56.8 |
| 1964 | 0.6 | 4.2 | 0.9 | 19.1 | 22.8 | 8.9 | 11.5 | 0.4 | 7.7 | 3.4 | 11.4 | 59.0 |
| 1965 | 0.6 | 4.2 | 1.0 | 19.2 | 21.4 | 8.8 | 10.1 | 0.4 | 8.5 | 4.1 | 10.1 | 56.7 |
| 1966 | 0.5 | 3.7 | 1.1 | 18.9 | 18.3 | 10.3 | 8.8 | 0.4 | 9.5 | 3.7 | 9.8 | 65.8 |
| 1967 | 0.5 | 4.7 | 0.9 | 19.1 | 22.0 | 11.0 | 11.0 | 0.4 | 8.4 | 4.7 | 10.0 | 82.1 |
| 1968 | 0.6 | 5.6 | 1.1 | 19.3 | 25.6 | 11.6 | 13.2 | 0.5 | 7.2 | 5.7 | 10.2 | 98.4 |
| 1969 | 0.6 | 5.6 | 1.1 | 20.8 | 28.5 | 12.6 | 12.8 | 0.6 | 12.0 | 4.6 | 10.7 | 86.8 |
| 1970 | 0.7 | 5.5 | 1.1 | 22.2 | 31.4 | 13.6 | 12.4 | 0.9 | 16.7 | 3.5 | 11.3 | 75.2 |
| 1971 | 0.7 | 6.7 | 1.2 | 24.0 | 32.0 | 12.0 | 13.0 | 1.0 | 12.0 | 4.9 | 12.0 | 89.0 |
| 1972 | 1.0 | 8.1 | 2.5 | 27.1 | 41.3 | 10.8 | 13.2 | 1.1 | 20.7 | 6.8 | 15.6 | 121.7 |
| 1973 | 1.3 | 11.9 | 2.7 | 40.1 | 53.4 | 15.3 | 17.7 | 2.4 | 29.7 | 8.2 | 18.3 | 122.0 |
| 1974 | 1.4 | 9.1 | 2.4 | 28.1 | 44.7 | 15.7 | 12.8 | 1.5 | 35.9 | 8.0 | 14.6 | 53.0 |
| 1975 | 1.4 | 9.4 | 3.0 | 33.4 | 47.9 | 11.3 | 14.3 | 1.2 | 28.0 | 9.6 | 16.6 | 66.0 |
| 1976 | 1.6 | 8.3 | 3.2 | 28.0 | 50.9 | 8.8 | 14.8 | 1.4 | 20.8 | 10.2 | 21.3 | 64.2 |
| 1977 | 1.6 | 9.3 | 3.2 | 23.8 | 55.5 | 6.8 | 18.4 | 1.1 | 16.5 | 9.3 | 21.8 | 80.0 |
| 1978 | 1.8 | 10.5 | 3.5 | 33.9 | 63.9 | 8.4 | 19.4 | 1.2 | 14.4 | 8.9 | 32.6 | 102.0 |
| 1979 | 2.2 | 13.4 | 3.4 | 54.0 | 80.0 | 12.8 | 24.0 | 3.3 | 14.0 | 10.4 | 44.0 | 142.0 |
| 1980 | 1.9 | 10.0 | 4.0 | 53.0 | 71.0 | 25.0 | 25.0 | 2.6 | 16.3 | 12.2 | 46.0 | 190.0 |

| | | | | | | | | | | | |
|---|---|---|---|---|---|---|---|---|---|---|---|
| | | | | | **World Equities** | | | | | | |
| | | | | Non-U.S. | | | | | | U.S. | |
| | Europe | | | Asia | | | Other | | | | |
| End of Year | Europe Total | Hong Kong | Japan | Singa-pore | Asia Total | Canada | Aus-tralia | Other Total | Non-U.S. Total | U.S. Total | World Equities Total |
| 1959 | 103.0 | | 14.6 | | 14.6 | 13.3 | 10.1 | 23.4 | 141.0 | 346.2 | 487.2 |
| 1960 | 135.1 | | 17.7 | | 17.7 | 13.2 | 14.2 | 27.4 | 180.2 | 345.0 | 525.2 |
| 1961 | 168.4 | | 20.5 | | 20.5 | 18.3 | 14.3 | 32.6 | 221.5 | 436.2 | 657.7 |
| 1962 | 146.6 | | 17.1 | | 17.1 | 17.1 | 14.3 | 31.4 | 195.0 | 383.5 | 578.5 |
| 1963 | 153.9 | | 23.1 | | 23.1 | 19.5 | 14.7 | 34.2 | 211.2 | 452.4 | 663.6 |
| 1964 | 149.9 | | 20.3 | | 20.3 | 24.3 | 17.4 | 41.7 | 211.9 | 523.5 | 735.4 |
| 1965 | 145.1 | | 18.5 | | 18.5 | 25.4 | 15.4 | 40.9 | 204.4 | 594.3 | 798.7 |
| 1966 | 150.8 | | 23.1 | | 23.1 | 23.1 | 15.8 | 38.9 | 212.8 | 534.6 | 747.4 |
| 1967 | 174.9 | | 27.5 | | 27.5 | 24.8 | 18.0 | 42.8 | 245.2 | 686.9 | 932.1 |
| 1968 | 199.0 | | 31.9 | | 31.9 | 31.4 | 20.2 | 51.6 | 282.4 | 789.4 | 1071.8 |
| 1969 | 196.7 | 3.5 | 38.1 | 2.2 | 43.8 | 32.4 | 23.5 | 55.9 | 296.4 | 710.7 | 1007.1 |
| 1970 | 194.5 | 4.2 | 44.3 | 2.1 | 50.6 | 37.5 | 26.7 | 64.2 | 309.2 | 700.9 | 1010.2 |
| 1971 | 208.5 | 6.8 | 53.0 | 3.4 | 63.2 | 42.8 | 21.0 | 63.8 | 335.5 | 827.5 | 1163.0 |
| 1972 | 269.9 | 17.8 | 80.7 | 10.7 | 109.2 | 56.9 | 23.4 | 80.3 | 459.5 | 991.2 | 1450.6 |
| 1973 | 322.9 | 10.9 | 154.0 | 7.0 | 171.9 | 55.1 | 25.1 | 80.3 | 575.1 | 791.4 | 1366.5 |
| 1974 | 227.2 | 4.3 | 118.0 | 3.7 | 126.0 | 40.5 | 22.0 | 62.5 | 415.8 | 545.1 | 960.9 |
| 1975 | 242.1 | 8.6 | 129.0 | 6.1 | 143.7 | 46.6 | 19.9 | 66.5 | 452.3 | 736.2 | 1188.4 |
| 1976 | 233.5 | 12.1 | 157.8 | 7.0 | 176.9 | 51.2 | 26.1 | 77.3 | 487.7 | 911.6 | 1399.3 |
| 1977 | 247.3 | 10.7 | 177.9 | 7.3 | 195.9 | 50.5 | 21.8 | 72.3 | 515.5 | 868.0 | 1383.4 |
| 1978 | 300.5 | 12.7 | 243.8 | 10.6 | 267.1 | 60.8 | 24.2 | 85.0 | 652.7 | 903.2 | 1555.8 |
| 1979 | 403.5 | 23.3 | 274.0 | 13.6 | 310.9 | 92.6 | 39.0 | 131.6 | 846.0 | 1062.7 | 1908.7 |
| 1980 | 457.0 | 38.0 | 357.0 | 24.3 | 419.3 | 113.0 | 60.0 | 173.0 | 1049.3 | 1380.6 | 2429.9 |

**Table II**  World Equities: Summary Statistics, 1960-1980

| Asset | Annual Returns in U.S. Dollars | | | Year-End Wealth Index 1959 = 1.00 | 1980 Year-End Value In Billions U.S. $ |
|---|---|---|---|---|---|
| | Compound Return (%) | Arithmetic Mean (%) | Standard Deviation (%) | | |
| Non-U.S. Equities: | | | | | |
| Europe | | | | | |
| Austria | 9.1 | 10.3 | 16.9 | 6.23 | 1.9 |
| Belgium | 9.2 | 10.1 | 13.8 | 6.39 | 10.0 |
| Denmark | 9.5 | 11.4 | 24.2 | 6.72 | 4.0 |
| France | 6.2 | 8.1 | 21.4 | 3.56 | 53.0 |
| Germany | 8.3 | 10.1 | 19.9 | 5.32 | 71.0 |
| Italy | 2.4 | 5.6 | 27.2 | 1.63 | 25.0 |
| Netherlands | 9.3 | 10.7 | 17.8 | 6.45 | 25.0 |
| Norway | 10.3 | 17.4 | 49.0 | 7.81 | 2.6 |
| Spain | 8.4 | 10.4 | 19.8 | 5.49 | 16.3 |
| Sweden | 8.4 | 9.7 | 16.7 | 5.40 | 12.2 |
| Switzerland | 10.2 | 12.5 | 22.9 | 7.74 | 46.0 |
| United Kingdom | 10.0 | 14.7 | 33.6 | 7.39 | 190.0 |
| Europe Total | 8.4 | 9.6 | 16.2 | 5.47 | 457.0 |
| Asia | | | | | |
| Hong Kong* | 24.6 | 40.3 | 61.3 | 11.24 | 38.0 |
| Japan | 15.6 | 19.0 | 31.4 | 20.86 | 357.0 |
| Singapore* | 23.2 | 37.0 | 66.1 | 9.96 | 24.3 |
| Asia Total | 15.9 | 19.7 | 33.0 | 22.29 | 419.3 |
| Other | | | | | |
| Australia | 9.8 | 12.2 | 22.8 | 7.12 | 60.0 |
| Canada | 10.7 | 12.1 | 17.5 | 8.47 | 113.0 |
| Other Total | 10.6 | 11.9 | 17.1 | 8.24 | 173.0 |
| Non-U.S. Total Equities | 10.6 | 11.8 | 16.3 | 8.23 | 1049.3 |
| U.S. Total Equities | 8.7 | 10.2 | 17.7 | 5.78 | 1380.6 |
| World Total Equities | 9.3 | 10.5 | 15.8 | 6.47 | 2429.9 |

*1970-1980.

include both capital appreciation and income.

Figure C graphically displays the cumulative wealth index results for some of the countries and portfolios. Asian equities were the best performers over the period, with $1.00 invested at the end of 1959 growing to $22.29 by the end of 1980. This extraordinary growth was not without substantial risk: The standard deviation of annual returns was 33.0 per cent for Asian equities, the highest of any equity portfolio. It should be noted that the return achieved by Asian equities—15.9 per cent per year compounded over the period— is not unprecedented in equity markets. The U.S. market, as measured by the Standard & Poor's index with dividends reinvested, returned 15.6 per cent per year over the 21-year period 1943-63. A similar return was earned in U.S. equities in 1908-28, but in that instance, the rise was followed by a crash.

European countries' compound annual returns ranged from a high of 10.3 per cent in Norway

to a low of 2.4 per cent in Italy. The European portfolio had a relatively low compound annual return of 8.4 per cent. Returns in the United States, Canada and Australia were higher at 8.7, 10.7 and 9.8 per cent per year, respectively. The world equity portfolio returned 9.3 per cent per year, with $1.00 invested at the end of 1959 growing to $6.47 by the end of 1980.

Tables III and IV show year-by-year total returns in per cent and cumulative wealth index values, respectively, for each country and for the various portfolios. Examination of the year-by-year data reveals some interesting market facts. One-year individual country returns ranged from a high of +211 per cent for Singapore in 1972 to a low of −60 per cent for Hong Kong in 1974. Italy's cumulative wealth index showed a loss over the period 1959-79; the 1980 bull market, however, pushed Italy to a gain for the entire period. At the end of 1970, approximately halfway through the period studied, Spain had

**Figure C:** U.S.-Dollar-Adjusted Cumulative Wealth Indexes of World Equities, 1960–1980 (year-end 1959 = 1.00)

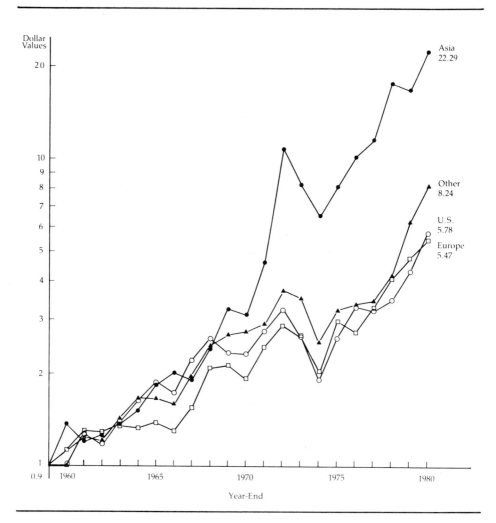

Year-End

the highest wealth index value; but that country turned out to be one of the worst performers over the 21-year period.

### Cross-Correlations

Table V presents cross-correlations of the equity series. *A priori*, we might expect substantial equity comovement to be related to geographical proximity, institutional currency relationships, partnership in trade, cultural similarity or similarity of the economic bases of the countries.

(Many institutional currency arrangements arose from the nineteenth century European colonial empires, which also created cultural alliances; other currency arrangements have arisen more recently to promote European unity and various national goals.)

The results show that European equities exhibit a good deal of comovement, with geographically adjacent Germany, Switzerland and the Netherlands forming a distinct "bloc." The United Kingdom, France, Belgium and the

**Figure D:** Market Values of Non-U.S. Bonds at the End of 1980 in Billions of U.S. Dollars
(Non-U.S. Bonds Total = $1,748.3 Billion)

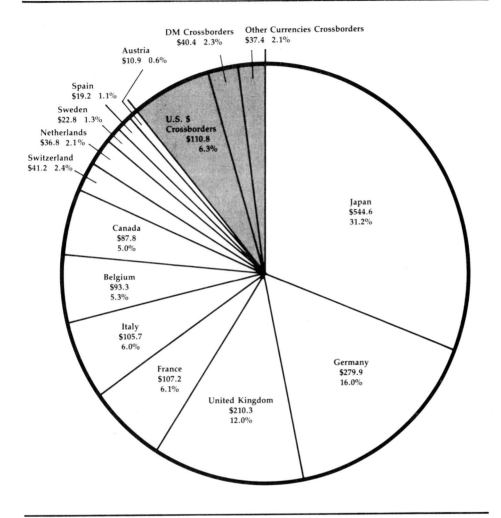

Netherlands, all of which face the trade routes of the English Channel and the North Sea, form a less distinct bloc. Countries that are culturally allied may have low equity correlations: Note in particular Norway and Sweden (−0.10), which have different economic bases (Norway is a resource economy, while Sweden is heavily industrial), and Germany and Austria (0.26). On the other hand, the three Asian countries exhibit very high cross-correlations. Finally, the United States, Canada and Australia form a bloc. This bloc of English-speaking countries also has high correlations with the United Kingdom, the present or former British colonies of Hong Kong and Singapore, and the Netherlands (a world trading center whose equity market is dominated by the multinational Royal Dutch/Shell Group).

### Bonds: Returns and Aggregate Market Values

The world bond market at the end of 1980 was dominated by non-U.S. bonds. Figure A shows the distribution of U.S. and non-U.S. bonds at that date. In Figure D, the non-U.S. bond market is broken down by country. The Japanese domestic bond market represents nearly one-third of the non-U.S. market and is half the size of the U.S. market. The vast majority (89.3 per cent) of the non-U.S. bond market consists of domestic bonds, with all "crossborder" categories comprising the balance.

Table VI summarizes the country-by-country U.S.-dollar-adjusted total (coupon plus capital appreciation) returns on a market-value-weighted portfolio of corporate and government bonds plus cash equivalents in each country. (The U.S. series excludes cash equivalents.) The returns thus measure the fixed-income market in each country and are not strictly comparable, since maturities and default premiums differ from one country to another. With this in mind, the best performing domestic bond market was that of Japan. Most other domestic bond markets had returns clustering (in U.S.-dollar-adjusted terms) around five per cent per year.

### Crossborder Bonds

We use the term "crossborder bond" to refer to any non-domestic bond. We consider a bond to be domestic if it meets both of the following criteria—(1) the currency of the bond is the currency of the borrower's home country and (2) the bond is primarily bought by nationals of the borrower's home country. The set of crossborder bonds subsumes the traditional designations of foreign bonds and Eurobonds. Every bond can thus be classified as domestic or crossborder.

This naming scheme corresponds to the way we believe risks are distributed in the world bond market. From the point of view of a U.S. investor, U.S. dollar crossborder bonds are exposed to political risk (sovereign risk, repatriation of funds risk, etc.) while U.S. dollar domestic bonds are not. Likewise, the German investor finds Deutschemark crossborder (but not domestic) bonds exposed to political risk. Exchange risk, on the other hand, is determined by whether the bond currency matches the currency with which the bondholder intends to buy goods.

Crossborder markets are not new, but the development of a large crossborder sector can be traced to the imposition of the Interest Equalization Tax by the United States in 1963. The Euro-bond market, which is the largest part of the crossborder sector today, enabled U.S. investors to avoid this tax. At first, the Eurobond market

was thin and contained a large proportion of low-quality issues. In the 1970s, this market came of age and in fact continued to grow, rather than decline (as might have been expected), after the Interest Equalization Tax was removed in 1974.

Table VI shows that over the 21-year period, U.S. dollar and Deutschemark crossborder bonds outperformed the domestic bond markets in those currencies by 1.7 and 0.1 percentage points per year, respectively. Since crossborder bonds expose the investor to political risk not faced by the typical (domestic) investor in domestic bonds of the same currency, we might expect that such a premium would be observed on crossborder bonds as a compensation for the extra risk. Arbitrage between domestic and crossborder sectors should, however, prevent the crossborder excess return from getting too high. The observed high excess return on U.S. dollar crossborder bonds may, then, be due to the probable greater default risk of the issues in that sector, particularly in the 1960s, rather than to a pure crossborder premium.

Tables VII and VIII present year-by-year total returns and cumulative wealth indexes, respectively, for all the categories of bonds. (Portfolios were not formed since market weights were not available.) The Dutch guilder, Japanese yen, Swiss franc and other crossborder currency sectors (studied over a much shorter period) had high returns, but these were largely the result of exchange appreciation against the dollar in 1975-78.

Table IX shows the cross-correlations of the bond categories. Crossborder and domestic bond returns for the same currency are very highly correlated because of the application of the same exchange adjustments to both series. Among domestic bond markets, most of the comovement is due to comovement in the currencies. The countries of Continental Europe (excluding Italy and Spain) are highly correlated, as are Canada and the United States.

### Relationships Between Equities, Bonds, Inflation and Exchange

Table X presents summary data on equity and bond returns, yields, and inflation and exchange rates, along with 1980 population and gross domestic product (GDP) statistics.

Examination of the first two columns reveals that the United States and the Scandinavian and Germanic countries have the highest per capita

**Table III** World Equities: Year-by-Year U.S.-Dollar-Adjusted Total Returns (in per cent)

| | | | | | | | | | | | | | |
|---|---|---|---|---|---|---|---|---|---|---|---|---|---|
| | | | | | | **World Equities** | | | | | | | |
| | | | | | | Non-U.S. | | | | | | | |
| | | | | | | Europe | | | | | | | |
| Year | Austria | Belgium | Denmark | France | Germany | Italy | Nether-lands | Norway | Spain | Sweden | Switzer-land | United Kingdom | |
| 1960 | 52.28 | −7.99 | 3.77 | 6.72 | 42.32 | 46.18 | 3.24 | 12.24 | 10.14 | 5.51 | 43.82 | 0.13 | |
| 1961 | 41.14 | 22.84 | 3.81 | 13.62 | 2.14 | 14.73 | 12.49 | 18.14 | 36.42 | 5.57 | 54.89 | 12.56 | |
| 1962 | −12.76 | −1.99 | 8.12 | 11.38 | −21.70 | −10.44 | −5.39 | −15.43 | 19.65 | 12.47 | −8.51 | 4.76 | |
| 1963 | −4.28 | 18.06 | 17.77 | −14.77 | 14.87 | −12.71 | 17.71 | 0.42 | 0.15 | 12.92 | −14.49 | 22.80 | |
| 1964 | 3.78 | 8.04 | 11.88 | −1.17 | 4.70 | −26.43 | 9.61 | 10.22 | 10.44 | 23.17 | −7.16 | −5.14 | |
| 1965 | −1.16 | −2.65 | 11.93 | −4.10 | −12.63 | 30.16 | −10.00 | 0.37 | 16.12 | 11.00 | −11.74 | 12.66 | |
| 1966 | −4.88 | −15.82 | 5.63 | −8.18 | −15.06 | 8.89 | −14.54 | −7.61 | 11.87 | −23.93 | −12.91 | −2.07 | |
| 1967 | 0.97 | 13.35 | −11.88 | 0.46 | 51.80 | −2.51 | 38.97 | 1.09 | −8.48 | 7.69 | 52.39 | 16.57 | |
| 1968 | 2.95 | 13.63 | 17.81 | 14.81 | 13.61 | 4.23 | 37.58 | 21.55 | 31.42 | 45.52 | 30.44 | 51.34 | |
| 1969 | 6.90 | 7.18 | 3.36 | 18.39 | 23.42 | 15.19 | −4.42 | 24.75 | 46.87 | 1.75 | 5.05 | −12.52 | |
| 1970 | 13.49 | 9.66 | −6.47 | −5.14 | −23.76 | −17.52 | −6.50 | 39.53 | −3.68 | −18.92 | −13.17 | −5.72 | |
| 1971 | 8.44 | 25.00 | 10.18 | 1.66 | 24.61 | −12.34 | 1.76 | 14.13 | 26.26 | 36.12 | 27.41 | 47.99 | |
| 1972 | 37.65 | 32.69 | 112.20 | 24.83 | 18.54 | 15.33 | 29.56 | 9.03 | 42.30 | 16.82 | 28.61 | 3.93 | |
| 1973 | 25.09 | 18.16 | 5.44 | 3.83 | −4.44 | 10.18 | −4.74 | 128.52 | 24.03 | 2.86 | −3.75 | −23.44 | |
| 1974 | 15.00 | −11.74 | −10.74 | −22.43 | 17.20 | −33.43 | −15.56 | −39.98 | −8.49 | 11.72 | −12.37 | −50.33 | |
| 1975 | −2.90 | 17.45 | 23.96 | 45.08 | 30.09 | −8.69 | 50.23 | −15.14 | 0.05 | 21.00 | 41.18 | 115.06 | |
| 1976 | 15.58 | 13.00 | 7.23 | −20.03 | 6.57 | −26.55 | 16.94 | 14.98 | −36.00 | 6.37 | 10.42 | −12.55 | |
| 1977 | −3.76 | 11.02 | 1.74 | 5.07 | 23.08 | −18.92 | 14.65 | −23.83 | −19.66 | −21.64 | 25.49 | 56.49 | |
| 1978 | 15.68 | 33.27 | 9.47 | 73.19 | 26.96 | 46.37 | 20.83 | 6.81 | 7.86 | 23.96 | 21.82 | 14.63 | |
| 1979 | 19.43 | 21.08 | −2.18 | 28.90 | −1.93 | 17.39 | 19.95 | 183.01 | 5.51 | 2.64 | 12.21 | 22.20 | |
| 1980 | −11.90 | −11.40 | 15.80 | −1.30 | −8.20 | 78.40 | 11.90 | −17.30 | 4.60 | 21.00 | −7.10 | 38.80 | |

| | | | | | | | | | | | |
|---|---|---|---|---|---|---|---|---|---|---|---|
| | | | | | **World Equities** | | | | | | |
| | | | | Non-U.S. | | | | | | U.S. | |
| | Europe | | Asia | | | Other | | | | | |
| Year | Europe Total | Hong Kong | Japan | Singa-pore | Asia Total | Canada | Aus-tralia | Other Total | Non-U.S. Total | U.S. Total | World Equities Total |
| 1960 | 13.65 | | 38.50 | | 38.50 | −1.16 | −0.07 | −0.69 | 13.84 | 0.83 | 4.60 |
| 1961 | 15.11 | | −13.03 | | −13.03 | 39.03 | 14.86 | 26.49 | 14.08 | 27.52 | 22.91 |
| 1962 | −2.35 | | 4.68 | | 4.68 | −6.84 | 0.95 | −3.43 | −1.86 | −9.29 | −6.79 |
| 1963 | 7.08 | | 8.78 | | 8.78 | 14.39 | 24.92 | 19.19 | 9.18 | 21.04 | 17.04 |
| 1964 | −2.13 | | 10.93 | | 10.93 | 24.36 | 5.17 | 16.12 | 2.25 | 16.71 | 12.11 |
| 1965 | 3.74 | | 21.39 | | 21.39 | 4.81 | −9.75 | −1.27 | 4.45 | 15.26 | 12.15 |
| 1966 | −5.92 | | 9.04 | | 9.04 | −9.24 | 4.87 | −3.92 | −4.17 | −8.21 | −7.18 |
| 1967 | 18.98 | | −4.85 | | −4.85 | 7.18 | 44.70 | 22.42 | 17.02 | 30.45 | 26.63 |
| 1968 | 35.05 | | 26.43 | | 26.43 | 26.61 | 28.62 | 27.46 | 32.76 | 14.95 | 19.63 |
| 1969 | 1.51 | | 34.15 | | 34.15 | 3.21 | 16.10 | 8.26 | 6.43 | −9.86 | −5.57 |
| 1970 | −9.04 | 21.31 | −6.35 | −5.43 | −4.09 | 15.81 | −19.14 | 1.10 | −6.40 | −1.00 | −2.59 |
| 1971 | 27.33 | 59.52 | 46.55 | 65.52 | 48.41 | 14.13 | −1.59 | 7.59 | 26.68 | 18.16 | 20.77 |
| 1972 | 16.45 | 161.66 | 126.56 | 211.04 | 134.88 | 33.12 | 21.06 | 29.15 | 41.17 | 17.71 | 24.48 |
| 1973 | −7.78 | −39.01 | −20.13 | −34.58 | −24.62 | −3.11 | −12.06 | −5.72 | −11.42 | −18.68 | −16.38 |
| 1974 | −23.34 | −60.33 | −15.65 | −46.69 | −19.75 | −26.52 | −32.97 | −28.54 | −22.99 | −27.77 | −25.76 |
| 1975 | 44.78 | 99.56 | 19.84 | 63.57 | 23.84 | 15.07 | 50.71 | 27.61 | 35.86 | 37.49 | 36.78 |
| 1976 | −7.56 | 40.55 | 25.80 | 13.83 | 26.17 | 9.71 | −10.00 | 3.81 | 4.83 | 26.68 | 18.36 |
| 1977 | 21.26 | −11.58 | 15.70 | 4.60 | 13.39 | −1.37 | 11.25 | 2.89 | 15.50 | −3.03 | 3.43 |
| 1978 | 25.51 | 18.61 | 53.33 | 45.31 | 51.13 | 20.55 | 22.24 | 21.06 | 34.62 | 8.53 | 18.25 |
| 1979 | 15.38 | 83.50 | −11.69 | 28.58 | −5.57 | 52.26 | 43.44 | 49.75 | 11.29 | 24.18 | 18.77 |
| 1980 | 14.53 | 69.90 | 29.70 | 61.20 | 34.09 | 22.00 | 52.20 | 30.95 | 24.27 | 33.22 | 29.25 |

GDP. (Consumer prices are generally higher in northern Europe than in the United States, lowering the estimate of the real prosperity of these European countries.) Comparing populations in Table X with equity market sizes in Table I shows that Singapore and Hong Kong have the largest per capita equity markets, reflecting these locales' importance as financial centers. The United States

**Table IV** World Equities: Cumulative Wealth Indexes of U.S.-Dollar-Adjusted Total Returns (year-end 1959 = 1.000)

| End of Year | Austria | Belgium | Denmark | France | Germany | Italy | Netherlands | Norway | Spain | Sweden | Switzerland | United Kingdom |
|---|---|---|---|---|---|---|---|---|---|---|---|---|
| 1959 | 1.000 | 1.000 | 1.000 | 1.000 | 1.000 | 1.000 | 1.000 | 1.000 | 1.000 | 1.000 | 1.000 | 1.000 |
| 1960 | 1.523 | 0.920 | 1.038 | 1.067 | 1.423 | 1.462 | 1.032 | 1.122 | 1.101 | 1.055 | 1.438 | 1.001 |
| 1961 | 2.149 | 1.130 | 1.077 | 1.213 | 1.454 | 1.677 | 1.161 | 1.326 | 1.503 | 1.114 | 2.228 | 1.127 |
| 1962 | 1.875 | 1.108 | 1.165 | 1.351 | 1.138 | 1.502 | 1.121 | 1.121 | 1.798 | 1.253 | 2.038 | 1.181 |
| 1963 | 1.795 | 1.308 | 1.372 | 1.151 | 1.307 | 1.311 | 1.293 | 1.126 | 1.800 | 1.415 | 1.743 | 1.450 |
| 1964 | 1.863 | 1.413 | 1.535 | 1.138 | 1.369 | 0.965 | 1.418 | 1.241 | 1.988 | 1.742 | 1.618 | 1.375 |
| 1965 | 1.841 | 1.376 | 1.718 | 1.091 | 1.196 | 1.256 | 1.276 | 1.246 | 2.309 | 1.934 | 1.428 | 1.550 |
| 1966 | 1.751 | 1.158 | 1.814 | 1.002 | 1.016 | 1.367 | 1.090 | 1.151 | 2.583 | 1.471 | 1.244 | 1.517 |
| 1967 | 1.768 | 1.312 | 1.599 | 1.006 | 1.542 | 1.333 | 1.515 | 1.164 | 2.364 | 1.584 | 1.895 | 1.769 |
| 1968 | 1.820 | 1.491 | 1.884 | 1.155 | 1.752 | 1.389 | 2.085 | 1.414 | 3.107 | 2.306 | 2.472 | 2.677 |
| 1969 | 1.946 | 1.598 | 1.947 | 1.368 | 2.162 | 1.600 | 1.993 | 1.764 | 4.563 | 2.346 | 2.597 | 2.342 |
| 1970 | 2.208 | 1.753 | 1.821 | 1.298 | 1.649 | 1.320 | 1.863 | 2.462 | 4.395 | 1.902 | 2.255 | 2.208 |
| 1971 | 2.395 | 2.191 | 2.006 | 1.319 | 2.054 | 1.157 | 1.896 | 2.810 | 5.549 | 2.589 | 2.873 | 3.267 |
| 1972 | 3.296 | 2.907 | 4.257 | 1.647 | 2.435 | 1.334 | 2.456 | 3.063 | 7.896 | 3.025 | 3.695 | 3.396 |
| 1973 | 4.124 | 3.435 | 4.489 | 1.710 | 2.327 | 1.470 | 2.340 | 7.000 | 9.794 | 3.111 | 3.556 | 2.600 |
| 1974 | 4.742 | 3.032 | 4.007 | 1.326 | 2.727 | 0.979 | 1.976 | 4.202 | 8.962 | 3.476 | 3.116 | 1.291 |
| 1975 | 4.605 | 3.561 | 4.967 | 1.924 | 3.548 | 0.894 | 2.968 | 3.565 | 8.967 | 4.206 | 4.400 | 2.777 |
| 1976 | 5.332 | 4.024 | 5.326 | 1.539 | 3.781 | 0.656 | 3.471 | 4.100 | 5.739 | 4.474 | 4.858 | 2.429 |
| 1977 | 5.122 | 4.468 | 5.419 | 1.617 | 4.654 | 0.532 | 3.979 | 3.123 | 4.611 | 3.505 | 6.097 | 3.801 |
| 1978 | 5.925 | 5.954 | 5.932 | 2.800 | 5.908 | 0.779 | 4.808 | 3.335 | 4.973 | 4.345 | 7.427 | 4.357 |
| 1979 | 7.076 | 7.209 | 5.803 | 3.609 | 5.794 | 0.914 | 5.768 | 9.439 | 5.247 | 4.460 | 8.334 | 5.324 |
| 1980 | 6.234 | 6.387 | 6.719 | 3.562 | 5.319 | 1.631 | 6.454 | 7.806 | 5.488 | 5.397 | 7.742 | 7.389 |

| | World Equities | | | | | | | | | U.S. | |
|---|---|---|---|---|---|---|---|---|---|---|---|
| | Non-U.S. | | | | | | | | | | |
| | Europe | Asia | | | | Other | | | | | |
| End of Year | Europe Total | Hong Kong* | Japan | Singapore* | Asia Total | Canada | Australia | Other Total | Non-U.S. Total | U.S. Total | World Equities Total |
| 1959 | 1.000 | | 1.000 | | 1.000 | 1.000 | 1.000 | 1.000 | 1.000 | 1.000 | 1.000 |
| 1960 | 1.137 | | 1.385 | | 1.385 | 0.988 | 0.999 | 0.993 | 1.138 | 1.008 | 1.046 |
| 1961 | 1.308 | | 1.205 | | 1.205 | 1.374 | 1.148 | 1.256 | 1.298 | 1.286 | 1.286 |
| 1962 | 1.278 | | 1.261 | | 1.261 | 1.280 | 1.159 | 1.213 | 1.275 | 1.166 | 1.198 |
| 1963 | 1.368 | | 1.372 | | 1.372 | 1.464 | 1.447 | 1.446 | 1.392 | 1.412 | 1.403 |
| 1964 | 1.339 | | 1.522 | | 1.522 | 1.821 | 1.522 | 1.679 | 1.423 | 1.648 | 1.572 |
| 1965 | 1.389 | | 1.847 | | 1.847 | 1.909 | 1.374 | 1.658 | 1.486 | 1.899 | 1.763 |
| 1966 | 1.307 | | 2.014 | | 2.014 | 1.732 | 1.441 | 1.593 | 1.424 | 1.743 | 1.637 |
| 1967 | 1.555 | | 1.916 | | 1.916 | 1.857 | 2.085 | 1.950 | 1.667 | 2.274 | 2.072 |
| 1968 | 2.100 | | 2.423 | | 2.423 | 2.351 | 2.681 | 2.485 | 2.213 | 2.614 | 2.480 |
| 1969 | 2.131 | 1.000 | 3.250 | 1.000 | 3.250 | 2.426 | 3.113 | 2.690 | 2.355 | 2.356 | 2.342 |
| 1970 | 1.939 | 1.213 | 3.044 | 0.946 | 3.117 | 2.810 | 2.517 | 2.720 | 2.204 | 2.332 | 2.281 |
| 1971 | 2.468 | 1.935 | 4.461 | 1.565 | 4.626 | 3.207 | 2.477 | 2.926 | 2.792 | 2.756 | 2.755 |
| 1972 | 2.874 | 5.063 | 10.106 | 4.869 | 10.866 | 4.269 | 2.999 | 3.780 | 3.942 | 3.244 | 3.429 |
| 1973 | 2.651 | 3.088 | 8.072 | 3.185 | 8.190 | 4.136 | 2.637 | 3.563 | 3.492 | 2.638 | 2.867 |
| 1974 | 2.032 | 1.225 | 6.808 | 1.698 | 6.573 | 3.039 | 1.768 | 2.546 | 2.689 | 1.905 | 2.129 |
| 1975 | 2.942 | 2.445 | 8.159 | 2.777 | 8.140 | 3.497 | 2.664 | 3.249 | 3.653 | 2.620 | 2.912 |
| 1976 | 2.720 | 3.436 | 10.264 | 3.162 | 10.271 | 3.837 | 2.398 | 3.373 | 3.830 | 3.319 | 3.446 |
| 1977 | 3.298 | 3.038 | 11.876 | 3.307 | 11.646 | 3.784 | 2.668 | 3.471 | 4.423 | 3.218 | 3.564 |
| 1978 | 4.139 | 3.604 | 18.209 | 4.805 | 17.600 | 4.562 | 3.261 | 4.202 | 5.954 | 3.493 | 4.215 |
| 1979 | 4.776 | 6.613 | 16.080 | 6.179 | 16.620 | 6.946 | 4.677 | 6.292 | 6.627 | 4.337 | 5.006 |
| 1980 | 5.470 | 11.235 | 20.856 | 9.960 | 22.286 | 8.474 | 7.119 | 8.239 | 8.235 | 5.778 | 6.470 |

* 1969 = 1.000.

**Table V**  World Equities: Cross-Correlations of Annual U.S.-Dollar-Adjusted Total Returns, 1960–1980

| Series | Austria | Belgium | Denmark | France | Germany | Italy | Nether-lands | Norway |
|---|---|---|---|---|---|---|---|---|
| Austria | −1.000 | | | | | | | |
| Belgium | 0.308 | 1.000 | | | | | | |
| Denmark | 0.224 | 0.387 | 1.000 | | | | | |
| France | 0.155 | 0.559 | 0.259 | 1.000 | | | | |
| Germany | 0.258 | 0.303 | 0.058 | 0.273 | 1.000 | | | |
| Italy | 0.180 | −0.104 | 0.156 | 0.398 | −0.004 | 1.000 | | |
| Netherlands | −0.012 | 0.567 | 0.342 | 0.484 | 0.537 | 0.031 | 1.000 | |
| Norway | 0.343 | 0.359 | −0.100 | 0.188 | −0.212 | 0.119 | 0.010 | 1.000 |
| Spain | 0.260 | 0.208 | 0.413 | 0.326 | −0.075 | 0.338 | −0.102 | 0.171 |
| Sweden | −0.038 | 0.311 | 0.281 | 0.277 | 0.285 | 0.131 | 0.429 | −0.100 |
| Switzerland | 0.454 | 0.465 | 0.134 | 0.444 | 0.700 | 0.129 | 0.658 | −0.021 |
| United Kingdom | −0.349 | 0.284 | 0.152 | 0.432 | 0.258 | 0.104 | 0.675 | −0.136 |
| Europe Total | −0.039 | 0.493 | 0.266 | 0.643 | 0.505 | 0.289 | 0.783 | −0.039 |
| Hong Kong | 0.127 | 0.447 | 0.743 | 0.387 | 0.131 | 0.324 | 0.729 | 0.046 |
| Japan | 0.216 | 0.331 | 0.831 | 0.361 | 0.302 | 0.307 | 0.284 | −0.257 |
| Singapore | 0.260 | 0.510 | 0.921 | 0.404 | 0.311 | 0.353 | 0.614 | −0.157 |
| Asia Total | 0.211 | 0.337 | 0.845 | 0.365 | 0.281 | 0.314 | 0.308 | −0.228 |
| Australia | −0.241 | 0.281 | 0.213 | 0.504 | 0.321 | 0.420 | 0.766 | 0.089 |
| Canada | 0.239 | 0.623 | 0.341 | 0.441 | −0.037 | 0.269 | 0.554 | 0.469 |
| Other Total | 0.029 | 0.544 | 0.329 | 0.528 | 0.157 | 0.363 | 0.743 | 0.358 |
| Non-U.S. Total Equities | 0.062 | 0.559 | 0.557 | 0.646 | 0.470 | 0.390 | 0.774 | −0.114 |
| U. S. Total Equities | −0.076 | 0.389 | 0.243 | 0.214 | 0.210 | 0.208 | 0.730 | 0.009 |
| World Total Equities | −0.042 | 0.483 | 0.358 | 0.384 | 0.322 | 0.281 | 0.804 | −0.045 |

| Series | Spain | Sweden | Switzer-land | United Kingdom | Europe Total | Hong Kong | Japan | Singa-pore |
|---|---|---|---|---|---|---|---|---|
| Spain | 1.000 | | | | | | | |
| Sweden | 0.313 | 1.000 | | | | | | |
| Switzerland | 0.127 | 0.233 | 1.000 | | | | | |
| United Kingdom | −0.039 | 0.301 | 0.454 | 1.000 | | | | |
| Europe Total | 0.178 | 0.471 | 0.712 | 0.882 | 1.000 | | | |
| Hong Kong | 0.418 | 0.376 | 0.563 | 0.487 | 0.598 | 1.000 | | |
| Japan | 0.337 | 0.340 | 0.240 | 0.171 | 0.374 | 0.707 | 1.000 | |
| Singapore | 0.585 | 0.439 | 0.584 | 0.338 | 0.547 | 0.898 | 0.927 | 1.000 |
| Asia Total | 0.338 | 0.337 | 0.244 | 0.198 | 0.391 | 0.759 | 0.997 | 0.952 |
| Australia | 0.090 | 0.282 | 0.432 | 0.674 | 0.731 | 0.667 | 0.184 | 0.512 |
| Canada | 0.260 | 0.312 | 0.350 | 0.360 | 0.505 | 0.791 | 0.231 | 0.598 |
| Other Total | 0.195 | 0.340 | 0.432 | 0.550 | 0.676 | 0.800 | 0.247 | 0.609 |
| Non-U.S. Total Equities | 0.242 | 0.522 | 0.643 | 0.716 | 0.905 | 0.785 | 0.688 | 0.826 |
| U.S. Total Equities | −0.115 | 0.398 | 0.454 | 0.617 | 0.627 | 0.814 | 0.216 | 0.579 |
| World Total Equities | −0.015 | 0.470 | 0.557 | 0.703 | 0.774 | 0.848 | 0.385 | 0.700 |

| Series | Asia Total | Aus-tralia | Canada | Other Total | Non-U.S. Total Equities | U.S. Total Equities | World Total Equities |
|---|---|---|---|---|---|---|---|
| Asia Total | 1.000 | | | | | | |
| Australia | 0.224 | 1.000 | | | | | |
| Canada | 0.280 | 0.577 | 1.000 | | | | |
| Other Total | 0.296 | 0.863 | 0.907 | 1.000 | | | |
| Non-U.S. Total Equities | 0.704 | 0.704 | 0.586 | 0.717 | 1.000 | | |
| U.S. Total Equities | 0.260 | 0.699 | 0.710 | 0.787 | 0.667 | 1.000 | |
| World Total Equities | 0.422 | 0.753 | 0.716 | 0.818 | 0.831 | 0.967 | 1.000 |

and Switzerland, likewise, have large equity markets relative to their populations. European countries have generally lower equity market sizes per capita than the non-European countries studied; but the European equity markets are very large relative to those markets not studied (which include most of Asia, Latin America and Africa).

## Yields and Inflation Rates within Countries

Economists, starting with Irving Fisher, have developed a self-consistent and elegant theory of prices and returns in a multisovereign world, based on the principles of economic equilibrium and rational expectations.[1] The intranational (within one country) components of this theory

1. Footnotes appear at end of article.

**Figure E:** U.S.-Dollar-Adjusted Cumulative Wealth Indexes of Selected Domestic Bond Markets, 1960–1980 (year-end 1959 = 1.00)

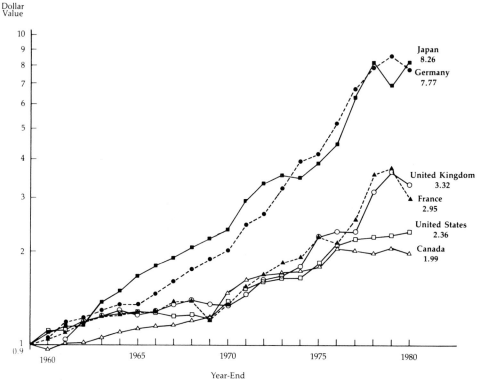

are the interest-inflation relationship, the expectations hypothesis for bond forward rates, and the capital asset pricing model (CAPM) for stocks.[2] Interest rates are postulated to consist of a relatively stable and relatively low real riskless rate of return plus the anticipated inflation rate over the life of the security, plus any interest rate risk (maturity) premiums that may exist. Thus we expect to observe a strong relationship between inflation rates and short-term yields in every country.

Table XI presents the year-by-year data. One can visually observe that short-term securities markets have more or less predicted short-term inflation rates, although there have been some notable exceptions. Japan in 1974 had a short-term yield of 5.8 per cent and an inflation rate of 24.6 per cent; that high real rate, however, did not persist, and Japanese inflation quickly fell to the level of the short-term yield. In the United States in early 1982, real rates are at a post-World War II high; we expect that they too will move toward their long-term mean (near zero per cent), with either rising inflation or falling yields, or both.

The long-term yields in Table XI tell a somewhat different story. Since they incorporate anticipated inflation over a long period, they are much less susceptible to rapid wide swings. As world inflation rates have risen over the 1960-80 period, long-term yields have risen in every country studied. But these yields do not (and theoretically should not) match year-to-year changes in the inflation rate. Countries that have had moderate inflation, such as Switzerland, have had modest increases in long-term yields, while most countries have exhibited dramatic increases in both numbers.

**Table VI**  World Bonds: Summary Statistics, 1960–1980

| Asset | Annual Returns in U.S. Dollars | | | Year-End 1980 Wealth Index 1959 = 1.00 |
|---|---|---|---|---|
| | Compound Return (%) | Arithmetic Mean (%) | Standard Deviation (%) | |
| Domestic Bonds: | | | | |
| Austria | 8.1 | 8.6 | 9.9 | 5.15 |
| Belgium | 7.7 | 8.1 | 9.4 | 4.75 |
| Canada | 3.3 | 3.5 | 6.3 | 1.99 |
| Denmark | 6.3 | 7.0 | 12.8 | 3.58 |
| France | 5.3 | 6.0 | 12.3 | 2.95 |
| Germany | 10.3 | 10.6 | 9.2 | 7.77 |
| Italy | 2.4 | 3.4 | 13.4 | 1.66 |
| Japan | 10.6 | 11.2 | 11.9 | 8.26 |
| Netherlands | 7.6 | 7.9 | 8.1 | 4.66 |
| Spain | 4.6 | 5.2 | 11.2 | 2.56 |
| Sweden | 6.2 | 6.4 | 5.9 | 3.57 |
| Switzerland | 8.4 | 9.1 | 12.4 | 5.48 |
| United Kingdom | 5.9 | 6.8 | 14.9 | 3.32 |
| United States | 4.2 | 4.3 | 5.4 | 2.36 |
| Crossborder Bonds: | | | | |
| Deutschemarks | 10.4 | 10.8 | 9.5 | 7.97 |
| Dutch Guilders* | 11.6 | 11.9 | 8.5 | 1.93 |
| Japanese Yen* | 18.0 | 19.8 | 19.2 | 2.71 |
| Swiss Francs* | 15.5 | 16.7 | 16.0 | 2.38 |
| U.S. Dollars | 5.9 | 6.0 | 4.4 | 3.34 |
| Other Currencies** | 5.7 | 5.8 | 2.5 | 1.25 |

*Returns measured over the period 1975–1980; wealth index 1974 = 1.00.
**Returns measured over the period 1977–1980; wealth index 1976 = 1.00.

## Inflation and International Exchange Rates

The international components of the equilibrium theory of prices and returns are based on the Law of One Price, which, in its simplest form, states that a good (physical or financial) cannot differ in price between two locales by more than the transport and transaction costs, or else arbitrage would take place to equalize the difference. Where there are governmental or other barriers to the flow of either goods or money, the Law of One Price breaks down. We can thus see to what extent the world capital market is integrated or segmented by observing the degree to which this law holds. A corollary of the Law of One Price is Purchasing Power Parity, which applies the law to market baskets of goods. Purchasing Power Parity asserts that, under ideal conditions, exchange rates instantaneously respond to local price level changes.

A number of applications of the Law of One Price to exchange rates, inflation rates and interest rates in an international setting can be expressed as parity theorems. First, expected changes in exchange rates are equal to expected differences in rates of inflation. (If, for example, U.S. expected inflation is 10 per cent and British expected inflation is 15 per cent, then the British pound is expected to decline by five per cent per

year in U.S. dollar terms.) Second, the difference in interest rates between two countries (for any maturity) will reflect the differences in expected inflation. (Continuing the above example, yields on British bonds should be five percentage points higher, for a given maturity, than U.S bond yields.) Third, as a consequence of the first two parity theorems, expected exchange rate changes are equal to the interest rate differential between two countries. Thus dollar-adjusted interest rates should be the same in every country.

The realism of these parity theorems over the long term can be assessed using the data in Table X. The countries with the highest inflation rates over the 1960-80 period have generally had the poorest exchange returns, casually confirming the inflation-exchange hypothesis. Japan, with an above-average exchange rate despite high inflation, is the most notable exception. Austria, Germany and Switzerland, which have experienced modest inflation, have had excellent currency performance against the dollar. Local currency short-term yields match inflation rates to a recognizable degree, with real rates negative in most of the larger markets over the period.

Table XI provides the data needed for a year-by-year examination of the inflation-exchange relationship. When inflation in a country increases relative to that in the United States, a

**Table VII** World Bonds: Year-by-Year U.S.-Dollar-Adjusted Total Returns (in per cent)

**World Bonds**

*Non-U.S. Domestic*

| Year | Austria | Belgium | Canada | Denmark | France | Germany | Italy | Japan | Nether-lands | Spain |
|------|---------|---------|--------|---------|--------|---------|-------|-------|--------------|-------|
| 1960 |         | −4.20   | −0.72  | −7.53   | 3.93   | 5.15    | 1.74  | 8.37  | 2.22         | 13.24 |
| 1961 |         | 7.31    | 2.75   | −7.57   | 5.18   | 11.42   | 5.35  | 6.18  | 8.68         | 9.80  |
| 1962 |         | 9.61    | −0.11  | 9.25    | 8.31   | 4.75    | 0.55  | −0.02 | 3.16         | 8.10  |
| 1963 |         | 2.81    | 4.09   | 18.44   | 4.76   | 6.49    | −1.94 | 19.24 | 1.07         | 1.30  |
| 1964 |         | 0.17    | 6.39   | −7.74   | 4.87   | 3.83    | 1.33  | 8.45  | 1.08         | 2.89  |
| 1965 | 4.09    | 6.01    | 1.82   | −5.17   | −2.40  | −0.08   | 12.74 | 12.24 | 0.43         | 0.54  |
| 1966 | 3.67    | 3.87    | 1.72   | 3.58    | 0.58   | 7.95    | 7.60  | 8.02  | 3.60         | −0.35 |
| 1967 | 3.41    | 8.40    | 0.46   | −4.58   | 8.15   | 10.20   | 5.96  | 6.25  | 7.25         | −9.89 |
| 1968 | 8.89    | 5.13    | 2.38   | 18.96   | 0.59   | 8.64    | 6.94  | 7.84  | 4.48         | 4.44  |
| 1969 | 7.13    | 1.80    | 0.64   | −7.75   | −13.13 | 8.73    | −0.80 | 6.65  | 0.10         | 4.04  |
| 1970 | 5.77    | 7.96    | 23.77  | 6.87    | 12.21  | 6.10    | −6.79 | 7.26  | 8.70         | −6.33 |
| 1971 | 18.68   | 23.51   | 10.11  | 21.42   | 14.61  | 21.93   | 25.58 | 23.30 | 19.12        | 20.29 |
| 1972 | 10.61   | 8.38    | 2.51   | 18.61   | 7.62   | 6.78    | 15.12 | 14.24 | 7.43         | 19.71 |
| 1973 | 15.30   | 10.57   | 2.37   | 7.01    | 10.00  | 22.95   | 2.92  | 6.43  | 13.27        | 13.35 |
| 1974 | 17.24   | 16.93   | 1.00   | 1.52    | 3.76   | 21.74   | −30.72| −1.35 | 21.75        | −6.88 |
| 1975 | 6.52    | 1.30    | 1.48   | 25.14   | 17.94  | 5.53    | 10.38 | 10.35 | 3.99         | 5.34  |
| 1976 | 27.05   | 16.47   | 16.30  | 4.05    | −5.36  | 25.31   | −24.53| 14.56 | 18.45        | −4.31 |
| 1977 | 17.99   | 17.64   | −1.69  | 5.62    | 15.96  | 30.01   | 12.82 | 42.70 | 15.92        | −12.10|
| 1978 | 28.48   | 32.69   | −2.82  | 42.27   | 43.56  | 16.84   | 23.00 | 30.26 | 25.32        | 28.73 |
| 1979 | 17.93   | 6.13    | 5.81   | 5.26    | 6.07   | 9.36    | 15.75 | −17.72| 7.17         | 24.28 |
| 1980 | −13.39  | −12.26  | −4.40  | −0.98   | −21.46 | −10.16  | −11.72| 22.25 | −7.32        | −7.62 |

**World Bonds**

| | *Non-U.S. Domestic* | | | *U.S. Domestic* | *Crossborder* | | | | | |
|------|--------|-----------------|-------------------|------------------|-------------------|------------------|------------------|-----------------|----------------|-----------------------|
| Year | Sweden | Switzer-land | United Kingdom | United States | Deutsche-marks | Dutch Guilders | Japanese Yen | Swiss Francs | U.S. Dollars | Other Curren-cies |
| 1960 | −0.76  | 3.52    | −0.47   | 10.74   | 9.54   |       |       |       | 3.74  |      |
| 1961 | 4.34   | 2.76    | 4.72    | 2.66    | 7.57   |       |       |       | 5.85  |      |
| 1962 | 8.19   | 1.86    | 13.19   | 5.94    | 6.00   |       |       |       | 8.39  |      |
| 1963 | 2.00   | 0.67    | 5.04    | 2.33    | 5.65   |       |       |       | 6.11  |      |
| 1964 | 2.96   | 0.46    | −1.18   | 4.15    | 4.30   |       |       |       | 6.22  |      |
| 1965 | 3.50   | 4.30    | 4.80    | −0.26   | 0.87   |       |       |       | 2.07  |      |
| 1966 | 6.40   | 0.66    | 5.27    | 1.09    | −0.62  |       |       |       | 0.69  |      |
| 1967 | 4.10   | 4.36    | −11.43  | −4.29   | 11.22  |       |       |       | 2.29  |      |
| 1968 | 9.91   | 5.98    | 1.55    | 2.21    | 7.81   |       |       |       | 5.97  |      |
| 1969 | 0.34   | −1.43   | 1.65    | −4.63   | 4.10   |       |       |       | −0.95 |      |
| 1970 | 7.29   | 3.68    | 8.64    | 14.36   | 8.92   |       |       |       | 4.17  |      |
| 1971 | 15.30  | 20.41   | 28.61   | 10.52   | 22.57  |       |       |       | 14.12 |      |
| 1972 | 8.06   | 7.26    | −12.53  | 5.81    | 13.93  |       |       |       | 10.94 |      |
| 1973 | 9.92   | 16.18   | −7.05   | 2.30    | 23.11  |       |       |       | 4.00  |      |
| 1974 | 14.81  | 30.22   | −2.63   | 0.17    | 21.90  |       |       |       | 1.87  |      |
| 1975 | −3.41  | 7.84    | 9.62    | 12.29   | 7.60   | 5.50  | 20.40 | 15.30 | 15.80 |      |
| 1976 | 12.83  | 22.82   | −9.06   | 15.58   | 26.30  | 18.77 | 15.95 | 23.76 | 14.16 |      |
| 1977 | −4.32  | 31.08   | 53.66   | 2.99    | 27.08  | 17.24 | 42.62 | 37.84 | 7.03  | 9.28 |
| 1978 | 17.84  | 37.74   | 6.64    | 1.17    | 21.37  | 23.01 | 32.65 | 29.74 | 4.10  | 6.39 |
| 1979 | 11.52  | 5.13    | 16.05   | 2.28    | 7.87   | 8.85  | −18.67| 2.35  | 2.31  | 2.33 |
| 1980 | 3.83   | −14.23  | 28.01   | 3.05    | −10.31 | −1.68 | 25.98 | −9.04 | 7.23  | 5.00 |

negative exchange return should be observed. The reader may make such comparisons directly. We note that while this rule is generally valid (especially over periods longer than one year), there are numerous exceptions. The inflation-interest relationship can also be explored by the reader using the local currency yield data in Table XI.

Referring back to Table X, we may examine the proposition that interest rates, converted to U.S. dollars, should be the same in every country. The 21-year compound annual dollar-adjusted bond returns in Table X range from 2.4 per cent for Italy to 10.6 per cent for Japan, suggesting that, at least over this turbulent period in the bond markets, there were substantial differences in (realized) returns among countries.

### Equity Expectation Parity

To the existing list of international parity theorems presented here we add Equity Expectation Parity. This is the proposition that beta-adjusted expected returns on stocks will be the same in every country. (If stock prices are set in a world CAPM framework, rather than locally, this theorem will hold.) We regressed U.S.-dollar-adjusted equity (country and regional) returns on the U.S.-dollar-adjusted world equity market portfolio. (The regressions were performed in excess return form—i.e., in excess of U.S. Treasury bill returns.) Table XII shows the results.

Alphas ranged from −1.92 for Italy to +20.58 for Hong Kong (in per cent per year). The alpha for the United States was −0.69, indicating below average beta-adjusted performance. Alphas approached significance for Hong Kong and Japan. Betas ranged from −0.27 for Norway to +2.81 for Hong Kong. The United States equity market had a world equity market beta of +1.08.

Table XII also shows correlations of each country's U.S.-dollar-adjusted equity returns with its dollar-adjusted bond returns and local inflation rates. The generally high correlation within a country between equity and bond returns reflects the application of the same exchange rate adjustment to each return series. The generally negative correlations between equities and inflation show that inflation hurts the stock market not just in the United States, but in most of the world. Many theories have been propounded to explain this relationship, but the mystery has not yet been solved.

### Do International Parity Theorems Hold?

The international parity theorems we have expounded here are the subject of intense debate. The work of Frenkel and others has generally supported the hypotheses.[3] Aliber found that the exchange-inflation relationship held more closely over the long term than in the short run.[4] (Officer has summarized the various views of this relationship in a review paper.[5]) Frenkel and

Levich have detected greater deviations from the interest-exchange relationship in domestic markets than in crossborder markets, attributing the finding to the greater degree of regulation in domestic markets (making crossborder markets more efficient).[6]

The efficiency of exchange markets themselves has also been investigated: Levich presents evidence that foreign exchange markets do not fully reflect all the available information, while Cornell leans toward an affirmation of market efficiency in the forward exchange market.[7] On the equity side, Stehle has shown that equity pricing is somewhat better explained by a world-market CAPM line than by local (within each country) CAPM lines.[8]

Our own view is that the set of theorems makes logical sense, and that barriers to international capital, goods and labor flows are likely to produce most of the observed deviations from the postulated relationships. We thus would not expect efficient-market-affirming results in the present international context. Black has propounded a theory of international capital market equilibrium with investment barriers, and we might expect a theory of this kind to reflect reality better than any set of purely efficient market hypotheses.[9]

### The Advantages of International Diversification

International diversification has the same advantages as diversification along any other dimension: If asset returns are imperfectly correlated, risk is reduced at a given level of expected return. Lessard and Solnik each have developed this idea in detail.[10] The cross-correlations of equities in Table V, and bonds in Table IX, along with the intracountry stock-bond correlations in Table XII, are low enough in general to suggest substantial gains purely from diversification.

A second argument for diversifying internationally is that segmentation in the world market may produce bargains. If securities are priced according to their local systematic risk, some of that risk becomes unsystematic and therefore diversifiable in a global context. Further, low past levels of U.S. investment in foreign markets may have led to underpricing in those markets; an investor might thus capture excess returns in non-U.S. securities. Regulations producing barriers to investment in a country may produce excess returns for an investor able to overcome those barriers.

A final argument for international investing is

**Table VIII** World Bonds: Cumulative Wealth Indexes of U.S.-Dollar-Adjusted Total Returns (year-end 1959 = 1.000)

## World Bonds

### Non-U.S. Domestic

| End of Year | Austria* | Belgium | Canada | Denmark | France | Germany | Italy | Japan | Netherlands | Spain |
|---|---|---|---|---|---|---|---|---|---|---|
| 1959 | | 1.000 | 1.000 | 1.000 | 1.000 | 1.000 | 1.000 | 1.000 | 1.000 | 1.000 |
| 1960 | | 0.958 | 0.993 | 0.925 | 1.039 | 1.052 | 1.017 | 1.084 | 1.022 | 1.132 |
| 1961 | | 1.028 | 1.020 | 0.855 | 1.093 | 1.171 | 1.072 | 1.151 | 1.111 | 1.243 |
| 1962 | | 1.127 | 1.019 | 0.934 | 1.184 | 1.227 | 1.078 | 1.150 | 1.146 | 1.344 |
| 1963 | | 1.159 | 1.061 | 1.106 | 1.240 | 1.307 | 1.057 | 1.372 | 1.158 | 1.362 |
| 1964 | 1.000 | 1.160 | 1.128 | 1.020 | 1.301 | 1.357 | 1.071 | 1.488 | 1.171 | 1.401 |
| 1965 | 1.041 | 1.230 | 1.149 | 0.968 | 1.270 | 1.356 | 1.207 | 1.670 | 1.176 | 1.409 |
| 1966 | 1.079 | 1.278 | 1.169 | 1.002 | 1.277 | 1.464 | 1.299 | 1.804 | 1.218 | 1.404 |
| 1967 | 1.116 | 1.385 | 1.174 | 0.956 | 1.381 | 1.613 | 1.377 | 1.916 | 1.307 | 1.265 |
| 1968 | 1.215 | 1.456 | 1.202 | 1.138 | 1.389 | 1.752 | 1.472 | 2.067 | 1.365 | 1.321 |
| 1969 | 1.302 | 1.482 | 1.210 | 1.049 | 1.207 | 1.905 | 1.460 | 2.204 | 1.366 | 1.374 |
| 1970 | 1.377 | 1.600 | 1.497 | 1.122 | 1.354 | 2.021 | 1.361 | 2.364 | 1.485 | 1.287 |
| 1971 | 1.634 | 1.976 | 1.649 | 1.362 | 1.552 | 2.464 | 1.710 | 2.915 | 1.769 | 1.549 |
| 1972 | 1.807 | 2.142 | 1.690 | 1.615 | 1.670 | 2.631 | 1.968 | 3.330 | 1.901 | 1.854 |
| 1973 | 2.084 | 2.369 | 1.730 | 1.728 | 1.837 | 3.326 | 2.025 | 3.544 | 2.153 | 2.101 |
| 1974 | 2.443 | 2.770 | 1.748 | 1.755 | 1.906 | 3.939 | 1.403 | 3.496 | 2.621 | 1.957 |
| 1975 | 2.602 | 2.806 | 1.773 | 2.196 | 2.248 | 4.157 | 1.549 | 3.858 | 2.726 | 2.061 |
| 1976 | 3.306 | 3.268 | 2.062 | 2.285 | 2.128 | 5.208 | 1.169 | 4.419 | 3.229 | 1.972 |
| 1977 | 3.901 | 3.844 | 2.028 | 2.413 | 2.467 | 6.771 | 1.319 | 6.307 | 3.743 | 1.734 |
| 1978 | 5.012 | 5.101 | 1.970 | 3.433 | 3.542 | 7.912 | 1.622 | 8.215 | 4.690 | 2.232 |
| 1979 | 5.911 | 5.414 | 2.085 | 3.614 | 3.757 | 8.652 | 1.878 | 6.760 | 5.027 | 2.774 |
| 1980 | 5.119 | 4.750 | 1.993 | 3.579 | 2.951 | 7.773 | 1.658 | 8.264 | 4.659 | 2.562 |

## World Bonds

| End of Year | Non-U.S. Domestic | | | U.S. Domestic | Crossborder | | | | | |
|---|---|---|---|---|---|---|---|---|---|---|
| | Sweden | Switzer-land | United Kingdom | United States | Deutsche-marks | Dutch Guilders** | Japanese Yen** | Swiss Francs** | U.S. Dollars | Other Curren-cies*** |
| 1959 | 1.000 | 1.000 | 1.000 | 1.000 | 1.000 | | | | 1.000 | |
| 1960 | 0.992 | 1.035 | 0.995 | 1.107 | 1.095 | | | | 1.037 | |
| 1961 | 1.035 | 1.064 | 1.042 | 1.137 | 1.178 | | | | 1.098 | |
| 1962 | 1.120 | 1.084 | 1.180 | 1.204 | 1.249 | | | | 1.190 | |
| 1963 | 1.143 | 1.091 | 1.239 | 1.232 | 1.320 | | | | 1.263 | |
| 1964 | 1.176 | 1.096 | 1.225 | 1.284 | 1.376 | | | | 1.341 | |
| 1965 | 1.218 | 1.143 | 1.284 | 1.280 | 1.388 | | | | 1.369 | |
| 1966 | 1.296 | 1.151 | 1.351 | 1.294 | 1.380 | | | | 1.379 | |
| 1967 | 1.349 | 1.201 | 1.197 | 1.239 | 1.535 | | | | 1.410 | |
| 1968 | 1.482 | 1.272 | 1.215 | 1.266 | 1.654 | | | | 1.494 | |
| 1969 | 1.487 | 1.254 | 1.235 | 1.207 | 1.722 | | | | 1.480 | |
| 1970 | 1.596 | 1.300 | 1.342 | 1.381 | 1.876 | | | | 1.542 | |
| 1971 | 1.840 | 1.566 | 1.726 | 1.526 | 2.299 | | | | 1.760 | |
| 1972 | 1.988 | 1.680 | 1.510 | 1.615 | 2.619 | | | | 1.952 | |
| 1973 | 2.185 | 1.951 | 1.403 | 1.652 | 3.225 | | | | 2.030 | |
| 1974 | 2.509 | 2.541 | 1.366 | 1.655 | 3.931 | 1.000 | 1.000 | 1.000 | 2.068 | |
| 1975 | 2.424 | 2.740 | 1.498 | 1.858 | 4.230 | 1.055 | 1.204 | 1.153 | 2.395 | |
| 1976 | 2.735 | 3.366 | 1.362 | 2.148 | 5.342 | 1.253 | 1.396 | 1.427 | 2.734 | 1.000 |
| 1977 | 2.617 | 4.412 | 2.093 | 2.212 | 6.789 | 1.469 | 1.991 | 1.967 | 2.926 | 1.093 |
| 1978 | 3.083 | 6.077 | 2.232 | 2.238 | 8.240 | 1.807 | 2.641 | 2.552 | 3.046 | 1.163 |
| 1979 | 3.439 | 6.389 | 2.590 | 2.289 | 8.888 | 1.967 | 2.148 | 2.612 | 3.117 | 1.190 |
| 1980 | 3.570 | 5.480 | 3.316 | 2.359 | 7.972 | 1.934 | 2.706 | 2.376 | 3.342 | 1.249 |

* 1964 = 1.000.
** 1974 = 1.000.
*** 1976 = 1.000.

**Table IX**  World Bonds: Cross-Correlations of Annual U.S.-Dollar-Adjusted Total Returns, 1960-1980

| Series | Austria | Belgium | Canada | Denmark | France | Germany | Italy |
|---|---|---|---|---|---|---|---|
| Austria | 1.000 | | | | | | |
| Belgium | 0.853 | 1.000 | | | | | |
| Canada | 0.244 | 0.159 | 1.000 | | | | |
| Denmark | 0.481 | 0.548 | −0.010 | 1.000 | | | |
| France | 0.544 | 0.716 | 0.010 | 0.693 | 1.000 | | |
| Germany | 0.823 | 0.771 | 0.179 | 0.217 | 0.427 | 1.000 | |
| Italy | 0.141 | 0.248 | −0.225 | 0.426 | 0.530 | −0.009 | 1.000 |
| Japan | 0.154 | 0.318 | −0.172 | 0.358 | 0.276 | 0.265 | 0.239 |
| Netherlands | 0.884 | 0.928 | 0.211 | 0.448 | 0.644 | 0.862 | 0.036 |
| Spain | 0.344 | 0.309 | −0.102 | 0.488 | 0.472 | 0.044 | 0.612 |
| Sweden | 0.586 | 0.630 | 0.264 | 0.418 | 0.281 | 0.338 | −0.039 |
| Switzerland | 0.882 | 0.895 | 0.037 | 0.475 | 0.662 | 0.854 | 0.075 |
| United Kingdom | −0.005 | 0.095 | −0.147 | 0.121 | 0.099 | 0.125 | 0.288 |
| United States | 0.150 | 0.049 | 0.632 | 0.228 | 0.146 | 0.098 | −0.132 |
| Deutschemark Crossborder | 0.853 | 0.810 | 0.215 | 0.342 | 0.546 | 0.938 | 0.018 |
| Dutch Guilder Crossborder | 0.935 | 0.980 | 0.289 | 0.463 | 0.665 | 0.872 | 0.233 |
| Japanese Yen Crossborder | −0.060 | 0.274 | −0.478 | 0.262 | 0.251 | 0.249 | 0.005 |
| Swiss Franc Crossborder | 0.749 | 0.842 | 0.105 | 0.421 | 0.673 | 0.905 | 0.286 |
| U.S. Dollar Crossborder | 0.172 | 0.154 | 0.250 | 0.442 | 0.169 | 0.157 | 0.083 |
| Other Crossborder | 0.194 | 0.434 | −0.619 | 0.173 | 0.341 | 0.634 | 0.114 |

| Series | Japan | Nether-lands | Spain | Sweden | Switzer-land | United Kingdom | United States |
|---|---|---|---|---|---|---|---|
| Japan | 1.000 | | | | | | |
| Netherlands | 0.244 | 1.000 | | | | | |
| Spain | −0.158 | 0.235 | 1.000 | | | | |
| Sweden | −0.183 | 0.631 | 0.440 | 1.000 | | | |
| Switzerland | 0.383 | 0.944 | 0.174 | 0.463 | 1.000 | | |
| United Kingdom | 0.500 | 0.033 | −0.128 | −0.238 | 0.134 | 1.000 | |
| United States | 0.095 | 0.166 | 0.072 | 0.059 | 0.104 | 0.076 | 1.000 |
| Deutschemark Crossborder | 0.293 | 0.903 | 0.158 | 0.400 | 0.901 | 0.025 | 0.242 |
| Dutch Guilder Crossborder | 0.360 | 0.996 | 0.274 | 0.462 | 0.968 | −0.198 | 0.025 |
| Japanese Yen Crossborder | 0.982 | 0.242 | −0.481 | −0.355 | 0.408 | 0.400 | −0.061 |
| Swiss Franc Crossborder | 0.594 | 0.858 | −0.047 | −0.032 | 0.949 | 0.104 | 0.115 |
| U.S. Dollar Crossborder | 0.325 | 0.178 | 0.117 | 0.036 | 0.167 | 0.168 | 0.715 |
| Other Crossborder | 0.944 | 0.443 | −0.553 | −0.554 | 0.610 | 0.666 | 0.160 |

| Series | Deutsche-mark Cross-Border | Dutch Guilder Cross-Border | Japanese Yen Cross-Border | Swiss Franc Cross-Border | U.S. Dollar Cross-Border | Other Cross-Border |
|---|---|---|---|---|---|---|
| Deutschemark Crossborder | 1.000 | | | | | |
| Dutch Guilder Crossborder | 0.931 | 1.000 | | | | |
| Japanese Yen Crossborder | 0.281 | 0.273 | 1.000 | | | |
| Swiss Franc Crossborder | 0.933 | 0.868 | 0.550 | 1.000 | | |
| U.S. Dollar Crossborder | 0.288 | −0.113 | 0.215 | 0.132 | 1.000 | |
| Other Crossborder | 0.624 | 0.500 | 0.917 | 0.786 | 0.683 | 1.000 |

the sheer size of the non-U.S. market. It is desirable as a matter of general principle to maintain as wide a horizon as possible so as not to exclude opportunities. The non-U.S. market has developed into a mature set of institutions surpassing the U.S. market in combined size. We believe that the U.S. investor should regard all investments, U.S. or foreign, traditional or non-traditional, as part of his opportunity set (excepting, perhaps, securities rendered totally unsuitable by tax laws or other international capital barriers).

If international parity theorems hold strictly, then exchange risk is not an issue in international investment; exchange rates adjust instantaneously to reflect true value, and the U.S. dollar investor faces exactly the same risk as the local currency investor. We believe that sufficient doubt has been cast on the "instantaneous" version of parity that we admit the possibility of uncompensated exchange risk in a given non-U.S. security. Over the long term, however, we expect that exchange risk would dampen (i.e., that the Law of One Price would hold better over the long run than over the short run). Furthermore, investors can diversify away a portion of exchange risk by investing in different countries, or hedge against

**Table X**  Comparative Data on 18 Countries

| Country | 1980 Population (millions) | 1980 GDP (billions of U.S. $)* | Exchange Rate in US $/FCU (end of 1980)** | Compound Annual Rates of Return, 1960-1980 | | | | |
|---|---|---|---|---|---|---|---|---|
| | | | | | Local Currency | | Exchange-Rate-Adjusted | |
| | | | | Exchange Return (%) | Inflation Rate (%) | Short-Term Yields (%) | Equity Returns (%) | Bond Returns (%) |
| Australia | 14.6 | 140.0 | 1.1815 | −3.0 | 6.4 | N/A | 9.8 | N/A |
| Austria | 7.5 | 76.3 | 0.0718 | 3.1 | 4.8 | 6.1 | 9.1 | 8.1 |
| Belgium | 9.9 | 110.9 | 0.0316 | 2.2 | 5.1 | 6.3 | 9.2 | 7.7 |
| Canada | 24.1 | 245.8 | 0.8386 | −1.1 | 5.3 | 5.9 | 10.7 | 3.3 |
| Denmark | 5.1 | 66.4 | 0.1663 | 0.7 | 7.6 | 7.7 | 9.5 | 6.3 |
| France | 53.7 | 571.3 | 0.2208 | 0.4 | 6.7 | 6.6 | 6.2 | 5.3 |
| Germany | 61.6 | 824.6 | 0.5074 | 3.7 | 3.8 | 4.3 | 8.3 | 10.3 |
| Hong Kong | 4.9 | 20.8 | 0.1957 | 0.4*** | N/A | N/A | 24.6*** | N/A |
| Italy | 57.1 | 323.6 | 0.0011 | −1.9 | 8.8 | 7.1 | 2.4 | 2.4 |
| Japan | 116.8 | 990.0 | 0.0049 | 2.8 | 7.2 | 5.6 | 15.6 | 10.6 |
| Netherlands | 14.1 | 161.4 | 0.4717 | 2.8 | 5.5 | 4.9 | 9.3 | 7.6 |
| Norway | 4.1 | 57.3 | 0.1935 | 1.6 | 6.2 | N/A | 10.3 | N/A |
| Singapore | 2.4 | 9.0 | 0.4819 | 1.8 | N/A | N/A | 23.2*** | N/A |
| Spain | 37.4 | 201.0 | 0.0126 | −1.3 | 10.3 | 6.3 | 8.4 | 4.6 |
| Sweden | 8.3 | 101.5 | 0.2288 | 0.8 | 6.5 | 5.8 | 8.4 | 6.2 |
| Switzerland | 6.3 | 97.4 | 0.5618 | 4.4 | 4.1 | 3.4 | 10.2 | 8.4 |
| United Kingdom | 55.9 | 405.1 | 2.3950 | −0.8 | 8.6 | 7.7 | 10.0 | 5.9 |
| United States | 226.5 | 2576.6 | — | — | 5.3 | 5.5 | 8.7 | 4.1 |

N/A = Not Available
* GDP = Gross Domestic Product.
** FCU = Foreign Currency Unit.
*** 1970-1980.

**Table XI**  Comparative Beginning-of-Year Local Currency Yields and Yearly Inflation and Exchange Returns for 14 Countries (in per cent)*

| Year | Austria | | | | Belgium | | | | Canada | | | | Denmark | | | |
|---|---|---|---|---|---|---|---|---|---|---|---|---|---|---|---|---|
| | LT Yield | ST Yield | Infla-tion Rate | Exch. Return | LT Yield | ST Yield | Infla-tion Rate | Exch. Return | LT Yield | ST Yield | Infla-tion Rate | Exch. Return | LT Yield | ST Yield | Infla-tion Rate | Exch. Return |
| 1960 | | 4.50 | 0.54 | −0.04 | 4.27 | 1.47 | 0.27 | 0.48 | 5.14 | 4.80 | 1.25 | −4.34 | 5.32 | 5.00 | 0.00 | 0.03 |
| 1961 | | 4.73 | 5.27 | 0.66 | 6.07 | 4.50 | 1.00 | −0.16 | 5.31 | 3.25 | 0.37 | −4.54 | 6.21 | 4.00 | 5.56 | 0.29 |
| 1962 | | 4.75 | 2.50 | 0.00 | 5.74 | 4.22 | 1.39 | 0.06 | 4.93 | 2.99 | 1.66 | −3.14 | 7.32 | 4.88 | 10.53 | −0.23 |
| 1963 | | 4.77 | 3.76 | 0.00 | 4.96 | 3.00 | 3.33 | −0.16 | 5.10 | 3.91 | 1.63 | −0.31 | 7.15 | 4.00 | 2.38 | −0.13 |
| 1964 | | 4.81 | 3.80 | 0.00 | 5.32 | 4.02 | 4.36 | 0.40 | 5.15 | 3.78 | 1.60 | 0.63 | 6.33 | 3.62 | 4.65 | −0.14 |
| 1965 | 6.35 | 4.89 | 5.41 | −0.08 | 6.43 | 4.75 | 3.82 | −0.02 | 5.03 | 3.82 | 2.98 | −0.11 | 7.47 | 4.88 | 6.67 | 0.44 |
| 1966 | 6.66 | 4.84 | 2.15 | −0.08 | 6.45 | 4.72 | 3.68 | −0.82 | 5.40 | 4.54 | 3.92 | −0.81 | 8.68 | 4.88 | 6.25 | −0.36 |
| 1967 | 7.08 | 5.05 | 4.21 | 0.12 | 6.76 | 5.77 | 3.38 | 0.85 | 5.76 | 4.96 | 3.77 | 0.30 | 7.47 | 4.88 | 9.80 | −7.32 |
| 1968 | 7.64 | 5.54 | 3.11 | 0.00 | 6.58 | 4.42 | 2.45 | −0.90 | 6.54 | 5.95 | 4.27 | 0.73 | 9.78 | 6.00 | 5.36 | −0.52 |
| 1969 | 7.45 | 5.85 | 2.87 | 0.00 | 6.65 | 4.65 | 4.15 | 0.83 | 7.27 | 6.24 | 4.55 | 0.00 | 8.84 | 6.50 | 5.08 | 0.12 |
| 1970 | 7.50 | 6.30 | 4.84 | 0.00 | 7.80 | 8.50 | 3.37 | −0.02 | 8.33 | 7.81 | 2.17 | 6.09 | 10.73 | 8.00 | 6.45 | 0.04 |
| 1971 | 7.77 | 6.56 | 5.03 | 9.15 | 7.79 | 6.95 | 5.33 | 11.01 | 6.99 | 4.44 | 4.11 | 0.90 | 11.19 | 8.00 | 6.06 | 6.05 |
| 1972 | 7.63 | 6.70 | 7.32 | 2.46 | 7.17 | 4.66 | 6.05 | 1.43 | 6.56 | 3.21 | 5.04 | 0.66 | 10.81 | 6.00 | 7.14 | 3.14 |
| 1973 | 7.59 | 6.75 | 7.69 | 16.58 | 7.21 | 4.37 | 7.03 | 6.78 | 7.12 | 3.65 | 9.08 | −0.02 | 10.34 | 6.00 | 10.67 | 8.86 |
| 1974 | 8.98 | 6.75 | 9.68 | 15.88 | 7.92 | 7.65 | 15.86 | 14.40 | 7.70 | 6.35 | 12.01 | 0.46 | 11.86 | 8.50 | 15.66 | 11.33 |
| 1975 | 10.18 | 7.19 | 7.14 | −7.45 | 9.03 | 10.63 | 11.23 | −8.63 | 8.77 | 7.12 | 10.19 | −2.48 | 15.09 | 9.50 | 5.21 | −8.54 |
| 1976 | 9.41 | 7.83 | 7.16 | 10.39 | 8.72 | 6.05 | 7.79 | 9.87 | 9.49 | 8.64 | 5.88 | 0.71 | 12.23 | 10.00 | 12.87 | 6.74 |
| 1977 | 8.55 | 8.06 | 4.57 | 10.79 | 10.84 | 6.42 | 9.23 | 8.47 | 8.14 | 9.10 | −7.79 | 14.48 | 13.50 | 12.28 | 0.17 | |
| 1978 | 8.87 | 8.06 | 3.50 | 13.22 | 9.85 | 8.60 | 3.86 | 14.38 | 8.77 | 7.17 | 8.67 | −7.72 | 17.00 | 15.20 | 7.81 | 13.51 |
| 1979 | 8.21 | 7.92 | 4.40 | 7.54 | 8.45 | 9.17 | 5.08 | 2.68 | 9.30 | 10.46 | 9.52 | 1.53 | 14.54 | 13.40 | 11.59 | −5.13 |
| 1980 | 7.96 | 7.43 | 6.61 | −9.98 | 9.51 | 14.35 | 7.57 | −11.01 | 10.26 | 13.66 | 11.20 | −2.23 | 15.82 | 17.00 | 9.97 | −10.81 |

| | France | | | | Germany | | | | Italy | | | | Japan | | | |
|---|---|---|---|---|---|---|---|---|---|---|---|---|---|---|---|---|
| Year | LT Yield | ST Yield | Infla-tion Rate | Exch. Return | LT Yield | ST Yield | Infla-tion Rate | Exch. Return | LT Yield | ST Yield | Infla-tion Rate | Exch. Return | LT Yield | ST Yield | Infla-tion Rate | Exch. Return |
| 1960 | 5.27 | 4.07 | 2.44 | −0.06 | 5.80 | 2.67 | 0.94 | −0.02 | 5.43 | 3.50 | 1.01 | 0.00 | | 7.30 | 2.88 | 0.29 |
| 1961 | 5.49 | 3.70 | 3.58 | 0.12 | 6.20 | 3.75 | 2.81 | 4.37 | 5.52 | 3.63 | 2.76 | 0.00 | 7.60 | 6.08 | 8.43 | −1.00 |
| 1962 | 5.56 | 3.58 | 4.32 | 0.06 | 6.00 | 2.00 | 2.56 | −0.04 | 5.50 | 3.63 | 5.61 | 0.00 | 7.84 | 6.08 | 4.44 | 1.01 |
| 1963 | 5.31 | 3.51 | 5.38 | 0.00 | 6.10 | 2.63 | 3.16 | 0.57 | 5.93 | 3.52 | 7.62 | −0.25 | 7.50 | 6.08 | 8.24 | −1.04 |
| 1964 | 5.36 | 4.66 | 2.36 | −0.04 | 6.00 | 2.63 | 2.42 | −0.05 | 6.73 | 3.63 | 5.79 | −0.37 | | 5.71 | 5.16 | 1.01 |
| 1965 | 5.45 | 4.16 | 2.50 | 0.04 | 6.40 | 3.88 | 3.94 | −0.71 | 7.20 | 3.63 | 3.45 | 0.00 | | 5.71 | 6.07 | −0.72 |
| 1966 | 6.28 | 4.48 | 2.81 | −0.04 | 7.70 | 4.75 | 2.88 | 0.71 | 6.68 | 3.63 | 2.16 | 0.00 | | 5.71 | 3.96 | −0.43 |
| 1967 | 6.79 | 5.68 | 3.28 | −1.01 | 7.70 | 2.75 | 0.59 | −0.54 | 6.61 | 3.52 | 3.65 | 0.12 | 6.86 | 5.71 | 5.72 | 0.14 |
| 1968 | 6.75 | 5.23 | 5.47 | 0.90 | 6.80 | 2.78 | 3.51 | −0.01 | 6.80 | 5.05 | 0.74 | 0.06 | 6.98 | 5.71 | 4.61 | 1.19 |
| 1969 | 7.42 | 8.41 | 5.69 | −0.81 | 6.30 | 2.78 | 1.98 | 8.39 | 6.65 | 5.05 | 4.04 | −0.31 | 7.05 | 5.71 | 5.75 | −0.04 |
| 1970 | 8.63 | 10.18 | 5.22 | −10.98 | 7.60 | 5.83 | 4.02 | 1.15 | 7.38 | 5.70 | 5.30 | 0.38 | 7.13 | 5.93 | 7.79 | 0.04 |
| 1971 | 8.26 | 7.73 | 5.86 | 0.69 | 8.20 | 5.83 | 5.73 | 11.61 | 9.10 | 6.57 | 4.53 | 4.92 | 7.24 | 5.80 | 5.38 | 13.63 |
| 1972 | 8.28 | 5.68 | 6.82 | 5.67 | 7.90 | 3.28 | 6.18 | 2.09 | 7.22 | 5.41 | 1.96 | 1.96 | 7.24 | 5.17 | 4.47 | 4.22 |
| 1973 | 8.78 | 7.30 | 8.24 | 1.93 | 8.60 | 4.30 | 7.24 | 18.44 | 7.44 | 6.00 | 11.68 | −4.19 | 6.40 | 4.15 | 16.49 | 7.85 |
| 1974 | 9.65 | 7.55 | 14.99 | 8.86 | 9.60 | 7.12 | 6.53 | 12.18 | 7.45 | 7.48 | 24.80 | −6.38 | 8.78 | 5.80 | 24.64 | −6.94 |
| 1975 | 11.21 | 11.60 | 9.94 | 5.93 | 9.80 | 5.19 | 5.51 | −8.11 | 12.15 | 13.40 | 11.49 | −5.00 | 9.60 | 6.83 | 8.41 | −1.38 |
| 1976 | 10.18 | 6.54 | 10.01 | −0.91 | 8.50 | 7.83 | 3.84 | 11.00 | 11.63 | 21.10 | 21.10 | −21.87 | 9.02 | 5.68 | 9.41 | 4.21 |
| 1977 | 11.04 | 10.40 | 9.19 | −9.75 | 7.60 | 5.48 | 3.61 | 12.23 | 13.95 | 17.74 | 15.19 | 0.35 | 8.73 | 5.68 | 6.21 | 22.02 |
| 1978 | 11.07 | 9.66 | 9.47 | 5.63 | 5.90 | 4.34 | 2.38 | 15.15 | 14.33 | 11.80 | 11.53 | 5.06 | 6.27 | 4.15 | 3.42 | 23.33 |
| 1979 | 8.96 | 6.56 | 11.53 | 12.56 | 6.80 | 4.33 | 5.28 | 5.57 | 13.70 | 10.88 | 17.71 | 3.24 | 6.09 | 3.39 | 4.92 | −18.82 |
| 1980 | 9.48 | 9.50 | 13.68 | 3.98 | 7.40 | 5.73 | 5.50 | −11.61 | 14.05 | 16.52 | 20.95 | −13.59 | 7.69 | 5.68 | 7.06 | 18.07 |

| | Netherlands | | | | Spain | | | | Sweden | | | | Switzerland | | | |
|---|---|---|---|---|---|---|---|---|---|---|---|---|---|---|---|---|
| Year | LT Yield | ST Yield | Infla-tion Rate | Exch. Return | LT Yield | ST Yield | Infla-tion Rate | Exch. Return | LT Yield | ST Yield | Infla-tion Rate | Exch. Return | LT Yield | ST Yield | Infla-tion Rate | Exch. Return |
| 1960 | 4.12 | 1.85 | 0.00 | 0.00 | 6.54 | 6.25 | 1.70 | 0.00 | 4.28 | 4.50 | 0.00 | 0.02 | 3.08 | 1.01 | 2.17 | 0.42 |
| 1961 | 4.33 | 1.54 | 2.04 | 4.72 | 5.79 | 4.60 | 0.63 | 0.25 | 5.36 | 4.50 | 2.17 | −0.10 | 3.02 | 1.50 | 2.99 | −0.25 |
| 1962 | 4.24 | 1.34 | 2.22 | 0.00 | 5.37 | 4.60 | 8.75 | 0.03 | 5.52 | 4.25 | 6.38 | −0.06 | 2.98 | 1.25 | 3.49 | −0.07 |
| 1963 | 4.25 | 2.02 | 3.90 | 0.00 | 5.08 | 4.60 | 6.61 | 0.04 | 4.89 | 2.80 | 2.00 | −0.23 | 3.12 | 1.88 | 3.93 | 0.09 |
| 1964 | 4.72 | 2.29 | 6.05 | 0.22 | 5.48 | 4.60 | 11.59 | 0.02 | 5.36 | 3.50 | 3.92 | 1.01 | 3.54 | 2.25 | 2.34 | 0.00 |
| 1965 | 5.33 | 3.77 | 4.92 | −0.53 | 5.75 | 4.60 | 9.90 | −0.07 | 6.02 | 4.80 | 5.66 | −0.62 | 4.07 | 2.75 | 4.58 | −0.07 |
| 1966 | 6.14 | 4.40 | 4.50 | −0.08 | 6.29 | 4.60 | 5.49 | −0.01 | 6.38 | 5.70 | 5.36 | 0.00 | 3.98 | 3.00 | 4.38 | −0.21 |
| 1967 | 6.54 | 5.06 | 4.13 | 0.50 | 7.01 | 4.60 | 6.87 | −13.92 | 6.35 | 6.00 | 3.39 | 0.29 | 4.53 | 3.75 | 3.71 | 0.05 |
| 1968 | 6.37 | 4.63 | 3.79 | −0.28 | 7.25 | 5.10 | 2.73 | −0.17 | 6.80 | 6.80 | 1.64 | −0.29 | 4.55 | 2.50 | 2.18 | 0.53 |
| 1969 | 6.58 | 4.77 | 6.98 | −0.50 | 7.53 | 5.10 | 3.23 | −0.35 | 6.19 | 5.25 | 4.84 | 0.19 | 4.33 | 3.50 | 2.28 | −0.37 |
| 1970 | 7.86 | 6.18 | 4.66 | 0.75 | 7.87 | 5.50 | 7.54 | 0.49 | 7.27 | 8.50 | 7.69 | 0.00 | 5.34 | 6.00 | 5.36 | 0.05 |
| 1971 | 7.68 | 6.08 | 8.16 | 10.40 | 9.71 | 6.50 | 8.55 | 5.61 | 7.32 | 8.25 | 7.14 | 6.27 | 5.70 | 4.50 | 6.50 | 10.24 |
| 1972 | 7.48 | 3.99 | 8.09 | 0.98 | 9.19 | 5.00 | 8.03 | 3.86 | 7.14 | 4.00 | 5.33 | 2.57 | 4.99 | 4.00 | 7.03 | 3.74 |
| 1973 | 7.49 | 3.19 | 8.12 | 14.23 | 8.48 | 5.00 | 13.99 | 11.62 | 7.34 | 2.75 | 7.59 | 3.39 | 5.27 | 4.75 | 10.78 | 16.34 |
| 1974 | 9.01 | 6.88 | 10.80 | 12.69 | 9.31 | 7.36 | 16.75 | 1.49 | 7.37 | 2.50 | 11.76 | 12.42 | 6.31 | 5.40 | 8.72 | 27.72 |
| 1975 | 9.09 | 6.97 | 9.53 | −6.77 | 11.77 | 5.00 | 14.68 | −6.12 | 8.17 | 8.75 | 9.47 | −6.95 | 7.17 | 7.00 | 4.01 | −3.05 |
| 1976 | 8.37 | 5.87 | 8.51 | 9.42 | 11.71 | 7.75 | 19.77 | −12.39 | 9.15 | 9.62 | 9.62 | 6.28 | 6.39 | 5.50 | 1.09 | 6.92 |
| 1977 | 8.11 | 5.84 | 4.99 | 7.76 | 12.06 | 7.00 | 26.95 | −15.68 | 9.61 | 9.50 | 12.28 | −11.63 | 4.81 | 4.00 | 1.27 | 22.52 |
| 1978 | 8.05 | 4.50 | 4.07 | 15.79 | 13.23 | 8.00 | 16.08 | 15.41 | 9.84 | 9.00 | 7.81 | 8.71 | 4.44 | 3.75 | 0.58 | 23.46 |
| 1979 | 7.74 | 9.39 | 4.57 | 3.33 | 13.49 | 15.00 | 15.69 | 5.99 | 10.09 | 5.75 | 8.70 | 3.59 | 3.33 | 1.00 | 5.09 | 2.53 |
| 1980 | 8.78 | 13.80 | 6.70 | −10.52 | 12.94 | 12.50 | 15.22 | −16.53 | 10.47 | 9.50 | 14.15 | −5.18 | 3.45 | 2.00 | 4.47 | −10.28 |

| | United Kingdom | | | | United States | | | | United Kingdom | | | | United States | | |
|---|---|---|---|---|---|---|---|---|---|---|---|---|---|---|---|---|
| Year | LT Yield | ST Yield | Infla-tion Rate | Exch. Return | LT Yield | ST Yield | Infla-tion Rate | Year | LT Yield | ST Yield | Infla-tion Rate | Exch. Return | LT Yield | ST Yield | Infla-tion Rate |
| 1960 | 5.33 | 3.37 | 2.22 | −0.28 | 4.14 | 2.66 | 1.48 | 1971 | 8.93 | 6.95 | 9.16 | 6.63 | 6.25 | 4.39 | 3.36 |
| 1961 | 6.17 | 4.35 | 4.35 | 0.28 | 3.93 | 2.13 | 0.67 | 1972 | 7.09 | 4.46 | 7.73 | −7.98 | 6.06 | 3.84 | 3.41 |
| 1962 | 6.25 | 5.40 | 2.60 | −0.28 | 4.00 | 2.73 | 1.22 | 1973 | 9.36 | 8.48 | 10.38 | −0.93 | 7.12 | 6.93 | 8.80 |
| 1963 | 5.14 | 3.72 | 2.03 | −0.28 | 4.01 | 3.12 | 1.65 | 1974 | 12.64 | 12.82 | 18.12 | 0.94 | 8.07 | 8.00 | 12.20 |
| 1964 | 5.24 | 3.72 | 4.48 | 0.00 | 4.25 | 3.54 | 1.19 | 1975 | 16.32 | 11.44 | 25.29 | −13.77 | 8.41 | 5.80 | 7.01 |
| 1965 | 6.38 | 6.63 | 4.52 | 0.28 | 4.30 | 3.93 | 1.92 | 1976 | 13.57 | 10.64 | 14.95 | −15.84 | 8.10 | 5.08 | 4.81 |
| 1966 | 6.59 | 5.52 | 3.87 | −0.28 | 4.76 | 4.76 | 3.35 | 1977 | 15.17 | 13.51 | 13.09 | 11.81 | 7.85 | 5.12 | 6.77 |
| 1967 | 6.63 | 6.53 | 2.19 | −13.94 | 4.99 | 4.21 | 3.04 | 1978 | 10.67 | 6.29 | 8.05 | 6.71 | 8.64 | 7.18 | 9.03 |
| 1968 | 7.31 | 7.48 | 5.58 | −0.72 | 5.53 | 5.21 | 4.72 | 1979 | 13.11 | 11.56 | 17.23 | 9.33 | 9.42 | 10.38 | 13.31 |
| 1969 | 8.01 | 6.78 | 5.08 | 0.48 | 6.39 | 6.58 | 6.11 | 1980 | 14.96 | 15.84 | 15.15 | 7.40 | 11.24 | 11.24 | 12.40 |
| 1970 | 8.91 | 7.95 | 7.74 | −0.24 | 6.96 | 6.53 | 5.49 | | | | | | | | |

*Government bond yields are used wherever possible for the long-term yields. For Japan (certain years prior to 1966) and Spain (all years) corporate bond yields are used instead. All short-term yields are government yields.

**Table XII**  Dollar-Adjusted Equity Returns: Regressions on World Equities and Correlations with Bonds and Inflation

| Country or Region | Excess Return Regressions of Country Equities on World Equity Portfolio* | | | | Correlation Coefficients of Equity Returns | |
|---|---|---|---|---|---|---|
| | Alpha (%) | Alpha T-Statistic | Beta | $R^2$ | With Dollar-Adjusted Bonds | With Local Inflation Rates |
| Austria | 4.86 | 1.15 | 0.01 | 0.000 | 0.224 | 0.048 |
| Belgium | 2.44 | 0.82 | 0.45 | 0.217 | 0.491 | −0.113 |
| Denmark | 2.91 | 0.53 | 0.60 | 0.106 | 0.338 | −0.199 |
| France | 0.17 | 0.04 | 0.50 | 0.099 | 0.606 | 0.106 |
| Germany | 2.41 | 0.53 | 0.45 | 0.079 | 0.277 | −0.285 |
| Italy | −1.92 | −0.31 | 0.41 | 0.014 | 0.265 | −0.076 |
| Netherlands | 0.65 | 0.25 | 0.90 | 0.636 | −0.041 | 0.021 |
| Norway | 13.39 | 1.16 | −0.27 | 0.000 | N/A | −0.126 |
| Spain | 4.73 | 0.96 | 0.04 | 0.000 | 0.526 | −0.662 |
| Sweden | 1.69 | 0.48 | 0.51 | 0.195 | 0.325 | −0.168 |
| Switzerland | 2.66 | 0.58 | 0.87 | 0.312 | 0.143 | −0.300 |
| United Kingdom | 1.76 | 0.31 | 1.47 | 0.466 | 0.515 | 0.348 |
| Europe Total | 0.14 | 0.06 | 0.80 | 0.590 | — | — |
| Hong Kong** | 20.58 | 1.88 | 2.81 | 0.702 | N/A | N/A |
| Japan | 9.49 | 1.36 | 0.81 | 0.123 | 0.410 | −0.499 |
| Singapore** | 18.26 | 1.16 | 2.59 | 0.476 | N/A | N/A |
| Asia Total | 9.61 | 1.33 | 0.92 | 0.153 | — | — |
| Australia | 1.52 | 0.42 | 1.02 | 0.521 | N/A | −0.119 |
| Canada | 2.75 | 0.95 | 0.77 | 0.488 | 0.170 | −0.104 |
| Other Total | 2.17 | 0.93 | 0.85 | 0.648 | — | — |
| Non-U.S. Total | 1.97 | 0.90 | 0.86 | 0.685 | — | — |
| United States Total | −0.69 | −0.63 | 1.08 | 0.934 | 0.210 | −0.130 |

*Returns are measured in excess of the U.S. Treasury bill return, which was 5.4 per cent compounded annually over 1960-1980 and 6.7 per cent compounded annually over 1970-80 (the period for which the Hong Kong and Singapore regressions were run). The dependent variable in each case is the country or region's dollar-adjusted equity market year-by-year return from Table III, less the contemporaneous one-year return on rolled-over 30-day U.S. Treasury bills. The independent variable in each case is the dollar-adjusted world equity market portfolio year-by-year return from Table III, less the same Treasury bill returns.
**1970-1980.

it completely in forward markets, incurring some transaction costs in the process.

We have not determined whether the world capital market is segmented or integrated. Since international investment occurs, markets cannot be totally segmented. But interest rates and equi-

ty returns (and, we might speculate, equity expectations) appear to differ substantially from country to country. We view the world market as partly segmented and partly integrated, moving in the direction of integration as investors expand their horizons and foreign markets grow. ■

## Footnotes

1. Irving Fisher, *The Theory of Interest* (New York: Macmillan, 1980).
2. The most comprehensive treatment of the three intranational theories taken as a unit is in Roger G. Ibbotson and Rex A. Sinquefield (foreword by Laurence B. Siegel), *Stocks, Bonds, Bills, and Inflation: The Past and The Future* (1982 Edition) (Charlottesville, Va.: Financial Analysts Research Foundation, 1982).
3. Jacob A. Frenkel and Harry G. Johnson, eds., *The Economics of Exchange Rates: Selected Readings* (Reading, Mass.: Addison-Wesley, 1978).
4. Robert Z. Aliber, *Exchange Risk and Corporate International Finance* (New York: John Wiley & Sons, 1978). See especially Chapters 5, 6 and 7 for tests of international parity theorems.

5. Lawrence H. Officer, "The Purchasing Power Parity Theory of Exchange Rates: A Review Article," *Staff Papers*, March 1976.
6. Jacob A. Frenkel and Richard M. Levich, "Transactions Costs and Interest Arbitrage: Tranquil Versus Turbulent Periods," *Journal of Political Economy*, November/December 1977, pp. 1209-1226.
7. Richard M. Levich, "The Efficiency of Markets for Foreign Exchange: A Review and Extension," in *International Financial Management*, Donald R. Lessard, ed. (Boston: Warren, Gorham & Lamont, 1979), pp. 243-276; Bradford Cornell, "Spot Rates, Forward Rates, and Market Efficiency," *Journal of Financial Economics*, August 1977, pp. 55-65.
8. Richard E. Stehle, "An Empirical Test of the Alternative Hypotheses of National and International

Pricing of Risky Assets,'' *Journal of Finance,* May 1977, pp. 493-502.

9. Fischer Black, ''International Capital Market Equilibrium with Investment Barriers,'' *Journal of Financial Economics,* December 1974, pp. 337-352.

10. Donald R. Lessard, ''World, National, and Industry Factors in Equity Returns: Implications for Risk Reduction Through International Diversification,'' *Journal of Finance,* May 1974, pp. 379-391; Bruno H. Solnik, ''Why Not Diversify Internationally?'' *Financial Analysts Journal,* July/August 1974, pp. 48-54.

## Appendix: Sources and Methodology

The methodologies for arriving at returns and aggregate values in the U.S. and non-U.S. equity and bond markets are described below. The work for U.S. and non-U.S. equities and U.S. bonds was relatively straightforward, proceeding largely from published sources (although we sampled a few sectors); thus these sections are short. For non-U.S. bonds, we sampled bond-by-bond price data for some sectors and derived returns from yields, coupons and maturities for others. We therefore explicate the non-U.S. bond methodology in detail.

### U.S. Equities

The source for our returns and values series for U.S. equities is Ibbotson and Fall's ''The U.S. Market Wealth Portfolio,'' *Journal of Portfolio Management,* Fall 1979, updated using the methodology described there. Our return series represents a market-value-weighted portfolio of the New York and American Stock Exchanges and NASDAQ over-the-counter stocks. The aggregate market value series for U.S. equities is the sum of the market values of the three components.

### Non-U.S. Equities

We collected monthly exchange-rate-adjusted stock index values and dividend yields from *Capital International Perspective* (published by Capital International S.A., Geneva) for all 17 countries. The return data in *Capital International Perspective* are for the stocks (generally large companies) listed therein as components of their indexes. We collected data starting with 1970 for Hong Kong and Singapore and 1960 for all the other countries. For a given month, we calculated the total return as the sum of the capital appreciation return (change in stock index value) and the income return (one-twelfth of the contemporaneous annual dividend yield). In the several instances where dividend yields were not available from *Capital International Perspective,* we obtained them from The Organization for Economic Cooperation and Development (OECD) *Interest Rates 1960-1974.* A few remaining unavailable dividend yields were interpolated. We then linked (compounded) the monthly returns to form annual total returns and cumulative total return indexes.

Yearly aggregate market values were collected from *Capital International Perspective* for Australia, Belgium, France, Germany, Italy, Japan, the Netherlands, Spain, Sweden, Switzerland and the United Kingdom. These values represent Capital International's estimate of the market value of all traded equities in a given country, not just those large stocks used to construct the stock performance index. We note that in some countries (notably Germany) sole proprietorships make up a large fraction of equities; these equities, along with partnerships and many small corporations, are not included in our aggregate market value data.

For Austria, Canada, Denmark, Hong Kong, Norway and Singapore, we collected aggregate market value data as of the end of 1980 from *Capital International Perspective.* We estimated earlier years' values as follows: The value at the end of year n − 1 is taken as the end-of-year n value divided by the year n total return relative, starting with the end of 1980 figure and working backward (''extrapolation by returns'').

### U.S. Bonds

The U.S. domestic bond series for 1969-72 consists of a market-value-weighted portfolio of Treasury notes and bonds, agencies, and intermediate and long-term corporates and preferred stocks. The total return and market value series for Treasury notes and bonds and both categories of corporates are taken from Ibbotson and Fall, as are the market values for preferred stocks. We calculated the return series for preferreds from High Grade Public Utility yields in *Moody's Public Utility Manual,* assuming an infinite maturity.

The market values for agencies were obtained from the annual *Flow of Funds Accounts,* published by The Board of Governors of the Federal Reserve System. To obtain return series for agencies, we constructed a one-bond portfolio using prices and coupons quoted in the *Bank and Quotation Record.* Our method was to ''purchase'' an agency bond with five years to maturity at the beginning of the year. The bond was then ''sold'' one year later.

The return was measured as the change in price plus the coupon.

Returns for 1973-80 are taken from the Lehman Brothers Kuhn Loeb Government/Corporate Bond Index. The aggregate market value at the end of 1980 is derived using the methodology of Ibbotson and Fall and includes municipal bonds (although the return series does not).

### Non-U.S. Domestic Bonds

For each non-U.S. country, the return on that country's domestic bonds is taken to be the market-value-weighted average of the return on the country's cash equivalents, corporate bonds and government bonds. Where either weights or returns were unavailable for a component, that component received a zero weight.

Year-end 1980 aggregate market values for bonds as displayed in the figures and tables are taken from Jeffrey D. Hanna and David Johnson's Salomon Brothers *International Bond Market Analysis* paper, ''How Big Is the World Bond Market?'' (October 15, 1981) for the countries (United States, Japan, West Germany, United Kingdom, France, Canada, Switzerland and the Netherlands) treated therein. Values for other countries are taken from the OECD *Financial Statistics: Part I* and The International Monetary Fund (IMP) *Government Finance Statistics Yearbook*.

#### Cash Equivalents

We calculated all cash returns as the yield on Treasury bills (or equivalent) lagged one year. The 1959 yields (1960 returns) for Austria, Denmark, Italy, Japan, Norway, Spain and Sweden, and the 1979 yields (1980 returns) for France and Switzerland, are official discount rates rather than market yields on Treasury bills. The sources of data are the OECD *Interest Rates 1960-1974* and *Financial Statistics: Part I* for 1960-1979 yields, and the IMF *International Financial Statistics* for 1959 yields.

Year-by-year aggregate market values for non-U.S. cash equivalents for weighting returns are taken from the IMF *Government Finance Statistics Yearbook*, Table G. Values for the years for which data were unavailable are estimated by geometric interpolation where possible and extrapolation by returns elsewhere.

#### Calculation of Bond Returns

The returns on non-U.S. corporate and government bonds are calculated from beginning and end-of-year yields and (actual or assumed) maturities. We assume that the coupon is equal to the beginning-of-year yield and that there is one coupon payment per year received at year-end.

### Non-U.S. Corporate Bonds

Yield data for non-U.S. corporate bonds were supplied by Wendy Freyer of R.G. Ibbotson & Company and are based on the OECD *Interest Rates 1960-1974* and OECD *Financial Statistics: Part I*. The year-end yield for all years except 1959 was used. For 1959, the yield on 1/31/60 (the date closest to year-end 1959 for which data were available) was used.

Secondary market yields on industrial and/or private sector bonds were used. Where secondary market yields were unavailable, primary market (issue) yields were used. Where no industrial or private sector yields were quoted in a given year, the country was omitted for that year.

To fill gaps in yield series, economically related series were used—Nippon Telephone and Telegraph bonds as a proxy for Japanese corporate bonds for 1963-65 and electricity supply services bonds as a proxy for Austrian corporate bonds for 1965-70.

We derived our maturity assumptions from the written description of the yield series in the relevant source. We assumed constant maturities for Austria (10 years), Belgium (seven years), Canada (12 years), France (15 years), Germany (four years), Italy (13.5 years), Japan (4.5 years), Spain (17.5 years) and the United Kingdom (20 years). For the Netherlands, we assumed a maturity of 10 years for 1959-65; 15 years for 1966, decreasing by one year each year through 1976; 4.5 years for 1977; four years for 1978; three years for 1979; and nine years for 1980.

Year-by-year aggregate market values of non-U.S. corporate bonds for weighting returns were supplied by Robert Ferguson of The First National Bank of Chicago (FNBC) and are based on OECD data. Missing years were filled in by adding or subtracting new issuance (from OECD *Financial Statistics: Part I*), geometric interpolation or extrapolation by returns.

### Non-U.S. Government Bonds

For non-U.S. government bonds, yield data for 1960-78 for all countries were obtained by Wendy Freyer from the OECD *Interest Rates 1960-1974* and OECD *Financial Statistics: Part I*. In addition, we used yields from OECD *Financial Statistics: Part I* for the United Kingdom for 1979 and 1980. The 1959 yields were collected from the IMF *International Financial Statistics*. Yields for 1979 and 1980 for all countries except the United Kingdom were obtained from International Monetary Fund data reported in *Moody's International Manual 1981*.

Based on written descriptions in the relevant

sources, we assumed constant maturities for Austria (10 years), Belgium (seven years), Canada (15 years), France (15 years), Germany (seven years), Japan (four years), the Netherlands (10 years), Switzerland (7.65 years) and the United Kingdom (10 years). For Denmark, we assumed a maturity of 38 years for 1959, decreasing by one year each year through 1975; for 1976, we assumed a maturity of six years, decreasing by one year for each year thereafter. For Italy, we assumed a maturity of 17.5 years for 1959-75 and seven years thereafter. For Sweden, we assumed a maturity of 7.5 years for 1959-64 and 10 years thereafter.

Year-by-year aggregate market values of non-U.S. government bonds for weighting returns are taken from the IMF *Government Finance Statistics Yearbook* and the OECD *Financial Statistics: Part I*. Missing years are filled in by geometric interpolation or extrapolation by returns.

## Crossborder Bonds

Robert Ferguson of The First National Bank of Chicago supplied us with bond-by-bond price, coupon and amount outstanding data on the universe of crossborder bonds for 1960-72. We calculated year-by-year total returns for each bond using the assumption that the coupon and capital gain were both received on the last day of each year (thus there is no reinvestment return). We included only bonds denominated in U.S. dollars (or Eurodollars) and Deutschemarks (or Euro-DM). We excluded other currency bonds because there were too few to eliminate sampling error. We excluded choice-of-currency bonds, bonds denominated in Units of Account, bonds with convertibility features, warrants and other non-bond attributes, Israeli savings series (which are redeemable at par before maturity by U.S. and other tourists in Israel), floating rate notes (which trade like cash), Cuban bonds in default, and bonds trading at very low prices (generally under $10). Then, using the previous year-end amounts outstanding supplied by FNBC as weights, we formed value-weighted portfolio returns for U.S. dollar and Deutschemark crossborder bonds for 1960-72.

For 1975-80, we obtained monthly bond-by-bond price and coupon data from a sample of bonds denominated in U.S. dollars, Deutschemarks, Japanese yen, Dutch guilders, Swiss francs and other currency sectors. Within each currency sector, bonds were selected using a sample stratified by maturity. Bond price and coupon data came from 19 sources. We calculated month-

ly returns and formed currency sector portfolios wherein the weight of each bond was equal to the market value (at previous month-end) of the bond's maturity category as a proportion of the market value of the whole currency sector, divided by the number of bonds in the maturity category. We then linked (compounded) the monthly portfolio returns to form the annual returns reported herein. To determine the relative sizes of the maturity categories for use in the above calculation, we aggregated bond maturity and amount outstanding data from numerous sources.

Year-end 1980 aggregate market values of crossborder bonds, by currency sector, are taken from Hanna and Johnson.

For 1973-74, we had no price data for crossborder bonds. We therefore calculated the arithmetic annual mean excess return of U.S. crossborder bonds over U.S. domestic bonds (see the section on U.S. bonds above) for the 19 years for which we had data, 1960-72 and 1975-80. This excess return, 1.70 per cent per year, was added to the U.S. domestic bond total return for each of the years 1973 and 1974 to produce U.S. dollar crossborder bond returns for those years. We performed a similar procedure for Deutschemark bonds for 1973-74, using the excess return of Deutschemark crossborder bonds over German domestic corporate bonds as presented herein. This excess return was 0.17 per cent per year.

## Other Statistics

All exchange rates were supplied as dollars per unit of foreign currency by L. Randolph Hood, Jr. of FNBC, based on DRI-FACS (Data Resources, Inc.) data. We converted these rates to returns (changes in exchange rate).

Inflation rates were obtained as consumer price indexes and converted to returns. The consumer price series for the United States came from the Bureau of Labor Statistics, U.S. Department of Labor. Data for all other countries were obtained from the OECD *Main Economic Indicators* for 1961-79 and from OECD *Financial Statistics: Part I* for 1980. For 1960, we only had data on the last three quarters of the year for non-U.S. countries. We calculated non-U.S. inflation rates for 1960, therefore, as the annualized rate over the three quarters.

Population and gross domestic product data were obtained from the 1982 *World Almanac*. The Hong Kong gross domestic product was taken from "Hong Kong," *Business Profile Series*, published by The Hongkong and Shanghai Banking Corporation.

# Why Does Stock Market Volatility Change Over Time?

G. WILLIAM SCHWERT*

## ABSTRACT

This paper analyzes the relation of stock volatility with real and nominal macroeconomic volatility, economic activity, financial leverage, and stock trading activity using monthly data from 1857 to 1987. An important fact, previously noted by Officer (1973), is that stock return variability was unusually high during the 1929–1939 Great Depression. While aggregate leverage is significantly correlated with volatility, it explains a relatively small part of the movements in stock volatility. The amplitude of the fluctuations in aggregate stock volatility is difficult to explain using simple models of stock valuation, especially during the Great Depression.

ESTIMATES OF THE STANDARD deviation of monthly stock returns vary from two to twenty percent per month during the 1857–1987 period. Tests for whether differences this large could be attributable to estimation error strongly reject the hypothesis of constant variance. Large changes in the ex ante volatility of market returns have important negative effects on risk-averse investors. Moreover, changes in the level of market volatility can have important effects on capital investment, consumption, and other business cycle variables. This raises the question of why stock volatility changes so much over time.

Many researchers have studied movements in aggregate stock market volatility. Officer (1973) relates these changes to the volatility of macroeconomic variables. Black (1976) and Christie (1982) argue that financial leverage partly explains this phenomenon. Recently, there have been many attempts to relate changes in stock market volatility to changes in expected returns to stocks, including Merton (1980), Pindyck (1984), Poterba and Summers (1986), French, Schwert, and Stambaugh (1987), Bollerslev, Engle, and Wooldridge (1988), and Abel (1988). Mascaro and Meltzer (1983) and Lauterbach (1989) find that macroeconomic volatility is related to interest rates.

Shiller (1981a,b) argues that the level of stock market volatility is too high relative to the ex post variability of dividends. In present value models such as Shiller's, a change in the volatility of either future cash flows or discount rates

* William E. Simon Graduate School of Business Administration, University of Rochester, and National Bureau of Economic Research. I received helpful comments from David Backus, Fischer Black, Marie Davidian, Harry DeAngelo, Beni Lauterbach, Ron Masulis, Grant McQueen, Robert Merton, Dan Nelson, Charles Plosser, Paul Seguin, Robert Stambaugh, Jerold Zimmerman, seminar participants at Yale University and at the Universities of Chicago, Michigan, Rochester, and Washington, and three anonymous referees. Ken French and René Stulz deserve special credit for their help. The Bradley Policy Research Center at the University of Rochester provided support for this research.

causes a change in the volatility of stock returns. There have been many critiques of Shiller's work, notably Kleidon (1986). Nevertheless, the literature on "excess volatility" has not addressed the question of why stock return volatility is higher at some times than at others.

This paper characterizes the changes in stock market volatility through time. In particular, it relates stock market volatility to the time-varying volatility of a variety of economic variables. Relative to the 1857–1987 period, volatility was unusually high from 1929 to 1939 for many economic series, including inflation, money growth, industrial production, and other measures of economic activity. Stock market volatility increases with financial leverage, as predicted by Black and Christie, although this factor explains only a small part of the variation in stock volatility. In addition, interest rate and corporate bond return volatility are correlated with stock return volatility. Finally, stock market volatility increases during recessions. None of these factors, however, plays a dominant role in explaining the behavior of stock volatility over time.

It is useful to think of the stock price, $P_t$ as the discounted present value of expected future cash flows to stockholders:

$$E_{t-1} P_t = E_{t-1} \sum_{k=1}^{\infty} \frac{D_{t+k}}{[1 + R_{t+k}]^k} \tag{1}$$

where $D_{t+k}$ is the capital gain plus dividends paid to stockholders in period $t + k$ and $1/[1 + R_{t+k}]$ is the discount rate for period $t + k$ based on information available at time $t - 1$. ($E_{t-1}$ denotes the conditional expectation.) The conditional variance of the stock price at time $t - 1$, $\text{var}_{t-1}(P_t)$, depends on the conditional variances of expected future cash flows and of future discount rates, and on the conditional covariances between these series.[1]

At the aggregate level, the value of corporate equity clearly depends on the health of the economy. If discount rates are constant over time in (1), the conditional variance of security prices is proportional to the conditional variance of the expected future cash flows. Thus, it is plausible that a change in the level of uncertainty about future macroeconomic conditions would cause a proportional change in stock return volatility.[2] If macroeconomic data provide information about the volatility of either future expected cash flows or future discount rates, they can help explain why stock return volatility changes over time. "Fads" or "bubbles" in stock prices would introduce additional sources of volatility.

Section I describes the time series properties of the data and the strategy for modeling time-varying volatility. Section II analyzes the relations of stock and bond return volatility with the volatility of inflation, money growth, and industrial production. Section III studies the relation between stock market volatility

---

[1] The variance of the sum of a sequence of ratios of random variables is not a simple function of the variances and covariances of the variables in the ratios, but standard asymptotic approximations depend on these parameters.

[2] For a positively autocorrelated variable, such as the volatility series in Table II, an unexpected increase in the variable implies an increase in expected future values of the series for many steps ahead. Given the discounting in (1), the volatility series will move almost proportionally. See Poterba and Summers (1986) for a simple model that posits a particular ARIMA process for the behavior of the time-varying parameters in a related context.

and macroeconomic activity. Section IV analyzes the relation between financial leverage and stock return volatility. Section V analyzes the relation between stock market trading activity and volatility. Finally, Section VI synthesizes the results from the preceding sections and presents concluding remarks.

## I. The Time Series Behavior of Stock and Bond Return Volatility

### A. *Volatility of Stock Returns*

Following French, Schwert, and Stambaugh (1987), I estimate the monthly standard deviation of stock returns using the daily returns to the Standard and Poor's (S&P) composite portfolio from January 1928 through December 1987. The estimates from February 1885 through December 1927 use daily returns on the Dow Jones composite portfolio. (See Schwert (1989d) for a more detailed description of these data.) The estimator of the variance of the monthly return is the sum of the squared daily returns (after subtracting the average daily return in the month):

$$\hat{\sigma}_t^2 = \sum_{i=1}^{N_t} r_{it}^2,\qquad(2)$$

where there are $N_t$ daily returns $r_{it}$ in month $t$.[3] Using nonoverlapping samples of daily data to estimate the monthly variance creates estimation error that is uncorrelated through time.[4]

Daily stock return data are not readily available before 1885. Also, macroeconomic data are rarely measured more often than monthly. To estimate volatility from monthly data, I use the following procedure:

(i) Estimate a 12th-order autoregression for the returns, including dummy variables $D_{jt}$ to allow for different monthly mean returns, using all data available for the series,

$$R_t = \sum_{j=1}^{12} \alpha_j D_{jt} + \sum_{i=1}^{12} \beta_i R_{t-i} + \varepsilon_t.\qquad(3a)$$

(ii) Estimate a 12th-order autoregression for the absolute values of the errors from (3a), including dummy variables to allow for different monthly standard deviations,

$$|\hat{\varepsilon}_t| = \sum_{j=1}^{12} \gamma_j D_{jt} + \sum_{i=1}^{12} \rho_i |\hat{\varepsilon}_{t-i}| + u_t.\qquad(3b)$$

---

[3] French, Schwert, and Stambaugh (1987) use one lagged cross-covariance in (2), and they make no adjustment for the mean return. Their estimator is not guaranteed to be positive. Indeed, for one month in the 1885–1927 period, the French, Schwert, and Stambaugh estimate of volatility is negative. The estimates from (2) are very similar to the French, Schwert, and Stambaugh estimates, except that they are always positive.

[4] If the data are normally distributed, the variance of the estimator $\hat{\sigma}_t$ is $\sigma_t^2/2N_t$, where $\sigma_t^2$ is the true variance (Kendall and Stuart (1969, p. 243)). Thus, for $N_t = 22$ and $\sigma_t = 0.04$, the standard error of $\hat{\sigma}_t$ is 0.006, which is small relative to the level of $\sigma_t$. Since this is a classic errors-in-variables problem, the autocorrelations of the estimates $\hat{\sigma}_t$ will be smaller than, but will decay at the same rate as, the autocorrelations of the true values $\sigma_t$.

(iii) The regressand $|\hat{\varepsilon}_t|$ is an estimate of the standard deviation of the stock market return for month $t$ similar to $\hat{\sigma}_t$ (although it uses one rather than 22 observations). The fitted values from (3b) $|\tilde{\varepsilon}_t|$ estimate the conditional standard deviation of $R_t$, given information available before month $t$.[5]

This method is a generalization of the 12-month rolling standard deviation estimator used by Officer (1973), Fama (1976), and Merton (1980) because it allows the conditional mean return to vary over time in (3a) and allows different weights for lagged absolute unexpected returns in (3b). It is similar to the autoregressive conditional heteroskedasticity (ARCH) model of Engle (1982). Davidian and Carroll (1987) argue that standard deviation specifications such as (3b) are more robust than variance specifications based on $\hat{\varepsilon}_t^2$. They also argue that iterated weighted least squares (WLS) estimates, iterating between (3a) and (3b), provide more efficient estimates. Following their suggestion, I iterate three times between (3a) and (3b) to compute WLS estimates.

Figure 1 plots the predicted standard deviations from monthly returns $|\tilde{\varepsilon}_{st}|$ for 1859–1987, along with the predicted standard deviations from daily returns $\tilde{\sigma}_t$ (from a 12th-order autoregression for $\hat{\sigma}_t$ as in (3b)) for 1885–1987. Volatility predictions from the daily data are much higher following the 1929 and 1987 stock market crashes because there were very large daily returns in October 1929 and October 1987. Otherwise, Figure 1 shows that the predicted volatility series are similar. Stock return volatility is persistent over time.

## B. *Volatility of Bond Returns*

If the underlying business risk of the firm rises, the risk of both the stock and the bonds of the firm should increase. Also, if leverage increases, both the stocks and the bonds of the firm become more risky. Thus, in many instances the risk of corporate stock and long-term corporate debt should change over time in similar ways.

Figure 2 plots the predicted standard deviations of long-term corporate bond returns $|\tilde{\varepsilon}_{rht}|$ for 1859–1987. It also shows the predicted standard deviations of stock returns $|\tilde{\varepsilon}_{st}|$ for comparison. Note that the scale of the right-hand bond return axis is about three times smaller than the scale of the left-hand stock return axis, showing that the standard deviation of monthly stock returns is about three times larger than for bond returns over this period. There are many similarities between predicted volatilities of stock and bond returns. In particular, volatility was very high from 1929 to 1939 compared with the rest of the 1859–1987 period. Moreover, bond returns were unusually volatile in the periods during and immediately following the Civil War (1861–1865). In recent times, the "OPEC oil shock" (1973–1974) caused an increase in the volatility of stock and bond returns.

Figure 3 plots the predicted standard deviations of short-term interest rates $|\tilde{\varepsilon}_{rst}|$ for 1859–1987. The volatility of $Int_t$ measures time variation in the ex ante

---

[5] Since the expected value of the absolute error is less than the standard deviation from a normal distribution, $E|\hat{\varepsilon}_{st}| = \sigma_t (2/\pi)^{1/2}$, all absolute errors are multiplied by the constant $(2/\pi)^{-1/2} \approx 1.2533$. Dan Nelson suggested this correction.

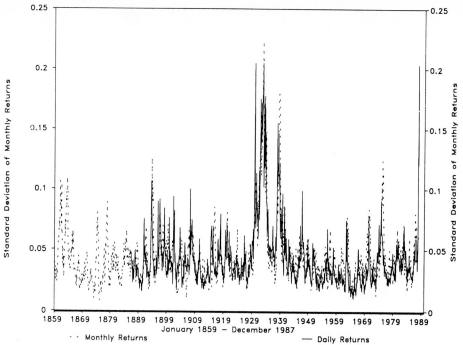

**Figure 1. Predictions of the monthly standard deviation of stock returns based on monthly data (– – –) for 1859–1987 and on daily data (——) for 1886–1987.** For monthly returns, a 12th-order autoregression with different monthly intercepts is used to model returns, and then the absolute values of the residuals are used to estimate volatility in month $t$. For daily returns, the returns in the month are used to estimate a sample deviation for each month. To model conditional volatility, a 12th-order autoregressive model with different monthly intercepts is used to predict the standard deviation in month $t$ based on lagged standard deviation estimates. This plot contains fitted values from the volatility regression models.

nominal interest rate, not risk, since these securities are essentially default free.[6] Note that the right-hand interest rate volatility scale is over 12 times smaller than the left-hand stock volatility scale. There are periods in the 19th century when short-term interest rate volatility rose for brief periods, many of which were associated with banking panics. (See Schwert (1989b).) It is clear from Figures 2 and 3 that long-term bond return and short-term interest rate volatility increased dramatically around 1979. There is not a similar increase in stock return volatility. As noted by Huizinga and Mishkin (1986), the Federal Reserve Board changed its operating procedures to focus on monetary aggregate targets at that time.

The plots in Figures 2 and 3 are consistent with the following simple story. Short-term interest rate and long-term bond return volatility have similarities due to inflation and monetary policy. Stock and long-term bond return volatility have similarities due to real financial and business risk.

Table I contains means, standard deviations, skewness, and kurtosis coeffi-

---

[6] See Fama (1976) for an analysis of the variability of short-term nominal interest rates.

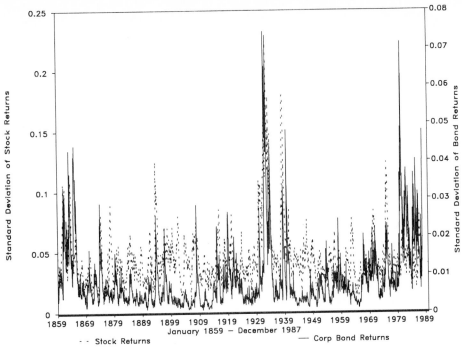

**Figure 2. Predictions of the monthly standard deviations of stock returns (−−−) and of high-grade long-term corporate bond returns (——) for 1859–1987.** A 12th-order autoregression with different monthly intercepts is used to model returns, and then the absolute values of the residuals are used to estimate volatility in month $t$. To model conditional volatility, a 12th-order autoregressive model with different monthly intercepts is used to predict the standard deviation in month $t$ based on lagged standard deviation estimates. This plot contains fitted values from the volatility regression models.

cients and autocorrelations of the estimates of stock return volatility based on monthly and daily data, $|\hat{\varepsilon}_{st}|$ and $\hat{\sigma}_t$. It also contains summary statistics for estimates of the volatility of short- and long-term bond returns, $|\hat{\varepsilon}_{rst}|$ and $|\hat{\varepsilon}_{rht}|$, inflation, $|\hat{\varepsilon}_{pt}|$, money growth, $|\hat{\varepsilon}_{mt}|$, and industrial production, $|\hat{\varepsilon}_{it}|$.[7]

Table II summarizes the autoregressions used to predict volatility. The sum of the autoregressive coefficients measures the persistence of the volatility series, where a value of unity implies nonstationarity. (See Engle and Bollerslev (1986) for a discussion of integrated conditional heteroskedasticity.) The $F$-test measures whether there is significant deterministic seasonal variation in the average volatility estimates. The coefficient of determination $R^2$ and the Box-Pierce (1970) statistic $Q(24)$ measure the adequacy of the fit of the model.

As suggested by the analysis in footnote 1, the estimates of volatility from daily data have much less error than the estimates from monthly data. The sample standard deviation of $|\hat{\varepsilon}_{st}|$ is about sixty percent larger than that of $\hat{\sigma}_t$ from 1885 to 1987, though the average values are similar. Moreover, the autocor-

---

[7] See Table AI in the Appendix for a brief description of the variables used in this paper.

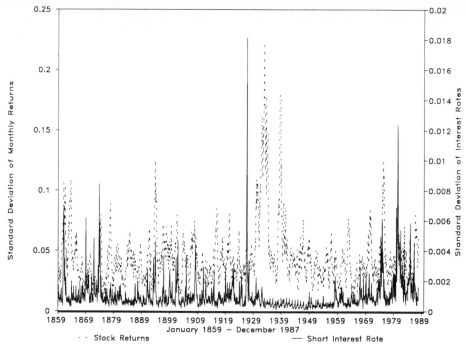

**Figure 3. Predictions of the monthly standard deviations of stock returns (---) and of short-term interest rates (——) for 1859–1987.** A 12th-order autoregression with different monthly intercepts is used to model returns or interest rates, and then the absolute values of the residuals are used to estimate volatility in month $t$. To model conditional volatility, a 12th-order autoregressive model with different monthly intercepts is used to predict the standard deviation in month $t$ based on lagged standard deviation estimates. This plot contains fitted values from the volatility regression models.

relations of $\hat{\sigma}_t$ are much larger than those of $|\hat{\varepsilon}_{st}|$, though they decay slowly for both series. This slow decay shows that stock volatility is highly persistent, perhaps nonstationary. (See Poterba and Summers (1986) and Schwert (1987) for further discussion.) The correlation between $|\hat{\varepsilon}_{st}|$ and $\hat{\sigma}_t$ is 0.56 from 1885 to 1987, and the correlation between the volatility predictions $|\tilde{\varepsilon}_{st}|$ and $\tilde{\sigma}_t$ is 0.78 from 1886 to 1987. The two methods of predicting volatility have similar time series properties.

The autocorrelations in Table I and the summary statistics for the estimated models in Table II are similar for all the volatility series. The autocorrelations are small (between 0.2 and 0.4), but they decay very slowly. This is consistent with conditional volatility being an integrated moving average process, so shocks to volatility have both permanent and transitory parts. The unit root tests in Table II show that most of the sums of the autoregressive coefficients are reliably different from unity using the tables in Fuller (1976). However, Schwert (1987, 1989a) shows that the Fuller critical values are misleading in situations such as this. The estimation error in the monthly volatility estimates biases the unit root

Table I

## Summary Statistics for Monthly Estimates of the Standard Deviations of Stock Returns, Bond Returns, and Growth Rates of the Producer Price Index, the Monetary Base, and Industrial Production, 1858–1987

The summary statistics are the means, standard deviations, skewness, kurtosis, and autocorrelations at lags 1, 2, 11, and 12 of the monthly standard deviation estimates and the Box-Pierce (1970) statistic for 24 lags of the autocorrelations $Q(24)$. A 12th-order autoregression with different monthly intercepts is used to model the growth rates, and then the absolute values of the errors from this model estimate the monthly standard deviations. The exception is the estimate of stock market volatility based on daily stock returns within the month. For further details, see equations (3a) and (3b) in the text and the data appendix.

| Volatility Series | Sample Period | Sample Size | Mean | Std. Dev. | Skewness | Kurtosis | Autocorrelations | | | | | |
|---|---|---|---|---|---|---|---|---|---|---|---|---|
| | | | | | | | $r_1$ | $r_2$ | $r_3$ | $r_{11}$ | $r_{12}$ | $Q(24)$ |
| Monthly stock returns | 1858–1987 | 1560 | 0.0444 | 0.0435 | 3.06 | 17.59 | 0.21 | 0.19 | 0.24 | 0.19 | 0.16 | 913 |
| Monthly stock returns | 1885–1987 | 1235 | 0.0455 | 0.0450 | 3.16 | 18.43 | 0.20 | 0.20 | 0.25 | 0.18 | 0.17 | 807 |
| Daily stock returns | 1885–1987 | 1235 | 0.0415 | 0.0272 | 3.16 | 14.29 | 0.69 | 0.58 | 0.51 | 0.44 | 0.44 | 5711 |
| Monthly short-term interest rates | 1858–1987 | 1560 | 0.0010 | 0.0141 | 5.42 | 53.21 | 0.43 | 0.34 | 0.19 | 0.14 | 0.16 | 1053 |
| Monthly high-quality long-term bond returns | 1858–1987 | 1560 | 0.0084 | 0.0116 | 3.25 | 13.76 | 0.42 | 0.32 | 0.34 | 0.25 | 0.22 | 2589 |
| Monthly medium-quality long-term bond returns | 1920–1987 | 816 | 0.0163 | 0.0223 | 5.25 | 47.94 | 0.40 | 0.25 | 0.33 | 0.26 | 0.24 | 1256 |
| PPI inflation rates | 1858–1987 | 1560 | 0.0127 | 0.0161 | 3.33 | 16.46 | 0.48 | 0.37 | 0.28 | 0.25 | 0.24 | 2586 |
| Monetary base growth rates | 1879–1987 | 1302 | 0.0080 | 0.0102 | 3.36 | 16.01 | 0.43 | 0.34 | 0.24 | 0.30 | 0.29 | 1549 |
| Industrial production growth rates | 1890–1987 | 1175 | 0.0184 | 0.0202 | 2.20 | 6.67 | 0.41 | 0.31 | 0.30 | 0.20 | 0.19 | 1486 |

Table II

## Summary Statistics for Autoregressive Predictive Models for the Volatility of Stock Returns, Bond Returns, and the Growth Rates of the Producer Price Index, the Monetary Base, and Industrial Production, 1859–1987

A 12th-order autoregression with different monthly intercepts is used to model the growth rates or returns, and then the absolute values of the errors from this model $|\hat{\epsilon}_t|$ estimate the monthly standard deviations. The exception is the estimate of stock market volatility based on daily stock returns within the month. The 12th-order autoregression for the volatility estimates is

$$|\hat{\epsilon}_t| = \sum_{j=1}^{12} \gamma_j D_{jt} + \sum_{i=1}^{12} \rho_i |\hat{\epsilon}_{t-1}| + u_t. \tag{3b}$$

This table shows the sum of the autoregressive coefficients ($\rho_1 + \cdots + \rho_{12}$), indicating the persistence of volatility. A $t$-test for whether the sum equals unity, indicating nonstationarity, is in parentheses below the sum. It also shows an $F$-test for the equality of the 12 monthly intercepts ($\gamma_1 = \cdots = \gamma_{12}$) and its $p$-value. Finally, it shows the coefficient of determination $R^2$ and the Box-Pierce (1970) $Q(24)$ statistic for the residual autocorrelations (which should be distributed as $\chi^2 (12)$ in this case).

| Volatility Series | Sum of AR Coefficients ($t$-test vs. one) | F-Test for Equal Monthly Intercepts ($p$-value) | $R^2$ | $Q(24)$ |
|---|---|---|---|---|
| Monthly stock returns | 0.8471 (−3.72) | 0.97 (0.475) | 0.132 | 45.8 |
| Daily stock returns | 0.9634 (−1.07) | 0.59 (0.838) | 0.524 | 60.2 |
| Monthly short-term interest rates | 0.7925 (−4.40) | 1.96 (0.028) | 0.371 | 19.5 |
| Monthly high-quality long-term bond returns | 0.8376 (−4.20) | 0.59 (0.835) | 0.260 | 59.4 |
| Monthly medium-quality long-term bond returns | 0.7769 (−3.47) | 6.78 (0.000) | 0.280 | 16.6 |
| PPI inflation rates | 0.8438 (−4.29) | 0.39 (0.961) | 0.271 | 53.1 |
| Monetary base growth rates | 0.7918 (−4.74) | 0.65 (0.787) | 0.220 | 37.0 |
| Industrial production growth rates | 0.8336 (−3.82) | 0.42 (0.948) | 0.219 | 46.9 |

estimates toward stationarity.[8] The results for the estimate of stock volatility from daily data $\hat{\sigma}_t$ support this conclusion since the sum of the autoregressive coefficients is closer to unity and the test statistic is small.

## C. Measurement Problems—The Effects of Diversification

Even though the set of stocks contained in the "market" portfolio changes over time, the behavior of volatility is not affected. There are few stocks in the sample

---

[8] Also see Pagan and Ullah (1988) for a discussion of the errors-in-variables problem associated with models like (3b).

in 1857, and they are all railroad stocks. Nevertheless, they represent most of the actively traded equity securities at that time. Also, railroads owned a wide variety of assets at that time. I have calculated tests for changes in stock volatility around the times when major changes in the composition of the portfolio occurred, and, surprisingly, there is no evidence of significant changes. Schwert (1989d) analyzes several alternative indices of United States stock returns for the 19th century and finds that the different portfolios have similar volatility after 1834. Though the number of securities and industries included has grown over time, the plot of stock return volatility in Figure 1 does not show a downward trend.

This conclusion contrasts with the analysis of unemployment, industrial production, and gross national product data by Romer (1986a,b, 1989). Also, when the Bureau of Labor Statistics has expanded the monthly sample used to calculate the CPI inflation series, there have been noticeable reductions in the volatility of measured inflation rates. Shapiro (1988) argues that the stability of stock return volatility between the 19th and 20th centuries supports Romer's conclusions that the higher level of volatility in pre-1930 macroeconomic data is primarily due to measurement problems. Nonetheless, it is perhaps surprising that stock return volatility is not higher in the 19th century due to measurement problems.

## II. Relations between Stock Market Volatility and Macroeconomic Volatility

### A. Volatility of Inflation and Monetary Growth

The stock returns analyzed above all measure nominal (dollar) payoffs. When inflation of goods' prices is uncertain, the volatility of nominal asset returns should reflect inflation volatility. I use the algorithm in equations (3a) and (3b) to estimate monthly inflation volatility from 1858 to 1987 for the PPI inflation rate. Figure 4 plots the predicted PPI inflation volatility $|\tilde{\varepsilon}_{pt}|$ from 1859 to 1987. Note that the right-hand PPI inflation volatility axis is about ⅔ smaller than the left-hand stock volatility axis. The volatility of inflation was very high around the Civil War (1860–1869), reflecting changes in the value of currency relative to gold after the U.S. went off the gold standard in 1862. Since the U.K. remained on the gold standard, this also represents volatility in the exchange rates between U.S. and U.K. currencies. The Spanish-American War (1898), World War I and its aftermath (1914–1921), and World War II (1941–1946) are also periods of high inflation uncertainty. Another increase in inflation volatility occurred during the 1973–1974 OPEC oil crisis. While inflation volatility increased during the 1929–1939 period, this change is minor compared with the volatility that occurred during wars.

Figure 5 plots the predicted volatility of the monetary base growth rates $|\tilde{\varepsilon}_{mt}|$ from 1880 to 1987. The volatility of money base growth rates rose during the bank panic and recession of 1893 and remained high until about 1900. The next sharp increase in volatility occurred during the bank panic of 1907. The period following the formation of the Federal Reserve System (1914–1923) was another period of high volatility. Finally, the period of the Great Depression (1929–1939)

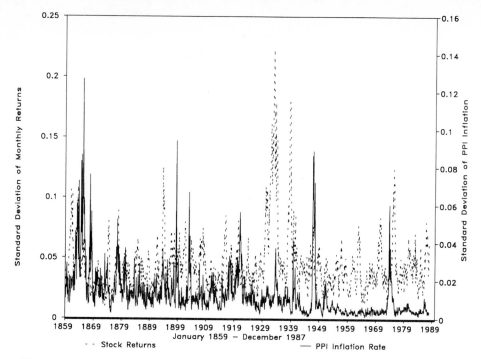

**Figure 4. Predictions of the monthly standard deviations of stock returns (– – –) and of producer price index inflation rates (——) for 1859–1987.** A 12th-order autoregression with different monthly intercepts is used to model returns or inflation rates, and then the absolute values of the residuals are used to estimate volatility in month $t$. To model conditional volatility, a 12th-order autoregressive model with different monthly intercepts is used to predict the standard deviation in month $t$ based on lagged standard deviation estimates. This plot contains fitted values from the volatility regression models.

was a period of very high volatility. Since the early 1950's, the volatility of the monetary base growth rate has been relatively low and stable.[9]

Both the PPI inflation rate and the monetary base growth rate exhibit much lower levels of volatility after World War II. In each case, the sample used to measure these variables has expanded over time, and there have been major institutional changes that have been intended to dampen macroeconomic fluctuations. Without detailed analysis similar to Romer's work on industrial production, unemployment, and gross national product, it is impossible to tell how important the changes in measurement techniques have been in reducing volatility.

Table III contains tests of the incremental predictive power of 12 lags of PPI inflation volatility $|\hat{\varepsilon}_{pt}|$ in a 12th-order vector autoregressive (VAR) system for

---

[9] It is surprising that the pattern of volatility is so different for the money base growth rate and the PPI inflation rate. Nevertheless, I have also analyzed the volatility of money supply ($M2$) growth and the Consumer Price Index (CPI) inflation rates since 1915, and they lead to similar conclusions. The lack of relation between monetary volatility and price volatility is an interesting question for future research.

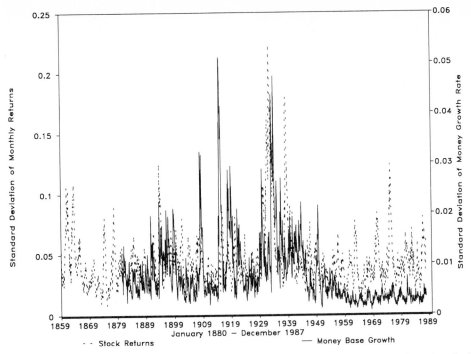

**Figure 5. Predictions of the monthly standard deviations of stock returns (– – –) and of money base growth rates (——) for 1880–1987.** A 12th-order autoregression with different monthly intercepts is used to model returns or money growth rates, and then the absolute values of the residuals are used to estimate volatility in month $t$. To model conditional volatility, a 12th-order autoregressive model with different monthly intercepts is used to predict the standard deviation in month $t$ based on lagged standard deviation estimates. This plot contains fitted values from the volatility regression models.

stock volatility, high-grade bond return volatility $|\hat{\varepsilon}_{rht}|$, and short-term interest volatility $|\hat{\varepsilon}_{rst}|$ that allows for different monthly intercepts. The VAR model uses both the monthly measure of stock return volatility $|\hat{\varepsilon}_{st}|$ and the daily measure $\hat{\sigma}_t$.[10] These VAR models are generalizations of the autoregressive model in (3b), but they include lagged values of other variables to help predict volatility. The $F$-tests in Table III measure the significance of the lagged values of the column variable in predicting the row variable, given the other variables in the model. $F$-statistics that are larger than the 0.01 critical value 2.28 are indicated with asterisks.

The largest $F$-statistics are on the main diagonal of these matrices, and the size of the statistics decreases away from the diagonal. For example, lagged stock

---

[10] Models using the volatility of medium-grade (Baa-rated) bond return volatility, $|\hat{\varepsilon}_{rmt}|$, instead of high-grade bond return volatility, yielded similar results for the post-1920 periods. Medium-grade bond volatility is more strongly related to the stock volatility and more weakly related to the short-term interest rate volatility, but the relations with the macroeconomic volatility series are generally similar. Because these data are only available from 1920 to 1987 and the results are similar, they are not reported.

volatility is the most important variable in predicting current stock volatility. Lagged bond return volatility also helps in most sample periods, and lagged short-term interest volatility contributes less. Likewise, stock volatility helps predict bond return volatility in most periods, but it rarely improves predictions of interest rate volatility. In most sample periods, short-term interest volatility helps predict bond return volatility and vice versa. Except for monthly stock volatility from 1953 to 1987, there is little evidence that inflation volatility helps to predict future asset return volatility.

The present value relation in (1) is forward-looking. In an efficient market, speculative prices will react in anticipation of future events. Thus, it is also interesting to see whether asset return volatility helps to forecast later volatility of macroeconomic variables. Except for long-term bond returns from 1859 to 1987, there is no evidence that either stock or bond return volatility helps to predict inflation volatility. Perhaps this is because the major changes in inflation volatility occur during wars, and there seems to be little effect of wars on stock or bond return volatility.

Table IV contains tests of the incremental predictive power of 12 lags of monetary base growth volatility $|\hat{\varepsilon}_{mt}|$ in a 12th-order VAR system similar to Table III. The relations among the measures of financial return volatility are similar to Table III. There is evidence that money growth volatility helps to predict the volatility of long-term bond returns from 1885 to 1919. Also, from 1885 to 1987, 1885 to 1919, and 1920 to 1952, there is evidence that money growth volatility helps to predict the volatility of stock returns measured using daily data. On the other hand, from 1920 to 1952 (and the sample periods that include this subperiod), both measures of stock return volatility help to predict the volatility of the base growth rate.

The relations between inflation or money growth volatility and the volatility of asset returns are not strong. It is surprising that these macroeconomic measures of nominal volatility are not more closely linked with the volatility of short- and long-term bond returns.

## B. Real Macroeconomic Volatility

Since common stocks reflect claims on future profits of corporations, it is plausible that the volatility of real economic activity is a major determinant of stock return volatility. In the present value model (1), the volatility of future expected cash flows, as well as discount rates, changes if the volatility of real activity changes.

Figure 6 contains a plot of the predicted volatility of the growth rates of industrial production $|\tilde{\varepsilon}_{it}|$.[11] Note that the right-hand industrial production volatility scale is about ⅔ smaller than the left-hand stock volatility scale. Summary statistics for these estimates are in Tables I and II. Industrial production volatility was high during the mid-1930's, during World War I, and especially

---

[11] I also examined the volatility of bank clearings data from Macaulay (1938) and the volatility of the liabilities of business failures data from Dun and Bradstreet (Citibase (1978)). Neither of these "real activity" variables was strongly related to stock volatility.

## Table III

## F-Tests from Vector Autoregressive Models for Stock, Bond, and Interest Rate Volatility, Including PPI Inflation Volatility, 1859–1987

A four variable, 12th-order vector autoregressive (VAR) model is estimated for stock, bond, interest rate, and PPI inflation volatility, including dummy variables for monthly intercepts. The $F$-tests reflect the incremental ability of the column variable to predict the respective row variables, given the other variables in the model. Measures of stock return volatility based on monthly data are used in the first four columns, and measures of stock return volatility based on daily data are used in the last four columns. The 0.05 and 0.01 critical values for the $F$-statistic with 12 and 200 degrees of freedom are 1.80 and 2.28, respectively. $F$-statistics greater than 2.28 are indicated with an asterisk.

| Dependent Variable | F-Tests with Monthly Stock Volatility | | | | F-Tests with Daily Stock Volatility | | | |
|---|---|---|---|---|---|---|---|---|
| | Stock | Bond | Interest | PPI | Stock | Bond | Interest | PPI |
| *1859–1987* | | | | | | | | |
| Stock | 2.07 | 1.46 | 1.30 | 0.50 | | | | |
| Bond | 0.80 | 10.82* | 0.94 | 1.36 | | | | |
| Interest | 0.86 | 2.65* | 12.68* | 0.94 | | | | |
| PPI | 1.93 | 6.42* | 0.68 | 5.70* | | | | |
| *1885–1987* | | | | | | | | |
| Stock | 9.33* | 2.89* | 0.89 | 0.95 | 67.92* | 6.77* | 1.65 | 2.10 |
| Bond | 5.83* | 15.74* | 1.98 | 1.14 | 2.83* | 14.06* | 3.75* | 1.27 |
| Interest | 1.67 | 3.87* | 21.99* | 0.65 | 0.84 | 2.29* | 21.39* | 0.61 |
| PPI | 2.16 | 1.04 | 0.60 | 31.91* | 1.04 | 1.13 | 0.83 | 28.83* |
| *1885–1919* | | | | | | | | |
| Stock | 1.16 | 1.24 | 0.41 | 0.72 | 8.86* | 4.31* | 2.99* | 1.26 |
| Bond | 1.41 | 8.05* | 1.25 | 0.51 | 0.71 | 6.03* | 1.20 | 0.86 |
| Interest | 2.41* | 1.51 | 3.34* | 0.48 | 0.94 | 1.20 | 4.57* | 1.95 |
| PPI | 1.33 | 1.04 | 1.65 | 3.67* | 1.14 | 0.70 | 0.59 | 3.29* |

**1920–1952**

| | | | | | | | | |
|---|---|---|---|---|---|---|---|---|
| Stock | 3.35* | 3.07* | 0.36 | 0.51 | 22.03* | 3.52* | 0.62 | 0.35 |
| Bond | 9.27* | 4.49* | 0.26 | 1.95 | 5.92* | 4.09* | 0.28 | 1.82 |
| Interest | 0.48 | 0.51 | 11.92* | 0.21 | 0.61 | 0.31 | 11.81* | 0.21 |
| PPI | 1.04 | 0.85 | 0.54 | 13.05* | 0.88 | 1.03 | 0.56 | 12.55* |

**1953–1987**

| | | | | | | | | |
|---|---|---|---|---|---|---|---|---|
| Stock | 1.26 | 1.05 | 1.63 | 3.65* | 6.50* | 1.51 | 0.72 | 1.55 |
| Bond | 2.00 | 3.17* | 3.20* | 1.36 | 3.27* | 3.09* | 3.97* | 1.52 |
| Interest | 1.67 | 5.23* | 5.25* | 1.99 | 0.99 | 5.04* | 4.39* | 1.90 |
| PPI | 0.63 | 0.35 | 0.76 | 19.16* | 0.96 | 0.41 | 0.87 | 16.72* |

## Table IV

### *F*-Tests from Vector Autoregressive Models for Stock, Bond, and Interest Rate Volatility, Including Monetary Base Growth Volatility, 1885–1987

A four variable, 12th-order vector autoregressive (VAR) model is estimated for stock, bond, interest rate, and monetary base growth volatility, including dummy variables for monthly intercepts. The *F*-tests reflect the incremental ability of the column variable to predict the respective row variables, given the other variables in the model. Measures of stock return volatility based on monthly data are used in the first four columns, and measures of stock return volatility based on daily data are used in the last four columns. The 0.05 and 0.01 critical values for the *F*-statistic with 12 and 200 degrees of freedom are 1.80 and 2.28, respectively. *F*-statistics greater than 2.28 are indicated with an asterisk.

| Dependent Variable | *F*-Tests with Monthly Stock Volatility | | | | *F*-Tests with Daily Stock Volatility | | | |
|---|---|---|---|---|---|---|---|---|
| | Stock | Bond | Interest | Base | Stock | Bond | Interest | Base |
| *1885–1987* | | | | | | | | |
| Stock | 7.85* | 2.60* | 0.78 | 0.93 | 62.39* | 5.83* | 1.00 | 4.83* |
| Bond | 5.36* | 16.92* | 1.79 | 2.25 | 2.76* | 15.88* | 3.39* | 1.36 |
| Interest | 1.41 | 3.50* | 22.30* | 1.07 | 0.88 | 2.04 | 22.61* | 0.60 |
| Base | 4.80* | 1.26 | 0.55 | 21.72* | 1.40 | 1.79 | 0.85 | 18.73* |
| *1885–1919* | | | | | | | | |
| Stock | 1.19 | 0.92 | 0.44 | 0.79 | 8.80* | 3.83* | 2.95* | 2.28* |
| Bond | 1.63 | 3.52* | 1.53 | 3.71* | 1.04 | 3.09* | 1.17 | 0.85 |
| Interest | 2.26 | 1.23 | 3.43* | 0.82 | 0.96 | 1.54 | 4.61* | 1.28 |
| Base | 1.98 | 0.87 | 1.46 | 2.96* | 0.92 | 3.21* | 1.03 | 2.47* |
| *1920–1952* | | | | | | | | |
| Stock | 2.82* | 3.16* | 0.40 | 0.88 | 23.21* | 3.64* | 0.86 | 2.44* |
| Bond | 7.80* | 4.03* | 0.26 | 1.11 | 4.78* | 3.60* | 0.27 | 1.16 |
| Interest | 0.40 | 0.38 | 11.99* | 0.39 | 0.56 | 0.22 | 12.08* | 0.42 |
| Base | 4.05* | 1.64 | 0.41 | 5.23* | 3.11* | 1.72 | 0.52 | 6.22* |
| *1953–1987* | | | | | | | | |
| Stock | 1.55 | 0.96 | 1.93 | 0.95 | 9.22* | 1.02 | 0.68 | 1.15 |
| Bond | 2.00 | 3.38* | 3.20* | 1.08 | 3.11* | 3.53* | 3.45* | 1.08 |
| Interest | 1.25 | 4.82* | 6.31* | 0.63 | 0.94 | 4.77* | 5.36* | 0.90 |
| Base | 0.83 | 0.68 | 1.43 | 1.63 | 1.11 | 0.85 | 1.26 | 1.74 |

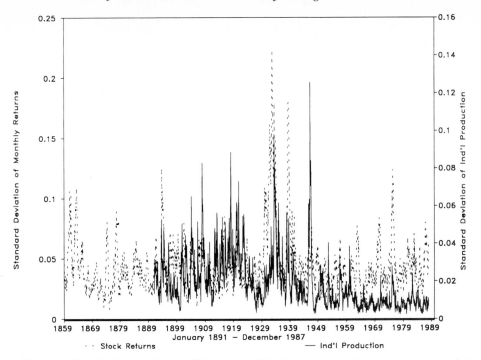

**Figure 6. Predictions of the monthly standard deviations of stock returns (– – –) and of industrial production growth rates (——) for 1891–1987.** A 12th-order autoregression with different monthly intercepts is used to model returns or industrial production growth rates, and then the absolute values of the residuals are used to estimate volatility in month $t$. To model conditional volatility, a 12th-order autoregressive model with different monthly intercepts is used to predict the standard deviation in month $t$ based on lagged standard deviation estimates. This plot contains fitted values from the volatility regression models.

during the post-World War II period. There is a small increase in volatility during the 1973–1974 recession. Romer (1986b) argues that data collection procedures cause part of the higher volatility of this series before 1929.

Table V contains tests of the incremental predictive power of 12 lags of industrial production volatility $|\hat{\varepsilon}_{it}|$ in a 12th-order VAR system similar to those in Tables III and IV. The results for the financial variables are similar to those reported in Table III. The $F$-statistics measuring the ability of industrial production volatility to predict financial volatility are small. There is somewhat stronger evidence that stock return volatility predicts industrial production volatility for the 1891–1987 and 1920–1952 periods.

Thus, there is weak evidence that macroeconomic volatility provides incremental information about future stock return volatility. There is somewhat stronger evidence that financial volatility helps to predict macroeconomic volatility. While many of the macroeconomic volatility series are high during 1929–1939, none increases by a factor of three as stock return volatility did. This "volatility puzzle" will remain after all the subsequent analysis.

Table V

## *F*-Tests from Vector Autoregressive Models for Stock, Bond, and Interest Rate Volatility, Including Industrial Production Growth Volatility, 1891–1987

A four variable, 12th-order vector autoregressive (VAR) model is estimated for stock, bond, interest rate, and industrial production growth volatility, including dummy variables for monthly intercepts. The *F*-tests reflect the incremental ability of the column variable to predict the respective row variables, given the other variables in the model. Measures of stock return volatility based on monthly data are used in the first four columns, and measures of stock return volatility based on daily data are used in the last four columns. The 0.05 and 0.01 critical values for the *F*-statistic with 12 and 200 degrees of freedom are 1.80 and 2.28, respectively. *F*-statistics greater than 2.28 are indicated with an asterisk.

| Dependent Variable | *F*-Tests with Monthly Stock Volatility | | | | *F*-Tests with Daily Stock Volatility | | | |
|---|---|---|---|---|---|---|---|---|
| | Stock | Bond | Interest | IP | Stock | Bond | Interest | IP |
| *1891–1987* | | | | | | | | |
| Stock | 9.47* | 2.66* | 0.85 | 1.03 | 64.93* | 6.25* | 1.25 | 2.24 |
| Bond | 5.12* | 15.66* | 1.85 | 0.49 | 2.68* | 14.41* | 3.43* | 0.99 |
| Interest | 1.43 | 3.63* | 21.87* | 0.51 | 0.81 | 2.11 | 21.92* | 0.62 |
| IP | 3.18* | 0.76 | 0.75 | 24.07* | 1.33 | 0.89 | 0.55 | 19.79* |
| *1891–1919* | | | | | | | | |
| Stock | 0.98 | 1.59 | 0.60 | 0.98 | 7.38* | 3.57* | 2.70* | 0.35 |
| Bond | 1.26 | 6.30* | 1.24 | 1.24 | 0.96 | 4.29* | 1.20 | 0.70 |
| Interest | 2.25 | 1.46 | 2.88* | 0.37 | 0.72 | 1.22 | 3.97* | 0.58 |
| IP | 0.95 | 0.85 | 0.66 | 3.27* | 1.72 | 1.70 | 0.67 | 2.73* |
| *1920–1952* | | | | | | | | |
| Stock | 3.82* | 3.32* | 0.39 | 1.29 | 22.36* | 3.74* | 0.65 | 0.72 |
| Bond | 8.46* | 4.20* | 0.27 | 0.79 | 5.18* | 3.50* | 0.23 | 0.66 |
| Interest | 0.52 | 0.38 | 12.25* | 0.48 | 0.72 | 0.20 | 12.21* | 0.56 |
| IP | 2.65* | 1.31 | 0.57 | 5.60* | 1.08 | 1.23 | 0.58 | 4.80* |
| *1953–1987* | | | | | | | | |
| Stock | 1.72 | 0.92 | 1.64 | 1.21 | 9.77* | 1.08 | 0.72 | 0.70 |
| Bond | 1.85 | 3.54* | 2.88* | 0.49 | 3.08* | 3.66* | 3.31* | 0.61 |
| Interest | 1.22 | 4.70* | 6.65* | 1.14 | 0.71 | 4.42* | 5.67* | 1.20 |
| IP | 1.42 | 0.79 | 0.22 | 3.48* | 0.77 | 1.02 | 0.29 | 3.37* |

### III. Volatility and the Level of Economic Activity

*A. Volatility During Recessions*

The previous tests analyzed the relations among various measures of volatility. There is also reason to believe that stock return volatility is related to the level of economic activity. For example, if firms have large fixed costs, net profits will fall faster than revenues if demand falls. This is often called "operating leverage."[12] Table VI contains a test of the relation between stock volatility and the level of macroeconomic activity. It contains estimates of the coefficient of a dummy variable added to equation (3b) equal to unity during recessions as defined by the National Bureau of Economic Research (NBER) and equal to zero otherwise. If this coefficient is reliably above zero, the volatility of the series is larger during recessions than during expansions.[13]

Table VI shows that volatility is higher during recessions since most of the estimates are positive and none is more than 1.2 standard errors below zero. Except for 1859–1919, all the estimates for stock volatility are more than 1.8 standard errors above zero. Moreover, the estimates of the percentage increase in volatility in recessions compared with expansions, in braces below the *t*-statistics, are large (up to 277 percent in 1920–1952 using the daily estimates of volatility). Along with the measures of stock market volatility $|\hat{\varepsilon}_{st}|$ and $\hat{\sigma}_t$, the volatility of industrial production $|\hat{\varepsilon}_{it}|$ shows the most reliable increases during recessions. There is weaker evidence that bond returns, short-term interest rates, and money growth rates have higher volatility during recessions.

Figure 7 shows the plot of predicted monthly stock volatility like Figure 1, except that the periods of NBER recessions are drawn as solid lines and expansions are drawn as dotted lines. It is clear from this plot that volatility is generally higher during recessions. This phenomenon is not limited to the Great Depression.

Thus, stock market volatility is related to the general health of the economy. One interpretation of this evidence is that it is caused by financial leverage. Stock prices are a leading indicator, so stock prices fall (relative to bond prices) before and during recessions. Thus, leverage increases during recessions, causing an increase in the volatility of leveraged stocks. The analysis below addresses this question directly.

*B. Volatility and Corporate Profitability*

I have also analyzed the relation between stock volatility and several measures of corporate profitability. Recently, Fama and French (1988b) and others have shown that variables such as dividend ($D/P$) or earnings yields ($E/P$) predict stock returns for horizons as far as five years into the future. Keim and Stambaugh (1986) and Fama and French (1989) show that spreads between the

---

[12] I am grateful to Fischer Black for suggesting this interpretation.

[13] Since the NBER announces the timing of recessions and expansions six to nine months *after* they have begun, this evidence does not imply that the recession variable can be used to help *predict* future volatility.

Table VI

# Estimates of the Relations Between Business Cycles and Financial and Macroeconomic Volatility, 1859–1987

Estimates of dummy variable coefficients are added to the autoregressive model for volatility. The $t$-statistics in parentheses use White's (1980) heteroskedasticity consistent standard errors. A dummy variable equal to one during months designated as recessions by the National Bureau of Economic Research is added to a regression containing 12 monthly dummy variables and 12 lags of volatility. The estimates represent the increase in average volatility during periods of recession. The percentage increase in volatility during recessions relative to expansions is in braces below the standard errors. The estimates in the first two columns use as much data as are available for the respective series. Coefficient estimates more than two standard errors from zero are indicated with an asterisk.

| Dependent Variable | 1859–1987 | 1859–1919 | 1920–1952 | 1953–1987 |
|---|---|---|---|---|
| Monthly stock returns | 0.0063* | −0.0014 | 0.0195* | 0.0139* |
| | (2.93) | (−0.55) | (3.09) | (3.12) |
| | {61%} | {−6%} | {234%} | {68%} |
| Daily stock returns | 0.0038* | 0.0014 | 0.0077* | 0.0037 |
| | (3.05) | (0.92) | (2.55) | (1.81) |
| | {99%} | {8%} | {277%} | {45%} |
| High-grade long-term bond returns | 0.00065 | 0.00019 | 0.00234 | 0.00160 |
| | (1.21) | (0.39) | (1.68) | (0.99) |
| | {42%} | {14%} | {161%} | {70%} |
| Short-term interest rates | 0.00008 | 0.00007 | 0.00004 | 0.00031 |
| | (1.22) | (0.88) | (0.33) | (1.41) |
| | {29%} | {15%} | {16%} | {134%} |
| PPI inflation rates | 0.00024 | −0.00070 | −0.00067 | −0.00052 |
| | (0.31) | (−0.58) | (−0.64) | (−1.16) |
| | {10%} | {−13%} | {−15%} | {−57%} |
| Monetary base growth rates | 0.0015* | 0.0017 | 0.0010 | −0.0002 |
| | (2.47) | (1.77) | (0.81) | (−0.51) |
| | {125%} | {54%} | {42%} | {−11%} |
| Industrial production growth rates | 0.0032* | 0.0011 | 0.0022 | 0.0026* |
| | (2.58) | (0.48) | (0.96) | (2.35) |
| | {83%} | {8%} | {30%} | {52%} |

yields on low versus high-grade long-term corporate debt also predict stock returns. Where such variables track time-varying expected returns, they may also predict time-varying volatility.

The relations between stock volatility with either dividend or earnings yields are sometimes positive and sometimes negative. These opposite associations suggest that there is no stable relation between earnings or dividend policy and stock volatility. To limit the number of reported results, I only summarize these tests here.

Table VII contains estimates of the coefficients of the spread between the yields on Baa- versus Aa-rated corporate bonds when added to the autoregressive models summarized in Table II. All of the estimates are positive, and several are more than two standard errors above zero. Thus, the difference between the

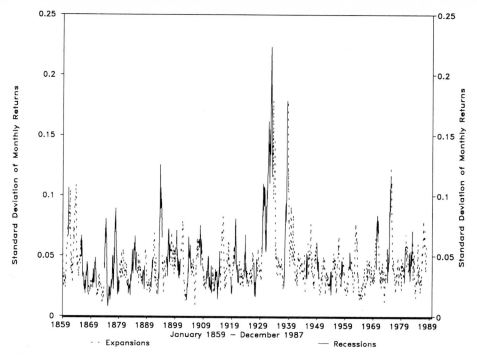

**Figure 7. Predictions of the monthly standard deviation of stock returns during NBER recessions (——) and during expansions (– – –) for 1859–1987.** A 12th-order autoregression with different monthly intercepts is used to model returns, and then the absolute values of the residuals are used to estimate volatility in month $t$. To model conditional volatility, a 12th-order autoregressive model with different monthly intercepts is used to predict the standard deviation in month $t$ based on lagged standard deviation estimates. This plot contains fitted values from the volatility regression model, shown separately for recessions and expansions.

yields on bonds of different quality is directly related to subsequently observed stock volatility. This is not surprising, since the difference in promised yields on bonds of different quality should be larger in periods when default risk is high.

## IV. Effects of Leverage on Stock Market Volatility

One explanation of time-varying stock volatility is that leverage changes as relative stock and bond prices change. In particular, the variance of the return to the assets of a firm $\sigma_{vt}^2$ is a function of the variances of the returns to the stock $\sigma_{st}^2$ and the bonds $\sigma_{bt}^2$ and the covariance of the returns $\text{cov}(R_{st}, R_{bt})$:

$$\sigma_{vt}^2 = (S/V)_{t-1}^2\ \sigma_{st}^2 + (B/V)_{t-1}^2\ \sigma_{bt}^2 + 2\ (S/V)_{t-1}\ (B/V)_{t-1}\ \text{cov}(R_{st}, R_{bt}), \quad (4)$$

where $(S/V)_{t-1}$ and $(B/V)_{t-1}$ represent the fraction of the market value of the firm due to stocks and bonds at time $t-1$. Consider a firm with riskless debt $(\sigma_{bt}^2 = \text{cov}(R_{st}, R_{bt}) = 0)$, where the variance of the assets of the firm $\sigma_v^2$ is constant

**Table VII**

## Estimates of the Relation Between the Standard Deviation of Stock Returns and the Corporate Bond Quality Yield Spreads, 1920–1987

The previous month's spread between the Moody's Baa long-term corporate bond yield and the Aa yield, $(y_{Baa} - y_{Aa})_{t-1}$, is included in an autoregressive model for volatility,

$$\sigma_{st} = \sum_{i=1}^{12} \alpha_i + \sum_{j=1}^{12} \beta_j \sigma_{st-j} + \gamma(y_{Baa} - y_{Aa})_{t-1} + u_t.$$

Only the coefficient of the yield spread $\gamma$ is shown. Asymptotic standard errors are in parentheses under the coefficient estimates. Coefficient estimates more than two standard errors from zero are indicated with an asterisk.

| Sample Period | Standard Deviation from Monthly Stock Returns | Standard Deviation from Daily Stock Returns |
|---|---|---|
| 1920–1987 | 14.83* | 3.937* |
| | (5.82) | (1.85) |
| 1920–1952 | 18.07* | 4.256 |
| | (8.00) | (2.15) |
| 1953–1987 | 5.649 | 3.950 |
| | (8.29) | (3.14) |

over time. The standard deviation of the stock return is $\sigma_{st} = \sigma_v (V/S)_{t-1}$. This shows how a change in the leverage of the firm causes a change in the volatility of stock returns.

Figure 8 plots the predictions of stock market volatility $\tilde{\sigma}_t$ from Figure 1 along with the estimates implied by changing leverage $(V/S)_{t-1}$ scaled to have a mean equal to the average of $\tilde{\sigma}_t$ for 1900–1987. Changing leverage explains a small portion of the increase in stock market volatility in the early 1930's and mid-1970's. It cannot explain most of the variation in $\tilde{\sigma}_t$.[14]

Christie (1982) proposes regression tests for the effects of changing leverage on the volatility of stock returns. He notes that, if the volatility of the value of the firm $\sigma_v$ is constant, (4) implies the regression model:

$$\sigma_{st} = \alpha_0 + \alpha_1 (B/S)_{t-1} + u_t, \tag{5}$$

where $\alpha_0 = \alpha_1 = \sigma_v$, in the riskless debt case. With risky consol bonds containing protective covenants, as modeled by Black and Cox (1976), Christie shows that $\alpha_0 = \sigma_v > \alpha_1$.

Table VIII contains generalized least squares (GLS) estimates of equation (5) for 1901–1987, 1901–1952, and 1953–1987. There is strong residual autocorrelation using ordinary least squares; hence, the GLS estimates use an ARMA(1,3)

---

[14] A plot using the monthly measure of volatility $|\tilde{e}_{st}|$ yields similar conclusions.

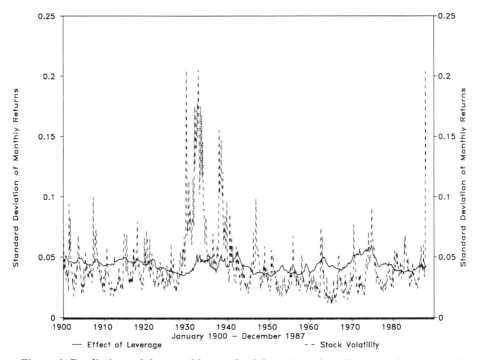

**Figure 8. Predictions of the monthly standard deviation of stock returns based on daily data (−−−) and the level of stock return volatility implied by changing financial leverage (——) for 1900–1987.** The daily returns in the month are used to estimate a sample standard deviation for each month. To model conditional volatility, a 12th-order autoregressive model with different monthly intercepts is used to predict the standard deviation in month $t$ based on lagged standard deviation estimates. This plot contains fitted values from the volatility regression model. The effect of leverage is estimated by assuming that the volatility of the assets of the firm is constant and that debt is riskless. Then, the standard deviation of stock returns changes in proportion to the value of the firm divided by the value of the stock $(V/S)_{t-1}$. When stock prices fall relative to bond prices, stock volatility increases. Thus, the "effect of leverage" plot is a time series of aggregate firm value (stock plus bond value) divided by stock value, scaled to have the same mean as the predictions of volatility from the regression model.

model for the errors. This is similar to the French, Schwert, and Stambaugh (1987) model for $\hat{\sigma}_t$. The results depend on the volatility measure and the sample period. For the daily volatility measure $\hat{\sigma}_t$, the intercept $\alpha_0$ is always greater than the slope $\alpha_1$, as predicted by the risky debt model. The estimates of $\alpha_0$ are between 0.03 and 0.04 per month, and they are over three standard errors from zero. This would be the estimate of firm volatility $\sigma_v$ in Christie's model. All the estimates of $\alpha_1$ are positive, showing that stock volatility rises when leverage rises. The standard errors are large, however, so the $t$-statistics testing $\alpha_1 = 0$, or testing $\alpha_1 = \alpha_0$, are small. The $t$-test in the last column of Table VIII tests the hypothesis that the slope equals the intercept ($\alpha_0 = \alpha_1$). The $p$-value in parentheses is for the two-sided alternative hypothesis ($\alpha_0 \neq \alpha_1$).

The estimates for the monthly volatility measure $|\tilde{\varepsilon}_{st}|$ for 1953–1987 are similar

**Table VIII**

**Estimates of the Relation Between the Standard Deviation of Stock Returns and Leverage, 1901–1987**

Regressions of stock volatility on debt/equity ratios,

$$\sigma_{st} = \alpha_0 + \alpha_1 \, (B/S)_{t-1} + u_t, \tag{5}$$

where $(B/S)_{t-1}$ is an estimate of the debt/equity ratio for the aggregate stock market portfolio at the end of month $t-1$. Generalized least squares estimates include an ARMA (1, 3) process for the errors. Asymptotic standard errors are in parentheses under the coefficient estimates. $S(u)$ is the standard deviation of the errors, $R^2$ is the coefficient of determination including the effects of estimating the ARMA (1, 3) process for the errors, and $Q(24)$ is the Box-Pierce (1970) statistic for 24 lags of the residual autocorrelations, which should be distributed as $\chi^2$ (20). The $t$-test for $\alpha_0 = \alpha_1$ tests whether the riskless debt model is an adequate approximation to the effect of leverage on stock return volatility, where $\alpha_0 > \alpha_1$ is implied by the risky debt model. Coefficient estimates more than two standard errors from zero are indicated with an asterisk. The $p$-values for the Box-Pierce statistic and for the two-sided alternative $\alpha_0 \neq \alpha_1$ are in parentheses under the test statistics.

| Sample Period | $\alpha_0$ | $\alpha_1$ | $S(u)$ | $R^2$ | $Q(24)$ | $t$-test $\alpha_0 = \alpha_1$ |
|---|---|---|---|---|---|---|
| | | Standard Deviation from Monthly Returns | | | | |
| 1901–1987 | 0.0269* | 0.0512* | 0.0424 | 0.165 | 56.2 | −0.87 |
| | (0.0101) | (0.0193) | | | (0.0000) | (0.383) |
| 1901–1952 | 0.0232 | 0.0700* | 0.0475 | 0.194 | 50.3 | −1.08 |
| | (0.0157) | (0.0300) | | | (0.0002) | (0.279) |
| 1953–1987 | 0.0315* | 0.0221 | 0.0336 | 0.055 | 16.9 | 0.45 |
| | (0.0066) | (0.0146) | | | (0.657) | (0.651) |
| | | Standard Deviation from Daily Returns | | | | |
| 1901–1987 | 0.0376* | 0.0154 | 0.0187 | 0.571 | 24.6 | 1.01 |
| | (0.0093) | (0.0147) | | | (0.216) | (0.311) |
| 1901–1952 | 0.0402* | 0.0168 | 0.0205 | 0.606 | 35.0 | 0.71 |
| | (0.0135) | (0.0225) | | | (0.020) | (0.479) |
| 1953–1987 | 0.0317* | 0.0101 | 0.0157 | 0.296 | 12.7 | 1.03 |
| | (0.0073) | (0.0147) | | | (0.890) | (0.301) |

to the daily estimates. For 1901–1952 and 1901–1987, however, the estimates of $\alpha_0$ are less than the estimates of $\alpha_1$, a result that is inconsistent with all the leverage models. Again, the standard errors are large, so the $t$-test for $\alpha_0 = \alpha_1$ is not large. These estimates of $\alpha_1$ are reliably above zero, showing that an increase in the debt/equity ratio $(B/S)_{t-1}$ leads to an increase in stock return volatility. These regressions also have strong residual autocorrelation. An obvious interpretation is that the volatility of the value of the firm $\sigma_{vt}$ is *not* constant over these samples. Rather, it rose at the same time that leverage rose during the Great Depression, so the large estimates of $\alpha_1$ are caused by omitting a correlated regressor. Again, this evidence shows that leverage alone cannot explain the historical movements in stock volatility.

## V. Stock Market Trading and Volatility

There are at least three theories that predict a positive relation between volatility and volume. First, if investors have heterogeneous beliefs, new information will cause both price changes and trading. Second, if some investors use price movements as information on which to make trading decisions, large price movements will cause large trading volume. Finally, if there is short-term "price pressure" due to illiquidity in secondary trading markets, large trading volume that is predominantly either buy or sell orders will cause price movements. There has been much previous research on the relation between volatility and trading volume, but most of it has focused on the behavior of individual securities. The time series behavior of volatility and trading volume for the aggregate stock market provides a different perspective on these questions.

## A. Trading Days and Volatility

French and Roll (1986) show that stock volatility is higher when stock exchanges are open for trading. In particular, they find that the variance of stock returns over weekends and holidays is much less than a typical one-day variance times the number of calendar days since trading last occurred. Most peculiarly, during 1968, when the NYSE closed on Wednesdays due to the "paper-work crunch," the variance of Tuesday to Thursday returns was not much larger than a one-day variance. This occurred even though the stock exchanges were the only economic institutions taking holidays. Table IX contains regressions,

$$\hat{\sigma}_{st} = \alpha_0 + \alpha_1 \sqrt{Days_t} + u_t, \tag{6}$$

where $Days_t$ is the number of trading days the NYSE was open during month $t$. If variance is proportional to trading time, $\alpha_1$ represents the standard deviation per trading day and $\alpha_0$ should equal zero. If volatility is unrelated to trading activity, the intercept $\alpha_0$ estimates the average monthly standard deviation and $\alpha_1$ should equal zero. Table IX contains GLS estimates of equation (6) for 1885–1987, 1885–1919, 1920–1952, and 1953–1987. These estimates do not provide strong support for either hypothesis, but the French-Roll scenario is more consistent with the data. All but one of the estimates of the trading time coefficient $\alpha_1$ are positive, and several are almost two standard errors above zero. On the other hand, many of the estimated intercepts are negative, and only one is more than two standard errors above zero. Thus, NYSE trading activity explains part of the variation in stock volatility. Nevertheless, this relation does not explain much of the variation in volatility through time.

## B. Trading Volume and Volatility

Another measure of stock trading activity is share trading volume. Karpoff (1987) surveys the extensive literature on the relation between volatility and volume. Table X contains estimates of the regression

$$\hat{\sigma}_{st} = \alpha_0 + \frac{\beta}{(1-\delta L)} Vol_t + u_t, \tag{7}$$

Table IX

## Estimates of the Relation Between the Standard Deviation of Stock Returns and the Square Root of the Number of Trading Days, 1885–1987

Regressions of stock volatility on the square root of the number of trading days per month,

$$\sigma_{st} = \alpha_0 + \alpha_1 \sqrt{Days_t} + u_t, \tag{6}$$

where $\sqrt{Days_t}$ is the square root of the NYSE trading days in the month. Generalized least squares estimates include an ARMA (1,3) process for the errors. Asymptotic standard errors are in parentheses under the coefficient estimates. $S(u)$ is the standard deviation of the errors, $R^2$ is the coefficient of determination including the effects of estimating the ARMA (1,3) process for the errors, and $Q(24)$ is the Box-Pierce (1970) statistic for 24 lags of the residual autocorrelations, which should be distributed as $\chi^2(20)$, with the $p$-value in parentheses under the test. Coefficient estimates more than two standard errors from zero are indicated with an asterisk.

| Sample Period | $\alpha_0$ | $\alpha_1$ | $S(u)$ | $R^2$ | $Q(24)$ |
|---|---|---|---|---|---|
| Standard Deviation from Monthly Returns | | | | | |
| 1885–1987 | −0.0276 | 0.0152* | 0.0418 | 0.142 | 56.1 |
| | (0.0357) | (0.0073) | | | (0.0003) |
| 1885–1919 | −0.0703 | 0.0224 | 0.0347 | 0.028 | 16.1 |
| | (0.0612) | (0.0122) | | | (0.708) |
| 1920–1952 | 0.0224 | 0.0065 | 0.0545 | 0.194 | 45.7 |
| | (0.0764) | (0.0152) | | | (0.0009) |
| 1953–1987 | −0.0514 | 0.0202 | 0.0336 | 0.055 | 16.3 |
| | (0.0567) | (0.0124) | | | (0.697) |
| Standard Deviation from Daily Returns | | | | | |
| 1885–1987 | 0.0341* | 0.0018 | 0.0186 | 0.538 | 21.9 |
| | (0.0150) | (0.0029) | | | (0.347) |
| 1885–1919 | 0.0251 | 0.0027 | 0.0157 | 0.226 | 10.9 |
| | (0.0231) | (0.0046) | | | (0.950) |
| 1920–1952 | 0.0632 | −0.0025 | 0.0231 | 0.622 | 38.7 |
| | (0.0318) | (0.0056) | | | (0.007) |
| 1953–1987 | −0.0038 | 0.0087 | 0.0157 | 0.300 | 13.1 |
| | (0.0225) | (0.0048) | | | (0.872) |

where $Vol_t$ is the growth rate of volume from month $t - 1$ to month $t$, and the errors $u_t$ follow an ARMA(1,3) process. This model relates stock volatility to a distributed lag of past share volume growth, where the coefficient of volume growth decreases geometrically.[15] The estimates in Table X also show a positive relation between stock volatility and trading activity. All the estimates of $\beta$ are more than two standard errors above zero. The estimates of $\delta$ are all positive. For the estimates of volatility based on daily data $\hat{\sigma}_t$, they are several standard

---

[15] This model was suggested by the pattern of regression coefficients in an unrestricted regression of volatility on current and four lags of volume growth. $L$ is the lag operator, $L^k X_t = X_{t-k}$.

**Table X**

## Estimates of the Relation Between the Standard Deviation of Stock Returns and Stock Market Trading Volume, 1885–1987

Distributed lag regressions of stock volatility on the growth rate of NYSE share trading volume ($Vol_t$),

$$\sigma_{st} = \alpha_0 + \frac{\beta}{(1 - \delta L)} \, Vol_t + u_t. \tag{7}$$

Generalized least squares estimates include an ARMA (1,3) process for the errors. Asymptotic standard errors are in parentheses under the coefficient estimates. The distributed lag model for the effect of current and lagged share volume growth on the monthly standard deviation of stock returns implies geometric decay. The implied coefficient for lag $k$ is $\beta\delta^k$. $L$ is the lag operator, $L^k X_t = X_{t-k}$. $S(u)$ is the standard deviation of the errors, $R^2$ is the coefficient of determination including the effects of estimating the ARMA (1,3) process for the errors, and $Q(24)$ is the Box-Pierce (1970) statistic for 24 lags of the residual autocorrelations, which should be distributed as $\chi^2(20)$, with the $p$-value in parentheses under the test. Coefficient estimates more than two standard errors from zero are indicated with an asterisk.

| Sample Period | $\alpha_0$ | $\beta$ | $\delta$ | $S(u)$ | $R^2$ | $Q(24)$ |
|---|---|---|---|---|---|---|
| | Standard Deviation from Monthly Returns | | | | | |
| 1885–1987 | 0.0454* | 0.0473* | 0.1561 | 0.0394 | 0.237 | 55.4 |
| | (0.0049) | (0.0038) | (0.0800) | | | (0.0000) |
| 1885–1919 | 0.0410* | 0.0331* | 0.3484* | 0.0328 | 0.127 | 19.2 |
| | (0.0023) | (0.0047) | (0.1320) | | | (0.509) |
| 1920–1952 | 0.0545* | 0.0629* | 0.0597 | 0.0502 | 0.316 | 40.9 |
| | (0.0150) | (0.0074) | (0.1188) | | | (0.004) |
| 1953–1987 | 0.0395* | 0.0539* | 0.3061 | 0.0324 | 0.124 | 19.9 |
| | (0.0025) | (0.0092) | (0.1684) | | | (0.462) |
| | Standard Deviation from Daily Returns | | | | | |
| 1885–1987 | −0.0246 | 0.0168* | 0.9984* | 0.0179 | 0.568 | 21.9 |
| | (0.0560) | (0.0019) | (0.0012) | | | (0.346) |
| 1885–1919 | 0.0372* | 0.0123* | 0.9536* | 0.0151 | 0.281 | 13.7 |
| | (0.0020) | (0.0023) | (0.0299) | | | (0.845) |
| 1920–1952 | 0.0484* | 0.0203* | 0.9007* | 0.0223 | 0.650 | 36.0 |
| | (0.0165) | (0.0037) | (0.1002) | | | (0.016) |
| 1953–1987 | 0.0351* | 0.0182* | 0.5952* | 0.0154 | 0.324 | 14.0 |
| | (0.0041) | (0.0044) | (0.2431) | | | (0.832) |

errors above zero. For the estimates of volatility based on monthly data $|\hat{\varepsilon}_{st}|$, the estimates of $\delta$ are closer to zero, though for 1885–1919 it is over two standard errors above zero. Thus, the evidence in Table X supports the proposition that stock market volatility is higher when trading activity is higher.

Table XI contains tests of the incremental predictive power of 12 lags of NYSE share volume growth $Vol_t$ in a 12th-order VAR system for stock volatility, high-grade bond return volatility $|\hat{\varepsilon}_{rht}|$, and short-term interest volatility $|\hat{\varepsilon}_{rst}|$ that allows for different monthly intercepts. This model is similar to those used in Tables III, IV, and V. The *F*-statistics measuring the ability of share volume growth to predict financial volatility are small, except for 1885–1919 and 1885–1987 using the daily measure of stock volatility $\hat{\sigma}_t$. There is little evidence that financial volatility helps to predict future trading volume growth, except for stock volatility from 1920 to 1952.

The main difference between the distributed lag models in Table X and the VAR models in Table XI is that the distributed lag models include the correlation of contemporaneous volume and volatility and the VAR models do not. The strong relations in Table X and the weak ones in Table XI point to a strong

### Table XI

### *F*-Tests from Vector Autoregressive Models for Stock, Bond, and Interest Rate Volatility, Including Growth in NYSE Share Trading Volume, 1885–1987

A four variable, 12th-order vector autoregressive (VAR) model is estimated for stock, bond, and interest rate volatility, and NYSE share trading volume growth (*Vol*), including dummy variables for monthly intercepts. The *F*-tests reflect the incremental ability of the column variable to predict the respective row variables, given the other variables in the model. Measures of stock return volatility based on monthly data are used in the first four columns, and measures of stock return volatility based on daily data are used in the last four columns. The 0.05 and 0.01 critical values for the *F*-statistic with 12 and 200 degrees of freedom are 1.80 and 2.28, respectively. *F*-statistics greater than 2.28 are indicated with an asterisk.

| Dependent Variable | *F*-tests with Monthly Stock Volatility | | | | *F*-tests with Daily Stock Volatility | | | |
|---|---|---|---|---|---|---|---|---|
| | Stock | Bond | Interest | *Vol* | Stock | Bond | Interest | *Vol* |
| *1885–1987* | | | | | | | | |
| Stock | 10.29* | 2.75* | 0.84 | 1.55 | 77.94* | 6.97* | 1.38 | 7.65* |
| Bond | 5.26* | 17.70* | 2.01 | 0.87 | 2.59* | 17.37* | 3.47* | 0.86 |
| Interest | 1.62 | 3.68* | 22.33* | 0.70 | 0.87 | 2.22 | 22.36* | 0.45 |
| *Vol* | 1.97 | 1.11 | 0.63 | 11.25* | 1.30 | 1.60 | 0.66 | 10.94* |
| *1885–1919* | | | | | | | | |
| Stock | 1.42 | 1.37 | 0.38 | 1.11 | 9.40* | 4.35* | 2.29* | 3.97* |
| Bond | 1.37 | 8.78* | 1.22 | 0.83 | 1.09 | 6.14* | 1.17 | 0.90 |
| Interest | 2.05 | 1.48 | 3.24* | 0.96 | 0.87 | 1.18 | 4.45* | 0.98 |
| *Vol* | 1.42 | 1.36 | 0.97 | 4.12* | 1.86 | 1.10 | 0.76 | 3.55* |
| *1920–1952* | | | | | | | | |
| Stock | 4.07* | 3.80* | 0.54 | 2.13 | 22.39* | 3.35* | 0.63 | 1.01 |
| Bond | 8.88* | 4.06* | 0.33 | 1.14 | 6.08* | 3.40* | 0.30 | 1.48 |
| Interest | 0.51 | 0.52 | 11.87* | 0.52 | 0.62 | 0.35 | 11.87* | 0.51 |
| *Vol* | 2.28* | 2.13 | 0.62 | 4.20* | 2.71* | 0.99 | 0.59 | 3.53* |
| *1953–1987* | | | | | | | | |
| Stock | 2.18 | 1.06 | 2.23 | 1.58 | 10.10* | 1.18 | 0.75 | 0.54 |
| Bond | 1.87 | 3.57* | 3.20* | 0.39 | 2.85* | 3.58* | 3.58* | 0.36 |
| Interest | 1.59 | 5.15* | 6.02* | 1.17 | 0.84 | 5.17* | 5.66* | 0.99 |
| *Vol* | 0.50 | 0.46 | 0.64 | 7.25* | 1.58 | 0.49 | 0.82 | 7.50* |

correlation between the "shocks" to volume and volatility. Unexpected changes in volatility and volume are highly positively correlated. Given the history of volatility, there is not much correlation between volatility and lagged values of trading volume.

In general, high trading activity and high volatility occur together. Of course, these regressions cannot show whether this relation is due to "trading noise" or to the flow of information to the stock market.

## VI. Summary and Conclusions

This paper analyzes many factors related to stock volatility, but it does not test for *causes* of stock price volatility. Rather, the hypotheses involve associations between stock volatility and other variables. For example, the analysis of the volatility of bond returns, inflation rates, money growth, and industrial production growth, along with stock volatility, seeks to determine whether these aggregate volatility measures change together through time. In most general equilibrium models, fundamental factors such as consumption and production opportunities and preferences would determine all these parameters (e.g., Abel (1988)). Nevertheless, the process of characterizing stylized facts about economic volatility helps to define the set of interesting questions, leading to tractable theoretical models.

### A. *Joint Effects of Leverage and Macroeconomic Volatility*

Most of the tests above analyze stock volatility along with one other factor. To summarize all these relations, Table XII contains estimates of the multiple regression:

$$\ln \tilde{\sigma}_{st} = \alpha_e + \alpha_r D_{rt} + \beta_1 \ln |\tilde{\varepsilon}_{pt}| + \beta_2 \ln |\tilde{\varepsilon}_{mt}|$$
$$+ \beta_3 \ln |\tilde{\varepsilon}_{it}| \tag{8}$$
$$+ \gamma \ln (V/S)_{t-1} + u_t.$$

In (8), $\alpha_e$ represents the constant term during expansions, and $(\alpha_e + \alpha_r)$ represents the constant term during recessions. The slope coefficients $\beta_1$ through $\beta_3$ represent the elasticities of stock return volatility with predicted inflation volatility, predicted money growth volatility, and predicted industrial production volatility, respectively. The coefficient $\gamma$ measures the effect of financial leverage on volatility. Table XII shows estimates of equation (8) for both measures of stock return volatility. There is no correction for autocorrelation in the errors from (8), although the standard errors use Hansen's (1982) heteroskedasticity and autocorrelation consistent covariance matrix.[16]

Equation (8) measures the contributions of macroeconomic conditional vola-

---

[16] Since many of the regressors in (8) are fitted values from first stage regressions (3b), the "generated regressors" problem discussed by Pagan (1984) is relevant here. In brief, to the extent that there are omitted variables that could be used to help to predict the volatility of some of these series, the coefficients of all of these second stage regressors will be biased. Experimentation with instrumental variables estimation, the technique recommended by Pagan, yielded similar results.

Table XII

## Estimates of the Relation of the Standard Deviation of Stock Returns to the Predicted Volatility of Macroeconomic Variables, and the Effect of Leverage, 1900–1987

The regression model,

$$\ln \tilde{\sigma}_{st} = \alpha_c + \alpha_r D_{rt} + \beta_1 \ln |\tilde{\varepsilon}_{pt}| + \beta_2 \ln |\tilde{\varepsilon}_{mt}| + \beta_3 \ln |\tilde{\varepsilon}_{it}| + \gamma \ln(V/S)_{t-1} + u_t, \qquad (8)$$

includes a constant $\alpha_c$ (not shown in this table), a dummy variable $D_{rt}$ equal to unity during NBER recessions, the logarithms of the predicted standard deviations of PPI inflation $|\tilde{\varepsilon}_{pt}|$, of money base growth $|\tilde{\varepsilon}_{mt}|$, and of industrial production $|\tilde{\varepsilon}_{it}|$, and the logarithm of leverage $(V/S)_{t-1}$. The predicted standard deviations are fitted values from the autoregressive models in Table II. The logarithm of the stock return volatility measures are the regressands. Asymptotic standard errors are in parentheses under the coefficient estimates. All tests use Hansen's (1982) heteroskedasticity and autocorrelation consistent covariance matrix, using 12 lags and leads and a damping factor of 0.7. $R^2$ is the coefficient of determination and $Q(24)$ is the Box-Pierce (1970) statistic for 24 lags of the residual autocorrelations, which should be distributed as $\chi^2(24)$ in this case, with the $p$-value in parentheses under the test. The column labeled Sum contains the sum of the coefficients of predicted volatilities. Coefficient estimates more than two standard errors from zero are indicated with an asterisk.

| Sample Period | Recessions $\alpha_r$ | Predicted Macroeconomic Volatility | | | | Leverage $\gamma$ | $R^2$ | $Q(24)$ |
|---|---|---|---|---|---|---|---|---|
| | | PPI $\beta_1$ | Base $\beta_2$ | IP $\beta_3$ | Sum | | | |
| | | Standard Deviation from Monthly Returns | | | | | | |
| 1900–1987 | 0.256* | −0.035 | 0.103 | 0.079 | 0.147 | 0.275 | 0.022 | 70.5 |
| | (0.120) | (0.076) | (0.072) | (0.059) | (0.088) | (0.440) | | (0.000) |
| 1900–1952 | 0.193 | −0.035 | 0.261* | 0.145 | 0.371* | −0.370 | 0.027 | 44.7 |
| | (0.148) | (0.096) | (0.088) | (0.079) | (0.131) | (0.634) | | (0.006) |
| 1953–1987 | 0.479* | 0.112 | −0.183 | 0.180* | 0.109 | 0.256 | 0.050 | 38.1 |
| | (0.082) | (0.128) | (0.133) | (0.083) | (0.179) | (0.644) | | (0.034) |
| | | Standard Deviation from Daily Returns | | | | | | |
| 1900–1987 | 0.182 | 0.087 | 0.210* | 0.031 | 0.328* | 0.091 | 0.208 | 2905 |
| | (0.096) | (0.045) | (0.062) | (0.043) | (0.068) | (0.316) | | (0.000) |
| 1900–1952 | 0.177 | 0.077 | 0.273* | 0.099 | 0.450* | −0.273 | 0.168 | 1795 |
| | (0.125) | (0.057) | (0.080) | (0.052) | (0.116) | (0.465) | | (0.000) |
| 1953–1987 | 0.248* | 0.151* | 0.119 | −0.009 | 0.262 | 0.047 | 0.120 | 540 |
| | (0.109) | (0.053) | (0.111) | (0.052) | (0.137) | (0.316) | | (0.000) |

tility factors, along with leverage, in explaining the time series variation in stock return volatility. From (4), $\sigma_{st}^2 \approx (V/S)_{t-1}^2 \sigma_{vt}^2$ since the variance of bond returns and the covariance of bond returns with stock returns will be much smaller than $\sigma_{vt}^2$. Thus, equation (8) is an approximation of (4), where the predicted volatilities of the macroeconomic factors affect firm volatility $\sigma_{vt}^2$. The sum of the elasticities $(\beta_1 + \beta_2 + \beta_3)$ measures the response of firm volatility to a one percent increase in the volatility of all the macroeconomic factors. The elasticity with leverage should be $\gamma = 1$.

The average level of volatility is much higher during recessions (consistent with Table VI). The column labeled "Recessions" in Table XII contains estimates of $\alpha_r$, the differential intercept during recessions. They are between 0.17 and 0.50 across the different measures of stock volatility and different periods, and many are reliably above zero. If the recession dummy variable proxies for variation in operating leverage, it is interesting that it remains important for stock volatility even when other factors are included.

The effect of financial leverage is small. The estimates using daily returns are reliably below unity. Perhaps this reflects the imperfect proxies for this and other regressors and the collinearity among them.

Most of the estimates of the predicted macroeconomic volatility coefficients are positive, and some are reliably above zero. For example, using the stock volatility measure from daily data ln $\hat{\sigma}_t$ for 1900–1952, all these coefficients are at least 1.35 standard errors above zero. The sum of these coefficients is 0.45, with a standard error of 0.12. Thus, if the volatility of inflation rates, money growth, and industrial production all increase one percent, stock volatility increases by 0.45 percent. Across both monthly and daily measures of stock volatility and across all subperiods, the coefficient estimates of predicted money base growth volatility are reliably positive most often.

### B. Summary

Many economic series were more volatile in the 1929–1939 Great Depression. Nevertheless, stock volatility increased by a factor of two or three during this period compared with the usual level of the series. (See Figure 1.) There is no other series in this paper that experienced similar behavior.

Second, there is evidence that many aggregate economic series are more volatile during recessions (Table VI). This is particularly true for financial asset returns and for measures of real economic activity. One interpretation of this evidence is that "operating leverage" increases during recessions.

Third, there is weak evidence that macroeconomic volatility can help to predict stock and bond return volatility (Tables III, IV, and V). The evidence is somewhat stronger that financial asset volatility helps to predict future macroeconomic volatility. This is not surprising since the prices of speculative assets should react quickly to new information about economic events.

Fourth, financial leverage affects stock volatility. When stock prices fall relative to bond prices, or when firms issue new debt securities in larger proportion to new equity than their prior capital structure, stock volatility increases (Table VIII). However, this effect explains only a small proportion of the changes in stock volatility over time (Figure 8).

Fifth, there seems to be a relation between trading activity and stock volatility. The number of trading days in the month is positively related to stock volatility, especially in 1953–1987 (Table IX). This reinforces the evidence in French and Roll (1986). Also, share trading volume growth is positively related to stock volatility (Tables X and XI).

### C. The Volatility Puzzle

Major episodes in United States economic history are associated with larger volatility, such as the Civil War, World War I, the Great Depression, World War

II, the OPEC oil shock, and the post-1979 period. The puzzle highlighted by the results in this paper is that stock volatility is not more closely related to other measures of economic volatility. For example, the volatility of inflation and money growth rates is very high during war periods, as is the volatility of industrial production. Yet the volatility of stock returns is not particularly high during wars.[17] There were many "financial crises" or "bank panics" during the 19th century in the United States that caused very high and volatile short-term interest rates. Schwert (1989b) shows that stock volatility increases for brief periods during and immediately following the worst panics, but there were no long-term effects on volatility.

On the other hand, the evidence in this paper reinforces the argument made by Officer (1973) that the volatility of stock returns from 1929 to 1939 was unusually high compared with either prior or subsequent experience. For many years macroeconomists have puzzled about the inability of their models to explain the data from the Great Depression. The results in this paper pose a similar challenge to financial economists. Moreover, based on evidence in Fama and French (1988a) and Poterba and Summers (1988), the 1929–1939 period plays a crucial role in the evidence for "mean reversion" in stock prices. I suspect that an analysis of Shiller's (1981a,b) variance bounds tests would reveal that the 1929–1939 period is responsible for the inference of "excess volatility" of stock prices. Indeed, the spirit of the preceding discussion suggests that stock volatility was inexplicably high during this period. I am hesitant to cede all this unexplained behavior to social psychologists as evidence of fads or bubbles.

Robert Merton has suggested that the Depression was an example of the so-called "Peso problem," in the sense that there was legitimate uncertainty about whether the economic system would survive. The Russian Revolution occurred only 12 years before the 1929 stock market crash, and there were major political and economic upheavals occurring throughout Europe in the interim. With the benefit of hindsight, we know that the U.S. and world economies came out of the Depression quite well. At the time, however, investors could not have had such confident expectations. Uncertainty about whether the "regime" had changed adds to the fundamental uncertainty reflected in past and future volatility of macroeconomic data. Hamilton's (1988) regime-switching model formalizes this notion. Schwert (1989b) and Turner, Startz, and Nelson (1989) use Hamilton's model to represent stock return volatility. It is not possible, however, to determine whether volatility was "too high" during the Depression without some model of the possible outcomes that did not occur. Thus, there remains a challenge to both theorists and empiricists to explain why this episode was so unusual.

## Appendix: Data Series Used in This Paper

### A. Common Stock Returns, 1857–1987

I use the monthly stock return index from Schwert (1989d). For 1926–1987, I use the returns including dividends to the value-weighted portfolio of all New

---

[17] If investors knew that the wars would have only short-term effects, it is likely that stock volatility would be affected less than the volatility of inflation or other macroeconomic variables.

Table AI
## Table AI
### Variables Used in This Paper

| Series | Description (Source) | Sample Period, Size |
|---|---|---|
| Stock | Monthly return to a value-weighted portfolio of New York Stock Exchange stocks (CRSP/Cowles/Macaulay/Smith and Cole) | 1/1857–12/1987 $T = 1572$ |
| $\sigma_t$ | Volatility of monthly stock returns from daily returns in the month (Dow Jones/Standard & Poor's) | 2/1885–12/1987 $T = 1235$ |
| Interest | Short-term interest rate on low risk debt instrument (CRSP/Macaulay) | 1/1857–12/1987 $T = 1572$ |
| $y_{Aa}$, Bond | Yield or return on high-grade long-term corporate debt (Moody's Aa/Macaulay) | 1/1857–12/1987 $T = 1572$ |
| $y_{Baa}$ | Yield on medium-grade long-term corporate debt (Moody's Baa) | 1/1919–12/1987 $T = 828$ |
| PPI | Inflation of producer price index for all commodities (BLS/Warren and Pearson) | 1/1857–12/1987 $T = 1572$ |
| Base | Growth rate of monetary base (high-powered money) (Friedman and Schwartz/NBER/Federal Reserve) | 7/1878–12/1987 $T = 1314$ |
| IP | Growth rate of the index of industrial production (seasonally adjusted - Federal Reserve) | 2/1889–12/1987 $T = 1187$ |
| $V/S$ | Market value of firm divided by the value of stock for S&P composite (Holland and Myers) | 1/1900–12/1987 $T = 1056$ |
| $Vol$ | NYSE share trading volume (S&P/NYSE) | 4/1881–12/1987 $T = 1280$ |
| $Days$ | Number of NYSE trading days per month (Dow Jones/S&P) | 2/1885–12/1987 $T = 1235$ |

York Stock Exchange (NYSE) stocks constructed by the Center for Research in Security Prices (CRSP) at the University of Chicago. For 1885–1925, I use the capital gain returns to the Dow Jones composite index (1972) and add the dividend yield from the value-weighted portfolio of NYSE stocks constructed by the Cowles Commission (1939, pp. 168–169), as corrected by Wilson and Jones (1987, p. 253, with erratum). For 1871–1885, I use the Cowles returns, corrected for the effects of time-averaging by Schwert (1989d). For 1857–1870, I use Macaulay's (1938, pp. A142–A161) index of railroad stock prices to calculate capital gain returns and then add an estimate of the dividend yield from Schwert (1989d). This is equivalent to adding a dividend yield of 0.56 percent per month (6.7 percent per year) to the percent changes in railroad stock prices.

### B. Short-Term Interest Rates, 1857–1987

For 1926–1987, I use the monthly yields on the shortest term U.S. Government security (with no special tax provisions) which matures after the end of the month from the Government Bond File constructed by CRSP. For 1857–1925, I use the four to six month commercial paper rates in New York from Macaulay (1938, Table 10, pp. A141–A161). The commercial paper yields are adjusted so that the level of the series is comparable to the Treasury yields, using the regression of CRSP yields on Macaulay yields from 1926 to 1937:

$$CRSP_t = -0.000761 + 0.9737368 \, Macaulay_t + u_t,$$

$$(.000085) \quad (0.0309330)$$

where standard errors are in parentheses under the coefficient estimates. This is equivalent to subtracting an average risk premium of 0.076 percent per month (0.91 percent per year) from the Macaulay yields to reflect a small default premium in commercial paper. The correlation between the CRSP and the Macaulay yields is 0.94 for 1926–1937.

## C. Long-Term Interest Rates, 1857–1987

The high-grade corporate bond yield for 1919–1987 is the Moody's Aa bond yield (Federal Reserve (1976a, Table 128, pp. 468–471) for 1919–1940, Federal Reserve (1976b, Table 12.12, pp. 720–721) for 1941–1947, and Citibase (1978) for 1948–1987). For 1857–1918, I use Macaulay's (1938, Table 10, pp. A141–A161) railroad bond yield index, adjusted to splice with the Moody's series using the average ratio of the yields during 1919, $(RR/Aa) = 0.964372$.

## D. Returns to Long-Term Corporate Bonds, 1857–1987

The capital gain or loss from holding the bond during the month is estimated from yields assuming that, at the beginning of the month, the bond has a 20-year maturity, a price equal to par, and a coupon equal to the yield, using the conventional bond pricing formula to calculate beginning and ending prices. The monthly income return is assumed to be one twelfth of the coupon. Since the Moody's yields are averages of the yields within the month, these returns are not comparable to returns based on end-of-month data. To correct for this problem, I estimate a first-order moving average process for the returns:

$$R^*_{bt} = \alpha + \varepsilon_t - \theta \, \varepsilon_{t-1},$$

and then the "corrected" returns are defined as $R_{bt} = \alpha + \varepsilon_t$. This correction eliminates the positive autocorrelation at lag one induced by the within-month aggregation of yields. (See Working (1960).) Note, however, that corrected returns are not good estimates of actual returns based on end-of-month prices since their cross-correlations with other variables are still affected by time aggregation of the yields.[18]

## E. Inflation Rates, 1857–1987

For 1890–1987, I use the Bureau of Labor Statistics' Producer Price Index (PPI) inflation rate, not seasonally adjusted. For 1857–1889, I use the inflation rate of the Warren and Pearson (1933) index of producer prices. I am grateful to Grant McQueen for making these data available to me.

---

[18] Schwert (1989d) develops a correction similar to this one for returns calculated from indexes of time-averaged stock prices.

### F. Stock Market Share Trading Volume, 1881–1987

Standard & Poor's (1986, p. 214) reports monthly NYSE share trading volume for 1883–1985.[19] Citibase (1978) contains similar data for 1986–1987. The NYSE provided data from April 1881 through 1882. I measure the number of trading days per month for 1885–1987 from the daily data on the Dow Jones indexes in Dow Jones (1972) and on the Standard & Poor's composite index in Standard & Poor's (1986, pp. 134–187).

### G. Financial Leverage, 1900–1987

Taggart (1986) discusses many estimates of the equity to total capital ratio ($S/V$) for public corporations in the United States for 1900–1979. Holland and Myers (1979) estimate the capital structure of corporations using National Income Accounts data on dividend and net interest payments from nonfinancial corporations. They capitalize these flows using the S&P dividend yield and the Moody's Baa bond yield, respectively. These data are available annually for 1929–1945 and quarterly for 1946–1987. For 1926, I use the estimate from Ciccolo and Baum (1986), based on the market value of debt and preferred and common stock for a sample of about 50 manufacturing firms. For 1900, 1912, and 1922, I multiply estimates of the book value of $S/V$ from Goldsmith, Lipsey, and Mendelson (1963, Tables III-4, and III-4b, pp. 140–141, 146–147) by the average ratio of these estimates divided by the Holland-Myers estimates for the years 1929, 1933, 1939, and 1945–1958, (HM/Goldsmith) = 1.226. Thus, I have annual estimates of $S/V$ for 1900, 1912, 1922, 1926, and 1929–1945 and quarterly estimates for 1946–1987.

I create a monthly series $(S/V)_t$ using the rates of return to the stock portfolio, $R_{st}$, described above and the returns to corporate bonds from Ibbotson (1986), $R_{bt}$. Before 1926, I estimate corporate bond returns using the yields on high-grade long-term bonds described above. I interpolate forward,

$$(S/V)_t^+ = \{S_{t-1}(1 + R_{st})/[S_{t-1}(1 + R_{st}) + B_{t-1}(1 + R_{bt})]\},$$

and backward,

$$(S/V)_t^- = \{S_{t+1}/(1 + R_{st+1})/[S_{t+1}/(1 + R_{st+1}) + B_{t+1}/(1 + R_{bt+1})]\}$$

and then use the average of these estimates for the monthly leverage estimate,

$$(S/V)_t = \{(S/V)_t^+ + (S/V)_t^-\}/2.$$

### H. Stock Return Volatility, 1885–1987

Following French, Schwert, and Stambaugh (1987), I use the daily returns to the Standard & Poor's composite portfolio for 1928–1987 to estimate the standard deviation of monthly stock returns. The estimate of the monthly standard

---

[19] The New York Stock Exchange was closed from August through mid-December, 1914 due to the outbreak of World War I. For purposes of this paper, I interpolate share volume growth during this period.

deviation is

$$\hat{\sigma}_t = \left\{ \sum_{i=1}^{N_t} r_{it}^2 \right\}^{1/2},$$

where $r_{it}$ is the return to the S&P portfolio on day $i$ in month $t$ (after subtracting the sample mean for the month) and there are $N_t$ trading days in month $t$. For 1885–1927 I use a comparable estimator based on the daily values of the Dow Jones composite portfolio. See Schwert (1989c,d) for more information about the daily stock returns and volatility estimates.

## I. Industrial Production, 1889–1987

For 1919–1987, I use the index of industrial production from the Federal Reserve Board (1986) and Citibase (1978). For 1889–1918, I use Babson's Index of the physical volume of business activity from Moore (1961, p. 130), adjusted to splice with the industrial production data using the average ratio of Babson to adjusted industrial production for 1919–1939 (7.372662). I am grateful to Grant McQueen for providing these data.

## J. Money Supply, 1867–1987

I use the monetary base (called high-powered money in Friedman and Schwartz (1963)). For 1867–1960, I use data from Friedman and Schwartz (1963, Table B-3, column (1), pp. 799–808) for the base. For 1961–1987, I use the seasonally adjusted monetary base reported by the Federal Reserve Board from Citibase (1978). These series are spliced using the average ratio of the respective series during 1960. Thus, the base data since 1960 are multiplied by 1.127538. The Friedman and Schwartz data are reported on a monthly basis beginning in May 1907. From June 1878 through April 1907, I use a monthly monetary base series from the National Bureau of Economic Research (NBER), multiplied by the average ratio of the Friedman and Schwartz series to the NBER series for 1878–1914, 1.006948. These data were provided by Professor Robert Barro. Thus, there are monthly data on growth rates of the base for 1878–1987.

### REFERENCES

Abel, Andrew, 1988, Stock prices under time-varying dividend risk: An exact solution in an infinite-horizon general equilibrium model, *Journal of Monetary Economics* 22, 375–393.

Black, Fischer, 1976, Studies of stock price volatility changes, in: *Proceedings of the 1976 Meetings of the Business and Economics Statistics Section*, American Statistical Association, 177–181.

———— and John C. Cox, 1976, Valuing corporate securities: Some effects of bond indenture provisions, *Journal of Finance* 31, 351–367.

Bollerslev, Tim, Robert F. Engle, and Jeffrey M. Wooldridge, 1988, A capital asset pricing model with time varying covariances, *Journal of Political Economy* 96, 116–131.

Box, George E. P. and David Pierce, 1970, Distribution of residual autocorrelations in autoregressive-integrated-moving average time series models, *Journal of the American Statistical Association* 65, 1509–1526.

Christie, Andrew A., 1982, The stochastic behavior of common stock variances: Value, leverage and interest rate effects, *Journal of Financial Economics* 10, 407–432.

Ciccolo, John C., Jr. and Christopher F. Baum, 1986, Changing balance sheet relationships in the

U.S. manufacturing sector, 1926–77, in Benjamin M. Friedman, ed: *The Changing Roles of Debt and Equity in Financing U.S. Capital Formation* (University of Chicago Press, Chicago), 81–109.

Citibase Economic Database, 1946–86 [machine-readable magnetic datafile], 1978 (Citibank, N.A., New York).

Cowles, Alfred III and Associates, 1939, *Common Stock Indexes*, 2nd ed., Cowles Commission Monograph no. 3 (Principia Press, Inc., Bloomington, IN).

Davidian, M. and R. J. Carroll, 1987, Variance function estimation, *Journal of the American Statistical Association* 82, 1079–1091.

Dow Jones & Co., 1972, *The Dow Jones Averages, 1885–1970*, Maurice L. Farrell, ed. (Dow Jones & Co., New York).

Engle, Robert F., 1982, Autoregressive conditional heteroskedasticity with estimates of the variance of United Kingdom inflation, *Econometrica* 50, 987–1007.

—— and Tim Bollerslev, 1986, Modeling the persistence of conditional variances, *Econometric Reviews* 5, 1–50.

Fama, Eugene F., 1976, Inflation uncertainty and expected returns on Treasury bills, *Journal of Political Economy* 84, 427–448.

—— and Kenneth R. French, 1988a, Permanent and transitory components of stock prices, *Journal of Political Economy* 96, 246–273.

—— and Kenneth R. French, 1988b, Dividend yields and expected stock returns, *Journal of Financial Economics* 22, 3–25.

—— and Kenneth R. French, 1989, Business conditions and expected returns on stocks and bonds, *Journal of Financial Economics*, Forthcoming.

Federal Reserve Board, 1976a, *Banking and Monetary Statistics, 1914–1941* (U.S. Government Printing Office, Washington, DC).

—— 1976b, *Banking and Monetary Statistics, 1941–1970* (U.S. Government Printing Office, Washington, DC).

—— 1986, *Industrial Production, 1986 Edition* (U.S. Government Printing Office, Washington, DC).

French, Kenneth R. and Richard Roll, 1986, Stock return variances: The arrival of information and the reaction of traders, *Journal of Financial Economics* 17, 5–26.

——, G. William Schwert, and Robert F. Stambaugh, 1987, Expected stock returns and volatility. *Journal of Financial Economics* 19, 3–29.

Friedman, Milton and Anna J. Schwartz, 1963, *A Monetary History of the United States, 1867–1960* (Princeton University Press, Princeton, NJ).

Fuller, Wayne A, 1976, *Introduction to Statistical Time Series* (John Wiley, New York).

Goldsmith, Raymond W., Robert E. Lipsey, and Morris Mendelson, 1963, *Studies in the National Balance Sheet of the United States, Vol. II* (Princeton University Press, Princeton, NJ).

Hamilton, James D., 1988, Rational-expectations econometric analysis of changes in regime: An investigation of the term structure of interest rates, *Journal of Economic Dynamics and Control* 12, 385–423.

Hansen, Lars P., 1982, Large sample properties of generalized method of moments estimators, *Econometrica* 50, 1029–1054.

Holland, Daniel M. and Stewart C. Myers, 1979, Trends in corporate profitability and capital costs, in R. Lindsay, ed.: *The Nation's Capital Needs: Three Studies* (Committee for Economic Development, New York).

Huizinga, John and Frederic S. Mishkin, 1986, Monetary policy regime shifts and the unusual behavior of real interest rates, *Carnegie-Rochester Conference Series on Public Policy* 24, 231–274.

Ibbotson Associates, 1986, *Stocks, Bonds, Bills, and Inflation: 1986 Yearbook* (Ibbotson Associates, Chicago).

Karpoff, Jonathan M., 1987, The relation between price changes and trading volume: A survey, *Journal of Financial and Quantitative Analysis* 22, 109–126.

Keim, Donald B. and Robert F. Stambaugh, 1986, Predicting returns in the stock and bond markets, *Journal of Financial Economics* 17, 357–390.

Kendall, Maurice G. and Alan Stuart, 1969, *The Advanced Theory of Statistics*, Vol. I, 3rd ed. (Hafner, New York).

Kleidon, Allan W., 1986, Variance bounds tests and stock price valuation models, *Journal of Political Economy* 94, 953–1001.

Lauterbach, Beni, 1989, Consumption volatility, production volatility, spot rate volatility and the returns on Treasury bills and bonds, *Journal of Financial Economics*, Forthcoming.

Macaulay, Frederick R., 1938, *The Movements of Interest Rates, Bond Yields and Stock Prices in the United States Since 1856* (National Bureau of Economic Research, New York).

Mascaro, Angelo and Allan H. Meltzer, 1983, Long- and short-term interest rates in a risky world, *Journal of Monetary Economics* 12, 485–518.

Merton, Robert C., 1980, On estimating the expected return on the market: An exploratory investigation, *Journal of Financial Economics* 8, 323–361.

Moore, Geoffrey H, ed., 1961, *Business Cycle Indicators, Vol. II, Basic Data on Cyclical Indicators* (Princeton University Press, Princeton, NJ).

Officer, Robert R., 1973, The variability of the market factor of New York Stock Exchange, *Journal of Business* 46, 434–453.

Pagan, Adrian, 1984, Econometric issues in the analysis of regressions with generated regressors, *International Economic Review* 25, 221–247.

―――― and Aman Ullah, 1988, The econometric analysis of models with risk terms, *Journal of Applied Econometrics* 3, 87–105.

Pindyck, Robert S., 1984, Risk, inflation, and the stock market, *American Economic Review* 74, 335–351.

Poterba, James M. and Lawrence H. Summers, 1986, The persistence of volatility and stock market fluctuations, *American Economic Review* 76, 1142–1151.

―――― and Lawrence H. Summers, 1988, Mean reversion in stock prices, *Journal of Financial Economics* 22, 27–59.

Romer, Christina D., 1986a, Spurious volatility in historical unemployment data, *Journal of Political Economy* 94, 1–37.

――――, 1986b, Is the stabilization of the postwar economy a figment of the data? *American Economic Review* 76, 314–334.

――――, 1989, The prewar business cycle reconsidered: New estimates of Gross National Product, 1869–1908, *Journal of Political Economy* 97, 1–37.

Schwert, G. William, 1987, Effects of model specification on tests for unit roots in macroeconomic data, *Journal of Monetary Economics* 20, 73–103.

――――, 1989a, Tests for unit roots: A Monte Carlo investigation, *Journal of Business and Economic Statistics* 7, 147–159.

――――, 1989b, Business cycles, financial crises and stock volatility, *Carnegie-Rochester Conference Series on Public Policy* 31, Forthcoming.

――――, 1989c, Stock volatility and the crash of '87, *Review of Financial Studies*, Forthcoming.

――――, 1989d, Indexes of United States stock prices from 1802–1987, *Journal of Business*, Forthcoming.

Shapiro, Matthew D., 1988, The stabilization of the U.S. economy: Evidence from the stock market, *American Economic Review* 78, 1067–1079.

Shiller, Robert J., 1981a, Do stock prices move too much to be justified by subsequent changes in dividends, *American Economic Review* 75, 421–436.

――――, 1981b, The use of volatility measures in assessing market efficiency, *Journal of Finance* 36, 291–304.

Smith, Walter B. and Arthur H. Cole, 1935, *Fluctuations in American Business, 1790–1860* (Harvard University Press, Cambridge).

Standard & Poor's, 1986, *Security Price Index Record, 1986 ed.* (Standard & Poor's Corp., New York).

Taggart, Robert A., 1986, Secular patterns in the financing of U.S. corporations, in Benjamin M. Friedman, ed.: *The Changing Roles of Debt and Equity in Financing U.S. Capital Formation* (University of Chicago Press, Chicago).

Turner, Christopher M., Richard Startz, and Charles R. Nelson, 1989, A Markov model of heteroskedasticity, risk and learning in the stock market, *Journal of Financial Economics*, Forthcoming.

Warren, G. F. and F. A. Pearson, 1933, Wholesale prices, 1720 to 1889, inclusive, in *Bulletin No. 572*, 111–114 (Bureau of Labor Statistics, U.S. Government Printing Office, Washington, DC).

White, Halbert, 1980, A heteroskedasticity-consistent covariance matrix estimator and a direct test for heteroskedasticity, *Econometrica* 48, 817–838.

Wilson, Jack W. and Charles P. Jones, 1987, A comparison of annual common stock returns: 1871–1925 with 1926–85, *Journal of Business* 60, 239–258.

Working, Holbrook, 1960, A note on the correlation of first differences of averages in random chains, *Econometrica* 28, 916–918.

# MEASURING SECURITY PRICE PERFORMANCE*

Stephen J. BROWN

*Bell Laboratories, Murray Hill, NJ 07974, USA*

Jerold B. WARNER

*University of Rochester, Rochester, NY 14627, USA*

Received January 1980, revised version received April 1980

Event studies focus on the impact of particular types of firm-specific events on the prices of the affected firms' securities. In this paper, observed stock return data are employed to examine various methodologies which are used in event studies to measure security price performance. Abnormal performance is introduced into this data. We find that a simple methodology based on the market model performs well under a wide variety of conditions. In some situations, even simpler methods which do not explicitly adjust for marketwide factors or for risk perform no worse than the market model. We also show how misuse of any of the methodologies can result in false inferences about the presence of abnormal performance.

## 1. Introduction and summary

The impact of particular types of firm-specific events (e.g., stock splits, earnings reports) on the prices of the affected firms' securities has been the subject of a number of studies. A major concern in those 'event' studies has been to assess the extent to which security price performance around the time of the event has been abnormal — that is, the extent to which security returns were different from those which would have been appropriate, given the model determining equilibrium expected returns.

Event studies provide a direct test of market efficiency. Systematically nonzero abnormal security returns which persist after a particular type of event are inconsistent with the hypothesis that security prices adjust quickly to fully reflect new information. In addition, to the extent that the event is unanticipated, the magnitude of abnormal performance at the time the event actually occurs is a measure of the impact of that type of event on the wealth of the firms' claimholders. Any such abnormal performance is consistent with market efficiency, however, since the abnormal returns would only have been

*Financial support for this research was provided to J.B. Warner by the Managerial Economics Research Center, University of Rochester, and the Institute for Quantitative Research in Finance, Columbia University. We are indebted to numerous colleagues for their help on this paper. We are especially grateful to Michael Gibbons and Michael Jensen for their assistance.

attainable by an investor if the occurrence of the event could have been predicted with certainty.

In this paper, observed stock return data are employed to examine various methodologies which are used in event studies to measure security price performance. Abnormal performance is introduced into this data. We assess the likelihood that various methodologies will lead to Type I errors — rejecting the null hypothesis of no abnormal performance when it is true, and Type II errors — failing to reject the null hypothesis of no abnormal performance when it is false. Our concern is with the power of the various methodologies. Power is the probability, for a given level of Type I error and a given level of abnormal performance, that the hypothesis of no abnormal performance will be rejected. Since a test's power indicates its ability to discern the presence of abnormal performance, then all other things equal, a more powerful test is preferred to a less powerful test.

The use of various methodologies is simulated by repeated application of each methodology to samples which have been constructed by random selection of securities and random assignment of an 'event-date' to each. Randomly selected securities should not, on average, exhibit any abnormal performance. Thus, for a large number of applications of a given methodology, we examine the frequency of Type I errors. Abnormal performance is then artificially introduced by transforming each sample security's return around the time it experiences a hypothetical event. Each methodology is then applied to a number of samples where the return data have thus been transformed. For each methodology, and for various levels of abnormal performance, this technique provides direct measures of the frequency of Type II errors. Since, for any given level of abnormal performance, the power of a test is equal to one minus the probability of a Type II error, this technique thus allows us to examine the power of the methodologies and the ability to detect abnormal performance when it is present.

*Overview of the paper*

General considerations which are relevant to measuring abnormal security price performance are discussed in section 2. Performance measures in event studies are classified into several categories: Mean Adjusted Returns, Market Adjusted Returns, and Market and Risk Adjusted Returns. In section 3, we specify methodologies which are based on each of these performance measures and which are representative of current practice. We then devise a simulation procedure for studying and comparing these methods, and their numerous variations.

Initial results are presented in section 4. For each methodology, the probability of Type I and Type II errors is assessed for both parametric and non-parametric significance tests. In addition, the distributional properties of the test statistics generated by each methodology are examined. We also focus on different ways in which actual event studies take into account the systematic risk of the sample securities. The risk adjustment methods we compare are based on market model residuals, Fama–MacBeth residuals, and what we call Control Portfolios.

In section 5, we discuss the effect of imprecise prior information about the timing of the event on the power of the tests. The use of the Cumulative Average Residual procedure suggested by Fama, Fisher, Jensen and Roll (1969) is also investigated.

In section 6, two forms of sample security 'clustering' are examined. We first look at the calendar time clustering of events, and examine the characteristics of the tests when all sample securities experience an event during the same calendar time period. We then examine how the tests are affected when all sample securities have higher than average (or lower than average) systematic risk.

Section 7 examines the effect of the choice of market index on the various tests. Section 8 reports additional simulation results. The sensitivity of earlier simulation results to the number of sample securities is investigated. Evidence is also presented on the likelihood that the various test methods will, for a given sample, lead to the same inference.

Our conclusions, along with a summary of the paper's major results, are presented in section 9; an appendix contains a more detailed discussion of the specific performance assessment methods used in the study.

## 2. Measuring abnormal performance: General considerations

### 2.1. Defining abnormal performance for a security

A security's price performance can only be considered 'abnormal' relative to a particular benchmark. Thus, it is necessary to specify a model generating 'normal' returns before abnormal returns can be measured. In this paper, we will concentrate on three general models of the process generating *ex ante* expected returns. These models are general representations of the models which have been assumed in event studies. For each model, the abnormal return for a given security in any time period $t$ is defined as the difference between its actual *ex post* return and that which is predicted under the assumed return-generating process, The three models are as follows.

### (1) *Mean Adjusted Returns*

The Mean Adjusted Returns model assumes that the *ex ante* expected return for a given security $i$ is equal to a constant $K_i$ which can differ across securities: $E(\tilde{R}_i)=K_i$. The predicted *ex post* return on security $i$ in time period $t$ is equal to $K_i$. The abnormal return $\varepsilon_{it}$ is equal to the difference between the observed return, $R_{it}$, and the predicted return $K_i$: $\varepsilon_{it} = R_{it} - K_i$.

The Mean Adjusted Returns model is consistent with the Capital Asset Pricing Model; under the assumption that a security has constant systematic risk and that the efficient frontier is stationary, the Asset Pricing Model also predicts that a security's expected return is constant.

### (2) Market Adjusted Returns

This model assumes that *ex ante* expected returns are equal across securities, but not necessarily constant for a given security. Since the market portfolio of risky assets $M$ is a linear combination of all securities, it follows that $E(\tilde{R}_{it}) = E(\tilde{R}_{mt}) = K_t$ for any security $i$. The *ex post* abnormal return on any security $i$ is given by the difference between its return and that on the market portfolio: $\varepsilon_{it} = R_{it} - R_{mt}$. The Market Adjusted Returns model is also consistent with the Asset Pricing model if all securities have systematic risk of unity.

### (3) Market and Risk Adjusted Returns

This model presumes that some version of the Capital Asset Pricing Model generates expected returns. For example, in the Black (1972) two-parameter Asset Pricing Model, $E(\tilde{R}_{it}) = E(\tilde{R}_{zt}) + \beta_i[E(\tilde{R}_{mt}) - E(\tilde{R}_{zt})] = K_{it}$ for any security $i$, where $R_{zt}$ is the return on a minimum variance portfolio of risky assets which is uncorrelated with the market portfolio. In the Black model, the abnormal return $\varepsilon_{it}$ is equal to $R_{it} - [R_{zt}(1 - \beta_i) + \beta_i R_{mt}]$.

For each of these three models, the return which will be realized on security $i$ in period $t$, $\tilde{R}_{it}$, is given by

$$\tilde{R}_{it} = K_{it} + \tilde{\varepsilon}_{it},$$

where $K_{it}$ is the expected return given by the particular model, and $\tilde{\varepsilon}_{it}$, which is unknown at the beginning of period $t$, is the component which is abnormal or unexpected.

### 2.2. Evaluating alternative performance measures

Under each model of the return generating process, there will be times when the realized return on a given security is different from that which was predicted. However, returns in an efficient market cannot systematically differ from those which are predicted. That is, the expected value of the unexpected component, $\tilde{\varepsilon}_{it}$, of a security's return cannot systematically differ from zero.

Let $I$ be an integer which is equal to 0 when no 'event' takes place, and equal to 1 when a particular event does take place. In an efficient market, the abnormal return measure $\varepsilon_{it}$, if correctly specified, must be such that

$$E(\tilde{\varepsilon}_{it}) = [E(\tilde{\varepsilon}_{it} \mid I = 0)]p(I = 0) + [E(\tilde{\varepsilon}_{it} \mid I = 1)]p(I = 1) = 0;$$

abnormal returns conditional on the event can systematically be non-zero, as can abnormal returns conditional on no event. The only restriction is that a security's abnormal return, weighted by its magnitude and probability of occurrence, have an expected value of zero. Under each model just discussed, the abnormal performance measure for every security has an unconditional mean of 0 if the model is correct. In that sense, the abnormal performance measures are unbiased for each model.

Of course, another major purpose of specifying the 'correct' model for expected returns is to reduce the variance of the abnormal return component $\varepsilon_{it}$. For example, in the Market and Risk Adjusted Returns model, a contemporaneous relationship between realized security returns and realized market returns is predicted by the *ex ante* model. In an event study, where the market return which was observed at the time of each firm's event is known, the variance of the abnormal component of returns will be lower if a model takes into account the *ex post* relationship between a security's return and that of the market. When the *ex post* return generating process is correctly specified, abnormal performance, which is just the difference between returns conditional on the event and returns unconditional on the event, should be easier to detect.[1] Thus, if the Capital Asset Pricing model is correct, then the Market and Risk Adjusted Returns method, by bringing to bear additional information about the determinants of realized returns, such as the security's systematic risk and the market's return, could increase the power of the tests over the Mean Adjusted Returns method.[2]

---

[1] Our definition of abnormal performance as the difference between conditional (expected) and unconditional (expected) returns is consistent with the abnormal performance metric used in studies where the event is associated with either good news ($I = 1$) or bad news ($I = 0$) [e.g., Ball and Brown (1968)]. In such studies, abnormal performance is often measured as the average of the deviation from unconditional returns when there is good news and the deviation from unconditional returns when there is bad news, where the deviation from unconditional returns when there is bad news is first multiplied by $-1$. It can be shown that this abnormal performance measure is equal to our definition of abnormal performance conditional on good news, multiplied by twice the probability of good news. If good news has probability 0.5, the two abnormal performance measures will be identical; in general, the two measures differ only by a factor of proportionality. See Patell (1979, p. 536) for a related discussion.

[2] This line of argument has been pushed still further. The Asset Pricing model allows a security's return to be contemporaneously related to additional 'factors' as well. For example, a security's realized return could be related to the return on the securities of a particular industry. Even though there is no 'industry factor' in the *ex ante* Asset Pricing model, under certain conditions taking into account such an *ex post* relationship leads to more powerful tests. For a further discussion, see Warner (1977, p. 259) and Langetieg (1978). Fama and MacBeth (1973, pp. 634–635) and Roll and Ross (1979) also discuss related issues in the context of multiple factor models.

## 2.3. On the role of simulation

Unfortunately, specifying a more precise model of the processs generating realized returns is not sufficient for that model to generate a more powerful test for abnormal performance. Even if the Capital Asset Pricing model is the correct specification of the return generating process, it does not follow that a performance measure based upon that model will dominate performance measures based on the Mean Adjusted Returns method.

First, there is measurement error in each of the variables upon which abnormal returns depend in the Asset Pricing model. Not only is a security's risk measured with error, but, as Roll (1977) has argued, the market portfolio cannot be observed directly. Such measurement error need not introduce any systematic bias in event studies.[3] However, with small samples, the measurement error in these variables may be so large that it renders inconsequential any potential efficiency gains from more precise specification of the return-generating process.[4]

Second, the efficiency of using a particular model of the return-generating process will depend critically on the appropriateness of the additional peripheral assumptions about the $\tilde{\varepsilon}_{it}$ which must be made in order to test the hypothesis of 'no abnormal performance' conditional on a particular event. For example, with each method, a test statistic such as a $t$-statistic must be computed and compared to the distribution of test statistics which is assumed to obtain under the null hypothesis. To the extent that the assumed sampling distribution under the null hypothesis differs from the true distribution, false inferences can result. If the assumed properties of the test statistic under the Mean Adjusted Returns Method are more appropriate than those under the Market and Risk Adjusted Returns Method, the Mean Adjusted Returns Method can be preferred even if the second method is 'correct'.

Finally, there are a variety of ways of measuring abnormal returns under different variants of the Asset Pricing model. These include market model residuals, Fama–MacBeth residuals, and control portfolios. The differences in the predictive ability of such alternative methods could be substantial; the usefulness of the Asset Pricing model is not independent of the specific method of implementing the Market and Risk Adjusted Returns model.

Even if it were possible to analytically derive and compare the properties of alternative methods for measuring abnormal performance in event studies, conclusions from the comparison would not necessarily be valid if the actual data used in event studies were generated by a process which differed from that which the comparison assumed. For this reason, the performance of the

---

[3]See Mayers and Rice (1979) for a more detailed discussion of how the unobservability of the true market portfolio affects the measures of abnormal performance. Bawa, Brown, and Klein (1979) present an extensive discussion of how measurement error can be taken into account by using the predictive distribution of returns [see also Patell (1976, p. 256)].

[4]Brenner (1979) makes a similar point.

alternative methods is an empirical question. To address the question, we will employ simulation techniques which use actual security return data (presumably generated by the 'true' process) to examine the characteristics of various methodologies for measuring abnormal performance.

## 3. The experimental design

### 3.1. Sample construction

Our study concentrates on abnormal performance measurement using monthly data.[5] To simulate methodologies based on the three general models just discussed, we first construct 250 samples, each containing 50 securities. The securities are selected at random and with replacement from a population consisting of all securities for which monthly return data are available on the files of the Center for Research in Security Prices (CRSP) at the University of Chicago.[6] For each security, we generate a hypothetical 'event' month. Events are assumed to occur with equal probability in each month from June 1944 through February 1971.[7] Events can occur in different

---

[5]For our simulation study, monthly data offers several advantages over daily data. The use of monthly data enables us to consider those studies which have employed Fama–MacBeth (1973) residuals; the data necessary for readily computing daily Fama–MacBeth residuals are not to our knowledge available, and such daily residuals have not been used in any event study.

Furthermore, the use of daily data involves complications whose treatment is largely beyond the scope of this paper. Daily stock returns depart more from normality than do monthly returns [Fama (1976, ch. 1)]. In addition, the estimation of parameters (such as systematic risk) from daily data is a non-trivial matter due to the non-synchronous trading problem [see Scholes and Williams (1977)]. Any conclusions from simulations using daily data could be sensitive to specific procedures we employed to handle the complications associated with non-normality and non-synchronous trading.

We have no strong reason to believe that our conclusions about the relative performance of various methods for measuring abnormal performance would be altered by the use of daily data. However, in the absence of problems such as non-normality and non-synchronous trading, all of the methods for measuring abnormal performance are potentially more powerful with daily data. First, daily returns have smaller standard deviations than do monthly returns. The mean standard deviation of monthly returns for randomly selected securities is about 7.8% [Fama (1976, p. 123)], whereas the corresponding mean standard deviation of daily returns will be approximately 1.8% if daily returns are serially independent. In addition, as we later indicate, the power of all the methodologies increases with knowledge about precisely when an event occurs; use of daily data is potentially useful in that it permits the researcher to take advantage of prior information about the specific day of the month on which an event took place. Performance measurement with daily data is the subject of a separate study we are currently undertaking.

[6]We used a combination congruential and Tausworthe (shift register) algorithm to generate uniformly distributed random numbers on the [0, 1) interval. See Marsaglia, Ananthanarayanan and Paul (1973) for a description of the algorithm.

[7]Given the other data requirements we will discuss, including the requirement that Fama–MacBeth residuals be computed, these are the calendar months whose selection maximizes the length of the calendar time period over which our simulations can be performed. With the exception of mutual funds, all CRSP listed securities are eligible for selection. Each CRSP security initially has the same probability of being selected, subject to data availability. A security can be selected more than once for inclusion in a given sample or in a different sample. In both cases, whenever a security already selected is again selected, it is treated as a 'different' security in the sense that a new event-date is generated.

calendar months for different securities. This set of sample securities and hypothetical event dates will be used in most of the present study.

Define month '0' as the month in which the firm has been assigned an event. For a given sample, we use 100 return observations on each security for the period around the time of the event. We use 100 months of data, from month $-89$ through month $+10$.[8]

### Introducing abnormal performance

Return data for the 250 samples which have been chosen is based on randomly selected securities and event dates, and, as indicated in section 2, should not systematically exhibit any abnormal performance. However, an important question we want to investigate is how different methodologies perform when some abnormal performance is present. It is thus necessary to specify a procedure for introducing a known level of abnormal performance into the sample securities.

A particular level of abnormal performance is artificially introduced into a given sample by transforming its actual return data. To introduce, say, $5\%$ abnormal performance for each security of a sample, 0.05 is added to the actual return on each sample security in the particular calendar month in which its event is assumed to occur. Abnormal performance is thus introduced by adding a constant to a security's observed return.[9]

---

[8]If a security does not have this 100 months of return data surrounding its event-date, it is not included in the sample. To handle such cases, we continue to select securities and event-dates until, for a given sample, we have found 50 securities with a sufficient amount of data. With this selection procedure, the probability of being included in our sample will depend upon the amount of data which is available for a security. For example, a security with continuous return data from 1935 through 1971 will be included with a higher frequency than one with a smaller amount of available data. Thus, our data requirements introduce a bias towards including only surviving companies; none of our simulation results suggest that the bias is of importance.

[9]Three points about the procedure for introducing abnormal performance are worth mentioning. First, note that the level of abnormal performance associated with an actual event could itself be stochastic; an event could thus affect not only the conditional mean of a security's return, but higher-order moments as well. Introducing a constant represents a simple case which enables us to focus on the detection of mean shifts when an event takes place, holding constant the conditional variance. The detection of mean shifts is the relevant phenomenon to study when investigating how well different methodologies pick up the impact of an event on the value of the firm.

Second, although it is not critical for our purposes, it should also be noted that if for a given security there is positive abnormal performance conditional on an event, there should also be negative abnormal performance conditional on no event. Otherwise, the unconditional expected return on the security will be abnormal, which is inconsistent with an efficient market. However, for simulations introducing positive abnormal performance in month '0', the appropriate downward adjustment to security returns in those months when the event does not occur is not obvious. The adjustment which leaves expected returns unaltered will depend upon the *ex ante* probability of the event, which in an actual event study is unobservable.

For all results reported in this paper, in order to leave mean returns unaltered across all levels of abnormal performance, for each sample security the observed return for each month in the

## 3.2. Abnormal performance measures for a given sample

For every sample, we have a set of security returns which is transformed to reflect various levels of abnormal performance. For each sample, we calculate performance measures based on the three models of the return-generating process discussed in section 2. The performance measures are briefly summarized here; further details are contained in the appendix.

(a) *Mean Adjusted Returns* — To implement this model, we focus on the returns to each sample security around the time of its event. We examine whether or not the returns on the sample securities in month '0' are statistically significantly different from the returns on the securities in the time period surrounding the event. As discussed below, several different significance tests are used. The Mean Adjusted Returns method is used by Masulis (1978).

(b) *Market Adjusted Returns* — Unlike the Mean Adjusted Returns methodology, this method takes into account marketwide movements which occurred at the same time that the sample firms experienced events. The variable of interest is the *difference* between the return on a sample security and the corresponding return on the market index. We initially use the Fisher Equally Weighted Index to represent the market portfolio, and we will later examine the results when the CRSP Value Weighted Index is employed. The performance measures are the differences between the sample security returns and the market index in month '0'. Again, the statistical significance of the measures is assessed in several different ways. The Market Adjusted Returns method is used by Cowles (1933) and Latane and Jones (1979).

(c) *Market and Risk Adjusted Returns* — This method takes into account both market-wide factors and the systematic risk of each sample security. Although we will examine a number of different variations of this

---

$(-89, +10)$ period is reduced by the level of abnormal performance divided by 100. Roughly speaking, this transformation presumes that for each sample security the *ex ante* probability of the event in any one month is 0.01. Simulations have also been carried out with no such adjustment, and the results do not appear to be sensitive to whether or not such an adjustment procedure is used.

Finally, it should be noted that our simulations are directly applicable to the case where there is 'good news' or 'bad news'. We are implicitly examining abnormal performance for those securities which had good news; if month '0' had unconditional abnormal performance equal to zero, then there need be no adjustment to returns in the $(-89, +10)$ period. Furthermore, we have also simulated a situation where, for a given sample security, good news (positive abnormal performance) or bad news (negative abnormal performance) occur with equal probability at month '0', and where the abnormal performance measure conditional on a bad news realization is multiplied by $-1$ before the null hypothesis of no abnormal sample security returns is tested. The results from such alternative simulations are quite similar to those reported in the paper, although there is a slight reduction in the degree of misspecification in the non-parametric tests.

method, we initially use the 'market model'.[10] For each sample security, we use ordinary least squares to regress its return over the period around the event against the returns on the Equally Weighted Index for the corresponding calendar months. The 'market model' regression which is performed yields a residual in each event related month for each sample security. The significance of the month '0' market model residuals is then examined.

*Detecting Type I and Type II errors for a given sample*

For a given sample, when no abnormal performance has been introduced we test whether or not, under each performance measure, the hypothesis of no abnormal performance is rejected. This null hypothesis should indeed be true if randomly selected securities do not, on average, exhibit any abnormal performance given a particular benchmark. We classify rejection of the null hypothesis here as a Type I error — rejecting it when it is true.

We then investigate how the methodologies perform when the null hypothesis is not true for the sample, that is, when the returns of the sample securities have been transformed to reflect abnormal performance. For a given level of abnormal performance introduced into every sample security, each methodology is applied and the hypothesis of no abnormal performance then tested. If the null hypothesis fails to be rejected, this is classified as a Type II error — failure to reject the null hypothesis of no abnormal performance when it is false.

## 4. Simulating the methodologies across samples: Procedure and initial results

Whether a particular performance measure happens to result in a Type I or Type II error for a given sample and a given level of abnormal performance yields little insight into the likelihood that a particular type of error will *systematically* be made with a given methodology. To get direct measures of the *ex ante* probability of Type I and Type II errors, the procedure of introducing abnormal performance and then testing for it must be applied to each of the 250 samples. For a specific level of abnormal performance introduced into each security of every sample, we examine the overall performance of a methodology when it is applied to each sample — that is, when the methodology is replicated 250 times. We concentrate on the frequency of Type I and Type II errors in these 250 trials.

For each methodology, table 1 shows the frequency with which the hypothesis of no abnormal performance in month '0' is rejected using several different significance tests. The results are reported for 0, 1, 5, 15 and 50% levels of abnormal performance introduced into each security of every sample

---

[10]See Fama (1976, chs. 3 and 4) for a discussion of the market model.

in month '0'.[11] The frequency of rejections is reported when the null hypothesis is tested at both the 0.05 and 0.01 significance levels using a one-tailed test.[12]

## 4.1. Rejection frequencies using t-tests

One set of significance tests for which results are reported in table 1 are t-tests.[13] When there is no abnormal performance, for all of the performance measurement methods the t-tests reject the null hypothesis at approximately the significance level of the test. For example, for the tests at the 0.05 level, the rejection rates range from 3.2% for the Market Adjusted Returns method

Table 1

A comparison of alternative performance measures. Percentage of 250 replications where the null hypothesis is rejected. One-tailed test. $H_0$: mean abnormal performance in month '0' = 0.0. Sample size = 50 securities.

| Method | Test level: $\alpha = 0.05$ | | | Test level: $\alpha = 0.01$ | | |
|---|---|---|---|---|---|---|
| | Actual level of abnormal performance in month '0' | | | | | |
| | 0% | 1% | 5% | 0% | 1% | 5% |
| *Mean Adjusted Returns* | | | | | | |
| t-test | 4.0 | 26.0 | 100.0 | 1.6 | 8.8 | 99.2 |
| Sign test | 0.8 | 6.4 | 96.0 | 0.0 | 1.6 | 90.8 |
| Wilcoxon signed rank test | 1.6 | 12.8 | 99.6 | 0.4 | 4.4 | 97.6 |
| *Market[a] Adjusted Returns* | | | | | | |
| t-test | 3.2 | 19.6 | 100.0 | 1.6 | 5.2 | 96.4 |
| Sign test | 0.0 | 9.2 | 99.2 | 0.0 | 2.0 | 97.6 |
| Wilcoxon signed rank test | 1.6 | 17.2 | 99.6 | 0.4 | 4.4 | 98.8 |
| *Market[a] and Risk Adjusted Returns* | | | | | | |
| t-test | 4.4 | 22.8 | 100.0 | 1.2 | 6.8 | 98.4 |
| Sign test | 0.4 | 7.2 | 99.6 | 0.0 | 2.4 | 98.0 |
| Wilcoxon signed rank test | 2.8 | 16.4 | 100.0 | 0.0 | 4.4 | 99.2 |

[a]Fisher Equally Weighted Index. Note that for 15 and 50% levels of abnormal performance, the percentage of rejections is 100% for all methods.

[11]The range of these levels of abnormal performance corresponds roughly to the range of estimated abnormal performance reported in Fama, Fisher, Jensen and Roll (1969, table 2). For example, for their sample of stock splits followed by divided increases, estimated abnormal performance ranged from about 1% in month '0' to 38% when the performance measure is cumulated over a 30-month period before and including month '0'.

[12]Throughout most of the paper, results will be reported for one-tailed tests. In a one-tailed test at any significance level $\alpha$, the critical value of the test statistic at or above which the null hypothesis is rejected is given by the $(1 - \alpha)$ fractile of the frequency distribution of the test statistic which is assumed to obtain under the null. In section 5, results for two-tailed tests will be discussed.

[13]The assumptions underlying the t-tests are discussed in the appendix. For an example of t-tests in event studies, see Jaffe (1974). Although different variations of the t-tests are examined in section 6, results for the initial simulations are not sensitive to the specific variation employed.

to 4.4% for the Market and Risk Adjusted Returns method; for tests at the 0.01 level of significance, the rejection rates for the three methods range from 1.2 to 1.6%.[14]

With 1% abnormal performance, using $t$-tests the Mean Adjusted Returns method rejects the null hypothesis in 26.0% of the 250 replications when testing at the 0.05 level of significance. This compares to a 22.8% rejection rate with the Market and Risk Adjusted Returns method, and a 19.6% rejection rate with the Market Adjusted Returns method. This result is striking: it suggests that the simplest method, the Mean Adjusted Returns method, is no less likely than either of the other two to detect abnormal performance when it is present.[15]

Furthermore, the results which obtain with 1% abnormal performance are robust with respect to seemingly minor variations in the simulation procedure. For example, the relative rankings of the tests do not seem to be very sensitive to the significance level at which the null hypothesis is tested: at the 0.01 level of significance, the Mean Adjusted Returns method rejects 8.8% of the time, compared to a rejection rate of 6.8% for the Market and Risk Adjusted Returns method and a 5.2% rate for the Market Adjusted Returns method. It should also be emphasized that our conclusions about the relative

[14]Even if the empirical sampling distribution of a particular test statistic corresponds exactly to the assumed theoretical distribution, the proportion of rejections when the null hypothesis is true will not be exactly equal to the test level: The proportion of rejections is itself a random variable with a sampling distribution. Suppose that, under the null hypothesis, the outcomes of the hypothesis tests for each of the 250 replications are independent. Then at the 0.05 test level, the proportion of rejections for such a Bernoulli process has a mean of 0.05 and a standard deviation of 0.014. If the proportion of rejections is normally distributed, then the percentage of rejections reported in table 1 for 0% abnormal performance should, if the test statistics are properly specified, be between 2 and 8% approximately 95% of the time when testing at the 0.05 level. At the 0.01 level, the proportion of rejections should be between 0 and 2.2% approximately 95% of the time.

In calculating the proportion of rejections to be observed under the null hypothesis, it should be kept in mind that our 250 samples or 'trials' cannot be regarded as literally independent. A given security can be included in more than 1 of the 250 replications. To investigate the degree of dependence, for each of the 250 samples we computed an equally weighted average return for the sample securities for event months $-89$ through $+10$. We then computed the 31125 pairwise correlation coefficients for the 250 samples. The correlation coefficient between sample 1 and sample 2, for example, is computed from the 100 equally weighted returns on each sample in event time.

The largest of the 31125 pairwise correlation coefficients is 0.42, and the smallest is $-0.34$. Using a two-tailed test, only 485, or about 1.5% of the correlation coefficients are significant at the 0.01 level, compared to an expected proportion of 1%. While the hypothesis that the samples are pairwise independent is rejected, the degree of linear dependence appears to be small.

[15]In comparing rejection frequencies across methodologies, it is necessary to gauge the magnitude of the differences in rejection proportions, either pairwise or jointly. If, for each replication, the results for two different test methods are independent of each other, then the difference in the proportion of rejections in 250 replications could be as large as about 4% merely due to chance; hence the difference between the 26.0% rejection rate for Mean Adjusted Returns need not be regarded as significantly different from the 22.8% rejection rate for the Market and Risk Adjusted Returns method.

performance of the Market Adjusted Returns and Market and Risk Adjusted Returns methods have not been induced by the use of the Equally Weighted Index. For example, with 1% abnormal performance, the rejection rate we obtain for the Market and Risk Adjusted Returns with the Equally Weighted Index is 22.8%; with the Value-Weighted Index, the rejection rate is even lower, 15.2%. Differences between the use of the Equally Weighted and Value Weighted Indices are examined in detail in section 7.[16]

When the level of abnormal performance is increased from 1 to 5% in each sample security, all three methods detect the abnormal performance almost all of the time: at the 0.05 significance level, all three methods reject the null hypothesis 100% of the time, and at the 0.01 level, the minimum rejection rate is 96.4% for the Market Adjusted Returns method. Similarly, when the level of abnormal performance is again increased first to 15% and then to 50%, all three methods reject virtually 100% of the time. While this high frequency of rejections suggests that the tests for abnormal performance are quite powerful when there is 5% or more abnormal performance, it should be kept in mind, as we will later discuss, that these results are critically dependent on the assumption that the precise time at which the abnormal performance occurs is known with certainty. Furthermore, as we will also discuss, the relatively favorable performance of the Mean Adjusted Returns method will not obtain under all experimental conditions.

## 4.2. Parametric vs. non-parametric significance tests

Implicit in the *t*-tests which are used to assess abnormal performance are a number of strong assumptions: for example, in order for the test statistics to be distributed Student-*t* in the Mean Adjusted Returns method, security returns must be normally distributed. If such an assumption is not met, then the sampling distribution of test statistics assumed for the hypothesis tests could differ from the actual distribution, and false inferences could result. If the distribution of the test statistic is misspecified, then the null hypothesis, when true, could be rejected with some frequency other than that given by the significance level of the test.

To examine the usefulness of significance tests which make less restrictive assumptions than the *t*-tests, we also employ two non-parametric tests of the

[16]In an Asset Pricing model context, there is no clear *a priori* justification for use of an equally weighted index. However, even if their use is viewed as an *ad hoc* procedure, the fact that such indices are employed in actual event studies [e.g., Fama, Fisher, Jensen and Roll (1969), Watts (1978)] suggests that the consequences of their use are of interest. In addition, there are strong reasons for reporting initial simulation results with the Equally Weighted Index. As we later discuss, some of the performance measures under study can actually be biased when used with the Value-Weighted Index. If we reported our initial simulation results using the Value-Weighted Index, biases associated with the use of that index would make it difficult to standardize the level of Type I errors across test methods; valid comparisons of the power of different methodologies would thus not be possible with our simulation procedure.

performance measures which have been used in actual event studies: (1) a sign test, and (2) a Wilcoxon signed rank test.[17] In the sign test for a given sample, the null hypothesis is that the proportion of sample securities having positive measures of abnormal performance (e.g., positive residuals) is equal to 0.5; the alternative hypothesis (for any particular level of abnormal performance) is that the proportion of sample securities having positive performance measures is greater than 0.5. In the Wilcoxon test, both the sign *and* the magnitude of the abnormal performance are taken into account in computing the test statistic.[18]

Table 1 indicates the frequency with which the two non-parametric tests reject the hypothesis of no abnormal performance in month '0' for each methodology and for 0, 1, 5, 15 and 50% abnormal performance. From the results with 0% abnormal performance, it appears that there is a serious problem with the use of these non-parametric tests: under the null hypothesis, the tests do not reject at the 'correct' level. For example, for tests at the 0.05 level, the rejection rates range from a low of 0% for the sign test in the Market Adjusted Returns method to a high of 2.8% for the Wilcoxon test used in conjunction with the Market and Risk Adjusted Returns method. For tests at the 0.01 level, four of the six rejection rates are equal to 0%, and the other two are equal to 0.4%. Compared to the significance level of the test, the sign and Wilcoxon tests do not appear to reject the null hypothesis often enough. Although they are used to avoid the problem of possible misspecification of the *t*-tests, it appears that the non-parametric tests themselves suffer from such a problem of misspecification.

*Distributional properties of the test statistics*

To further examine the properties of the *t*, sign, and Wilcoxon tests, in table 2 we report summary measures for the actual frequency distribution of each test statistic, based on the 250 replications. Even when there is no abnormal performance, in many cases there appear to be significant differences between the empirical sampling distribution of the test statistic and the distribution which is assumed for the hypothesis tests. That such differences are substantial implies that tests for abnormal security price performance can be misleading and must be interpreted with great caution.

For the *t*-tests, the differences between the actual and assumed distribution of the test statistics seem small. For example, when there is no abnormal performance, the average *t*-statistics are approximately 0, ranging from a low of −0.13 in the Mean Adjusted Returns method to a high of −0.04 in the Market Adjusted Returns method. There is also evidence that the *t*-statistics

---

[17]See, for example, Kaplan and Roll (1972), Ball, Brown and Finn (1977), and Collins and Dent (1979).

[18]Details of the calculation of these test statistics are contained in the appendix.

are leptokurtic and slightly skewed to the right. However, at the 0.05 significance level it is only for the Mean Adjusted Returns method that the Kolmogorov–Smirnov test rejects the hypothesis that the distribution of $t$-values is indeed $t$. For both the Mean Adjusted Returns and Market and Risk Adjusted Returns methods, it also appears that the $t$-tests result in slightly 'too many' extreme negative $t$-values.[19]

For the sign and Wilcoxon tests, in large samples the test statistics should be distributed unit normal. However, table 2 indicates that the mean of the test statistics is generally significantly less than 0 under the null hypothesis; the mean test statistics ranges from a low of $-0.52$ for the sign test in the Market and Risk Adjusted Returns method to a high of $-0.42$ for the Wilcoxon test in Market and Risk Adjusted Returns method; the $\chi^2$ and Kolmogorov–Smirnov tests reject the hypothesis of normality with mean 0 for all the tests.

Our finding for the non-parametric tests that the average test statistic is significantly negative is not difficult to explain: the sign and Wilcoxon tests assume that the distribution of a security specific performance measure (such as a market model residual) is symmetric, with half of the observations above the mean and half below the mean. However, there is evidence of right skewness in security specific performance measures such as market model residuals [Fama, Fisher, Jensen and Roll (1969, p. 6)]. With fewer positive than negative performance measures, the median performance measure will

---

[19]There are two related points about the frequency distributions of the $t$-statistics, summarized in table 2, which should be mentioned. First, note that the $t$-statistics in the Mean Adjusted Returns method have an estimated variance of 1.32, higher than the variance of the $t$-statistics of either of the other methods. The higher variance is indicative of the troubling behavior of the Mean Adjusted Returns $t$-tests in the left-hand tail region. There, 21 of the 250 $t$-statistics fall in the 5% left-hand tail of a $t$ distribution, compared to an expected number of 12.5, and 41 of the test statistics fall in the 10% lower tail of a $t$ distribution, compared to an expected number of 25. This large fraction of test statistics in the lower tail region implies that a test of the hypothesis that there is no abnormal performance (compared to an alternative hypothesis that abnormal performance is negative) will result in rejection of that hypothesis at a rate almost twice that of the significance level of the test when the null hypothesis is true. Similar left-hand tail behavior is obtained in later simulations where the Value-Weighted Index is employed for computing market model residuals. Use of the Jaffe–Mandelker dependence adjustment procedure, which we will later discuss, also yields such left-hand tail behavior in the $t$-statistics even when market model residuals are computed from the Equally Weighted Index.

Second, note that when there is 1% abnormal performance, the distributions of the $t$-statistics for all methods are quite different from the $t$ distribution, which is the distribution which should obtain under the null hypothesis; that there are such differences merely indicates that the $t$-tests do in fact pick up abnormal performance when it is present. When there is abnormal performance, one could also compare the distributions of test statistics to the non-central $t$, which is the distribution which would be expected under the alternative hypothesis if the test statistics were correctly specified. However, since even the null distributions are at least slightly misspecified, it also seems reasonable to anticipate some misspecification in the distribution which should obtain under the alternative hypothesis. Given such misspecification, analytically deriving power functions under the assumptions of the various tests is not a reliable way of understanding the actual power functions for the tests. A simulation technique such as ours is necessary.

Table 2

Summary measures for the actual frequency distribution of each test statistic, based on the 250 replications. Upper and lower lines indicate 0 and 1% abnormal performance, respectively.

| Method | Mean | Variance | t-statistic for mean | $\beta_1 = \mu_3^2/\mu_2^3$ | Kurtosis | Pearson skewness | $\chi^2$ statistic (20 equally spaced intervals) | $\chi^2$ statistic (9 tail region intervals)[a] | Kolmogorov–Smirnov D-statistic |
|---|---|---|---|---|---|---|---|---|---|
| *Mean Adjusted Returns* | | | | | | | | | |
| t-test values 0% abnormal performance | −0.13 | 1.32 | −1.80 | 0.02 | 3.20 | 0.06 | 29.0 | 24.1 | 0.09 |
| 1% abnormal performance | 0.92 | 1.30 | 12.8 | 0.03 | 3.18 | 0.07 | 284.0 | 280.0 | 0.33 |
| Sign test values | −0.51 | 0.83 | −8.89 | 0.00 | 3.01 | 0.03 | 325.0 | 90.2 | 0.29 |
| | 0.25 | 0.79 | 4.45 | 0.00 | 3.01 | 0.02 | 282.0 | 13.0 | 0.20 |
| Wilcoxon test values | −0.42 | 0.96 | −6.87 | 0.01 | 2.78 | 0.05 | 88.2 | 64.5 | 0.18 |
| | 0.66 | 0.96 | 9.14 | 0.00 | 2.75 | 0.01 | 107.0 | 60.7 | 0.25 |
| *Market Adjusted Returns* | | | | | | | | | |
| t-values | −0.04 | 1.04 | −0.59 | 0.01 | 4.18 | 0.04 | 13.6 | 5.65 | 0.06 |
| | 0.92 | 1.06 | 14.1 | 0.04 | 4.17 | 0.06 | 246.8 | 212.2 | 0.35 |
| Sign test values | −0.52 | 0.87 | −8.83 | 0.11 | 2.71 | 0.24 | 304.5 | 86.6 | 0.26 |
| | 0.39 | 0.79 | 6.84 | 0.05 | 2.98 | 0.12 | 283.1 | 27.5 | 0.24 |
| Wilcoxon test values | −0.43 | 1.01 | −6.66 | 0.02 | 2.79 | 0.07 | 75.1 | 81.5 | 0.17 |
| | 0.69 | 1.01 | 1.08 | 0.05 | 2.93 | 0.12 | 149.1 | 103.9 | 0.30 |

*Market and Risk Adjusted Returns*

| | | | | | | | | | |
|---|---|---|---|---|---|---|---|---|---|
| t-values | −0.05 | 1.01 | −0.77 | 0.07 | 3.72 | 0.09 | 20.1 | 9.06 | 0.06 |
| | 0.91 | 1.03 | 14.1 | 0.08 | 3.61 | 0.10 | 259.4 | 227.0 | 0.34 |
| Sign test values | −0.48 | 0.82 | −8.51 | 0.10 | 2.93 | 0.18 | 347.7 | 84.3 | 0.29 |
| | 0.48 | 0.73 | 8.91 | 0.00 | 3.01 | 0.03 | 287.1 | 18.8 | 0.30 |
| Wilcoxon test values | −0.42 | 1.02 | −6.66 | 0.00 | 2.77 | 0.00 | 79.9 | 61.5 | 0.18 |
| | 0.72 | 0.97 | 11.6 | 0.02 | 2.78 | 0.07 | 166.6 | 115.1 | 0.30 |

[a]For tests concentrating on the tail regions, the 9 intervals are: 0–0.01, 0.01–0.02, 0.02–0.05, 0.05–0.1, 0.1–0.9, 0.9–0.95, 0.95–0.98, 0.98–0.99, 0.99–1.0.

Upper percentage points

| | 0.95 | 0.99 |
|---|---|---|
| $\chi^2(8)$ | 15.5 | 20.1 |
| $\chi^2(19)$ | 30.1 | 36.2 |
| $D$ ($N = 250$) | 0.086 | 0.103 |
| $\beta_1$ (assuming normality, $N = 250$) | 0.063 | 0.129 |
| Kurtosis (normality, $N = 250$) | 3.52 | 3.87 |

be negative even when the average performance measure is equal to 0. The non-parametric tests will tend to reject the null 'too often' (compared to the significance level of the test) when testing for negative abnormal performance and 'not often enough' when testing for positive abnormal performance.[20]

The non-parametric tests could, in principle, take asymmetry in the distribution of the performance measure into account and test the null hypothesis that the proportion of positive performance measures is equal to some number other than 0.5. However, such a test would first require a procedure for determining the proportion of positive security-specific performance measures which obtains in the absence of abnormal performance. We know of no event study which has employed such a test.[21]

### 4.3. Different risk adjustment methods

In the initial simulations reported in table 1, we concluded that tests which used risk-adjusted returns were no more powerful than tests which used returns which had not been adjusted for systematic risk. However, that conclusion was predicated on the assumption that the 'market model residual' method we chose represented the appropriate method of risk adjustment. To investigate the robustness of those earlier results, it is useful to simulate other risk adjustment methods which have also been used in actual event studies. We will examine two alternative methods; specific details of each method are discussed in the appendix.

*Fama–MacBeth Residuals* — Instead of computing a market model residual for each sample security, a 'Fama–MacBeth' (1973) residual is computed instead. Average residuals are then computed and abnormal performance is assessed in the same way as with the Market Model Residual method.[22]

Market model residuals are an appropriate performance measure if security returns are multivariate normal. For Fama–MacBeth residuals to be

---

[20]Even a small degree of asymmetry will lead to such a result. For example, if a sample of 50 securities has 27 negative and 23 positive market model residuals in month '0', the test statistic in the sign test will be approximately $-0.5$. This is about equal to the average value of $-0.48$ reported in table 2. Note that the use of continuously compounded (rather than arithmetic) returns is likely to reduce the extent of the asymmetry in market model residuals.

[21]Residual based techniques focusing on median (rather than mean) residuals could presumably use estimation procedures other than ordinary least squares to perform the market model regressions [see Bassett and Koenker (1978), and Cornell and Dietrich (1978)]. However, even if the non-parametric tests were properly calibrated by focusing on differences from medians, it is not obvious that the tests would be more powerful (against specific alternatives) than the $t$-tests, particularly since the $t$-tests, with their additional restrictions, seem reasonably well specified. But it should be kept in mind that there do exist distributions of the security-specific performance measures for which tests such as the sign test will be more efficient, particularly distributions with sufficiently heavy tails. See Lehman (1975, pp. 171–175) for a further discussion of the power of the $t$, sign, and Wilcoxon tests.

[22]Fama–MacBeth residuals have been used by, for example, Jaffe (1974) and Mandelker (1974).

an appropriate performance measure, it is also necessary for equilibrium expected returns to be generated according to the Black (1972) version of the Asset Pricing model. A comparison of the performance of the market model and Fama–MacBeth residual techniques will indicate the benefits, if any, which are associated with the restrictive assumptions (and additional data requirements) implicit in using the Fama–MacBeth residuals.

*Control Portfolios* — This method forms the sample securities into a portfolio with an estimated $\beta$ of 1. Regardless of the risk level of each sample security, the portfolio thus formed should have the same risk as the market portfolio. Those securities comprising the market portfolio become a 'control portfolio' in the sense that the market portfolio has the same risk level as the sample securities, but is not experiencing the 'event' under study. The performance measure for month '0' is the difference between the return on a portfolio of sample securities (formed so that $\hat{\beta} = 1$) and the average return on the market portfolio in the calendar months in which the sample securities experience events.

Variations of the Control Portfolio technique have been used by, for example, Black and Scholes (1973), Gonedes, Dopuch and Penman (1976), Warner (1977) and Watts (1978).[23] By concentrating on the difference in mean returns, this method makes no particular assumption about which version of the Asset Pricing model is correct.

*Simulation results for alternative risk adjustment methods*

To compare the different methods for risk adjustment, table 3 indicates the simulation results for 250 replications of each risk adjustment method with 0, 1 and 5% levels of abnormal performance. Two important results emerge from the simulation.

Compared to using Market Model residuals, the use of Fama–MacBeth residuals does not increase the power of the tests. Earlier, for example, using the Equally Weighted Index and with 1% abnormal performance, the Market Model Residual method rejected 22.8% of the time; the rejection rate using Fama–MacBeth residuals is 21.6%. Even if the Black model is corrent, there appears to be sufficient measurement error in the parameter estimates on which Fama–MacBeth residuals are based so that the tests based on those residuals are no more useful than those based on the multivariate normality assumption of the Market Model. Furthermore, use of the Control Portfolio method also results in no increase in the proportion of rejections which take place under the alternative hypotheses: With 1% abnormal performance, the Control Portfolio method rejects the null hy-

---

[23]The Control Portfolio technique has also been used to control for factors other than systematic risk. See Gonedes, Dopuch and Penman (1976, p. 113) for a discussion.

pothesis in 18.0% of the 250 replications. These results for alternative risk adjustment procedures are consistent with our earlier conclusion that the Mean Adjusted Returns method performs no worse than those methods which explicitly adjust for systematic risk.[24]

Table 3

Different methods for risk adjustment. Percentage of 250 replications where the null hypothesis is rejected ($\alpha = 0.05$). One-tailed $t$-test results. $H_0$: mean abnormal performance in month '0' = 0.0. Sample size = 50 securities.

| Method | Actual level of abnormal performance in month '0' | | | Mean $t$-statistic with 1% abnormal performance |
|---|---|---|---|---|
| | 0% | 1% | 5% | |
| *Methods making no explicit risk adjustment* | | | | |
| Mean Adjusted Returns | 4.0 | 26.0 | 100.0 | 0.92 |
| Market Adjusted Returns | 3.2 | 19.6 | 100.0 | 0.92 |
| *Methods with market and risk-adjusted returns* | | | | |
| Market Model Residuals | 4.4 | 22.8 | 100.0 | 0.91 |
| Fama–MacBeth Residuals | 4.0 | 21.6 | 100.0 | 0.89 |
| Control Portfolio | 4.4 | 18.0 | 100.0 | 0.86 |

## 5. The use of prior information

The simulations which have been performed thus far make the strong assumption that the time at which abnormal security price performance occurs is known with complete certainty. However, if it is only known when, for example, the *Wall Street Journal* announced that the 'event' had taken place, then the calendar date of the event cannot be pinpointed exactly and the date itself becomes a random variable; in that case, abnormal returns for a number of periods before the 'announcement date' will typically be scrutinized for evidence of 'abnormal' performance. Similarly, even when it can be established with certainty when the event occurred, one is often concerned with whether or not there exists a profitable trading rule which could be implemented conditional on an event. In such a situation, it is necessary to study abnormal price performance for the period following time '0'.

---

[24]We have also examined the properties of the test statistics generated with Fama–MacBeth residuals and the Control Portfolio method. For both methods, the distribution of $t$-statistics is reasonably close to Student-$t$, and the properties of the test statistics are very similar to those reported in table 2 for the market model residual methodology.

## 5.1. *Assessing abnormal performance when its precise date is unknown*

We now examine how uncertainty about the precise date of the abnormal performance affects the power of the tests. For every security in each of the 250 samples, abnormal performance is generated in one specific month in the interval from month $-10$ through $+10$. The event month of abnormal performance can differ across securities; for a given security, the event month of abnormal performance is a drawing from a uniform distribution.[25] In this experiment, 0, 1, 5, 15% and 50% abnormal performance is introduced for each security for one month in the $(-10, +10)$ interval. This experimental situation corresponds to one where abnormal performance occurs (a) at some time in the 21-month interval up to and including month '0', or (b) at some time in the 21-month interval including and following the event. The null hypothesis to be tested is that the mean level of abnormal performance over the entire 21-month interval is equal to 0.

Table 4 shows the frequency with which each test method results in a rejection of the null hypothesis of no abnormal performance. The results are dramatic: even at high levels of abnormal performance, the hypothesis of no abnormal performance often fails to be rejected. For example, with 5% abnormal performance, the rejection rates range from 16.0% with the Control Portfolio method to a high of 28.4% with the Mean Adjusted Returns method. With 15% abnormal performance, the rejection rates increase and are on the order of 70 to 80% for the various test methods; however, these rejection rates are still much lower than those obtained in the earlier simulations, where the precise date of abnormal performance was known with certainty. There, using $t$-tests even 5% abnormal performance was detected 100% of the time by all of the test methods.[26]

To further illustrate how prior information can be used to increase the power of the tests, in table 4 we also show the results of a simulation where all abnormal performance occurs in the $(-5, +5)$ interval and is uniformly distributed. When prior information can be used to narrow the time interval in which the abnormal performance could have occurred, in this case from $(-10, +10)$ to $(-5, +5)$, the rejection rates increase substantially in the presence of a given level of abnormal performance. With 5% abnormal performance, the rejection rates increase from 28.4 to 35.2% for the Mean Adjusted Returns method, and from 24.4 to 39.6% using Market Model residuals.

---

[25]When other distributions (e.g., normal, exponential) were used, the qualitative conclusions of this section remained unchanged.

[26]Furthermore, the rejection rates in table 4 cannot be markedly increased if the researcher is merely willing to tolerate a slightly higher probability of Type I error — that is, if one is willing to conduct the hypothesis test at a higher significance level. For example, in the Mean Adjusted Returns method, the rejection rate with 5% abnormal performance is 28.4%. To obtain a rejection rate of 50%, the significance level would have to be increased to about 0.20; to obtain a 75% rejection rate, the significance level would have to be increased to about 0.35.

Table 4

Alternative performance measures when the precise date of the abnormal performance is unknown.[a] Percentage of 250 replications where the null hypothesis is rejected ($\alpha = 0.05$). One-tailed $t$-test results using Equally Weighted Index. $H_0$: mean abnormal performance in the interval $(-10, +10) = 0.0$

| Method | Actual level of abnormal performance in interval $(-10, +10)$ | | | | |
| --- | --- | --- | --- | --- | --- |
| | 0% | 1% | 5% | 15% | 50% |
| Mean Adjusted Returns | 7.6 | 9.2 | 28.4 | 82.0 | 100.0 |
| | (9.2) | (13.6) | (35.2) | (94.4) | (100.0) |
| Market Adjusted Returns | 3.6 | 5.6 | 18.4 | 73.2 | 100.0 |
| | (5.2) | (6.8) | (35.2) | (96.4) | (100.0) |
| Market Model Residuals | 7.2 | 10.8 | 24.4 | 86.4 | 100.0 |
| | (7.6) | (10.4) | (39.6) | (96.8) | (100.0) |
| Fama–MacBeth Residuals | 3.6 | 5.2 | 16.4 | 74.8 | 100.0 |
| | (8.8) | (15.6) | (45.6) | (97.6) | (100.0) |
| Control Portfolio | 4.8 | 6.4 | 16.0 | 70.0 | 100.0 |
| | (5.6) | (6.8) | (32.0) | (91.2) | (100.0) |

[a]For each security, abnormal performance is introduced for one month in the interval $(-10, +10)$ with each month having an equal probability of being selected. The rejection rates shown in brackets are for the case where (1) for each security, abnormal performance is introduced for one month in the $(-5, +5)$ interval, with each month having an equal probability of being selected, and (2) the null hypothesis is that the mean abnormal performance in the $(-5, +5)$ interval is equal to 0.

Table 5

The behavior of two-tailed tests. Percentage of replications, for the 0.025 significance level, where a one-tailed $t$-test rejects the null hypothesis of no abnormal performance. This rejection rate is identical to the percentage of replications where a two-tailed test at the 0.05 level rejects the null and detects positive abnormal performance. Rejection rates from table 4, for a one-tailed test with $\alpha = 0.05$, are shown in brackets. $H_0$: mean abnormal performance in the interval $(-10, +10) = 0.0$.[a]

| Method | Actual level of abnormal performance in interval $(-10, +10)$ | | | |
| --- | --- | --- | --- | --- |
| | 0% | 1% | 5% | 15% |
| Mean Adjusted Returns | 4.8 | 5.6 | 17.6 | 74.4 |
| | (7.6) | (9.2) | (28.4) | (82.0) |
| Market Adjusted Returns | 1.0 | 2.4 | 9.2 | 58.0 |
| | (3.6) | (5.6) | (18.4) | (73.2) |
| Market Model Residuals | 3.2 | 5.2 | 18.4 | 78.8 |
| | (7.2) | (10.8) | (24.4) | (86.4) |
| Fama-MacBeth Residuals | 2.0 | 2.0 | 9.2 | 60.4 |
| | (3.6) | (5.2) | (16.4) | (74.8) |
| Control Portfolio | 2.0 | 2.4 | 8.0 | 48.4 |
| | (4.8) | (6.4) | (16.0) | (70.0) |

[a]For each security, abnormal performance is introduced for one month in the $(-10, +10)$ interval, with each month having an equal probability of being selected.

*Rejection rates for two-tailed significance tests*

There is yet another assumption about prior information which all of our simulations make and whose consequences can also be studied: the hypothesis tests we perform throughout this paper are one-tailed tests. An implicit assumption in such tests is that the sign of the abnormal performance is also known. However, if one cannot use prior information to impose this restriction, the appropriate test is two-tailed. For a given significance level, the power of the tests is thus reduced.[27]

In table 5, we report rejection rates for one-tailed tests conducted at both the 0.05 and 0.025 significance levels. The rejection rate for a one-tailed test at the 0.025 level also represents the percentage of replications in which a two-tailed test at the 0.05 level will pick up positive abnormal performance. Thus, comparing the rejection rates for one-tailed tests at the 0.05 and 0.025 levels is equivalent to comparing the frequency with which one-tailed and two-tailed tests, each conducted at the 0.05 level, will lead the researcher to conclude that positive abnormal performance is present.

When the sign of the abnormal performance is not known *a priori*, the ability to discern abnormal performance is reduced markedly. For example, with 5% abnormal performance in the $(-10, +10)$ interval, a two-tailed test at the 0.05 significance level picks up positive abnormal performance 17.6% of the time for the Mean Adjusted Returns method, compared to a rate of 28.4% for the corresponding one-tailed test. With 15% abnormal performance in the $(-10, +10)$ interval, a two-tailed test with that method detects positive abnormal performance in 74.4% of the replications, compared to a rate of 82.0% for a one-tailed test. While such results are hardly surprising, they serve to underscore the importance of using all available prior information in testing for abnormal performance.

## 5.2. Using cumulative average residuals

One method frequently used to investigate abnormal performance when there is incomplete prior information about when it occurs is the 'cumulative average residual' (CAR) technique employed by Fama, Fisher, Jensen and Roll (1969).[28] The technique focuses on the average market model residuals of the sample securities for a number of periods around the event. The

---

[27]Similarly, to obtain a particular rejection frequency when there is abnormal performance of a given sign and magnitude, the level of Type I error must be increased in moving from a one-tailed to a two-tailed test. For example, two-tailed tests would have to be conducted at the 0.1 level to pick up positive abnormal performance with the same frequency as that which has been reported throughout this paper for one-tailed testes at the 0.05 significance level.

[28]A similar technique involves construction of an Abnormal Performance Index [e.g., Ball and Brown (1968)]. In simulations not reported here, the abnormal performance measures of Ball–Brown, Pettit, and Beaver–Dukes [see Ohlson (1978, p. 184) for a description of these measures] were also examined. The properties of the confidence bands traced out by such alternative metrics were similar to those discussed for the CARs.

cumulative average residual for a given event-related month $t$ is defined as the value of the cumulative average residual in the previous event-month plus the current value of the average residual, $AR_t$,

$$CAR_t = CAR_{t-1} + AR_t. \tag{1}$$

Examining the CAR of a set of sample securities as of any given event-related month $t$ is a way of looking at whether or not the values of the average residuals, starting from the month of cumulation and up to that point, are systematically different from 0.[29]

To simulate the CAR technique for various levels of abnormal performance, we use the values of the average market model residuals which were obtained for the simulations reported in table 4, where abnormal performance is uniformly distributed in the $(-10, +10)$ interval. For a given sample and a given level of abnormal performance, we take the average market model residuals and begin cumulating them in month $-10$; cumulation then continues for every month through month $+10$. For each sample, the procedure yields a set of 21 cumulative average residuals, one for each event-related month from $-10$ through $+10$. For a given event-related month, repeated application of the procedure to each of the 250 samples yields 250 cumulative average residuals.

*Cumulative average residuals when there is no abnormal performance*

To understand the properties of CARs under the null hypothesis, in fig. 1 we trace selected fractiles of the 250 CARs in each event-related month for the case where no abnormal performance is introduced. As the figure indicates, the 0.05 and 0.95 fractiles of the 250 CARs depart more and more from 0 as the cumulation process continues. By the end of month $+10$, the 0.95 fractile takes on a value of over $9\%$, and the 0.05 fractile takes on a value of about $-9\%$. This suggests that the CAR for a given sample could appear to wander a great deal from 0, even in the absence of abnormal performance.[30]

The behavior of the CAR is consistent with a simple explanation. As eq. (1) indicates, the CAR for a given sample is by construction a random walk.[31] Like any process which follows a random walk, the CAR can easily

[29]Examining the CAR as of any event month is equivalent to examining the significance of the mean average residual over the cumulation period. However, looking at the entire set of event-time CARs on a month by month basis is not very meaningful unless the significance test explicitly takes into account the fact that CARs are, by construction, highly serially dependent.

[30]In table 2, we presented evidence that average residuals were skewed to the right. The slight apparent downward drift in the 0.5 fractile of the CAR would thus be expected.

[31]CARs will be a random walk if the average residuals in event time are independent and identically distributed. A confidence band such as that traced out by the 0.05 and 0.95 fractiles in fig. 1 should increase with the square root of the number of months over which cumulation takes place.

give the *appearance* of 'significant' positive or negative drift, when none is present. However, even if no abnormal performance were present, neither the seemingly significant upward drift indicated by the 0.95 fractile or the downward drift of the 0.05 fractile could be considered outside of the realm of chance. Indeed, in 5% of the 250 samples, the value of the CAR exceeds the values taken on by the 0.95 fractile reported in fig. 1; in another 5% of the samples, the value of the CAR is less than that taken on by the 0.05 fractile. The pattern of CAR fractiles in fig. 1 serves to underscore the necessity for statistical tests on the performance measures, since merely looking at a picture of CARs can easily result in Type I errors.

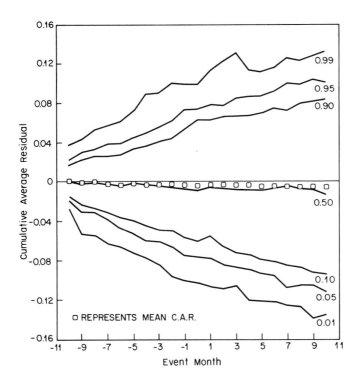

Fig. 1. Fractiles of cumulative average residual under null hypothesis of no abnormal performance.

*Cumulative average residuals when abnormal performance is present*

In fig. 2, we show selected fractiles of the CARs for the case where 5% abnormal performance occurs for each sample security, and the month of abnormal performance is uniformly distributed in the (−10, +10) interval.

The value of each fractile as of month +10 is higher by approximately 0.05 than the corresponding value in fig. 1, when no abnormal performance was present; however, the 0.5 fractile, that is, the median CAR as of month +10 still falls well within the bounds which were shown in fig. 1, and which obtain under the null hypothesis. Moreover, since for a given sample the

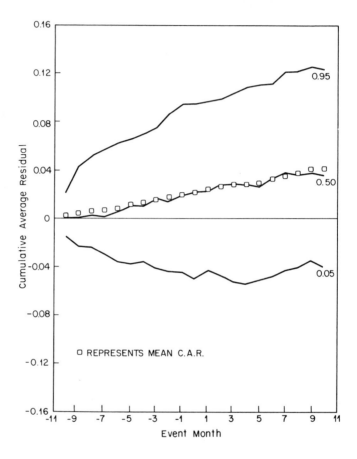

Fig. 2. Fractiles of cumulative average residual with 5% excess return distributed uniformly on months −10 to +10.

month of abnormal performance is uniformly distributed across securities and not on average large in any one month, CAR plots for the individual samples would tend to show a pattern not strikingly different from what would be expected under the null hypothesis. In such a case, there is little information which the CAR for the sample provides in helping to decide whether abnormal performance is present.

However, in fig. 3 we show fractiles of CARs when 5% abnormal performance occurs in month '0' for all sample securities. Although the fractiles at the end of the cumulation period take on values similar to those shown in fig. 2, there is an apparent 'spike' at month '0'; such a spike shows up not only in the selected fractiles, but in the CAR plot for any given

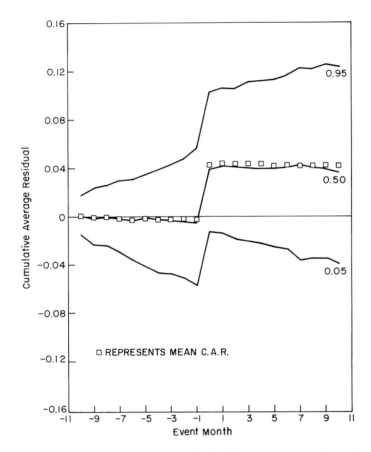

Fig. 3. Fractiles of cumulative average residual with 5% excess return in month zero.

sample. Given some prior information that month '0' is of particular interest to focus on, the existence of such a spike in the CAR pattern could reasonably suggest to the researcher that a hypothesis test for abnormal performance in month '0' rather than the entire ($-10$, $+10$) period would be appropriate. The test on month '0' picks up abnormal performance 100% of the time, as indicated in table 1, whereas the test in the ($-10$, $+10$) interval only yields the rejection rate of 24.4% shown in table 4. Thus, when the timing of the abnormal performance is not uniform over the period under study, the precise pattern of estimated abnormal returns is conveniently summarized by a CAR plot; the pattern can provide useful information beyond that given by the value of the CAR at the end of an arbitrary 'cumulation period'.[32]

## 6. The effect of clustering

### 6.1. Event month clustering

The securities of a sample will frequently each experience an event during the same calendar time period. For example, as Schwert (1978) and Foster (1980) discuss, government regulation or mandated accounting procedures will often have a simultaneous impact on a number of different securities whose price performance around the time of an event is being examined. We refer to the close or simultaneous spacing of events as event month clustering.

Clustering has implications for the characteristics of the test methods being examined in this paper. The general impact of clustering is to lower the number of securities whose month '0' behavior is independent. The month '0' dependence is important for two reasons. First, if performance measures such as the deviation from historical mean returns or market model residuals are positively correlated across securities in calendar time, then such clustering will increase the variance of the performance measures (e.g., the average residual) and hence lower the power of the tests. Secondly, the month '0' dependence in security-specific performance measures must explicitly be taken into account in testing the null hypothesis of no abnormal performance. Otherwise, even in the absence of abnormal performance, the null

---

[32]Our discussion of CAR plots touches on a deeper set of issues which arises in connection with all tests for abnormal performance: *a priori*, the researcher often does not know when the abnormal performance would have occurred, nor perhaps even the frequency distribution of the time of the abnormal performance. Lacking that information, the choice of time period over which to conduct the hypothesis test is arbitrary, and one's inferences can be sensitive to the choice.

For example, if for all securities the abnormal performance occurs in month '0' or a few months surrounding it, a hypothesis test conducted over the entire $(-10, +10)$ period is less likely to pick up abnormal performance than one concentrating on month '0'. Conversely, if the event month of abnormal performance is uniformly distributed over the $(-10, +10)$ period, but the hypothesis test is performed for month '0', the abnormal performance is also less likely to be detected. In general, the hypothesis test should give weights to event months which are the same as those implicit in the actual frequency distribution of the time of abnormal performance. However, in the absence of a plausible *a priori* reason for doing so, it is dangerous to infer the frequency distribution of the time of abnormal performance by merely looking at CAR plots and the estimated level of abnormal performance in each event-related month: if one puts enough weight on 'outliers', the null can always be rejected even when it is true.

hypothesis will be rejected too frequently if security specific performance measures are positively correlated.[33]

*Inducing clustering in event-dates of the sample securities*

To examine the effect of clustering, we must specify a new procedure for generating event-dates. For each of the securities in a given sample, month '0' is restricted to fall in a particular calendar time month which is common to all securities in the sample. The month is randomly selected. For each sample, a new calendar month is selected.[34] The effect of clustering is simulated with the same levels of abnormal performance which were used previously: 0, 1, 5 and 15%. All abnormal performance is generated in month '0'.

*Testing for abnormal performance when there is clustering*

For each performance measurement method, *t*-tests for month '0' abnormal performance are conducted using three different methods, each of which is discussed in the appendix. The *t*-tests are first conducted under the assumption that the performance measures (e.g., residuals) are independent across securities. The *t*-tests are also performed using two different methods for taking into account cross-sectional dependence.

One procedure, which we call 'Crude Dependence Adjustment', focuses on the series of event-time average performance measures (e.g., average residuals). A second, more complicated method we simulate has been employed by Jaffe (1974) and Mandelker (1974); that method forms various portfolios of sample securities in calendar time; as discussed in the appendix, the portfolios are formed so as to make their performance measures independent and homoscedastic, and the hypothesis test is actually performed on the independent performance measures of the portfolios. In table 6, we present simulation results for the different tests. From the numbers presented in the table, several results are apparent.

First, event-month clustering has a substantial impact on rejection frequencies for the Mean Adjusted Returns method. For example, when the *t*-tests ignore cross-sectional dependence in security specific performance measures,

---

[33]This consequence of the independence assumption has recently been discussed by, for example, Beaver (1979) and Collins and Dent (1978). Note that for the simulations presented thus far, cross-sectional dependence is unimportant because the degree of clustering is small: Since event dates are independent draws from a uniform distribution comprised of over 300 different calendar months, the likelihood that many securities in a given sample will have a common event date is small. Previous simulations have been performed both with and without dependence adjustment of the types to be discussed in this section; the differences in Type I error frequencies under the null hypothesis are generally small.

[34]The month is between June 1944 and March 1968. For a given sample, any month in that period has an equal probability of being selected; for the purpose of maintaining sample to sample independence, the selection of calendar months is carried out without replacement.

the Mean Adjusted Returns method rejects the null hypothesis 32.4% of the time when there is no abnormal performance;[35] this compares to rejection rates of about 3% using either Crude Dependence Adjustment or the Jaffe–Mandelker procedure. Clustering also reduces the power of the Mean Adjusted Returns method against specific alternative hypotheses: with highly correlated security specific performance measures, the variance of the mean

Table 6

The effect of event-month clustering.[a] Percentage of 250 replications where the null hypothesis is rejected ($\alpha = 0.05$). One-tailed $t$-test results. $H_0$: mean abnormal performance in month '0' = 0.0.

| Method | Actual level of abnormal performance in month '0' | | |
|---|---|---|---|
| | 0% | 1% | 5% |
| *Mean Adjusted Returns* | | | |
| No Dependence Adjustment | 32.4 | 44.4 | 74.0 |
| Crude Adjustment | 3.2 | 4.8 | 31.6 |
| Jaffe–Mandelker | 3.6 | 5.6 | 34.4 |
| *Market Adjusted Returns* | | | |
| No Dependence Adjustment | 3.6 | 22.8 | 99.6 |
| Crude Adjustment | 4.0 | 23.6 | 99.6 |
| Jaffe–Mandelker | 5.2 | 24.4 | 99.6 |
| *Market Model Residuals* | | | |
| No Dependence Adjustment | 4.0 | 23.2 | 99.2 |
| Crude Adjustment | 5.6 | 24.8 | 99.6 |
| Jaffe–Mandelker | 6.0 | 26.8 | 99.6 |
| *Fama–MacBeth Residuals* | | | |
| No Dependence Adjustment | 4.0 | 25.2 | 100.0 |
| Crude Adjustment | 4.8 | 24.4 | 98.8 |
| Jaffe–Mandelker | 4.8 | 26.4 | 99.2 |
| *Control Portfolio* | | | |
| Crude Adjustment | 4.4 | 23.2 | 99.2 |

[a]For a given replication, month '0' falls on the same calendar date for each security. The calendar date differs from replication to replication. Equally Weighted Index.
[b]Methodology not readily adapted to other dependence adjustment procedures.

[35]Event month clustering is not the only stochastic process generating events which would lead to 'too many' rejections for the Mean Adjusted Returns method. When there is no clustering, but the event tends to occur only in those months when the market return is abnormally high, then rejection rates using Mean Adjusted Returns will also be too high with a one-tailed test for positive abnormal performance. Furthermore, in an actual event study involving only one security, an analogous situation arises. For that case, the Mean Adjusted Returns method will not yield the probability of Type I error assumed in the hypothesis tests if the market return at the time of the event happened to have been abnormally high (or abnormally low).

performance measure, computed across sample securities, is higher, and the power of the tests is expected to be lower. With 5% abnormal performance, the Mean Adjusted Returns method rejects the null hypothesis 31.6% of the time using Crude Dependence Adjustment, and 34.4% of the time using the Jaffe–Mandelker procedure. These numbers are much lower than the rejection rate of 100% we obtained in the analogous earlier simulation without clustering.

Secondly, in marked contrast to the results for the Mean Adjusted Returns method, clustering appears to have little impact on rejection frequencies for any of the other performance measurement methods, and thus our earlier conclusions about the relatively favorable performance of Mean Adjusted Returns do not apply if there is clustering. When the null hypothesis is true, for our simulations it makes little difference whether or not cross-sectional dependence is taken into account. For example, in the Market Adjusted Returns method, the rejections rate with no dependence adjustment is 3.6%, compared to rejection rates of 4.0% using Crude Dependence Adjustment and 5.2% with the Jaffe–Mandelker procedure.

Furthermore, when abnormal performance is present, the rejection rates when there is clustering are not markedly different from those when there is no clustering: With 1% abnormal performance, the rejection rates with clustering are on the order of 20 to 25%, slightly higher than was the case in earlier simulations without clustering. It thus appears that for all methods taking into account market-wide factors, with the Equally Weighted Index the degree of cross-sectional dependence in the performance measures is negligible for randomly selected securities.[36] However, in an actual event study, a sample of securities whose events are clustered in calendar time may be nonrandom; the sample securities might be drawn from a common industry group having positively correlated performance measures. In such a case, the power of the tests is reduced even if a particular methodology abstracts from the market, and taking into account cross-sectional dependence in order to assure the 'correct' proportion of rejections is appropriate in such a case.

Third, it appears that the differences in simulation results between the Crude Adjustment procedure and the Jaffe–Mandelker procedure are small. In the presence of abnormal performance, there is a slight increase in rejection frequencies with the Jaffe–Mandelker procedure, and the increase

---

[36]Note that our finding of negligible cross-sectional dependence is specific to the Equally Weighted Index. With that index, randomly selected securities would not be expected to exhibit systematic positive cross-sectional dependence in performance measures. For example, if all securities in the market had positively correlated market model residuals, then the market model has really not abstracted from marketwide influences. With the Value Weighted Index, the unweighted average of pairwise covariances between residuals can be positive; in fact, simulations of clustering with the Value Weighted Index result in rejection rates under the null of about 15% (for $\alpha = 0.05$) when cross-sectional dependence is ignored.

takes place for every test method. The increase is consistent with our discussion in the appendix, where we suggest that the Jaffe–Mandelker procedure will be more precise than Crude Dependence Adjustment.

## 6.2. Security risk clustering

Another form of clustering which is pertinent to our study is clustering by systematic risk: a particular sample may consist of securities which tend to have higher than average (or lower than average) systematic risk. Since for individual securities there is a positive empirical relationship between the variance of returns and systematic risk (as well as between market model residual variance and systematic risk),[37] it seems reasonable to expect that tests for abnormal performance will be more powerful for low risk securities than for high risk securities; the intuition is simply that a given level of abnormal performance should be easier to detect when 'normal' fluctuations in sample security returns (and the standard errors of parameter estimates such as $\hat{\beta}$) are small rather than large.

### Security risk clustering: Sample selection procedure

To see the effect of security risk clustering, we construct two sets of 250 samples, where all 500 samples have 50 securities each. We call the first 250 samples low-risk samples, and the second 250 samples high-risk samples.

The samples are constructed as follows. Securities are picked and event dates generated as discussed in section 3. In addition to data availability requirements imposed earlier, it is also required that a security have data from event-months $-149$ through $-90$. Based on an estimate of $\beta$ in that 60-month period, a security is assigned to a sample in either the high-risk or low-risk set, depending on whether its estimated $\beta$ is greater than 1 or less than 1.[38] The procedure of picking securities and event dates, and then of assigning securities to samples based on $\hat{\beta}$, is continued until both the low-risk set of samples and the high-risk set of samples each has 250 samples of 50 securities.

### Simulation results for risk-clustered samples

For each set of 250 samples, various methodologies are simulated as in previous experiments not involving either security-risk or event-month clus-

---

[37]See Fama (1976, pp. 121–124). Note that empirically there is also a negative relationship between $\hat{\beta}$ (and hence variance of returns) and firm size. We have not examined the separate, independent effect of firm size on the power of the tests. However, to the extent that $\beta$ merely proxies for firm size, tests for abnormal performance would be expected to be more powerful for large firms than for small firms.

[38]By selecting on the basis of previous $\hat{\beta}$, the expected value of the measurement error in $\hat{\beta}$ over the $(-89, -11)$ period should be zero for both the high-$\hat{\beta}$ and low-$\hat{\beta}$ samples. See Black, Jensen and Scholes (1972) for a discussion.

Table 7

The effect of clustering by risk.[a] Percentage of 250 replications where the null hypothesis is rejected ($\alpha = 0.05$). One-tailed t-test results. $H_0$: mean abnormal performance in month '0' = 0.0.

| Method | Rejection rates | | | | Mean t-statistics | | | |
|---|---|---|---|---|---|---|---|---|
| | Abnormal performance 0% | | Abnormal performance 1% | | Abnormal performance 0% | | Abnormal performance 1% | |
| | $\beta<1$ | $\beta>1$ | $\beta<1$ | $\beta>1$ | $\beta<1$ | $\beta>1$ | $\beta<1$ | $\beta>1$ |
| Mean Adjusted Returns | 6.8 | 6.0 | 26.8 | 24.4 | −0.03 | −0.02 | 1.18 | 0.89 |
| Market Adjusted Returns | 7.6 | 7.2 | 31.6 | 24.8 | −0.02 | 0.07 | 1.14 | 0.99 |
| Market Model Residuals | 8.0 | 5.6 | 29.6 | 21.6 | −0.02 | 0.01 | 1.18 | 0.91 |
| Fama–MacBeth Residuals | 8.4 | 5.6 | 30.0 | 20.0 | 0.02 | −0.02 | 1.19 | 0.88 |
| Control Portfolio | 8.4 | 5.2 | 17.6 | 14.0 | 0.11 | 0.03 | 0.74 | 0.54 |

| | Mean $\hat{\beta}$ ($N = 12500$) |
|---|---|
| 250 samples with $\hat{\beta}<1$ | 0.81 |
| 250 samples with $\hat{\beta}>1$ | 1.24 |

[a]CRSP Equally Weighted Index. There are 500 samples, each having 50 securities. $\bar{\beta}<1$ refers to the 250 samples formed from securities with estimated $\beta$s less than 1. $\hat{\beta}>1$ refers to the 250 samples formed from securities with estimated $\beta$s greater than 1.

tering. In table 7, for both the low-$\hat{\beta}$ set of samples and the high-$\hat{\beta}$ set of samples, we show rejection rates and mean $t$-statistics when various methodologies are applied to each set of 250 samples, and when all abnormal performance is introduced in month '0'.

When there is no abnormal performance, neither the rejection rates nor the mean $t$-statistics seem particularly out of line for any of the test methods. It is a bit surprising that the Market Adjusted Returns method does not reject 'too often' for the $\hat{\beta} > 1$ samples and 'not often enough' when $\hat{\beta} < 1$; however, it should be kept in mind that the rejection proportions shown in the table are merely estimates of the true proportions; in addition, there is some overlap in the sets of samples in the sense that individual securities in the high-$\hat{\beta}$ set can have true $\beta$s less than 1, and securities in the low-$\hat{\beta}$ set can have $\beta$s greater than 1.

With 1% abnormal performance, for all test methods both the rejection rates and the mean $t$-statistics are higher for the $\hat{\beta} < 1$ set of samples than for the $\hat{\beta} > 1$ set of samples. But the rejection rates for the high-$\hat{\beta}$ and low-$\hat{\beta}$ samples are generally not markedly different from each other, averaging 27.1% (across test methods) for the $\hat{\beta} < 1$ samples and 21.0% for the $\hat{\beta} > 1$ samples. Nor are these rejection rates much different from the 21.6% average rejection rate (across test methods) we obtained earlier for samples where the average $\hat{\beta}$ was approximately 1. Furthermore, the Mean Adjusted Returns method continues to perform well, rejecting the null 26.8% of the time for the $\hat{\beta} < 1$ samples, and 24.4% of the time for the $\hat{\beta} > 1$ samples.

Our risk clustering simulations also provide some new insight into the relative efficacy of various test methods. A careful look at table 7 reveals that while the rejection rates and mean $t$-statistics for the Control Portfolio method are indeed higher for $\hat{\beta} < 1$ sample than for $\hat{\beta} > 1$ samples when there is abnormal performance, both sets of numbers are lower than for previous samples with $\hat{\beta}$s averaging 1. For example, using the Control Portfolio method, the mean $t$-statistic in our earlier results was 0.86 with 1% abnormal performance; the figures are 0.74 and 0.54, respectively, for the $\hat{\beta} < 1$ and $\hat{\beta} > 1$ sets of samples. While the relative rankings of most of the test methods are not very sensitive to sample security $\beta$, the version of the Control Portfolio method we have simulated performs noticeably worse, relative to both itself and to the other methods, when $\beta$ departs from 1.

The unfavorable performance of the Control Portfolio method when average $\hat{\beta}$ is different from 1 is related to the manner in which the methodology forms portfolios.[39] The Control Portfolio method we simulate is likely to involve short selling of some sample securities when average $\hat{\beta}$ is much different from 1. With short selling, the weights applied to the two subportfolios of sample securities will be vastly different from each other, and the variance of returns on the portfolio thus formed will be quite large;

---

[39]Gonedes, Dopuch and Penman (1976) and Gonedes (1978) discuss a related issue.

compared to a situation where each subportfolio has the same positive weight, the performance measure, which is the difference between portfolio returns and market returns, will also have a higher variance.

In addition, portfolio residual variance tends to be lowest when $\beta$ is 1 [Black, Jensen and Scholes (1972, table 2)]. Portfolios of sample securities which have $\beta$s much different from 1 will have greater estimation error in subportfolio $\beta$ and hence greater estimation error in calculating appropriate weights for subportfolios. This will also increase the variance of the performance measure and lower the power of the tests.

## 7. The choice of market index

Simulation results reported thus far have been based on use of the Equally Weighted Index. However, while the Equally Weighted Index is often employed in actual event studies, the Asset Pricing Model provides no justification for its use: the Asset Pricing model specifies an *ex ante* relationship between security expected returns and systematic risk measured with respect to the Value-Weighted Index. To examine the sensitivity of our earlier results to the choice of market index, we replicate the experiment reported in table 4 using the Value-Weighted (rather than the Equally Weighted) Index. As in the table 4 simulations, the event-month of abnormal performance is a drawing from a uniform distribution in the interval from month $-10$ through $+10$. For each methodology, results using the Value Weighted Index, along with the corresponding earlier results for the Equal Weighted Index, are reported in table 8.

### 7.1. Estimates of systematic risk using different market indices

One way in which the simulation results using the Value-Weighted Index differ from those using the Equally Weighted Index is related to the estimates of sample security systematic risk. To focus on the differences, which will play an important role in our discussion, for each of the 250 replications the average and standard deviation of the market model $\beta$s using each index are computed; summary statistics are shown at the bottom of table 8.

For the Equally Weighted Index, the mean of the 250 average $\beta$s is equal to 0.993, which is insignificantly different from 1. That the average $\hat{\beta}$ is approximately equal to 1 is hardly surprising, since our simulation procedure involves random selection of securities.

However, with the Value-Weighted Index, estimates of sample security $\beta$s are systematically different from 1. With that Index, the mean of the 250 average $\beta$s is 1.13, with a standard deviation of 0.031. At the 0.01 level of significance, the hypothesis that the mean average $\beta$ is equal to 1 must be rejected.

Table 8

The effect of the choice of market index. Percentage of 250 replications where the null hypothesis is rejected ($\alpha=0.05$). One-tailed $t$-test results. $H_0$: mean abnormal performance in interval $(-10, +10)=0.0$. $VW=$CRSP Value Weighted Index. $EW=$Equally Weighted Index.

| Method | Actual level of abnormal performance in the interval $(-10, +10)$[a] | | | | | | | |
| | 0% | | 1% | | 5% | | 15% | |
| | VW | EW | VW | EW | VW | EW | VW | EW |
|---|---|---|---|---|---|---|---|---|
| Mean Adjusted Returns | 7.6 | 7.6 | 9.2 | 9.2 | 28.4 | 28.4 | 82.0 | 82.0 |
| Market Adjusted Returns | 20.4 | 3.6 | 24.0 | 5.6 | 44.8 | 18.4 | 94.8 | 73.2 |
| Market Model Residuals | 4.0 | 7.2 | 6.0 | 10.8 | 18.8 | 24.4 | 76.4 | 86.4 |
| Fama–MacBeth Residuals | 1.2 | 3.6 | 2.0 | 5.2 | 7.2 | 16.4 | 54.8 | 74.8 |
| Control Portfolio | 14.0 | 4.8 | 15.6 | 6.4 | 29.6 | 16.0 | 78.0 | 70.0 |

[a]For each security, abnormal performance is introduced for one month in the interval $(-10, +10)$, with each month having an equal probability of being selected.

Summary Statistics, Systematic Risk Estimates

| | VW | EW |
|---|---|---|
| Mean estimate of $\beta$ | 1.13 | 0.993 |
| Average cross-sectional standard deviation of $\beta$ | 0.49 | 0.43 |
| Standard deviation of average $\beta$s for the 250 samples | 0.031 | 0.027 |

There is no necessity for $\hat{\beta}$s computed from a value-weighted (rather than an equally weighted) index to have an unweighted average of 1; the only requirement is that the value-weighted average of all security $\hat{\beta}$s (computed with respect to the value-weighted index) be equal to 1. For randomly selected securities, an unweighted average $\hat{\beta}$ greater than 1 would be expected if securities with low value weights have relatively high $\hat{\beta}$s, and vice versa. Hence an average $\hat{\beta}$ of 1.13 results from a particular cross-sectional distribution of $\beta$, and does not imply that our selection procedure is somehow biased toward including high risk securities.

## 7.2. Type I errors with the value-weighted index

Our finding that the unweighted average of $\hat{\beta}$s computed from the Value-Weighted Index is not equal to 1, along with the fact that not all securities have the same value weights in the market portfolio, turns out to have significant implications for the behavior of one performance measurement method under study: the Market Adjusted Returns method implicitly assumes that security $\beta$s average to one, and looks at the average differences between security returns and those on the Value-Weighted Market Index. However, since average $\beta$ is greater than 1, an equally weighted portfolio of randomly selected stocks is expected to have returns which are greater than those of the Value-Weighted Index. The unweighted average difference between security returns and returns on the Value-Weighted Market Index will tend to be positive for any sample of randomly selected securities. Using the Value-Weighted Index, the Market Adjusted Returns method will reject the null hypothesis 'too often'.

This potential problem with the Market Adjusted Returns method does not result from the use of the Value-Weighted Index itself. Rather, a potential bias is induced by the failure to appropriately value weight security returns and security specific performance measures.[40] To our knowledge no

---

[40]For the Market Model Residuals method, under the null hypothesis there is no bias inherent in not value-weighting the residuals: Since for every security the expected value of the residuals is zero, the average residual is expected to be zero for any set of weights applied to the individual residuals. On the other hand, for the Market Adjusted Returns method, some securities have performance measures which on average will be positive, (e.g., $\beta > 1$) and others have performance measures which will be negative (e.g., $\beta < 1$). Equal weighting of the security specific performance measures will not guarantee an average performance measure of zero because the number of securities with positive performance measures is greater than the number with negative performance measures.

For Fama–MacBeth residuals, there could well be biases in our simulations with the Value-Weighted Index. Note that Fama–MacBeth residuals are computed on the basis of estimates of $\gamma_0$ and $\gamma_1$ derived from the Equally-Weighted Index. If a security's $\hat{\beta}$ is computed from the Value-Weighted Index, and Fama–MacBeth residuals then calculated from $\hat{\gamma}_0$ and $\hat{\gamma}_1$ based on the Equally Weighted Index, there is no reason for a security's Fama–MacBeth residual to have an expected value of 0 under the null hypothesis of no abnormal performance. Furthermore, deriving estimates of $\gamma_0$ and $\gamma_1$ for the Value-Weighted Index would require more than a mere replication of the Fama–MacBeth procedure; the use of value-weighting procedures (e.g., for portfolio formation) would also be indicated.

event study employing the Market Adjusted Returns method has used such value-weighting. Furthermore, as a practical matter the bias can be substantial. As table 8 indicates, when there is no abnormal performance, the Market Adjusted Returns method rejects the null hypothesis a whopping 20.4% of the time using the Value-Weighted Index, and the mean $t$-statistic for 250 replications is 0.77; if the hypothesis test is performed at the 0.1 rather than the 0.05 level, the rejection rate increases to 27.2%.[41]

From table 8, it also appears that the Control Portfolio method exhibits a positive bias in the performance measure. For that methodology, the rejection rate under the null hypothesis is 14.0% (for $\alpha = 0.05$), and the mean $t$-statistic is 0.36. However, the problem of 'too many' rejections when using the Value-Weighted Index cannot be attributed to the failure to value-weight the security-specific performance measures; this is because the Control Portfolio method, unlike the Market Adjusted Returns method, applies weights to securities such that the portfolio thus formed has a $\beta$ of 1 and an expected return equal to that of the Value-Weighted Market Index.[42]

### 7.3. Type II errors with the value-weighted index

Because some of the performance measurement methods do not, under the null hypothesis, reject at the significance level of the test when used with the Value-Weighted Index, legitimate comparisons of the power of the tests for the Equally Weighted versus Value-Weighted Index are not possible for those methods, since the probability of Type I errors differs according to the index being used. However, the one method which does not suffer from 'too high' a frequency of Type I errors using the Value-Weighted Index is the Market Model Residuals method. Some clue as to the relationship between

[41]The rejection frequencies reported in table 8 for the Market Adjusted Returns method will not always be applicable because the magnitude of the bias in the method is critically dependent on several parameters of the experimental situation. For example, for randomly selected securities, the propensity for rejecting 'too often' under the null will be positively related to sample size and the length of time over which abnormal performance is being measured: if a given performance measure, averaged over sample securities, is positive, whether one can reject the null hypothesis that the average performance measure is zero depends on the number of independent observations over which the average is computed. For example, when the null hypothesis being tested is that month '0' (rather than months $-10$, $+10$) abnormal performance is 0, the rejection rates using the Value-Weighted Index are not much different from those which obtained in simulations using the Equally Weighted Index.

Note also that the bias in the Market Adjusted Returns method is not always positive. The sign of the bias is related to the systematic risk of the sample securities. If the value-weighted average $\hat{\beta}$ is greater than 1, the bias will be positive; if it is less than 1, it will be negative.

[42]The computation of the test statistic in the Control Portfolio method is discussed in the appendix. The distributional properties of the test statistic in repeated sampling will depend upon the sampling properties of the weights which are estimated and applied to the returns on individual securities; the properties could differ according to the index employed, particularly since the degree of measurement error in $\hat{\beta}$ (and hence in the weights) can be a function of the index. Conditions on the weights sufficient for the test statistic to be distributed Student-$t$ have not to our knowledge been discussed in the event study literature.

the power of the tests and the specific market index is provided by the results for that method.

As shown in table 8, for each of several different levels of abnormal performance, the rejection rates using Market Model Residuals are higher with the Equally Weighted Index than with the Value-Weighted Index. With 1% abnormal performance, the rejection rates are 10.8 and 6.0%, respectively; with 5% abnormal performance, the rejection rates are 24.4 and 18.8%, respectively.

It thus appears that use of the Equally Weighted Index is no less likely, and in fact slightly more likely, to pick up abnormal performance than use of the Value-Weighted Index. Such a finding is consistent with the argument that the returns on randomly selected securities are on average more highly correlated with the Equally Weighted Index than the Value-Weighted Index. If for a majority of sample securities the precision with which $\beta$ and hence residuals are measured is higher with the Equally Weighted Index, abnormal performance would be easier to detect using that benchmark.

## 8. Additional simulation results

### 8.1. Simulation results for different sample sizes

All results reported thus far in this paper are for sample sizes of 50 securities. However, it is of interest to examine the sensitivity of our results to sample size. For the case where all sample securities experience abnormal performance in month '0', table 9 reports simulation results for sample sizes of 12, 25, and again for 50 securities.[43]

As would be expected, the power of the tests increases with sample size. However, the rejection frequencies are not especially sensitive to the number of sample securities. For example, with the Mean Adjusted Returns method, doubling the sample size from 12 to 25 securities increases the rejection frequency with 1% abnormal performance from 14.0 to 15.2%. Doubling sample size again to 50 securities increases the rejection frequency to 26.0%. Furthermore, the relatively favorable performance of the Mean Adjusted Returns method seems to be independent of sample size, and the rejection frequencies still do not appear to be dramatically different than those for methods which adjust returns for market performance and risk.

### 8.2. The relationship among the tests

In many of the simulations we have performed, the rejection frequencies are not dramatically different for different methodologies. However, even if

---

[43]When we attempt to examine larger samples as well, the computing costs were found to be prohibitively high. For sample sizes of 100, the cost of performing just a third of the 250 replications was in excess of $1,000.

two methods have the same rejection frequency for any level of abnormal performance, this does not imply that the two methods will always lead a researcher to the same conclusion. For example, if each of two methods rejects the null hypothesis in 50 of the 250 samples, the samples on which the first method rejects the null hypothesis need not be the same as the samples on which the second method rejects the null hypothesis.[44] To assess the likelihood that the various methods will lead to results which are consistent

Table 9

The effect of sample size on rejection frequencies. Percentage of 250 replications where the null hypothesis is rejected ($\alpha = 0.05$). One-tailed $t$-test results. $H_0$: mean abnormal performance in month '0' = 0.0. Equally Weighted Index.

| Method | Actual level of abnormal performance in month '0' | | |
| --- | --- | --- | --- |
| | 0% | 1% | 5% |
| *Mean Adjusted Returns* | | | |
| $N = 12$ | 5.2 | 14.0 | 79.2 |
| $N = 25$ | 6.0 | 15.2 | 94.8 |
| $N = 50$ | 4.0 | 26.0 | 100.0 |
| *Market Adjusted Returns* | | | |
| $N = 12$ | 2.8 | 8.4 | 72.4 |
| $N = 25$ | 3.6 | 13.2 | 91.6 |
| $N = 50$ | 3.2 | 19.6 | 100.0 |
| *Market Model Residuals* | | | |
| $N = 12$ | 3.2 | 9.6 | 72.4 |
| $N = 25$ | 4.4 | 13.6 | 91.6 |
| $N = 50$ | 4.4 | 22.8 | 100.0 |
| *Fama–MacBeth Residuals* | | | |
| $N = 12$ | 2.8 | 8.4 | 56.8 |
| $N = 25$ | 4.8 | 15.2 | 93.2 |
| $N = 50$ | 4.0 | 21.6 | 100.0 |
| *Control Portfolio* | | | |
| $N = 12$ | 2.8 | 8.4 | 56.8 |
| $N = 25$ | 2.4 | 12.8 | 84.8 |
| $N = 50$ | 4.4 | 18.0 | 100.0 |

for a given sample, it is necessary to examine the results of our earlier hypothesis tests in more detail. In table 10, for the case where all abnormal performance occurs in month '0', we indicate the frequency with which the results of the hypothesis tests for a given sample are the same for different methodologies.

[44]Charest (1978), Langetieg (1978), and Brenner (1979) have all conducted event studies where the results of the hypothesis tests appear to be somewhat sensitive to the particular test method which is used.

When the null hypothesis is true, it appears that the test methods typically lead to results which are somewhat, but not perfectly consistent. For example, in the simulations we presented in table 1, under the null hypothesis the Mean Adjusted Returns method rejected in 4.0% of the samples, and the Market Adjusted Returns method rejected the null hypothesis in 3.2% of the 250 samples. However, as indicated in table 10, the frequency with which *both* methods reject the null hypothesis when it is true

Table 10

The relationship among the tests. For 1% abnormal performance in month '0', the table shows the frequency (in 250 replications) with which a given combination of methods resulted in (a) at least one rejection ($R \geq 1$), and (b) an inconsistency (one rejection, one failure to reject; $R = 1$). The third entry is the frequency with which both methods reject the null hypothesis when it is true ($R = 0$). The number in parentheses is the product of the individual rejection frequencies which obtained for each method under the null hypothesis. $H_0$: mean abnormal performance in month '0' $= 0.0$ ($\alpha = 0.05$). One-tailed $t$-test results. Equally Weighted Index.

| | Market Adjusted Returns | Market Model Residuals | Fama– MacBeth Residuals | Control Portfolios |
|---|---|---|---|---|
| **Mean Adjusted Returns** | | | | |
| $R \geq 1$ | 45.6% | 48.8 | 47.6 | 44.0 |
| $R = 1$ | 33.2 | 33.2 | 33.6 | 33.2 |
| $R = 0$ | 1.6(0.13) | 2.0(0.18) | 1.6(0.16) | 1.2(0.18) |
| **Market Adjusted Returns** | | | | |
| $R \geq 1$ | | 42.4 | 41.2 | 37.6 |
| $R = 1$ | | 25.2 | 25.6 | 22.4 |
| $R = 0$ | | 2.4(0.15) | 2.8(0.13) | 2.8(0.14) |
| **Market Model Residuals** | | | | |
| $R \geq 1$ | | | 44.4 | 40.8 |
| $R = 1$ | | | 25.2 | 26.4 |
| $R = 0$ | | | 3.2(0.18) | 2.4(0.19) |
| **Fama–MacBeth Residuals** | | | | |
| $R \geq 1$ | | | | 39.6 |
| $R = 1$ | | | | 25.6 |
| $R = 0$ | | | | 2.8(0.18) |

is 1.6%, which is approximately 10 times the frequency which would be expected if the two methods were independent. Furthermore, for all of the pairwise combinations of methods shown in table 10, it appears that the results of the hypothesis tests are also highly correlated; the frequency with which two given methods reject the null hypothesis when it is true ranges from 1.2 to 3.2%. This high correlation suggests that rejecting the null hypothesis using two different methods is much more likely than would be expected by assuming independence of the test methods.

When the null hypothesis is not true, the test methods are still not perfectly consistent. With 1% abnormal performance, the likelihood that one method will reject the null hypothesis but the other will fail to reject ranges from 22.4 to 33.6%; inconsistencies between two methods seem least likely for the combination of Control Portfolios and Market Adjusted Returns.

Our finding that the test methods are not always consistent when there is abnormal performance opens up the possibility that there are sets of methodologies which, when used jointly, are more likely to detect abnormal performance than any one method alone. For example, as table 10 indicates, with 1% abnormal performance, the frequency with which *at least* one of two methods rejects the null hypothesis of no abnormal performance ranges from 37.6 to 48.8%, which is higher than the rejection rates which typically obtain for the individual tests. However, we hasten to add that the higher rejection rates are not themselves evidence of a more powerful test. It should be kept in mind that the significance level of the test (that is, the probability of *falsely* rejecting at least one of two null hypotheses) also increases when methodologies are used in combination with each other. The probability of at least one Type I error increases with the number of tests, and cannot be assessed unless the dependence of the tests is taken into account.

## 9. Summary and conclusions

In this paper, observed monthly stock return data were employed to examine various methodologies with which event studies measure security price performance. Abnormal performance was artificially introduced into this data. Our conclusions about the performance of the different methodologies can be summarized as follows.

### 9.1. Simulation results for the 'no clustering' case

Initially, we simulated a situation where securities and event dates were randomly selected, and event dates for different securities were not clustered in calendar time. When abnormal performance was present, the differences between methodologies based on Mean Adjusted Returns, Market Adjusted Returns, and Market and Risk Adjusted Returns were quite small; the simplest methodology, Mean Adjusted Returns, picked up abnormal performance no less frequently than did the other methodologies, and the power of the tests did not appear to be enhanced using risk adjustment procedures suggested by the Asset Pricing model. For example, when 1% abnormal performance was introduced in month '0' for every security in a sample of 50, each of the methodologies rejected the null hypothesis of no abnormal month '0' performance about 20% of the time when performing a one-tailed *t*-test at the 0.05 level of significance. Such a result also indicates that if the researcher is working with a sample size of 50 and the event under study is not expected *a priori* to have changed the value of the affected securities by 1% or more, the use of monthly data is unlikely to detect the event's impact.

*The use of prior information*

With 5% or more abnormal performance in month '0', rejection rates for a sample size of 50 were 100% for all of the methodologies. However, that simulation result does not imply that an event study using monthly data will always pick up 5% or more abnormal performance using a sample size of 50: if the researcher is unable to identify the specific time at which the abnormal performance would have occurred, the power of the tests for abnormal performance falls off dramatically. For example, we simulated a situation where each of 50 sample securities had 5% abnormal performance in a particular month surrounding month '0', but the precise month was uncertain and different across securities. When the time of the abnormal performance could only be narrowed to an 11 month 'window', the null hypothesis of no abnormal performance over the window was rejected only 30 to 40% of the time with the different methodologies. Thus, unless the time of the abnormal performance can be narrowed using prior information, the null hypothesis often fails to be rejected even when the sample securities experience high levels of abnormal performance.

## 9.2. Performance measurement when event dates or systematic risk estimates are clustered

*Calendar time clustering of events*

Our conclusions about the relatively favorable performance of the Mean Adjusted Returns method were found to be highly sensitive to the specification of the stochastic process generating events. For example, when we simulated a situation in which event dates were randomly selected, but clustered in calendar time, the Mean Adjusted Returns method performed very poorly compared to those methods which explicitly adjusted for market performance and for systematic risk. In the extreme example of clustering we examined, all securities of a given sample were assigned a common event date, and the *t*-tests were adjusted to take into account cross-sectional dependence in the security-specific performance measures. The Mean Adjusted Returns method detected 5% abnormal performance in month '0' only about 35% of the time, compared to rejection rates of 98.8 to 100.0% for all the other test methods. On the basis of such results, it is difficult to argue that the use of the Mean Adjusted Returns method will always be appropriate. When there is event month clustering, methodologies which incorporate information about the market's realized return perform substantially better than Mean Adjusted Returns.

*Sample security risk clustering*

Within the class of methodologies which adjust for marketwide factors, we examined several alternatives. These included a one-factor market model, a two-factor model utilizing Fama–MacBeth residuals, and a Control Portfolio technique in which the return on a portfolio of sample securities was compared to that of another portfolio with the same estimated systematic risk. For randomly selected securities, which were of 'average' risk, the differences between these methodologies were small, regardless of whether or not there was calendar time clustering of events. However, when securities were not randomly selected, and sample security systematic risk estimates were systematically 'clustered' and different from 1, an important difference between the methodologies emerged: with systematic risk clustering, the Control Portfolio method was much less likely to pick up a given level of abnormal performance than either a one-factor or a two-factor model. In fact, when there was risk clustering but not event month clustering, even the simple Mean Adjusted Returns method outperformed the seemingly complicated Control Portfolio method. Thus, under plausible conditions the researcher can actually be made worse off using explicit risk adjustment procedures.

### 9.3. Additional simulation results

#### The choice of market index

Although use of the Equally Weighted Index is an *ad hoc* procedure, that index led to no notable difficulties in our simulations; however, improper use of the Value-Weighted Index was shown to cause considerable problems which have not been recognized in extant event studies. For example, when some methodologies (including the widely used 'Control Portfolio' methodology) were used with the Value-Weighted Index, the null hypothesis was rejected too often, in some cases over 20% of the time (when testing at the 0.05 significance level) even when there was no abnormal performance. Furthermore, we find no evidence that the use of the Value-Weighted Index increases the power of the tests.

#### The appropriate statistical test

For methodologies using the Equally Weighted Index, and for many of those using the Value-Weighted Index, we found that $t$-tests focusing on the average month '0' performance measure (e.g., the average residual) are reasonably well-specified. Although stated significance levels should not be taken literally, when the null hypothesis is true the $t$-tests typically reject at approximately the significance level of the test; the differences between the empirical frequency distribution of the test statistics and the $t$-distribution are generally not large.

On the other hand, certain non-parametric tests used in event studies are not correctly specified. We indicated how the sign and Wilcoxon tests will not give the 'correct' number of rejections unless asymmetry in the distribution of security specific performance measures is taken into account; as far as we can determine, no event study using non-parametric tests has recognized how sensitive the tests can be to departures from the symmetry assumption.

### 9.4. The bottom line: What's the best methodology?

Our goal in this paper has not been to formulate the 'best' event study methodology, but rather, to compare different methodologies which have actually been used in event studies and which constitute current practice. Even among the methods we have studied, it is difficult to simulate every conceivable variation of each methodology, and every plausible experimental situation; while we cannot, therefore, indicate the 'best' methodology (given some set of criteria), our simulations do provide a useful basis for discriminating between alternative procedures.

A 'bottom line' that emerges from our study is this: beyond a simple, one-factor market model, there is no evidence that more complicated methodologies convey any benefit. In fact, we have presented evidence that more complicated methodologies can actually make the researcher worse off, both compared to the market model and to even simpler methods, like Mean Adjusted Returns, which make no explicit risk adjustment. This is not to say that existing techniques cannot be improved; indeed, our results have led us to suggest a number of ways in which such improvements can be made. But even if the researcher doing an event study has a strong comparative advantage at improving existing methods, a good use of his time is still in reading old issues of the *Wall Street Journal* to more accurately determine event dates.

### Appendix: Methodologies for measuring security price performance

In this appendix, we discuss in more detail the different methods for measuring security price performance which are used in the study. For all of the methodologies, securities are selected as discussed in section 3. For a given security $i$, its monthly arithmetic return, $R_{it}$, is available over a period beginning in the 89th month prior to the event ($t = -89$) and terminating at the end of the tenth month following the event ($t = +10$). There are two observation periods over which return behavior is examined: a single month (month 0) and a series of event-related months (typically, months $-10$ through $+10$). For a particular level of abnormal performance, a given method computes the performance measures for individual securities in each of the 250 samples and, for each sample, assesses the statistical significance of those measures.[45]

### A.1. Mean adjusted returns

For each security $i$, the mean $K_i$, and standard deviation $\sigma(R_i)$ of its return in months $-89$ through $-11$ are estimated:

$$\hat{K}_i = \frac{1}{79} \sum_{t=-89}^{-11} R_{it},$$  (A.1)

$$\hat{\sigma}(R_i) = \left[ \frac{1}{78} \sum_{t=-89}^{-11} (R_{it} - \hat{K}_i)^2 \right]^{\frac{1}{2}}.$$  (A.2)

The measure of abnormal performance for a given security in a given event-related month, $A_{it}$, is the difference between its realized return and the estimate of its mean return in the $(-89, -11)$ period, where this difference is standardized by the estimated standard deviation of the security's return in the $(-89, -11)$ period,[46]

$$A_{it} = (R_{it} - \hat{K}_i)/\hat{\sigma}(R_i).$$  (A.3)

---

[45]For all statistical tests reported in the paper, the $(-10, +10)$ period is ignored in estimating parameters such as the variance of the various performance measures. The simulations presented in tables 1 through 3 have also been replicated using the additional returns from the $(-10, +10)$ period. The additional 21 months of data provided by this period do not appear to have a marked impact on the rejection frequencies or on the distributional properties of the test statistics under the null hypothesis.

However, in an actual event study, the results can be sensitive to the inclusion (or exclusion) of the period surrounding the event. If high levels of abnormal performance are present, then including observations from around the time of the event gives more weight to apparent 'outliers', tending to increase the variance of the security-specific performance measures, and, as borne out by simulations not reported here, lowering the power of the tests. In addition, if there are abnormal returns in the event period, it is difficult to infer 'normal' returns, particularly if the period of the abnormal performance is long and includes an amount of data which is substantial relative to the total available. For a further discussion of reasons to exclude the 'event' period, see Brown, Durbin and Evans (1975). Note that if the event period is excluded in computing parameter estimates which are then used to predict returns into that period, the variance of the performance measure can be adjusted to reflect the predictive nature of the excess returns [see Patell (1976)]. However, event studies typically make no such adjustment; to be consistent with those studies, our simulations, as discussed in this appendix, also make no such adjustment.

[46]The standardization is similar to that which is performed in the Jaffe–Mandelker procedure. Earlier, we noted that the $t$-statistics for the Mean Adjusted Returns method had too much mass in the left-hand tail. That behavior becomes more pronounced without the standardization, making comparisons of power difficult because the level of Type I error is not constant across methodologies.

For month '0', and every month, this procedure yields one performance measure for each of the $N$ securities in the sample.

### The t-tests

The $t$-test for month '0' examines whether or not the average value of the performance measure in month '0' (i.e., the average month '0' standardized difference) is equal to 0. Except when otherwise specified, the $t$-test in the Mean Adjusted Returns method takes into account cross-sectional dependence in the security specific performance measures via a procedure we call Crude Dependence Adjustment.

For all methods using Crude Dependence Adjustment, the standard deviation of the month '0' average performance measure is estimated from the values of the average performance measures in months $-49$ through $-11$. Any cross-sectional dependence in the performance measures is thus taken into account. If the average performance measures for each event-related month are normal, independent,[47] and identically distributed, then under the null hypothesis the ratio of the month '0' average performance measure to the estimated standard deviation is distributed Student-$t$ with 38 degrees of freedom.

With Crude Dependence Adjustment, the test statistic is given by

$$\frac{\frac{1}{N}\sum_{i=1}^{N} A_{i0}}{\left[\frac{1}{38}\left(\sum_{t=-49}^{-11}\left[\left(\frac{1}{N}\sum_{i=1}^{N} A_{it}\right)-A^{*}\right]^{2}\right)\right]^{\frac{1}{2}}},$$  (A.4)

where

$$A^{*}=\left[\sum_{t=-49}^{-11}\sum_{i=1}^{N} A_{it}\right]\cdot\frac{1}{39N}.$$  (A.5)

In the $t$-test for abnormal performance in the $(-10, +10)$ interval, the numerator in (4) becomes

$$\frac{1}{21N}\sum_{t=-10}^{+10}\sum_{i=1}^{N} A_{it},$$  (A.6)

---

[47]Note that, in general, the average performance measures will not literally be independent, which is one reason we refer to our procedure as a crude one. For example, suppose security A had an event in January and security B had an event in March of the same year. Then the average standardized difference in event months spread two months apart ($-2$ and 0, $-1$ and $+1$, etc.) will be calculated on the basis of observations from the same calendar month, and which are likely to be positively correlated. That the Mean Adjusted Returns method does not appear to reject the null hypothesis 'too often' suggests that the degree of dependence is small with this procedure.

and the denominator is the same as that shown in (4), divided by $\sqrt{21}$. This test statistic is also assumed to be distributed Student-$t$ with 38 degrees of freedom.

### Non-parametric tests

The test statistic in the sign test for month '0' abnormal performance is given by

$$Z = \frac{|P - 0.5| - 1/2N}{\sqrt{(0.5(0.5)/N)}},$$  (A.7)

where $P$ is the proportion of $A_i$'s in month '0' having positive signs.[48] The test statistic is assumed unit normal under the null hypothesis. The Wilcoxon test is carried out as in Lehmann (1975, pp. 128–129).

### A.2. Market adjusted returns

For month '0', the performance measure for a given sample security is the difference between its return and the corresponding return on the market index,

$$A_{it} = R_{it} - R_{mt}.$$  (A.8)

An assumption sufficient for using such a performance measure is that the systematic risk for each sample security is equal to 1. In that case, the expected value of the difference between the return on a security and the return on the market index should, in an asset pricing model framework, be equal to zero.[49] The significance of the month '0' and months $(-10, +10)$ abnormal performance is assessed exactly as in the Mean Adjusted Returns method. For the month '0' $t$-test, the performance measure for a sample is the average difference.

### A.3. Market model residuals

For each security in the sample, we regress its return in months $-89$ through $-11$ against the returns on the market portfolio during the corresponding calendar months. This 'market model' regression yields a 'residual' in each event-related month for each security. For a given security, the market model residual is its measure of abnormal performance. For the

---

[48]The sign of $Z$ is equal to the sign of the difference between $P$ and 0.5.

[49]For the average difference to be zero, it is not necessary for *all* sample securities to have $\beta = 1$. It is required only that the average $\beta$ be equal to 1.

$t$-test on month '0', the performance measure is the average market model residual. Thus, we examine the significance of

$$\frac{1}{N} \sum_{i=1}^{N} A_{i0}, \tag{A.9}$$

where

$$A_{it} = R_{it} - \hat{\alpha}_i - \hat{\beta}_i R_{mt}. \tag{A.10}$$

Because residual cross-correlation in calendar time is likely to be small (and would generally be even smaller in event time), simulations with Market Model Residuals make no dependence adjustment, unless otherwise stated. For procedures making no dependence adjustment, the significance test on the average residual (or average security specific performance measure) is carried out under the assumption that residuals (or other performance measures) are uncorrelated across securities. The standard deviation of the average performance measure is estimated on the basis of the standard deviation of the performance measure of each sample security in the $(-89, -11)$ period. For month '0', the test statistic is given by

$$\frac{\frac{1}{N} \sum_{i=1}^{N} A_{i0}}{\frac{1}{N} \left( \sum_{i=1}^{N} \left[ \frac{1}{77} \sum_{t=-89}^{-11} \left( A_{it} - \left( \sum_{t=-89}^{-11} \frac{A_i}{79} \right) \right)^2 \right] \right)^{\frac{1}{2}}}, \tag{A.11}$$

which is distributed Student-$t$ with 78 degrees of freedom for the assumed normal and independent $A_{it}$s.

### A.4. Fama–MacBeth residuals

For each security in the sample, we again use the market model to compute an estimate of its systematic risk over the period from $-89$ through $-11$. Using that estimate, we then compute a 'Fama–MacBeth' residual for each security for each month from $-10$ through $+10$,

$$A_{it} = R_{it} - \hat{\gamma}_1 - \hat{\gamma}_2 \hat{\beta}_i. \tag{A.12}$$

For a given month $t$, the Fama–MacBeth residual for security $i$, $A_{it}$, is the return on the security, net of the effect of marketwide factors captured by estimates of $\gamma_1$ and $\gamma_2$. We refer to the $A_{it}$s as 'Fama–MacBeth' residuals because the estimates of $\gamma_1$ and $\gamma_2$ which we use were derived by Fama and

MacBeth (1973).[50] For a given month, these coefficients reflect, respectively, the constant and the slope term in a cross-sectional regression of average portfolio return on average portfolio $\hat{\beta}$. The estimates $\hat{\gamma}_1$ and $\hat{\gamma}_2$ differ from calendar month to calendar month. However, for a given calendar month, they are the same for all securities, and should correspond to the return on the zero beta portfolio and the slope of the market line, respectively.[51]

The month '0' performance measure for a given security is its Fama–MacBeth residual. As with market model residuals, the performance measure for the *t*-test is the average Fama–MacBeth residual, and its statistical significance is assessed exactly as in that method. The test statistic is given in (A.11), unless otherwise stated.

### A.5. Control portfolios

This method forms a portfolio of sample securities where the portfolio has approximately the same estimated systematic risk as the market index. The month '0' performance measure for this method is the difference between the return on that portfolio of sample securities and the average return on the market index in the months when securities experienced events.

The procedure we use to construct portfolios and estimate weights is as follows:

*Portfolio Construction* — Two portfolios are formed from the sample securities. Each portfolio is assigned half of those securities. The first portfolio consists of 'low-$\hat{\beta}$' sample securities. The second portfolio consists of 'high-$\hat{\beta}$' sample securities. The composition of each portfolio is determined by a market model regression for each of the securities in the sample for the months $-89$ through $-50$. The securities are ranked according to their estimated $\hat{\beta}$s and, based on the rankings, securities are assigned to either the high-$\hat{\beta}$ or low-$\hat{\beta}$ portfolio.

*Estimation of Weights* — For each month in event-related time, we estimate the returns on each of two portfolios. The first is the equally weighted portfolio of high-$\hat{\beta}$ securities. The second is the equally weighted portfolio of low-$\hat{\beta}$ securities. For each equally weighted portfolio, we estimate its $\beta$, based on data from months $-49$ through $-11$. In this way, $\hat{\beta}$s used for forming portfolios and $\hat{\beta}$s used for estimating weights will be independent. Given the two estimates of $\beta$, we estimate a unique set of weights

---

[50]The estimates of $\gamma_1$ and $\gamma_2$ which we use are those reported in Fama (1976, pp. 357–360). The methodology for estimating those coefficients is discussed both there and in Fama and MacBeth (1973). In the original Fama–MacBeth article, $\gamma_1$ and $\gamma_2$ are referred to as $\gamma_0$ and $\gamma_1$, respectively.

[51]See Fama (1976, ch. 9). Brenner (1976) presents evidence that the Fama–MacBeth estimates of $\gamma_1$ are not uncorrelated with the market return.

Bawa, Vijay, Stephen Brown and Roger Klein, 1979, Estimation risk and optimal portfolio choice (North-Holland, New York).

Beaver, William H., 1979, Econometric properties of alternative security return metrics, Unpublished manuscript (Stanford University, Stanford, CA).

Black, Fischer, 1972, Capital market equilibrium with restricted borrowing, Journal of Business 45, July, 444–454.

Black, Fischer and Myron Scholes, 1973, The behavior of security returns around ex-dividend days, Unpublished manuscript (Massachusetts Institute of Technology, Cambridge, MA).

Black, Fischer, Michael Jensen and Myron Scholes, 1972, The capital asset pricing model: Some empirical tests, in: M. Jensen, ed., Studies in the theory of capital markets (Praeger, New York).

Brenner, Menachem, 1976, A note on risk, return, and equilibrium: Empirical tests, Journal of Political Economy 84, April, 407–409.

Brenner, Menachem, 1979, The sensitivity of the efficient market hypothesis to alternative specifications of the market model, Journal of Finance 34, Sept., 915–929.

Brown, R.L., J. Durbin and J.M. Evans, 1975, Techniques for testing the constancy of regression relationships over time, Journal of the Royal Statistical Society Series B 37, 149–192.

Charest, Guy, 1978, Split information, stock returns, and market efficiency, Journal of Financial Economics 6, June/Sept., 265–296.

Collins, Daniel W. and Warren T. Dent, 1978, Econometric testing procedures in market based accounting research, Unpublished manuscript (Michigan State University, East Lansing, MI).

Collins, Daniel W. and Warren T. Dent, 1979, The proposed elimination of full cost accounting in the extractive petroleum industry, Journal of Accounting and Economics 1, March, 3–44.

Cornell, Bradford and J. Kimball Dietrich, 1978, Mean-absolute-deviation versus least squares regression estimation of beta coefficients, Journal of Financial and Quantitative Analysis 13, March, 123–131.

Cowles, Alfred, 1933, Can stock market forecasters forecast?, Econometrica 1, 309–324.

Fama, Eugene F., 1976, Foundations of finance (Basic Books, New York).

Fama, Eugene F. and James D. MacBeth, 1973, Risk, return and equilibrium: Empirical tests, Journal of Political Economy 71, May/June, 607–636.

Fama, Eugene F., Lawrence Fisher, Michael Jensen and Richard Roll, 1969, The adjustment of stock prices of new information, International Economic Review 10, Feb., 1–21.

Foster, George, 1980, Accounting policy decisions and capital market research, Journal of Accounting and Economics, forthcoming.

Gonedes, Nicholas J., 1978, Corporate signaling, external accounting, and capital market equilibrium: Evidence on dividends, income and extraordinary items, Journal of Accounting Research 16, Spring, 26–79.

Gonedes, Nicholas J., Nicholas Dopuch and Stephen J. Penman, 1976, Disclosure rules, information-production, and capital market equilibrium: The case of forecast disclosure rules, Journal of Accounting Research 14, Spring, 89–137.

Jaffe, Jeffrey F., 1974, Special information and insider trading, Journal of Business 47, July, 410–428.

Kaplan, Robert S. and Richard Roll, 1972, Investor evaluation of accounting information: Some empirical evidence, Journal of Business 45, April, 225–257.

Langetieg, Terence C., 1978, An application of a three factor performance index to measure stockholder gains from merger, Journal of Financial Economics 6, Dec., 365–384.

Latane, Henry A. and Charles P. Jones, 1979, Standardized unexpected earnings — 1971–1977, Journal of Finance 34, 717–724.

Lehmann, E.L., 1975, Nonparametrics: Statistical methods based on ranks (Holden-Day, San Francisco, CA).

Mandelker, Gershon, 1974, Risk and return: The case of merging firms, Journal of Financial Economics 1, Dec., 303–335.

Marsaglia, G., K. Ananthanarayanan and N. Paul, 1973, Random number generator package — 'Super duper', Mimeo. (School of Computer Science, McGill University, Montreal).

Masulis, Ronald W., 1978, The effects of capital structure change on security prices, Unpublished Ph.D. dissertation (University of Chicago, Chicago, IL).

Mayers, David and Edward M. Rice, 1979, Measuring portfolio performance and the empirical content of asset pricing models, Journal of Financial Economics 7, March, 3–28.

Officer, Robert R., 1971, A time series examination of the market factor of the New York stock exchange, Ph.D. dissertation (University of Chicago, Chicago, IL).

Ohlson, James A., 1978, On the theory of residual analyses and abnormal performance metrics, Australian Journal of Management 3, Oct., 175–193.

Ohlson, James A., 1979, Residual (API) analysis and the private value of information, Journal of Accounting Research 17, Autumn, 506–527.

Patell, James M., 1976, Corporate forecasts of earnings per share and stock price behavior: Empirical tests, Journal of Accounting Research 14, Autumn, 246–276.

Patell, James M., 1979, The API and the design of experiments, Journal of Accounting Research 17, Autumn, 528–549.

Roll, Richard, 1977, A critique of the asset pricing theory's tests; Part I: On past and potential testability of the theory, Journal of Financial Economics 4, March 129–176.

Roll, Richard and Stephen A. Ross, 1979, An empirical investigation of the arbitrage pricing theory, Unpublished manuscript (University of California, Los Angeles, CA).

Scholes, Myron and Joseph Williams, 1977, Estimating betas from non-synchronous data, Journal of Financial Economics 5, Dec., 309–328.

Schwert, G. William, 1978, Measuring the effects of regulation: evidence from capital markets, Unpublished manuscript (University of Rochester, Rochester, NY).

Udinsky, Jerald and Daniel Kirshner, 1979, A comparison of relative predictive power for financial models of rates of return, Journal of Financial and Quantitative Analysis 14, June, 293–315.

Warner, Jerold B., 1977, Bankruptcy, absolute priority, and the pricing of risky debt claims, Journal of Financial Economics 4, May, 239–276.

Watts, Ross L., 1978, Systematic 'abnormal' returns after quarterly earnings announcements, Journal of Financial Economics 6, June/Sept., 127–150.

# STOCK RETURN VARIANCES
## The Arrival of Information and the Reaction of Traders*

### Kenneth R. FRENCH

*University of Chicago, Chicago, IL 60637, USA*

### Richard ROLL

*University of California, Los Angeles, CA 90024, USA*
*Goldman, Sachs & Co., New York, NY 10004, USA*

Received March 1985, final version received January 1986

Asset prices are much more volatile during exchange trading hours than during non-trading hours. This paper considers three explanations for this phenomenon: (1) volatility is caused by public information which is more likely to arrive during normal business hours; (2) volatility is caused by private information which affects prices when informed investors trade; and (3) volatility is caused by pricing errors that occur during trading. Although a significant fraction of the daily variance is caused by mispricing, the behavior of returns around exchange holidays suggests that private information is the principle factor behind high trading-time variances.

## 1. Introduction

Equity returns are more volatile during exchange trading hours than during non-trading hours. For example, the variance of returns from the open to the close of trading on an average day is over six times larger than the variance of close-to-open returns over a weekend, even though the weekend is eleven times longer. On an hourly basis, the variance when the exchanges are open is between 13 and 100 times larger, depending on the non-trading period being considered.

The phenomenon has been pointed out by several authors including Fama (1965), Granger and Morgenstern (1970), Oldfield and Rogalski (1980), and Christie (1981), but it has not generated much attention. We believe it is important. It represents an empirical puzzle whose solution may provide a deeper understanding of information processing in financial markets.

*This paper has benefited from the comments of seminar participants at Boston College, the University of British Columbia, the University of Chicago, Dartmouth College, Harvard University, Northwestern University, Purdue University and Stanford University. We are also grateful to Craig Ansley, Merton Miller, Steven Ross, Robert Stambaugh, William Schwert, Jerold Warner (the referee), and especially, Douglas Diamond and Eugene Fama for comments on an earlier draft.

We consider three possible explanations for the observed variance pattern. The first possibility is that more public information arrives during normal business hours. Under this hypothesis, most return volatility is caused by things like judicial decisions and tender offers and these announcements are clustered during the trading day. The second explanation assumes that most return volatility is caused by private information and that this information only affects prices through the trading of informed investors. If the informed investors are more likely to trade when the exchanges are open, return variances will be high during this period.

The third possibility we consider is that the process of trading introduces noise into stock returns. For example, perhaps investors over-react to each other's trades. This trading noise would increase return variances when the exchanges are open.

To determine the relative importance of these three explanations, we examine the behavior of returns around business days when the New York and American Stock Exchanges were closed. If high trading-time variances are caused by the arrival of public information during the business day, return variances should not fall simply because the exchanges are closed. On the other hand, both the trading noise hypothesis and the private information hypothesis predict that return variances will be unusually low around exchange holidays. We find that the two-day return variance around exchange holidays is only slightly larger than the variance of a normal one-day return.

Our exchange holiday results are consistent with both the private information hypothesis and the trading noise hypothesis. To discriminate between these hypotheses we compare daily return variances with variances for longer holding periods. If daily returns are independent, the variance for a long holding period will equal the cumulated daily variances within the period. However, if daily returns are affected by trading noise, the longer holding period variance will be smaller than the cumulated daily variance.

These tests suggest that, on average, between 4% and 12% of the daily return variance is caused by mispricing. However, even if we assume that all of the mispricing occurs during the trading day, it has a small impact on the relation between trading and non-trading variances. It appears that the large difference between these variances is caused by differences in the arrival and incorporation of information during trading and non-trading periods.

## 2. Trading and non-trading variances

If hourly stock return variances were constant across trading and non-trading periods, the variance of weekend returns (i.e., Friday close to Monday close) would be three times the variance of weekday returns (e.g., Tuesday close to Wednesday close). In this section we examine this proposition and we

Table 1

Average ratios of multiple-day variances relative to single-day variances for all NYSE and AMEX stocks and for quintiles of stocks sorted by equity value.[a]

| | | All stocks | Smallest quintile[a] | 2 | 3 | 4 | Largest quintile |
|---|---|---|---|---|---|---|---|
| Two-day holidays | Average ratio[b] | 1.247 | 1.301 | 1.199 | 1.239 | 1.217 | 1.281 |
| | Standard error[c] | 0.066 | 0.068 | 0.054 | 0.052 | 0.097 | 0.100 |
| | Standard deviation[d] | 1.354 | 1.446 | 1.270 | 1.371 | 1.149 | 1.351 |
| | Number of firms[e] | 1962.5 | 390.3 | 392.3 | 392.4 | 393.5 | 394.1 |
| | Average sample size[f] | 10.0 | 10.0 | 10.0 | 10.0 | 10.0 | 10.0 |
| Weekends | Average ratio | 1.107 | 1.122 | 1.108 | 1.119 | 1.105 | 1.082 |
| | Standard error | 0.012 | 0.010 | 0.016 | 0.014 | 0.014 | 0.017 |
| | Standard deviation | 0.385 | 0.412 | 0.379 | 0.435 | 0.337 | 0.286 |
| | Number of firms | 2055.3 | 411.2 | 410.8 | 410.6 | 411.2 | 411.5 |
| | Average sample size | 92.8 | 92.5 | 92.8 | 92.9 | 93.0 | 93.0 |
| Holiday weekends | Average ratio | 1.117 | 1.111 | 1.122 | 1.099 | 1.122 | 1.130 |
| | Standard error | 0.092 | 0.053 | 0.085 | 0.071 | 0.106 | 0.151 |
| | Standard deviation | 1.219 | 1.176 | 0.992 | 1.276 | 1.232 | 1.014 |
| | Number of firms | 2055.7 | 411.3 | 410.8 | 410.9 | 411.2 | 411.5 |
| | Average sample size | 11.1 | 11.0 | 11.1 | 11.1 | 11.1 | 11.1 |

[a] Stocks are sorted into quintiles based on their equity values at the beginning of ten two-year subperiods between 1963–1982.

[b] The average ratio comparing the variance of two-, three-, and four-calendar-day returns with the variance of one-day returns. This estimate is the average of the ten subperiod averages.

[c] The standard error of the reported average ratio. This standard error is based on the distribution of the ten subperiod average ratios.

[d] The average cross-sectional standard deviation. The ratios for individual firms are used to estimate the standard deviation for each subperiod. The reported standard deviation is the average of the ten subperiod standard deviations.

[e] The average number of firms in each subperiod.

[f] The average number of multiple-day returns for each stock in each subperiod.

report on the relation between firm size and the trading/non-trading variance differential.

Our tests use the daily returns provided by the Center for Research in Security Prices for all common stocks listed on the New York and American Stock Exchanges between 1963 and 1982. We break this twenty-year period into ten two-year subperiods. For each stock, we calculate return variances for weekdays, weekends, holidays, and holiday weekends during each subperiod. These estimates are used to compute multiple-to-single-day variance ratios for each stock in each subperiod.

The first column of table 1 reports grand averages of the estimated variance ratios. The grand averages are calculated by first averaging the variance ratios across the stocks within each subperiod and then averaging the ten subperiod averages. The grand averages are consistent with the evidence in earlier papers.

The variance of the total return over a weekend or a holiday is only slightly higher than the variance of the total return over a normal weekday. For example, the variance for a three-day weekend return is only 10.7% higher than the variance for a normal one-day return.

Table 1 also reports standard errors of the grand averages. These standard errors, which are based on the distribution of the ten subperiod averages, range from 0.04 for weekends to 0.29 for holiday weekends. Under the assumption that the subperiod averages are independent and identically distributed, the grand averages are many standard errors below 2.0, 3.0, or 4.0.

One can imagine many factors that might affect the way investors acquire and react to information about particular firms. For example, perhaps firms in some industries are closely monitored by financial analysts, while little private information is collected about firms in other industries. In this study, we concentrate on firm size as a potential factor because it is easy to observe and because the rewards from acquiring and using firm-specific information are probably a function of this variable.

To examine whether the relation between trading and non-trading variances is a function of firm size, we sort firms into quintiles based on their equity values at the beginning of each subperiod. The averages of the subperiod averages for the quintiles are reported in columns 2 through 6 in table 1. There is no obvious relation between the estimated variance ratios and firm size. For example, the average two-day variance ratio for the smallest firms (column 2) is 1.30 with a standard error of 0.07 and the average ratio for the largest firms (column 6) is 1.28 with a standard error of 0.10.

To see what the estimated variance ratios imply about the difference between trading and non-trading variances, assume that

(a) returns are intertemporally uncorrelated,
(b) the exchange is open six hours per day (the present situation),
(c) there are just two uniform regimes, trading and non-trading hours; returns are identically distributed within these regimes but have different variances between them.

(These assumptions are made at this point merely for temporary illustrative convenience. We relax them later.)

Let $\sigma_T^2$ be the variance of returns *per hour* during trading and let $\sigma_N^2$ be the variance per hour at other times. Since there are 66 non-trading hours over the weekend and 18 non-trading hours in a normal business day, the average weekend-to-weekday variance ratio for all firms implies

$$66\sigma_N^2 + 6\sigma_T^2 = 1.107\left(18\sigma_N^2 + 6\sigma_T^2\right). \tag{1}$$

Thus, based on the weekend variance ratio,

$$\sigma_T^2 = 71.8\sigma_N^2;$$

the hourly variance when the New York exchanges are open is roughly seventy times the hourly variance when they are closed. We can make similar transformations with the average variance ratios for two- and four-day holidays. Using the averages for all stocks in table 1 gives:

| Non-trading interval | Hourly trading to non-trading variance ratio |
|---|---|
| Mid-week holidays | 13.2 |
| Weekends | 71.8 |
| Holiday Weekends | 99.6 |

Trading hours are more volatile than non-trading hours. Among non-trading hours, weekends have lower volatility than normal holidays and holiday weekends have the lowest volatility of all.

## 3. Possible explanations

There seem to be two general explanations for the empirical phenomenon that prices are more variable during exchange trading hours. The obvious possibility is that information arrives more frequently during the business day. The second possible explanation is that trading somehow induces volatility.

To examine the first possibility, it is useful to divide information into two categories: public information and private information. Public information is information that becomes known at the same time that it affects stock prices. Examples of this information include changes in the weather, Supreme Court decisions, and the outcome of the World Series. Information produced by firms, such as financial reports, or by the government, such as United States Department of Agriculture crop forecasts, is included in this category if no one trades on the information before it is released.

Private information is at the other end of the spectrum. While public information affects prices before anyone can trade on it, private information only affects prices through trading. Much of the information produced by investors and security analysts is in this category.

Obviously, most information falls in the continuum between public and private information. However, this artificial dichotomy is useful because it allows us to develop and test several hypotheses about the variance pattern we observe.

Our first hypothesis is that the higher trading-time volatility occurs because public information is more likely to appear during normal business hours. This explanation is plausible since most public information is probably a by-product of normal business activities.

The private information hypothesis is similar. Under this hypothesis, return variances are higher during trading hours because most private information is incorporated into prices during this period. There are two possible reasons for this. First, the production of private information may be more common when the exchanges are open. For example, security analysts are more likely to work at this time. Activities such as visiting corporate headquarters, examining company documents, and making recommendations to clients are all easier to do during the business day. In addition, the benefits of producing private information are larger when the exchanges are open and the information can be acted on quickly and conveniently.

Even if private information is produced at a constant rate during both trading and non-trading periods, trades based on this information could lead to high trading-time variances. Consider the effect of private information that is produced after the New York exchanges close. Since this information can only affect prices through the trading of informed investors, the price reaction is delayed until this trading occurs. If the informed investors trade on the New York exchanges, their information cannot affect prices until the exchanges open.

The fact that private information only affects prices when markets are open appears to offer a simple, yet general, explanation for high trading-time variances. However, this story will not explain the results in table 1 unless we assume that private information affects returns for more than one trading day. All of the estimates in table 1 are based on close-to-close returns, which include both a non-trading period and a trading period. If non-trading information is completely revealed in prices during the next trading day, it will affect the 'right' close-to-close return. For example, if private information produced during the weekend only affects Monday's return and information produced during a weeknight only affects the next day's return, the weekend-to-weekday variance ratios in table 1 accurately reflect the private information produced during each period. Unless private information affects prices for more than one trading day, the hypothesis that informed investors only trade when the exchanges are open cannot explain the low variance ratios in table 1.

To summarize, the private information hypothesis says that the variance pattern we observe occurs either because most private information is produced during normal business hours or because informed investors usually trade when the exchanges are open and they trade on their information for more than one day.

The second general explanation for high trading-time variances is that the process of trading introduces noise into stock returns. Suppose each day's return can be broken into two components: an information component that reflects a rational assessment of the information arriving that day, and an independent or positively correlated error component.[1] If the daily pricing error occurs during the trading period, it will increase the trading-time variance. It is important to note that under this hypothesis at least some trading noise (the error component in the daily return) is not corrected during the trading day in which it occurs. If all trading noise were corrected quickly, the noise would increase intra-day return variances, but it would not affect our close-to-close returns.

In summary, the hypotheses to be examined are:

(H.1)  High trading-time volatility is caused by public information which is more likely to be observed during normal business hours.

(H.2)  High trading-time volatility is caused by private information which is more likely to affect prices when the exchanges are open.

(H.3)  High trading-time volatility is caused by pricing errors that occur during trading.

## 4. Tests of the hypotheses

In this section we examine the predictions of the three hypotheses. It is important to recognize that the hypotheses are not mutually exclusive. In fact, the observed variance pattern might be caused by all three factors simultaneously. Our goal is to provide some sense of the empirical importance of each explanation.

### 4.1. Exchange holidays

The New York and American Stock Exchanges were closed on Wednesdays during the second half of 1968 because of a paperwork backlog. The exchanges were also closed on many of the election days in our sample period. These exchange holidays give us an excellent opportunity to examine the relative importance of our three hypotheses.[2]

Under the public information hypothesis, the return variance for a business day should not depend on whether the exchanges are open or closed. Therefore, this hypothesis predicts that stock return variances will not be reduced by the exchange holidays in 1968. The prediction of the public information hypothesis for election holidays is less clearcut. One might expect unusually high variances on election days since election results are publicly observable

---

[1] In the discussion below, we add a third component that arises because of the bid/ask spread.

[2] French (1980) also uses returns around the 1968 exchange holidays to make inferences about the exchange holidays.

information. However, perhaps the exchanges close on election days because less public information is available.

The private information hypothesis predicts that return variances will be reduced by both the election day closings and the exchange holidays in 1968. The size of this reduction depends on the interval used to compute returns. Since private information only affects prices when informed investors trade, the reduction in the variance should be large during the period that the exchanges are closed. For example, the variance of the return from the close of trading on Tuesday to the open on Thursday should be unusually low if the exchanges are closed on Wednesday.

Much of the reduction in the variance will be eliminated if the next day's trading is included in the return. The information that would have affected prices on Wednesday will affect prices during trading on Thursday instead. However, the variance for the two-day close-to-close return from Tuesday to Thursday should still be less than twice the variance of a normal one-day return. This difference may persist for two reasons. First, private information may affect prices for more than one trading day. The information that would have been revealed through trading on Wednesday and Thursday may not be fully incorporated in prices if trading is limited to Thursday. Second, less private information may be produced when the markets are closed. Exchange holidays reduce the value of private information. Informed investors either must delay acting on their information – and run the risk that someone else will discover it – or they must find a less convenient way to trade. Because of its reduced value, less private information will be produced when the exchanges are closed.

If we increase the holding period to one week, the private information hypothesis predicts that the effect of the exchange holiday on the total variance should be even smaller. Equivalently, the variance for the days following an exchange holiday should be larger than normal. Adding more trading days to the return interval allows more time for the private information to affect prices. Also, with less information produced on the exchange holiday, more will be produced on succeeding days. There are two reasons for this production effect. First, with more information available to produce, the cost of generating any particular amount should fall. Second, some of the information that is not produced privately because the exchanges are closed might become publicly observable after a few days.

Hypothesis H.3 makes a simpler prediction. If high trading-time variances are caused by trading noise, the variance should fall when the exchanges are closed and the variance that is lost should not be recovered.

Table 2 presents evidence to test these predictions. The first section of this table reports daily variance ratios comparing the two-day returns for exchange holidays in 1968 (from Tuesday close to Thursday close) with a normal one-day variance estimated between January 1963 and December 1982. The

Table 2

Daily and weekly variance ratios for exchange holidays.

| | | All stocks | Smallest quintile[a] | 2 | 3 | 4 | Largest quintile |
|---|---|---|---|---|---|---|---|
| | | *Daily variance ratios* | | | | | |
| Exchange holidays in 1968 | Average ratio[b] | 1.145 | 1.077 | 1.043 | 1.180 | 1.239 | 1.274 |
| | Standard deviation[c] | 0.882 | 0.857 | 0.647 | 0.979 | 0.944 | 1.001 |
| | Number of firms | 2083 | 597 | 455 | 374 | 342 | 315 |
| | Average sample size[d] | 22.7 | 22.8 | 22.7 | 22.6 | 22.7 | 22.85 |
| Election holidays | Average ratio[e] | 1.165 | 1.131 | 1.073 | 1.186 | 1.159 | 1.332 |
| | Standard deviation | 1.079 | 1.222 | 1.065 | 1.040 | 0.799 | 1.118 |
| | Number of firms | 2026 | 572 | 426 | 367 | 347 | 314 |
| | Average sample size | 8.5 | 8.2 | 8.2 | 8.1 | 8.7 | 9.5 |
| | | *Weekly variance ratios* | | | | | |
| Exchange holidays in 1968 | Average ratio[f] | 0.821 | 0.901 | 0.802 | 0.772 | 0.793 | 0.784 |
| | Standard deviation | 0.559 | 0.667 | 0.484 | 0.422 | 0.511 | 0.612 |
| | Number of firms | 2093 | 600 | 457 | 376 | 344 | 316 |
| | Average sample size | 20.6 | 20.7 | 20.6 | 20.5 | 20.7 | 20.8 |
| Election holidays | Average ratio | 0.839 | 0.876 | 0.776 | 0.889 | 0.779 | 0.868 |
| | Standard deviation | 0.614 | 0.707 | 0.627 | 0.678 | 0.501 | 0.527 |
| | Number of firms | 1188 | 278 | 221 | 192 | 229 | 268 |
| | Average sample size | 8.5 | 8.3 | 8.3 | 8.3 | 8.6 | 8.8 |

[a] Firms are sorted into quintiles based on their relative equity values when they are first listed in the CRSP daily master file.

[b] Average variance ratio comparing two-day exchange holiday returns with single-calendar-day returns between January 1963 and December 1982.

[c] Cross-sectional standard deviation of the individual firm ratios.

[d] Average number of exchange holidays for each firm.

[e] Average variance ratio comparing two-day exchange holiday returns with single-calendar-day returns from 1962–1969, 1972, 1976, and 1980.

[f] Average ratio comparing the return variance for weeks containing exchange holidays with the return variance for weeks containing five trading days.

results are surprising. The average ratio across all stocks is 1.145. The averages for the size portfolios range from 1.043 for the second quintile to 1.274 for the fifth quintile. In other words, these point estimates indicate that, on average, the variance for the *two-day* exchange holiday returns is only 14.5% higher than the variance for normal one-day returns.

To get an idea about the reliability of these estimates, we construct similar ratios using the returns for Wednesday and Thursday during each half year from 1963 to 1982. For example, we compute a two-day variance for each stock using all of the Wednesday–Thursday returns observed during the first half of 1963. This variance is compared to the one-day variance estimated between July of 1963 and December of 1982. The ratio of these variances is averaged across stocks to get the average ratio for the first half of 1963. This process is repeated for each of the 39 half years in our sample. (The second half of 1968 is not included because it contains the Wednesday holidays.) The averages (which are not shown) range from 1.18 for the second half of 1964 to 4.32 for the second half of 1974, with a grand average of 2.00. It appears that the low 1968 variance ratio, 1.14, is not caused by chance, but by the exchange holiday.

The first section of table 2 also reports average daily variance ratios for election days. During our sample period, the exchanges closed for elections in 1962–1969, 1972, 1976, and 1980. Therefore, we compare the two-day election returns with one-day returns from those years. The average variance ratio for all stocks is 1.165. The portfolio averages range from 1.073 for the second quintile to 1.333 for the fifth quintile.

To check the reliability of the daily election ratios in table 2, we construct similar ratios using combined Tuesday–Wednesday returns for non-election weeks. Each replication involves one observation from each of the eight election years. For example, the first Tuesday–Wednesday pair of each election year is used in the first replication and the second pair is used in the second replication. This procedure generates a total of 45 replications, with average variance ratios ranging from 1.61 for the thirtieth Tuesday–Wednesday pair each year to 2.62 for the first pair. The grand average is 1.98. Again, it does not appear that the election holiday variance ratio of 1.17 is caused by chance. There appears to be a strong relation between the low variance ratios and the exchange holidays.

The daily variance ratios for election holidays and exchange holidays in 1968 are consistent with both the private information hypothesis and the trading noise hypothesis. However, these ratios provide little support for the public information hypothesis, which predicts that the two-day exchange holiday variance should be twice the one-day variance.

Weekly variance ratios in the second section of table 2 offer some evidence about the relative importance of private information and trading noise. Under the trading noise hypothesis, exchange holidays should cause a permanent reduction in the cumulated return variance. On the other hand, the private information hypothesis predicts that most of the lost variance will be recovered; when the holding period is increased there is more time to incorporate private information into prices and to discover information that was not produced on the exchange holiday.

To test these predictions, we compare the returns for weeks that include exchange holidays with the returns for normal five-trading-day weeks. For example, the weekly return for a Wednesday holiday in 1968 is measured from the close of trading on Tuesday to the close of trading on the following Tuesday. The five-trading-day variance is estimated using returns from Tuesday close to Tuesday close over all five-trading-day weeks in the full 1962–1982 sample period. The election week returns are measured from Monday close to Monday close and they are compared with weekly returns for 1962–1969, 1972, 1976, and 1980.

The weekly variance ratios in table 2 are consistent with the trading noise hypothesis. Across all stocks, the average weekly ratio for exchange holidays in 1968 is 0.82, and the average election week ratio is 0.84. However, neither of these estimates is very reliable. Simulated weekly variance ratios for the exchange holidays in 1968, which are constructed like the simulated daily ratios above, vary between 0.54 and 2.04. Simulated election week variances range from 0.76 to 1.53. The standard deviations of the simulated average ratios are 0.35 and 0.14, respectively. It is difficult to draw meaningful inferences from the weekly exchange holiday ratios.

## 4.2. Autocorrelations

The exchange holiday results support both the private information hypothesis and the trading noise hypothesis. We can obtain more information about the relative importance of these hypotheses by examining the autocorrelations of the daily returns. Neither public information nor private information will generate observable serial correlation. In principle, information may induce autocorrelation by changing the level of expected returns. However, the variance of expected returns is almost certainly so small that autocorrelation from this source is unobservable in realized returns for individual stocks.

Under the trading noise hypothesis, stock returns should be serially correlated. It is difficult to characterize short-run autocorrelations without a specific mispricing model. However, unless market prices are unrelated to the objective economic value of the stock, pricing errors must be corrected in the long run. These corrections would generate negative autocorrelations.

Two other factors may induce serial correlation under all three hypotheses. Close-to-close returns, such as those reported by CRSP, contain measurement error because each closing trade may be executed at any price within the bid/ask spread. If these measurement errors are independent from day to day, they will induce negative first-order autocorrelation. For example, suppose today's closing price is on the bid side of the market. Then today's observed return is negatively biased and tomorrow's observed return is positively biased. If today's price is on the ask side, the pattern is reversed but the observed returns are still negatively correlated.[3]

---

[3] If daily bid/ask errors are not independent, they can induce negative autocorrelations beyond lag 1. The autocorrelations in table 3 use all of the prices in the CRSP daily master file. These prices include both trade prices and the mean of bid and ask prices when a stock did not trade during a day. To control for one potential source of dependence, we have also estimated the autocorrelations using just trade prices. Deleting returns involving bid/ask prices has only one noticeable effect – the first-order autocorrelations increase slightly. For example, the average first-order autocorrelation across all stocks increases from 0.003 to 0.009.

Systematic variation in expected returns can also induce serial correlation. For example, the day of the week effects documented by French (1980) induce positive autocorrelations at every fifth lag (5, 10, 15, etc.) and negative autocorrelations at all other lags. Day of the month effects documented by Ariel (1984) also imply non-zero autocorrelations. However, since the variance of daily realized returns is much larger than the variance of daily expected returns, autocorrelation from this source will have little effect on our results.[4]

Because the predictions of the trading noise hypothesis are not precise, we are not interested in a detailed study of the autocorrelation structure of daily returns. However, the general behavior of the autocorrelations can help us discriminate between the trading noise hypothesis and the information hypotheses. In summary, we expect that measurement error from the bid/ask spread will lead to negative first-order autocorrelation under all three hypotheses. Neither the public nor the private information hypothesis predicts any other serial correlation, while the trading noise hypothesis predicts that daily returns will be negatively correlated beyond lag one.

Table 3 shows average autocorrelations for lags between one and fifteen days. The general procedure used to compute these averages is similar to the procedure used in table 1. Autocorrelations are estimated for individual stocks during each two-year subperiod. The first column of table 3 reports grand averages that are calculated by averaging the autocorrelations across all of the stocks within each subperiod and then averaging the ten subperiod averages. Columns 2 through 6 report the average autocorrelations for firms that have been sorted into quintiles based on their equity values at the beginning of each subperiod. Table 3 also includes standard errors of the autocorrelation estimates. These standard errors are based on the distribution of the ten subperiod averages, under the assumption that these averages are independent and identically distributed.[5]

The results in table 3 are generally consistent with the predictions of the trading noise hypothesis. All of the estimated autocorrelations from lag 2 to lag 12 are negative. Although the estimates are small in absolute magnitude, many are more than three standard errors from zero. The persistence of the negative autocorrelations suggests that trading noise is not completely corrected for at least two weeks.

The behavior of the first-order autocorrelations in table 3 is surprising. We expected measurement error within the bid/ask spread to induce negative

---

[4] To examine this issue in more detail, we have recomputed the autocorrelations reported in table 3 below using returns which are adjusted for day-of-the-week effects. This adjustment does not alter any of our inferences.

[5] Under the assumption that returns are serially independent, the expected value of the estimated autocorrelations for each firm is $-1/(T-1)$, where $T$ is the number of observations used in the estimate. [See Moran (1948).] Therefore, we increase the individual autocorrelation estimates by $1/(T-1)$ before computing the subperiod and full period averages.

Table 3

Average daily autocorrelations in percent for all NYSE and AMEX stocks and for quintiles of stocks sorted by equity value.[a]

| Lag | All stocks | Smallest quintile | 2 | 3 | 4 | Largest quintile |
|---|---|---|---|---|---|---|
| 1 | 0.33 (0.87) | −6.42 (1.55) | −1.66 (1.07) | 1.17 (0.83) | 2.49 (0.84) | 5.44 (1.01) |
| 2 | −1.15 (0.15) | −1.94 (0.24) | −1.43 (0.20) | −1.28 (0.15) | −0.75 (0.14) | −0.40 (0.26) |
| 3 | −1.15 (0.15) | −1.35 (0.16) | −1.39 (0.23) | −1.26 (0.19) | −1.00 (0.21) | −0.81 (0.22) |
| 4 | −0.68 (0.23) | −0.85 (0.16) | −0.66 (0.19) | −0.62 (0.29) | −0.49 (0.28) | −0.78 (0.34) |
| 5 | −0.28 (0.23) | −0.44 (0.17) | −0.15 (0.28) | −0.05 (0.22) | −0.15 (0.27) | −0.59 (0.39) |
| 6 | −0.95 (0.24) | −0.84 (0.24) | −0.72 (0.25) | −0.84 (0.29) | −0.92 (0.26) | −1.38 (0.29) |
| 7 | −0.64 (0.25) | −0.53 (0.19) | −0.53 (0.30) | −0.50 (0.27) | −0.63 (0.26) | −0.98 (0.32) |
| 8 | −0.37 (0.24) | −0.14 (0.15) | −0.42 (0.23) | −0.31 (0.30) | −0.25 (0.25) | −0.73 (0.40) |
| 9 | −0.45 (0.19) | −0.34 (0.13) | −0.47 (0.16) | −0.27 (0.17) | −0.57 (0.20) | −0.60 (0.40) |
| 10 | −0.26 (0.15) | −0.12 (0.12) | −0.10 (0.15) | −0.15 (0.18) | −0.38 (0.19) | −0.51 (0.24) |
| 11 | −0.52 (0.18) | −0.27 (0.10) | −0.54 (0.13) | −0.58 (0.21) | −0.57 (0.23) | −0.65 (0.32) |
| 12 | −0.20 (0.22) | −0.35 (0.12) | −0.18 (0.20) | −0.21 (0.24) | −0.10 (0.28) | −0.19 (0.31) |
| 13 | −0.15 (0.20) | −0.11 (0.12) | 0.02 (0.18) | −0.03 (0.20) | −0.14 (0.28) | −0.47 (0.35) |
| 14 | 0.15 (0.25) | 0.28 (0.13) | 0.05 (0.17) | 0.18 (0.24) | 0.14 (0.27) | 0.10 (0.50) |
| 15 | 0.42 (0.15) | 0.28 (0.12) | 0.38 (0.17) | 0.49 (0.17) | 0.43 (0.21) | 0.52 (0.28) |

[a] The autocorrelations and standard errors (in parentheses) are reported in percent. Autocorrelations are estimated for individual firms during each of ten two-year subperiods between 1963 and 1982. These autocorrelations are averaged to compute subperiod averages. Each reported autocorrelation is the average of ten subperiod averages. The standard error is based on the distribution of the ten subperiod averages. Approximately 500 returns are used to estimate the autocorrelations for each firm in each subperiod. On average, there are about 380 firms in each quintile during each subperiod.

are not. In fact, the first-order autocorrelation for the largest quintile of stocks is 5.4%, with a standard error of 1.0%.

Although they are surprising, the positive autocorrelations also support the trading noise hypothesis. If we rule out the possibility that the reported prices contain positively correlated measurement errors, we are unable to imagine any sensible explanation of these results that does not involve trading noise. For example, suppose traders over-react to new information and this over-reaction persists for more than one day. Then tomorrow's pricing error is positively correlated with both today's information component and today's pricing error. Alternatively, suppose the market does not incorporate all information as soon as it is released. Then today's pricing error is negatively correlated with today's information and tomorrow's error is positively correlated with today's information. The positive correlation between today's information and tomorrow's error could generate positively autocorrelated returns. Since negative first-order autocorrelation induced by the bid/ask spread is smaller for the larger firms, it dominates the error-induced positive autocorrelation only in the first and second quintiles.

The results in table 3 are consistent with the trading noise hypothesis. However, since the average autocorrelations are small in absolute magnitude, it is hard to gauge their economic significance. To estimate the importance of the trading noise hypothesis, we compare daily return variances with variances for longer holding period returns. If daily returns were independent, the variance for a long holding period would equal the cumulated daily variances within the period. On the other hand, if daily returns are temporarily affected by trading noise, the longer period variance will be smaller than the cumulated daily variances.

This comparison presumes that the relative importance of both pricing errors and bid/ask errors is reduced as the holding period is increased. For example, suppose mispricing is corrected within three weeks. Then pricing errors that occur during the first ten weeks of each three-month holding period have no effect on the three-month return and errors that occur during the last three weeks have a reduced effect. If pricing errors are corrected within three weeks and bid/ask errors are corrected overnight, most of the three-month return reflects a rational assessment of the information arriving during the three-month period. When the holding period is extended to six months, this approximation becomes even more accurate. By comparing the variance of long holding period returns (which reflect information) with the variance implied by daily returns (which reflect information, pricing errors, and bid/ask errors), we can estimate the fraction of the daily variance that is caused by rational assessments of information.[6]

Table 4 reports average actual-to-implied variance ratios for holding periods of two trading days; one, two, and three weeks; and one, three, and six months. The general procedure used to compute these average ratios is similar to the procedure used in tables 1 and 3. We first compute actual-to-implied

---

[6]This comparison was suggested to us by Eugene Fama. Perry (1982) uses a similar approach to examine the process generating stock returns.

Table 4

Actual-to-implied variance ratios for all NYSE and AMEX stocks and for quintiles of stocks sorted by equity value.

| | | All stocks | Smallest quintile[a] | 2 | 3 | 4 | Largest quintile |
|---|---|---|---|---|---|---|---|
| Two trading days | Average ratio[b] | 0.999 | 0.933 | 0.979 | 1.007 | 1.021 | 1.048 |
| | Standard error[c] | 0.010 | 0.015 | 0.011 | 0.010 | 0.009 | 0.013 |
| | Number of firms[d] | 1900.2 | 362.6 | 374.6 | 373.9 | 386.8 | 402.3 |
| | Average sample size[e] | 250.5 | 249.0 | 250.3 | 250.8 | 251.0 | 251.0 |
| One week | Average ratio | 0.966 | 0.853 | 0.928 | 0.979 | 1.005 | 1.053 |
| | Standard error | 0.017 | 0.025 | 0.019 | 0.018 | 0.018 | 0.019 |
| | Number of firms | 1899.6 | 362.1 | 374.5 | 373.9 | 386.8 | 402.3 |
| | Average sample size | 103.6 | 102.7 | 103.6 | 103.9 | 104.0 | 104.1 |
| Two weeks | Average ratio | 0.943 | 0.803 | 0.900 | 0.959 | 0.995 | 1.045 |
| | Standard error | 0.024 | 0.026 | 0.025 | 0.025 | 0.027 | 0.025 |
| | Number of firms | 1899.5 | 362.0 | 374.5 | 373.9 | 386.8 | 402.3 |
| | Average sample size | 51.5 | 50.9 | 51.5 | 51.7 | 51.8 | 51.8 |
| Three weeks | Average ratio | 0.929 | 0.784 | 0.888 | 0.953 | 0.985 | 1.024 |
| | Standard error | 0.022 | 0.026 | 0.026 | 0.023 | 0.024 | 0.024 |
| | Number of firms | 1899.5 | 362.0 | 374.4 | 373.9 | 386.8 | 402.2 |
| | Average sample size | 34.0 | 33.5 | 34.0 | 34.1 | 34.2 | 34.2 |
| One month | Average ratio | 0.906 | 0.773 | 0.874 | 0.931 | 0.959 | 0.983 |
| | Standard error | 0.022 | 0.023 | 0.027 | 0.025 | 0.020 | 0.024 |
| | Number of firms | 1898.9 | 361.7 | 374.3 | 373.9 | 386.8 | 402.2 |
| | Average sample size | 23.6 | 23.0 | 23.6 | 23.8 | 23.8 | 23.9 |
| Three months | Average ratio | 0.894 | 0.752 | 0.876 | 0.949 | 0.942 | 0.941 |
| | Standard error | 0.045 | 0.032 | 0.043 | 0.051 | 0.055 | 0.066 |
| | Number of firms | 1895.3 | 359.8 | 373.6 | 373.5 | 386.6 | 401.8 |
| | Average sample size | 7.7 | 7.3 | 7.7 | 7.8 | 7.9 | 7.9 |
| Six months | Average ratio | 0.883 | 0.731 | 0.862 | 0.931 | 0.929 | 0.907 |
| | Standard error | 0.102 | 0.062 | 0.086 | 0.109 | 0.117 | 0.129 |
| | Number of firms | 1554.2 | 203.4 | 291.8 | 324.8 | 350.5 | 383.7 |
| | Average sample size | 4.0 | 4.0 | 4.0 | 4.0 | 4.0 | 4.0 |

[a]Stocks are sorted in quintiles based on their equity value at the beginning of ten two-year subperiods between 1963–1982.

[b]Average ratio comparing the actual holding period variance with the variance implied by single-trading-day returns under the assumption that the one-day returns are independent. The reported ratio is the average of ten subperiod averages.

[c]The standard error of the reported average ratio. This standard error is based on the distribution of the ten subperiod average ratios.

[d]The average number of firms in each subperiod.

[e]The average number of multiple-day returns for each stock in each subperiod.

variance ratios for each stock in each two-year subperiod. This is done in four steps. For example, to estimate the weekly actual-to-implied variance ratio for a given stock in a particular two-year subperiod, we first calculate the average trading day return during the 104 weeks in that period. Next, we cumulate the daily squared deviations around this average. Then under the assumption that the daily returns are independent, we estimate the implied weekly variance by dividing this total by 104. Finally, we divide the actual weekly variance by the implied variance. The same procedure is used to estimate variance ratios for other holding periods.[7]

The first column of Table 4 reports grand averages that are calculated by averaging the estimated variance ratios across all the stocks within each subperiod and then averaging the ten subperiod averages. The averages for stocks that have been sorted into quintiles based on their equity values at the beginning of each subperiod are reported in columns 2 through 6. Table 4 also includes standard errors that are based on the distribution of the ten sub-period averages, under the assumption that the subperiod averages are independent and identically distributed.

The results in table 4 indicate that a significant fraction of the daily variance is caused by pricing and bid/ask errors. The six-month actual-to-implied variance ratio for all firms is 0.88. The six-month averages for the smallest and largest quintiles are 0.73 and 0.91, respectively. Based on these point estimates, 27% of the daily variance for the first quintile and 9% of the daily variance for the fifth quintile is eliminated in the long run. One would draw nearly identical inferences from the three-month variance ratios. This supports the assumption that bid/ask and pricing errors have relatively little effect on three- and six-month holding period returns.

Since both the pricing errors and the bid/ask errors are temporary, the six-month ratios in table 4 only allow us to make an estimate of their combined effect. However, by assuming that the variance of the bid/ask errors is zero, these ratios place an upper bound on the point estimate of the relative variance of the pricing errors. We can estimate a lower bound for this variance by combining the results in tables 3 and 4.

Suppose each day's return is made up of three independent components: a rational information component ($X_t$), a mispricing component ($Y_t$), and a bid/ask error ($Z_t$),

$$R_t = X_t + Y_t + Z_t. \tag{2}$$

---

[7] These ratios may be affected by two sources of bias. Both the actual and implied variances are estimated with error. Since we are using the ratio of these estimates our measure is biased upward. However, simulations suggest that this bias is negligible. The second source of bias may be more important. We are assuming that the expected returns are constant over each estimation period. Violations of this assumption will have little effect on the implied variances since they are based on daily variance estimates. However, changing expected returns could positively bias the actual long-term variance estimates. To reduce this effect, we limit each estimation period to two years and we limit the holding periods to a maximum of six months.

Also, suppose that the daily information components are independent and identically distributed with variance var($X_t$). The bid/ask error in the daily return depends on the error in the current price ($e_t$), and the error in the previous day's price ($e_{t-1}$),

$$Z_t = e_t - e_{t-1}. \tag{3}$$

If the daily price errors ($e_t$) are independent and identically distributed, the variance and first-order autocovariance of the bid/ask errors equal

$$\text{var}(Z_t) = 2\,\text{var}(e_t) \tag{4}$$

and

$$\text{cov}(Z_t, Z_{t-1}) = -\text{var}(e_t) = -\text{var}(Z_t)/2. \tag{5}$$

Therefore, the first-order autocorrelation of the bid/ask errors is $-0.5$.[8]

If pricing and bid/ask errors have a negligible effect on six-month returns, the six-month variance ratios in table 4 can be written as

$$V_6 = \text{var}(X_t)/\text{var}(R_t), \tag{6}$$

where var($X_t$) and var($R_t$) are the variances of the daily information component and the total daily return, respectively. Using eq. (5) and the assumption that the daily information components are serially independent, the first-order autocorrelation of the daily returns is

$$\begin{aligned}
\rho_R &= \text{cov}(R_t, R_{t-1})/\text{var}(R_t) \\
&= [\text{cov}(Y_t, Y_{t-1}) + \text{cov}(Z_t, Z_{t-1})]/\text{var}(R_t) \\
&= [\rho_{Y1}\text{var}(Y_t) - \text{var}(Z_t)/2]/\text{var}(R_t).
\end{aligned} \tag{7}$$

Eqs. (6) and (7) can be combined to obtain an expression for the relative variance of the pricing errors,

$$\text{var}(Y_t)/\text{var}(R_t) = (1 - V_6 + 2\rho_R)/(1 + 2\rho_{Y1}). \tag{8}$$

Unfortunately, we cannot observe $\rho_{Y1}$, the autocorrelation of the pricing errors. However, since this autocorrelation must be less than 1.0, eq. (8) gives a lower bound for the point estimate of the relative variance,

$$\text{var}(Y_t)/\text{var}(R_t) > (1 - V_6 + 2\rho_R)/3. \tag{9}$$

---

[8] This bid/ask spread phenomenon is examined in more detail by Cohen et al. (1983) and Roll (1984).

Using the average first-order autocorrelations in table 3 and the average six-month variance ratios in table 4, the upper and lower bounds on our point estimates of the relative pricing error variance for all stocks and for each quintile are:

| | All stocks | Smallest quintile | 2 | 3 | 4 | Largest quintile |
|---|---|---|---|---|---|---|
| Upper bound | 11.7% | 26.9% | 13.8% | 6.9% | 7.1% | 9.3% |
| Lower bound | 4.1% | 4.7% | 3.5% | 3.1% | 4.0% | 6.7% |

The lower bound is roughly constant across the five portfolios. This similarity is not limited to the lower bound. Differences in the relative pricing error variances will be small as long as the autocorrelation of these errors is approximately the same across portfolios.

### 4.3. Implications

The estimates in tables 3 and 4 suggest that a non-trivial fraction of the daily variance is caused by mispricing. However, pricing errors have a negligible effect on the weekend-to-weekday variance ratios in table 1. Suppose we adjust those ratios under a set of assumptions that magnifies the impact of mispricing. Specifically, assume that the variance of the weekday pricing errors and the variance of the weekday bid/ask errors are as large as the variance of weekend errors. Then the weekday and weekend returns ($R_{1t}$ and $R_{3t}$, respectively) can be written as

$$R_{1t} = X_{1t} + Y_t + Z_t, \tag{10}$$

$$R_{3t} = X_{3t} + Y_t + Z_t. \tag{11}$$

Based on the average ratio for all firms in table 1, the variance of $R_{3t}$ is 10.7% larger than the variance of $R_{1t}$,

$$\mathrm{var}(X_{3t} + Y_t + Z_t) = 1.107\,\mathrm{var}(X_{1t} + Y_t + Z_t). \tag{12}$$

The average six-month variance ratio for all firms in table 4 is 0.88. To magnify the effect of mispricing further, assume that this ratio applies to the weekend variance,

$$\mathrm{var}(X_{3t}) = 0.883\,\mathrm{var}(X_{3t} + Y_t + Z_t). \tag{13}$$

Under the assumption that the information and mispricing components are independent, eqs. (12) and (13) can be combined to eliminate the bid/ask and pricing error variances,

$$\text{var}(X_{3t}) = 1.123 \, \text{var}(X_{1t}).  \tag{14}$$

Eliminating the effect of these errors increases the average weekend-to-weekday variance ratio for all firms by less than 2%. This effect varies from less than 1% for the largest quintile of stocks to less than 6% for the smallest quintile. Bid/ask and pricing errors also have a negligible effect on the two- and four-day variance ratios in table 1 and on the exchange holiday ratios in table 2.

It appears that the low daily variance ratios are caused by a reduction in the arrival of information when the exchanges are closed. Moreover, the exchange holiday variances suggest that private information causes most stock price changes.[9]

## 5. Summary and conclusions

Asset returns display a puzzling difference in volatility between exchange trading hours and non-trading hours. For example, we estimate that the per hour return variance was about 70 times larger during a trading hour than during a weekend non-trading hour, on average, over all stocks listed on the New York and American Exchanges from January 1963 through December 1982.[10]

We consider three factors that might explain the high trading-time variances. First, the arrival of public information may be more frequent during the business day. Second, private information may be much more likely to affect prices when the New York exchanges are open. Third, the process of trading may induce volatility.

Our results indicate that, on average, approximately 4 to 12% of the daily variance is caused by mispricing. However, even if we assume that pricing errors are generated only when the exchanges are open, these errors have a trivial effect on the difference between trading and non-trading variances. We conclude that this difference is caused by differences in the flow of information during trading and non-trading hours. Moreover, small return variances over exchange holidays suggest that most of this information is private.

## Appendix

If we are willing to ignore sampling error (and just assume that sample estimates are population values), we can deduce additional information about

---

[9] In the appendix we develop some implications under the assumption that the information and error components are not independent.

[10] This estimate is based on the variance ratio for weekends in table 1.

the correlation between information and mispricing and about the quantity of information produced on a non-market business day (such as a Wednesday in 1968).

First, define $W_t = Y_t + Z_t$ as the sum of the mispricing component and the bid/ask error. Define $X_t$ as the information-induced return for one day. The variance ratio for table 4 can be written as

$$a = \text{var}(X)/\text{var}(X + W). \qquad (A.1)$$

Solving (A.1) with a = 0.883 (from table 4),

$$\sigma_X/\sigma_W = \frac{\rho_{XW} + \sqrt{\rho_{XW}^2 + 0.1325}}{0.1325}, \qquad (A.2)$$

where $\rho_{XW}$ is the contemporaneous correlation between $X$ and $W$, and $\sigma$ is the standard deviation. Thus, if there is *no* correlation between information and mispricing ($\rho_{XW} = 0$),

$$\sigma_X/\sigma_W = 2.75.$$

In principle, we could have a low information-to-mispricing variance ratio. For example, if $\rho_{XW} = -1$, $\sigma_X/\sigma_W$ is only 0.48. At the other extreme, if $\rho_{XW} = +1$, $\sigma_X/\sigma_W = 15.6$.

The variance ratios for business days which are not trading days can be written as

$$b = \text{var}(kX + W)/\text{var}(X + W), \qquad (A.3)$$

where $k^2 - 1$ $(1 \le k \le \sqrt{2})$ is the information produced during a business-day-exchange holiday. For $b = 1.145$ (from table 2) and $\sigma_{XW} = 0$, (A.1) and (A.3) imply $K = 1.079$; i.e., only about 16 percent of a normal business day's information was produced on the 1968 Wednesday business days which were exchange holidays.

Going one step further, we can combine (A.1) and (A.3) to eliminate $\sigma_{XW}$. This provides an expression for the ratio of mispricing to information variance as a function of $k$,

$$q = \frac{\text{var}(W)}{\text{var}(X)} = \frac{ak^2 + (1 - a)k - b}{a(k - 1)} = k + \frac{1}{a} + \frac{1 - b}{a(k - 1)}. \qquad (A.4)$$

We note that $\partial q/\partial k = 1 + ((b - 1)/a(k - 1)^2)$, which is positive because $b > 1$. The function $q$ has a zero at $k_L = \{(a - 1) + [(a - 1)^2 + 4ab]^{1/2}\}/2a$. For values of $k$ greater than $k_U = \{(2a - 1) + [(2a - 1)^2 + 4a(b - a)]^{1/2}\}/2a$, the mispricing variance exceeds the information variance, i.e., $q > 1$.

Table A.1

Exchange holiday information consistent with information variance exceeding mispricing variance
(% of normal day).

| Actual-to-implied variance ratio, $a$ | Ratio of two-day exchange holiday return variance to normal day return variance, $b$ | | | | | |
|---|---|---|---|---|---|---|
| | 1.05 | 1.10 | 1.15 | 1.20 | 1.25 | 1.30 |
| | Information produced on exchange holiday as a percentage of information produced, on a normal day, consistent with information variance exceeding mispricing variance[a] | | | | | |
| 0.75 | 5.78 to 9.88 | 11.59 to 19.56 | 17.41 to 29.07 | 23.26 to 38.44 | 29.12 to 47.68 | 34.99 to 56.82 |
| 0.80 | 5.60 to 9.86 | 11.21 to 19.48 | 16.84 to 28.90 | 22.48 to 38.15 | 28.13 to 47.26 | 33.80 to 56.25 |
| 0.85 | 5.43 to 9.84 | 10.87 to 19.40 | 16.32 to 28.73 | 21.78 to 37.87 | 27.24 to 46.86 | 32.72 to 55.70 |
| 0.90 | 5.27 to 9.82 | 10.55 to 19.32 | 15.84 to 28.87 | 21.13 to 37.60 | 26.43 to 46.46 | 31.73 to 55.17 |
| 0.95 | 5.13 to 9.79 | 10.27 to 19.24 | 15.40 to 28.40 | 20.54 to 37.34 | 25.69 to 46.08 | 30.83 to 54.66 |

[a] The lower and upper bounds are given by

$$K_L = 100\{(a-1) + [(a-1)^2 + 4ab]^{1/2}\}/2a \text{ and } K_U = 100\{(2a-1)^2 + 4a(b-a)]^{1/2}\}/2a.$$

The information variance exceeds the mispricing variance only when $\cdot k$ is between $k_U$ and $k_L$. For our estimated parameters, $k_L = 1.074$ and $k_U = 1.130$. Under the assumption that the estimated values are population values, the information variance would exceed the mispricing variance if the information produced on a 1968 Wednesday was between 15.3 and 27.7 percent of that produced on a normal day. In fact, depending on the values of $a$ and $b$, the range can be even narrower than $k_U - k_L$ because the implied correlation coefficient in (A.3) must lie between $-1$ and $+1$. From (A.1), the correlation between the information and mispricing components is obtained using the solution to (A.4),

$$\rho_{XW} = (1 - a - aq)/2a\sqrt{q}. \tag{A.5}$$

For instance, $q = 0$ is clearly ruled out by (A.5) unless $a = 1$. Thus, the lower bound on $k$ must exceed $k_L$.

In general, the restriction on the correlation, $-1 \leq \rho_{XW} \leq 1$, implies from (A.5)

$$1 + \sqrt{1/a} > \sqrt{q} > \sqrt{1/a} - 1. \tag{A.6}$$

For our estimates $a = 0.883$, $b = 1.145$, $\sqrt{q}$ has a lower bound of 0.06419, implying a lower bound on $k$ of 1.0745 (which is slightly higher than $k_L$).

There are sampling errors in the estimates of $a$ and $b$. Thus, although the range of $k$ where the information variance is larger than the mispricing variance is rather narrow for our point estimates, it could be much larger for other values of $a$ and $b$. Table A.1 gives the range $100(k_U^2 - 1)$ to $100(k_L^2 - 1)$

for other values of $a$ and $b$ which could be conceivable given the sampling error.

As the other variance ratio $b$ increases, the interval widens. But even for $b = 1.30$, the information variance is larger than the mispricing variance only if the amount of information produced on a 1968 Wednesday is *less* than about 56 percent of the information produced on a normal business day.

The results are rather insensitive to the variance ratio $a$. Also, for all the values in the table, the correlation between $X$ and $W$ is negative. It ranges from $-0.33$ for $a = 0.75$, $b = 1.05$, to $-0.47$ for $a = 0.95$, $b = 1.30$.

## References

Ariel, Robert A., 1986, A monthly effect in stock returns, Journal of Financial Economics, forthcoming.

Christie, Andrew A., 1981, On efficient estimation and intra-week behavior of common stock variances, Unpublished working paper, April (University of Rochester, Rochester, NY).

Cohen, Kalman J., Gabriel, A. Hawawini, Steven F. Maier, Robert A. Schwartz and David K. Whitcomb, 1983, Friction in the trading process and the estimation of systematic risk, Journal of Financial Economics 12, Aug., 263–278.

Fama, Eugene F., 1965, The behavior of stock market prices, Journal of Business 38, Jan., 34–105.

French, Kenneth R., 1980, Stock returns and the weekend effect, Journal of Financial Economics 8, March, 55–70.

Granger, Clive W.J. and Oskar Morgenstern, 1970, Predictability of stock market prices (Heath-Lexington, Lexington, MA).

Moran, P.A.P., 1948, Some theorems on time series, Biometrika 35, 255–260.

Oldfield, George S., Jr. and Richard J. Rogalski, 1980, A theory of common stock returns over trading and non-trading periods, Journal of Finance 35, June, 729–751.

Perry, Phillip R., 1982, The time-variance relationship of security returns: Implications for the return generating stochastic process, Journal of Finance 37, June, 857–870.

Roll, Richard, 1984, A simple implicit measure of the bid/ask spread in an efficient market, Journal of Finance 39, Sept., 1127–1139.

# II

# EFFICIENT CAPITAL MARKETS

**1** Roberts, H., "Stock Market 'Patterns' and Financial Analysis: Methodological Suggestions," *Journal of Finance*, 14 (March 1959), pp. 1–10.

**2** Jensen, M. C., and G. A. Bennington, "Random Walks and Technical Theories: Some Additional Evidence," *Journal of Finance*, 25 (May 1970), pp. 469–482.

**3** Patell, J. M., and M. A. Wolfson, "The Intraday Speed of Adjustment of Stock Prices to Earnings and Dividend Announcements," *Journal of Financial Economics*, 13 (June 1984), pp. 223–252.

**4** Mikkelson, W. H., and M. M. Partch, "Stock Price Effects and Costs of Secondary Distributions," *Journal of Financial Economics*, 14 (June 1985), pp. 165–194.

**5** Bradley, M., A. Desari, and E. H. Kim, "Synergistics Gains from Corporate Acquisitions and Their Division between the Stockholders of Target and Acquiring Firms," *Journal of Financial Economics*, 21 (May 1988), pp. 3–40.

**6** Seyhun, H. N., "Insiders' Profits, Cost of Trading and Market Efficiency," *Journal of Financial Economics*, 16 (June 1986), pp. 198–212.

**7** Lloyd-Davies, P., and M. Canes, "Stock Prices and the Publication of Second-Hand Information," *Journal of Business*, 51 (January 1978), pp. 43–56.

The term "efficient capital markets" has several related meanings. There is a large literature that defines and models prices set in efficient markets (or rational expectations equilibrium). Since the focus of this book is on the empirical evidence on capital markets, we have chosen papers that illustrate a variety of tests of efficiency.

**Roberts (1959)** is an illustration of the random walk model for stock prices. He makes the simple point that changes in stock prices caused by the arrival of new information should be random, so the level of stock prices follows a random walk. Of course, this assumes that expected returns to stocks are constant over time, or at least do not vary much compared with the size of price changes caused by new information. The most important contribution of Roberts's paper is to show that the accumulation of random shocks creates apparent patterns, similar to the behavior of actual stock prices. Such plots have led technical analysts to look for "heads-and-shoulders," "resistance levels," and other types of patterns, yet by construction future changes in the level of a random walk are completely unpredictable. Thus, **Roberts (1959)** is one of the earliest papers on *weak form market efficiency.* As Fama (1970) defines it, weak form efficiency means that prices reflect all information available in past prices.

**Jensen and Bennington (1970)** study a particular type of technical trading method called the "relative strength" rule. The importance of this paper is not that it debunked a popular trading method. Instead, this paper lays out methodological problems that arise in the analysis of many similar types of trading rules. *Sample selection bias,* caused by using the same sample of returns to find the "best" trading rule and then calculating significance tests on the same data, overstates the reliability of the evidence in favor of the trading rule. *Risk adjustment* is important because risky securities should have higher expected returns in equilibrium, and many trading rules like relative strength have a tendency to select risky securities. *Transaction costs* are important because they reduce the profitability of the rule compared with passive, buy-and-hold investment strategies.

*Semistrong form market efficiency* means that asset prices reflect public information. **Patell and Wolfson** (1984) use intraday stock prices to study the speed of adjustment to the release of information about dividends and earnings. They find that prices adjust within 15 minutes of the announcement, so on average abnormal returns are not available. They note that the standard deviation of returns stays abnormally high for 4 to 6 hours after the announcement, which may reflect further information gathering triggered by the news release. They also show that during the 15 minutes after the announcement there is a stronger than normal tendency for prices to move in the same direction. (Usually there is a strong tendency for price changes to be negatively correlated between trades because of variation between the bid and ask prices of the specialist.) Thus, while the price adjustment is not instantaneous, it is very quick, and most of the "abnormal" behavior is due to market microstructure (the details of the transaction process.)

**Mikkelson and Partch** (1985) study the effects of secondary distributions—sales of large blocks of stock to many investors in an organized set of transactions. They find no abnormal price movement around the trade date for registered distributions where the seller has advertised in advance through a Securities and Exchange Commission (SEC) filing that the sale is going to occur. On the other hand, on the announcement day of the registration there is a larger price drop the more likely it is that the seller has reliable information about the company. They also find that larger trades are associated with larger price drops on the announcement day. Not surprisingly, information that a blockholder wants to sell a large amount of stock causes a drop in price. **Mikkelson and Partch** find a similar price drop for unregistered secondary distributions where the announcement date and the trade date are the same.

**Bradley, Desai, and Kim (1988)** study the reaction of daily stock prices for firms that are targets of tender offers. Because tender offers usually involve large premiums for target shares, and because there is a rich set of interesting corporate finance questions involved, this paper is a good example of an event study. The authors study the effects on prices when there are multiple bidders seeking control of the target firm, and they study the effects on the price of the bidding firm's stock.

**Seyhun (1986)** studies the behavior of stock prices around trades by insiders. Corporate officers, directors, and very large blockholders are required to file reports of trading in their company's stock with the SEC. The SEC then publishes a summary of this data for public dissemination. Seyhun finds that stock prices rise after insider purchases and fall after sales, but there are no abnormal returns net of transaction costs available to noninsiders from using the information filed with the SEC. Thus, not surprisingly, there is reliable evidence that official insiders have more information than is reflected in stock prices. (So the market is not *strong form efficient*—market prices do not reflect all private information.) Of course, this is also implied by the evidence in **Mikkelson and Partch (1985)** that the identity of the seller in a secondary distribution plays an important role in explaining the drop in price. Frankly, few people have ever seriously suggested that markets should be strong form efficient; Fama (1970) included that part of the definition of efficiency for completeness. After all, someone has to discover (or produce) information first, so it is impossible for prices to reflect information before it exists.

There has been much research focusing on "anomalies" with respect to the efficient markets hypothesis (e.g., Jensen (1978) and **Schwert (1983)** summarize the contents of two special issues of the *Journal of Financial Economics* devoted to such anomalies). We include one paper that at first glance shows semistrong form efficiency, but at a deeper level raises questions about the process by which information gets incorporated in prices. **Lloyd-Davies and Canes (1978)** analyze the reaction of daily stock prices to publication of stories in the "Heard on the Street" column of the *Wall Street Journal*. They find there is a strong announcement day effect (favorable stories causing price increases and unfavorable stories causing decreases).[1] There is weak evidence of a small effect on the day after the story, but the evidence is generally consistent with semistrong form efficiency. The puzzle highlighted by **Lloyd-Davies and Canes** is that the "Heard on the Street" column is essentially a summary of research reports written by security analysts that were available to investors through brokerage firms up to 6 weeks before the *Wall Street Journal* published its story. Either the extra publicity associated with the *Wall Street Journal* story caused the price reaction, or the writer of the column creates information by being a "superanalyst" and picking analysts' reports that are particularly insightful.

[1]After the sample period used by **Lloyd-Davies and Canes,** Foster Winans was prosecuted by the Securities and Exchange Commission because he leaked information about his "Heard on the Street" columns. The people who used these tips apparently made money by trading before the story was published.

# STOCK-MARKET "PATTERNS" AND FINANCIAL ANALYSIS: METHODOLOGICAL SUGGESTIONS

HARRY V. ROBERTS*

*University of Chicago*

## INTRODUCTION

OF ALL ECONOMIC time series, the history of security prices, both individual and aggregate, has probably been most widely and intensively studied. While financial analysts agree that underlying economic facts and relationships are important, many also believe that the history of the market itself contains "patterns" that give clues to the future, if only these patterns can be properly understood. The Dow theory and its many offspring are evidence of this conviction. In extreme form such theories maintain that *only* the patterns of the past need be studied, since the effect of everything else is reflected "on the tape."

A common and convenient name for analysis of stock-market patterns is "technical analysis." Perhaps no one in the financial world completely ignores technical analysis—indeed, its terminology is ingrained in market reporting—and some rely intensively on it. Technical analysis includes many different approaches, most requiring a good deal of subjective judgment in application. In part these approaches are purely empirical; in part they are based on analogy with physical processes, such as tides and waves.

In light of this intense interest in patterns and of the publicity given to statistics in recent years, it seems curious that there has not been widespread recognition among financial analysts that the patterns of technical analysis may be little, if anything, more than a statistical artifact. At least, it is safe to say that the close resemblance between market behavior over relatively long time periods and that of simple chance devices has escaped general attention,

* I am indebted to Lawrence West and Arnold Moore for help in the preparation of this paper.

Reprinted for private circulation from

THE JOURNAL OF FINANCE

Vol. XIV, No. 1, March 1959

PRINTED IN U.S.A.

though the role of chance variation in very short time periods has often been recognized. One possible explanation is that the usual method of graphing stock prices gives a picture of successive *levels* rather than of *changes,* and levels can give an artificial appearance of "pattern" or "trend." A second is that chance behavior itself produces "patterns" that invite spurious interpretations.

More evidence for this assertion about stock-market behavior is still needed, but almost all the fragmentary evidence known to me is consistent with it. The major published evidence from recent years is a paper about British stock indexes (and American commodity prices) by the British statistician, M. G. Kendall, which appeared in 1953.[1] I have done similar, though less comprehensive, work with recent American data, for both indexes and individual companies, which has been entirely consistent with Kendall's findings. If, for example, weekly *changes* of the Dow Jones Index are examined statistically, it is apparent that these changes behave very much as if they had been generated by an extremely simple chance model. The history of market *levels* behaves very much as if levels had been generated by a *cumulation* of results given by the chance model.

These general conclusions have been reached, probably repeatedly, long before Kendall's study. Thus Holbrook Working, writing in 1934, said:

It has several times been noted that time series commonly possess in many respects the characteristics of series of cumulated random numbers. The separate items in such time series are by no means random in character, but the changes between successive items tend to be largely random. This characteristic has been noted conspicuously in sensitive commodity prices. . . . King has concluded that stock prices resemble cumulations of purely random changes even more strongly than do commodity prices.[2]

Indeed, the main reason for this paper is to call to the attention of financial analysts empirical results that seem to have been ignored in the past, for whatever reason, and to point out some methodological implications of these results for the study of securities.

From the point of view of the scholar, much more research is needed to establish more precisely the limits to which these generalizations can be carried. For example, do they apply to changes for periods other than weekly? (In my own explorations they have

1. Maurice G. Kendall, "The Analysis of Economic Time Series. I," *Journal of the Royal Statistical Society* (Ser. A), CXVI (1953), 11–25.

2. Holbrook Working, "A Random-Difference Series for Use in the Analysis of Time Series." *Journal of the American Statistical Association,* XXIX (1934), 11.

worked fairly well for both longer and shorter periods.) How well do they apply to individual securities? (Most work has been done on indexes.) What slight departures from the chance model are detectable? Perhaps the traditional academic suspicion about the stock market as an object of scholarly research will be overcome, and this work will be done.[3] This paper, however, is concerned with the methodological problems of the financial analyst who cannot afford to ignore evidence that is easily obtainable from the most casual empirical analysis. From his point of view there should be great interest in the possibility that, to a first approximation, stock-market behavior may be statistically the simplest, by far, of all economic time series.

This paper will describe the chance model more precisely, discuss briefly the common-sense interpretation of the model, and outline a number of methodological suggestions for financial analysts.

## THE CHANCE MODEL

Kendall found that changes in security prices behaved nearly as if they had been generated by a suitably designed roulette wheel for which each outcome was statistically independent of past history and for which relative frequencies were reasonably stable through time. This means that, once a person accumulates enough evidence to make good estimates of the relative frequencies (probabilities) of different outcomes of the wheel, he would base his predictions only on these relative frequencies and pay no attention to the pattern of recent spins. Recent spins are relevant to prediction only insofar as they contribute to more precise estimates of relative frequencies. In a gambling expression, this roulette wheel "has no memory."

The chance model just described insists on independence but makes no commitment about the relative frequencies, or probabilities, of different outcomes except that these must be stable over time. A frequency distribution of past changes is a good basis for estimating these probabilities, so long as the independence assumption holds. For concreteness in demonstration, we shall assume that weekly changes of a particular index behave as if they were independent observations on a normal distribution, with mean $+0.5$ and standard deviation $5.0$. The details of constructing such a roulette wheel need not concern us here. We shall, in fact, employ for our purpose a published table of random numbers that can be modified easily to

---

3. Holbrook Working has worked for many years on the behavior of commodities markets, and full publication of his findings is still forthcoming.

conform to the specifications stated above.[4] Assuming that the series starts at 450, we obtain a hypothetical year's experience graphed in Figures 1 and 2.

To even a casual observer of the stock market, Figure 2 is hauntingly realistic, even to the "head-and-shoulders" top. Probably all the classical patterns of technical analysis can be generated artificially by a suitable roulette wheel or random-number table. Figure 1 gives much less evidence of patterns, although intensive and imaginative scrutiny would undoubtedly suggest some. The only *persistent*

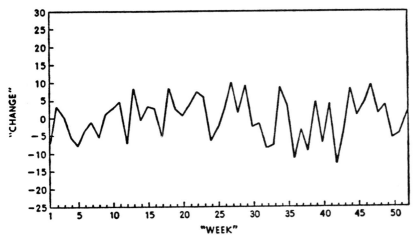

FIG. 1.—Simulated market changes for 52 weeks

patterns of Figure 1 (and its continuation beyond 52 weeks) are (1) the relative frequency of different outcomes and (2) the clustering tendency for similar outcomes. The clustering phenomenon runs contrary to intuitive feelings about chance and raises temporary hopes about predictability. These hopes, however, can be crushed by theoretical analysis that shows clustering to give no information beyond that contained in the relative frequencies.

Figures 3 and 4 give the corresponding diagrams for the Dow Jones Industrial Index for 1956. The general resemblance between Figures 3–4 and Figures 1–2 is unmistakable, although no pains were taken to devise a "roulette" wheel that would simulate closely the actual history of 1956. The major difference in detail between Figures 1 and 3 is that Figure 3 shows greater dispersion. We prob-

4. The RAND Corporation, *A Million Random Digits with 100,000 Normal Deviates* (Glencoe, Ill.: Free Press, 1955).

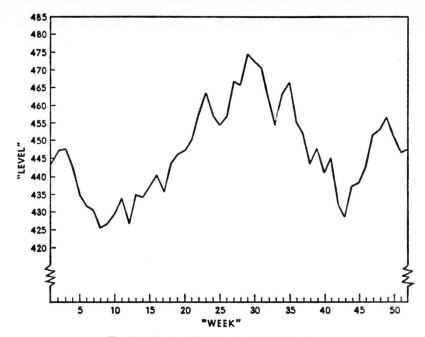

FIG. 2.—Simulated market levels for 52 weeks

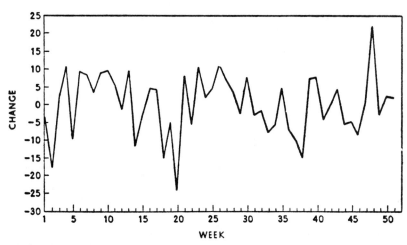

FIG. 3.—Changes from Friday to Friday (closing) January 6, 1956—December 28, 1956. Dow Jones Industrial Index.

ably could have imitated Figure 3 more closely by using a somewhat larger standard deviation than 5 in constructing the artificial series. It is well, however, to avoid giving the wrong impression by showing *too* striking a parallel in all details. Two artificial series constructed by precisely the same method typically differ from each other just as would two brothers or two years of market history. To put it differently, the chance model cannot duplicate history in any sense other than that in which one evening in a gambling casino duplicates an-

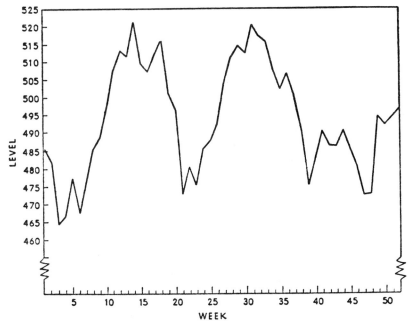

FIG. 4.—Friday closing levels, December 30, 1955—December 28, 1956. Dow Jones Industrial Index.

other. For relatively short periods of history like 52 weeks, there can be substantial differences. In fact, however, the dispersion of Figure 3 is almost surely greater than that of Figure 1 by more than we would expect from the same chance mechanism. We subsequently obtained a better simulation by using a standard deviation of 7 rather than 5.

### MEANING OF THE CHANCE MODEL

There are two common reactions to this chance model: (1) while "chance" may be important in extremely short-run stock-market movements, it is inconceivable that the longer-term movement should be a cumulation of short-term "chance" development; (2) once one reflects on the situation, it is obvious that a simple chance model must hold. We shall discuss each reaction briefly.

The first reaction stems partly from a misunderstanding of the term "chance." The chance model of the previous section was meant to illustrate the possibility of constructing a simple mechanical device that would duplicate many of the characteristic features of stock-market movements. Even if the statistical behavior of the market and the mechanical device were completely indistinguishable, it might still be possible to attain a degree of predictability better than that given by knowledge of past relative frequencies alone. To attain such predictability, however, more would be needed than the past history of market prices: e.g., economic theory and knowledge of economic facts might suggest relationships of market prices with other economic variables that might be of predictive value. It seems more likely that economic analysis could give predictive insight into stock-market behavior than that physical analysis could help with a real roulette wheel. Even completely deterministic phenomena, such as the decimal expansions of irrational numbers (e.g., $e$ and $\pi$), appear to be "chance" phenomena to an observer who does not understand the underlying mechanism. Phenomena that can be described only as "chance" today, such as the emission of alpha particles in radioactive decay, may ultimately be understood in a deeper sense.

In another sense the reaction against "chance" is sound. Much more empirical work is needed, and it seems likely that departures from simple chance models will be found—if not for stock-market averages, then for individual stocks; if not for weekly periods, then for some other period; if not from the independence assumption, then from the assumption of a stable underlying distribution; etc. Indeed, the analytical proposals of this paper are based on the assumption that such departures will occasionally be found. Holbrook Working has discovered such departures in his commodity market research.[5]

As to the second reaction, that the chance model is obvious, there is a plausible rationale. "If the stock market behaved like a mechanically imperfect roulette wheel, people would notice the imperfections and by acting on them, remove them." This rationale is appealing, if for no other reason than its value as counterweight to the popular view of stock market "irrationality," but it is obviously incomplete.

5. Holbrook Working, "New Ideas and Methods for Price Research," *Journal of Farm Economics*, XXXVIII (1956), 1427–36.

For example, why should not observation of market imperfection lead to greater imperfection rather than less? All we can do is to suggest the importance of the study of such questions.

## SUGGESTIONS FOR FINANCIAL ANALYSIS

This section is devoted to statistical suggestions to financial analysts and others who make their living by the study of the market. The fundamental suggestion, of course, is to analyze price *changes* as well as price *levels*. Initially, the weekly change seems worth using, but other time periods may also be useful. This suggestion seems trivial, but it is not. If the simple chance hypothesis is correct, then the statistical behavior of changes, which are independent, is much simpler than that of levels, which are not. There already exists, for example, a body of statistical techniques for analysis of independent data: in fact, modern statistical theory has been largely built up on the assumption of independence. Much of it also assumes, as we did for convenience in the artificial example, that the underlying distribution is a normal distribution in the technical sense of that term. The assumption of normality usually seems far less crucial to the applicability of statistical methods than does that of independence, and some statistical techniques, called "non-parametric," do not make the normality assumption.

If one graphs weekly changes without any formal statistical analysis, he will have taken the most important single step. So long as the stock or stock index behaves like a reasonably good roulette wheel, the visual impression will be similar to that of Figures 1 and 3. If there is a really fundamental shift in the underlying situation, it can be detected visually more readily by an analysis of changes than of levels. Conversely, if there has been no fundamental shift, a graph of changes will be much less likely to give the impression that there has been a shift.

There are formal statistical techniques to supplement visual analysis (though never to replace it entirely, since graphical study is always partial insurance against misapplication of statistical analysis). The most popular field of applied statistics—industrial quality control—draws on these techniques extensively. Though there would undoubtedly be many differences in detail, a financial analyst should find much of interest and relevance in methods of quality control.[6]

6. W. Allen Wallis and Harry V. Roberts, *Statistics: A New Approach* (Glencoe, Ill.: Free Press, 1956), chaps. 16, 18; A. Hald, *Statistical Theory with Engineering Applications* (New York: John Wiley & Sons, Inc., 1952), chap. 13; Eugene L. Grant, *Statistical Quality Control* (rev. ed.; New York: McGraw-Hill Book Co., Inc., 1952).

We shall illustrate briefly how these ideas might be applied in financial analysis. For concreteness, we begin with the data given graphically in Figure 3.

1. The first question is that of independence: Can we regard these weekly changes as independent? Purely to illustrate one test of independence, we shall apply a test based on runs above and below zero. If we denote a positive change by "+" and a negative change by "−", Figure 3 yields the following sequence of +'s and −'s.

$$- - + + - + + + + + + - + - - + + - - - + - + + + + + +$$
$$- + - - - - + - - - + + - - + - - - + + - + +$$

A "run" is a consecutive sequence of the same symbol: e.g., − −, + +, −, and + + + + + + are the first four runs. We count 24 runs, which does not differ significantly from the expected number of 26.41.[7]

There are many tests for independence, and experience will show the most useful ones for this kind of application. I would guess that the mean-square successive difference[8] would prove useful. This has the virtue of providing a descriptive measure of the degree of independence or dependence, as well as a test that gives simply an all-or-none verdict or a significance level. A slight degree of dependence may not invalidate subsequent analysis of the kind proposed here, while substantial dependence may open the way for forecasts that exploit the observed pattern, just as one might do by careful study of a defective roulette wheel.

The idea of "rational subgroups" commonly used in industrial practice may be useful,[9] particularly in relating changes for different intervals of time, such as days and weeks.

2. If substantial dependence is found, it may be directly useful for forecasting, using the well-known methods of autoregression. Dependence may also suggest useful avenues for investigation. A sharp jump in the level of price changes for a particular stock, for example, might be found to coincide with a change in management. The company's history since that change would then be the object of an analysis like that described in the preceding paragraph.

3. If a close approximation to independence is found for any moderately large number of weeks (say at least 52, as a rule of thumb), set up "control limits" to aid visual analysis in the future.

7. For mechanical details see Wallis and Roberts, *op. cit.*

8. *Ibid.*

9. Grant, *op. cit.*

These limits can be calculated in many ways.[10] If a point falls outside the control limits, this gives a signal for the analyst to search for an explanation beyond the series itself: e.g., company developments, economic changes, governmental actions. So long as points stay within the limits, there is no need for special attention, although there may also be supplemental warning signals based on gradual shifts that cause trends but do not immediately throw points outside control limits. There will be risks of failing to search when a search is warranted and of searching when nothing is to be found. These risks can be evaluated and the control limits determined accordingly. The aim of the procedure is to economize the time of the financial analyst, who cannot possibly be simultaneously in close contact with the many individual companies that he must be familiar with. It should tend to avoid the numerous false signals that are so strongly suggested by examination of levels rather than changes.

This outline of statistical procedure is meant only to be suggestive. The general nature of the statistical attack is obvious, but the details will be supplied with practical experience guided by sound statistical theory. It may be found, for example, that it is wiser to analyze changes of logarithms or square roots of levels than absolute changes, especially when long periods of time are examined. But much is to be gained simply by viewing a familiar problem from a new vantage point, and minor statistical refinements or blemishes may not be crucial.

These statistical suggestions are only a preliminary to the real work of the financial analyst. which extends far beyond the tape itself and draws on knowledge and skills, including statistical knowledge and skills, that are not discussed here. There is every reason to believe, however, that this method of looking at the tape will facilitate all that takes place afterward. Further statistical analysis, such as multiple regression, will be sounder if based on independent changes rather than dependent levels. Judgment and intuition will proceed more soundly if not hindered by an unnecessary grappling with market "patterns."

10. Wallis and Roberts, *op. cit.*; Hald, *op. cit.*; and Grant, *op. cit.*

# RANDOM WALKS AND TECHNICAL THEORIES: SOME ADDITIONAL EVIDENCE

Michael C. Jensen and George A. Benington[*]

## I. Introduction

THE RANDOM WALK and martingale efficient market theories of security price behavior imply that stock market trading rules based solely on the past price series cannot earn profits greater than those generated by a simple buy-and-hold policy[1]. A vast amount of statistical testing of the behavior of security prices indicates very little evidence of any important dependencies in security price changes through time.[2] Technical analysts or chartists, however, have insisted that this evidence does not imply their methods are invalid and have argued that the dependencies upon which their rules are based are much too subtle to be captured by simple statistical tests. In an effort to meet these criticisms Alexander (1961, 1964) and later Fama and Blume (1966) have examined the profitability of various "filter" trading rules based only on the past price series which purportedly capture the essential characteristics of many technical theories. These studies indicate the "filter" rules do not yield profits net of transactions costs which are higher than those earned by a simple buy-and-hold strategy. Similarly, James (1968) and Van Horne and Parker (1967) have found that various trading rules based upon moving averages of past prices do not yield profits greater than those of a buy-and-hold policy.

Robert A. Levy (1967a, b) has reported empirical results of tests of variations of a technical portfolio trading rule variously called the "relative strength" or "portfolio upgrading" rule. The rule is based solely on the past price series of common stocks, and yet his results seem to indicate that some of the variations of the trading rule perform "significantly" better than a simple buy-and-hold strategy. On the basis of this evidence Levy (1967a) concludes that ". . . the theory of random walks has been refuted." In an invited comment Jensen (1967) pointed out that Levy's results do not support a conclusion as strong as this. In that "Comment" it was pointed out that due to several errors the results reported by Levy overstated the excess returns earned by the profitable trading rules over the returns earned by the buy-and-hold comparison. (These arguments will not be repeated here; the interested reader may consult the original articles for the specific criticisms.) Nevertheless, even after correction for these errors Levy's results still indicated some of the trading rules earned substantially more than the buy-and-hold returns, and

* Assistant Professor and Director of Computing Services respectively at the College of Business Administration, University of Rochester. This Research was supported by the Security Trust Company, Rochester, New York. We wish to express our appreciation to David Besenfelder for his help in the computer programming effort.

1. Cf. Cootner (1964), Fama (1965), Mandelbrot (1966) and Samuelson (1965).

2. For example, cf. Fama (1965), Roll (1968), and the papers in Cootner (1964).

*Reprinted from* THE JOURNAL OF FINANCE, Vol. XXV, No. 2, May, 1970

Jensen (1967) indicated that even these results were inconclusive because of the existence of a subtle form of selection bias.

In his Ph.D. thesis, Levy (1966) reports the results of tests of the profitability of some 68 variations of various trading rules of which very few that were based only on past information yielded returns higher than that given by a buy-and-hold policy.[3] All these rules were tested on the same body of data[4] used in showing the profitability of the additional rules reported by Levy (1967a). Likewise, given enough computer time, we are sure that we can find a mechanical trading rule which "works" on a table of *random numbers*—provided of course that we are allowed to test the rule on the *same* table of numbers which we used to discover the rule. We realize of course that the rule would prove useless on any other table of random numbers, and this is exactly the issue with Levy's results.

As pointed out in the "Comment," the only way to discover whether or not Levy's results are indicative of substantial dependencies in stock prices or are merely the result of this selection bias is to replicate the rules on a different body of data. In a "Reply" Levy (1968) states that additional testing of one of the rules on another body of data[5] yielded returns of 31% per annum. He did not report the buy-and-hold returns for this sample; he did report the returns on the S & P 500-stock index over the same period as slightly less than 10% per annum, and claims the trading rule returns when adjusted[6] to a risk level equal to that of the S & P ". . , would have produced nearly 16% . . .".

The purpose of this paper is to report the results of an extensive set of tests of two of Levy's rules which seemed to earn substantially more than a buy-and-hold policy for his sample of 200 securities in the period 1960-1965.

## II. The Trading Rule

The "relative strength" trading rule as defined by Levy is as follows:

Define $\bar{P}_{jt}$ to be the average price of the j'th security over the 27 weeks prior to and including time t. Let $PR_{jt} = P_{jt}/\bar{P}_{jt}$ be the ratio of the price at time t to the 27 week average price at time t. (1) Define a percentage X $(0 < X < 100)$ and a "cast out rank" K, and invest an equal dollar amount in the X% of the securities under consideration having the largest ratio $PR_{jt}$ at time t. (2) in weeks $t + \tau$ $(\tau = 1, 2, \ldots)$ calculate $PR_{j,t+\tau}$ for all securities, rank them from low to high, and sell all securities currently held with ranks greater than K. (3) Immediately reinvest all proceeds from these sales in the X% of the securities at time $t + \tau$ for which $PR_{j,t+\tau}$ is greatest.

Levy found that the two policies with $(X = 10\%, K = 160)$ and $(X = $

3. The results for 20 of these rules, none of which show higher returns after transactions costs than the (correct) buy-and-hold returns of 13.4% [cf. Jensen (1967)], are reported in another article by Levy (1967c).

4. Weekly closing prices on 200 securities listed on the New York Stock Exchange in the 5-year period from October, 1960 to October, 1965.

5. The daily closing prices of 625 New York Stock Exchange securities over the period July 1, 1962 to November 25, 1966.

6. No description of his adjustment method was provided.

5%, K = 140) yielded the maximum returns for his sample (20% and 26.1% unadjusted for risk, while the buy-and-hold returns were 13.4%). We have replicated his tests for these two rules for seven non-overlapping 5-year time periods and for 3 to 5 non-overlapping randomly chosen samples of securities within each time period. The results are presented below.

### III. The Data

The data for this study were drawn from the University of Chicago Center for Research in Security Prices Monthly Price Relative File.[7] The file contains monthly closing prices, dividends and commission rates on every security on the New York Stock Exchange over the period January, 1926 to March, 1966. In total the file contains data on 1,952 securities and allows one to construct a complete series of (1) dividends and prices adjusted for all capital changes and (2) the actual round lot commission rate on each security for each month.

### IV. The Analysis

In order to keep the broad parameters of our replication as close as possible to the original framework used by Levy, we divided the 40-year period covered by our file into the seven non-overlapping time periods (equal in length to Levy's) given in Table 1. (Note that the last period, October 1960-September 1965, is almost identical to Levy's.) After enumerating all securities listed on the N.Y.S.E. at the beginning of *each* of these periods (see Table 1) we randomly ordered them into subsamples of 200 securities each (the same size sample as that used by Levy).

TABLE 1

SAMPLE INTERVALS AND NUMBER OF SECURITIES LISTED ON THE
N.Y.S.E. AT THE BEGINNING OF EACH TIME PERIOD

| Time Period* | Number of Securities Listed on N.Y.S.E. at Beginning of Period |
|---|---|
| (1)  Oct. 1930-Sept. 1935 | 733 |
| (2)  Oct. 1935-Sept. 1940 | 722 |
| (3)  Oct. 1940-Sept. 1945 | 788 |
| (4)  Oct. 1945-Sept. 1950 | 866 |
| (5)  Oct. 1950-Sept. 1955 | 1010 |
| (6)  Oct. 1955-Sept. 1960 | 1044 |
| (7)  Oct. 1960-Sept. 1965 | 1110 |

* The first 7 months of these periods are used in establishing the initial rankings for the trading rules. Thus the first returns are calculated for May of the following year. All return data are reported for the interval May 1931 through September 1935, etc.

Thus we obtained 29 separate samples of 200 securities each[8] for use in replicating the trading rule—where Levy had one observation on 200 securities we have 29 observations. These 29 independent samples allow us to obtain a very good estimate of the ability of the trading rules to earn profits superior to that of the buy-and-hold policy in any given time period and over

7. Now distributed by Standard Statistics Inc.

8. Except for the third time period in which there were only 788 securities listed giving us 4 samples for that time period of 197 securities each.

many different time periods. Note also that we have eliminated one additional source of bias in Levy's procedure by not requiring (as he did) that the securities be listed over the entire 5-year sample period. No investor can possibly accomplish this when actually operating a trading rule since he cannot know ahead of time which firms will stay in business and which will not.

*The Trading Profits vs. the B & H Returns.*—The average returns earned over all seven time periods for all 29 samples by each of the trading rules and the buy-and-hold (B & H) policy are given in Table 2. The returns on the

TABLE 2
AVERAGE RETURNS AND PERFORMANCE MEASURES OVER ALL
PERIODS FOR VARIOUS POLICIES*

| | Average Annual Return** | | Average Performance Measure δ |
|---|---|---|---|
| Policy | Net of Trans. Costs | Gross of Trans. Costs | |
| (1) | (2) | (3) | (4) |
| Buy-and-Hold*** | .107 | .111 | −.0018 |
| (X = 10%, K = 160) | .107 | .125 | −.0049 |
| (X = 5%, K = 140) | .093 | .124 | −.0254 |

* Calculated over all portfolios in Tables 4 and 5.
** Continuously compounded.
*** Weighted Average. Weights are proportional to number of trading rule portfolios in each period.

B & H policy given in Table 2 are the weighted average returns which would have been earned by investing an equal dollar amount in every security listed on the N.Y.S.E. at the beginning of each of the 7 periods under consideration (assuming that all dividends were reinvested in their respective securities when received'). The returns net of commissions account for the actual transactions costs involved in the initial purchase and final sale (but ignore the transactions costs on the reinvestment of dividends as do the return calculations on the trading rule portfolios).

We can see from Col. 3 of Table 2 that before allowance for commissions costs the trading rules earned approximately 1.4% more than the B & H policy. However, from Col. 2 of Table 2 we see that after allowance for commissions[10] the trading rules earned returns roughly equivalent to or less than the B & H policy. We shall see below however that the trading rules generate portfolios with greater risk than the B & H policy so that after allowance for the differential risk the rules performed somewhat worse than the B & H

9. If a security was delisted during a particular time period the proceeds were assumed to have been reinvested in the Fisher Investment Performance Index (cf. Fisher [1966]) which was constructed to approximate the returns from a buy-and-hold policy including all securities on the N.Y.S.E.. This procedure is unlikely to cause serious bias and saves a considerable amount of computer time. The weights used in calculating the average B & H returns are proportional to the number of trading rule portfolios in each period. This procedure was followed in order to make the B & H average comparable to the trading rule average in which (due to the differing sample sizes) the time periods receive different weights. The simple averages for each time period are given in Tables 3 and 4.

10. Calculated at the actual round lot rate applying to each security at the time of each trade.

policy. Thus at first glance the results of Levy's trading rule simulation on 200 securities are not substantiated in our replication on 29 independent samples of 200 securities selected over a 35 year time interval.

Fama and Blume (1966) and more recently Smidt (1968) have argued persuasively that these results (the higher returns before allowance for transactions costs and returns comparable or lower than the B & H policy after allowance for transactions costs) are just what we would expect in an efficient market in which traders acting upon information are subject to transactions costs. We can expect outside traders to remove dependencies in security prices only up to the limits imposed by the transactions costs. Any dependencies which are not large enough to yield extraordinary profits after allowance for the costs of acting upon them are thus consistent with the economic meaning of the theory of random walks.

Tables 3 and 4 present the summary statistics of the replication of Levy's trading rules for each time period. Columns 3 and 4 contain the annual returns net and gross of actual transactions costs generated by the trading rule when applied to each sample of 200 securities[11] and for the buy-and-hold comparison. The last line of each panel gives the average values of the trading rule statistics for each sample for the period summarized in the panel.

After transactions costs the (X = 10%, K = 160) trading rule earned more than the B & H policy in only 13 of the 29 cases and the B & H policy showed higher returns in 16 of the 29 cases (see Col. 3 of Table 3). Thus, even ignoring the risk issues, the rule was not able to generate systematically higher returns than the B & H policy. Table 4 shows that the (X = 5%, K = 140) policy performed even less well, yielding a score of 12 to 17 in favor of the B & H policy.

Note also panel 7 of Tables 3 and 4 which gives the results for a time period almost identical to Levy's. The trading rule returns on all 5 portfolios are far smaller than the 20% and 26% respectively he reported. In fact 12.9% is the highest return we obtained in this period and 5 of the 10 rules earned less than the B & H policy. This is additional evidence that Levy's original high returns were spurious and probably attributable to the selection bias discussed earlier.

As before, gross of transactions costs, both trading rules performed much better relative to the B & H policy; with the (X = 10%, K = 160) policy earning higher returns than the B & H policy in 19 of the 29 cases and the (X = 5%, K = 140) policy yielding higher returns in 18 of the 29 cases.

In addition comparison of the mean portfolio return (net of transactions costs) with the B & H return in each subperiod indicates that the B & H returns were higher in 4 out of the 7 periods for the (X = 10%, K = 160) rule and 5 out of the 7 periods for the (X = 5%, K = 140) rule. Gross of transactions costs the B & H policy yielded higher returns in 4 of 7 periods for the (X = 10%, K = 160) policy and 3 of 7 periods for the (X = 5%, K = 140) policy.

---

11. The data is monthly. Thus the $PR_{jt}$ is defined as the ratio of the price at the end of month t to the average of the closing prices for months $t - 6$ through month t. The trading rule is then applied at one month intervals for the remainder of the period.

TABLE 3
SUMMARY STATISTICS FOR B & H AND TRADING RULE PORTFOLIOS
FOR VARIOUS TIME PERIODS
(Trading Rule is Levy's (X = 10%, K = 160) Policy)

| Time Period | Portfolio | Continuously Compounded Annual Rate of Return | | Std. Dev.* | Beta | Delta |
| | | Net of Trans. Costs | Gross of Trans. Costs | | | |
|---|---|---|---|---|---|---|
| (1) | (2) | (3) | (4) | (5) | (6) | (7) |
| May 31 to | B & H | 0.047 | 0.051 | 0.157 | 0.942 | −0.017 |
| Sep 35 | 1. | 0.088 | 0.100 | 0.137 | 0.774 | 0.027 |
| [1] | 2. | −0.013 | 0.009 | 0.112 | 0.617 | −0.066 |
| | 3. | −0.032 | −0.013 | 0.151 | 0.860 | −0.093 |
| Portfolio Average | | 0.014 | 0.032 | 0.133 | 0.750 | −0.044 |
| May 36 to | B & H | −.031 | −0.027 | 0.109 | 0.929 | 0.004 |
| Sep 40 | 1. | −0.081 | −0.067 | 0.095 | 0.769 | −0.057 |
| [2] | 2. | −0.048 | −0.032 | 0.106 | 0.802 | −0.020 |
| | 3. | −0.103 | −0.085 | 0.104 | 0.829 | −0.078 |
| Portfolio Average | | −0.078 | −0.062 | 0.101 | 0.800 | −0.052 |
| May 41 to | B & H | 0.300 | 0.306 | 0.058 | 1.032 | −0.043 |
| Sep 45 | 1. | 0.290 | 0.316 | 0.059 | 0.969 | −0.032 |
| | 2. | 0.320 | 0.347 | 0.067 | 1.048 | −0.032 |
| [3] | 3. | 0.237 | 0.260 | 0.056 | 0.881 | −0.049 |
| | 4. | 0.259 | 0.290 | 0.071 | 1.178 | −0.116 |
| Portfolio Average | | 0.277 | 0.303 | 0.063 | 1.019 | −0.057 |
| May 46 to | B & H | 0.032 | 0.036 | 0.049 | 0.950 | 0.012 |
| Sep 50 | 1. | 0.021 | 0.037 | 0.055 | 0.996 | −0.000 |
| | 2. | 0.002 | 0.019 | 0.053 | 0.933 | −0.017 |
| [4]) | 3. | 0.031 | 0.047 | 0.054 | 0.983 | 0.010 |
| | 4. | 0.006 | 0.021 | 0.053 | 0.952 | −0.014 |
| Portfolio Average | | 0.015 | 0.031 | 0.054 | 0.966 | −0.005 |
| May 51 to | B & H | 0.157 | 0.161 | 0.031 | 0.989 | −0.004 |
| Sep 55 | 1. | 0.164 | 0.179 | 0.039 | 1.139 | −0.016 |
| | 2. | 0.204 | 0.219 | 0.041 | 1.179 | 0.013 |
| [5] | 3. | 0.150 | 0.170 | 0.041 | 1.162 | −0.030 |
| | 4. | 0.162 | 0.178 | 0.037 | 1.026 | −0.002 |
| | 5. | 0.179 | 0.196 | 0.033 | 0.919 | 0.026 |
| Portfolio Average | | 0.172 | 0.188 | 0.038 | 1.085 | −0.002 |

* Standard deviation of the monthly returns.

TABLE 3 (Cont'd)

| Time Period | Portfolio | Continuously Compounded Annual Rate of Return | | Std. Dev. | Beta | Delta |
|---|---|---|---|---|---|---|
| | | Net of Trans. Costs | Gross of Trans. Costs | | | |
| (1) | (2) | (3) | (4) | (5) | (6) | (7) |
| May 56 to | B & H | 0.090 | 0.095 | 0.033 | 0.968 | 0.012 |
| Sep 60 | 1. | 0.272 | 0.281 | 0.048 | 0.829 | 0.174 |
| | 2. | 0.125 | 0.141 | 0.046 | 1.067 | 0.040 |
| [6] | 3. | 0.110 | 0.128 | 0.044 | 1.122 | 0.024 |
| | 4. | 0.201 | 0.216 | 0.048 | 1.096 | 0.104 |
| | 5. | 0.083 | 0.099 | 0.041 | 1.076 | 0.002 |
| Portfolio Average | | 0.158 | 0.173 | 0.045 | 1.038 | 0.069 |
| May 61 to | B & H | 0.096 | 0.101 | 0.039 | 0.956 | 0.014 |
| Sep 65 | 1. | 0.129 | 0.146 | 0.048 | 1.044 | 0.040 |
| | 2. | 0.087 | 0.105 | 0.042 | 0.922 | 0.008 |
| [7] | 3. | 0.101 | 0.120 | 0.051 | 1.161 | 0.010 |
| | 4. | 0.063 | 0.081 | 0.046 | 1.032 | −0.019 |
| | 5. | 0.103 | 0.123 | 0.044 | 0.953 | 0.021 |
| Portfolio Average | | 0.097 | 0.115 | 0.046 | 1.022 | 0.012 |

*An Alternative Comparison and a Test of Significance.*—Tables 3 and 4 contain the B & H returns calculated for an initial equal dollar investment in *every* security on the exchange at the beginning of each period. We have also calculated the B & H returns which would have been realized on *each sample* of 200 securities. The differences between these B & H returns and the trading rule returns for each sample in each time period are given in Table 5. The results are substantially the same as those reported in Tables 3 and 4 in terms of the number of instances in which the trading rules earned higher returns than the B & H policy (see last two lines of Table 5 for a summary).

The mean difference between the B & H and trading rule returns is given for each policy (both net and gross of transactions costs) in Table 5 along with the standard deviation of the differences. The "t" values given at the bottom of Table 5 (none of which is greater than 1.5) indicate that none of the differences is significantly different from zero. Thus even ignoring the issue of differential risk between the B & H and trading rule policies the trading rules do not earn significantly more than the B & H policy.

## V. Risk and the Performance of the Trading Rules

In order to compare the riskiness of the portfolios generated by the trading rules with the risk of the B & H policy we have calculated the standard deviation of the monthly returns (after transactions costs), and these are given in column 5 of Tables 3 and 4. Except for the first two subperiods the standard deviations of the trading rule portfolios are uniformly higher than that for the B & H policy. Thus, for equal expected returns a risk averse

TABLE 4

Summary Statistics for B & H and Trading Rule Portfolios
for Various Time Periods

(Trading Rule is Levy's (X = 5%, K = 160) Policy)

| Time Period | Portfolio | Continuously Compounded Annual Rate of Return | | Std. Dev. | Beta | Delta |
| | | Net of Trans. Costs | Gross of Trans. Costs | | | |
|---|---|---|---|---|---|---|
| (1) | (2) | (3) | (4) | (5) | (6) | (7) |
| May 31 to | B & H | 0.047 | 0.051 | 0.157 | 0.942 | −0.017 |
| Sep 35 | 1. | −0.154 | −0.125 | 0.138 | 0.728 | −0.223 |
| [1] | 2. | −0.054 | −0.017 | 0.128 | 0.672 | −0.110 |
| | 3. | −0.047 | −0.017 | 0.151 | 0.822 | −01.08 |
| Portfolio Average | | −0.085 | −0.053 | 0.139 | 0.741 | −0.147 |
| May 36 to | B & H | −0.031 | −0.027 | 0.109 | 0.929 | 0.004 |
| Sep 40 | 1. | −0.142 | −0.121 | 0.102 | 0.806 | −0.124 |
| [2] | 2. | −0.021 | 0.004 | 0.141 | 0.962 | 0.016 |
| | 3. | −0.157 | −0.127 | 0.103 | 0.761 | −0.143 |
| Portfolio Average | | −0.107 | −0.081 | 0.116 | 0.843 | −0.083 |
| May 41 to | B & H | 0.300 | 0.306 | 0.058 | 1.032 | −0.043 |
| Sep 45 | 1. | 0.309 | 0.352 | 0.072 | 1.094 | −0.053 |
| | 2. | 0.326 | 0.368 | 0.084 | 1.160 | −0.059 |
| [3] | 3. | 0.203 | 0.237 | 0.066 | 0.995 | −0.110 |
| | 4. | 0.246 | 0.292 | 0.081 | 1,329 | −0.170 |
| Portfolio Average | | 0.271 | 0.312 | 0.076 | 1.145 | −0.098 |
| May 46 to | B & H | 0.032 | 0.036 | 0.049 | 0.950 | 0.012 |
| Sep 50 | 1. | −0.021 | 0.005 | 0.056 | 1.004 | −0.042 |
| | 2. | −0.004 | 0.016 | 0.056 | 0.958 | −0.024 |
| [4] | 3. | 0.038 | 0.060 | 0.059 | 1.021 | 0.017 |
| | 4. | −0.003 | 0.019 | 0.056 | 0.965 | −0.023 |
| Portfolio Average | | 0.002 | 0.025 | 0.057 | 0.987 | −0.018 |
| May 51 to | B & H | 0.157 | 0.161 | 0.031 | 0.989 | −0.004 |
| Sep 55 | 1. | 0.155 | 0.178 | 0.038 | 1.074 | −0.015 |
| | 2. | 0.155 | 0.178 | 0.042 | 1.136 | −0.023 |
| [5] | 3. | 0.188 | 0.213 | 0.046 | 1.228 | −0.007 |
| | 4. | 0.132 | 0.160 | 0.036 | 0.949 | −0.019 |
| | 5. | 0.221 | 0.241 | 0.039 | 0.868 | 0.067 |
| Portfolio Average | | 0.170 | 0.194 | 0.040 | 1.051 | 0.001 |

TABLE 4 (Cont'd)

| Time Period | Portfolio | Continuously Compounded Annual Rate of Return | | Std. Dev. | Beta | Delta |
|---|---|---|---|---|---|---|
| | | Net of Trans. Costs | Gross of Trans. Costs | | | |
| (1) | (2) | (3) | (4) | (5) | (6) | (7) |
| May 56 to | B & H | 0.090 | 0.095 | 0.033 | 0.968 | 0.012 |
| Sep 60 | 1. | 0.245 | 0.258 | 0.046 | 0.822 | 0.152 |
| | 2. | 0.158 | 0.181 | 0.058 | 1.174 | 0.064 |
| [6] | 3. | 0.135 | 0.159 | 0.051 | 1.205 | 0.043 |
| | 4. | 0.242 | 0.263 | 0.056 | 1.170 | 0.135 |
| | 5. | 0.080 | 0.106 | 0.046 | 1.139 | −0.004 |
| Portfolio Average | | 0.172 | 0.193 | 0.052 | 1.102 | 0.078 |
| May 61 to | B & H | 0.096 | 0.101 | 0.039 | 0.956 | 0.014 |
| Sep 65 | 1. | 0.101 | 0.130 | 0.053 | 1.087 | 0.013 |
| | 2. | 0.091 | 0.119 | 0.047 | 0.956 | 0.010 |
| [7] | 3. | 0.123 | 0.149 | 0.060 | 1.296 | 0.023 |
| | 4. | 0.078 | 0.107 | 0.053 | 1.092 | −0.009 |
| | 5. | 0.073 | 0.104 | 0.052 | 1.019 | −0.010 |
| Portfolio Average | | 0.093 | 0.122 | 0.053 | 1.090 | 0.005 |

investor choosing among portfolios on the basis of mean and standard deviation would not be indifferent between them. This brings us to a serious issue.

If securities markets are dominated by risk-averse investors and risky assets are priced so as to earn more on average than less risky assets then any portfolio manager or security analyst will be able to earn above average returns if he systematically selects a portfolio with higher than average risk; so too will a mechanical trading rule. Jensen (1967) has pointed out that there is good reason to believe that Levy's trading rules will tend to select such an above average risk portfolio during time periods in which the market is experiencing generally positive returns. Thus it is important in comparing the returns of the trading rule to those of the B & H policy to make explicit allowance for any differential returns due solely to different degrees of risk.

*A Portfolio Evaluation Model.*—Jensen (1969) has proposed a model for evaluating the performance of portfolios which takes explicit account of the effects of differential riskiness in comparing portfolios. The model is based upon recent mean-variance general equilibrium models of the pricing of capital assets proposed by Sharpe (1964), Lintner (1965), Mossin (1966), and Fama (1968). The measure of performance, $\delta_j$ for any portfolio j in any given holding period suggested by Jensen is

$$\delta_j = R_j - [R_F + (R_M - R_F)\beta_j] \tag{1}$$

where

$R_j$ = the rate of return on portfolio j.
$R_F$ = the riskless rate of interest.

$R_M$ = the rate of return on a market portfolio consisting of an investment in each outstanding asset in proportion to its value.

$\beta_J = \dfrac{\text{cov}(R_J, R_M)}{\sigma^2(R_M)}$ = the systematic risk of the j'th portfolio.

We shall not review the details of the derivation of (1) here; the interested reader is referred to Jensen (1969). However, Figure 1 gives a graphical in-

TABLE 5

DIFFERENCES BETWEEN B & H AND TRADING RULE RETURNS.
(B & H RETURNS CALCULATED FOR EACH SUBSAMPLE OF 200 SECURITIES.)

| | B & H Returns—Trading Rule Returns | | | |
| | [X = 10%, K = 160] | | [X = 5%, K = 140] | |
| Period | Net of Trans. Costs | Gross of Trans. Costs | Net of Trans. Costs | Gross of Trans. Costs |
|---|---|---|---|---|
| (1) | (2) | (3) | (4) | (5) |
| | −0.024 | −0.032 | 0.218 | 0.193 |
| 1 | 0.057 | 0.040 | 0.098 | 0.066 |
| | 0.079 | 0.065 | 0.094 | 0.069 |
| | 0.035 | 0.024 | 0.096 | 0.078 |
| 2 | 0.033 | 0.021 | 0.006 | −0.015 |
| | 0.074 | 0.061 | 0.128 | 0.103 |
| | 0.012 | −0.008 | −0.007 | −0.044 |
| 3 | −0.013 | −0.033 | −0.019 | −0.054 |
| | 0.039 | 0.021 | 0.073 | 0.044 |
| | 0.058 | 0.034 | 0.071 | 0.032 |
| | 0.012 | 0.0 | 0.054 | 0.032 |
| 4 | 0.030 | 0.016 | 0.036 | 0.019 |
| | 0.008 | −0.004 | 0.001 | −0.017 |
| | 0.020 | 0.008 | 0.029 | 0.010 |
| | −0.016 | −0.027 | −0.007 | −0.026 |
| | −0.032 | −0.043 | 0.017 | −0.002 |
| 5 | 0.003 | −0.012 | −0.035 | −0.055 |
| | −0.012 | −0.024 | 0.018 | −0.006 |
| | −0.017 | −0.029 | −0.059 | −0.074 |
| | −0.177 | −0.181 | −0.150 | −0.158 |
| | −0.034 | −0.045 | −0.067 | −0.085 |
| 6 | −0.022 | −0.035 | −0.047 | −0.066 |
| | −0.100 | −0.110 | −0.141 | −0.157 |
| | −0.004 | −0.016 | −0.001 | −0.023 |
| | −0.033 | −0.045 | −0.005 | −0.029 |
| | 0.002 | −0.011 | −0.002 | −0.025 |
| 7 | 0.003 | −0.011 | −0.019 | −0.040 |
| | 0.035 | 0.022 | 0.020 | −0.004 |
| | 0.005 | −0.010 | 0.035 | 0.009 |
| Mean Difference = $\bar{d}$ | .001 | −.013 | .015 | −.008 |
| Std. Dev. = $\sigma(\bar{d})$ | .050 | .048 | .075 | .072 |
| $t(\bar{d}) = \bar{d}/(\sigma(\bar{d})/\sqrt{29})$ | 1.07 | −1.46 | 1.08 | −.60 |
| Number (−) | 12 | 18 | 13 | 18 |
| Number (+) | 17 | 11 | 16 | 11 |

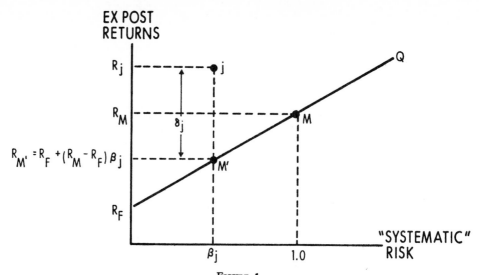

FIGURE 1
The Measure of Performance $\delta_j$, for a Hypothetical Portfolio

terpretation of the measure of performance $\delta_j$. The point M represents the realized returns on the market portfolio and its "systematic" risk (which from the definition of $\beta$, can be seen to be unity). The point $R_F$ is the riskless rate and the equation of the line $R_F MQ$ is

$$E(R|R_M, \beta) = R_F + (R_M - R_F)\beta. \tag{2}$$

If the asset pricing model is valid, the line $R_F MQ$ given by eq. (2) gives us the locus of expected returns on any portfolio conditional on the ex post market returns and the systematic risk of the portfolio, $\beta$, in the absence of any forecasting ability by the portfolio manager. Thus the line $R_F MQ$ represents the trade off between risk and return which existed in the market over this particular holding period. The point j represents the ex post returns $R_j$ on a hypothetical portfolio j over this holding period, and $\beta_j$ is its systematic risk. The vertical distance between the risk-return combination of any portfolio j and the line $R_F MQ$ in Figure 1 is the measure of performance of portfolio j.

In the absence of any forecasting ability by the portfolio manager the expected value of $\delta_j$ is zero. That is we expect the realized returns of the portfolio to fluctuate randomly about the line $R_F MQ$ through successive holding intervals. If $\delta_j > 0$ systematically, the portfolio has earned returns higher than that implied solely by its level of risk, and therefore the manager can be judged to have superior forecasting ability. If $\delta_j < 0$ systematically, the portfolio has earned returns less than that implied by its level of risk, and if the model is valid this can only be explained by the absence of forecasting ability and the generation of large expenses by the manager (see Jensen [1969, pp. 227f]).

The measure $\delta_j$ may also be interpreted in the following manner: Let M' be a portfolio consisting of a combined investment in the riskless asset and the market portfolio M such that its risk is equal to $\beta_j$. Now $\delta_j$ may be interpreted as the difference between the return realized on the j'th portfolio and the return $R_M$, which could have been earned on the equivalent risk market portfolio M'. If $\delta_j > 0$, the portfolio j has yielded the investor a return greater than the return on a combined investment in M and F with an identical level of systematic risk.

The measures of systematic risk for each of the portfolios generated by the trading rules and for the B & H policy are given in column 6 of Tables 3 and 4, and the measures of performance $\delta_j$ are given in column 7. The market returns and risk free rates used in these estimates are given in Table 6. The

TABLE 6

MARKET AND RISKLESS RETURNS USED IN ESTIMATING
THE PERFORMANCE MEASURES $\delta_j$

| Period | Market Return* | Riskless Rate** |
|---|---|---|
| 1) May 1931-Sept. 1935 | .064 | .0334 |
| 2) May 1936-Sept. 1940 | −.039 | .0108 |
| 3) May 1941-Sept. 1945 | .296 | .0080 |
| 4) May 1946-Sept. 1950 | .020 | .0104 |
| 5) May 1951-Sept. 1955 | .149 | .0206 |
| 6) May 1956-Sept. 1960 | .075 | .0296 |
| 7) May 1961-Sept. 1965 | .079 | .0344 |

* Continuously compounded returns on Fisher Investment Performance Index (Fisher [1966]), obtained from most recent Monthly Price Relative Tape distributed by Standard Statistics, Inc.

** Continuously compounded yield to maturity (at the beginning of the period) of a government bond maturing at the end of the period estimated from yield curves presented in the U. S. Treasury Bulletin, except for the first two periods. The rate for the first period is the average yield on long-term government bonds at the beginning of the period taken from the *Eighteenth Annual* Report of the Federal Reserve Board—1931 (Washington, D.C., 1932), p. 79. The rate for the second period is the average yield on U.S. Treasury 3-5 year notes taken from the *Twenty-Third Annual Report of the Board of Governors of the Federal Reserve System—1936* (Washington, D.C., 1937), p. 118.

average $\delta$'s for the B & H policy and the trading rule portfolios over all periods are given in column 4 of Table 2. The $\bar{\delta}$ for the B & H policy (after transactions costs) over all 7 periods was −.0018; that is the B & H policy earned on average .18% per year (compounded continuously) less than that implied by its level of risk and the asset pricing model.

On the other hand the average $\delta$ for the trading rules (net of transactions cost) was −.49% and −2.54% respectively for the (X = 10%, K = 160) and (X = 5%, K = 140) policies. That is, after explicit adjustment for the systematic riskiness of the two policies, they earned −.49% and −2.54% less than that implied by their level of risk and the asset pricing model. In addition the average $\delta$ for the portfolios was greater than the $\delta$ for the B & H policy in only 2 periods for both of the trading rules (see Tables 3 and 4). Since the point at issue is whether or not the trading rules perform *significantly better* than the B & H policy the fact that they don't on the average even perform as well means we need not bother with any formal tests of significance.

## VI. Summary and Conclusions

Our replication of two of Levy's trading rules on 29 independent samples of 200 securities each over successive 5 year time intervals in the period 1931 to 1965 does not support his results. After allowance for transactions costs the trading rules did not on the average earn significantly more than the B & H policy. Furthermore, since the trading rule portfolios were on the average more risky than the B & H portfolios this simple comparison of returns is biased in favor of the trading rules. After explicit adjustment for the level of risk it was shown that net of transactions costs the two trading rules we tested earned on average −.31% and −2.36% less than an equivalent risk B & H policy. Given these results we conclude that with respect to the performance of Levy's "relative strength" trading rules the behavior of security prices on the N.Y.S.E. is remarkably close to that predicted by the efficient market theories of security price behavior, and Levy's (1967a) conclusion that ". . . the theory of random walks has been refuted," is not substantiated.

## REFERENCES

1. Sidney S. Alexander. "Price Movements in Speculative Markets: Trends or Random Walks," *Industrial Management Review,* II (May, 1961), 7-26.
2. Sidney S. Alexander. "Price Movements in Speculative Markets: Trends or Random Walks, Number 2," *Industrial Management Review,* V (Spring, 1964), 25-46.
3. Paul H. Cootner, (ed.). *The Random Character of Stock Market Prices.* (Cambridge, Mass.: M.I.T. Press, 1964).
4. Eugene Fama. "The Behavior of Stock-Market Prices," *Journal of Business,* XXXVII (January, 1965), 34-105.
5. Eugene Fama, and Marshall Blume. "Filter Rules and Stock Market Trading," *Journal of Business,* XXXIX (January, 1966), 226-41.
6. Eugene Fama. "Risk, Return, and Equilibrium: Some Clarifying Comments," *Journal of Finance* (March, 1968), 29-40.
7. Lawrence Fisher. "Some New Stock Market Indexes," *Journal of Business,* XXXIX, Part 2 (January, 1966), 191-225.
8. F. E. James, Jr. "Monthly Moving Averages—An Effective Investment Tool?," *Journal of Financial and Quantitative Analysis* (September, 1968), 315-326.
9. Michael C. Jensen. "Random Walks: Reality or Myth—Comment," *Financial Analysts Journal* (November-December, 1967), 77-85.
10. Michael C. Jensen. "Risk, the Pricing of Capital Assets, and the Evaluation of Investment Portfolios," *Journal of Business,* 42 (April, 1969), 167-247.
11. Robert A. Levy. "An Evaluation of Selected Applications of Stock Market Timing Techniques, Trading Tactics and Trend Analysis," (Unpublished Ph.D. dissertation, The American University, 1966).
12. Robert A. Levy. "Random Walks: Reality or Myth," *Financial Analysts Journal,* (November-December, 1967a).
13. Robert A. Levy. "Relative Strength as a Criterion for Investment Selection," *Journal of Finance,* XXII (December, 1967b), 595-610
14. Robert A. Levy. "The Principle of Portfolio Upgrading," *The Industrial Management Review* (Fall, 1967c), 82-96.
15. Robert A. Levy. "Random Walks: Reality or Myth—Reply," *Financial Analysts Journal,* (January-February, 1968), 129-132.
16. John Lintner. "Security Prices, Risk, and Maximal Gains from Diversification," *Journal of Finance,* XX (December, 1965), 587-616.
17. Benoit Mandelbrot. "Forecasts of Future Prices, Unbiased Markets and 'Martingale' Models," *Journal of Business,* XXXIX, Part 2 (January, 1966), 242-55.
18. Jan Mossin. "Equilibrium in a Capital Asset Market," *Econometrica,* XXXIV (October, 1966), 768-83.
19. Richard Roll. "The Efficient Market Model Applied to U.S. Treasury Bill Rates," (Unpublished Ph.D. dissertation, University of Chicago, 1968)

20. Paul A. Samuelson. "Proof That Properly Anticipated Prices Fluctuate Randomly," *Industrial Management Review*, VI (Spring, 1965), 41-49.
21. William F. Sharpe. "Capital Asset Prices: A Theory of Market Equilibrium under Conditions of Risk," *Journal of Finance, XIX* (September, 1964), 425-42.
22. Seymour Smidt. "A New Look at the Random Walk Hypothesis," *Journal of Financial and Quantitative Analysis* (September, 1968), 235-261.
23. J. C. Van Horne and G. G. C. Parker. "The Random Walk Theory: An Empirical Test," *Financial Analysts Journal* (November-December, 1967), 87-92.

# THE INTRADAY SPEED OF ADJUSTMENT OF STOCK PRICES TO EARNINGS AND DIVIDEND ANNOUNCEMENTS*

James M. PATELL and Mark A. WOLFSON

*Stanford University, Stanford, CA 94305, USA*

Received February 1983, final version received December 1983

This paper examines the effects of Broad Tape news releases of earnings and dividend announcements on three aspects of intraday stock price behavior: mean returns, return variance, and serial correlation in consecutive price changes. The initial price reaction is evident in the first pair of price changes following the release (i.e., within a few minutes, at most). The returns earned by simple trading rules dissipate within five to ten minutes, although significant returns are detected in the overnight period and at the opening of trading on the next day. Disturbances in the variance and serial correlation persist for several hours and extend into the following trading day. As a class, dividend announcements induce much less activity than do earnings, although the response to dividend changes is comparable to the earnings announcement effect.

## 1. Introduction

This paper examines the effects of earnings and dividend announcements on the intraday behavior of stock prices. Most characterizations of an efficient securities market imply that publicly available information should be assimilated by traders and reflected in prices 'very quickly'. By analyzing the consecutive price changes surrounding the minute at which announcements appear on the Dow Jones News Service (the Broad Tape), we attempt to measure the speed with which announcement-induced effects first appear and the interval required for their eventual dissipation.

Our tests focus on three aspects of the intraday stock price process: (1) changes in the mean level of the price process (i.e., average intraday returns); (2) the variance of the multinomial distributions of one-hour and overnight price changes; (3) the serial dependence of consecutive price changes. In each case, we compare the price changes observed during announcement periods to

*Financial support for this project was provided by the Stanford Program in Accounting and by the Kaiser Foundation Health Plan, Inc. We gratefully acknowledge the research assistance provided by Theodore Day, Alison Kirby, William Speer and James Starr, the assistance of Mihir Bhattacharya and Mark Rubinstein in facilitating our use of the data base underlying this study, and the helpful comments of Rick Antle, Gary Biddle, Joel Demski, Eugene Fama, George Foster, Nicholas Gonedes, Nils Hakansson, Robert Holthausen, David Larcker, Richard Leftwich, Charles Plosser, Stephen Ross, Katherine Schipper, G. William Schwert, Jerold Warner (the referee) and Jerold Zimmerman.

Journal of Financial Economics 13 (1984) 223–252. North-Holland

the empirical distributions of observations from non-announcement periods. Our operational definition of 'full adjustment' is the absence of significant differences between the test and control samples, and we use exclusively non-parametric statistical procedures in order to avoid the imposition of particular distribution assumptions.

To detect changes in the level of the price process, we test trading strategies that are conditioned upon the comparison of announced earnings numbers to their most recent Value Line forecasts and announced dividends to the previous dividend declarations. Our results indicate that these simple trading rules cease to earn statistically significant returns within ten to fifteen minutes of the news release. However, for the earnings announcements we also find significantly elevated returns during the overnight period following the release and at the opening of trading on the next day. It is important to note that the power of these tests, like that of all trading rule tests of market efficiency, depends critically upon the optimality of the trading strategy; the poorer the trading rule, the more quickly the market will appear to assimilate information.

The earnings announcements in our sample also are associated with large increases in the variance of intraday returns which persist for up to four hours after the disclosure. Smaller but still significant variance increases extend into the following day. Dividend announcements, as a class, do not appear to induce large increases in the intraday price change variance, but significant disturbances can be detected at the announcement of dividend *changes*.

The time series properties of intraday stock prices are quite different from those of the daily, weekly, or monthly return series analyzed in most empirical studies. For example, sequential price changes exhibit negative correlation or a 'reversal tendency', rather than the serial independence or random walk observed in longer sampling intervals. We find large disturbances in the correlation pattern immediately following the release of earnings numbers and dividend changes; the major portion of the announcement effect dissipates within sixty to ninety minutes, although, as in the variance tests, statistically significant departures continue into the following day.

In section 2, we relate our analyses to prior theoretical and empirical research on intraday price behavior. Section 3 contains a description of our data. In sections 4, 5 and 6, we present the designs and results of the mean return, return variance, and serial correlation experiments, respectively. Section 7 briefly summarizes the study.

## 2. Measuring the intraday speed of adjustment

### 2.1. Trading rules

Dann, Mayers and Raab (1977) performed extensive tests of a trading strategy devised by Grier and Albin (1973) that is based on the notion that large block trades may signal predictable dependencies in subsequent stock prices. The trading rule exploits these dependencies by purchasing at the block price those stocks that experienced an open-to-block price reduction of at least 4.56 percent, and then selling the shares at the closing price that day.[1] In addition to incorporating transaction costs and the effects of total dollar investment levels, Dann et al. demonstrated the sensitivity of the trading rule to delays in investor response. They found that virtually all of the potential trading profits dissipated within five minutes of the block trade and that the prices themselves became unbiased estimates of closing prices approximately fifteen minutes after the block transactions. In section 4, we conduct tests that yield similar estimates for the announcement day duration of the significant returns to simple trading rules based on earnings and dividend disclosures, and we extend the analysis to include the overnight and following day trading periods.

### 2.2. Variance tests

While the mean returns earned by simple trading rules provide a rough measure of the duration of profitable trading opportunities and thus are of both practical and academic interest, the documentation of the effects of information arrival on other parameters of the price process may further guide the modeling of market microstructure. Hillmer and Yu (1979) devised a cumulative sum technique that could, in theory, be used to measure the speed of adjustment of any 'market behavior variable'; they used it to detect temporary shifts in the mean and the variance of stock price changes and in the frequency of transactions. As examples, Hillmer and Yu measured adjustment intervals for five specific events, including two earnings reports. They observed no change in the expected value of stock returns during the five adjustment periods, but they interpreted their results as indicating significant increases in return variance which lasted from three to six hours, with the effects sometimes beginning prior to the disclosure.[2]

Our experimental design differs from that of Hillmer and Yu in two basic respects. First, Hillmer and Yu computed a separate adjustment interval for each event, whereas we compute aggregate cross-sectional statistics for large samples of earnings and dividend announcements. Each approach has its advantages. In return for allowing each event to induce an idiosyncratic price adjustment, the Hillmer and Yu technique must estimate the adjustment parameters from a single observed price series. In contrast, we assume that

---

[1] A −5.23 percent filter was also tested.

[2] The five events were the cancellation of the B-1 bomber, as observed in the stock prices of Rockwell International and Boeing, earnings reports for IBM and General Motors, and a defense contract grant for Todd Shipyards. Todd's stock trades infrequently, and the variance effect for this firm was estimated to last nineteen hours.

homogeneous classes of firms and events (e.g., earnings announcements, dividend declarations, or various subsets thereof) induce similar price adjustment characteristics, and we pool observations to obtain relatively efficient estimates. At a more fundamental level, Hillmer and Yu derived their test statistics from parametric assumptions that are appropriate for daily or longer sampling intervals but that are restrictive when applied to intraday price data. Specifically, they assumed (albeit tentatively) that consecutive price changes are independently and identically distributed. Our analysis indicates that these assumptions do not fit the intraday stock price process, and we construct non-parametric procedures which exploit the observed empirical properties.

### 2.3. Intraday time series properties

While stock prices appear to follow a random walk process when sampled at weekly or monthly intervals, small departures from a random walk can be detected in daily return series.[3] When the sampling interval is reduced to sequential price changes within a day, however, a distinctly different stochastic process becomes evident. Consecutive changes in transaction prices exhibit strong negative serial correlation; our tests indicate that it is more than twice as likely that a price increase will be followed by a price decrease rather than by a further increase, and conversely.

Working (1954, 1958) was among the first to examine the intraday price change process for commodity futures contracts. He referred to the observed negative first-order serial correlation as 'price jiggling', and he also recognized a linkage between larger price changes and the arrival of unexpected information. Smidt (1965) found similar evidence of significant negative serial correlation in intraday price changes for soybean futures, and in Smidt (1968), he discussed conditions under which the demand for liquidity would induce negative serial correlation, while 'the gradual adjustment of prices to new information' would lead to consecutive price changes in the same direction (p. 252). The serial correlation portion of our study examines this hypothesis in detail.

Niederhoffer and Osborne (1966) extended their prior work on intraday stock price behavior [Osborne (1962, 1965), Niederhoffer (1965, 1966)] in a study that documented strong negative serial correlation in consecutive price changes; reversals (two consecutive changes of opposite sign) outnumbered continuations (two consecutive changes of the same sign) by about three to one. They attributed the reversal process to the functioning of an auction market in which traders may place either limit orders (orders to buy or sell at a specific price) or market orders (orders to buy or sell immediately at the best

---

[3]See Cootner (1964) and Fama (1965, 1970).

available price).[4] After any crossing limit orders have been executed, the specialist's book will contain a lower panel of buy-limit orders and an upper panel of sell-limit orders, separated by the bid–ask spread. As buy-market orders arrive, they are executed at the asking price, and as sell-market orders arrive, they are executed at the bid price. Consecutive buy-market orders do not cause a change in the recorded transaction price because they are executed at the same asking price, and only the eventual arrival of a sell-market order triggers a change in the recorded price. Consecutive sell-market orders have the same effect. If (a) there are sufficient limit orders, relative to market orders, at the bid and asking prices, and (b) no new limit orders arrive which narrow the bid–ask spread, then all of the recorded *changes* in transaction prices will be reversals.

Clearly, violations of conditions (a) and (b) occur frequently, and successive price changes in the same direction are observed. Violations of condition (b) still generally result in the expected number of reversals exceeding the expected number of continuations. Violations of condition (a) are likely to occur either when many market orders arrive on one side or when many limit orders on one side are cancelled. The rationale for our serial correlation tests associates such events with the arrival of significant information.

Further empirical evidence of negative serial correlation in consecutive stock price changes has been provided by Simmons (1971), Carey and Sherr (1974), Garbade and Lieber (1977), Epps (1979) and Smidt (1979). In addition, several stochastic process models of transaction price behavior have appeared; see, for example, Garman (1976), Garbade and Lieber (1977) and Oldfield, Rogalski, and Jarrow (1977).[5] The role of the specialist as an economic agent was considered at length by Baumol (1965), and a variety of models of the specialist's activities have been developed; see Barnea (1974, 1976), Schwartz and Whitcomb (1976), Beja and Hakansson (1979), Garbade and Silber (1979) and Goldman and Beja (1979). All of these studies incorporated, to some extent, elements that can lead to a reversal process in consecutive transaction price changes, and Beja and Hakansson further considered the manner in which new information generates buy and sell orders and eventually becomes impounded in observed prices.

## 2.4. Earnings 'anomalies'

Many researchers have documented apparent opportunities for systematic trading profits that persist for two to three *months* after the date of certain

---

[4]More precisely, a limit buy order is to be executed at or below the stated price, and a limit sell order is to be executed at or above the stated price.

[5]See also Osborne (1965) for a very complete representation of the institutional features of the trading process in a dynamic analog model.

types of earnings announcements. In a comprehensive review paper, Ball (1978) examined the experimental designs and empirical evidence in twenty such studies, and several more analyses have appeared since; see Charest (1978), Watts (1978), Latané and Jones (1979), Beaver and Landsman (1981), Nichols and Brown (1981), Reinganum (1981) and Rendleman et al. (1982). Most of these studies share several design characteristics. First, they use an explicit asset-pricing model to estimate equilibrium expected returns against which 'abnormal' realized post-announcement returns can be identified. Many of the studies note that apparent anomalies may indicate model misspecification rather than market inefficiency. Second, more extreme deviations from (models of) expected earnings generate larger abnormal profits; most of the studies examine only these large forecast errors (i.e., 20 to 40 percent of forecasted earnings).[6] Third, many authors note that the apparent strength of the anomalies varies through time, and differences in sampling periods can cause large differences in empirical findings.

Our intraday tests differ from the anomalies studies on all three counts, and thus our results cannot conclusively support or refute their findings. We do not use an explicit asset pricing model; our test procedures compare announcement date price changes to the empirical distributions of price changes in non-announcement periods in order to test for significant differences. In effect, we assume that certain parameters of these distributions remain stationary in the absence of disclosures and that they return to the same values after adjusting to informative news releases. Our sample consists of 96 firms whose size and option exchange listing guarantee a close following by analysts; only 24 of our usable earnings announcements differed from their publicly available Value Line forecasts by more than 20 percent. Finally, our data base includes over 400,000 price change observations, but it spans only fourteen months in 1976–77. Although we examine price behavior through the end of the second day following announcements, we cannot powerfully test the possibility that small daily effects may become statistically significant when accumulated over long periods. For all of these reasons, our results cannot be compared directly to those of the anomalies studies.

## 3. Data

### 3.1. Announcements

Our announcement sample consists of 571 earnings and dividend disclosures released by 96 firms during 1976 and 1977; the composition of the sample is displayed in table 1.[7] During this period, 93 of the firms were listed on the New

---

[6] Rendleman et al. is a notable exception.

[7] The firms' names are listed in the appendix to Patell and Wolfson (1982).

Table 1

Announcement sample composition.

| Time of release | Single earnings announcements | Single dividend announcements | Earnings and dividend[a] | Total |
|---|---|---|---|---|
| Before trading | 58 | 18 | 3 | 79 |
| 10:00–11:00 | 41 | 25 | 8 | 74 |
| 11:00–12:00 | 39 | 33 | 11 | 83 |
| 12:00– 1:00 | 45 | 32 | 6 | 83 |
| 1:00– 2:00 | 31 | 27 | 3 | 61 |
| 2:00– 3:00 | 23 | 33 | 9 | 65 |
| 3:00– 4:00 | 19 | 8 | 4 | 31 |
| During trading | 198 | 158 | 41 | 397 |
| After trading | 49 | 39 | 7 | 95 |
| Total | 305 | 215 | 51 | 571 |

[a] These announcements are categorized by the earnings announcement time.

York Stock Exchange (NYSE), two were listed on the American Stock Exchange (AMEX), and one switched from over-the-counter trading to an AMEX listing. Selection of these firms is based solely on the availability of intraday stock price data. These data were originally obtained from the Chicago Board Options Exchange (CBOE), and the sample firms constituted the entire population of the CBOE at that time. We should stress, however, that only *stock* prices are used in our tests.

We used the *Wall Street Journal Index* to identify the publication date of all quarterly and annual earnings announcements (including forecasts and preliminary announcements) and all dividend declarations issued by the CBOE firms. An initial sample of 796 announcements was identified, and the hour and minute of each news release were collected manually from copies of the Dow Jones News Service, also known as the Broad Tape. Our inability to locate either the announcement time on the Broad Tape or the necessary copy of the Broad Tape itself removed approximately 140 announcements from the test sample, although these announcements were retained to ensure their exclusion from various control samples. Several announcements were lost because they appeared on dates on which the stock exchanges were closed. Sixteen announcements were removed when examination of the stock price data base indicated that they had triggered trading halts.[8] Finally, we retained only those earnings releases that were the first announcement, whether formal or preliminary, to appear after the end of the relevant fiscal quarter or year.

[8]Although only sixteen trading-halt announcements occur in the sample, they exert a disproportionately large effect in many of the tests both because of the intensity of the trading activity following the halt and because this activity is postponed to a point when typical announcement effects have disappeared. We thank Richard Leftwich for convincing us of the potential importance of this problem.

Thus, 58 earnings forecasts and redundant earnings announcements do not appear in the test sample, although they are excluded from control period observations.

Because Broad Tape monitors are placed at each trading station on the Exchange floor, the Broad Tape disclosure time should closely approximate the minute at which the announcement itself first becomes public information upon which trades can be predicated.[9] Almost all of the earnings and dividend announcements appearing on the Broad Tape are published in the next business day's *Wall Street Journal* (WSJ).[10] However, the Broad Tape operates from 8:00 a.m. EST to approximately 6:30 p.m., and thus announcements can appear up to two hours before trading begins at 10:00 a.m., or as many as two and one-half hours after trading ends at 4:00 p.m.[11] Therefore, some announcements are publicly available for trading purposes on the day preceding WSJ publication while others cannot be acted upon (at least for U.S. exchange trading) until trading begins on the WSJ date.

Most earnings announcements appear on the Broad Tape in releases of one to four paragraphs, and each release or release segment ends with a notation of the hour and minute of the broadcast. Dividend declarations usually appear in shorter releases, and brief dividend announcements for several firms are occasionally blocked together on the Tape with a single time notation. Some of our sample news releases contained both an earnings and a dividend announcement; in others, the two announcements appeared in different time-stamped segments of the same story, separated by five to thirty minutes. In a few cases, firms issued clearly distinct earnings and dividend releases on the same day, separated by as many as five hours. In order to compare the relative effects of earnings and dividend announcements, we restrict our test samples to dates on which only one earnings or dividend disclosure occurred, i.e., the announcements in the first two columns of table 1.

## 3.2. Intraday stock prices

The intraday stock price data for the 295 trading days covered by this study (August 23, 1976 through October 21, 1977) were compiled from the CBOE/Berkeley Options Transactions Data Base, which provides a nearly complete time-stamped (to the second) stock price history. The stock price data are 'nearly' complete in the sense that stock prices were recorded each time a new bid or asking price was quoted for any put or call option written on a

---

[9]Information may become public prior to Broad Tape disclosure in an indirect fashion through the price or volume effects of transactions by insiders.

[10]For less than one percent of our sample, the delay was two or more business days.

[11]See Patell and Wolfson (1982) for a more complete description of the operation of the Broad Tape and for tests of the 'market wisdom' that bad news is more likely to appear after trading than during trading. The announcements in this sample and in a second sample for 1979 generally support that contention.

particular stock, and each time a put or call option transaction occurred. Consequently, if a stock price changed twice during a period in which no new bid or asking prices were quoted and no transactions were recorded for any put or call options written on that stock, the first price change is not recorded.[12] This phenomenon should not have a systematic effect on the mean return or variance tests, which require knowledge of the price level at a particular time, although the possible consequences for the serial correlation tests are less clear. Both the mean and the variance tests examine overnight price changes (opening price less previous day's closing price), which were corrected for all cash and stock dividends and stock splits recorded in the *Daily Stock Price Records* or *Moody's Dividend Record*.

### 3.3. Earnings expectations

In order to approximate trading strategies based on investors' expectations of earnings, we obtained *Value Line Investment Survey* forecasts of the quarterly and annual earnings per share amounts. The *Investment Survey* is published weekly; analyses of approximately 1700 firms are included and updated on a quarterly basis. Each analysis contains, among many other items, predictions of the next four quarterly and the next annual earnings per share figures. For each earnings announcement, we collected the relevant quarterly or annual forecast from the most recent *Survey* issue preceding the disclosure date. The elapsed interval between the Value Line publication date and the Broad Tape disclosure date ranged from 3 to 91 days, with a median of 53 days. We also examined the *Survey* issue following each earnings announcement and performed any restatements necessary to place the earnings per share forecast and outcome on a comparable basis with respect to dilution, extraordinary items, etc.

Brown and Rozeff (1978) conducted extensive comparisons of the relative accuracy of Value Line forecasts and various univariate time series models, for both quarterly and annual earnings per share. They summarized their results as providing convincing evidence of Value Line's superiority over the time series models. In our sample, the deviations of actual earnings from Value Line forecasts were symmetrically distributed about zero, with an average absolute value of 14 percent of the Value Line prediction.

## 4. Effects on mean intraday returns

To address the questions of whether any profitable trading opportunities exist immediately surrounding earnings and dividend announcements, and if

---

[12]More generally, if the stock price assumed $k$ different values during a period containing no option quotations or transactions, the first $k - 1$ are not recorded. For a complete description of the price data, see Bhattacharya and Rubinstein (1978).

so, for how long they last, we examine the average returns earned by feasible (post-release) strategies that depend upon the data disclosed. We should stress at the outset that our trading rules are extremely simple and may seriously understate the potential returns to more sophisticated traders acting on the most current public information available on the announcement date. As in any trading strategy study of market efficiency, the power of a test depends upon the keenness of the strategy.[13] Any deviation from the optimal ex ante trading strategy will artificially reduce the apparent gains and make the market appear more efficient.

A complete trading strategy dictates the amount to be invested in each long or short position (perhaps as a function of the data disclosed) and the interval over which to maintain the position (a holding period that is either too short or too long may reduce the estimated adjustment interval by reducing the signal-to-noise ratio). Further complications may be introduced by the existence of the reversal process in intraday prices. By definition, in a random walk price process knowledge of past prices cannot be used to earn future profits. In a reversal process, however, a floor trader may be able to exploit the observed price series, perhaps in conjunction with the content of the disclosure, to increase any trading profits that may exist. For all of these reasons, our test results represent a lower bound on the magnitude and duration of the announcement-induced mean returns. On the other hand, we do not incorporate transactions costs or the sensitivity of the results to the size of the investment; both were included in the Dann et al. study and both serve to reduce potential economic gains.[14]

We perform two related tests of the significance of the intraday returns. The first is a Wilcoxon single-sample test which compares the announcement date returns to a norm of zero. We also compare the announcement period returns to those of control samples constructed by matching five of the firm's non-announcement days to each disclosure date and implementing the strategy at exactly the same time as the actual earnings or dividend release. The non-announcement dates are selected at random after excluding the day of and the day following the Broad Tape release date for all earnings, dividend, and forecast announcements listed in the *Wall Street Journal Index*.[15] We then compute one-sided coverage probabilities for a Mann–Whitney test of the hypothesis that the announcement sample returns are stochastically larger than

---

[13] See Ohlson (1979) and Patell (1979) for an extensive discussion.

[14] Dann et al. also note that brokers or specialists may be able to avoid transaction costs or to transact at advantageous prices.

[15] For those announcements whose Broad Tape disclosure times were not found, we exclude the trading day prior to and the day of WSJ publication. When necessary for computational reasons, an upper limit of 600 observations is imposed on the control sample.

Table 2

Intraday price changes accompanying earnings announcements: Trade on sign of Value Line forecast error.

| Holding period[a] | Announcement sample | | Control sample | | Wilcoxon probability[b] | Mann–Whitney probability[c] |
|---|---|---|---|---|---|---|
| | Number of observations | Average percent return | Number of observations | Average percent return | | |
| Announcement day | | | | | | |
| −180 to −150 | 84 | 0.009 | 376 | −0.024 | 0.456 | 0.334 |
| −150 to −120 | 104 | 0.015 | 470 | −0.058 | 0.295 | 0.067 |
| −120 to − 90 | 126 | 0.022 | 582 | −0.025 | 0.444 | 0.196 |
| − 90 to − 60 | 143 | 0.064 | 600 | 0.039 | 0.037 | 0.388 |
| − 60 to − 30 | 163 | 0.059 | 600 | 0.005 | 0.057 | 0.109 |
| − 30 to    0 | 177 | 0.054 | 600 | 0.029 | 0.206 | 0.521 |
| 0 to + 30 | 182 | 0.225 | 600 | −0.021 | 0.0001 | 0.0001 |
| + 5 to + 35 | 182 | 0.088 | 600 | −0.034 | 0.067 | 0.078 |
| + 10 to + 40 | 181 | 0.062 | 600 | −0.033 | 0.288 | 0.298 |
| + 15 to + 45 | 181 | 0.054 | 600 | −0.042 | 0.397 | 0.323 |
| + 20 to + 50 | 180 | 0.028 | 600 | −0.021 | 0.548 | 0.659 |
| + 30 to + 60 | 177 | 0.008 | 600 | −0.029 | 0.622 | 0.373 |
| + 45 to + 75 | 170 | −0.009 | 600 | 0.015 | 0.524 | 0.590 |
| + 60 to + 90 | 167 | 0.039 | 600 | −0.016 | 0.176 | 0.115 |
| + 90 to +120 | 153 | 0.016 | 600 | 0.020 | 0.281 | 0.329 |
| +120 to +150 | 139 | −0.068 | 600 | 0.007 | 0.954 | 0.958 |
| +150 to +180 | 122 | 0.107 | 596 | 0.025 | 0.316 | 0.539 |
| Overnight 0 to +1 | 189 | 0.093 | 600 | 0.025 | 0.040 | 0.072 |
| Day +1 from open | | | | | | |
| 0 to + 30 | 190 | 0.129 | 600 | −0.009 | 0.007 | 0.035 |
| + 15 to + 45 | 190 | −0.015 | 600 | 0.013 | 0.813 | 0.789 |
| + 30 to + 60 | 190 | 0.017 | 600 | −0.032 | 0.492 | 0.114 |
| + 60 to + 90 | 190 | 0.002 | 600 | −0.015 | 0.583 | 0.416 |
| + 90 to +120 | 190 | 0.040 | 600 | −0.011 | 0.090 | 0.111 |

[a] Holding periods are measured in minutes relative to the announcement, except overnight returns, which are from close to open.

[b] One-sided coverage probabilities for the Wilcoxon one-sample test of the null hypothesis of zero returns against the alternative hypothesis that the announcement sample returns are positive.

[c] One-sided coverage probabilities for the Mann–Whitney U-test of the null hypothesis of equal returns against the alternative hypothesis that the announcement sample returns are stochastically larger.

the control sample returns (i.e., that the distribution of returns is 'shifted upward').[16]

## 4.1. Earnings

The earnings announcement trading rule compares the announced earnings per share figure to the most recent Value Line forecast. Stocks are bought if

[16] The Wilcoxon test is robust with respect to cross-sectional differences in the dispersion of firms' return distributions, whereas the Mann–Whitney test presumes that the dispersion of price changes is constant both among firms and between the test and control samples. Our results in section 5 indicate an increase in price change variability on the announcement date, and Pratt (1966) has shown that when this phenomenon is coupled with the different sizes of our test and control samples, the Mann–Whitney significance levels may be overstated slightly.

earnings exceed the forecast and sold if earnings fall short, and each stock is assigned an equal weight in computing the test statistics. Table 2 and fig. 1 display the average returns earned by the trading rule in three intervals: various 30 minute holding periods during the announcement day (aligned in relation to the minute of the release), the evening of the announcement day, and five thirty minute periods beginning at the opening of trading on the day following the release. We actually conduct the tests from the beginning of day −1 through the end of day +2, but we find no consistently significant results beyond those reported in the tables.

We do not detect significant returns at any time during day −1 or the evening preceding the announcement date, and the data are omitted from table 2 and fig. 1. There is, however, some suggestion of activity beginning 60 to 90 minutes before the release. The 30 minute period beginning at the minute of the announcement exhibits a significant positive return (approximately one quarter of one percent) that is four to five times larger than those in surrounding periods. The average 30 minute return beginning five minutes later is considerably smaller (approximately one tenth of one percent), as in the Dann et al. study, although it is still significant at the ten percent level. The returns

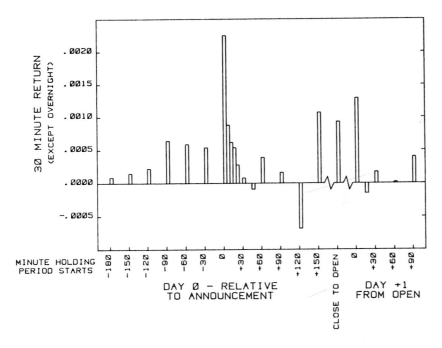

Fig. 1. Intraday returns accompanying earnings announcements: Trading on sign of Value Line forecast error.

Table 3

Trading day and overnight returns accompanying earnings announcements: Trade on sign of Value Line forecast error.

| Holding period | Number of observations | Average percent return | Wilcoxon probability[a] | Mann–Whitney probability[b] |
|---|---|---|---|---|
| Open to close day −1 | 191 | −0.034 | 0.536 | 0.491 |
| Overnight −1 to 0 | 190 | −0.001 | 0.587 | 0.748 |
| Open to close day 0 | 190 | 0.439 | 0.0007 | 0.0004 |
| Overnight 0 to +1 | 189 | 0.093 | 0.040 | 0.072 |
| Open to close day +1 | 190 | 0.174 | 0.106 | 0.143 |
| Overnight +1 to +2 | 183 | 0.022 | 0.323 | 0.684 |
| Open to close day +2 | 185 | 0.005 | 0.405 | 0.378 |

[a] One-sided coverage probabilities for the Wilcoxon one-sample test of the null hypothesis of zero returns against the alternative hypothesis that the announcement sample returns are positive.

[b] One-sided coverage probabilities for the Mann–Whitney U-test of the null hypothesis that the announcement sample returns are equal to those of a randomly selected non-announcement sample (with 595–600 observations in all periods) against the alternative hypothesis that the announcement sample returns are stochastically larger.

measured over the next 10 to 60 minutes then fall back to the pre-announcement level. The sample size also declines as the end of trading cuts off later intervals for announcements appearing in the afternoon. We should note that because of the overlapping holding periods, the rows in the central portion of table 2 do not constitute independent tests.[17]

The evening following the announcement provides an opportunity for news to be disseminated to investors who are unable to execute intraday trading strategies, and their actions may affect the overnight price change and the opening trades of the next day. This possibility was not explored in the Dann et al. analysis. Our sample of (appropriately signed) overnight price changes following earnings announcements appears to be significantly positive, as do the price changes in the first thirty minutes of day +1. No other periods through the evening following day +2 exhibit significant returns.

Except for the overnight period, all of the entries in table 2 and fig. 1 refer solely to 30 minute returns. The positive overnight and following day returns may appear to suggest that longer intraday holding intervals would yield more significant results. However, in the tests reported in table 3, we extend the holding period to the full six-hour trading day, and we find the same general picture. The returns during the announcement day are strongly significant, the overnight returns from day 0 to day +1 are significant, and those for day +1

[17]Because of the negative serial correlation in intraday price changes, even statistics for non-overlapping periods may be mutually dependent.

Table 4

Intraday price changes accompanying announcements of dividend changes: Trade on sign of dividend change.

| Holding period[a] | Announcement sample | | Control sample | | Wilcoxon probability[b] | Mann–Whitney probability[c] |
|---|---|---|---|---|---|---|
| | Number of observations | Average percent return | Number of observations | Average percent return | | |
| Announcement day | | | | | | |
| −180 to −150 | 16 | 0.044 | 79 | 0.018 | 0.382 | 0.417 |
| −150 to −120 | 17 | 0.064 | 83 | −0.026 | 0.382 | 0.320 |
| −120 to −90 | 23 | 0.081 | 113 | −0.059 | 0.149 | 0.084 |
| −90 to −60 | 26 | 0.072 | 128 | −0.017 | 0.061 | 0.054 |
| −60 to −30 | 29 | 0.108 | 141 | −0.062 | 0.045 | 0.073 |
| −30 to 0 | 31 | 0.032 | 150 | 0.015 | 0.236 | 0.494 |
| 0 to +30 | 35 | 0.384 | 170 | −0.028 | 0.003 | 0.0001 |
| +5 to +35 | 34 | 0.172 | 166 | 0.027 | 0.058 | 0.143 |
| +10 to +40 | 34 | −0.040 | 165 | 0.030 | 0.705 | 0.707 |
| +15 to +45 | 34 | −0.146 | 165 | 0.033 | 0.908 | 0.966 |
| +20 to +50 | 34 | −0.066 | 165 | 0.034 | 0.736 | 0.873 |
| +30 to +60 | 34 | −0.117 | 165 | 0.020 | 0.933 | 0.986 |
| +45 to +75 | 34 | −0.080 | 165 | 0.013 | 0.867 | 0.877 |
| +60 to +90 | 32 | −0.068 | 155 | 0.031 | 0.813 | 0.949 |
| +90 to +120 | 27 | 0.102 | 131 | 0.044 | 0.151 | 0.191 |
| +120 to +150 | 22 | 0.017 | 108 | −0.094 | 0.359 | 0.220 |
| +150 to +180 | 20 | 0.023 | 98 | 0.041 | 0.298 | 0.585 |
| Overnight 0 to +1 | 35 | 0.221 | 169 | −0.011 | 0.034 | 0.083 |
| Day +1 from open | | | | | | |
| 0 to +30 | 42 | −0.017 | 170 | −0.049 | 0.692 | 0.552 |
| +15 to +45 | 42 | −0.041 | 170 | −0.021 | 0.595 | 0.449 |
| +30 to +60 | 42 | 0.014 | 170 | 0.008 | 0.452 | 0.474 |
| +60 to +90 | 42 | −0.002 | 170 | −0.057 | 0.508 | 0.280 |
| +90 to +120 | 42 | −0.058 | 170 | −0.024 | 0.716 | 0.524 |

[a]Holding periods are measured in minutes relative to the announcement, except overnight returns, which are from close to open.

[b]One-sided coverage probabilities for the Wilcoxon one-sample test of the null hypothesis of zero returns against the alternative hypothesis that the announcement sample returns are positive.

[c]One-sided coverage probabilities for the Mann–Whitney U-test of the null hypothesis of equal returns against the alternative hypothesis that the announcement sample returns are stochastically larger.

are significant at the 10 to 15 percent level. The returns in the overnight period preceding day +2 and for day +2 itself are insignificant.

If we restrict attention to relatively extreme deviations from expected earnings, the sample size becomes quite small; only 24 of the usable announcements differed from their Value Line forecasts by more than 20 percent (14 above and 10 below). The returns for days −1 and +1 and for all of the overnight periods are similar to those reported in table 3 in all respects: mean and median returns, interquartile ranges, and significance levels. The average return for the Broad Tape disclosure date increases to 1.068 percent (versus 0.439 percent for the entire sample of 190 observations), with a Wilcoxon significance level of 0.004. The average return for day +2 is higher than that of the full sample (0.343 percent versus 0.005 percent), although it is significant at only the 17 percent level, perhaps because of the reduced sample size.

## 4.2. Dividends

The information content of dividend declarations may differ from that of earnings announcements in two important ways. First, most earnings announcements appear in long releases that contain many potentially informative items in addition to the earnings disclosure itself.[18] Dividend announcements, on the other hand, are usually only one or two lines long, containing the dividend amount and the dates of declaration, ex-dividend trading, and payment. Second, because a dividend amount equal to the previous declaration is the maximum likelihood estimate for most firms, announcements of dividend *changes* may be substantially more 'surprising'. Seventy-seven of the firms in our sample issued at least one announcement of a dividend change (increase, decrease, extra, or special) during the fourteen month test period. Table 4 contains the average returns attained by buying the stock of those firms that announced dividend increases or special dividends, and selling those that decreased or skipped a dividend.[19] Despite the reduced sample size, the pattern of price response is quite similar to that accompanying earnings releases: weak pre-announcement movement, a statistically striking surge at the minute of the disclosure, and a tapering off in 10 to 15 minutes. The overnight effect is also positive, although none is apparent at the opening of trading on the next day. The remaining sample of unchanged dividend announcements exhibits no significant returns at any time during the announcement period.

## 5. Effects on intraday return variance

The purpose of the variance tests is to determine the duration of the increased variability of stock returns that accompanies earnings and dividend disclosures. As in the previous section, we draw inferences concerning the speed of adjustment by comparing the distributional properties of announcement and non-announcement return samples. The non-announcement distributions are approximated by compiling the multinomial frequencies of one-hour and overnight price changes for each firm, measured during periods that exclude all earnings, earnings forecast, and dividend releases. We do not, however, exclude the dates of other events such as news articles on contract negotiations, product introductions, etc. To the extent that these events induce effects similar to those accompanying earnings and dividend announcements, we may bias our results toward a shorter adjustment interval.

We define an extreme price change as one that falls in either of the five percent tails of the multinomial distribution for the appropriate one-hour or

---

[18] Other informative items in the earnings news release also introduce noise in a trading strategy based solely on the earnings number.

[19] Almost all of the dividend changes were increases or special dividends.

overnight trading period. Because transaction price changes are restricted to multiples of one-eighth of one dollar, a sampling interval of at least one hour is necessary in order to 'spread out' the price change distributions so that tail areas approximating five percent coverage probability can be discerned. If transaction prices were continuous, (almost) exactly ten percent of the observations would be labeled extreme. However, application of a 'five percent or fewer' cut-off rule to each end of the discrete price change distributions typically results in less than ten percent of the observations lying in the critical regions; for the sample as a whole, the average is 6.05 percent. Of course, there is some cross-sectional variation about the average, and furthermore, most of the sample firms' frequency distributions share a common characteristic: midday one-hour price changes tend to be smaller in absolute value than those occurring early or late in the day. Therefore, separate critical values are computed for each hour for each firm. The relative proportion of observations falling in the tails thus provides an estimate of the binomial probability, $P_{it}$, of an extreme value in that firm-hour.

In order to aggregate across firm-hours, we use a generalized form of the Normal approximation to the binomial test. The probability of an extreme value in any particular firm-hour is $P_{it}$, and the expected number of extreme values in any sample is the sum of the $P_{it}$ values for the included firm-hours. In large samples, the following statistic is an approximate standard Normal variate:

$$Z = \left( X - 0.5 - \sum_{i,t} P_{it} \right) \Big/ \sqrt{\sum_{i,t} P_{it}(1.0 - P_{it})},$$

where $X$ is the observed number of extreme values, and the summations are taken over the firm-hours included in the test sample.[20] Because we are considering the one-sided alternative hypothesis that the probability of extreme values increases during announcement periods, a Z-statistic of 2.33 is significant at the one percent level.

To compute the number of extreme values accompanying disclosures, we first locate the hour of the announcement and then compare the size of the price change for that hour to the reference distribution for that firm in that hour of the day. The various hourly intervals preceding and following the announcement are treated in the same fashion, as is the overnight period. In this way, announcements appearing before or after trading hours may be included in the tests.[21] Table 5 presents the number of extreme price changes in each one-hour or overnight period, extending from ten periods before to fifteen periods after the Broad Tape disclosure.

---

[20] The numerator of the Z-statistic is reduced by 0.5 as a correction for continuity.

[21] The test results are essentially unchanged if non-trading-period releases are excluded.

The earnings announcement sample achieves a $Z$-statistic of 19.4 during the hour of the release; approximately one-third of the price changes are extreme. The frequency of extreme returns remains significantly elevated for four hours following earnings announcements, and the data suggest some activity in the hour preceding the news release. Although none of the periods from +5 to

Table 5

Extreme price changes in one-hour and overnight periods surrounding earnings and dividend[a] announcements.

| Period relative to announcement | Earnings announcements[b] | | | Dividend announcements[b] | | |
|---|---|---|---|---|---|---|
| | Extreme price changes | | Binomial significance[c] | Extreme price changes | | Binomial significance[c] |
| | Actual | Expected | | Actual | Expected | |
| − 10 | 19 | 17.7 | 0.425 | 11 | 12.5 | 0.284 |
| − 9 | 23 | 18.6 | 0.174 | 11 | 12.5 | 0.284 |
| − 8 | 28 | 18.5 | 0.015 | 19 | 13.0 | 0.057 |
| − 7 | 20 | 18.2 | 0.371 | 14 | 12.7 | 0.595 |
| − 6 | 26 | 18.4 | 0.044 | 12 | 12.9 | 0.659 |
| − 5 | 27 | 18.0 | 0.019 | 16 | 12.7 | 0.206 |
| − 4 | 15 | 17.3 | 0.758 | 14 | 12.6 | 0.390 |
| − 3 | 21 | 17.8 | 0.248 | 12 | 12.6 | 0.629 |
| − 2 | 25 | 18.6 | 0.079 | 12 | 12.5 | 0.618 |
| − 1 | 28 | 18.5 | 0.015 | 13 | 13.1 | 0.567 |
| 0 | 98 | 18.0 | 0.0000 | 16 | 12.6 | 0.198 |
| + 1 | 51 | 18.3 | 0.0000 | 10 | 12.8 | 0.832 |
| + 2 | 30 | 17.9 | 0.0020 | 10 | 12.6 | 0.819 |
| + 3 | 32 | 17.2 | 0.0002 | 17 | 12.4 | 0.113 |
| + 4 | 31 | 17.7 | 0.0008 | 12 | 12.5 | 0.610 |
| + 5 | 22 | 18.5 | 0.236 | 16 | 12.4 | 0.181 |
| + 6 | 22 | 18.5 | 0.233 | 11 | 12.9 | 0.755 |
| + 7 | 21 | 17.9 | 0.261 | 14 | 12.6 | 0.397 |
| + 8 | 20 | 18.3 | 0.390 | 15 | 13.0 | 0.330 |
| + 9 | 24 | 17.9 | 0.084 | 20 | 12.9 | 0.029 |
| +10 | 23 | 17.2 | 0.095 | 11 | 12.6 | 0.729 |
| +11 | 11 | 17.8 | 0.963 | 18 | 12.8 | 0.089 |
| +12 | 23 | 18.7 | 0.181 | 19 | 12.7 | 0.047 |
| +13 | 19 | 18.6 | 0.512 | 18 | 13.4 | 0.125 |
| +14 | 23 | 15.6 | 0.034 | 14 | 10.6 | 0.174 |
| +15 | 19 | 14.7 | 0.156 | 11 | 10.2 | 0.456 |
| Total observations each period | | 242–300 | | | 170–214 | |

[a]An extreme price change is one that falls in either of the five percent tails of the price change distribution estimated from a sample of price changes for the appropriate firm and trading period on non-announcement days.

[b]Single announcement per day samples. Announcements appearing after the close of trading are included.

[c]One-sided coverage probabilities for the generalized Normal approximation to the binomial test of the hypothesis that the probability of an extreme price change during the test period is equal to the non-announcement control period frequency for that firm-hour (sample average = 0.0605).

+ 10 is individually significant, the observed number of extreme price changes exceeds the expected number in each. If we aggregate these six intervals to yield a total sample of 1,780 price changes, 132 extreme changes occur while only 108.4 are expected; the approximate binomial significance level is one percent. Overall, these statistics depict a very strong reaction at the announcement, the major portion of which decays within two hours, but with detectable traces that linger into the following day. Fig. 2 graphically displays the decay rate.

The columns of table 5 labeled 'Dividend announcements' contain all of the dividend disclosures, rather than only dividend changes, and the difference in response between the earnings and dividend samples is dramatic. None of the dividend intervals exhibits strongly significant increases in variance, and many of the immediate post-announcement periods contain fewer extreme price changes than expected by chance. However, if we again restrict attention to announcements of dividend changes, the hour of the release achieves an approximate significance level of 14 percent, although the sample size is small. Subsequent periods are not significant, even when pooled though period + 10.

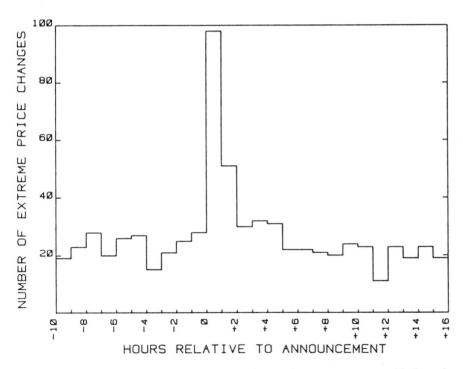

Fig. 2. Extreme intraday price changes accompanying earnings announcements; this figure is based on the first two columns of table 5.

Table 6

Serial correlation coefficients for consecutive intraday
stock price changes: Non-announcement period.

| Order (lag) | Mean[a] | Median[a] |
|---|---|---|
| 1 | −0.4186 | −0.4145 |
| 2 | +0.2511 | +0.2220 |
| 3 | −0.1609 | −0.1221 |
| 4 | +0.1288 | +0.0908 |
| 5 | −0.1001 | −0.0675 |
| 6 | +0.0836 | +0.0491 |
| 7 | −0.0804 | −0.0525 |
| 8 | +0.0747 | +0.0433 |
| 9 | −0.0667 | −0.0434 |
| 10 | +0.0598 | +0.0332 |

[a]The sample contains 96 firms; each is weighted
equally in the mean. Observations on days 0 and +1
relative to all earnings, dividend, and earnings forecast
announcements are excluded.

## 6. Serial correlation tests

As noted in section 2, many prior studies have documented negative
first-order serial correlation in consecutive intraday stock price changes. Table
6 contains our sample's average and median values of consecutive price change
autocorrelation coefficients for lags one through ten.[22] The decaying magnitudes and alternating signs are characteristic of a first-order autoregressive
process with a negative parameter.

In order to provide a more complete frame of reference, table 7 contains the
relative frequencies of price change reversals measured over intervals of
different duration. In consecutive price changes, reversals occur slightly more
than twice as often as continuations, but as the sampling interval increases, the
reversal frequency decreases markedly; 56.8 percent of the one-hour price
changes are reversals, in comparison to only 50.5 percent of the three-hour
price changes. Indeed, at the daily level a small positive serial correlation in
price changes obtains. This evolution of the price change process from reversal
to random walk is consistent with the model presented by Garbade and Lieber
(1977). The Z-statistics shown in table 7 are large-sample standard Normal
approximations to the binomial test of the hypothesis that the probability of a
reversal is 0.50.

We should note, however, that the reversal frequencies and serial correlation
coefficients are not cross-sectional constants; there is considerable variation in
the magnitudes of these parameters across firms. While the median reversal

[22]The statistics in tables 6 and 7 are computed from observations only in the non-announcement
periods.

Table 7

Relative frequency of reversals in intraday stock price changes: Non-announcement period.

| Interval[a] | Observations | Percent reversals | Z-statistic[b] |
|---|---|---|---|
| Consecutive changes | 434,327 | 69.07 | 251.42 |
| One hour | 75,076 | 56.80 | 37.28 |
| Two hours | 32,251 | 54.70 | 16.87 |
| Three hours | 16,227 | 50.53 | 1.35 |
| Day | 19,968 | 48.56 | −4.07 |

[a] Intervals are non-overlapping; for example, the three two-hour trading intervals within the day are 10:00–12:00, 12:00–2:00, and 2:00–4:00. The day interval is close to close. Observations on days 0 and +1 relative to all earnings, dividend, and earnings forecast announcements are excluded.

[b] Standard Normal approximation to a binomial test of the hypothesis that the probability of a reversal is 0.50. Critical one-sided values of the Z-statistic are:

| Probability | Critical Z |
|---|---|
| 0.200 | 0.85 |
| 0.100 | 1.29 |
| 0.050 | 1.65 |
| 0.010 | 2.33 |
| 0.001 | 3.11 |

frequency is 68 percent, ten firms exhibit reversal frequencies above 80 percent, and ten exhibit frequencies below 55 percent. However, all 96 firms display the same pattern shown in table 6, and the rank order of firms with respect to the size of the coefficients is similar across lags.[23]

Our experiments seek to determine the extent to which financial disclosures 'interrupt' the reversal process in sequential price changes and the speed with which the reversal process 'recovers'. The relative frequencies of reversals and continuations immediately surrounding the minute at which the announcements appeared on the Broad Tape are compared to the frequencies in non-announcement periods. Chi-squared tests of two-by-two contingency tables then provide a method for determining when the reversal process is first affected and the elapsed interval until the process becomes statistically indistinguishable from its normal pattern.[24] By extending the tests to include price

[23] Despite the cross-sectional variation, our pooled value of 0.6907 for the consecutive change reversal frequency is virtually identical to the value of 0.6868 reported by Smidt (1979) in a study of transactions data for twelve securities during 1977.

[24] As in the previous tests, the non-announcement control sample excludes the days of and following all earnings, dividend, and earnings forecasts, but no other news events. Although the inclusion of other events introduces a potential bias toward a shorter adjustment interval, the bias should be small; approximately 33,000 announcement period price change observations are removed from the total of 468,000, but the reversal frequency in the remaining control sample increases by only one-tenth of one percent.

changes preceding the disclosure, we may also detect any 'anticipatory' price change activity.

Fig. 3 illustrates the numbering convention for the price change sequences. Sequence number 0 compares the price change 'containing' or 'bracketing' the announcement to the preceding change; i.e., sequence 0 ends with the first new price after the announcement. Sequence 1 compares the first price change entirely after the announcement to the change bracketing the announcement.

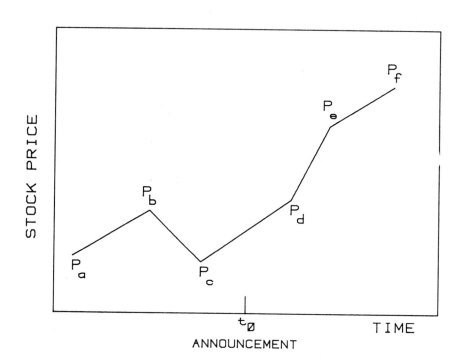

| PRICE CHANGE SEQUENCE NUMBER | SIGN COMPARISON | REVERSAL OR CONTINUATION |
|---|---|---|
| -1 | $(P_C - P_B)$ vs $(P_B - P_A)$ | REVERSAL |
| 0 | $(P_D - P_C)$ vs $(P_C - P_B)$ | REVERSAL |
| +1 | $(P_E - P_D)$ vs $(P_D - P_C)$ | CONTINUATION |
| +2 | $(P_F - P_E)$ vs $(P_E - P_D)$ | CONTINUATION |

Fig. 3. Illustration of price change sequence numbers.

Table 8 contains the relative frequencies of continuations in price sequences surrounding earnings and dividend announcements. In table 8, attention is restricted to the single-announcement samples containing only those releases that appeared during trading hours. It is evident that the relative frequency of continuations increases immediately following earnings announcements and remains significantly elevated through the seventh sequential price change. The strength of the announcement effect is much greater for earnings than for dividend declarations; only the first two price changes for dividends exhibit a marginally significant positive departure from the non-announcement continuation rate.

Table 8

Relative frequencies of continuations in consecutive intraday stock price changes surrounding disclosures.

| Price change sequence number | Earnings announcements[a] | | | Dividend announcements[a] | | |
|---|---|---|---|---|---|---|
| | Number of observations | Percent continuations | Chi-squared[b] | Number of observations | Percent continuations | Chi-squared[b] |
| − 6 | 86 | 36.0 | 0.83 | 76 | 32.9 | 0.06 |
| − 5 | 94 | 33.0 | 0.10 | 84 | 33.3 | 0.13 |
| − 4 | 106 | 35.8 | 0.98 | 103 | 34.0 | 0.32 |
| − 3 | 119 | 34.5 | 0.54 | 115 | 33.0 | 0.15 |
| − 2 | 131 | 41.2 | 6.03 | 120 | 32.5 | 0.08 |
| − 1 | 144 | 36.8 | 2.06 | 124 | 31.5 | 0.00 |
| 0 | 155 | 40.0 | 5.56 | 129 | 29.5 | 0.07 |
| + 1 | 168 | 53.0 | 37.20 | 139 | 37.4 | 2.44 |
| + 2 | 181 | 51.9 | 36.40 | 144 | 39.6 | 4.65 |
| + 3 | 169 | 45.0 | 14.95 | 140 | 32.9 | 0.16 |
| + 4 | 163 | 44.2 | 12.77 | 131 | 33.6 | 0.32 |
| + 5 | 154 | 45.5 | 14.54 | 121 | 25.6 | 1.36 |
| + 6 | 147 | 46.9 | 16.90 | 108 | 36.1 | 1.13 |
| + 7 | 138 | 40.6 | 5.58 | 98 | 33.7 | 0.23 |
| + 8 | 132 | 37.9 | 2.67 | 87 | 31.0 | 0.01 |
| + 9 | 125 | 39.2 | 3.63 | 80 | 30.0 | 0.00 |
| + 10 | 120 | 38.3 | 2.75 | 69 | 39.1 | 1.81 |

[a] Single announcement per day samples.

[b] Chi-squared statistic (adjusted for continuity) for two-by-two contingency table test of equality between the relative frequencies of continuations on the announcement date and in a non-announcement control period ($N = 434,327$; percent continuations $= 30.93$). Critical values of the chi-squared statistic with one degree of freedom are:

| Probability | Critical $\chi^2$ |
|---|---|
| 0.200 | 1.64 |
| 0.100 | 2.71 |
| 0.050 | 3.84 |
| 0.010 | 6.64 |
| 0.001 | 10.83 |

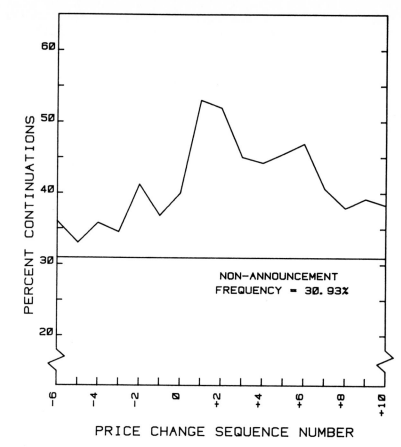

Fig. 4. Relative frequency of price change continuations surrounding earnings announcements: Operational time.

We observe that the continuation rate preceding earnings announcements is elevated at the 0, −1, and −2 sequences.[25] An increase at the zeroth sequence is expected even in the absence of any 'anticipatory' trading, if the probabilities of good or bad news appearing on the Broad Tape are independent of previous price changes. In this case, the serial dependence in the zeroth

[25] The number of observations at sequence number 2 may exceed that at sequence number 1, and the number 1 observations may exceed the number 0 observations for the following reason. Occasionally, an announcement appears within a minute or two of precisely 10:00 EST and precedes the first price quote on the tape. The ensuing first quote is not compared to the preceding day's closing price, and therefore there is no starting point against which the next price change can be labeled a continuation or reversal. Thus some observations available for sequence number 2 are lost for number 1. Similarly, announcements occurring before the second price of the day are unavailable for the zeroth sequence.

sequence is weakened as the probabilities of a price increase or decrease move toward the probabilities of good or bad news, and the probability of a continuation should rise toward fifty percent. The elevated continuation rate in earlier price changes may occur because we have not obtained the earliest release time for some earnings announcements that were transmitted in two or more separate segments, or because of prior availability from other sources. Fig. 4 displays the evolution of the continuation rate for the earnings sample.

Table 8 and fig. 4 examine the price change process in operational time (number of elapsed price changes) rather than in real time ( number of elapsed minutes). Operational time provides a convenient standard because the frequency of price changes varies through the day as well as across firms.

Table 9

Relative frequencies of continuations in consecutive intraday stock price changes surrounding disclosures: Temporal partition.

| Interval[a] (minutes) relative to announcement | Earnings announcements[b] | | | Dividend announcements[b] | | |
|---|---|---|---|---|---|---|
| | Number of observations | Percent continuations | Chi-squared[c] | Number of observations | Percent continuations | Chi-squared[c] |
| − 180 to − 120 | 250 | 31.2 | 0.00 | 289 | 29.1 | 0.38 |
| − 120 to − 60 | 438 | 31.7 | 0.10 | 304 | 31.9 | 0.10 |
| − 60 to − 30 | 219 | 32.9 | 0.30 | 185 | 34.6 | 1.00 |
| − 30 to − 0 | 319 | 36.4 | 4.16 | 211 | 31.3 | 0.00 |
| 0 to 15 | 345 | 60.3 | 137.73 | 80 | 40.0 | 2.67 |
| 15 to 30 | 288 | 45.5 | 27.88 | 112 | 38.4 | 2.58 |
| 30 to 45 | 248 | 44.8 | 21.56 | 120 | 29.2 | 0.10 |
| 45 to 60 | 228 | 38.6 | 5.92 | 146 | 34.9 | 0.92 |
| 60 to 90 | 346 | 39.3 | 10.98 | 252 | 34.5 | 1.36 |
| 90 to 120 | 290 | 33.4 | 0.75 | 238 | 31.1 | 0.00 |
| 120 to 150 | 274 | 33.2 | 0.57 | 170 | 40.6 | 6.98 |
| 150 to 180 | 255 | 34.1 | 1.07 | 154 | 37.7 | 2.96 |
| 180 to 210 | 212 | 36.3 | 2.64 | 144 | 29.2 | 0.13 |
| 210 to 240 | 165 | 35.2 | 1.19 | 119 | 31.1 | 0.00 |
| 240 to 300 | 223 | 33.6 | 0.64 | 182 | 32.4 | 0.13 |

[a] The zeroth price change sequence (i.e., the price change which brackets the announcement) is excluded from all intervals.

[b] Single announcement per day samples.

[c] Chi-squared statistic (adjusted for continuity) for two-by-two contingency table test of equality between the relative frequencies of continuations on the announcement date and in a non-announcement control period ($N = 434,327$; percent continuations $= 30.93$). Critical values of the chi-squared statistic with one degree of freedom are:

| Probability | Critical $\chi^2$ |
|---|---|
| 0.200 | 1.64 |
| 0.100 | 2.71 |
| 0.050 | 3.84 |
| 0.010 | 6.64 |
| 0.001 | 10.83 |

However, the chronological speed of adjustment is of interest both because it allows comparison of our results with other studies and because it involves the aggregation of observations. In table 8, the post-announcement decay in the significance levels of the chi-squared statistics is due both to the drop in the continuation rate and to the decreased sample sizes occurring near the end of the day. The chi-squared statistic will decline as the sample size falls even if the continuation rate remains at a constant elevated level. For example, if the final three sequences (i.e., numbers 8, 9, and 10) of the earnings sample are pooled, they achieve a chi-squared value of 9.67 which is significant at the one percent level, although none of the individual sequences is significant at the five percent level. In table 9, we divide the announcement period into discrete real-time intervals, and all price changes occurring within an interval are pooled to yield an average continuation frequency. We also increase the duration of the pre-announcement and later post-announcement intervals so that the sample sizes remain comparable; the first hour following the announcement is divided into fifteen minute intervals and the other periods extend either thirty or sixty minutes. Table 9 contains the chi-squared statistics and fig. 5 illustrates the earnings announcement continuation frequency as a function of elapsed time.

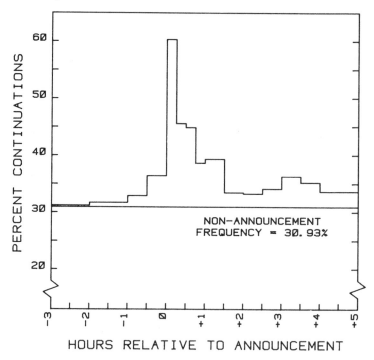

Fig. 5. Relative frequency of price change continuations surrounding earnings announcements: Real time.

As fig. 5 illustrates, the continuation frequency rises sharply at the earnings announcement, and although it then declines within fifteen minutes of the release, samples of comparable size remain significantly above the non-announcement level until approximately ninety minutes have elapsed.[26] Note, however, that in a pattern similar to the variance tests, the major portion of the increase in the continuation rate decays quickly, but the rate lies uniformly above the control frequency through the end of the announcement day. If the observations from +90 through +300 minutes are pooled, the continuation rate is 34.2 percent with a chi-squared statistic that is significant at the one percent level.

When we apply our test procedures to the consecutive price changes at the opening of the day following earnings announcements, the first price change sequence exhibits an average continuation rate of 45.0 percent, significantly (0.001) above the overall non-announcement norm of 30.9 percent.[27] Although the opening sequence of the non-announcement sample (which excludes days 0 and +1) also exhibits an increased continuation frequency of 35.8 percent, direct comparison of these sets of observations yields a chi-squared statistic of 6.55.[28] When the observations are aggregated into thirty minute intervals, the announcement continuation frequencies consistently lie two to five percentage points above the corresponding control sample frequencies for the first two hours of the day, although none of the individual thirty minute blocks is significant. If we further pool all of the observations over the first two hours to yield an announcement sample size of 1,362 sequences with a continuation rate of 35.1 percent (versus the 30.8 percent control rate for the first two hours of all non-announcement days), the difference is significant at the 0.001 level.

In both tables 8 and 9, dividend declarations exhibit a much smaller (but still detectable) effect on the continuation rate than do earnings announcements. The pooled continuation frequency during the first thirty minutes following dividend releases is 39.1 percent, which is significant at approximately the two percent level. As in the mean and variance tests, the subsample of dividend change announcements is associated with much stronger dis-

---

[26]Although fig. 5 gives the impression of a constant frequency during an interval, it is generally true that both the number of price changes and the continuation frequency are higher at the beginning than at the end of each post-announcement interval. Note that the zeroth price sequence, which contains one price change after the release and one before, is excluded from all of the real time intervals in order to sharpen the distinction between pre- and post-announcement activity.

[27]Only announcements that appeared during trading are included in this computation and the ensuing discussion. However, we find similar effects in the sample of announcements that appeared after the close of trading on day 0, for which the open on day +1 is the first trading possibility. For example, the continuation rate for the post-trading announcements in the first sequence on day +1 is 44.1 percent.

[28]Garbade and Sekaran (1981) examined opening trades using procedures essentially identical to those described in Garbade and Lieber (1977). They found no significant differences between opening and subsequent trades with respect to the mean and variance of the stock price process.

turbances in the serial correlation pattern. In the 79 price change sequences occurring in the first thirty minutes following these news releases, the continuation frequency is 51.9 percent, with a chi-squared statistic of 15.3. As with the earnings announcements, the rate remains elevated throughout the rest of the day; the pooled continuation frequency from $+90$ through $+300$ minutes is 36.3 percent, with a chi-squared statistic of 5.82.

In the tests reported in tables 8 and 9, we combined observations from all 96 firms to determine the non-announcement control frequency and to construct the announcement samples. However, as discussed earlier, the reversal frequency does vary cross-sectionally, and it is possible that cross-sectional aggregation distorts the test results. To accommodate this variation, we stratify the sample firms into seven groups of roughly equal size: those with non-announcement reversal frequencies above 80 percent, those between 75 percent and 80 percent, those between 70 percent and 75 percent, and so on until the seventh group contains those below 55 percent. Chi-squared contingency tests are conducted within each stratum, and the resulting statistics summed to yield an overall chi-squared test statistic with seven degrees of freedom. The results of this procedure, the details of which are not reported here, are entirely consistent with those reported in table 9.

## 7. Summary

Two phenomena emerge strongly and consistently throughout the analysis. First, the price reaction to earnings and dividend announcements begins very quickly. The reaction is evident in the first pair of price changes (i.e., within at most a few minutes) of the appearance of the news release on Broad Tape monitors. All three sets of experiments hint at some activity in the hour or two preceding the Broad Tape news release, but by far the largest portion of the price response occurs in the first five to fifteen minutes after the disclosure.

Second, dividend announcements as a class induce a much weaker response than do earnings. However, the price reaction to announcements of dividend *changes* is similar to that of earnings announcements, in both magnitude and duration. Unchanged dividends have essentially no effect. We should also recall that earnings announcements are embedded in long press releases that contain many other bits of potentially relevant information, while dividend declarations seldom mention anything but the dividend. Therefore, an inference about the relative information content of earnings and dividend numbers per se may be unwarranted.

The issue of the duration of the announcement effects is much more delicate, for a variety of reasons. We have noted at several points that our estimates of the adjustment interval are functions of the power of the statistical tests. As discriminatory power falls, the apparent speed of adjustment increases. All of our tests are essentially non-parametric, and thus they avoid particular assumptions about asset pricing models or distributional forms. We do assume stationarity, in the sense that we compare announcement samples to non-announcement controls and use their eventual similarity as an indication of full adjustment. Of course, these tests are less powerful than more detailed parametric procedures *if* the required parametric assumptions are, in fact, met. The validity of various sets of assumptions is one of the important issues in the debate over apparent pricing anomalies or market inefficiencies. Moreover, many of the relevant parametric asset pricing models would be very difficult to estimate on an intraday basis. Notwithstanding these disclaimers, parametric tests that are both correctly specified and more powerful are likely to suggest longer adjustment intervals.

We should emphasize that our sample firms are large, actively traded, and closely watched. Several investment services predict both the date and content of these firms' forthcoming earnings announcements. It is possible that the adjustment intervals would be significantly longer for smaller firms, or for other, less regular announcements made by our sample firms. By the same token, however, a lower level of trading activity would make the measurement of these intervals more difficult. In addition, a larger and more diverse sample of firms could yield a higher proportion of extreme deviations from estimates of market expectations. Our limited examination of large forecast errors and the more pronounced reaction to dividend changes, as opposed to all dividend announcements, suggest a variety of special samples that might exhibit longer adjustment periods.

Finally, we must consider the relation between the mean return tests where trading profits largely disappear in five to ten minutes (although we do detect significant mean returns in the overnight period and at the opening of trading on the following day), and the variance and serial correlation tests where disturbances persist for several hours after public disclosure and extend well into the following day. Of course, these differences do not constitute a discrepancy if the increases in variance and continuation rate do not offer the promise of a better trading strategy. It is quite possible that different parameters of the price process adjust at different rates. However, the variance and serial correlation results may also highlight the naiveté of our trading rules and the possibility that sophisticated, well-informed traders could reap larger gains for longer periods. The three experimental designs simply may differ among themselves with respect to discriminatory power, and the specification of the trading rule is an obvious candidate for further refinement.

In conclusion, our empirical results are consistent with the notion that the stock market impounds publicly available information 'very quickly'. In the broader context of the intraday price process, a host of interesting hypotheses can be generated, but the design of well-structured experiments will require further developments in the theory of market microstructure. The influence of information arrival is one of the most challenging problems in modeling market behavior, and we hope that the empirical features described here aid in the construction of such models.

# References

Ball, Ray, 1978, Anomalies in relationships between securities' yields and yield-surrogates, Journal of Financial Economics 6, 103–126.

Barnea, Amir, 1974, Performance evaluation of New York Stock Exchange specialists, Journal of Financial and Quantitative Analysis 9, 511–535.

Barnea, Amir, 1976, Reply: Specialists' performance and serial dependence of stock price changes, Journal of Financial and Quantitative Analysis 11, 909–911.

Baumol, William J., 1965, The stock market and economic efficiency (Fordham University Press, New York).

Beaver, William H. and Wayne R. Landsman, 1981, Note on the behavior of residual security returns for winner and loser portfolios, Journal of Accounting and Economics 3, 233–241.

Beja, Avraham and Nils H. Hakansson, 1979, From orders to trades: Some alternative market mechanisms, in: Edward Bloch and Robert A. Schwartz, eds., Impending changes for securities markets: What role for the exchanges? (JAI Press, Greenwich, CT).

Bhattacharya, Mihir and Mark Rubinstein, 1978, CBOE/Berkeley options transactions data base: Users' manual (University of California, Berkeley, CA).

Brown, Lawrence D. and Michael S. Rozeff, 1978, The superiority of analyst forecasts as measures of expectations: Evidence from earnings, Journal of Finance 33, 1–16.

Carey, Kenneth J. and Lawrence A. Sherr, 1974, Market and price factors in transaction-to-transaction price change behavior of common stocks, Applied Economics 6, 45–58.

Charest, Guy, 1978, Dividend information, stock returns and market efficiency – II, Journal of Financial Economics 6, 297–330.

Cootner, Paul H., 1964, The random character of stock market prices (M.I.T. Press, Cambridge, MA).

Dann, Larry Y., David Mayers and Robert J. Raab, Jr., 1977, Trading rules, large blocks and the speed of price adjustment, Journal of Financial Economics 4, 3–22.

Epps, Thomas W., 1979, Comovements in stock prices in the very short run, Journal of the American Statistical Association 74, 291–298.

Fama, Eugene F., 1965, The behavior of stock-market prices, Journal of Business 38, 34–105.

Fama, Eugene F., 1970, Efficient capital markets: A review of theory and empirical work, Journal of Finance 25, 383–423.

Garbade, Kenneth D. and Zvi Lieber, 1977, On the independence of transactions on the New York Stock Exchange, Journal of Banking and Finance 1, 151–172.

Garbade, Kenneth D. and Chandra P. Sekaran, 1981, Opening prices on the New York Stock Exchange, Journal of Banking and Finance 5, 345–355.

Garbade, Kenneth D. and William L. Silber, 1979, Structural organization of secondary markets: Clearing frequency, dealer activity and liquidity risk, Journal of Finance 34, 577–593.

Garman, Mark B., 1976, Market microstructure, Journal of Financial Economics 3, 257–275.

Goldman, M. Barry and Avraham Beja, 1979, Market prices vs. equilibrium prices: Returns' variance, serial correlation, and the role of the specialist, Journal of Finance 34, 595–607.

Grier, Paul C. and Peter S. Albin, 1973, Nonrandom price changes in association with trading in large blocks, Journal of Business 46, 425–433.

Hillmer, S.C. and P.L. Yu, 1979, The market speed of adjustment to new information, Journal of Financial Economics 7, 321–345.

Latané, Henry A. and Charles P. Jones, 1979, Standardized unexpected earnings – 1971–77, Journal of Finance 34, 717–724.

Nichols, William D. and Stewart L. Brown, 1981, Assimilating earnings and split information: Is the capital market becoming more efficient?, Journal of Financial Economics 9, 309–315.

Niederhoffer, Victor, 1965, Clustering of stock prices, Operations Research 13, 258–265.

Niederhoffer, Victor, 1966, A new look at clustering of stock prices, Journal of Business 39, 309–313.

Niederhoffer, Victor and M.F.M. Osborne, 1966, Market making and reversal on the stock exchange, Journal of the American Statistical Association 61, 897–916.

Ohlson, James A., 1979, Residual (API) analysis and the private value of information, Journal of Accounting Research 17, 506–527.

Oldfield, George S., Richard J. Rogalski and Robert A. Jarrow, 1977, An autoregressive jump process for common stock returns, Journal of Financial Economics 5, 389–418.

Osborne, M.F.M., 1962, Periodic structure in the brownian motion of stock prices, Operations Research 10, 345–379.

Osborne, M.F.M., 1965, The dynamics of stock trading, Econometrica 33, 38–113.

Patell, James M., 1979, The API and the design of experiments, Journal of Accounting Research 17, 528–549.

Patell, James M. and Mark A. Wolfson, 1982, Good news, bad news, and the intraday timing of corporate disclosures, The Accounting Review 57, 509–527.

Pratt, John W., 1964, Robustness of some procedures for the two-sample location problem, Journal of the American Statistical Association 59, 665–680.

Reinganum, Marc R., 1981, Misspecification of capital asset pricing: Empirical anomalies based on earnings' yields and market values, Journal of Financial Economics 9, 19–46.

Rendleman, Robert J., Jr., Charles P. Jones and Henry A. Latané, 1982, Empirical anomalies based on unexpected earnings and the importance of risk adjustments, Journal of Financial Economics 10, 269–287.

Schwartz, Robert A. and David K. Whitcomb, 1976, Comment: Assessing the impact of stock exchange specialists on stock volatility, Journal of Financial and Quantitative Analysis 11, 901–908.

Simmons, Donald M., 1971, Common-stock transaction sequences and the random-walk model, Operations Research 19, 845–861.

Smidt, Seymour, 1965, A test of the serial independence of price changes in soybean futures, Food Research Institute Studies 2, 117–136.

Smidt, Seymour, 1968, A new look at the random walk hypothesis, Journal of Financial and Quantitative Analysis 3, 235–261.

Smidt, Seymour, 1979, Continuous vs. intermittent trading on auction markets, Journal of Financial and Quantitative Analysis 14, 837–866.

Watts, Ross L., 1978, Systematic 'abnormal' returns after quarterly earnings announcements, Journal of Financial Economics 6, 127–150.

Working, Holbrook, 1954, Price effects of scalping and day trading, Proceedings of the Chicago Board of Trade Annual Symposium, 114–143.

Working, Holbrook, 1958, A theory of anticipatory prices, American Economic Review 48, 188–199.

# STOCK PRICE EFFECTS AND COSTS OF SECONDARY DISTRIBUTIONS

Wayne H. MIKKELSON and M. Megan PARTCH*

*University of Oregon, Eugene, OR 97403-1208, USA*

Received February 1984, final version received July 1984

This study does not support the view that a large number of shares can be sold at the prevailing market price and at a small cost. A significant stock price decrease is observed at the initial announcement of secondary distributions. The price declines are greater for offerings by officers and directors and for larger offerings, but are significant for all types of sellers and for large and small offerings. There is no significant price decline at the offering when secondaries are announced in advance. Underwriting and other selling costs are substantial and are positively related to relative offering size.

## 1. Introduction

An unresolved issue is whether a large block of common stock can be sold at the prevailing market price and at a small cost. News of an offering can be associated with a decrease in share price if (1) the sale causes the market to revise downward its assessment of the firm's prospects or (2) demand for the firm's shares is not perfectly elastic. In addition, there can be substantial costs associated with the selling effort that reduce the net proceeds of the sale.

This paper investigates the stock price effects and costs associated with large block sales of common stock in the form of secondary distributions. We focus on secondary distributions because they are offerings of substantial size and are not associated with a change in the firm's assets or capital structure. Thus, the price effects and costs of the sale of shares can be measured in the absence of confounding changes in assets or capital structure.

This study is closely related to Scholes' (1972) investigation of secondary distributions. Our study differs from Scholes' in that we examine returns around the earliest announcement date as well as around the offering date. We

*We have received helpful comments from participants of finance workshops at Northwestern University, the University of California at Los Angeles, the University of Alberta, the University of Chicago, the University of Iowa, the University of Oregon, and Washington University. We are grateful for the helpful comments and suggestions given to us by A. Christie, L. Dann, E. Fama, P. Healy, A. Hess, R. Holthausen, M. Hopewell, R. Leftwich, R. Ruback, M. Ryngaert, P. Wier, and especially D. Mayers, the referee.

investigate registered and non-registered offerings separately, since offerings registered with the Securities and Exchange Commission (SEC) are disclosed in advance of the offering and non-registered secondaries are not. We also document the selling costs of secondary distributions, including (1) the under-writing spread, (2) other expenses incurred by the seller, and (3) the difference between the offering price and the closing market price on the day of the sale.

Our results do not support the view that a shareholder can sell a large number of shares within a short period of time at approximately the prevailing market price and at a small cost. We find that secondary offerings are associated with a significant decrease in share price. The average two-day abnormal stock return at the earliest public disclosure of the offerings is $-1.96\%$ for non-registered secondaries and $-2.87\%$ for registered secondaries. We find no statistically significant abnormal stock return at the actual offering date for registered distributions. Further, the selling costs of secondaries are substantial. The average total selling costs of non-registered secondaries are 5% of the pre-announcement value of the shares offered for sale. Sellers of registered secondaries incur total costs of 6.7%. These costs, in addition to the price decline at the initial announcement, indicate that secondary distributions have a large negative effect on the wealth of the selling shareholders.[1]

We investigate whether the stock price response to the announcement of the offering depends on the characteristics of the selling shareholder(s) and/or the size of the offering. Our analysis provides evidence on Scholes' hypothesis that the market infers unfavorable information about the firm from the secondary offering. We examine the relation between the magnitude of the stock price change at the announcement of registered offerings and various characteristics of the offerings disclosed in the prospectuses. Like Scholes, we find that the category of selling shareholder is related to the stock price response. The stock price response is not related to the seller's pre- or post-offering ownership stake nor to the dollar value of the offering. Among the categories of sellers, the average price decrease is largest for secondaries by officers and directors, sellers most likely perceived to hold inside information about the firm. However, we also find a statistically significant negative price response for *all* categories of sellers. The pervasiveness of this result suggests that the characteristics of the selling shareholders that we examine cannot explain completely the price response to secondary offerings, and suggests that the *event* of a sale is a source of the market's perception of unfavorable information.

Scholes also examines whether at the offering date there is a temporary decrease in share price, which he calls a price pressure effect, that depends on the size of the offering. He finds no relation between the price change on the

---

[1] Ryngaert (1983) finds similar price effects and underwriting costs for a sample of registered secondaries that predates our sample of secondary offerings.

offering date and offering size.[2] Our analysis differs in that we distinguish, as do Kraus and Stoll (1972), between a permanent stock price effect at the announcement of the offering that is due to less than perfectly elastic demand (a supply effect) and a temporary price effect at the offering that reflects compensation for costs incurred by buyers of a secoⁿdary (a liquidity cost effect).

We test for a supply effect by examining the relation between the initial announcement price effect and the relative size of the offering. We find that the price response to the initial disclosure of secondaries is related to the size of offering, measured relative to the total number of shares outstanding, even when we control for certain characteristics of the selling stockholder. This evidence could be interpreted as consistent with less than perfectly elastic demand for a firm's shares. However, because the variables we use to characterize the sellers may not capture fully the market's perception of unfavorable information, the evidence is also consistent with the interpretation that size is a proxy for unfavorable information. We also examine whether the relation between the price effect and relative offering size depends on characteristics that we conjecture are determinants of the elasticity of demand. These tests provide no support for a supply effect. Thus, we cannot conclude that we have uncovered evidence of a supply effect.

We investigate a liquidity cost effect by looking for evidence of a price recovery after the offering date, and by examining whether underwriting and other costs of secondaries depend on the selling effort required to find buyers of a large quantity of shares. No evidence is found of a price recovery immediately following the offering date of secondaries. However, the underwriting spread for both registered and non-registered secondaries is related positively to the size of the offering, measured relative to either total shares outstanding or average daily trading volume. Since larger distributions presumably require greater selling effort, this evidence supports the notion that underwriting spreads are in part compensation for the selling effort associated with secondary offerings. As Kraus and Stoll (1972) suggest, compensation for liquidity costs of a secondary offering appears to be in the form of underwriting compensation rather than a price recovery following the offering date.

The next section discusses secondary distributions. Section 3 describes the samples of secondary offerings and presents our empirical methods. Section 4

---

[2]Related evidence is provided by several other studies. Kraus and Stoll (1972) study daily and intraday stock returns at the time of large block trades. They find price changes that are related to the size of the block. Hess and Frost (1982) examine share price behavior at the issuance date of primary stock offerings by public utility companies, and fail to uncover any evidence of a price effect related to offering size. Asquith and Mullins (1983) examine share price behavior at the announcement of primary and secondary offerings of common stock. They find some evidence that the stock price effects are related to the size of the offering, but their tests do not control for the asset structure or capital structure effects of primary offerings nor for the characteristics of the selling shareholder in secondary offerings.

provides evidence on average stock returns, and examines potential explanations of the stock price effects. Evidence on underwriting compensation and other costs is presented in section 5. A summary and conclusions are presented in section 6.

## 2. Secondary distributions of common stock

The secondary distributions examined in this study are sales of outstanding securities that take place off the exchange, usually after the close of trading, and generally at a price less than or equal to that day's closing price on the exchange. Secondary offerings require the approval of the exchange(s) on which the securities are listed. According to Rule 393 of the New York Stock Exchange, for example, approval of a secondary is based on the judgment of exchange officials that the block of securities cannot be absorbed in the normal course of trading.

The seller of a secondary distribution may be required to register the offering with the SEC. The Securities Act of 1933 requires the registration of a public offering of a firm's outstanding securities, if the seller has a control relationship with the firm.[3] Registration involves filing a prospectus in advance of the actual offering that contains information about the selling shareholder, the securities being sold, the terms of the offering and the selling arrangements. A report of the proposed secondary offering usually appears in *The Wall Street Journal* on the day following the filing of the prospectus.

The first public disclosure of non-registered secondary distributions is typically on the news tape of the exchange or on a news service wire shortly before the distribution becomes effective. The initial announcement may occur before or after the close of trading on the offering date. The tape reveals the identity of the firm whose shares are being sold, the number of shares offered, the dealer discount and whether the seller is reserving the right to stabilize share price. Although the seller's identity is reported to the exchange in the application for permission to offer a secondary, the identity of the seller in a non-registered offering typically is not reported by the exchange, or disclosed to buyers by the selling agents. Potentially important differences between registered and non-registered secondary offerings are (1) the length of time between the initial public disclosure and the beginning of the offering and (2) the information about the offering that is publicly disclosed by the time of the offering. Because of these fundamental differences, we analyze registered and non-registered offerings separately.

---

[3] Federal regulation states that ʻthe term 'control' means the possession, direct or indirect, of the power to direct or cause the direction of the management and policies of a person, whether through the ownership of voting securities, by contract, or otherwise'. (See 17 CFR 230.40J at paragraph 3342.)

## 3. Description of samples and empirical methods

### 3.1. Selection criteria

Initially, all underwritten secondary distributions of common stock that occurred between 1972 and 1981 are identified in the semi-annual issues of the *Investment Dealers' Digest* containing the Corporate Financing Directory. Nearly 2000 secondary distributions were reported during this ten-year period.

The final samples satisfy the following selection criteria: (1) secondary offerings are not made in combination with primary offerings of securities; (2) the shares are listed on either the New York Stock Exchange (NYSE) or the American Stock Exchange (ASE) at the time of the offering; (3) no other news about the company was reported in *The Wall Street Journal* on the date of the initial announcement; and (4) certain data requirements are met. For registered secondaries, the data requirements include obtaining an offering prospectus and identifying the date of first public disclosure. For the non-registered sample we require that there not be any material inconsistencies between the number of shares offered or the offering date as reported by the *Investment Dealers' Digest* and the *SEC Statistical Bulletin*. Finally, two non-registered offerings that were announced in *The Wall Street Journal* prior to the offering are eliminated.

These selection criteria determine final samples of 146 registered offerings and 321 non-registered offerings. Table 1 reports the total number of offerings

Table 1

Total number of secondary distributions of common stock at the four stages of sample formation (1972–1981).

| Sample | Registered offerings | Non-registered offerings |
|---|---|---|
| (1) Initial sample of all underwritten secondary and combination offerings | 1464 | 516 |
| (2) Secondary offerings | 390 | 516 |
| (3) Secondary offerings for NYSE/ASE firms | 183 | 360 |
| (4) Final sample of secondary offerings | 146[a] | 321[b] |

[a] Registered offerings are excluded from the final sample if (1) other potentially important news about the company was reported in *The Wall Street Journal* on the announcement date (13 offerings), (2) an offering prospectus could not be obtained (20 offerings), or (3) neither an announcement in *The Wall Street Journal* nor the filing date with the SEC could be identified (4 offerings).

[b] Non-registered offerings are excluded from the final sample if (1) other potentially important news about the firm was reported in *The Wall Street Journal* on the announcement date (20 offerings), (2) there were any material inconsistencies between data reported in the *Investment Dealers' Digest* and the *SEC Statistical Bulletin* (17 offerings), or (3) the offering was announced in *The Wall Street Journal* before the sale (2 offerings).

Table 2

Number of registered and non-registered secondary distributions of common stock by year.

| Year | Registered offerings | Non-registered offerings |
|------|---------------------|--------------------------|
| 1972 | 60 | 71 |
| 1973 | 16 | 84 |
| 1974 | 7 | 27 |
| 1975 | 11 | 25 |
| 1976 | 17 | 21 |
| 1977 | 8 | 23 |
| 1978 | 12 | 21 |
| 1979 | 3 | 15 |
| 1980 | 8 | 15 |
| 1981 | 4 | 19 |
| 1972–81 | 146 | 321 |

remaining at the four stages of sample formation. More than 1000 registered offerings are excluded because they were made in combination with a primary offering of securities, usually common stock. Table 2 reports the distribution of offerings in the final samples by calendar year. Approximately one-half of the distributions in the final samples occurred in 1972 or 1973.[4]

## 3.2. Characteristics of the samples

Selected descriptive statistics for the samples of registered and non-registered offerings are presented in table 3. The first four rows present statistics on the absolute size of the offering. In terms of both the number of shares offered and the dollar value of the shares offered, the registered offerings are considerably larger than the non-registered offerings. Relative measures of the size of offering presented in rows 5 and 6 indicate that on average the number of shares offered in registered distributions represents 8.1% of the total number of shares outstanding and in non-registered distributions represents 2.7% of total shares outstanding.[5] Rows 7 and 8 indicate that the number of shares offered is substantial relative to average daily trading volume measured over the six months preceding the month of the first public disclosure of the offering. The average ratio of shares offered to average daily trading volume is

[4] Secondary distributions were used frequently in the latter part of our sample period. However, they were very often accompanied by a primary offering of shares and thus are excluded.

[5] Scholes' sample consists of 73 registered offerings and 272 non-registered offerings made in the period from July 1961 through December 1965. The average ratio of shares offered divided by shares outstanding is 2.2% for his sample of 345 secondaries. For our two samples combined, the average ratio is 4.4%. The average dollar value of secondaries is $4.7 million for Scholes' sample and is $12.3 million for our two samples combined.

Table 3

Selected summary statistics for 146 registered and 321 non-registered secondary distributions of common stock (1972–1981).[a]

| Descriptive measure | Mean | Median | Standard deviation | Minimum | Maximum |
|---|---|---|---|---|---|
| *Number of shares offered (000)* | | | | | |
| (1)  Registered offerings | 828 | 462 | 1492 | 70 | 13357 |
| (2)  Non-registered offerings | 152 | 117 | 130 | 13 | 1124 |
| *Value of shares offered (000)[b]* | | | | | |
| (3)  Registered offerings | $31593 | $14000 | $50448 | $691 | $296000 |
| (4)  Non-registered offerings | $3486 | $2276 | $3624 | $125 | $21694 |
| *Shares offered / shares outstanding* | | | | | |
| (5)  Registered offerings | 0.081 | 0.053 | 0.077 | 0.001 | 0.473 |
| (6)  Non-registered offerings | 0.027 | 0.023 | 0.019 | 0.001 | 0.098 |
| *Shares offered / average daily trading volume* | | | | | |
| (7)  Registered offerings | 96.5 | 60.79 | 104.0 | 3.1 | 811.5 |
| (8)  Non-registered offerings | 29.7 | 19.91 | 28.8 | 1.0 | 190.9 |
| *Shares offered / shares held by institutional investors* | | | | | |
| (9)  Registered offerings | 5.69 | 0.632 | 27.0 | 0.001 | 300.0 |
| (10)  Non-registered offerings | 1.62 | 0.186 | 16.9 | 0.001 | 295.3 |

[a] For the registered secondaries, summary statistics are calculated using data collected from the offering prospectuses and from the *Security Owner's Stock Guide*. Summary statistics for the non-registered offerings are calculated using data from the *Security Owner's Stock Guide*, the *Investment Dealers' Digest* and the *SEC Statistical Bulletin*.

[b] Dollar value is calculated using the offer price.

96.5 for registered distributions, more than three times the average ratio of 29.7 for non-registered distributions. In addition, as indicated in rows 9 and 10, the average size of registered offerings is also greater when the size of the offering is measured relative to the number of shares held by institutional investors in the month prior to the first public disclosure of the offering.

When information on the selling shareholders is available, an offering is classified into one of the categories of selling stockholders listed in table 4. For registered distributions, the offering prospectus is examined to identify the selling stockholder. When there are two or more sellers of different types, the secondary is classified according to the type of stockholder selling the largest number of shares in the distribution. An exception to this classification rule is that a secondary is placed in the directors and officers category if any of the sellers is a director or an officer.[6] The identity of the selling stockholder in

[6] In the sample of 146 registered secondaries, there are 89 offerings by a single seller, and 57 offerings by more than one type of shareholder. Of the 36 offerings by multiple sellers involving officers and directors, there are 18 cases where officers and directors sold more shares than the other selling shareholders.

Table 4

Distribution by category of the principal selling stockholder(s) of 146 registered and 321 non-registered secondary distributions of common stock (1972–1981) (proportions in parentheses).

| Category of principal selling stockholder(s) | Number of registered offerings[a] | Number of non-registered offerings[b] |
|---|---|---|
| (1) Directors(s) or officer(s) | 53(0.37) | 6(0.03) |
| (2) Individual(s) | 25(0.17) | 8(0.04) |
| (3) Corporation | 20(0.14) | 11(0.05) |
| (4) Investment company, bank or insurance company | 10(0.07) | 155(0.71) |
| (5) Trust, estate, foundation, university or government | 38(0.25) | 16(0.07) |
| (6) Various[c] | 0 | 22(0.10) |
| (7) No information | 0 | 103(0.00)[d] |
| Total sample | 146(1.0) | 321(1.0) |

[a] Source: Offering prospectus.

[b] Source: *SEC Statistical Bulletin*.

[c] This term is used by the SEC; its precise meaning is unclear.

[d] The offerings with no information on the type of selling stockholder are excluded from the calculation of sample proportions. The sample proportions are based on a sample of 218 offerings.

non-registered secondaries is not publicly disclosed at the time of the sale. However, the *SEC Statistical Bulletin* classifies completed offerings by type of selling stockholder. These classifications were reported only through 1976, so it is not possible to classify the selling stockholder for non-registered secondary distributions after 1976.

Table 4 presents the distributions of registered and non-registered offerings by category of the principal selling stockholder. The distributions appear to reflect the SEC's registration requirements. For example, 37% of the registered offerings are sales by directors or officers, while only 3% of the non-registered offerings are classified into this category. On the other hand, only 7% of the registered secondaries represent sales by insurance companies, banks or investment companies, but 71% of the non-registered offerings are sales by this category of stockholder. The relatively greater proportion of corporations and individuals offering registered rather than non-registered distributions suggests that these sellers tend to have a control relationship with the firm, as defined by federal regulation. The low proportion of registered offerings by insurance companies, banks and investment companies suggests that selling stockholders who are not required to register generally do not view registration as beneficial to their selling effort.[7]

[7] The definition of control (footnote 3 above) leaves considerable ambiguity as to the type of seller actually required to register a secondary offering. It does not appear possible to identify precisely secondaries that are registered voluntarily.

### 3.3. Estimation of daily prediction errors

Daily prediction errors, or excess returns, are estimated around the date of the first public disclosure of the sale [the announcement date (AD)], as well as around the date the offering begins [the distribution date (DD)]. For 124 of the 146 registered secondaries, the announcement date is the date of announcement in *The Wall Street Journal*. For the remaining 22 cases, the announcement date is defined as the trading day following the date of registration with the SEC.[8] For non-registered secondaries, the announcement date is also the distribution date, since there are no announcements in advance of the offerings. Thus, for these distributions prediction errors are examined around a single date. The prediction error for the common stock of firm $j$ on day $t$ is defined as

$$PE_{jt} = R_{jt} - \left( \hat{\alpha}_j + \hat{\beta}_j R_{mt} \right), \tag{1}$$

where $R_{jt}$ is the continuously compounded rate of return for the common stock of firm $j$ on day $t$, and $R_{mt}$ is the continuously compounded rate of return for the CRSP equally weighted index on day $t$. The coefficients $\hat{\alpha}_j$ and $\hat{\beta}_j$ are ordinary least squares estimates of firm $j$'s market model parameters. The estimation period includes the 140 days that end 61 days before the announcement date of the secondary and the 140 days that begin 61 days after the distribution date, a total of 280 trading days.

Prediction errors are calculated for each day in the event period that begins 60 trading days before the announcement date and ends 60 trading days after the distribution date. The event period is 121 trading days for all non-registered offerings but differs for the registered offerings, varying from 123 to 247 days.

The average prediction error on event day $t$ for a sample of $N$ secondary distributions is

$$APE_t = \frac{1}{N} \sum_{j=1}^{N} PE_{jt}. \tag{2}$$

A test of statistical significance is conducted to determine whether the average standardized prediction error equals zero. Each standardized prediction error ($SPE_{jt}$) is defined as

$$SPE_{jt} = PE_{jt}/S_{jt}, \tag{3}$$

---

[8] These 22 observations include 15 not reported in *The Wall Street Journal* and seven where the registration date preceded the earliest published report by more than one trading day.

where

$$
S_{jt} = \left[ V_j^2 \left\{ 1 + \frac{1}{ED} + \frac{\left( R_{m_t} - \overline{R}_m \right)^2}{\displaystyle\sum_{i=1}^{ED} \left( R_{mi} - \overline{R}_m \right)^2} \right\} \right]^{1/2}
\tag{4}
$$

In (4), $V_j^2$ is the residual variance of firm $j$'s market model regression, $ED$ is the number of days in the period used to estimate the market model, $R_{mt}$ is the market return on day $t$, and $\overline{R}_m$ is the mean market return in the estimation period. The average standardized prediction error is

$$
ASPE_t = \frac{1}{N} \sum_{j=1}^{N} SPE_{jt}.
\tag{5}
$$

The individual daily prediction errors are assumed to be distributed normal, so each $SPE_{jt}$ is distributed Student $t$ with variance equal to $ED/(ED-2)$. Under the Central Limit Theorem, $ASPE_t$ is distributed normal with a variance equal to $[ED/(ED-2)(N)]$, assuming that the individual prediction errors are cross-sectionally independent. Since $ED$ is large, $ED/(ED-2)$ is very close to one and the variance of $ASPE_t$ approximately equals $1/N$. For each day, the following $Z$-statistic is computed:

$$
Z = \sqrt{N} \left( ASPE_t \right),
\tag{6}
$$

which has a unit normal distribution under the hypothesis that the mean standardized prediction error equals zero.[9]

---

[9] Our choice of statistical test is based on the simulation results presented by Brown and Warner (1984). For samples of 50 securities, Brown and Warner find that the mean excess return is distributed very close to normal, which supports our application of the Central Limit Theorem. In addition, when events are not clustered in calendar time, Brown and Warner find that the assumption of cross-sectional independence in estimating the variance of mean excess returns results in test statistics that are well-specified under the null hypothesis and are more powerful than procedures that do not assume cross-sectional independence. This supports our procedure of standardizing daily prediction errors before aggregating cross-sectionally. This method gives greater weight to the prediction errors that are measured more precisely (lower standard error of prediction errors) and presumably eliminates heteroscedasticity among prediction errors of different firms.

## 4. Evidence on stock price effects

### 4.1. Average prediction errors

Table 5 presents summary statistics of daily prediction errors for 21 trading days centered around the date of the earliest public disclosure of registered and non-registered secondaries. Column 1 designates the trading day, where day 0 is the announcement date. Columns 2 and 4 present the average daily prediction errors, and columns 3 and 5 present the proportion of negative prediction errors for each day.

Table 5

Daily average prediction errors and proportions of negative prediction errors for 21 trading days around the date of the earliest public disclosure of 146 registered and 321 non-registered secondary distributions of common stock (1972–1981).

| Trading day (1) | Registered distributions | | Non-registered distributions | |
|---|---|---|---|---|
| | Average prediction error[b] (2) | Proportion negative[c] (3) | Average prediction error[b] (4) | Proportion negative[c] (5) |
| −10 | −0.31%[d] | 0.59[d] | −0.09% | 0.53 |
| −9 | 0.39[e] | 0.49 | 0.11 | 0.49 |
| −8 | 0.21 | 0.47 | 0.05 | 0.53 |
| −7 | 0.08 | 0.49 | −0.05 | 0.50 |
| −6 | 0.09 | 0.51 | 0.07 | 0.48 |
| −5 | −0.25 | 0.58 | −0.22[d] | 0.56[d] |
| −4 | −0.17 | 0.58 | −0.21[e] | 0.55 |
| −3 | −0.07 | 0.53 | −0.18 | 0.53 |
| −2 | −0.23 | 0.55 | 0.10 | 0.50 |
| −1 | −1.31[e] | 0.71[e] | −0.40[e] | 0.58[e] |
| 0[a] | −1.56[e] | 0.72[e] | −0.40[e] | 0.61[e] |
| 1 | 0.09 | 0.49 | −1.56[e] | 0.73[e] |
| 2 | 0.33[d] | 0.49 | −0.73[e] | 0.62[e] |
| 3 | 0.38[d] | 0.47 | −0.41[e] | 0.58[e] |
| 4 | 0.37[e] | 0.41[d] | −0.46[e] | 0.57[e] |
| 5 | 0.19 | 0.48 | −0.15 | 0.59 |
| 6 | −0.20 | 0.56 | −0.15[e] | 0.57[d] |
| 7 | 0.01 | 0.49 | 0.01 | 0.52 |
| 8 | 0.19 | 0.52 | −0.15 | 0.55 |
| 9 | 0.05 | 0.48 | 0.09 | 0.50 |
| 10 | 0.02 | 0.53 | −0.13 | 0.50 |

[a] Day 0 is the announcement date for registered secondaries and is the distribution date for non-registered secondaries.

[b] The null hypothesis for each day is that the average standardized prediction error equals zero.

[c] The null hypothesis for each day is that the proportion of negative prediction errors equals 0.50. The test statistic is the Wilcoxon signed-ranks statistic described by Daniel (1978).

[d] Significant at the 0.05 level.

[e] Significant at the 0.01 level.

The average prediction errors in column 2 and the proportion of negative prediction errors in column 3 indicate a pronounced negative change in the value of common stock at the announcement of registered secondaries. The average two-day prediction error for the day preceding the announcement date (day $-1$) and the announcement date (day 0) is $-2.87\%$. The average prediction errors on days $-1$ and 0 are both significant at the 0.01 level and 83% of the two-day prediction errors are negative.[10]

The disclosure of non-registered secondaries also has a negative effect on stock price. The average two-day prediction error for the distribution date (day 0) and the day following the distribution date (day 1) is $-1.96\%$. Both average prediction errors in this two-day period are significant at the 0.01 level. Days 0 and 1 comprise the two-day period of interest for non-registered distributions, since these offerings typically are disclosed and begin after the close of trading on the distribution day. It is not surprising, therefore, that the largest negative average prediction error is observed on day 1. For this day, the average prediction error is $-1.56\%$, and 73% of the prediction errors are negative. Buyers of non-registered secondaries on average appear to earn negative returns, since the average percentage discount of the offer price from the closing price on day 0 is only 0.2%, as reported below in table 11.

The average prediction errors observed on days 2, 3 and 4 for non-registered secondaries are troublesome. Each of these three average prediction errors is less than $-0.40\%$ and is significant at the 0.01 level. This suggests market inefficiency. An alternative explanation of the negative and significant returns on days 2 through 4 is that in some cases the offering date reported in the *Investment Dealers' Digest* and in the *SEC Statistical Bulletin* precedes the true offering date. However, we have no reason to suspect that the reported offering dates are incorrect. In addition, for the three subsamples of offerings with a standardized prediction error less than $-1.5$ on day 2, 3 or 4, respectively, the average standardized prediction errors on day 1 are negative and significant at the 0.01 level. This finding is consistent with an explanation based on incorrect dates only if news of the offering is leaked in advance. Finally, the negative returns on days 2, 3 and 4 do not appear to be related to the actual distribution of shares, since approximately 90% of the non-registered secondaries are completed by the end of day 1. Therefore, we do not have a satisfactory explanation at this time for the significant negative average prediction errors following day 1.

Table 6 presents the average prediction errors for the eleven trading days centered around the distribution date of registered secondaries. Eight of the eleven average prediction errors are negative, but no single average prediction

---

[10] Test statistics are not adjusted to account for a possible increase in variance of returns around the announcement date. However, if every firm's variance of daily returns increases by the same proportion, the standard error of returns must increase by more than four times to change the inference that the day $-1$ and day 0 average prediction errors are significant at the 0.05 level.

Table 6

Daily average prediction errors and proportions of negative prediction errors for 11 trading days around the distribution date of 146 registered secondary distributions of common stock (1972–1981).

| Trading day (1) | Average prediction error[b] (2) | Proportion negative[c] (3) |
|---|---|---|
| − 5 | − 0.14% | 0.56 |
| − 4 | 0.07 | 0.46 |
| − 3 | 0.29 | 0.48 |
| − 2 | − 0.08 | 0.55 |
| − 1 | − 0.30 | 0.60 |
| 0[a] | − 0.12 | 0.57 |
| 1 | − 0.12 | 0.53 |
| 2 | 0.10 | 0.47 |
| 3 | − 0.21 | 0.48 |
| 4 | − 0.31 | 0.57 |
| 5 | − 0.03 | 0.45 |

[a] Day 0 is the distribution date of the secondary offering.

[b] The null hypothesis tested for each day is that the average standardized prediction error equals zero. None of the average standardized prediction errors is significant at the 0.05 level.

[c] The null hypothesis for each day is that the proportion of negative prediction errors equals 0.50. The test statistic is the Wilcoxon signed-ranks statistic described by Daniel (1978). None of the test statistics is significant at the 0.05 level. The lowest $p$-value is 0.127 on day 0.

error is significant at the 0.05 level. Only the average prediction error on day − 1 is significant at the 0.10 level. In addition, for each day the signed-ranks test statistic is insignificant at the 0.10 level. On the distribution date, the average prediction error is only − 0.12% and 57% of the prediction errors are negative. Thus, there is no evidence of statistically significant changes in share price on the day of or immediately following the distribution date of registered offerings.

The average prediction errors for several intervals of trading days around the announcement date and the distribution date are reported in table 7. For registered offerings, the average prediction error for the eleven days surrounding the announcement date is − 2.23%, and is significant at the 0.01 level. The average prediction error in the interval from six trading days after the announcement date to six days before the distribution date, a period that is of different length for each registered secondary, is only − 1.02%, and is not statistically significant at the 0.10 level. The average prediction error is − 0.85% for the eleven days centered around the distribution date for these offerings, and is also not significant at the 0.10 level. Thus, the sum of the average prediction errors for registered secondaries from five trading days before the announcement date to five trading days after the distribution date is − 4.10%.

Table 7

Average prediction errors for several intervals around the announcement date (AD) and the distribution date (DD) of 146 registered and 321 non-registered secondary distributions of common stock (1972–1981).

| Interval of trading days (1) | Registered distributions | | Non-registered distributions | |
|---|---|---|---|---|
| | Average interval prediction error[a] (2) | Z-value[b] (3) | Average interval prediction error[a] (4) | Z-value[b] (5) |
| AD − 49, AD − 39 | 0.12% | 0.26 | −0.38% | −1.23 |
| AD − 38, AD − 28 | 0.42 | 0.66 | −0.21 | −0.83 |
| AD − 27, AD − 17 | 1.14 | 2.09 | −0.48 | −1.75 |
| AD − 16, AD − 6 | −0.17 | −0.44 | −0.42 | −1.27 |
| AD − 5,   AD + 5 | −2.23 | −3.70 | −4.62 | −11.62 |
| AD + 6,   DD − 6[c] | −1.02 | −0.55 | d | |
| DD − 5,   DD + 5 | −0.85 | −1.29 | e | |
| DD + 6,   DD + 16 | 0.78 | 2.29 | −0.54 | −0.94 |
| DD + 17, DD + 27 | 0.35 | 1.28 | 0.43 | 0.95 |
| DD + 28, DD + 38 | 0.46 | 0.90 | 0.02 | 0.08 |
| DD + 39, DD + 49 | 0.05 | 0.19 | −0.07 | −0.11 |

[a] The average interval prediction error ($AIPE$) equals the sum of the daily average prediction errors ($APE$) in the specified interval of days.

$$AIPE_{D_1, D_2} = \sum_{t=D_1}^{D_2} APE_t,$$

where $D_1$ and $D_2$ are the first and last days in the interval of interest.

[b] The null hypothesis for each interval is that the average cumulative standardized prediction error equals zero. The Z-values reported above do not change materially when calculated as the average prediction error divided by an estimate of the standard deviation adjusted for first-, second- and third-order autocorrelation in the prediction errors.

[c] Only 119 registered secondaries are represented in this interval because in 27 cases the announcement date and distribution date are less than 11 days apart.

[d] This interval contains zero days.

[e] The distribution date is the date of earliest public disclosure (AD).

During the comparable eleven-day period for non-registered secondaries, the average prediction error is −4.62%.[11]

Significant negative stock price effects are confined primarily to intervals that contain the announcement date. No negative average prediction error that is significant at the 0.05 level is observed for any interval that precedes the announcement date or follows the distribution date for registered secondaries.

[11] If we combine our samples of registered and non-registered secondaries, as Scholes does, the average prediction error on the offering date is −0.31% and the average prediction error for the eleven days surrounding the offering date is −3.43%. Scholes reports an average return of −0.55% on the offering date and −1.69% for the eleven days around the offering date for his sample of secondaries.

For non-registered secondaries, the average prediction errors for the eleven-day periods that immediately precede and follow the eleven-day interval around the announcement date are not significant at the 0.10 level.

Significant positive returns are observed in the period following the distribution of shares in registered secondaries. The cumulative average prediction error over days 6 through 16 is 0.78%, and the cumulative average prediction error for the interval from days 6 through 49 is 1.64%. Both are significant at the 0.01 level. However, since these positive returns do not begin until six days after the sale, it seems unlikely that they are associated with a price recovery that is related to a decrease in price around the announcement and distribution dates. There is no evidence of a price recovery for the non-registered secondaries. The cumulative average prediction error is $-0.54\%$ over days 6 through 16 and is $-0.20\%$ for the interval from day 6 through 49.[12]

In summary, we find a significant negative stock price response to the earliest public disclosure of both registered and non-registered secondary distributions. The small negative price change observed at the distribution date of registered secondaries is not significantly different from zero. Thus, the significant price impact of secondaries occurs in response to news of the offerings, rather than at the time of the actual sale of shares. In the remainder of this section we present evidence that is relevant to possible explanations of the stock price effects.

### 4.2. Potential determinants of the announcement date price effects

We examine two potential explanations of the stock price effects of secondary distributions. The first is the notion that the decrease in share price reflects the market's belief that the seller has unfavorable information about the firm, or at a minimum that the seller has no favorable information. The second explanation is that the decrease in share price is due to a supply effect, i.e., movement along a downward sloping transaction, or excess, demand curve for a firm's shares.[13]

*Price effect due to unfavorable information.*   Several characteristics of a seller or of a secondary distribution are potential determinants of the market's percep-

---

[12] Scholes reports an average prediction error of $-0.8\%$ for registered secondaries and of $-1.4\%$ for non-registered secondaries over the fourteen days that follow the offering date. He argues that given a commission of approximately 1%, an investor is essentially indifferent between buying shares in a secondary offering and paying no commission or buying the shares several days after the offering and paying a commission. Our results do not support this statement. Over the sixteen days following the offering date, the average prediction error for registered secondaries is 0.2% and for nonregistered secondaries is $-3.9\%$.

[13] The concept of a transaction, or excess, demand curve is presented in Hirshleifer (1980). A transaction demand curve relates share price and the quantity of shares demanded by investors in excess of shares already owned.

tion that the seller possesses unfavorable information about the firm. First, the market's perception may depend on the seller's relation to the firm. For example, Scholes (1972) suggests that an individual involved in a firm's decision-making, such as an officer or director, is viewed more likely to possess inside information than other shareholders. Therefore, we test the following proposition:

> The relative decrease in stock price at the initial announcement is greater for offerings by officers or directors than for offerings by other types of sellers.

This proposition is tested using the classification of registered offerings described in section 3.2.

Second, the market's perception that the seller holds unfavorable information may depend on the seller's proportional ownership of the firm's shares. The seller's incentive and ability to be informed about the firm's prospects is greater, the larger the ownership stake. For example, the holder of a sufficiently large block of shares who can exercise some influence over the firm's activities is likely to be informed about the firm through direct communication with management. A second proposition we test is:

> The relative decrease in stock price at the initial announcement is greater, the larger is the proportion of the firm's shares held by the seller prior to the offering.

Third, investors' view of whether the seller holds unfavorable information may depend on the seller's proportional ownership of the firm's shares following the secondary offering. The smaller is the seller's post-offering ownership stake, the smaller is any decrease in the selling stockholder's wealth due to unfavorable information that is divulged after the offering. Therefore, the market is more likely to perceive that the seller possesses unfavorable information if the seller retains none or only a small proportion of the firm's shares after the offering. We test the following proposition:

> The relative decrease in stock price at the initial announcement is greater, the smaller is the seller's post-offering ownership stake of the firm's shares.

To test the two propositions concerning the seller's ownership in the firm, the number of shares held and the number of shares offered by the principal seller were collected from the offering prospectus of each registered secondary.

Fourth, dollar value of the secondary offering may also be a determinant of the market's perception that the seller holds unfavorable inside information. Controlling for other possible determinants, the larger is the dollar value of the offering, the greater is the incentive of the seller to be informed about the firm's prospects and to act on unfavorable inside information. A fourth proposition is:

> The relative decrease in stock price at the initial announcement is greater, the larger is the dollar value of the offering.

The number of shares offered and the offer price are collected from the prospectus of each registered secondary.

*Supply effect on share price due to less than perfectly elastic demand.* If a firm's shares do not have sufficiently close substitutes, so that demand is less than perfectly elastic, a potential price effect of a secondary offering is due to movement along a downward sloping excess demand curve. This effect reflects neither the transactions costs of selling shares nor a change in the market's assessment of the firm's earnings prospects. Instead, a supply effect represents a change in equilibrium price due to the characteristics of demand for a firm's shares, and implies that the marginal market valuation of the last share offered is below the current market price. This corresponds to what Kraus and Stoll (1972) call a 'distribution effect due to different investor preferences for a given security'.

A supply effect implies that the price response to a secondary depends on the size of the offering and on the elasticity of demand for the firm's shares. In addition, in an efficient market a supply effect occurs at the initial announcement, since a supply effect represents a change in equilibrium price. Therefore, we test the following proposition:

> The relative decrease in stock price at the initial announcement is greater, the larger is the number of shares offered relative to the number of shares outstanding.

A difficulty with testing this proposition is that a negative relation between the price response and the size of the offering is also consistent with the unfavorable information hypothesis, since offering size can be a proxy for unfavorable information. However, a supply effect suggests that the elasticity of demand as well as the size of the offering affect the price response. We attempt to distinguish a supply effect from an unfavorable information effect by investigating whether the relation between the price response and offering size depends on factors we conjecture are related to demand elasticity.

### 4.3. Cross-sectional tests of the propositions

Table 8 reports the estimates of the coefficients of weighted least squares regressions of the two-day announcement period prediction error for registered secondaries on (1) an index variable that equals one if the seller is classified as

Table 8

Estimated coefficients for weighted least squares regressions of the two-day announcement period prediction errors on proxies for the market's assessment of unfavorable information and for relative offering size for 146 registered secondary distributions of common stock (1972–1981) (*t*-statistics are in parentheses).[a]

| | Independent variables[b] | | | | | | |
| | Const. (1) | *TYPE* (2) | *STAKE* (3) | *KEEP* (4) | ln(*DVAL*) (5) | *SIZE1* (6) | *F*-stat.[c] |
|---|---|---|---|---|---|---|---|
| (1) | 0.012 (0.56) | −0.016 (−2.27) | 0.076 (0.55) | −0.083 (−0.59) | −0.002 (−1.14) | −0.144 (−0.56) | 14.43 (6,140) |
| (2) | 0.004 (0.20) | −0.016 (−2.47) | −0.045 (−1.10) | 0.029 (0.57) | −0.002 (−0.83) | | 15.56 (5,141) |
| (3) | 0.013 (0.62) | −0.019 (−3.21) | | | −0.003 (−1.22) | −0.076 (−1.94) | 21.81 (4,142) |

[a] The dependent and independent variables are divided by the standard error of the two-day prediction error.

[b] Independent variables are defined as follows: *TYPE* = index variable equal to one if seller is an officer or director and equal to zero otherwise, *STAKE* = proportional ownership position of principal seller prior to the offering, *KEEP* = proportional ownership position of principal seller after the offering, *DVAL* = dollar value of the offering, and *SIZE1* = number of shares offered divided by the number of shares outstanding.

[c] The *F*-statistic tests the hypothesis that all the coefficients (including the intercept) are different from zero. Degrees of freedom are in parentheses under the *F*-statistic.

an officer or director and equals zero otherwise (*TYPE*), (2) the pre-offering proportional ownership stake of the seller (*STAKE*), (3) the post-offering ownership position of the seller (*KEEP*), (4) the natural logarithm of the dollar value of the offering (*DVAL*) and (5) the number of shares offered divided by shares outstanding (*SIZE1*). The dependent and independent variables are divided by the standard error of the predicted two-day announcement period stock return to adjust for unequal variances of prediction errors across firms. These tests do not include non-registered secondaries, because *TYPE*, *STAKE* and *KEEP* are not disclosed in the announcement of these offerings.

Row 1 of table 8 presents the coefficient estimates of a multiple regression on all five independent variables. Only the coefficient on the dummy variable for the type of seller has a *t*-statistic that is significant at the 0.05 level. Since the variable *SIZE1* in most cases equals the difference between the variables *STAKE* and *KEEP*, *SIZE1* is excluded from the regression reported in row 2.[14] Again, only the coefficient on type of seller (*TYPE*) is significant. When the variables *STAKE* and *KEEP* are excluded, the coefficients on relative

[14] *SIZE1* equals *STAKE* minus *KEEP* for the 89 offerings by a single seller.

Table 9

Estimated coefficients for weighted least squares regressions of the two-day announcement period prediction errors on the relative size and the log of dollar value of the offering for registered secondary distributions of common stock (1972–1981) (*t*-statistics are in parentheses).[a]

| Sample of secondaries | Sample size | Independent variables[b] | | | F-stat.[c] |
|---|---|---|---|---|---|
| | | Const. | *SIZE1* | ln(*DVAL*) | |
| (1) Registered offerings by sellers other than officers and directors | 93 | 0.021 (0.90) | −0.082 (−1.86) | −0.003 (−1.45) | 12.45 (3, 90) |
| (2) Registered offerings by sellers other than officers and directors | 93 | −0.012 (−2.92) | −0.077 (−1.75) | | 17.42 (2, 91) |
| (3) Registered offerings by sellers in the trust and estates category | 38 | 0.036 (0.89) | −2.11 (−2.01) | −0.004 (−1.08) | 6.12 (3, 35) |
| (4) Registered offerings by sellers in the trusts and estates category | 38 | −0.077 (−1.12) | −0.166 (−1.73) | | 8.56 (2, 36) |

[a] The dependent and independent variables are divided by the standard error of the two-day prediction error.

[b] Independent variables are defined as follows: *SIZE1* = number of shares offered divided by the number of shares outstanding, and *DVAL* = dollar value of the offering.

[c] The *F*-statistic tests the hypothesis that all the coefficients (including the intercept) are different from zero. Degrees of freedom are in parentheses under the *F*-statistic.

offering size (*SIZE1*) and on type of seller (*TYPE*) are significant at the 0.10 and 0.01 levels, respectively.[15]

The significant coefficient on type of seller (*TYPE*) is consistent with a price effect due to the market's inference of unfavorable information. However, the statistically insignificant coefficients for the pre-offering ownership position (*STAKE*), the post-offering ownership position (*KEEP*) and the dollar value of the offering (*DVAL*) do not support a price effect due to unfavorable information. The negative coefficient on the relative offering size (*SIZE1*) can be interpreted in two ways. First, *SIZE1* is related to each of the variables *STAKE*, *KEEP* and *DVAL*, and is possibly a proxy for the effects of unfavorable information. The second interpretation is that the coefficient on *SIZE1* represents an effect due to less than perfectly elastic demand.

We attempt to distinguish between a supply effect and an unfavorable information effect. First, we estimate the cross-sectional relation between the

---

[15] Scholes finds no relation between prediction errors and measures of *SIZE1* for his combined sample of registered and non-registered secondaries. Scholes' results differ from ours for at least two reasons: (1) the dependent variable in his regression is the *single-day* prediction error on the *offering* date, and (2) Scholes does not control for other potential determinants of price effects and estimates simple regressions on *SIZE1* and *DVAL*, respectively.

initial announcement two-day prediction errors and *SIZE1* for subsamples of offerings that are least likely to be associated with a price effect due to unfavorable information. Offerings by officers and directors are excluded from these subsamples, since the evidence in table 8 indicates that sales by officers and directors are associated with a significantly greater price decrease than sales by other types of shareholders. Table 9 shows that for the sample that excludes offerings by officers and directors, the coefficient on *SIZE1* is significant at the 0.10 level both in a regression that includes the dollar value of the offering, and in a simple regression. For the sample of 38 secondaries in the trusts or estates category, the coefficient on *SIZE1* is significant at the 0.05 level in the multiple regression including the dollar value of the offer, and is significant at the 0.10 level in the simple regression. These results provide weak support for a supply effect. However, even for these offerings *SIZE1* may be a determinant of the market's perception of unfavorable information.

Second, since a supply effect implies that the price response is related not only to the relative size of the offering, but also to the elasticity of demand for a firm's shares, we attempt to control for possible differences in elasticity of demand across firms. We classify secondaries according to characteristics that are related to firm size or trading activity. We conjecture that demand for a firm's shares is less elastic for (1) smaller firms, (2) lower priced shares, (3) shares with lower average daily trading volume, and (4) shares with a smaller proportion of ownership by institutional investors. The conjecture implies that the relation between the announcement period prediction error and the relative size of secondary offerings depends on these factors.

For both the registered and non-registered samples, we test whether the cross-sectional relation between the announcement period prediction error and *SIZE1* differs between subsamples of offerings grouped according to one of these four characteristics.[16] That is, we test for equality of the coefficients on *SIZE1* between subsamples.[17] In none of the eight tests is the *F*-statistic significant at the 0.10 level. The relation between the announcement period

---

[16] The market value of the equity, calculated as the offer price times the number of shares outstanding in the month prior to the announcement, is used as a proxy for firm size. The number of shares outstanding is reported in the *Security Owner's Stock Guide*. Average daily trading volume is calculated over the six months prior to the month of the first public disclosure, using monthly trading volume reported in the *Security Owner's Stock Guide*. Shares held by institutional investors were collected for the month prior to the disclosure of the offering from the *Security Owner's Stock Guide*.

[17] Our test of equality of coefficients on *SIZE1* is presented in Johnston (1972, pp. 192–199). For each of the four characteristics conjectured to be associated with demand elasticity, we sort the secondaries into two samples, for example the smallest third of the firms ($S$) and the largest third of the firms ($L$). Unrestricted regressions (i) (small firms) and (ii) (large firms) are estimated on the subsamples,

$$PE = \alpha_S + \beta_S (SIZE1), \tag{i}$$

$$PE = \alpha_L + \beta_L (SIZE1), \tag{ii}$$

For the unrestricted model, the total sum of squared residuals, denoted $SS_u$, equals the sum of squared residuals from the two simple regressions given above. (*Continued on next page*)

prediction error and the relative size of the offering (*SIZE1*) does not depend on any of the four variables that we conjecture are related to determinants of demand elasticity. These results do not support a supply effect.

Even though the identity of the seller and the relative size of the offering are related to the price response, there is evidence that secondaries are associated with a negative stock price reaction regardless of the characteristics of the offering that we hypothesize are important. Table 10 reports average prediction errors at the announcement of registered secondaries for the five categories of sellers defined in table 4 and for quartiles of secondaries grouped by relative size of offering (*SIZE1*). Column 4 presents two-day average prediction errors for days −1 and 0, where day 0 is the announcement date.

The two-day average prediction errors range from −2.44% for secondaries by individuals to −3.40% for secondaries by directors and officers. The two-day average prediction error is −2.57% for secondaries by sellers other than officers or directors.[18] The *Z*-values in column 6 indicate that the average prediction errors are significant at the 0.01 level for all seller types.[19] For

---

Next a restricted regression model (iii) is estimated on the combined samples of small and large firms, where only the intercept term is allowed to vary between the two subsamples,

$$PE = \alpha + \alpha'(D) + \beta(SIZE1),$$    (iii)

where $D$ is an index variable that equals one for subset $S$ firms and equals zero otherwise. The sum of squared residuals of the restricted model is denoted $SS_R$.

To test for a difference in the coefficients on *SIZE1* between the two subsamples, we compute the following *F*-statistic:

$$F = (SS_R - SS_u)/[SS_u/(N_S + N_L - 4)],$$    (iv)

where $N_S$ and $N_L$ are the numbers of small and large firms in subsets $S$ and $L$, respectively. A significant *F*-statistic implies a reduction in the sum of squared residuals due to allowing the coefficient on *SIZE1* to vary across the subsamples of firms.

[18] The prediction errors of subsamples of secondaries grouped by the type of selling stockholder are also analyzed using a non-parametric test, the Mann–Whitney U-test. The results are very similar to the *Z*-values reported in table 10.

[19] The results in table 10 do not appear to be sensitive to our particular method of classifying sellers. Other classification schemes we investigated lead to similar results. These other procedures include (1) redefining the officer and director category to include their family members, trusts for their benefit, corporations controlled by them and non-profit institutions on whose boards they sit; (2) re-assigning officers and directors to other categories if there were multiple sellers involved and other sellers sold more shares than the officers and directors; and (3) classifying sellers based on information in the *SEC Statistical Bulletin*, as did Scholes. Based on the SEC seller categories, we also find the largest price response to sales by corporations, and the smallest price response to sales by trusts and estates, consistent with Scholes' findings. However, the average two-day prediction error is significant at the 0.01 level for each seller category.

In addition, we consider the possibility that the identity of the seller may not always be known at the initial public disclosure of registered secondaries. If the published report precedes the SEC filing date and the seller's identity is not revealed by *The Wall Street Journal*, then it is likely that the seller's identity is not known at the time of the first public disclosure of the secondary.

To determine the importance of these differences in disclosure, we partition the 53 observations in the officer and director category into two groups. The first group of 41 observations includes those where the identity of the seller is known at the announcement. The second group includes the 12 observations where the report in *The Wall Street Journal* precedes the SEC filing and does not disclose the seller's identity. The difference between the two-day average prediction errors for these two groups is not significant at the 0.10 level.

Table 10

Two-day announcement period common stock average prediction errors and proportions of negative two-day prediction errors for 146 registered secondary distributions of common stock classified by the type of selling stockholder and by offering size (1972–1981).

| Sample of secondaries[a] (1) | Number of observations (2) | Average number of shares offered ÷ shares outstanding (SIZE1) (3) | Average two-day prediction error (4) | Proportion negative (5) | Z-value[b] (6) |
|---|---|---|---|---|---|
| Officers and directors | 53 | 0.099 | −3.40% | 0.85 | −8.47 |
| All other sellers | 93 | 0.076 | −2.57 | 0.82 | −8.36 |
| Individuals | 25 | 0.014 | −2.44 | 0.80 | −4.05 |
| Corporations | 20 | 0.143 | −2.90 | 0.85 | −4.27 |
| Banks, insurance companies and investment companies | 10 | 0.070 | −2.65 | 0.90 | −2.52 |
| Trusts, estates, universities and foundations | 38 | 0.064 | −2.47 | 0.79 | −5.41 |
| Size quartile 1 | 36 | 0.189 | −3.94 | 0.92 | −6.96 |
| Size quartile 2 | 37 | 0.075 | −2.83 | 0.78 | −5.84 |
| Size quartile 3 | 37 | 0.041 | −2.73 | 0.81 | −6.52 |
| Size quartile 4 | 36 | 0.019 | −2.00 | 0.81 | −4.48 |

[a] The classification of sellers is based on information disclosed in the offering prospectus, as described in section 3.2.

[b] The null hypothesis is that the average standardized prediction error for the two-day announcement period equals zero.

subsets of secondaries grouped by relative offering size, the average prediction error ranges from −3.94% for the largest offerings (quartile 1) to −2.00% for the smallest offerings (quartile 4). The average prediction errors are significant at the 0.01 level in all quartiles.

In column 5 we report the proportion of negative two-day prediction errors in each subset of secondary offerings. Among the subsamples grouped by type of seller the smallest proportion is 0.79, and among the size subsamples the smallest proportion is 0.78. These proportions, along with two-day average prediction errors in column 4, suggest that a negative price response is pervasive across the sample.[20]

[20] Scholes (1972) also compares average prediction errors of different seller types for his combined sample of registered and non-registered secondaries. Scholes calculates average prediction errors, by seller type, for 21 days surrounding the actual date of the offering. We see two possible problems with this procedure. First, it is likely that the identity of most sellers of registered offerings is disclosed *prior* to the time interval examined by Scholes. For example, for

The uniformly negative price effects presented in table 10 suggest two implications about the information conveyed by the sale of securities. First, the market's perception of who holds inside information may be quite broad. Second, the event of a secondary offering may convey unfavorable information since it suggests that the seller, or the selling agent, is unable to find a buyer willing to acquire a substantial block of shares at or above the current market price. For example, Bradley and Wakeman (1983) suggest that a firm's decision not to repurchase a block of shares and to allow it to be sold in a secondary distribution conveys unfavorable information about the firm's value. Moreover, a secondary offering generally distributes shares held by one or a few investors among a larger number of investors, and can be viewed as the opposite of stock purchases that result in the accumulation of a substantial block of shares by a single investor.[21] A secondary may reduce the likelihood of an attempt to acquire control of the firm.

## 5. Underwriting and other costs of secondaries

The evidence reported in the preceding section shows that on average the news of a secondary distribution is met with a decrease in share price. Other potentially important wealth effects on the sellers are the underwriting and other costs associated with secondary distributions. In this section we document that these costs are substantial, suggesting that holders of shares cannot sell a large number of shares within a short period of time at a small cost. In addition, we examine whether costs are predominantly payments to underwriters or price discounts to the buyers of shares.

### 5.1. Descriptive statistics

Table 11 presents a summary of the dollar and percentage costs for the samples of registered and non-registered secondaries. The costs of secondaries include the underwriting spread (row 1), other expenses incurred by the seller (row 2) and the difference between the offer price and the market value of the

---

119 of the 146 registered secondaries in our sample, the announcement date precedes the offering date by more than ten trading days. Second, it is unclear that the identity of most sellers of non-registered secondaries is known by ten days *after* the offering date. Neither the exchange nor the selling agent reveal the identity of the seller. In addition, very few sellers of non-registered secondaries appear to be insiders, and therefore are not required to report the sale as an insider transaction. For example, in our sample only 3% of the sellers are officers or directors.

[21] Mikkelson and Ruback (1984) find positive stock price effects for target firms when another firm files a Schedule 13D disclosing that a 5% or greater ownership position has been attained. For a sample of 184 filings where no plans to acquire control were disclosed, the average reported ownership position is 12.0% of the target firm's shares and the average two-day prediction error of the target firms is 1.73%.

Table 11

Summary of the average underwriting and other costs of 146 registered and 321 non-registered secondary distributions of common stock (1972–1981).

| | Registered offerings[a] | | | | Non-registered offerings[a] | | | |
|---|---|---|---|---|---|---|---|---|
| | Cost in millions | | Cost as percent of value of offering | | Cost in millions | | Cost as percent of value of offering | |
| Type of cost | Mean (1) | Median (2) | Mean (3) | Median (4) | Mean (5) | Median (6) | Mean (7) | Median (8) |
| (1) Underwriting spread | $1.19 | $0.65 | 4.9% | 4.7% | $0.15 | $0.10 | 4.7% | 4.4% |
| (2) Other reported expenses | 0.19 | 0.12 | 1.1 | 0.8 | b | b | b | b |
| (3) Discount in offer price[c] | 0.13 | 0.0 | 0.6 | 0.0 | 0.01 | 0.0 | 0.2 | 0.0 |
| (4) Sum of costs: (1) + (2) + (3) | $1.44 | $0.85 | 6.7% | 6.0% | $0.16 | $0.11 | 5.0% | 4.6% |

[a] The average offering sizes are $31.6 million and $3.5 million for the registered and non-registered offerings, respectively.

[b] These data are unavailable.

[c] The discount is the difference between the market value of the shares at the close of trading on the offering date and the offer price.

shares offered at the close of trading on the offering date (row 3).[22] Columns 1 and 5 present the average total dollar magnitudes and columns 2 and 6 present the median magnitudes. Columns 3 and 7 contain the average percentage costs measured relative to the total dollar value of the offering. Median percentages are reported in columns 4 and 8.

The largest component of the costs of both registered and non-registered secondaries is the underwriting spread, the difference between the seller's and underwriter's proceeds. The average underwriting compensation relative to the total dollar value of the offering is approximately 5% for both types of offerings. The costs of registered offerings are very similar to the proportional costs for various size categories of underwritten primary offerings of common stock reported by Smith (1977). For example, the 34 registered secondary offerings between $20 million and $50 million have an average underwriting spread of 4.28%, and other costs on average are 0.7% of the value of the offering. For 156 primary offerings in this size bracket, Smith reports an

---

[22] Other costs are not itemized in the offering prospectus. But according to the SEC documentation of the Registered Offering Statistics data base, other expenses reported in the offering prospectus include the SEC filing fee, state taxes, transfer fees, printing and engraving expenses, legal fees, accounting and auditing fees, engineering fees and miscellaneous expenses.

average underwriting spread of 4.3% and average proportional other expenses of 0.4%. Underwriting spreads are lower for non-registered than for registered secondaries in all categories of offering size. For example, the average underwriting spread is 2.79% for the four non-registered offerings between $20 million and $50 million. Most non-registered offerings in our sample are between $2 million and $5 million. The average underwriting spread is 4.44% for the 129 non-registered offerings in this category and is 6.18% for the 30 registered offerings in this category.

The relative discount between the offer price and the market price at the close of trading on the offering date is 0.6% for the registered offerings and is 0.2% for the non-registered offerings. Although on average the offering occurs at a discount, for 59% of registered and 55% of non-registered offerings the offering price equals the closing price.

The costs presented in table 11 are substantial. The average total cost of registered offerings is 6.7% of the value of the offering. This includes the underwriting spread, other selling costs and the discount between the closing and offering prices. The average total cost of non-registered offerings is 5.0%, which includes the underwriting spread and the discount between the closing and offering prices. Therefore, in addition to the significant stock price effects at the initial announcement, the underwriting and other costs of secondaries are an important part of the wealth effect of a secondary offering on the selling shareholder. A potential determinant of underwriting costs is investigated below.

## 5.2. Underwriting and the costs of liquidity

Another possible price effect associated with the actual sale of a large number of shares is a liquidity cost effect, a temporary price decline reflecting compensation to the buyer for providing liquidity to the seller. Buyers may require compensation for (1) an undesired portfolio composition due to acquiring the shares upon short notice, (2) the transactions costs of adjusting portfolio composition to accommodate the shares or (3) the costs of reselling the shares. One form of compensation to the buyers is selling the shares at a discount relative to market price. Kraus and Stoll (1972) call this a 'distribution effect due to short-run liquidity costs.'

We differentiate a liquidity cost effect from a supply effect, and our distinction is similar to that drawn by Kraus and Stoll (1972). A liquidity cost effect on share price represents compensation to the marginal buyer through a temporary deviation from the equilibrium price at the offering, and a price recovery following the sale of shares. A supply effect represents a change in equilibrium price and does not imply a price recovery. Therefore, for registered secondaries a supply effect is expected to occur in response to the initial announcement in an efficient market. In contrast, a liquidity cost effect is expected to occur at the offering, since this effect represents compensation to the buyers.

The average daily stock returns in the first few days following the distribution date of registered secondaries (table 6) and non-registered secondaries (table 5) show no evidence of a price recovery that supports a liquidity cost effect.[23] The only evidence of positive returns is observed six or more days after registered offerings. This is in contrast to Kraus and Stoll's finding of a price decline and a partial price recovery by the close of trading following large block trades they classify as sales.

There are two possible reasons that we do not detect a temporary decrease in price associated with secondaries. First, the price decline and recovery may be observable only in intraday price changes. Second, as pointed out by Kraus and Stoll, there may be no compensation to the buyers of underwritten secondaries because underwriters provide liquidity to sellers by locating investors willing to buy all of the shares at the prevailing market price, and guaranteeing the net proceeds of the sale.

It may be costly to identify investors willing to buy at the current market price when the relative offering size is large. That is, the relative size of a secondary offering is a possible determinant of selling costs that are reflected in the underwriting spread. One view of this relation is that the marginal costs of search for buyers increase with the relative size of the offering. A second view is that underwriters provide assurance to potential buyers about the accuracy of information about the sale. The costs of providing this assurance may depend on the relative size of the offering, since offering size is a possible determinant of the market's perception of unfavorable information. Therefore, we test the following proposition:

> The relative underwriting spread of a secondary is positively related to the relative size of the offering.

That is, an effect of an increase in relative size of the offering is an increase in underwriting costs per share.

Table 12 presents estimates of cross-sectional regressions of underwriting spread per share on the relative size of the offering and on the natural log of the total dollar value of the offering ($DVAL$). We measure offering size relative to the number of shares outstanding ($SIZE1$) as well as relative to average daily trading volume measured over the six months preceding the announce-

---

[23] We do not have an explanation for the significant positive average prediction errors on the second, third and fourth trading days that follow the announcement date of registered secondaries (table 5). The pattern of returns suggests a price recovery, but it is unclear how these returns can be interpreted as compensation to the eventual buyers or as a liquidity cost effect. We are unaware of a theory that predicts positive stock returns between the announcement and distribution dates of secondaries.

Table 12

Estimated coefficients for regressions of the underwriting spread on measures of size and natural log of the dollar value of the offering for 146 registered secondaries and 321 non-registered secondary distributions of common stock (1972–1981) (*t*-statistics are in parentheses).

| | Independent variables[a] | | | | | |
| Sample | Const. (1) | SIZE1 (2) | SIZE2 (3) | ln(DVAL) (4) | $R^2$ | F-stat.[b] |
|---|---|---|---|---|---|---|
| (1) Registered secondaries | 0.123 (19.64) | 0.056 (5.18) | | −0.088 (−12.78) | 0.58 | 98.18 (3,143) |
| (2) Registered secondaries | 0.126 (19.63) | | 0.00003 (3.90) | −0.008 (−12.62) | 0.55 | 86.49 (3,143) |
| (3) Non-registered secondaries | 0.110 (14.29) | 0.220 (4.64) | | −0.009 (−8.76) | 0.21 | 41.73 (3,318) |
| (4) Non-registered secondaries | 0.108 (14.30) | | 0.0002 (5.42) | −0.009 (−8.69) | 0.23 | 46.38 (2,319) |

[a] Independent variables are defined as follows: *SIZE1* = number of shares offered divided by number of shares outstanding, *SIZE2* = number of shares offered divided by average daily trading volume for the six months preceding the month of the announcement, and *DVAL* = dollar value of the offering.

[b] The *F*-statistic tests the hypothesis that all the coefficients (including the intercept) are different from zero. Degrees of freedom are in parentheses under the *F*-statistic.

ment month (*SIZE2*). Motivation for the second independent variable (*DVAL*) is provided by Smith (1977), who reports that underwriting spread decreases by incrementally smaller amounts as the dollar value of primary offerings of common stock increases. We investigate whether there is a positive association between underwriting spread and the relative size of the offering, controlling for the effect of the dollar value of the offering.

The positive and significant coefficients reported in columns 2 and 3 suggest that in both the registered and non-registered samples there is a positive relation between underwriting spread and the relative size of the offering, regardless of the measure of size.[24] The coefficients on the log of the dollar value of the offering presented in column 4 are negative and significant, consistent with the summary data presented in Smith (1977).

The regressions reported in table 12 are also estimated using a dependent variable that measures the sum of the underwriting spread and the proportional discount between the offer price and the closing market price on the offering date. The new dependent variable equals the difference between the

---

[24] To investigate the view that underwriters provide assurance to buyers about the accuracy of information, an index variable is added to the regressions reported in rows 1 and 2 in table 12. The variable equals one if the seller is classified as an officer or director and equals zero otherwise. Presumably the effort required in assuring investors about the accurate disclosure of information is greater for secondaries by officers and directors. We find, however, that the coefficient on this index variable is not significant at the 0.10 level.

closing market price and the offering price net of underwriting spread, divided by the closing market price. The coefficients for *SIZE1* and *SIZE2* are positive and significant at the 0.01 level in each regression, and are not sufficiently different from the results in table 12 to warrant a detailed presentation.

The positive relation between underwriting spread and relative offering size, demonstrated in table 12, suggests that for secondary distributions a component of underwriting compensation is related to the costs of selling shares. This holds under the assumption that the effort underwriters expend providing liquidity to sellers increases with the relative size of the offering. Furthermore, given Kraus and Stoll's finding of an intraday price recovery following large block transactions, one can argue that without underwriting secondary distributions completed within the same amount of time would be associated with larger price discounts than are observed in our samples.[25] Therefore, our failure to find a large average discount between closing price and offering price or a price decline and recovery around the offering date does not necessarily imply that liquidity costs are unimportant for secondaries.

## 6. Summary and conclusions

This study reports significant negative average stock returns at the earliest public announcement of secondary distributions of common stock and documents the substantial underwriting and other costs involved. The average two-day risk-adjusted stock return at the initial announcement is $-2.87\%$ for registered secondaries and is $-1.96\%$ for non-registered secondaries. Average underwriting compensation is approximately 5% of the value of the offering for both registered and non-registered secondaries. Average total selling costs are 6.7% for registered offerings and are 5.0% for non-registered offerings. Overall, our evidence does not support the view that a shareholder can sell a large quantity of shares within a short period of time at the prevailing market price and at a small cost.

[25] Scholes (1972, p. 208) states that the seller incurs similar costs in selling shares through a secondary versus selling shares in the open market after news of the sale is divulged. For our sample of non-registered secondaries, on average the seller incurs costs of 5.0% (see table 11). If the seller waits until the market fully incorporates news of the secondary, say five days after the offering, the average additional price decrease is $-3.0\%$. Therefore, if the commission costs of selling shares are less than 2.0%, the total costs incurred by the seller appear to be lower when shares are sold in the market, even if the market has fully incorporated news of the sale. An alternative view of these data is that on average the commission and liquidity costs of selling a large number of shares without the services of an underwriter are at least 2.0%; otherwise sellers would not choose an underwritten secondary as the method to sell shares.

The seller of a registered secondary on average incurs cost of 6.7% and does not avoid a price effect due to news of the offering, since these offerings are announced in advance. The substantial decrease in wealth borne by the sellers of registered offerings suggests that there are substantial costs of selling the shares without the services of an underwriter. It is unclear why a shareholder sells shares through a registered secondary offering, if the costs of selling the shares in the market are only the normal commission costs of a large block transaction.

We analyze various characteristics of sellers of registered secondary offerings that may determine the stock price response to the initial announcement. We find evidence that the decrease in stock price is greater for offerings by officers or directors, consistent with an effect that reflects the market's inference that the seller holds unfavorable information about the firm. The announcement period stock price response is not significantly related to the seller's pre-offering or post-offering ownership stake nor to the dollar value of the offering. We also find weak evidence of a negative relation between the announcement period stock return and the size of the offering measured relative to total shares outstanding. This evidence could be interpreted as consistent with less than perfectly elastic demand for shares. However, this result is also consistent with a relation between relative offering size and the market's perception that the seller holds unfavorable information.

Perhaps the most striking finding of our study is that significant negative stock price effects are observed for all types of secondaries. Regardless of the type of seller or the size of the offering, news of a secondary is met with a decrease in share price. One interpretation is that the market's perception of investors with inside information is much broader than just corporate insiders. A second interpretation is that unfavorable information is conveyed by the event of a sale. That is, a secondary informs the market that the seller, or a selling agent, was unsuccessful in locating a buyer willing to acquire the entire block of shares at or above the prevailing market price. Thus, information that reduces share price possibly is conveyed by the characteristics of the buyer(s) of a concentrated holding of shares, as well as by the method of sale and the particular characteristics of the offering.

No evidence of a temporary price decrease that reflects compensation to the buyers is observed in daily stock returns immediately following the distribution date. We find, however, that the underwriting spread of secondaries is related positively to the relative size of the offering, controlling for the effect of dollar value of the offering. This is consistent with the argument that the underwriting spread in part reflects compensation for the underwriters' selling effort or liquidity services, and that selling effort depends on relative offering size. Therefore, even though we find no evidence of a decrease in share price followed by a price recovery for secondary offerings, we cannot conclude that the costs of liquidity are unimportant. The evidence is consistent with Kraus and Stoll's suggestion that the selling effort of underwriters in secondaries mitigates the temporary decrease in share price that otherwise would be associated with the sale of a large quantity of shares within a short period of time.

Finally, the significant stock price effects and substantial costs of offering shares in a secondary distribution raise three questions that we leave unanswered. First, what benefits to the selling shareholders offset the costs of secondaries? For example, it is unclear what factors motivate a shareholder to sell shares in a secondary offering when the average sum of underwriting and other costs exceeds 5% of the value of the offering and the average price response to the announcement of the offering is less than $-2\%$. Second, can the selling stockholder, or the firm whose shares are being sold, take actions to reduce the stock price effects? For example, as Black and Scholes (1974) propose, the selling stockholder may be able to convey a credible signal to market participants that the sale is not motivated by private information. Our results, however, indicate that significant price effects are associated with both small and large offerings, with registered and non-registered offerings and with offerings by all types of sellers. Third, how do the costs of a secondary compare to the costs of alternative methods of selling a large number of shares?

# References

Asquith, P. and D. Mullins, 1983, Equity issues and stock price dilution, Unpublished paper (Harvard Business School, Cambridge, MA).

Black, F. and M. Scholes, 1974, From theory to a new financial product, Journal of Finance 29, 399–412.

Bradley, M. and L. Wakeman, 1983, The wealth effects of targeted share repurchases, Journal of Financial Economics 11, 301–328.

Brown, S. and J. Warner, 1985, Using daily stock returns: The case of event studies, Journal of Financial Economics 14, 3–31.

Daniel, W.W., 1978, Applied nonparametric statistics (Houghton Mifflin, Boston, MA).

Hess, A. and P. Frost, 1982, Tests for price effects of new issues of seasoned securities, Journal of Finance 37, 11–26.

Hirshleifer, J., 1980, Price theory and applications, 2nd ed. (Prentice Hall, New York).

Investment Dealers' Digest, 1972–1982, Corporate financing directory (The Dealers' Digest Publ. Co., New York).

Johnston, J., 1972, Econometric methods, 2nd ed. (McGraw-Hill, New York).

Kraus, A. and H. Stoll, 1972, Price impacts of block trading on the New York Stock Exchange, Journal of Finance 27, 569–588.

Mikkelson, W. and R. Ruback, 1984, Corporate investments in common stock, Unpublished paper (College of Business, University of Oregon, Eugene, OR, and Sloan School of Management, M.I.T., Cambridge, MA).

Ryngaert, M., 1983, An examination of large scale security transactions, Unpublished paper (Graduate School of Business, University of Chicago, Chicago, IL).

Security Owner's Stock Guide, 1971–1981 (Standard and Poor's, New York).

Scholes, M., 1972, The market for securities: Substitution versus price pressure and the effects of information on share price, Journal of Business 45, 179–211.

Smith, C., 1977, Alternative methods for raising capital: Rights versus underwritten offerings, Journal of Financial Economics 5, 273–307.

# SYNERGISTIC GAINS FROM CORPORATE ACQUISITIONS AND THEIR DIVISION BETWEEN THE STOCKHOLDERS OF TARGET AND ACQUIRING FIRMS*

Michael BRADLEY

*University of Michigan, Ann Arbor, MI 48109, USA*

Anand DESAI

*University of Florida, Gainesville, FL 32611, USA*

E. Han KIM

*University of Michigan, Ann Arbor, MI 48109, USA*

Received August 1984, final version received December 1987

This paper documents that a successful tender offer increases the combined value of the target and acquiring firms by an average of 7.4%. We also provide a theoretical analysis of the process of competition for control of the target and empirical evidence that competition among bidding firms increases the returns to targets and decreases the returns to acquirers, that the supply of target shares is positively sloped, and that changes in the legal/institutional environment of tender offers have had no impact on the total (percentage) synergistic gains created but have significantly affected their division between the stockholders of the target and acquiring firms.

## 1. Introduction

There is empirical evidence that corporate acquisitions effected through tender offers are wealth-increasing transactions for the stockholders of both the target and acquiring firms [Dodd and Ruback (1977) and Bradley (1980)]. Moreover, Bradley, Desai, and Kim (1983) show that these gains are not due to the market's reassessment of previously undervalued securities. They docu-

*This paper is a substantially revised version of earlier drafts entitled 'Specialized Resources and Competition in the Market for Corporate Control' (September 1982) and 'Determinants of the Wealth Effects of Corporate Acquisitions via Tender Offers: Theory and Evidence' (September 1983). We have received valuable comments and criticism from participants of finance workshops at Buffalo, Berkeley–Stanford, Concordia, Indiana, Michigan, Minnesota, Northwestern, NYU, Ohio State, Purdue, Rutgers, SMU, Toronto, UCLA, USC, VPI, Washington University, Wharton, and Wisconsin/Madison. In addition we would like to thank Cliff Ball, Robert Comment, Gregg Jarrell, Stanley Kon, Richard Leftwich (a referee of earlier drafts), John McConnell, Philip Perry, Myron Scholes, an anonymous referee of the most recent draft and, especially, Michael Jensen (the editor) for their helpful comments. This research was supported by Michigan Business School Summer Research Grants.

Journal of Financial Economics 21 (1988) 3–40. North-Holland

ment that the positive revaluation of the target's shares is permanent only if the offer is successful, i.e., only if the resources of the two firms are combined. This evidence is consistent with the synergy theory of tender offers, which posits that the acquisition of control over the target enables the acquirer to redeploy the combined assets of the two firms toward higher-valued uses.

None of the above studies, however, documents the magnitude of the synergistic gains that result from successful acquisitions achieved through tender offers. Indeed, whether or not such acquisitions result in synergistic gains is still a contentious issue in the literature. For example, Roll (1986) has proposed the 'Hubris Hypothesis', which posits that the gains to target shareholders represent wealth transfers from acquiring firms' shareholders and not necessarily synergistic gains. To test this hypothesis, it is necessary to measure synergistic gains using matched pairs of target and acquiring firms. None of the earlier studies impose this requirement on their samples.

In this paper, we estimate the magnitude of the synergistic gains, using the revaluation of the combined wealth of target-firm and acquiring-firm share-holders as a basis. We also examine the factors that determine the division of these gains between the stockholders of the two firms and document how the division and the total gains created have changed with the changing environment of the tender offer process.

This paper is organized as follows. In section 2 we estimate the synergistic gains created by successful tender offers. In section 3 we analyze how these gains are divided between the stockholders of the target and acquiring firms. Section 3 also summarizes our analysis of competition among bidding firms, which is presented more fully in the appendix. We present our empirical results on competition and the division of gains in section 4. A summary and concluding remarks are presented in section 5.

## 2. Synergistic gains

### 2.1. Definition of synergy

We assume that a tender offer is an attempt by the bidding firm to exploit a profit opportunity created by a change in economic conditions. This change may be the result of an exogenous change in supply and/or demand, techno-logical innovations, or purposeful investments by the bidding firm. The value created by the combination may result from more efficient management, economies of scale, improved production techniques, the combination of complementary resources, the redeployment of assets to more profitable uses, the exploitation of market power, or any number of value-creating mecha-nisms that fall under the general rubric of corporate synergy. We define the total synergistic gain from a successful tender offer as the sum of the change in the wealth of the stockholders of the target and acquiring firms:

$$\Delta \Pi = \Delta W_{\text{T}} + \Delta W_{\text{A}}, \tag{1}$$

where

$\Delta \Pi$   = total synergistic gain,
$\Delta W_{\mathrm{T}}$ = change in target-firm shareholders' wealth, and
$\Delta W_{\mathrm{A}}$ = change in acquiring-firm stockholders' wealth.

This definition assumes that corporate acquisitions effected through inter-firm tender offers have no effect on the wealth of the senior claimants (e.g., bondholders and other creditors) of the firms involved. Kim and McConnell (1977) and Asquith and Kim (1982) provide evidence that is consistent with this assumption for a sample of firms involved in corporate mergers.

## 2.2. Sample description

Our study is based on a sample of successful tender offer contests occurring over the period 1963–1984. We identify the beginning of a tender offer contest with the announcement of a bid for a given target. If there is only one bid, the contest ends when the offer is executed. The average duration between the announcement and the execution of a tender offer is three to four weeks. If additional bids are made by the same or another firm while the initial bid is outstanding, our definition of the contest is extended through the execution of the last bid made. The duration of a contest is also extended if a subsequent bid is made within 14 trading days of the expiration of a previous bid.

The primary data base consists of 921 interfirm tender offers, reflecting contests for 721 target firms between October 1958 and December 1984.[1] From this data base we select our sample according to the following criteria: (1) The winning bidder in each contest purchased at least some of the outstanding target shares, (2) the acquisition took place after 1963, and (3) the shares of *both* the target and acquiring firms were traded on the New York Stock Exchange (NYSE) or the American Stock Exchange (AMEX) at the time of the acquisition. The first criterion is imposed because our definition of synergistic gains applies only to successful tender offers.[2] The last two criteria enable us to use the CRSP (Center for Research in Security Prices) daily stock return data to calculate the total synergistic gain from an acquisition.

These selection criteria reduce our initial sample of 721 tender offer contests to 236. Summary statistics for the percentage of target shares held, sought, and

---

[1] Tender offers through 1977 were identified with the help of the data bases compiled by Bradley (1980) and Dodd and Ruback (1977). Relevant information for all offers was collected and/or verified with citations in the *Wall Street Journal* (index and newspaper).

[2] Rather than imposing some arbitrary cut-off point for the definition of a successful tender offer, we include in our sample all offers in which the bidding firm bought any number of target shares. The smallest percentage of shares purchased is 2.0. Although this may appear small, one should recognize that the control of a corporation lies along a continuum from none for those who own no shares to complete for those who own 100% of the firm's voting shares. From this perspective, the acquisition of even 2.0% may significantly alter the power of voting coalitions and affect the operations of the firm.

Table 1

Descriptive statistics of the percentage of target shares held, sought, and purchased by the acquiring firms in 236 successful tender offer contests effected over the period 1963–1984.[a]

| | Percent of target shares[b] | | |
| | Held | Sought | Purchased |
|---|---|---|---|
| Mean | 9.8 | 66.2 | 60.4 |
| Standard deviation | 18.2 | 32.2 | 30.2 |
| Median | 0 | 67.2 | 62.8 |
| Minimum | 0 | 5.4 | 2.0 |
| Maximum | 78.0 | 100.0 | 100.0 |

[a] We define a successful tender offer as one in which the bidding firm buys some (however few) of the target shares pursuant to the terms of the bid.
[b] The denominator of all these percentages is the total number of shares outstanding.

purchased in the 236 successful tender offers are reported in table 1. Of the 236 acquiring firms, 155 held no target shares prior to the offer. The 236 acquiring firms sought, on average, 66.2% of the target shares. The mean as well as the median fraction of target shares ultimately purchased in our total sample is in excess of 50%. Thus the 'typical' acquiring firm in our sample held no target shares prior to the offer but held a majority of the outstanding target shares upon successful execution of the offer.

### 2.3. Methodology

Our estimates of the gains created by tender offers are based on market model prediction errors. Under the assumption of multivariate normality, the abnormal return (prediction error) to firm $i$ on day $t$ can be written as

$$AR_{it} = R_{it} - \hat{\alpha}_i - \hat{\beta}_i R_{mt},\qquad(2)$$

where

$AR_{it}$ = abnormal return to firm $i$ on day $t$,
$R_{it}$ = realized return to firm $i$ on day $t$,
$\hat{\alpha}_i, \hat{\beta}_i$ = market model parameter estimates, and
$R_{mt}$ = return to the equally-weighted CRSP market portfolio on day $t$.

The market model parameter estimates for each target firm are obtained using a maximum of 240 trading days of daily returns data beginning 300 days before the announcement of the first tender offer bid in the contest. Estimates for the acquiring firms are obtained using 240 trading days of returns data beginning 300 days before the first bid made for the target by this firm.[3]

For each of the 472 firms in our sample, we cumulate the daily abnormal return over a contest-specific interval to obtain the cumulative abnormal return ($CAR$). The $CAR$ is computed from five trading days before the announcement of the first bid through five days after the announcement of the ultimately successful bid. We begin to cumulate the $CAR$ five days before the announcement of the initial bid in order to capture any anticipatory price behavior (leakage of information) that may occur before the actual public announcement.

Ideally, we would like to extend our $CAR$ window until the day just before the offer is executed. Reliable execution dates are not available, however, for most of the offers in our sample. The postannouncement interval of five trading days is consistent with the requirement in the 1968 Williams Amendment that tendered shares can be withdrawn within seven calendar days (five trading days). The seven-calendar-day withdrawal period was extended to 15 business days in 1970, and starting in 1978 the regulation required that all tender offers remain open for 20 business days.

We do not extend the $CAR$ window through the execution of the offer because this would cause a downward bias in the measured returns to target shareholders. This downward bias stems from the necessary condition for a successful tender offer that the offer price, $P_T$, be greater than the expected postexecution price of the remaining target shares, $P_E$. (See the appendix.) The premium ($P_T - P_E$) can be likened to a dividend paid to tendering

---

[3] In a recent paper Loderer and Mauer (1986) argue that the market model parameter estimates for acquiring firms will be biased if the estimation period is confined to the period just before the acquisition. Specifically, they argue that the estimate of the constant $\alpha$ will be biased upward because many acquiring firms initiate acquisition programs – indeed, investment programs in general – following a period of earnings growth. This overstimate of $\alpha$ for acquiring firms will result in a negative bias in the market model residuals (prediction errors) after the acquisition. Clearly, whether using preoffer data biases the estimate of the constant is an empirical issue.

To examine this issue, we estimated the market model parameters for the acquiring firms twice: first, using preoffer data as described above, and second, using 240 days beginning 20 days following the execution of the offer. The mean of the preoffer $\alpha$'s is $-0.01\%$ ($\sigma = 0.13\%$) and the mean of the postoffer $\alpha$'s is $-0.02\%$ ($\sigma = 0.13\%$). Although the mean of the preoffer $\alpha$'s is larger (a less negative number) than the mean of the postoffer $\alpha$'s, neither estimate is significantly different from zero or significantly different from the other. Moreover, if the preoffer $\alpha$'s are systematically greater than the postoffer $\alpha$'s, a linear regression of preoffer $\alpha$'s on the postoffer $\alpha$'s should yield either a slope coefficient greater than one and/or a positive constant. Contrary to this prediction, a simple linear regression yields the following results:

$$\text{Pre } \alpha_i = -0.00012 + 0.126 \text{ Post } \alpha_i, \qquad R^2 = 0.015.$$
$$(t = -1.4) \ (t = 1.9)$$

With these results and because our typical estimation period for cumulative abnormal returns is only 11 days, we feel that our results will not be significantly biased by using the preoffer $\alpha$'s. We should note that the Loderer and Mauer analysis is based on monthly data whereas ours is based on daily data. Perhaps the misestimation of the $\alpha$ of acquiring firms is important (significant) only when monthly data are used.

stockholders. As such, the target shares will trade 'cum-dividend' after the announcement until just before the execution and 'ex-dividend' after the execution. The 'cum-dividend' return is the relevant measure of the gain to target stockholders.

Ending the $CAR$ window before the execution of the offer subjects our estimates to two potential biases. On the one hand, there is still a positive probability of failure after the end of the $CAR$ window, and hence, our estimate of returns might be downward biased. On the other hand, to the extent that the market assigns a positive probability that the outstanding offer will be topped by a higher-valued bid, the measure will be an overestimate. We feel that the choice of five trading days after the announcement of the ultimately successful offer as the end of the window represents a reasonable tradeoff between these possible sources of bias.[4]

[4] We recognize that our $CAR$ statistic is but one measure of the increase in the wealth of target stockholders. An alternative measure has been proposed by Jensen (1985) and Comment and Jarrell (1987). These authors employ what has become known as the blended premium ($BP$), which is defined as

$$BP = [(F)(P_T - P_0) + (1 - F)(P_E - P_0)]/P_0,$$

where $F$ is the fraction of target shares purchased at $P_T$ and $P_0$ is the pre-offer market price of the target shares.

As mentioned above, the necessary data for some of the variables in this equation are not available. However, for the 52 tender offers in our sample that were effected over the period 1981–1984, we were able to obtain all the necessary data from Robert Comment and Gregg Jarrell. For each of the offers in this subsample, we calculate a blended premium, using the closing price six days prior to the public announcement of the offer as a measure of $P_0$.

The mean $BP$ for these 52 firms is 43.03%. In comparison, our $CAR$ measure for this portfolio of firms is 35.34% (see table 2). A simple linear regression of $CAR$ on $BP$ yields the following results:

| | | |
|---|---|---|
| Model: | $CAR = \gamma_0 + \gamma_1 (BP)$ | |
| Coefficient: | 0.018 0.779 | |
| Standard error: | 0.019 0.037 | |
| $R^2$ and $F$-statistic: | 0.902 442.3 | |

Although the estimate of the constant ($\gamma_0$) in this regression is insignificantly different from zero, the estimate of the slope coefficient ($\gamma_1$) is significantly less than 1.0. Thus, both the regression results and the difference in means indicate that our $CAR$ measure is systematically less than $BP$ by roughly 7.7%.

There are a number of reasons why we would expect $CAR$ to be systematically less than $BP$. As discussed above, there still may be a positive probability that the outstanding offer will be unsuccessful even five days after the announcement of the ultimately successful offer, which is the end of our $CAR$ window. If this were the reason for the discrepancy, however, we would expect to see the $CAR$ to single-bidder targets rise after our cutoff date. No such increase is observed (see table 3 and fig. 2). Moreover, there are at least two computational reasons why $CAR$ is systematically less than $BP$, and these explanations can easily account for the 7.7% difference.

First, $CAR$ is, by design, net of market movements. The average duration of the offers in this sample is 22 trading days or one trading month. The average monthly return to the CRSP equally-weighted market portfolio between 1981 and 1984 is roughly 1.7%. Since the average Beta of the firms in this sample is 0.996, 1.7% of the 7.7% difference between $BP$ and $CAR$ can be attributed to general market movements.

A second reason for the disparity between $CAR$ and $BP$ is that the former is a sum of (abnormal) returns whereas the latter is essentially a continuously compounded return. Given that

Our *CAR* algorithm generates an 11-day window for all but 15 tender offers in which there is only one bidder. For tender offer contests in which there is more than one bidder, the window for targets varies, with a mean of 43 trading days and a standard deviation of 52 trading days.

Using these variable-window *CAR*s, we estimate the dollar gain to the target and acquiring firms in each tender offer contest $i$ as

$$\Delta \hat{W}_{\mathrm{T}i} = W_{\mathrm{T}i} \cdot CART_i, \qquad \Delta \hat{W}_{\mathrm{A}i} = W_{\mathrm{A}i} \cdot CARA_i, \tag{3}$$

where

$W_{\mathrm{T}i}$     = market value of the target equity as of the end of six trading days prior to the first announcement for the target, minus the value of the target shares held by the acquirer,

$CART_i$ = cumulative abnormal return to the target firm from five trading days before the announcement of the first bid through five trading days after the announcement of the ultimately successful bid,

$W_{\mathrm{A}i}$     = market value of the acquiring firm as of the end of six days prior to the first announcement made by the acquiring firm,

$CARA_i$ = cumulative abnormal return to the acquiring firm from five trading days before the announcement of the first offer made by this firm through five trading days after the announcement of the ultimately successful bid.

Conceptually, an empirical measure of the total percentage synergistic gains created by the $i$th tender offer would be a weighted average of *CART* and *CARA*. Since *CART* and *CARA* are based on different event windows, however, they are not directly comparable. Moreover, we have no information on the statistical properties of such a weighted average.

To circumvent these statistical problems, our estimate of the total percentage synergistic gains is based on the *CAR* to a value-weighted *portfolio* of the $i$th target and the $i$th acquiring firm, where the weights used are $W_{\mathrm{T}i}$ and $W_{\mathrm{A}i}$ as defined above. Market model parameter estimates for each of the 236 value-weighted portfolios are obtained using 240 trading days of portfolio returns beginning 300 days before the first tender offer bid in the contest. The

---

the returns to the targets are predominantly positive over the tender offer period, it follows that the sum of the daily (abnormal) returns will be strictly less than a continuously compounded return. For example, the sum of 2% per day for 22 days is 44%, whereas the continuously compounded return of 2% for 22 days is 55%.

In sum, our *CAR* measure is less than the *BP* measure used by Jensen and by Comment and Jarrell. However, it is not at all clear which is superior. One obvious advantage of the *CAR* statistic is that it has known statistical properties and therefore can be used in hypothesis testing.

combined percentage synergistic gain created by a successful tender offer, $CARC_i$, is measured by cumulating the abnormal returns to this portfolio from five trading days before the announcement of the first bid through five days after the announcement of the ultimately successful bid. Using this percentage measure, we estimate the total dollar synergistic gain, $\Delta\hat{\Pi}_i$, as

$$\Delta\hat{\Pi}_i = \Pi_i \cdot CARC_i, \tag{4}$$

where

$$\Pi_i = W_{Ti} + W_{Ai}.$$

## 2.4. Estimate of synergistic gains

Table 2 reports our measures of the synergistic gains created by tender offers, as well as the changes in the wealth of the stockholders of the target and acquiring firms. The data in the last column of the top panel of table 2 (labeled *Combined*) show that the combined value of the target and acquiring firms increased, on average, by 7.43%, with 75% of the combined revaluations being positive. Our estimate of this percentage synergistic gain is statistically greater than zero ($z = 19.95$).[5]

The mean total dollar gain created by the acquisitions in our sample is $117 million (expressed in December 1984 dollars). Since the distribution of our

---

[5] This $z$-statistic is computed following Patell's (1976) eq. (11). Specifically, we compute the standardized abnormal return to the $i$th portfolio on day $t$, $SAR_{it}$, defined as

$$SAR_{it} = AR_{it} \left/ \left[ \sigma_i \left( 1 + \frac{1}{T_i} + \frac{(R_{mt} - \overline{R}_m)^2}{\sum_\tau (R_{m\tau} - \overline{R}_m)^2} \right)^{1/2} \right] \right.,$$

where

$\sigma_i$ = standard deviation of the residuals in the market model estimation period,
$T_i$ = number of days in the estimation period, and
$\overline{R}_m$ = mean return to the market portfolio over the estimation period.

The $SAR_{it}$ is then used to obtain the standardized $CAR_i$ over $K_i$ event days:

$$SCAR_i = \left[ \sum_{t=1}^{K_i} SAR_{it} \right] \left/ \sqrt{K_i} \right. .$$

Finally, the $z$-statistic for the portfolio of $N_p$ firms in the sample is computed as

$$z = \sum_{i=1}^{N_p} SCAR_i \left/ \left[ \sum_{i=1}^{N_p} ((T_i - 2)/(T_i - 4)) \right]^{1/2} \right. .$$

Table 2

Mean percentage and dollar synergistic gains to 236 successful tender offer contests effected between 1963 and 1984 for combined, target, and acquiring firms. All dollar figures are stated in millions of 1984 dollars.[a]

| | Subperiod | | | Total |
|---|---|---|---|---|
| | 7/63–6/68 | 7/68–12/80 | 1/81–12/84 | 7/63–12/84 |
| No. of contests | 51 | 133 | 52 | 236 |
| *Combined* | | | | |
| % $CARC$ | 7.78[b] | 7.08[b] | 8.00[b] | 7.43[b] |
| $\$\Delta\hat{\Pi}$ | 91.08 | 87.45 | 218.51 | 117.11 |
| % Positive | 78 | 74 | 73 | 75 |
| *Targets* | | | | |
| % $CART$ | 18.92[b] | 35.29[b] | 35.34[b] | 31.77[b] |
| $\$\Delta\hat{W}_T$ | 70.71 | 71.59 | 233.53 | 107.08 |
| % Positive | 94 | 98 | 90 | 95 |
| *Acquirers* | | | | |
| % $CARA$ | 4.09[b] | 1.30 | −2.93[b] | 0.97[b] |
| $\$\Delta\hat{W}_A$ | 24.96 | 31.80 | −27.28 | 17.30 |
| % Positive | 59 | 48 | 35 | 47 |

[a] $\Delta\hat{W}_T = W_T * CART$; $\Delta\hat{W}_A = W_A * CARA$; and $\Delta\hat{\Pi} = (W_T + W_A) * CARC$; where $W_T$ = preoffer market value of target equity, excluding shares held by the acquirer; $W_A$ = preoffer market value of equity of acquiring firm; $CART$ = cumulative abnormal return from five days before the first offer to five days after the last offer made for this target; $CARA$ = cumulative abnormal return from five days before the first offer to five days after the last offer made by this bidding firm; $CARC$ = cumulative abnormal return to the value-weighted portfolio of the target and the acquiring firm, measured over the same interval as $CART$.
[b] Significantly different from zero at the 0.01 level.

dollar measure $\Delta\hat{\Pi}$ is extremely leptokurtic and skewed to the right (the skewness and kurtosis coefficients are 6.70 and 62.38, respectively), we conduct the nonparametric Wilcoxon Signed Rank test to test if the median $\Delta\hat{\Pi}$ of $26.9 million for the total sample is statistically greater than zero. This test yields a $z$-statistic of 9.30, which is significant at the 1% level.

Table 2 also reports data for three subperiods: 1963–1968, 1968–1980, and 1981–1984. Although this division is somewhat arbitrary, there have been some dramatic changes in the tender offer process during the 22-year period under study, and these three subperiods correspond roughly to the three distinct regimes that have existed in the legal and institutional environment of tender offers since 1963.

The first period (1963–1968) is important because before 1968, cash tender offers were free of government regulation. They were considered private transactions between the acquiring firm and the stockholders of the target firm. In July 1968 Congress passed the Williams Amendment, which brought the tender offer within the purview of the Securities and Exchange Commission (SEC). In the same year, Virginia enacted the first state antitakeover statute; by 1978, 36 states had enacted their own takeover regulations. By isolating the offers that occurred in the unregulated period, we can examine the effects of government regulation on the magnitude and division of the synergistic gains from tender offers.

The last period (1981–1984) is distinguished by three factors that have drastically changed the environment in which tender offers take place. First is the avowed laissez-faire attitude of the Reagan Administration toward corporate takeovers in general.[6] Second is the development of sophisticated tactics to repel takeovers (poison pills, targeted share repurchases, lock-up provisions, and supermajority and fair-price amendments). The third factor is the advent of investment banking firms that specialize in raising funds to finance corporate takeovers. We are interested in how these recent developments in the market for corporate control have affected the gains created by tender offers.

The data in the top panel of table 2 indicate that the percentage synergistic gains created by tender offers have remained remarkably constant, between 7% and 8%, over the three subperiods. The dollar gains, however, have increased dramatically from the first two subperiods to the third; expressed in December 1984 dollars, the average synergistic gain has grown from $91 million and $87 million in the first two subperiods to $219 million in the 1981–1984 subperiod.

This increase in the dollar synergistic gains, but not in the percentage synergistic gains, is due to the increase in the size of target firms. The mean preoffer market value of targets increased from $379 million in the first period to $550 million in the last period, while the average size of acquiring firms actually dropped from $1,624 million to $1,477 million.

The increase in the size of the target firms in the third period may be due to the laissez-faire attitude of the Reagan Administration and innovative financing methods of investment banking firms. Also, the popularity of two-tier offers has reduced the cash outlays required of bidding firms.[7] These developments in the takeover arena have made it easier for bidding firms to seek control of larger targets.

In the next section we identify the factors that determine how the synergy gains created by tender offers are divided between the stockholders of the target and acquiring firms. The data presented in the last two panels of table 2 allow us to draw some preliminary conclusions on this issue.

---

[6]See the Economic Report of the President, 1985, especially ch. 6.

[7]In the typical two-tier offer, the bidding firm makes a cash offer for a fraction of the target shares (usually 51% or more) and agrees to purchase the remainder if the offer is successful. Often, the remaining shares are purchased by an exchange of securities. Thus, the cash outlay for the shares purchased through a fractional tender offer is less than the outlay necessary for an any-or-all cash offer.

The overwhelming conclusion is that target stockholders capture the majority of the gains from tender offers. Ninety-five percent of the targets in the total sample experienced a positive abnormal return. The average abnormal return is 32% and the ratio of the mean dollar gain to targets to the mean dollar total gain ($\Delta \hat{W}_T / \Delta \hat{\Pi}$) is 91%. In contrast, the average abnormal return to acquiring firms is 0.97%, only 47% of the observations are positive, and the ratio of the mean dollar gain to the mean total gain ($\Delta \hat{W}_A / \Delta \hat{\Pi}$) is 15%. Whether measured as rates of return or dollar gains, the lion's share of the gains from tender offers is captured by target shareholders.

The data in table 2 also indicate that the returns to acquiring firms have decreased over time, whereas the returns to targets have increased. The mean abnormal return to acquiring firms is 4.09% ($z = 5.88$) in the first period and $-2.93\%$ ($z = -2.79$) in the last. In contrast, the mean abnormal return to targets has increased from 18.92% ($z = 26.2$) to 35.34% ($z = 26.2$).

In sum, the data in table 2 compel the following conclusions:

(1) Successful tender offers generate significant synergistic gains and lead to a more efficient allocation of corporate resources.[8]
(2) The stockholders of both target and acquiring firms realize significant positive abnormal returns. However, most of the gains are captured by the stockholders of target firms.
(3) Both the rate of return and dollar gains to target stockholders have increased over time, whereas the returns to the stockholders of acquiring firms have decreased. In fact, in the most recent subperiod, acquiring firms actually suffered a significant abnormal loss.

## 3. A model of the division of the gains from interfirm tender offers

In the previous section we documented that corporate acquisitions made through tender offers generate significantly positive synergistic gains. In this section we attempt to identify the factors that determine the division of the synergistic gains between the stockholders of the target and acquiring firms. We begin by reviewing the important legal and institutional aspects of this capital market transaction. We then summarize and extend our analysis of the tender offer process, which is presented in the appendix. This summary and extension provide a framework within which we develop implications regarding the division of the gains from tender offers.

---

[8]We recognize that, theoretically, the gains from tender offers may stem from the creation of market power and not necessarily from increased allocative efficiency. However, the work of Eckbo (1983, 1985) and Stillman (1983) indicates that corporate acquisitions have no measurable effect on the degree of market power in the economy.

## 3.1. Regulation of tender offers

As discussed earlier, interfirm cash tender offers were not regulated by federal securities law until July 1968 when Congress passed the Williams Amendment and brought cash tender offers within the purview of the SEC.[9] Provisions of the Williams Amendment require bidding firms to provide detailed information about how the tender offer will be financed and what changes in the operations of the target will be made if the offer is successful. The regulations also specify a minimum number of days that a tender offer must remain open and a minimum number of days before the target shares can be purchased. Target stockholders who have tendered their shares to one bidding firm are allowed to withdraw their shares if a higher-valued offer is made by another firm before the required number of days for the initial offer has elapsed. Furthermore, if an outstanding offer is revised upward, then all target stockholders, even those who tendered their shares at the previous terms, must receive the higher price.

The 'disclosure and delay' requirements of federal regulations make the tender offer process similar to an open auction for the target shares. The regulations force bidding firms to reveal information about the target company and delay the offer long enough so that other potential bidding firms can discover this information. Moreover, the delay and withdrawal provisions of the regulations allow target stockholders to take advantage of competing offers similar to that which occurs in open auction markets. The delay requirements permit further production of information that may generate higher-valued bids, and the withdrawal privilege allows target stockholders to recontract and tender their shares to the firm that makes the highest-valued offer.[10]

## 3.2. Assumptions

To be consistent with the institutional setting of the tender offer process, we assume that competition for the target shares is effected through a tatônnement process. We also assume that there are no transactions costs in bidding, that target shareholders are wealth maximizers, and that managers of bidding firms seek to maximize their shareholders' wealth.

From the evidence presented in section 2, we view a tender offer as an attempt by the bidding firm to gain control of the target resources and to

---

[9]Stock tender offers (exchange offers) are regulated under the original Securities and Exchange Act of 1933 because the transaction typically involves the issuance of new stock.

[10]Fifty-one (22%) of the offers in our sample were effected prior to the passage of the Williams Amendment and were thus free of its constraints. However, voluntary practices and/or the rules of the NYSE or AMEX during the 1960s produced offers not unlike those in the post-Williams era. Thus, in most of the pre-Williams offers in our sample the bidding firm was identified, target stockholders were given at least one week to tender their shares, and oversubscribed offers were effected on a pro-rata basis.

allocate the combined resources of the two firms to higher-valued uses. We assume that to generate synergistic gains the bidding firm must secure control, which requires acquisition of at least $N_C$ of the $N_0$ target shares outstanding.[11] We do not analyze the determinants of $N_C$. Rather, we assume that $N_C$ is target-specific. We can, however, speculate on several factors that would affect its magnitude. The most obvious include the number of target shares outstanding, the concentration of these shares among the target stockholders, the predisposition of the target stockholders toward the takeover, and provisions in the firm's charter about the number of shares (votes) required to make fundamental changes in the firm's operations.

### 3.3. The tender offer process

In the appendix we present an analysis of the tender offer process within the context of the above assumptions and institutional and legal setting. We demonstrate that competition among rival management teams, including the managers of the target firm, ensures that the total value of the successful offer must be greater than or equal to the next-highest-valued allocation of the target resources.[12] Thus, given competition by target managers, the minimum value of the offer is bounded by the total preoffer market value of the target shares.

Our analysis implies a certain structure for the bidding process. In the appendix we show that a successful tender offer must be front-end loaded, i.e.,

$$P_T > P_E, \tag{5}$$

where

$P_T$ = front-end price, and

$P_E$ = back-end price.[13]

We also show that the winning bid in a tender offer contest will be the bid that maximizes the difference between $P_T$ and $P_E$. By this criterion, bidding

---

[11] It cannot be the case that the bidding firm can simply 'package' its value-creating ideas and sell them to the target firm. If this were possible, the bidding firm would never bother with the costly process of acquiring the target shares through a public tender offer. The control assumption is consistent with the finding of Bradley, Desai, and Kim (1983) that the permanent positive revaluation of target shares requires a successful acquisition of the target shares by the bidding firm.

[12] In this respect our notion of competition in the market for corporate control parallels that of Ruback (1983).

[13] If the bidding firm makes a partial offer without specifying the back-end price, we define $P_E$ as the market's expectation of the postacquisition price of the target shares not purchased.

firms have an incentive to minimize $P_E$, regardless of their valuation of the target firm. In the appendix, we argue that the minimum $P_E$ will be determined by statutes and legal standards. Thus, rival bidders will compete for control of the target by setting the back-end price to the minimum 'allowable' level and bidding for a controlling interest with their front-end price.

There is empirical evidence to support this view of the bidding process. As predicted by our analysis, the vast majority of successful tender offers are front-end loaded. Of the 52 tender offer contests for which we have estimates of $P_T$ and $P_E$ (see footnote 4), 32 satisfy the condition $P_T > P_E$. In 19 cases the two prices are (nominally) equivalent. Only in two instances is $P_T < P_E$; in one case the back-end price is \$.25 higher and in the other it is \$1.00 more. Note that the estimate of $P_E$ is the (ex-post) market price of unpurchased target shares two days after the execution of the front-end offer. Thus, nominally equivalent front- and back-end prices do not vitiate our prediction that successful tender offers must be front-end loaded. The time value of money between the execution of the front and back ends makes the present value of $P_E$ less than $P_T$. Moreover, general market movements between these two dates could account for the two aberrant cases where our measure of $P_E$ is greater than $P_T$.[14]

Also, there is evidence that of the three parameters of a tender offer, rival bidding firms typically compete with each other on the front-end price, $P_T$, rather than on the back-end price, $P_E$, or the fraction of target shares sought, $F$. In our sample of 236 tender offer contests, we can identify a total of 408 bids: 236 initial bids and 172 revised bids. Of these 172 revised bids, 127 (74%) involved an increase only in $P_T$. Four bids involved an increase in the fraction of shares sought, $F$, alone and 28 bids involved an increase in both $P_T$ and $F$. In the remaining 13 bids, the changes in $P_T$ and $F$ were in the opposite directions.

Our analysis of the tender offer process in the appendix is based on two unrealistic assumptions: (1) there are no tax consequences from tendering and (2) target stockholders have homogeneous beliefs about the outcome of the offer and about the postexecution market price of the target shares not purchased. These assumptions imply that all target stockholders have the same reservation price and hence the supply of target shares is perfectly elastic.

---

[14] In section 4.1 we provide further evidence that successful tender offers are front-end loaded. Data reported in that section show that the *CAR* to the targets of single-bidder tender offers begins to decline 18 days after the announcement of the ultimately successful bid. This period roughly coincides with the average duration of the tender offers in our sample. We interpret this price decline as the ex-dividend effect discussed above. The ex-dividend effect will result in a price decline of the target shares on the execution date only if $P_T > P_E$. Bradley (1980) and Comment and Jarrell (1987) also provide evidence that the average front-end price in successful tender offers is significantly greater than the average back-end price.

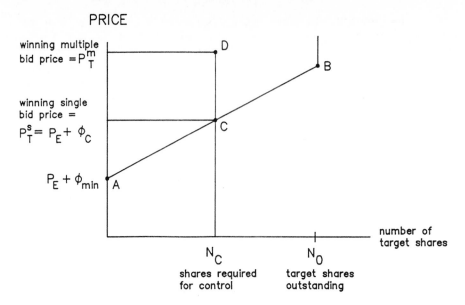

Fig. 1. The postannouncement supply of target shares with heterogeneous capital-gains tax positions and/or expectations about future takeover bids. $P_E$ = back-end price of the outstanding offer, $\phi_i$ = premium demanded by the owner of the $i$th share, $P_T^s$ = winning price in a single-bidder acquisition = the minimum price to elicit $N_C$ shares, $P_T^m$ = winning price in a multiple-bidder acquisition, $ABC$ = postannouncement supply of target shares.

Relaxing these two assumptions requires us to modify inequality (5) as follows: The owner of the $i$th target share will not tender unless

$$P_T > P_E + \phi_i, \tag{6}$$

where $\phi_i$ is the premium demanded by the owner of the $i$th share above $P_E$. The premium $\phi_i$ varies across target shareholders and represents differences in capital-gains tax positions and in expectations regarding the possibility of future acquisition activity. When tendering shares results in a realization of taxable gains, the shareholder loses an option to defer the capital-gains tax to a future date [Rosenfeld (1982)]. With heterogeneous capital-gains tax positions among target shareholders, the option will have a different value for different shareholders; hence, the premium $\phi_i$ will vary across target shareholders.

Another component of $\phi_i$ stems from differing expectations about the outcome of an outstanding offer and the probability of receiving future takeover bids. For example, all market participants may not agree that the outstanding offer represents the highest-valued bid that will be made. Some target stockholders may believe there is a positive probability that a higher-valued bidder might materialize after they tender their shares and the outstanding offer is executed.[15] From this perspective, $\phi_i$ may be thought of as the premium individual $i$ must be paid to give up the (expected) benefit from a subsequent, higher-valued takeover bid.

Given the vector $\phi_i$, the supply of target shares will be upward sloping as represented by the line $ACB$ in fig. 1. We also assume that all bidders know the minimum price required to elicit $N_C$ shares but do not know each other's maximum offer price. The minimum price required to elicit $N_C$ target shares is denoted in fig. 1 by $P_E + \phi_C$, where $\phi_C$ is the premium demanded by the owner of the $N_C$th share. This reservation price of the marginal tendering shareholder determines the minimum synergistic gain ($MSG$) that a bidding firm must be able to generate to win control of the target firm and still make a profit.

When only one firm can create synergistic gains in excess of $MSG$, that firm will bid $P_T^s = P_E + \phi_C$ and win control of the target. (See point $C$ in fig. 1.) If at least one more firm can generate synergistic gains in excess of $MSG$, an auction will ensue. As discussed above, rival bidding firms will compete by raising $P_T$. Thus, competition among bidding firms will move the target stockholders vertically off their supply curve (e.g., to point $D$ in fig. 1) and, as a consequence, the offer will be oversubscribed.[16]

Because the successful offer price in a multiple-bidder contest, $P_T^m$, will be greater than the offer price in a successful single-bidder offer, i.e., $P_T^m > P_T^s$ (compare points $D$ and $C$ in fig. 1), the dollar gains to target stockholders will be greater in multiple-bidder contests than in single-bidder contests. Specifically, the dollar gains can be written as

$$\Delta W_T = (P_T - P_0)(N_C) + (P_E - P_0)(N_0 - N_C), \tag{7}$$

where $P_0$ is the preoffer market price of target shares. The first term on the right side of eq. (7), $(P_T - P_0)(N_C)$, represents the premium paid to target stockholders for the shares purchased on the front end. The second term, $(P_E - P_0)(N_0 - N_C)$, represents the premium paid for the remaining shares on the back end. Because $P_T^m > P_T^s$ and by the assumption that the other terms in eq. (7) are independent of the occurrence of a multiple-bidder contest, $\Delta W_T$ will be greater in a multiple-bidder contest than in a single-bidder offer.

---

[15]Of course if a higher-valued bid materializes before the offer is executed, provisions in the Williams Amendment allow target stockholders to withdraw their shares from the lower bidder and tender them to the higher bidder.

[16]Consistent with this implication, the frequency of oversubscribed offers is greater in our multiple-bidder sample (90%) than in our single-bidder sample (67%).

This prediction in dollar terms will hold also in percentage terms if we make certain independence assumptions about the occurrence of a multiple-bidder contest and the preoffer values of the target and bidding firms. Specifically, assuming that the occurrence of a multiple-bidder contest is independent of the preoffer value of the target, $W_T$, it follows that the rate of return to target stockholders will be greater in multiple-bidder contests than in single-bidder contests. Moreover, assuming that $\Delta \Pi$, the total synergistic gains created by the combination, and $W_A$, the preoffer value of the acquiring firm, are independent of the occurrence of a multiple-bidder contest, it follows that the rate of return to acquirers will be greater in single-bidder contests than in multiple-bidder contests.

An alternative hypothesis is that multiple-bidder contests arise when the initial bid is 'too low' and that there is no difference between the premiums ultimately paid for targets in single- and multiple-bidder contests. According to this scenario, the gains to the targets of multiple-bidder contests would start out low on the announcement of the initial bid and rise to the level of the gains in single-bidder offers. The eventual gains to both targets and acquirers would be unaffected by the number of bidding firms.

Finally, an upward sloping supply of target shares implies a positive relation between the return to target stockholders and the fraction of shares purchased. Consider once again fig. 1. By our analysis, successful single-bidder acquisitions will take place along the (positively sloped) line $ACB$ and the successful price in multiple-bidder acquisitions will always lie above this supply curve. Thus, the gain (return) to target stockholders will be positively related to the number (fraction) of target shares purchased.

## 4. Empirical evidence on the determinants of the division of the gains from tender offers

We begin our empirical analysis by examining the time series of cumulative abnormal returns (*CAR*s) to the portfolios of 236 targets and 236 acquiring firms, classified by the observed level of competition among bidding firms. Although the time-series analysis provides insights into the intertemporal behavior of the returns from tender offers, it is unidimensional and hence does not allow us to examine the simultaneous effects of the factors identified by our analysis. Furthermore, when the first bid for the target shares is announced, the eventual outcome of the bid is uncertain. This uncertainty is resolved over time when either new information about the acquisition is revealed to the market or when competing, higher-valued bids for the target are announced. The period over which this uncertainty is resolved varies across the sample, and the *CAR*s to the portfolios cannot account for these differences. Thus, we also conduct cross-sectional analyses using the variable window return measures defined in section 2.

## 4.1. Time-series analysis

The time series of *CAR*s are computed for three portfolios of the target firms: 163 targets of single-bidder tender offers, 73 targets of multiple-bidder tender offer contests, and the total sample of 236 targets. Similarly, three *CAR* series are computed for the corresponding portfolios of the acquiring firms.

To be classified as a multiple-bidder contest, a tender offer contest must involve an identifiable second bidder – i.e., the firm's name is mentioned in the press and it must be actively seeking target shares by engaging in at least one of the following activities: (1) making a formal tender offer or a merger proposal, (2) negotiating a merger possibility with the target management, or (3) announcing its plans to make a bid. The activities of competing bidding firms were obtained from citations in the *Wall Street Journal*.[17]

For each portfolio $p$ consisting of $N_t$ firms on day $t$, the abnormal return for day $t$ is defined as

$$AR_{pt} = (1/N_t) \sum_{i=1}^{N_t} AR_{it}.$$  (8)

The $K$-day *CAR* for each portfolio is defined as

$$CAR_{pK} = \sum_{t=-\tau}^{K-\tau-1} AR_{pt},$$  (9)

where $\tau$ is the number of days before the relevant event day. To test the significance of this $K$-day cumulative abnormal return to the portfolio, we compute a standardized portfolio cumulative abnormal return, $SCAR_{pK}$, in a manner analogous to the $SCAR_i$ computation described in footnote 5. This $SCAR_{pK}$ has a $t$-distribution with 238 degrees of freedom.

The *CAR* series for the three portfolios of the target firms in our sample are presented in table 3 and plotted in fig. 2. The *CAR* series are cumulated from event day $-20$ through event day $+80$, where event day 0 is the day on which

---

[17]Classifying a tender offer as a single- or multiple-bidder contest based on the number of identifiable bidding firms becomes ambiguous when an initial bidding firm revises its bid and there is no identifiable competing bidder. On the one hand, the revision may have been triggered by the realization (on the part of the bidding firm) that the initial offer was too low to induce the target shareholders to tender their shares. On the other hand, it may have been a response to a competing offer by another firm or the anticipation thereof that we were unable to identify. Since it is impossible to distinguish between these two cases, the empirical tests were run twice. One set of results is based on a multiple/single-*bidder* classification (the number of firms bidding for the target); a second set of results is based on a multiple/single-*bid* classification scheme (the number of bids made for the target). Since the results are qualitatively indistinguishable, we report results based only on the multiple/single-*bidder* classification.

Table 3

Percentage abnormal returns ($AR$) and cumulative abnormal returns ($CAR$) to the portfolio of target firms involved in 236 tender offer contests, 163 single-bidder contests and 73 multiple-bidder contests between 1963 and 1984.

| Event day | Single-bidder subsample | | | | Multiple-bidder subsample | | | | Total sample | | | |
|---|---|---|---|---|---|---|---|---|---|---|---|---|
| | $NT$[a] | $NP$[b] | $AR$ | $CAR$ | $NT$ | $NP$ | $AR$ | $CAR$ | $NT$ | $NP$ | $AR$ | $CAR$ |
| −20 | 163 | 72 | −0.13 | −0.13 | 71 | 33 | 0.11 | 0.11 | 234 | 105 | −0.05 | −0.05 |
| −15 | 163 | 87 | 0.19 | 0.38 | 71 | 30 | −0.27 | 1.46 | 234 | 117 | 0.05 | 0.70 |
| −10 | 162 | 78 | 0.28 | 1.26 | 73 | 39 | 1.60 | 4.04 | 235 | 117 | 0.69 | 2.12 |
| −5 | 162 | 85 | 0.21 | 3.01 | 73 | 44 | 0.60 | 6.12 | 235 | 129 | 0.33 | 3.97 |
| −4 | 160 | 83 | 1.09 | 4.10 | 73 | 40 | 0.92 | 7.04 | 233 | 123 | 1.03 | 5.01 |
| −3 | 162 | 94 | 0.98 | 5.08 | 73 | 38 | 1.09 | 8.13 | 235 | 132 | 1.01 | 6.02 |
| −2 | 159 | 103 | 1.57 | 6.64 | 73 | 44 | 1.46 | 9.59 | 232 | 147 | 1.53 | 7.56 |
| −1 | 147 | 101 | 2.63 | 9.27 | 72 | 52 | 2.27 | 11.86 | 219 | 153 | 2.51 | 10.07 |
| 0 | 163 | 139 | 14.67 | 23.95 | 73 | 66 | 14.12 | 25.98 | 236 | 205 | 14.50 | 24.57 |
| 1 | 135 | 95 | 4.71 | 28.66 | 56 | 41 | 4.42 | 30.40 | 191 | 136 | 4.63 | 29.19 |
| 2 | 156 | 78 | 0.79 | 29.44 | 61 | 29 | 0.81 | 31.21 | 217 | 107 | 0.79 | 29.99 |
| 3 | 159 | 72 | 0.69 | 30.14 | 66 | 29 | 0.96 | 32.17 | 225 | 101 | 0.77 | 30.76 |
| 4 | 159 | 80 | 0.13 | 30.27 | 71 | 41 | 1.79 | 33.96 | 230 | 121 | 0.65 | 31.41 |
| 5 | 160 | 76 | 0.05 | 30.33 | 70 | 34 | 0.88 | 34.85 | 230 | 110 | 0.31 | 31.71 |
| 10 | 162 | 79 | −0.28 | 30.46 | 70 | 32 | −0.07 | 37.82 | 232 | 111 | −0.22 | 32.72 |
| 15 | 160 | 76 | −0.12 | 30.40 | 68 | 37 | 0.53 | 40.94 | 228 | 113 | 0.07 | 33.63 |
| 20 | 152 | 71 | −0.43 | 29.17 | 70 | 35 | 0.09 | 41.70 | 222 | 106 | −0.27 | 33.02 |
| 30 | 130 | 59 | −0.24 | 27.84 | 69 | 33 | −0.18 | 44.92 | 199 | 92 | −0.22 | 33.19 |
| 40 | 117 | 45 | −0.25 | 26.65 | 63 | 30 | 0.09 | 46.12 | 180 | 75 | −0.13 | 32.85 |
| 50 | 108 | 50 | 0.25 | 25.80 | 59 | 27 | −0.13 | 45.47 | 167 | 77 | 0.12 | 32.06 |
| 60 | 97 | 41 | −0.06 | 26.04 | 53 | 33 | 0.17 | 44.70 | 150 | 74 | 0.02 | 31.95 |
| 70 | 89 | 41 | −0.06 | 26.14 | 43 | 19 | 0.01 | 44.26 | 132 | 60 | −0.04 | 31.87 |
| 80 | 84 | 42 | −0.35 | 24.65 | 41 | 24 | 0.46 | 45.50 | 125 | 66 | −0.08 | 31.28 |

[a] $NT$ = total number of firms.
[b] $NP$ = number of firms with positive abnormal returns.

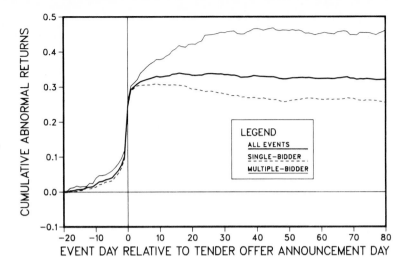

Fig. 2. Cumulative abnormal returns to the portfolio of target firms involved in 236 contests, 163 single-bidder contests and 73 multiple-bidder contests, 1963–1984. Event day relative to tender offer announcement day.

the announcement of the first offer for the target appeared in the *Wall Street Journal*.

The *CAR* for the portfolio of all 236 target firms from event day $-5$ through event day $+5$ is 28.07% with a *t*-statistic of 51.24, showing once again that an acquisition by tender offer is a wealth-increasing event for the stockholders of the target firm.

The *AR* and the *CAR* of the single-bidder subsample on day 0 (14.67% and 23.95%) are approximately equal to those of the multiple-bidder subsample (14.12% and 25.98%). Thus when a target receives an initial offer, the average value of this offer does not depend on whether it will be followed by other bids. Only when competing bids are actually announced do additional returns accrue to the targets of multiple-bidder contests. The additional returns are reflected in the gradual rise of the *CAR* series for the multiple-bidder sample. The difference in the *CAR* between the multiple-bidder and single-bidder subsamples reaches about 20% by day $+40$.[18] Clearly, target shareholders earn greater returns from multiple-bidder contests than from single-bidder offers.

These findings are not consistent with the alternative hypothesis that multiple-bidder contests arise because the initial bid was too low. Rather, they

---

[18]Some of this difference can be attributed to the postexecution drop in the price of the remaining target shares. Of the 163 single-bidder offers, 119 (or 73%) were executed within 40 trading days of the initial announcement. By contrast, only 32 of the 73 multiple-bidder offers (44%) were executed during this 40-day period. Since the time-series analysis cannot account for the differences in the duration of the tender offers in the sample, formal tests for the effect of competition on the returns to targets and acquirers must await the cross-sectional tests in the next section.

Table 4

Percentage abnormal returns ($AR$) and cumulative abnormal returns ($CAR$) to the portfolio of acquiring firms involved in 236 tender offer contests, 163 single-bidder contests and 73 multiple-bidder contests between 1963 and 1984.

| Event day | Single-bidder subsample | | | | Multiple-bidder subsample | | | | Total sample | | | |
|---|---|---|---|---|---|---|---|---|---|---|---|---|
| | $NT$[a] | $NP$[b] | $AR$ | $CAR$ | $NT$ | $NP$ | $AR$ | $CAR$ | $NT$ | $NP$ | $AR$ | $CAR$ |
| −20 | 163 | 84 | 0.12 | 0.12 | 73 | 33 | −0.07 | −0.07 | 236 | 117 | 0.06 | 0.06 |
| −15 | 163 | 74 | −0.17 | 0.20 | 73 | 30 | −0.22 | −0.66 | 236 | 104 | −0.19 | −0.06 |
| −10 | 163 | 85 | 0.25 | 0.66 | 73 | 36 | 0.14 | −0.05 | 236 | 121 | 0.22 | 0.44 |
| −5 | 163 | 79 | 0.12 | 1.05 | 73 | 32 | −0.30 | 0.23 | 236 | 111 | −0.01 | 0.80 |
| −4 | 163 | 73 | 0.04 | 1.09 | 73 | 39 | 0.14 | 0.37 | 236 | 112 | 0.07 | 0.87 |
| −3 | 163 | 92 | 0.50 | 1.59 | 73 | 38 | 0.34 | 0.71 | 236 | 130 | 0.45 | 1.32 |
| −2 | 163 | 84 | 0.50 | 2.09 | 72 | 29 | 0.23 | 0.95 | 235 | 113 | 0.42 | 1.74 |
| −1 | 163 | 86 | 0.19 | 2.29 | 72 | 28 | −0.39 | 0.56 | 235 | 114 | 0.02 | 1.76 |
| 0 | 163 | 80 | 0.62 | 2.91 | 73 | 30 | −0.65 | −0.09 | 236 | 110 | 0.23 | 1.99 |
| 1 | 162 | 76 | −0.16 | 2.75 | 71 | 34 | −0.41 | −0.51 | 233 | 110 | −0.24 | 1.75 |
| 2 | 163 | 79 | 0.16 | 2.91 | 73 | 34 | −0.33 | −0.83 | 236 | 113 | 0.01 | 1.76 |
| 3 | 163 | 73 | −0.24 | 2.67 | 73 | 35 | −0.12 | −0.96 | 236 | 108 | −0.20 | 1.55 |
| 4 | 163 | 73 | 0.17 | 2.84 | 72 | 39 | 0.05 | −0.91 | 235 | 112 | 0.13 | 1.69 |
| 5 | 163 | 66 | −0.35 | 2.50 | 73 | 36 | 0.49 | −0.43 | 236 | 102 | −0.09 | 1.60 |
| 10 | 163 | 93 | 0.02 | 2.71 | 73 | 38 | 0.20 | −1.13 | 236 | 131 | 0.08 | 1.53 |
| 15 | 163 | 77 | 0.31 | 3.33 | 73 | 33 | 0.15 | −1.04 | 236 | 110 | 0.26 | 1.98 |
| 20 | 163 | 83 | 0.37 | 3.69 | 73 | 33 | 0.04 | −0.17 | 236 | 116 | 0.27 | 2.51 |
| 30 | 163 | 72 | −0.03 | 3.29 | 73 | 32 | −0.35 | 0.56 | 236 | 104 | −0.13 | 2.46 |
| 40 | 163 | 80 | 0.12 | 2.97 | 73 | 30 | −0.21 | 0.64 | 236 | 110 | 0.02 | 2.26 |
| 50 | 163 | 77 | −0.01 | 2.70 | 73 | 34 | −0.08 | 0.42 | 236 | 111 | −0.03 | 2.00 |
| 60 | 163 | 81 | −0.08 | 2.73 | 73 | 37 | −0.20 | 0.61 | 236 | 118 | −0.12 | 2.09 |
| 70 | 163 | 80 | −0.08 | 2.22 | 73 | 37 | −0.11 | −0.55 | 236 | 117 | −0.09 | 1.37 |
| 80 | 163 | 73 | −0.04 | 2.02 | 73 | 36 | 0.16 | 0.70 | 236 | 109 | 0.02 | 1.62 |

[a] $NT$ = total number of firms.
[b] $NP$ = number of firms with positive abnormal returns.

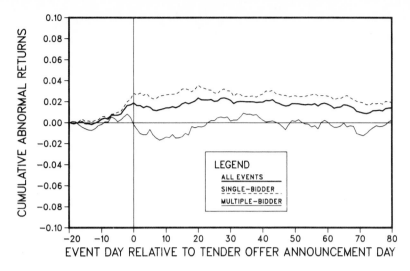

Fig. 3. Cumulative abnormal returns to the portfolios of acquiring firms involved in 236 contests, 163 single-bidder contests and 73 multiple-bidder contests, 1963–1984. Event day relative to tender offer announcement day.

suggest that the premiums paid to the target shareholders in multiple-bidder contests are, as implied by our model, above the supply curve of target shares.

The *CAR* series for the three portfolios of acquiring firms are presented in table 4 and plotted in fig. 3. Event day 0 is the day of the announcement of the first offer made by the acquiring firm. The *CAR* to the portfolio of all 236 acquiring firms from event day $-5$ through $+5$ is 0.79% with a *t*-statistic of 1.69. This is not significantly different from zero at the 5% level. However, the *CAR* from day $-5$ through day $+20$ is 1.70% ($t = 2.36$), which is significant at the 5% level. Thus, unlike for target firms, there is mixed evidence concerning the returns to acquiring firms.

Classifying the portfolios of acquiring firms by the level of competition reveals that the *CAR* from day $-5$ through day $+20$ to the single-bidder portfolio is 2.8% ($t = 2.94$), whereas the return to the multiple-bidder portfolio is $-0.70$% ($t = -0.56$) over the same period. Thus, significant positive returns accrue to the stockholders of acquiring firms in single-bidder tender offers but not in multiple-bidder contests.

To examine the behavior of the *CAR*s to the multiple-bidder portfolio more closely, we divide the sample into two groups: first-bidder, ultimately successful acquirers, and those acquirers who entered the contest after some other firm initiated the bidding process. Of the 73 acquirers in the multiple-bidder portfolio, 24 are first-bidder acquirers, and 49 are late-bidder acquirers. The *CAR* from day $-5$ to day $+1$ for the portfolio of first-bidder acquirers is

2.0%, whereas the *CAR* for the portfolio of late-bidder acquirers is $-2.5\%$ over the same interval. Apparently, the market's reaction to the first bid of first-bidder acquirers in multiple-bidder contests is similar to its reaction to bids made in single-bidder tender offers. Thus the negative *CAR* from day $-5$ to day $+1$ to the portfolio of acquirers in multiple-bidder contests is due primarily to the negative returns to late-bidder acquirers, more commonly known as white knights. In other words, our data indicate that the average white knight pays 'too much' for the target it acquires.

In sum, our time-series analysis indicates that the net effect of multiple-bidder contests is to increase the returns to target firms and decrease the returns to acquiring firms. The market's average reaction to the bid that initiates a tender offer contest does not depend on whether the bid eventually leads to a multiple-bidder contest. This is true for both target and bidding firms. Only when competing bids are actually made do we observe greater returns to target shareholders and a dissipation of the initial gains to the stockholders of bidding firms.

### 4.2. Cross-sectional analysis

In this section we use variable-window *CAR*s to examine the cross-sectional differences in the returns to the stockholders of target and acquiring firms. Specifically, we examine the effects of (1) changes in the tender offer environment, (2) competition, and (3) the fraction of target shares purchased on the rates of return to these stockholders. We also examine the effects of the above variables on the total value-weighted percentage synergistic gains.

Our cross-sectional regression model is given by eq. (10) and the variables are defined in table 5,

$$CAR = \gamma_0 + \gamma_1 T_1 + \gamma_2 T_2 + \gamma_3 M + \gamma_4 F. \tag{10}$$

The dummy variables $T_1$ and $T_2$ indicate the time period (environment) in which the tender offer is made. $T_1$ equals one if the offer is made between July 1, 1968 and December 1980, and zero otherwise. It is included to account for the effect of the passage of the Williams Amendment. $T_2$ equals one if the offer is made after December 1980, and zero otherwise. It is included to account for the changes in the acquisitions arena that have occurred in the 1980s.

The dummy variable $M$, which equals one if the offer is made in a multiple-bidder contest and zero otherwise, reflects the level of competition. We restrict our analysis of competition to a simple single/multiple-bidder classification instead of the number of bidders, because our multiple-bidder sample consists of 65 contests with two bidding firms and only 8 with more

Table 5

Weighted least-squares estimates of the effects of time-period, multiple-bidder contests, and fraction of shares purchased on the abnormal returns to the stockholders of the targets ($CART$), acquirers ($CARA$), and combined ($CARC$) involved in 236 successful tender offers between 1963 and 1984 ($t$-statistics in parentheses).[a]

Model:   $CAR = \gamma_0 + \gamma_1 T_1 + \gamma_2 T_2 + \gamma_3 M + \gamma_4 F.$

| Dependent Variable | $\hat{\gamma}_0$ | $\hat{\gamma}_1$ | $\hat{\gamma}_2$ | $\hat{\gamma}_3$ | $\hat{\gamma}_4$ | $F$-statistic |
|---|---|---|---|---|---|---|
| $CART$ | 0.098 (3.89) | 0.080 (3.22) | 0.053 (1.40) | 0.130 (4.23) | 0.167 (4.26) | 14.84[b] |
| $CARA$ | 0.035 (2.65) | −0.025 (−2.07) | −0.055 (−3.43) | −0.017 (−1.32) | 0.005 (0.27) | 4.20[c] |
| $CARC$ | 0.069 (4.60) | (−0.012) (−0.87) | −0.018 (−0.91) | 0.024 (1.35) | 0.006 (0.28) | 0.66[d] |

[a] $CART$ = cumulative abnormal return to the target shares from five trading days before the announcement of the first bid through five trading days after the announcement of the ultimately successful bid; $CARA$ = cumulative abnormal return to the acquiring firm from five trading days before the announcement of the first offer made by this firm through five trading days after the announcement of the ultimately successful bid; $CARC$ = cumulative abnormal return to the value-weighted portfolio of the target and the acquiring firms from five trading days before the announcement of the first offer made for the target through five days after the announcement of the ultimately successful bid; $T_1$ = dummy variable that equals one if the offer is made between July 1, 1968 and December 1980, and zero otherwise; $T_2$ = dummy variable that equals one if the offer is made after December 1980, and zero otherwise; $M$ = dummy variable that equals one if the offer is made in a multiple-bidder contest, and zero otherwise; $F$ = fraction of target shares purchased in the offer by the successful bidder.

[b] Significant at the 0.01 level.

[c] Significant at the 0.05 level.

[d] Insignificantly different from zero.

than two bidding firms. Our analysis in section 3 indicates that the estimate of $\gamma_3$ will be positive for targets and negative for acquirers.

The final independent variable included in our regression model is $F$, the fraction of target shares purchased by the successful bidding firm. A positively sloping supply of target shares implies that the return to target stockholders will be positively related to $F$.[19]

Finally, to account for the possibility of heteroskedasticity in the data, all observations are divided by the standard error of the $K_i$-day $CAR$. This is equivalent to using weighted least squares to estimate the regression parameters, where the standard error of the firm's $CAR$ is the relevant weight. This

[19] We perform all our cross-sectional tests using two definitions of $F$. In the first, the denominator is simply the total number of shares outstanding; in the second, we adjust the denominator by subtracting the number of shares held by the acquirer (prior to the offer) from the total number of shares outstanding. The results are virtually identical using these alternative measures. In the text we only report results based on the first definition.

standard error is computed as the square root of the sum of the variances of the prediction errors over the $K_i$ days.[20]

### 4.2.1. Returns to target stockholders

The results of our regression analysis for the sample of target firms are reported in the first row of table 5. The estimates of $\gamma_0$ and $\gamma_1$ are both statistically greater than zero. These statistics imply that the average abnormal return to target stockholders is significantly positive ($\hat{\gamma}_0 = 9.8\%$, $t = 3.89$) and even more so after the passage of the Williams Amendment ($\hat{\gamma}_1 = 8.0\%$, $t = 3.22$).[21] The point estimate of $\gamma_2$ is also positive ($\hat{\gamma}_2 = 5.3\%$, $t = 1.40$) but is not significantly different from zero.[22]

The estimated coefficient of the single/multiple-bidder dummy variable is significantly greater than zero ($\hat{\gamma}_3 = 13.0\%$, $t = 4.23$). Consistent with the earlier results, the marginal impact of a multiple-bidder contest is to increase the return to the target stockholders.

The estimated coefficient on the fraction of target shares purchased, $F$, is significantly positive ($\hat{\gamma}_4 = 16.7\%$, $t = 4.26$). This is consistent with a positively sloping supply of target shares.

### 4.2.2. Returns to the stockholders of acquiring firms

The second row of table 5 reports the results of our cross-sectional regression analysis for acquiring firms.[23] The estimate of the constant is significantly

---

[20]Specifically, the standard error of $CAR$ is given by $(\sum_t^{K_i}\sigma_i^2 C_{it})^{1/2}$, where $C_{it} = (1 + 1/T + ((R_{mt} - \bar{R}_m)^2/\sum_\tau^T (R_{m\tau} - \bar{R}_m)^2))$, $\sigma_i$ is the standard deviation of the residuals from the estimation period of $T$ days, and $\bar{R}_m$ is the mean return on the market over the estimation period.

[21]This result is consistent with the findings of Jarrell and Bradley (1980). They find that the passage of the Williams Amendment is associated with an increase in the returns to targets and a decrease in the returns to acquirers.

[22]The lack of statistical significance of the estimate of $\gamma_2$ may be due to the positive relation between the second time-period dummy variable, $T_2$, and the multiple/single-bidder dummy variable, $M$. The simple correlation between these two independent variables is 0.18 ($P = 0.007$). Multicollinearity between two independent variables biases the $t$-statistics of the estimated coefficients toward zero.

[23]Earlier studies suggest that the average rate of return to all acquiring firms may not be an appropriate measure of the gains from tender offers because of the disparity between the values of the target and acquiring firms. The acquisition of a very small firm by a very large firm may have an imperceptible effect on the return to the acquiring firm regardless of the profitability of the acquisition. Consistent with this observation, Asquith, Bruner, and Mullins (1983) show that the measured returns to acquiring firms are positively related to a dummy variable that indicates whether the target is at least 10% of the value of the acquiring firm. Jarrell (1983) generalizes this finding and shows that the return to acquiring firms is a continuous positive function of the relative value of the target. Kim and McConnell (1977) and Asquith and Kim (1982) limit their analysis to acquisitions involving targets that are at least 10% of the value of their respective acquiring firms. Thus, the regressions for acquiring firms were run on two data sets: the entire 236-observation sample and a subsample in which the targets are at least 10% of the value of their acquirers. (There are 171 tender offer events in which the relative size of the target is 10% or more.) Because none of our empirical results are materially different for the reduced sample, we report only results for the total sample.

positive ($\hat{\gamma}_0 = 3.5\%$, $t = 2.65$) which indicates that the average return to acquiring firms in single-bidder tender offers effected before passage of the Williams Amendment was significantly positive. The estimates of $\gamma_1$ and $\gamma_2$ are both significantly negative ($\hat{\gamma}_1 = -2.5\%$, $t = -2.07$ and $\hat{\gamma}_2 = -5.5\%$, $t = -3.43$, respectively). Thus, bidding firms earn significantly lower returns in the post-Williams Amendment era. Moreover, the estimate of $\gamma_2$ is less than the estimate of $\gamma_1$, which is consistent with our earlier results in table 2 that the returns to acquiring firms have decreased over time and that in the most recent subperiod acquiring firms actually suffered a significant loss.

The point estimate of the coefficient on the single/multiple-bidder dummy variable ($\gamma_3 = -1.7\%$, $t = -1.32$) shows that the marginal impact of multiple-bidder contests is to reduce the returns to acquiring firms, but this estimate is not significantly different from zero.[24] Note that higher returns to targets from multiple-bidder contests do not translate into corresponding lower returns to acquiring firms unless the total synergistic gains are the same in multiple-bidder and single-bidder contests. We return to this issue in the next subsection.

Finally, we note without much elaboration that the return to acquiring firms is unrelated to $F$, the fraction of shares purchased; the estimate of $\gamma_4$ has a $t$-statistic of 0.27. By our analysis this relation (estimate) should be negative: all else constant, the greater $F$, the greater the returns to targets and the smaller the returns to acquirers. However, this implication is based on the assumption that the total synergy created and the preoffer values of the target and acquiring firms are all independent of $F$. Violation of any of these independence assumptions would negate the prediction of a negative relation between $F$ and $CARA$. No attempt was made to pursue this issue further.

To provide a more intuitive presentation of the separate effects of regulation and competition on the returns to acquiring firms, we report the $CARA$ by time period and our multiple/single-bidder classification in table 6. The data show that acquiring firms gained most (4.62%, $z = 5.99$) in single-bidder contests effected during the unregulated period of 1963–1968; they lost the most ($-5.10\%$, $z = -2.87$) in multiple-bidder contests effected in the most recent period (1981–1984).

Perhaps the most notable of the data reported in table 6 is that the 52 acquiring firms in the most recent period (1981–1984) realized a significant abnormal loss of $-2.93\%$ ($z = -2.79$). This period is associated with an increase in the extent and degree of Congressional regulations, the tolerance of Reagan Administration towards large-scale mergers, the advent of investment banking firms that specialize in raising funds to finance takeover battles, and the development of sophisticated defensive tactics. We believe that all of these

---

[24] Once again we note that the multicollinearity between $T_2$ and $M$ biases the $t$-statistics of the estimated coefficients of each toward zero. See footnote 22.

Table 6

Percent mean abnormal return to acquirers involved in 236 successful tender offers between 1963 and 1984, by time period and multiple/single-bidder classification (*z*-statistics in parentheses).

| | Subperiod | | | Total |
|---|---|---|---|---|
| | 7/63–6/68 | 7/68–12/80 | 1/81–12/84 | 7/63–12/84 |
| Single bidder | 4.62[a] | 1.74[b] | −1.08 | 2.00[a] |
| | (5.99) | (2.04) | (−1.14) | (4.11) |
| | $N = 42$ | $N = 93$ | $N = 28$ | $N = 163$ |
| Multiple bidder | 1.62 | 0.27 | −5.10[a] | −1.33 |
| | (1.05) | (0.22) | (−2.87) | (−1.44) |
| | $N = 9$ | $N = 40$ | $N = 24$ | $N = 73$ |
| Total | 4.09[a] | 1.30 | −2.93[a] | 0.97[a] |
| | (5.88) | (1.58) | (−2.79) | (2.61) |
| | $N = 51$ | $N = 133$ | $N = 52$ | $N = 236$ |

[a]Significant at the 0.01 level.
[b]Significant at the 0.01 level.

factors have contributed to an increase in competition among bidding firms. Consistent with this conjecture, the data in the table indicate an increasing trend in the relative frequency of multiple-bidder contests over time; 18%, 30%, and 46%, in subperiods 1963–1968, 1968–1980, and 1981–1984, respectively. Obviously, an increase in competition among bidders does not explain negative returns to acquirers. However, if every successful bidder is pushed to its maximum valuation of the target, there is a greater probability that overvaluations will occur and the acquirer's shareholders will suffer a capital loss. This adverse effect was most severe during the period 1981–1984, when the shareholders on average lost 5.10% ($z = -2.87$) as a result of successful acquisitions in multiple-bidder contests.

In light of these results, we note our earlier finding [Bradley, Desai, and Kim (1983)] that the *un*successful bidders in multiple-bidder contests during the period 1963–1980 on average lost 8% of their preoffer value. In contrast, the data in table 6 show that the average gain to the successful bidders in multiple-bidder contests during the same period (1963–1980) is not significantly different from zero. Thus, it appears that once a firm finds itself in a bidding war, it is better to win than lose, even though in winning, the firm's stockholders may suffer a capital loss.

On the basis of our time-series analysis in section 4.1, we conjectured that the low returns to acquiring firms in multiple-bidder contests are driven by the negative returns to so-called white knights. The results of our cross-sectional analysis reinforce this conclusion. As reported in table 6, the mean *CARA* of the 73 successful bidders in our multiple-bidder sample is −1.33% ($z = -1.44$). The mean *CARA* to the 24 first-bidder acquirers is 0.81% ($z = 0.41$), whereas the mean *CARA* for the 49 late-bidder acquirers (white knights) is −2.38%

($z = -2.05$). Clearly, the evidence is consistent with our contention that white knights, on average, pay 'too much' for the targets they acquire.

### 4.2.3. Total percentage synergistic gains

The results of our cross-sectional regression analysis for the relative synergistic gains ($CARC$) are presented in the third row of table 5. The data show that only the estimate of $\gamma_0$ is significantly different from zero. The estimate of the constant indicates that the average unregulated, single-bidder tender offer results in an increase in the combined values of the two firms.

The estimate of the coefficient on the multiple/single-bidder dummy variable is positive but the $t$-statistic is only 1.35. We interpret this as weak evidence that competition among bidding firms generates additional information that leads to a higher-valued allocation of the combined resources of the two firms.[25] Alternatively, it may be that the potential for large synergistic gains attracts multiple bidders. At any rate, the positive relation between our measure of synergistic gains and our multiple/single-bidder dummy variable partially explains the lack of a significant negative relation between the returns to acquiring firms and the multiple/single-bidder dummy variable.

Finally, neither of the estimated coefficients on the time dummy variables is significantly different from zero. This suggests that the effects of increased regulation, developments in the investment banking industry, and the use of defensive tactics have been a zero sum game. That is, the increased gains to the stockholders of target firms have come at the expense of the gains to the stockholders of acquired firms.

## 5. Summary and conclusions

This paper provides a theoretical and empirical analysis of interfirm tender offers. We analyze the mechanics of the tender offer process and demonstrate how this capital market transaction allocates corporate resources to their highest-valued use. Our empirical analysis documents the synergistic gains created by tender offers and how these gains are divided between the stockholders of the target and acquiring firms.

Our analysis of the tender offer process, which is presented in the appendix, demonstrates that a successful tender offer must be front-end loaded. More importantly, we show that two-tier, front-end loaded tender offers are not coercive and do not impede the (optimal) allocation of the target resources. Indeed, we argue that all successful offers, even partial and any and all offers,

---

[25] The positive correlation between the time-period dummy variables ($T_1$ and $T_2$) and the multiple/single-bidder dummy variable ($M$) biases the $t$-statistics of the estimated coefficients toward zero.

are front-end loaded. We also argue that although there are three parameters of any tender offer, rival bidding firms compete on the front-end offer price rather than the back-end price or the fraction of shares sought. The data are consistent with both conjectures.

On the basis of this characterization of the tender offer process, we show that the bidding firm that can effect the highest-valued reallocation of the target resources can always fashion the highest-valued (winning) bid. We also show that target managers are always able to structure an intrafirm tender offer that can defeat a value-decreasing interfirm tender offer. Thus, the management team that can effect the highest-valued allocation of the target resources will acquire (maintain) control of the target.

Our empirical investigation is based on an exhaustive sample of successful tender offers effected between 1963 and 1984 in which both the target and acquiring firms were listed on either the NYSE or AMEX at the time of the acquisition. The average synergistic gain created by the 236 offers in our sample is $117 million (in December 1984 dollars), representing a 7.4% increase in the combined wealth of the stockholders of the target and acquiring firms. This finding is consistent with the synergy hypothesis advanced by Bradley, Desai, and Kim (1983) and inconsistent with Roll's (1986) 'Hubris Hypothesis'.

We find that target stockholders have captured the lion's share of the gains from tender offers, and their share of the gains has increased significantly since the passage of the Williams Amendment in 1968. Acquiring firms, on the other hand, realized a significant positive gain only during the unregulated period 1963–1968 and, in fact, suffered a significant loss during the most recent subperiod, 1981–1984. We also find that the total percentage synergistic gains from tender offers have remained remarkably constant over time. Thus, government regulations and other changes that have occurred in the tender offer environment have been a zero sum game: the increase in the gains to the target stockholders has come at the expense of the stockholders of acquiring firms.

Our empirical analysis confirms our contention that competition among bidding firms increases the returns to targets and decreases the returns to acquirers. However, competition is not a zero sum game: total synergistic gains are larger in multiple-bidder acquisitions. Thus, the targets of multiple-bidder contests realize greater gains not only at the expense of the shareholders of acquiring firms but also from the greater synergistic gains that accompany these transactions.

We find that competition among bidding firms reduces the average gain to acquirers to a level that is not significantly different from zero. This adverse effect of competition is most severe for late-bidder acquirers, more commonly known as white knights. On average, the white knights in our sample pay 'too much' for the targets they acquire.

Our data also show that the return to target firms is positively related to the fraction of target shares purchased. This is consistent with our contention that tax considerations and/or heterogeneous expectations among target shareholders generate a positively sloped supply of target shares.

In sum, our theoretical analysis implies that interfirm tender offers are efficient mechanisms to channel corporate resources to higher-valued uses. Our empirical results are consistent with this implication. We therefore see no justification for the continuing efforts by those in Washington to 'reform' the tender offer process.[26] Rather, we believe that public policy should be directed toward facilitating this capital market transaction.

## Appendix: An analysis of the tender offer process[27]

The objective of this appendix is to demonstrate analytically the contentions made in section 3.3. To this end, we develop a stylized model of the tender offer process that is consistent with existing legal and institutional constraints.[28] We analyze the mechanics of the tender offer process and demonstrate how market forces arise to solve various problems posed by this capital market transaction. Specifically, we show (1) how bidding firms use front-end loaded offers to solve the free-rider problem and (2) how the potential for competing bids by target managers solves the prisoner's dilemma and ensures that successful tender offers will be value-increasing transactions for target stockholders. More important, we demonstrate how market forces ensure that the management team that can effect the highest-valued allocation of the target resources will acquire (maintain) control of the target. Although some of these issues have been discussed elsewhere in the literature, we do provide some new insights into the mechanics of the tender offer and the process of competition in the market for corporate control.

### A.1. Tender offers and the free-rider problem

### A.1.1. The problem

The free-rider problem associated with tender offers has been analyzed by several authors.[29] The issue can be illustrated by means of a simple numerical example. Consider an all-equity target firm with ten shares outstanding, each selling at $40: a $400 firm. Assume that if a potential acquiring firm were to

---

[26]Lehn and Jones (1987) document that over the past three years, at least 74 bills have been introduced by more than 100 senators or congressmen to further regulate corporate takeovers.

[27]This appendix is a revised version of a model developed in Bradley and Kim (1984). In revising this portion of the paper, we have benefited greatly from helpful discussions with Elazar Berkovitch.

[28]For alternative modeling of tender offers, see Berkovitch and Khanna (1986), Fishman (1986), Khanna (1986), and Shleifer and Vishny (1986).

[29]See Bradley (1980) and Grossman and Hart (1980).

secure control of the target, it could reallocate the firm's resources in such a way that the market value of the target firm's assets would increase to $600. Thus the acquisition would generate a $200 synergistic gain.

Assume that in an attempt to exploit the available synergies, a potential acquirer makes the following offer. It will purchase five of the outstanding target shares (a controlling interest) at $50 per share (a 25% premium). If the offer is successful, the market price per share will rise to $60 ($= \$600/10$). If fewer than five shares are tendered, the offer will be withdrawn and the target's share price will fall back to the preoffer level of $40 per share.[30]

If we assume that the target stockholders behave as atomistic wealth maximizers, their optimal response to this offer is clear. They will hold on to their shares because the payoff will be greater if they wait until others tender their shares and the value of the target is increased by the takeover. As a consequence, no one will tender, even though by tendering they would all realize a substantial capital gain. This result is nothing more than a manifestation of the free-rider problem. The inability of target stockholders to write and enforce a contract that all will tender leads each separately not to tender. Each hopes that the others will tender so that the value of the target will be increased by the takeover, but none will tender for $50 if the postexecution market value of the target shares is (expected to be) $60. Those who do not tender will hope to free ride on those who do, but because all target stockholders will feel this way, no shares will be tendered.

### A.1.2. The solution

The obvious solution to the free-rider problem is for the bidding firm to make a two-tier bid and front-end load the offer. Specifically, the bidding firm must set $P_T$, the offer price, greater than $P_E$, the (expected) postoffer price. In our example, the bidding firm could offer to buy five shares at $60 and stipulate that if five shares (a controlling block) were obtained, it would effect a takeout merger and redeem the remaining five shares for $50 a piece.

The dominating response for any target stockholder to this revised bid is to tender. By assumption, if the offer is unsuccessful, each stockholder's wealth will remain at its preoffer level. If the offer is successful and a target stockholder does not tender, however, he will forego the takeover premium, $P_T - P_E$. Since all target stockholders will evaluate the offer in the same manner, all will tender and the offer will be successful.

The implication of the foregoing analysis is clear. A necessary condition for a successful tender offer is that it be front-end loaded, i.e., $P_T > P_E$. By front-end loading the offer, the bidding firm provides an incentive for target stockholders to tender and thus solves the free-rider problem.

---

[30] Bradley, Desai, and Kim (1983) document that the market price of the shares of a target of an unsuccessful tender offer falls back to the pretender offer level if the target is not taken over within the next five years.

## A.2. The prisoner's dilemma and corporate raiders

### A.2.1. The problem

Critics of the tender offer process often claim that front-end loaded offers are coercive in that target stockholders have no real choice but to tender under such terms. Further, critics argue that the coercive nature of front-end loaded, two-tier offers allows so-called corporate raiders to acquire the assets of a target for something less than their preoffer market value. To illustrate this point, we return to the numerical example in which the hypothetical target has 10 shares outstanding, each worth $40. Assume that a potential corporate raider makes the following two-tier bid. The raider will pay $50 per share (a 25% premium) for five target shares. Having obtained control of the target, it will then redeem the remaining target shares for $20 per share. If fewer than five shares are tendered, the offer will be withdrawn. In terms of our earlier notation, $P_T = \$50$ and $P_E = \$20$.

The 'corporate-raiding' aspect of the above offer lies in the fact that the bidding firm is attempting to buy a $400 firm for $350: $250 on the front end and $100 on the back end. Table 7 illustrates the payoff matrix faced by a target stockholder with two shares. The two possible responses are to hold or to tender. Without any loss in generality, we consider three possible aggregate market responses: fewer than five shares are tendered, in which case the offer will be withdrawn and the price of the target shares will fall to their preoffer level; exactly five shares are tendered and all are accepted by the bidding firm; and all outstanding shares are tendered and, following federal regulations, five shares are accepted on a pro-rata basis. The entries in table 7 reflect the changes from preoffer wealth of $80.

Reading the entries across the first row of table 7, if the stockholder does not tender and the offer is unsuccessful, his wealth will be unaffected. If the offer is successful, however, he will lose $40. Each of his two shares will be redeemed in the back end of the offer for $20.

If the stockholder tenders and the offer is unsuccessful, his wealth will be unaffected. If exactly five shares are tendered, the stockholder will receive $100: $50 for each share tendered. This will increase his wealth by $20. If all outstanding shares are tendered, the offer will be executed on a pro rata basis and the stockholder will receive $50 for one share (the front end) and $20 for the other (the back end). Thus, he will receive $70 for his two-share portfolio for a net loss of $10.

The entries in table 7 indicate that the dominant strategy is to tender: if the offer is successful, the shareholder's wealth will be greater; and if the offer is unsuccessful, his wealth will be no different. Thus, each target stockholder acting in his self-interest will tender all of his shares. As a result, the offer will be successful and the acquiring firm will have obtained a $400 firm for $350.

Table 7

Wealth changes for a target stockholder (owning two shares) contingent on aggregate stockholder response and his individual response. Rows indicate stockholder response; columns indicate aggregate stockholder response; and cells indicate change in wealth. *Assumptions*: Target is an all-equity firm with ten shares outstanding and stockholder owns two shares with a preoffer value of $40 each. Tender offer is for 50% of the target shares; offer (front-end) price is $50; (implicit) back-end price is $20; pro-rata execution.

| Individual shareholder response | Aggregate shareholder response | | |
|---|---|---|---|
| | Unsuccessful offer | Successful offer | |
| | Fewer than five shares tendered | Five shares tendered | All other shares tendered |
| Hold | 0 | $ − 40 | $ − 40 |
| Tender | 0 | $ + 20 | $ − 10 |

The preceding numerical example is general in its application. As long as $P_T > P_E$, target stockholders will find it in their interest to tender. Note that this tendering decision is independent of $P_0$, the preoffer market price of the target shares. Once a firm receives a takeover bid the behavior of the target stockholders is determined by the relation between $P_T$ and $P_E$ and is independent of $P_0$.

The potential for a corporate raider to acquire the target assets at less than their market value stems from the inability of the target stockholders to act collectively. The presumption is that it is prohibitively costly for the target stockholders to write and enforce a contract that guarantees that no one will tender and attempt to realize the 25% front-end premium.

### A.2.2. Institutional / legal solutions to the Prisoner's Dilemma

Clearly, if target stockholders could act collectively or if arbitrageurs could secure a controlling block of the firm's shares, front-end loaded offers would pose no problem (dilemma). Under these circumstances, the target stockholders or market arbitrageurs would collectively analyze the entire value of each bid according to the equation

$$V = [F \times P_T] + [(1 - F) \times P_E],$$

where $F$ is the fraction of target shares purchased on the front end. That is, they would evaluate each bid in terms of the fraction of shares purchased at the offer price and the fraction purchased (redeemed) at the back-end price. They would then tender collectively to the bidder who offered the highest-valued total bid. Thus, collective action on the part of target stockholders or arbitrageurs could solve the prisoner's dilemma.

Another solution to the prisoner's dilemma stems from the legal/institutional constraints imposed on bidding firms in setting the back-end or takeout price, $P_E$. Note that corporate 'raiding' requires bidding firms to be able to set $P_E$ below the preoffer price, $P_0$. The latitude afforded bidding firms in setting the back-end price ($P_E$) is governed by state statutes and charter provisions. Many states have fair-price *statutes* dictating that the back-end price cannot be lower than the front-end price. Fair-price *charter amendments* impose the same constraints on bidders.[31] Finally, target stockholders can seek an appraisal remedy from the courts if the back-end price is less than 'fair'. The appraisal remedy exists to prevent the exploitation of a minority by a majority of a firm's stockholders. For example, suppose that a bidding firm secures a majority of the firm's shares in the front end of a two-step tender offer. Appraisal statutes exist to insure that the majority will not 'cash out' the minority at an 'unfair' price. In sum, these legal and institutional arrangements impose a limit on the minimum $P_E$ that the bidder can set, and thereby limit the extent to which corporate raiders can ply their trade.

### A.2.3. A market solution to the prisoner's dilemma

Even when target stockholders cannot act collectively or they are not 'protected' by legal/institutional sanctions, there will be a market solution to

---

[31] The constraints imposed by fair-price statutes and fair-price amendments do not vitiate our necessary condition for a successful tender offer that $P_T$ be greater than $P_E$. Even when these legal and institutional constraints require the back-end price to be nominally equal to the front-end price, there are economic forces at work that make even these offers front-end loaded.

To begin with, fair-price provisions are relevant only in two-step takeovers. Thus, one way to negate their effects is for bidding firms to buy a controlling interest in the target at the stated offer price and never buy the remaining target shares. In other words, the bidding firm could secure a controlling interest in the target and run it as a subsidiary. As long as the bidding firm does not buy the remaining shares in a two-step takeover, fair-price provisions cannot guarantee that the back-end market price will be as great as the front-end offer price.

A second reason why fair-price provisions do not affect our necessary condition for a successful offer is the time value of money. If there is a significant delay between the first and the second steps of a two-step takeover, the value of the front end will be greater than the (present) value of the back end even if the dollar amounts of the two are the same.

Finally, transactions costs may make the front-end price more valuable than the back-end price even when the two are nominally the same. Typically, target stockholders who tender to the front end of a two-step offer do not pay brokerage fees. However, if a significant number of shares are purchased in the front end and, as a result, the major exchanges delist the firm's stock, target stockholders will have to incur transactions costs to have their shares redeemed at the back-end price.

In sum, although fair-price provisions constrain the degree to which bidding firms can effect a front-end loaded acquisition, these constraints do not negate our necessary condition for a successful offer. For many of these same reasons, even any-and-all offers, in which the bidding firm is willing to buy all target shares at a given price, are, for all intents and purposes, front-end loaded offers. For a further analysis of the constraints imposed on bidding firms in setting the back-end or takeout price, see Bradley and Rosenzweig (1986 a, b).

the prisoner's dilemma. Recall that in section A.2.1, the bid of the 'raider' was $50 each for five shares on the front end and $20 each for the remaining five shares on the back end; and that in the absence of an alternative bid, target stockholders were induced to tender their shares to this bidder.

Consider now a share repurchase (an intrafirm tender offer) with the following terms. The target managers will pay $60 each for all shares tendered up to five shares. If more than five shares are tendered, they will effect the offer on a pro-rata basis, and hence, the *implicit* back-end price of this offer is $20. The question now becomes; how will target stockholders respond to these two competing bids?

We employ the logic of game theory to deduce the 'optimal' response by target stockholders. Assume first that target stockholders believe that the 'raider' will be successful; i.e., the 'raider' will be successful in attracting at least five of the ten target shares. (Note that in our example we assume that the 'raider' will be able to secure control of the target with five shares. To be technically correct we should be talking about securing 51% of the outstanding target shares.) With these beliefs, target stockholders will also believe that the target management will purchase every share tendered at $60. Consequently, they will not tender to the raider; instead, they will tender to the target management. Clearly, this does not constitute a Nash equilibrium.

Assume now that target stockholders believe that the target managers will be successful in their share repurchase program. Under this set of beliefs, target stockholders will tender to the target managers and the repurchase program will in fact succeed. This is a Nash equilibrium – the beliefs of target stockholders are fulfilled.

Table 8 illustrates the response/outcome payoff matrix facing our two-share target stockholder in the wake of the bid by the 'raider' and the intrafirm tender offer. The entries in the table illustrate that tendering to the share repurchase is the dominant strategy. The obvious outcome of this game is that all target stockholders will tender their shares to the repurchase program and, as indicated in the table, aggregate stockholder wealth will be unchanged.

• The importance of the preceding numeric example lies in its generality. Target managers are always able to structure an intrafirm tender offer that dominates the bid of a corporate raider who attempts to acquire the target at below its preoffer market value. The potential for such a dominating intrafirm tender offer solves the prisoner's dilemma.[32] As a result, value-decreasing bids will never be successful and therefore probably are never made.

---

[32]Another defensive mechanism available to target management is to liquidate the firm and pay out the proceeds as a liquidating dividend. Thus, the firm's liquidation value represents the ultimate lower bound for the value of a successful raiding bid. Kim and Schatzberg (1987) examine a sample of firms that voluntarily liquidated and document that the shareholder wealth increased by an average of 34 percent.

Table 8

Wealth changes for a target stockholder (owning two shares) contingent on aggregate stockholder response and his individual response. Rows indicate stockholder response; columns indicate aggregate shareholder response; and cells indicate change in wealth. *Assumptions*: Target is an all-equity firm with ten shares outstanding and stockholder owns two shares with a preoffer value of $40 each. One tender offer outstanding: bidder offers to buy 50% of the target shares for $50 on the front end and $20 on the back end; a repurchase program outstanding: offer to repurchase up to 50% of the target shares for $60 (on the front end) with an implicit back-end price of $20; pro-rata execution.

| Individual shareholder response | Aggregate market response | | | | |
|---|---|---|---|---|---|
| | Repurchase successful | | Bidder successful | | Neither offer successful |
| | 50% tendered | All other shares tendered | 50% tendered | All other shares tendered | |
| Hold | $ − 40 | $ − 40 | $ − 40 | $ − 40 | 0 |
| Tender to bidder | − 40 | − 40 | + 20 | − 10 | 0 |
| Tender repurchase | + 40 | 0 | + 40 | + 40 | 0 |

## A.3. Tender offers with synergistic gains

The analysis presented in the preceding section implies that only value-increasing tender offers will be made. In this section we argue that if there is more than one firm that can effect a value-increasing allocation of the target resources, the firm that can effect the highest synergistic gain will win control of the target. To see this, consider two firms that are able to effect synergistic gains by combining with the target. Assume that bidder 1 can increase the value of the target to $500 and bidder 2 can increase its value to $600. As we will see, both firms will attempt to set as high a front-end price as possible and will try to minimize its back-end price. As discussed earlier, the minimum $P_E$ that a bidding firm can set is determined by legal and institutional factors. Thus we assume that the minimum $P_E$ is specific to the target – as opposed to the bidding firm. For expositional convenience, we assume that the minimum $P_E$ that either bidder can set is the preoffer value of the target firm, which is $40 in our example. With a $40 back-end price, bidder 1 can offer $60 on the front end (for five shares) and bidder 2 can offer $80. The question now becomes: if both bidding firms make their respective maximum offers, how would target stockholders respond?

It is clear that there is no dominant strategy for target stockholders to pursue. There is no unique Nash equilibrium. If target stockholders believe that bidder 1 will win, the optimal strategy is to tender to bidder 1. However, if they believe bidder 2 will win, they will tender to bidder 2. In short, with front-end loaded tender offers it is always better to have tendered to the winning bidder. Thus, each target stockholder will tender to the bidding firm that he believes will win.

Given the above assumptions, bidder 2 (the one that can effect the highest-valued synergy) can make the following revised bid. It can make a firm commitment to purchase up to five (51%) of the target shares for $1 more than bidder 1's offer price ($61), regardless of the number of shares tendered to bidder 1. We now examine the possible equilibria of this revised game.

Assume that target stockholders believe that bidder 2 will win the contest. With this set of beliefs, target stockholders will tender to bidder 2 and bidder 2 will in fact win. This is a Nash equilibrium.

Now assume that target stockholders believe that bidder 1 will win the contest (secure 51% of the target shares). Under these circumstances target stockholders would eschew bidder 1's offer and tender to bidder 2's firm commitment to buy up to 51% of the shares at $61 per share. Since, by assumption, target stockholders believe that bidder 1 will receive at least 51%, they will also believe that bidder 2 will purchase every share tendered for $61 each. Thus, when target stockholders believe that bidder 1 will win, they will tender to bidder 2 instead. Consequently, this is not a Nash equilibrium. Thus, by the above analysis, the only set of beliefs that are consistent with the outcome of the 'game' is that bidder 2, the higher-valued bidder with the firm commitment offer, will win the tender offer contest.

Note that bidder 1 (the lower-valued bidder) will never make an offer with a front-end price greater than $60 a share, nor will it make an unconditional (firm-commitment) offer at $60 a share. Given a minimum back-end price of $40, the acquisition of five shares at greater than $60 a share will result in a value-decreasing transaction for its shareholders. (Recall that bidder 1 can effect only $100 in total synergistic gains.) Moreover, it will never offer a firm commitment at $60 a share, because bidder 1 knows that every share it purchases at $60 will be worth only $40 when bidder 2 inevitably gains control of the target.

The analysis of this appendix generates several important implications. First, in tender offer contests, the successful bidder will be the one that can effect the highest synergistic gains. Second, the total value of the winning offer must be at least equal to the next-highest-valued allocation of the target resources, which is bounded from below by the preoffer market value of the target shares. Thus, successful tender offers will be value-increasing transactions for the stockholders of target firms and will result in the optimal allocation of the target resources.

## References

Asquith, P., R. Bruner, and D. Mullins, 1983, The gains to bidding firms from merger, Journal of Financial Economics 11, 121–140.

Asquith, P. and E.H. Kim, 1982, The impact of merger bids on the participating firms' security holders, Journal of Finance 37, 1209–1228.

Berkovitch, E. and N. Khanna, 1986, A theory of acquisition markets: Mergers versus tender offers: Golden parachutes and greenmail, Working paper (University of Michigan, Ann Arbor, MI).

Bradley, M., 1980, Interfirm tender offers and the market for corporate control, Journal of Business 53, 345–376.

Bradley, M. and E.H. Kim, 1984, The advent and mechanics of the tender offer: An analysis of ownership structure and prisoner's dilemma, Proceedings of Seminar on the Analysis of Security Prices 29, 277–302.

Bradley, M. and M. Rosenzweig, 1986a, Defensive stock repurchases, Harvard Law Review 99, 1378–1430.

Bradley, M. and M. Rosenzweig, 1986b, Defensive stock repurchases and the appraisal remedy, Yale Law Journal 96, 322–338.

Bradley, M., A. Desai, and E.H. Kim, 1983, The rationale behind interfirm tender offers: Information or synergy?, Journal of Financial Economics 11, 183–206.

Comment, R. and G. Jarrell, 1987, Two-tier and negotiated tender offers: The imprisonment of the free-riding shareholder, Journal of Financial Economics 19, 283–310.

Dodd, P. and R. Ruback, 1977, Tender offers and stockholder returns, Journal of Financial Economics 5, 351–373.

Eckbo, B.E., 1983, Horizontal mergers, collusion, and stockholder wealth, Journal of Financial Economics 11, 241–274.

Eckbo, B.E., 1985, Mergers and the market concentration doctrine: Evidence from the capital market, Journal of Business 58, 325–349.

Economic report of the President, Feb. 1985.

Fishman, M., 1986, A theory of preemptive takeover bidding, Working paper (Northwestern University, Evanston, IL).

Grossman, S. and O. Hart, 1980, Takeover bids, the free rider problem, and the theory of the corporation, Bell Journal of Economics 11, 42–64.

Jarrell, G., 1983, Do acquirers benefit from corporate acquisitions?, Working paper (University of Chicago, Chicago, IL).

Jarrell, G. and M. Bradley, 1980, The economic effects of federal and state regulations of cash tender offers, Journal of Law and Economics 23, 371–407.

Jensen, M.C., 1985, When Unocal won over Mesa, shareholders and society lost, The Financier 9, 30–52.

Khanna, N., 1986, Optimal bidding for tender offers, Working paper (University of Michigan, Ann Arbor, MI).

Kim, E.H. and J. McConnell, 1977, Corporate merger and the 'co-insurance' of corporate debt, Journal of Finance 32, 349–365.

Kim, E.H. and J. Schatzberg, 1987, Voluntary corporate liquidations, Journal of Financial Economics 19, 311–328.

Lehn, K. and J.W. Jones, 1987, The legislative politics of hostile corporate takeovers, Paper presented at the conference on political economy and business (Washington University, St. Louis, MO).

Loderer, C.F. and D.C. Mauer, 1986, Acquiring firms in corporate mergers· The postmerger performance, Working paper (Purdue University, W. Lafayette, IN).

Patell, J.M., 1976, Corporate forecasts of earnings per share and stock price behavior: Empirical tests, Journal of Accounting Research 14, 246–276.

Roll, R., 1986, The Hubris hypothesis of corporate takeovers, Journal of Business 59, 197–216.

Rosenfeld, A., 1982, Repurchase offers, information adjusted premiums and shareholder response, MERC monograph series MP-8201 (University of Rochester, Rochester, NY).

Ruback, R., 1983, Assessing competition in the market for corporate control, Journal of Financial Economics 11, 141–153.

Shleifer, A. and R.W. Vishny, 1986, Large shareholders and corporate control, Journal of Political Economy 94, 461–488.

Stillman, R., 1983, Examining antitrust policy towards horizontal mergers, Journal of Financial Economics 11, 225–240.

# INSIDERS' PROFITS, COSTS OF TRADING, AND MARKET EFFICIENCY*

## H. Nejat SEYHUN

*The University of Michigan, Ann Arbor, MI 48109, USA*

Received November 1984, final version received October 1985

This study investigates the anomalous findings of the previous insider trading studies that any investor can earn abnormal profits by reading the *Official Summary*. Availability of abnormal profits to insiders, availability of abnormal profits to outsiders who imitate insiders, determinants of insiders' predictive ability, and effect of insider trading on costs of trading for other investors are examined by using approximately 60,000 insider sale and purchase transactions from 1975 to 1981. Implications for market efficiency and evaluation of abnormal profits to active trading strategies are discussed.

## 1. Introduction

Numerous studies, such as Lorie and Niederhoffer (1968), Pratt and DeVere (1970), Jaffe (1974), and Finnerty (1976) among others, conclude that insiders earn significant abnormal profits by trading the securities of their own firms.[1] Estimates of insiders' abnormal profits in these studies vary from 3% to 30% during holding periods of eight months to three years. Surprisingly, insider trading studies also report that even uninformed *outsiders* can earn significant abnormal profits by imitating insiders: Outsiders can purchase stock following insiders' stock purchases, sell stock following insiders' stock sales using publicly available insider trading information, and thereby also earn 3% to 30% abnormal profits.

The conclusion that abnormal profits can be earned by trading on the basis of publicly available information contradicts the efficient markets hypothesis which maintains that security prices respond rapidly to public information,

*This paper is based on a Ph.D. dissertation written at the University of Rochester. I am grateful to my dissertation committee, G. William Schwert (chairman), Clifford W. Smith, and Jerold B. Warner for their guidance and encouragement. Helpful comments were received from Michael Bradley, Susan Chaplinsky, Eugene Fama, Michael Jensen, Han Kim, Richard Leftwich, Wayne Mikkelson, Jay Ritter, and an anonymous referee.

[1] Individuals who are officers, directors, and owners of 10% or more of any equity class of securities are defined as insiders by the Securities and Exchange Act of 1934.

Journal of Financial Economics 16 (1986) 189–212. North-Holland

thus precluding any systematic profit opportunities. The efficient markets hypothesis is a central tenet of financial economics and it is supported by a large body of evidence.[2] This study reinvestigates stock price behavior following insiders' transactions and attempts to reconcile the efficient markets hypothesis with the previously reported availability of abnormal profits to outsiders.

Recent studies by Banz (1981) and Reinganum (1981) document that the use of the Capital Asset Pricing Model results in potential biases in measuring expected returns to securities. Consequently, the results of the previous insider trading studies using the CAPM must be interpreted with caution. The methodology used in this study avoids this bias. Furthermore, previous insider trading studies generally assume that all insider trading information becomes publicly available within two months. This assumption can lead to a potential bias against market efficiency: In efficient markets, stock price reaction is expected to occur at the time information becomes public. If some transactions are published with a more than two month delay, then the stock price reaction is also expected to occur with a more than two month delay. To evaluate the abnormal returns available to outsiders, this study uses the actual dates insiders first report their transactions to the Securities and Exchange Commission (SEC) and the dates insider trading information is published in the *Official Summary*. The profitability of insider trading is evaluated by examining approximately 60,000 insider transactions during the period 1975 to 1981. The data are analyzed separately for buy and sell decisions, type of insiders, and dollar volume of insider trading.

A generally overlooked implication of profitable trading by informed investors is that there is a loser for each winner, since informed traders' abnormal profits reduce the opposing traders' realized returns dollar for dollar. An investor who attempts to exploit a perceived profit opportunity must also bear the risk of potential losses to opposing informed traders. If the informed traders impose significant losses on the opposing uninformed traders, then ignoring informed traders' abnormal profits can lead to an overstatement of the realizable abnormal returns to any trading rule.

The significance of the costs imposed by the informed traders on the uninformed traders has not been empirically examined, since the informed traders' abnormal profits are not readily observable. Studies by Glosten and Milgrom (1985), Copeland and Galai (1983), Treynor (1981), and Bagehot (1971) hypothesize a positive relation between the informed traders' abnormal profits and the bid–ask spread in that security. Profitable trading by informed traders imposes abnormal losses on all opposing traders, including the market-maker. Consequently, the market-maker is forced to charge a higher

---

[2] See Fama (1970) for a review of theory and early evidence on the efficient markets hypothesis.

bid–ask spread to all traders to help offset his systematic losses to informed traders. In this study, the significance of the uninformed traders' expected losses to the informed traders is investigated by examining the relation between the bid–ask spread and insiders' abnormal profits.

The paper is organized as follows: Section 2 discusses the relation between profitable trading by informed traders and the bid–ask spread. The insider trading data and the sample characteristics are discussed in section 3. Section 4 explains the empirical methodology, and section 5 presents the results. Conclusions and implications are in section 6.

## 2. Informed traders' abnormal profits and bid–ask spread

If some traders are better informed than others, then the market-maker in a security experiences an adverse selection problem. If he were to set a single price to buy and sell any amount of securities on demand, on average, he would neither gain from nor lose to uninformed investors, since trading by uninformed investors is not related to abnormal future stock price movements by definition. However, he would systematically lose to the informed traders. He would inadvertently buy stock from the informed traders prior to abnormal stock price declines and sell stock to the informed traders prior to abnormal stock price increases, thereby resulting in inventory positions that are negatively correlated with future abnormal stock price movements. In effect, the informed traders' abnormal profits would come at the market-maker's expense.

If the market-maker cannot distinguish the informed traders from the uninformed traders prior to trading, then he would be forced to charge all traders for the expected value of their possible non-public information. He would lower his bid (purchase) price to reflect possible unfavorable information and raise his ask (sale) price to reflect possible favorable information of the informed traders. The informed traders would still purchase stock from the market-maker if they expect the stock price to rise above the ask price, or sell stock to the market-maker if they expect the stock price to fall below the bid price. Therefore, even with a positive bid–ask spread, the market-maker continues to incur net losses to the informed traders. However, his losses to the informed traders are now offset by his gains from the uninformed traders, who now pay a higher bid–ask spread to trade with the market-maker. A higher bid–ask spread means that the expected traders' abnormal profits come at the expense of the uninformed traders who trade for reasons other than profiting from information.

The market-maker's response to informed traders implies a positive relation between the bid–ask spread and the informed traders' abnormal profits. The bid–ask spread would be higher than otherwise, if the informed traders possess more valuable information when they trade or account for a greater proportion of the overall trading volume.[3] In effect, the market-maker's bid–ask spread reflects his expected losses to *all* informed traders.

Ignoring the relation between the bid–ask spread and the expected loss to informed traders can lead to an overstatement of the realizable return to any active trading rule. If it is assumed that investors can always trade at the current stock price without ever paying the bid–ask spread, then their realizable return will be overstated by an amount equal to their expected loss to informed traders. This study provides the first empirical test of the hypothesized positive relation between the bid–ask spread and the expected loss to informed traders. If the evidence indicates a significant positive relation between the bid–ask spread and the expected loss to informed traders, then an allowance for the expected loss to informed traders can be made by including the bid–ask spread for a 100-share transaction as an additional cost of trading. The bid–ask spread for a 100-share transaction would overestimate the expected loss to informed traders to the extent that it reflects other costs of market-making. However, if the informed investors trade larger volumes of stock to exploit more valuable information, then the bid–ask spread for a 100-share transaction can also underestimate the expected loss to informed traders from their larger volume transactions.

## 3. Data and sample characteristics

The insider trading data used in this study come from a computer tape compiled by the Securities and Exchange Commission (SEC). The tape summarizes more than 1.5 million insider transactions in all publicly held firms from 1975 to 1981. This study analyzes a sample of transactions in 790 firms on the daily returns file of the Center for Research in Security Prices (CRSP). The 190 firms listed on option exchanges on January 1, 1977 are included in the sample. The remaining 600 firms are chosen by stratified random sampling based on the size of firms' equity. Out of 790 firms, 21 did not report any insider trading between 1975 and 1981. Consequently, the actual number of firms analyzed is 769.

Table 1, panel A shows a breakdown of the insider trading sample by firm size. The sample analyzed in this study contains a total of 59,148 open market sales and purchases.[4] Total dollar value of insiders' transactions exceeds $11 billion, 58% of which occurs in the largest firm size group. Panel B shows a

---

[3] Other factors that can affect the size of the bid–ask spread, such as the competition facing the market-maker or costs of maintaining inventories, are analyzed in Demsetz (1968), Tinic (1972), Tinic and West (1972), Benston and Hagerman (1974), Stoll (1978), and Amihud and Mendelson (1980) among others.

[4] Numerous consistency checks on dates, prices, and shares were performed to eliminate approximately 1000 transactions containing apparent data errors. Also, transactions involving less than 100 shares are excluded.

Table 1

Distribution of the number of firms, dollar value, and number of transactions, grouped by the average size of equity of the firm and the identity of insiders (dollar figures are in $ million). Sample period is from 1975 to 1981.

| | Panel A: Grouping by firm size | | | | | |
| --- | --- | --- | --- | --- | --- | --- |
| | Less than $25 million | Between $25 and $50 million | Between $50 and $250 million | Between $250 million and $1 billion | More than $1 billion | All firms |
| Number of firms | 104 | 68 | 173 | 267 | 157 | 769 |
| Total dollar value of transactions | $152 | $182 | $1,287 | $2,990 | $6,490 | $11,101 |
| Number of transactions | 4,141 | 3,010 | 10,552 | 23,267 | 18,178 | 59,148 |
| Ratio of purchases to sales | 2.09 | 1.27 | 0.79 | 0.57 | 0.59 | 0.70 |

| | Panel B: Grouping by identity of insiders | | | | | |
| --- | --- | --- | --- | --- | --- | --- |
| | Officers | Directors | Officer-directors | Chairmen of boards of directors | Large share-holders | All insiders |
| Total dollar value of transactions | $806 | $1,889 | $571 | $408 | $7,427 | $11,101 |
| Number of transactions | 21,913 | 17,486 | 6,520 | 3,400 | 9,829 | 59,148 |

breakdown of the insider trading sample by the identity of insiders: officers, directors, officer-directors, chairmen of the boards of directors, and large shareholders. Officers trade most frequently, followed by directors, large shareholders, officer-directors, and chairmen of the boards of directors. The large shareholder group also trades the largest dollar volume of stock, accounting for 67% of the overall dollar volume of trading.

## 4. Empirical methodology

### 4.1. Benchmark selection

Among the recent insider trading studies, Jaffe (1974) and Finnerty (1976) use variants of the Capital Asset Pricing Model (CAPM) to estimate abnormal returns to securities. Work by Banz (1981) and Reinganum (1981) shows that the CAPM based residuals are on average positive for small firms, and negative for large firms. This systematic bias in CAPM residuals can lead to biases in estimating abnormal returns in insider trading studies. If insiders have predominantly more purchases than sales in small firms, then the positive CAPM residuals in small firms will be associated with insider purchases. Similarly, if insiders have predominantly more sales than purchases in large firms, then the negative CAPM residuals in large firms will be associated with insider sales.

Table 1 shows the ratio of insiders' stock purchases to sales for different size firms. In small firms, insiders have approximately twice as many purchases as sales. In large firms, the ratio of insiders' purchases to sales falls to about 0.6. This evidence suggests that even if insider trading conveys no information, biases in the CAPM can indeed result in finding positive abnormal returns following insider purchases and negative abnormal returns following insider sales. Consequently, the conclusions of the previous insider trading studies using the CAPM benchmark may overstate the abnormal returns realized from insider trading.

This study uses the market-model to measure the expected returns to securities. The market-model is a statistical model based on the joint normality of the distribution of security returns. Given parameter stationarity, the market-model prediction errors have an expected value of zero for firms of any size, thereby avoiding the bias introduced by CAPM.

## 4.2. Abnormal returns and significance tests

Based on the market-model, the prediction error $PE_{i,t}$ for security $i$ on day $t$, from 199 days before to 300 days after each event day is calculated as follows:[5]

$$PE_{i,t} = \left( r_{i,t} - \left( \hat{\alpha}_i + \hat{\beta}_i r_{m,t} \right) \right) W \quad \text{for} \quad t = -199, 300, \tag{1}$$

where $r_{i,t}$ is the with-dividend return to security $i$ on day $t$, and $r_{m,t}$ is the with-dividend return to value-weighted portfolio of all New York Stock Exchange and American Stock Exchange stocks on day $t$. To account for potential changes in market parameters, two sets of parameters $\hat{\alpha}_i$ and $\hat{\beta}_i$ are estimated using ordinary least squares regression of $r_{i,t}$ on $r_{m,t}$ with 250 pre-event and 250 post-event daily return data, always excluding the period from 199 days before to 300 days after the event day. The pre-event estimates are used to calculate the prediction errors between days $-199$ and $-1$, and post-event estimates are used to calculate the prediction errors between days 0 and 300. The last insider trading day in each month is taken as the event day. The parameter $W$ is equal to one if the number of buyers exceed the number

---

[5]See Fama (1976, ch. 4) for a discussion of the market-model. The event study methodology is pioneered by Fama, Fisher, Jensen and Roll (1969).

of sellers in that month, or minus one if the number of sellers exceed the number of buyers. If the number of buyers equals the number of sellers, that month is excluded. An insider is considered a buyer if he buys more shares than he sells or a seller if he sells more shares than he buys. Insiders who buy as many shares as they sell are ignored.

Successive, non-overlapping one-month and two-month periods are used to classify insiders' transactions. The overall results are similar and only two-month period results are reported. The two-month period results are chosen for extensive analysis to economize on data processing costs.

The average portfolio prediction error for event day $t$, $APE_t$, is calculated by averaging all prediction errors for that event day. This test statistic incorporates any possible cross-sectional dependencies of prediction errors at a given calendar day,

$$APE_t = \frac{1}{K_t} \sum_{i=1}^{K_t} PE_{i,t} \quad \text{for} \quad t = -199,300, \tag{2}$$

where $K_t$ is the number of prediction errors on event day $t$.

The significance of the average portfolio prediction errors is measured by standardizing the average portfolio prediction errors by their sample standard error $\hat{\sigma}(APE)$,

$$t(APE_t) = APE_t/\hat{\sigma}(APE). \tag{3}$$

The sample standard error of $APE_t$, $\hat{\sigma}(APE)$, is calculated from 199 days before to 300 days after the event day, by taking into account the serial correlation of the $APE_t$'s. Empirical examination of the $APE$ series shows a stationary, third-order autoregressive process. Thus,

$$APE_t = \delta + \phi_1 APE_{t-1} + \phi_2 APE_{t-2} + \phi_3 APE_{t-3} + u_t. \tag{4}$$

The standard error of the $APE$ series, $\hat{\sigma}(APE)$, is computed by solving the Yule–Walker equations corresponding to eq. (4).[6] The $t$-statistic in eq. (3) has a Student-$t$ distribution with 493 degrees of freedom when $APE_t$ is a stationary normal process. The cumulative daily average prediction error from event day $t_1$ to event day $t_2$, $CAPE(t_1, t_2)$, is calculated by summing the daily average prediction errors,

$$CAPE\ (t_1, t_2) = \sum_{t=t_1}^{t_2} APE_t. \tag{5}$$

The significance of the cumulative daily average prediction error is measured

---

[6]For a discussion of autoregressive processes, see Nelson (1973). For the overall sample, the partial autocorrelation coefficients of the $APE_t$ in eq. (4) are 0.38 ($t$-statistic 8.4) at first lag, 0.16 ($t$-statistic 3.5) at second lag, and 0.10 ($t$-statistic 2.2) at third lag.

by standardizing each cumulative daily average prediction error by its sample standard error,[7]

$$t\big(CAPE(t_1, t_2)\big) = CAPE(t_1, t_2)\big/\hat{\sigma}\big(CAPE(t_1, t_2)\big). \tag{6}$$

## 5. Empirical results

### 5.1. Profitability of insider trading

The cumulative daily average prediction errors are plotted separately for sales and purchases in fig. 1. The cumulative daily average prediction errors and their $t$-statistics computed from eq. (5) and (6), respectively, are shown in table 2. For the overall sample, the prediction errors for sales are multiplied by minus one before averaging with purchases. Consequently, abnormal stock price rises following insiders' purchases and abnormal stock price declines following insiders' sales are measured as positive abnormal returns in the overall sample.

If insiders purchase stock prior to an announcement of favorable information, then insiders' purchases will be *followed* by positive abnormal returns. If insiders also refrain from purchasing stock until after unfavorable information is announced, then insiders' purchases will be *preceded* by negative abnormal returns. Similar considerations hold for insiders' sale transactions. Table 2 shows that, during the 100 days following the insider trading day, stock prices rise abnormally by 3.0% ($t$-statistic 4.4) for purchases and decline abnormally by 1.7% ($t$-statistic $-2.7$) for sales. This suggests that insiders purchase stock prior to the release of favorable information and sell stock prior to the release of unfavorable information.[8] During the 100 days prior to the insider trading day, stock prices decline abnormally by 1.4% ($t$-statistic $-2.1$) for purchases and rise abnormally by 2.5% ($t$-statistic 4.0) for sales. This suggests that insiders also tend to refrain from purchasing stock until after unfavorable information is released, and from selling stock until after favorable information is released. Fig. 1 indicates that most of the abnormal stock price adjustment occurs during the 100 days following the insider trading day. For the overall sample, the stock price adjustment between days 101 and 300 is 0.8% ($t$-statistic 0.9), which is insignificantly different from zero.

---

[7] The standard error of the cumulative daily average prediction error, $\hat{\sigma}(CAPE(t_1, t_2))$, is calculated from the general formula for the variance of a sum,

$$\hat{\sigma}\big(CAPE(t_1, t_2)\big) = \left[\sum_{j=t_1}^{t_2} \sum_{k=t_1}^{t_2} \mathrm{cov}\big(APE_j, APE_k\big)\right]^{1/2},$$

where the covariances of the $APE$ are computed from the Yule–Walker equations corresponding to eq. (4).

[8] During the first 40 days following the insider trading day, stock prices rise abnormally for 55% of the purchases and only 45% of the sales. The $t$-statistics for the hypothesis that the true proportions are 50% are 7.5 for purchases and $-9.4$ for sales.

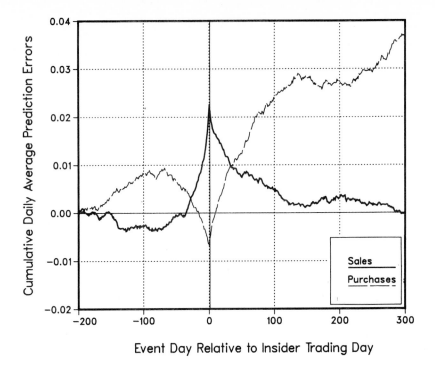

Fig. 1. Cumulative daily average prediction errors from 199 days before to 300 days after the insider trading day, for a portfolio of 769 firms traded by insiders during 1975 to 1981, separated by sale and purchase transactions.

Insiders' abnormal profits do not appear to be especially large. However, insider trading is regulated by the Securities and Exchange Act of 1934. Insiders can be sued for violating their fiduciary responsibilities to their shareholders if they trade on material non-public information prior to the public announcement of the information.[9] Consequently, insiders would not be expected to trade for their own account immediately prior to highly profitable but also publicized corporate events such as mergers and tender offers.

Estimates of insiders' abnormal profits presented in table 2 are smaller than the estimates in the previous insider trading studies. For example, Jaffe (1974) estimates insiders' gross abnormal profits to be 2% over two months and 5%

---

[9]Section 10 of the Securities and Exchange Act of 1934 prohibits fraud in purchase or sale of securities. Section 16(a) requires the reporting of insiders' transactions. Section 16(b) requires the profits from purchases and sales within six months of each other to be returned to the corporation. Section 16(c) prohibits short sales by insiders. Section 32 as amended in 1975 provides penalties up to $10,000 fine and five years of imprisonment for violating any provision of the securities law.

Table 2

Percentage cumulative daily average prediction errors, *CAPE*, and their *t*-statistics in parentheses, for 769 firms traded by insiders from 1975 to 1981 for selected periods around the insider trading day, denoted as day 0.

| Event period | *CAPE* for overall sample | *CAPE* for purchases | *CAPE* for sales |
|---|---|---|---|
| Day −100 through 0 | −2.1 (−3.3) | −1.4 (−2.1) | 2.5 (4.0) |
| Day −20 through 0 | −1.3 (−4.8) | −0.7 (−2.4) | 1.7 (6.2) |
| Day 1 through 20 | 1.0 (3.7) | 1.1 (3.8) | −0.9 (−3.3) |
| Day 1 through 50 | 1.6 (3.6) | 1.9 (4.0) | −1.5 (−3.4) |
| Day 1 through 100 | 2.3 (3.7) | 3.0 (4.4) | −1.7 (−2.7) |
| Day 101 through 300 | 0.8 (0.9) | 1.3 (1.4) | −0.5 (−0.6) |
| Day 1 through 300 | 3.1 (2.8) | 4.3 (3.7) | −2.2 (−2.0) |
| Sample size | 15,083 | 6,244 | 8,839 |

over eight months following intensive trading periods. An outsider who imitates insiders with a two-month delay also earns 5% over the next eight months. This implies that Jaffe finds 7% abnormal returns over a ten-month period. Finnerty (1976) finds between 4.8% and 8.3% abnormal returns over an eleven-month period. Pratt and DeVere (1970) examine the returns to firms purchased by three or more insiders and sold by none, and firms sold by three or more insiders and purchased by none. Pratt and DeVere find that firms purchased outperform firms sold by 17.5% after one year, 28.6% after two years, and 32.4% after three years.

In an attempt to reconcile the differences with the previous studies, the tests in table 2 are replicated using different models of expected returns, different estimating periods, and different classification criterion for insiders. As alternative benchmark models, the Scholes and Williams (1977) estimates of the market-model parameters, the mean-returns adjusted model, and the Sharpe–Lintner version of the CAPM are used. The results based on the Scholes–Williams model and the mean-returns adjusted model agree closely with the market-model which suggests that the results are not sensitive to a particular measure of expected returns. The results using only the pre-event periods to estimate expected returns to securities are similar to fig. 1. Using dollar volume of insider sales and purchases instead of number of insiders to classify a given month as a purchase or sale month also gives similar results. Classifying insider trading months on the basis of the net number of insiders (calculated as the absolute value of purchasers minus sellers in each month) does not reveal significant differences in abnormal returns to insiders.

In contrast, using the CAPM benchmark to measure the expected returns to securities increases the measured abnormal returns during the 300 days following the insider trading day from 3.1% to 4.3%. This evidence is consistent with the upward bias in CAPM based abnormal returns. The exact magnitude of the bias due to CAPM during other time periods would depend on the strength of the small firm effect and the distribution of the sale and purchase transactions across firms. Also, using the period immediately prior to the insider trading day to estimate the market-model parameters increases the measured abnormal returns from 3.1% up to about 7%. This is not surprising since fig. 1 indicates that using the period immediately prior to the insider trading day would cause estimates of expected returns to be downward biased for purchases and upward biased for sales. These tests suggest that the failure of the CAPM to properly measure expected returns, as well as inappropriate choice of estimation periods, can result in larger estimates of abnormal profits following insider transactions.

## 5.2. Bid–ask spread and expected loss to insiders

As discussed earlier, the market-maker's response to profitable trading by informed traders is to raise the bid–ask spread. Recent studies by Schultz (1983) and Stoll and Whaley (1983) show that there is a negative monotonic relation between firm size and the bid–ask spread. For small firms (average equity value of $3.4 million), Schultz estimates the bid–ask spread plus the commission fee to be 11.4%. Stoll and Whaley estimate that the bid–ask spread falls from 2.9% to 0.7% as firm size increases from about $15 million to more than $3 billion. Consequently, the hypothesized positive relation between the bid–ask spread and expected loss to insiders implies a negative relation between the firm size and expected loss to insiders. Fixed costs of market-making combined with lower trading volume in small firms also implies larger bid–ask spreads in small firms. However, if the fixed cost of market-making is largely responsible for differences in bid–ask spreads across firms, then no relation between firm size and expected loss to informed traders would be expected.

The relation between the firm size and expected losses to insiders is investigated by using regression analysis. Including insider transactions from successive calendar months induces autocorrelation of the residuals which is taken

Table 3

Generalized least squares regression of the cumulative daily average prediction errors, and ordinary least squares regression of the probability of trading against insiders, on the average size of the equity of the firm.[a] The $t$-statistics for the estimated coefficients are shown in parentheses. Sample period is from 1975 to 1981.

| Model number | Model | Sample size | F-statistics |
|---|---|---|---|
| (1) | $CAPE(1,50) = 0.130 - 0.0057LV$<br>$\quad\quad\quad\quad\quad (8.3)\quad (-7.4)$ | 15,083 | $54.0^b$ |
| (2) | $CAPE(1,50) = 0.045 - 0.015V2 - 0.023V3 - 0.035V4 - 0.036V5$<br>$\quad\quad\quad\quad\quad (9.1)\quad (-2.0)\quad (-4.0)\quad (-6.6)\quad (-6.6)$ | 15,083 | $15.5^b$ |
| (3) | $CAPE(1,100) = 0.200 - 0.0092\,LV$<br>$\quad\quad\quad\quad\quad\quad (8.1)\quad (-7.3)$ | 15,083 | $53.0^b$ |
| (4) | $CAPE(1,100) = 0.070 - 0.021V2 - 0.041V3 - 0.056V4 - 0.058V5$<br>$\quad\quad\quad\quad\quad\quad (7.2)\quad (-1.7)\quad (-4.4)\quad (-6.7)\quad (-6.6)$ | 15,083 | $15.5^b$ |
| (5) | $Probability = 0.122 - 0.0054LV$<br>$\quad\quad\quad\quad\quad (6.0)\quad (-5.2)$ | 769 | $26.5^b$ |
| (6) | $Probability = 0.036 + 0.0095V2 - 0.017V3 - 0.025V4 - 0.028V5$<br>$\quad\quad\quad\quad\quad (6.5)\quad (1.0)\quad\quad (-2.5)\quad (-4.0)\quad (-4.0)$ | 769 | $9.0^b$ |

[a] $CAPE(1,50)$ and $CAPE(1,100)$ are the cumulative daily average prediction errors from 1 day to 50 days, and 1 day to 100 days following the insider trading day, respectively. $LV$ is the natural log of the average value of equity between 1975 and 1981. $V2 = 1$ if value of equity is greater than or equal to $25 million and less than $50 million, otherwise $V2 = 0$. $V3 = 1$ if value of equity is greater than or equal to $50 million and less than $250 million, otherwise $V3 = 0$. $V4 = 1$ if value of equity is greater than or equal to $250 million and less than $1 billion, otherwise $V4 = 0$. $V5 = 1$ if value of equity is greater than or equal to $1 billion, otherwise $V5 = 0$. Value of equity is less than $25 million, if $V2 = V3 = V4 = V5 = 0$. *Probability* is probability of trading against insiders, calculated as the absolute value of the net dollar value of insider trading divided by the total dollar value of trading in that security from 1975 to 1981.

[b] Significant at 1% level.

into account by using generalized least squares. The prediction errors across firms at a given calendar day are expected to be uncorrelated, since multiplying the prediction errors for sale transactions by minus one randomizes the prediction errors.[10]

Table 3 shows regression of insiders' abnormal profits on firm size. Models (1) and (3) indicate negative relations between the abnormal returns to insiders and the natural log of the firm size, both significant at the 1% level. Using the dummy variable models (2) and (4), insiders' abnormal profits in different size firms are readily observable. The cumulative daily average prediction errors from 1 day to 50 days following the insider trading day decrease from 4.5% to 0.9% as firm size increases from less than $25 million to more than $1 billion. Similarly, the cumulative daily average prediction errors from 1 day to 100

---

[10] In addition to the market model, regressions are replicated using the mean-returns adjusted model, Scholes–Williams model, and CAPM. The results are similar and are not shown.

days following the insider trading day decrease from 7.0% to 1.2% as firm size increases from less than $25 million to more than $1 billion. This evidence suggests that, conditional on trading, insiders in small firms earn substantially greater abnormal returns than the insiders in large firms. Consequently, conditional on trading, insiders in small firms also impose substantially greater costs on the uninformed traders than the insiders in large firms.

Table 3 also provides information on the probability of trading against insiders, defined as the ratio of dollar volume of insider trading to all trading in that security. Model (5) in table 3 shows a negative relation between the probability of trading against insiders and the log of firm size. This relation is significant at the 1% level. The dummy variable model (6) indicates that the probability of trading against an insider declines from about 4% for firms less than $25 million to about 0.8% for firms greater than $1 billion. Thus, the evidence indicates that the probability of trading against insiders also declines with increasing firm size.

The results in table 3 indicate that the expected losses to insiders fall with the size of the firm. Insiders' abnormal profits, conditional on trading, as well as the probability of trading against insiders decline with the size of the firm. To the extent insider trading is positively correlated with trading by all informed traders, this evidence is consistent with the hypothesis that informed traders impose significant costs on uninformed traders, and the bid–ask spread reflects the expected loss to informed traders.

A precise imputation of the expected loss to informed traders requires measurement of the expected abnormal profits of *all* informed traders, an empirically infeasible task. This study takes the bid–ask spread for a 100-share transaction as an approximate measure of the expected loss to informed traders. With competition, the bid–ask spread would not differ from the expected loss to informed traders by more than other costs of market-making. For example, if the bid–ask spread were less than the expected loss to informed traders, then the market-maker could not survive. If the bid–ask spread were to exceed the expected loss to informed traders by more than the other costs of market-making, then other potential market-makers would find it profitable to undercut the market-maker by placing simultaneous buy orders at his bid price and sell orders at his ask price.

Market efficiency studies generally assume that informed traders are a negligibly small part of the market, and therefore, the expected loss to informed traders may be ignored. The evidence presented in this study shows a significant positive relation between the bid–ask spread and the expected loss to insiders. This evidence suggests that the expected loss to informed traders is significant and is incorporated into the prices of securities. This finding implies that the expected loss to informed traders must also be taken into account to evaluate the realizable abnormal returns to active trading strategies. An approximate allowance for the expected loss to informed traders can be made by including the bid–ask spread as an additional cost of trading. Such an example is Phillips and Smith (1980) who evaluate the efficiency of the listed options market by including the bid–ask spread as an additional cost of trading for active trading strategies.

### 5.3. Determinants of insiders' abnormal profits

Previous insider trading studies have not investigated the sources of insiders' superior predictive ability. Most studies examine intensive trading months, defined as the difference between number of buyers and sellers. Jaffe (1974) also examines large dollar volume of trading by insiders, but concludes that the dollar volume of trading by insiders is not related to the value of insider information. An exception is found by Scholes (1972), who reports differences in the quality of information for different secondary sellers.

The tests presented in tables 4 and 5 investigate the determinants of insiders' superior predictive ability. This investigation also provides a check on the robustness of the negative relation between the expected loss to insiders and firm size. Generalized least squares regressions are used to account for serial correlation of the residuals. The dependent variable is the estimate of insiders' abnormal profit, the cumulative daily average prediction error. The independent variables are dummy variables for sales transactions and types of insiders, dollar volume of insider trading, proportion of firm traded, net number of insiders trading, and value of the firm.

Model (1) in table 4 shows a regression of the cumulative daily average prediction errors from 1 day to 50 days after the insider trading day on a dummy variable for sales transactions. The regression confirms the earlier result that insiders can reliably forecast future abnormal stock price changes, and purchase stock prior to abnormal price increases and sell stock prior to abnormal price decreases. Model (2) shows a regression of cumulative daily average prediction errors on types of insiders. All insiders are grouped into one of five categories: officers, directors, officer-directors, chairmen of the board of directors, and large shareholders. A given month is classified as an officer trading month, if officers trade the most dollar volume during that month.[11] The coefficient of the officer-director group is significantly positive at the 1% level, suggesting that on average officer-directors trade on more valuable information than officers. Differences between all insiders are significant at the 5% level. These tests indicate that insiders who are more familiar with the overall operations of the firm trade on more valuable information.

Model (3) shows a regression of the cumulative daily average prediction errors from 1 day to 50 days after the insider trading day, on the dollar value

---

[11]Similar results are obtained by classifying insider trading months on the basis of the frequency rather than the dollar value of insiders' transactions.

of trading. The slope coefficient in model (3) is insignificantly different from zero, which suggests that the dollar value of insider trading is not related to the value of insider information. This finding is similar to Jaffe (1974) and Scholes (1972) who also fail to find a relation between dollar volume of trading and value of insider information. A likely explanation for this result can be found in tables 1, 3, 4, and 5. Table 1 indicates that insiders in large firms and large shareholders in all firms account for most of the dollar value of trading. Table 3 and model (2) of tables 4 and 5 suggest that insiders in large firms and large shareholders in all firms trade on less valuable information. Consequently, the lack of information content of the large dollar volume transactions is likely to be due to the fact that the large dollar volume of transactions proxies for large firms and large shareholders: Insiders in large firms and large shareholders in all firms who happen to trade the large dollar volume transactions, also trade on less valuable information.

Model (4) in table 4 uses the natural log of the dollar value of trade. Taking the log of the dollar value of trade puts relatively less weight on extremely large dollar value transactions. The regression indicates that insiders' abnormal profits increase with the log of the dollar value of the transactions. The coefficient of the log of dollar value of trading is significantly positive at slightly above the 1% level. Model (5) uses the natural log of the proportion of the firm traded. Model (5) also indicates a positive relation between the insiders' abnormal profit and the log of proportion of the firm traded which is significant at the 1% level. Models (4) and (5) suggest that insiders trade larger dollar volume of stock to exploit more valuable information. However, dollar volume of trading increases less than linearly with the value of insider information.

Model (6) uses the natural log of the dollar value of trading and the natural log of firm size as explanatory variables. The coefficient of the dollar value of trading remains significantly positive, while the coefficient of firm size remains significantly negative. In fact, including firm size increases the significance of the dollar value of trading: For a given firm, insiders respond to more valuable information by trading a greater dollar volume of stock. Model (7) uses the natural log of the proportion of the firm traded and log of firm size. Once again, the proportion of the firm traded is positively related to insiders' abnormal profits, while firm size is negatively related to insiders' abnormal profits. Both coefficients are significant at the 1% level.

Types of insiders are included as additional explanatory variables in models (8) and (9). Inclusion of the types of insiders does not diminish the explanatory power of the firm size or the dollar value of insider trading. The magnitude and the significance of the estimated coefficients for firm size and dollar value of trade agree closely across models (6) and (8). Similarly, the magnitude and the significance of the estimated coefficients for firm size and the proportion of the firm traded agree closely across models (7) and (9). This evidence suggests that

Table 4

Generalized least squares regression of the cumulative daily average prediction errors from 1 day to 50 days following the insider trading day, on purchase versus sale decisions, type of insiders, dollar volume and log of dollar value of insider trading, log of proportion of the firm traded. net number of insiders, and the log of the value of the firm.[a] The t-statistics for estimated coefficients are shown in parentheses. Sample period is from 1975 to 1981.

| Model number | Model | F-statistics |
|---|---|---|
| (1) | $CAPE(1,50) = 0.020 - 0.033S$ <br> $\quad\quad\quad\quad\quad (9.8)\ (-13.2)$ | $174.7^{b}$ |
| (2) | $CAPE(1,50) = 0.012 + 0.004DIR + 0.012OD + 0.007CB + 0.004SH$ <br> $\quad\quad\quad\quad\quad (5.9)\quad (1.4)\quad\quad (3.1)\quad\quad (1.5)\quad\quad (0.9)$ | $2.6^{c}$ |
| (3) | $CAPE(1,50) = 0.016 - 0.0002T$ <br> $\quad\quad\quad\quad\quad (11.9)\ (-0.9)$ | $0.8$ |
| (4) | $CAPE(1,50) = 0.001 + 0.0013LT$ <br> $\quad\quad\quad\quad\quad (0.2)\quad (2.5)$ | $6.1^{c}$ |
| (5) | $CAPE(1,50) = 0.046 + 0.033LP$ <br> $\quad\quad\quad\quad\quad (9.2)\quad (6.3)$ | $40.7^{b}$ |
| (6) | $CAPE(1,50) = 0.122 - 0.0068LV + 0.0026LT$ <br> $\quad\quad\quad\quad\quad (7.9)\quad (-8.4)\quad\quad (4.7)$ | $37.8^{b}$ |
| (7) | $CAPE(1,50) = 0.120 - 0.0045LV + 0.0022LP$ <br> $\quad\quad\quad\quad\quad (8.0)\quad (-5.3)\quad\quad (3.8)$ | $34.0^{b}$ |
| (8) | $CAPE(1,50) = 0.118 - 0.0067LV + 0.0028LT + 0.001DIR + 0.007OD + 0.001CB - 0.005SH$ <br> $\quad\quad\quad\quad\quad (7.4)\quad (-8.1)\quad\quad (4.7)\quad\quad (0.4)\quad\quad (1.7)\quad\quad (0.3)\quad (-1.1)$ | $13.6^{b}$ |
| (9) | $CAPE(1,50) = 0.119 - 0.0042LV + 0.0023LP + 0.001DIR + 0.007OD + 0.002CB - 0.003SH$ <br> $\quad\quad\quad\quad\quad (7.5)\quad (-4.9)\quad\quad (3.7)\quad\quad (0.5)\quad\quad (1.8)\quad\quad (0.4)\quad (-0.7)$ | $12.3^{b}$ |
| (10) | $CAPE(1,50) = 0.012 + 0.006NI2 - 0.006NI3 + 0.016NI4 + 0.017NI5 + 0.016NI6$ <br> $\quad\quad\quad\quad\quad (7.6)\quad (2.1)\quad\quad (1.4)\quad\quad (1.7)\quad\quad (2.1)\quad\quad (2.3)$ | $2.7^{c}$ |
| (11) | $CAPE(1,50) = 0.041 + 0.003NI2 - 0.002NI3 + 0.005NI4 + 0.012NI5 + 0.010NI6 + 0.003LP$ <br> $\quad\quad\quad\quad\quad (7.6)\quad (1.2)\quad\quad (0.3)\quad\quad (0.9)\quad\quad (1.4)\quad\quad (1.4)\quad\quad (5.6)$ | $7.5^{b}$ |

[a] $CAPE(1,50)$ is the cumulative daily average prediction errors from 1 day to 50 days following the insider trading day. $S = 1$ if a sale, or 0 if a purchase. In models (2) through (11), $CAPE(1,50)$ for sales are normalized by multiplying by $-1$. $DIR = 1$ if trader is a director, otherwise $DIR = 0$. $OD = 1$ if trader is an officer-director, otherwise $OD = 0$. $CB = 1$ if trader is the chairman of the board of directors, otherwise $CB = 0$. $SH = 1$ if trader is a large shareholder, otherwise $SH = 0$. Trader is an officer if $DIR = OD = CB = SH = 0$. $LV$ is the natural log of the average value of equity, $T$ is dollar volume of trading (in $ million), $LT$ is the natural log of the dollar value of trade, and $LP$ is the natural log of the proportion of the firm traded. $NI2 = 1$ if net number of insiders equals 2, otherwise $NI2 = 0$. $NI3 = 1$ if net number of insiders equals 3, otherwise $NI3 = 0$. $NI4 = 1$ if net number of insiders equals 4, otherwise $NI4 = 0$. $NI5 = 1$ if net number of insiders equals 5, otherwise $NI5 = 0$. $NI6 = 1$ if net number of insiders is greater than or equal to 6, otherwise $NI6 = 0$. Net number of traders equals 1 if $NI2 = NI3 = NI4 = NI5 = NI6 = 0$.

[b] Significant at 1% level.

[c] Significant at 5% level.

Table 5

Generalized least squares regression of the cumulative daily average prediction errors from 1 day to 100 days following the insider trading day, on purchase versus sale decisions, type of insiders, dollar volume and log of dollar value of insider trading, log of proportion of the firm traded, net number of insiders, and the log of the value of the firm.[a] The $t$-statistics for estimated coefficients are shown in parentheses. Sample period is from 1975 to 1981.

| Model number | Model | $F$-statistics |
|---|---|---|
| (1) | $CAPE(1,100) = 0.030 - 0.045S$<br>$\quad\quad\quad\quad\quad (9.7)\quad (-13.3)$ | $177.2^{b}$ |
| (2) | $CAPE(1,100) = 0.015 + 0.008DIR + 0.018OD + 0.018CB + 0.004SH$<br>$\quad\quad\quad\quad\quad (5.0)\quad (2.1)\quad\quad (3.1)\quad\quad (2.4)\quad\quad (0.6)$ | $3.4^{b}$ |
| (3) | $CAPE(1,100) = 0.022 - 0.0002T$<br>$\quad\quad\quad\quad\quad (10.4)\quad (-0.7)$ | $0.4$ |
| (4) | $CAPE(1,100) = -0.001 + 0.0022LT$<br>$\quad\quad\quad\quad\quad (-0.2)\quad (2.7)$ | $7.4^{b}$ |
| (5) | $CAPE(1,100) = 0.065 + 0.0047LP$<br>$\quad\quad\quad\quad\quad (8.7)\quad (6.0)$ | $36.6^{b}$ |
| (6) | $CAPE(1,100) = 0.195 + 0.011LV + 0.0038LT$<br>$\quad\quad\quad\quad\quad (7.7)\quad (-8.2)\quad (4.7)$ | $37.8^{b}$ |
| (7) | $CAPE(1,100) = 0.200 - 0.007LV + 0.0031LP$<br>$\quad\quad\quad\quad\quad (7.8)\quad (-5.5)\quad (3.7)$ | $33.2^{b}$ |
| (8) | $CAPE(1,100) = 0.185 - 0.011LV + 0.0041LT + 0.005DIR + 0.011OD + 0.009CB - 0.009SH$<br>$\quad\quad\quad\quad\quad (7.2)\quad (-7.9)\quad (4.7)\quad\quad (1.2)\quad\quad (1.8)\quad\quad (1.2)\quad\quad (-1.2)$ | $13.9^{b}$ |
| (9) | $CAPE(1,100) = 0.187 - 0.007LV + 0.0033LP + 0.005DIR + 0.011OD + 0.010CB - 0.006SH$<br>$\quad\quad\quad\quad\quad (7.3)\quad (-5.1)\quad (3.6)\quad\quad (1.3)\quad\quad (2.0)\quad\quad (1.3)\quad\quad (-0.9)$ | $12.3^{b}$ |
| (10) | $CAPE(1,100) = 0.017 + 0.010N12 + 0.011N13 + 0.018N14 + 0.014N15 + 0.029N16$<br>$\quad\quad\quad\quad\quad (6.5)\quad (2.4)\quad\quad (1.9)\quad\quad (2.2)\quad\quad (1.2)\quad\quad (3.0)$ | $3.3^{b}$ |
| (11) | $CAPE(1,100) = 0.057 + 0.006N12 + 0.005N13 + 0.011N14 + 0.006N15 + 0.020N16 + 0.004LP$<br>$\quad\quad\quad\quad\quad (6.8)\quad (1.5)\quad\quad (0.9)\quad\quad (1.3)\quad\quad (0.5)\quad\quad (2.0)\quad\quad (5.1)$ | $7.0^{b}$ |

[a]$CAPE(1,100)$ is the cumulative daily average prediction errors from 1 day to 100 days following the insider trading day. $S = 1$ if a sale, or 0 if a purchase. In models (2) through (11), $CAPE(1,100)$ for sales are normalized by multiplying by $-1$. $DIR = 1$ if trader is a director, otherwise $DIR = 0$. $OD = 1$ if trader is an officer-director, otherwise $OD = 0$. $CB = 1$ if trader is the chairman of the board of directors, otherwise $CB = 0$. $SH = 1$ if trader is a large shareholder, otherwise $SH = 0$. Trader is an officer if $DIR = OD = CB = SH = 0$. $LV$ is the natural log of the average value of equity, $T$ is dollar volume of trading ( in $ million), $LT$ is the natural log of the dollar value of trade, and $LP$ is the natural log of the proportion of the firm traded. $N12 = 1$ if net number of insiders equals 2, otherwise $N12 = 0$. $N13 = 1$ if net number of insiders equals 3, otherwise $N13 = 0$. $N14 = 1$ if net number of insiders equals 4, otherwise $N14 = 0$. $N15 = 1$ if net number of insiders equals 5, otherwise $N15 = 0$. $N16 = 1$ if net number of insiders is greater than or equal to 6, otherwise $N16 = 0$. Net number of traders equals 1 if $N12 = N13 = N14 = N15 = N16 = 0$.

[b]Significant at 1% level.

the types of insiders, dollar volume of trading, and firm size are separate determinants of insiders' abnormal profits.

Model (10) shows a regression of insiders' abnormal profits on the net number of insiders, defined as the absolute value of the difference between the number of buyers and sellers. The magnitude of insiders' abnormal profits generally increases with the net number of insiders, and the differences among abnormal returns to the net number of insiders are significant at the 5% level. This result is similar to a finding by Jaffe (1974). Model (11) also includes the natural log of the proportion of the firm traded as an additional explanatory variable. Both the coefficient and the significance of the proportion of the firm traded remain unchanged from model (5). However, in model (11), the net number of insiders variable is no longer significant. This evidence suggests that the significance of the net number of insiders is due largely to a proxy effect for the proportion of the firm traded.

The regressions in table 5 use the cumulative average prediction errors from 1 day to 100 days following the insider trading day as a measure of insiders' abnormal profits. The magnitudes of the estimated coefficients in table 5 are somewhat higher than in table 4 while the significance levels of the estimated coefficients are comparable. Differences between table 4 and table 5 are most notable for the identity of insider regression. Model (2) suggests that the chairmen of the boards of directors as well as the officer-directors trade on more valuable information than officers. Differences in abnormal returns to all insiders are significant at the 1% level in model (2). The other regressions indicate that sales versus purchases, dollar volume of trading, proportion of the firm traded, and firm size remain as significant determinants of insiders' predictive ability. Once again, the significance of the net number of insiders is due largely to a proxy effect for the proportion of the firm traded.

The evidence presented in tables 4 and 5 suggests several conclusions. First, it appears that insider information arises as a result of insiders' association with the firm, since insiders who are closer to day-to-day decision-making trade on more valuable information. Second, the significant negative relation between insiders' abnormal profits and firm size is not diminished when other determinants of insider trading are considered. Most profitable insider trading occurs in small firms. Third, insiders can distinguish the differences in the value of their information and trade a larger volume of stock when they have more valuable information. The failure of the previous insider trading studies to find a positive relation between dollar volume of trading and value of insider information appears to be due to the fact that the large dollar volume of transactions proxies for large firms and large shareholders.

The evidence presented in tables 4 and 5 also provides additional support for the hypothesis that the bid–ask spread reflects the expected loss to informed traders. If the fixed costs of market-making are mostly responsible for determining the bid–ask spreads, then the bid–ask spread is expected to

Table 6

Insiders' open market transactions from 1975 to 1981, grouped by the number of calendar days between the insider trading day, the day insiders' reports are first received by the SEC and the availability day of the *Official Summary*. Numbers in parentheses are the fraction of the total sample of 59,148 transactions.

| Event period | Delay less than or equal to 30 days | Delay between 30 and 60 days | Delay between 60 and 90 days | Delay over 90 days |
|---|---|---|---|---|
| Trade day to report day | 38,791 (0.66) | 15,676 (0.27) | 1,507 (0.03) | 3,174 (0.05) |
| Report day to availability of *Official Summary* | 1,389 (0.02) | 38,246 (0.65) | 18,560 (0.31) | 953 (0.02) |
| Trade day to availability of *Official Summary* | 134 (0.0) | 9,487 (0.16) | 31,272 (0.53) | 18,255 (0.31) |

fall with the dollar volume of trade, since a given cost is averaged over a greater number of shares. If the expected loss to informed traders is a significant factor in determining the bid–ask spread, then the bid–ask spread is expected to rise with the dollar volume of trade, since tables 4 and 5 indicate that market-maker's expected loss to informed traders rises with the dollar volume of trade. The available evidence shows that the bid–ask spread indeed rises with the dollar volume of trade.[12]

A word of caution is in order at this point. The coefficients of determination of the regressions shown in tables 4 and 5 are about 1%. This indicates that characteristics of the *reported* insider transactions explain a small proportion of the variance of abnormal returns. One interpretation of the small coefficient of determination is that insider trading regulations deter insiders from trading freely on the basis of their privileged information. Insiders would have incentive to refrain from trading, or hide their most important information transactions by trading through friends and relatives to avoid potential sanctions by the SEC. Non-reported trading by insiders or trading by informed traders who are not classified as insiders are likely to be more sensitive to the value of their information.

## 5.4. Market efficiency

This study also examines the availability of abnormal profits to outsiders following the first day insiders' reports are received by the Securities and Exchange Commission and the day the *Official Summary* becomes publicly

---

[12] For example, Mikkelson and Partch (1985) report that the underwriting spread increases with the relative size of the secondary offerings.

Table 7

Percentage cumulative daily average prediction errors and their *t*-statistics in parentheses for 769 firms traded by insiders from 1975 to 1981 around the day insiders' reports are first received by the SEC and the day the *Official Summary* is available.

| | Cumulative daily average prediction errors | |
|---|---|---|
| Event period | Insiders' reports are received by SEC; day 0 is last day of month | *Official Summary* is available on day 0 |
| Day 1 through 20 | 0.5 (3.2) | 0.3 (1.9) |
| Day 1 through 50 | 0.8 (3.5) | 0.7 (2.4) |
| Day 1 through 100 | 1.4 (4.3) | 1.2 (3.0) |
| Day 1 through 300 | 1.9 (3.4) | 1.1 (1.7) |
| Sample size | 10,221 | 8,302 |

available.[13] Table 6 shows that there are substantial delays in reporting and publishing insiders' transactions. For example, the delay between the insider trading day and the availability day of the *Official Summary* exceeds 90 days for 31% of the transactions and 60 days for 84% of the transactions. To prevent biasing the tests against market efficiency, only the reported transactions as of the last day of each month are used to form portfolios. Similarly, for the publication day tests, only the published transactions in the *Official Summary* are used to form portfolios for any calendar month.

Table 7 shows the cumulative daily average prediction errors for selected periods around the day insider reports are received by the SEC and the availability day of the *Official Summary*. The cumulative daily average prediction errors are also plotted in fig. 2. The methodology used to measure the magnitude and significance of the cumulative daily average prediction errors is identical to the trading day tests. Table 7 indicates that if an outsider trades on the basis of insiders' transactions as soon as insiders' reports are received by the SEC, he can earn 1.4% after 100 days and 1.9% after 300 days. If the outsider waits until after the *Official Summary* is available, then the gross abnormal return is only 1.1% during the next 300 days. Fig. 2 indicates that the decline in abnormal return following the dissemination of insider trading

---

[13] Since no publication dates appear on the *Official Summary*, the date the *Official Summary* is received by the Rush–Rhees Library of the University of Rochester is used as the availability date. Due to delays in postal delivery, the actual availability date may be as much as a week to ten days earlier than the delivery date to the Rush–Rhees Library.

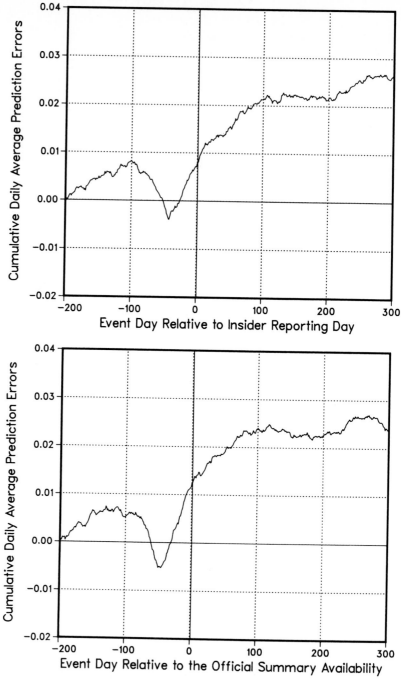

Fig. 2. Cumulative daily average prediction errors from 199 days before to 300 days after the first day insiders' reports are received by the SEC and the availability day of the *Official Summary* to a portfolio of 769 firms traded by insiders during 1975 to 1981.

information is attributable to the stock price adjustment following the insider trading day.

To evaluate the realizable abnormal profits from imitating insiders, outsiders' gross abnormal profits are compared to the bid–ask spread for 100-shares plus the commission fee for a round trip transaction. The bid–ask spread plus the commission fee is taken to be 6.8% for firms less than $25 million, 5.2% for firms between $25 and $50 million, 3.7% for firms between $50 and $250 million, 3.2% for firms between $250 million and $1 billion, and 2.7% for firms greater than $1 billion.[14] Net of these trading costs, abnormal returns to outsiders following either the reporting day or the publication day are nonpositive. In addition, abnormal profits to outsiders using more selective trading rules based on identity of insiders, dollar volume of trading, proportion of the firm traded, and firm size are examined. More selective trading rules also reveal no significantly positive abnormal profits to outsiders net of the trading costs. This evidence is consistent with market efficiency. Insiders can predict future abnormal stock price changes, however, following the public dissemination of insider trading information, outsiders cannot earn abnormal profits net of trading costs.

## 6. Conclusions and implications

The evidence presented in this study indicates that insiders can predict abnormal future stock price changes. Insiders purchase stock prior to an abnormal rise in stock prices and sell stock prior to an abnormal decline in stock prices. Furthermore, different insiders possess differences in quality of information. Insiders who are expected to be more knowledgeable with the overall affairs of the firm, such as chairmen of the boards of directors or officer-directors, are more successful predictors of future abnormal stock price changes than officers or shareholders alone. Evidence also suggests that insiders can discern the differences in the value of their information and trade greater volumes of stock to exploit more valuable information.

The evidence presented in this study also shows that as a percentage of stock price, the expected loss to insiders and firm size are negatively correlated. This finding is consistent with the hypothesis that the expected loss to informed traders is reflected in the bid–ask spread for a given security, since smaller firms have larger percentage bid–ask spreads. An implication of this evidence is that ignoring the expected loss to informed traders, especially in small firms, can lead to an overstatement of the realizable abnormal return to any active trading strategy. An allowance for the expected loss to informed traders can be

---

[14] Estimates of trading costs correspond to Stoll and Whaley estimates for their firm size groups 1, 2, 6, 9, and 10. See Stoll and Whaley (1983, p. 73).

made by deducting the bid–ask spread from the gross abnormal return to any active trading strategy. This evidence also suggests that some recent anomalies concerning the efficient markets hypothesis can disappear if the expected loss to informed traders is taken into account by including the bid–ask spread as an additional cost of trading.

In this study, the realizable return to outsiders is examined following the first day insiders' reports are received by the SEC and the day the *Official Summary* becomes publicly available. Following the public dissemination of insider trading information, the abnormal return to outsiders net of the bid–ask spread plus the commission fee is non-positive. Examining more selective trading rules based on types of insiders, dollar volume of trading, proportion of the firm traded, and firm size also shows that no significantly positive abnormal return to outsiders net of the trading costs. This evidence is consistent with market efficiency: Outside investors cannot use the publicly available information about insiders' transactions to earn abnormal profits.

## References

Amihud, Y. and H. Mendelson, 1980, Dealership market: Market making with inventory, Journal of Financial Economics 8, 31–53.

Bagehot, W. (pseud), 1971, The only game in town, Financial Analyst Journal 2, 12–14.

Banz, R.W., 1981, The relationship between return and market value of common stocks, Journal of Financial Economics 9, 3–18.

Benston, G.J. and R.L. Hagerman, 1974, Determinants of bid–asked spreads in over-the-counter market, Journal of Financial Economics 1, 353–374.

Copeland, T.E. and D. Galai, 1983, Information effects on the bid–ask spread, Journal of Finance 38, 1457–1470.

Demsetz, H., 1968, The cost of transacting, Quarterly Journal of Economics 82, 33–53.

Fama, E.F., 1970, Efficient capital markets: A review of theory and empirical work, Journal of Finance 25, 383–417.

Fama, E.F., 1976, Foundation of finance (Basic Books, New York).

Fama, E.F., L. Fisher, M.C. Jensen and R. Roll, 1969, The adjustment of stock prices to new information, International Economic Review 10, 1–21.

Finnerty, J.E., 1976, Insiders and market efficiency, Journal of Finance 31, 1141–1148.

Glosten, L.L. and P.R. Milgrom, 1985, Bid, ask and transaction prices in a specialist market with heterogeneously informed traders, Journal of Financial Economics 14, 71–100.

Jaffe, J.F., 1974, Special information and insider trading, Journal of Business 47, 410–428.

Lorie, J.H. and V. Niederhoffer, 1968, Predictive and statistical properties of insider trading, Journal of Law and Economics 11, 35–51.

Mikkelson, W.H. and M.M. Partch, 1985, Stock price effects and costs of secondary distributions, Journal of Financial Economics 14, 165–194.

Nelson, C.R., 1973, Applied time series analysis (Holden-Day, San Francisco, CA).

Phillips, S.M. and C.W. Smith, Jr., 1980, Trading costs for listed options: The implications for market efficiency, Journal of Financial Economics 8, 179–201.

Pratt, S.P. and C.W. DeVere, 1970, Relationship between insider trading and rates of return for NYSE common stocks, 1960–1966, in: J. Lorie and R. Brealey, eds., Modern developments in investment management (Praeger, New York).

Reinganum, M.R., 1981, Misspecification of capital asset pricing: Empirical anomalies based on earnings' yields and market values, Journal of Financial Economics 9, 19–46.

Scholes, M.S., 1972, The market for securities: Substitution versus price pressure and the effects of information on share price, Journal of Business 45, 179–211.

Scholes, M.S. and J. Williams, 1977, Estimating betas from non-synchronous data, Journal of Financial Economics 5, 309–328.

Schultz, P., 1983, Transactions costs and the small firm effect: A comment, Journal of Financial Economics 12, 81–88.

Stoll, H.R., 1978, The supply of dealer services in securities markets, Journal of Finance 33, 1133–1151.

Stoll, H.R. and R.E. Whaley, 1983, Transactions costs and the small firm effect, Journal of Financial Economics 12, 57–79.

Tinic, S.M., 1972, The economics of liquidity services, Quarterly Journal of Economics 86, 79–93.

Tinic, S.M. and R.R. West, 1972, Competition and the pricing of dealer service in the over-the-counter stock market, Journal of Financial and Quantitative Analysts 7, 1707–1728.

Treynor, J., 1981, What does it take to win the trading game?, Financial Analysts Journal, 55–60.

**Peter Lloyd-Davies***

*University of Rochester*

**Michael Canes***

*American Petroleum Institute*

# Stock Prices and the Publication of Second-Hand Information

## Introduction

Considerable evidence has accumulated over the past 10 years suggesting that the stock market adjusts in an efficient manner to the arrival of new information. Claims by technical analysts that excess returns may be earned by studying price movements have found little support in studies by Fama and Blume (1966), Jensen and Benington (1970), and others.[1] Investigations of price movements accompanying economic events (e.g., Ball and Brown [1968] on earnings announcements, Fama et al. [1969] on stock splits) likewise have offered little hope that trading based on these announcements will be profitable. Perhaps most significantly, the gross returns earned by professional portfolio managers do not appear to be higher, given the risk level, than the returns from a naive strategy of buying and holding the market portfolio (see, e.g., Sharpe 1966; Jensen 1968, 1969).

Some economists have expressed satisfaction with these results on grounds that efficiently determined stock prices give better signals for resource allocation than prices that do not reflect

This paper presents evidence on the effects of secondary dissemination of stock analysts' recommendations after primary dissemination to analysts' clients. The evidence suggests that such secondary dissemination significantly affects stock prices and that the effect is not reversed within the subsequent 20 trading days. One inference is that stock analysts provide economically valuable information to clients, and a second is that primary dissemination of such information does not always bring about a full stock-price adjustment, contrary to the claims of the strong form of the efficient market hypothesis.

* We gratefully acknowledge the assistance of Myron Scholes of the University of Chicago, who provided us with the daily return data used in our computations.

1. A certain amount of short-lived positive serial correlation seems to exist in daily returns but not enough to power a trading strategy.

(*Journal of Business*, 1978, vol. 51, no. 1)

available information. Others are perplexed, however, at an implied inefficiency—namely, the existence of the security-analysis industry. If prices reflect all information that analysts are examining, why then are investors willing to pay for their services? There are several possible answers. One is that analysts' recommendations are based on inside information that is not yet reflected in prices. This leaves unexplained the apparent lack of consistent superior performance by professionally managed portfolios. A second is that investors are irrational in the sense that they know they are getting nothing for something. The empirical literature in economics, however, gives reason to believe that investors who pay for research do so to economize rather than squander resources. Still another possibility arises from the past pricing system for security research. Under the regime of fixed brokerage commissions on the New York Stock Exchange (NYSE), the marginal cost of research to the investor was often zero, offered as a "free" service to attract clients. But security analysis also was sold apart from brokerage services, so that the pricing structure alone cannot explain the existence of such analysis. Finally, the purchase of research might be rationalized as a consumption rather than an investment activity. Possibly, it is prestigious to hold an account with a research-oriented brokerage house, and there may be an element of fun in using such research to try to beat the market (just as rational consumers may read the daily racing form and use it to play the horses). In these circumstances, such research could survive even if it provided no inside information to customers.

In all of the above cases, purchasers of security research would be expected to act upon the information received. This raises a number of empirical questions; and we here address four: (1) Do prices adjust when an analyst revises his recommendation about a stock? (2) Does the rate of adjustment depend upon the extent to which the recommendation is disseminated? (3) Do recommendations to buy have different effects from recommendations to sell? (4) Are analysts' recommendations self-fulfilling prophecies, that is, do they give rise to higher (lower) returns than normal when announced but lower (higher) returns than normal later on?

The strongest form of the efficient market hypothesis predicts that an analyst's recommendation would result in no adjustment at all. A weaker version would allow the recommendation to carry information but predict that prices will adjust as soon as the analyst's clients have access to the information. Under this version, clients act as arbitrageurs, purchasing undervalued stock in anticipation of abnormal returns. As long as a stock is undervalued, clients continue to purchase, and ultimately the information contained in the recommendation is completely reflected in the price.

There is, however, an objection to this argument. As an analyst's clients buy a particular stock on his recommendation, their portfolios become more and more unbalanced; that is, they begin to assume increasing amounts of diversifiable risk. This increasing risk can bring their arbitrage operation to a halt before the abnormal returns are eliminated, since at some point the abnormal returns become fair returns for an abnormal risk.[2] Thus, a single-investor arbitrage model may not be applicable in a world of uncertainty, where generally the risks from buying or selling short large quantities of one stock cannot be fully insured by compensating portfolio adjustments. Unlike the case of perfect certainty, investors' demand curves for individual securities are downward sloping, and so even investors with inside information have finite demands for undervalued stocks.

Under these conditions, prices will not completely adjust until the information is known to more than a few analysts' clients. Thus, as the information becomes more widespread, further price adjustments will occur.

Recommendations to buy may have different effects from recommendations to sell. The sale of stock may force an investor to incur capital gains taxes, whereas the sale of other assets to finance the purchase of stock can be carried out so as to minimize tax liabilities. Further, without short sales, an investor can sell only stocks already in his portfolio, whereas no such constraint affects his ability to buy. If he chooses to sell short a stock not in his portfolio, he then is penalized by receiving no interest on the proceeds, whereas no such penalty applies to purchases. For all these reasons, analysts' sell recommendations should have smaller impact on stock prices than buy recommendations.

If analysts' recommendations convey no inside information but investors act on them, then the recommendations will be self-fulfilling prophecies. On the other hand, since the returns on a stock are ultimately determined by the firm's cash flows, any abnormal price increase (decrease) that results from a spurious recommendation must be followed by abnormally low (high) returns later on. Evidence that initial stock-price adjustments are later reversed would suggest that analysts can affect stock prices even though there is no real economic content to their recommendations.

### The Test

To answer the questions posed in the previous section, we sought to obtain not only data on analysts' recommendations to their clients but also data on the dissemination of these recommendations to other investors.

---

2. See Lloyd-Davies (1975) for a detailed discussion of this process.

We therefore examined the effect on market prices of the publication of analysts' recommendations in the *Wall Street Journal* column "Heard on the Street." This column has been published in its present format since late 1969. In a typical column, several Wall Street analysts' opinions about a number of stocks are presented. Often several analysts comment on the same stocks, and on some but not all occasions their opinions are presented as recommendations for purchases or sales. The opinions of the analysts often are published with comments solicited from the corporations involved. The author of the column generally seeks out instances where analysts have recently revised their recommendations. For obvious reasons, the analysts are careful to ensure that their clients receive the information before it goes to the *Wall Street Journal*. The interval between the clients' receipt of the recommendation and publication in the *Journal* is fairly short—on the order of a few days to 1 week or 2, and variable. Generally, *Wall Street Journal* publication of an analyst's recommendation is its first public exposure.[3] The author does not editorialize about the analysts' statements, and a large number of different analysts are quoted at one time or another.[4] For these reasons, the publication of a recommendation in the column does not represent an endorsement by the *Wall Street Journal;* any price movement that accompanies publication is then a result of the dissemination of the original recommendation rather than an endorsement by another knowledgeable party.

To avoid ambiguity, we eliminated from consideration all cases in which the analysts quoted were not unanimous in recommending either a purchase or a sale of the stock. (No weight was attached to the opinion of a firm's management.) Our sample covers 1970 and 1971 and consists of 597 buy recommendations and 188 sell recommendations, almost all from the NYSE.

The technique used to examine the effect of the publication of an analyst's recommendation is the now familiar market residual technique pioneered by Fama et al. (1969). The daily return (continuously compounded) on each stock was regressed on the return on a portfolio of equal dollar investments in all NYSE and American Exchange (AMEX) stocks (rebalanced daily),[5] using 2 years of daily data from 1968 to 1969. The regression line was then used as a predictor of actual rates of return on the stock in question, conditional upon the perfor-

---

3. The information about the way the column is prepared comes from personal interviews with Charles Elia, the principal author of this column, on April 8, 1974, and December 30, 1976.

4. In our sample of 785 recommendations, we recorded opinions by over 90 different analysts.

5. Consideration was given to the possibility of constraining the intercept of the regression to conform to the equilibrium condition of the capital asset pricing model. This would provide more efficient estimates of the beta coefficients if the specification of the traditional capital asset pricing model (CAPM) is correct. There is reason to doubt this, however (see Black, Jensen, and Scholes 1972), and it was felt that the unconstrained estimation would be more robust.

mance of the market, from 20 days preceding the appearance of the recommendation in the *Journal* through the 20 trading days subsequent to it. The difference between the actual and predicted return represents the residual return that is not explained by the movement in the general level of stock prices. Our null hypothesis is that this residual is drawn from a distribution with a zero mean, that is, that the appearance of the analyst's recommendation in the *Journal* has no systematic effect on the price of the stock recommended.

**The Results**

The residuals obtained in this manner were averaged over all stocks recommended for purchase or sale for each day relative to the appearance of the recommendation in the *Journal*. These average residuals are presented in figure 1a and b and in table 1. A quick glance at the figures shows considerable support for the hypothesis that the appearance of the report in the *Journal* affects the stock price. There is on

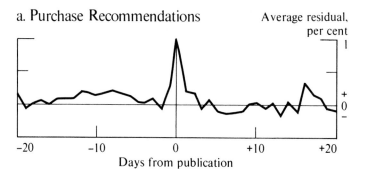

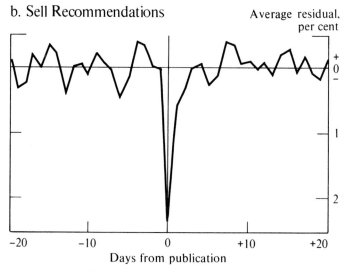

FIG. 1.—Daily average residuals

TABLE 1          Daily Average Residuals, Standard Deviations of Residuals

| Day | Buy Recommendations (597) | | | Sell Recommendations (188) | | |
|---|---|---|---|---|---|---|
| | Average Residual (%) | SD of Residual (%) | $t$ | Average Residual (%) | SD of Residual (%) | $t$ |
| −20 | .159 | 1.844 | 2.099 | .137 | 2.920 | .642 |
| −19 | −.013 | 1.894 | −.169 | −.332 | 2.233 | −2.038 |
| −18 | .026 | 2.054 | .306 | −.236 | 2.482 | −1.301 |
| −17 | .085 | 1.880 | 1.105 | .207 | 2.577 | 1.099 |
| −16 | .006 | 1.787 | .078 | .034 | 2.324 | .198 |
| −15 | .090 | 1.825 | 1.205 | .340 | 2.519 | 1.851 |
| −14 | .102 | 2.016 | 1.239 | .205 | 2.407 | 1.165 |
| −13 | .117 | 2.157 | 1.320 | −.415 | 2.571 | −2.213 |
| −12 | .212 | 2.151 | 2.411 | .016 | 2.372 | .089 |
| −11 | .186 | 2.060 | 2.212 | .052 | 2.764 | .257 |
| −10 | .153 | 2.152 | 1.738 | −.124 | 3.719 | −.456 |
| −9 | .168 | 2.022 | 2.033 | .236 | 2.322 | 1.392 |
| −8 | .203 | 1.880 | 2.644 | .053 | 2.783 | .260 |
| −7 | .171 | 1.995 | 2.092 | −.009 | 2.605 | −.049 |
| −6 | .144 | 2.054 | 1.712 | −.473 | 2.247 | −2.886 |
| −5 | .055 | 2.234 | .600 | −.148 | 2.410 | −.841 |
| −4 | .067 | 2.211 | .736 | .399 | 2.991 | −1.828 |
| −3 | .081 | 1.914 | 1.035 | .331 | 3.817 | 1.188 |
| −2 | −.017 | 2.194 | −.184 | .020 | 3.227 | .086 |
| −1 | .278 | 2.297 | 2.959 | −.010 | 2.710 | −.048 |
| 0 | .923 | 2.360 | 9.552 | −2.374 | 3.297 | −9.874 |
| 1 | .205 | 2.059 | 2.434 | −.546 | 3.261 | −2.297 |
| 2 | .187 | 1.865 | 2.449 | −.293 | 2.585 | −1.554 |
| 3 | −.049 | 1.812 | −.664 | .007 | 2.804 | .034 |
| 4 | .063 | 1.842 | .836 | .088 | 2.465 | .488 |
| 5 | −.082 | 1.825 | −1.096 | −.221 | 2.515 | −1.206 |
| 6 | −.132 | 1.818 | −1.778 | −.137 | 2.664 | −1.704 |
| 7 | −.127 | 2.003 | −1.550 | .391 | 2.542 | 2.109 |
| 8 | −.106 | 1.904 | −1.356 | .351 | 2.272 | 2.117 |
| 9 | .015 | 1.981 | .187 | .077 | 2.455 | .428 |
| 10 | .020 | 1.862 | .267 | .109 | 2.106 | .712 |
| 11 | −.027 | 1.876 | −.347 | −.008 | 2.295 | −.048 |
| 12 | .019 | 1.707 | .276 | .073 | 2.387 | .419 |
| 13 | −.168 | 1.820 | −2.253 | −.112 | 1.787 | −.860 |
| 14 | .045 | 1.975 | .559 | .207 | 2.214 | 1.284 |
| 15 | −.072 | 2.019 | −.871 | .298 | 2.089 | 1.957 |
| 16 | .336 | 2.167 | 3.784 | −.028 | 2.554 | −.148 |
| 17 | .156 | 1.860 | 2.053 | .166 | 2.306 | .989 |
| 18 | .102 | 2.063 | 1.202 | −.075 | 2.157 | −.473 |
| 19 | −.070 | 1.882 | −.904 | −.169 | 2.651 | −.872 |
| 20 | −.077 | 1.906 | −.981 | .123 | 2.209 | .765 |

average an abnormal return of slightly less than 1% (0.923%) on the day a stock receives a favorable mention in the column and a negative return of over 2% (−2.374%) if the stock receives an unfavorable mention.[6]

6. The *Wall Street Journal* is a morning newspaper which is available to investors prior to the opening of trading. Thus, publication occurs before, not after, that day's stock price changes. However, because of lack of data, we do not know when during the day the adjustments take place.

Figure 2*a* and *b* shows the cross-sectional distributions of residuals for each sample on the day of publication. They are both significantly skewed,[7] the purchase recommendations to the right and the sells to the left. This suggests that the samples probably contain a mixture of observations, some of which are taken seriously by investors and others which have relatively little impact.

We attempted to test the statistical significance of the daily average

## a. Purchase Recommendations

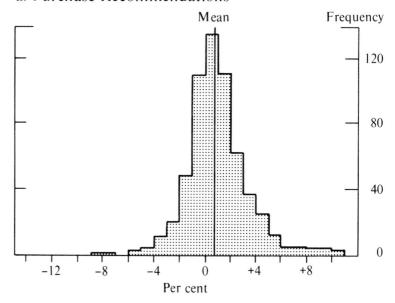

## b. Sell Recommendations

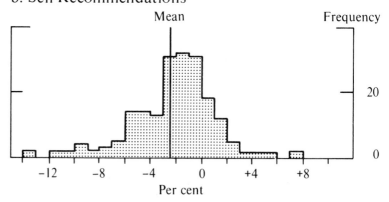

Fig. 2.—Cross-sectional distribution of residuals

7. The ratio of the third central moment to the cube of the standard deviation is 0.620 for the purchase recommendations and −0.644 for the sells. The probability of getting statistics this high (low) from a normal distribution is less than 1%.

residuals. Unfortunately, it is difficult to describe the sampling behavior of this statistic because the elements in the average may come from quite different distributions, and these distributions may be correlated in unknown ways. For example, the residuals for two stocks that were mentioned on 2 different days may be reasonably considered to be statistically independent. But on many days we have several sample points and these are sometimes firms in the same industry, so the hypothesis of independence among residuals may be unrealistic.[8] The simplest approach is to ignore this problem and to assume that all observations are independent drawings from the same normal distribution. We may then calculate a cross-sectional standard deviation for each of the days (given in fig. 3a and b and table 1), divide by the square root of the sample size to get the standard deviation of the sample average, and form a t-statistic (given in table 1). For both samples, the t-statistic is numerically greater than 9, which confirms the first impres-

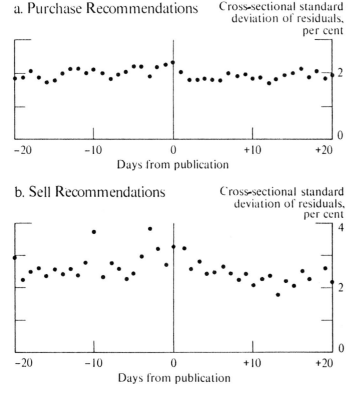

FIG. 3.—Cross-sectional standard deviations of residuals

8. Among the purchase sample there are over three recommendations on average per date; among the sells, over two recommendations per date. Both distributions are highly skewed; i.e., there are a few dates with a large number of recommendations.

sion that the probability of obtaining such a large value by chance is virtually nil.

A slightly more refined approach would make allowances for the fact that the individual firm residuals come from distributions with different variances. We deflated each residual by its standard deviation around the time-series regression line and then took an average. For the purchase recommendations, we found that the residual on the day of publication was on average 0.539 SD above zero, and for sell recommendations, it was 1.317 SD below zero. On the day a stock receives a buy recommendation, it has about a 70% probability of rising in value, while on the day a stock receives a sell recommendation, it has about a 90% probability of falling in value. If we treat the residuals, deflated by their standard deviations, as independent and identically distributed with a unit variance, we may form a $t$-statistic to give us the probability of the distribution having a zero mean. For the purchase recommendations, this is $0.539 \times \sqrt{598}$, which is over 13, and for the sell recommendations, it is $1.317 \times \sqrt{188}$, which is over 18. This lends more support to the notion that dissemination of an analyst's recommendation among the investing public has a significant impact on price. It seems most unlikely that these results are entirely produced by our ignoring the small degree of cross-sectional correlation between residuals of different firms.[9]

One possible explanation for our results is that publication of analysts' recommendations in the *Journal* sometimes constitutes new information. Although clients know the recommendations of those analysts to whom they subscribe, there need be no investor preaware of the recommendations of all of the analysts quoted. Thus, our results might simply reflect investor response to the new information that several analysts were offering similar recommendations on a stock.

To test this, we compared the behavior of the residuals for all 1970 recommendations (496) with the subset of single analyst's recommendations (433). The results for the two were 0.81% versus 0.76% for the buy sample and $-2.11\%$ versus $-1.91\%$ for the sells. Thus, more weight is accorded multiple than single analyst's recommendations, but that alone does not explain our results.

We now turn to differences in the performances of the buy and sell samples. The cumulative average residuals (fig. 4a and b) show strikingly different patterns. The total price movements are similar in both cases, but the buy sample shows most of the abnormal price performance occurring before the publication of the recommendation and a

9. There is also the problem that security returns are not normally distributed, as documented amply by Mandelbrot (1963) and Fama (1965). But the calculated variances seem quite stable, which argues against the Stable Paretian hypothesis, and the central-limit theorem suggests that the average residual may be approximately normal even if the individual residuals are not.

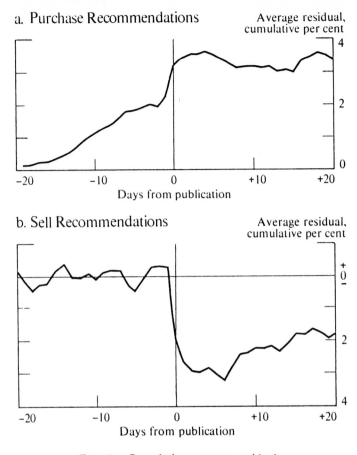

a. Purchase Recommendations

Average residual, cumulative per cent

Days from publication

b. Sell Recommendations

Average residual, cumulative per cent

Days from publication

FIG. 4.—Cumulative average residuals

relatively small movement on the day of publication itself. The sell sample, however, shows no tendency for the price to move down before publication and a much larger shift on the day of publication. One inference consistent with this difference is that an analyst's clients are more likely to act on a buy than a sell recommendation, perhaps for reasons given in the introductory section.

We found support for another explanation of the difference between the two samples. On average, columns with purchase recommendations discussed more stocks than columns with sell recommendations. One possible reason is that the sell recommendations reflected more important news items which were given greater prominence in the column. We therefore collected data on the number of stocks discussed in the column (as proxy for the importance of each item) for a subsample of 496 stocks in 1970 and used this to explain the size of the residual. The dependent variable used is the day 0 residual for buy recommendations and the negative of the day 0 residual for sell recommendations. We also used a dummy variable which took the value of 1 for a purchase recommendation and 0 for a sell. The results of the regression are as follows (*t*-statistics in parentheses):

$$\text{Residual} = 2.38 - 1.09 \text{ Buy/Sell} - 0.05 \text{ Number}$$
$$\phantom{\text{Residual} = } (8.54) \quad (-3.61) \qquad\quad (-3.43)$$

Both variables are statistically significant, although the $R^2$ is only .06.

The size of the residual on the day of publication may be expected to vary according to the credibility of the analyst, the number of clients who have already received the recommendation, and how strong the recommendation is. Most analysts were not quoted frequently enough for us to run separate tests on them. We did, however, run cross-sectional regressions with dummy variables for some of the larger firms. Our expectation for these firms was that the residual would be smaller on the day of publication since a greater number of investors already would have acted on the information. The results of the regression are:

$$\text{Residual} = 2.34 - 1.03 \text{ Buy/Sell} - 0.3 \text{ Number}$$
$$\phantom{\text{Residual} = } (7.69) \quad (-3.36) \qquad\quad (-1.43)$$

$$+ .76 \text{ Hutton} - .86 \text{ Merrill, Lynch} - 0.17 \text{ Bache}$$
$$\phantom{+} (0.83) \qquad\quad (-1.24) \qquad\qquad (-0.20)$$

$$- 0.64 \text{ Paine, Webber} - 0.75 \text{ Standard \& Poor}$$
$$\phantom{-} (-1.28) \qquad\qquad\quad (-1.76)$$

$$- 0.26 \text{ Argus} - 1.47 \text{ Moodys} - 0.17 \text{ Walston.}$$
$$\phantom{-} (-0.51) \qquad\; (-0.81) \qquad\quad (-0.41)$$

Almost all the coefficients are negative, although not very significantly. In our judgment, the sample size for each analyst is too small to draw strong inferences, but the results are consistent with our expectations.

The differences among analysts no doubt contribute to the somewhat higher than normal cross-sectional standard deviations on the date of publication. For the purchase recommendations, the standard deviation is 2.360%, which is the highest of the 41 days considered, and for the sells it is 3.297%, which is the third highest. (The sell sample happens to consist of riskier stocks than the buy sample; the average standard deviation from the time-series regression line in that sample is 1.94% as opposed to 1.73% for the buy sample.)[10] By taking the same samples of firms but using different dates, we were able to calculate

10. The cross-sectional variance may be thought of as an estimator of the average second moment around the group mean. If the individual means are different, then the cross-sectional variance will always be greater than the average variance—as seen in this case.

"normal" values of these cross-sectional standard deviations,[11] which came out to be 1.88% for the buys and 2.15% for the sells. The standard deviations for the sell sample seem to be almost uniformly above this value, particularly before publication, and so are the standard deviations of the buy residuals before publication. This probably is related to the differences in lags between the client's receipt of the recommendation and publication in the *Journal* and to differences in credibility, number of clients, and strength of recommendations.

The behavior of the average residuals prior to the day of publication should be interpreted cautiously. In part this behavior is explained by selection bias, since a stock sometimes is brought to the attention of the author of the column by abnormal price behavior that then prompts him to seek an explanation from Wall Street analysts. At other times, the author decides to publish a previously received recommendation about a stock when abnormal price behavior is observed. In some cases, however, he may discover or already have in hand a recommendation which in fact is unrelated to the abnormal behavior. The high degree of serial correlation in the residuals (0.40 for the buy sample and 0.22 for the sell sample) probably is due largely to the variation among stocks in the lag between an analyst's notification of his clients and publication of the recommendation in the *Journal*.

Consider finally the behavior of the average residuals in the 20 trading days following publication. The price adjustment does not seem to take place on day 0 but seems to persist for the next 2 days. (The *t*-values for those days given in table 1 are all quite high.) Under these circumstances, traders could profit by delaying a purchase for a couple of days following a sell recommendation or by delaying a sale for a couple of days following a purchase recommendation. The quantities involved, however, are fairly small—on the order of 0.4% following a purchase recommendation and 0.8% following sale recommendation—and therefore could not be used to power a trading rule if commissions had to be paid. In both samples there is some tendency for the cumulative average residual to adjust in the opposite direction during the next 18 days, although the daily variance is sufficiently high that we cannot take this as firm evidence that the market overreacts and then adjusts. But there is also no evidence that the cumulative average residual returns to prepublication levels, which would be indicated if analysts' recommendations had no real economic content. The evidence on this, however, is weak since the return to prepublication levels might not take place for months, by which time there would be too much noise in the returns to have confidence in the results.

11. We reduced all the dates by 200 trading days, estimated residuals for 41 consecutive days, calculated daily cross-sectional standard deviations, and averaged them.

## Conclusions

On the basis of the evidence reported above, we find that stock prices do adjust to revisions in analysts' recommendations. Further, we reject the hypothesis that purchase or sell recommendations r leased to a small group of investors are immediately and fully reflected in the stock price. Instead, it appears that subsequent dissemination of the information has a significant impact on the price. This is consistent with the idea expressed earlier that a few investors with inside information will not eliminate all abnormal returns because of the abnormal risks that such a portfolio shift on their part would entail. Our evidence also gives some indication that investors who use analysts' services are getting something of value. In other words, there is here some evidence that analysts' recommendations do provide inside information and are not mere self-fulfilling prophecies.

At the same time, information readily available for 25¢ by reading "Heard on the Street" appears to be very quickly incorporated into stock prices, and the information in the column cannot be used to power a trading rule when transactions costs must be paid. Thus, the evidence of this paper does not point to an unexploited opportunity for profit, which is perhaps a fundamental test of market efficiency.

We leave unexplained the apparent inconsistency between this study and others which have concluded that analysts' recommendations are worthless. Our sample size is quite large, and our results are not caused by a few chance outliers.[12] We would expect open competition for the services of securities analysts to cause them to price their research so that no net abnormal returns are earned, but it is hard to see why such services should persist if they do not provide abnormal returns before expenses. For this reason, we find it easier to accept evidence that the industry does have a real economic product than to explain its existence if it does not.

## References

Ball, R., and Brown, P. 1968. An empirical evaluation of accounting income numbers. *Journal of Accounting Research* 6 (Fall): 159–78.

Black, F.; Jensen, M.; and Scholes, M. 1972. The capital asset pricing model: some empirical tests. In M. C. Jensen (ed.), *Studies in the Theory of Capital Markets*. New York: Praeger.

Fama, E. 1965. The behavior of stock market prices. *Journal of Business* 38 (January): 34–105.

Fama, E., and Blume, M. 1966. Filter rules and stock market trading. *Journal of Business* 39 (January): 226–41.

Fama, E.; Fisher, L.; Jensen, M.; and Roll, R. 1969. The adjustment of stock prices to new information. *International Economic Review* 10 (February): 1–21.

12. We ran the tests on 1970 and 1971 data separately and got virtually identical results.

Jensen, M. 1968. The performance of mutual funds in the period 1945–64. *Journal of Finance* 23 (May): 389–416.

Jensen, M. 1969. Risk, the pricing of capital assets, and the evaluation of investment portfolios. *Journal of Business* 42 (April): 167–247.

Jensen, M., and Benington, G. 1970. Random walks and technical theories: some additional evidence. *Journal of Finance* 25 (May): 469–82.

Lloyd-Davies, P. 1975. Speculation, market efficiency and pareto optimality in an uncertain capital market. Working Paper Series, No. 7537, University of Rochester, Graduate School of Management, September.

Mandelbrot, B. 1963. The variation of certain speculative prices. *Journal of Business* 36 (October): 394–419.

Sharpe, W. 1966. Mutual fund performance. *Journal of Business* 39 (January): 119–38.

# PORTFOLIO THEORY AND ASSET PRICING

**1** Bloomfield, T., R. Leftwich, and J. B. Long, "Portfolio Strategies and Performance," *Journal of Financial Economics*, 5 (November 1977), pp. 201–218.

**2** Fama, E. F., "A Note on the Market Model and the Two-Parameter Model," *Journal of Finance*, 28 (December 1973), pp. 1181–1185.

**3** Roll, R., "A Critique of the Asset Pricing Theory's Tests; Part I: On Past and Potential Testability of the Theory," *Journal of Financial Economics*, 4 (March 1977), pp. 129–176.

**4** Gibbons, M. R., S. A. Ross, and J. Shanken, "A Test of the Efficiency of a Given Portfolio," *Econometrica*, 57 (September 1989), pp.1121–1152.

**5** Breeden, D. T., M. R. Gibbons, and R. H. Litzenberger, "Empirical Tests of the Consumption-Oriented CAPM," *Journal of Finance*, 44 (June 1989), pp. 231–262.

**6** Shanken, J., "The Arbitrage Pricing Theory: Is It Testable?" *Journal of Finance*, 37 (December 1982), pp. 1129–1140.

**7** Schwert, G. W., "Size and Stock Returns, and Other Empirical Regularities," *Journal of Financial Economics*, 12 (June 1983), pp. 3–12.

**8.** Amihud, Y., and H. Mendelson, "Asset Pricing and the Bid-Ask Spread," *Journal of Financial Economics*, 17 (December 1986), pp. 223–249.

Portfolio theory and the asset pricing models that evolved from it are probably the most important historical developments in the economics of capital markets. Indeed, Harry Markowitz (1959) and William Sharpe (1964) were cowinners of the 1990 Nobel Prize in Economics, along with Merton Miller. The idea that *diversification* of asset holdings reduces the risk of a portfolio, with no adverse effect on expected returns, changed the focus of capitals markets research away from the analysis of individual securities and toward the selection of assets that reduce overall portfolio risk. This also allowed the definition of security risk as the marginal contribution by the security to the risk of the portfolio. Along with the important idea of market equilibrium — aggregate supply equals aggregate demand — portfolio theory led to asset pricing models where the trade-off of expected return for marginal risk was the same for all securities — the *Capital Asset Pricing Model (CAPM)*.

Most textbooks on investments or capital markets devote several chapters to diversification, portfolio theory, and asset pricing models. In keeping with the focus of this book, we have selected papers that present empirical evidence on the validity or usefulness of these theories.

**Bloomfield, Leftwich, and Long (1977)** examine several popular methods for constructing "optimal" portfolios of New York Stock Exchange stocks. If the means, variances, and covariances of stock returns were known, there are well-known mathematical methods for finding the investment proportions to use to combine a set of stocks into a portfolio with the lowest possible variance or standard deviation for a given mean return (an *efficient* portfolio.)[1] In reality, however, these parameters are not known and must be estimated from historical data or other information about the stocks. **Bloomfield, Leftwich, and Long** show that because of estimation errors, the portfolios formed used "optimal" investment proportions no better than equal-weighted portfolios of the same number of stocks. Since the effort needed to calculate "optimal" weights is large, these results imply that simple diversification methods are likely to be cost-effective compared with more complex techniques.

**Fama (1973)** is a short note that explains the difference between the "market model" regression equation and the Capital Asset Pricing Model. Assuming multivariate normality of security returns, the "market model" is a *time series* regression model of asset return $R_{it}$ on market portfolio return $R_{mt}$,

$$R_{it} = \alpha_{im} + \beta_{im} R_{mt} + \varepsilon_{it}, \quad t=1, \ldots, T \qquad (1)$$

with a slope coefficient $\beta_{im} = \text{cov}(R_{it}, R_{mt}) / \sigma^2(R_{mt})$. The CAPM is a *cross-sectional* model relating expected stock returns $E(R_i)$ to the relative marginal risk coefficient $\beta_{im}$,

$$E(R_i) = R_f + [E(R_m) - R_f] \beta_{im}, \quad i=1, \ldots, N \qquad (2)$$

where $R_f$ is the return to a risk-free asset. Fama shows that the CAPM (2) implies that the intercept in the market model (1) is related to the slope coefficient, $\alpha_{im} = (1 - \beta_{im}) R_f$. This paper is useful in teaching students the difference between the statistical market model and the economic CAPM.

**Roll (1977)** surveys the theory and empirical evidence on the tests of the Capital Asset Pricing Model. He is highly critical of the tests because they use a proxy for the "market portfolio" consisting of New York Stock Exchange stocks. (Indeed, the earliest tests all used an equal-weighted portfolio of NYSE stocks.) The CAPM says that the correct portfolio to use is the value-weighted portfolio of all marketable assets, the aggregate supply of assets. **Roll** shows how approximation error can lead to incorrect inferences.

**Gibbons, Ross, and Shanken (1989)** summarize much of the earlier literature on tests of the CAPM (or tests that a particular portfolio is mean-variance efficient.) They also develop new, simpler tests that have exact statistical distributions and interesting geometric interpretations. This paper is a current example of the large literature on multivariate tests of the CAPM, including Gibbons (1982), Stambaugh (1982), Shanken (1985).

[1]Note that this use of the word "efficient" is completely unrelated to the concept of efficient capital markets.

**Breeden, Gibbons, and Litzenberger (1989)** perform tests of Breeden's (1979) consumption CAPM, where risk is measured by the covariance of security returns with aggregate consumption. They summarize many prior tests of this model and focus on the measurement problems in the consumption data.

**Shanken (1982)** discusses the empirical implications of the Arbitrage Pricing Theory (APT) developed by Ross (1976). He argues that the tests of the APT that used factor analysis to identify unobserved factors are not valid. He shows that observationally equivalent transformations of the data have very different interpretations. Thus, like **Roll (1977)**, he shows that asset pricing model tests can be difficult to interpret.

**Schwert (1983)** summarizes a set of papers published in a special issue of the *Journal of Financial Economics* that show systematic departures from the CAPM. In particular, average risk-adjusted returns to stocks of small firms are too high (the "small-firm effect"), average risk-adjusted returns to stocks with high earnings/price ratios are too high (the "E/P effect"), and the small-firm effect is very strong during the first few days in January. He reviews the economic and statistical arguments for why these results might be spurious, but decides that none of these explanations is conclusive.

**Amihud and Mendelson (1986)** depart from the focus on portfolio risk as the primary basis for differences in expected returns across assets. Instead, they focus on the effects that differential transaction costs have on expected returns. Since investors are interested in returns net of costs, assets with higher costs will be traded less frequently and will have higher gross returns to offset the higher costs. The tests using NYSE stocks with different bid-ask spreads find strong support for this model. Since small firms' stocks tend to be illiquid, **Amihud and Mendelson** find that most of the evidence for the small-firm effect can be explained by the higher spreads.

# PORTFOLIO STRATEGIES AND PERFORMANCE

Ted BLOOMFIELD, Richard LEFTWICH and John B. LONG, Jr.*

*Graduate School of Management, University of Rochester, Rochester, NY 14627, U.S.A.*

Received July 1977, revised version received August 1977

The relative performance of several portfolio selection strategies is assessed empirically. These strategies vary in sophistication from a 'naive' strategy of maintaining equal dollar investments in each stock available to a strategy that periodically uses updated parameter estimates to calculate new optimal proportions of portfolio value to be invested in the stocks available. Although it is to be expected *a priori* that relatively sophisticated strategies will perform at least as well as the more naive strategies, implementation costs will clearly differ across strategies and across investor-specific parameters such as total portfolio value. Thus estimation of the various strategies' performance gross of these costs is a necessary consideration in rational strategy selection by any given investor.

## 1. Introduction

Since the seminal work of Markowitz[1] almost 25 years ago, theoretical and empirical studies of optimal portfolio choice[2] have defined optimality in terms of mean-variance efficiency. If an investor can borrow and lend at a 'riskless' rate of interest in addition to investing in risky securities, this characterization of portfolio choice takes a particularly simple form. Mean-variance efficiency is attained in this case by combining riskless borrowing or lending with an investment in the 'tangency portfolio' of risky securities – that portfolio whose expected rate of return in excess of the riskless rate is greatest as a fraction of the standard deviation of its rate of return, i.e., the portfolio with the maximum 'reward-to-variability' ratio. If there were no transaction costs and if investors had identical expectations, market equilibrium theory predicts that the relative dollar quantities ('weights') of individual stocks in the tangency portfolio would be proportional to the stocks' total values and thus these weights would be trivial to compute.

*We wish to thank the referee, Eugene Fama, and Michael C. Jensen for their helpful comments.
[1]See Markowitz (1952, 1956, 1959).
[2]See, for example, Johnson and Shannon (1974, 1975), Blume (1970), Evans (1970), Cohen and Pogue (1967), Sharpe (1967), and Tobin (1958).

Actual implementation of portfolio startegies designed to maximize the reward-to-variability ratio does involve non-negligible transaction costs which increase with the number of different stocks in the portfolio. This provides an incentive to restrict the set of stocks from which a tangency portfolio is chosen. Restricting portfolio size, however, involves not only a potential efficiency loss, but also non-trivial costs of computing portfolio weights. Market equilibrium theory does not offer the simple solution here that it does in the case of no transaction costs. Even if transaction costs are ignored, equilibrium theory does not imply that the tangency portfolio associated with a restricted set of stocks consists of those stocks held in proportion to their market values. The tangency portfolio weights mut be estimated and that estimation is both costly and subject to error.[3] There is, however, a trade-off between estimation costs and estimation accuracy. Thus, in addition to restrictions on portfolio size, two other potential cost reduction techniques are (a) using cruder and less expensive estimation procedures and (b) reducing the frequency of incorporating 'new' data into portfolio weight estimates. The magnitude of the gross efficiency losses associated with use of any of these techniques is an empirical question.

In this paper, we empirically assess the performance (before transaction and estimation costs) of five different portfolio strategies that employ one or more of the cost reduction techniques mentioned above. With one exception, these strategies are all designed to approximate continuous investment in the tangency portfolio for the universe of stocks to which the strategies are applied. Using monthly return data on over 800 stocks and measuring the performance of the alternative strategies over three non-overlapping five year intervals, our basic conclusion is that, for any given 'nominal portfolio size' (the number of stocks available for inclusion in the portfolio), the use of the more sophisticated (and expensive) techniques for estimating optimal weights and/or more frequent 'up-dating' of optimal weights does not result in significant improvements in portfolio efficiency. On the other hand, our results are entirely consistent with the well-documented relation between portfolio size and portfolio efficiency. For all of the strategies considered, the larger the nominal portfolio size, the more efficient is the chosen portfolio.

Our basic conclusion – that 'fine tuning' portfolio weights doesn't pay – is contrary to the conclusion of recent papers by Johnson and Shannon (1974, 1975). Using quarterly data on 50 stocks for an eight-year period, they conclude that frequent (quarterly) re-estimation of optimal portfolio weights using sophisti-

---

[3]In the absence of a simple equilibrium rule like 'weights proportional to total values', tangency portfolio weights must be based on estimates of the means, variances, and co-variances of stock returns. In practice, these distribution parameters are estimated from historical data and the estimates are subject to error though they may be unbiased. Even if the parameter estimates are unbiased, however, the process of converting them into portfolio weights may be such that the weights are not unbiased. If, for example, an unbiased parameter estimate is squared, the result is not an unbiased estimate of the square of the parameter.

cated estimation techniques (regression and quadratic programming) resulted in dramatic improvements in portfolio efficiency when compared to a 'naive' strategy of simply maintaining equal portfolio weights. They also found, however, that without quarterly up-dating of portfolio weights, the performance of the optimized strategy was worse than that of the equally weighted portfolio strategy. This would imply either that there is significant non-stationarity in the joint distribution of security returns or that the market is inefficient. Neither of these implications is entirely consistent with the bulk of empirical evidence on security return behavior.[4] Our own results, based on a much larger sample of securities and time intervals, indicate that Johnson and Shannon's results are specific to their particular sample and are not generally representative. In any case, we have defined our portfolio strategies to conform closely to those evaluated by Johnson and Shannon and by others [e.g., Cohen and Pogue (1967)][5] in order to facilitate comparisons of results.

The plan of the paper is as follows: In section 2 we provide detailed descriptions of the five portfolio strategies we consider, the data base on which the strategies are evaluated, and the procedures we use to compute the various statistics that summarize the strategies' performance. Section 3 describes the empirical results, and section 4 summarizes the conclusions we draw from those results. Appendices A and B describe two alternative algorithms used to estimate security weights in the tangency portfolio.

## 2. Methodology

### 2.1. Definition of strategies

The five strategies defined below were chosen to reflect varying degrees of complexity in the estimation of portfolio weights and varying frequences of up-dating the weights. With the exception of Strategy A, all of the strategies are designed to select the 'tangency portfolio' from the stock universe to which they are applied and to maintain continuous investment in that portfolio. The effects of restricting the number of stocks available for inclusion in the portfolio (the 'nominal portfolio size') are assessed by applying each strategy to randomly selected security sets of size $n$, where $n$ takes the values 3, 5, 7, ..., 17, and 50.[6]

---

[4]For an overview of this evidence, see Fama (1976).

[5]Except for the rebalancing frequency [monthly in our study, quarterly in Johnson and Shannor (1974, 1975), and annually in Cohen and Pogue (1967)], there are at least two strategies common to all studies: (a) investment in equally weighted portfolios, and (b) investment in portfolios that are estimated to be efficient via the Sharpe (1963) single-index model. Unfortunately, the significance of Cohen and Pogue's results is extremely weak since the performance of alternative strategies was measured using only seven years of annual returns.

[6]Several studies [e.g., Evans and Archer (1968)] have found that most of the potential dispersion reduction gains from increased portfolio sizes are achieved by the time $n$ is increased to 15–20.

Since short sales are not allowed,[7] some of the strategies may assign zero weights to some stocks in the set of stocks to which they are applied and thus the 'actual portfolio size' for some replications of the experiment may be less than the nominal portfolio size. This empirical relation between nominal and actual portfolio size for each strategy is one of the performance characteristics we summarize in the following analysis.

The particular strategies we employ are:

*Strategy A.* Rebalance monthly to equal weights on all stocks available for inclusion.

Strategy A serves both as reference point for evaluation of the other strategies and as a strategy that involves no estimation costs.

*Strategy B.* At the beginning of each five-year evaluation period estimate the weights for the tangency portfolio from the stocks available for inclusion. Rebalance monthly to those estimated weights during the evaluation period.

Strategy B involves relatively complex computations (explained in appendix A) in the estimation of portfolio weights. It also involves, however, a very low frequency of re-estimation or 'up-dating' of the weights.

*Strategy C.* Same as Strategy B except that the tangency portfolio weights are re-estimated at the beginning of each month using the latest data then available.

Comparison of the performance of Strategies B and C will provide some evidence about the effect of more frequent up-dating of estimated portfolio weights.

*Strategy D.* Same as Strategy B except that portfolio weights are estimated using the simplified algorithm explained in appendix B.

*Strategy E.* Same as Strategy C except that the simplified estimation algorithm in appendix B is used.

The simplified estimation algorithm used in Strategies D and E is based on an assumption that all securities have the same ratio of expected excess return to $\beta$. This algorithm is considerably less expensive to compute than the algorithm used in Strategies B and C. The essential features of all of the strategies are summarized in table 1.

[7]All of the previously mentioned empirical studies of the performance of portfolios estimated to be mean-variance efficient have used this assumption. It should be noted, however, that much of the complexity of estimating efficient portfolio weights is due solely to this assumption.

Table 1

Summary of portfolio formation strategies.

| Strategy | Weighting scheme for stocks | Frequency of rebalancing | Frequency of revision of weights |
|---|---|---|---|
| A | Equal weights | Monthly | Nil |
| B | Optimal weights (as in appendix A) | Monthly | Nil |
| C | Optimal weights (as in appendix A) | Monthly | Monthly |
| D | Modified optimal weights (as in appendix B) | Monthly | Nil |
| E | Modified optimal weights (as in appendix B) | Monthly | Monthly |

## 2.2. The data

Three contiguous five-year intervals were selected as 'evaluation periods' and, for each evaluation period, the thirty months immediately preceding it was defined as an 'estimation period' for purposes of computing portfolio weights in Strategies B and D and initial weights in Strategies C and E. Monthly rates of return on securities and a monthly 'risk-free rate' series were obtained from the University of Rochester Security Data Base which is a merger of the University of Chicago CRSP file with other financial data files. [8] For each evaluation

[8]Subsequent to our research, we discovered the risk-free rate series compiled by Bildersee (1975) based on monthly Treasury Bill prices. The Security Data Base risk-free rate is significantly higher than that calculated by Bildersee for the time periods we investigated. As yet, we have not been able to reconcile the differences between the series. The extent of the differences for the time periods described in table 2 is summarized below:

Average risk-free rate (% per month).

|  | Bildersee | Security data base |
|---|---|---|
| *Period 1* | | |
| Estimation (30 months) | 0.278 | 0.340 |
| Evaluation (59 months) | 0.409 | 0.551 |
| *Period 2* | | |
| Estimation | 0.183 | 0.300 |
| Evaluation | 0.232 | 0.304 |
| *Period 3* | | |
| Estimation | 0.100 | 0.170 |
| Evaluation | 0.197 | 0.299 |

In principle, use of a higher risk-free rate results in selecting portfolios with higher mean return and higher standard deviation for Strategies B, C, D and E. This does not introduce any systematic bias into our comparisons of the relative performance of these strategies. Strategy A portfolios are independent of the risk-free rate. Johnson and Shannon (1974) used a constant 5% per annum as the risk-free rate in their study.

period, all stocks having returns continuously available throughout the period and its associated estimation period were included in the test population.

To assure broad coverage of the test population, a two-stage sampling procedure was used. First, the test population for each evaluation period was randomly partitioned into non-overlapping subsamples of size 50. Then, when evaluating the strategies for small nominal portfolio sizes ($3 \leq n \leq 17$), 20 samples of size $n$ were drawn from each of the size-50 subsamples formed in the first stage. Evaluation of the strategies for a nominal portfolio size of 50 was done by applying the strategies to all of the first-stage size 50 samples. The above characteristics of the test population are summarized in table 2.

Table 2

Data base details.

| Period | Estimation period | Evaluation period | Stocks available | Samples of size 50 |
|--------|-------------------|-------------------|------------------|--------------------|
| 1 | Feb. 63 – July 65 | Aug. 65 – June 70 | 823 | 16 |
| 2 | March 58 – Aug. 60 | Sept. 60 – July 65 | 877 | 17 |
| 3 | April 53 – Sept. 55 | Oct. 55 – Aug. 60 | 893 | 17 |

## 2.3. Performance measurement for small portfolio sizes

The performance of the strategies for small nominal portfolio sizes ($3 \leq n \leq 17$) was measured only over evaluation period 1 (Aug. 1965 – June 1970). For that evaluation period the test population was randomly partitioned into 16 non-overlapping samples of 50 stocks each. These samples were indexed by $j = 1, 2, ..., 16$. To evaluate the strategies' performance for a particular nominal portfolio size $n$, 20 subsamples (indexed by $i = 1, 2, ..., 20$) of size $n$ were drawn in the following way from each of the 16 size-50 samples: From the $j$th size-50 sample, a random subsample of size $n$ was drawn without replacement. The identities on the $n$ stocks were noted and they were returned to the 50-stock sample. Repeating this procedure an additional 19 times yielded the 20 subsamples of size $n$ from the $j$th size-50 sample. When applied to all 16 size-50 samples, 320 size-$n$ subsamples were generated. These subsamples were indexed by $(i, j, n), i = 1, 2, ..., 20; j = 1, 2, ..., 16; n = 3, 5, 7, ..., 17$.

When applied to the stock universe $(i, j, n)$, the rate of return to Strategy $X (X = A, B, C, D, E)$ in month $t$ of the evaluation period was denoted by $R_t (X, i, j, n)$. From these rates of return the following summary statistics were computed:

$$AV(X, i, j, n) = \frac{1}{59} \sum_{t=1}^{59} R_t(X, i, j, n),$$

Table 3

Grand average values[a] - Nominal portfolio sizes 3 to 17 - Period August 1965 to June 1970.

| Strategy | Statistic | Nominal portfolio size | | | | | | | |
|---|---|---|---|---|---|---|---|---|---|
| | | 3 | 5 | 7 | 9 | 11 | 13 | 15 | 17 |
| A | $\overline{AV}$ | 0.458 | 0.471 | 0.490 | 0.514 | 0.476 | 0.493 | 0.513 | 0.499 |
| | $\overline{SD}$ | 6.620 | 5.989 | 5.689 | 5.608 | 5.491 | 5.397 | 5.338 | 5.309 |
| B | $\overline{AV}$ | 0.392 | 0.385 | 0.391 | 0.386 | 0.339 | 0.376 | 0.381 | 0.380 |
| | $\overline{SD}$ | 7.089 | 6.559 | 6.270 | 6.071 | 5.816 | 5.684 | 5.613 | 5.528 |
| C | $\overline{AV}$ | 0.541 | 0.514 | 0.544 | 0.628 | 0.494 | 0.526 | 0.618 | 0.599 |
| | $\overline{SD}$ | 8.016 | 7.771 | 7.647 | 6.826 | 7.262 | 7.117 | 7.080 | 6.994 |
| D | $\overline{AV}$ | 0.414 | 0.424 | 0.445 | 0.458 | 0.427 | 0.433 | 0.449 | 0.439 |
| | $\overline{SD}$ | 6.465 | 5.894 | 5.512 | 5.388 | 5.226 | 5.124 | 5.054 | 5.014 |
| E | $\overline{AV}$ | 0.494 | 0.484 | 0.512 | 0.541 | 0.514 | 0.524 | 0.521 | 0.528 |
| | $\overline{SD}$ | 6.510 | 5.886 | 5.598 | 5.446 | 5.317 | 5.237 | 5.143 | 5.117 |

[a]Cell entries for $\overline{AV}$ and $\overline{SD}$ are percentage rates of return per month.

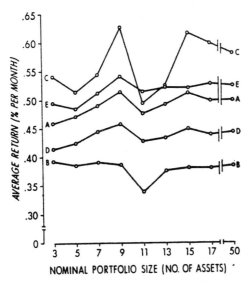

Fig. 1. The relation in evaluation period 1, for each strategy, between average monthly return and nominal portfolio size.

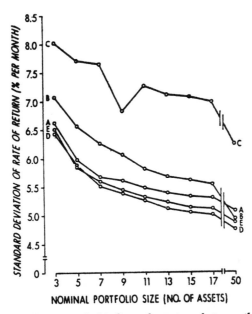

Fig. 2. The relation in evaluation period 1, for each strategy, between the standard deviation of monthly returns and nominal portfolio size.

and

$$SD(X, i, j, n) \equiv \left[ \frac{1}{59} \sum_{t=1}^{59} (R_t(X, i, j, n) - AV(X, i, j, n))^2 \right]^{\frac{1}{2}},$$

for $X = A, B, C, D, E$; $i = 1, 2, \ldots, 20$; $j = 1, 2, \ldots, 16$; and $n = 3, 5, 7, \ldots, 17$. For each strategy and portfolio size, these statistics were then averaged across $i$ and $j$ to yield

$$\overline{AV}(X, n) \equiv \frac{1}{320} \sum_{i=1}^{20} \sum_{j=1}^{16} AV(X, i, j, n),$$

and

$$\overline{SD}(X, n) \equiv \frac{1}{320} \sum_{i=1}^{20} \sum_{j=1}^{16} SD(X, i, j, n).$$

Table 4

Average actual portfolio sizes for alternative nominal portfolio sizes and portfolio selection strategies.

| Nominal portfolio size | Portfolio selection strategy | | | | |
|---|---|---|---|---|---|
| | A | B | C | D | E |
| 3 | 3.0 | 2.0 | 1.7 | 2.9 | 3.0 |
| 5 | 5.0 | 3.1 | 2.6 | 4.9 | 5.0 |
| 7 | 7.0 | 4.1 | 3.2 | 6.8 | 6.9 |
| 9 | 9.0 | 4.8 | 3.9 | 8.8 | 8.9 |
| 11 | 11.0 | 5.5 | 4.3 | 10.8 | 10.9 |
| 13 | 13.0 | 6.2 | 4.8 | 12.7 | 12.9 |
| 15 | 15.0 | 6.8 | 5.2 | 14.7 | 14.9 |
| 17 | 17.0 | 7.1 | 5.6 | 16.6 | 16.9 |

The values of these averages are reported in table 3 and are depicted in figs. 1 and 2. Table 4 gives the average actual portfolio size for each startegy and nominal portfolio size.

## 2.4. Performance measurement for the large portfolio size

When evaluating the strategies' performance for the nominal portfolio size of 50, all three of the evaluation periods were used. The symbol $R_t(X, j, k)$ denotes the rate of return in month $t$ of evaluation period $k$ for Strategy $X$ when it is applied to the $j$th 50-stock subsample of period $k$'s test population. Using this notation, the following statistics were computed:

$$AV(X, j, k) = \frac{1}{59} \sum_{t=1}^{59} R_t(X, j, k),$$

and

$$SD(X,j,k) = \left[\frac{1}{59} \sum_{t=1}^{59} (R_t(X,j,k) - AV(X,j,k))^2\right]^{\frac{1}{2}},$$

for $X = A, B, C, D, E$; $j = 1, 2, \ldots, 16$ for $k = 1$; and $j = 1, 2, \ldots, 17$ for $k = 2, 3$. For each strategy and each evaluation period, these statistics were then averaged across the 50-stock subsamples to obtain $\overline{AV}(X, k)$ and $\overline{SD}(X, k)$, where $X = A, B, C, D, E$ and $k = 1, 2, 3$, These averages are reported in table 5. Table 5 also gives the cross-sectional sample standard deviation of $AV$ and $SD$,

Table 5

Performance for 50-stock universes.[a]

| Period | Strategy | AV | | SD | |
|--------|----------|----------------------|--------------|---------------------|---------------|
| | | $\overline{AV}$ | $\sigma(AV)$ | $\overline{SD}$ | $\sigma(SD)$ |
| 1 | A | 0.498 | 0.142 | 5.08 | 0.30 |
| | B | 0.384 | 0.328 | 4.94 | 0.72 |
| | C | 0.582 | 0.495 | 6.25 | 0.65 |
| | D | 0.443 | 0.150 | 4.76 | 0.32 |
| | E | 0.525 | 0.101 | 4.88 | 0.27 |
| 2 | A | 1.063 | 0.142 | 4.14 | 0.21 |
| | B | 0.974 | 0.201 | 4.02 | 0.30 |
| | C | 1.084 | 0.288 | 4.42 | 0.53 |
| | D | 1.094 | 0.145 | 3.98 | 0.22 |
| | E | 1.059 | 0.138 | 4.01 | 0.20 |
| 3 | A | 1.005 | 0.133 | 3.38 | 0.20 |
| | B | 1.138 | 0.311 | 3.22 | 0.46 |
| | C | 1.233 | 0.285 | 3.51 | 0.47 |
| | D | 0.956 | 0.161 | 3.37 | 0.18 |
| | E | 0.935 | 0.157 | 3.39 | 0.20 |

[a]Cell entries for $AV$ and $SD$ are percentage rates of return per month.

Table 6

Average actual portfolio sizes for alternative strategies for nominal portfolio size of 50 stocks.

| Period | No. of samples | Portfolio selection strategy | | | | |
|--------|----------------|------|------|------|------|------|
| | | A | B | C | D | E |
| 1 | 16 | 50 | 14.3 | 10.4 | 48.9 | 49.6 |
| 2 | 17 | 50 | 19.6 | 10.8 | 49.2 | 49.6 |
| 3 | 17 | 50 | 14.9 | 14.4 | 49.7 | 49.3 |

within each period for each strategy, e.g., $\sigma(AV)$ for Strategy C in period 1 was computed as

$$\left[\frac{1}{16}\sum_{j=1}^{16}(AV(C,j,1)-\overline{AV}(C,1))^2\right]^{\frac{1}{2}}$$

Table 6 gives the average actual portfolio sizes for each strategy in each of the evaluation periods.

## 3. Results

In section 1, three factors affecting estimation and transaction costs were mentioned; (i) portfolio size, (ii) the complexity of the scheme for estimating portfolio weights, and (iii) the frequency of up-dating portfolio weights. The results reported in tables 3 and 5 show variations in average portfolio performance (before estimation and transaction costs) resulting from attempts to reduce costs by restricting portfolio size, using crude estimation techniques, and low frequencies of up-dating portfolio weights. In interpreting these results the following general observations should be kept in mind:

(a) The columns of table 3 are not statistically independent. Both because of overlaps in different size portfolios for a given strategy and because of cross-sectional dependence in the returns of individual securities, it is expected, for instance, that the performance of Strategy B for $n = 5$ will be positively correlated with B's performance for $n = 13$.

(b) In table 3, the performances of different strategies for any given nominal portfolio size are not independent. For some pairs of strategies (e.g., B and C, D and E), the portfolio overlap is such that their returns probably have a very high cross-sectional correlation. The same observation applies, of course, to comparisons of different strategies within a given evaluation period in table 5.

(c) The '$\overline{SD}$' statistics reported in tables 3 and 5 are estimates of the time-series dispersion in monthly strategy returns. The $\sigma(\cdot)$ statistics reported in table 5 are measures of the cross-sectional (across the 50-stock subsamples) dispersion in the $AV$ and $SD$ statistics for each strategy.

### 3.1. The effects of restricting portfolio size

With the exception of the somewhat erratic behavior of Strategy C, all strategies exhibited a monotonic decline in the dispersion of their monthly rates of return as nominal portfolio size was increased. In moving from $n = 3$ to $n = 17$, there was about a 20% reduction in $\overline{SD}$ for all strategies (except C). Increasing $n$ from 17 to 50 resulted in a further 5% reduction for all strategies except B and C, for which the reduction was about 10%. In no case did average monthly return appear to be systematically related to portfolio size.[9]

Inspection of tables 4 and 6 suggests that the deviant behavior of Strategy C (and, to a lesser extent, Strategy B) can be attributed to its relatively small average actual portfolio size when compared to its nominal portfolio size. This difference between nominal and actual portfolio sizes was emphasized by Johnson and Shannon (1974, 1975). When comparing the performance of equally weighted portfolios with the performance of a strategy involving sophisticated estimation of tangency portfolio weights and frequent updating, they found that, with equal nominal portfolio sizes, the two strategies had approximately the same level of dispersion in their monthly rates of return. The average actual portfolio size for the sophisticated strategy, however, was substantially less than its nominal size, i.e., the strategy greatly reduced the number of securities in the portfolio without increasing the variance of portfolio returns. If this empirical result were generally representative, it would indicate a potentially significant benefit of the sophisticated strategy. Johnson and Shannon's result, however, is not at all confirmed in our study. In tables 3 and 5, Strategies B and C (the two strategies with low actual sizes relative to nominal sizes) have consistently higher dispersion in their monthly returns than do the other strategies. As indicated by the $\sigma(\cdot)$ measures in table 5, Strategies B and C also exhibited much more performance variability across the disjoint 50-stock subsamples than did the other strategies.

## 3.2. The effects of crude estimation techniques

Among the strategies (B–E) that involve some deliberate attempt to replicate the performance of the tangency portfolio, Strategy D is a crude, low estimation cost analog of Strategy B (B and D both involve a low estimation frequency) and, similarly, Strategy E is the analog of Strategy C (C and E are the high estimation frequency strategies). Except for the comparison of B and D in evaluation period 3 for a nominal portfolio size of 50, the 'sophisticated' strategies (B and C) had consistently higher dispersion in their monthly rates of return than did their cruder analogs. Although this was probably due to the smaller actual portfolio sizes of the sophisticated strategies, it was not a result that could have been confidently predicted a priori. Indeed, the latest evidence available prior to our study [see the discussion of Johnson and Shannon (1974, 1975) in section 3.1] indicated the reverse – that in spite of lower actual portfolio sizes, sophisticated estimation techniques do not increase the dispersion of returns.

---

[9]Although the rank correlation between portfolio size and average monthly return is significant at the $\alpha = 0.20$ level (two-tailed test) for Strategies A, B, and E ($\rho = 0.65$ for A, $\rho = -0.63$ for B, and $\rho = 0.70$ for E), the relation is probably spurious. The difference between the maximum and minimum (across portfolio sizes) average monthly returns is less than 0.06% for each of these strategies.

In terms of average monthly returns, there was no statistically significant difference between the performance of the sophisticated strategies and their crude analogs when applied to small security universe ($3 \leq n \leq 17$). The standard deviation of the difference in the monthly returns of Strategies B and D when applied to the same stock universe (similarly for C and E) would be smallest if their returns were perfectly correlated. In that case the standard deviation of the difference in monthly returns would simply be the absolute value of the difference in the strategies' individual standard deviations. Even under this extreme assumption, however, the results in table 3 indicate no significant difference in average monthly returns. If the same extreme assumption (perfect cross-sectional correlation) is used to estimate the significance of the results for 50-stock universes reported in table 5, the results are ambiguous. Strategy D has a 'significantly' higher average return than Strategy B in periods 1 and 2 and vice versa in period 3. There is no significant difference in the average returns on Strategies C and E for periods 1 and 2 and Strategy C does better in period 3.

Strategy A involves no estimation costs at all and, in that sense, is the crudest strategy of all. On an *a priori* basis, however, Strategy A is not strictly comparable to the other strategies since it does not involve any deliberate attempt to replicate the tangency portfolio. Nevertheless, in our study, Strategy A was not significantly dominated in terms of mean-variance efficiency by any of the other strategies. Indeed, the largest (though probably not significant) difference between A's performance and that of the other strategies appears in the comparison of A and B for the small portfolio sizes and, in that case, A appears to dominate B.

### 3.3. The effects of low frequency estimation

One of the techniques for reducing estimation costs is to reduce the frequency of re-estimating portfolio weights on the basis of more recent data. Strategy B is the low estimation frequency analog of Strategy C and, similarly, Strategy D is the low frequency analog of Strategy E.

Judging from the performance statistics in tables 3 and 5, the most consistently observed effect of low estimation frequencies is a reduction in the dispersion of monthly returns. This is most pronounced (as might be expected because of lower actual portfolio sizes) in the comparison of Strategies B and C. Evidently, the month-to-month variability in the portfolio weights for Strategies C and E introduced more variability in monthly strategy returns than it removed by having more 'up-to-date' estimates of efficient weights.

The average monthly returns of Strategy B were lower for all portfolio sizes and evaluation periods than the average returns of the high estimation frequency Strategy C. Even under the extreme assumption of perfect cross-sectional correlation (explained above in section 3.2), however, the difference in B and C's returns is 'significant' only for size-50 portfolios in periods 2 and 3. Because of the relatively small difference in the dispersion of Strategies D and E's monthly returns, the extreme assumption of perfect cross-sectional correlation implies that the average returns of Strategy E (a high frequency strategy) are 'significantly' greater then the average returns of Strategy D for small portfolio sizes. This pattern is reversed, however, for size-50 portfolios in two out of the three evaluation periods.

## 4. Interpretation and conclusion

On the basis of our empirical measurements of the performance of alternative portfolio strategies we conclude that:

(a) The choice of the size of the security universe to which any given strategy is applied is a non-trivial matter. Increasing the size of the security universe clearly reduces the dispersion of monthly rates of return to the portfolio strategy. Just as clearly, however, the transaction and estimation costs of implementing the strategy will, for most investors, be an increasing function of the security universe size.

(b) To the extent that they are significantly more expensive to implement than relatively naive strategies, strategies that involve complex (and purportedly more accurate) calculations of 'optimal' portfolio weights are not worth employing. The complex strategies we evaluated exhibited consistently greater dispersion in their monthly returns than did their more naive analogs applied to the same stock universes. At the same time, the average monthly returns (before implementation costs) of the complex strategies were not significantly greater than those of the cruder strategies. Ironically, this failure of the complex strategies probably is due to their complexity. Given the 'true' values of the security return distribution parameters (means, variances, and covariances) the complex strategies would, by construction, yield more accurate estimates of tangency portfolio weights than the more naive strategies. Because they are much more complicated functions of the distribution parameters, however, the weight estimators in the complex strategies are more sensitive to measurement errors in those parameters. Thus, in the process of arriving at portfolio weights, 'noise' in estimates of the distribution parameters is magnified more in the complex strategies than in the naive strategies and, at least in our simulations, this noise was more than enough to offset the potential superiority of the complex strategies.

(c) Frequent up-dating of 'optimal' portfolio weights increases the dispersion of returns without significantly or unambiguously increasing the average level of returns (before transaction and estimation costs). This is to be expected if the joint distribution of monthly security returns is relatively stationary and does not exhibit significant serial dependence. To the extent that frequent up-dating of calculated portfolio weights is costly, our results indicate at least that the optimal up-dating interval is longer than one month.

## Appendix A[10]

From time series regressions of monthly stock returns on monthly returns to an 'index portfolio', estimates of the following parameters are obtained:

(i) $\beta_j$ = the 'beta' of stock $j$,
(ii) $v_j$ = the residual variance from the regression for stock $j$,
(iii) $\mu_j$ = the expected excess of stock $j$'s return above the risk-free rate of return,
(iv) $\sigma_I^2$ = the variance of the rate of return on the index portfolio.

It is assumed in the algorithm below that the covariance structure of stock returns is given by

$$\sigma_{ij} = \beta_i^2 \sigma_I^2 + v_i, \qquad i = j,$$
$$= \beta_i \beta_j \sigma_I^2, \qquad i \neq j,$$

where $\sigma_{ii}$ is the variance of stock $i$'s return and $\sigma_{ij}$ is the covariance between the returns of stocks $i$ and $j$. It is also assumed that $\mu_j > 0$ for at least one stock.

In fig. 3, the 'tangency' portfolio is represented by $T$, the point where a straight line from the risk-free asset $(0, r_F)$ is tangent to the 'efficient frontier', $BC$, of the set of feasible stock portfolios.

The problem of determining the composition of the tangency portfolio is then equivalent to the problem of finding the portfolio $P$ that maximizes the angle $\theta$ subject to the constraints

$$\mu_P = \theta \sigma_P, \tag{1}$$

$$\beta_P = \sum_{j=1}^{N} X_j \beta_j, \tag{2}$$

$$\sum_{j=1}^{N} X_j = 1, \tag{3}$$

$$X_j \geq 0, \qquad j = 1, \ldots, N, \tag{4}$$

where $\mu_P$ and $\sigma_P$ are given by

$$\mu_P \equiv \sum_{j=1}^{N} X_j \mu_j, \tag{5}$$

$$\sigma_P \equiv \left\{ \sum_{j=1}^{N} X_j^2 v_j + \beta_P^2 \sigma_I^2 \right\}^{\frac{1}{2}}, \tag{6}$$

---

[10]Although developed independently, the algorithm described in appendix A is equivalent to an algorithm proposed by Elton, Gruber, and Padberg (1976).

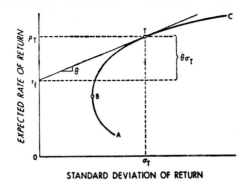

Fig. 3.   Curve *ABC* is the 'efficient frontier'. Point *T* is the 'tangency portfolio' and $\rho_T$ and $\sigma_T$ are its expected rate of return and standard deviation $r_F$ is the risk-free rate, and $\theta$ is the tangency portfolio's reward-to-variability ratio.

and where $X_j$ is the proportion of total portfolio value invested in stock $j$. The Lagrangean for this problem is

$$L = \theta + \lambda_1(\mu_P - \theta\sigma_P) + \lambda_2\left(\beta_P - \sum_{j=1}^{N} X_j\beta_j\right) + \lambda_3\left(1 - \sum_{j=1}^{N} X_j\right), \qquad (7)$$

where $\mu_P$ and $\sigma_P$ are given by (5) and (6). Some of the necessary conditions for maximization of $\theta$ are then

$$L_\theta = 1 - \lambda_1\sigma_P = 0, \qquad (8)$$

$$L_{\beta_P} = \lambda_2 - \lambda_1\theta\beta_P\sigma_I^2\sigma_P^{-1} = 0, \qquad (9)$$

$$L_{X_j} = \lambda_1\mu_j - \lambda_1\theta X_j v_j\sigma_P^{-1} - \lambda_2\beta_j - \lambda_3 \leq 0, \quad j = 1, ..., N, \qquad (10)$$

$$X_j L_{X_j} = 0, \qquad\qquad\qquad\qquad j = 1, ..., N, \qquad (11)$$

where in (8)–(11) and in all that follows it is assumed that all variables are evaluated at their optimal values. Taken together with (1)–(6), (8)–(11) imply that $\lambda_3 = 0$ and that

$$X_j = \sigma_P(\lambda_1\theta)^{-1}\left[\frac{\lambda_1\mu_j - \lambda_2\beta_j}{v_j}\right], \quad \lambda_1\mu_j - \lambda_2\beta_j \geq 0,$$

$$= 0, \qquad\qquad\qquad\quad \lambda_1\mu_j - \lambda_2\beta_j < 0, \qquad (12)$$

or

$$X_j = a\left(\frac{\mu_j}{v_j}\right) - b\left(\frac{\beta_j}{v_j}\right), \quad a\mu_j - b\beta_j \geq 0,$$

$$= 0, \qquad\qquad\qquad a\mu_j - b\beta_j > 0, \qquad (13)$$

where

$$a \equiv \theta^{-1}\sigma_P \quad \text{and} \quad b \equiv \lambda_2 \sigma_P / \lambda_1 \theta. \tag{14}$$

Let $J$ be the index set such that $X_j > 0$ if $j \in J$ and $X_j = 0$ if $j \notin J$. Then, since $\sum_{j \in J} X_j = 1$ and $\sum_{j \in J} X_j \beta_j = \beta_P = (\lambda_2 \sigma_P / \lambda_1 \theta)(\sigma_I^2)^{-1}$ [from (9)] $= b(\sigma_I^2)^{-1}$ [from (14)], the ratio $\gamma \equiv b/a$ can be solved for, and

$$X_j = (a/v_j)(\mu_j - \gamma \beta_j), \qquad j \in J, \tag{15}$$

where

$$\gamma = \left\{ \sum_{j \in J} \left( \frac{\beta_j^2 \sigma_I^2}{v_j} \right) \left( \frac{\mu_j}{\beta_j} \right) \right\} \Big/ \left\{ 1 + \sum_{j \in J} \left( \frac{\beta_j^2 \sigma_I^2}{v_j} \right) \right\}. \tag{16}$$

All that now remains is to find the optimal index set $J$. This can be accomplished by the following algorithm:

(i) Index the stocks such that

$$\mu_1 / |\beta_1| \geq \mu_2 / |\beta_2| \geq \ldots \geq \mu_N / |\beta_N|.$$

(ii) Let $\gamma_j$ be defined as $\gamma$ computed from (16) for the index set $J = \{1, 2, \ldots, j\}$.

(iii) The optimal index set is $J = \{1, 2, \ldots, k\}$ where $k$ is the smallest index for which $\mu_{k+1} - \gamma_k \beta_{k+1} \leq 0$ unless $\mu_N - \gamma_N \beta_N > 0$ in which case $J = \{1, 2, \ldots, N\}$.

Given $J$, the optimal portfolio weights are then computed from (15) with $a$ chosen so that $\sum_{j \in J} X_j = 1$.

In actual application of the algorithm to small security universes (e.g., $N = 3$), it may be the case that all estimated mean excess returns are negative, i.e., $\mu_j < 0, j = 1, \ldots, N$. In these cases, we used the rule of placing all funds in the risk-free asset. In our study, this situation occurred only in period 1 for Strategies B and C. In the case of Strategy B it occurred only for $N = 3$ and then only for 5 out of the 320 size-3 universe sampled. For Strategy C, which involved monthly reestimation of portfolio weights and hence 18,880 applications of the algorithm for each value of $N$, the situation arose in 6.5% of the applications for $N = 3$; 2% for $N = 5$; 0.7% for $N = 7$; 0.4% for $N = 9$; 0.2% for $N = 11$; 0.04% for $N = 13$; 0.04% for $N = 15$; and 0.03% for $N = 17$.

## Appendix B

If it is assumed that all stocks plot on the 'security market line', i.e., that

$$\frac{\mu_1}{\beta_1} = \frac{\mu_2}{\beta_2} = \ldots = \frac{\mu_N}{\beta_N}, \tag{17}$$

then from (15) and (16) in appendix A

$$X_j = K\frac{\beta_j}{v_j}, \quad \beta_j > 0,$$

$$= 0, \quad \beta_j \le 0,$$

(18)

where $K$ is chosen so that

$$\sum_{j=2}^{N} X_j = 1.$$

In all applications of this simplified algorithm, there was never a case in which $\beta_j < 0$, $j = 1, ..., N$. Had there been such a case, however, the implied investment rule would be to put all funds in the risk-free asset.

# References

Bildersee, J.S., 1975, Some new bond indexes, Journal of Business 48, 506–525.

Blume, M.E., 1970, Portfolio theory: A step towards its practical application, Journal of Business 43, 152–173.

Cohen, K.J. and J.A. Pogue, 1967, An empirical evaluation of alternative portfolio-selection models, Journal of Business 40, 166–193.

Elton, E.J., M.G. Gruber and M.W. Padberg, 1976, Simple criteria for optimal portfolio selection, Journal of Finance 31, 1341–1357.

Evans, J.L., 1970, An analysis of portfolio maintenance strategies, Journal of Finance 25, 561–571.

Evans, J.L. and S.H. Archer, 1968, Diversification and the reduction of dispersion: An empirical analysis, Journal of Finance 23, 761–767.

Fama, E.F., 1976, Foundations of finance (Basic Books, New York).

Johnson, K.H. and D.S. Shannon, 1974, A note on diversification and reduction of dispersion, Journal of Financial Economics 1, 365–372.

Johnson, K.H. and D.S. Shannon, 1975, Portfolio maintenance strategies revisited, Atlantic Economic Journal 3, 25–35.

Markowitz, H., 1952, Portfolio selection, Journal of Finance 7, 77–91.

Markowitz, H., 1956, The optimization of a quadratic function subject to linear constraints, Naval Research Logistics Quarterly 3, 111–133.

Markowitz, H., 1959, Portfolio selection: Efficient diversification of investments (Wiley, New York).

Sharpe, W.F., 1963, A simplified model for portfolio analysis, Management Science 9, 277–293.

Sharpe, W.F., 1967, Portfolio analysis, Journal of Financial and Quantitative Analysis 2, 76–84.

Tobin, J., 1958, Liquidity preference as behavior towards risk, Review of Economic Studies 25, 65–86.

# A NOTE ON THE MARKET MODEL AND THE TWO-PARAMETER MODEL

EUGENE F. FAMA*

IN [5] I showed the equivalence of the two-parameter models of capital market equilibrium of Sharpe [9] and Lintner [7]. I also pointed out errors that these authors made in applying the conditions on equilibrium expected returns of the two-parameter model to a world in which returns are generated by the so-called "market model." As noted recently by Beja [2], some of my comments on the market model were incorrect. This paper attempts to set the record straight.

What I will say is not new. Every statistical result can be found in Cramér [4, chs. 21, 22, 24, and 29] and Anderson [1, ch. 2]. But application of these results to the relationships between the two-parameter model of equilibrium expected returns and the market model involves subtleties sufficient, I think, to make reconsideration of the issues worthwhile.

## I. THE TWO-PARAMETER MODEL

In the Sharpe-Lintner model, the capital market is assumed to be perfect in the sense that investors are price-takers, and there are no transactions costs, information costs, or taxes. Investors are assumed to behave as if they choose among portfolios on the basis of maximum expected utility. Moreover, given the amount of funds to be invested, the expected utility associated with any portfolio is assumed to be solely a function of the mean and variance of the distribution of the one-period percentage return on the portfolios. This can be shown to imply either that investor utility functions are well approximated by quadratic functions of percentage return or that the joint distribution of the one-period percentage returns on assets is multivariate normal.[1] The marginal expected utility of expected return is assumed to be positive, and investors are assumed to be risk-averse in the sense that the marginal expected utility of variance of return is negative. These assumptions imply the *efficient set theorem:* The optimal portfolio for any investor must be efficient in the sense that no other portfolio with the same or higher expected return has lower variance of return.

To get testable implications about the measurement of risk and market equilibrium relationships between risk and expected return, the Sharpe-Lintner model then assumes that any investor can borrow or lend as much as he likes

* Graduate School of Business, University of Chicago. This research was supported by a grant from the National Science Foundation. The comments of F. Black, N. Gonedes, W. Sharpe, and A. Zellner are gratefully acknowledged.

1. When the model is based on normality, the explicit assumption is usually just that the distribution of the return on any portfolio is normal. But this is equivalent to assuming that every linear combination of asset returns has a normal distribution, which implies that the joint distribution of security returns is multivariate normal. (Anderson [1, p. 37].)

*Reprinted from* THE JOURNAL OF FINANCE, Vol. XXVIII, No. 5, December, 1973

at a risk-free rate of interest and that there is complete agreement or "homogeneous expectations" among investors with respect to portfolio return distributions. It then follows that in a market equilibrium all efficient portfolios are combinations of riskless borrowing or lending with the market portfolio m, with m defined by the weights

$$x_{im} = \frac{\text{total market value of all units of asset i}}{\text{total market value of all assets}}, \quad i = 1, 2, \ldots, N,$$

invested in each of the N available assets. The relationship between the expected return on asset i, $E(\tilde{R}_i)$, and its risk in the market portfolio m is[2]

$$E(\tilde{R}_i) = R_f + [E(\tilde{R}_m) - R_f]\beta_i \tag{1}$$

where

$$\beta_i \equiv \frac{\text{cov}(\tilde{R}_i, \tilde{R}_m)}{\sigma^2(\tilde{R}_m)}. \tag{2}$$

Equation (1) says that the expected return on asset i is the riskless rate of interest $R_f$ plus a risk premium that is $\beta_i$ times the difference between $E(\tilde{R}_m)$, the expected return on the market portfolio, and $R_f$.

The parameter $\beta_i$ is a measure of the risk of asset i relative to the total risk of the market portfolio m. That is, in the two-parameter world, the total risk of m can be measured by the variance of its return, $\sigma^2(\tilde{R}_m)$, and, since $\tilde{R}_m = \sum_i x_{im}\tilde{R}_i$,

$$\sigma^2(\tilde{R}_m) = \sum_i\sum_j x_{im}x_{jm}\,\text{cov}(\tilde{R}_i, \tilde{R}_j) = \sum_i x_{im}\,\text{cov}(\tilde{R}_i, \tilde{R}_m). \tag{3}$$

Thus, $\text{cov}(\tilde{R}_i, \tilde{R}_m)$ is the risk of asset i in m in the sense that it determines the contribution of i to $\sigma^2(\tilde{R}_m)$. The parameter $\beta_i$ is then the risk of i in m, measured relative to the total risk of m.[3]

## II. The Market Model

The market model is

$$\tilde{R}_i = \alpha_i + \beta_i\tilde{R}_m + \tilde{\epsilon}_i, \quad i = 1, 2, \ldots, N, \tag{4}$$

with the additional assumptions that $E(\tilde{\epsilon}_i) = 0$ and $\tilde{\epsilon}_i$ and $\tilde{R}_m$ are independent, which together imply that the conditional expectation of $\tilde{R}_i$ given $R_m$ is

$$E(\tilde{R}_i|R_m) = \alpha_i + \beta_i R_m. \tag{5}$$

It is also usually assumed that the disturbances $\tilde{\epsilon}_i$ are uncorrelated across assets.[4]

---

2. Tildes ($\sim$) are used to denote random variables.

3. Since the papers of Sharpe and Lintner, there has been much work, both theoretical and empirical, on the two-parameter model. For a detailed discussion, see Jensen [6].

4. When an explicit link with the Sharpe-Lintner model of expected returns is desired, (4) is written as

$$\tilde{R}_i = R_f(1 - \beta_i) + \beta_i\tilde{R}_m + \tilde{\epsilon}_i.$$

In empirical work, time subscripts are added to $\tilde{R}_i$, $R_f$, $\tilde{R}_m$, and $\tilde{\epsilon}_i$ and it is assumed that $\tilde{\epsilon}_i$ and $\tilde{R}_m$ are serially uncorrelated and that (4) is a stationary process in the sense that $\beta_i$ and

We examine now the extent to which the market model is implied, first by the simple assumption that the joint density of $\tilde{R}_i$ and $\tilde{R}_m$ is continuous and then by the somewhat stronger assumption that the joint distribution of all security returns is multivariate normal. The final section considers the links between the market model and the two-parameter model.

If the joint density $f(R_i, R_m)$ of $\tilde{R}_i$ and $\tilde{R}_m$ is continuous, then the values of $\alpha_i$ and $\beta_i$ that minimize

$$\sigma^2(\tilde{\epsilon}_i) = E\{[\tilde{R}_i - \alpha_i - \beta_i \tilde{R}_m]^2\} = \int_{R_i} \int_{R_m} (R_i - \alpha_i - \beta_i R_m)^2 \, f(R_i, R_m) dR_m dR_i \tag{6}$$

are Cramér [4], Ch. 21, Section 21.6,

$$\beta_i = \frac{\text{cov}(\tilde{R}_i, \tilde{R}_m)}{\sigma^2(\tilde{R}_m)} \qquad \text{and} \qquad \alpha_i = E(\tilde{R}_i) - \beta_i E(\tilde{R}_m). \tag{7}$$

Moreover, with these values of $\alpha_i$ and $\beta_i$, it is always true that $E(\tilde{\epsilon}_i) = 0$ and that

$$\text{cov}(\tilde{\epsilon}_i, \tilde{R}_m) = \text{cov}(\tilde{R}_i - \alpha_i - \frac{\text{cov}(\tilde{R}_i, \tilde{R}_m)}{\sigma^2(\tilde{R}_m)} \tilde{R}_m, \tilde{R}_m)$$

$$= \text{cov}(\tilde{R}_i, \tilde{R}_m) - \text{cov}(\tilde{R}_i, \tilde{R}_m) = 0.$$

Thus, in spite of the fact that $\tilde{R}_m$ (which is just $\sum_i x_{im} \tilde{R}_i$) contains $\tilde{\epsilon}_i$, the two are uncorrelated.[5]

But $\text{cov}(\tilde{\epsilon}_i, \tilde{R}_m) = 0$ does not imply that $\tilde{\epsilon}_i$ and $\tilde{R}_m$ are independent, just that they are uncorrelated. The disturbance $\tilde{\epsilon}_i$ in (4) could, for example, be heteroscedastic.[6] In addition, $E(\tilde{\epsilon}_i) = 0$ does not imply that for all $R_m$, $E(\tilde{\epsilon}_i | R_m) = 0$, which is required if (5) is to hold. Thus, the conditional expectation of $\tilde{R}_i$ given $R_m$ is not necessarily a linear function of $R_m$.[7]

Now suppose that the joint distribution of asset returns is multivariate normal. Then for any asset i, the joint distribution of $\tilde{R}_i$ and $\tilde{R}_m$ is bivariate normal. To see this, consider the following transformations of the vector of asset returns:

---

the distributions of $\tilde{R}_m$ and $\tilde{\epsilon}_i$ are constant through time. Since this paper is concerned with the relationship between the market model and the static version of the two-parameter model, these time series assumptions of the market model are not considered.

5. This contradicts my statement in the last paragraph of page 38 of [5]. The point is noted by Beja [2] and by Black, Jensen, and Scholes [3, fn. 1, p. 118].

6. In this connection, note that $\sigma^2(\tilde{\epsilon}_i)$ in (6) is not to be interpreted as $\sigma^2(\tilde{R}_i | R_m)$, the variance of $\tilde{R}_i$ conditional on $\tilde{R}_m$. The averaging in (6) is with respect to both $\tilde{R}_i$ and $\tilde{R}_m$.

7. In the statistics literature, the function $R_i(R_m) = \alpha_i + \beta_i R_m$, with $\alpha_i$ and $\beta_i$ given by (7), is called the *linear* regression function of $R_i$ on $R_m$. As noted earlier, these values of $\alpha_i$ and $\beta_i$ minimize $\sigma^2(\tilde{\epsilon}_i)$ in (6). The conditional expectation $E(\tilde{R}_i | R_m)$, interpreted as a function of $R_m$, is called *the* regression function of $R_i$ on $R_m$. It has the property that among *all* functions $g(R_m)$ it minimizes $E\{[\tilde{R}_i - g(\tilde{R}_m)]^2\}$, where, as in $\sigma^2(\tilde{\epsilon}_i)$ of (6), the expectation is with respect to both $\tilde{R}_i$ and $\tilde{R}_m$. (Cramér [4, Ch. 21, Section 21.5].)

$$
\begin{bmatrix} \tilde{R}_1 \\ \cdot \\ \cdot \\ \cdot \\ \cdot \\ \tilde{R}_{N-1} \\ \tilde{R}_m \end{bmatrix} = \begin{bmatrix} 1 & 0 & 0 & \cdot & \cdot & 0 \\ 0 & 1 & 0 & \cdot & \cdot & 0 \\ & & 1 & & & \\ \cdot & \cdot & & \cdot & & \cdot \\ \cdot & \cdot & & & \cdot & \cdot \\ \cdot & \cdot & & & & \cdot \\ x_{1m} & x_{2m} & x_{3m} & \cdot & \cdot & x_{Nm} \end{bmatrix} \begin{bmatrix} \tilde{R}_1 \\ \cdot \\ \cdot \\ \cdot \\ \cdot \\ \cdot \\ \tilde{R}_N \end{bmatrix} \qquad (8)
$$

If the vector of asset returns $\tilde{R} \equiv [\tilde{R}_1, \ldots, \tilde{R}_N]'$ is multivariate normal, then $[\tilde{R}_1, \ldots, \tilde{R}_{N-1}, \tilde{R}_m]'$ is multivariate normal since it is a linear transformation of $\tilde{R}$. It follows that $\tilde{R}_i$ and $\tilde{R}_m$ are bivariate normal. (Anderson [1, Ch. 2].)

Bivariate normality of $\tilde{R}_i$ and $\tilde{R}_m$ implies that the conditional expectation $E(\tilde{R}_i|R_m)$ is (5) with $\alpha_i$ and $\beta_i$ given by (7). Moreover, bivariate normality of $\tilde{R}_i$ and $\tilde{R}_m$ and absence of correlation between $\tilde{\epsilon}_i$ and $\tilde{R}_m$ in (4) imply that $\tilde{\epsilon}_i$ and $\tilde{R}_m$ are independent.[8]

But with or without multivariate normality of the joint distribution of asset returns, one cannot assume that for all $j \neq i$, $\text{cov}(\tilde{\epsilon}_i, \tilde{\epsilon}_j) = 0$ since from (3), (4) and (7)

$$
\tilde{R}_m = \sum_i x_{im}\tilde{R}_i = \sum_i x_{im}\alpha_i + \sum_i x_{im}\beta_i \tilde{R}_m + \sum_i x_{im}\tilde{\epsilon}_i
$$

$$
= \sum_i x_{im}\left[ E(\tilde{R}_i) - \frac{\text{cov}(\tilde{R}_i, \tilde{R}_m)}{\sigma^2(\tilde{R}_m)} E(\tilde{R}_m) \right] + \sum_i x_{im} \frac{\text{cov}(\tilde{R}_i, \tilde{R}_m)}{\sigma^2(\tilde{R}_m)} \tilde{R}_m + \sum_i x_{im}\tilde{\epsilon}_i
$$

$$
= E(\tilde{R}_m) - \frac{\sigma^2(\tilde{R}_m)}{\sigma^2(\tilde{R}_m)} E(\tilde{R}_m) + \frac{\sigma^2(\tilde{R}_m)}{\sigma^2(\tilde{R}_m)} \tilde{R}_m + \sum_i x_{im} \tilde{\epsilon}_i.
$$

Thus,

$$
\tilde{R}_m = \tilde{R}_m + \sum_i x_{im}\tilde{\epsilon}_i \qquad (10)
$$

and

$$
\sum_i x_{im}\tilde{\epsilon}_i = 0. \qquad (11)
$$

In short, there is always an exact linear relationship among the disturbances $\tilde{\epsilon}_i$ of the market model.[9]

## III. The Two-Parameter Model and the Market Model

In the Sharpe-Lintner two-parameter model, (1) is the relationship between expected return and risk, and $\beta_i = \text{cov}(\tilde{R}_i, \tilde{R}_m)/\sigma^2(R_m)$ is the appropriate measure of the risk of asset $i$ in the market portfolio $m$ whether or not the

---

8. These implications of multivariate normality were first pointed out to me by Donald L. Garren. Roll [8, p. 272, fn. 4] notes that bivariate normality of $\tilde{R}_i$ and $\tilde{R}_m$ implies (5).

9. This point is implicit in (8). In transforming the return vector $\tilde{R} = [\tilde{R}_1, \ldots, \tilde{R}_N]'$ into $[\tilde{R}_1, \ldots, \tilde{R}_{N-1}, \tilde{R}_m]'$, one security (arbitrarily chosen as the N'th) is lost. Its return is implied by $\tilde{R}_m$ and the returns on the other $N - 1$ securities. Equivalently, the covariance matrices of $\tilde{R}$ and $[\tilde{R}_1, \ldots, \tilde{R}_{N-1}, \tilde{R}_m]'$ are nonsingular but that of $[\tilde{R}, \tilde{R}_m]' = [\tilde{R}_1, \ldots, \tilde{R}_N, \tilde{R}_m]'$ is singular.

stochastic process generating returns is taken to be the market model.[10] With equations (10) and (11), however, we can make more precise Sharpe's notion that, in the context of equation (4), $\beta_i$ is a measure of the "systematic risk" of asset i, while $\sigma^2(\tilde{\epsilon}_i)$ is a measure of its "unsystematic risk." Since $\sum_i x_{im}\tilde{\epsilon}_i = 0$, regardless of whether there are many or few assets in the market, $\tilde{\epsilon}_i$ is indeed "diversified away" in the market portfolio. The contribution of the disturbances from (4) to the risk or variance of the return on the market portfolio is always literally zero, and $\beta_i$ always completely captures the contribution of asset i to $\sigma^2(\tilde{R}_m)$.

Finally, what does the preceding analysis suggest concerning natural links between the market model and the two-parameter model of capital market equilibrium? First, suppose the two-parameter model is derived from the assumption of quadratic utility functions and assume also that the joint density of $R_i$ and $\tilde{R}_m$ is continuous. Then, the linear regression coefficient $\beta_i$ that minimizes $\sigma^2(\tilde{\epsilon}_i)$ in the market model equation (4) is identical to the risk measure $\beta_i = \text{cov}(\tilde{R}_i, \tilde{R}_m)/\sigma^2(\tilde{R}_m)$ that is relevant for the two-parameter model. Moreover, $E(\tilde{\epsilon}_i) = 0$ and $\tilde{\epsilon}_i$ and $\tilde{R}_m$ are uncorrelated. But the market model assumptions that $\tilde{\epsilon}_i$ and $\tilde{R}_m$ are independent and that (5) holds are not necessarily valid.

If the two-parameter model is derived from the assumption that the joint distribution of asset returns is multivariate normal, the link with the market model is much more natural. Then it is necessarily true that $\tilde{\epsilon}_i$ and $\tilde{R}_m$ are independent and that $E(\tilde{R}_i|R_m) = \alpha_i + \beta_i R_m$.

In this case, and in every other, however, the market model assumption that the disturbances $\tilde{\epsilon}_i$ are uncorrelated across all assets cannot hold. The weighted average of the $\tilde{\epsilon}_i$ in the market portfolio in always identically zero.

## REFERENCES

1. T. W. Anderson. *An Introduction to Multivariate Statistical Analysis.* New York: John Wiley and Sons, Inc., 1958.
2. Avraham Beja. "On Systematic and Unsystematic Components of Financial Risk," *Journal of Finance*, Vol. 27, No. 1 (March, 1972), pp. 37-45.
3. F. Black, M. C. Jensen and M. Scholes. "The Capital Asset Pricing Model: Some Empirical Tests," in M. C. Jensen (ed.), *Studies in the Theory of Capital Markets.* New York: Praeger, 1972.
4. Harald Cramér. *Mathematical Methods of Statistics.* Princeton, N.J.: Princeton University Press, 1946.
5. Eugene F. Fama. "Risk, Return, and Equilibrium: Some Clarifying Comments," *Journal of Finance*, Vol. 23, No. 1 (March, 1968), pp. 29-40.
6. Michael C. Jensen. "Capital Markets: Theory and Evidence," *Bell Journal of Economics and Management Science*, Vol. 3, No. 2, (Autumn, 1972), pp. 357-398.
7. John Lintner. "Security Prices, Risk, and Maximal Gains from Diversification," *Journal of Finance*, Vol. 20, No. 5 (December, 1965), pp. 587-616.
8. Richard Roll. "Bias in Fitting the Sharpe Model to Time Series Data," *Journal of Financial and Quantitative Analysis*, Vol. 4, No. 3 (September, 1969), pp. 271-289.
9. Willam F. Sharpe. "Capital Asset Prices: A Theory of Market Equilibrium under Conditions of Risk," *Journal of Finance*, Vol. 19, No. 4 (September, 1964), pp. 425-442.

10. This contradicts the statements of the last paragraph of p. 38 of [5].

# A CRITIQUE OF THE ASSET PRICING THEORY'S TESTS

## Part I: On Past and Potential Testability of the Theory*

### Richard ROLL**

*University of California, Los Angeles, CA 90024, U.S.A.*

Received June 1976, revised version received October 1976

Testing the two-parameter asset pricing theory is difficult (and currently infeasible). Due to a mathematical equivalence between the individual return/'beta' linearity relation and the market portfolio's mean-variance efficiency, any valid test presupposes complete knowledge of the true market portfolio's composition. This implies, inter alia, that every individual asset must be included in a correct test. Errors of inference inducible by incomplete tests are discussed and some ambiguities in published tests are explained.

> If the horn honks and the mechanic concludes that the whole electrical system is working, he is in deep trouble . . .
>
> Pirsig (1974)

## 1. Introduction and summary

The two-parameter asset pricing theory is testable *in principle*; but arguments are given here that: (a) No correct and unambiguous test of the theory has appeared in the literature, and (b) there is practically no possibility that such a

---

*This is Part I of a three-part study. Parts II and III are summarized in the introduction here, but will appear in later issues. A copy of the complete paper can be obtained by writing the author at: Graduate School of Management, University of California, Los Angeles, CA 90024, USA.

**This paper was written while the author was at the Centre d'Enseignement Supérieur des Affaires, France. Eugene Fama, Michael C. Jensen, John B. Long, Jr., Stephen Ross and Bruno H. Solnik provided many useful comments and Patricia Porter provided excellent secretarial service. While the paper was being written, Fama pointed out that his new book (1976) contains some of the same analysis and conclusions. New papers by Stephen Ross (forthcoming) and John B. Long (1976) contain results emphasized, and formerly believed to have been discovered, here. The reader will be able to verify, however, that most of this material is non-redundant.

To the authors criticised here: these papers were singled out because they are the best and most widely read on the subject. I have written some papers in this area too and have taught the subject to a number of unsuspecting students. So, the absence of detailed self-criticism should be attributed to the greater importance of the other papers and does not imply any personal prescience. None was present.

---

test can be accomplished in the future. This broad indictment of one of the three fundamental paradigms of modern finance will undoubtedly be greeted by my colleagues, as it was by me, with scepticism and consternation. The purpose of this paper is to eliminate the scepticism. (No relief is offered for the consternation.)

Here are the paper's conclusions:

(1) There is only a single testable hypothesis associated with the generalized two-parameter asset pricing model of Black (1972). This hypothesis is: 'the market portfolio is mean-variance efficient'.

(2) All other so-called implications of the model, the best known being the linearity relation between expected return and 'beta', follow from the market portfolio's efficiency and are not independently testable. There is an 'if and only if' relation between return/beta linearity and market portfolio mean-variance efficiency.

(3) In *any* sample of observations on individual returns, regardless of the generating process, there will always be an infinite number of ex-post mean-variance efficient portfolios. For each one, the sample 'betas' calculated between it and individual assets will be exactly linearly related to the individual sample mean returns. In other words, if the betas are calculated against such a portfolio, they will satisfy the linearity relation *exactly* whether or not the true market portfolio is mean-variance efficient. (The same properties also hold ex ante, of course). These results are implied in earlier literature [e.g., Ross (1972)], but I do not believe that their full consequences have been adequately explored previously. Some of these consequences are:

(4) The theory is not testable unless the exact composition of the true market portfolio is known and used in the tests. This implies that the theory is not testable unless *all* individual assets are included in the sample.

(5) Using a proxy for the market portfolio is subject to two difficulties. First the proxy itself might be mean-variance efficient even when the true market portfolio is not. This is a real danger since *every* sample will display efficient portfolios that satisfy perfectly all of the theory's implications. For example, suppose there exist 1000 assets but only 500 are used in the sample. For the sample, there will exist well-diversified portfolios of the 500 assets that seem to be reasonable proxies for the market and for which observed returns are exactly linearly related cross-sectionally to observed betas. On the other hand, the chosen proxy may turn out to be inefficient; but obviously, this alone implies nothing about the true market portfolio's efficiency. Furthermore, most reasonable proxies will be very highly correlated with each other and with the true market whether or not they are mean-variance efficient. This high correlation will make it seem that the exact composition is unimportant, whereas it can cause quite different inferences.

(6) As a case in point, a detailed discussion is provided of the papers by Fama and MacBeth (1973), Black, Jensen, and Scholes (1972) and Blume and Friend (1973), in the context of their rejection of the Sharpe–Lintner model. It is shown that their tests results are fully compatible with the Sharpe–Lintner model and a specification error in the measured 'market' portfolio. A misspecification would have created bias *and* non-stationarity in the fitted cross-sectional risk/return lines even if there were a constant riskless return. For the Black, Jensen and Scholes data, for example, there was a mean-variance efficient 'market' proxy that supported the Sharpe–Lintner model *perfectly* and that had a correlation of 0.895 with the market proxy actually employed. However, it cannot be ascertained without further analysis whether this other portfolio satisfied all the requirements of a good market proxy (such as positive proportions invested in all assets).

The market portfolio identification problem constitutes a severe limitation to the testability of the two-parameter theory. No two investigators who disagree on the market's measured composition can be made to agree on the theory's test results. However, suppose that advances in electronic monitoring of human capital and other non-traded assets make the market portfolio's true composition knowable; or more realistically, suppose a given composition is just agreed upon by everyone relevant. How should the mean-variance efficiency of this known composition portfolio be tested? Part II of the paper (to appear in a later issue) investigates the peculiar econometric problems associated with such testing, viz.:

(7) A direct test of the proxy's mean-variance efficiency is difficult computationally because the full sample covariance matrix of individual returns must be inverted and statistically because the sampling distribution of the efficient set is generally unknown. Some possible solutions to the statistical problems are presented. They include tests based on the fact that the market portfolio must have positive proportions invested in all assets; large sample distribution-free tests; and tests based on the sampling distribution of the efficient set assuming Gaussian returns.

(8) Testing for the proxy's efficiency by using the return/beta linearity relation also poses empirical difficulties:
   (a) The two-parameter theory does not make a prediction about parameter values but only about the form (linear) of the cross-sectional relation. Thus, econometric procedures designed to obtain accurate parameter estimates are not very useful.
   (b) Specifically, the widely-used portfolio grouping procedure can support the theory even when it is false. This is because individual asset deviations from exact linearity can cancel out in the formation of

portfolios. (Such deviations are not necessarily related to betas.) Some simulated data given by Miller and Scholes (1972) were used as an example of such an occurrence. Deviations in these data were known to be related to generating process asymmetry which would not have been detectable in grouped observations.

(9) Several others tests are proposed for the linearity relations. These include:

(a) An Aitken-type procedure that gives unbiased cross-sectional tests with individual assets, and

(b) a procedure that exploits asymptotic exact linearity by measuring the rate of decrease of cross-sectional residual variance with respect to increasing time-series sample size.

In Part III of the paper (to appear in a future issue), some of the common uses of the two-parameter theory are called into question:

(10) Deviations from the return/beta linearity relation are frequently linked with some other phenomenon. The validity of such linkages is criticised using the Jensen measure of portfolio performance as an example. If the 'market' proxy used in the calculations is exactly (not significantly different from) ex-post efficient, *all* of the individual Jensen performance measures gross of expenses will be identically (not significantly different from) zero. They can be (significantly) non-zero only if the proxy market portfolio is (significantly) not efficient. But if the proxy market portfolio is not efficient, what is the justification for using it as a benchmark in performance evaluation?

(11) The beta itself is criticised as a risk measure on two grounds: first, that it will always be (significantly) positively related to observed average individual returns if the market index is on (not significantly off) the positively sloped section of the ex-post efficient frontier, *regardless of investors' attitudes toward risk*; and second, that it depends, non-monotonically, on the particular market proxy used. About the second point: if two investors happen to choose two different 'market' portfolios, both of which are mean-variance efficient, the same security might have a beta of 1.5 for the first investor and 0.5 for the second. This is intuitively obvious since beta is supposed to be a *relative* measure of risk. But less obvious is the fact that if both investors increase the proportions this security represents in their 'markets', its beta will change and it can increase for one investor and decrease for another.

An appendix to this part (I) contains a compact analytic derivation of the efficient set propositions and includes a few original results (e.g., identity of the efficient portfolio that maximizes cross-sectional variation in beta).

## 2. The testable feature of asset pricing theory and the features that have been 'tested'

### 2.1. Efficient set mathematics

We should begin any quantitative enquiry by setting forth the relationships that are mutually and logically equivalent. The mathematics of the mean-variance efficient set serves just such a purpose, for it exposes several logically-equivalent relations among mean returns and covariances (which are the building blocks of the asset pricing theory). The mathematics is mostly available elsewhere [see, e.g., Sharpe (1970), Merton (1972), Black (1972), Szegö (1975), Fama (1976), Long (1976)] and a compact statement of all the familiar results plus some new ones is provided in the appendix.

The efficient set mathematics has been discussed most usually in terms of *ex-ante* returns and covariances. To emphasize the purely mathematical nature of the results, however, I should like to state it in terms of an observed sample of returns on $N$ assets. No presumption is made about the population that generated this sample. It can be any probability law imaginable. Furthermore, no mention need be made about equilibrium, risk aversion, homogeneous anticipations, or anything else like that. There are only two assumptions:

(A.1)   The sample product–moment covariance matrix, $V$, is non-singular.

(A.2)   At least one asset had a different sample mean return from others.

These are very weak assumptions. (A.1) simply rules out assets whose returns were constant during every period in the sample and it excludes any pair of linear combinations of assets that were perfectly correlated during the sample period. (A.2) merely requires some sample variation in the critical variable of interest. After all, it is cross-sectional variation in the mean return which asset pricing theory strives to explain.

Given the sample covariance matrix and the arithmetic sample mean returns (expressed as an $N \times 1$ column vector $R$), the sample frontier of efficient ex-post portfolios can be easily obtained. This frontier enumerates all the portfolios that had minimal sample variance for each given level of mean sample return. Suppose we choose one of these portfolios, say portfolio $m$, with sample return $r_m$, which lies on the positively-sloped part of the efficient frontier. (That is, there is no other portfolio with the same sample variance that had a higher mean return.) Then the following statements are true:

(S.1)   There exists a unique portfolio, denoted $z$, that had a correlation of zero with $m$ during the sample period and that lies on the negatively-sloped segment of the sample efficient frontier; this implies that the sample return of $m$ was greater than that of $z$, $r_m > r_z$. (For a formal proof, see the appendix, Corollary 3.)

(S.2)  For any arbitrary asset or portfolio, say $j$, the sample mean return is equal to a weighted average of $r_z$ and $r_m$ where the weight of $m$ is *exactly* the sample linear regression slope coefficient of $j$ on $m$, i.e.,

$$r_j \equiv (1 - \beta_j)r_z + \beta_j r_m, \qquad \text{for all } j, \tag{1}$$

where

$$\beta_j \equiv \frac{\text{sample covariance of } j \text{ and } m}{\text{sample variance of } m}$$

(Proof: Appendix, Corollary 6).

Statement (S.1) is related to the following facts:

(S.3)  Every portfolio on the positively-sloped segment of the sample efficient set was positively correlated with every other one (Corollary 4).

(S.4)  Every sample efficient portfolio except the global minimum sample variance portfolio has an orthogonal portfolio with finite mean return (Corollary 3).

It is easy to see that (S.3) and (S.4) imply that $r_m > r_z$ because we have chosen $m$ to lie in the positively-sloped segment of the sample efficient frontier.
  Proposition S.2, on the other hand follows from:

(S.5)  The investment proportions of any sample efficient portfolio can be expressed as a weighted average of the proportions in any other two sample efficient portfolios whose means are different (Corollary 5).

Given (S.5), it is a simple matter to prove (1); see the appendix or, e.g., Black (1972, p. 450). In fact, a more general proposition than (1) follows readily from (S.5). Let $A$ and $B$ be *any* two arbitrary sample efficient portfolios, ex-post correlated or not, but with different sample mean returns. Then:

(S.6)  The mean return on any arbitrary asset, $j$, is given exactly by

$$r_j \equiv (1 - \beta_j')r_A + \beta_j' r_B, \qquad \text{for all } j \tag{2}$$

(Corollary 6.A).

In eq. (2) $\beta'_j$ is the multivariate *sample* slope coefficient for $B$ from the regression of $r_j$ on $r_A$ and $r_B$. Furthermore, this regression coefficient has a simple form,

$$\beta'_j = (\sigma_{jB} - \sigma_{AB})/(\sigma_{BB} - \sigma_{AB}),$$

where $\sigma_{ik}$ is the sample covariance of $i$ and $k$. It is easy to see that (1) is merely a special case of (2) that obtains when $A$ is chosen to be $B$'s orthogonal sample portfolio.

Expression (2) can be considered a logical equivalent to assumptions (A.1) and (A.2). In other words, given an observed non-singular sample covariance matrix and at least two different sample mean returns, every observed mean return has exactly the relation shown in (2). Equivalently, every observed sample 'beta' conforms exactly to the rearrangement of (1),

$$\beta_j \equiv (r_j - r_z)/(r_m - r_z). \tag{3}$$

A converse statement is also true:

(S.7)  Let $\beta$ be the $(N \times 1)$ column vector of simple regression slope coefficients computed between individual assets and some portfolio $m$. Then the vector of mean returns $R$ is an exact linear function of the vector $\beta$ only if $m$ is a sample efficient portfolio; i.e., in general,

$$R \equiv r_z \iota + (r_m - r_z)\beta, \tag{4}$$

if and only if $r_m$ is ex-post efficient [$r_z$ is the mean return on $m$'s corresponding efficient orthogonal portfolio and $\iota$ is the unit vector, see Ross (1972, 1973)].

It follows that mean returns are *not* exact linear functions of betas when $m$ is not efficient. This does not imply that mean returns are necessarily related to non-linear functions of beta. They are just not *exactly* linear. For example, the relation

$$R = \alpha + g\beta$$

is a possibility if $m$ is inefficient; where $\alpha$ is a vector whose elements are non-constant but are unrelated to the elements of $\beta$, and $g$ is a scalar constant.

Before going on to the theory of asset pricing, it is well to emphasize the nature of these mathematical relations. Identity symbols have been used in (1) through (4) because they really are identities. Given the choice of $m$ as ex-post efficient, these expressions hold exactly. They do not, therefore, provide any information about the state of nature or about the process that generated the sample. The underlying probability law might be anything and the relations above would always be observed ex-post. This has relevant implications for testing the asset pricing theory, as we shall see.

## 2.2. A review of some asset pricing theory tests

Three widely-quoted empirical papers on asset pricing theory are Black, Jensen and Scholes (1972), Blume and Friend (1973), and Fama and MacBeth (1973).[1] Let us examine what they said they were testing: The statement in Fama and MacBeth is very clear. They refer to a portfolio $m$ which is on the ex-ante efficient frontier as seen by a single investor. This leads to the derivation of an equation identical to (1) but with investors' subjective parameters instead of sample parameters. The resulting equation [Fama–MacBeth (1973, p. 610)]

> '. . . has three testable implications: (C.1) the relationship between the expected returns on a security and its risk in any efficient portfolio $m$ is linear. (C.2) $\beta_i$ is a complete measure of the risk of security $i$ in the efficient portfolio $m$; no other measure of the risk of $i$ appears in (6) [eq. (1) here]. (C.3) in a market of risk-averse investors, higher risk should be associated with higher return; that is $E(\tilde{R}_m) - E(\tilde{R}_0) > 0$.' [$R_0$ is the same as $r_z$ here.]

Given that the word 'risk' has replaced the parameter $\beta$, we have already seen that Fama and MacBeth's (C.1), (C.2), and (C.3) are simply implications of the fact that $m$ is assumed ex-ante efficient.[2] If $m$ is known to be efficient, these relations are not independently testable. They are tautological. When $m$ is efficient, the expected return *must* be linear in $\beta$ and $E(\tilde{R}_m)$ must exceed $E(\tilde{R}_0)$. Incidentally, given the assumption that $m$ is efficient, their last inequality has nothing to do with risk aversion. It is purely the mathematical implication of the assumption about $m$ and the definition of $\beta$. It is totally independent of investor preferences since it follows from the mathematical property (S.1). Conversely, if Fama and MacBeth's (C.1) is true, and ex-ante $\beta$ is an exact linear function of ex-ante expected return, then $m$ must be ex-ante mean-variance efficient.

It is clear from the authors' discussion that they are aware of these internal

---

[1]There are other interesting papers containing similar tests, e.g., Petit and Westerfield (1974) and Modigliani, Pogue, Scholes and Solnik (1972). Petit and Westerfield's test of the asset pricing theory is actually identical to Black, Jensen and Scholes' although Petit and Westerfield seem to deny this. Modigliani, Pogue, Scholes and Solnik carry out a similar test for eight *different* European stock markets. Palacios (1973) and Rosa (1975) present detailed investigations for Spain and France respectively. Roll (1973) gives a comparative test of the asset pricing theory and the optimal growth model using the same methodology. See also Fama and MacBeth (1974a). Fama and MacBeth (1974b) investigate the extension of asset pricing theory into a multi-period context. Roll and Solnik (1975) apply the methodology to exchange rates.

[2](C.2), the statement that no other risk measure except $\beta$ is important, presupposes that $\beta$ measures risk. Whether it measures risk or not, however, it is the only variable on the right side of (1). ($r_z$ and $r_m$ are constant cross-sectionally.) Thus, it is the only cross-sectional explanatory variable of any kind.

relations. For example, on page 609 they state, '... there are conditions on expected returns that are implied by the fact that in a two-parameter world investors hold efficient portfolios.' But on page 610 they make a statement inconsistent with the facts and with their own knowledge of the mathematics: 'To test conditions (C.1)–(C.3) we must identify some efficient portfolio *m*.' Of course, if *m* is identified as efficient, there is no need to test (C.1)–(C.3). (See also the self-contradictory second paragraph on p. 614.)

But there are testable hypotheses in the Fama–MacBeth paper. The hypotheses really are:

(H.1) Investors regard as *optimal* those particular investment portfolios that are mean-variance efficient.

Assuming identical probability assessments by all investors, this hypothesis leads to:

(H.2) The 'market portfolio' is ex-ante efficient.

The 'market portfolio' is defined as a value-weighted combination of all assets (p. 611). Fama and MacBeth credit Black (1972) with deducing (H.2) given (H.1) and given homogeneous investor expectations. The Black proof is quite simple: Since all investors have identical beliefs and hold efficient portfolios, every investor holds a linear combination of two arbitrary efficient portfolios. Since the market portfolio is by construction a linear combination of the portfolios of individual investors, it is also a linear combination of these two efficient portfolios and is therefore also efficient [because the linear combination of any two efficient portfolios is also efficient by the basic mathematical property of the efficient set, (S.5)]. Interestingly, Black states that Lintner (1969) '... has shown that removing [the] assumption [of homogeneous anticipations] does not change the structure of capital asset prices in any significant way' (p. 445). Nevertheless, Black's proof of the market portfolio's efficiency does require homogeneity. This might be relaxed in a more general (and as yet unknown) proof; but Fama (1976, ch. 7) has argued that, in fact, no equilibrium model with non-homogeneous anticipations is testable.[3]

---

[3]On page 447 at the beginning of his discussion of efficient portfolios, Black makes a statement that seems to be in conflict with the results here. He claims that Cass and Stiglitz (1970) have shown

'... that if the returns on securities are not assumed to be joint normal, but are allowed to be arbitrary, then the set of efficient portfolios can be written as a weighted combination of two basic portfolios *only* for a special class of utility functions' (italics added).

It is clear from his subsequent discussion that Black was referring to *mean-variance* efficient portfolios. Thus, his statement is false. Efficient mean-variance portfolios can *always* be constructed as a 'weighted combination of two basic portfolios'. Furthermore Cass and Stiglitz never claimed the contrary. What they did was to enumerate the set of utility functions for

In both the Black paper and the Fama–MacBeth paper there exists a bit of unfortunate wording about the efficient set mathematics and about optimal investment choices. At first, it might seem that the resulting confusion would be only minor. But when it comes to empirical testing and to specifying exactly those relations that are empirically rejectable and are valid scientific hypotheses, this possible confusion is of great significance.

The only viable (i.e., rejectable) hypothesis that we have so far been able to uncover is (H.2), the market portfolio is mean-variance efficient.[4] The assumptions which are sufficient for this result are rather strong: Perfect capital markets, homogeneous anticipations, two-parameter probability distributions of returns. But there is also another assumption that has received little attention in the literature: namely, the market portfolio must be identifiable.

This last assumption is very important when we consider that there will always be *some* portfolio which is ex-post efficient and will bring about exact observed linearity among ex-post sample mean returns and ex-post sample betas. If we do not know the composition of the market portfolio, we might by chance select a proxy that is close to mean-variance efficient. In fact, it may be hard to find a highly-diversified portfolio that is sufficiently far inside the ex-post efficient frontier to permit the detection of statistically significant departures from mean return/beta exact linearity. We will return to this point later. First, let us see what some of the other papers have been testing.

The widely-quoted paper by Black, Jensen, and Scholes (1972) makes no mention of the possible efficiency of the market portfolio and its importance for the linear relation between return and 'beta'. In fact, however, the authors modestly claim that their '. . . main emphasis has been to test the strict traditional form of the asset pricing model' (p. 113), by which they mean the original Sharpe (1964), Lintner (1965) model similar to (1), but with $r_z$ replaced by a 'riskless' return. [This model results from the asset pricing theory assumptions listed above, and used by Black to derive (1), plus the extra assumption that investors can borrow and lend as much as they like at a riskless interest rate.] Black, Jensen, and Scholes explicitly deny that they have provided tests of any other hypothesis. However, the Black model is clearly in the backs of their minds and on page 81 they even go so far as to provide a historical glimpse of Black's theoretical progress by asserting that he 'was able' to derive his model

which all investors would construct their *optimal* portfolios as a weighted average of two basic portfolios. Under a restrictive set of preferences, each investor would regard a mean-variance efficient portfolio as optimal; but as Cass and Stiglitz show, there are other investor preferences which would lead to 'separation' (or the choice of an optimal portfolio which is a weighted combination of two others), under which the optimal portfolio is *not* mean-variance efficient. [See also Hakansson (1969), Jacob (1970) and Ross (1976). The last reference gives separation results for probability distributions instead of utility functions.]

[4]Fama and MacBeth also provide an ingenious time-series test of market competition, given the hypothesis (H.2). However, this part of their paper is about a different set of hypotheses than our subject here.

'after we had observed this phenomena' (that mean returns are linearly related to calculated beta coefficients but supposedly with a different slope and intercept than those implied by the Sharpe–Lintner theory). The graphs plotted by Black, Jensen, and Scholes appear to portray a very linear mean return/beta relation over long sample periods. Unlike Fama and MacBeth, however, no formal test of linearity is provided. (It must not have seemed necessary given the authors' goal.) Thus, no formal information is given on the possible efficiency of the measured market portfolio, nor about the hypothesis (H.2).

A direct test of linearity was provided by one of the authors [Jensen (1972a, 1972b)], who, using the same data as those used by Black, Jensen and Scholes, presented results from a regression similar to the one later computed by Fama and MacBeth. In fact, the fitted equations are nearly identical in form but the measurement methods were somewhat different and the 'market' portfolios used in calculating betas were different.[5] This was evidently sufficient to create some disparity between the two sets of results. We cannot ascertain the exact extent of the disparity because the sub-periods reported in the two papers were not identical. At least the signs of coefficients on squared beta terms were in agreement, being negative during the longer sample periods. The statistical significance of these negative signs is less clear. For example, the coefficient given by Fama–MacBeth for the squared beta term during 1946–55 was $-0.0076$ (p. 623). The same coefficient given by Jensen for an overlapping period, July 1948 to March 1957, was $-0.0055$. The associated $t$-statistics were far apart, however, Fama–MacBeth's was $-2.16$ whereas Jensen's was only $-0.524$.[6] This difference may very well be due to Fama and MacBeth's presumably more powerful test but there is no way to be sure without a complete replication.

It might be worthwhile carrying out such a replication because the linearity is directly related to the market portfolio's efficiency. We can already be sure that the 'market' portfolios used by Jensen and by Fama and MacBeth did not lie exactly on the sample efficient frontier. If they had been exactly efficient, the relation between the mean return vector and the vector of sample betas would have been exactly linear and it was not.[7] But it is not necessary for the basic hypothesis (H.2) (the market portfolio is *ex-ante* efficient) that the observed market portfolio be exactly *ex-post* efficient in every period. It only needs to be efficient over 'sufficiently' long periods. Now both Jensen and Fama–MacBeth find no significant non-linearity over the longest sample period nor do they find

---

[5]Cf. Jensen (1972b, pp. 385–388) with Fama and MacBeth (1973, pp. 615–617).

[6]Jensen reported a $t$-statistic with respect to a non-zero theoretical value which he derived from Merton's (1973) continuous time model. The number above is his $t$-statistic for a hypothesized coefficient of zero.

[7]Actually, this is not entirely true for Fama–MacBeth since they did not use *concurrent* sample mean returns and betas. Thus, some deviation from linearity might have been observed in their results, even if the 'market' portfolio had been exactly sample efficient, because the sample betas might not have been stationary. Part II of this paper will examine the importance for testing the basic hypothesis of attempting to purge measurement errors from sample betas. (This was the reason Fama and MacBeth did not use concurrent observations.)

any significance for non-beta 'measures of risk' such as standard deviation. Although this is consistent with their market portfolio proxies having been sample efficient over the long term, it is also consistent with their proxies having been inefficient (as we will soon see).

Interestingly, Fama and MacBeth offer a possible explanation for the significance of non-linear beta terms during some sample periods: viz., they suggest that there are omitted variables from the theory for which the non-linear terms act as proxies. Of course, their results are also consistent with the simpler explanation that the Fama–MacBeth 'market' portfolio was not exactly ex-post efficient in every sub-period. This alone implies that non-linear terms could be significant. It is also true that the non-exact ex-post efficiency of the market might induce significance in individual standard deviations (i.e., in non-portfolio risk measures).

### 2.3. Tests of the Sharpe–Lintner model

Let us now turn to an ancillary examination of the evidence offered by Black, Jensen and Scholes and by others against the original Sharpe–Lintner theory. It will be useful to have the following supplementary results from the efficient set mathematics.

Given the following additional assumption:

(A.3)   There exists an asset whose return was a constant, $r_F$, during the sample period.

Then:

(S.7)   The sample efficient set (in the mean-variance space) is a parabola with a tangent on the return axis at $r_F$.

(S.8)   Suppose we denote the 'risky efficient set' as the ensemble of portfolios with minimum variance *excluding* asset $F$. Then results (S.1) through (S.6) still hold for the portfolios composing this 'risky efficient set'.

In particular, for any ex post portfolio composed entirely of risky assets and lying on the positively-sloped segment of the 'risky efficient set', sample mean returns on all assets are exact linear functions of sample betas as portrayed by eq. (1); sample mean $r_z$ in (1) is the return on a portfolio lying on the negatively-sloped segment of the risky efficient set whose return was uncorrelated with the return on $m$ during the sample period.

In other words, we have the familiar diagram shown in fig. 1, where $m$, $m^*$ and $z$ are all portfolios composed of risky assets only and are all on the sample risky efficient boundary. The portfolio $m^*$ is the sample 'tangent' portfolio whose return, according to Corollary 3.A of the appendix, is determined by the riskless return, $r_F$, and of some simple functions of the mean return vector of individual assets and of the sample covariance matrix. Portfolio $z$ has been chosen to have zero sample correlation with portfolio $m$, a feat that is always possible for any position of $m$.

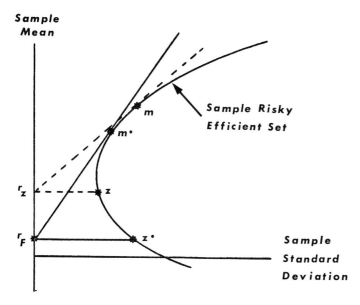

Fig. 1. The sample risky efficient set, sample market proxy and sample zero-beta portfolio.

Now let us consider the sample linearity property between mean return and beta. First, if portfolio $m$ is used to compute beta, we must have the mathematical result already found,

$$r_j = r_z + (r_m - r_z)\beta_j, \qquad \text{for all } j. \tag{5a}$$

On the other hand we might choose portfolio $m^*$ to compute the betas. This will produce a different set of sample betas because $m$ and $m^*$ are not perfectly correlated. Denoting these second betas by $\beta_j^*$, we must have also another linearity relation,

$$r_j = r_F + (r_{m^*} - r_F)\beta_j^*, \qquad \text{for all } j. \tag{5b}$$

What about $z^*$, the *risky* efficient portfolio that is uncorrelated with $m^*$? Since it too must be usable in yet another linearity relation with the $\beta^*$'s, it must have the same mean return as $r_F$. In fact, it is quite easy to prove that this is so.[8] Furthermore, since there is an infinite number of efficient risky portfolios along the positively-sloped boundary, there is an infinite number of these linearity relations, all equally satisfied exactly (but all with different beta vectors). In particular, $r_z$ and $r_m$ would have their own $\beta_z^*$ and $\beta_m^*$ in (5b) and would satisfy the second linearity relation above. *Note that $\beta_z^*$ must be non-zero* because efficient orthogonal portfolios are unique. Thus, even though $m$ and $z$ are uncorrelated, $m^*$ and $z$ must be correlated. Furthermore, although $m^*$'s orthogonal portfolio is constrained to have the same sample return as the riskless return, there is no such restriction on portfolio $z$. Depending on the relative positions of $m$ and $m^*$, $r_z$ can be greater or less than $r_F$.[9]

Armed with these purely logical results which are true for any sample satisfying assumptions (A.1), (A.2), and (A.3), let us turn to the published tests of the original Sharpe–Lintner theory. First, what are the principal hypotheses of this theory? They are:

(H.3)   Investors can borrow or lend at the riskless rate, $r_F$.

(H.1)   (Same as before.) They consider that mean-variance efficient portfolios are optimal.

Thus, each individual would compose his portfolio of the riskless asset $F$ and his subjective tangent portfolio $m^*$. If investors had homogeneous probability assessments, they would all have the same tangent portfolio. Thus:

(H.4)   The ex-ante efficient tangent portfolio is the market portfolio of all assets.

Of course, since there seems to be little possibility of rejecting (H.3) or even (H.1) with direct information, we are left with (H.4) as the testable hypothesis.

Black, Jensen, and Scholes rejected the Sharpe–Lintner theory as a result of the following 'test': First, a 'market' portfolio was chosen and sample betas were calculated via a procedure designed carefully to remove measurement error. Then, the cross-sectional mean return/beta linearity relation was esti-

---

[8]By Corollary 3.A of the appendix, a tangent drawn to any point $p$ on the efficient frontier intersects the return axis at the level of the mean return on $p$'s orthogonal portfolio. Since $m^*$ is, by definition, located at the tangency drawn from $r_F$, we must have $r_F = r_{z^*}$. In the mean-*variance* space, there is a little-known analogous property: a line from any point $p$ on the efficient frontier that passes through the global minimum variance position also intersects the return axis at the level of $p$'s orthogonal portfolio. In general, if $p$ is efficient, every portfolio orthogonal to $p$ will have return $r_z = (a - br_p)/(b - cr_p)$ where $a$, $b$, and $c$ are the 'efficient set constants' (see appendix, Definition A.9).

[9]$r_z$ will exceed $r_F$ if and only if $r_m > r_{m^*}$.

mated in the form

$$r_j - r_F = \hat{\gamma}_0 + \hat{\gamma}_1 \beta_j + \hat{\varepsilon}_j, \tag{6}$$

where $\hat{\varepsilon}_j$ is the estimated residual.

The basic results were that $\hat{\gamma}_0$ exceeded zero, that $\hat{\gamma}_1$ was less than $r_m - r_F$, and that $\hat{\gamma}_0$ was highly variable from one sub-period to another. This led them to reject hypothesis (H.4).

Given our preceding analysis of the efficient set mathematics, we are entitled to be suspicious of their conclusion. Unless Black, Jensen, and Scholes were successful in choosing $m^*$ (in fig. 1) for their market portfolio, their results are fully compatible with the original Sharpe–Lintner model. This is readily seen in the two ex-post equations (5a) and (5b). Suppose, for example, that their 'market' portfolio was really $m$ rather than $m^*$. Then solve (5b) for $j = z$ and use this to replace $r_z$ in (5a). The result is

$$r_j - r_F = \beta_z^*(r_{m^*} - r_F) + [r_m - r_F - \beta_z^*(r_{m^*} - r_F)]\beta_j.$$

Now we have already seen that $\beta_z^*$ *must* be non-zero[10] and that the Sharpe–Lintner theory implies $r_{m^*} > r_F$ ex-ante (and ex-post asymptotically with increasing time-series sample size and with stationarity). Thus, the estimated coefficient $\hat{\gamma}_0$ in (6) is seen to be equal to $\beta_z^*(r_{m^*} - r_F)$ given validity of the Sharpe–Lintner theory and efficiency of the measured 'market' portfolio $m$. Furthermore, since Black, Jensen, and Scholes' constant term, $\hat{\gamma}_0$, is a function of the true tangent portfolio, $m^*$, whose return is a random variable, we should *expect* to see an intertemporal variation in their constant term even when $r_F$ is a fixed number. There will be an offsetting variation in $\hat{\gamma}_1$, the slope of (6).

No calculations were made by Black, Jensen, and Scholes to ascertain whether their market portfolio was in fact close (statistically) to the ex-post tangent portfolio over long periods. But we can be absolutely certain that it was not! Why? Because the pure mathematics of the efficient set tell us that the relation (5b) is *exactly* satisfied in every ex-post sample for which assumptions (A.1), (A.2), and (A.3) were true. Assumption (A.3), a constant return existed, was indeed approximately satisfied during all their sample periods. Thus, we can be sure that for each sample period there was a portfolio $m^*$ whose associated sample beta vector was a linear function of the mean return vector and for which the coefficients of (6) satisfied $\hat{\gamma}_0 = 0$. Since the sample beta vector calculated by Black, Jensen, and Scholes differed significantly from the vector that satisfied (5b) and did not approach that vector as the time series sample size increased,

---

[10]As a reminder, $\beta_z^*$ is defined the sample analog of $\text{Cov}(r_z, r_m)/\text{Var}(r_{m^*})$; i.e., the beta for the *proxy* zero-beta portfolio ($z$) computed against the *true* market portfolio ($m^*$). N.B.: This 'zero-beta' portfolio has a beta of zero only against $m$. It has a non-zero beta against *all* other efficient portfolios.

we know that their 'market' portfolio was not statistically close to the tangent portfolio.[11]

On the other hand, one should note also that an ex-post verification of (5b) would not have implied that (A.3) was valid. In other words, the purely mathematical proposition (5b) can be observed even if investors are totally prohibited from access to a riskless asset. Consider the following scenario as an example: Investors are totally excluded from riskless borrowing and lending. Nevertheless, the government publishes each period a number called the riskless rate of interest. It follows that each period there will exist some portfolio $m^*$ whose associated betas along with the published number exactly satisfy (5b). This observed $m^*$ will not necessarily be the market portfolio, of course. How can we distinguish empirically this scenario from the Sharpe–Lintner model where riskless borrowing and lending is fully permissible? We cannot do so from the linearity relation (6) *alone*. We must have independent information on the true market portfolio's identity. Only then can we determine whether this particular portfolio is or is not the tangent portfolio and thereby distinguish between the two scenarios.

In summary, even if Black, Jensen, and Scholes had been unable to reject the hypothesis that $\hat{\gamma}_0$ equals zero and that there is a linear beta/mean return trade-off, they would not have been entitled to support the Sharpe–Lintner theory. They shouldn't have rejected the theory either upon not finding $\hat{\gamma}_0 = 0$. Their test is simply without rejecting power for hypothesis (H.4).

Black, Jensen, and Scholes realized that using a misspecified 'market' portfolio would result in a measured $\hat{\gamma}_0$ from (6) not equal to zero. However, they thought mistakenly that the $\hat{\gamma}_0$ would have to be constant even with the misspecification (cf. their page 115). This was a critical oversight, for it led to a professional consensus that the Sharpe–Lintner theory was false. It seems probable (at least to me) that such an opinion would have been held less widely if the market index' composition had been correctly perceived as *the* critical variable in understanding the test results; that is, if we had realized that a readjustment of the market portfolio's proportions might have reconciled the test results as well to Sharpe's and Lintner's theory as to Black's.

It may occur to the reader that the Black, Jensen, and Scholes paper tested a joint hypothesis: the Sharpe–Lintner theory *and* the hypothesis that the portfolio they used as the 'market' proxy was the true market portfolio. This joint hypothesis was indeed tested and it was rejected. We can conclude therefrom that either

(a) the Sharpe–Lintner theory is false, or
(b) the portfolio used by Black, Jensen, and Scholes was not the true market portfolio, or
(c) both (a) and (b).

---

[11]In the next section their results are used to actually calculate the mean and variance of this sample tangent portfolio (see table 1).

There lies the trouble with joint hypotheses. One never knows what to conclude. Indeed, it would be possible to construct a joint hypothesis to reconcile *any* individual hypothesis to *any* empirical observation. In the present case, fortunately, there is at least the information that (b) is false. The portfolio used by Black, Jensen, and Scholes was certainly not the true market portfolio; but whether it was statistically close to the true market portfolio [thus leading to conclusion (a)] or whether it was closer than the Sharpe–Lintner assumptions are to reality is beyond our capacity to know.

As for the other papers, Fama and MacBeth present tests of the Sharpe–Lintner theory which are similar in spirit, form, and conclusion to those of Black, Jensen, and Scholes (see their section VI, pages 630–633). The explicit stated hypothesis is that $\hat{\gamma}_0$ from (6) be insignificantly different from zero.[12] Their conclusion is that '. . . the most efficient tests of the S–L (Sharpe–Lintner) hypothesis . . . support the negative conclusions of others' (p. 633), (because $\hat{\gamma}_0$ was found to be significantly different from zero). Probably because of the nature of their methodology, Fama and MacBeth, unlike Black, Jensen, and Scholes, did not consider the variability of $\hat{\gamma}_0$ as an additional piece of condemning evidence against the Sharpe–Lintner hypothesis. Thus, they did not draw Black, Jensen, and Scholes' second erroneous inference.[13]

Blume and Friend (1973) provide an equivalent set of empirical results but interpret them quite differently. They begin by explicitly stating the Black model [essentially eq. (1)], and they take a similar tack in asserting that the observed zero-beta return, $r_z$, must equal the riskless rate, $r_F$,[14] in order for the Sharpe–Lintner hypothesis to be supported. They also find that the observed estimate of $r_z$ is significantly different from $r_F$ and thus reject the Sharpe–Lintner hypothesis.

They are clearly bothered by this conclusion, however, because they are convinced that a nearly riskless interest rate *did* exist. They state that: 'If returns are measured in real terms, the only risk in holding governments of appropriate maturities would stem from unexpected changes in the price level . . . [and] . . . this risk . . . has been very small' (p. 20). The second step in the argument leading to their inquietude is the conclusion that if a riskless asset *does* exist, the intertemporal variance in the zero-beta portfolio's return (i.e., in $r_z$) must be

---

[12]On page 630, they state: 'In the Sharpe–Lintner two-parameter model of equilibrium one has, in addition to conditions (C.1)–(C.3), the hypothesis that $E(\hat{\gamma}_0) = R_{ft}$.' (This is equivalent to Black, Jensen, and Scholes' model because Fama and MacBeth did not subtract $R_{ft}$ from both sides of the linearity relation.)

[13]The first inference was $\hat{\gamma}_0$'s significant positivity. BJS stated clearly that misspecification in the market proxy portfolio could cause this. The second inference was intertemporal variation in $\hat{\gamma}_0$. They incorrectly thought that misspecification could not cause this. It was really this second crucial inference which induced them to state that the Sharpe–Lintner model was rejected by the data.

[14]This is, of course, equivalent to $\hat{\gamma}_0$ being zero in eq. (6).

zero (see their discussion on pages 22–23),[15] and they claim to have demonstrated the falsity of this empirical implication in their earlier article (1970).

This leads to an interesting conclusion: namely, the 'return generating process' corresponding to Black's model '. . . cannot explain the observed returns of all financial assets . . .. Nonetheless . . . it may be . . . adequate . . . for a subset of all financial assets, such as common stocks on the NYSE . . .. If this be so, the minimum variance zero-beta portfolio consisting only of common stocks would not be *the* zero-beta portfolio of the capital asset pricing model. However, . . . the expected return on all zero-beta assets and in particular a zero-beta portfolio consisting only of common stocks must be the same, namely the risk-free rate if such an asset exists' (pp. 22–23, italics theirs).

Blume and Friend have been quoted here at some length because their article illustrates the confusion that can arise from an insufficient understanding of efficient set mathematics. Some of their statements might very well be true; for example, that a riskless asset exists and that 'the zero-beta portfolio consisting only of common stocks would not be *the* zero-beta portfolio [of the global market]'. This last phrase might have led them to a correct understanding, for they seemed to be considering two 'market' portfolios, one consisting only of equities and one consisting of all assets in existence. Their mistake was brought about by concluding that two such distinct 'market' proxy portfolios would be associated with zero-beta (or orthogonal) portfolios having the *same* mean return and that this return must be equal to the riskless rate of interest. That conclusion is false. For example, suppose we consider the possibility that both the equities-only portfolio *and* the global all-assets portfolio are both mean-variance efficient. If these two portfolios had different mean returns and are not perfectly correlated, then the mean returns of their associated zero-beta portfolios *must* differ. Of course, if the Sharpe–Lintner hypothesis is valid, the global market portfolio's associated zero-beta portfolio would have an expected return equal to the riskless interest rate. This would imply nothing whatever about the equities-only zero-beta portfolio, the one actually used by Blume and Friend in their tests.

Blume and Friend conclude with some statements that illustrate the dangers of ad hoc theorizing. Their results supposedly (1) 'indicate a negative differential between the required rates of return on high-grade corporate bonds and on stock on a risk-adjusted basis', and (2) indicate that the supposed differential '. . . is consistent either with segmentation of markets, inadequacies of the return generating model used in this paper,[16] or a deficient short sales mechanism' (p. 32). Since corporate bonds were not included in the empirical work,[17] the first statement must be due to the observation that $\hat{\gamma}_0$ was not zero, i.e., that the

---

[15]Their argument is a bit clouded by being couched in the framework of the 'return generating process', but the inference above is indeed there.

[16]The generating model corresponds to Black's theory.

[17]A brief mention of bonds was contained in their note 24, page 31.

measured zero-beta return exceeded significantly the measured riskless return. This observation is perfectly consistent with *non*-segmented markets, with the Black model *or* the Sharpe–Lintner model, and with *perfect* short selling opportunities; in other words, with the precisely opposite set of circumstances to those postulated in their second statement.

One page earlier, Blume and Friend assert that '. . . the observed risk-return tradeoff would certainly have been highly non-linear in all periods' if corporate bonds had been '. . . included in the analysis' (p. 31). The evidence offered to support this is that corporate bonds indexes have measured betas close to zero, a fact that has no relevance for linearity.

If bonds had been included in the analysis, they might have been included in a new 'market' proxy and a new observed efficient set would have been obtained. The resulting linearity, or lack thereof, would have been completely dependent on the ex-post efficiency of this new market portfolio. If bonds were not made part of the market portfolio proxy, the risk-return tradeoff would still have been linear, including the bonds' returns and betas, unless the market proxy was significantly not ex-post mean-variance efficient. If it was significantly not efficient, there was no justification for its use as a proxy.

Blume and Friend conclude from their analysis: '. . . Even without allowing for the tax advantages of debt financing, the cost of bond financing may have been substantially smaller than the risk-adjusted cost of stock financing and probably smaller than the risk-adjusted cost of internal financing' (pp. 31–32). We suddenly encounter a conclusion about an important economic quantity (internal financing) upon literally its first and only mention in the entire paper, and we are told that is dearer than bond financing on a risk-adjusted basis. Still reeling, we come to the final paragraph and its assessment that '. . . in the current state of testing of the capital asset theory, the evidence points to segmentation of markets as between stocks and bonds, even though there are few legal restrictions which would have this effect' (p. 32)!

In summarizing all these empirical exercises about the Sharpe–Lintner theory, one is obliged to conclude that not a single paper contains a valid test of the theory. In fact, as Fama (1976, ch. 9) has recently concluded, there has been *no* unambiguous test of this theory in the published literature. Furthermore, it is easy to see that the prospect is dim for the ultimate achievement of such a test. We can well imagine that the critical issue of contention will always be the *identity* of the true market portfolio. Some portfolio will always occupy the Sharpe–Lintner tangency position; but whether the position will be occupied by a value-weighted average of all the assets in existence seems to be a difficult question.

In summarizing the three major papers in a broader context, two of them contained a formal test of efficiency for the market portfolio proxy. This test was the explicit inclusion of non-linear beta terms in the cross-sectional risk-return relation. Both Fama and MacBeth and Blume and Friend concluded that the non-linear terms were insignificantly different from zero. What does this tell us about the major hypothesis (H.2) of generalized asset pricing theory? In so far as we are ignorant of how close their proxy market portfolios were to the real thing, it tells us nothing at all. On the other hand, if we are willing to *assume* a close approximation between real and proxy markets, then the test results do not reject the basic hypothesis that the true market portfolio is efficient. (I shall argue in the next section, however, that such a 'good' approximation should be confronted with a strong dose of scepticism.)

Black, Jensen, and Scholes did not present a formal test of the linearity relation and thus gave no formal evidence about *their* proxy's efficiency. [Jensen (1972a, 1972b) did do this with the same data, however.] Their other stated test, of the Sharpe–Lintner theory, is certainly open to question since no information was provided about the proxy market's relation to the Sharpe–Lintner tangency. (In fact, we know there was a difference between the ex-post Sharpe–Lintner tangency portfolio and Black, Jensen, and Scholes' 'market'. See above.) Therefore, for the Black, Jensen, Scholes paper taken in isolation from Jensen's addition, no hypothesis *whatever* was tested unambiguously.

## 3. Measuring the market and testing the theories

### 3.1. The Sharpe–Lintner case

As mentioned earlier in connection with Black, Jensen, and Scholes' conclusions, there has been in the literature some consideration of mis-measuring the market portfolio. Black, Jensen, and Scholes thought that a mis-specified market would cause a bias in the cross-sectional risk-return intercept from the Sharpe–Lintner prediction, but that the intercept would be intertemporally constant. But as we have seen, an incorrect market portfolio can cause *both* a bias *and* variation of the intercept over time, even when the Sharpe–Lintner theory is the true state of nature.

Mayers (1973) also considered the question of omitted (and non-marketable) assets and reached a similar conclusion with respect to the empirical implications: '. . . the primary testable propositions of the extended [Mayers] model are the linearity of the risk-expected return relationships . . . and the implication that no other variables . . . should be systematically related to expected return' [Mayers (1973, p. 266)].

These conclusions about the empirical implications of Mayers' model are very interesting for the following reason (among others): his derived risk coefficient, though denoted by the symbol '$\beta$', is not the simple regression slope coefficient of the other models. For a given marketable asset, Mayers' beta depends on that marketable asset's return covariance with aggregate non-marketable assets' returns. This implies that a mean-variance efficient marketable portfolio for one investor need not necessarily be mean-variance efficient for another; and thus, there is no longer a mathematical equivalence between mean-variance efficiency and beta/expected return linearity.

It is not clear whether this makes the Mayers model more or less easily testable. The problem of non-identifiability of the market portfolio (in this case, of the marketable market portfolio) is still present since its return also appears in Mayers' linearity relation. In addition, there is a new problem in measuring the return to aggregate nonmarketable capital. On the other hand, if these measurement problems were resolved, the Mayers model may be more easily testable because the linearity relation is more structured – it requires a particular relation between marketable and non-marketable aggregate portfolio returns. Furthermore, the testability of this structure does not seem to be hindered by a mathematical equivalence to the mean-variance efficiency of either portfolio.

Returning now to the simpler Sharpe–Lintner theory, despite the overwhelming importance for testing of measuring the market return properly, references to the consequences of doing it improperly are rather rare. In a typical reference, Petit and Westerfield simply say that the market '. . . is commonly measured by a stock market index, such as the Fisher Link Relative Index or the Standard and Poor's 500 . . .' (p. 581), and they pick yet a third proxy for their own calculations (the Fisher Combination Investment Performance Index). Blume and Friend also use this latter index and make no mention of its being only a proxy. Curiously, they do mention that the all-equities 'zero-beta' portfolio may be only an approximation (p. 23), but, as already noted, they draw an incorrect inference from this fact and they make no reference to the one-to-one relation between an error in the market proxy and an error in the zero-beta proxy.

Fama and MacBeth used 'Fisher's Arithmetic Index, an equally weighted average of all stocks listed on the New York Stock Exchange' (p. 614). This index is not even close to a value-weighted index and should never be suggested as a market proxy. But Fama and MacBeth make no mention of possible error in the proxy's measurement, despite the fact that their paper comes closest to a systematic exploitation of the efficient set mathematics and its implications. Given Fama's more recent statements (1976), it is safe to say that he would not choose this index again.

One analysis of mis-measurement of the market portfolio was presented by Miller and Scholes (1972, pp. 63–66). They report an experiment which had an important influence on the research of others. It is often mentioned in conversations and sometimes in print. For example, in his review article, Jensen (1972a) states that Miller and Scholes '. . . conclude that the improper measurement of the market portfolio returns does not seem to be causing substantial problems' (p. 365).

Miller and Scholes studied the following problem: Suppose that individual returns are generated by a process containing a 'true' market index, $m^*$,

$$\tilde{R}_i = \beta_i \tilde{R}_{m^*} + \tilde{\eta}_i, \tag{7}$$

where $\beta_i$ is constant and $\tilde{\eta}_i$ is a random variable with zero mean.

Suppose also that only a proxy index, $m$, is identifiable and that its returns satisfy the same equation,

$$\tilde{R}_m = \beta_m \tilde{R}_{m^*} + \tilde{\eta}_m. \tag{8}$$

Miller and Scholes then ask the question, what would be the large sample value of $\hat{\gamma}_1$ in a cross-sectional model of the form

$$\bar{R}_i = \hat{\gamma}_0 + \hat{\gamma}_1 \hat{b}_i + \hat{\varepsilon}_j, \tag{9}$$

where $\bar{R}_i$ is the time-series sample mean of $\tilde{R}_i$, $\hat{b}_i$ is the simple least-squares time-series regression slope coefficient of the individual return $\tilde{R}_i$ on the *proxy* market, $\tilde{R}_m$ and $\hat{\varepsilon}_j$ is the estimated residual. They show under quite general conditions that $\hat{\gamma}_1$ will be asymptotic to

$$\beta_m \bar{R}_{m^*} [r^2(\hat{b}_i, \beta_i)/r^2(R_m, R_{m^*})].$$

The term in brackets contains two squared correlation coefficients, a cross-sectional one between true and estimated beta and a time-series one between true and proxy market return.[18]

Miller and Scholes went on to an empirical analysis. Having first estimated the cross-sectional model (9) using an all-equities proxy for the market, they re-estimated (9) with a 25% bond index and then with a 50% bond index. The coefficients $\hat{\gamma}_1$ '. . . were virtually unchanged . . .' (p. 66) in the three cases. They state that empirically '. . . the correlation between the old and new indexes was very close to one' (p. 66), i.e., that $r^2(R_m, R_{m^*}) \approx 1$ if $R_{m^*}$ is taken as the 'old' index. Also, the old and new 'coefficients of risk' were almost perfectly correlated, $r^2(\hat{b}_i, \beta_i) \approx 1$. This implied that the old and new estimates of $\gamma_1$ were proportional by the factor $\beta_m$ which is the beta of the new proxy index with respect to the old proxy.

Conclusion: if the market proxy is perfectly correlated with the true market, the resulting cross-sectional model would yield a $\hat{\gamma}_1$ exactly proportional to the $\gamma_1$ computed by using the true market. It is easy to see, therefore, that the Sharpe–Lintner basic hypothesis (H.4) would be supported by the data, and by this test procedure, if it were true.[19]

The key to understanding the nature and significance of this conclusion is the

---

[18]Note that the $\gamma_0$ would be intertemporally constant in the Miller–Scholes framework. Thus, their model is consistent with the Black, Jensen, Scholes interpretation of $\hat{\gamma}_0$, which is misleading in the case of a mis-measured market proxy portfolio.

[19]A simple way to see this is as follows: Suppose the returns in (7) and (8) are *excess* returns, that $\eta_m \equiv 0$, and that the Sharpe–Lintner (H.4) is valid. Then the cross-sectional model (9) would yield the asymptotic result, $\hat{\gamma}_0 = 0$ and $\hat{\gamma}_1 = \bar{R}_m$, where $\bar{R}_m$ is the market proxy excess mean return. Then it would appear from the data that the market proxy is efficient and equal to the Sharpe–Lintner tangent portfolio.

perfect correlation between the proxy and the true market. Of course, if such a perfect correlation were the state of nature (and everyone knew it), the mean-standard deviation efficient frontier would be a line composed of various combinations of the proxy and true markets. This alone implies the existence of a riskless return, one particular linear combination, and it also implies an infinity of Sharpe–Lintner tangent portfolios, any one of which would support (H.4) in the cross-sectional tests.

Since the mere presence of perfect correlation between the true and proxy markets implies the Sharpe–Lintner result, how are the Miller–Scholes results to be reconciled with the results of Black, Jensen, and Scholes, Blume and Friend and Fama and MacBeth, all of whom rejected the Sharpe–Lintner theory. Miller and Scholes actually anticipated an econometric reconciliation which will be discussed in detail in the next section. There exist other explanations and one very simple possibility will be discussed next.

Actually, Miller and Scholes (and others)[20] only found *almost* perfect correlation between two *proxy* market portfolios. The demonstration of such a correlation for the *true* market was beyond their (and is beyond our) econometric ingenuity for the simple reason that the true market portfolio is unknown. This suggests a reconciliation of the body of empirical results based on either (a) the true market is not *perfectly* correlated with the measured proxies, or (b) perfect correlation only exists among inefficient portfolios. Explanation (b) is inconsistent with equilibrium unless there are restrictions on short-selling. Even if there were such restrictions, however, the computation of sample betas with an inefficient portfolio would give an asymptotically (time-series-wise) not exactly-linear mean return beta relation. It would therefore seem unlikely that this particular explanation has much validity.

To understand explanation (a), we need to know the effect of market proxy correlation on the deviation between the Sharpe–Lintner implications and the observed results. For example, referring again to fig. 1, where $m^*$ is the true market portfolio and $m$ is the proxy, what is the relation between the distance $r_z - r_F$ on the one hand and the correlation between $\tilde{r}_{m^*}$ and $\tilde{r}_m$ on the other hand? From the geometry alone, we observe that this must depend upon the curvature of the risky efficient set and on its distance from the return axis. It also must depend on the absolute and relative positions of $m$ and $m^*$. If both are located far out on the positive segment of the efficient frontier, they might be nearly perfectly correlated and yet imply a large and significant difference between the returns $r_F$ and $r_z$ on their orthogonal portfolios.

Some simple numerical examples may serve to illustrate the possible magnitudes involved. There are two hypothetical states of nature contained in the two examples in table 1. The numbers are not just made up, however. Those

[20]See, for example, Fisher (1966). Table 4.5 (p. 81) of Lorie and Brealey (1972), gives correlation coefficients for five commonly-used indexes, for data from the mid-20's to the mid-60's, ranging between 0.906 and 0.985.

in the 'Given' panel come directly from Black, Jensen, and Scholes' tables 5 and 7 (1972) – for Example 1 – and from Morgan's table 3 (1975) – for Example 2. Example 1 contains ex-post results calculated from monthly returns for 1931–65. Example 2 also contains ex-post numbers but for 5-day intervals from July 1962 through December 1972.[21] Only the 3.0 riskless interest rate in Example 2 is a

Table 1

Examples of the ex-post risky efficient set and of sample correlation among efficient portfolios.

| Quantity | Symbol | Numerical values (%/annum) | |
| --- | --- | --- | --- |
| | | Example 1 (BJS results) | Example 2 (Morgan results) |
| *Given:* | | | |
| Riskless return | $r_F$ | 1.920 | 3.0 |
| Market proxy return | $r_m$ | | |
|   Mean | | 18.96 | 15.54 |
|   Standard deviation | | 106.9 | 101.4 |
| Return on market proxy's efficient orthogonal portfolio | $r_z$ | | |
|   Mean | | 5.976 | 4.067 |
|   Standard deviation | | 51.10 | 52.14 |
| *Implied by the above:* | | | |
| Global minimum variance portfolio | $r_0$ | | |
|   Mean | | 8.392 | 6.469 |
|   Standard deviation | | 46.10 | 33.12 |
| Sharpe–Lintner tangent portfolio | $r_{m^*}$ | | |
|   Mean | | 12.34 | 12.75 |
|   Standard deviation | | 58.49 | 77.74 |
| Correlation coefficient between market proxy's return and return on S–L tangent portfolio | $\rho$ | 0.8952 | 0.9860 |

pure assumption. The source paper provided no measure of the riskless return and 3 percent was chosen as a reasonable but conservative figure for the period.

Given one additional and strong assumption, estimates for the global minimum variance and Sharpe–Lintner tangent portfolios are implied by the riskless return, the market proxy and the market proxy's orthogonal (zero-beta) efficient

---

[21]The BJS and Morgan numbers have been made comparable by using suitable annualisation multipliers. The BJS numbers were multiplied by 1200 and the Morgan numbers by 36500/7. Morgan gave several different measures of $m$ and $z$. I used the numbers in the first column of his table 3, p. 371, and the first of each pair. To obtain the standard deviation of the market proxy, I assumed that his 'risk premium: mean/std. error' was computed as

$$[(r_m - r_z)\sqrt{522}]/\sqrt{(\sigma_z^2 + \sigma_m^2)}, \qquad 522 = \text{sample size}.$$

I am indebted to him for private correspondence that certified the validity of this assumption.

portfolio that were provided in the source papers. The crucial assumption is that the market proxy and its associated zero-beta portfolio are actually located on the ex-post efficient frontier.[22] If $m$ and $z$ are both efficient, the variance of each one is related to its mean by the efficient set quadratic equation, (A.11) of the appendix, which contains the three 'efficient set constants', $a$, $b$ and $c$. In addition, since $m$ and $z$ were orthogonal by construction, their means are related by a third expression (A.15) which is the general equation relating the mean returns of orthogonal efficient portfolios. Since this expression also contains the efficient set constants, there results a non-linear system of three equations in the three unknowns, $a$, $b$ and $c$. Usually, as in the case of our examples here, the system has a unique solution. Once the three efficient set constants are determined, all the other information of table 1 is computable in a straightforward way. The Sharpe–Lintner tangent portfolio's return requires additionally that the riskless interest rate be assigned a value.

The examples' relevance derives from the tangent portfolio and its correlation with the proxy market portfolio. In Example 1, Black, Jensen, and Scholes' data indicate that the Sharpe–Lintner tangent portfolio had an average monthly return of 12.3 (percent per annum) from 1931–65 and that its ex-post correlation with their market proxy was on the order of 90 percent. Notice that the tangent return was only 65 percent of the market proxy return, despite the significant correlation. Also note that the Black, Jensen, and Scholes zero-beta proxy returned 5.976 (percent per annum) on average. As mentioned previously, this finding was used by them to deny the validity of Sharpe–Lintner theory (because 5.976 was significantly greater than 1.920, the estimated riskless return).

There is a possible way to examine the validity of their conclusion. Using the same data, a different consistency check of the Sharpe–Lintner model would involve the individual asset investment proportions in the observed tangency portfolio. If any of these were significantly negative, the tangency portfolio would not satisfy the qualities of a market portfolio, which must have positive investments in all assets. [23] The suggested exercise (it has not yet been done by anyone, to my knowledge), has been termed a 'consistency check' rather than a 'test' of the Sharpe–Lintner theory because of the many assets omitted from the Black, Jensen, and Scholes sample. The omission of even a single asset can in principle cause an observed tangency portfolio to alter in composition

---

[22]There are several reasons why this is a strong assumption and why the results of table 1 should only be considered as examples. In both the Black, Jensen, Scholes and the Morgan papers, the samples consisted only of equities. Thus, it is very unlikely that the market proxy was exactly mean-variance efficient. Even if the samples had included all assets, the zero-beta measured portfolios were probably not precisely on the ex-post mean-variance boundary because the full covariance matrix was never inverted to find the efficient set constants. For example, Morgan estimated the efficient set by using a sample of 89 portfolios of 6 securities each (p. 365). This estimate of the efficient set would have differed, although perhaps in only a minor way, from the efficient set computed using the 534 ($89 \times 6$) individual stocks.

[23]I am indebted to Michael C. Jensen for suggesting this procedure.

from totally positive to some negative proportions. (The alteration is not merely an allocation of the former weight of the omitted asset to the remaining assets because the entire efficient set can change.) Nevertheless, the calculation would be worthwhile because it would at least provide an insight into the possibility of incorrect inferences arising from market proxy portfolio misspecification within the Black, Jensen, and Scholes universe of securities. Unfortunately, the calculation cannot be reported here because it requires the full sample covariance matrix and the sample mean return vector of individual assets. These are not in my possession.

The Morgan data, which cover a later period than the Black, Jensen, and Scholes data, imply an even higher correlation between the market proxy and the Sharpe–Lintner ex-post tangency portfolios. This is due partly to a lower mean return of the market proxy and partly to a larger *assumed* riskless return which has caused the tangent portfolio to lie closer to the proxy.[24] However, the same qualitative conclusions obtain: Efficient portfolios are highly correlated and the Sharpe–Lintner theory is consistent with the data and a mis-specified market index.

Recall that *all* efficient portfolios on the positively-sloped segment are positively correlated. It is also true that the correlation increases with increasing mean returns of the two portfolios in question (holding constant the difference between their means). In the two numerical examples of table 1, for instance, all efficient portfolios with returns between 14 and 49 percent for Example 1 and with returns between 12 and 36 percent for Example 2 had *squared* correlations with the market proxy greater than 90 percent.

The implications of this are clear: Any hypothesis, such as Sharpe–Lintner, that makes a specific prediction about the position of the market portfolio, is likely to be highly susceptible to a type II error – being rejected when it is true. Heuristically, a small error in measuring the market's composition can cause an error in testing the theory. The market proxy may be almost perfectly correlated with the true market and yet a significant difference can emerge between the proxy zero-beta return and the true zero-beta return (or the riskless return).

### 3.2. The generalized asset pricing theory case

For testing the Sharpe–Lintner hypothesis (H.4), the identifiability of the market portfolio is a serious problem. For the more general asset pricing hypothesis (H.2), it is perhaps even a more serious problem. For (H.4), we can at least get an idea of the consequences of a mis-specified market portfolio by *assuming* that the proxy market is efficient. Then, the ex-post tangent portfolio can be calculated as in the above examples and its return and reasonableness can be

---

[24]The effect of the riskless rate assumption is easy to assess. For an assumption of 2% rather than 3%, the correlation between market proxy and tangent portfolio would have been 0.9587. For 4%, the correlation would have been 0.9999. Thus a considerable range of assumptions for the riskless rate would have given the same general impression.

judged against external criteria. For example, it might have been expected that the true market portfolio had less variance and less return than the Black, Jensen, and Scholes and the Morgan all-equities proxies, perhaps because equities are more variable than the average asset. Or, if the all-equities proxies had been combined with bonds, human capital, and real estate in reasonable proportions, the resulting mixture might have been closer to the observed tangent portfolio. Naturally, such possibilities are mere conjectures. They are not testable hypotheses, again for the simple reason that the true market portfolio has an unknown composition.

For the more general hypothesis (H.2), such judgements based on common-sense interpretation of the results are likely to be unavailable. (H.2) merely requires that the true market be somewhere on the positively-sloped segment of the mean-variance efficient frontier. For relatively small (time-series) sample sizes, this hypothesis is highly susceptible to a type I error, being acceptable when it is false; but as the number of time-series observations increases, the hypothesis will almost surely be rejected, even when it is true. To see why, first consider the fact that the true market portfolio has a positive proportion invested in every individual asset. This implies that every reasonable candidate for the market proxy must have totally positive investment proportions. In many cases, in fact, the investment proportions are either the positive constant $1/N$ for the included assets (and zero for excluded assets), or the proportions display little cross-sectional variation. We know, therefore, that all such candidates for the proxy market portfolio must lie in a relatively small region of the mean-variance space.

Suppose, for example, that the true efficient set is given by the curve labeled '$I$' in fig. 2. In this particular example, efficient portfolios between $A$ and $B$ are assumed to have totally positive investment proportions. As shown in the appendix, Theorem 3, an efficient set like $I$, whose global minimum variance portfolio has totally positive investment proportions, will occur if the variance of every individual asset exceeds its covariances with all other individual assets (if $\sigma_j^2 > \sigma_{ij}$ for all $j \neq i$). Above the point $A$ and below the point $B$, at least one asset has negative investment proportions. Suppose the asset that leaves the efficient set at point $A$ is indexed $j$. Then the curve $I_{-j}$ would be the efficient set if $j$ did not exist. $I$ and $I_{-j}$ are tangent at a single point at most. (There might have been no finite tangency because $j$ might have had a positive or a negative weight in all portfolios on $I$.)[25] But since the weight is assumed negative above $A$ and positive below $A$, it must be zero at $A$. Since it is zero everywhere on $I_{-j}$, $A$ must be a tangency. ($I$ and $I_{-j}$ obviously cannot cross since they are minima.)

---

[25]The curve $I_{-j}$, with one omitted asset, is offered as an expositional example. In general, there will be more than one omitted asset from any empirical sample and so there will be no common point between the true efficient frontier and the sample efficient frontier, except in an unusual circumstance (the unusual circumstance being that *all* omitted assets have their zero investment proportions at a common point on the true efficient set).

If (H.2) is true, the true market portfolio must lie on the boundary $I$ between $A$ and $B$, say at $m^*$. If $m$ is chosen as the market proxy, all empirical tests will support (H.2) because the proxy $m$ does indeed lie on the reduced efficient boundary $I_{-j}$ which lacks asset $j$. Although proxy portfolio $m$ is inefficient globally (since it lies below $I$), this fact will not be detectable by any test using the reduced subset without $j$.

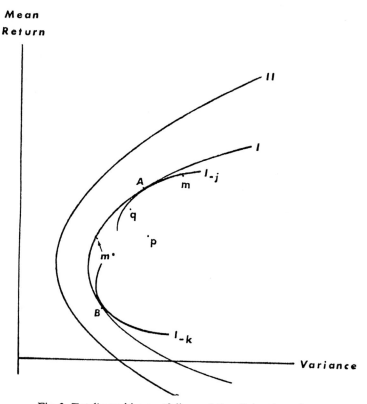

Fig. 2. Totally positive portfolios and the efficient boundary.

Thus (H.2) will be supported correctly, but for the wrong reason. On the other hand, suppose that the true market is really inefficient and lies within $I$ at the point labelled $p$. Then the same exact test with market proxy $m$ will support (H.2) incorrectly. In fact, it seems that this is the greatest danger. For any subset of assets, there exists an 'efficient frontier' whose constituent portfolios will satisfy all empirical tests of (H.2). As long as the investment proportions in the subset of assets are totally positive somewhere along this reduced boundary, a 'reasonable' market proxy will be available and it will support (H.2) since it will be subset efficient.

On the other hand, the geometry makes evident that a type II error is also quite possible. Suppose that portfolio $q$ has been chosen as the market proxy and that (H.2) is true and that $m^*$ is truly efficient and lies on $I$. In this case, a large sample will almost surely reject (H.2) since the proxy does not even lie on the reduced efficient set $I_{-j}$. Note that this will occur even when the proxy is highly correlated with the true market $m^*$ and is also highly correlated with a proxy which is subset efficient.

The empirical situation is aggravated by this likelihood of a high correlation between the true market and the proxy, whether (H.2) is true or false. Such a high correlation is bound to make it seem that the exact identity of the market is of relatively minor significance and the temptation will be great to modify the market proxy slightly to obtain the *desired* result, whether it be rejection or acceptance of (H.2). In fact, if the identity of the true market is a matter of dispute among different researchers, there may be no way to settle the validity of (H.2) with any size of sample. The only exception would seem to be when (H.2) is false, the true state of nature is depicted by efficient set II in fig. 2 and the sample contains every asset. In this case, *no* totally-positive portfolio is efficient and large (time-series) samples would reject (H.2) unambiguously.

In principle, such a test is easy to construct. As shown in the appendix, the investment proportions for portfolios that lie on the ex-post efficient boundary are given by the $N \times 1$ vector

$$X = B\begin{pmatrix} r \\ 1 \end{pmatrix},$$

where $B$ is an $(N \times 2)$ matrix of constants that depend only on the mean returns and sample covariances of the $N$ individual assets, and $r$ is the mean return of the ex-post efficient portfolio whose investment proportions are given by $X$. Since $B$ contains constants, the test simply involves computing $X$ at two points – at the minimum and maximum observed individual returns, $r_{min}$ and $r_{max}$, to obtain

$$X_{min} \equiv B\begin{pmatrix} r_{min} \\ 1 \end{pmatrix} \quad \text{and} \quad X_{max} \equiv B\begin{pmatrix} r_{max} \\ 1 \end{pmatrix}.$$

Then if there is a single element that is significantly negative in both $X_{min}$ and $X_{max}$, (H.2) is false. This follows because every totally positive portfolio lies between $r_{min}$ and $r_{max}$. Thus, if all efficient portfolios in this interval have one or more significantly negative investment proportions, there is no totally positive mean-variance efficient portfolio. Unfortunately, this 'test' is only valid in principle. The full covariance matrix of all individual assets is required to compute the matrix $B$. Furthermore, the sampling variation of $B$ would generally be unknown. Finally, the cost of collecting data *for every* existing asset would be prohibitive.

In summary of this section, the sole viable hypothesis of generalized asset pricing theory is (H.2) – the true market portfolio is ex-ante efficient. This hypothesis offers a non-trivial challenge to our econometric ingenuity and the challenge has not yet been satisfactorily met. The problem can be summarised by noting that in a given sample there are always portfolios which do not reject (H.2) and that little external information is available on the true market portfolio's exact composition. Furthermore, even a small mis-specification of the proxy's composition can lead to the wrong conclusion. What might seem a trivial mis-specification in an ordinary statistical application can be of crucial importance for testing (H.2).

## Appendix

### The efficient set mathematics[26]

The efficient set (or efficient portfolio frontier) is composed of portfolios with minimum variance at each possible level of mean return. Ex-ante variances and mean returns of individual assets must be estimated or subjectively determined. The ex-post efficient set is a sample statistic, the set of minimum sample variance portfolios.

Given the characteristics of individual assets, a portfolio is completely characterized by the proportions invested in its constituent securities,

$$X_p = \|x_{ip}\|,$$

where $x_{ip}$ is the proportion of portfolio $p$ invested in asset $i$, and $X_p$ is a vector subject to the constraint

$$X_p' \iota = 1, \tag{A.1}$$

$\iota$ denoting the unit vector. When speaking of a single portfolio, we will suppress the subscript $p$ on the vector $X$.

The parameters of the efficient set problem are the mean return vector of individual assets,

$$R = \|r_i\|,$$

[26]As mentioned in the text, most of the results in this appendix have appeared previously. See particularly Merton (1972), which is the original full analytic treatment of the efficient set mathematics. Szegö (1975) seems to be the only other relatively complete treatment but Sharpe (1970), Black (1972) and Fama (1976) also contain many of the same results. I have made no attempt to ascribe originality.

and the covariance matrix of individual returns,

$$V = \|\sigma_{ij}\|.$$

These can be either population values or they can be sample product moments. The mathematics that follows does not require a distinction, merely a set of numbers $R$ and $V$. Any portfolio's mean and variance are given by

$$r_p = X'R, \tag{A.2}$$

$$\sigma_p^2 = X'VX. \tag{A.3}$$

Similarly, the covariance of any two arbitrary portfolios (say $p_1$ and $p_2$) is given by

$$\sigma_{p_1 p_2} = X'_{p_1} V X_{p_2}. \tag{A.4}$$

*Necessary and sufficient condition for a portfolio to be efficient*

The efficient set is found by minimizing $\sigma_p^2$ subject to the two constraints (A.1) and (A.2). The Lagrangian is

$$L = X'VX - \lambda_1(X'R - r_p) - \lambda_2(X'\iota - 1),$$

where $\lambda_1$ and $\lambda_2$ are undetermined multipliers. The first extremum conditions are the vector

$$VX = \tfrac{1}{2}(\lambda_1 R + \lambda_2 \iota), \tag{A.5}$$

plus the constraints (A.1) and (A.2).

If the joint distribution of individual returns is non-degenerate, the covariance matrix is positive definite (and non-singular), and all efficient portfolios satisfy

$$X = \tfrac{1}{2} V^{-1} (R \; \iota) \begin{pmatrix} \lambda_1 \\ \lambda_2 \end{pmatrix}. \tag{A.6}$$

Non-degeneracy simply implies that no two distinct linear combinations of assets are perfectly correlated and that no asset has zero variance. We shall see later how to find the efficient set when this condition is not satisfied. When the probability distribution *is* non-degenerate, the second-order conditions for a minimum are satisfied because the covariance matrix is positive definite.

*The equation of the efficient set*

Different efficient portfolios are determined by different values of the multipliers in eq. (A.6). The result can be written in a more intuitive way, however, as shown in the following:

*Theorem 1. If no linear combination of assets has zero variance and at least two assets have different mean returns, the investment proportions of a mean-variance efficient portfolio whose mean return is $r_p$ are given by the vector*

$$X = V^{-1}(R\iota)A^{-1}\begin{pmatrix} r_p \\ 1 \end{pmatrix}, \tag{A.7}$$

*where the $(2 \times 2)$ matrix $A$ is defined as*

$$A \equiv (R\iota)'\, V^{-1}(R\iota). \tag{A.8}$$

*Proof.* The assumptions in the 'if' clause guarantee that $V$ is positive definite and that $(R\iota)$ has rank two. This implies that $A$ is non-singular and positive definite. Then pre-multiplying eq. (A.6) by $(R\iota)'$ gives

$$\tfrac{1}{2}\begin{pmatrix} \lambda_1 \\ \lambda_2 \end{pmatrix} = A^{-1}(R\iota)'\, X,$$

and by using constraints (A.1) and (A.2), this simplifies to

$$\tfrac{1}{2}\begin{pmatrix} \lambda_1 \\ \lambda_2 \end{pmatrix} = A^{-1}\begin{pmatrix} r_p \\ 1 \end{pmatrix}.$$

Substitution for $\tfrac{1}{2}\begin{pmatrix} \lambda_1 \\ \lambda_2 \end{pmatrix}$ in eq. (A.6) then gives eq. (A.7).  Q.E.D.

The matrix $A$ is the fundamental matrix of information about the basic data contained in the means and covariances of individual assets. As we shall see, the elements of $A$ contain sufficient information to prove all the important results of the efficient set mathematics. Since $A$ is $2 \times 2$ and symmetric, it contains only three distinct constants.

*Definition*

$$a = R'V^{-1}R, \quad b = R'V^{-1}\iota, \quad c = \iota'V^{-1}\iota, \tag{A.9}$$

are the 'efficient set constants' contained in the matrix

$$A \equiv \begin{pmatrix} a & b \\ b & c \end{pmatrix}.$$

For example:

*Corollary 1. The variance of any mean-variance efficient portfolio is related to its mean by the parabola*

$$\sigma_p^2 = (r_p\ 1)A^{-1}\begin{pmatrix} r_p \\ 1 \end{pmatrix}, \tag{A.10}$$

*which can be written in scalar notation as*

$$\sigma_p^2 = (a - 2br_p + cr_p^2)/(ac - b^2). \tag{A.11}$$

*Proof.* The efficient investment proportions given by eq. (A.7) can be used in the general formula for a portfolio's variance, (A.3), to give

$$\sigma_p^2 = (r_p\ 1)A^{-1}(R\ \imath)'V^{-1}\ VV^{-1}(R\ \imath)A^{-1}(r_p\ 1)'$$

$$= (r_p\ 1)A^{-1}\ AA^{-1}(r_p\ 1)'. \qquad \text{Q.E.D.}$$

*The minimum variance portfolio*

One portfolio of special interest is the global minimum variance portfolio. Its mean and variance are found easily from the minimum of eq. (A.10).

*Corollary 2. The global minimum variance is*

$$\sigma_0^2 = 1/c. \tag{A.12}$$

*The portfolio with this variance has mean return*

$$r_0 = b/c, \tag{A.13}$$

*and its investment proportions are given by*

$$X_0 = V^{-1}\imath/c. \tag{A.14}$$

*It is positively correlated with all portfolios and assets and its covariance with all individual assets and all portfolios is a fixed constant, $\sigma_0^2$, which is its own variance.*

*Proof.* Eq. (A.13) is obtained from the zero of the first derivative of eq. (A.11),

$$0 = -b - cr_0.$$

This gives a minimum if the second derivative of eq. (A.11),

$$2c/(ac - b^2),$$

is positive. From eq. (A.9), we note that $c$ must be positive since it is a quadratic form of the positive definite matrix $V^{-1}$. The denominator is positive because it is the determinant of $A$ which is also positive definite.

Eq. (A.12) is obtained by substituting eq. (A.13) in the general formula for the variance of efficient portfolios, (A.11). Similarly, substituting eq. (A.13) into eq. (A.7) gives

$$X_0 = V^{-1}(R\,\imath) \begin{pmatrix} c & -b \\ -b & a \end{pmatrix} \begin{pmatrix} b/c \\ 1 \end{pmatrix} \Big/ (ac - b^2)$$

$$= V^{-1}(R\,\imath) \begin{pmatrix} 0 \\ 1/c \end{pmatrix}$$

$$= V^{-1}\imath/c.$$

which is eq. (A.14).

The last statement about the covariance of the minimum-variance portfolio is obtained as follows: Let $X_j$ be any arbitrary vector of investment proportions. Then the covariance between this portfolio, $j$, and the global minimum variance portfolio is

$$\sigma_{j0} = X'_j V X_0 = X'_j \imath/c = 1/c. \qquad \text{Q.E.D.}$$

Heuristically, the minimum variance portfolio *must* be positively correlated with all other portfolios. If it were not, a further combination would result in another portfolio whose variance was even smaller. A heuristic reason for the constancy of the covariance is more subtle; but consider the following: Find the minimum variance portfolio that could be obtained from any arbitrary pair of assets. It can be verified readily that this minimum coincides with one or the other assets if and only if their covariance equals one of their variances. The same thing is true when one of this arbitrary pair is the global minimum variance portfolio. Since it is indeed the minimum, *its* variance must equal the arbitrary covariance (which is thus seen to be constant and independent of the second asset).

*Efficient portfolios and correlation*

*Corollary 3.   For every efficient portfolio except the global minimum variance portfolio there exists a unique orthogonal efficient portfolio with finite mean. If the first efficient portfolio has mean $r_p$, its orthogonal portfolio has mean $r_z$ given by*

$$r_z = (a - br_p)/(b - cr_p). \tag{A.15}$$

*Furthermore, portfolio z always lies on the opposite-sloped segment of the efficient set from portfolio p.*

*Proof.* By using eq. (A.7) in eq. (A.4), we can obtain the covariance between any arbitrary pair of efficient portfolios, say between $p$ and $q$, as

$$\sigma_{qp} = (r_q 1) A^{-1} \begin{pmatrix} r_p \\ 1 \end{pmatrix}. \tag{A.16}$$

If $p$ and $q$ are orthogonal, this covariance is zero. Thus, putting $q = z$ gives the equation

$$(r_z\, 1) \begin{pmatrix} c & -b \\ -b & a \end{pmatrix} \begin{pmatrix} r_p \\ 1 \end{pmatrix} = 0,$$

from which eq. (A.15) follows directly. [Note that the determinant of $A$ has been eliminated from eq. (A.16).] Uniqueness is obvious from eqs. (A.7) and (A.15).

The second part of the corollary follows by noting that if $r_z$ is on the negatively sloped efficient set segment, its return must be smaller than the return on the global minimum variance portfolio, i.e., $r_z < b/c$. Then from eq. (A.15), $(a - b r_p)/(b - c r_p) < b/c$. If the return on $r_p$ also satisfied $r_p < b/c$ then $b - c r_p$ would be positive and we would have

$$a - b r_p < (b/c)(b - c r_p),$$

or $a - b^2/c < 0$. But since $c$ is positive, this is a contradiction because $ac - b^2$ is recognized as the determinant of $A$, which is positive. Thus, $r_p$ must exceed $b/c$ and be on the positively-sloped segment.     Q.E.D.

The geometry of these orthogonal portfolios is useful, as can be seen in the following:

*Corollary 3.A. In the return-variance space, the line passing between the efficient portfolio p and the global minimum variance portfolio intersects the return axis at $r_z$. In the return-standard deviation space, the tangent to the efficient set at $r_p$ intersects the return axis at $r_z$.*

*Proof.* In the mean-variance space, the slope of the line connecting portfolios $p$ and $0$ is

$$(r_p - r_0)/(\sigma_p^2 - \sigma_0^2),$$

and its intercept on the return axis is

$$r_p - \sigma_p^2 \{(r_p - r_0)/(\sigma_p^2 - \sigma_0^2)\}.$$

Substituting for $r_0$ and $\sigma_0^2$ from eqs. (A.13) and (A.12) and simplifying, this expression reduces to $(br_p - a)/(cr_p - b)$ which is $r_z$ in eq. (A.15). Thus the first statement is proven. To prove the second, it is easiest to use the first derivative of eq. (A.11). This provides an expression for the tangent to the efficient set in the mean-standard derivation space. Multiplying this tangent by $\sigma_p$ and subtracting the result from $r_p$ gives eq. (A.15).      Q.E.D.

*Corollary 4.   All portfolios on the positively-sloped segment of the efficient set are positively correlated.*

*Proof.*   From eq. (A.16) we can see that any two efficient portfolios, $p$ and $q$, will be negatively correlated if and only if

$$a - b(r_p + r_q) + c\, r_p r_q < 0,$$

which implies that

$$a - br_p < r_q(b - cr_p).$$

If $p$ is on the positively-sloped efficient segment, $b - cr_p < 0$, and thus $r_q < r_z$, where $z$ is $p$'s orthogonal portfolio. But $z$ must lie on the negatively-sloped segment, from Corollary 3. Thus, $q$ is also on the negatively-sloped segment since its return is smaller than $r_z$.      Q.E.D.

It is easy to see by the same argument that all portfolios on the negatively-sloped segment are positively correlated too. Only portfolios that lie sufficiently far apart, and on opposite sides of the efficient set, are negatively correlated. Heuristically, if investors do wish to minimize variance and maximize expected returns, all investors who agree on the probability distribution would hold positively correlated portfolios.

*The separation or 'two-fund' theorem*

*Corollary 5* ('Two-Fund Theorem').   *The investment proportions vector of every mean-variance efficient portfolio is a linear combination of the proportions vectors of two other efficient portfolios whose means are different.*

*Proof.*   From eq. (A.7), the investment proportions are seen to be linear in the mean return. This is so because the $(N \times 2)$ matrix, $B \equiv V^{-1}(R\,\mathbf{1})A^{-1}$, contains only constants ($N$ is the number of individual assets). Thus, if $p_1$, $p_2$ and $p_3$ are efficient portfolios and $\alpha$ is a constant given by $\alpha \equiv (r_3 - r_2)/(r_1 - r_2)$, then

$$X_{p_3} = B\begin{pmatrix} r_3 \\ 1 \end{pmatrix} = B\begin{pmatrix} \alpha r_1 + (1-\alpha)r_2 \\ 1 \end{pmatrix}$$

$$= \alpha X_{p_1} + (1-\alpha)X_{p_2}, \qquad \text{Q.E.D.}$$

According to Corollary 5, if we identify two efficient portfolios, all others can be constructed as a linear combination of these two. We might as well pick two portfolios whose means and variances are easy to compute. One would certainly be the global minimum variance portfolio with mean and variance given by eqs. (A.13) and (A.12). Its investment proportions, eq. (A.14), are simply the sums of the rows of the inverse covariance matrix, $V^{-1}$ (normalized by the sum of all elements of $V^{-1}$). A second easily-computable efficient portfolio is the one with mean return $r_1 \equiv a/b$. Its variance is $\sigma_1^2 = a/b^2$ and its investment proportions are

$$X_1 = V^{-1}R/b. \tag{A.17}$$

From Corollary 3, eq. (A.15), we observe that this portfolio's orthogonal portfolio has a mean of zero.[27] Thus, its associated covariance vector is *proportional* to the mean return vector. Its investment proportions are very easy to compute as can be seen in eq. (A.17).

*Relations among individual asset parameters*
*Corollary 6. The covariance vector of individual assets with any portfolio can be expressed as an exact linear function of the individual mean returns vector if and only if the portfolio is efficient.*

*Proof of Sufficiency.* The vector of covariances between individual assets and a particular efficient portfolio is given by $VX$, where $X$ is the portfolio's investment proportions vector. From eq. (A.7), this implies

$$VX = (R\ \iota)A^{-1}\begin{pmatrix} r_p \\ 1 \end{pmatrix}. \tag{A.18}$$

Since $A^{-1}\begin{pmatrix} r_p \\ 1 \end{pmatrix}$ contains two constants, $VX$ is linear in $R$.    Q.E.D.

Although eq. (A.18) is perfectly acceptable as a result, it can be rewritten in a more traditional and perhaps more recognizable form. Note that the $(2 \times 1)$

[27] I am indebted to Eugene Fama for pointing out this fact.

vector $A^{-1}\binom{r_p}{1}$ can be simplified as

$$\begin{pmatrix} cr_p - b \\ -br_p + a \end{pmatrix} / (ac - b^2) = \frac{cr_p - b}{ac - b^2} \begin{pmatrix} 1 \\ -r_z \end{pmatrix} = \frac{\sigma_p^2}{r_p - r_z} \begin{pmatrix} 1 \\ -r_z \end{pmatrix},$$

where $z$ is $p$'s orthogonal portfolio. Substitution back into eq. (A.18) gives

$$R = r_z 1 + (r_p - r_z)\beta, \tag{A.19}$$

where $\beta \equiv VX/\sigma_p^2$ is the vector of simple regression slope coefficients of individual assets on efficient portfolio $p$ (the 'betas'). Since the covariances are linear in the mean return, of course the 'betas' are too.

*Proof of Necessity.*    Let the vector of covariances with an arbitrary portfolio $m$ be an exact linear function of the mean returns,

$$VX_m = \alpha_1 R + \alpha_2 1,$$

where $\alpha_1$ and $\alpha_2$ are arbitrary constants. Then the vector $X_m$ is equal to

$$X_m = \alpha_1 V^{-1} R + \alpha_2 V^{-1} 1$$

$$= \alpha_1 b X_1 + \alpha_2 c X_0,$$

where $X_1$ is the vector of investment proportions for special efficient portfolio 1 [see eq. (A.17)], and $X_0$ is the vector of proportions for the global minimum variance portfolio ($b$ and $c$ are two of the three efficient set constants).

Since the constraint (A.1) must apply to all such vectors, including the vector $X_m$, we must have

$$\alpha_1 b + \alpha_2 c = 1.$$

Thus $X_m$ is a weighted average of two efficient vectors $X_1$ and $X_0$ and, by Corollary 5, $X_m$ also is efficient.    Q.E.D.

A slightly more general form of the linearity property can be obtained. Let us suppose that portfolios $A$ and $B$ are chosen arbitrarily and that the *multivariate* regression coefficients are computed between individual asset returns and these two portfolios' returns. Then:

*Corollary 6.A.*[28]    *Let vectors of multivariate regression coefficients be calculated between individual asset returns (as dependent variables) and the returns o*

---

[28]I am indebted to John B. Long, Jr. for pointing out a previous error in this corollary.

*two imperfectly-correlated portfolios A and B (as explanatory variables). Then both multivariate regression coefficient vectors are exact linear functions of the mean return vector if and only if A and B are efficient. Furthermore,*

(a)  *the coefficient vector for asset j on portfolio A is given by*

$$(VX_A - \sigma_{AB}\mathbf{i})/(\sigma_A^2 - \sigma_{AB}) = (R - r_{B\mathbf{i}})/(r_A - r_B), \tag{A.20}$$

*and similarly for portfolio B with the A and B subscripts interchanged; and*

(b)  *the two coefficient vectors sum to the unit vector.*

*Proof of Sufficiency.* If statement (a) is true, the proof of exact linearity is identical to the proof of Corollary 6 because (A.20) shows that the multivariate coefficient vector is linear in the covariance vector $VX_A$. Since a linear function of a linear function is also linear, the result follows immediately.

To prove parts (a) and (b), first note that the usual multivariate coefficient of $A$ obtained by regressing $j$ on $A$ and $B$ would have been

$$\beta_j' \equiv \frac{\sigma_{jA}\sigma_B^2 - \sigma_{jB}\sigma_{AB}}{\sigma_A^2\sigma_B^2 - \sigma_{AB}^2}. \tag{A.21}$$

But since $A$ and $B$ are mean-variance efficient, this multivariate coefficient can be simplified. Noting from eq. (A.19) that $\sigma_{jB} = \sigma_B^2(r_j - r_{z_B})/(r_B - r_{z_B})$, where $z_B$ is $B$'s orthogonal portfolio, and noting analogous expressions for $\sigma_{jA}$ and $\sigma_{AB}$, eq. (A.21) can be rewritten as

$$\beta_j' = \frac{(r_j - r_{z_A})(r_B - r_{z_B}) - (r_j - r_{z_B})(r_B - r_{z_A})}{(r_A - r_{z_A})(r_B - r_{z_B}) - (r_A - r_{z_B})(r_B - r_{z_A})},$$

or

$$\beta_j' = \frac{r_j - r_B}{r_A - r_B} = \frac{\sigma_{jA} - \sigma_{AB}}{\sigma_A^2 - \sigma_{AB}}. \tag{A.22}$$

This proves part (a). Since the same development can be made in behalf of portfolio $B$, the multivariate coefficient against $B$ must be $(r_j - r_A)/(r_B - r_A) = 1 - \beta_j'$. This proves part (b). Q.E.D.

*Proof of Necessity.* Let both multivariate coefficient vectors be exact linear functions of the mean return vector. Using the general definition (A.21) of multivariate coefficients and the same procedure as that contained in the necessity proof of Corollary 6, it can be shown that the vectors $W_A$ and $W_B$, defined by

$$W_A \equiv (X_A - \beta_{AB}X_B)/(1 - \beta_{AB}),$$

and

$$W_B \equiv (X_B - \beta_{BA} X_A)/(1 - \beta_{BA}),$$

are efficient. (Here, $\beta_{AB} = \sigma_{AB}/\sigma_B^2$.)

Adding the two equations in order to eliminate $X_B$ gives

$$W_A(1 - \beta_{AB}) + W_B \beta_{AB}(1 - \beta_{BA}) = X_A(1 - \beta_{BA}\beta_{AB}).$$

Since the coefficients of $W_A$ and $W_B$ sum to $1 - \beta_{BA}\beta_{AB}$, $X_A$ is a linear combination of two efficient vectors and is therefore also efficient (by Corollary 5). An identical development proves the efficiency of vector $X_B$. Since $A$ and $B$ are efficient, statements (a) and (b) are true.     Q.E.D.

Suppose that some non-efficient portfolio $q$ has been used to estimate a vector of betas. There exists an efficient portfolio $p$ that has the same mean return, $r_p = r_q$, and for which eq. (A.19) is satisfied. But the betas of eq. (A.19) are $VX_p/\sigma_p^2$ whereas the betas estimated with portfolio $q$ are $\hat{\beta} \equiv VX_q/\sigma_q^2$. Using the estimates $\hat{\beta}$, (A.19) can be rewritten as

$$R \equiv r_z + (r_q - r_z)\hat{\beta} + \frac{r_q - r_z}{\sigma_q^2} V(X_p/k - X_q), \tag{A.23}$$

where $k = \sigma_p^2/\sigma_q^2$. The expression (A.23) is linear in the vector $\hat{\beta}$ if and only if the last term is a constant vector. But if $q$ is not efficient, then $k < 1$. This implies that the last term can be constant only if $r_p \neq r_q$, which is a contradiction. (This is actually an equivalent proof to that used for Corollary 6; but it has the advantage that the deviations from a linear return-beta relation caused by using an inefficient base portfolio are given explicit display.)

One feature of eq. (A.23) is of particular interest: It would be quite possible that a subset of the elements of $X_p$ and $X_q$ be equal; and if the returns and betas for this particular subset were calculated, they would be exactly linearly related when taken alone. Thus the full set of data is not *continuously* non-linear even when the base portfolio is *in*efficient.

To reiterate, an efficient set calculated from a subset of assets will pass through portfolios that are inefficient globally. But since such portfolios are efficient for the subset, their associated subset of betas will be exactly linear in the subset of mean returns.

*Corollary 7. The proportion invested in a given individual asset changes monotonically along the efficient frontier.*

*Proof.* By inspection from eq. (A.7). (The gradient vector of $X$ with respect to $r_p$ is a constant vector.)

This corollary implies that if an individual asset represents a non-zero proportion in any efficient portfolio, it is held in *all* efficient portfolios except at most one. It is either held in positive amount or sold short in all others. N.B. It is mathematically possible that some assets are positively (or negatively) represented in all efficient portfolios and even that the individual proportion is a constant.

The gradient vector of eq. (A.7) can be written as

$$\partial X/\partial r_p = \sigma_0^2 V^{-1}(R/r_0 - \imath)/(r_1 - r_0), \tag{A.24}$$

where $r_1$ and $r_0$ are means of, respectively, the special efficient portfolio 1 (see Corollary 5), and of the global minimum variance portfolio. $\sigma_0^2$ is the global minimum variance. The gradient vector of the covariance between individual assets and efficient portfolios is $\partial(VX)/\partial r$ and thus it is also monotonic. Since $r_1 > r_0$ if $r_0$ is positive, we see that as the efficient portfolio's return increases, the covariance between a given asset and the portfolio increases (is zero, or decreases) when the asset's mean return is larger (equal to, or smaller) than the return on the global minimum variance portfolio.

In contrast, the *betas* computed with efficient portfolios are *not* monotonic. In fact:

*Corollary 7.A.*   *To every individual asset, there corresponds a unique pair of orthogonal portfolios which provides the maximum and minimum betas for that asset. These portfolios have returns*

$$r = r_{z_j} \pm \sigma_0 \sigma_{z_j} \sqrt{|A|}, \tag{A.25}$$

*where $z_j$ is the efficient portfolio whose return is orthogonal to the return of asset $j$, $\sigma_0^2$ is the global minimum variance, and A is the efficient set information matrix (A.8).*

*Proof.*   The beta of any individual asset with efficient portfolio $p$ is given by

$$\beta_j = (r_j \; 1)A^{-1}(r_p \; 1)'/\sigma_p^2. \tag{A.26}$$

Differentiating with respect to $r_p$ gives a function whose zero is a quadratic equation in $r_p$. Some tedious algebra simplifies the result to (A.25). (Note that $\sigma_p^2$ is a function of $r_p$.)

To prove that the maximum and minimum beta efficient portfolios are orthogonal, simply use (A.4). Their covariance is

$$(r_z + K \; 1)A^{-1}(r_z - K \; 1)',$$

where

$$K = \sqrt{(\sigma_{z_j}^2 \sigma_0^2 |A|)}.$$

In scalar notation, this reduces to

$$(a - 2br_{z_j} + cr_{z_j}^2 - cK^2)/|A|,$$

and since

$$\sigma_{z_j}^2 \equiv (a - 2br_{z_j} + cr_{z_j}^2)/|A| = cK^2/|A|,$$

the covariance is zero.      Q.E.D.

An asset whose return is greater than the return on the minimum variance portfolio will be positively correlated with all efficient portfolios on the positive segment. This implies that its maximum-beta efficient portfolio will have return $r_{z_j} + \sigma_0 \sigma_{z_j} \sqrt{|A|}$, and its minimum-beta efficient portfolio will have return equal to the smaller root of eq. (A.25).[29]

A straightforward application of l'Hôpitals' rule to eq. (A.26) shows that every individual beta converges to zero as the efficient portfolio's return grows indefinitely large (or small). (This does not violate the fact that the weighted average beta is always one because the investment proportions grow indefinitely large in absolute value.) As an implication, the cross-sectional variance in beta is determined by the particular efficient portfolio used in the computation. When the global minimum variance portfolio is used, all betas are equal to 1.0 and their cross-sectional variance is zero. At an infinite return, all betas converge to zero and again their cross-sectional variance is zero. Naturally, there must exist an efficient portfolio whose associated betas have a maximum cross-sectional variation:

*Corollary 7.B. The maximum cross-sectional variance in beta is given by either one of the two efficient portfolios whose returns are*

$$r_p = r_0 \pm \sigma_0^2 \sqrt{|A|}, \tag{A.27}$$

*where $r_0$ and $\sigma_0^2$ are the mean and variance of the global minimum variance portfolio and A is the efficient set information matrix (A.8).*

---

[29]As an example, for the Black, Jensen, and Scholes data of table 1 in the paper, an asset with the same return as the proxy market, $r_j = 18.96$ percent, would have had a maximum beta of 1.66 and a minimum of $-0.659$ over all efficient portfolios. (Assuming that the BJS market proxy and *its* zero beta portfolio were in fact efficient.) The two efficient portfolios that would have provided these maximum and minimum betas had returns of 11.6 and 0.375 percent, respectively.

*Proof.* It is possible to prove this result directly from the definition of beta, but the algebra is tedious. A shorter proof uses the fact that all beta vectors computed for efficient portfolios are exactly linear in the mean return vector (see Corollary 6). From the linearity relation (A.19), we must have

$$\beta = (R - r_z \imath)/(r_p - r_z), \tag{A.28}$$

and the cross-sectional variance in beta is therefore

$$\text{Var}(\beta) = \text{Var}(R)/(r_p - r_z)^2. \tag{A.29}$$

The cross-sectional variance of individual returns, $\text{Var}(R)$, is a constant with respect to movements along the efficient set. Thus, $\text{Var}(\beta)$ is maximized when $|r_p - r_z|$ is minimized. From Corollary 3, we note that $r_z$ is a simple function of $r_p$ [eq. (A.15)]. The first derivative of $r_p - r_z$ with respect to $r_p$ gives a quadratic equation in $r_p$ whose solution is eq. (A.27).     Q.E.D.

It is evident that the two portfolios which satisfy eq. (A.27) lie symmetrically on oppositely-sloped segments of the efficient frontier. The elements of their two associated beta vectors must therefore be equal and of opposite sign.[30] They are also orthogonal. These are the only orthogonal efficient portfolios whose variances are equal and by Corollary 3.A, their variance is $2\sigma_0^2$.

## *The efficient set when the minimum variance is zero*

A special problem arises when the least risky portfolio has zero variance.[31] This could be caused by the existence of a riskless asset but the possibilities for its occurrence are much broader. In general, it occurs if the covariance matrix of returns is only positive *semi-definite*; that is, if there exists a vector of investment proportions $X_F$ such that $X_F' V X_F = 0$.

Since $V$ is no longer of full rank, its singularity precludes the direct calculation of the investment proportions vector. The simplest and most intuitive way to find them is to proceed in two steps as follows. First, find the efficient set parabola for the restricted group composed of all mutually non-degenerate assets. This means that any non-risky assets and one member of each pair of perfectly-correlated assets must first be discarded. A 'risky efficient set' is constructed from the remaining assets. For example, if the original $N$ assets had covariance

---

[30]Continuing the numerical example with the Black, Jensen and Scholes data (table 1), the efficient portfolios with returns 13.44 and 3.44 percent would have maximized the cross-sectional beta variance.

[31]Mathematically speaking, there is nothing to preclude several zero-variance portfolios with different mean returns. Of course rational asset pricing would preclude such an event since in the absence of restrictions on short-selling, an infinite return could be obtained without a risk.

matrix $V$ with rank $L < N$, $N-L$ rows and columns of $V$ would be discarded to obtain an $L \times L$ covariance matrix, $V_L$, with full rank. *It is obvious that all the results found previously for V when it had rank N must apply to the restricted set of L assets whose covariance matrix is* $V_L$. In particular, Theorem 1 and Corollaries 1–7 all apply to the reduced space of $L$ assets. A reduced 'risky efficient set' can be derived; the betas calculated against portfolios that lie on this 'risky efficient set' are linear in the reduced vector of mean returns. The minimum variance among portfolios of the $L$ assets is $1/\iota' V_L^{-1} \iota$; and so on.

This implies:

*Theorem 2. Let an efficient set be computed from the L assets whose covariance matrix is non-singular. Then the global efficient set is composed of*

$$\alpha X_L = \alpha \sigma_0^2 V_L^{-1}[(R_L - r_F \iota)/(r_0 - r_F)], \tag{A.30}$$

*as investment proportions in the L assets and* $1 - \alpha\iota' X_L$ *in the zero-variance asset F. The scalar α is positive for efficient portfolios on the positive (negative) segment if* $r_F$ *is less (greater) than the return* $r_0$ *on the minimum variance portfolio of the L assets.* $\sigma_0^2$ *is this minimum variance.*

*Proof.* Since the global minimum variance is zero, the efficient set is composed of line segments in the mean-standard deviation space. This means that there is some tangent to the reduced ($L$ asset) mean-standard deviation efficient set which passes through $r_F$ and gives the global efficient set. From Corollary 3.A, we see that the return at the tangency point must be the solution to

$$r_F = (br_\tau - a)/(cr_\tau - b),$$

where $a$, $b$, and $c$ are the three 'efficient set constants' for the $L$ assets only. This equation is reversible, which implies

$$r_\tau = (br_F - a)/(cr_F - b).$$

Substituting $r_\tau$ in (A.7) gives the $X_L$ investment proportions vector used in (A.30).

The last part of the theorem is established by noting that

$$r_F - r_\tau = (a - 2br_F + cr_F^2)/(cr_F - b).$$

The numerator is positive since $|A_L| = ac - b^2 > 0$.

Thus $r_\tau \gtreqless r_F$ implies $r_F \lesseqgtr b/c = r_0$.      Q.E.D.

An alternative proof proceeds directly from the variance of the reduced set of efficient portfolios. In other words, we can find the minimum with respect to $r_p$ of

$$\alpha^2 \sigma_p^2,$$

subject to

$$r = \alpha r_p + (1-\alpha) r_F.$$

Using the efficient set variance formula for $\sigma_p^2$, the first derivative of $\alpha^2 \sigma_p^2$ is zero when

$$(r_p - r_F)(cr_p - b) - (a - 2br_p + cr_p^2) = 0,$$

and this reduces to

$$r_p = (br_F - a)/(cr_F - b).$$

*Corollary.* When $V$ is singular, all positive-variance efficient portfolios are perfectly correlated.

*Proof.* Theorem 2 shows that the vector $\alpha X_L$ of investments in the reduced $L$ asset space is proportional for all positive variance efficient portfolios. The remaining investment, $1 - \alpha \iota' X_L$, is placed in a zero-variance asset. Thus, the returns on all efficient portfolios are exactly linearly related.    Q.E.D.

*Qualitative results for investment proportions vectors*

The sign pattern of the investment proportions vector of an efficient portfolio is an important datum in several contexts. For example, the interdiction of short-selling would leave a region of the efficient frontier unchanged if and only if that region were characterized by totally non-negative investment proportions, $X \geqq 0$.

Perhaps more importantly, there may exist no efficient vector such that $X > 0$. This means that *no* efficient portfolio has positive investments in all individual assets; which would imply, in turn, that the 'market' portfolio (composed of all assets) could not be efficient. If the reader thinks there must be *some* efficient portfolio whose $X$ vector is positive, the counter-example in the footnote is offered.[32] There seems to be no necessary economic reason to con-

---

[32]Let three assets have mean return vector and covariance matrix,

$$R' = (1\ 2\ 3) \quad \text{and} \quad V = \begin{pmatrix} 2 & 2 & 2 \\ 2 & 5 & 6 \\ 2 & 6 & 10 \end{pmatrix}.$$

Using eq. (A.7), it can be verified readily that every efficient portfolio contains a *zero* investment in the second asset.

sider such examples pathological. In particular, the argument that such mean (anticipated) returns must be out of equilibrium presupposes that investors regard mean-variance efficiency as optimal.

When the global minimum variance is zero, the entire efficient set is composed of linear combinations of $X_F$ and $X_L$ (see Theorem 2 above). Suppose that $F$ is a single riskless individual asset. Then we can restrict our attention to $X_L \gtrless 0$. When the global minimum variance is positive, things are slightly more complicated because a totally positive vector $X$ might occur anywhere within the range $[r_{\max}, r_{\min}]$, i.e., between the maximum and minimum individual asset returns.

A beginning to this problem is suggested by the following:

*Theorem 3 [Debreu–Herstein (1953)]. Suppose the covariance matrix is non-negative. Then if the global minimum variance portfolio has totally positive investment proportions, the variance of every individual asset is larger than each of its associated covariances.*

*Proof.* Suppose we put $V^{-1} = sI - Q$. Where $I$ is the $(N \times N)$ identity matrix and $Q > 0$. Debreu and Herstein showed that $V \geq 0$ if and only if $s$ is larger than the largest eigenvalue of $Q$. This implies that in the matrix $sI - Q$, all diagonal elements are positive and all off-diagonal elements are negative. Furthermore, they also showed (p. 603), that if the sum of every row of $sI - Q$. is positive, and if $d_{ij}$ is the cofactor of its $i$th row and $j$th column, then $d_{ii} > d_{ij}$ for all $i \neq j$ [see also Quirk and Saposnik (1968, pp. 210–211)].          Q.E.D.

This result can be interpreted as follows. The weights $X_0$ of the global minimum variance portfolio are proportional to the sums of the rows of $V^{-1}$ [see (A.14)]. Thus a necessary condition for $X_0 > 0$ is that each of $V$'s diagonal elements exceeds every off-diagonal element in the same row. Heuristically, such a condition implies weak correlation among every pair of assets. For any pair, say $i$ and $j$, we must have not only $\sigma_i^2 \sigma_j^2 > \sigma_{ij}^2$ (which is always satisfied when $V$ is non-singular), but also $\sigma_i^2 > \sigma_{ij}$ and $\sigma_j^2 > \sigma_{ij}$. The minimal variance formed by every combination of two assets must be associated with a positive investment in both assets. Viewed geometrically, the locus of portfolios formed from every pair of assets is bowed outward toward the return axis *between* them. It seems likely that this result can be generalized to the case when $V$ contains some negative covariances but I have not been able to find a proof.

Since the global minimum variance portfolio has strictly positive proportions in this case, by Corollary 7 above there must be a finite range of efficient portfolios with strictly positive investment proportions in its neighborhood.

In fact, every efficient portfolio, whose return $r_p$ satisfies

$$(R \ \iota) A^{-1} \binom{r_p}{1} > 0,$$

has a totally positive investment proportions vector [cf. Debreu and Herstein (1953, p. 601)]. This condition is equivalent to

$$(R - r_z i)(r_p - r_0) > 0,$$

where $r_z$ is $p$'s orthogonal portfolio and 0 is the global minimum variance portfolio. From the geometry Corollary 3.A, it is easy to see that $(R - r_z i)(r_p - r_0)$ is strictly positive for some $r_p$ in $r_{min} \leq r_p \leq r_{max}$. Since in the present case the global minimum variance portfolio is totally positive, $r_{min} < r_0 < r_{max}$, and there is a finite range where the vector is positive. If the covariance matrix satisfies the conditions of Theorem 3, we must have the following bounds on orthogonal portfolios association with $r_{max}$ and $r_{min}$:

$$r_{z_{max}} \geq r_{min} \quad \text{and} \quad r_{z_{min}} \leq r_{max}.$$

Unfortunately, this result does not constitute a necessary condition for the existence of *some* totally positive efficient proportions vector. Examples are easy to construct where the global minimum variance portfolio has negative investment proportions but where another efficient portfolio is totally positive. Typically, this would occur when $r_0$ is outside the range $[r_{max}, r_{min}]$ and when there are relatively strong positive correlations among individual assets. In other words, when there are certain assets whose variances are inferior to some of their associated covariances. It is only for sufficiently strong correlations that $X$ becomes non-positive everywhere (as in the example of footnote 32).

## References

Black, F., 1972, Capital market equilibrium with restricted borrowing, Journal of Business 45, 444–454.

Black, F., M.C. Jensen and M. Scholes, 1972, The capital asset pricing model: Some empirical tests, in: M.C. Jensen, ed., Studies in the theory of capital markets (Praeger, New York).

Blume, M.E. and I. Friend, 1973, A new look at the capital asset pricing model, Journal of Finance 28, 19–34.

Cass, D. and J.G. Stiglitz, 1970, The structure of investor preference and asset returns, and separability in portfolio allocation: A contribution to the pure theory of mutual funds, Journal of Economic Theory 2, 122–160.

Debreu, G. and I.N. Herstein, 1953, Non-negative square matrices, Econometrica 21, 597–607.

Fama, E.F., 1976, Foundations of finance (Basic Books, New York).

Fama, E.F. and J.D. MacBeth, 1973, Risk, return and equilibrium: Empirical tests, Journal of Political Economy 81, 607–636.

Fama, E.F. and J.D. MacBeth, 1974a, Long-term growth in a short-term market, Journal of Finance 39, 857–885.

Fama, E.F. and J.D. MacBeth, 1974b, Tests of the multi-period two-parameter model, Journal of Financial Economics 1, 43–66.

Fisher, L., 1966, Some new stock market indices, Journal of Business 23, 191–225.

Friend, I. and M. Blume, 1970, Measurement of portfolio performance under uncertainty, American Economic Review 60, 561–575.

Hakansson, N.H., 1969, Risk disposition and the separation property in portfolio selection, Journal of Financial and Quantitative Analysis 4, 401–416.

Jacob, N., 1970, The measurement of market similarity for securities under uncertainty, Journal of Business 43, 328–340.

Jensen, M.C., 1972a, Capital markets: Theory and evidence, Bell Journal of Economics and Management Science 3, 357–398.

Jensen, M.C., 1972b, The foundations and current state of capital market theory, in: M.C. Jensen, ed., Studies in the theory of capital markets (Praeger, New York).

Lintner, J., 1965, The valuation of risk assets and the selection of risky investments in stock portfolios and capital budgets, Review of Economics and Statistics 47, 13–47.

Lintner, J., 1969, The aggregation of investor's diverse judgements and preferences in purely competitive security markets, Journal of Financial and Quantitative Analysis 4, 347–400.

Long, J.B., 1976, Mean-variance efficiency and portfolio choice in the context of differential taxation of dividends and capital gains, unpublished manuscript (Graduate School of Management, University of Rochester, NY).

Lorie, J.F. and R. Brealey, 1972, Modern developments in investment management (Praeger, New York).

Mayers, D., 1973, Nonmarketable assets and the determination of capital asset prices in the absence of a riskless asset, Journal of Business 46, 258–267.

Merton, R.C., 1972, An analytic derivation of the efficient portfolio frontier, Journal of Financial and Quantitative Analysis 7, 1851–1872.

Merton, R.C., 1973, An inter-temporal capital asset pricing model, Econometrica 41, 867–887.

Miller, M.H. and M. Scholes, 1972, Rates of return in relation to risk: A re-examination of some recent findings, in: M.C. Jensen, ed., Studies in the theory of capital markets (Praeger, New York).

Modigliani, F., G. Pogue, M. Scholes and B. Solnik, 1972, Efficiency of European capital markets and comparison with the American market, Proceedings of the First International Conference on Stock Exchanges, CISMEC.

Morgan, I.G., 1975, Prediction of return with the minimum variance zero-beta portfolio, Journal of Financial Economics 2, 361–376.

Palacios, J., 1973, The stock market in Spain: Tests of efficiency and capital market theory, unpublished dissertation (Stanford University, CA).

Petit, R.R. and R. Westerfield, 1974, Using the capital asset pricing model and the market model to predict security returns, Journal of Financial and Quantitative Analysis 9, 579–605.

Pirsig, R.M., 1974, Zen and the art of motorcycle maintenance (William Morrow, New York).

Quirk, J. and R. Saposnik, 1968, Introduction to general equilibrium theory and welfare economics (McGraw-Hill, New York).

Roll, R., 1973, Evidence on the 'growth–optimum' model, Journal of Finance 28, 551–566.

Roll, R. and B.S. Solnik, 1975, A pure foreign exchange asset pricing model, Journal of International Economics (forthcoming).

Rosa, J.J., 1975, Rentabilité, risque et equilibre à la bourse de Paris, Working Paper 7508 (Institut Orléanais de Finance).

Ross, S.A., 1972, The arbitrage theory of capital asset pricing, Working Paper 2–73 (Rodney L. White Center for Financial Research, University of Pennsylvania, Philadelphia, PA), forthcoming in Econometrica.

Ross, S.A., 1973, Return, risk and arbitrage, Working Paper 17–73a (Rodney L. White Center for Financial Research, University of Pennsylvania, Philadelphia, PA).

Ross, S.A., 1976, Mutual fund separation in financial theory – The separating distributions, Working Paper 1–76 (Rodney L. White Center for Financial Research, University of Pennsylvania, Philadelphia, PA).

Ross, S.A., forthcoming, A note on the capital asset pricing model (CAPM), short-selling restrictions, and related issues, Journal of Finance.

Sharpe, W.F., 1964, Capital asset prices: A theory of market equilibrium under conditions of risk, Journal of Finance 19, 425–442.

Sharpe, W.F., 1970, Portfolio theory and capital markets, (McGraw-Hill, New York).

Szegö, G.P., 1975, Nuovi risultati analitici nella teoria della selezione del portafoglio (C.N.R., Comitato Scienze Economiche, Sociologiche e Statistiche).

# A TEST OF THE EFFICIENCY OF A GIVEN PORTFOLIO

By Michael R. Gibbons, Stephen A. Ross, and Jay Shanken[1]

A test for the ex ante efficiency of a given portfolio of assets is analyzed. The relevant statistic has a tractable small sample distribution. Its power function is derived and used to study the sensitivity of the test to the portfolio choice and to the number of assets used to determine the ex post mean-variance efficient frontier.

Several intuitive interpretations of the test are provided, including a simple mean-standard deviation geometric explanation. A univariate test, equivalent to our multivariate-based method, is derived, and it suggests some useful diagnostic tools which may explain why the null hypothesis is rejected.

Empirical examples suggest that the multivariate approach can lead to more appropriate conclusions than those based on traditional inference which relies on a set of dependent univariate statistics.

Keywords: Asset pricing, CAPM, multivariate test, portfolio efficiency.

## 1. INTRODUCTION

The modern theory of finance has always been rooted in empirical analysis. The mean-variance capital asset pricing model (CAPM) developed by Sharpe (1964) and Lintner (1965) has been studied and tested in more papers than can possibly be attributed here. This is only natural; the quality and quantity of financial data, especially stock market price series, are the envy of other fields in economics.

The theory is generally expressed in terms of its first-order conditions on the risk premium. Expected returns on assets are linearly related to the regression coefficients, or betas, of the asset returns on some index of market returns. In other words, risk premiums in equilibrium depend on betas. The standard tests of the CAPM are based on regression techniques with various adaptations. For some notable examples, see Black, Jensen, and Scholes (1972) and Fama and MacBeth (1973). Usually, cross-sectional regressions are run of asset returns on estimated beta coefficients, and estimates of the slope are reported. Often the data are grouped to reduce measurement errors, and sometimes the estimation is done at a sequence of time points to create a time series of estimates from which the precision of the overall average can be determined.

Roll (1977, 1978), among others, has raised serious doubts whether these procedures are, in fact, tests of the CAPM. Insofar as proxies are used for the market portfolio, the Sharpe-Lintner theory is not being tested. Furthermore, as Roll emphasizes, the regression tests are probably of quite low power, and

[1] We are grateful to Ted Anderson, Fischer Black, Douglas Breeden, Michael Brennan, Gary Chamberlain, Dave Jobson, Allan Kleidon, Bruce Lehmann, Paul Pfleiderer, Richard Roll, and two anonymous referees as well as the seminar participants at Duke University, Harvard University, Indiana University, Stanford University, University of California at San Diego, University of Illinois at Urbana, and Yale University for helpful comments. We appreciate the research assistance of Ajay Dravid, Jung-Jin Lee, and Tong-sheng Sun. Financial support was provided in part by the National Science Foundation and the Stanford Program in Finance. This paper supersedes an earlier paper with the same title by Stephen Ross.

grouping may lower the power further. These objections leave the empirical testing of the CAPM in an odd state of limbo. If the proxy is not a valid surrogate, then as tests of the CAPM the existing empirical investigations are somewhat beside the point.[2] On the other hand, if the proxy is valid, then the small sample distribution and power of the tests are unknown.

This is unfortunate and indicative of a missed opportunity. The CAPM is one of many financial theories which suggest quite specific hypotheses couched in terms of observables. The rich data available for testing these hypotheses are an incentive to develop tests which are explicitly directed at them. In this paper we develop a canonical example of such a test using multivariate statistical methods. The problem we consider is the central one addressed in tests of the CAPM. Since the theory is equivalent to the assertion that the market portfolio is mean-variance efficient, we wish to test whether any particular portfolio is ex ante mean-variance efficient.

While the paper is organized into seven sections, it also can be viewed as consisting of three parts. The first part (Sections 2 through 4) considers a multivariate statistic for testing mean-variance efficiency and examines the properties of such a test. The second part (Sections 5 and 6) studies the relation between this multivariate test and alternative approaches based on a set of univariate statistics. The third part (Sections 7 and 8) concludes the paper by extending the framework to related hypotheses and providing suggestions for future research. A more detailed summary of each section follows.

In Section 2 we recall a necessary condition for the efficiency of some portfolio. We use this implication as a null hypothesis that can be tested using a statistic which has a tractable finite sample distribution under both the null and alternate hypotheses. In addition, we relate this statistic to three alternative approaches which are based on asymptotic approximations. In the third section the multivariate test is given a geometric interpretation in the mean-standard deviation space of portfolio theory. The method and geometry are then applied to a data set from one of the classic empirical papers in modern finance; we reaffirm and complement the findings of Black, Jensen, and Scholes (1972). The fourth section turns to issues relating to the power of the test. Here we consider the sensitivity of the test to the choice of the portfolio which is examined for efficiency and the effect of the number of assets used to determine the ex post efficient frontier. A new data base is analyzed in this section, and we demonstrate that one's conclusions regarding the efficiency of a given index can be altered by the type of assets used to construct the ex post frontier.

The fifth section attempts to contrast actual empirical results when the multivariate method is used versus informal inference based on a set of dependent univariate statistics. Here we provide examples where the multivariate test rejects even though none of the univariate statistics seem to be significant. We also have

---

[2] Recent work by Kandel and Stambaugh (1987) and Shanken (1987b) do consider tests of the CAPM conditional on an assumption about the correlation between the proxy and the true market portfolio.

the reverse situation where there are a seemingly large number of "significant" univariate statistics; yet, the multivariate test fails to reject at the traditional levels of significance. In this section we also introduce another data set which allows us to re-examine the size-effect anomaly. Section 6 develops an alternative interpretation of the multivariate test. The statistic is equivalent to the usual calculation for a $t$ statistic on an intercept term in a *univariate* simple regression model, with the ex post efficient portfolio used as the dependent variable and the portfolio whose ex ante efficiency is under examination as the explanatory variable. This section also develops some useful diagnostics for explaining why the null hypothesis may not be consistent with the data. Most of the empirical work in this section focuses on the size effect only in the month of January.

Section 7 extends the analysis to a case where one wishes to investigate the potential efficiency of some linear combination of a set of portfolios, where the weights in the combination are not specified. This turns out to be a minor adaptation of the work in Section 2.

## 2. TEST STATISTIC FOR JUDGING THE EFFICIENCY OF A GIVEN PORTFOLIO

We assume throughout that there is a given riskless rate of interest, $R_{ft}$, for each time period. Excess returns are computed by subtracting $R_{ft}$ from the total rates of return. Consider the following multivariate linear regression:

$$(1) \qquad \tilde{r}_{it} = \alpha_{ip} + \beta_{ip}\tilde{r}_{pt} + \tilde{\varepsilon}_{it} \qquad \forall i = 1, \dots, N,$$

where $\tilde{r}_{it} \equiv$ the excess return on asset $i$ in period $t$; $\tilde{r}_{pt} \equiv$ the excess return on the portfolio whose efficiency is being tested; and $\tilde{\varepsilon}_{it} \equiv$ the disturbance term for asset $i$ in period $t$. The disturbances are assumed to be jointly normally distributed each period with mean zero and nonsingular covariance matrix $\Sigma$, conditional on the excess returns for portfolio $p$. We also assume independence of the disturbances over time. In order that $\Sigma$ be nonsingular, $\tilde{r}_{pt}$ and the $N$ left-hand side assets must be linearly independent.

If a particular portfolio is mean-variance efficient (i.e., it minimizes variance for a given level of expected return), then the following first-order condition must be satisfied for the given $N$ assets:

$$(2) \qquad \mathscr{E}(\tilde{r}_{it}) = \beta_{ip}\mathscr{E}(\tilde{r}_{pt}).$$

Thus, combining the first-order condition in (2) with the distributional assumption given by (1) yields the following parameter restriction, which is stated in the form of a null hypothesis:

$$(3) \qquad H_0: \alpha_{ip} = 0, \qquad \forall i = 1, \dots, N.$$

Testing the above null hypothesis is essentially the same proposal as in the work by Black, Jensen, and Scholes (1972), except that they replace $\tilde{r}_{pt}$ by a portfolio which they call the market portfolio and refer to their test as a test of the CAPM. In addition, they do not report the joint significance of the estimated values for $\alpha_{ip}$ across all $N$ equations; instead, they report $N$ univariate $t$ statistics based on each equation.

Given the normality assumption, the null hypothesis in (3) can be tested using "Hotelling's $T^2$ test," a multivariate generalization of the univariate $t$-test (e.g., see Malinvaud (1980, page 230)). A brief derivation of the equivalent $F$ test is included for completeness and as a means of introducing some notation that will be needed later. If we estimate the multivariate system of (1) using ordinary least squares for each individual equation, the estimated intercepts have a multivariate normal distribution, conditional on $r_{pt}$ ($\forall t = 1, \ldots, T$), with

$$(4) \qquad \sqrt{T/\left(1 + \hat{\theta}_p^2\right)} \, \hat{\alpha}_p \sim N\left\{ \sqrt{T/\left(1 + \hat{\theta}_p^2\right)} \, \alpha_p; \Sigma \right\},$$

where $T \equiv$ number of time series observations on returns; $\hat{\alpha}_p' \equiv (\hat{\alpha}_{1p} \hat{\alpha}_{2p} \ldots \hat{\alpha}_{Np})$; $\hat{\theta}_p \equiv \bar{r}_p / s_p$; $\bar{r}_p \equiv$ sample mean of $\tilde{r}_{pt}$; and $s_p^2 \equiv$ sample variance of $\tilde{r}_{pt}$ without an adjustment for degrees of freedom. Furthermore, $\hat{\alpha}_p$ and $\hat{\Sigma}$ are independent with $(T-2)\hat{\Sigma}$ having a Wishart distribution with parameters $(T-2)$ and $\Sigma$. These facts imply (see Morrison (1976, page 131)) that $(T(T-N-1)/N(T-2))W_u$ has a noncentral $F$ distribution with degrees of freedom $N$ and $(T-N-1)$, where

$$(5) \qquad W_u \equiv \hat{\alpha}_p' \hat{\Sigma}^{-1} \hat{\alpha}_p / \left(1 + \hat{\theta}_p^2\right)$$

and $\hat{\Sigma} \equiv$ unbiased residual covariance matrix.[3] (The corresponding statistic based on the maximum likelihood estimate of $\Sigma$ will be denoted as $W$.) The noncentrality parameter, $\lambda$, is given by

$$(6) \qquad \lambda \equiv \left[ T/\left(1 + \hat{\theta}_p^2\right) \right] \alpha_p' \Sigma^{-1} \alpha_p.$$

Under the null hypothesis that $\alpha_p$ equals zero, $\lambda = 0$, and we have a central $F$ distribution. More generally, the distribution under the alternative provides a way to study the power of the test; more will be said about this in a later section. It is also interesting to note that under the null hypothesis the $W_u$ statistic has a central $F$ distribution unconditionally, for the parameters of this central $F$ do not depend on $\tilde{r}_{pt}$ in any way. However, we do not know the unconditional distribution of $\hat{\alpha}_p$ or $W_u$ under the alternate, for the conditional distribution depends on the sample values of $\tilde{r}_{pt}$ through $\hat{\theta}_p^2$.

Generally, the normality assumption has been viewed as providing a "good working approximation" to the distribution of monthly stock returns (see Fama (1976, Chapter 1) for a summary of the relevant empirical work). There is some evidence, however, that the true distributions are slightly leptokurtic relative to the normal distribution. While departures from normality of the disturbances in (1) will affect the small-sample distribution of the test statistic, simulation evidence by MacKinlay (1985) suggests that the $F$ test is fairly robust to such misspecifications.[4] This is important, since the application of standard asymptotic tests to the efficiency problem can result in faulty inferences, given the sample sizes often used in financial empirical work.

---

[3] We assume that $N$ is less than or equal to $T - 2$ so that $\hat{\Sigma}$ is nonsingular.

[4] Tests for normality of the residuals of the size and industry portfolios, which are used below, do reveal excess kurtosis and some skewness as well. These results are available on request to the authors.

TABLE 1

A COMPARISON OF FOUR ASYMPTOTICALLY EQUIVALENT TESTS OF EX ANTE EFFICIENCY OF A
GIVEN PORTFOLIO. THE $W$ STATISTIC IS DISTRIBUTED AS A TRANSFORM OF A CENTRAL $F$
DISTRIBUTION IN FINITE SAMPLES. THE WALD TEST, THE LIKELIHOOD RATIO TEST (LRT),
AND THE LAGRANGE MULTIPLIER TEST (LMT) ARE MONOTONE TRANSFORMS OF $W$, AND
EACH IS DISTRIBUTED AS CHI-SQUARE WITH $N$ DEGREES OF FREEDOM AS $T$ APPROACHES
INFINITY.

| $N$ | $T$ | $P$-Value Using Exact Distribution of $W$ | $P$-Values Using Asymptotic Approximations | | |
|---|---|---|---|---|---|
| | | | Wald | LRT | LMT |
| 10 | 60 | .05 | .008 | .027 | .071 |
| 20 | 60 | .05 | .000 | .007 | .094 |
| 40 | 60 | .05 | .000 | .000 | .173 |
| 58 | 60 | .05 | .000 | .000 | .403 |
| 10 | 120 | .05 | .023 | .038 | .060 |
| 20 | 120 | .05 | .005 | .023 | .070 |
| 40 | 120 | .05 | .000 | .003 | .094 |
| 58 | 120 | .05 | .000 | .000 | .122 |
| 118 | 120 | .05 | .000 | .000 | .431 |
| 10 | 240 | .05 | .035 | .044 | .055 |
| 20 | 240 | .05 | .109 | .035 | .059 |
| 40 | 240 | .05 | .003 | .017 | .069 |
| 58 | 240 | .05 | .000 | .006 | .079 |
| 118 | 240 | .05 | .000 | .000 | .123 |
| 238 | 240 | .05 | .000 | .000 | .451 |
| 10 | 60 | .10 | .025 | .061 | .122 |
| 20 | 60 | .10 | .000 | .019 | .146 |
| 40 | 60 | .10 | .000 | .000 | .216 |
| 58 | 60 | .10 | .000 | .000 | .404 |
| 10 | 120 | .10 | .056 | .081 | .111 |
| 20 | 120 | .10 | .017 | .053 | .122 |
| 40 | 120 | .10 | .000 | .010 | .147 |
| 58 | 120 | .10 | .000 | .000 | .175 |
| 118 | 120 | .10 | .000 | .000 | .432 |
| 10 | 240 | .10 | .076 | .090 | .106 |
| 20 | 240 | .10 | .048 | .075 | .111 |
| 40 | 240 | .10 | .009 | .041 | .122 |
| 58 | 240 | .10 | .001 | .018 | .133 |
| 118 | 240 | .10 | .000 | .000 | .178 |
| 238 | 240 | .10 | .000 | .000 | .452 |

Note: $N$ is the number of assets used together with portfolio $p$ to construct the ex post frontier, and $T$ is the
number of time series observations.

Table I illustrates this problem for the Wald, likelihood ratio, and Lagrange
multiplier tests, each of which is asymptotically distributed as chi-square with $N$
degrees of freedom as $T \rightarrow \infty$.[5] Since the small-sample distribution of $W$ is
known (assuming normality), the implied realization of $W$ can be inferred from
the information in the first three columns of Table I (i.e., $N$, $T$, and the
hypothetical $p$-value). The implied asymptotic $p$-values given in the last three

[5] Jobson and Korkie (1982) also discuss these three tests using a simulation. They approximate the
distribution of the likelihood ratio test with an $F$ distribution based on Rao's (1951) work. In their
1985 paper they recognize that a small sample distribution is available under the null hypothesis.

columns are then obtained using the fact that each test statistic is a monotonic function of $W$.[6]

Consistent with the results of Berndt and Savin (1977), the $p$-values are always lowest for the Wald test and highest for the Lagrange multiplier test with the likelihood ratio test in between. Clearly, the asymptotic approximation becomes worse as the number of assets, $N$, approaches the number of time series observations, $T$. Shanken (1985) reaches similar conclusions based on an approximation when the riskless asset is not observable.

### 3. A GEOMETRIC INTERPRETATION OF THE TEST STATISTIC, $W$

So far, the primary motivation for the $W$ statistic has been its well-known distributional properties. For rigorous statistical inference such results are an absolute necessity. Just as important, though, is the development of a measure which allows one to examine the economic significance of departures from the null hypothesis. Fortunately, our test has a nice geometric interpretation.

It is shown in the Appendix that:

$$(7) \qquad W = \left[ \frac{\sqrt{1 + \hat{\theta}^{*2}}}{\sqrt{1 + \hat{\theta}_p^2}} \right]^2 - 1 \equiv \psi^2 - 1,$$

where $\hat{\theta}^*$ is the ex post price of risk (i.e., the maximum excess sample mean return per unit of sample standard deviation) and $\hat{\theta}_p$ is the ratio of ex post average excess return on portfolio $p$ to its standard deviation (i.e., $\hat{\theta}_p \equiv \bar{r}_p/s_p$). Note that $\psi$ cannot be less than one since $\hat{\theta}^*$ is the slope of the ex post frontier based on all assets used in the test (including portfolio $p$).

The curve in Figure 1a represents the (ex post) minimum-variance frontier of the risky assets. When a riskless investment is available, the frontier is a straight line emanating from the origin and tangent to the curve at $m$. $\hat{\theta}^*$ is the slope of the tangent line whereas $\hat{\theta}_p$ is the slope of the line through $p$.

An examination of (7) suggests that $\psi^2$ should be close to one under the null hypothesis. When $\hat{\theta}^*$ is sufficiently greater than $\hat{\theta}_p$, the return per unit of risk for portfolio $p$ is much lower than the ex post frontier tradeoff, and we will reject the hypothesis that portfolio $p$ is ex ante mean-variance efficient. In Figure 1a $\psi$ is just the distance along the ex post frontier up to any given risk level, $\sigma$, divided by the similar distance along the line from the origin through $p$.

The reader may wonder why the test is based on the square of the slopes as opposed to the actual slopes. The reason is straightforward. Our null hypothesis only represents a necessary condition for ex ante efficiency. This condition is satisfied even if portfolio $p$ is on the negative sloping portion of the minimum-variance frontier for all assets (including the risk-free security). Thus, only the

---

[6] The relations are $LRT = T \ln(1 + W)$ and $LMT = TW/(1 + W)$. Shanken (1985) has discussed this result for the case where the riskless asset does not exist. A proof of the result in the case where the riskless asset does exist is available upon request to the authors. Berndt and Savin (1977) discuss similar relationships among alternative asymptotic tests in a more general setting.

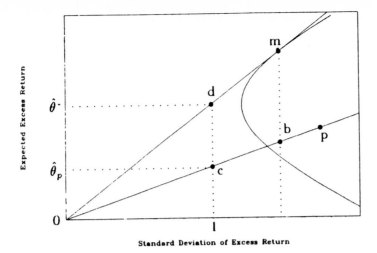

1a.) Geometric intuition for W. Note the distance Oc
     is $\sqrt{1 + \hat{\theta}_p^2}$, and the distance Od is $\sqrt{1 + \hat{\theta}^{*2}}$.

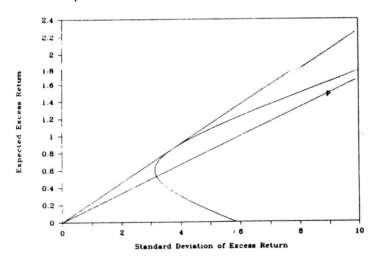

1b.) *Ex post* efficient frontier based on 10 beta-sorted
     portfolios and the CRSP Equal-Weighted Index
     using monthly data, 1931-1965. Point p repre-
     sents the CRSP Equal-Weighted Index.

FIGURE 1.—Various plots of ex post mean variance efficient frontiers.

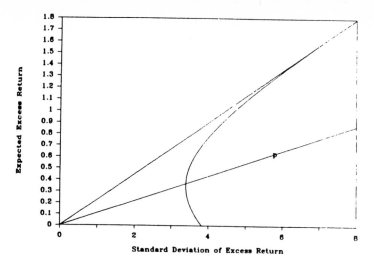

1c.) *Ex post* efficient frontier based on 12 industry portfolios and the CRSP Value-Weighted Index using monthly data, 1926-1982. Point p represents the CRSP Value-Weighted Index.

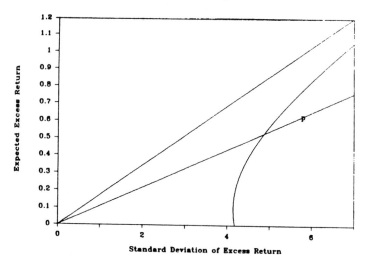

1d.) *Ex post* efficient frontier based on 10 size-sorted portfolios and the CRSP Value-Weighted Index using monthly data, 1926-1982. Point p represents the CRSP Value-Weighted Index.

FIGURE 1.—Continued.

TABLE II

SUMMARY STATISTICS ON BETA-SORTED PORTFOLIOS BASED ON MONTHLY DATA, 1931–65
($T = 420$). ALL SIMPLE EXCESS RETURNS ARE NOMINAL AND IN PERCENTAGE FORM, AND THE
CRSP EQUAL-WEIGHTED INDEX IS PORTFOLIO $p$. THE FOLLOWING PARAMETER ESTIMATES
ARE FOR THE REGRESSION MODEL: $\tilde{r}_{it} = \alpha_{ip} + \beta_{ip}\tilde{r}_{pt} + \tilde{\varepsilon}_{it}$ $\forall i = 1,\ldots,10$ AND $\forall t = 1,\ldots,420$,
WHERE $R_i^2$ IS THE COEFFICIENT OF DETERMINATION FOR EQUATION $i$.

| Portfolio Number | $\hat{\alpha}_{ip}$ | $s(\hat{\alpha}_{ip})$ | $\hat{\beta}_{ip}$ | $s(\hat{\beta}_{ip})$ | $R_i^2$ |
|---|---|---|---|---|---|
| 1 | −0.19 | 0.17 | 1.54 | 0.02 | 0.94 |
| 2 | −0.19 | 0.10 | 1.37 | 0.01 | 0.97 |
| 3 | −0.06 | 0.09 | 1.24 | 0.01 | 0.98 |
| 4 | −0.09 | 0.07 | 1.17 | 0.01 | 0.98 |
| 5 | −0.06 | 0.07 | 1.06 | 0.01 | 0.98 |
| 6 | 0.05 | 0.07 | 0.92 | 0.01 | 0.97 |
| 7 | 0.03 | 0.07 | 0.86 | 0.01 | 0.97 |
| 8 | 0.12 | 0.07 | 0.74 | 0.01 | 0.96 |
| 9 | 0.14 | 0.08 | 0.63 | 0.01 | 0.92 |
| 10 | 0.22 | 0.09 | 0.51 | 0.01 | 0.85 |

NOTE: For this sample period $\hat{\theta}_p$ and $\hat{\theta}^*$ are 0.166 and 0.227, respectively. These imply a value for $W_u$ equal to 0.023, which has a $p$-value of 0.476. Under the hypothesis that the CRSP Equal-Weighted Index is efficient, $\mathcal{E}(W_u)$ is 0.024 and $SD(W_u)$ is 0.011.

absolute value of the slope is relevant for our null hypothesis, and our test is then based on the squared values.

Figure 1b is based on a data set that is very similar to the one used by Black, Jensen, and Scholes (1972) (hereafter, BJS).[7] Using monthly returns on 10 beta-sorted portfolios from January, 1931 through December, 1965, $\hat{\theta}^* = 0.227$ while the CRSP Equal-Weighted Index, which is portfolio $p$, has $\hat{\theta}_p = 0.166$. To judge whether these two slopes are statistically different, we can calculate ($\psi^2 - 1$), which is 0.02333. Based on the results in Section 2, we can use a central $F$ distribution with degrees of freedom 10 and 409 to judge the statistical significance of this difference in slopes. The resulting $F$ statistic is 0.96, which has a $p$-value of 0.48. Our multivariate test confirms the conclusion reached by BJS for their overall time period in that the ex ante efficiency of the CRSP Equal-Weighted Index cannot be rejected; equivalently, if this Index is taken as the true market portfolio, then the Sharpe-Lintner version of the CAPM cannot be rejected. Table II provides some summary statistics on the beta-sorted portfolios that were used for Figure 1b. Table II, when compared with Table II in BJS, verifies that our data base is very similar to the one used by BJS.

BJS provide various scatter plots of average returns versus estimated betas to judge the fit of the data to the expected linear relation if the CRSP Equal-Weighted

---

[7] While BJS relied on the data from the Center for Research in Security Prices (hereafter, CRSP) at the University of Chicago, it is not possible to replicate their data. The CRSP tapes are continually revised to reflect data errors, and one would need the same version of the CRSP file to perfectly duplicate a data base. For example, we were able to find more firms per year than reported in Table 1 of BJS because of corrections to the data base. Also we relied on Ibbotson and Sinquefield (1979) for the return of US Treasury Bills as the riskless rate. This latter data base was not used by BJS. However, we followed the grouping procedure outlined in BJS in forming the 10 portfolios that were used in constructing Figure 1 and Table II.

Index is efficient. We view figures like our Figure 1b as complementary to these scatter plots, for they summarize the multivariate test in a manner familiar to financial economists. The advantage of the scatter plots in BJS is that they may provide some information as to which asset or which set of assets is least consistent with the hypothesis that the index is efficient; figures like Figure 1b really do not provide such information. On the other hand, the scatter plots in BJS can be difficult to interpret due to heteroscedasticity across the different portfolios as well as contemporaneous cross-sectional dependence. Section 6 will suggest some other types of diagnostic information based on the multivariate framework.

To understand further the behavior of our measure of efficiency, $\psi^2$, its small sample distribution given in Section 2 is helpful. Since a linear transform of $\psi^2$ has a central $F$ distribution with degrees of freedom $N$ and $(T - N - 1)$, we can use the first two moments of the central $F$ to calculate:

$$(8) \qquad \mathscr{E}(\psi^2 - 1) = \left[ \frac{N}{T - N - 3} \right]$$

and

$$(9) \qquad SD(\psi^2 - 1) = \left[ \frac{1}{T - N - 3} \right] \sqrt{\frac{2N(T - 3)}{T - N - 5}} \, .$$

The first moment for $\psi^2$ only exists if $T > N + 3$ while the second moment for $\psi^2$ only exists if $T > N + 5$. These last two equations for the moments can be applied to the BJS data set for 1931–1965 where $N = 10$ and $T = 420$, so $\mathscr{E}(\psi^2 - 1)$ and the standard deviation of $\psi^2$ are 0.024 and 0.011, respectively. As the realized value of $\psi^2 - 1$ is less than its expectation, it is not surprising that the ex ante efficiency of the Equal-Weighted Index cannot be rejected for this time period.

This measure, $\psi$, is a new variant of the geometry developed to examine portfolio performance. In past procedures the efficient frontier has been taken as given, and a distance such as $mb$ in Figure 1a has been used as a measure of $p$'s performance. Note that $mb$ is simply the return differential of the ex post optimal portfolio over $p$, computed at the sample standard deviation of the ex post optimal portfolio. Another suggestion has been to use the difference in their slopes $\hat{\theta}^* - \hat{\theta}_p$ as a measure of $p$'s relative performance. How the true ex ante frontier is to be known is unclear, and if the ex post frontier is used, then we face the statistical problem of this paper.

### 4. THE POWER OF THE MULTIVARIATE TEST FOR EFFICIENCY

The empirical illustration in the previous section fails to reject the ex ante efficiency of the Equal-Weighted Index when using 10 beta-sorted portfolios as in BJS.[8] Such a result may occur because the null hypothesis is in fact true, or it

---

[8] We have also examined our data base using the same subperiods as in BJS. When we aggregate the results of the multivariate test across these four subperiods, we can reject ex ante efficiency at usual levels of significance. This confirms the conclusions reached by BJS.

may be due to the use of a test which is not powerful enough to detect economically important deviations from efficiency of the Index. Questions of power for various types of test statistics have been a long standing concern among financial economists (e.g., see Roll (1977), among others). This section will focus on the power of the multivariate test.

From Section 2 we know that under both the null and alternate hypotheses a simple transform of $W$, or $\psi^2$, has an $F$ distribution with degrees of freedom $N$ and $T - N - 1$. The $F$ distribution is noncentral with the noncentrality parameter given by equation (6); under the null hypothesis the noncentrality parameter is zero. It deserves emphasis that the $F$ distribution under the alternative is conditional on the returns of portfolio $p$ since the noncentrality parameter depends on $\hat{\theta}_p^2$. Thus, we will be studying the power function conditional on a value for $\hat{\theta}_p^2$, not the unconditional power function.

The probability of rejecting a false null hypothesis increases as the noncentrality parameter increases, holding constant the numerator and denominator degrees of freedom (Johnson and Kotz (1970, page 193)). Studying the factors that affect the noncentrality parameter, $\lambda$, will give some guidance about the power of the multivariate test. From equation (6) we can see that $\lambda$ is a weighted sum of squared deviations about the point $\alpha_p = 0$. The weighting matrix is the inverse of the covariance matrix of the ordinary least squares estimators for $\alpha_p$. Thus, estimated departures from the null are weighted according to the variability of the estimator and the cross-sectional dependence among the estimators.

The noncentrality parameter can also be given an intuitive economic interpretation. The derivation of equation (23) in the Appendix would hold for the population counterparts of the sample estimates, so it is also true that $\alpha_p' \Sigma^{-1} \alpha_p = \theta^{*2} - \theta_p^2$. It follows directly that

$$\lambda = \left[ T / \left( 1 + \hat{\theta}_p^2 \right) \right] \left( \theta^{*2} - \theta_p^2 \right).$$

Not surprisingly, the power of the test will increase as the ex ante *in*efficiency of portfolio $p$ increases as measured in terms of the slope of the relevant opportunity sets. If $\hat{\theta}_p^2$ increases, the precision of the estimator for $\alpha_p$ declines, so the power of the test decreases.

Figure 2 summarizes how the power of the test is affected by $\theta^*$ and $\theta_p$. When the proportion of potential efficiency (i.e., $\theta_p / \theta^*$) is equal to one, the null hypothesis is true. As this proportion approaches zero, the given portfolio is becoming less efficient. Figure 2 is based on values for the significance level, $N$, and $T$ that are common for existing empirical work on asset pricing models; we have used $N = 10$ or $20$ and $T = 60$ or $120$ and a five percent significance level. Empirical work on the CRSP Indexes reports estimates of $\theta_p$ between 0 and 0.4. We have used this range to guide our selection of a grid for $\theta_p$ and $\theta^*$. In addition, Figure 2 is based on the assumption that $\hat{\theta}_p = \theta_p$ to eliminate one of the parameters that affect $\lambda$; this assumption suggests that our calculations of power are for situations where the sample is representative of the underlying population.

Even within the range of parameters that we consider, the probability of rejecting the null hypothesis ranges from five percent to nearly 100 percent depending on the difference between the two relevant measures of slope. For

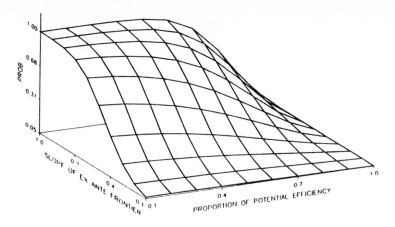

2a.) N = 10 and T = 60.

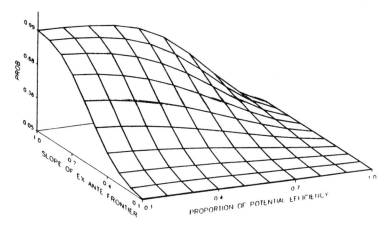

2b.) N = 20 and T = 60.

FIGURE 2.—Sensitivity of the power of the test to the choice of the index. Each figure is based on a different combination of the number of assets ($N$) and the number of time series observations ($T$). In all cases a critical level of five percent is used.

example, if $\theta_p$ equals .2 (which is high relative to the average from 1926–1982) and if $N = 20$ and $T = 60$, then the probability of rejecting a false null hypothesis ranges from ten percent (for $\theta^* = .3$) to 98 percent (for $\theta^* = 1.0$).

Given the data bases that are available, an empiricist is always faced with the question of the appropriate sizes for $N$ and $T$. For example, with the CRSP monthly file we have a data base which extends back to 1926 for every firm on the New York Stock Exchange. This would permit the empiricist to use around 700 time series observations (i.e., $T$) and well over 2000 firms (i.e., $N$). However, the actual $N$ used may be restricted by $T$ to keep estimates of covariance matrices nonsingular, and the actual $T$ used is constrained by concerns over

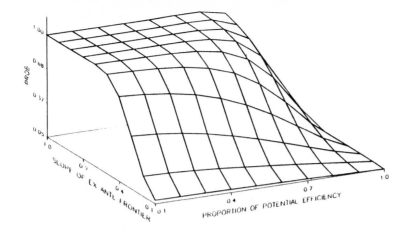

2c.) N = 10 and T = 120.

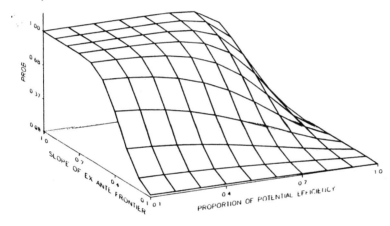

2d.) N = 20 and T = 120.

FIGURE 2.—Continued.

stationarity. It is not uncommon to see published work where $T$ is around 60 monthly observations and $N$ is between 10 and 20. While these numbers for $N$ and $T$ are common, we are not aware of any formal attempts to study the appropriate values to select. We will now examine this issue in the context of the specific hypothesis of ex ante efficiency. While the analysis is focused on an admittedly special case, our hope is that it may shed some light on other cases as well.

To get more intuition about the impact of $N$ on equation (6), consider a case in which $\Sigma$ has a constant value down the diagonal and a constant (but different) value for all off-diagonal elements. Since $\Sigma$ represents the contemporaneous covariances across assets after the "market effect" has been removed, such a structure includes the Sharpe (1963) diagonal model as a special case when the off-diagonal terms are zero. The more general case where the off-diagonal terms are constant but are nonzero is motivated by the work of Elton and Gruber (1973) and Elton, Gruber, and Urich (1978).[9] Under this structure we can parameterize $\Sigma$ as:

$$(10) \qquad \Sigma = (1 - \rho)\omega^2 I_N + \rho\omega^2 \iota_N \iota_N',$$

where $\rho \equiv$ the correlation between $\tilde{\varepsilon}_{it}$ and $\tilde{\varepsilon}_{jt}$; $\omega^2 \equiv$ the variance of $\tilde{\varepsilon}_{it}$; $I_N \equiv$ an identity matrix of dimension $N$; and $\iota_N' \equiv$ a $1 \times N$ vector of 1's. The inverse[10] of this patterned matrix is (Graybill (1983)):

$$\Sigma^{-1} = \frac{1}{(1 - \rho)\omega^2} \left[ I_N - \frac{\rho}{1 + (N - 1)\rho} \iota_N \iota_N' \right].$$

Substituting the above equation for $\Sigma^{-1}$ in equation (6) gives:

$$(11) \qquad \lambda = \frac{T/(1 + \hat{\theta}_p^2)}{(1 - \rho)\omega^2} \left[ N\mu_2 - \frac{N^2\rho}{(1 - \rho) + N\rho} \mu_1^2 \right].$$

where $\mu_1 \equiv (\iota_N' \alpha_p)/N$ and $\mu_2 \equiv (\alpha_p' \alpha_p)/N$. One could view $\mu_1$ as a measure of the "average" misspecification across assets while $\mu_2$ indicates the noncentral dispersion of the departures from the null hypothesis across assets.

When $N$ is relatively large and $\rho$ is not equal to zero, equation (11) implies:

$$(12) \qquad \lambda/N \cong \frac{T/(1 + \hat{\theta}_p^2)}{(1 - \rho)\omega^2} (\mu_2 - \mu_1^2) = \frac{T/(1 + \hat{\theta}_p^2)}{(1 - \rho)\omega^2} \text{VAR}(\alpha_p),$$

where $\text{VAR}(\alpha_p)$ denotes the cross-sectional variance of the elements of $\alpha_p$. Thus, $\lambda$ is approximately proportional to $N$ and $T$.[11] Alternatively, if either $\rho = 0$ or $\mu_1 = 0$, then $\lambda$ is exactly proportional to $N$ and $T$.[12] Unfortunately, this is still not adequate to determine the impact of changing $N$ and $T$, for these two parameters affect not only the noncentrality parameter but also the degrees of freedom.

We have evaluated the power of the multivariate test for various combinations of $\lambda$, $N$, and $T$.[13] These numerical results provide some guidance on the proper

---

[9] Strictly speaking, the Sharpe diagonal model allows for heteroscedasticity in the disturbances of the market model equations; our formulation assumes homoscedasticity. Also, the constant correlation model of Elton and Gruber is usually applied to the correlation matrix for total returns; we are assuming constant correlation after the market effect has been removed.

[10] Necessary and sufficient conditions for this inverse to exist are that $\rho \neq 1$ and $\rho \neq (1 - N)^{-1}$; see Graybill (1983, page 190–191). In addition, the matrix should be positive definite; this would require that $\rho > -1/(N - 1)$.

[11] In general, since $\rho < 1$, $\lambda/N$ is less than or equal to the right side of (12) when $\rho \geq 0$.

[12] If the Equal-Weighted Index is portfolio $p$, then we would expect $\mu_1$ to approach zero as $N$ becomes large.

[13] These numerical calculations require evaluation of a noncentral $F$ distribution and an inverse of a central $F$ distribution. The latter calculation relied on the MDFI subroutine provided by IMSL. The former calculations are based on a subroutine written by J. M. Bremner (1978), and a driver program written by R. Bohrer and T. Yancey of the University of Illinois at Champaign-Urbana. Each subroutine was checked by verifying its output with the published tables reported in Tang (1938) and Titu (1967).

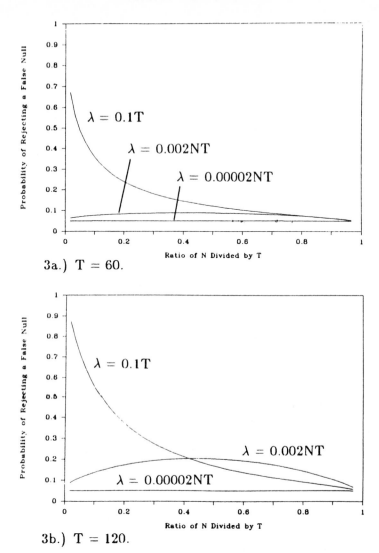

3a.) T = 60.

3b.) T = 120.

FIGURE 3.—Sensitivity of the power of the test to the choice of the number of assets ($N$) gives a fixed number of time series observations ($T$).

choice of $N$ and $T$. We assumed that $\lambda$ is proportional to $NT$, and Figure 3 provides various values for the constant of proportionality.[14] We selected this constant of proportionality based on equation (11) when $\rho = 0$. In this case, the constant is $\mu_2/[\omega^2(1 + \hat{\theta}_p^2)]$. We then replaced $\mu_2$ and $\omega^2$ with the cross-sectional averages of $\hat{\alpha}_{ip}^2$ and $\hat{\sigma}_i^2$, respectively, from an actual data set. We also know that $\hat{\theta}_p$ is 0.166 for the CRSP Equal-Weighted Index (1931–1965) and 0.109 for the

[14] MacKinlay (1987) studies the power of the test using alternative parameterizations of the noncentrality parameter.

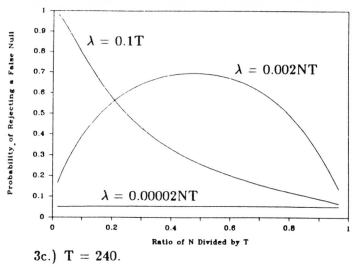

3c.)  T = 240.

FIGURE 3.—Continued.

CRSP Value-Weighted Index (1926–1982). This provides a rough guide to typical values for the constant of proportionality. The constant is 0.004 using the beta-sorted portfolios, and it is 0.002 using a set of industry portfolios. For size-sorted portfolios the constant is 0.004 using all months and 0.763 for monthly data only using January. (The details on how the industry portfolios and size-sorted portfolios were created will be provided later in this paper.)

In Figure 3, we look at cases where the constant is 0.00002 and 0.002, which are small relative to the above calculations. For purposes of comparison, Figure 3 also includes a case where $\lambda$ is not affected by $N$; instead we set $\lambda = .1T$. This represents a situation where an investigator has one asset that violates the null hypothesis, and all the remaining assets that are added are consistent with the efficiency of some given portfolio $p$. While Figure 3 is based on specific values for the constant of proportionality, the general pattern that is observed is consistent with a wide range of choices that we tried but did not report here.[15]

For a fixed number of time series observations, Figure 3 demonstrates that there may be an important decision to be made by the empiricist. Even though the noncentrality parameter increases as $N$ increases, it is not necessarily appropriate to choose the maximum $N$ possible. Given our particular parameterization of the problem, it appears that $N$ should be roughly a third to one half of $T$, or when five years of monthly data are used, 20 to 30 assets may be appropriate. When the constant is very low, the power is so small for all possible values of $N$

---

[15] We were not able to evaluate the noncentral $F$ for very high values of $\lambda$, so we have little knowledge about the shape of the power function when the constant of proportionality is high. If the constant is large enough, it is conceivable that a corner solution of setting $N = T - 2$ may be appropriate.

that it is not an important decision. Alternatively, if the noncentrality parameter is proportional to $T$ and not affected by $N$, clearly setting $N = 1$ is the preferred strategy. In this case adding securities does not provide more information about departures from the null hypothesis; however, additional securities increase the number of unknown parameters to be estimated. It deserves emphasis that these conclusions about the proper choice of $N$ may not be appropriate for all possible situations and models.

The choices of $N$ and $T$ are not the only decisions facing the empiricist in designing the econometric analysis. Since $N$ must always be less than $T$ (unless highly structured covariance matrices are entertained), the empiricist must also decide how to select the assets to maximize the power of the test. Given $N$ and $T$ we wish to maximize the quadratic form $\alpha'_p \Sigma^{-1} \alpha_p$, or equivalently $\theta^*$; however, these parameters are unobservable. A common approach is to use beta-sorted portfolios. While dispersion in betas is useful in decreasing the asymptotic standard error in estimates of the expected return on the zero-beta asset (Gibbons (1980) and Shanken (1982)), such sorting need not maximize departures from the null hypothesis as measured by $\lambda$.[16]

Empirical examples presented below illustrate the effect that different asset sets can have on the outcome of the test. First, we consider a set of 12 industry portfolios.[17] An industry grouping seems reasonable on economic grounds and also captures some of the important correlations among stocks. To measure the return from a "buy-and-hold" investment strategy, the relative market values of the securities are used to weight the returns. Almost every monthly return on the CRSP tape from 1926 through 1982 is included, which should minimize problems with survivorship bias.[18] Table III provides some summary statistics on the industry portfolios.

The multivariate $F$ statistic rejects the hypothesis of ex ante efficiency at about the one percent significance level. The relevant $F$ statistic is 2.13 with degrees of freedom 12 and 671; its $p$-value is 0.013.[19] To complement these numerical results, Figure 1c, which is similar to Figures 1a and 1b, provides a geometrical summary.

---

[16] In fact, for a given set of $N$ securities, the multivariate test is invariant to how we group these assets into $N$ portfolios; we could form $N$ portfolios so that they have very little dispersion in their beta values with no impact on the power. This follows from the well-known result in the multivariate statistics literature that our test is invariant to linear transformations of the data (Anderson (1984, pages 321–323)). Of course, the selection of the original subset of assets to be analyzed is important even though the way they are aggregated into portfolios is not (given that the number of portfolios is the same as the number of original assets).

[17] For the details of the data base, see Breeden, Gibbons, and Litzenberger (1987), who developed these data for tests of the consumption-based asset pricing model. The industry grouping closely follows a classification used by Sharpe (1982).

[18] However, all firms with a SIC number of 39 (i.e., miscellaneous manufacturing industries) are excluded to avoid any possible problems with a singular covariance matrix when the CRSP Value-Weighted Index is used as portfolio $p$.

[19] While not reported here, we also analyzed this data set across various subperiods. Based on five year subperiods, the $p$-value for the $F$ statistic is less than five percent in 7 out of 11 cases, is less than 10 percent in 9 out of 11 cases, and rejects when aggregated across the subperiods. Thus, the rejection of the overall period is confirmed by the subperiods as well.

To understand this low $p$-value, consider the fact that for this time period $\hat{\theta}_p = 0.109$ while the slope of the opportunity set using the ex post optimal portfolio, $\hat{\theta}^*$, is more than double with a value of 0.224. With these numbers we can calculate $\psi^2$ as 1.038. For $N = 12$ and $T = 684$, $\mathscr{E}(\tilde{\psi}^2)$ is 1.018 with $SD(\tilde{\psi}^2)$ of 0.007. Thus, the realized value of $\psi^2$ is nearly three standard deviations from its expected value if the CRSP Value-Weighted Index is truly ex ante efficient.

Perhaps of greater interest is the fact that the multivariate test rejects the null hypothesis at the one percent level even though all 12 univariate $t$ statistics fail to reject at even the five percent level. The next section builds on such contrasting results by analyzing why univariate test may be difficult to summarize across different assets.

## 5. THE PROBLEM WITH UNIVARIATE TESTS

Table II suggests that high beta portfolios earn too little and low beta portfolios too much if the Equal-Weighted Index is presumed to be efficient; similar evidence was used by BJS to garner support for the zero-beta version of the CAPM. Yet, this pattern is difficult to interpret. The upper triangular portion of Table IV provides the sample correlation matrix of the market model residuals based on the regressions that are summarized in Table II. A very distinctive pattern emerges in that the residuals of portfolios with similar betas are positively correlated while those of portfolios with very different betas are negatively correlated. Based on the variance-covariance matrix for $\hat{\alpha}_p$ in equation (4), it is clear that the estimators for $\alpha_{ip}$ will have the same pattern of correlation. Thus, it is difficult to infer whether the observed pattern in estimated values of $\alpha_{ip}$'s is

### TABLE III

SUMMARY STATISTICS ON INDUSTRY-SORTED PORTFOLIOS BASED ON MONTHLY DATA, 1926–82 ($T = 684$). ALL SIMPLE EXCESS RETURNS ARE NOMINAL AND IN PERCENTAGE FORM, AND THE CRSP VALUE-WEIGHTED INDEX IS PORTFOLIO $p$. THE FOLLOWING PARAMETER ESTIMATES ARE FOR THE REGRESSION MODEL: $\tilde{r}_{it} = \alpha_{ip} + \beta_{ip}\tilde{r}_{pt} + \tilde{\varepsilon}_{it}$ $\forall i = 1,\ldots,12$ AND $\forall t = 1,\ldots,684$, WHERE $R_i^2$ IS THE COEFFICIENT OF DETERMINATION FOR EQUATION $i$.

| Industry Portfolio | $\hat{\alpha}_{ip}$ | $s(\hat{\alpha}_{ip})$ | $\hat{\beta}_{ip}$ | $s(\hat{\beta}_{ip})$ | $R_i^2$ |
|---|---|---|---|---|---|
| Petroleum | 0.17 | 0.14 | 0.93 | 0.02 | 0.69 |
| Financial | −0.05 | 0.09 | 1.19 | 0.02 | 0.89 |
| Consumer Durables | 0.03 | 0.09 | 1.29 | 0.02 | 0.90 |
| Basic Industries | 0.00 | 0.00 | 1.09 | 0.01 | 0.94 |
| Food and Tobacco | 0.12 | 0.07 | 0.76 | 0.01 | 0.83 |
| Construction | −0.17 | 0.12 | 1.20 | 0.02 | 0.85 |
| Capital Goods | 0.10 | 0.08 | 1.08 | 0.01 | 0.91 |
| Transportation | −0.17 | 0.14 | 1.20 | 0.02 | 0.78 |
| Utilities | 0.05 | 0.09 | 0.74 | 0.02 | 0.76 |
| Trade and Textiles | 0.00 | 0.00 | 0.94 | 0.02 | 0.77 |
| Services | 0.43 | 0.37 | 0.80 | 0.06 | 0.19 |
| Recreation | −0.03 | 0.13 | 1.22 | 0.02 | 0.78 |

NOTE: For this sample period $\hat{\theta}_g$ and $\hat{\theta}^*$ are 0.109 and 0.224, respectively. These imply a value for $W_u$ equal to 0.038, which has a $p$-value of 0.013. Under the hypothesis that the CRSP Value-Weighted Index is efficient, $\mathscr{E}(\tilde{W}_u)$ is 0.018 and $SD(\tilde{W}_u)$ is 0.007.

TABLE IV

SAMPLE CORRELATION MATRIX OF RESIDUALS FROM MARKET MODEL REGRESSIONS USING EXCESS RETURNS.

THE UPPER TRIANGULAR PORTION OF THE TABLE IS BASED ON 10 BETA-SORTED PORTFOLIOS FOR THE DEPENDENT VARIABLES AND THE CRSP EQUAL-WEIGHTED INDEX FOR PORTFOLIO $p$. ALL MONTHLY DATA FROM 1931–65 ($T = 420$) ARE USED. TABLE II SUMMARIZES THE OTHER PARAMETER ESTIMATES FOR THIS REGRESSION MODEL. THE LOWER TRIANGULAR PORTION OF THE TABLE IS BASED ON 10 SIZE-SORTED PORTFOLIOS FOR THE DEPENDENT VARIABLES AND THE CRSP VALUE-WEIGHTED INDEX FOR PORTFOLIO $p$. ALL MONTHLY DATA FROM 1926–82 ($T = 684$) ARE USED. TABLE V SUMMARIZES THE OTHER PARAMETER ESTIMATES FOR THIS REGRESSION MODEL.

| | | | | | Portfolio Number: | | | | |
| 1 | 2 | 3 | 4 | 5 | 6 | 7 | 8 | 9 | 10 |
|---|---|---|---|---|---|---|---|---|---|
| | .52 | .39 | .03 | −.32 | −.51 | −.64 | −.60 | −.64 | −.50 |
| .62 | | .38 | .01 | −.16 | −.35 | −.50 | −.52 | −.53 | −.55 |
| .72 | .68 | | .08 | −.06 | −.25 | −.37 | −.43 | −.46 | −.49 |
| .70 | .66 | .75 | | −.06 | −.07 | −.11 | −.13 | −.32 | −.22 |
| .63 | .66 | .70 | .72 | | .21 | .25 | .12 | .03 | −.16 |
| .63 | .61 | .68 | .65 | .72 | | .34 | .36 | .26 | .06 |
| .52 | .41 | .57 | .55 | .62 | .67 | | .43 | .46 | .23 |
| .39 | .39 | .51 | .46 | .50 | .59 | .52 | | .49 | .27 |
| .28 | .35 | .21 | .27 | .26 | .36 | .27 | .30 | | .56 |
| −.54 | −.59 | −.68 | −.66 | −.68 | −.68 | −.61 | −.66 | −.38 | |

NOTE: For the upper triangular portion of the table, portfolio 1 consists of firms with the highest values for historical estimates of beta while portfolio 10 contains the firms with the lowest values. For the lower triangular portion of the table, portfolio 1 is a value-weighted portfolio of firms whose market capitalization is in the lowest decile of the NYSE while portfolio 10 contains firms in the highest decile.

due to correlation in the estimation error or to the actual pattern in the true parameters.

Other examples from empirical work in financial economics could also be cited where univariate tests are difficult to interpret. Since the work of Banz (1981) and Reinganum (1981), the "size effect" has received a great deal of attention. (For more information about this research see Schwert (1983), who summarizes the existing evidence and also provides a useful bibliography.) While most of the research in this area now focuses on returns in January, we begin by looking at the original evidence which did not distinguish between January and non-January returns.

We have created a data base of monthly stock returns using the CRSP file. Firms were sorted into 10 portfolios based on the relative market value of their total equity outstanding. In other words, we ranked firms by their market values in December, 1925 (say), and we then formed 10 portfolios where the first portfolio contains all those firms in the lowest decile of firm size and the tenth portfolio consists of companies in the highest decile of firm size on the New York Stock Exchange. Each of the ten portfolios is value-weighted, and the firms are not resorted by their market values for five years. Thus, the returns on these 10 portfolios from January, 1926 through December, 1930 represent the returns from a buy-and-hold strategy without any rebalancing for five years; this portfolio formation was adopted to represent a low transaction cost investment strat-

TABLE V

SUMMARY STATISTICS ON SIZE-SORTED PORTFOLIOS BASED ON MONTHLY DATA, 1926–82 ($T = 684$). ALL SIMPLE EXCESS RETURNS ARE NOMINAL AND IN PERCENTAGE FORM, AND THE CRSP VALUE-WEIGHTED INDEX IS PORTFOLIO $p$. THE FOLLOWING PARAMETER ESTIMATES ARE FOR THE REGRESSION MODEL: $\tilde{r}_{it} = \alpha_{ip} + \beta_{ip}\tilde{r}_{pt} + \tilde{\varepsilon}_{it}$ $\forall i = 1,\ldots,10$ AND $\forall t = 1,\ldots,684$, WHERE $R_i^2$ IS THE COEFFICIENT OF DETERMINATION FOR EQUATION $i$.

| Portfolio Number | $\hat{\alpha}_{ip}$ | $s(\hat{\alpha}_{ip})$ | $\hat{\beta}_{ip}$ | $s(\hat{\beta}_{ip})$ | $R_i^2$ |
|---|---|---|---|---|---|
| 1 | 0.28 | 0.24 | 1.59 | 0.04 | 0.68 |
| 2 | 0.34 | 0.18 | 1.45 | 0.03 | 0.78 |
| 3 | 0.25 | 0.14 | 1.40 | 0.02 | 0.84 |
| 4 | 0.18 | 0.13 | 1.36 | 0.02 | 0.85 |
| 5 | 0.19 | 0.10 | 1.27 | 0.02 | 0.89 |
| 6 | 0.18 | 0.09 | 1.25 | 0.02 | 0.91 |
| 7 | 0.08 | 0.07 | 1.18 | 0.01 | 0.93 |
| 8 | 0.08 | 0.06 | 1.17 | 0.01 | 0.95 |
| 9 | 0.00 | 0.00 | 1.16 | 0.01 | 0.96 |
| 10 | −0.01 | 0.05 | 0.94 | 0.00 | 0.98 |

NOTE: Portfolio 1 is a value-weighted portfolio of firms whose market capitalization is in the lowest decile of the NYSE while portfolio 10 contains firms in the highest decile. For this sample period $\theta_p$ and $\theta^*$ are 0.109 and 0.172, respectively. These imply a value for $W_u$ equal to 0.017, which has a $p$-value of 0.301. Under the hypothesis that the CRSP Value-Weighted Index is efficient, $\mathscr{E}(\tilde{W}_u)$ is 0.015 and $SD(\tilde{W}_u)$ is 0.007.

egy. The resorting and rebalancing occurred in December of 1925, 1930,..., 1980. Table V summarizes the behavior of the returns on these portfolios for the entire time period.

Given the existing evidence on the size effect, some readers may find it somewhat surprising that, in the overall period from 1926 through 1982, the multivariate test fails to reject efficiency of the CRSP Value-Weighted Index at the usual levels of significance. The first row of Table VI reports the statistic and its corresponding $p$-value; Figure 1d provides a geometrical interpretation for this overall period.[20]

The correlation matrix of the market model residuals of the size portfolios exhibits a distinctive pattern. The lower triangular portion of Table IV provides this information based on the overall period. However, the pattern is identical across every ten year subperiod reported in Table VI, and a similar pattern is also described by Brown, Kleidon, and Marsh (1983, page 47) and Huberman and Kandel (1985b). The correlation is positive and high among the low decile firms. The correlation declines as one compares portfolios from very different deciles. Even more striking is the fact that the highest decile portfolio has negative sample correlation with all other decile portfolios. (In some of the subperiods, this negative correlation occurred for the ninth decile as well.) Thus, if we observe that the lowest decile performs well (i.e., estimated alphas that are positive), we would then expect that the highest decile would do poorly (and vice versa). This is the case, for example, in the period 1946–1955, where five out of

[20] The subperiod results in Table VI are consistent with the conclusions of Brown, Kleidon, and Marsh (1983) who find the size effect is not constant across all subperiods.

TABLE VI

Testing the ex ante efficiency of the CRSP Value-Weighted Index (i.e., portfolio $p$) relative to 10 size-sorted portfolios. All simple excess returns are nominal and in percentage form. Overall period is based on all monthly data from 1926–82. The following model is estimated and tested: $\tilde{r}_{it} = \alpha_{ip} + \beta_{ip}\tilde{r}_{pt} + \tilde{\varepsilon}_{it}$ $\forall i = 1, \ldots, 10$ and $\forall t = 1, \ldots, T$. $H_0$: $\alpha_{ip} = 0$ $\forall i = 1, \ldots, 10$.

| Time Period ($T$) | $\theta_p$ | $\theta^\bullet$ | $W_u$ (P-Value) | Number of $\|t(\hat{\alpha}_{ip})\| \geq 1.96$ |
|---|---|---|---|---|
| 1926–1982 (684) | 0.109 | 0.172 | 0.018 (0.301) | 1 |
| 1926–1935 (120) | 0.065 | 0.354 | 0.119 (0.227) | 0 |
| 1936–1945 (120) | 0.146 | 0.286 | 0.059 (0.765) | 0 |
| 1946–1955 (120) | 0.308 | 0.469 | 0.113 (0.264) | 5 |
| 1956–1965 (120) | 0.216 | 0.604 | 0.302 (0.001) | 1 |
| 1966–1975 (120) | −0.019 | 0.408 | 0.164 (0.065) | 0 |
| 1976–1982 (84) | 0.093 | 0.538 | 0.275 (0.039) | 9 |

NOTE: $\theta_p$ is the ratio of the sample average excess return on the CRSP Value-Weighted Index divided by its sample standard deviation, and $\theta^\bullet$ is the maximum value possible of the ratio of the sample average excess return divided by the sample standard deviation. $W = (\theta^{\bullet 2} - \theta_p^2)/(1 + \theta_p^2)$, and it is distributed as a transform of a central $F$ distribution with degrees of freedom 10 and $T - 11$ under the null hypothesis. $W$ should converge to zero as $T$ approaches infinity if the CRSP Value-Weighted Index is ex ante efficient. By converting the $p$-values for the $W_u$ statistics to an implied realization for a standardized normal random variable, the results across the 6 subperiods can be summarized by summing up the 6 independent and standardized normals and dividing by the square root of 6 as suggested in Shanken (1985). This quantity is 2.87 which implies a rejection across the subperiods at the usual levels of significance.

ten portfolios have significant alphas (at the five percent level), but the multivariate test cannot reject the efficiency of the Value-Weighted Index.

Even though summarizing the results of univariate tests can be difficult, applied empirical work continues to report such statistics. This is only natural, for univariate tests are more intuitive (perhaps because they are used more) and seem to give more diagnostic information about the nature of the departure from the null hypothesis when it is rejected. Part of the goal of this paper is to provide some intuition behind multivariate tests. Section 3 has already done this to some extent by demonstrating that the multivariate test can be viewed as a particular measurement in mean-standard deviation space of portfolio theory. The next section shows that the multivariate test is equivalent to a "$t$ test" on the intercept in a particular regression which should be intuitive. A way to generate diagnostic information about the nature of the departures from the null hypothesis is also provided.

### 6. ANOTHER INTERPRETATION OF THE TEST STATISTIC, $W$

The hypothesis that $\alpha_{ip} = 0$ $\forall i$ is violated if and only if some linear combination of the $\alpha$'s is zero; i.e., if and only if some portfolio of the $N$ assets has a nonzero intercept when its excess returns are regressed on those of portfolio $p$. With this in mind, it is interesting to consider the portfolio which, in a given sample, maximizes the square of the usual $t$ statistic for the intercept. It is well known in the literature on multivariate statistics that this maximum value is Hotelling's $T^2$ statistic, our $TW_u$. In this section we focus on the composition of the maximizing portfolio, $a$, and its economic interpretation.

Thus, let $\tilde{r}_{at} \equiv a'\tilde{r}_{2t}$, where $\tilde{r}_{2t}$ is an $N \times 1$ vector with typical element $\tilde{r}_{it}$ $\forall i = 1, \ldots, N$. Let $\hat{\alpha}_p$ be the $N \times 1$ vector of regression intercept estimates. Then $\hat{\alpha}_a = a'\hat{\alpha}_p$ and $\widehat{VAR}(\hat{\alpha}_a) = (1 + \hat{\theta}_p^2)a'\hat{\Sigma}a/T$ by (4) above.[21] Therefore,

$$(13) \qquad t_a^2 = \left[ \frac{\hat{\alpha}_a}{\widehat{SD}(\hat{\alpha}_a)} \right]^2 = \frac{(a'\hat{\alpha}_p)^2}{\widehat{VAR}(a'\hat{\alpha}_p)} = \frac{T(a'\hat{\alpha}_p)^2}{(1 + \hat{\theta}_p^2)a'\hat{\Sigma}a}.$$

Since we can multiply $a$ by any scalar without changing the value of $t_a^2$, we shall adopt the normalization that $a'\hat{\alpha}_p = c$, where $c$ is any constant different from zero. With this normalization, $T(a'\hat{\alpha}_p)^2$ and $(1 + \hat{\theta}_p^2)$ in (13) are fixed given the sample. Hence, maximizing $t_a^2$ is equivalent to the following minimization problem:

$$\min_{a} : \qquad a'\hat{\Sigma}a$$

$$\text{subject to:} \qquad a'\hat{\alpha}_p = c.$$

Since the above problem is similar to the standard portfolio problem, the form of the solution is:

$$a = \frac{c}{\hat{\alpha}_p'\hat{\Sigma}^{-1}\hat{\alpha}_p} \hat{\Sigma}^{-1}\hat{\alpha}_p.$$

Substituting this solution for $a$ into equation (13), $t_a^2$ becomes:

$$t_a^2 = \frac{T\hat{\alpha}_p'\hat{\Sigma}^{-1}\hat{\alpha}_p}{1 + \hat{\theta}_p^2}.$$

Combining this equation with (5) establishes that $t_a^2 = TW_u$. Not surprisingly, the distribution of $t_a$ is not Student $t$, for portfolio $a$ was formed after examining the data.

The derivation of $t_a^2$ suggests some additional information to summarize empirical work on ex ante efficiency. Given the actual value of $a$ based on the sample, one will know the particular linear combination which led to the rejection of the null hypothesis. If the null hypothesis is rejected, then $a$ may give us some constructive information about how to create a better model.

Portfolio $a$ has an economic basis as well. When this portfolio is combined properly with portfolio $p$, the combination turns out to be ex post efficient. In

---

[21] Since we are working with returns in excess of the riskless rate, $\iota_N'a$ need not equal 1, for the riskless asset will be held (long or short) so that all wealth is invested.

other words, for some value of $k$,

(14) $\qquad \tilde{r}_t^* = (1 - k)\tilde{r}_{pt} + k\tilde{r}_{at},$

where $\tilde{r}_t^*$ is the return on this ex post efficient portfolio. For convenience, we set $c$ so that the sample means of $\tilde{r}_{pt}$, $\tilde{r}_{at}$, and $\tilde{r}_t^*$ are all equal. The equivalence of these three means requires that:

$$c \equiv \bar{r}_p \frac{\hat{\alpha}_p' \hat{\Sigma}^{-1} \hat{\alpha}_p}{\hat{\alpha}_p' \hat{\Sigma}^{-1} \bar{r}_2}.$$

For the remainder of the paper, we will refer to portfolio $a$ as the "active" portfolio. In many applications of our methodology, portfolio $p$ will be a "passive" portfolio, i.e., a buy-and-hold investment strategy. While our methods are applicable to situations where portfolio $p$ is not passive, certainly in its application to tests of the CAPM, portfolio $p$ will be passive. In such a setting portfolio $a$ is naturally interpreted as an active portfolio, for it represents a way to improve the efficiency of portfolio $p$. The terminology of "active" and "passive" has been used by Treynor and Black (1973), among others.

To establish this relation between the ex post efficient portfolio and portfolios $a$ and $p$, we first recall the equation for the weights of an efficient portfolio, $w^*$. Using equation (22) in the Appendix and setting $m$ in that equation to $\bar{r}_p$:

(15) $\qquad w^* = \frac{\bar{r}_p}{\bar{r}' \hat{V}^{-1} \bar{r}} \hat{V}^{-1} \bar{r}.$

$\hat{V}$ can be parameterized as:

$$\hat{V} = \begin{bmatrix} s_p^2 & s_p^2 \hat{\beta}_p' \\ s_p^2 \hat{\beta}_p & \hat{\beta}_p \hat{\beta}_p' s_p^2 + \hat{\Sigma} \end{bmatrix}.$$

Using the formula for the inverse of a partitioned matrix (see equation (24) in the Appendix) on the last expression and substituting this into equation (15) for $\hat{V}^{-1}$, equation (14) can be derived after some tedious, but straightforward, algebra.

The previous paragraphs have established that the square of the usual $t$ statistic for the estimated intercept, $\hat{\alpha}_a$, equals the $T^2$ test statistic, $TW_u$. A similar result can be established as well for the ex post efficient portfolio with the same sample mean as portfolio $p$, i.e., the estimated intercept, $\hat{\alpha}^*$, from regressing $\tilde{r}_t^*$ on $\tilde{r}_{pt}$ has a squared $t$ statistic, $t^{*2}$, which is identical to $t_a^2$. Since we will not use this result in what follows, we only note the fact here without proof.[22]

To illustrate the usefulness of the active portfolio interpretation, we return to the example of Section 5 where the size effect (across all months) is examined. The second column of Table V is roughly consistent with the findings of Brown,

[22] The two key facts used in the proof are that $\alpha^* = k\alpha_a$ and $SD(\tilde{\varepsilon}_t^*) = kSD(\tilde{\varepsilon}_{at})$, where $\tilde{\varepsilon}_t^*$ is the disturbance in the regression of $\tilde{r}_t^*$ on $\tilde{r}_{pt}$; these equalities hold for the estimates as well as the parameters. Since $t^*$ is essentially a ratio of $\hat{\alpha}^*$ and $\widehat{SD}(\hat{\varepsilon}_t^*)$, $k$ cancels. The two key facts can be established by working with the moments of $\tilde{r}_t^*$ based on equation (14).

TABLE VII

DESCRIPTIVE INFORMATION ABOUT THE ACTIVE PORTFOLIO, $a$. THESE STATISTICS ARE BASED ON SIZE-SORTED PORTFOLIOS USING MONTHLY RETURNS, 1926–82 ($T = 684$). ALL SIMPLE EXCESS RETURNS ARE NOMINAL AND IN PERCENTAGE FORM, AND THE CRSP VALUE-WEIGHTED INDEX IS PORTFOLIO $p$.

|  | Monthly Returns in all Months ($T = 684$) | Monthly Returns in only January ($T = 57$) | Monthly Returns Excluding January ($T = 627$) |
|---|---|---|---|
| $\hat{\alpha}_a$ | 0.05 | 1.36 | 0.05 |
| $t_a^2$ | 11.97 | 71.57 | 11.09 |
| $k$ | 7.56 | 0.87 | 7.95 |
| $a_1$ | $-0.02$ | 0.09 | $-0.04$ |
| $a_2$ | 0.04 | 0.07 | $-0.01$ |
| $a_3$ | 0.04 | 0.08 | 0.03 |
| $a_4$ | 0.00 | 0.07 | $-0.02$ |
| $a_5$ | 0.06 | 0.03 | 0.12 |
| $a_6$ | 0.08 | $-0.04$ | 0.06 |
| $a_7$ | 0.01 | 0.10 | 0.03 |
| $a_8$ | 0.10 | 0.04 | 0.09 |
| $a_9$ | 0.04 | $-0.52$ | 0.01 |
| $a_{10}$ | 0.60 | $-0.16$ | 0.63 |
| $a_{RF}$ | 0.12 | 1.25 | 0.09 |
| $\Sigma a_i$ | 1.00 | 1.00 | 1.00 |

NOTE: Portfolio 1 is a value-weighted portfolio of firms whose market capitalization is in the lowest decile of the NYSE while portfolio 10 contains firms in the highest decile. The portion of wealth invested in the riskless asset is denoted by $a_{RF}$.

Kleidon, and Marsh in that the estimated alphas are approximately monotonic in the decile size rankings. However, such a result does not imply that an optimal portfolio should give large weight to small firms. As Dybvig and Ross (1985) point out, alphas only indicate the direction of investment for marginal improvements in a portfolio. The portfolio that is globally optimal may have a very different weighting scheme than is suggested by the alphas. A comparison of Tables V and VII verifies this.

For example, the portion of the active portfolio invested in the portfolio of the smallest firms (i.e., $a_1$) has a sign which is opposite that of its estimated alpha. Furthermore, the active portfolio suggests spreading one's investment fairly evenly across the portfolios in the bottom 9 deciles and then investing a rather large proportion in the portfolio of large firms, not small firms. Table VII also reports $\hat{\alpha}_a$, $t_a^2$, and $k$ for the overall period. Note that as $k$ is much greater than one ($k = 7.56$), the ex post efficient portfolio has a huge short position in the value-weighted index. Since this index is dominated by the largest firms, the net large firm position in the efficient portfolio is therefore actually negative. It is interesting that ex post efficiency is achieved by avoiding (i.e., shorting) large firms rather than aggressively investing in small firms.

The reader should keep in mind that Tables IV through VI and the second column of Table VII have examined the size effect across all months. Based on just these results, the size effect seems to be less important than perhaps originally thought. However, if the data are sorted by January returns versus

TABLE VIII

SUMMARY STATISTICS ON SIZE-SORTED PORTFOLIOS BASED ON JANUARY RETURNS, 1926–82 ($T = 57$). ALL SIMPLE EXCESS RETURNS ARE NOMINAL AND IN PERCENTAGE FORM, AND THE CRSP VALUE-WEIGHTED INDEX IS PORTFOLIO $p$. THE FOLLOWING PARAMETER ESTIMATES ARE FOR THE REGRESSION MODEL: $\tilde{r}_{it} = \alpha_{ip} + \beta_{ip}\tilde{r}_{pt} + \tilde{\varepsilon}_{it}$ $\forall i = 1, \ldots, 10$, WHERE $R_i^2$ IS THE COEFFICIENT OF DETERMINATION FOR EQUATION $i$.

| Portfolio Number | $\hat{\alpha}_{ip}$ | $s(\hat{\alpha}_{ip})$ | $\hat{\beta}_{ip}$ | $s(\hat{\beta}_{ip})$ | $R_i^2$ |
|---|---|---|---|---|---|
| 1 | 6.12 | 0.87 | 1.67 | 0.18 | 0.62 |
| 2 | 4.60 | 0.67 | 1.52 | 0.14 | 0.69 |
| 3 | 3.43 | 0.47 | 1.44 | 0.10 | 0.80 |
| 4 | 2.88 | 0.49 | 1.44 | 0.10 | 0.80 |
| 5 | 1.79 | 0.34 | 1.19 | 0.07 | 0.85 |
| 6 | 1.79 | 0.30 | 1.21 | 0.06 | 0.88 |
| 7 | 0.85 | 0.20 | 1.16 | 0.04 | 0.94 |
| 8 | 0.80 | 0.23 | 1.17 | 0.05 | 0.92 |
| 9 | 0.31 | 0.17 | 1.05 | 0.03 | 0.95 |
| 10 | −0.52 | 0.10 | 0.94 | 0.02 | 0.98 |

NOTE: Portfolio 1 is a value-weighted portfolio of firms whose market capitalization is in the lowest decile of the NYSE while portfolio 10 contains firms in the highest decile. For this sample period $\hat{\theta}_p$ and $\hat{\theta}^*$ are 0.259 and 1.197, respectively. These imply a value for $W_u$ equal to 1.256, which has a $p$-value of 0.000. Under the hypothesis that the CRSP Value-Weighted Index is efficient, $\mathcal{E}(\hat{W}_u)$ is 0.219 and $SD(\hat{W}_u)$ is 0.111.

non-January returns, the multivariate approach confirms the importance of the size effect—at least for the month of January. Table VIII summarizes the sample characteristics of our 10 size-sorted portfolios when using only returns in January from 1926 through 1982. A comparison of Tables V and VIII reveals that the size effect is much more pronounced in January than in other months; this is consistent with the work by Keim (1983). This impression from the univariate statistics is confirmed by the multivariate test of ex ante efficiency, for the $F$ test is 5.99 with a $p$-value of zero to three decimal places. In contrast, the $F$ test based on all months excluding January is 1.09 with a $p$-value of 0.36. The weights of the active portfolio, $a$, are presented in the last two columns of Table VII for January versus non-January months. As in the first column of Table VII, the active portfolio is not dominated by small firms. For the month of January, one's investment should be evenly spread (roughly speaking) across the eight portfolios in the bottom deciles (or smaller firms); however, firms in the top two deciles (or larger firms) should be shorted.[23] Results for non-January months are similar to those based on all monthly data.

The evidence in Table VII suggests that the optimal active portfolio is not dominated by small firms even in the month of January—at least based on the ex post sample moments. Nevertheless, in the marketplace we see the development of mutual funds which specialize in holding the equities of just small firms.[24]

[23] The active portfolio for the month of January involves a rather large position in the riskless asset ($a_{RF}$ equals 1.25). This investment in the riskless security is necessary to maintain a sample mean return on the active portfolio equal to that of the CRSP Value-Weighted Index.

[24] Examples of such funds include The Small Company Portfolio of Dimensional Fund Advisors and the Extended Market Fund of Wells Fargo Investment Advisors.

Such funds suggest that efficient portfolios may be achieved by combining indexes like the S&P 500 (or the CRSP Value-Weighted Index) with a portfolio of small firms. We now turn to an examination of the ex ante efficiency of such a linear combination in the next section. A multivariate statistical test of such an investment strategy turns out to be a simple extension of the test developed in Section 2.

### 7. TESTING THE EFFICIENCY OF A PORTFOLIO OF $L$ ASSETS

If a portfolio of $L$ other portfolios is efficient, then there exist parameter restrictions on the joint distribution of excess returns similar to those considered earlier. Specifically, if $\tilde{r}_{xt} = \sum_{j=1}^{L} x_j \tilde{r}_{jt}$ (where $\sum_{j=1}^{L} x_j = 1$) and if $\tilde{r}_{xt}$ is efficient, then

$$(16) \qquad \mathcal{E}(\tilde{r}_{it}) = \sum_{j=1}^{L} \delta_{ij} \mathcal{E}(\tilde{r}_{jr}),$$

where the $\delta_{ij}$'s are the coefficients in the following regression:

$$(17) \qquad \tilde{r}_{it} = \delta_{i0} + \sum_{j=1}^{L} \delta_{ij} \tilde{r}_{jt} + \tilde{\eta}_{it} \qquad \forall i = 1, \ldots, N.$$

(We will assume that the stochastic characteristics of $\tilde{\eta}_{it}$ are the same as those of $\tilde{\varepsilon}_{it}$ in equation (1).) Conversely, (16) implies that some portfolio of the given $L$ portfolios is on the minimum variance frontier (Jobson and Korkie (1982)). Thus, a necessary condition for the efficiency of a linear combination $(\tilde{r}_{1t}, \tilde{r}_{2t}, \ldots, \tilde{r}_{Lt})$ with respect to the total set of $N + L$ risky assets is:

$$(18) \qquad H_0: \qquad \delta_{i0} = 0 \qquad \forall i = 1, \ldots, N.$$

The above null hypothesis follows when the parameter restriction given by (16) is imposed on (17).

In this case, $[T/N][(T - N - L)/(T - L - 1)](1 + \bar{r}_p' \hat{\Omega}^{-1} \bar{r}_p)^{-1} \hat{\delta}_0' \hat{\Sigma}^{-1} \hat{\delta}_0$ has a noncentral $F$ distribution with degrees of freedom $N$ and $(T - N - L)$, where $\bar{r}_p$ is a vector of sample means for $\tilde{r}_{pt} \equiv (\tilde{r}_{1t}, \tilde{r}_{2t}, \ldots, \tilde{r}_{Lt})$, $\hat{\Omega}$ is the sample variance-covariance matrix for $\tilde{r}_{pt}$, $\delta_0$ has a typical element $\delta_{i0}$, and $\hat{\delta}_0$ is the least squares estimator for $\delta_0$ based on the $N$ regression equations in (17) above. Further, the noncentrality parameter is given by $[T/(1 + \bar{r}_p' \hat{\Omega}^{-1} \bar{r}_p)] \delta_0' \Sigma^{-1} \delta_0$. Under the null hypothesis (18), the noncentrality parameter is 0.

For an application of the methodology developed in this section, we return to the results based on the size-sorted portfolios using returns only during the month of January. In the previous section, we found that we could reject the ex ante efficiency of the CRSP Value-Weighted Index. It could be that there exists a linear combination of the lowest decile portfolio and the Value-Weighted Index which is efficient. To consider such a case, we set $L = 2$ and $N = 9$. (Since portfolio 1 has become a regressor in a system like (17), we can no longer use it as a dependent variable.) The $F$ statistic to test hypothesis (18) is 1.09 with a

$p$-value of 0.39, so we cannot reject efficiency of this combination at the usual levels of significance. Of course, this inference ignores the obvious pre-test bias.

Throughout this paper we have assumed that there is an observable riskless rate of return, in which case the efficient frontier is simply a line in mean-standard deviation space. Suppose, now, that we wish to determine whether a set of $L+1$ portfolios $(L \geq 1)$ spans the minimum-variance frontier determined by these portfolios and the $N$ other assets. The $N + L + 1$ asset returns are assumed to be linearly independent. If we observe the return on the "zero-beta" portfolio (which in practice we do not), this spanning hypothesis (with $L = 1$) naturally arises in the context of the zero-beta version of the CAPM due to Black (1972).[25]

To formulate the test for spanning for any $L \geq 1$, consider the system of regression equations,

$$(19) \qquad R_{it} = \delta_{i0} + \sum_{j=1}^{L+1} \delta_{ij} \tilde{R}_{jt} + \bar{\eta}_{it} \qquad \forall i = 1, \ldots, N,$$

where $\tilde{R}_{it}$ denotes total returns, not excess returns. Huberman and Kandel (1985a) observe that the spanning hypothesis is equivalent to the following restrictions:

$$(20) \qquad \delta_{i0} = 0 \qquad \forall i = 1, \ldots, N$$

and

$$(21) \qquad \sum_{j=1}^{L+1} \delta_{ij} = 1 \qquad \forall i = 1, \ldots, N.$$

Imposing (21) on the parameters in (19) and letting $\tilde{r}_{it}$ denote returns in excess of the returns on portfolio $L+1$, we derive (17). Thus, the problem of testing (20) in the context of (17) is identical to that of testing (18) in the riskless case above. All we have learned about testing the riskless asset case is equally relevant to the spanning problem, provided that "excess returns" are interpreted appropriately. Perhaps most importantly, the exact distribution of our test statistic is known under both the null and alternative hypotheses, permitting evaluation of the power of the test. Note that this test of spanning imposes (21) and then assesses whether the intercepts in the resulting regression model are equal to zero.[26] In contrast, Huberman and Kandel (1985a) propose a joint $F$ test of (20)

[25] More generally, suppose the $L+1$st portfolio is uncorrelated with each of the first $L$ portfolios and has minimum variance among all such orthogonal portfolios. A simple generalization of the argument in Fama (1976, page 373) establishes that $\delta_{iL+1} = 1 - \sum_{j=1}^{L} \delta_{ij}$ for all $i$. It then follows (details are available on request) from the results of Huberman and Kandel (1985a) that the $L+1$ portfolios span the minimum-variance frontier if and only if some combination of the first $L$ portfolios is on the frontier. Thus, a test of the latter hypothesis can be conducted as in this section provided that the minimum-variance orthogonal portfolio is observable.

[26] An intermediate approach would be to first test (21) directly and then, provided the null is not rejected, proceed to test (20). Once again, the test of (21) is an $F$ test, and the exact distribution under the alternative may be determined along the lines of our earlier analysis. Of course, this test statistic does require that we observe the return on the $L+1$ spanning portfolios.

and (21) against an unrestricted alternative; however, the distribution of this statistic has not been studied under the alternative.

## 8. SUMMARY AND FUTURE RESEARCH

While this paper focuses on a particular hypothesis from modern finance, this apparently narrow view is adopted to gain better insight about a broad class of financial models which have a very similar structure to the one that we examine. The null hypothesis of this paper is a central hypothesis common to all risk-based asset pricing theories.[27] The nature of financial data and theories suggests the use of multivariate statistical methods which are not necessarily intuitive. We have attempted to provide some insight into how such tests function and to explain why they may provide different answers relative to univariate tests that are applied in an informal manner. In addition, we have studied the power of our suggested statistic and have isolated factors which will change the power of the test. There are at least two natural extensions of this work, and we now discuss each in turn.

First, the multivariate test considered here requires that the number of assets under study always be less than the number of time series observations. This restriction is imposed so that the sample variance-covariance matrix remains nonsingular. A test statistic which could handle situations with a large number of assets would be interesting.[28]

Second, we have not been very careful to specify the information set on which the various moments are conditioned. Gibbons and Ferson (1985), Grossman and Shiller (1982), and Hansen and Singleton (1982, 1983) have emphasized the importance of this issue for empirical work on positive models of asset pricing. Our methods provide a test of the ex ante *unconditional* efficiency of some portfolio—that is, when the opportunity set is constructed from the unconditional moments, not the conditional moments. When the riskless rate is changing (as it is in all of our data sets), then our methods provide a test of the *conditional* efficiency of some portfolio given the riskless rate. Of course, such an interpretation presumes that our implicit model for conditional moments given the riskless rate is correct. Ferson, Kandel, and Stambaugh (1987) and Shanken (1987a) provide more detailed analysis of testing conditional mean-variance efficiency.[29]

---

[27] If there is no riskless asset, then the null hypothesis becomes nonlinear in the parameters, for the intercept term is proportional to $(1 - \beta_{ip})$. Gibbons (1982) has explored this hypothesis using statistics which only have asymptotic justification. These statistics have been given an elegant geometric interpretation by Kandel (1984). While we still do not have a complete characterization of the small sample theory, Shanken (1985, 1986) has provided some useful bounds for the finite sample behavior of these tests.

[28] See Affleck-Graves and McDonald (1988) for some preliminary work on this problem.

[29] As Hansen and Richard (1987) emphasize, efficiency relative to a given information set need not imply efficiency relative to a subset. This implication does hold given some additional (and admittedly restrictive) assumptions, however. Let the information set, $I$, include the riskless rate, and let $p$ be efficient, given $I$. Assume betas conditional on $I$ are constant and $\mathscr{E}(\tilde{r}_{it}|r_{pt}, I)$ is linear in $r_{pt}$. It follows that $\mathscr{E}(\tilde{r}_{it}|r_{pt}, I) = \beta_{ip}r_{pt}$, and by iterated expectations $\mathscr{E}(\tilde{r}_{it}|r_{pt}, R_{ft}) = \beta_{ip}r_{pt}$, where $R_{ft}$ is the riskless rate. Thus, $p$ is on the minimum-variance frontier, given $R_{ft}$, and the methods of this paper are applicable.

*Graduate School of Business, Stanford University, Stanford, CA, U.S.A.,*

*School of Organization and Management, Yale University, New Haven, CT, U.S.A.,*

*and*

*Simon School of Business Administration, University of Rochester, Rochester, NY, U.S.A.*

*Manuscript received April, 1986; final revision received November, 1988.*

## APPENDIX

### DERIVATION OF EQUATION (7)

To understand the derivation of (7), first consider the basic portfolio problem:

$$\text{min:} \quad w'\hat{V}w$$

subject to $w'\bar{r} = m$, a mean constraint, where $w \equiv$ the vector of $N + 1$ portfolio weights; $\hat{V} \equiv$ the variance-covariance matrix of $N + 1$ assets; and $\bar{r} \equiv$ the vector of $N + 1$ sample mean excess returns. Without loss of generality, we assume that $p$ itself is the first component of our excess return vector. Thus, $\bar{r}' = (\bar{r}_p, \bar{r}_2')$ where $\bar{r}_2$ is a column vector of mean excess returns on the original $N$ assets. The first-order conditions for this problem are:

$$(22) \qquad w = \varphi \hat{V}^{-1}\bar{r}$$

and

$$\varphi = \frac{m}{\bar{r}'\hat{V}^{-1}\bar{r}},$$

where $\varphi$ is the Lagrange multiplier. Hence,

$$\left[ \frac{\text{mean}}{\text{standard deviation}} \right]^2 = \frac{m^2}{w'\hat{V}w}$$

$$= \frac{m^2}{\left[ \dfrac{m}{\bar{r}'\hat{V}^{-1}\bar{r}} \right]^2 \bar{r}'\hat{V}^{-1}\bar{r}}$$

$$= \bar{r}'\hat{V}^{-1}\bar{r}$$

$$\equiv \theta^{*2}.$$

Finally, to arrive at (7) we need to establish that:

$$(23) \qquad \hat{\alpha}_p'\hat{\Sigma}^{-1}\hat{\alpha}_p = \theta^{*2} - \theta_p^2,$$

where in contrast to the rest of the paper $\hat{\Sigma}$ is now the maximum likelihood estimator. The last equality follows from rewriting the elements of $\hat{V}$ in terms of $s_p^2$, $\hat{\beta}_p$, and $\hat{\Sigma}$ and then finding $\hat{V}^{-1}$ using the formula for a partitioned inverse. These steps lead to:

$$(24) \qquad \hat{V}^{-1} = \begin{bmatrix} s_p^{-2} + \hat{\beta}_p'\hat{\Sigma}^{-1}\hat{\beta}_p & -\hat{\beta}_p'\hat{\Sigma}^{-1} \\ -\hat{\Sigma}^{-1}\hat{\beta}_p & \hat{\Sigma}^{-1} \end{bmatrix}.$$

Then straightforward algebra yields:

$$\bar{r}'\hat{V}^{-1}\bar{r} = \left( \bar{r}_p^2/s_p^2 \right) + \left[ \left( \bar{r}_2 - \hat{\beta}_p\bar{r}_p \right)'\hat{\Sigma}^{-1}\left( \bar{r}_2 - \hat{\beta}_p\bar{r}_p \right) \right].$$

Since $\hat{\alpha}_p = \bar{r}_2 - \hat{\beta}_p \bar{r}_p$ and since the first term on the left-hand side of the above equation is $\theta^{*2}$ and the first term on the right-hand side is $\hat{\theta}_p^2$, we can rewrite the last equation as:

$$\theta^{*2} = \theta_p^2 + \hat{\alpha}_p' \hat{\Sigma}^{-1} \hat{\alpha}_p$$

or

$$\hat{\alpha}_p' \hat{\Sigma}^{-1} \hat{\alpha}_p = \theta^{*2} - \theta_p^2.$$

Thus,

$$W = \frac{\theta^{*2} - \theta_p^2}{1 + \theta_p^2} = \psi^2 - 1,$$

and the equality given in (7) has been justified.

## REFERENCES

AFFLECK-GRAVES, J., AND B. McDONALD (1988): "Multivariate Tests of Asset Pricing: The Comparative Power of Alternative Statistics," Working Paper, University of Notre Dame.

ANDERSON, T. W. (1984): *An Introduction to Multivariate Statistical Analysis*, Second Edition. New York: John Wiley.

BANZ, R. W. (1981): "The Relationship between Return and Market Value of Common Stock," *Journal of Financial Economics*, 9, 3–18.

BERNDT, E. R., AND N. E. SAVIN (1977): "Conflict among Criteria for Testing Hypotheses in the Multivariate Linear Regression Model," *Econometrica*, 45, 1263–1277.

BLACK, F. (1972): "Capital Market Equilibrium with Restricted Borrowing," *The Journal of Business*, 45, 444–454.

BLACK, F., M. C. JENSEN, AND M. SCHOLES (1972): "The Capital Asset Pricing Model: Some Empirical Findings," in *Studies in the Theory of Capital Markets*, ed. by M. C. Jensen. New York: Praeger.

BREEDEN, D. T., M. R. GIBBONS, AND R. H. LITZENBERGER (1987): "Empirical Tests of the Consumption-Oriented CAPM," Research Paper #879, Graduate School of Business, Stanford University, Stanford, CA.

BREMNER, J. M. (1978): "Mixtures of Beta Distributions, Algorithm AS 123," *Applied Statistics*, 27, 104–109.

BROWN, P., A. W. KLEIDON, AND T. A. MARSH (1983): "New Evidence on the Nature of Size-Related Anomalies in Stock Prices," *Journal of Financial Economics*, 12, 33–56.

DYBVIG, P. H., AND S. A. ROSS (1985): "The Analytics of Performance Measurement Using a Security Market Line," *Journal of Finance*, 40, 401–416.

ELTON, E. J., AND M. J. GRUBER (1973): "Estimating the Dependence Structure of Share Prices—Implications for Portfolio Selection," *Journal of Finance*, 28, 1203–1232.

ELTON, E. J., M. J. GRUBER, AND T. J. URICH (1978): "Are Betas Best?" *Journal of Finance*, 33, 1375–1384.

FAMA, E. F. (1976): *Foundations of Finance*. New York: Basic Books.

FAMA, E. F., AND J. D. MACBETH (1973): "Risk, Return, and Equilibrium: Empirical Tests," *Journal of Political Economy*, 81, 607–636.

FERSON, W., S. KANDEL, AND R. STAMBAUGH (1987): "Tests of Asset Pricing with Time-Varying Expected Risk Premiums and Market Betas," *Journal of Finance*, 42, 201–220.

GIBBONS, M. R. (1980): "Estimating the Parameters of the Capital Asset Pricing Model—A Minimum Expected Loss Approach," Research Paper #565, Graduate School of Business, Stanford University, Stanford, CA.

——— (1982): "Multivariate Tests of Financial Models: A New Approach," *Journal of Financial Economics*, 10, 3–28.

GIBBONS, M. R., AND W. FERSON (1985): "Testing Asset Pricing Models with Changing Expectations and an Unobservable Market Portfolio," *Journal of Financial Economics*, 14, 217–236.

GRAYBILL, F. A. (1983): *Matrices with Applications in Statistics*, Second Edition. Belmont, CA: Wadsworth.

GROSSMAN, S., AND R. SHILLER (1982): "Consumption Correlatedness and Risk Measurement in Economies with Non-Traded Assets and Heterogeneous Information," *Journal of Financial Economics*, 10, 195–210.

HANSEN, L., AND S. RICHARD (1987): "The Role of Conditioning Information in Deducing Testable Restrictions Implied by Dynamic Asset Pricing Models," *Econometrica*, 55, 587–614.

HANSEN, L., AND K. SINGLETON (1982): "Generalized Instrumental Variables Estimation of Nonlinear Rational Expectations Models," *Econometrica*, 50, 1269–1286.

——— (1983): "Stochastic Consumption, Risk Aversion, and the Temporal Behavior of Stock Market Returns," *Journal of Political Economy*, 91, 249–265.

HUBERMAN, G., AND S. KANDEL (1985A): "Likelihood Ratio Tests of Asset Pricing and Mutual Fund Separation," Graduate School of Business, University of Chicago, Chicago, IL.

——— (1985b): "A Size Based Stock Returns Model," Graduate School of Business, University of Chicago, Chicago, IL.

IBBOTSON, R., AND R. SINQUEFIELD (1979): *Stocks, Bonds, Bills and Inflation: Historical Returns (1926–1978)*. Charlottesville, VA: Financial Analysts Research Foundation.

JOBSON, J. D., AND B. KORKIE (1982): "Potential Performance and Tests of Portfolio Efficiency," *Journal of Financial Economics*, 10, 433–466.

——— (1985): "Some Tests of Linear Asset Pricing with Multivariate Normality," *Canadian Journal of Administrative Sciences*, 2, 114–138.

JOHNSON, N. L., AND S. KOTZ (1970): *Continuous Univariate Distributions*, Volume 2. New York: John Wiley.

KANDEL, S. (1984): "The Likelihood Ratio Test Statistic of Mean-Variance Efficiency without a Riskless Asset," *Journal of Financial Economics*, 13, 575–592.

KANDEL, S., AND R. STAMBAUGH (1987): "On Correlations and Inferences about Mean-Variance Efficiency," *Journal of Financial Economics*, 18, 61–90.

KEIM, D. B. (1983): "Size-Related Anomalies and Stock Return Seasonality: Further Empirical Evidence," *Journal of Financial Economics*, 12, 13–32.

LINTNER, J. (1965): "The Valuation of Risk Assets and the Selection of Risky Investment in Stock Portfolios and Capital Budgets," *Review of Economics and Statistics*, 47, 13–37.

MACBETH, J. (1975): "Tests of Two Parameter Models of Capital Market Equilibrium," Ph.D. Dissertation, Graduate School of Business, University of Chicago, Chicago, IL.

MACKINLAY, A. C. (1985): "An Analysis of Multivariate Financial Tests," Ph.D. Dissertation, Graduate School of Business, University of Chicago, Chicago, IL.

——— (1987): "On Multivariate Tests of the CAPM," *Journal of Financial Economics*, 18, 341–372.

MALINVAUD, E. (1980): *Statistical Methods of Econometrics*, Third Edition. Amsterdam: North Holland Publishing.

MERTON, R. (1973): "An Intertemporal Capital Asset Pricing Model," *Econometrica*, 41, 867–887.

MORRISON, D. F. (1976): *Multivariate Statistical Methods*, Second Edition. New York: McGraw-Hill.

RAO, C. R. (1951): "An Asymptotic Expansion of the Distribution of Wilks Criterion," *Bulletin of the Institute of International Statistics*, 33, 33–38.

REINGANUM, M. R. (1981): "Misspecification of Capital Asset Pricing: Empirical Anomalies Based on Earnings Yields and Market Values," *Journal of Financial Economics*, 9, 19–46.

ROLL, R. (1977): "A Critique of the Asset Pricing Theory's Tests—Part 1: On Past and Potential Testability of the Theory," *Journal of Financial Economics*, 4, 129–176.

——— (1978): "Ambiguity When Performance is Measured by the Securities Market Line," *Journal of Finance*, 33, 1051–1069.

SCHWERT, G. W. (1983): "Size and Stock Returns, and Other Empirical Regularities," *Journal of Financial Economics*, 12, 3–12.

SHANKEN, J. (1982): "An Analysis of the Traditional Risk-Return Model," Ph.D. Dissertation, Graduate School of Industrial Administration, Carnegie-Mellon University, Pittsburgh, PA.

——— (1985): "Multivariate Tests of the Zero-Beta CAPM," *Journal of Financial Economics*, 14, 327–348.

——— (1986): "Testing Portfolio Efficiency when the Zero-Beta Rate Is Unknown: A Note," *Journal of Finance*, 41, 269–276.

——— (1987a): "The Intertemporal Capital Asset Pricing Model: An Empirical Investigation," Working Paper, University of Rochester.

——— (1987b): "Multivariate Proxies and Asset Pricing Relations: Living with the Roll Critique," *Journal of Financial Economics*, 18, 91–110.

SHARPE, W. F. (1963): "A Simplified Model of Portfolio Analysis," *Management Science*, 9, 277–293.

———— (1964): "Capital Asset Prices: A Theory of Market Equilibrium under Conditions of Risk," *Journal of Finance*, 19, 425–442.

———— (1982): "Factors in New York Stock Exchange Security Returns, 1931–79," *Journal of Portfolio Management*, 8, 5–19.

SILVEY, S. D. (1975): *Statistical Inference*. London: Chapman and Hall.

STAMBAUGH, R. F. (1982): "On the Exclusion of Assets from Tests of the Two-Parameter Model: A Sensitivity Analysis," *Journal of Financial Economics*, 10, 237–268.

TANG, P. C. (1938): "The Power Function of the Analysis of Variance Tests with Tables and Illustrations of Their Use," *Statistical Research Memoirs*, 2, 126–150.

TIKU, M. L. (1967): "Tables of the Power of the F-Test," *Journal of the American Statistical Association*, 62, 525–539.

TREYNOR, J. L., AND F. BLACK (1973): "How to Use Security Analysis to Improve Portfolio Selection," *Journal of Business*, 46, 66–86.

# Empirical Tests of the Consumption-Oriented CAPM

DOUGLAS T. BREEDEN, MICHAEL R. GIBBONS, and
ROBERT H. LITZENBERGER*

## ABSTRACT

The empirical implications of the consumption-oriented capital asset pricing model (CCAPM) are examined, and its performance is compared with a model based on the market portfolio. The CCAPM is estimated after adjusting for measurement problems associated with reported consumption data. The CCAPM is tested using betas based on both consumption and the portfolio having the maximum correlation with consumption. As predicted by the CCAPM, the market price of risk is significantly positive, and the estimate of the real interest rate is close to zero. The performances of the traditional CAPM and the CCAPM are about the same.

IN AN INTERTEMPORAL ECONOMY, Rubinstein (1976), Breeden and Litzenberger (1978), and Breeden (1979) demonstrate that equilibrium expected excess returns are proportional to their "consumption betas." This contrasts with the market-oriented capital asset pricing model (hereafter, CAPM) derived in a single-period economy by Sharpe (1964) and Lintner (1965). While tests of the CAPM by Black, Jensen, and Scholes (1972), Fama and MacBeth (1973), Gibbons (1982), and others find a positive association between average excess returns and betas using a proxy for the market portfolio, the relation is not proportional. This paper studies similar empirical issues for the consumption-oriented capital asset pricing model (hereafter, CCAPM).

Even though the relevant market portfolio includes all assets, most empirical research focuses on common stocks for which accurately measured data are available. In contrast, reported consumption data are estimates of the relevant consumption flows, and the data are subject to measurement problems not found with stock indexes. In this paper the tests of the CCAPM incorporate some adjustments for these measurement problems.

The outline of the paper is as follows. Section I provides an alternative derivation of the CCAPM. Section II examines four econometric problems associated with measured consumption: the durables problem, the problem of

*Duke University; Stanford University and visiting the University of Chicago (1988-1989); and University of Pennsylvania, respectively. We are grateful for the comments we have received from seminar participants at a number of universities. Special thanks go to Eugene Fama, Wayne Ferson, Bruce Lehmann, Bill Schwert, Jay Shanken, Kenneth Singleton, René Stulz, and an anonymous referee. Over the years this paper has benefited also from research assistance by Susan Cheng, Hal Heaton, Chi-Fu Huang, Charles Jacklin, and Ehud Ronn. Financial support was provided in part to all authors by the Stanford Program in Finance. Breeden (1981-1982) and Gibbons (1982-1983) acknowledge with thanks financial support provided for this research by Batterymarch Financial Management.

measured consumption as an integral of spot consumption rates, the problem that consumption data are reported infrequently, and the problem of pure sampling error in consumption measures. Time series properties of consumption measures are also discussed in Section II. Section III analyzes the empirical characteristics of estimated consumption betas for various stock and bond portfolios. The composition of the portfolio whose return has the highest correlation with the growth rate of real, per capita consumption is also discussed in Section III. This portfolio is used in some of the tests of the model. Section IV presents empirical tests of the consumption and market-oriented CAPMs based on their implications for unconditional moments. Section V concludes the paper with a review of the results obtained.

## I. A Synthesis of the CCAPM Theory

The Rubinstein (1976) derivation of the CCAPM assumes that, over a discrete time interval, the joint distribution of all assets' returns with each individual's optimal consumption is normal. More generally, Breeden and Litzenberger (1978) derive the CCAPM in a discrete-time framework for the *subset of assets* whose returns are jointly lognormally distributed with aggregate consumption. Breeden's (1979) continuous-time derivation of the CCAPM applies instantaneously to all assets, based on the assumption that assets' returns and individuals' optimal consumption paths follow diffusion processes. In all these papers, utility functions are time additive.

Since the CCAPM is well known, a standard review is unnecessary. The following synthesis provides a theoretical basis that is more relevant for the subsequent empirical work. In particular, theoretical predictions are derived for easily estimated models which are based on unconditional moments of returns using discretely sampled data.

Let $\{\tilde{R}_{it}, i = 1, \cdots, M\}$ be the rates of return on risky assets from time $t - 1$ to time $t$. $M$ may be less than the number of all risky assets in the economy. Let $\tilde{R}_{zt}$ be the rates of return on a portfolio whose return is uncorrelated with the growth rate in aggregate consumption. All individuals are assumed to have time-additive, monotonically increasing, and strictly concave von Neumann-Morgenstern utility functions for lifetime consumption. Identical beliefs, a fixed population with infinite lifetimes, a single consumption good, and capital markets that permit an unconstrained Pareto-optimal allocation of consumption are also assumed. From the first-order conditions for individual $k$'s optimal consumption and portfolio plan, it follows that

$$\mathscr{E}[(\tilde{R}_{it} - \tilde{R}_{zt})[U^{k'}(\tilde{C}_t^k)/U^{k'}(C_{t-1}^k)] \mid \phi_{t-1}] = 0, \forall \ i, k, \tag{1}$$

where $\phi_{t-1}$ describes the full information set at time $t - 1$. This relation holds for any sampling interval. This is well known (e.g., see Lucas (1978)).

An individual achieves an optimal portfolio by adjusting the portfolio weights and consumption plans until relation (1) holds for all assets. Breeden and Litzenberger (1978) show that, in a capital market that permits an unconstrained Pareto-optimal allocation of consumption, each individual's consumption at a given date is an increasing function of *aggregate* consumption. Furthermore, each individual's optimal marginal utility of consumption at a given date $t$ is equal to a scalar, $a_k$, times a monotonically decreasing function of aggregate consumption, $g\,(C_t,t)$, which is identical for all individuals. The assumption that all individuals have the same subjective rate of time preference implies that the time dependence of the aggregate marginal utility function is the same for all dates, so $g\,(C_t,t) = f\,(C_t)$. Thus, in equilibrium in a Pareto-efficient capital market, the growth rate in the marginal utility of consumption would be identical for all individuals and equal to the growth rate in the "aggregate marginal utility" of consumption. That is,

$$\frac{U'(C_t)}{U'(C_{t-1})} = \frac{f(C_t)}{f(C_{t-1})} \cong 1 - [-C_{t-1}f'(C_{t-1})/f(C_{t-1})]c_t^*, \qquad (2)$$

where $c_t^*$ is the growth rate in aggregate consumption per capita and where the approximation follows from a first-order Taylor series. The term in square brackets is aggregate relative risk aversion evaluated at $C_{t-1}$. If we take relative risk aversion as approximately constant and denote it as $b$, we can combine (1) with these approximations in (2) and find (ignoring the approximations)[1]

$$\mathscr{E}\{(\tilde{R}_{it} - \tilde{R}_{zt})(1 - b\tilde{c}_t^*)|\phi_{t-1}\} = 0. \qquad (3)$$

Since (3) is zero conditional on any information, it also holds in terms of unconditional expectations:

$$\mathscr{E}\{(\tilde{R}_{it} - \tilde{R}_{zt})(1 - b\tilde{c}_t^*)\} = 0. \qquad (4)$$

The return on an asset may be stated as a linear function of the growth rate in aggregate consumption per capita, $c_t^*$, plus a disturbance. This disturbance term is assumed to be uncorrelated with $\tilde{c}_t^*$ for a proper subset of assets ($i = 1, \cdots, M$). These conditions, combined with the assumption of constant unconditional consumption betas and alphas, imply

$$\tilde{R}_{it} = \alpha_{ci}^* + \beta_{ci}^*\tilde{c}_t^* + \tilde{u}_{it}^*, \quad \forall i = 1, \cdots, M,$$

$$\mathscr{E}\{\tilde{u}_{it}^*\} = 0 \quad \text{and} \quad \mathscr{E}\{\tilde{u}_{it}^*\tilde{c}_t^*\} = 0, \qquad (5)$$

where $\beta_{ci}^* \equiv \text{cov}(\tilde{R}_{it}, \tilde{c}_t^*)/\text{var}(\tilde{c}_t^*)$, $\alpha_{ci}^* \equiv \mu_i - \beta_{ci}^*\mathscr{E}\{\tilde{c}_t^*\}$, and $\mu_i \equiv \mathscr{E}\{\tilde{R}_{it}\}$. Asterisks indicate parameters in relation to true consumption growth. Later asterisks are removed to indicate parameters in relation to measured consumption growth.

For a zero consumption beta portfolio consisting of just the $M$ assets,

$$\tilde{R}_{zt} = \gamma_0 + \tilde{\mu}_{zt}^*,$$

$$\mathscr{E}\{\tilde{u}_{zt}\} = 0,$$

$$\mathscr{E}\{\tilde{u}_{zt}\tilde{c}_t^*\} = 0. \qquad (6)$$

Substituting the right-hand side (hereafter, RHS) of (5) and (6) into relation (4) gives the CCAPM:

$$\mu_i - \gamma_0 = \gamma_1^*\beta_{ci}^*, \quad \forall\ i = 1, \cdots, M, \qquad (7)$$

---

[1] The approximation can be avoided by making an additional distributional assumption that $\text{cov}(\tilde{u}_{it}^*, \tilde{X}_t) = 0$, where $X_t \equiv f\,(\hat{c}_t)/f\,(\hat{c}_{t-1})$ and $\tilde{u}_{it}^*$ is defined in (5) below. All the following results go through, and $\gamma_1^* \equiv \text{cov}(\tilde{c}_{t1} - \tilde{X}_t)/E\,(\tilde{X}_t)$. The market price of consumption beta risk, $\gamma_1^*$, appears in equation (7) below.

where $\gamma_1^* \equiv b \, \mathrm{var}(\tilde{c}_t^*)/[1 - b\mathscr{E}\,(\tilde{c}_t^*)]$. The market price of consumption beta risk, $\gamma_1^*$, increases as the variability of consumption increases. If $[1 - b\mathscr{E}\,(\tilde{c}_t^*)] > 0$ and $\mathscr{E}\,(\tilde{c}_t^*) > 0$, then $\gamma_1^*$ also increases as relative risk aversion increases.

This model only gives the CCAPM for a proper subset of assets—those assets that have a conditionally linear relation with $c_t^*$ over the measurement interval. Assets which do not satisfy (5) still are priced according to their joint distributions of payoffs with consumption, but higher order co-moments with consumption are required for pricing over discrete intervals. Since in the continuous-time model all assets' returns and consumption are locally jointly normally distributed, the CCAPM applies to all assets as long as returns can be measured over instantaneous intervals. However, since the available data are measured discretely, the CCAPM in (7) is more useful for empirical tests.

In continuous time with time-additive utility, Breeden (1979) demonstrates that Merton's (1973) intertemporal multi-beta asset pricing model is equivalent to a single-beta CCAPM. However, Cornell (1981) emphasizes that the conditional consumption beta in such a representation need not be constant. The tests presented in this paper are tests of restrictions on the unconditional co-moments of assets returns and consumption growth. As Grossman and Shiller (1982) point out, such tests do not ignore Cornell's (1981) concerns about changes in the conditional moments. An advantage of tests based on unconditional moments is that a specification of the changes in conditional moments is not required. To the extent that changes in the conditional moments could be modeled, the resulting tests may be more powerful. For examples of such tests see Gibbons and Ferson (1985), Hansen and Singleton (1983), and Litzenberger and Ronn (1986). Since the CCAPM has predictions for conditional and unconditional expectations, failure to reject the "unconditional CCAPM" is a necessary, but not sufficient, condition for acceptance of the model.

## II. Econometric Problems Associated with Measured Consumption

In this section, a distinction is made between the appropriate theoretical definition of aggregate consumption per capita and the consumption reported by the Department of Commerce. Four measurement problems are examined: 1) the reporting of expenditures, rather than consumption, 2) the reporting of an integral of consumption rates, rather than the consumption rate at a point in time, 3) infrequent reporting of consumption data relative to stock returns, and 4) reporting aggregate consumption with sampling error since only a subset of the total population of consumption transactions is measured.

The CCAPM prices assets with respect to changes in aggregate consumption between two points in time. In contrast, the available data on aggregate "consumption" provide total expenditures on goods and services over a period of time. These differences between consumption in theory and its measured counterpart suggest the first two problems. First, goods and services need not be consumed in the same period that they are purchased. Second, measured aggregate consumption is closer to an integral of consumption over a period of time than to "spot" consumption (at a point in time). This second problem creates a "summation bias."

While returns on stocks are available on an intraday basis, corresponding consumption data are not available. Currently, only quarterly data are provided back to 1939, and monthly reporting begins in 1959. Infrequent reporting of aggregate expenditures on consumption is the measurement problem analyzed in the third subsection. The fourth subsection demonstrates that sampling error in aggregate consumption does not bias the statistical tests.

## A. Description of the Consumption Data

Exploring the empirical implications of the CCAPM for a long sample period requires aggregate consumption data from different sources. The tables in Sections III and IV focus on a time series for consumption that requires "splicing" the data at two points. Each of these three data sources is discussed in turn.

As is discussed later, powerful tests of any asset pricing model require precise estimations for the relevant betas. Precision of the estimators improves if the variability of the consumption measure increases, holding everything else constant. Since consumption was quite variable in the 1930s, we want to include this time period in our empirical work.[2] Unfortunately, aggregate consumption data are not available, except for annual sampling intervals, from 1929 to 1939. However, nominal personal income less transfer payments is available on a monthly basis from the U.S. Department of Commerce,[3] and these income numbers are used to approximate quarterly consumption for this decade.

From 1929 to 1939 a regression of annual consumption data on personal income yields

$$z_{1t} = 0.00186 + 0.56z_{2t} + \hat{v}_t, \qquad R^2 = 0.94, \qquad (8)$$
$$\phantom{z_{1t} = }(0.39) \qquad (11.51)$$

where $z_{1t} \equiv$ annual growth of real nondurables and services consumption per capita, $z_{2t} \equiv$ annual growth of real personal income less transfer payments per capita, and $t$-statistics are in parentheses. The data for the above regression are deflated by the average level of the Consumer Price Index (CPI) from the U.S. Bureau of Labor Statistics. The population numbers, which are used to calculate per capita values, are from the *Statistical Abstract of the United States* and reflect the resident population of the U.S. The monthly numbers on personal income less transfer payments are used to infer the consumption numbers based on the above regression equation. From these monthly estimates of consumption, quarterly growth rates are constructed.

From 1939 through 1958 the spliced consumption data rely on quarterly expenditures on nondurable goods and services based on national income accounting. From 1939 through 1946, the data are deflated by the average level of the monthly CPI for the relevant quarter. From 1947 through 1958, real consumption data are available from the Commerce Department. Only seasonally

---

[2] There is no doubt that part of the unusual volatility of consumption during the 1930s is due to data construction, not variation in true consumption.

[3] For both the annual and monthly data, see *National Income and Product Statistics of the United States, 1929–46*. This appeared as a supplement to the *Survey of Current Business*, July 1947.

adjusted numbers for consumption are available.[4] Average total U.S. population during a quarter as reported by the Commerce Department is used to calculate the per capita numbers. Various issues of *Business Conditions Digest, Business Statistics,* and *The National Income and Product Accounts of the United States* report the relevant data.

The consumption data from 1959 to 1982 are constructed in essentially the same manner as that from 1947 to 1958.[5] However, since the government started publishing monthly numbers during this latter period, these monthly numbers are used to compute growth in real consumption per capita over a quarter. For example, growth in a first quarter is based on expenditures during March, relative to expenditures during the prior December.

In later sections, the term "spliced" consumption data refers to the data base constructed in the above manner, which combines the quarterly observations on monthly income data from 1929 to 1938, the quarterly consumption expenditures from 1939 to 1958, and the quarterly observations on the monthly consumption expenditures from 1959 to 1982.

For the whole time period (1929–1982), the consumption data are based on expenditures on nondurables plus services, following Hall (1978). This is an attempt to minimize the measurement problem associated with expenditures versus current consumption of goods and services. No attempt is made to extract the consumption flow from durable goods.[6] While monthly sampling of consumption data is available after 1958, most of the tables do not rely on this information. As the sampling interval decreases, "nondurables" become more durable. However, some of the calculations have been repeated using monthly sampling intervals, and these results are summarized in the text and footnotes.

## B. Interval versus Spot Consumption (the Summation Bias)

Ignoring other measurement problems, the reported ("interval") consumption rate for a quarter is the integral of the instantaneous ("spot") consumption rates during the quarter. The CCAPM relates expected quarterly returns on assets (e.g., from January 1 to March 31) and the covariances of those returns with the change in the spot consumption rate from the beginning of the quarter to the end of the quarter. This subsection derives the relation between the desired population covariances (and betas) of assets' returns relative to spot consumption changes and the population covariances (and betas) of assets' returns relative to changes in interval consumption. The variance of interval consumption changes is shown to have only two thirds the variance of spot consumption changes, while the autocorrelation of interval consumption is 0.25 due to the integration of spot

---

[4] Since the seasonal adjustment smoothes expenditures, such an adjustment may be desirable if the transformed expenditures better resemble actual consumption. Of course, seasonal adjustment is inappropriate if it removes seasonals in true consumption.

[5] The only exception to this occurs for the population number for December 1978. This number is adjusted from the published tables because there is an obvious typographical error.

[6] Alternative treatments for this measurement problem exist in the literature. For example, Marsh (1981) postulates a latent variable model to estimate the parameters of the CCAPM. A more recent attempt is made by Dunn and Singleton (1986), using an econometric approach that relies on the specification of preferences for the representative economic agent.

rates. These latter results are reported by Working (1960) and generalized by Tiao (1972). Similar results on time aggregation have been used in studies of stock prices and corporate earnings (Lambert (1978) and Beaver, Lambert, and Morse (1980)). In an independent and contemporaneous paper, Grossman, Melino, and Shiller (1987) derive maximum-likelihood estimates of CCAPM parameters, explicitly accounting for time aggregation of consumption data. Our bias corrections are much simpler but give similar results.

Without loss of generality, consider a two-quarter period with $t = 0$ being the beginning of the first quarter and $t = T$ being the end of the first quarter. All discussion will analyze annualized consumption rates, so $T = 0.25$ for a quarter. Initially, let the change in the spot consumption rate over a quarter be the cumulative of $n$ discrete changes, $\{\tilde{\Delta}_1^C, \tilde{\Delta}_2^C, \cdots, \tilde{\Delta}_n^C\}$ for the first quarter, and $\{\tilde{\Delta}_{n+1}^C, \tilde{\Delta}_{n+2}^C, \cdots, \tilde{\Delta}_{2n}^C\}$ for the second quarter. That is, $\tilde{C}_T = C_0 + \sum_1^n \tilde{\Delta}_i^C$. Similarly, let the wealth at time $T$ from buying one share of an asset at time 0 (and reinvesting any dividends) equal its initial price plus $n$ random increments $\{\tilde{\Delta}_i^a\}: P_T = P_0 + \sum_1^n \tilde{\Delta}_i^a$.[7]

Changes in consumption, $\tilde{\Delta}_i^C$, are assumed to be homoscedastic and serially uncorrelated. Similar assumptions are made for the asset's return, $\tilde{\Delta}_i^a$, with variance $\sigma_a^2$. The contemporaneous covariation of an asset's return with consumption changes is $\sigma_{ac}$, and noncontemporaneous covariances are assumed to be zero. The variance of the change in the spot consumption from the beginning of a quarter to the end of the quarter is $\text{var}(\tilde{C}_T - \tilde{C}_0) = \text{var}(\sum_1^n \tilde{\Delta}_i^C) = \sigma_C^2 T$.

The first quarter's *reported* annualized consumption, $C_{Q1}$, is a summation of the consumption during the quarter, annualized by multiplying by 4 (or $1/T$):

$$C_{Q1} = (1/T) \sum_{j=1}^n C_j \Delta t = (1/T) \sum_{j=1}^n (C_0 + \sum_{i=1}^j \Delta_i^C) \Delta t. \tag{9}$$

The annualized consumption rate for the second quarter, $C_{Q2}$, is the same as (9), but with the first summation for $j$ being $n + 1$ to $2n$.

Continuous movements in consumption and asset prices can be approximated by letting the number of discrete movements per quarter, $n$, go to infinity ($\Delta t \to 0$). Doing this, the change in reported consumption becomes[8]

$$C_{Q2} - C_{Q1} = \int_0^T (t/T) \Delta_t^C \, dt + \int_T^{2T} ((2T - t)/T) \Delta_t^C \, dt. \tag{10}$$

---

[7] The summation bias is developed for price changes and consumption changes, not rates of return and consumption growth rates. When the prior period's price and consumption are fixed, the results of this section apply. However, in tests involving unconditional moments, the prior period's price and consumption are random. Since it is difficult to derive a closed-form solution for the summation bias in terms of rates, the subsequent analysis ignores this distinction.

[8] To see this, represent $C_{Q2}$ and $C_{Q1}$ as in (9) and take the difference:

$$C_{Q2} - C_{Q1} = (1/T) \left\{ \sum_1^{n+1} \Delta_i^C + \sum_1^{n+2} \Delta_i^C + \cdots + \sum_1^{2n} \Delta_i^C \right\} \Delta t$$

$$-(1/T) \left\{ \sum_1^1 \Delta_i^C + \sum_1^2 \Delta_i^C + \cdots + \sum_i^n \Delta_i^C \right\} \Delta t$$

$$= n^{-1} \{\Delta_2^C + 2\Delta_3^C + \cdots + (n - 1)\Delta_n^C + n\Delta_{n+1}^C + (n - 1)\Delta_{n+2}^C + \cdots + \Delta_{2n}^C\}.$$

Letting $n$ become large gives equation (10).

Given the independence of spot consumption change over time, (10) implies that the variance of reported annualized consumption changes is

$$\mathrm{var}(\tilde{C}_{Q2} - \tilde{C}_{Q1}) = \int_0^T ((t/T)^2 \sigma_C^2) \, dt$$

$$+ \int_T^{2T} ((2T - t)/T)^2 \sigma_C^2 \, dt = (2/3)\sigma_C^2 T. \tag{11}$$

Thus, the population variance of reported (interval) consumption changes for a quarter is two thirds of the population variance for changes in the spot consumption from the beginning of a quarter to the end of the quarter. The averaging caused by the integration leads to the lower variance for reported consumption.

Next, consider the covariance of an asset's quarterly return with quarterly changes in the consumption. The covariance of the change in spot consumption from the beginning of a quarter to the end of the quarter with an asset's return over the same period is $\sigma_{aC} T$, given the i.i.d. assumption. With reported, interval consumption data, the covariance can be computed from (10):

$$\mathrm{cov}(\tilde{C}_{Q2} - \tilde{C}_{Q1}, \tilde{P}_{2T} - \tilde{P}_T) = T^{-1} \int_T^{2T} (2T - t)\sigma_{aC} \, dt = T\sigma_{aC}/2. \tag{12}$$

Thus, from (12) the population covariance of an asset's quarterly return with reported (interval) consumption is half the population covariance of the asset's return with spot consumption changes.

Given (11) and (12), betas measured relative to reported quarterly consumption changes are ¾ times the corresponding betas with spot consumption:

$$\beta_{ac}^{sum} = \frac{(1/2)\sigma_{aC} T}{(2/3)\sigma_C^2 T} = (3/4)\beta_{ac}^{spot}. \tag{13}$$

Since the CCAPM relates quarterly returns to "spot betas," the subsequent empirical tests multiply the mean-adjusted consumption growth rates by ¾ to obtain unbiased "spot betas." The ¾ relation of interval betas to spot betas in (17) is a special case of the multiperiod differencing relation: $\beta_{ac}^{sum} = \beta_{ac}^{spot} [K - (1/2)]/[K - (1/3)]$, where $K$ is the differencing interval. Thus, monthly data sampled quarterly (i.e., $K = 3$) should give interval betas that are $(5/2)/(8/3) = 0.9375$ times the spot betas. When quarterly consumption growth rates are calculated from monthly data, the quarterly numbers are mean adjusted and multiplied by 0.9375.

Although changes in spot consumption are uncorrelated, changes in reported, interval consumption rates have positive autocorrelation. To see this, use (10) to compute the covariance of the reported consumption change from $Q1$ to $Q2$ with the reported change from $Q2$ to $Q3$, noting that all covariance arises from the time overlap from $T$ to $2T$:

$$\mathrm{cov}(\tilde{C}_{Q3} - \tilde{C}_{Q2}, \tilde{C}_{Q2} - \tilde{C}_{Q1}) = \int_T^{2T} ((t - T)(2T - t)/T^2)\sigma_C^2 \, dt = (1/6)\sigma_C^2 T. \tag{14}$$

The first-order autocorrelation in reported consumption is 0.25 since

$$\rho_1 = \text{cov}(\tilde{C}_{Q3} - \tilde{C}_{Q2}, \tilde{C}_{Q2} - \tilde{C}_{Q1})/\text{var}(\tilde{C}_{Q2} - \tilde{C}_{Q1}) = \frac{(1/6)\sigma_C^2 T}{(2/3)\sigma_C^2 T} = 0.25. \quad (15)$$

By similar calculations, higher order autocorrelation is zero. Table I presents the time series properties of reported *unspliced* quarterly consumption growth rates. First-order autocorrelation of quarterly real consumption growth for the entire 1939–1982 period is estimated to be 0.29, which is insignificantly different from the theoretical value of 0.25 at usual levels of significance. Higher order autocorrelations are not significantly different from zero. Thus, the model for reported consumption is not rejected by the sample autocorrelations.

Monthly growth rates of real consumption from 1959 to 1982 exhibit negative autocorrelation of −0.28, which is significantly different from zero and from the hypothesized 0.25. This may be caused by vagaries such as bad weather and strikes in major industries, which cut current consumption temporarily but are followed by catch-up purchases. Quarterly growth rates in consumption computed from the monthly series again have positive autocorrelation of 0.13, more closely in line with the value 0.0625 (or 1/16) predicted by the summation bias.[9] The longer the differencing interval, the less affected the data are by temporary fluctuations and measurement errors in consumption.

Chen, Roll, and Ross (1986) and Hansen and Singleton (1983) use monthly data on unadjusted consumption growth. Since those data's autocorrelation statistics suggest significant departures from the random-walk assumption, the statistics they present warrant re-examination. The use of larger differencing intervals should be fruitful.

## C. Infrequent Reporting of Consumption: The Maximum Correlation Portfolio

Since the returns on many assets are available for a longer time and are reported more frequently than consumption, more precise evidence on the CCAPM can be provided if only returns were needed to test the theory. Fortunately, Breeden's (1979, footnote 8) derivation of the CCAPM justifies the use of betas measured relative to a portfolio that has maximum correlation with growth in aggregate consumption, in place of betas measured relative to aggregate consumption. This result is amplified below, as it is shown that securities' betas measured relative to this maximum correlation portfolio (hereafter, MCP) are equal to their consumption betas divided by the consumption beta of the MCP. If a riskless asset exists, then the consumption beta of the MCP can be changed by adjusting leverage. Our MCP excludes the riskless asset, resulting in a consumption beta of 2.9.

In the following, the first $M$ assets have a linear relation with consumption as in equation (5). The CCAPM holds with respect to these $M$ assets when betas are measured relative to the MCP obtained from these $M$ assets. Second, for *any* subset $N$ (where $N \leq M$) of these $M$ assets, the CCAPM holds for that subset when betas are measured relative to the MCP obtained from these $N$ assets.

---

[9] The derivation of this prediction is similar to the derivation of equation (15).

Table I

# Time Series Properties of Percentage Changes in Real, Per Capita Consumption of Nondurable Goods and Services

Data are seasonally adjusted as reported by the Department of Commerce in the *Survey of Current Business*. $T$ denotes the number of observations, while $\bar{c}$ and $\widehat{SD}(c)$ are the sample mean and standard deviation, respectively. Under the hypothesis that the observations are serially uncorrelated, the asymptotic standard errors for the sample autocorrelations are $1/\sqrt{T}$, as given by $SD^*(\hat{\rho}_k)$. Under the hypothesis that $\rho_1 = 0.25$ and $\rho_k = 0\ \forall\ |k| > 1$, $SD(\rho_1)$ and $SD(\rho_k)$ report the asymptotic standard errors using the results of Bartlett (1946). The test statistic for the joint hypothesis that all autocorrelations are zero for lags 1 through 12 is given by $Q_{12}$, the modified Box-Pierce $Q$-statistic. $Q_{12}$ is asymptotically distributed as chi-square with 12 degrees of freedom. The $p$-value is the probability of drawing a $Q_{12}$ statistic larger than the current value under the null hypothesis.

| Time Period | $T$ | $\bar{c}$ | $\widehat{SD}(c)$ | $\hat{\rho}_1$ | $\hat{\rho}_2$ | $\hat{\rho}_3$ | $\hat{\rho}_4$ | $\hat{\rho}_8$ | $SD^*$ $(\hat{\rho}_k)$ | $\widehat{SD}$ $(\hat{\rho}_1)$ | $\widehat{SD}$ $(\hat{\rho}_k)$ | $Q_{12}$ | $p$-Value |
|---|---|---|---|---|---|---|---|---|---|---|---|---|---|
| | | | | | Panel A: Quarterly Consumption Data | | | | | | | | |
| 39Q2–82Q4 | 175 | 0.00543 | 0.00951 | 0.29 | 0.03 | −0.00 | 0.07 | 0.02 | 0.08 | 0.07 | 0.08 | 23.93 | 0.02 |
| 39Q2–52Q4 | 55 | 0.00665 | 0.01517 | 0.30 | 0.03 | −0.04 | 0.08 | 0.08 | 0.13 | 0.12 | 0.14 | 11.26 | 0.51 |
| 53Q1–67Q4 | 60 | 0.00463 | 0.00549 | 0.21 | 0.09 | 0.11 | −0.01 | −0.22 | 0.13 | 0.12 | 0.14 | 11.25 | 0.51 |
| 68Q1–82Q4 | 60 | 0.00511 | 0.00487 | 0.36 | 0.01 | 0.26 | 0.09 | −0.31 | 0.13 | 0.12 | 0.14 | 25.95 | 0.01 |
| | | | | | Panel B: Monthly Consumption Data | | | | | | | | |
| 1959–1982 | 287 | 0.00178 | 0.00447 | −0.28 | −0.02 | −0.14 | −0.12 | −0.19 | 0.06 | 0.05 | 0.06 | 43.09 | 0.00 |
| 1959–1970 | 143 | 0.00199 | 0.00467 | −0.31 | −0.11 | 0.18 | −0.08 | −0.17 | 0.08 | 0.08 | 0.09 | 33.49 | 0.00 |
| 1971–1982 | 144 | 0.00156 | 0.00427 | −0.24 | 0.07 | 0.09 | −0.16 | −0.16 | 0.08 | 0.08 | 0.09 | 20.56 | 0.06 |
| | | | | | Panel C: Quarterly Sampling of Monthly Consumption Data | | | | | | | | |
| 59Q2–82Q4 | 95 | 0.00521 | 0.00568 | 0.13 | −0.13 | 0.20 | 0.04 | −0.17 | 0.10 | 0.09 | 0.11 | 13.42 | 0.34 |
| 59Q2–70Q4 | 47 | 0.00576 | 0.00506 | 0.13 | −0.15 | 0.13 | −0.03 | −0.04 | 0.15 | 0.13 | 0.15 | 10.61 | 0.56 |
| 71Q1–82Q4 | 47 | 0.00468 | 0.00623 | 0.12 | −0.07 | 0.22 | −0.10 | −0.26 | 0.14 | 0.13 | 0.15 | 11.40 | 0.50 |

The following notation will be used throughout the paper. Let $\mu$ be the $N \times 1$ vector unconditional expected returns, let $\mathbf{1}$ be an $N \times 1$ vector of ones, and let $\beta_c^*$ be the $N \times 1$ vector of unconditional consumption betas. Let $\tilde{R}_{mcp}$ be the return on the MCP that excludes the riskless asset, let $\beta_{c,nb}^*$ be the unconditional consumption beta of this "no borrowing" MCP, and let $\beta_{mcp}$ be the $N \times 1$ vector of unconditional MCP betas. The $N \times N$ unconditional covariance matrix for returns is $\mathbf{V}$, which is assumed to be nonsingular.

Consider the following portfolio problem: find the minimum-variance portfolio that has a consumption beta of $\beta_{c,nb}^*$ (i.e., with no borrowing). The consumption beta of a portfolio is the product of its correlation coefficient with consumption and the portfolio's standard deviation, divided by the standard deviation of consumption. By constraining the consumption beta to be fixed and then minimizing variance, the resulting portfolio has the maximum correlation with consumption, i.e., the MCP. Mathematically, the MCP solves

$$\min_{\{\mathbf{w}\}}: \mathbf{w}'\mathbf{V}\mathbf{w} + 2\lambda(\beta_{c,nb}^* - \mathbf{w}'\beta_c^*), \qquad (16)$$

where $\lambda$ is a Lagrange multiplier. The weights (i.e., $\mathbf{w}$) in the MCP are not constrained to unity since the risky assets may be combined with a riskless asset without any effect on the correlation coefficient, the variance, or the consumption beta. Alternatively, if the weights obtained sum to the value $S$, those same weights multiplied by $1/S$ sum to unity and have the same correlation with consumption. Thus, the existence or nonexistence of a riskless asset does not affect the MCP analysis.

The first-order conditions imply

$$\mathbf{w}_{mcp} = \lambda \mathbf{V}^{-1}\beta_c^*. \qquad (17)$$

Since $\beta_{c,nb}^* = \mathbf{w}_{mcp}'\beta_c^*$, $\lambda = \beta_{c,nb}^*/(\beta_c^{*'}\mathbf{V}^{-1}\beta_c^*)$. Pre-multiplying (17) by $\mathbf{w}_{mcp}'\mathbf{V}$ and simplifying implies $\mathbf{w}_{mcp}'\mathbf{V}\mathbf{w}_{mcp} = \lambda\beta_{c,nb}^*$. The MCP betas of risky assets are

$$\beta_{mcp} = \frac{\mathbf{V}\mathbf{w}_{mcp}}{\mathbf{w}_{mcp}'\,\mathbf{V}\mathbf{w}_{mcp}} = \frac{\lambda\beta_c^*}{\lambda\beta_{c,nb}^*} = \beta_c^*/\beta_{c,nb}^*, \qquad (18)$$

using the facts just derived.

In words, (18) states that assets' betas measured relative to the MCP are proportional to their betas relative to true consumption. Substituting (18) into the zero-beta CCAPM and using the CCAPM to get the expected excess return on the MCP implies

$$\mu - \gamma_0\mathbf{1} = \beta_{mcp}(\mu_{mcp} - \gamma_0), \qquad (19)$$

Where $\mu_{mcp} \equiv \mathscr{E}(\tilde{R}_{mcp,t})$. Thus, the CCAPM may be restated (and tested) in terms of the MCP, and the testable implication is that the MCP is ex ante mean-variance efficient. Obviously, any zero-consumption beta portfolio also has a zero beta relative to the MCP.

The above result also suggests an intuitive interpretation of the portfolio weights for the MCP. Equation (17) implies

$$\mathbf{w}_{mcp} = \lambda \mathbf{V}^{-1}\beta_c^* = \theta \mathbf{V}^{-1}\mathbf{V}_{ac}^*, \qquad (20)$$

where $\theta \equiv \lambda/\mathrm{var}(\tilde{c}) = \dfrac{\beta_{c,nb}^*}{(\beta_c^{*'}\mathbf{V}^{-1}\beta_c^*)\mathrm{var}(\tilde{c}^*)}$ and $\mathbf{V}_{ac}^*$ is the $N \times 1$ vector of covariances of returns with consumption. From (20), the MCP's weights are proportional to the coefficients in a multiple regression of consumption on the various risky assets' returns, with $\theta$ being the factor of proportionality. Actually, $\theta$ equals $\beta_{c,nb}^*$ divided by the coefficient of determination $(R^2)$ of the multiple regression just described. To see this, note that the weights in the multiple regression, $\mathbf{w}_c^*$, are $\mathbf{w}_c^* = \mathbf{V}^{-1}\mathbf{V}_{ac}^*$, and the $R^2$ in the regression is

$$R^2 = (\mathbf{w}_c^{*'}\mathbf{V}\mathbf{w}_c^*)/\mathrm{var}(\tilde{c}^*) = (\beta_c^{*'}\mathbf{V}^{-1}\beta_c^*)\mathrm{var}(\tilde{c}^*), \tag{21}$$

which shows that $\theta = \beta_{c,nb}^*/R^2$. If there is a riskless asset, a unit beta MCP has weights that equal the regression's coefficients divided by the $R$-squared value of the regression (with any residual wealth in the riskless asset). Betas with respect to such a unit-beta MCP equal the assets' direct consumption betas (see equation (18)).

The optimization problem of (16) does not involve a constraint on means, so a MCP is not tautologically a mean-variance efficient portfolio. However, the CCAPM does imply mean-variance efficiency of that MCP in equilibrium. This implication is tested later in our paper.

## D. Sampling Error In Reported Consumption

In this section the problem of pure sampling error in reported consumption is examined. These errors are assumed to be random and uncorrelated with economic variables. Continue with $\tilde{c}_t^*$ as the true growth rate of real consumption from $t-1$ to $t$, and let $\tilde{c}_t$ be the reported growth rate. The measurement error, $\tilde{\epsilon}_t$, is such that

$$\tilde{c}_t = \tilde{c}_t^* + \tilde{\epsilon}_t \tag{22}$$

$$\mathcal{E}(\tilde{\epsilon}_t) = 0, \qquad \mathrm{cov}(\tilde{\epsilon}_t, \tilde{c}_t^*) = 0,$$

$$\mathrm{cov}(\tilde{\epsilon}_t, \tilde{R}_{it}) = 0, \qquad \forall \; i = 1, \cdots, N. \tag{23}$$

Substituting (22) into the CCAPM of (7) gives

$$\mu_i - \gamma_0 = \gamma_1^* \, \beta_{ci}^* = \gamma_1^* \mathrm{cov}(\tilde{R}_{it}, \tilde{c}_t - \tilde{\epsilon}_t)/\mathrm{var}(\tilde{c}_t^*)$$

$$= \gamma_1^* \, \frac{\mathrm{var}(\tilde{c}_t)\mathrm{cov}(\tilde{R}_{it}, \tilde{c}_t)}{\mathrm{var}(\tilde{c}_t^*)\mathrm{var}(\tilde{c}_t)} = \gamma_1\beta_{ci}, \tag{24}$$

where $\beta_{ci}$ is the beta asset of $i$ with respect to reported consumption, and $\gamma_1 \equiv \gamma_1^*[\mathrm{var}(\tilde{c}_t)/\mathrm{var}(\tilde{c}_t^*)]$. As long as the variance of the measurement error is positive, the variance of measured consumption exceeds the variance of true consumption. From (24), the slope coefficient, $\gamma_1$, in the relation between excess returns and betas with reported consumption is biased upward as an estimate of the price of risk, $\gamma_1^*$.

Sampling error in reported consumption does not cause a bias in the coefficients of a multiple regression of consumption growth on risky asset returns. However, the coefficient of determination for such a regression is downward biased. While the portfolio weights of the MCP are calculated by taking ratios of the regression coefficients divided by this $R^2$, the downward bias in $R^2$ affects all the weights in a proportional fashion. Thus, this has no effect on the subsequent tests.

Some other important measurement errors in aggregate consumption data involve interpolation (i.e., expenditures for all items are sampled every month), to which the analysis of this subsection is not applicable. This problem is similar to one faced by Fama and Schwert (1977, 1979) in their analysis of components of the CPI. Unfortunately, the interpolation problems with consumption are exacerbated by the summation bias, and it is difficult to disentangle the two effects. For example, either problem leads to serial correlation in consumption, noncontemporaneous correlation between aggregate consumption and returns, and more serious effects as sampling interval becomes shorter.[10] If the summation bias were not present, presumably an approach similar to that in Scholes and Williams (1977) would be appropriate. Perhaps the combination of interplation and summation bias explains the pattern of serial correlations in monthly data on consumption growth (see Panel B of Table I). Interpolation is yet another reason for avoiding monthly sampling intervals.

## III. Empirical Characteristics of Consumption Betas and the MCP

Since existing empirical research on the CCAPM is not extensive, we summarize how consumption betas vary across different assets. Several types of assets will be studied, including government and corporate bonds and equities.

Monthly returns on individual securities are gathered from the Center for Research in Security Prices (CRSP) at the University of Chicago. Twelve portfolios of these stocks are formed by grouping firms using the first two digits of their SIC numbers. The grouping closely followed a classification used by Sharpe (1982), with the major exception being that Sharpe's "consumer goods" category is subdivided. This subdivision should increase the dispersion of consumption betas in the sample. While other groupings of stocks have been suggested (e.g., see Stambaugh (1982)), Sharpe's scheme is selected because the industry portfolios are reasonable and capture some important correlation patterns among stocks. Table II provides more details on the classification scheme. To represent the return on a "buy and hold" strategy, relative market values are used to weight the returns in a given portfolio. Every return on the CRSP tape from 1926 through 1982 is included, which should minimize problems with survivorship bias.[11]

---

[10] Interpolation should result in serial correlation in the residuals in regressions of returns on consumption growth. (Equation (26) below is such a regression.) Yet, when we examine the residuals, the autocorrelations are not striking. On the other hand, when we run a multiple regression of returns on a leading value of consumption, current consumption, and lagged consumption, we do get an interesting pattern. Generally, the coefficient on the lead value is insignificant, the coefficient on current consumption is significant and positive, and the coefficient on lagged consumption is significant and negative. Usually, the absolute value of the coefficient on the lagged value is about half the value of the coefficient on current consumption. However, as we note in the text, the significance of the coefficient on lagged consumption is predictable if only a summation bias is present.

[11] However, all firms with a SIC number of 39 (i.e., miscellaneous manufacturing industries) are excluded to avoid any possible problems with a singular covariance matrix when the CRSP value-weighted index is added to the sample.

Table II

**Estimated Betas Relative to 1) Growth in Real, Per Capita Consumption[a], 2) Maximum-Correlation Portfolio for Consumption, and 3) CRSP Value-Weighted Index**

NA denotes not available. The maximum correlation portfolio (MCP) is constructed from the seventeen assets given in Table III. The weights of the MCP are determined by maximizing the sample correlation between the return on the portfolio and the growth rate of real consumption; see Table III for more details.

| Asset (SIC Codes) | Number of Firms | | | Spliced Consumption, Quarterly 1929–1982 ($T = 215$) | | | Max.-Correlation Cons. Portfolio, Monthly 1926–1982 ($T = 684$) | | | CRSP Value-Weighted Index Monthly 1926–1982 ($T = 684$) | | |
|---|---|---|---|---|---|---|---|---|---|---|---|---|
| | 1/26 | 6/54 | 12/82 | $\hat{\beta}_c$ | $t(\hat{\beta})$ | $R^2$ | $\hat{\beta}_{MCP}$ | $t(\hat{\beta})$ | $R^2$ | $\hat{\beta}_{CRSP}$ | $t(\hat{\beta})$ | $R^2$ |
| U.S. Treasury bills | — | — | — | −0.11 | −1.27 | 0.01 | 0.03 | 3.86 | 0.02 | 0.01 | 2.04 | 0.01 |
| Long-term govt. bonds | NA | NA | NA | −0.01 | −0.02 | 0.00 | 0.07 | 2.53 | 0.01 | 0.07 | 4.93 | 0.03 |
| Long-term corp. bonds | NA | NA | NA | 0.24 | 0.91 | 0.00 | 0.07 | 2.52 | 0.01 | 0.08 | 6.62 | 0.06 |
| Junk bond premium | NA | NA | NA | 2.45 | 6.85 | 0.18 | 0.63 | 18.52 | 0.33 | 0.33 | 20.45 | 0.38 |
| Petroleum (13, 29) | 46 | 51 | 69 | 4.31 | 6.37 | 0.16 | 1.41 | 20.61 | 0.38 | 0.92 | 38.63 | 0.69 |
| Finance & real estate (60–69) | 16 | 43 | 234 | 5.85 | 6.30 | 0.16 | 1.50 | 18.81 | 0.34 | 1.19 | 75.95 | 0.89 |
| Consumer durables (25, 30, 36, 37, 50, 55, 57) | 69 | 157 | 180 | 6.86 | 6.80 | 0.18 | 1.79 | 22.03 | 0.42 | 1.29 | 80.79 | 0.91 |

| | | | | | | | | | | | |
|---|---|---|---|---|---|---|---|---|---|---|---|
| Basic industries (10, 12, 14, 24, 26, 28, 33) | 94 | 207 | 194 | 5.45 | 6.95 | 0.18 | 1.48 | 21.98 | 0.41 | 1.09 | 100.80 | 0.94 |
| Food & tobacco (1, 20, 21, 54) | 64 | 103 | 81 | 3.25 | 5.69 | 0.13 | 0.99 | 18.62 | 0.34 | 0.76 | 58.15 | 0.83 |
| Construction (15–17, 32, 52) | 5 | 28 | 53 | 7.36 | 7.06 | 0.19 | 1.57 | 19.16 | 0.35 | 1.20 | 61.22 | 0.85 |
| Capital goods (34, 35, 38) | 39 | 120 | 191 | 5.31 | 6.74 | 0.18 | 1.45 | 21.10 | 0.39 | 1.08 | 85.90 | 0.92 |
| Transportation (40–42, 44, 45, 47) | 78 | 85 | 46 | 5.15 | 4.97 | 0.10 | 1.27 | 13.52 | 0.21 | 1.19 | 49.04 | 0.78 |
| Utilities (46, 48, 49) | 24 | 102 | 176 | 3.73 | 6.10 | 0.15 | 1.04 | 19.40 | 0.35 | 0.75 | 46.34 | 0.76 |
| Textiles & trade (22, 23, 31, 51, 53, 56, 59) | 46 | 101 | 119 | 5.63 | 7.84 | 0.22 | 1.66 | 30.49 | 0.58 | 0.95 | 48.73 | 0.78 |
| Services (72, 73, 75, 80, 82, 89) | 3 | 4 | 57 | 4.21 | 4.18 | 0.08 | 1.65 | 12.97 | 0.20 | 0.80 | 12.82 | 0.19 |
| Leisure (27, 58, 70, 78, 79) | 12 | 31 | 59 | 7.35 | 6.95 | 0.18 | 1.85 | 23.03 | 0.44 | 1.22 | 49.82 | 0.78 |
| CRSP value-weighted | NA | NA | NA | 4.92 | 7.06 | 0.19 | 1.37 | 23.73 | 0.45 | 1.00 | — | — |

[a] The spliced consumption data are scaled to adjust for the summation bias problem. Real growth in per capita consumption is multiplied by 0.75 for observations between 1939Q2 and 1959Q1, and by 0.9375 otherwise.

While methods which handle data on individual securities rather than aggregate portfolios could be dveloped, this route was not followed.[12] The dimensionality of the parameter space is enormous when analyzing a large cross-section of securities, and conventional methods for statistical inference may become unreliable. Also, a grouping procedure by industry decreases the number of statistics to be reported—probably without a disastrous loss of information.

Several types of assets should be represented, for Stambaugh (1982) finds the statistical results are not robust to the assets under study. Short-term Treasury bills, long-term government bonds, and high-grade long-term corporate bonds are included using the data in Ibbotson and Sinquefield (1982). In addition, the recent work by Chen, Roll, and Ross (1986) suggests that the difference in returns is between low-grade long-term corporate bonds (or "junk" bonds) and long-term government bonds is useful in explaining expected returns, so these returns are included as well.[13] To capture the spread between junk bonds and government bonds, a return is calculated on a portfolio which buys junk bonds by shorting long-term government bonds and then invests in short-term T-bills.[14] This portfolio's return is referred to as the "junk bond premium." Returns on junk bonds relative to government bonds primarily reflect changes in investors' perceptions concerning the probability of default. This is related to their perceptions of current and future economic conditions, which should be related to consumption growth. In fact, our statistical analysis shows a strong relation between junk bond returns and real consumption growth.

Returns are expressed in real terms and on a simple basis without continuously compounding. Returns are deflated by the Consumer Price Index, as reported by the U.S. Bureau of Labor Statistics on a monthly basis for the entire sample period. For purposes of testing the CAPM, the CRSP value-weighted index is used as the proxy for the market portfolio.[15]

Table II reports estimated betas for various assets. (The construction of the MCP is described below.) The table reveals that different measures of risk are highly correlated. In fact, the correlation between the market betas and the consumption betas (or the MCP betas) is 0.96 (or 0.94). Of course, while the risk measures are highly correlated, the rankings of the risk measures for the various assets are not exactly the same.

As discussed by Breeden (1980), industries' consumption betas should be related to price and income elasticities of demand and to supply elasticities. Goods with high income elasticities of demand should have high consumption

---

[12] Using different econometric methods, Mankiw and Shapiro (1985) have analyzed a version of the CCAPM using individual securities. However, they only rely on quarterly consumption data from 1959 to 1982.

[13] We are grateful to Roger Ibbotson, who made these data available to us. Since Ibbotson's data ended in 1978, the data are extended through 1982 using the monthly return on a mutual fund which is managed by Vanguard. This portfolio, the High Yield Bond Fund, is based on an investment strategy very similar to the one used by Ibbotson in constructing his return series.

[14] The investment in short-term T-bills is convenient but not necessary. The asset pricing models are specified assuming that the assets are held with some net capital invested.

[15] See Roll (1977) for a discussion of the potential consequences of selecting a proxy for the true market portfolio. The reader should keep in mind that one usual form of the consumption-based theory includes the market portfolio as part of the statement. Nevertheless, the theoretical results hold when any security replaces the market portfolio (Breeden (1979)).

betas, ceteris paribus. This appears to be borne out in the data, for consumer durables, construction, and recreation and leisure all have high consumption betas. While the services portfolio may have a high income elasticity, it does not have a high consumption beta. However, the number of firms in that portfolio is quite low (<5) for the first thirty years, and the $R$-squared is also low (0.08). Goods with lower income elasticities of demand, such as utilities, petroleum, food and agriculture, and transportation, have the lowest consumption betas of the stock portfolios.

Section II.*C* discusses the usefulness of a maximum correlation portfolio. Equation (20) suggests a way to calculate the weights in an MCP. Table III reports the results of running a regression of consumption growth on the returns from the twelve industry portfolios, four bond portfolios, and the CRSP value-weighted index for the period 1929–1982. Consumption growth is adjusted so that the summation bias in the estimated covariances between consumption and the returns on assets is removed. Table III gives the coefficients after they are rescaled so that they sum to one hundred percent, for the MCP in Section IV does not use the riskless asset.

The composition of the MCP in Table III helps to explain why Chen, Roll, and Ross (1986) found such an unimportant role for aggregate consumption. The MCP gives large absolute weights to long-term government bonds (−31%), the

### Table III

### Estimated Weights for the Maximum-Correlation Portfolio for Consumption Based on Spliced Quarterly Data from 1929–1982

All data are in real terms. (Consumption growth is scaled to adjust for the summation bias). The coefficient of determination for the above regression is 0.25, and the $F$-statistic for testing the joint significance of all the coefficients is 3.93 with a $p$-value of 0.0001. Before running real consumption growth on the returns, the data are mean adjusted. Then consumption growth is multiplied by two for observations between 1939Q2 and 1959Q1, and by 1.2 otherwise.

| Asset | Weight | $t$-Statistic |
|---|---|---|
| U.S. Treasury bills | 0.01 | 0.02 |
| Long-term government bonds | 0.54 | 1.05 |
| Long-term corporate bonds | −0.31 | −0.64 |
| Junk bond premium | 0.59 | 2.71 |
| Petroleum | 0.27 | 1.13 |
| Banking, finance and real estate | −0.17 | 0.38 |
| Consumer durables | 0.10 | 0.44 |
| Basic industries | 0.33 | 0.90 |
| Agriculture, food, and tobacco | −0.35 | −1.45 |
| Construction | −0.11 | −0.80 |
| Capital goods | 0.03 | 0.11 |
| Transportation | −0.29 | −2.25 |
| Utilities | 0.18 | 0.72 |
| Textiles, retail stores, and wholesalers | 0.49 | 2.69 |
| Services | 0.08 | 1.39 |
| Recreation and leisure | 0.13 | 1.17 |
| CRSP value-weighted index | −0.51 | −0.38 |
| | 1.00 | |

junk bond premium (59%), and the CRSP index (−51%). Since these three variables were included as factors in Chen, Roll, and Ross (1986), aggregate consumption may be dominated as an additional factor given multicollinearity and measurement error.

The weights reported in Table III seem extreme, for the MCP involves large short positions in assets. Placing restrictions on the estimated weights would eliminate the extreme positions but could sacrifice some consistency with the underlying theory. The collinearity among the assets makes it difficult to estimate any single weight with precision, but the fitted value from the regression may be useful for our purposes. To see how the MCP tracks consumption growth, the following regression is run using spliced quarterly data from 1929 to 1982 (again, consumption has been scaled so that the reported beta is free of the summation bias):[16]

$$R_{MCP,t} = 0.00828 + 2.90c_t' + \hat{u}_{MCP,t}, \ R^2 = 0.33, \tag{25}$$
$$\phantom{R_{MCP,t} = }(2.62) \qquad (10.19)$$

where $t$-statistics are given in parentheses. Since the MCP places no funds in the minimum-variance zero-beta portfolio, it need not have a unit beta. Even though the correlation between the MCP and consumption growth is 0.57, the theory of Section II. *C* still predicts that the MCP should be mean-variance efficient relative to the assets that it contains. Furthermore, the estimated risk measures when using actual consumption growth versus the MCP give similar rankings, and the sample correlation between the two sets of betas in Table II is 0.98.

Unlike the CRSP value-weighted index, the MCP has fixed weights since the entire sample period is used in the estimation reported in Table III. Constant weights are appropriate for the empirical work focuses on unconditional moments.[17] Moreover, estimating the weights by subperiods is not practical since quarterly data limit the number of available observations.

To better understand the MCP, Table IV compares it with the CRSP value-weighted index, a portfolio that has been studied extensively. According to Table III, the CRSP index has a negative weight in the MCP (−51%), yet the two portfolios are positively correlated. For the overall period, the correlation is 0.67. Furthermore, the MCP has roughly half the mean and standard deviation as the proxy for the market. Risk aversion combined with the CAPM predicts that the

---

[16] For observations between 1939Q2 and 1959Q1, $c_t' = 0.75(c_t - \bar{c})$. Otherwise, $c_t' = 0.9375 \ (c_{it} - \bar{c})$, where $\bar{c}$ is the sample mean of $c_t$ for the entire time period. By reducing the sizes of the consumption growth deviations, the slope coefficient is scaled up so as to be consistent (at least with regard to the summation bias).

[17] Even if second moments change conditional on predetermined information, working with a constant weight MCP is still appropriate for investigations involving unconditional moments. However, certain forms of heteroscedasticity may pose a problem for our statistical inference even in large samples. There is evidence of heteroscedasticity. We divided the overall period into four subperiods (1929Q2–1939Q1, 1939Q2–1947Q1, 1947Q2–1959Q1, and 1959Q2–1982Q4) and examined the constancy of the covariance matrix across all four periods. The covariance matrix is 18 × 18 involving the returns on seventeen assets in Table III and consumption growth. Using a likelihood-ratio test and an asymptotic approximation involving the $F$-distribution (Box (1949)), the $F$-statistic is 3.378 with degrees of freedom of 513 and 43165.7. The $p$-value is less than 0.001.

## Table IV

### Descriptive Statistics on Real Returns from Treasury Bills, the CRSP Value-Weighted Index, and the Maximum-Correlation Portfolio (MCP) for Consumption Based on Monthly Data, 1926–1982

The sample means are annualized by multiplying by 12. The sample standard deviations are annualized by multiplying by $\sqrt{12}$. (Since returns on T-bills are serially correlated, the annualized standard deviation is not the approximate standard deviation for annual holding periods.) Correlations between the CRSP return and the MCP return for the four periods are 0.67, 0.75, 0.59, and 0.41, respectively. The maximum-correlation portfolio (MCP) is constructed from the seventeen assets given in Table III. The weights of the MCP are determined by maximizing the sample correlation between the return on the portfolio and the growth rate of real consumption; see Table III for more details.

| Date | Number of Observations | Mean of T-bills | $t$-Statistic for Mean of T-bills | Standard Deviation |
|---|---|---|---|---|
| 1926–1982 | 684 | 0.0013 | 0.48 | 0.0204 |
| 1926–1945 | 240 | 0.0100 | 1.77 | 0.0253 |
| 1946–1965 | 240 | −0.0082 | −1.74 | 0.0211 |
| 1966–1982 | 204 | 0.0023 | 0.89 | 0.0106 |

| Date | Number of Observations | Mean of CRSP Return | $t$-Statistic for Mean of CRSP Return | Standard Deviation |
|---|---|---|---|---|
| 1926–1982 | 684 | 0.0767 | 2.88 | 0.2013 |
| 1926–1945 | 240 | 0.1002 | 1.61 | 0.2782 |
| 1946–1965 | 240 | 0.1039 | 3.70 | 0.1257 |
| 1966–1982 | 204 | 0.0172 | 0.44 | 0.1615 |

| Date | Number of Observations | Mean of MCP Return | $t$-Statistic for Mean of MCP Return | Standard Deviation |
|---|---|---|---|---|
| 1926–1982 | 684 | 0.0370 | 2.83 | 0.0987 |
| 1926–1945 | 240 | 0.0598 | 1.98 | 0.1351 |
| 1946–1965 | 240 | 0.0382 | 2.62 | 0.0651 |
| 1966–1982 | 204 | 0.0086 | 0.46 | 0.0786 |

mean of the market is positive, and the CCAPM makes the same prediction about the mean of the MCP. The point estimates for both portfolios are consistent with these predictions. However, when the standard deviation of the return is large in 1926–1945, the mean of the MCP is marginally significant while the market proxy is not.

## IV. Testing the CCAPM and the CAPM

The usefulness of the risk measures in predicting expected returns is examined in this section. Two issues are studied. First, does expected return increase as the risk increases? Second, is the relation between risk and return linear? These two issues are synonymous with the question of mean-variance efficiency for a given portfolio. In addition, estimates of the expected real return on the zero-beta portfolio will be compared with the real return on a nominally riskless bill.

The empirical implications of the CCAPM in terms of aggregate consumption are examined first. Then the empirical results are extended by testing the mean-variance efficiency of the maximum-correlation portfolio. Finally, the CAPM is studied by testing the ex ante efficiency of the CRSP index.

Since the relevant econometric methodology is detailed by Gibbons (1982), only a brief development is provided here. In the case of the CCAPM, a regression similar to the market model is assumed to be a well-specified statistical model. That is, the joint distribution between the return on an asset and real growth in per capita consumption, $\tilde{c}_t$, is such that the disturbance term in the following regression has mean zero and is uncorrelated with $\tilde{c}_t$. Such an assumption justifies the following regression model:

$$\tilde{R}_{it} = \alpha_{ci} + \beta_{ci}\tilde{c}_t' + \tilde{u}_{it}, \qquad \forall \ i = 1, \cdots, N, \quad t = 1, \cdots, T. \tag{26}$$

Further, it is assumed that

$$\mathscr{E}(\tilde{u}_{is}\tilde{u}_{jt}) = \begin{cases} \sigma_{ij} & \forall \ s = t, \\ 0 & \text{otherwise.} \end{cases} \tag{27}$$

Since $\tilde{c}_t'$ has already been mean-adjusted, $\mu_i$ is equal to $\alpha_{ci}$.[18] Also, $\tilde{c}_t'$ has been scaled so that the summation bias is avoided.

Using the CCAPM as modified in Section II. $D$ to account for sampling error in consumption provides

$$\mu_i = \gamma_0 + \gamma_1\beta_{ci}. \tag{28}$$

The theoretical relation in (28) imposes a parameter restriction on (26) of the form:

$$\alpha_{ci} = \gamma_0 + \gamma_1\beta_{ci}. \tag{29}$$

Pooling the time-series regressions in (26) across all $N$ assets and then imposing the parameter restriction given in (29) provides a framework in which to estimate the expected return on the zero-beta portfolio, $\gamma_0$, and the market price of beta risk, $\gamma_1$. In addition, the parameter restriction may be tested.

There are various econometric methods for estimating the above model. Many of these are asymptotically (as $T$ approaches infinity) equivalent to a full maximum-likelihood procedure. In the past, these alternatives have been selected because of computational considerations. However, results by Kandel (1984) and extended by Shanken (1985) make full maximum likelihood easy to implement.[19]

---

[18] Consumption growth is adjusted by its sample mean, not the unknown population mean. Our statistical inference that follows is conditional on the sample mean equal to its population counterpart. We overstate the significance of our tests as a result.

[19] Shanken (1982) shows that the full maximum-likelihood estimator may have desirable properties as the number of assets, $N$, used in estimating the model becomes large.

Shanken establishes that the full maximum-likelihood estimators for $\gamma_0$ and $\gamma_1$ can be found by minimizing the following function:

$$L(\gamma_0, \gamma_1) = (1/(1 + (\gamma_1^2/s_c^2)))\mathbf{e}'(\gamma)\hat{\boldsymbol{\Sigma}}^{-1}\mathbf{e}(\gamma), \qquad (30)$$

where

$\mathbf{e}(\gamma) \equiv \bar{\mathbf{R}} - \gamma_0\mathbf{1}_N - \gamma_1\hat{\beta}_c,$

$\hat{\boldsymbol{\Sigma}} \equiv T^{-1}\sum_{t=1}^{T}\hat{\mathbf{u}}_t\hat{\mathbf{u}}_t',$

$s_c^2 \equiv T^{-1}\sum_{t=1}^{T}c_t'^2;$

$\hat{\beta}_c \equiv N \times 1$ vector with typical element $\hat{\beta}_{ci}$, where $\hat{\beta}_{ci}$ is the usual unrestricted ordinary least-squares estimator of $\beta_{ci}$ in (26),

$\hat{\mathbf{u}}_t \equiv N \times 1$ vector with typical element $\hat{u}_{it}$, where $\hat{u}_{it}$ is the residual in (26) when ordinary least squares is performed, and

$\bar{\mathbf{R}} \equiv N \times 1$ vector with typical element $\bar{R}_i$, the sample mean of the return on asset $i$.

The concentrated-likelihood function is proportional to equation (30),[20] in which $\gamma_0$ and $\gamma_1$ are the only unknowns.

The first-order conditions for minimizing (30) involve a quadratic equation. The concentrated-likelihood function for the overall time period is graphed in Figure 1, a and b. Figure 1b suggests that, in the neighborhood of the maximum-likelihood estimates, $\gamma_0$ is estimated more precisely than $\gamma_1$ and there is negative correlation between the two estimates. Figure 1a has a coarser grid than Figure 1b. Figure 1a suggests that higher values for $\hat{\gamma}_1$ will not dramatically affect the maximized value of the likelihood function, but lower values for $\hat{\gamma}_1$ will have an impact.

Table V provides the point estimates of $\gamma_0$ and $\gamma_1$ along with the asymptotic standard errors. The subperiods in Table V correspond to the points where the data are spliced (see Section II. $A$). Unlike many studies on asset pricing models, the estimates of the expected return on the zero-beta asset are quite small. With the exception of the first subperiod, the point estimates are less than or equal to fifteen basis points (annualized), and in many cases the rate is negative (but only significant and negative in the second subperiod). This suggests that one implication of a riskless asset version of the CCAPM is consistent with the data. Table IV provides some information about the ex post real return on short-term Treasury bills during this time period, and in all cases the estimate of $\gamma_0$ is smaller than the sample mean in Table IV. Another implication of the CCAPM is that the market price of risk should be positive, for the expected return increases as the risk increases. This implication is verified for all periods, and

---

[20] Shanken derives this result by first maximizing the likelihood function with respect to $\beta_{ci}$ and $\sigma_{ij}$. These estimators depend on $\gamma_0$ and $\gamma_1$. Shanken then substitutes the estimators for $\beta_{ci}$ and $\sigma_{ij}$ back into the original likelihood function, which then depends on only $\gamma_0$ and $\gamma_1$. This new function is the concentrated-likelihood function. After some algebra he discovers that maximizing the concentrated-likelihood function is equivalent to minimizing (30) above. Note that full maximum likelihood refers to maximizing the likelihood function with respect to $\sigma_{ij}$ as well as $\gamma_0$, $\gamma_1$, and $\beta_{ci}$.

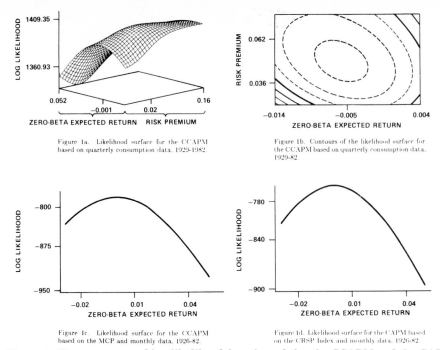

Figure 1a. Likelihood surface for the CCAPM based on quarterly consumption data, 1929-1982.

Figure 1b. Contours of the likelihood surface for the CCAPM based on quarterly consumption data, 1929-82.

Figure 1c. Likelihood surface for the CCAPM based on the MCP and monthly data, 1926-82.

Figure 1d. Likelihood surface for the CAPM based on the CRSP Index and monthly data, 1926-82.

**Figure 1. The concentrated log likelihood functions, $l$, for the CCAPM and the CAPM.** The relevant parameters of these functions are the expected annualized return on the "zero-beta" portfolio, $\gamma_0$, and the expected annualized premium for consumption-beta risk, $\gamma_1$.

the point estimate is statistically significant in most rows of Table V.[21] While the magnitude of the estimate of $\gamma_1$ seems large, Section II.*D* shows that $\gamma_1$ is biased upwards relative to $\gamma_1^*$ by the variance of the sampling error in reported consumption. Reflecting the large standard errors in some subperiods, the variation in $\hat{\gamma}_1$ across subperiods is striking. Since $\gamma_1$ does reflect the variance in measurement error for consumption, the high value of $\hat{\gamma}_1$ in the earlier subperiods (except 1929–1939) may be the result.

The CCAPM also implies that the relation between expected returns and betas is linear, or the null hypothesis is the equality given in (29). This null hypothesis is tested against a vague alternative that the equality does not hold.

Gibbons (1982) suggests a likelihood ratio for testing hypotheses like (29). Such an approach relies on an asymptotic distribution as $T$ becomes large. However, the methodology may have undesirable small sample properties, espe-

---

[21] In addition to the full maximum-likelihood procedure, the two step GLS estimator suggested in Gibbons (1982) was used. This estimator is not as desirable as the full maximum-likelihood approach as the number of securities approaches infinity, and it should be downward biased due to a phenomenon similar to errors-in-variables for simple regressions. Since consumption betas are measured less precisely than market betas, the difference between the full maximum likelihood and two-step GLS should be larger in this application than in past tests of the CAPM. In fact, the GLS estimate of $\gamma_1$ is usually half the value reported in Table V. On the other hand, the simulations by Amsler and Schmidt (1985) suggest that the finite sample behavior of the GLS estimator is better than the maximum-likelihood alternative. Since the sign of the estimate from either approach is the same across any row in Table V and since the significance from zero is the same across any row (except for one subperiod), the GLS results are not reported, but they are available on request to the authors.

**Table V**

## Estimating and Testing the CCAPM Using Aggregate Consumption Data

All data are annualized and in real terms ($\tilde{R}_{it}$), and consumption growth ($\tilde{c}'_t$) is adjusted to correct for the summation bias. The model is fit to seventeen assets (twelve industry portfolios, four boud portfolios, and the CRSP value-weighted index). The econometric model is

$$\tilde{R}_{it} = \alpha_{ci} + \beta_{ci}\tilde{c}'_t + \tilde{u}_{it},$$
$$\mathcal{E}(\tilde{u}_t\tilde{u}'_s) = \Sigma \text{ if } t = s, 0 \text{ otherwise.}$$
$$H_0: \alpha_{ci} = \gamma_0 + \gamma_1\beta_{ci}, \forall i = 1, \cdots, 17.$$

The data are annualized by multiplying the quarterly returns by 4 and monthly returns by 12. $F(\beta_{ci} = \beta_{cj})$ is the $F$-statistic for testing the hypothesis that $\beta_{ci} = \beta_{cj}$ $\forall$ $i \neq j$, while $F(\beta_{ci} = 0)$ tests the hypothesis that $\beta_{ci} = 0$, $\forall i = 1, \cdots, 17$. Both $\hat{\gamma}_0$ and $\hat{\gamma}_1$ are estimates from a full maximum-likelihood procedure, and their respective standard errors (given in parentheses below the estimates) are based on the inverse of the relevant information matrix. The likelihood ratio (LR) provides a test of the null hypothesis that expected returns are linear in consumption betas as implied by the CCAPM. The likelihood ratio is adjusted by Bartlett's (1938) correction. In all cases, $p$-value is the probability of seeing a higher statistic than the one reported under the null hypothesis. If the test statistics are independent across subperiods, then the last four rows can be aggregated into one summary measure. In the case of the likelihood-ratio test, the overall results yield a $\chi^2_{60}$ random variable with a realization equal to 69.06. (This yields a $p$-value equal to 0.198.) For the $F$-statistic, the overall results yield a standardized normal random variable with a realization equal to 0.68, which implies 0.25 as a $p$-value.

| Date | Number of Observations | F-test: Betas Equal (p-Value) | F-test: Betas = Zero (p-Value) | $\hat{\gamma}_0$ (SE($\hat{\gamma}_0$)) | $\hat{\gamma}_1$ (SE($\hat{\gamma}_1$)) | LR Test of $H_0$ (p-Value) |
|---|---|---|---|---|---|---|
| Panel A: Spliced Quarterly Consumption Data, Adjusted for Summation Bias, 1929–1982 | | | | | | |
| 1929Q2– 1982Q4 | 215 | 3.874 (<0.001) | 3.912 (<0.001) | −0.0061 (0.0044) | 0.0478 (0.0133) | 28.03 (0.021) |
| 1929Q2– 1939Q1 | 40 | 4.319 (0.001) | 4.241 (0.001) | 0.0484 (0.0091) | 0.0329 (0.0189) | 26.45 (0.034) |
| 1939Q2– 1947Q1 | 32 | 0.502 (0.908) | 1.410 (0.261) | −0.2558 (0.0859) | 0.5850 (0.2507) | 6.84 (0.962) |
| 1947Q2– 1959Q1 | 48 | 1.006 (0.476) | 1.182 (0.334) | −0.0699 (0.0469) | 0.2928 (0.1865) | 14.82 (0.464) |
| 1959Q2– 1982Q4 | 95 | 2.257 (0.009) | 2.277 (0.008) | 0.0015 (0.0028) | 0.0187 (0.0062) | 20.95 (0.138) |
| Panel B: Unspliced Quarterly Consumption Data, Adjusted for Summation Bias, 1947–1982 | | | | | | |
| 1947Q2– 1982Q4 | 144 | 1.342 (0.182) | 1.695 (0.052) | −0.0325 (0.0256) | 0.2136 (0.1430) | 19.87 (0.177) |
| 1959Q2– 1982Q4 | 96 | 1.398 (0.165) | 1.450 (0.137) | −0.0007 (0.0040) | 0.0528 (0.0179) | 16.29 (0.363) |
| Panel C: Unspliced Monthly Consumption Data, Adjusted for Summation Bias, 1959–1982 | | | | | | |
| 1959 Feb– 1982 Dec | 287 | 1.316 (0.186) | 1.581 (0.069) | −0.0008 (0.0034) | 0.0804 (0.0263) | 10.47 (0.789) |

cially when the number of assets is large (Stambaugh (1982)). The simulation by Amsler and Schmidt (1985) indicates that Barlett's (1938) correction, which was suggested by Jobson and Korkie (1982), improves the small sample performance of the likelihood ratio even when the number of assets is large. This correction is applied in all of the following tables.[22]

For the overall period using spliced data, the linear equality between reward and risk implied by the CCAPM is rejected at the traditional levels of significance. The last column of Table V reports the statistic in Panel A. This rejection is confirmed by Shanken's (1985, 1986) lower bound statistic, which suggests that the inference is robust to the asymptotic approximation of the likelihood ratio.[23] However, as noted at the bottom of Table V, aggregation of the results for each subperiod fails to reject the CCAPM at traditional levels of significance. The subperiod of 1929–1939 is the most damaging to the model. Given the nature of the consumption data used for this time period (see Section II. *A*), such behavior is troubling, for the rejection of the CCAPM may be due to measurement problems. On the other hand, the *F*-statistics given in the third and fourth columns of Table V suggest another interpretation. These *F*-statistics examine the joint significance of the risk measures across the assets as well as the significance of the dispersion of the risk measures across the assets. If all the risk measures were equal, then tests of (29) would lack power, and $\gamma_0$ and $\gamma_1$ would not be identified. In the first subperiod the risk measures are estimated with the most precision, and as a result tests against the null are more powerful.

Panel A of Table V is based on spliced quarterly consumption data. That is, monthly income predicts consumption for 1929–1939, and monthly consumption forms the basis of the quarterly numbers from 1959 to 1982. The above statistics are also calculated using the unspliced quarterly data from 1947 to 1982 with quarterly sampling intervals and on unspliced monthly data from 1959 to 1982 with monthly sampling intervals. The spliced data are considered first because the time series is longer and the measurement problems are less severe for quarterly observations than for monthly.

However, the results based on the spliced data are the least favorable to the CCAPM. Panels B and C in Table V suggest that the linearity hypothesis is *never* rejected with the unspliced monthly numbers and the unspliced quarterly numbers. Shanken's upper bound test confirms this result except for the subperiod 1947Q2-1982Q4. Also, the market price of consumption beta risk is also higher (with one exception) for the unspliced results.[24]

---

[22] The Lagrange multiplier test (suggested by Stambaugh (1982)) and the CSR test (suggested by Shanken (1986)) were also computed for all time periods without dramatically different results and not reported here. Both tests are monotonic transforms of the likelihood ratio (Shanken (1985)). The choice of which statistic to report is somewhat arbitrary. Since the geometric interpretation of the likelihood ratio follows, this statistic is reported in the tables.

[23] For all results we confirmed the inferences with Shanken's (1985, 1986) tests which have upper or lower bounds based on *finite sample* distributions. If the null hypothesis is not rejected with the upper bound, then it would not be rejected using an exact distribution. Similarly, if one rejects with the lower bound, such a result holds with a finite sample distribution.

[24] These results are consistent with those of Wheatley (1986), who re-examined Hansen and Singleton's (1983) tests of the CCAPM. Using 1959–1981 data, Wheatley showed by simulation that measurement error in consumption biased their test statistics. After correcting for that bias, he was unable to reject the CCAPM.

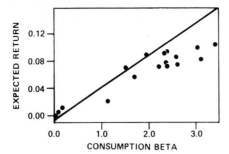

Figure 2a. 1929Q2 1982Q4.

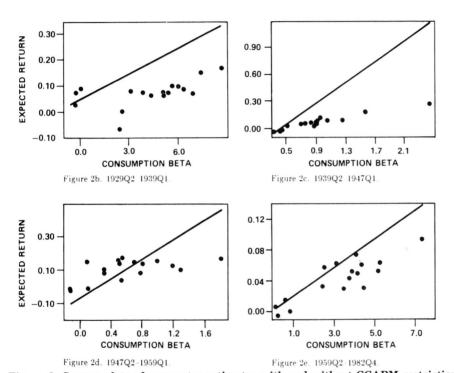

Figure 2b. 1929Q2 1939Q1.

Figure 2c. 1939Q2 1947Q1.

Figure 2d. 1947Q2–1959Q1.

Figure 2e. 1959Q2–1982Q4.

**Figure 2. Scatter plots of parameter estimates with and without CCAPM restriction.** All data are annualized and in real terms, and consumption growth is adjusted to correct for summation bias. Seventeen assets (twelve industry portfolios, four bond portfolios, and the CRSP value-weighted index) are used. The intercept and slope of the solid straight line in each plot are determined by the maximum-likelihood estimates for the expected return on the "zero-beta" asset and premium for consumption-beta risk, respectively (*not* the ordinary least squares fit of the points). All points should fall on this line if the CCAPM is true. The seventeen points on each plot represent unrestricted estimates of expected return, $E(\tilde{R}_{it})$, and consumption beta, $\beta_{ci}$. (Note that the scale varies across the scatter plots.)

Except for the subperiod 1929–1939 (and its effect on the results for the overall time period), Table V provides positive support for the CCAPM. To provide a more intuitive interpretation of the empirical results, Figure 2 informally examines the deviations for the null hypothesis. Figure 2 plots the unrestricted mean returns against the unrestricted estimates of betas. The straight line represents the relation estimated by maximum likelihood. Despite the rejection of the theory by formal tests, the relation between expected returns and betas is reasonably linear[25]—perhaps more than could have been anticipated given the poor quality of the consumption data. In some of the plots (e.g., Figure 2d), a straight line fit to the points would be flat. Given the measurement error in the consumption betas, this flatness is expected. To better understand the "empirical validity" of the CCAPM, the efficiency of the maximum-correlation portfolio will now be considered.

Section II. *C* demonstrates that the MCP is ex ante mean-variance efficient under the CCAPM. This result is derived when the covariance matrix among returns on securities and consumption growth is known, which is not the case here. Thus, all the statistical inference concerning the ex ante efficiency of the MCP is conditional on the portfolio being the desired theoretical construct. Estimation error in the portfolio weights is ignored.

Following Gibbons (1982), consider testing the efficiency of any portfolio $p$ when the riskless asset is not observed. Assume that the following regression is well specified in the sense that the error term has a zero mean and is uncorrelated with $\tilde{R}_{pt}$:

$$\tilde{R}_{it} = \alpha_{pi} + \beta_{pi}\tilde{R}_{pt} + \tilde{u}_{it}. \tag{31}$$

If portfolio $p$ is efficient, then the following parameter restriction holds:

$$\alpha_{pi} = \gamma(1 - \beta_{pi}), \tag{32}$$

where $\gamma$ is the expected return on the portfolio which is uncorrelated with p. Similar to the econometric model of (26) and (29) above, (31) and (32) are combined and then estimated by a full maximum-likelihood procedure. Furthermore, when (32) is treated as a null hypothesis, both a likelihood ratio and an asymptotic $F$ are calculated. In the tests that follow, the maximum-correlation portfolio or the CRSP index is used as portfolio $p$.[26]

Figure 1, c and d, graphs the concentrated-likelihood function relative to possible estimates of the expected return on the zero-beta portfolio in the case of the MCP and CRSP index, respectively. Table VI summarizes the statistical results for both portfolios as well. Like Table V, the third column of Table VI indicates a small expected return on the zero-beta asset. Further, the point estimate when using the MCP never exceeds that when using the CRSP index. Also, the overall period rejects the efficiency of either the maximum-correlation portfolio or the CRSP index, as indicated by the last column of the table. (This rejection would occur even without relying on asymptotic theory to approximate the sampling distribution, for the lower bound test also rejects.) Unlike Table V, the rejection of the model does not stem from just the first subperiod. These

---

[25] Like beauty, perceived linearity is in the eyes of the beholder. One reviewer of this paper thought the graphs in Figure 2 revealed remarkable nonlinearities.

[26] Panels A and B of Table VI are based on sixteen assets, not seventeen as in Table V. The regressions using the CRSP index as the dependent variable have been excluded because otherwise the covariance matrix of the residuals would be singular.

**Table VI**

**Estimating and Testing the Mean-Variance
Efficiency of the Maximum-Correlation
Portfolio (MCP) and the CRSP Value-Weighted
Index, 1926–1982**

All returns ($\tilde{R}_{it}$) are annualized and in real terms. The model is fit to sixteen assets (twelve industry and four bond portfolios). The econometric model is

$$\tilde{R}_{it} = \alpha_{pi} + \beta_{pi}\tilde{R}_{pt} + \tilde{u}_{it},$$
$$\mathcal{E}(\tilde{u}_t \tilde{u}'_s) = \Sigma \text{ if } t = s, 0 \text{ otherwise.}$$
$$H_0: \alpha_{pi} = \gamma(1 - \beta_{pi}), \forall i = 1, \cdots, 16.$$

$\tilde{R}_{pt}$ is either the return on MCP or a CRSP index. The maximum correlation portfolio (MCP) is constructed from the seventeen assets given in Table III. The weights of the MCP are determined by maximizing the sample correlation between the return on the portfolio and the growth rate of real consumption; see Table III for more details. The data are annualized by multiplying the monthly returns by 12. $\tilde{\gamma}$ is an estimate from a full maximum-likelihood procedure, and the standard errors (given in parentheses below the estimates) are based on the inverse of the relevant information matrix. The likelihood ratio (LR) provides a test of the null hypothesis that a given portfolio is efficient. The ratio is adjusted by Bartlett's (1938) correction. The *p*-value is the probability of seeing a higher statistic than the one reported under the null hypothesis. If the tests are independent across subperiods, then the last three rows in each panel can be aggregated into one summary measure based on either the likelihood ratio or the *F*-test. These aggregate test statistics always have *p*-values less than 0.0001.

| Date | Number of Observations | $\hat{\gamma}$ (SE($\hat{\gamma}$)) | LR Test (*p*-Value) |
|---|---|---|---|
| *Panel A: Mean-Variance Efficiency Tests on the MCP* | | | |
| 1926–1982 | 684 | −0.0009 (0.0027) | 26.86 (0.029) |
| 1926–1945 | 240 | 0.0064 (0.0054) | 49.21 (<0.001) |
| 1946–1965 | 240 | −0.0151 (0.0049) | 40.96 (<0.001) |
| 1966–1982 | 204 | 0.0016 (0.0024) | 19.25 (0.203) |
| *Panel B: Mean-Variance Efficiency Tests on CRSP Index* | | | |
| 1926–1982 | 684 | 0.0000 (0.0027) | 26.77 (0.031) |
| 1926–1945 | 240 | 0.0076 (0.0053) | 49.98 (<0.001) |
| 1946–1965 | 240 | −0.0125 (0.0047) | 36.62 (0.001) |
| 1966–1982 | 204 | 0.0016 (0.0024) | 19.23 (0.204) |

stronger rejections are probably due to the increased number of observations, which provides more precision. The joint significance of the betas across assets, as well as the significance of the dispersion of the betas across assets, is unrelated in Table VI, but it is much higher than the comparable $F$-statistics reported in Table V. Unfortunately, the test of efficiency of the MCP assumes that the portfolio weights are estimated without error, which is obviously not the case. If this measurement error were taken into account, the $p$-value would increase (see Kandel and Stambaugh (1988)).

The likelihood ratio test in Table VI can be given a geometrical interpretation based on the position of either the MCP or the CRSP index relative to the ex post efficiency frontier (Kandel 1984)). The mean-variance frontier is a parabola. A line joining the points corresponding to any given frontier portfolio and the minimum-variance portfolio intersects the mean axis at a point corresponding to the expected return of all portfolios having a zero beta relative to the frontier portfolio. When graphed with the variance on the horizontal axis, the slope of this line is equal to half the slope of the tangent at the point corresponding to the frontier portfolio (Gonzales-Gaviria (1973), pp. 58–61).

Building on this geometric relation, Figure 3 presents a graphical interpretation of the test statistic based on the ex post frontier. The maximum-likelihood estimates of the expected return on a portfolio having a zero beta relative to a test portfolio $p$ (either MCP or CRSP in Figure 3) is denoted as $\gamma$. A line joining the mean axis at $\hat{\gamma}$ and the ex post minimum variance portfolio intersects the ex post frontier at a point ($A$ or $B$ in Figure 3) corresponding to the frontier portfolio having ex post zero-beta portfolios whose mean returns are equal to $\hat{\gamma}$. Let $x$ equal the slope of this line. This portfolio would be the test portfolio, $p$, if and only if the test portfolio were ex post mean-variance efficient. Now consider a line joining the point corresponding to the test portfolio, $p$, and $\hat{\gamma}$. Denote the slope of this line by $y$. The LRT is equal to $T \ln(x/y)$ and is directly testing whether the slope of the second line is significantly less than the slope of the first line. A significantly lower slope for the second line implies rejection of the null hypothesis that the test portfolio is ex ante mean-variance efficient. The results of Table IV suggest that the two lines in either Figure 3a or 3b do have statistically different slopes.

Figure 3 also provides a comparison of the inefficiency of the MCP versus the CRSP index. For example, Figure 3a provides the unconstrained ex post frontier as well as a parabola which represents the maximum-likelihood estimate of the frontier assuming that the MCP is efficient. Figure 3b provides similar information in the case of the CRSP index. The scales of Figure 3a and 3b are equal, and there is little difference between the frontier constrained so that MCP is efficient versus a case where the CRSP index is efficient. Figure 3c, which has a very fine grid, is provided to see the difference between the two constrained frontiers.

Based on Table VI and Figure 3, the relative merits of the CCAPM versus the CAPM are difficult to discern. The inefficiency of either the MCP or the CRSP index is about the same. The two models are hard to compare because they are inherently non-nested hypotheses, which makes formal inference difficult. How-

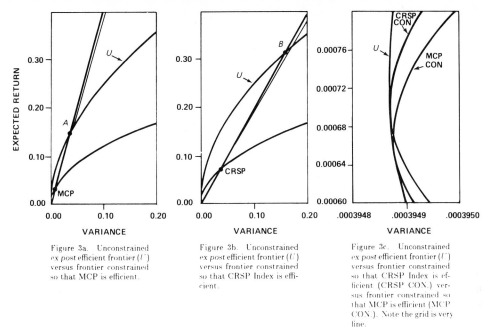

Figure 3a. Unconstrained *ex post* efficient frontier (*U*) versus frontier constrained so that MCP is efficient.

Figure 3b. Unconstrained *ex post* efficient frontier (*U*) versus frontier constrained so that CRSP Index is efficient.

Figure 3c. Unconstrained *ex post* efficient frontier (*U*) versus frontier constrained so that CRSP Index is efficient (CRSP CON.) versus frontier constrained so that MCP is efficient (MCP CON.). Note the grid is very fine.

**Figure 3. A geometrical interpretation of the likelihood-ratio test, LRT, of ex ante efficiency for the MCP and CRSP value-weighted index based on monthly real returns, 1926–1982.** The sample means and variances are annualized by multiplying by twelve. The LRT equals $T \ln(x/y)$. $x$ is the slope of the straight line that passes through the maximum-likelihood estimate of the expected return on the zero-beta portfolio, $\hat{\gamma}$, and the global minimum variance point of the ex post frontier. $y$ is the slope of the straight line that passes through $\hat{\gamma}$ and the test portfolio (either the MCP or CRSP index). The ex post frontier is based on sixteen assets (twelve industry portfolios and four bond portfolios) and either the MCP or CRSP index.

ever, the apparent inefficiency of the MCP is overstated since the portfolio weights are estimated with error.

## V. Conclusion

This paper tests the consumption-oriented CAPM and compares the model with the market-oriented CAPM. Two econometric problems peculiar to consumption data are analyzed. First, real consumption reported for a quarter is an integral of instantaneous consumption rates during the quarter, rather than the consumption rate on the last day of the quarter. This "summation bias" lowers the variance of measured consumption growth and creates positive autocorrelation, even when the true consumption rate has no autocorrelation. This summation bias also underestimates the covariance between measured consumption and asset returns by half the true values, with the result that measured consumption betas are ¾ of their true values. The empirical work accounts of these problems.

A second major econometric problem is the paucity of data points for consumption growth rates. Some tests use the consumption data (adjusted for the summation bias). However, alternative tests are based on the returns of the portfolio of assets (the "MCP") that is most highly correlated with the growth rate of real consumption. The CCAPM implies that expected returns should be linearly related to betas calculated with respect to the MCP. Interestingly, the MCP has a correlation of 0.67 with the CRSP value-weighted index. Apart from stocks, a major component of the MCP is the return on a "junk bond" portfolio. Thus, the correlation between average returns and the sensitivity of returns on various assets to junk bond returns, which has been discussed by Chen, Roll, and Ross (1983), may be attributed to the correlation between junk bond returns and real growth in consumption.

A number of tests of the consumption-oriented CAPM are examined. Unlike past studies on asset pricing, the estimated return on the zero-beta asset is quite small. Except for one subperiod, all the estimates are less than or equal to fifteen basis points (annualized). This suggests that some of the implications of a riskless real asset version of the CCAPM are consistent with the data. Another implication of the CCAPM is that the market price of risk should be positive; in other words, the expected return increases as the risk increases. This implication is verified for all periods, and the point estimate is statistically significant in most of the subperiods.

Based on the quarterly consumption data for the overall period, the linear equality between reward and risk implied by the CCAPM is rejected at the 0.05 level. However, a plot suggests that the relation is reasonably linear given the poor quality of the consumption data. Analysis by subperiods reveals that the time period from 1929 through 1939 seems to be the most damaging to the model. In fact, when the model is estimated by subperiods and then the results are aggregated across subperiods, no rejection occurs at the usual levels of significance. The first subperiod may be rejecting the model because the risk measures are estimated more precisely due to the large fluctuations in consumption and asset returns in the 1930s. The added precision should increase the power of tests. On the other hand, the quality of the data for this time period is particularly suspicious. While the CCAPM is by no means a perfect description of the data, we found the fit better than we anticipated.

For the overall period (1926–1982), the mean-variance efficiency is rejected for both the CRSP value-weighted index and the portfolio with maximum correlation with consumption (the MCP). This rejection occurs in a number of time periods, not just the 1929–1939 subperiod. Given that the estimated risk measures for both models are highly correlated, this similarity in the performances by the CAPM and the CCAPM is predictable. Since these tests permit the use of monthly, not quarterly, data, the rejection could be attributed to the increased power of the tests due to additional observations. On the other hand, the statistical significance of the rejection of the efficiency of the MCP is overstated since the portfolio weights are unknown and had to be estimated.

### REFERENCES

Amsler, C. and P. Schmidt, 1985, A Monte Carlo investigation of the accuracy of multivariate CAPM tests, *Journal of Financial Economics* 14, 359–376.

Bartlett, M., 1938, Further aspects of the theory of multiple regression, *Proceedings of the Cambridge Philosophical Society* 34, 33–47.

———, 1946, On the theoretical specification and sampling properties of autocorrelated time series, *Supplement to the Journal of the Royal Statistical Society* 8, 27–41.

Beaver, W., R. Lambert, and D. Morse, 1980, The information content of security prices, *Journal of Accounting and Economics* 2, 3–28.

Black, F., 1972, Capital market equilibrium with restricted borrowing, *Journal of Business* 45, 444–454.

———, M. Jensen, and M. Scholes, 1972, The capital asset pricing model: Some empirical findings, in M. Jensen, ed.: *Studies in the Theory of Capital Markets* (Praeger, New York).

Box, G., 1949, A general distribution theory for a class of likelihood criteria, *Biometrika* 36, 317–346.

Breeden, D., 1979. An intertemporal asset pricing model with stochastic consumption and investment opportunities, *Journal of Financial Economics* 7, 265–296.

———, 1980, Consumption risk in futures markets, *Journal of Finance* 35, 503–520.

——— and R. Litzenberger, 1978, Prices of state-contingent claims implicit in option prices, *Journal of Business* 51, 621–651.

Chen, N., R. Roll, and S. Ross, 1986, Economic forces and the stock market, *Journal of Business* 59, 383–404.

Cornell, B., 1981. The consumption based asset pricing model: A note on potential tests and applications, *Journal of Financial Economics* 9, 103–108.

Dunn, K. and K. Singleton, 1986, Modeling the term structure of interest rates under nonseparable utility and durability of goods, *Journal of Financial Economics* 17, 27–56.

Fama, E., 1976, *Foundations of Finance* (Basic Books, New York).

——— and J. MacBeth, 1973, Risk, return and equilibrium: Empirical tests, *Journal of Political Economy* 81, 607–636.

——— and G. Schwert, 1977, Asset returns and inflation, *Journal of Financial Economics* 5, 115–146.

——— and G. Schwert, 1979, Inflation, interest, and relative prices, *Journal of Business* 52, 183–209.

Ferson, W., 1983, Expected real interest rates and consumption in efficient financial markets: Empirical tests, *Journal of Financial and Quantitative Analysis* 18, 477–498.

Gibbons, M., 1982. Multivariate tests of financial models: A new approach, *Journal of Financial Economics* 10, 3–27.

——— and W. Ferson, 1985, Testing asset pricing models with changing expectations and an unobservable market portfolio, *Journal of Financial Economics* 14, 217–236.

Gonzales-Gaviria, N., 1973, Inflation and capital asset market prices: Theory and tests, Ph.D. dissertation, Graduate School of Business, Stanford University.

Grossman, S. and R. Shiller, 1982, Consumption correlatedness and risk measurement in economies with non-traded assets and heterogeneous information, *Journal of Financial Economics* 10, 195–210.

———, A. Melino, and R. Shiller, 1987, Estimating the continuous-time consumption-based asset-pricing model, *Journal of Business and Economic Statistics* 5, 315–328.

Hall, R., 1978, Stochastic implications of the life cycle-permanent income hypothesis: Theory and evidence, *Journal of Political Economy* 86, 971–987.

Hansen, L. and K. Singleton, 1982, Generalized instrumental variables estimation of nonlinear rational expectations models, *Econometrica* 50, 1269–1286.

——— and K. Singleton, 1983, Stochastic consumption, risk aversion, and the temporary behavior of asset returns, *Journal of Political Economy* 91, 249–265.

Ibbotson, R. and R. Sinquefield, 1982, *Stocks, Bonds, Bills and Inflation: Updates (1926–1982)* (R. G. Ibbotson Associates Inc., Chicago, IL).

Jobson, J. and R. Korkie, 1982, Potential performance and tests of portfolio efficiency, *Journal of Financial Economics* 10, 433–466.

Kandel, S., 1984, The likelihood ratio test statistic of mean-variance efficiency without a riskless asset, *Journal of Financial Economics* 13, 575–592.

——— and R. Stambaugh, 1988, A mean-variance framework for tests of asset pricing models, Unpublished manuscript, Graduate School of Business, University of Chicago.

Lambert, R., 1978, The time aggregation of earnings series, Unpublished manuscript, Graduate School of Business, Stanford University.

Lintner, J., 1965, The valuation of risk assets and the selection of risky investments in stock portfolios and capital budgets, *Review of Economics and Statistics* 47, 13–37.

Litzenberger, R. and E. Ronn, 1986, A utility-based model of common stock returns, *Journal of Finance* 41, 67–92.

Lucas, R., 1978, Asset prices in an exchange economy, *Econometrica* 46, 1429–1445.

Mankiw, N. and M. Shapiro, 1985, Risk and return: Consumption beta versus market beta, Unpublished manuscript, Cowles Foundation, Yale University.

Marsh, T., 1981, Intertemporal capital asset pricing model and the term structure of interest rates, Ph.D. dissertation, University of Chicago.

Merton, R., 1973, An intertemporal capital asset pricing model, *Econometrica* 41, 867–887.

Roll, R., 1977, A critique of the asset pricing theory's test—Part 1: On past and potential testability of the theory, *Journal of Financial Economics* 4, 129–176.

Rubinstein, M., 1976, The valuation of uncertain income streams and the pricing of options, *Bell Journal of Economics and Management Science* 7, 407–425.

Scholes, M. and J. Williams, 1977, Estimating betas from nonsynchronous data, *Journal of Financial Economics* 5, 309–327.

Shanken, J., 1982, An asymptotic analysis of the traditional risk-return model, Unpublished manuscript, School of Business Administration, University of California, Berkeley.

———, 1985, Multivariate tests of the zero-beta CAPM, *Journal of Financial Economics* 14, 327–348.

———, 1986, Testing portfolio efficiency when the zero-beta rate is unknown: A note, *Journal of Finance* 41, 269–276.

Sharpe, W., 1964, Capital asset prices: A theory of market equilibrium under conditions of risk, *Journal of Finance* 19, 425–442.

———, 1982, Factors in New York Stock Exchange security returns, 1931–1979, *Journal of Portfolio Management* 8, 5–19.

Stambaugh, R., 1982, On the exclusion of assets from tests of the two-parameter model: A sensitivity analysis, *Journal of Financial Economics* 10, 237–268.

Stulz, R., 1981, A model of international asset pricing, *Journal of Financial Economics* 9, 383–406.

Tiao, G., 1972, Asymptotic behavior of temporal aggregates of time series, *Biometrika* 59, 525–531.

Wheatley, S. 1986, Some tests of the consumption based asset pricing model, Unpublished manuscript, School of Business Administration, University of Washington, Seattle.

Working, H., 1960, A note of the correlation of first differences of averages in a random chain, *Econometrica* 28, 916–918.

# The Journal of FINANCE

| VOL. XXXVII | DECEMBER 1982 | No. 5 |
|---|---|---|

# The Arbitrage Pricing Theory: Is it Testable?

JAY SHANKEN*

### ABSTRACT

This paper challenges the view that the Arbitrage Pricing Theory (APT) is inherently more susceptible to empirical verification than the Capital Asset Pricing Model (CAPM). The usual formulation of the testable implications of the APT is shown to be inadequate, as it precludes the very expected return differentials which the theory attempts to explain. A recent competitive-equilibrium extension of the APT may be testable in principle. In order to implement such a test, however, observation of the return on the true market portfolio appears to be necessary.

THE CAPITAL ASSET PRICING Model (CAPM) has, for many years, been the major framework for analyzing the cross-sectional variation in expected asset returns. The main implication of the theory is that expected return should be linearly related to an asset's covariance with the return on the market portfolio:

$$E_i = \gamma_0 + \gamma_1 \beta_i$$

where

$$\beta_i = \sigma_{im}/\sigma_m^2 \qquad (1)$$

is the "beta coefficient" of asset $i$, $E_i$ its expected return, and $\gamma_0$ and $\gamma_1$ are constants that do not depend on $i$.

This simple relation has been the focus of intensive empirical scrutiny for more than a decade. Roll [16], in an influential article, suggests that the CAPM is testable in principle, but he argues that "(a) No correct and unambiguous test has appeared in the literature, and (b) There is practically no possibility that such a test can be accomplished in the future." These conclusions are a consequence of our inability to observe the exact composition of the true market portfolio.

The Arbitrage Pricing Theory (APT) of Ross [18, 19] has been proposed as a testable alternative, and perhaps the natural successor to the CAPM (Ross [21], p. 894). An important intuition in modern portfolio theory is that it is the

* University of California at Berkeley. Thanks to David Babbel, Michael Brennan, Greg Connor, Ken Dunn, Mark Rubinstein, Jeff Skelton, Sheridan Titman, participants in seminars at Berkeley and Stanford and especially Jim Ohlson and Rex Thompson for their helpful comments.

covariability of an asset's return with the return on other assets, rather than its total variability, that is important from the perspective of a risk averse investor who holds a well-diversified portfolio of many assets. Ross's seminal contribution was his insight that this intuition can be transformed into a theory of asset pricing with implications similar to (1).

Whereas derivation of the CAPM requires very specific technical assumptions (quadratic utility or multivariate normality of returns, for example), Ross's theory exploits the concept of a "large" (many assets) security market, consistent with the intuition described above. The market portfolio plays no special role in this theory. Rather, it is the covariability of an asset's return with those random factors which systematically influence the returns on most assets, that is reflected in the expected return relation. This ability of the APT to accommodate several sources of "systematic risk" has been considered by many an advantage in comparison with the CAPM.

Brennan [1] has described the APT as "a minimalist model of security market equilibrium" that is "logically prior to our other utility based models, and should be tested before the predictions of stronger utility specifications are considered." The body of empirical literature concerned with testing the APT is growing at a rapid rate. In addition to the early work of Gehr [8] are studies by Chen [5], Roll and Ross [17], Oldfield and Rogalski [14], P. Brennan [2], Gibbons [9], Reinganum [15], and Brown and Weinstein [3]. The goal of this paper is to provide a critical perspective on this important area of empirical research. Our concern is not with the particular experimental designs and statistical methods used. We address the more fundamental question of what it means to test the APT. The arguments presented below challenge the view that the APT is inherently more susceptible to empirical verification than the CAPM.

The paper is organized as follows. Section I provides an overview of the Ross APT. Section II discusses the inadequacy of the usual formulation of the testable implications of the theory. Section III considers the interpretation of empirical investigations of the APT. Section IV summarizes the main conclusions. Technical arguments have been placed in appendices.

## I. An Overview of the Ross APT

The APT assumes returns conform to a $K$-factor linear model ($K < N$):

$$R_i = E_i + \beta_{i1}\delta_1 + \cdots + \beta_{iK}\delta_K + \epsilon_i \qquad i = 1, N$$

$R_i$ is the random return on asset $i$, and $E_i$ its expected return. The $\delta_k$ are mean zero common factors and the $\epsilon_i$ are mean zero asset specific disturbances assumed to be uncorrelated with the $\delta_k$ and with each other. In the language of factor analysis, the $\beta_{ik}$ are the factor loadings. $N$ is the number of assets under consideration. In matrix notation,

$$R = E + B\delta + \epsilon \qquad (2)$$

where $R$, $E$, and $\epsilon$ are $N \times 1$, $B$ is $N \times K$, and $\delta$ is $K \times 1$. Let $D$ be the diagonal covariance matrix of $\epsilon$.

A decomposition as in (2) will hold whenever returns are regressed on an arbitrary set of random variables measured as deviations from the mean. In general, however, the $\epsilon_i$ will be correlated, thereby violating the factor model definition. An example is the usual "market model" in which $\delta$ is the return on a market proxy (see Fama [7], Chapter 3). There is considerable empirical evidence documenting correlation between market model disturbances (see King [12]). Sometimes it is convenient to treat the disturbances as if they were uncorrelated, however. This is often referred to as the Sharpe single index model. Only in this case does the market model constitute a factor model ($K = 1$) in the strict sense used here.

A special case that conveys the basic idea behind the APT, but is too restrictive to be of practical interest, occurs when $\epsilon \equiv 0$, i.e., there are no asset-specific disturbances. In this case, absence of riskless arbitrage implies the existence of a constant $\gamma_0$ and a $K$-vector $\gamma_1$ such that

$$E = \gamma_0 1_N + B\gamma_1 \tag{3}$$

Ross's argument is as follows. Consider an arbitrage portfolio with no systematic risk; i.e., an $N$-vector $X$ such that

$$X'1_N = 0 \quad \text{and} \quad X'B = 0$$

Assuming $\epsilon \equiv 0$ in (2),

$$X'R = X'E$$

Since the portfolio requires no net investment and is riskless we must have, in the absence of arbitrage,

$$X'E = 0$$

In the language of linear algebra, *any* vector orthogonal to $1_N$ and the columns of $B$ is orthogonal to $E$. It follows that $E$ must be a linear combination of $1_N$ and the columns of $B$, as stated in (3).

When asset specific disturbances are introduced, the situation is complicated considerably. In this case, zero investment and zero systematic risk imply

$$X'R = X'E + X'\epsilon$$

If $N$ is "large" and the arbitrage portfolio is well diversified, then laws of large numbers suggest that the asset specific risk will be *approximately* diversified away so that

$$X'R \approx X'E \quad \text{and hence} \quad X'E \approx 0$$

Even if we overlook the approximation, there is a technical problem. We have considered a well diversified $X$, while the linear algebra leading to (3) requires that $X'E = 0$ for *any* $X$ orthogonal to $1_N$ and $B$.

Ross [18] still manages to prove a result in the spirit of (3) for the general model with asset specific disturbances. The result is considerably weaker than (3), however. Specifically, as the number of assets under consideration approaches infinity, the sum of squared deviations from (3) converges; i.e., there exist $\gamma_0$ and $\gamma_1$ such that

$$\sum_{i=1}^{\infty}[E_i - \gamma_0 - \beta_i\gamma_1]^2 < \infty \tag{4}$$

where $\beta_i$ is the $i^{th}$ row of $B$. In order that (4) hold, "most" of the deviations from linearity must be "small," although any particular deviation may be "large."[1]

A test of the APT must, of course, be implemented with a finite set of data. Since any finite sum of squared deviations is clearly finite, (4) is not an empirically testable condition. We should like to know, therefore, whether any empirically testable bound on the deviations is implied by the theory. The arguments in Appendix A suggest that this is not the case. What, then, have empirical investigations of the APT actually tested? This is considered in the next section.

## II. The Usual Empirical Formulation

Empirical investigations of the APT have attempted to test the following proposition:

> *If* a set of asset returns conforms to a $K$-factor model, *then* the expected return vector is equal to a linear combination of a unit vector and the factor loading vectors                                                                          (5)

i.e., If (2) then (3).

We shall refer to (5) as the empirical formulation of the APT. Given the discussion of Section I, we know that *(5) is not literally an implication of the APT*. Nonetheless, it might be viewed as a reasonable representation of the *intuitive* content of the theory. Its rejection could not be equated with rejection of the theory. Its acceptance in an empirical test would be consistent with the theory, however, and might (power considerations aside) be interpreted as evidence in favor of the theory. A theory that cannot be rejected is not necessarily preferable to the CAPM, though.

Proponents of the APT have emphasized that, in contrast to the CAPM, the APT may be tested by merely observing subsets of the set of all returns (Roll and Ross [17], p. 1080).[2] Provided that observable returns conform to a factor model, the matrix of factor loadings can be estimated by the statistical technique of factor analysis (see Morrison [13], Chapter 9). The number of factors must be known in advance, though they need not be observable. There is an issue of uniqueness, however. If $A$ is any $K \times K$ nonsingular matrix, then $B$ and $\delta$ in (2) may be replaced by $BA$ and $A^{-1}\delta$. The factor model definition is still satisfied, but with factors $A^{-1}\delta$ and loading matrix $BA$. As Roll and Ross ([17], p. 1084) note, this is of no concern from the perspective of the APT. The empirical formulation of the APT in (5) is a statement about the relation between the expected return vector $E$ and the space spanned by the loading vectors and a unit vector.[3] Since that space is unaltered when $B$ is replaced by $BA$, there is really no

---

[1] Formally: for every $\varepsilon > 0$, there exists an integer $M$ such that for all $i > M$, $|E_i - \gamma_0 - \beta_i\gamma_1| < \varepsilon$.

[2] As Roll and Ross note, "the APT yields a statement of relative pricing on subsets of the universe of assets." This contrasts with the CAPM which is a preference based equilibrium model, not an arbitrage model. See Huberman [10] for a clarification of the no-arbitrage condition underlying the APT.

[3] The space spanned by a given set of vectors is the set of all vectors which are linear combinations of those given vectors.

problem. The particular factor analytic estimation technique used simply chooses some basis for that space.

In light of the difficulties in measuring the true market portfolio, a theory which permits estimation of the appropriate risk measures without observation of the corresponding "factors" is certainly appealing. Some might argue that this apparent immunity from measurement problems more than compensates for the ambiguity surrounding the approximate nature of the risk-return relation. Another source of ambiguity should be considered, however.

Let us say that two sets of securities are *equivalent* if the corresponding sets of obtainable portfolio returns are identical. In this case, the two sets of securities are merely different packagings of the same underlying returns. Given perfect markets with no transaction costs, investors would be indifferent between equivalent sets. This simple idea plays an important role in many applications of arbitrage theory (for example, the Modigliani-Miller theory of corporate capital structure, and the theory of option pricing). The return on the equity of a firm may be viewed as the return on a portfolio whose components correspond to the underlying assets (long positions) and liabilities (short positions) of the firm. Alternative packagings of the underlying returns may, of course, be obtained by forming portfolios of stocks. The empirical formulation of the APT in (5) does not discriminate between different packagings. It would seem natural, therefore, to inquire as to the relation between the factors in the respective factor models for two equivalent sets of securities.

If, intuitively, we identify factors with the pervasive forces in the economy, then we might expect the same set of factors to be obtained from equivalent sets of securities. This is not the case, however. The basic idea may be illustrated with a simple example. Consider two securities which conform to the following 1-factor model:

$$R_1 = E_1 + \delta + \epsilon_1$$
$$R_2 = E_2 - \delta + \epsilon_2 \tag{6}$$

where

$$\text{var}(\delta) = 1 \quad \text{and} \quad \text{var}(\epsilon_1) = \text{var}(\epsilon_2) = \sigma^2 > 0$$

Let $R_1^* = R_1$ and $R_2^* = \alpha R_1 + (1 - \alpha) R_2$. Thus $R_2^*$ is the return on a portfolio of the initial securities. $R_2^*$ may be written as

$$R_2^* = [\alpha E_1 + (1 - \alpha) E_2] + (2\alpha - 1)\delta + [\alpha\epsilon_1 + (1 - \alpha)\epsilon_2]$$

Now $\text{cov}[\epsilon_1, \alpha\epsilon_1 + (1 - \alpha)\epsilon_2] = \alpha\sigma^2$. Unless $\alpha = 0$, $R_1^*$ and $R_2^*$ will not conform to a 1-factor model with factor $\delta$. The disturbance term for $R_2^*$, relative to $\delta$, is a mixture of $\epsilon_1$ and $\epsilon_2$, and is not uncorrelated with $\epsilon_1$.

Consider the covariance between $R_1^*$ and $R_2^*$:

$$\text{cov}(R_1^*, R_2^*) = \alpha\text{var}(R_1) + (1 - \alpha)\text{cov}(R_1, R_2)$$
$$= \alpha(1 + \sigma^2) + (1 - \alpha)(- 1)$$

Let $\alpha = 1/(2 + \sigma^2)$, so that $\text{cov}(R_1^*, R_2^*) = 0$. Since $\alpha \neq 0$, $R_1^*$ and $R_2^*$ violate the

1-factor model. But any set of uncorrelated returns conforms to the simplest possible factor model: a 0-factor model. To see this, write $R_1^*$ and $R_2^*$ as

$$R_1^* = E_1^* + \epsilon_1^*$$

$$R_2^* = E_2^* + \epsilon_2^* \tag{7}$$

where $E_i^* = E(R_i^*)$ and $\epsilon_i^* = R_i^* - E_i^*$, $i = 1, 2$. By the choice of $\alpha$, $\text{cov}(\epsilon_1^*, \epsilon_2^*) = 0$. Therefore (7) is a legitimate factor model with $K = 0$. It is easily verified that $\{R_1, R_2\}$ and $\{R_1^*, R_2^*\}$ are equivalent sets.[4]

It has been shown that equivalent sets of securities need not conform to the same factor model. In particular, the number of factors in the respective models need not be the same. Therefore, this is not an instance of the phenomenon described earlier, which involved an arbitrary invertible transformation of one set of factors into another basis for the same factor space.[5] Whereas that phenomenon poses no problem, the present consideration does. The empirical formulation of the APT in (5), together with (6), implies the existence of $\gamma_0$ and $\gamma_1$ such that[6]

$$\begin{bmatrix} E_1 \\ E_2 \end{bmatrix} = \gamma_0 \begin{bmatrix} 1 \\ 1 \end{bmatrix} + \gamma_1 \begin{bmatrix} 1 \\ -1 \end{bmatrix} \tag{8}$$

On the other hand, (5) and (7) imply the existence of $\gamma_0^*$ such that

$$\begin{bmatrix} E_1^* \\ E_2^* \end{bmatrix} = \gamma_0^* \begin{bmatrix} 1 \\ 1 \end{bmatrix} \tag{9}$$

But equivalence means that $R_1$ and $R_2$ are equal to portfolios of $R_1^*$ and $R_2^*$, so that $E_1 = E_2 = \gamma_0^*$ as well. (8) and (9) will not be consistent unless $\gamma_1 = 0$ and $\gamma_0 = \gamma_0^*$.

Let us summarize the observations above. First, equivalent sets of securities may conform to very different factor structures. Second, the usual empirical formulation of the APT, when applied to these structures, may yield different and inconsistent implications concerning expected returns for a given set of securities. The implications will be consistent if and only if all of the securities have the same expected return. While the example above considered only two securities, the conclusions apply, aside from a few mild technical restrictions, to any *finite* set of securities (see Appendix B).[7]

In light of these observations, (5) cannot be considered an adequate formulation of the empirical content of a testable theory of asset pricing. It rules out the very expected return differentials which the theory seeks to explain.[8] We have already noted that the exact risk-return relation of (5) is not literally an implication of the Ross APT. The positing of such a relation might, therefore, be considered the main source of difficulty. But our observations concerning the factor models of

---

[4] $R_2$ may be recovered by shorting $\alpha/(1 - \alpha)$ units of $R_1^*$ and buying $1/(1 - \alpha)$ units of $R_2^*$.

[5] The factor space is the set of random variables which are linear combinations of the given factors.

[6] The case $N = 2$ is clearly without content and is considered for the purpose of illustration only. The same conclusions hold for any finite $N$. See Appendix B.

[7] Note that the CAPM suggests no particular relation between the expected returns of uncorrelated securities, since their covariances with the market may vary.

[8] Ingersoll [11] has made a similar assertion independently.

equivalent sets of securities are disturbing (and revealing) quite apart from this issue.

The phenomenon is actually more general than the previous discussion might suggest. The following proposition is proved in Appendix B: given a vector of returns $R$ and (almost) any other vector of random variables $\delta$, there exists an equivalent set of securities with return vector $R^*$, which conforms to a factor model with factors $\delta$. Given this undesirable degree of flexibility, how are we to identify the "true" factors? Indeed, does such a phrase have a well-defined meaning? The securities we observe in the market constitute a particular packaging of the underlying returns in the economy. Are we to assume that the "relevant" factor model is the one which corresponds to this particular packaging? These issues are addressed in the following section.

## III. Interpreting Empirical Studies of the APT

Given a vector of security returns, suppose that, using the best available statistical methods, we are unable to reject the expected return relation (3). Should this be interpreted as evidence in support of the APT? The following discussion suggests that such an interpretation may be inappropriate. Let $\delta$ be the return on a mean-variance efficient portfolio of securities, and let $R$ be a vector of returns on a proper subset of the securities which enter $\delta$.[9] The proposition of Appendix $B$ implies the existence of an equivalent vector of returns $R^*$, which conforms to a one-factor model with $\delta$ as the factor.

Suppose the vector of returns used in an empirical test happens to be $R^*$. Note that the factor loadings on $\delta$ are just the usual beta coefficients with respect to $\delta$. Since $\delta$ is mean-variance efficient, the expected return relation (3) must hold exactly (see Fama [7], Roll [16], or Ross [20]). An empirical test of the APT based on $R^*$ necessarily will appear to support the theory (given a large enough sample of data). It would generally be wrong to attribute any *economic* significance to such a result, however, since the validity of (3), in this case, is simply a *mathematical* consequence of the mean-variance efficiency of $\delta$.

The scenario described above might seem a bit improbable. It is intended more to illustrate what is possible than what is likely. What does seem plausible is that some of the factors in a given factor model representation of returns might be highly correlated with the return on a mean-variance efficient portfolio. In that case, it would not be surprising to find some of those factors "priced" in an APT empirical investigation. Such an empirical result would be of questionable economic significance, however.

These remarks are very close in spirit to the "Roll Critique" of tests of the CAPM. Roll argues that empirical investigations of the CAPM which use proxies for the true market portfolio are really tests of the mean-variance efficiency of those proxies, not tests of the CAPM. The CAPM implies that a particular portfolio, the market portfolio, is efficient. The theory is not testable unless *that* portfolio is observable and used in the tests.

Similarly, it is argued here that factor-analytic empirical investigations of the

[9] If $\delta$ consisted solely of securities in $R$, then $\Sigma$ (see Appendix B) would be singular.

APT are not necessarily tests of that theory. In the case of the APT, we are confronted with the task of identifying the relevant factor structure, rather than the true market portfolio.[10] Whereas we have a reasonably clear notion of what is meant by "the true market portfolio," it is not clear in what sense, if any, a uniquely "relevant factor structure" exists. We noted in Section II that there are, in general, many factor structures corresponding to equivalent sets of securities. The APT does not appear to provide a criterion for singling out one structure as the "relevant" one.

The recent work of Connor [6] on "Asset Pricing in Factor Economies" is pertinent in this regard. Building on the earlier work of Ross, Connor obtains an exact pricing relation by introducing assumptions about the aggregate structure of the economy. As he notes, his theory relies on principles of competitive equilibrium rather than on an arbitrage technique. Significant, from our present perspective, is the central role played by the market portfolio. A crucial condition in the Connor "equilibrium APT" is that *idiosyncratic risk, defined relative to a given factor structure, is completely diversified away in the market portfolio.* It is important to appreciate the relative nature of this condition. The same economy might satisfy the condition with respect to one factor representation of returns and fail to satisfy it with respect to an alternative representation.

This diversification condition provides us with a basis for evaluating and interpreting factor-analytic investigations of the APT. We argued earlier against attaching much economic significance to factor-analytic results. Suppose, however, it can be shown that the factors (implicitly) identified in a factor analysis explain all of the variation in the return on the market portfolio.[11] In this case, it might be appropriate to interpret the results of the investigation as reflecting on the validity of the "equilibrium APT."[12] Without observing the return on the true market portfolio, however, it is unlikely that the diversification condition can ever be conclusively verified in practice. Thus the "equilibrium APT" appears to be subject to substantially the same difficulties encountered in testing the CAPM.

Additional insight into the relation between Connor's work and the inadequacy of the usual empirical formulation of the APT may be obtained by reconsidering the case of the 0-factor model, i.e., a set of mutually uncorrelated returns. If there are no "systematic factors," then all risk is, by definition, idiosyncratic. The condition that idiosyncratic risk be diversified away in the market portfolio requires, in this case, that the variance of the market return be zero. Given the substantial variation in all commonly observed market proxies, we can reject this condition with some confidence. Thus, from the perspective of the "equilibrium

---

[10] An alternative would be to abandon the notion of a "relevant" factor structure, and view the APT as having implications for approximate asset pricing relative to any set of "factors." The implied degree of approximation would presumably differ for different sets of factors. Appendix A notes some problems with the view, but is, by no means, conclusive.

[11] See Shanken and Tajirian [22] for some empirical evidence related to this condition.

[12] Connor employs a more general concept of "factor structure" than that used here and in the empirical APT literature. Since he does not require that the factor model disturbances be uncorrelated, the empirical implications of his work are not limited to factors obtained (implicitly) by factor analysis.

APT," the existence of a 0-factor representation of returns (appropriately) fails to take on any economic significance.

## IV. Summary and Conclusions

It is generally accepted that the Capital Asset Pricing Model (CAPM) is not truly testable in a strict sense. Much of this acceptance can be attributed to the persuasive analysis of Roll, who argues that the CAPM is not testable unless the market portfolio of all assets is used in the empirical test. The Arbitrage Pricing Theory (APT) of Ross has been proposed as a testable alternative to the CAPM. Its proponents suggest that it suffices to merely consider subsets of the universe of existing assets to test the APT. The rapidly growing volume of empirical analysis purporting to test the theory indicates that this view has achieved a significant level of acceptance in the finance research community. Our previous observations suggest that this acceptance may not be warranted.

Ross's theory does not (even in the limit as the number of assets $\rightarrow \infty$) imply an exact linear risk-return relation. The testability of the theory could reasonably be questioned on this ground alone. Perhaps of greater concern is the inadequacy of the usual empirical formulation of the intuitive content of the theory. This formulation states that if a (large) set of asset returns conforms to a factor model, then the expected return vector should be equal to a linear combination of the loading vectors and a unit vector. This proposition is appealing in that it appears to capture the spirit of the theory, and is susceptible to statistical testing via factor analytic methods. But taken literally, it is actually equivalent to the proposition that all securities have the same expected return.

This surprising conclusion is a consequence of a previously unnoticed property of the factor model representation of returns. The factor model can be manipulated rather arbitrarily by repackaging a given set of securities. A new set of returns and a corresponding factor model can be produced, with virtually any prespecified random variables as the factors. By itself, therefore, factor analysis is not an adequate tool for identifying the random components of returns that should be relevant to asset pricing.

This conclusion is compatible with the recent work of Connor, who extends the earlier work of Ross. Connor's competitive equilibrium analysis highlights the role of certain aggregate features of the economy in asset pricing. Factor analysis is merely concerned with statistical correlations and is blind to aggregate economic considerations. The failure of the usual empirical formulation of the APT to discriminate between alternative factor representations on the basis of such considerations is its fundamental weakness. Unfortunately, since the market portfolio plays a prominent role in Connor's "equilibrium APT," it appears to be subject to substantially the same difficulties encountered in testing the CAPM.

## Appendix A

In this appendix it is argued that Ross's APT does not imply an empirically testable bound on the sum of squared deviations in (4). It is necessary to first review some essential features of the proof in Ross [18]. Consider the problem of minimizing the variance of an arbitrage portfolio with no systematic risk and expected return $c > 0$; i.e.,

$$\text{minimize } X'DX$$

subject to

$$X'1_N = 0$$

$$X'\beta = 0$$

$$\text{and} \quad X'E = c \tag{A.1}$$

More specifically, consider an infinite sequence of such problems implicitly indexed by $N$, the number of assets in the subset under consideration. Let $a$ be the minimum variance obtained in (A.1). Given some mild assumptions on preferences and boundedness of the elements of $D$, Ross shows that utility maximization implies the sequence of $a$ values must be bounded away from zero. Intuitively, a sequence of $a$'s approaching zero would constitute a sort of arbitrage opportunity in the limit.

Now let

$$e \equiv E - \gamma_0 1_N - \gamma_1 \beta$$

with $\gamma_0$ and $\gamma_1$ chosen so as to minimize the expression $e'D^{-1}e$. $\gamma_0$ and $\gamma_1$ so defined are identical to the coefficients from a generalized least squares regression of $E$ on $1_N$ and $\beta$ with nonsingular covariance matrix $D$. $e$ is the corresponding vector of residuals. A key result in Ross's analysis (Ross [18], p. 349, 357) is that

$$e'D^{-1}e = c^2/a \tag{A.2}$$

If the elements of $D$ are bounded above, say by $u$, then

$$e'e \leq uc^2/a \tag{A.3}$$

It might appear that (A.3) provides an upper bound on the finite sum of squared deviations $e'e$, which could conceivably be tested. But (A.2) and (A.3) are purely algebraic facts, devoid of any economic content. The economics enters when we recall that utility maximization implies the sequence of $a$'s is bounded away from zero. It follows from (A.3) that the sum of squared deviations remains bounded above as the number of assets approaches infinity. Therefore, the theory yields an economic restriction on the expected returns in an infinite sequence of economies. There does not appear to be a restriction on any particular economy in the sequence.

## Appendix B

This appendix generalizes the results of the two asset example of Section II. Let $R$ be an $N$-vector of security returns with positive-definite covariance matrix $V$. Let $\delta$ be a $K$-vector of mean zero random variables jointly distributed with $R$. As noted in Section I, we can regress each of the components of $R$ on $\delta$ to obtain the following representation:

$$R = E + B\delta + \epsilon \qquad \text{(B.1)}$$

where $E(\delta) = E(\epsilon) = 0$, so that $E = E(R)$. Let $\sum$ be the covariance matrix of $\epsilon$. In general, $\sum$ will not be diagonal, so that (B.1) is not a factor model representation. We shall assume $\sum$ is positive definite. While this rules out some potential random vectors $\delta$, it is a fairly general assumption which should encompass many cases. In particular, in the $K = 0$ case $\sum = V$ and hence is positive definite.

Let $Q$ be an $N \times N$ nonsingular matrix such that

$$Q'Q = \sum^{-1}$$

Such a matrix always exists, given our assumptions (this fact is used to show that a generalized least squares regression is equivalent to an ordinary least squares regression on transformed variables (see Theil [23], p. 23). Assume that the row sums of $Q$ are all nonzero (if we imagine that the parameters of $\sum$ have been generated by some random continuous process, then the row sums will be nonzero with probability one). Let $D$ be the diagonal matrix with $i^{th}$ entry equal to the reciprocal of row sum $i$ of matrix $Q$, and let $P \equiv DQ$. Then $P1_N = 1_N$, i.e., the row sums of $P$ are all equal to one.

Premultiplication of a return vector by $P$ generates a vector of portfolio returns. Transforming the representation (B.1) we obtain

$$R^* = E^* + B^*\delta + \epsilon^*$$

where

$$R^* = PR, \qquad E^* = PE, \qquad B^* = PB \quad \text{and} \quad \epsilon^* = P\epsilon \qquad \text{(B.2)}$$

$P$ has been constructed so that

$$\text{Var}(\epsilon^*) = P \sum P' = DQ \sum Q'D' = D^2$$

is diagonal. Therefore, the representation (B.2) is a legitimate $K$-factor model. The usual empirical formulation of the APT (see (5) of Section II) implies that there exist $\gamma_0$ and $\gamma_1$ such that

$$E^* = \gamma_0 1_N + B^*\gamma_1 \qquad \text{(B.3)}$$

Premultiplication of both sides of (B.3) by $P^{-1}$ gives

$$P^{-1}E^* = \gamma_0 P^{-1}1_N + P^{-1}B^*\gamma_1$$

Using (B.2) and noting that $P1_N = 1_N$ implies $P^{-1}1_N = 1_N$, we obtain

$$E = \gamma_0 1_N + B\gamma_1 \qquad \text{(B.4)}$$

(B.4) is the usual APT expected return relation, with risk measured relative to the random vector $\delta$. Since $\delta$ is essentially arbitrary, many such relations may be deduced for the same expected return vector $E$. The existence of many distinct representations for $E$ is not, in itself, a problem (recall that in the mean-variance context, a different representation exists for each mean-variance efficient portfolio of the securities in $R$). To the contrary, it might appear that the APT may be tested using any random vector $\delta$. Unfortunately, this view is untenable, since it leads to a logical contradiction.

This may be seen by letting $K = 0$ in the argument leading to (B.4); i.e., let $\delta$ be the empty set (vector). In this case, we have the existence of a single number $\gamma_0$, such that

$$E = \gamma_0 1_N \tag{B.5}$$

Thus the empirical formulation of the APT, from which (B.5) was deduced, rules out the very expected return differentials which the theory attempts to explain.

## REFERENCES

1. M. Brennan. "Discussion." *Journal of Finance* 36 (May 1981), 352–3.
2. P. Brennan. "A Test of the Arbitrage Pricing Model." Unpublished manuscript, University of British Columbia, Vancouver, Canada, 1981.
3. S. Brown and M. Weinstein. "A New Approach to Testing Asset Pricing Models: The Bilinear Paradigm." Unpublished manuscript, Bell Laboratories, Holmdell, NJ: 1982.
4. G. Chamberlain and M. Rothschild. "Arbitrage and Mean-Variance Analysis on Large Asset Markets." Unpublished manuscript, University of Wisconsin, 1981.
5. N. Chen. "Some Empirical Tests of the Theory of Arbitrage Pricing." Working Paper No. 69, University of Chicago, 1982.
6. G. Connor. "Asset Pricing in Factor Economies." Doctoral dissertation, Yale University, 1982.
7. E. Fama. *Foundations of Finance*. New York: Basic Books, Inc., 1976.
8. A. Gehr. "Some Tests of the Arbitrage Pricing Theory." *Journal of the Midwest Finance Association*, 1975.
9. M. Gibbons. "Empirical Examination of the Return Generating Process of the Arbitrage Pricing Theory." Unpublished manuscript, Stanford University, 1981.
10. G. Huberman. "A Simple Approach to Arbitrage Pricing Theory." Working Paper No. 44, University of Chicago, 1980.
11. J. Ingersoll. "Some Results in the Theory of Arbitrage Pricing." Working Paper No. 67, University of Chicago, 1982.
12. B. King. "Market and Industry Factors in Stock Price Behavior." *Journal of Business* 39 (1966), 139–90.
13. D. Morrison. *Multivariate Statistical Methods*. 2nd edition. New York: McGraw-Hill, 1976.
14. G. Oldfield and R. Rogalski. "Treasury Bill Factors and Common Stock Returns." *Journal of Finance* 36 (May 1981), 337–50.
15. M. Reinganum. "The Arbitrage Pricing Theory: Some Empirical Results." *Journal of Finance* 36 (May 1981), 313–21.
16. R. Roll. "A Critique of the Asset Pricing Theory's Tests." *Journal of Financial Economics* (May 1977), 129–76.
17. —— and S. Ross. "An Empirical Investigation of the Arbitrage Pricing Theory." *Journal of Finance* 35 (December 1980), 1073–1103.
18. S. Ross. "The Arbitrage Theory of Capital Asset Pricing." *Journal of Economic Theory*, December 1976, 341–60.
19. ——. "Return, Risk, and Arbitrage." In I. Friend and J. Bicksler (eds.), *Risk and Return in Finance*. Cambridge: Ballinger, 1977.
20. ——. "The Capital Asset Pricing Model (CAPM), Short-Sale Restrictions and Related Issues." *Journal of Finance* 32 (March 1977), 177–83.
21. ——. "The Current Status of the Capital Asset Pricing Model (CAPM)." *Journal of Finance* 33 (June 1978), 885–901.
22. J. Shanken and A. Tajirian. "Equity Factors and the Market Portfolio." Unpublished manuscript, University of California, Berkeley, 1982.
23. H. Theil. *Principles of Econometrics*. New York: John Wiley & Sons, Inc., 1971.

# SIZE AND STOCK RETURNS, AND OTHER EMPIRICAL REGULARITIES

G. William SCHWERT*

*University of Rochester, Rochester, NY 14627, USA*

## 1. Introduction

The recent plethora of papers documenting size, turn-of-the-year and earnings/price ratio 'effects' on stock returns represents an unusual coincidence of interest among a broad group of financial economists. This special issue of the *Journal of Financial Economics* contains some of the papers on the 'size effect' and other empirical regularities. These introductory remarks survey the papers in this issue, as well as some related papers, and attempt to put the research on the 'size effect' in perspective.

There are seven papers in this issue of the *Journal* that relate in different ways to the 'size effect'; that is, that average returns to small firms' stocks are substantially higher than any known capital asset pricing model predicts. These papers provide substantial new information about the 'size effect'. In particular, we now know that a large part of the high return occurs in the first few days of January and it exists in Australia as well as in the United States. We also know that transaction costs are higher for small firms' stocks than for larger firms' stocks, and that this does not seem to explain all of the 'size effect'. Finally, we know that the magnitude of the 'size effect' varies over time and it is related to other evidence concerning high average returns to stocks with low earnings/price ratios. The papers in this issue document some unexplained empirical regularities that will probably puzzle financial economists for at least the next several years.

## 2. Why is this topic interesting? Cross-sectional differences in expected returns

All of the papers in this issue are concerned with systematic cross-sectional differences among stock returns. The simple observation that there are systematic differences is neither novel nor exciting; this phenomenon

*Andrew Christie, Kenneth French, Bulent Gultekin, Michael Jensen, Allan Kleidon, John Long, Terry Marsh, William Meckling, Charles Plosser, Richard Roll, Richard Ruback, Clifford Smith, Jerold Warner, Robert Whaley, and Jerold Zimmerman provided valuable criticism of earlier drafts, although they are not responsible for the views expressed in this paper. Financial support from the Batterymarch Financial Management Corporation is gratefully acknowledged.

0304-405x/83/$3.00 © Elsevier Science Publishers B.V. (North-Holland)

motivates the various capital asset pricing models (CAPMs) that have interested financial economists for many years. However, the systematic cross-sectional differences that are examined here do not seem to be predicted by any of these models.

Standard asset pricing models are based on the proposition that individuals are risk averse. These models predict a positive relation between an asset's risk and its expected return. Asset pricing models have such an important place in contemporary finance that they are used as a pedagogic device to measure the opportunity cost of capital in most graduate finance courses.

The statistical evidence supporting the positive relation between risk and expected return is surprisingly weak. In tests of the Sharpe (1964), Lintner (1965), and Black (1972) capital asset pricing models, the statistical association between risk and average returns is often only marginally significant. For example, in Fama and MacBeth (1973) the $t$-statistic testing the hypothesis that the slope of the risk-return relation is zero is 2.57 for the 1935–68 sample period, but it is only 1.92, 0.70, and 1.73 for the 1935–45, 1946–55, and 1956–68 subperiods, respectively.

While there are many possible explanations for these empirical results, the weak statistical association between average returns and risk provides an interesting benchmark for measuring the strength of other types of differences in average returns among securities. For example, the association between firm size and average stock returns is about as strong as the association between risk and average returns. For this perspective, it is not surprising that there has been a growth in papers on the 'size effect' and other empirical regularities in average stock returns.

## 3. Empirical evidence on the 'size effect'

Banz (1981, p. 14) uses a methodology similar to Fama and MacBeth (1973) and finds a negative association between average returns to stocks and the market value of the stocks after controlling for risk. The $t$-statistic for whether the 'size effect' coefficient equals zero is $-2.54$ for the 1936–75 period, and it is $-1.88$ and $-1.91$ for the 1936–55 and 1956–75 subperiods, respectively. Thus, the statistical association between the 'size' of the firm and average stock returns is comparable to the association between average return and risk.

This peculiar empirical finding prompted a number of researchers to ask whether the 'size effect' is related to other empirical anomalies apparent in stock return data. For example, Reinganum (1981a, p. 45) finds: 'After controlling returns for any $E/P$ effect, a strong firm size effect still emerged. But, after controlling returns for any market value effect, a separate $E/P$ effect was not found'. Thus, Reinganum concludes that the 'size effect' subsumes the evidence of Basu (1977), who finds that stocks with high earnings/price ($E/P$) ratios have higher average risk-adjusted returns than low $E/P$ stocks.

The papers by Banz (1981) and Reinganum (1981a) have drawn a lot of attention, as evidenced by the large number of papers that attempt to explain the existence of the 'size effect'.[1] I will group these papers into three categories in the subsequent discussion: (a) papers that look for an explanation of the findings of Banz (1981) and Reinganum (1981a) in measurement or statistical testing errors; (b) papers that provide more detailed characterizations of the 'size effect'; and (c) papers that propose an economic explanation of the evidence.

## 3.1. The 'size effect' as a statistical artifact

A number of papers have analyzed the statistical tests in the papers by Banz (1981) and Reinganum (1981a). In particular, Roll (1981) suggests that the stocks of small firms are traded less frequently than the stocks of larger firms so that estimates of systematic risk from daily stock returns will be biased downward. Both Roll and Reinganum (1982) conclude, however, that the bias in risk estimates due to non-synchronous trading cannot explain the magnitude of the risk-adjusted average returns found by Reinganum (1981a).

Christie and Hertzel (1981) argue that the 'size effect' could be due to non-stationarity in the risk measures. The risk of the stock of a levered firm increases as the stock value decreases. Historical estimates that assume risk is constant over time understate the risk of levered stocks whose value has fallen; hence, average risk-adjusted returns for stocks with low current value should be positive because risk is underestimated. Nevertheless, adjusting for this bias in risk estimates does not eliminate the 'size effect'.

In this issue, Basu (1983) re-examines Reinganum's (1981a) results using a different sample period and a different procedure for creating portfolios of stocks ranked on both size and earnings/price ratios. Basu also uses a variety of procedures to control for risk and finds that returns to stocks of firms with low market value are riskier than the stocks of large firms. In one of his tests, Basu sorts stocks into portfolios with different $E/P$ ratios but similar market value and concludes that high $E/P$ stocks earn statistically significant positive risk-adjusted returns. On the other hand, when stocks are sorted into portfolios with different market value but similar $E/P$ ratios, Basu finds no significant risk-adjusted returns related to market value for the 1963–80 period. Thus, it seems that Basu's results contradict Reinganum's (1981a) conclusion that the 'size effect' subsumes the '$E/P$ effect'. Finally, Basu notes that there is some interaction between size and $E/P$ ratios in the sense that

---

[1]The references to this paper contain 19 papers dated 1981 or later that pertain to the 'size effect'; seven of these papers are contained in this issue of the *Journal of Financial Economics*.

the magnitude of risk-adjusted returns is largest for small firms with high $E/P$ ratios. Basu concludes that both the '$E/P$ effect' and the 'size effect' probably are an indication of deficiencies in the capital asset pricing model, not a sign of market inefficiency.[2]

Recently, Roll (1982) and Blume and Stambaugh (1983) examine the effects of the different portfolio strategies implicit in alternative estimators of risk-adjusted returns to portfolios of small firms' stocks. They conclude that the annualized arithmetic average daily risk-adjusted returns calculated by Reinganum (1981a) are about twice as large as the risk-adjusted returns to a portfolio that is purchased at the beginning of the year and held for an entire year. The use of compounded arithmetic average returns is similar to a portfolio strategy that involves daily rebalancing to attain equal weights for the stocks in the portfolio. On the other hand, a buy-and-hold strategy involves no rebalancing within the measurement interval. Since the magnitude of the 'size effect' is apparently sensitive to the technique used to calculate average risk-adjusted returns, both Roll (1982) and Blume and Stambaugh (1983) question the empirical importance of this phenomenon.

In sum, several papers have attempted to explain the anomalous results of Banz (1981) and Reinganum (1981a) by showing that risk estimates are biased downward or average return estimates are biased upward for small firms' stocks. While it is true that the magnitude of the 'size effect' is affected by these statistical issues, none of these papers have been able to completely explain the evidence on the 'size effect'.

### 3.2. Further characterization of the 'size effect'

In this issue, Keim (1983) and Brown, Kleidon and Marsh (1983) provide new evidence on the time series behavior of the 'size effect'. Keim notes that the average risk-adjusted return to a portfolio of small firms' stocks is large in January and much smaller for the rest of the year. About half of the annual 'size effect' occurs in January, and about 25 percent of the annual 'size effect' occurs during the first five trading days of January. Therefore, Keim finds that the 'size effect' exhibits seasonality analogous to the earlier findings of Officer (1975) and Rozeff and Kinney (1976) for aggregate market portfolio returns.

Brown, Kleidon and Marsh (1983) examine the behavior of the 'size effect' over time. Using data from 1967–79, they find that the risk-adjusted average returns to portfolios ranked on size are linearly related to the logarithm of the size variable, but that the magnitude and sign of that relation are not

---

[2]Ball (1978) discusses tests of market efficiency that use the CAPM to measure equilibrium expected returns. Ball argues that significant abnormal returns to trading strategies that involve relatively stable portfolios of securities are evidence of errors in the CAPM, not evidence of inefficient capital markets. Thus, tests using $E/P$ ratios, such as Basu (1977), probably indicate poor estimates of expected returns from the CAPM.

constant within the 1967–79 sample period. In particular, the 'size effect' seems to imply a negative excess return for small firms' stocks between 1969–73 and a positive excess return between 1974–79. Brown, Kleidon and Marsh speculate about the types of explanations that are consistent with a time-varying 'size effect', but find no explanation that seems likely to fit both Keim's (1983) evidence and their own.

### 3.3. Economic explanations for the 'size effect' — and the lack thereof

### 3.3.1. Tax effects

As a result of Keim's (1983) finding that a large part of the differential risk-adjusted returns to small firms' stocks occurs in the first week of January, several papers attempt to explain the 'turn-of-the-year effect'. A natural hypothesis to consider is that some investors sell securities at the end of the calendar year to establish short-term capital losses for income tax purposes. If this 'selling pressure' depresses stock prices prior to the end of the year, the increase in prices during the first week of the subsequent year superficially seems reasonable. This conjecture has become so commonplace that it was discussed in the 'Heard on the Street' column in the *Wall Street Journal* on December 27, 1982.

Roll (1983) and Reinganum (1983) examine the extent to which the 'January size effect' can be explained by the tax-loss-selling-pressure hypothesis. Both Roll and Reinganum find that the magnitude of the price increase in the first week of January is positively related to the magnitude of short-term capital losses that could have been realized at the end of the previous year. They conjecture that the effect is largest for small firms because small firms' stock returns are more volatile, and because tax-exempt investors, such as pension funds, have relatively small holdings in small firms' stocks. Also, the transaction costs of trading in small firms' stocks are larger than for stocks of larger firms. On the other hand, in this issue, Reinganum finds that average stock returns are high during the first five trading days of the calendar year, even for stocks that show capital gains over the previous year. He also finds that average returns to small firms' stocks are high relative to larger firms' stocks for the entire month of January. This difference is not limited to the first five trading days. Thus, Reinganum concludes that the 'January size effect' cannot be completely explained by tax-loss-selling.

### 3.3.2. International evidence on tax effects

Several papers examine the 'January size effect' using international data. In this issue, Brown, Keim, Kleidon and Marsh (1983) analyze the returns to Australian stocks, since the typical fiscal year end for tax purposes is June 30 in Australia. Using monthly data from 1958 to 1981, they find that average returns to most Australian stocks are substantially larger in January and July than in the other ten months. The 'size effect' does not appear to be seasonal, however, because the average return to the smallest decile of stocks is about 4 percent per year greater than any of the other size portfolios and this difference does not seem to vary across months. Thus, while stock returns are seasonal in Australia, as noted previously by Officer (1975), and there does seem to be a 'size effect', the 'size effect' is not obviously related to the end of the tax year. Brown, Keim, Kleidon and Marsh conclude that tax-loss-selling probably does not explain the 'January size effect' found in U.S. data.

Other papers that examine the relation between firm size, tax-loss-selling, and seasonality in stock returns include Gultekin and Gultekin (1982) and Berges, McConnell and Schlarbaum (1982). Gultekin and Gultekin examine average monthly returns to market portfolios of a number of different countries. They find seasonality in most countries, with a predominance of high average returns in January when the tax year ends in these countries. Berges, McConnell and Schlarbaum examine monthly returns to 391 stocks traded on the Toronto and Montreal Stock Exchanges from 1950 through 1980. They estimate average returns to five portfolios ranked on the market value of outstanding stock and find higher average returns in January, especially for small firms' stocks. However, this phenomenon seems to exist both before and after 1972, when Canada first imposed a capital gains tax. Therefore, Berges, McConnell and Schlarbaum agree with Reinganum (1983) that tax-loss-selling does not completely explain the 'January size effect'.

### 3.3.3. Transaction costs

In this issue, Stoll and Whaley (1983) and Schultz (1983) examine the magnitude of transaction costs for stocks of firms in different size categories. Stoll and Whaley examine monthly returns to New York Stock Exchange (NYSE)-listed stocks from 1960 through 1979 for ten portfolios ranked on market value of the stock. They note that small firms' stocks tend to have lower prices and higher bid–ask spreads, so transaction costs are relatively high for these stocks. Adding together estimates of the bid–ask spread and the commission rate, round-trip transaction costs average 6.8 percent for the smallest decile of firms and 2.7 percent for the largest decile of firms. Stoll and Whaley estimate risk-adjusted returns to the small firm portfolio net of transaction costs and find that a round-trip transaction every three months is sufficient to eliminate the 'size effect'. If round-trip transactions occur once per year, the average abnormal return is about 4.5 percent per year after transaction costs with a $t$-statistic of 1.75.

Schultz (1983) examines daily returns to New York and American Stock

Exchange stocks from 1963 through 1979. Since American Stock Exchange (AMEX) stocks generally have lower market values than NYSE-listed stocks. most of the firms in the smallest decile portfolio are listed on the AMEX. Consistent with the results of Stoll and Whaley (1983), Schultz finds the average round-trip transaction costs for the small firm portfolio are about 11.4 percent. Nevertheless, for holding periods of one year, the small firm portfolio earns average risk-adjusted returns of about 31 percent per year net of transaction costs. This 'size effect' has a *t*-statistic of 2.8. Schultz also estimates average transaction costs for each month and finds no evidence of seasonality that could explain the 'January size effect' found by Keim (1983). Therefore, Schultz concludes that transaction costs cannot explain the high average returns to small firms' stocks.

### 3.3.4. Other modifications of the CAPM

A number of papers have examined the relations between the 'size effect' and other variables that might be related to expected returns. For example, Cook and Rozeff (1982) examine the relations between firm size, dividend yield, and co-skewness. The latter variables have been proposed to account for effects of taxation and of skewness preference, respectively, on the specification of the capital asset pricing model. Keim (1982) analyzes the relation between dividend yield and firm size. Lakonishok and Shapiro (1982) examine the relation between firm size and the standard deviation of the stock return on the premise that standard deviation is an appropriate measure of risk if investors hold undiversified portfolios. Reinganum (1981b) examines the relation between firm size and the risk-adjusted returns from a version of the arbitrage pricing model of Ross (1976). While it is difficult to summarize the methodology and results of all these papers, none of these papers find a satisfactory explanation of the 'size effect'.

## 4. Where do we go from here?

The search for an explanation of this anomaly has been unsuccessful. Almost all authors of papers on the 'size effect' agree that it is evidence of misspecification of the capital asset pricing model, rather than evidence of inefficient capital markets. On the other hand, none of the attempts to modify the CAPM to account for taxation, transaction costs, skewness preference, and so forth have been successful at discovering the 'missing factor' for which size is a proxy. Thus, our understanding of the economic or statistical causes of the apparently high average returns to small firms' stocks is incomplete. It seems unlikely that the 'size effect' will be used to measure the opportunity cost of risky capital in the same way the CAPM is used because it is hard to understand why the opportunity cost of capital should be substantially higher for small firms than for large firms. It is especially hard to understand why the cost of capital should be higher for small firms during the first week of January. Therefore, it is unlikely that the 'size effect' will be taken into account in teaching capital budgeting or performance evaluation for investment portfolios.

The evidence on the 'size effect' probably will influence the use of the CAPM in 'event studies', especially in cases where new information is released in early January or cases where the sample is concentrated on firms of a given size. For example, studies of whether large firms are differentially affected by political costs would probably want to take account of the 'size effect' in estimating abnormal returns associated with information events. Of course, if historical average returns or the market model are used to calculate 'normal' returns to stocks, the 'size effect' is not a problem as long as the seasonality of stock returns is taken into account.

In short, I believe that the 'size effect' will join the 'weekend effect' that has been documented by French (1980) and Gibbons and Hess (1981) as an empirical anomaly. French and Gibbons and Hess find that average returns to stocks are negative from the close of trading on Friday to the close of trading on Monday. While these anomalies are statistically significant, they have not been explained using conventional economic models.

Where do we go from here? I suspect that empirical researchers will continue to search for the variable or combination of variables that will make the 'size effect' go away. However, to successfully explain the 'size effect', new theory must be developed that is consistent with rational maximizing behavior on the part of all actors in the model. As several authors have noted, the attempts to use institutional factors such as differential taxation or transaction costs to explain the 'size effect' seem to suggest the existence of profitable trading strategies for tax-exempt institutional investors that face relatively low costs of transacting. In equilibrium, these profits should be competed away, so that more sophisticated models are necessary to explain this apparent empirical regularity. Given the variety of plausible hypotheses that have been tried with at best partial success, I am not optimistic that we will understand the causes of the 'size effect' soon.

I also suspect that researchers will continue to measure the extent to which the 'size effect' is related to other anomalous differences in average returns to financial assets such as the '$E/P$ effect'. However, evidence on the similarity of two anomalies is not likely to help us understand either one.

The papers in this issue of the *Journal of Financial Economics* set a standard for future papers on the 'size effect'. Each paper contains carefully done empirical research. As a result, much more is known about the association between firm size and average stock returns, and we know that a variety of plausible hypotheses do not explain the 'size effect'. This work provides us with facts that are difficult to understand given our current knowledge about capital markets. I hope these empirical regularities will stimulate future research on the aspects of capital market institutions that will explain what now seem to be anomalies. New models of asset pricing that can explain the empirical evidence on the 'size effect', while maintaining the assumption of rational maximizing behavior, would be a significant step forward in financial research.

# References

Ball, Ray, 1978, Anomalies in relationships between securities' yields and yield-surrogates, Journal of Financial Economics 6, 103–126.

Banz, Rolf W., 1981, The relationship between return and market value of common stock, Journal of Financial Economics 9, 3–18.

Basu, Sanjoy, 1977, Investment performance of common stocks in relation to their price-earnings ratios: A test of the efficient market hypothesis, Journal of Finance 32, 663–682.

Basu, Sanjoy, 1983, The relationship between earnings' yield, market value and the return for NYSE common stocks: Further evidence, Journal of Financial Economics 12, this issue.

Berges, Angel, John J. McConnell and Gary G. Schlarbaum, 1982, An investigation of the turn-of-the-year effect, the small firm effect, and the tax-loss-selling-pressure hypothesis in Canadian stock returns, Manuscript (Purdue University, West Lafayette, IN).

Black, Fischer, 1972, Capital market equilibrium with restricted borrowing, Journal of Business 45, 444–455.

Blume, Marshall E. and Robert F. Stambaugh, 1983, Biases in computed returns: An application to the size effect, Manuscript (University of Pennsylvania, Philadelphia, PA).

Brown, Philip, Donald B. Keim, Allan W. Kleidon and Terry A. Marsh, 1983, Stock return seasonalities and the 'tax-loss selling' hypothesis: Analysis of the arguments and Australian evidence, Journal of Financial Economics 12, this issue.

Brown, Philip, Allan W. Kleidon and Terry A. Marsh, 1983, New evidence on the nature of size related anomalies in stock prices, Journal of Financial Economics 12, this issue.

Christie, Andrew A. and Michael Hertzel, 1981, Capital asset pricing 'anomalies': Size and other correlations, Manuscript (University of Rochester, Rochester, NY).

Cook, Thomas J. and Michael S. Rozeff, 1982, Size, dividend yield and co-skewness effects on stock returns: Some empirical tests, Manuscript (University of Iowa, Iowa City, IA).

Fama, Eugene F. and James D. MacBeth, 1973, Risk, return and equilibrium: Empirical tests Journal of Political Economy 81, 607–636.

French, Kenneth R., 1980, Stock returns and the weekend effect, Journal of Financial Economics 8, 55–70.

Gibbons, Michael R. and Patrick J. Hess, 1981, Day of the week effects and asset returns, Journal of Business 54, 579–596.

Gultekin, Mustafa N. and N. Bulent Gultekin, 1982, Stock market seasonality and the turn of the tax year effect: International evidence, Manuscript (University of Pennsylvania, Philadelphia, PA).

Keim, Donald B., 1982, Dividend yields and stock returns: Implications of abnormal January returns, Manuscript (University of Pennsylvania, Philadelphia, PA).

Keim, Donald B., 1983, Size related anomalies and stock return seasonality: Further empirical evidence, Journal of Financial Economics 12, this issue.

Lakonishok, Josef and Alan C. Shapiro, 1982, Partial diversification as an explanation of the small firm effect: An empirical analysis, Manuscript (University of Southern California, Los Angeles, CA).

Lintner, John, 1965, The valuation of risk assets and the selection of risky investments in stock portfolios and capital budgets, Review of Economics and Statistics 47, 13–37.

Officer, Robert R., 1975, Seasonality in the Australian capital markets: Market efficiency and empirical issues, Journal of Financial Economics 2, 29–52.

Reinganum, Marc R., 1981a, Misspecification of capital asset pricing: Empirical anomalies based on earnings yields and market values, Journal of Financial Economics 9, 19–46.

Reinganum, Marc R., 1981b, The arbitrage pricing theory: Some empirical results, Journal of Finance 36, 313–321.

Reinganum, Marc R., 1982, A direct test of Roll's conjecture on the firm size effect, Journal of Finance 37, 27–35.

Reinganum, Marc R., 1983, The anomalous stock market behavior of small firms in January: Empirical tests for tax-loss selling effects, Journal of Financial Economics 12, this issue.

Roll, Richard, 1981, A possible explanation of the small firm effect, Journal of Finance 36, 879–888.

Roll, Richard, 1982, On computing mean returns and the small firm premium, Working paper no. 22-82 (Graduate School of Management, University of California, Los Angeles, CA).

Roll, Richard, 1983, Vas ist das? The turn of the year effect and the return premium of small firms, Journal of Portfolio Management, 9, 18–28.

Ross, Stephen A., 1976, The arbitrage theory of capital asset pricing, Journal of Economic Theory 13, 341–360.

Rozeff, Michael S. and William R. Kinney, Jr., 1976, Capital market seasonality: The case of stock returns, Journal of Financial Economics 3, 379–402.

Schultz, Paul, 1983, Transaction costs and the small firm effect: A comment, Journal of Financial Economics 12, this issue.

Sharpe, William F., 1964, Capital asset prices: A theory of market equilibrium under conditions of risk, Journal of Finance 19, 425–442.

Stoll, Hans R. and Robert E. Whaley, 1983, Transaction costs and the small firm effect, Journal of Financial Economics 12, this issue.

# ASSET PRICING AND THE BID–ASK SPREAD*

## Yakov AMIHUD

*Tel Aviv University, Tel Aviv, Israel*
*New York University, New York, NY 10006, USA*

## Haim MENDELSON

*University of Rochester, Rochester, NY 14627, USA*

Received August 1985, final version received April 1986

This paper studies the effect of the bid–ask spread on asset pricing. We analyze a model in which investors with different expected holding periods trade assets with different relative spreads. The resulting testable hypothesis is that market-observed expected return is an increasing and concave function of the spread. We test this hypothesis, and the empirical results are consistent with the predictions of the model.

## 1. Introduction

Liquidity, marketability or trading costs are among the primary attributes of many investment plans and financial instruments. In the securities industry, portfolio managers and investment consultants tailor portfolios to fit their clients' investment horizons and liquidity objectives. But despite its evident importance in practice, the role of liquidity in capital markets is hardly reflected in academic research. This paper attempts to narrow this gap by examining the effects of illiquidity on asset pricing.

Illiquidity can be measured by the cost of immediate execution. An investor willing to transact faces a tradeoff: He may either wait to transact at a favorable price or insist on immediate execution at the current bid or ask price. The quoted ask (offer) price includes a premium for immediate buying, and the bid price similarly reflects a concession required for immediate sale. Thus, a natural measure of illiquidity is the spread between the bid and ask

*We wish to thank Hans Stoll and Robert Whaley for furnishing the spread data, and Manny Pai for excellent programming assistance. We acknowledge helpful comments by the Editor, Clifford W. Smith, by an anonymous referee, by Harry DeAngelo, Linda DeAngelo, Michael C. Jensen, Krishna Ramaswamy and Jerry Zimmerman, and especially by John Long and G. William Schwert. Partial financial support by the Managerial Economics Research Center of the University of Rochester, the Salomon Brothers Center for the Study of Financial Markets, and the Israel Institute for Business Research is acknowledged.

Journal of Financial Economics 17 (1986) 223–249. North-Holland

prices, which is the sum of the buying premium and the selling concession.[1] Indeed, the relative spread on stocks has been found to be negatively corre- lated with liquidity characteristics such as the trading volume, the number of shareholders, the number of market makers trading the stock and the stock price continuity.[2]

This paper suggests that expected asset returns are increasing in the (rela- tive) bid–ask spread. We first model the effects of the spread on asset returns. Our model predicts that higher-spread assets yield higher expected returns, and that there is a clientele effect whereby investors with longer holding periods select assets with higher spreads. The resulting testable hypothesis is that asset returns are an increasing and concave function of the spread. The model also predicts that expected returns net of trading costs increase with the holding period, and consequently higher-spread assets yield higher net returns to their holders. Hence, an investor expecting a long holding period can gain by holding high-spread assets.

We test the predicted spread–return relation using data for the period 1961–1980, and find that our hypotheses are consistent with the evidence: Average portfolio risk-adjusted returns increase with their bid–ask spread, and the slope of the return–spread relationship decreases with the spread. Finally, we verify that the spread effect persists when firm size is added as an explanatory variable in the regression equations. We emphasize that the spread effect is by no means an anomaly or an indication of market in- efficiency; rather, it represents a rational response by an efficient market to the existence of the spread.

This study highlights the importance of securities market microstructure in determining asset returns, and provides a link between this area and mainstream research on capital markets. Our results suggest that liquidity- increasing financial policies can reduce the firm's opportunity cost of capital, and provide measures for the value of improvements in the trading and exchange process.[3] In the area of portfolio selection, our findings may guide investors in balancing expected trading costs against expected returns. In sum, we demonstrate the importance of market-microstructure factors as determi- nants of stock returns.

In the following section we present a model of the return–spread relation and form the hypotheses for our empirical tests. In section 3 we test the

---

[1] Demsetz (1968) first related the spread to the cost of transacting. See also Amihud and Mendelson (1980, 1982), Phillips and Smith (1982), Ho and Stoll (1981, 1983), Copeland and Galai (1983), and West and Tinic (1971). For an analysis of transaction costs in the context of a fixed investment horizon, see Chen, Kim and Kon (1975), Levy (1978), Milne and Smith (1980), and Treynor (1980).

[2] See, e.g., Garbade (1982) and Stoll (1985).

[3] See, e.g., Mendelson (1982, 1985, 1986, 1987), Amihud and Mendelson (1985, 1986) for the interaction between market characteristics, trading organization and liquidity.

predicted relationship, and in section 4 we relate our findings to the firm size anomaly. Our concluding remarks are offered in section 5.

## 2. A model of the return–spread relation

In this section we model the role of the bid–ask spread in determining asset returns. We consider $M$ investor types numbered by $i = 1, 2, \ldots, M$, and $N + 1$ capital assets indexed by $j = 0, 1, 2, \ldots, N$. Each asset $j$ generates a perpetual cash flow of $\$d_j$ per unit time ($d_j > 0$) and has a relative spread of $S_j$, reflecting its trading costs. Asset 0 is a zero-spread asset ($S_0 = 0$) having unlimited supply. Assets are perfectly divisible, and one unit of each positive-spread asset $j$ ($j = 1, 2, \ldots, N$) is available.

Trading is performed via competitive market makers who quote assets' bid and ask prices and stand ready to trade at these prices. The market makers bridge the time gaps between the arrivals of buyers and sellers to the market, absorb transitory excess demand or supply in their inventory positions, and are compensated by the spread, which is competitively set. Thus, they quote for each asset $j$ an ask price $V_j$ and a bid price $V_j(1 - S_j)$, giving rise to two price vectors: an ask price vector $(V_0, V_1, \ldots, V_N)$ and a bid price vector $(V_0, V_1(1 - S_1), \ldots, V_N(1 - S_N))$.[4]

A type-$i$ investor enters the market with wealth $W_i$ used to purchase capital assets (at the quoted ask prices). He holds these assets for a random, exponentially distributed time $T_i$ with mean $E[T_i] = 1/\mu_i$, liquidates his portfolio by selling it to the market makers at the bid prices, and leaves the market. We number investor types by increasing expected holding periods, $\mu_1^{-1} \le \mu_2^{-1} \le \cdots \le \mu_M^{-1}$, and assets by increasing relative spreads, $0 = S_0 \le S_1 \le \cdots \le S_N < 1$. Finally, we assume that the arrivals of type-$i$ investors to the market follow a Poisson process with rate $\lambda_i$, with the interarrival times and holding periods being stochastically independent.

In statistical equilibrium, the number of type-$i$ investors with portfolio holdings in the market has a Poisson distribution with mean $m_i = \lambda_i/\mu_i$ [cf. Ross (1970, ch. 2)]. The market makers' inventories fluctuate over time to accommodate transitory excess demand or supply disturbances, but their *expected* inventory positions are zero, i.e., market makers are 'seeking out the market price that equilibrates buying and selling pressures' [Bagehot (1971, p. 14); see also Garman (1976)]. This implies that the expected sum of investors' holdings in each positive-spread asset is equal to its available supply of one unit.

Consider now the portfolio decision of a type-$i$ investor facing a given set of bid and ask prices, whose objective is to maximize the expected discounted net

---

[4] Competition among market makers drives the spread to the level $S_j$ of trading costs. In a different scenario, $V_j$ may be viewed as the sum of the market price and the buying transaction cost, and $V_j(1 - S_j)$ as the price net of the cost of a sell transaction.

cash flows received over his planning horizon. The discount rate $\rho$ is the spread-free, risk-adjusted rate of return on the zero-spread asset. Let $x_{ij}$ be the quantity of asset $j$ acquired by the type-$i$ investor. We call the vector $\{x_{ij}, j = 0, 1, 2, \ldots, N\}$ 'portfolio $i$'. The expected present value of holding portfolio $i$ is the sum of the expected discounted value of the continuous cash stream received over its holding period and the expected discounted liquidation revenue. This sum is given by

$$
E_{T_i}\left\{\int_0^{T_i} e^{-\rho y}\left[\sum_{j=0}^{N} x_{ij} d_j\right] dy\right\} + E_{T_i}\left\{e^{-\rho T_i} \sum_{j=0}^{N} x_{ij} V_j(1 - S_j)\right\}
$$

$$
= (\mu_i + \rho)^{-1} \sum_{j=0}^{N} x_{ij}\left[d_j + \mu_i V_j(1 - S_j)\right].
$$

Thus, for *given* vectors of bid and ask prices, a type-$i$ investor solves the problem

$$
\max \sum_{j=0}^{N} x_{ij}\left[d_j + \mu_i V_j(1 - S_j)\right], \tag{1}
$$

subject to

$$
\sum_{j=0}^{N} x_{ij} V_j \le W_i \quad \text{and} \quad x_{ij} \ge 0 \quad \text{for all} \quad j = 0, 1, 2, \ldots, N, \tag{2}
$$

where condition (2) expresses the wealth constraint and the exclusion of investors' short positions.[5] Under our specification, the usual market clearing conditions read

$$
\sum_{i=1}^{M} m_i x_{ij} = 1, \qquad j = 1, 2, \ldots, N \tag{3}
$$

(recall that $m_i$ is the expected number of type-$i$ investors in the market).

When an $M \times (N + 1)$ matrix $X^*$ and an $(N + 1)$-dimensional vector $V^*$ solve the $M$ optimization problems (1)–(2) such that (3) is satisfied, we call $X^*$ an equilibrium allocation matrix and $V^*$ – an equilibrium ask price vector [the corresponding bid price vector is $(V_0^*, V_1^*(1 - S_1), \ldots, V_N^*(1 - S_N))$]. The

---

[5]In our context, the use of short sales cannot eliminate the spread effect, since short sales by themselves entail additional transaction costs. Note that a constraint on short positions is necessary in models of tax clienteles [cf. Miller (1977), Litzenberger and Ramaswamy (1980)]. Clearly, market makers are allowed to have transitory long or short positions, but are constrained to have zero expected inventory positions [cf. Garman (1976)].

above model may be viewed as a special case of the linear exchange model [cf. Gale (1960)], which is known to have an equilibrium allocation and a unique equilibrium price vector. Our model enables us to derive and interpret the resulting equilibrium in a straightforward and intuitive way as follows.

We define the expected *spread-adjusted return* of asset $j$ to investor-type $i$ as the difference between the gross market return on asset $j$ and its expected liquidation cost per unit time:

$$r_{ij} = d_j/V_j - \mu_i S_j, \tag{4}$$

where $d_j/V_j$ is the gross return on security $j$, and $\mu_i S_j$ is the *spread-adjustment*, or expected liquidation cost (per unit time), equal to the product of the liquidation probability per unit time by the percentage spread. Note that the spread-adjusted return depends on *both* the asset $j$ and the investor-type $i$ (through the expected holding period).

For a given price vector $V$, investor $i$ selects for his portfolio the assets $j$ which provide him the highest spread-adjusted return, given by

$$r_i^* = \max_{j=0,1,2,\ldots,N} r_{ij}, \tag{5}$$

with $r_1^* \leq r_2^* \leq r_3^* \leq \cdots \leq r_M^*$, since, by (4), $r_{ij}$ is a non-decreasing function of $i$ for all $j$. These inequalities state that the spread-adjusted return on a portfolio increases with the expected holding period. That is, investors with longer expected holding periods will earn higher returns *net* of transaction costs.[6]

The *gross* return required by investor $i$ on asset $j$ is given by $r_i^* + \mu_i S_j$, which reflects both the required spread-adjusted return $r_i^*$ and the expected liquidation cost $\mu_i S_j$. The equilibrium gross (market-observed) return on asset $j$ is determined by its highest-valued use, which is in the portfolio $i$ with the minimal required return, implying that

$$d_j/V_j^* = \min_{i=1,2,\ldots,M} \left\{ r_i^* + \mu_i S_j \right\}. \tag{6}$$

Eq. (6) can also be written in the form

$$V_j^* = \max_{i=1,2,\ldots,M} \left\{ d_j/(r_i^* + \mu_i S_j) \right\}, \tag{7}$$

[6] This is consistent with the suggestions that while the illiquidity of investments such as real estate [Fogler (1984)] coins [Kane (1984)] and stamps [Taylor (1983)] excludes them from short-term investment portfolios, they are expected to provide superior performance when held over a long investment horizon (the same may apply to stock-exchange seats) [Schwert (1977)]. See also Day, Stoll and Whaley (1985) on the clientele of small firms, and Elton and Gruber (1978) on tax clienteles.

implying that the equilibrium value of asset $j$, $V_j{}^*$, is equal to the present value of its perpetual cash flow, discounted at the gross return $(r_i{}^* + \mu_i S_j)$. Alternatively, $V_j{}^*$ can be written as the difference between (i) the present value of the perpetual cash stream $d_j$ and (ii) the present value of the expected trading costs for all the present and future holders of asset $j$, where both are discounted at the spread-adjusted return of the holding investor. To see this, assume that the available quantity of asset $j$ is held by type-$i$ investors; then (7) can be written as

$$V_j{}^* = d_j/r_i{}^* - \mu_i V_j{}^* S_j/r_i{}^*,$$

where the first term is, obviously, (i). As for the second, the expected quantity of asset $j$ sold per unit time by type-$i$ investors is $\mu_i$, and each sale incurs a transaction cost of $V_j{}^* S_j$; thus, $\mu_i V_j{}^* S_j/r_i{}^*$ is the expected present value (discounted at $r_i{}^*$) of the transaction-cost cash flow.

The implications of the above equilibrium on the relation between returns, spreads and holding periods are summarized by the following propositions.

*Proposition 1 (clientele effect).   Assets with higher spreads are allocated in equilibrium to portfolios with (the same or) longer expected holding periods.*

*Proof.*   Consider two assets, $j$ and $k$, such that in equilibrium asset $j$ is in portfolio $i$ and asset $k$ is in portfolio $i+1$ (recall that $\mu_i \geq \mu_{i+1}$). Applying (5), we obtain $r_{ij} \geq r_{ik}$ and $r_{i+1,k} \geq r_{i+1,j}$; thus, substituting from (4), $d_j/V_j{}^* - \mu_i S_j \geq d_k/V_k{}^* - \mu_i S_k$ and $d_k/V_k{}^* - \mu_{i+1} S_k \geq d_j/V_j{}^* - \mu_{i+1} S_j$, implying that $(\mu_i - \mu_{i+1})(S_k - S_j) \geq 0$. It follows that if $\mu_i > \mu_{i+1}$, we must have $S_k \geq S_j$. The case of non-consecutive portfolios immediately follows.   Q.E.D.

*Proposition 2 (spread–return relationship).   In equilibrium, the observed market (gross) return is an increasing and concave piecewise-linear function of the (relative) spread.*

*Proof.*   Let $f_i(S) = r_i{}^* + \mu_i S$. By (6), the market return on an asset with relative spread $S$ is given by $f(S) \equiv \min_{i=1,2,\ldots,M} f_i(S)$. Now, the proposition follows from the fact that monotonicity and concavity are preserved by the minimum operator, and that the minimum of a finite collection of linear functions is piecewise-linear.   Q.E.D.

Proposition 2 is the main testable implication of our model. Intuitively, the positive association between return and spread reflects the compensation required by investors for their trading costs, and its concavity results from the clientele effect (Proposition 1). To see this, recall that transaction costs are amortized over the investor's holding period. The longer this period, the

Table 1

An example of the equilibrium relation between asset bid–ask spreads, returns and values (see section 2). There are 10 assets ($j$), each generating \$1 per period, with relative bid–ask spreads $S_j$ (= dollar spread divided by asset value) ranging from 0 to 0.045 (column 2), and 4 investor types ($i$) with expected holding periods, $\mu_i^{-1}$, of 1/12, 1/2, 1 and 5 periods.[a] The return on the zero-spread asset is $\rho$; all returns are measured in excess of $\rho$. A type-$i$ investor chooses the assets $j$ which maximize his spread-adjusted return, $r_{ij}$, given by the difference between the gross market return on asset $j$ and its expected liquidation cost per unit time. The equilibrium solution gives the excess spread-adjusted returns, $r_{ij} - \rho$, in columns 3–6, where the boxes highlight the assets with the highest excess spread-adjusted return for each investor-type. The equilibrium portfolio for each investor-type is composed of the boxed assets. Column 7 shows the assets' equilibrium excess gross returns observed in the market, which include the expected liquidation cost to their holders. Column 8 shows the resulting asset values, obtained by discounting the perpetuity by the respective equilibrium market return, as a fraction of the value of the zero-spread asset.

| | | Investor type, $i$ | | | | Market return in excess of $\rho$, the return on the zero-spread asset | Value of asset $j$ relative to that of the zero-spread asset, $V_j/V_0$ |
| | | 1 | 2 | 3 | 4 | | |
| | Relative bid–ask spread, $S_j$ | Length of holding period, $\mu_i^{-1}$ | | | | | |
| Asset, $j$ | | 1/12 | 1/2 | 1 | 5 | | |
| | | Excess spread-adjusted return, $r_{ij} - \rho$ | | | | | |
| (1) | (2) | (3) | (4) | (5) | (6) | (7) | (8) |
| 0 | 0 | 0 | 0 | 0 | 0 | 0 | 1 |
| 1 | 0.005 | 0 | 0.05 | 0.055 | 0.059 | 0.06 | 0.943 |
| 2 | 0.01 | 0 | 0.10 | 0.11 | 0.118 | 0.12 | 0.893 |
| 3 | 0.015 | −0.05 | 0.10 | 0.115 | 0.127 | 0.13 | 0.885 |
| 4 | 0.02 | −0.10 | 0.10 | 0.12 | 0.136 | 0.14 | 0.877 |
| 5 | 0.025 | −0.155 | 0.095 | 0.12 | 0.140 | 0.145 | 0.873 |
| 6 | 0.03 | −0.21 | 0.09 | 0.12 | 0.144 | 0.15 | 0.870 |
| 7 | 0.035 | −0.265 | 0.085 | 0.12 | 0.148 | 0.155 | 0.866 |
| 8 | 0.04 | −0.324 | 0.076 | 0.116 | 0.148 | 0.156 | 0.865 |
| 9 | 0.045 | −0.383 | 0.067 | 0.112 | 0.148 | 0.157 | 0.864 |

[a] Investors have the same wealth, and the expected number of investors of each type is 1.

smaller the compensation required for a given increase in the spread. Since in equilibrium higher-spread securities are acquired by investors with longer horizons, the added return required for a given increase in spread gets smaller. In terms of our model, longer-holding-period portfolios contain higher-spread assets and have a lower slope $\mu_i$ for the return–spread relation.

A simple numerical example can illustrate the spread–return relation. Assume $N = 9$ positive-spread assets and $M = 4$ investor types whose expected holding periods are $1/\mu_1 = 1/12$, $1/\mu_2 = 1/2$, $1/\mu_3 = 1$, and $1/\mu_4 = 5$. For simplicity we set $\lambda_i = \mu_i$, implying that the expected number of investors of each type $i$ is $m_i = 1$. Assets yield $d_j = \$1$ per period, and all investors have equal wealth. The relative spread of asset $j$ is $S_j = 0.005j$, $j = 0, 1, 2, \ldots, 9$; thus, asset percentage spreads range from zero to 4.5%.

Using this data, we solve (1)–(3) and obtain the results in table 1 and figs. 1 and 2. Note that the additional excess return per unit of spread goes down

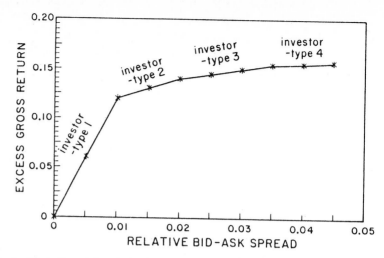

Fig. 1. An illustration of the relation between observed market return in excess of the return on the zero-spread asset (the excess gross return) and the relative bid–ask spread (see the numerical example of section 2 and table 1, column 7). There are 10 assets, each generating $1 per period, with relative bid–ask spreads (= dollar spread divided by asset value) ranging from 0 to 0.045, and 4 investor types with expected holding periods ranging from 1/12 to 5 periods. Investors have equal wealth, and the expected number of investors of each type is 1. The relation between asset returns and bid–ask spreads is piecewise-linear, increasing and concave, with each linear section corresponding to the portfolio of a different investor type.

from $\mu_1 = 12$ in portfolio 1 to $\mu_2 = 2$ for portfolio 2, then to $\mu_3 = 1$ in portfolio 3, and finally to $\mu_4 = 0.2$ in portfolio 4. The behavior of the excess market return as a function of the spread is shown in fig. 1, which demonstrates both the positive compensation for higher spread and the clientele effect which moderates the excess returns, especially for the high-spread assets. This figure summarizes the main testable implications of our model: The observed market return should be an increasing and concave function of the relative spread. The piecewise-linear functional form suggested by our model provides a specific and detailed set of hypotheses tested in the next section. The effect of the spread on asset values (or prices) is demonstrated in fig 2: the equilibrium values are decreasing and convex in the spread.

While the above model provides a lucid demonstration of the spread–return (or spread–price) relation, our main results do not hinge on its specific form, and hold as well under different specifications. Consider $(N + 1)$ assets, each generating the same stochastic (gross) cash flow given by the process $\{ X(t), t \geq 0 \}$. Assume that each transaction in asset $j$ entails a cost of $\$c_j$, with $0 = c_0 < c_1 < c_2 < \cdots < c_N$ (asset 0 having zero spread). There are $M$ investor types numbered by $i = 1, 2, \ldots, M$, and the transaction epochs of type-$i$ investors follow a renewal process with given parameters (depending on $i$).[7]

---

[7]An investor could be viewed as owning a number of portfolios with different liquidation horizons, without changing the results.

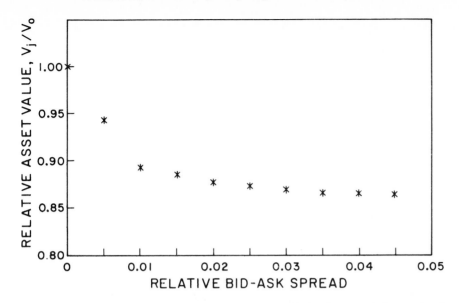

Fig. 2. The relation between asset values and bid–ask spreads for the numerical example of section 2 (see table 1, column 8, and fig. 1). The figure depicts the value of each asset $j$ relative to the value of the zero-spread asset, $V_j/V_0$, as a function of the bid–ask spread relative to the asset's value. Asset values are a decreasing function of the spread.

Denote the highest price a type-$i$ investor will pay for asset $j$ by $V_{ij}$. When the price of each asset $j$ is determined by its highest-valued use, we have $V_j = \max_{i=1,2,\ldots,M} V_{ij}$ with $V_{ij} = V_{i0} - c_j\theta_i$, where $\theta_i$ is the value (for investor-type $i$) of \$1 at each transaction epoch. Letting $f_i(c) = V_{i0} - c\theta_i$, and following the arguments of Proposition 2, we obtain that the price [given by $\max_{i=1,2,\ldots,M} f_i(c)$] is decreasing and convex in $c$. Further, it can be shown that the price is a decreasing and convex function of the relative transaction cost, thus demonstrating the robustness of our results. Qualitatively, similar results will hold as long as a longer investment horizon mitigates the burden of transaction costs by enabling their amortization over a longer holding period.

The next section presents empirical tests of our main testable hypotheses (Proposition 2).

## 3. Empirical tests

This section presents an empirical examination of the relation between expected returns and bid–ask spreads of NYSE stocks, focusing on the particular functional relationship predicted by our model. Specifically, our hypothesis is that expected return is an increasing and concave function of the spread.

### 3.1. The data and the derivation of the variables

Our data consist of monthly securities returns provided by the Center for Research in Security Prices and relative bid–ask spreads collected for NYSE stocks from *Fitch's Stock Quotations on the NYSE*. The relative spread is the dollar spread divided by the average of the bid and ask prices at year end. The actual spread variable used, $S$, is the average of the beginning and end-of-year relative spreads for each of the years 1960–1979 [the data is the same as in Stoll and Whaley (1983)].

The relationship between stock returns, relative risk[8] ($\beta$) and spread[9] is tested over the period 1961–1980. Following the methodology developed by Black, Jensen and Scholes (1972), Fama and MacBeth (1973) and Black and Scholes (1974), we first formed portfolios by grouping stocks according to their spread and relative risk, and then tested our hypotheses by examining the cross-sectional relation between average excess return, spread and relative risk over time. We divided the data into twenty overlapping periods of eleven years each, consisting of a five-year $\beta$ estimation period $E_n$, a five-year portfolio formation period $F_n$, and a one-year cross-section test period $T_n$ ($n = 1, 2, \ldots, 20$).[10] The three subperiods of each eleven-year period are now considered in detail:

(i) *The beta estimation period $E_{\cdot}$* was used to estimate the $\beta$ coefficients from the market model regressions

$$R_{jt}^{e} = \alpha_j + \beta_j R_{mt}^{e} + \varepsilon_{jt}, \qquad t = 1, \ldots, 60,$$

where $R_{jt}^{e}$ and $R_{mt}^{e}$ are the month-$t$ excess returns (over the 90-day T-bill rates) on stock $j$ and on the market,[11] respectively, and $\beta_j$ is the estimate of the relative risk[12] of stock $j$.

(ii) *The portfolio formation period $F_n$* was used to form the test portfolios and estimate their $\beta$ and spread parameters. All stocks traded through the

---

[8] By the CAPM, the $\beta$ risk is the major determinant of asset returns. Our analysis in section 2 dealt with certainty-equivalent rates of return.

[9] The cost of transacting also includes brokerage commissions. In Stoll and Whaley (1983), the correlation between portfolio spreads and brokerage fees was 0.996, hence we omitted the latter.

[10] To illustrate, $E_1 = 1951$–1955, $F_1 = 1956$–1960, $T_1 = 1961$; $E_2 = 1952$–1956, $F_2 = 1957$–1961, $T_2 = 1962$; $\ldots E_{20} = 1970$–1974, $F_{20} = 1975$–1979, $T_{20} = 1980$.

[11] Throughout this study, $R_m$ and the test portfolios are equally weighted. See Black, Jensen and Scholes (1972), Fama and MacBeth (1973) and Stoll and Whaley (1983, p. 71).

[12] Jensen (1968) has shown that the measure of relative risk, $\beta_j$, may be used for a holding period of any length (p. 189).

entire eleven-year period $n$ and for which the spread was available for the last year of $F_n$ were ranked by that spread and divided into seven equal groups. Within each of the seven spread groups, stocks were ranked by their $\beta$ coefficients, obtained from $E_n$, and divided into seven equal subgroups. This yields 49 $(7 \times 7)$ equal-sized portfolios,[13] with significant variability of the spreads as well as the betas within the spread groups. Then, we estimated $\beta$ for each portfolio from the market model regression over the months of $F_n$,

$$R^e_{pt} = \alpha_p + \beta_p R^e_{mt} + \varepsilon_{pt}, \qquad t = 1,\ldots,60, \quad p = 1,\ldots,49,$$

where $R^e_{pt}$ is the average[14] excess return of the securities included in portfolio $p$ in month $t$. Finally, we calculated the portfolio spread $S_{pn}$ by averaging the spreads (of the last year of $F_n$) across the stocks in portfolio $p$. Each portfolio $p$ in period $n$ is thus characterized by the pair $(\beta_{pn}, S_{pn})$ ($p = 1, 2, \ldots, 49$, $n = 1, 2, \ldots, 20$). Altogether, we have 980 $(= 49 \times 20)$ portfolios.

(iii) *The cross-section test period* $T_n$ was used to test the relation between $R^e_{pn}$, $\beta_{pn}$ and $S_{pn}$ across portfolios, where $R^e_{pn}$ is the average monthly excess return on the stocks in portfolio $p$ in $T_n$, the last year of period $n$.[15]

Table 2 presents summary statistics for the 49 portfolio groups, classified by spread and $\beta$. Note that both $\beta$ and the excess return increase with the spread. The correlation coefficients between the portfolio excess returns $R^e_p$, the portfolio betas $\beta_p$ and the spreads $S_p$, presented in table 3, show that both $\beta_p$ and $S_p$ are positively correlated with excess returns; the correlation between $R^e_p$ and the spread over the twenty-year period is about twice as high as that between $R^e_p$ and $\beta$. Also, note the high positive correlation between $\beta$ and the spread.

## 3.2. Test methodology

We now turn to test the major hypothesis of model, namely, that expected return is an increasing and concave function of the relative spread. This is a classical case of covariance analysis and pooling of cross-section and time-series data [see Kmenta (1971, ch. 12-2), Maddala (1977, ch. 14), Judge et al. (1980, ch. 8)], where the estimation model has to allow for differences over cross-sec-

---

[13] The long trading-period requirement might have eliminated from our sample the riskier and higher-spread stocks, thus reducing the variability of the data. Throughout, 'equal' portfolios may differ from one another by one security due to indivisibility.

[14] Throughout, averaging means arithmetic averaging.

[15] Note that our test is predictive in nature, using estimates of risk and spread which are available at the beginning of the test period. See Fama (1976, 349–351).

Table 2

Average relative bid-ask spread, monthly excess return, relative risk ($\beta$) and firm size for the 49 portfolios for the 20 test-period years 1961–1980. Portfolios are indexed by the spread group $i$ ($i = 1$ for the smallest spread) and by the beta group $j$ ($j = 1$ for the smallest beta). Portfolio composition changes every year and the sample size ranges between 619 and 900 stocks.

The relative bid-ask spread of a stock is its dollar spread divided by the average of the bid and ask prices at year end. The portfolio spread is the average relative spread of stocks in the portfolio.

The portfolio (monthly) excess return is the 12-month arithmetic average of the monthly average returns on the stocks in the portfolio in excess of that month's Treasury-Bill rate.

The portfolio beta is the average relative risk ($\beta$) coefficient for the stocks in the portfolio, estimated over the 5 years preceding the test period. Size is the market value of the firm's equity in millions of dollars at the end of the year preceding the test period, averaged over the firms included in the portfolio.

| Spread group, $i$ | | Beta group, $j$ | | | | | | | | Mean |
|---|---|---|---|---|---|---|---|---|---|---|
| | | 1 | 2 | 3 | 4 | 5 | 6 | 7 | | |
| 1 | Spread | 0.004765 | 0.004850 | 0.004860 | 0.004789 | 0.004878 | 0.004891 | 0.004980 | | 0.00486 |
| | Excess return | 0.002706 | 0.001306 | 0.003380 | 0.004409 | 0.003427 | 0.005416 | 0.003781 | | 0.00349 |
| | Beta | 0.54001 | 0.67797 | 0.75890 | 0.77867 | 0.83231 | 0.91651 | 1.08973 | | 0.799 |
| | Size | 4089.8 | 3245.5 | 3231.9 | 2317.3 | 1430.0 | 1418.8 | 595.7 | | 2333 |
| 2 | Spread | 0.007435 | 0.007445 | 0.007463 | 0.007414 | 0.007508 | 0.007412 | 0.007452 | | 0.00745 |
| | Excess return | 0.003174 | 0.003543 | 0.003549 | 0.004995 | 0.003050 | 0.006424 | 0.011061 | | 0.00511 |
| | Beta | 0.55369 | 0.71874 | 0.81652 | 0.84596 | 0.90668 | 1.02999 | 1.21992 | | 0.870 |
| | Size | 780.2 | 880.3 | 741.5 | 707.6 | 656.1 | 605.9 | 282.7 | | 665 |
| 3 | Spread | 0.009392 | 0.009386 | 0.009400 | 0.009375 | 0.009339 | 0.009350 | 0.009425 | | 0.00939 |
| | Excess return | 0.001838 | 0.003165 | 0.006707 | 0.002619 | 0.004473 | 0.006133 | 0.005063 | | 0.00429 |
| | Beta | 0.56069 | 0.67271 | 0.79543 | 0.89866 | 1.00357 | 1.04518 | 1.20940 | | 0.884 |
| | Size | 476.2 | 502.1 | 695.9 | 370.1 | 363.9 | 293.3 | 227.1 | | 418 |

| | | | | | | | | |
|---|---|---|---|---|---|---|---|---|
| **4** | Spread | 0.011470 | 0.011473 | 0.011411 | 0.011464 | 0.011449 | 0.011487 | 0.011411 | 0.01145 |
| | Excess return | 0.003217 | 0.002447 | 0.005296 | 0.004521 | 0.008505 | 0.008033 | 0.009178 | 0.00589 |
| | Beta | 0.58821 | 0.69158 | 0.84828 | 0.92208 | 0.99515 | 1.07535 | 1.26739 | 0.913 |
| | Size | 331.9 | 362.7 | 370.6 | 248.4 | 250.5 | 192.4 | 174.5 | 276 |
| **5** | Spread | 0.014015 | 0.013913 | 0.013955 | 0.013998 | 0.013883 | 0.013969 | 0.013988 | 0.01396 |
| | Excess return | 0.002583 | 0.004340 | 0.003318 | 0.006763 | 0.008076 | 0.011460 | 0.010266 | 0.00669 |
| | Beta | 0.60153 | 0.71197 | 0.82031 | 0.92906 | 1.04923 | 1.12224 | 1.28927 | 0.932 |
| | Size | 243.1 | 257.3 | 213.6 | 166.3 | 149.2 | 146.2 | 111.3 | 184 |
| **6** | Spread | 0.017662 | 0.017513 | 0.017699 | 0.017759 | 0.017789 | 0.017763 | 0.017967 | 0.01774 |
| | Excess return | 0.003637 | 0.006937 | 0.007209 | 0.007415 | 0.011254 | 0.010877 | 0.012516 | 0.00855 |
| | Beta | 0.65522 | 0.73861 | 0.87193 | 0.94479 | 1.07714 | 1.16769 | 1.33498 | 0.970 |
| | Size | 135.6 | 131.1 | 127.1 | 113.1 | 91.2 | 89.9 | 72.8 | 109 |
| **7** | Spread | 0.032890 | 0.029385 | 0.031614 | 0.031472 | 0.031647 | 0.033169 | 0.034385 | 0.03208 |
| | Excess return | 0.006683 | 0.008876 | 0.008044 | 0.007405 | 0.012335 | 0.013384 | 0.014929 | 0.01024 |
| | Beta | 0.76132 | 0.88340 | 0.99811 | 1.12656 | 1.23899 | 1.33249 | 1.46259 | 1.115 |
| | Size | 75.2 | 67.8 | 57.5 | 54.7 | 44.0 | 47.8 | 37.3 | 55 |
| **Mean** | Spread | 0.013947 | 0.013424 | 0.013772 | 0.013753 | 0.013792 | 0.014006 | 0.014230 | 0.01385 |
| | Excess return | 0.003405 | 0.004373 | 0.005357 | 0.005447 | 0.007303 | 0.008818 | 0.009542 | 0.00632 |
| | Beta | 0.60867 | 0.72785 | 0.84421 | 0.92083 | 1.01472 | 1.09849 | 1.26761 | 0.926 |
| | Size | 876 | 778 | 777 | 568 | 426 | 399 | 214 | 577 |

Table 3

Correlation coefficients between the annual average portfolio spread $S_p$, excess return $R_p^e$ and beta $\beta_p$ for the entire sample period 1961–1980 and for its two 10-year subperiods, 1961–1970 and 1971–1980. Portfolio spread is the average bid–ask spread as a fraction of the year-end average of the bid and ask prices for all securities in the portfolio. Excess returns are the average monthly returns in excess of the monthly T-Bill rate.

| Period | Correlation coefficient between | | | Number of observations |
|---|---|---|---|---|
| | $R_p^e$ and $S_p$ | $R_p^e$ and $\beta_p$ | $\beta_p$ and $S_p$ | |
| 1961–80 | 0.239 | 0.123 | 0.361 | 980 |
| 1961–70 | 0.179 | 0.132 | 0.163 | 490 |
| 1971–80 | 0.285 | 0.118 | 0.540 | 490 |

tional units (portfolios) and over time. This is done by employing two sets of dummy variables: The first set consists of 48 portfolio dummy variables, defined by $DP_{ij} = 1$ if the portfolio is in group $(i, j)$ and zero otherwise; $i = 1, 2, \ldots, 7$ is the spread-group index and $j = 1, 2, \ldots, 7$ is the $\beta$-group index, with $DP_{7,7} \equiv 0$. By construction, the spread increases in $i$, and $\beta$ increases in $j$. A second set of dummy variables, defined by $DY_n = 1$ in year $n$ ($n = 1, 2, \ldots, 19$) and zero otherwise, accounts for differences in returns between years.

An important implication of our model is that the slope of the return–spread relation declines as we move to higher-spread groups. To allow for different slope coefficients across spread groups, we decomposed the spread variable $S_{pn}$ into seven variables $S_{pn}^i$ ($i = 1, 2, \ldots, 7$) defined by $S_{pn}^i = S_{pn}$ if in spread group $i$ ($i = 1, 2, \ldots, 7$) and zero otherwise. Due to the high correlation between $S_{pn}^i$ and $\sum_{j=1}^7 DP_{ij}$, we constructed the mean-adjusted spread variables, $\hat{S}_{pn}^i = S_{pn}^i - \bar{S}^i$ if portfolio $(p, n)$ is in group $i$ and zero otherwise, where $\bar{S}^i$ is the mean spread for the $i$th spread group. The means of $\hat{S}_{pn}^i$ are zero and their correlations with $\sum_{j=1}^7 DP_{ij}$ are zero. Replacing $S_{pn}^i$ by the mean-adjusted variables thus leads to a separation between the level effects among groups (captured by $DP_{ij}$) and the slope effects within spread groups (captured by $\hat{S}_{pn}^i$).

Using the above variables, we carried out the pooled cross-section and time-series estimation of our model:

$$R_{pn}^e = a_0 + a_1 \beta_{pn} + \sum_{i=1}^7 b_i \hat{S}_{pn}^i + \sum_{i=1}^7 \sum_{j=1}^7 c_{ij} DP_{ij} + \sum_{n=1}^{19} d_n DY_n + \varepsilon_{pn}, \quad (8)$$

where $a_0$, $a_1$, $b_i$, $c_{ij}$ and $d_n$ are coefficients and the $\varepsilon_{pn}$ are the residuals. The slope coefficients $b_i$ measure the response of stock returns to increasing the spread *within* spread group $i$, and the dummy coefficients $c_{ij}$ measure the difference between the mean return on portfolio $(i, j)$ and that of portfolio $(7, 7)$ which corresponds to the highest spread and $\beta$ group.

The sums $\sum_{i=1}^{7} c_{ij}$ measure the differences in mean returns between $\beta$ groups $j$, while $\sum_{j=1}^{7} c_{ij}$ measure the differences in mean returns between spread groups $i$. Thus, for any given $\beta$, model (8) represents a piecewise-linear functional form of the return–spread relation. This follows the Malinvaud (1970, pp. 317–318) and Kmenta (1971, pp. 468–469) methodology for estimating non-linear relationships, which groups the data based on the values of the explanatory variable, and fits a piecewise linear curve using two sets of variables: group dummies to capture differences between group means, and products of the explanatory variable by the group dummies to allow for the different slopes.

Estimation of the pooled model (8) using OLS is problematic due to the possibility of cross-sectional heteroskedasticity and cross-sectional correlations among residuals across portfolio groups. While the estimated OLS coefficients are unbiased and consistent, their estimated variances are not, leading to biased test statistics. This calls for a generalized least squares (GLS) estimation procedure. Given that the variance–covariance matrix of the residuals in (8) is $\sigma^2 V$, where $\sigma^2$ is a scalar and $V$ is a symmetric positive-definite matrix, the GLS procedure uses a matrix $Q$ satisfying $Q'Q = V^{-1}$ to transform all the regression variables by pre-multiplication. The variance–covariance matrix $V$ was assumed to be block diagonal (reflecting independence between years), where the diagonal blocks consist of twenty identical $49 \times 49$ positive definite matrices $U$. Then, $V = I \otimes U$, where $I$ is the $20 \times 20$ identity matrix and $\otimes$ denotes the Kronecker product. To obtain the $49 \times 49$ matrix $U$, we first estimated model (8) by OLS and then used the data month by month to obtain the residuals $\hat{\varepsilon}_{pm}$ ($p = 1, 2, \ldots, 49$) for each month $m$ ($m = 1, 2, \ldots, 240$). Then, we estimated $U$ by averaging the resulting 240 monthly variance–covariance matrices – the resulting estimate of the variance–covariance matrix $V$ is known to be consistent [cf. Kmenta (1971, ch. 12)]. The transformation matrix $Q$ was calculated using the Choleski decomposition method. The variables of model (8) were then pre-multiplied by the transformation matrix $Q$, and the transformed version of model (8) was estimated to provide the GLS results.

## 3.3. The results

We first ran a simple OLS regression of the excess returns on $\beta$, the spread and the nineteen-year dummy variables:

$$R^{e}_{pn} = 0.0040 + \underset{(9.17)}{0.00947} \beta_{pn} + \sum_{n=1}^{19} d_n DY_n + e_{pn},$$

and

$$R^{e}_{pn} = 0.0036 + \underset{(6.18)}{0.00672}\beta_{pn} + \underset{(6.83)}{0.211}S_{pn} + \sum_{n=1}^{19} d_{n}DY_{n} + e_{pn}.$$

(*t*-statistics are in parentheses.) The results show that excess returns are increasing in both $\beta$ and the spread. The coefficient of $S_{pn}$ implies that a 1% increase in the spread is associated with a 0.211% increase in the monthly risk-adjusted excess return. The coefficient of $\beta$ declines when the spread variable is added to the equation, indicating that part of the effect which could be attributed to $\beta$ may, in fact, be due to the spread.[16] The coefficient of $\beta$ is 0.00672, very close to 0.00671, which is the average monthly excess return on common stocks for this period.

Next, we estimated the detailed model (8) using both OLS and GLS. The slope coefficients of the spread variables are presented in table 4, and the coefficients of $DP_{ij}$ are given in table 5. To estimate the pattern of the dummy coefficients, we employed the model

$$c_{ij} = \alpha + \sum_{i=1}^{6} \gamma_{i}DS_{i} + \sum_{j=1}^{6} \delta_{j}DB_{j} + e_{ij}, \tag{9}$$

where the spread dummy $DS_{i}$ ($i = 1, \ldots, 6$) is one if the portfolio is in spread group $i$ and zero otherwise, and the $\beta$ dummy $DB_{j}$ ($j = 1, \ldots, 6$) is one if the portfolio is in $\beta$ group $j$ and zero otherwise. Thus, the coefficients $\gamma_{i}$ in (9) measure the difference between the average return of spread group $i$ and that of the seventh (highest) spread group, and the coefficients $\delta_{j}$ measure the corresponding differences between $\beta$ groups.

The estimates of (8)–(9) presented in tables 4 and 6 support our two hypotheses:

(i) The coefficients $\gamma_{i}$ of $DS_{i}$ in model (9) are negative and generally increasing in $i$, implying that risk-adjusted excess returns increase with the spread. The difference in the monthly mean excess return between the two extreme spread groups is 0.857% when estimated by OLS and 0.681% when estimated by GLS.

(ii) The slope coefficients of the spreads, $b_{i}$, are positive and generally decreasing as we move to higher spread groups. This is consistent with the hypothesized concavity of the return–spread relation, reflecting the lower sensitivity of long-term portfolios to the spread.

---

[16] Given the strong positive correlation between $S_{pn}$ and $\beta_{pn}$, the omission of $S_{pn}$ from the regression equation which tests the CAPM results in an upward bias in the estimated coefficient of $\beta$; see Kmenta (1971, p. 392).

Table 4

Estimated regressions of the portfolio monthly excess returns, $R^c$, on the mean-adjusted spread variables $\hat{S}^i$ and relative risk, $\beta$, for the years 1961–1980, using ordinary least squares and generalized least squares estimation methods. The regression model (8)[a] applies pooled cross-section and time-series estimation.

The coefficient of $\hat{S}^i$ reflects the response of stock returns to an increase in the bid–ask spread within spread group $i$, where $i = 1$ corresponds to the lowest-spread group.

(*t*-values are in parentheses).

| Independent variable | Ordinary least squares coefficients | Generalized least squares coefficients | | |
|---|---|---|---|---|
| | Entire period 1961–1980 | Entire period 1961–1980 | Subperiod 1961–1970 | Subperiod 1971–1980 |
| $\hat{S}_1$ | 3.641 (2.76) | 1.310 (1.16) | 0.080 (0.05) | 2.303 (1.27) |
| $\hat{S}_2$ | 3.242 (3.50) | 1.747 (2.56) | 0.975 (0.91) | 2.505 (2.41) |
| $\hat{S}_3$ | 2.854 (3.93) | 1.660 (3.01) | 0.934 (1.10) | 2.27 (2.80) |
| $\hat{S}_4$ | 1.657 (3.06) | 0.482 (1.16) | −0.149 (0.21) | 0.983 (1.69) |
| $\hat{S}_5$ | 2.224 (5.69) | 1.206 (3.84) | 0.922 (1.67) | 1.500 (3.47) |
| $\hat{S}_6$ | 1.365 (5.28) | 0.650 (2.96) | 0.838 (2.21) | 0.475 (1.50) |
| $\hat{S}_7$ | 0.605 (5.28) | 0.256 (2.56) | 0.176 (1.49) | 0.489 (2.49) |
| $\beta$ | −0.0058 (2.53) | −0.000 (0.10) | −0.002 (0.47) | −0.003 (0.72) |

[a] The regression model is

$$R^e_{pn} = a_0 + a_1\beta_{pn} + \sum_{i=1}^{7} b_i\hat{S}^i_{pn} + \sum_{i=1}^{7}\sum_{j=1}^{7} c_{ij}DP_{ij} + \sum_{n=1}^{19} d_n DY_n + \varepsilon_{pn}, \qquad (8)$$

where $R^e_{pn}$ is the average excess return for portfolio $p$ in year $n$, $\beta_{pn}$ is the average portfolio relative risk, $\hat{S}^i_{pn}$ is the mean-adjusted spread within spread group $i$ ( = the deviation of the spread of portfolio $p$ in year $n$ from the mean spread of its spread group, $i$), $DP_{ij}$ are the portfolio-group dummy variables ( = 1 in portfolio group $(i, j)$, zero otherwise), $DY_n$ are the year dummy variables ( = 1 in year $n$, 0 otherwise), and $\varepsilon_{pn}$ are the residuals. The GLS estimated coefficients of the portfolio-group dummies $DP_{ij}$ are reported in table 5.

The effect of the relative risk is measured in model (8) by both $\beta$ and the dummy variables and is further summarized by the $DB_j$ coefficients of model (9). The emerging pattern is that (spread-adjusted) excess returns increase with $\beta$ as depicted by the significant negative and increasing coefficients $\delta_j$. The effect of $\beta$ is captured mainly through the dummies rather than the coefficient $a_1$, which is highly insignificant in the GLS estimation. Finally, we estimated

Table 5

Generalized least squares estimates of the difference between the mean monthly excess return of the portfolio with the highest spread and beta – portfolio (7, 7), the 49th portfolio – and the mean monthly excess returns of each of the other 48 portfolios. These are the estimated coefficients of the 48 portfolio dummy variables $DP_{ij}$ in the pooled cross-section and time-series regression model (8), using GLS, over the entire period 1961–1980.
$t$-statistics for all unmarked table entries are greater than 1.96, implying that the estimated coefficient is significant at better than the 2.5% level (one-tail test).

| Spread group, $i$ | Beta group, $j$ | | | | | | | |
|---|---|---|---|---|---|---|---|---|
| | 1 (low) | 2 | 3 | 4 | 5 | 6 | 7 (high) | Mean |
| 1 (low) | −0.0117 | −0.0132 | −0.0111 | −0.0100 | −0.0111 | −0.0091 | −0.0108 | −0.0110 |
| 2 | −0.0113 | −0.0109 | −0.0109 | −0.0094 | −0.0115 | −0.0079 | −0.0033[b] | −0.0093 |
| 3 | −0.0127 | −0.0113 | −0.0078[a] | −0.0118 | −0.0100 | −0.0082 | −0.0094 | −0.0102 |
| 4 | −0.0113 | −0.0120 | −0.0091 | −0.0099 | −0.0059[a] | −0.0064 | −0.0052[b] | −0.0085 |
| 5 | −0.0120 | −0.0101 | −0.0111 | −0.0077 | −0.0062[a] | −0.0030[b] | −0.0041[b] | −0.0077 |
| 6 | −0.0108 | −0.0074[a] | −0.0072 | −0.0070 | −0.0032[b] | −0.0035[b] | −0.0020[b] | −0.0059 |
| 7 (high) | −0.0080 | −0.0049[b] | −0.0063 | −0.0068 | −0.0019[b] | −0.0013[b] | 0.0000 | −0.0042 |
| Mean | −0.0111 | −0.0100 | −0.0091 | −0.0089 | −0.0071 | −0.0056 | −0.0050 | |

[a]$1.645 < t < 1.96$, implying significance at better than the 5% level (one-tail test).
[b]$t < 1.645$, insignificant at the 5% level (one-tail test).

models (8)–(9) for the two ten-year subperiods, with generally the same pattern of results.

Detailed tests of our main hypotheses are presented in table 7. In 7(B), we test the significance of the spread effect by omitting all spread-related variables and examine the resulting increase in the unexplained variance. In 7(C) we test whether the mean excess returns of all spread groups are equal by eliminating all spread-related dummy variables. The significance of the non-linearities was tested in two ways: First we replaced all the spread-related variables (eliminating the $\hat{S}_{pn}^i$ and replacing the $DP_{ij}$ with six $\beta$ dummies) by the original spread variable $S_{pn}$ [see 7(D)]. Then we tested the equality of the slope coefficients across spread groups by re-estimating model (8), replacing the variables $\hat{S}^1$ through $\hat{S}^7$ by their sum [see 7(E)]. In all four cases, the $F$-tests for the changes in the sum of squared residuals reject the null hypotheses at better than the 0.01 level. Thus, our hypotheses are fully supported by the data.

## 4. Firm size, spread and return

The well-known negative relationship between spread and firm size suggests that our findings may bear on the 'small-firm anomaly': Banz (1981) and Reinganum (1981a, b) found a negative relation between risk-adjusted mean

Table 6

Regression estimates of the difference between the mean return of the spread and beta groups and the mean return of the highest-spread and highest-beta portfolio. The estimation model is

$$c_{ij} = \alpha + \sum_{i=1}^{6} \gamma_i DS_i + \sum_{j=1}^{6} \delta_j DB_j + e_{ij}, \qquad (9)$$

where $c_{ij}$ are the dummy coefficients estimated from model (8) (table 5); $DS_i = 1$ for the $i$th spread group and zero otherwise; and $DB_j = 1$ for the $j$th beta group and zero otherwise. Spreads are increasing in $i$, and betas are increasing in $j$.
($t$-statistics are in parentheses).

| Independent variable | Estimated regression coefficients | | | |
| | Entire 1961–1980 period | | Subperiods | |
| | From OLS regression | From GLS regression | 1961–1970 GLS | 1971–1980 GLS |
| --- | --- | --- | --- | --- |
| $DS_1$ | −0.00857 (9.05) | −0.00681 (7.74) | −0.00730 (7.46) | −0.00397 (3.33) |
| $DS_2$ | −0.00654 (6.90) | −0.00517 (5.88) | −0.00578 (5.91) | −0.00267 (2.24) |
| $DS_3$ | −0.00729 (7.70) | −0.00599 (6.82) | −0.00556 (5.69) | −0.00483 (4.05) |
| $DS_4$ | −0.00552 (5.83) | −0.00439 (4.99) | −0.00446 (4.56) | −0.00301 (2.53) |
| $DS_5$ | −0.00461 (4.86) | −0.00359 (4.08) | −0.00335 (3.42) | −0.00272 (2.28) |
| $DS_6$ | −0.00252 (2.66) | −0.00172 (1.95) | −0.00246 (2.52) | 0.00051 (0.42) |
| $DB_1$ | −0.00964 (10.18) | −0.00614 (6.98) | −0.00669 (6.84) | −0.00454 (3.81) |
| $DB_2$ | −0.00767 (8.10) | −0.00500 (5.68) | −0.00495 (5.06) | −0.00421 (3.53) |
| $DB_3$ | −0.00626 (6.61) | −0.00411 (4.67) | −0.00325 (3.32) | −0.00434 (3.64) |
| $DB_4$ | −0.00568 (6.00) | −0.00398 (4.53) | −0.00260 (2.66) | −0.00485 (4.07) |
| $DB_5$ | −0.00336 (3.55) | −0.00214 (2.43) | −0.00098 (1.00) | −0.00293 (2.46) |
| $DB_6$ | −0.00147 (1.56) | −0.00065 (0.74) | 0.00017 (0.18) | −0.00121 (1.01) |

returns on stocks and their market value, indicating either a misspecification of the CAPM or evidence of market inefficiency [see Schwert (1983) for a comprehensive review]. Thus, it is instructive to estimate the effects of a firm-size variable and to test its significance vis-a-vis our variables.

We re-estimated our models adding a new explanatory variable – $SIZE$, the market value of the firm's equity in millions of dollars at the end of the year

Table 7

Tests of hypotheses on the return–spread relation. All regressions are estimated by GLS.

| Model[a] | Degrees of freedom of the model | SSR, sum of squared residuals | Difference from model (A)[b] | | | F-statistic |
|---|---|---|---|---|---|---|
| | | | DF | SSR | MS | |
| (A) | 75 | 76.7877 | – | – | – | – |
| (B) | 26 | 85.5489 | 49 | 8.7612 | 0.1788 | 2.10 |
| (C) | 33 | 83.3506 | 42 | 6.5629 | 0.1563 | 1.84 |
| (D) | 27 | 84.7339 | 48 | 7.9462 | 0.1655 | 1.95 |
| (E) | 69 | 78.4249 | 6 | 1.6372 | 0.2729 | 3.21 |

[a] The regression models are as follows.

*Model (A)* – the full model:

$$R_{pn}^e = a_0 + a_1 \beta_{pn} + \sum_{i=1}^{7} b_i \hat{S}_{pn}^i + \sum_{i=1}^{7} \sum_{j=1}^{7} c_{ij} DP_{ij} + \sum_{n=1}^{19} d_n DY_n + \varepsilon_{pn}, \qquad (8)$$

where $p = 1, 2, \ldots, 49$, $n = 1, 2, \ldots, 20$, and $DP_{77} \equiv 0$.

*Model (B)* – a restricted model for testing the existence of any spread effect:

$$R_{pn}^e = a_0 + a_1 \beta_{pn} + \sum_{j=1}^{6} \gamma_j DB_j + \sum_{n=1}^{19} d_n DY_n + \varepsilon_{pn}.$$

*Model (C)* – a restricted model for testing the equality of mean excess returns across spread groups:

$$R_{pn}^e = a_0 + a_1 \beta_{pn} + \sum_{i=1}^{7} b_i \hat{S}_{pn}^i + \sum_{j=1}^{6} \gamma_j DB_j + \sum_{n=1}^{19} d_n DY_n + \varepsilon_{pn}.$$

*Model (D)* – a restricted model for testing the non-linearity of the return–spread relation:

$$R_{pn}^e = a_0 + a_1 \beta_{pn} + a_2 S_{pn} + \sum_{j=1}^{6} \gamma_j DB_j + \sum_{n=1}^{19} d_n DY_n + \varepsilon_{pn}.$$

*Model (E)* – a restricted model testing the equality of the slope coefficients across spread groups:

$$R_{pn}^e = a_0 + a_1 \beta_{pn} + a_2 \left( \sum_{i=1}^{7} \hat{S}_{pn}^i \right) + \sum_{i=1}^{7} \sum_{j=1}^{7} c_{ij} DP_{ij} + \sum_{n=1}^{19} d_n DY_n + \varepsilon_{pn}.$$

The regression variables are:

$R_{pn}^e$ = average portfolio excess return (the dependent variable) for portfolio $p$ in year $n$,
$\beta_{pn}$ = average portfolio relative ($\beta$) risk,
$S_{pn}$ = average portfolio relative spread,
$\hat{S}_{pn}^i$ = mean-adjusted spread (the deviation of the spread $S_{pn}$ of portfolio $p$ in year $n$ from the mean spread of its spread group, $i$),
$DP_{ij}$ = portfolio group dummy; one in portfolio group $(i, j)$, zero otherwise,
$DY_n$ = year dummy; one in year $n$, zero otherwise,
$DB_j$ = $\beta$ group dummy; one in $\beta$ group $j$, zero otherwise. $DB_j = \sum_{i=1}^{7} DP_{ij}$ ($j = 1, 2, \ldots, 6$).

[b] Data for the $F$-test on each of the restricted models:

$DF$ = difference in the number of degrees of freedom between the full and restricted model,
$SSR$ = difference in the sum of squares between the full and restricted model,
$MS$ = $SSR/DF$, the mean square.

just preceding the test period. As seen in table 2, there is a negative relationship between *SIZE* and both spread and $\beta$. The effect of firm size on stock returns was tested by incorporating *SIZE* in all our models, but its estimated effect was negligible and highly insignificant.

To allow for a possible non-linear effect (as other studies do), we replaced *SIZE* by its natural logarithm and examined the impact of adding log(*SIZE*) to our regression equations. First, we estimated the simple linear model

$$R^e_{pn} = 0.0082 + 0.0060\beta_{pn} + 0.158S_{pn} + 0.0006\log(SIZE)_{pn}$$
$$(5.05) \qquad (3.44) \qquad (1.56)$$

$$+ \sum_{n=1}^{19} d_n DY_n + e_{pn}.$$

The results indicate that the risk and spread effects prevail, whereas the size effect is insignificant. We then re-estimated our detailed model (8) with the added variable log(*SIZE*) using GLS over the entire sample period and its two ten-year subperiods. The results in table 8(B) suggest that the size effect is insignificant, and it remains insignificant when the only spread variable appearing in the regression equation is $S_{pn}$ [see 8(C)]. The coefficient of log(*SIZE*) becomes significant only when all the spread-related variables are altogether omitted [table 8(D)]. Finally, we performed an *F*-test for the significance of our set of spread variables given log(*SIZE*). The test produced $F = 2.02$, significant at better than the 0.01 level. Thus, while our spread variables render the size effect insignificant, they remain highly significant even with log(*SIZE*) in the regression equation. In sum, our results on the return-spread relation cannot be explained by a 'size effect' even if, the latter exists. In fact, any 'size effect' may be a consequence of a spread effect, with firm size serving as a proxy for liquidity. And, rather than suggesting an 'anomaly' or an indication of market inefficiency, our return–spread relation represents a rational response by an efficient market to the existence of the spread.

A number of studies have attempted to explain the size effect in terms of the bid–ask spread. Stoll and Whaley (1983) suggested that investors' valuations are based on returns net of transaction costs, and observed that the costs of transacting in small-firm stocks are relatively higher. They thus subtracted these costs from the measured returns and tested for a small-firm effect. Using an interesting empirical procedure based on arbitrage portfolios, they found that if round-trip transactions occurred every three months, the size effect was eliminated. They thus concluded that the CAPM, applied to after-transaction-cost returns over an appropriately chosen holding period, cannot be rejected.

Table 8

Effects of firm size on portfolio returns, controlling for the effects of the bid–ask spread, over the period 1961–1980 and its two 10-year subperiods.

| Model[a] | Sample period | Definition of size variable | Estimates for the size variable | | Spread variables included in the regression equation |
|---|---|---|---|---|---|
| | | | Coefficient | $t$-value | |
| (A) | 1961–80 | $SIZE$ | $-0.23 \times 10^{-6}$ | 0.74 | all[b] |
| (B) | 1961–80 | log($SIZE$) | $-0.000650$ | 1.52 | all[b] |
| (B) | 1961–70 | log($SIZE$) | $-0.000916$ | 1.46 | all[b] |
| (B) | 1971–80 | log($SIZE$) | $-0.000216$ | 0.34 | all[b] |
| (C) | 1961–80 | log($SIZE$) | $-0.00032$ | 1.08 | $S$ ($a_2 = 0.153$, $t = 2.51$) |
| (D) | 1961–80 | log($SIZE$) | $-0.00057$ | 2.0 | none |

[a] The models used are as follows.

*Model (A)* is obtained by adding $SIZE$ to (8), i.e.,

$$R_{pn}^e = a_0 + a_1 \beta_{pn} + \sum_{i=1}^{7} b_i \hat{S}_{pn}^i + \sum_{i=1}^{7} \sum_{j=1}^{7} c_{ij} DP_{ij} + \psi \cdot SIZE_{pn} + \sum_{n=1}^{19} d_n DY_n + \varepsilon_{pn}.$$

*Model (B)* is obtained by adding log($SIZE$) to (8), i.e., replacing $SIZE_{pn}$ in (A) by log($SIZE_{pn}$).

*Model (C)* includes log($SIZE$) and the spread variable $S_{pn}$:

$$R_{pn}^e = a_0 + a_1 \beta_{pn} + a_2 S_{pn} + \sum_{j=1}^{6} \gamma_j DB_j + \eta \cdot \log(SIZE_{pn}) + \sum_{j=1}^{19} d_n DY_n + \varepsilon_{pn}.$$

*Model (D)* is obtained by omitting $S_{pn}$ from model (C).

The regression variables are:

$R_{pn}^e$ = average excess return for portfolio $p$ in year $n$ (the dependent variable),
$\beta_{pn}$ = average portfolio relative ($\beta$) risk,
$S_{pn}$ = average portfolio relative spread,
$\hat{S}_{pn}^i$ = mean-adjusted spread (the deviation of the spread $S_{pn}$ of portfolio $p$ in year $n$ from the mean spread of its spread group, $i$),
$DP_{ij}$ = portfolio group dummy; one in portfolio group ($i$, $j$), zero otherwise,
$DB_j$ = $\beta$-group dummy; one in $\beta$-group $j$, zero otherwise. $DB_j = \sum_{i=1}^{7} DP_{ij}$ ($j = 1,2,\ldots,6$).
$DY_n$ = year dummy; one in year $n$, zero otherwise,
$SIZE_{pn}$ = average market value of the equity of firms in portfolio $p$ in the year just preceding $n$, in millions of dollars.

[b] Results obtained by adding the size variable to the full model (8).

This conclusion was challenged by Schultz (1983), who claimed that transaction costs do not completely explain the size effect. Extending Stoll and Whaley's sample to smaller AMEX firms, Schultz found that small firms earn positive excess returns after transaction costs for holding periods of one year. He thus concluded that transaction costs cannot explain the violations of the CAPM. This criticism, however, hardly settles the issue, and in fact highlights a basic problem. Given the higher returns and higher spreads of small firms' stocks, it is always possible to find an investment horizon which nullifies the abnormal return after transaction costs. But then, finding that a horizon of one year does not eliminate the size effect is insufficient to determine whether or not transaction costs are the proper explanation.

Our examination of the relation between stock returns and bid–ask spreads is based on a theory which produces well-specified hypotheses. In the context of our model, the after-transaction-cost return, as defined in the above studies, is not meaningful. Stoll–Whaley and Schultz consider this key variable to be a property of the security, and calculate it by subtracting the transaction cost from the gross return, implicitly assuming the same holding period. for all stocks. By our model, the spread-adjusted return depends not only on the stock's return and spread, but also on the holding horizon of its specific clientele [see (4)]. Thus, their method is inapplicable to test our hypotheses on the return–spread relation.

The different objective guiding our empirical study has shaped its different methodology and structure. Stoll–Whaley and Schultz aim at explaining the 'small firm' anomaly through the bid–ask spread, hence their portfolio construction and test procedure are governed by firm size.[17] We start from a theoretical specification of the return–spread relation, and the objective of our empirical study is to test the explicit functional form predicted by our model. Thus, our empirical results are disciplined by the theory and in fact the test procedure is called for by the theory.

A second issue raised by Schultz (1983) is the seasonal behavior of the size effect, which is particularly pronounced in the month of January.[18] In the context of our study, there is a question whether liquidity has a seasonal. A test of this hypothesis requires data on monthly bid–ask spreads which was unavailable to us. Given our data of a single spread observation per year, we are unable to carry out a powerful test incorporating seasonality, a topic which is worthy of further research.

An empirical issue in the computation of returns on small firms is the possible upward bias due to the bid–ask spread, suggested by Blume and Stambaugh (1983), Roll (1983) and Fisher and Weaver (1985). Blume and Stambaugh estimate the bias to be $\frac{1}{4}S^2$, where $S$ is the relative spread. Given the magnitudes of the spreads and the excess returns, this difference is negligible. Indeed, we re-estimated models (8)–(9), applying the Blume–

---

[17]Stoll–Whaley and Schultz subordinate their study of the bid–ask effect to the small-firm classification, a procedure which is natural for studying the small-firm anomaly. Our portfolio-construction method is motivated by the prediction that stock returns are a function of the bid–ask spread and $\beta$, and is designed specifically to test this hypothesis.

[18]Lakonishok and Smidt (1984) found that the small-firm effect prevails at the turn-of-the-year when returns are measured net of transaction costs, using the high and low prices as proxies for the ask and bid prices.

Stambaugh and Fisher–Weaver approach and obtained similar results which uniformly supported our hypotheses.[19]

## 5. Conclusion

This paper studies the effect of securities' bid–ask spreads on their returns. We model a market where rational traders differ in their expected holding periods and assets have different spreads. The ensuing equilibrium has the following characteristics: (i) market-observed average returns are an increasing function of the spread; (ii) asset returns to their holders, net of trading costs, increase with the spread;[20] (iii) there is a clientele effect, whereby stocks with higher spreads are held by investors with longer holding periods; and (iv) due to the clientele effect, returns on higher-spread stocks are less spread-sensitive, giving rise to a concave return–spread relation. We design a detailed test on the behavior of observed returns, and our results support the theory. The robustness and statistical significance of our results are very encouraging, especially when compared to the Fama–MacBeth (1973) benchmark. These results do not point at an anomaly or market inefficiency; rather, they reflect a rational response by investors in an efficient market when faced with trading friction and transaction costs.

The higher yields required on higher-spread stocks give firms an incentive to increase the liquidity of their securities, thus reducing their opportunity cost of capital. Consequently, liquidity-increasing financial policies may increase the value of the firm. This was demonstrated for our numerical example in fig. 2, which depicts the relation between asset values and their bid–ask spreads. Applying our empirical results, consider an asset which yields $1 per month, has a bid–ask spread of 3.2% (as in our high-spread portfolio group) and its proper opportunity cost of capital is 2% per month, yielding a value of $50. If the spread is reduced to 0.486% (as in our low-spread portfolio group), our estimates imply that the value of the asset would increase to $75.8, about a 50% increase, suggesting a strong incentive for the firm to invest in increasing the liquidity of the claims it issues. In particular, phenomena such as 'going public' (compared to private placement), standardization of the contractual forms of securities, limited liability, exchange listing and information disclosures may be construed as investments in increased liquidity. It is of interest to examine to what extent observed corporate financial policies can be explained by the liquidity-increasing motive. Such an investigation could

---

[19] To illustrate, the coefficient of $DS_1$ in model (9), which reflects the difference in returns between the highest and lowest spread groups, was $-0.00765$ ($t = 8.15$) by the OLS method and $-0.00587$ ($t = 6.73$) by GLS.

[20] Recall that, in the context of our model, net returns cannot be defined as stock characteristics, since they depend on both the stock and the owning investor. Our result is that despite their higher spread, the net return on high-spread stocks to their holders is higher.

create a link between securities market microstructure and corporate financial policies, and constitutes a natural avenue for further research.

This also suggests that a more comprehensive model of the return–spread relation could consider supply response by firms. Rather than set the spread exogenously, as in our model, firms may engage in a supply adjustment, increasing the liquidity of their securities at a cost. In equilibrium, the marginal increase in value due to improved liquidity will equal the marginal cost of such an improvement. Then, differences in firms' ability to affect liquidity will be reflected in differences in bid–ask spreads and risk-adjusted returns across securities.[21]

We believe that this paper makes a strong case for studying the role of liquidity in asset pricing in a broader context. The generality of our analysis is limited in that we do not consider the difference between marginal liquidity and total liquidity, and the associated relation between liquidation uncertainty and holding period uncertainty. This issue deserves further attention. In our model, all assets are liquidated at the end of the investor's holding period. Thus, there is no distinction between the liquidity of an asset when considered by itself and its liquidity in a portfolio context, nor is it necessary to consider the dispersion of possible holding periods for each asset in the portfolio. In a more general model, each investor may be faced with a sequence of stochastic cash demands occurring at random points in time. The investor would then have to determine the quantities of each security to be liquidated at each point in time. In such a setting, an investor's portfolio is likely to include an array of assets with both low and high spreads, whose proportions will reflect both the distribution of the amounts to be liquidated and the dispersion of his liquidation times. Then, there would be a distinction between the liquidity of an asset and its marginal contribution to the liquidity of an investor's portfolio. A study along these lines should focus on the interrelationship between total and marginal liquidity and its effect on asset pricing.

Further research could also be carried out on the interplay between liquidity and risk, and on the relation between asset returns and a more comprehensive set of liquidity characteristics. And finally, it is of interest to pursue the link between corporate financial theory and the theory of exchange, possibly leading to a unified framework which will enhance our understanding of organizations and markets.

## References

Amihud, Yakov and Haim Mendelson, 1980, Dealership market: Market-making with inventory, Journal of Financial Economics 8, 31–53.

Amihud, Yakov and Haim Mendelson, 1982, Asset price behavior in a dealership market, Financial Analysts Journal 29, 50–59.

[21] Even if some firms could issue an unlimited supply of zero-spread securities, our results show that there will still be differentials in investors' net yields.

Amihud, Yakov and Haim Mendelson, 1985, An integrated computerized trading system, in: Y. Amihud, T.S. Ho and R.A. Schwartz, eds., Market making and the changing structure of the securities industry (Lexington Heath, Lexington, MA) 217–235.

Amihud, Yakov and Haim Mendelson, 1986a, Liquidity and stock returns, Financial Analysts Journal 42, 43–48.

Amihud, Yakov and Haim Mendelson, 1986b, Trading mechanisms and stock returns: An empirical investigation, Working paper.

Bagehot, Walter, 1971, The only game in town, Financial Analysts Journal 27, 12–14.

Banz, Rolf W., 1981, The relationship between return and market value of common stocks, Journal of Financial Economics 9, 3–18.

Benston, George and Robert Hagerman, 1974, Determinants of bid–ask spreads in the over-the-counter market, Journal of Financial Economics 1, 353–364.

Black, Fischer, Michael C. Jensen and Myron Scholes, 1972, The capital asset pricing model: Some empirical tests, in: Michael C. Jensen, ed., Studies in the theory of capital markets (Praeger, New York) 79–121.

Black, Fischer and Myron Scholes, 1974, The effects of dividend yield and dividend policy on common stock prices and returns, Journal of Financial Economics 1, 1–22.

Blume, Marshall E. and Robert F. Stambaugh, 1983, Biases in computing returns: An application to the size effect, Journal of Financial Economics 12, 387–404.

Chen, Andrew H., E. Han Kim and Stanley J. Kon, 1975, Cash demand, liquidation costs and capital market equilibrium under uncertainty, Journal of Financial Economics 2, 293–308.

Day, Theodore, E., Hans R. Stoll and Robert E. Whaley, 1985, Taxes, financial policy and small business (Lexington Heath, Lexington, MA) forthcoming.

Demsetz, Harold, 1968, The cost of transacting, Quarterly Journal of Economics 82, 35–53.

Elton, Edwin J. and Martin J. Gruber, 1978, Taxes and portfolio composition, Journal of Financial Economics 6, 399–410.

Fama, Eugene F., 1976, Foundations of finance (Basic Books, New York).

Fama, Eugene F. and James MacBeth, 1973, Risk, return and equilibrium: Empirical tests, Journal of Political Economy 81, 607–636.

Fisher, Lawrence and Daniel G. Weaver, 1985, Improving the measurement of returns of stocks, portfolios, and equally-weighted indexes: Avoiding or compensating for 'biases' due to bid–ask spread and other transient errors in price, Mimeo.

Fogler, H. Russel, 1984, 20% in real estate: Can theory justify it?, Journal of Portfolio Management 10, 6–13.

Gale, David, 1960, The theory of linear economic models (McGraw-Hill, New York).

Garbade, Kenneth, 1982, Securities markets (McGraw-Hill, New York).

Garman, Mark B., 1976, Market microstructure, Journal of Financial Economics 3, 257–275.

Ho, Thomas and Hans Stoll, 1981, Optimal dealer pricing under transactions and return uncertainty, Journal of Financial Economics 9, 47–73.

Ho, Thomas and Hans Stoll, 1983, The dynamics of dealer markets under competition, Journal of Finance 38, 1053–1074.

Jensen, Michael C., 1968, Risk, the pricing of capital assets, and the evaluation of investment portfolios, Journal of Business 42, 167–247.

Judge, George G., William E. Griffiths, R. Carter Hill and Tsoung-Chao Lee, 1980, The theory and practice of econometrics (Wiley, New York).

Kane, Alex, 1984, Coins: Anatomy of a fad asset, Journal of Portfolio Management 10, 44–51.

Kmenta, Jan, 1971, Elements of econometrics (Macmillan, New York).

Lakonishok, Josef and Seymour Smidt, 1984, Volume, price and rate of return for active and inactive stocks with applications to turn-of-the-year behavior, Journal of Financial Economics 13, 435–455.

Levy, Haim, 1978, Equilibrium in an imperfect market: A constraint on the number of securities in a portfolio, American Economic Review 68, 643–658.

Litzenberger, Robert H. and Krishna Ramaswamy, 1980, Dividends, short selling restrictions, tax-induced investor clienteles and market equilibrium, Journal of Finance 35, 469–482.

Maddala, G.S., 1977, Econometrics (McGraw-Hill, New York).

Malinvaud, E., 1970, Statistical methods of econometrics (Elsevier, New York).

Mendelson, Haim, 1982, Market behavior in a clearing house, Econometrica 50, 1505–1524.

Mendelson, Haim, 1985, Random competitive exchange: Price distributions and gains from trade, Journal of Economic Theory 37, 254–280.

Mendelson, Haim, 1986, Exchange with random quantities and discrete feasible prices, Working paper (Graduate School of Management, University of Rochester, Rochester, NY).

Mendelson, Haim, 1987, Consolidation, fragmentation and market performance, Journal of Financial and Quantitative Analysis, forthcoming.

Miller, Merton H., 1977, Debt and taxes, Journal of Finance 32, 261–275.

Milne, Frank and Clifford W. Smith, Jr., 1980, Capital asset pricing with proportional transaction costs, Journal of Financial and Quantitative Analysis 15, 253–265.

Phillips, Susan M. and Clifford W. Smith, Jr., 1980, Trading costs for listed options: The implications for market efficiency, Journal of Financial Economics 8, 179–201.

Reinganum, Marc R., 1981a, Misspecification of capital asset pricing: Empirical anomalies based on earnings yields and market values, Journal of Financial Economics 9, 19–46.

Reinganum, Marc R., 1981b, The arbitrage pricing theory: Some empirical evidence, Journal of Finance 36, 313–320.

Roll, Richard, 1983, On computing mean return and the small firm premium, Journal of Financial Economics 12, 371–386.

Ross, S.M., 1970, Applied probability models with optimization applications (Holden-Day, San Francisco, CA).

Schwert, G. William, 1977, Stock exchange seats as capital assets, Journal of Financial Economics 6, 51–78.

Schwert, G. William, 1983, Size and stock returns, and other empirical regularities, Journal of Financial Economics 12, 3–12.

Schultz, Paul, 1983, Transaction costs and the small firm effect: A comment, Journal of Financial Economics 12, 81–88.

Stoll, Hans R. and Robert E. Whaley, 1983, Transaction costs and the small firm effect, Journal of Financial Economics 12, 57–79.

Stoll, Hans, 1985, Alternative views of market making, in: Y. Amihud, T. Ho and R. Schartz, eds., Market making and the changing structure of the securities industry (Lexington Heath, Lexington, MA) 67–92.

Treynor, Jack, 1980, Liquidity, interest rates and inflation, Unpublished manuscript.

West, Richard R. and Seha M. Tinic, 1971, The economics of the stock market (Praeger, New York).

# IV

# TIME-VARYING EXPECTED RETURNS

**1** Fama, E. F., and G. W. Schwert, "Asset Returns and Inflation," *Journal of Financial Economics*, 5 (November 1977), pp. 115-146.

**2** Stambaugh, R. F., "The Information in Forward Rates: Implications for Models of Term Structure," *Journal of Financial Economics*, 21 (May 1988), pp. 41-70.

**3** Fama, E. F., and K. R. French, "Business Conditions and Expected Returns on Stocks and Bonds," *Journal of Financial Economics*, 25 (November 1989), pp. 23-49.

Much of the early literature on efficient capital markets also assumed that the distribution of asset returns is the same in each period. For example, the random walk model for stock prices would only be true in an efficient market if expected returns to stocks were constant over time. While much of the evidence is consistent with that model, there has been a growing literature that shows predictable variation in asset returns. This could be evidence of market inefficiency, or it could be that equilibrium expected returns are not constant over time.

**Fama and Schwert (1977)** show that returns to short- and long-term bonds, to real estate, and to human capital move about one to one with the short-term Treasury bill yield, so the risk premiums on these assets are unrelated to the level of interest rates. The risk premium on NYSE stocks, however, is reliably negatively related to interest rates from 1953 to 1971. For monthly returns, about 3 percent of the variation in excess returns to stocks is explained by the level of the short-term interest rate. **Fama and Schwert** also show that common stocks are negatively related to unexpected inflation during this period.

**Stambaugh (1988)** discusses much of the recent empirical work on the behavior of prices of default-free bonds for different maturities. In particular, he shows that Fama's (1984) evidence that forward interest rates predict future returns on Treasury bills is consistent with a two-factor version of the Cox, Ingersoll, and Ross (1985) term structure model. Moreover, he shows that the term structure tends to be upward-sloping during expansions and downward-sloping during recessions — also see Fama (1986). He argues that this may be related to increased uncertainty about future consumption opportunities during recessions.

**Fama and French (1989)** extend their earlier work on the predictability of expected returns to stocks [Fama and French (1988a,b)] using dividend yields, default yield spreads on corporate bonds, and term yield spreads on government bonds to predict future holding period returns to common stocks, corporate bonds, and government bonds. They find similar patterns of variation in these classes of assets from 1927 to 1987.

These are only a few of many papers documenting time-varying expected returns — see also Keim and Stambaugh (1986), French, Schwert, and Stambaugh (1987), Campbell (1987), and Fama (1991). The message in this fast-growing literature is that most of the variation in daily or monthly stock returns is unpredictable, but expected returns do appear to vary slowly over time. The challenge for future research is to provide better economic explanations for the measured variation in risk premiums.

# ASSET RETURNS AND INFLATION[*]

## Eugene F. FAMA

*Graduate School of Business, University of Chicago, Chicago, IL 60637, U.S.A.*

## G. William SCHWERT

*Graduate School of Management, University of Rochester, Rochester, NY 14627, U.S.A.*

Received June 1977, revised version received September 1977

We estimate the extent to which various assets were hedges against the expected and unexpected components of the inflation rate during the 1953–71 period. We find that U.S. government bonds and bills were a complete hedge against expected inflation, and private residential real estate was a complete hedge against both expected and unexpected inflation. Labor income showed little short-term relationship with either expected or unexpected inflation. The most anomalous result is that common stock returns were negatively related to the expected component of the inflation rate, and probably also to the unexpected component.

The recent episode of high inflation rates has focused interest on the question of which assets, if any, provide effective hedges against inflation. In this paper we examine the qualities of a variety of assets as hedges against the expected and unexpected components of the inflation rate.

## 1. Hedging against inflation: Theory

Irving Fisher (1930) noted that the nominal interest rate can be expressed as the sum of an expected real return and an expected inflation rate. The proposition that expected nominal returns contain market assessments of expected inflation rates can be applied to all assets. Thus, if the market is an efficient or rational processor of the information available at time $t-1$, it will set the price of any asset $j$ so that the expected nominal return on the asset from $t-1$ to $t$ is the sum of the appropriate equilibrium expected real return and the best possible assessment of the expected inflation rate from $t-1$ to $t$. Formally,

$$E(\tilde{R}_{jt}|\phi_{t-1}) = E(\tilde{r}_{jt}|\phi_{t-1}) + E(\tilde{\Delta}_t|\phi_{t-1}), \tag{1}$$

[*]The comments of Nicholas Gonedes, Michael Jensen, John Long, William Meckling, Charles Plosser, Harry Roberts, Richard Roll, Michael Rozeff, and Clifford Smith are gratefully acknowledged. This research is supported by the National Science Foundation.

where $\tilde{R}_{jt}$ is the nominal return on asset $j$ from $t-1$ to $t$, $E(\tilde{r}_{jt}|\phi_{t-1})$ is the appropriate equilibrium expected real return on the asset implied by the set of information $\phi_{t-1}$ available at $t-1$, $E(\tilde{\Delta}_t|\phi_{t-1})$ is the best possible assessment of the expected value of the inflation rate $\tilde{\Delta}_t$ that can be made on the basis of $\phi_{t-1}$, and tildes denote random variables.

The story meant to be conveyed by eq. (1) is that the market uses $\phi_{t-1}$ to correctly assess the expected inflation rate and to determine the appropriate equilibrium expected real return on asset $j$, including perhaps a risk adjustment which differentiates the expected return on asset $j$ from that on other assets. The market then sets the price of the asset so that its expected nominal return is the sum of the equilibrium expected real return and the correctly assessed expected inflation rate.

As a quantity theorist Fisher felt that the real and monetary sectors of the economy are largely independent. Thus, he hypothesized that the expected real return in (1) is determined by real factors, like the productivity of capital, investor time preferences, and tastes for risk, and that the expected real return and the expected inflation rate are unrelated. This assumption is convenient for our purposes because it allows us to study asset return–inflation relationships without introducing a complete general equilibrium model for expected real returns.

Given some way to measure the expected inflation rate, $E(\tilde{\Delta}_t|\phi_{t-1})$, tests of the joint hypotheses that the market is efficient and that the expected real return and expected inflation rate vary independently can be obtained from estimates of the regression model,

$$\tilde{R}_{jt} = \alpha_j + \beta_j E(\tilde{\Delta}_t|\phi_{t-1}) + \tilde{\varepsilon}_{jt}. \tag{2}$$

Since a regression estimates the conditional expected value of the dependent variable as a function of the independent variable, an estimate of the regression coefficient $\beta_j$ which is statistically indistinguishable from 1.0 is consistent with the hypothesis that the expected nominal return on asset $j$ varies in one-to-one correspondence with the expected inflation rate. Since the expected real return on the asset is its expected nominal return minus the expected inflation rate, an estimate of $\beta_j$ which is indistinguishable from 1.0 is also consistent with the hypothesis that the expected real return on the asset and the expected inflation rate are unrelated.

We are also interested in the extent to which asset returns at $t$ reflect the unanticipated component of the inflation rate between $t-1$ and $t$, $\tilde{\Delta}_t - E(\tilde{\Delta}_t|\phi_{t-1})$. To this end, we expand (1) as follows:

$$E(\tilde{R}_{jt}|\phi_{t-1}, \Delta_t) = E(\tilde{r}_{jt}|\phi_{t-1}) + E(\tilde{\Delta}_t|\phi_{t-1})$$
$$+ \gamma_j[\Delta_t - E(\tilde{\Delta}_t|\phi_{t-1})]. \tag{3}$$

Estimates of (3) can be based on the regression model,

$$\bar{R}_{jt} = \alpha_j + \beta_j E(\bar{\Delta}_t | \phi_{t-1}) + \gamma_j [\Delta_t - E(\bar{\Delta}_t | \phi_{t-1})] + \bar{\eta}_{jt}. \tag{4}$$

An estimate of the regression coefficient $\gamma_j$ which is statistically indistinguishable from 1.0 is consistent with the hypothesis that on average the nominal return to asset $j$ varies in one-to-one correspondence with the unexpected inflation rate.

Fisher's model says that all assets should have a coefficient $\beta_j = 1.0$ for the expected inflation rate in (4), but to obtain hypotheses about the coefficient $\gamma_j$ for the unexpected inflation rate, we must rely largely on intuition, and our intuition about $\gamma_j$ is different for different assets. For example, since the nominal value of a treasury bill which matures at time $t$ is fixed at $t-1$, the return on the bill from $t-1$ to $t$ cannot react to the unexpected rate of inflation from $t-1$ to $t$. On the other hand, there is a general belief that real estate and common stocks are hedges against inflation, unanticipated as well as anticipated, so that $\gamma_j$ for these assets should be positive. It is also widely believed [see, for example, Kessel and Alchian (1960)] that income from human capital adjusts to both anticipated and unanticipated inflation, although possibly with a lag. For longer-term bonds, whose cash payoffs are fixed in nominal terms, the signs and magnitudes of $\gamma_j$ in (3) and (4) depend on how the unanticipated inflation rate is related to changes in the discount rates that the market will use to price bonds in the future, a link that we investigate in some detail.

Since the unexpected rate of inflation is, by definition, uncorrelated with the expected rate of inflation, eq. (4) produces tests of the Fisher hypothesis that $\beta_j = 1.0$ which are identical to those that would be obtained from (2). We concentrate on models based on (4). When the tests suggest that $\beta_j = 1.0$, we say that the asset is a *complete hedge against expected inflation*: The expected nominal return on the asset varies in one-to-one correspondence with the expected inflation rate, and the expected real return on the asset is uncorrelated with the expected inflation rate. When $\gamma_j = 1.0$, the asset is a *complete hedge against unexpected inflation*. When the tests suggest that $\beta_j = \gamma_j = 1.0$, we say that the asset is a *complete hedge against inflation*: The nominal return on the asset varies in one-to-one correspondence with both the expected and unexpected components of the inflation rate, and the *ex post* real return on the asset is uncorrelated with the *ex post* inflation rate.

The fact that an asset is a complete hedge against expected and/or unexpected inflation does not imply that the real return on the asset has zero variance or even a small variance. Noninflation factors can generate variation in nominal returns which can be large or small relative to the variation in nominal returns associated with the expected and unexpected components of the inflation rate. In terms of equation (4), an asset might be a complete hedge against inflation, that is, both $\beta_j$ and $\gamma_j$ equal to 1.0, but inflation might 'explain' a small fraction of the variation in the asset's nominal return; that is, the variance of the disturbance $\bar{\eta}_{jt}$, which in this case is the variance of the asset's real return, might be large relative to the variance of the expected and unexpected components of the inflation rate.

## 2. The data

### 2.1. The rate of inflation

We use the Bureau of Labor Statistics Consumer Price Index (CPI) to estimate the rate of inflation. The rate of inflation, $\Delta_t$, is defined as the natural logarithm of the ratio of the values of the CPI at $t$ and $t-1$. Given the assumption that the purpose of investment is eventual consumption, the use of an inflation rate for consumption goods is appropriate – a point clearly recognized by Fisher (1930, ch. I) in his development of the theory.

In 1953 the Bureau of Labor Statistics increased the coverage of the CPI sample of goods and the frequency with which prices of individual goods are collected. Thus, the CPI data since January 1953 provide a more current and comprehensive measure of inflation than did earlier data. In August 1971 the government imposed price controls which discouraged increases in quoted prices of goods. The effective prices of goods and services increased during this period because of longer average purchase delays and increases in other costs of search in purchasing goods. When price controls were phased out in 1973 and 1974, the changes in the measured prices of goods in the CPI probably overstated the true inflation rate, as producers switched to prices as a means of rationing output among consumers. Thus, it is likely that from August 1971 until sometime in late 1974 the CPI was not a good measure of the cost to consumers of obtaining goods and services, so for the most part we concentrate on the period from January 1953 through July 1971. Fama and Schwert (1977b) discuss in detail the time series behavior of the CPI and its major components during this period.

### 2.2. Returns on assets

The return on an asset is the change in the price of the asset from $t-1$ to $t$ plus the cash flow paid to owners of the asset during the period, all relative to the price of the asset at $t-1$. For common stocks, we use returns on an equally-weighted portfolio of all New York Stock Exchange (NYSE) stocks and on a value-weighted portfolio of NYSE stocks, labeled $s_{et}$ and $s_{vt}$, respectively. Both series are from the Center for Research in Security Prices of the University of Chicago. Like the inflation rate, the common stock returns are continuously compounded. In general, continuous compounding is used in calculating asset returns.

Returns on U.S. treasury bills with one to six months to maturity, denoted $B_{1t}$ through $B_{6t}$, are derived from the Salomon Brothers quote sheets. The details of the calculations are described in Fama (1976b, ch. 6). Data for bills with one to three months to maturity are available since January 1953, while data for bills with four to six months to maturity are available since March 1959. Since bills pay no coupons, the return on a bill depends only on the change in its price from $t-1$ to $t$.

Returns on longer-term U.S. government bonds are based on indices constructed by Bildersee (1974). We use his indices to compute returns to bonds with from one to two years to maturity, $D_{1t}$; from two to three years to maturity, $D_{2t}$; from three to four years to maturity, $D_{3t}$; and from four to five years to maturity, $D_{4t}$. The statistical properties of these bond returns are analyzed in Fama and Schwert (1977a).

The return to privately held residential real estate, $r_t$, is measured as the rate of inflation of the Home Purchase Price component of the CPI. The Home Purchase Price index is based on the purchase prices of homes with mortgages newly insured by the FHA. To control for fluctuation in the quality of units in the sample, average prices for different quality classes are combined with fixed weights and the index is expressed as a price per square foot. However, the data have some deficiencies. The index is available only as a three month moving average. The FHA reports the sale price at the time the home is insured, so a lag of one to three months may occur between the date when the price is determined and the date when it is reflected in the index. In addition, there is a one month lag between the time that the FHA collects the data and the time when they show up in the CPI. Finally, FHA-insured housing is not a representative sample of all owner-occupied residential real estate. Nevertheless, the Home Purchase Price index seems to be the best available quality adjusted index of transaction prices for real estate.[1]

Ideally, we would like to have a measure of the return to real estate net of expenses but including the value of the service flows to owner-occupied housing. Owner-occupied housing differs from other assets such as stocks and bonds in that the 'dividend' return on housing is received in kind, so the relevant data are not available. Our hope is that our measure of the capital gain return to real estate, $r_t$, provides an adequate proxy for the variation of the total return to real estate, though not of the level of the total return.

Finally, since there is a general presumption that nominal income from human capital changes to reflect inflation, we include it in our tests. All of our other asset returns include changes in capital values, but these are not available for

[1]The Home Purchase Price index is described in 'Housing Costs in the Consumer Price Index', *Monthly Labor Review* (February 1956), pp. 189–196, and 'Housing Costs in the Consumer Price Index', *Monthly Labor Review* (April 1956), pp. 442–446. B.L.S. Bulletin No. 1517, 'The Consumer Price Index, History and Techniques' (1966), describes the construction of the entire CPI in detail.

human capital. The income variable we use is the rate of change of labor income per capita of the labor force,

$$h_t = \ln(H_t/L_t) - \ln(H_{t-1}/L_{t-1}) \tag{5}$$

where $H_t$ is the sum of wages and salary disbursements plus the proprietors' income portion of seasonally adjusted personal income, as reported monthly in the *Survey of Current Business*, and $L_t$ is the seasonally adjusted monthly total civilian labor force collected by the Bureau of the Census of the Department of Commerce. Since $h_t$ is the rate of change in income per capita, it must adjust to reflect the inflation rate if real labor income is to be independent of the price level. The arguments are detailed in Fama and Schwert (1977a).

### 2.3. Statistical properties of the data

Table 1 shows estimates of the first twelve autocorrelations of the CPI inflation rate and the nominal returns on the different assets for monthly data from January 1953 to July 1971. The sample autocorrelations of the monthly holding period returns to treasury bills ($B_{1t}$, $B_{2t}$, $B_{3t}$), are large for all twelve lags, which suggests that the expected monthly nominal returns on bills change through time. The sample autocorrelations of the returns to real estate, $r_t$, and the inflation rate, $\Delta_t$, are similar at all twelve lags and reliably different from zero. On the other hand, the autocorrelations of the returns on the government bond portfolios ($D_{1t}$, $D_{2t}$, $D_{3t}$, $D_{4t}$), the NYSE common stock portfolios ($s_{vt}$, $s_{et}$), and the income variable, $h_t$, are generally close to zero at all lags except lag one. In short, the behavior of the autocorrelations of nominal returns differs across assets.

Table 2 shows estimates of the first twelve autocorrelations of the monthly real returns on the assets for the January 1953 to July 1971 period. The real return is the nominal return minus the observed CPI inflation rate for the period. Except for some small positive autocorrelation at lag one, and sometimes at lags 2 and 12 (the seasonal lag), the autocorrelations of the real returns are close to zero.

The combination of the heterogeneous autocorrelations of the nominal returns on different assets in table 1 with the relatively homogeneous autocorrelations of real returns in table 2 is consistent with the proposition that the nominal returns on all assets vary with the inflation rate, but the persistent positive autocorrelation of the inflation rate is more evident in the nominal returns on assets that have smaller standard deviations. In other words, the inflation-related variation in asset returns shows up better in the time series behavior of the nominal returns on assets that are subject to less non-inflation variation. Then, because the inflation-related variation in nominal returns is common to all assets, all real returns are serially uncorrelated.

Table 1

Means, standard deviations and autocorrelations of monthly nominal rates of return, January 1953 – July 1971.[a]

| Asset | $\rho_1$ | $\rho_2$ | $\rho_3$ | $\rho_4$ | $\rho_5$ | $\rho_6$ | $\rho_7$ | $\rho_8$ | $\rho_9$ | $\rho_{10}$ | $\rho_{11}$ | $\rho_{12}$ | Mean | Standard deviation |
|---|---|---|---|---|---|---|---|---|---|---|---|---|---|---|
| **Treasury bills** | | | | | | | | | | | | | | |
| $B_{1t}$ | 0.97 | 0.95 | 0.93 | 0.91 | 0.88 | 0.85 | 0.83 | 0.81 | 0.78 | 0.74 | 0.72 | 0.70 | 0.0026 | 0.0013 |
| $B_{2t}$ | 0.91 | 0.88 | 0.86 | 0.83 | 0.81 | 0.76 | 0.74 | 0.73 | 0.71 | 0.68 | 0.66 | 0.64 | 0.0029 | 0.0014 |
| $B_{3t}$ | 0.83 | 0.79 | 0.78 | 0.75 | 0.73 | 0.67 | 0.63 | 0.64 | 0.63 | 0.57 | 0.57 | 0.57 | 0.0031 | 0.0015 |
| **Government bonds** | | | | | | | | | | | | | | |
| $D_{1t}$ | 0.25 | 0.09 | 0.13 | 0.12 | 0.12 | 0.04 | -0.05 | 0.01 | 0.00 | -0.01 | 0.06 | 0.06 | 0.0031 | 0.0044 |
| $D_{2t}$ | 0.16 | 0.09 | 0.07 | 0.09 | 0.01 | 0.02 | -0.11 | -0.05 | -0.03 | -0.06 | 0.00 | 0.02 | 0.0031 | 0.0066 |
| $D_{3t}$ | 0.18 | 0.11 | 0.05 | 0.10 | -0.01 | -0.02 | -0.11 | -0.10 | -0.04 | -0.05 | -0.02 | -0.03 | 0.0029 | 0.0080 |
| $D_{4t}$ | 0.15 | 0.05 | 0.08 | 0.11 | -0.07 | -0.04 | -0.11 | -0.09 | -0.01 | -0.04 | -0.06 | 0.00 | 0.0026 | 0.0096 |
| **Real estate** | | | | | | | | | | | | | | |
| $r_t$ | 0.39 | 0.21 | 0.06 | 0.13 | 0.13 | 0.21 | 0.21 | 0.18 | 0.18 | 0.25 | 0.29 | 0.25 | 0.0017 | 0.0036 |
| **Labor income** | | | | | | | | | | | | | | |
| $h_t$ | 0.09 | 0.11 | -0.02 | 0.14 | 0.08 | 0.10 | 0.02 | -0.03 | -0.05 | -0.07 | 0.00 | -0.12 | 0.0032 | 0.0059 |
| **Common stocks** | | | | | | | | | | | | | | |
| $s_{ut}$ | 0.11 | 0.01 | 0.01 | 0.14 | 0.09 | -0.03 | -0.09 | -0.11 | 0.07 | -0.17 | 0.00 | 0.01 | 0.0089 | 0.0362 |
| $s_{et}$ | 0.19 | 0.08 | -0.01 | 0.11 | 0.06 | 0.04 | -0.14 | -0.21 | 0.01 | -0.09 | 0.04 | 0.00 | 0.0102 | 0.0425 |
| **Inflation** | | | | | | | | | | | | | | |
| $\Delta_t$ | 0.37 | 0.36 | 0.27 | 0.30 | 0.28 | 0.28 | 0.25 | 0.33 | 0.35 | 0.33 | 0.26 | 0.36 | 0.0019 | 0.0023 |

[a]Sample autocorrelations are estimated as regression coefficients. The asymptotic standard error of $\rho_t$ is 0.07 under the hypothesis that the true autocorrelations are all equal to zero.

Table 2

Means, standard deviations and autocorrelations of monthly real rates of return, January 1953 – July 1971.[a]

| Asset | $\rho_1$ | $\rho_2$ | $\rho_3$ | $\rho_4$ | $\rho_5$ | $\rho_6$ | $\rho_7$ | $\rho_8$ | $\rho_9$ | $\rho_{10}$ | $\rho_{11}$ | $\rho_{12}$ | Mean | Standard deviation |
|---|---|---|---|---|---|---|---|---|---|---|---|---|---|---|
| Treasury bills | | | | | | | | | | | | | | |
| $B_{1t}$ | 0.11 | 0.12 | −0.02 | −0.01 | −0.02 | −0.02 | −0.07 | 0.05 | 0.10 | 0.10 | 0.03 | 0.19 | 0.0007 | 0.0020 |
| $B_{2t}$ | 0.13 | 0.14 | −0.02 | −0.03 | −0.01 | −0.06 | −0.08 | 0.03 | 0.06 | 0.12 | 0.04 | 0.18 | 0.0010 | 0.0020 |
| $B_{3t}$ | 0.15 | 0.14 | −0.03 | −0.06 | −0.01 | −0.08 | −0.09 | 0.01 | 0.05 | 0.11 | 0.03 | 0.17 | 0.0012 | 0.0020 |
| Government bonds | | | | | | | | | | | | | | |
| $D_{1t}$ | 0.17 | 0.07 | 0.04 | 0.01 | 0.07 | −0.03 | −0.12 | −0.05 | −0.05 | −0.03 | 0.03 | 0.05 | 0.0012 | 0.0047 |
| $D_{2t}$ | 0.14 | 0.12 | 0.02 | 0.04 | −0.01 | 0.00 | −0.13 | −0.07 | −0.05 | −0.05 | 0.00 | 0.04 | 0.0012 | 0.0068 |
| $D_{3t}$ | 0.18 | 0.14 | 0.03 | 0.07 | −0.02 | −0.02 | −0.12 | −0.10 | −0.03 | −0.03 | 0.00 | −0.01 | 0.0010 | 0.0083 |
| $D_{4t}$ | 0.15 | 0.08 | 0.07 | 0.09 | −0.07 | −0.03 | −0.11 | −0.09 | 0.00 | −0.03 | −0.05 | 0.02 | 0.0007 | 0.0099 |
| Real estate | | | | | | | | | | | | | | |
| $r_t$ | 0.14 | −0.03 | −0.16 | −0.16 | −0.02 | 0.04 | 0.05 | 0.01 | −0.02 | 0.05 | 0.09 | 0.13 | −0.0002 | 0.0034 |
| Labor income | | | | | | | | | | | | | | |
| $h_t$ | 0.16 | 0.15 | 0.00 | 0.10 | 0.03 | 0.10 | 0.03 | −0.02 | −0.03 | −0.06 | 0.03 | −0.12 | 0.0013 | 0.0061 |
| Common stocks | | | | | | | | | | | | | | |
| $s_{et}$ | 0.14 | 0.02 | 0.03 | 0.14 | 0.10 | −0.03 | −0.09 | −0.10 | 0.08 | −0.16 | 0.00 | 0.01 | 0.0070 | 0.0366 |
| $s_{ut}$ | 0.21 | 0.09 | 0.00 | 0.11 | 0.07 | 0.04 | −0.13 | −0.20 | 0.02 | −0.09 | 0.04 | 0.00 | 0.0084 | 0.0430 |

[a]The asymptotic standard error of $\rho_1$ is 0.07 under the hypothesis that the true autocorrelations are all equal to zero.

Table 3

Average, annualized, percent, nominal returns on assets and average CPI inflation rates.[a]

| Variable | Period | | | | |
|---|---|---|---|---|---|
| | 1/53–12/57 | 1/58–12/62 | 1/63–12/67 | 1/68–7/71 | 8/71–12/75 |
| Inflation | | | | | |
| $\Delta_t$ | 1.3 | 1.3 | 2.2 | 5.1 | 7.1 |
| Treasury bills | | | | | |
| $B_{1t}$ | 1.9 | 2.2 | 3.7 | 5.5 | 5.7 |
| $B_{2t}$ | 2.1 | 2.7 | 4.0 | 5.9 | 6.0 |
| $B_{3t}$ | 2.3 | 3.0 | 4.1 | 6.1 | 6.4 |
| Government bonds | | | | | |
| $D_{1t}$ | 2.3 | 3.5 | 3.6 | 6.1 | N.A. |
| $D_{2t}$ | 2.7 | 3.6 | 3.2 | 5.7 | N.A. |
| $D_{3t}$ | 2.6 | 3.7 | 2.9 | 5.1 | N.A. |
| $D_{4t}$ | 2.4 | 3.3 | 2.6 | 4.5 | N.A. |
| Real estate | | | | | |
| $r_t$ | 1.0 | 0.6 | 1.7 | 5.9 | 6.2 |
| Labor income | | | | | |
| $h_t$ | 2.2 | 3.4 | 5.2 | 4.7 | 6.1 |
| Common stocks | | | | | |
| $s_{vt}$ | 12.3 | 12.8 | 12.5 | 3.0 | 1.6 |
| $s_{et}$ | 10.5 | 14.4 | 18.5 | 3.3 | −0.6 |

[a]Average nominal returns and inflation rates are annualized from monthly average returns like those in table 1. For bills ($B_{1t}$, $B_{2t}$, $B_{3t}$) and bonds ($D_{1t}$, $D_{2t}$, $D_{3t}$, $D_{4t}$) this means that instruments of a given maturity are purchased and sold each month, and then the average monthly returns are annualized, that is, multiplied by 1,200. Data for the bond portfolios are not available (N.A.) for the latest subperiod.

A general picture of the qualities of different assets as inflation hedges is also provided by table 3, which shows average annualized percent inflation rates and nominal asset returns for subperiods. For the real estate variable ($r_t$) and for each of the three treasury bills ($B_{1t}$, $B_{2t}$, $B_{3t}$), the subperiod ordering of average nominal returns corresponds exactly to the ordering of average inflation rates. The correspondence between the ordering of average returns and average inflation rates is not so exact for the four government bond portfolios ($D_{1t}$, $D_{2t}$, $D_{3t}$, $D_{4t}$), but the tendency for average returns to follow the average inflation rate is still noticeable. The average rates of change of income per capita ($h_t$) generally move with average inflation rates, but $\bar{h}$ is relatively high during the 1963 to 1967 subperiod when the average inflation rate is relatively low. Finally, a phenomenon that perplexes us throughout this study is the apparent inverse relationship between stock returns ($s_{vt}$, $s_{et}$) and inflation rates since 1953.

Note, however, that in spite of their inverse relationship with inflation rates, average returns on stocks are higher for the overall period than average returns on other assets, a fact which is more evident in tables 1 and 2. Note also that, with the exception of the last subperiod in table 3, average returns on bills and bonds are greater than the average inflation rate, so that real returns on these instruments are generally positive. Moreover, average returns on bills increase with maturity, a pattern which is less evident in the bond returns. Finally, the fact that the average returns to private residential real estate shown in table 3 are generally less than the average inflation rates does not necessarily imply negative average real returns to real estate since our measure of the real estate return covers only capital gains.

Tables 1 to 3 provide a useful introduction to the properties of different assets as inflation hedges, but the picture that emerges is impressionistic. The tests that follow provide more precise measures of the relationships between asset returns and the two components of the inflation rate, expected and unexpected.

## 3. Tests of assets as hedges against expected inflation

### 3.1. A measure of expected inflation

To implement tests of assets as hedges against expected and unexpected inflation using the model in (4), an empirical measure of the expected inflation rate, $E(\bar{\Delta}_t | \phi_{t-1})$, based on data available at time $t-1$, is needed. The nominal return or interest rate on a treasury bill which matures at time $t$, $B_t$, is known at $t-1$. Fama (1975) notes that if the expected real return on the bill is constant through time, and if the bill market is efficient, the nominal return on the bill is equal to the constant expected real return plus the expected inflation rate,

$$B_t = E(\tilde{r}) + E(\bar{\Delta}_t | \phi_{t-1}). \tag{6}$$

Thus, the expected inflation rate is

$$E(\bar{\Delta}_t | \phi_{t-1}) = -E(\tilde{r}) + B_t. \tag{7}$$

Tests of (7) can be obtained from estimates of

$$\bar{\Delta}_t = \alpha + \beta B_t + \tilde{\varepsilon}_t, \tag{8}$$

where the proposition of (7) is that $\beta = 1.0$ and $E(\tilde{\varepsilon}_t | \phi_{t-1}) = 0$; that is, all variation in the nominal return $B_t$ set at $t-1$ reflects variation in $E(\bar{\Delta}_t | \phi_{t-1})$, the best possible assessment at $t-1$ of the expected value of the inflation rate to be observed at $t$. The unexpected component of the inflation rate is then just the disturbance $\tilde{\varepsilon}_t$ in (8).

The estimate of (8) using monthly data for the January 1953 – July 1971 period is shown in table 4. Consistent with the hypothesis of (7), the estimate of $\beta$ is 0.98 with a standard error of 0.10, and the first three autocorrelations of the residuals, $\rho_1(\hat{e})$, $\rho_2(\hat{e})$, and $\rho_3(\hat{e})$, are close to zero. Table 4 also shows the estimate of the regression of the quarterly inflation rate on the return to maturity or interest rate on a three month treasury bill, $B_{3t}$, set at the beginning of the quarter. The estimate of the slope coefficient $\hat{\beta}$ is close to one with a small standard error, $R^2$ is 0.48, and the residuals seem to be serially uncorrelated. Finally, the regression of the semiannual inflation rate on $B_{6t}$, the return to maturity or interest rate on a six month treasury bill set at the beginning of the six month period, indicates that $B_{6t}$ is a good proxy for the semiannual expected inflation rate. The estimate of $\beta$ is 1.06 with a standard error of 0.10, $R^2$ is 0.82, and the residuals do not seem to be autocorrelated.

A more detailed discussion of the interest rate–inflation model of eqs. (6) to (8) is in Fama (1975) and Fama and Schwert (1977b). For our purposes, the important empirical finding is that estimates of eq. (8) are consistent with the proposition that changes in the interest rate, $B_t$, correspond to changes in the expected inflation rate, $E(\tilde{\Delta}_t | \phi_{t-1})$. Thus, we use the nominal return or interest rate on a treasury bill which matures at the end of period $t$ as a proxy for the expected inflation rate for period $t$, and the unexpected inflation rate is measured as $\Delta_t - B_t$, the difference between the inflation rate realized *ex post* and the *ex ante* interest rate. The empirical analog of eq. (4) is then[2]

$$\tilde{R}_{jt} = \alpha_j + \beta_j B_t + \gamma_j (\Delta_t - B_t) + \tilde{\eta}_{jt}. \tag{9}$$

Finally, the proxies for the expected and unexpected monthly inflation rates have very different time series properties. The autocorrelations of $B_{1t}$ in table 1 are close to 1.0 at lower-order lags and only decay slowly at higher-order lags, which is suggestive of a non-stationary process such as a random walk. Thus, the proxy for the expected inflation rate wanders slowly over time with little affinity for any particular value. In contrast, since the estimated regression of $\Delta_t$ on $B_{1t}$ in table 4 produces a slope coefficient $\hat{\beta} = 0.98$, the residuals from the regression have time series properties almost identical to those of $\Delta_t - B_{1t}$. Thus from the monthly results in table 4 we can conclude that $\Delta_t - B_{1t}$ has the properties required of a proxy for the unexpected inflation rate; that is, $\Delta_t - B_{1t}$ is serially uncorrelated and uncorrelated with the proxy for the expected inflation rate. The inflation rate, which is just the sum of its expected and unexpected components, is therefore approximately a random walk plus serially uncor-

---

[2]There is some evidence that inflation can be predicted slightly better by using additional information available at time $t-1$, such as lags of the inflation rate [see, for example, Hess and Bicksler (1975) or Nelson and Schwert (1977)]. Taking account of such complications does not materially affect the results.

Table 4

Interest rates as measures of expected inflation, $\Delta_t = \alpha + \beta B_t + \epsilon_t$ (standard errors in parentheses).[a]

| Interest rate[b] $B_t$ | Period | Sample size $T$ | $\alpha$ | $\beta$ | $R^2$ | $S(\ell)$ | $\rho_1(\ell)$ | $\rho_2(\ell)$ | $\rho_3(\ell)$ |
|---|---|---|---|---|---|---|---|---|---|
| Monthly, $B_{1t}$ | 1/53–7/71 | 223 | −0.0007 (0.0003) | 0.98 (0.10) | 0.29 | 0.0020 | 0.10 | 0.12 | −0.02 |
| Quarterly, $B_{3t}$ | 1/53–6/71 | 74 | −0.0023 (0.0011) | 0.93 (0.11) | 0.48 | 0.0038 | 0.00 | 0.04 | 0.10 |
| Semi-annual, $B_{6t}$[c] | 7/59–6/71 | 24 | −0.0097 (0.0024) | 1.06 (0.10) | 0.82 | 0.0038 | 0.00 | −0.04 | 0.16 |

[a] The coefficients of determination, $R^2$, are adjusted for degrees of freedom. $S(\ell)$ is the standard error of the regression residuals, and $\rho_\ell(\ell)$ is the residual autocorrelation at lag $\tau$.

[b] $B_t$ is the return or interest rate on a treasury bill which matures at the end of period $t$. It is known at the beginning of the period.

[c] Returns on six-month bills are only available since March 1959.

related noise. This is consistent with the autocorrelations of the inflation rate in table 1 which are much less than one but do not decay as the lag is increased.[3]

## 3.2. Tests based on monthly data

Estimates of eq. (9) for monthly data from January 1953 to July 1971 are shown in table 5. The estimates of $\beta_j$, the coefficient for the expected inflation proxy in (9), are close to one for treasury bills ($B_{2t}$, $B_{3t}$), the government bond portfolios ($D_{1t}$, $D_{2t}$, $D_{3t}$, $D_{4t}$), and real estate ($r_t$). Although the estimates of $\beta_j$ for the returns to two and three month bills are more than two standard errors above one, the standard errors of the coefficients are underestimated in this case because the residuals and the expected inflation proxy are both positively auto-correlated [cf. Theil (1971, pp. 254–257)]. The estimate of $\beta_j$ for the income variable, $h_t$, is 0.51 with a standard error of 0.31, so we cannot comfortably reject the hypothesis that $\beta_j = 1$. However, since there is a wide range of alternative hypotheses that also can't be rejected, table 5 does not provide much evidence that labor income is a hedge against the monthly expected inflation rate.

Since the regressions for treasury bill and bond returns yield coefficient estimates for $B_{1t}$ that are close to 1.0 and coefficients for $\Delta_t - B_{1t}$ that are generally within one standard error of zero, the time series properties of the residuals from these regressions correspond to the properties of the premiums on bills and bonds, that is, the differences between their one month returns and the return on a one month bill. The non-trivial autocorrelations of these premiums, evident in the residual autocorrelations in table 5, are documented and discussed in Fama (1976a).

However, these residual autocorrelations gain additional interest in our work. Since $B_{1t}$ in (9) is the proxy for the expected inflation rate in eqs. (1) to (4), the residual autocorrelations in the regressions for bills and bonds in table 5 can be interpreted as variation in expected real returns which is independent of variation in the expected inflation rate. Thus, the residual autocorrelations are evidence of the type of independent variation of expected real returns and the expected inflation rate which allows (2) and (4) to provide meaningful measures of variation in expected nominal returns in response to variation in the expected inflation rate. On the other hand, the large first-order residual autocorrelation for the real estate return $r_t$ in table 5 is less interesting since it is probably a consequence of the fact that the Home Purchase Price index on which $r_t$ is based is a three month moving average.

Given an asset whose expected return varies directly with $B_{1t}$, we can expect the large autocorrelations of $B_{1t}$ to have a more noticeable effect on the time series behavior of the asset's return when the proxy for the expected inflation rate

---

[3]Box and Jenkins (1976, pp. 123–124 and 200–201) describe such a process and the behavior of its sample autocorrelations.

Table 5

Hedges against monthly expected and unexpected inflation, $R_{jt} = a_j + \beta_j B_{1t} + \gamma_j(\Delta_t - B_{1t}) + \eta_{jt}$ (standard errors in parentheses); 1/53 – 7/71, T = 223.

| Asset $R_{jt}$ | $a_j$ | $\beta_j$ | $\hat{\gamma}_j$ | $R^2$ | $S(\hat{\eta}_j)$ | $\rho_1(\hat{\eta}_j)$ | $\rho_2(\hat{\eta}_j)$ | $\rho_3(\hat{\eta}_j)$ |
|---|---|---|---|---|---|---|---|---|
| $B_{2t}$ | 0.0002 (0.0001) | 1.04 (0.02) | 0.01 (0.01) | 0.94 | 0.0003 | 0.34 | 0.20 | 0.18 |
| $B_{3t}$ | 0.0002 (0.0001) | 1.08 (0.03) | 0.02 (0.02) | 0.85 | 0.0006 | 0.28 | 0.13 | 0.20 |
| $D_{1t}$ | 0.0001 (0.0006) | 1.11 (0.22) | −0.11 (0.14) | 0.10 | 0.0042 | 0.20 | 0.02 | 0.07 |
| $D_{2t}$ | 0.0002 (0.0010) | 1.03 (0.34) | −0.15 (0.22) | 0.03 | 0.0065 | 0.14 | 0.07 | 0.06 |
| $D_{3t}$ | 0.0002 (0.0012) | 0.94 (0.41) | −0.26 (0.27) | 0.02 | 0.0079 | 0.18 | 0.09 | 0.06 |
| $D_{4t}$ | −0.0001 (0.0015) | 0.90 (0.50) | −0.36 (0.33) | 0.01 | 0.0096 | 0.15 | 0.04 | 0.08 |
| $r_t$ | −0.0012 (0.0005) | 1.19 (0.16) | 0.31 (0.11) | 0.21 | 0.0032 | 0.22 | −0.01 | −0.17 |
| $h_t$ | 0.0020 (0.0009) | 0.51 (0.31) | 0.16 (0.20) | 0.01 | 0.0059 | 0.09 | 0.11 | −0.03 |
| $s_{et}$ | 0.0228 (0.0055) | −5.52 (1.85) | −0.77 (1.22) | 0.03 | 0.0356 | 0.06 | −0.02 | −0.03 |
| $s_{6t}$ | 0.0235 (0.0064) | −5.70 (2.17) | −2.35 (1.44) | 0.03 | 0.0418 | 0.13 | 0.07 | −0.05 |

is a large component of the variance of the asset's return. This is observed in the results for real estate, bills, and bonds in tables 1 and 5. In the regressions of table 5, the coefficients of determination, $R^2$, are large for the monthly returns on two and three month bills while the $R^2$ statistics are relatively small for real estate and the government bond portfolios. In table 1, the autocorrelations of the bill returns are likewise larger than those for real estate and bonds.

Having discussed the results for assets whose expected returns seem to vary directly with our proxy for the expected inflation rate, we turn now to the prime counterexample. In table 5, the estimates of $\beta_J$ for $s_{et}$ and $s_{vt}$, the returns to the NYSE common stock portfolios, are both approximately $-5.5$, with standard errors of about 2.0. We can reject the hypothesis that common stocks are a hedge against the expected monthly inflation rate. The negative relationship between common stock returns and expected inflation rates has also been noted by Lintner (1975), Body (1976), Nelson (1976), and Jaffe and Mandelker (1976), among others. The anomalous behavior of common stock returns is analyzed in more detail in section 4.

### 3.3. Tests based on quarterly and semiannual data

The Fisher hypothesis that expected nominal returns should vary directly with the expected inflation rate can be applied to any time interval over which the variables might be measured. Table 6 shows estimates of eq. (9) based on quarterly and semiannual returns and inflation rates. The nominal return or interest rate on a three month bill observed at the beginning of each quarter, $B_{3t}$, is the proxy for the expected quarterly inflation rate. The *ex ante* six month bill rate, $B_{6t}$, is likewise taken as the proxy for the semiannual expected inflation rate. Since data for six month bills are not available prior to March 1959, the semiannual tests only cover the second half of 1959 through the first half of 1971.

The quarterly and semiannual results in table 6 are similar to the monthly results in table 5. Government bonds and real estate are complete hedges against the expected inflation rate since the estimates of $\beta_J$, the coefficient of the expected inflation proxy in (9), are close to one for these assets. Quarterly labor income is positively related to the quarterly expected inflation proxy while semiannual labor income is negatively related to the semiannual expected inflation proxy, but both coefficient estimates have large standard errors. Although the standard errors of the coefficients get progressively larger, common stock returns show negative relationships with the quarterly and semiannual expected inflation proxies similar in magnitude to those observed in the monthly data.

## 4. Tests of assets as hedges against unexpected inflation

### 4.1. Tests based on monthly data

In the monthly tests of table 5, the estimates of $\gamma_j$, the regression coefficient in

(9) that measures the quality of an asset as a hedge against the unexpected component of the inflation rate, are mostly less than one standard error from zero. The only estimate of $\gamma_j$ which is more than two standard errors from zero is obtained when the return to real estate, $r_t$, is the dependent variable in the regression. Thus, there is some evidence that real estate is a partial hedge against unexpected monthly inflation. Apparently it is not a complete hedge since the estimate of $\gamma_j$ for real estate is reliably less than unity.

There is a suggestive pattern in the relationships between the unexpected inflation proxy and the returns to the government bond portfolios. The estimates of $\gamma_j$ for $D_{1t}$, $D_{2t}$, $D_{3t}$ and $D_{4t}$ are all negative and they increase in absolute value with term to maturity. An explanation for this result, having to do with the information that current unexpected inflation contains about future expected inflation, is explored later. Current unexpected inflation seems to have a negative effect on the nominal returns to NYSE common stocks, but the standard errors of the estimates of $\gamma_j$ are large relative to the values of the coefficients.

Table 6

Hedges against quarterly and semiannual expected and unexpected inflation,
$R_{jt} = \hat{a}_j + \hat{\beta}_j B_t + \hat{\gamma}_j (\Delta_t - B_t) + \hat{\eta}_{jt}$ (standard errors in parentheses).

| Asset $R_{jt}$ | $\hat{a}_j$ | $\hat{\beta}_j$ | $\hat{\gamma}_j$ | $R^2$ | $S(\hat{\eta}_j)$ | $\rho_1(\hat{\eta}_j)$ | $\rho_2(\hat{\eta}_j)$ | $\rho_3(\hat{\eta}_j)$ |
|---|---|---|---|---|---|---|---|---|
| | | | (A) Quarterly data: 1/53–6/71, $T = 74$ | | | | | |
| $B_{1t}$ | −0.0002 (0.0002) | 0.95 (0.02) | 0.05 (0.02) | 0.97 | 0.0007 | 0.17 | 0.06 | 0.29 |
| $D_{1t}$ | −0.0026 (0.0023) | 1.21 (0.23) | −0.50 (0.25) | 0.29 | 0.0080 | 0.11 | 0.06 | −0.07 |
| $D_{2t}$ | −0.0041 (0.0037) | 1.23 (0.38) | −0.93 (0.40) | 0.17 | 0.0130 | 0.11 | 0.03 | −0.09 |
| $D_{3t}$ | −0.0054 (0.0045) | 1.18 (0.46) | −1.33 (0.49) | 0.15 | 0.0158 | 0.18 | 0.00 | −0.07 |
| $D_{4t}$ | −0.0069 (0.0054) | 1.19 (0.55) | −1.47 (0.58) | 0.12 | 0.0187 | 0.16 | −0.05 | −0.05 |
| $r_t$ | −0.0032 (0.0019) | 1.15 (0.19) | 0.56 (0.20) | 0.35 | 0.0065 | −0.20 | 0.03 | −0.02 |
| $h_t$ | 0.0049 (0.0031) | 0.45 (0.32) | −0.32 (0.33) | 0.02 | 0.0108 | 0.19 | 0.18 | −0.15 |
| $s_{vt}$ | 0.0572 (0.0199) | −4.88 (2.04) | −4.11 (2.14) | 0.09 | 0.0693 | 0.01 | −0.08 | −0.10 |
| $s_{at}$ | 0.0549 (0.0247) | −4.95 (2.54) | −6.50 (2.66) | 0.09 | 0.0861 | 0.04 | −0.02 | −0.13 |

Table 6 (continued)

| Asset $R_{Jt}$ | $\hat{a}_J$ | $\beta_J$ | $\hat{\gamma}_J$ | $R^2$ | $S(\hat{\eta}_J)$ | $\rho_1(\hat{\eta}_J)$ | $\rho_2(\hat{\eta}_J)$ | $\rho_3(\hat{\eta}_J)$ |
|---|---|---|---|---|---|---|---|---|
| \multicolumn{9}{c}{(B) Semiannual data: 7/59–6/71, $T = 24$} |
| $B_{1t}$ | 0.0025 (0.0017) | 0.84 (0.06) | 0.23 (0.11) | 0.92 | 0.0020 | 0.44 | 0.46 | 0.09 |
| $B_{2t}$ | 0.0018 (0.0013) | 0.89 (0.04) | 0.15 (0.09) | 0.95 | 0.0016 | 0.35 | 0.37 | 0.00 |
| $B_{3t}$ | 0.0027 (0.0013) | 0.88 (0.04) | 0.16 (0.08) | 0.95 | 0.0015 | 0.07 | 0.35 | −0.09 |
| $D_{1t}$ | −0.0110 (0.0089) | 1.08 (0.29) | −1.15 (0.59) | 0.38 | 0.0106 | 0.03 | −0.27 | 0.12 |
| $D_{2t}$ | −0.0158 (0.0143) | 1.03 (0.47) | −1.75 (0.95) | 0.19 | 0.0170 | 0.01 | −0.38 | 0.11 |
| $D_{3t}$ | −0.0183 (0.0185) | 0.88 (0.61) | −2.37 (1.24) | 0.12 | 0.0220 | 0.01 | −0.44 | 0.05 |
| $D_{4t}$ | −0.0212 (0.0223) | 0.79 (0.73) | −2.75 (1.49) | 0.09 | 0.0266 | −0.03 | −0.47 | 0.03 |
| $r_t$ | −0.0054 (0.0073) | 1.27 (0.24) | 1.14 (0.49) | 0.60 | 0.0087 | −0.21 | 0.39 | −0.15 |
| $h_t$ | 0.0367 (0.0125) | −0.13 (0.41) | 1.40 (0.84) | 0.04 | 0.0149 | 0.08 | −0.10 | 0.01 |
| $s_{vt}$ | 0.1169 (0.0990) | −4.26 (3.25) | −2.09 (6.62) | 0.00 | 0.1178 | −0.20 | −0.18 | −0.04 |
| $s_{et}$ | 0.1222 (0.1266 | −4.87 (4.15) | −4.38 (8.46) | −0.01 | 0.1506 | −0.03 | −0.19 | −0.05 |

## 4.2. Tests based on quarterly and semiannual data

The quarterly and semiannual results in table 6 suggest more pronounced relationships between unexpected inflation rates and asset returns. The negative relationship between the common stock returns, $s_{et}$ and $s_{vt}$, and the unexpected inflation proxy shows up more reliably, at least in the results for quarterly data. For the returns on the government bond portfolios ($D_{1t}$, $D_{2t}$, $D_{3t}$ and $D_{4t}$), the estimates of $\gamma_J$ get progressively more negative as one goes from the monthly regressions in table 5 to the quarterly and semiannual regressions in table 6, and in all cases, the absolute magnitude of $\hat{\gamma}_J$ increases with term to maturity.

On the other hand, for quarterly and semiannual labor income, the estimates of $\gamma_J$, the coefficient of the unexpected inflation proxy in (9), are very different from each other, although both estimates have large standard errors. Indeed, a coherent explanation for the monthly, quarterly, and semiannual estimates of eq. (9) for the labor income variable, $h_t$, is not evident. Perhaps a more detailed analysis of the relationship between inflation and labor income, emphasizing the 'wage lag' hypothesis of Kessel and Alchian (1960) or 'Phillips Curve' phenomena, would yield more consistent results. Or perhaps there are unidentified problems in the way the labor income variable is measured. In any case, our results show little relationship between nominal labor income and the expected and unexpected components of inflation measured over periods of up to six months.

There is a more interesting story in the measured relationships between the return to real estate, $r_t$, and unexpected inflation rates. In tables 5 and 6, the estimates of $\gamma_j$ for the return to real estate are largest for semiannual data (1.14), next largest for quarterly data (0.56), and smallest for monthly data (0.31). All of these estimates are more than two standard errors above zero. One interpretation of these results is that real estate provides a better hedge against longer-term unexpected inflation. However, an alternative explanation, based on measurement problems in the real estate data, seems more plausible. Moreover, it suggests that real estate is a complete hedge against expected and unexpected inflation, even on a monthly basis.

The Home Purchase Price index from which $r_t$ is calculated is computed as a three month moving average, and since the actual transaction dates typically occur from one to three months prior to the time they are reflected in the index, the correlation between $r_t$ and unexpected inflation rates is spuriously spread over six months. However, looking at longer holding periods has the effect of overcoming most of the non-synchronous measurement of $r_t$ and unexpected inflation.

The lags built into the measurement of $r_t$ do not have a similar attenuating effect on the estimates of $\beta_j$, the coefficient for the interest rate in (9), which are all relatively close to unity for the real estate variable, even in the monthly data of table 5. This result is probably due to the fact that the interest rate, our proxy for the expected inflation rate, is a slowly wandering series whose level shows much persistence through time (see table 1). Thus, even though it is a little out of date, the 'expected' inflation rate portion of the measured real estate return is probably highly correlated with the expected inflation rate which is built into the current interest rate.

An alternative approach to estimating the effects of nonsynchronous measurement of $r_t$ and the monthly unexpected inflation rate is provided by the model

$$\tilde{r}_t = \alpha + \beta \, B_{1t} + \sum_{i=0}^{6} \gamma_i (\varDelta_{t-i} - B_{1t-i}) + \tilde{\varepsilon}_t. \tag{10}$$

As noted earlier, our proxy for the unexpected monthly inflation rate, $(\varDelta_t - B_{1t})$, is serially uncorrelated, so the seven unexpected inflation rates in eq. (10) are uncorrelated. Since there is reason to believe that the current measured return to real estate, $r_t$, is composed of price changes which have occurred over the last three to six months, we expect some of the coefficients of lagged unexpected inflation rates in (10) to be positive. The estimate of eq. (10) using monthly data from July 1953 to July 1971 is

$$r_t = -0.0009 + 1.22B_{1t} + 0.27(\Delta_t - B_{1t}) + 0.31(\Delta_{t-1} - B_{1t-1})$$
$$(0.0005)\ (0.16)\quad (0.11)\qquad\qquad (0.11)$$

$$+ 0.22(\Delta_{t-2} - B_{1t-2}) - 0.06(\Delta_{t-3} - B_{1t-3}) + 0.23(\Delta_{t-4} - B_{1t-4})$$
$$(0.11)\qquad\qquad .(0.11)\qquad\qquad\qquad (0.11)$$

$$- 0.10(\Delta_{t-5} - B_{1t-5}) + 0.01(\Delta_{t-6} - B_{1t-6}) + \varepsilon_t,$$
$$(0.11)\qquad\qquad (0.11)$$

where standard errors are in parentheses. The $F$-statistic for the hypothesis that $\gamma_1 = \gamma_2 = \ldots = \gamma_6 = 0$ is 3.01, which is greater than the 0.01 fractile of the $F$-distribution with 6 and 208 degrees of freedom.

Moreover, applying the analysis of Scholes and Williams (1977) indicates that the sum of the estimators of the coefficients of current and lagged unexpected inflation rates in (10) is a consistent estimator of the contemporaneous relationship between the true return to real estate and the unexpected monthly inflation rate when there are no dating errors in $\Delta_t - B_{1t}$, but there are lagged dating errors in $r_t$. The sum of the estimated coefficients of unexpected inflation rates

$$\sum_{i=0}^{6} \hat{\gamma}_i = 0.88,$$

is close to one, with a standard error (calculated as the square root of the sum of the variances of the individual coefficients) equal to 0.29.

In short, once we take account of the measurement errors in the real estate return, either in the manner of (10) or by working with semi-annual data, estimates of $\beta_j$ and $\gamma_j$ in (9) are both close to unity. These results are consistent with the hypothesis that real estate is a complete hedge against inflation, expected and unexpected. That is, the nominal return to real estate varies directly with both the expected and unexpected components of the inflation rate, so that the real return to real estate (the nominal return minus the inflation rate) is unrelated to the inflation rate.

Note, however, that being a complete hedge against inflation does not imply that the inflation adjusted return to real estate is certain. For example, the coefficient of determination in the semiannual regression in table 6 suggests that about 40 percent of the variance of the semiannual real estate return is left unexplained by the combined effects of the expected and unexpected components of the semiannual inflation rate.

## 5. Short-term bills as hedges against longer-term inflation

Table 6 also shows estimates of (9) for quarterly and semiannual data where the dependent variables are the returns from strategies of rolling over a sequence of shorter-term bills. For example, the quarterly return to one month treasury bills, labeled $B_{1t}$ in part A of table 6, is the sum of the three monthly returns on one month bills during the quarter. The semiannual returns on one, two, and three month bills, $B_{1t}$, $B_{2t}$, and $B_{3t}$, used in part B of table 6, are likewise obtained by rolling over the relevant shorter-term bills during the six month period. Thus, the six-month version of $B_{2t}$ involves three consecutive two month bills, while $B_{3t}$ is obtained by purchasing two consecutive three month bills.

Since short-term bill returns contain assessments of expected inflation rates which are updated within longer holding periods, the strategy of rolling over short-term bills provides a hedge against changes in expected inflation rates during longer holding periods. For example, the return to maturity on a three month bill cannot adjust to intraquarter changes in expectations about inflation, whereas month to month reassessments of the expected inflation rate are built into the quarterly return on a sequence of one month bills.

In statistical terms, the *ex ante* interest rate or return on a three month bill contains measurement error as an estimate of the sequence of one month expected inflation rates impounded in the quarterly return on three successive one month bills. Likewise, the *ex ante* interest rate or return on a six month bill contains measurement error as a measure of the expected inflation rates impounded in strategies of rolling over one, two, or three month bills during the six month period. This measurement error perhaps explains why for the short-term bills the estimates of $\beta_j$, the coefficient of the longer-term interest rate, are several standard errors less than unity in both the quarterly and semiannual regressions in table 6.

The returns to strategies of rolling over shorter-term bills produce estimates of $\gamma_j$, the coefficient of the unexpected inflation proxy in (9), which are all positive and more than two standard errors from zero. Although we now seem to be dealing with unexpected quarterly and semiannual inflation rates, this result is again traceable to the fact that rolling over shorter-term bills provides a moving hedge against changes in expected inflation rates which is not obtained when a longer-term bill is purchased and held to maturity.

For example, a sequence of six one month bills takes advantage of the market's monthly reassessments of expected inflation rates, whereas the return on a six month bill held to maturity does not benefit from such updates of inflation expectations, However, our proxy for the unexpected semiannual inflation rate is just $\Delta_t - B_{6t}$, the *ex post* six month inflation rate minus the interest rate on a six month bill set at the beginning of the semiannual period. Even if $B_{6t}$ fully reflects all of the information about the inflation rate for the coming six months which is available at the beginning of the period, $\Delta_t - B_{6t}$ is nevertheless at least partially attributable to changes in expectations about inflation that take place within the semiannual period. Since these intraperiod changes in expected inflation rates are built into the returns to strategies of rolling over shorter-term bills, they account for the positive estimates of $\gamma_j$ for the returns to these strategies. The estimates of $\gamma_j$ are far from unity because only a small part of the variation in the longer-term unexpected inflation rate is due to the shorter-term reassessments of expected inflation rates that are captured by the rollover strategies.

## 6. Common stocks and inflation

### 6.1. Theoretical considerations

Various arguments can be given for why common stocks might be helped or hurt by unanticipated inflation. For example, Kessel (1956) argues that unanticipated inflation is to the benefit of the stockholders of firms that are net debtors. In more general terms, unanticipated inflation should benefit the common stock of firms that have made more long-term commitments to pay fixed nominal amounts than to receive them. The net debtor–creditor hypothesis is difficult to implement empirically since a firm might have long-term contracts to purchase labor, raw materials, and capital, to sell its own products, and to borrow money to finance its operations. Nevertheless, this hypothesis and others [see, for example, Lintner's (1975) discussion of the tax effects of inflation] provide some theoretical possibilities for explaining the effects of unanticipated inflation on the returns to common stocks.

On the other hand, like others who have investigated the topic, for example, Lintner (1975), Nelson (1976), and Jaffe and Mandelker (1976), we have no explanation for the negative relationship between common stock returns and the *expected* component of the inflation rate. There are two possibilities. Some as yet unidentified phenomenon might cause equilibrium expected real returns to stocks to be negatively related to expected inflation rates, Or the market might be inefficient in impounding available information about future inflation into stock prices.

We now examine the relationship between stock returns and the expected inflation rate from a different perspective and in somewhat more detail. The additional results improve our understanding of the statistical nature of the phenomenon, but we remain unable to identify its economic origins.

### 6.2. Some additional tests

Using data for the January 1953 to July 1971 period, the estimated regression of the monthly return to the value-weighted portfolio of NYSE common stocks on the one month treasury bill rate is

$$s_{vt} = 0.0234 - 5.50B_{1t} + \hat{\varepsilon}_t, \qquad \bar{R}^2 = 0.03, \quad S(\hat{\varepsilon}) = 0.0356.$$
$$\quad (0.0054) \; (1.85)$$
(11)

Thus, the estimated relationship between the expected nominal return on stocks for month $t$ and our proxy for the expected inflation rate for month $t$ (the one month bill rate set at the end on month $t-1$) is

$$E(\tilde{s}_{vt}|B_{1t}) = 0.0234 - 5.5B_{1t}. \qquad (12)$$

If the return on a one month bill exceeds 0.0042, that is, 0.42 percent per month, eq. (12) assesses a negative expected nominal return on the portfolio of NYSE common stocks. During the twenty-three month period from January 1969 through November 1970, $B_{1t}$ was always greater than 0.0042, implying that expected nominal returns on NYSE stocks were negative during this period. For example, in Febuary 1970, $B_{1t}$ was 0.0063, which implies an expected nominal return on stocks of approximately $-1.17$ percent for this month.

While market efficiency does not rule out a negative relationship between expected returns on common stocks and expected inflation rates, it does rule out situations where risky assets (common stocks) have lower expected returns than less risky assets such as treasury bills or even cash. It is of some interest, then, to test more systematically the extent to which the negative relationship between interest rates and expected returns to common stocks can be used for profit. We examine the following trading strategy:

(a) Using thirty-six months of data starting in January 1953, estimate the regression of the return to the value-weighted portfolio of common stocks, $s_{vt}$, on the one month treasury bill rate, $B_{1t}$.

(b) Use the estimates of the regression parameters along with the interest rate on one month treasury bills observed at the end of the thirty-sixth month to assess $\hat{s}_{vt}$, the expected return on the common stock portfolio for the thirty-seventh month.

(c) If this prediction of the return on stocks is less than the treasury bill return, $\hat{s}_{vt} < B_{1t}$, buy the treasury bill in that month, so that the return on the strategy is $R_{pt} = B_{1t}$. Otherwise, buy the stock portfolio, so that $R_{pt} = s_{vt}$.

(d) Update the estimates of the stock return–interest rate relationship in step (a) by dropping the oldest month and adding the most recent month (always using the most recent three years' worth of data for estimation), and repeat steps (b) and (c).

The strategy is in operation for each month from January 1956 through December 1975. Note that since the treasury bill rate which is being used to predict stock returns for month $t$ is available at the beginning of the month, the strategy is of interest irrespective of one's attitude toward our proposition that the bill rate is a good proxy for the expected inflation rate.

Table 7 summarizes the returns on the strategy, $R_{pt}$, in comparison to the returns from a policy of buying and holding the portfolio of NYSE common stocks in each period, $s_{vt}$, and in comparison to the returns from holding a sequence of one month treasury bills, $B_{1t}$. In calculating $R_{pt}$, $s_{vt}$, and $B_{1t}$, there are no adjustments for transactions costs. Table 7 also summarizes the returns, $R_{pt}^*$, on the strategy under the assumption that a switch between bills and stocks involves a one percent cost.

In many ways the strategy of switching between stocks and bills seems to do well vis-à-vis the policy of buying and holding stocks. The standard deviations of the monthly returns to the strategy are lower than those from the stocks only policy, reflecting the fact that the variability of the returns on the switching strategy is low when bills are held. Ignoring transactions costs, the average return on the switching strategy for the overall period is 8.4 percent per year versus 7.1 percent for the stocks only policy. When the overall period is divided into three subperiods, the switching strategy provides higher average returns than the stocks only policy in two of the three comparisons. When four subperiods are examined, the switching strategy provides larger average returns in three of them.

However, other evidence in table 7 is less favorable to the strategy of switching between stocks and bills. When an adjustment is made for the higher transactions costs of the switching strategy, the comparison of average returns is reversed. The buy and hold policy then shows larger average returns than the switching strategy for the overall period and for most of the subperiods. Thus, the switching strategy does not seem to be a practical prescription for beating the market.

More interesting for understanding the economics of the pricing process is the statistical evidence in table 7 that, even when transactions costs are ignored, the switching strategy is not reliably better than the policy of buying and holding common stocks. The $t$-statistics for the differences between the average returns from buying and holding stocks and the average returns from switching between stocks and bills are never much different from zero. Even for the latest subperiods, when the switching strategy works best, the $t$-statistics are close to $-1.0$. In subperiods when the stocks only policy does better, the $t$-statistics for the average return differences are close to 1.0. For the overall period, the $t$-statistic on the difference between the average return to stocks and the average return to the switching strategy is $-0.54$.

These results are important. Regressions like (11) indicate that there is a reliable negative relationship between the level of the expected returns on common stocks and the level of the treasury bill rate. Equivalently, given that the coefficient of the interest rate in (11) is about three standard errors below zero, there is little doubt that the risk premium on stocks, the difference between the expected returns on stocks and bills, varies inversely with the interest rate. However, regressions like (11) explain little of the variance of stock returns ($R^2$ is only 0.03), which in turn means relatively large standard errors for the estimated regression coefficient of the interest rate. This shows up in the tests of

Table 7

Comparisons of returns to stocks ($s_{et}$), bills ($B_{1t}$), and an expected inflation trading strategy ($R_{pt}$).[a]

| Period | T | Average annualized percent returns | | | | Standard deviations of monthly returns | | | | Trading strategy switches | | $t(\bar{s}_e - R_p)$ |
|---|---|---|---|---|---|---|---|---|---|---|---|---|
| | | $\bar{s}_e$ | $R_p$ | $R_p{}^*$ | $\bar{B}_1$ | $S(s_e)$ | $S(R_p)$ | $S(R_p{}^*)$ | $S(B_1)$ | Number of months in bills | Number of switches | |
| 1/56–12/75 | 240 | 7.1 | 8.4 | 6.2 | 4.0 | 0.0407 | 0.0241 | 0.0243 | 0.0015 | 100 | 46 | −0.54 |
| 1/56–12/61 | 72 | 11.8 | 13.1 | 10.6 | 2.3 | 0.0328 | 0.0244 | 0.0250 | 0.0006 | 39 | 16 | −0.44 |
| 1/62–12/68 | 84 | 9.4 | 5.6 | 3.1 | 3.7 | 0.0355 | 0.0234 | 0.0239 | 0.0007 | 28 | 18 | 1.06 |
| 1/69–12/75 | 84 | 0.7 | 7.2 | 5.5 | 5.7 | 0.0503 | 0.0245 | 0.0242 | 0.0012 | 45 | 12 | −1.13 |
| 1/56–12/60 | 60 | 9.4 | 11.0 | 8.0 | 2.4 | 0.0338 | 0.0238 | 0.0243 | 0.0006 | 27 | 16 | −0.44 |
| 1/61–12/65 | 60 | 12.4 | 8.0 | 5.2 | 3.0 | 0.0341 | 0.0266 | 0.0255 | 0.0005 | 12 | 14 | 1.22 |
| 1/66– 7/71 | 67 | 4.6 | 6.4 | 4.9 | 5.0 | 0.0421 | 0.0229 | 0.0234 | 0.0009 | 30 | 7 | −0.35 |
| 8/71–12/75 | 53 | 1.6 | 8.7 | 6.9 | 5.7 | 0.0518 | 0.0241 | 0.0241 | 0.0014 | 27 | 8 | −0.94 |

[a] The standard deviations shown are for monthly continuously compounded returns. Average annualized percent returns are average continuously compounded monthly returns multiplied by 1200. The standard deviations used in calculating the $t$-statistics, $t(\bar{s}_e - R_p)$, are based on the time series of the difference $s_{et} - R_{pt}$.

the trading strategy which indicate that the regressions are not reliably identifying periods when the expected returns on stocks are less than the returns on bills.[4]

Thus, although there is good evidence that the expected risk premium on stocks varies inversely with the interest rate, the parameters of the relationship are not estimated with sufficient precision to allow reliable inferences that there are periods when the expected risk premium is negative. The reliable negative relationship between expected stock returns and the *ex ante* interest rate (which we like to interpret as a proxy for the expected inflation rate) remains an economic enigma, but we cannot as yet reliably conclude that it is evidence of a market inefficiency.

## 7. Effects of changes in the interest rate

### 7.1. Government bonds

The results in tables 5 and 6 indicate that the holding period returns to portfolios of government bonds are negatively related to the current unexpected inflation proxy. One possible explanation is that current unexpected inflation contains information about future expected inflation, which in turn affects future expected nominal returns on bonds. If there is an unanticipated rise in expected future inflation rates, current prices of bonds fall in order to raise future expected nominal returns. Moreover, the monthly expected inflation rate proxy, $B_{1t}$, follows a process somewhat like a random walk, so any change in the expected inflation rate is expected to persist.[5] Since long-term bonds have more future periods requiring adjustments in expected nominal returns, unanticipated changes in expected future inflation rates have a greater effect on the current *ex post* returns to longer-term bonds. Fama (1976a) provides a formal development of this argument and supporting empirical evidence.

Recalling that $B_{t+1}$ and $B_t$ are observed at the end of periods $t$ and $t-1$, respectively, the change in the treasury bill rate, $(B_{t+1} - B_t)$, measures the change in the expected inflation rate from $t-1$ to $t$ plus any change in the expected real return to bills. If the market uses more information than that contained in past

---

[4]We have also tested the strategy of switching between stocks and bills with different conventions concerning the number of preceding months used to generate the time series of estimates of the stock return–interest rate relationship. When compared with other options that were tried, the results in table 7, which are based on estimates from thirty-six months of preceding data, are relatively favorable to the switching strategy.

[5]The extrapolative time series model (a first-order moving average process for the first differences of the monthly inflation rate) used by Nelson (1976) and Nelson and Schwert (1977) to predict the monthly CPI inflation rate also implies that the expected inflation rate follows a random walk. Thus, any change in the expected inflation rate is permanent, and the change in the expected inflation rate is proportional to the current unexpected inflation rate.

Table 8

Effects of changes in expectations of inflation (standard errors in parentheses).

| Asset $R_{jt}$ | $\hat{a}_j$ | $\hat{\beta}_j$ | $\hat{\gamma}_j$ | $\hat{\delta}_j$ | $R^2$ | $S(\varepsilon_j)$ | $\rho_1(\varepsilon_j)$ | $\rho_2(\varepsilon_j)$ | $\rho_3(\varepsilon_j)$ |
|---|---|---|---|---|---|---|---|---|---|
| (A) Monthly data: 1/53–7/71, $T = 223$ | | | | | | | | | |
| $R_{jt} = \hat{a}_j + \hat{\beta}_j B_{1t} + \hat{\gamma}_j(\Delta_t - B_{\theta t}) + \hat{\delta}_j(B_{1t+1} - B_{1t}) + \varepsilon_{jt}$ | | | | | | | | | |
| $B_{2t}$ | 0.0003 (0.0001) | 1.03 (0.02) | 0.01 (0.01) | −0.40 (0.07) | 0.95 | 0.0003 | 0.33 | 0.19 | 0.20 |
| $B_{3t}$ | 0.0003 (0.0001) | 1.06 (0.03) | 0.01 (0.02) | −0.91 (0.11) | 0.89 | 0.0005 | 0.18 | 0.17 | 0.20 |
| $D_{1t}$ | 0.0006 (0.0006) | 0.94 (0.19) | −0.15 (0.13) | −5.94 (0.78) | 0.29 | 0.0037 | 0.04 | −0.04 | 0.03 |
| $D_{2t}$ | 0.0010 (0.0009) | 0.77 (0.31) | −0.22 (0.20) | −8.89 (1.23) | 0.22 | 0.0059 | −0.03 | 0.03 | 0.03 |
| $D_{3t}$ | 0.0011 (0.0011) | 0.62 (0.38) | −0.34 (0.25) | −10.76 (1.51) | 0.20 | 0.0072 | 0.02 | 0.03 | 0.04 |
| $D_{4t}$ | 0.0009 (0.0014) | 0.56 (0.46) | −0.45 (0.30) | −11.88 (1.85) | 0.16 | 0.0088 | 0.01 | 0.01 | 0.04 |
| $r_t$ | −0.0012 (0.0005) | 1.20 (0.17) | 0.32 (0.11) | 0.41 (0.67) | 0.20 | 0.0032 | 0.22 | 0.00 | −0.17 |
| $h_t$ | 0.0019 (0.0009) | 0.53 (0.31) | 0.17 (0.20) | 0.58 (1.25) | 0.00 | 0.0059 | 0.08 | 0.10 | −0.03 |
| $s_{vt}$ | 0.0243 (0.0055) | −6.03 (1.84) | −0.91 (1.21) | −17.70 (7.43) | 0.05 | 0.0352 | 0.08 | −0.04 | −0.03 |
| $s_{et}$ | 0.0249 (0.0064) | −6.21 (2.17) | −2.49 (1.43) | −17.54 (8.77) | 0.05 | 0.0416 | 0.15 | 0.05 | −0.05 |
| (B) Quarterly data: 1/53–6/71, $T = 74$ | | | | | | | | | |
| $R_{jt} = \hat{a}_j + \hat{\beta}_j B_{3t} + \hat{\gamma}_j(\Delta_t - B_{3t}) + \hat{\delta}_j(B_{3t+1} - B_{3t}) + \varepsilon_{jt}$ | | | | | | | | | |
| $D_{1t}$ | 0.0014 (0.0012) | 0.91 (0.12) | −0.18 (0.13) | −4.47 (0.32) | 0.81 | 0.0042 | −0.08 | −0.06 | −0.14 |
| $D_{2t}$ | 0.0023 (0.0021) | 0.74 (0.21) | −0.43 (0.22) | −7.16 (0.55) | 0.76 | 0.0070 | −0.08 | −0.19 | −0.14 |
| $D_{3t}$ | 0.0022 (0.0026) | 0.60 (0.27) | −0.74 (0.28) | −8.51 (0.69) | 0.73 | 0.0090 | 0.02 | −0.19 | −0.10 |
| $D_{4t}$ | 0.0018 (0.0034) | 0.54 (0.35) | −0.79 (0.36) | −9.66 (0.90) | 0.66 | 0.0116 | −0.04 | −0.22 | −0.05 |
| $r_t$ | −0.0039 (0.0019) | 1.20 (0.19) | 0.50 (0.20) | 0.80 (0.50) | 0.37 | 0.0064 | −0.16 | 0.09 | −0.03 |
| $h_t$ | 0.0031 (0.0031) | 0.59 (0.31) | −0.46 (0.33) | 1.95 (0.81) | 0.08 | 0.0105 | 0.05 | 0.13 | −0.18 |
| $s_{vt}$ | 0.0619 (0.0204) | −5.24 (2.07) | −3.75 (2.17) | −5.21 (5.38) | 0.08 | 0.0693 | 0.02 | −0.08 | −0.09 |
| $s_{et}$ | 0.0614 (0.0254) | −5.44 (2.57) | −6.00 (2.70) | −7.17 (6.68) | 0.09 | 0.0860 | 0.06 | −0.01 | −0.11 |

inflation rates to form expectations of future inflation rates, the change in the expected inflation rate which is incorporated in $(B_{t+1} - B_t)$ reflects more information than is in the current unexpected inflation rate. To test this hypothesis, estimates of

$$\tilde{R}_{jt} = \alpha_j + \beta_j B_t + \gamma_j (\varDelta_t - B_t) + \delta_j (B_{t+1} - B_t) + \tilde{\varepsilon}_{jt} \tag{13}$$

are presented in table 8. Note again that the proxy for the current unexpected inflation rate, $(\varDelta_t - B_t)$, is contemporaneous with $(B_{t+1} - B_t)$. Thus, if the market uses information beyond that contained in past inflation rates to form expectations of future inflation rates, we expect that $\gamma_j$ in (13) will be equal to zero and $\delta_j$ will be negative for assets such as government bonds and bills whose payoffs are fixed in nominal terms.

The estimates of (13) from monthly data, shown in part A of table 8, are consistent with the hypothesis that $\gamma_j$ is zero and $\delta_j$ is negative for bills and bonds. For these assets, none of the estimates of $\gamma_j$, the coefficient for the unexpected inflation proxy, is as much as two standard errors from zero; all of the estimates of $\delta_j$, the coefficient of the change in the one month treasury bill rate, are more than six standard errors below zero, and the estimates of $\delta_j$ become progressively more negative with increases in term to maturity.

The estimates of (13) from quarterly data, shown in part B of table 8, also produce significant negative estimates of $\delta_j$, which is now the coefficient of the change from one quarter to the next in the three month treasury bill rate, our proxy for the change in the quarterly expected inflation rate. For the quarterly returns on the bond portfolios, the estimates of $\delta_j$ are all more than ten standard errors below zero. The estimates of $\gamma_j$, the coefficient of the quarterly unexpected inflation proxy, are closer to zero in table 8 than in table 6, where the regression model does not include the change in the treasury bill rate, but the standard errors of $\hat{\gamma}_j$ are also smaller in table 8, so $\hat{\gamma}_j$ is still more than two standard errors from zero for the longer-term bond portfolio returns, $D_{3t}$ and $D_{4t}$.

In short, $(B_{t+1} - B_t)$, our proxy for the unanticipated change in the expected inflation rate from time $t-1$ to time $t$, shows strong negative relationships with the *ex post* returns to government bonds from $t-1$ to $t$, and the magnitude of the effect increases with term to maturity. The effect of our proxy for the unexpected inflation rate, $(\varDelta_t - B_t)$, on the *ex post* nominal returns to the bond portfolios is mitigated when the change in the treasury bill rate is included in the regression model, but the effect of the unexpected inflation proxy does not disappear. This could be due in part to variation in the expected real returns on bills which contaminates $(B_{t+1} - B_t)$ as a measure of the unanticipated change in the expected inflation rate and prevents the change in the interest rate from fully neutralizing the effects of the unexpected inflation proxy, $(\varDelta_t - B_t)$. Moreover, to the extent that there is predictability in the changes in the expected inflation rate, that is, if the expected inflation rate is not exactly a random walk, then there is additional error in $(B_{t+1} - B_t)$ as a measure of the unanticipated change in the expected inflation rate.[6]

### 7.2. Other assets

There is no reason to hypothesize that changes in the expected inflation rate from $t-1$ to $t$, as approximated by $(B_{t+1} - B_t)$, will have any specific effect on the *ex post* returns at time $t$ to assets whose future cash payoffs are not fixed in nominal terms. Since cash payoffs on such assets can adjust to reflect current expectations about inflation, expected real payoffs may be independent of the expected inflation rate, in which case $\delta_j$ in (13) is equal to zero.

In the tests on monthly data in table 8, the estimates of $\delta_j$ for the real estate return, $r_t$, and for labor income, $h_t$, are less than one standard error from zero. However, in the quarterly data both variables produce estimates of $\delta_j$ that are positive and fairly large relative to their standard errors. Since the $t$-statistic on $\delta_j$ in the regression for the quarterly real estate return is only 1.6, we are inclined to attribute most of the deviation of the coefficient from zero to chance. On the other hand, the $t$-statistic for $\delta_j$ in the quarterly labor income regression is in excess of 2.0. On a statistical basis, this is more impressive, but the result is nevertheless somewhat strange, given that the estimate of the coefficient of $B_{3t}$, 0.58, is somewhat less than 1.0. In other words, labor income for quarter $t$ seems to adjust in advance to changes in the three month expected inflation rate, $B_{3t+1} - B_{3t}$, while adjusting only partially to the expected inflation rate impounded in $B_{3t}$ at the beginning of the quarter. In short, the quarterly labor income regressions in table 8, like the earlier results for labor income, leave us with a confused picture of the qualities of human capital as a hedge against inflation.

Finally, the estimates of $\delta_j$ for monthly common stock returns in part A of table 8 are negative and more than two standard errors below zero. The point estimates indicate that an increase from the end of month $t-1$ to the end of month $t$ in the one month bill rate is associated with a lowering of common stock returns for month $t$ which is, on average, about seventeen times as large as the increase in the interest rate. Moreover, given that $B_{1t}$ behaves much like a random walk, and given that the expanded model in table 8 also produces negative estimated coefficients for the interest rate $B_{1t}$, an increase in the interest rate also reduces expected returns on stocks in the future since the higher level of $B_{1t+1}$ is expected to persist.

This extreme picture of the double effect of a change in the interest rate on stock returns is attenuated by the results for quarterly data in table 8 where the estimated coefficients for the change in the quarterly bill rate, $B_{3t+1} - B_{3t}$,

[6]Some evidence on the existence of these possible sources of contamination of $(B_{t+1} - B_t)$ as a measure of the change in the expected inflation rate is in Hess and Bicksler (1975), Fama (1976a, 1976c), and Nelson and Schwert (1977).

though still substantially negative, are not large relative to their substantial standard errors. However, as in earlier tables, the estimates of the regression coefficient for the unexpected inflation rate $\Delta_t - B_t$, though not always large relative to their standard errors, are consistently negative. On balance, we conclude that table 8 makes a net contribution to the overall impression that common stocks are, on several counts, rather perverse inflation hedges, at least in the period since 1953.

## 8. Implications for multiperiod models of market equilibrium

Our results provide some of the first empirical clues about how multiperiod considerations might cause equilibrium expected returns on assets to deviate from the predictions of the Sharpe (1964) – Lintner (1965) – Black (1972) models of market equilibrium. The regression results suggest that expected nominal returns on real estate, bonds, and bills vary directly with the level of the expected inflation rate (as proxied by the nominal interest rate), so that the expected real returns on these assets are unrelated to the expected inflation rate. On the other hand, expected nominal returns to common stocks are negatively related to the level of the expected inflation rate, which implies an even stronger negative relationship between the expected inflation rate and the expected real returns on stocks. Thus, the portfolio opportunity set facing investors changes through time in that the differences between the expected real returns on stocks and the expected real returns on other assets vary with the level of the nominal interest rate.

According to the analyses of Fama (1970), Merton (1973), Long (1974), and Fama and MacBeth (1974), changes through time in the portfolio opportunity set can become a problem for the Sharpe–Lintner–Black models when (i) there are relationships between asset returns realized at $t$ and the characteristics of the portfolio opportunity set that turns up at $t$, and (ii) these relationships differ across assets. When these two conditions are met, different assets do not provide equivalent hedges against changes in the opportunity set. Their differential properties as hedges can lead to differences among the expected returns on assets from $t-1$ and $t$ above and beyond the differences implied by the 'market risks' of the assets, whereas in the Sharpe–Lintner–Black models, market risk is the sole determinant of differences in expected returns.

In our tests, the key variable for changes in the portfolio opportunity set from $t-1$ to $t$ is the change in the interest rate, our proxy for the change in the level of the expected inflation rate, since this change seems to imply changes in the structure of expected real returns on assets from $t$ to $t+1$. The evidence in table 8 is that the nominal returns from $t-1$ to $t$ on common stocks and on government debt instruments are related to the change in the interest rate, and the relationships are not the same across assets. For example, the returns on the government debt instruments are progressively more sensitive to the change in the interest rate the longer is the term to maturity of the instrument. Thus, different assets seem to have different qualities as hedges against the changes in the portfolio opportunity set that are related to changes in the interest rate, which is the sort of thing that can give rise to differential expected returns on assets from $t-1$ to $t$ beyond those predicted by the simple versions of the Sharpe–Lintner–Black models.

## 9. Conclusions

### 9.1. Summary of results

The evidence suggests that, of all the assets examined, only private residential real estate is a complete hedge against both expected and unexpected inflation during the 1953–71 period. On average, the nominal real estate return moves in one-to-one correspondence with both the expected and unexpected components of the inflation rate, so that the *ex post* real return to real estate is unrelated to the *ex poste* inflation rate.

Government debt instruments, bonds and bills, are complete hedges against expected inflation. The expected nominal returns on these instruments vary directly with the expected inflation rate so that their expected real returns are unrelated to the expected inflation rate.

At least for time intervals up to six months in length, human capital is at best a partial hedge against expected and unexpected inflation. However, the estimates of the relationships between labor income and expected and unexpected inflation rates are consistent with such wide ranges of values for the coefficients that the regression results do not provide convincing evidence on the qualities of human capital as an inflation hedge. More qualitative evidence for longer subperiods, like that in table 3, suggests that labor income tends to move with the inflation rate, but even in these rough tests the correspondence is not always consistent across subperiods.

Common stock returns are negatively related to the expected inflation rate during the 1953–71 period. Although the results are less consistent, common stock returns also seem to be negatively related to the unexpected inflation rate and to changes in the expected inflation rate. Thus, contrary to long-held beliefs, but in line with accumulating empirical evidence, common stocks are rather perverse as hedges against inflation. However, little of the variation in stock returns is accounted for by their negative measured relationships with expected and unexpected inflation rates. Moreover, our attempts to construct trading rules based on the stock return–expected inflation rate relationship do not lead to the conclusion that expected returns on stocks have sometimes wandered so low during periods of high expected inflation as to be below treasury bill rates.

## 9.2. Relation to previous studies

Fama (1975, 1976a) documents the properties of treasury bills as hedges against expected inflation rates. This paper extends his analysis by examining longer-term bills as hedges against shorter-term expected inflation rates, by examing the ability of a succession of short-term bills to hedge against expected and unexpected inflation rates over longer holding periods, and by analyzing the effects of changes in expectations of future inflation rates on the holding period returns to longer-term bills.

The analysis of private residential real estate and of the Bildersee (1974) government bond portfolios as hedges against expected and unexpected inflation does not seem to have a precedent. In Fama and Schwert (1977a), we suggest that human capital might have been a hedge against inflation during the 1953–72 period, but the results reported here do not strongly support that conjecture.

The negative relationship observed between the returns to common stocks and expected inflation rates confirms and extends the evidence of Lintner (1975), Jaffe and Mandelker (1976), Body (1976), and Nelson (1976). This finding stands out even more in our work since the other assets that we examine are at least partial hedges against expected inflation. While the negative relationship of common stock returns with expected inflation rates does not account for a large portion of the variation in common stock returns, and although it does not seem to imply profitable trading rules, the existence of the relationship is nonetheless anomalous.

## References

Bildersee, John, 1974, Some new bond indexes extended and expanded results, Working Paper no. 2-74, Jan. (Rodney White Center for Financial Research, University of Pennsylvania, Philadelphia, PA).

Black, Fischer, 1972, Capital market equilibrium with restricted borrowing, Journal of Business 45, July, 444–455.

Body, Zvi, 1976, Common stocks as a hedge against inflation, Journal of Finance 31, May, 459–470.

Box, G.E.P. and G.M. Jenkins, 1976, Time series analysis, rev. ed. (Holden-Day, San Francisco, CA).

Fama, Eugene F., 1970, Multiperiod consumption–investment decisions, American Economic Review 60, March, 163–174.

Fama, Eugene F., 1975, Short-term interest rates as predictors of inflation, American Economic Review 65, June, 269–282.

Fama, Eugene F., 1976a, Inflation uncertainty and expected returns on treasury bills, Journal of Political Economy 84, June, 427–448.

Fama, Eugene F., 1976b, Foundations of finance (Basic Books, New York).

Fama, Eugene F., 1976c, Forward rates as predictors of future spot rates, Journal of Financial Economics 3, Oct., 362–377.

Fama, Eugene F. and James MacBeth, 1974, Tests of the multi-period two parameter model, Journal of Financial Economics 1, May, 43–66.

Fama, Eugene F. and G. William Schwert, 1977a, Human capital and capital market equilibrium, Journal of Financial Economics 4, Jan., 95–125.

Fama, Eugene F. and G. William Schwert, 1977b, Inflation, interest and relative prices, Working Paper no. 7720, May (Graduate School of Management, University of Rochester, Rochester, NY) forthcoming in the Journal of Business.

Fisher, Irving, 1930, The theory of interest (MacMillan, New York).

Hess, Patrick J. and James L. Bicksler, 1975, Capital asset prices versus time series models as predictors of inflation: The expected real rate of interest and market efficiency, Journal of Financial Economics 2, Dec., 341–360.

Jaffe, Jeffrey and Gershon Mandelker, 1976, The 'Fisher effect' for risky assets: An empirical investigation, Journal of Finance 31, May, 447–458.

Kessel, Reuben, 1956, Inflation-caused wealth redistribution: A test of a hypothesis, American Economic Review 46, March, 128–141.

Kessel, Reuben and Armen Alchian, 1960, The meaning and validity of the inflation-induced lag of wages behind prices, American Economic Review 50, March, 45–66.

Lintner, John, 1965, The valuation of risk assets and the selection of risky investments in stock portfolios and capital budgets, Review of Economics and Statistics 47, Feb., 13–37.

Lintner, John, 1975, Inflation and security returns, Journal of Finance 30, May, 259–280.

Long, John B., 1974, Stock prices, inflation and the term structure of interest rates, Journal of Financial Economics 1, July, 131–170.

Merton, Robert C., 1973, An intertemporal capital asset pricing model, Econometrica 41, Sept., 867–887.

Nelson, Charles R., 1976, Inflation and rates of return on common stocks, Journal of Finance 31, May, 471–483.

Nelson, Charles R. and G. William Schwert, 1977, On testing the hypothesis that the real rate of interest is constant, American Economic Review 67, June, 478–486.

Scholes, Myron and Joseph Williams, 1977, Estimating betas with nonsynchronous data, Working paper (University of Chicago, Chicago, IL) forthcoming in the Journal of Financial Economics.

Sharpe, William F., 1964, Capital asset prices: A theory of market equilibrium under conditions of risk, Journal of Finance 19, Sept., 425–442.

Theil, Henri, 1971, Principles of econometrics (Wiley, New York).

# THE INFORMATION IN FORWARD RATES
## Implications for Models of the Term Structure

### Robert F. STAMBAUGH*

*University of Chicago, Chicago, IL 60637, USA*

Received November 1986, final version received June 1987

Term-structure models from Cox, Ingersoll, and Ross (1985) imply that conditional expected discrete-period returns on discount instruments are linear functions of forward rates. Tests reject a single-latent-variable model of expected returns on U.S. Treasury bills, but two or three latent variables appear to describe expected returns on bills of all maturities. Expected returns estimated using two-latent-variables exhibit variation with business cycles similar to what Fama (1986) observes for forward rates. Inverted term structures precede recessions and upward-sloping structures precede recoveries.

## 1. Introduction

Empirical work in finance during the past ten years has devoted increased attention to variation through time in expected asset returns. Evidence produced by numerous studies, viewed collectively, indicates that returns on many types of assets can be predicted by a variety of variables observed ex ante.[1] A number of studies use variation in expected returns to make inferences about theories of the relative pricing of assets, e.g., Hansen and Singleton (1982, 1983), Hansen and Hodrick (1983), Gibbons and Ferson (1985), Campbell (1987), and Ferson, Kandel, and Stambaugh (1987). These studies illustrate that asset pricing theories often provide a richer set of empirical implications when expected returns are changing.

Forward rates for U.S. Treasury bills can reliably predict returns on bills of various maturities [e.g., Fama (1976, 1984a) and Startz (1982)]. For example,

*I thank Nai-fu Chen, Eugene Fama, Wayne Ferson, Campbell Harvey, Gur Huberman, Ravi Jagannathan, Krishna Ramaswamy, John Campbell (the referee), René Stulz (the editor), and participants in workshops at the University of Chicago, Duke University, University of Michigan, University of Minnesota, University of Pennsylvania, Vanderbilt University, and National Bureau of Economic Research for helpful discussions and comments. Financial support was provided by the Center for Research in Security Prices, and much of the research was conducted while the author was a Batterymarch Fellow.

[1]A partial list includes Fama and Schwert (1977), Hall (1981), Huizinga and Mishkin (1984), Keim and Stambaugh (1986), Campbell (1987), French, Schwert, and Stambaugh (1987), and Fama and French (1988).

Fama (1984a) regresses monthly bill returns in excess of the one-month rate on forward premiums (forward rates in excess of the one-month rate) and finds reliable predictive power for bills having maturities of two to six months, with up to 39% of the variance explained for two-month bills. Fama submits (p. 520) that 'the rich patterns of variation in expected returns uncovered here stand as challenges to be explained by more explicit models of market equilibrium'.

This study asks whether the information about expected Treasury bill returns in forward rates is consistent with various models of the term structure, primarily the one- and two-factor general equilibrium models developed by Cox, Ingersoll, and Ross (1985). The role of forward premiums as predictors of discrete-period excess returns is developed within the framework of Cox, Ingersoll, and Ross (hereafter CIR). Two convenient properties of the CIR models are exploited. First, the continuously compounded yield on a discount bond is a linear function of the relevant underlying state variables. Second, the dynamic processes of those state variables imply linear conditional expectations of future values given current values. Together these properties imply that forward premiums are linear predictors of excess returns. The likely effects of measurement error make the proposed investigation of expected returns more reasonable than an examination of other implications (such as perfect correlation of price changes in the one-factor model).

Restrictions on expected returns implied by the CIR models are tested using a multivariate latent-variable specification and the generalized method of moments (GMM) approach of Hansen (1982) and Hansen and Singleton (1982). The number of latent variables required to describe expected excess returns equals the number of state variables that enter the CIR pricing relation. A single-variable model of the term structure is rejected, but the evidence suggests that two, perhaps three, latent variables are sufficient to describe the expected excess returns on bills with maturities from two to twelve months.[2] This inference is obtained, however, only after steps are taken to avoid possible spurious effects due to measurement error. Tests on data more susceptible to problems of measurement error make it appear that the number of latent variables required to describe expected excess returns is no less than the number of maturities considered.

Fama (1986) concludes that although the term structure of expected returns on Treasury bills, as measured by the structure of forward rates, has been humped on average over the past 20 years, periods of upward-sloping term

---

[2]Brennan and Schwartz (1980,1982), using a different approach, conclude that there are probably three factors present in prices of U.S. and Canadian Government bonds of various maturities. Rather than examining expected returns, they examine the deviations between actual bond prices and bond prices implied by a specific model containing two state variables represented by the short rate and the consol rate. Brennan and Schwartz conclude that the correlation structure of these deviations across different bonds indicates the presence of a third factor.

structures tend to coincide with periods of economic expansion and periods of humps tend to surround recessions. This study finds that a two-latent-variable model also produces shifts in the term structure of expected returns that appear to be related to the business cycle. Specifically, downward-sloping term structures tend to precede peaks and upward-sloping structures tend to precede troughs. One interpretation of such behavior in expected returns, implied by a model proposed by Rubinstein (1974) and reconsidered by Breeden (1986), involves differences between variances of expected aggregate consumption at different dates in the future.

## 2. Conditional expected returns in the Cox–Ingersoll–Ross models

In addition to providing a framework for modeling the term structure of interest rates in a general equilibrium setting, CIR also develop several specific models as illustrations. Two of these models are particularly suited to analyzing expected returns in discrete time.

In the first model, production opportunities in the economy depend on a single state variable summarized by the equilibrium (instantaneous) rate of interest $r(t)$, which follows the process

$$dr = \kappa(\theta - r)\,dt + \sigma\sqrt{r}\,dz_1, \tag{1}$$

with $\kappa\theta \geq 0$ and $\sigma > 0$, and where $dz_1$ is the increment of a standard Wiener process.[3] Let $P(\tau, t)$ denote the price at time $t$ of a default-free discount bond with time to maturity $\tau$ and face value equal to unity, and define $p(\tau, t) \equiv \ln P(\tau, t)$. Then $p(\tau, t)$ is given by

$$p(\tau, t) = \alpha(\tau) + \beta(\tau)r(t), \tag{2}$$

where $\alpha(\tau)$ and $\beta(\tau)$ also depend on $\kappa, \theta, \sigma$, and a constant risk premium parameter, $\lambda$.[4]

The second model introduces a distinction between nominal and real values and assumes that the price level $\pi(t)$ follows the process

$$d\pi = y\pi\,dt + \sigma_\pi\pi\sqrt{y}\,dz_2, \tag{3}$$

and that the expected inflation rate $y(t)$ follows the process

$$dy = \kappa_2(\theta_2 - y)\,dt + \sigma_2\sqrt{y}\,dz_3, \tag{4}$$

---

[3]See Marsh and Rosenfeld (1983) and Oldfield and Rogalski (1987) for empirical investigations of the validity of the process in (1).

[4]See Cox, Ingersoll, and Ross (1985, pp. 390–394).

where $dz_2$ and $dz_3$ are increments of Wiener processes (assumed to be uncorrelated with $dz_1$) and $\mathrm{cov}(y, \pi) \equiv \rho \sigma_2 \sigma_\pi y \pi$. If $P(\tau, t)$ now represents the nominal price of a discount bond with maturity $\tau$ that is default-free in nominal terms, then $p(\tau, t)\ [= \ln P(\tau, t)]$ is given by

$$p(\tau, t) = \alpha^*(\tau) + \beta(\tau)r(t) + \delta(\tau)y(t), \qquad (5)$$

where $\beta(\tau)$ is the same as in (2) and $\alpha^*(\tau)$ and $\delta(\tau)$ also depend on $\kappa$, $\theta$, $\sigma$, $\lambda$, $\sigma_\pi$, $\kappa_2$, $\theta_2$, $\sigma_2$, and $\rho$.[5] [The real price of a bond that is default-free in real terms (an index bond) is still given by (2).]

A convenient characteristic of both (2) and (5) is that, for a given maturity, the relation between $p(\tau, t)$ and the state variables is linear with constant coefficients. Such a property might be conjectured for more general models. For example, Oldfield and Rogalski (1987) apply a no-arbitrage approach [e.g., Vasicek (1977) and Richard (1978)] to obtain relations of the general form

$$p(\tau, t) = a_0(\tau) + \sum_{i=1}^{K} a_i(\tau)x_i(t), \qquad (6)$$

where the $a$'s are constants for a given $\tau$ and the $x$'s are realizations of $K$ state variables (factors).[6] As those authors point out, however, obtaining such a relation through the no-arbitrage approach requires joint assumptions about the processes governing the factors as well as the risk 'prices' associated with the factors. In general, one cannot be sure that such assumptions are consistent with an underlying model of equilibrium.[7] This study entertains (6) as an empirical representation of the term structure but recognizes that, beyond the one- and two-factor CIR models in (2) and (5), theoretical support is tenuous.

The square root processes in (1) and (4) possess the convenient property that conditional expectations of the state variables are linear functions of their past realizations.[8] That is, if $x(t) \equiv [r(t)\ \ y(t)]'$, then

$$E\{x(t+1)|x(t)\} = d_1 + D_2 x(t), \qquad (7)$$

---

[5]See Cox, Ingersoll, and Ross (1985, pp. 401–404), where the process for $y$ is given by their 'Model 2'.

[6]Richard (1978) assumes the same dynamics as in (1), (3), and (4), and he obtains the pricing relation in (5) using the no-arbitrage approach. Richard also makes assumptions about the functional forms of the prices of risk, whereas Cox, Ingersoll, and Ross make an assumption about individuals' utility functions and derive such prices endogenously.

[7]See Cox, Ingersoll, and Ross (1985, pp. 397–398) for a discussion of this point.

[8]These properties are given by Cox, Ingersoll, and Ross (1985, p. 392). The bivariate relation in (7) follows immediately, given the assumed independence of $dz_1$ and $dz_3$ (and $D_2$ is in fact diagonal). The conditional distribution of $x(t+1)$ is bivariate noncentral chi-square [see Johnson and Kotz (1972, pp. 230–231)].

where $d_1$ and $D_2$ are constant. The deviations from these conditional means are heteroskedastic, however. In models with more than two factors, eq. (7) is assumed to describe conditional expectations of a $K \times 1$ vector of state variables, $x$. For other than the CIR models described above, such an assumption is not necessarily consistent with (6) as an equilibrium pricing relation. The remainder of this section shows that (7), when combined with the pricing equations represented generally by (6), implies that conditional expected excess returns over discrete periods are linear functions of forward premiums.

Let $H(\tau, t+1)$ denote the continuously compounded rate of return from $t$ to $t+1$ (one month) on a bill with $\tau$ months to maturity at $t$, and let $h(\tau, t+1)$ denote the return in excess of the one-month rate. That is,

$$h(\tau, t+1) = H(\tau, t+1) - H(1, t+1)$$

$$= p(\tau - 1, t+1) - p(\tau, t) + p(1, t) \qquad (8)$$

[noting that $p(0, t+1) = 0$]. Let $F(\tau, t)$ denote the forward rate for the month ending at $t + \tau$ observed at the end of month $t$, and define the forward premium $f(\tau, t)$ as the forward rate in excess of the one-month rate. That is,

$$f(\tau, t) = F(\tau, t) - H(1, t+1)$$

$$= p(\tau - 1, t) - p(\tau, t) + p(1, t). \qquad (9)$$

Let $h(t+1) \equiv [h(\tau_1^h, t+1), \ldots, h(\tau_N^h, t+1)]'$ denote an $N \times 1$ vector of excess returns, where the $N$ maturities are held constant for all $t$. Given (8) and the pricing relation in (6), $h(t+1)$ can be written as

$$h(t+1) = c_1 + C_2 x(t+1) + C_3 x(t), \qquad (10)$$

where $c_1$, $C_2$, and $C_3$ are constant. Let $f(t) \equiv [f(\tau_1^f, t), \ldots, f(\tau_M^f, t)]'$ denote an $M \times 1$ vector of forward premiums, where the $M$ maturities are held constant for all $t$ but may be different from the maturities used in constructing $h(t+1)$. Given (6) and (9), $f(t)$ can be written as

$$f(t) = g_1 + G_2 x(t), \qquad (11)$$

where $g_1$ and $G_2$ are constant. Assume $M \geq K$, where $K$ is the dimension of $x$ (number of state variables), and assume that $G_2$ has full column rank.[9] Then there exist $g_1^*$ and $G_2^*$ (not unique if $M > K$) such that

$$x(t) = g_1^* + G_2^* f(t). \qquad (12)$$

---

[9]The latter condition will hold in the CIR models.

Combining (7), (10), and (12) gives the result

$$E\{h(t+1)|f(t)\} = b_1 + B_2 f(t),$$  (13)

where

$$b_1 = c_1 + C_2 d_1 + [C_2 D_2 + C_3] g_1^*,$$  (14)

and

$$B_2 = [C_2 D_2 + C_3] G_2^*.$$  (15)

The $N \times M$ matrix $B_2$ in (13) has rank of at most $K$, the number of state variables, since $G_2^*$ in (15) has dimensions $K \times M$. In other words, at least $M - K$ of the forward premiums are redundant for determining conditional expected excess returns. The linear relation in (13), with the accompanying rank condition on $B_2$, serves as the primary focus of this study's empirical work.

## 3. Empirical considerations

The previous section discusses expectations of excess returns conditioned on forward premiums, but the selection of forward premiums as the conditioning variables is arbitrary. For example, the same models allow conditional expected excess returns to be stated as linear functions of yields to maturity. Forward premiums are selected primarily to provide a link to previous studies that document variation in expected excess returns on Treasury bills [Fama (1984a, 1986)].

The condition that the rank of $B_2$ in (13) is at most $K$ can be viewed as a restriction on the coefficient matrix in the multivariate regression,

$$h(t+1) = b_1 + B_2 f(t) + u(t+1), \qquad t = 1, \dots, T.$$  (16)

Tests of similar rank restrictions are discussed by Hansen and Hodrick (1983) and by Gibbons and Ferson (1985). [See also Campbell (1987).] To derive testable rank restrictions, those studies assume expectations conditioned on the set of information variables are linear with constant coefficients and the conditional betas of the underlying pricing relation are constant, although these assumptions are not necessarily part of the pricing theory being tested. The essential point of the previous section is that the CIR models imply such econometric restrictions.

Although the models of the term structure discussed above lead to apparently testable implications about the behavior of expected excess returns, a strict interpretation of these models produces less appealing implications. For example, the vector of yield changes should lie in a $K$-dimensional subspace (e.g., yield changes should be perfectly correlated across maturities in the one-factor model). Similarly, the covariance matrix of $u(t+1)$ in (16) should have rank of at most $K$. Such strong implications surely fail in the data, but rejecting the models on these grounds is probably unreasonable. Given the likely quotation errors, the averaging of bid and ask prices, and other imperfections in the price data, it seems reasonable to design statistical tests that allow for the presence of measurement error.

Although measurement error can render some of the strictest implications of the CIR models empirically uninteresting, the implications about expected returns can offer legitimate tests if one makes assumptions about the nature of the measurement errors. The approach here makes three assumptions. First, measurement errors in both $h(t+1)$ and $f(t)$ add noise to $u(t+1)$ sufficient to give the covariance matrix of $u(t+1)$ full rank. A specific distribution for the measurement errors is not assumed, and in general $u(t+1)$ remains non-normal and heteroskedastic.[10] Second, if $f(t)$ denotes the observed forward premiums and $f^*(t)$ denotes the true (unobservable) forward premiums, assume that

$$\mathrm{E}\{\, f^*(t)|f(t)\} = w_1 + W_2\, f(t), \tag{17}$$

where $w_1$ and $W_2$ are constant. Third, assume that the measurement errors in $h(t+1)$ are uncorrelated with $f(t)$. These assumptions preserve the original properties of (16), except that the disturbance covariance matrix becomes nonsingular. The rank of the coefficient matrix $B_2$ is still at most $K$. Thus, the relation between expected excess returns and forward rates can still be used to test the models. Satisfying the assumption that errors in $h(t+1)$ are uncorrelated with $f(t)$ requires some care in selecting the data used to construct excess returns and forward rates. As will be seen, inferences about the rank of $B_2$ are sensitive to violations of this assumption.

Since both the continuously compounded returns and forward premiums used here to investigate (16) are stated in excess of the one-month rate, the distinction between real and nominal values disappears insofar as measuring bill prices. The real/nominal distinction is important, however, in defining the characteristics of the bills being investigated. The bills used here are nominally default-free, as opposed to index bonds. Thus, for example, rejection of $K = 1$ would reject a one-factor CIR model in which a distinction between real and

---

[10]Another approach is to allow specific assumptions about the distribution of measurement errors to determine the stochastic specification of the econometric model. Brown and Dybvig (1986), in an investigation of the one-factor CIR model, assume that the measurement errors are normally and identically distributed and use this specification to obtain maximum likelihood estimates of the model's parameters.

nominal values is either not recognized or assumed to be unimportant. A rejection of $K = 1$ would not reject the same model if the real/nominal distinction is important. When inflation is appended to such a model in the manner described in the previous section, then the rank of $B_2$ equals two when the bills used are nominally default-free.[11]

The rank restriction on $B_2$ is not the only restriction on (16) imposed by a particular pricing model. For example, in the absence of measurement errors, the coefficients in (16) are functions (albeit complicated) of four parameters in the one-factor CIR model and of nine parameters in the two-factor CIR model. The introduction of additional unknown parameters to account for measurement errors, such as $w_1$ and $W_2$ in (17), further complicates the analysis, but imposing additional restrictions in (16) might prove to be an interesting direction for future work.

## 4. Data and empirical results

### 4.1. The unique role of the matched-maturity forward premium

The data set to be investigated first was constructed by Fama (1984a) using the U.S. Government Securities File of the Center for Research in Security Prices (CRSP) at the University of Chicago. This data set provides month-end prices of U.S. Treasury bills for each of six maturities from one to six months. The data begin in March 1959 and have been updated by CRSP through 1985. Each month, the bill with maturity closest to six months is selected. This bill is then followed to maturity, providing in subsequent months the prices for maturities of five months, four months, etc. The prices, which are averages of bid and ask quotations, are then used to compute both excess returns and forward premiums for each of five maturities from two to six months. Since there are both five excess returns ($N$) and five forward premiums ($M$), the coefficient matrix $B_2$ in (16) has dimensions $5 \times 5$.

Before proceeding directly to formal tests of the rank of the coefficient matrix $B_2$ in (16), a more descriptive examination of this hypothesis is presented. Fama (1984a) estimates, for each of five maturities, regressions of the form

$$h(\tau, t+1) = b_{1,\tau} + b_{2,\tau} f(\tau, t) + u(\tau, t+1). \tag{18}$$

In other words, the maturity used in computing the forward premium is the same as that used in computing the excess return. A useful starting point for this study is to ask whether the forward premium with the same maturity

---

[11]Gibbons and Ramaswamy (1986) use a different approach to test a model with inflation uncertainty where (2) prices an index bond.

Table 1

Correlations between excess returns and forward premiums on Treasury bills with maturities of two to six months, March 1959 to November 1985. $h(\tau, t+1)$ is the excess return on a bill with $\tau$ months to maturity at the end of month $t$, and $f(\tau, t)$ is the forward premium for month $t + \tau$ observed at the end of month $t$.

| Excess return $h(\tau, t+1)$ | Forward premium | | | | |
|---|---|---|---|---|---|
| | $f(2, t)$ | $f(3, t)$ | $f(4, t)$ | $f(5, t)$ | $f(6, t)$ |

*Panel A.* Forward premiums with matching maturities; the five maturities used to construct the forward rates are the same as those used to compute the excess returns (i.e., the same set of bills is used to compute both forward rates and excess returns).

| | | | | | |
|---|---|---|---|---|---|
| $h(2, t+1)$ | 0.48 | 0.30 | 0.29 | 0.32 | 0.19 |
| $h(3, t+1)$ | 0.29 | 0.34 | 0.27 | 0.28 | 0.21 |
| $h(4, t+1)$ | 0.20 | 0.26 | 0.32 | 0.19 | 0.16 |
| $h(5, t+1)$ | 0.19 | 0.23 | 0.29 | 0.31 | 0.19 |
| $h(6, t+1)$ | 0.16 | 0.19 | 0.25 | 0.28 | 0.26 |

*Panel B.* Forward premiums with nonmatching maturities; the forward-rate maturity is in each case about one week less than the maturity used to compute the excess return (i.e., a different set of bills is used to compute the forward rates).

| | | | | | |
|---|---|---|---|---|---|
| $h(2, t+1)$ | 0.25 | 0.25 | 0.26 | 0.28 | 0.14 |
| $h(3, t+1)$ | 0.17 | 0.26 | 0.30 | 0.26 | 0.19 |
| $h(4, t+1)$ | 0.07 | 0.18 | 0.29 | 0.17 | 0.12 |
| $h(5, t+1)$ | 0.11 | 0.18 | 0.30 | 0.27 | 0.20 |
| $h(6, t+1)$ | 0.12 | 0.15 | 0.29 | 0.27 | 0.20 |

contains more information, in terms of correlation, about the expected excess return than does a forward premium for another maturity. In the one-factor CIR model, for example, a single forward premium for any maturity is sufficient to capture all of the information in the current term structure. In that case, there would be no particular reason to select the forward premium whose maturity matches that of the excess return. We do observe, however, that forward premiums are not perfectly correlated across maturities; indeed, for the overall March 1959 to November 1978 period, the pairwise correlations among forward premiums for the five maturities range from only 0.49 to 0.66.

Panel A of table 1 displays the sample correlations between excess returns and forward premiums for all of the possible pairings. In virtually all cases, for the overall period and both subperiods, the correlation between the excess return for a given maturity and the forward premium for any of the five maturities is highest when the maturity of the forward premium matches that of the excess return. That is, the largest number in each row tends to lie on the diagonal. The only exceptions occur for $h(6, t+1)$ in the overall period and in the first subperiod, in which cases the correlation is highest for $f(5, t)$. All of the other cases suggest that the forward premium with the matching maturity possesses the greatest ability to forecast next month's excess return.

Table 2

Regressions of excess returns on forward premiums for Treasury bills with maturities of two to six months, March 1959 to November 1985. $h(\tau^h, t+1)$ is the excess return on a bill with $\tau^h$ months to maturity at the end of month $t$, and $f(\tau, t-s)$ is the forward rate for the one-month period ending at $t - s + \tau$. The $t$-statistics reflect comparisons of the coefficient estimates to zero and are computed using heteroskedasticity-consistent estimates of standard errors.

$$h(\tau^h, t+1) = b_1 + \sum_{\tau=2}^{6} b_\tau f(\tau, t-s) + u(t+1).$$

| Months to maturity $\tau^h$ | Estimated coefficients | | | | | | | | | | | | $R^2$ | $\rho_1(u)^b$ |
|---|---|---|---|---|---|---|---|---|---|---|---|---|---|---|
| | $\hat{b}_1{}^a$ | $\hat{b}_2$ | $\hat{b}_3$ | $\hat{b}_4$ | $\hat{b}_5$ | $\hat{b}_6$ | $t(\hat{b}_1)$ | $t(\hat{b}_2)$ | $t(\hat{b}_3)$ | $t(\hat{b}_4)$ | $t(\hat{b}_5)$ | $t(\hat{b}_6)$ | | |
| *Panel A.*   Forward premiums with matching maturities, not lagged ($s = 0$); the five values of $\tau^h$ match exactly the five values of $\tau$ | | | | | | | | | | | | | | |
| 2 | 0.17 | 0.58 | −0.04 | −0.00 | 0.10 | −0.05 | 2.43 | 4.70 | −0.34 | −0.01 | 1.49 | −0.75 | 0.236 | 0.14 |
| 3 | 0.11 | 0.15 | 0.46 | 0.04 | 0.18 | −0.04 | 0.89 | 0.75 | 2.49 | 0.22 | 1.48 | −0.29 | 0.134 | 0.13 |
| 4 | −0.04 | −0.10 | 0.33 | 0.80 | 0.03 | −0.05 | −0.23 | −0.33 | 1.19 | 2.99 | 0.16 | −0.27 | 0.107 | 0.12 |
| 5 | −0.12 | −0.24 | 0.06 | 0.73 | 0.70 | −0.03 | −0.51 | −0.61 | 0.17 | 2.16 | 2.99 | −0.11 | 0.118 | 0.14 |
| 6 | −0.30 | −0.32 | −0.23 | 0.71 | 0.62 | 0.52 | −1.06 | −0.66 | −0.53 | 1.80 | 2.27 | 1.49 | 0.106 | 0.13 |
| *Panel B.*   Forward premiums with nonmatching maturities, not lagged ($s = 0$); each value of $\tau$ is about one week less than a value of $\tau^h$ | | | | | | | | | | | | | | |
| 2 | 0.24 | 0.13 | 0.14 | 0.12 | 0.15 | −0.13 | 2.79 | 0.82 | 0.63 | 0.54 | 1.59 | −1.65 | 0.107 | 0.29 |
| 3 | 0.19 | −0.09 | 0.23 | 0.41 | 0.18 | −0.07 | 1.36 | −0.46 | 0.64 | 1.16 | 1.36 | −0.52 | 0.103 | 0.15 |
| 4 | 0.07 | −0.37 | 0.13 | 1.02 | 0.10 | −0.10 | 0.35 | −1.30 | 0.25 | 2.04 | 0.47 | −0.54 | 0.097 | 0.14 |
| 5 | −0.03 | −0.47 | −0.21 | 1.10 | 0.54 | 0.10 | −0.11 | −1.40 | −0.32 | 1.72 | 2.13 | 0.43 | 0.116 | 0.17 |
| 6 | −0.13 | −0.46 | −0.53 | 1.24 | 0.70 | 0.24 | −0.46 | −1.16 | −0.68 | 1.60 | 2.40 | 0.89 | 0.110 | 0.14 |
| *Panel C.*   Lagged forward premiums ($s = 1$); the same sets of bills are used to compute excess returns and forward premiums, but the forward premiums are lagged one month | | | | | | | | | | | | | | |
| 2 | 0.19 | 0.12 | 0.35 | −0.02 | −0.01 | −0.00 | 3.14 | 1.15 | 3.27 | −0.19 | −0.25 | −0.01 | 0.116 | 0.29 |
| 3 | 0.24 | −0.07 | 0.24 | 0.01 | 0.18 | 0.09 | 2.21 | −0.39 | 1.36 | 0.08 | 1.93 | 0.70 | 0.059 | 0.16 |
| 4 | 0.14 | −0.33 | 0.30 | 0.10 | 0.39 | −0.00 | 0.90 | −1.15 | 1.17 | 0.41 | 2.79 | −0.00 | 0.045 | 0.12 |
| 5 | 0.16 | −0.55 | 0.36 | 0.04 | 0.48 | 0.28 | 0.76 | −1.28 | 0.97 | 0.11 | 2.58 | 1.08 | 0.058 | 0.15 |
| 6 | 0.18 | −0.70 | 0.39 | −0.18 | 0.69 | 0.30 | 0.68 | −1.34 | 0.93 | −0.45 | 2.73 | 0.97 | 0.052 | 0.11 |

[a]The numbers in this column are multiplied by 1,000.

[b]$\rho_1(u)$ is the estimated first-order autocorrelation of the residuals.

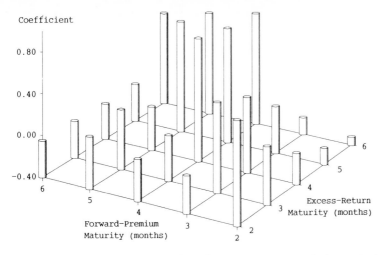

Fig. 1. Plot of coefficients estimated in regressions of excess returns on matched-maturity forward premiums of Treasury bills with maturities of two to six months, March 1959 to November 1985.

Perhaps a more striking illustration of the above phenomenon occurs when the excess return for each maturity is regressed simultaneously on the five forward premiums. Panel A of table 2 reports results of the regression

$$h(\tau^h, t+1) = b_1 + \sum_{\tau=2}^{6} b_\tau f(\tau, t) + u(t+1), \qquad (19)$$

for $\tau^h = 2, \ldots, 6$. With few exceptions, the coefficient on the forward premium for month $t + \tau^h$ is more than two standard errors above zero, but the coefficients for the other forward premiums are not reliably different from zero. [The $t$-statistics reported are based on heteroskedasticity-consistent estimates of the standard errors. See White (1980) and Hsieh (1983).] Fig. 1 plots the estimated coefficients on the five forward premiums for each of the five excess-return regressions in the overall period. The pattern of larger coefficients for the matched-maturity forward premiums is illustrated by the taller symbols on the diagonal of the grid, although adjacent values are also large in the regressions with excess returns of maturities five and six.

### 4.2. Possible explanations and alternative sets of forward premiums

The dominant contribution of the matched-maturity forward premium in the above results might be viewed as casual evidence against the one-factor CIR model of the term structure. As noted earlier, that model assigns no unique role to the matched-maturity premium – any other maturity should serve as well. In contrast, fig. 1 suggests that each of the forward premiums plays a unique role in predicting one of the excess returns, and this observation is confirmed more formally in the latent-variable tests presented below. One could argue that such results are consistent with a model in which a larger number of state variables are important for pricing. If each of the state variables is highly autocorrelated, then the matched-maturity forward premium is likely to have the greatest predictive ability. If $x_i(t)$ is approximately equal to the conditional expectation of $x_i(t+1)$, then the right-hand side of (6) gives a good approximation to the expected value of $p(\tau-1, t+1)$. In that case, comparing (8) and (9) reveals that the conditional expectation of $h(\tau, t+1)$ is approximately $f(\tau, t)$, since the conditional expectation of $p(\tau-1, t+1)$ is approximately $p(\tau-1, t)$. Forward premiums for other maturities do not possess this property. Thus, with a large number of highly autocorrelated state variables, the matched-maturity forward premium could play a unique role in predicting the excess return.

There is, however, a second possible explanation for these empirical regularities. From (8) and (9), observe that both $h(\tau, t+1)$ and $f(\tau, t)$ contain the (log) prices $p(\tau, t)$ and $p(1, t)$. As Fama (1984a) notes, measurement errors in these prices can produce spurious, self-fulfilling components of predicted excess returns. This possibility is investigated here by constructing an alternative set of forward premiums using bills different from those used to compute excess returns. Although the measurement errors in two disjoint sets of bill prices are not necessarily independent, this approach might provide some information about which, if either, of the above two explanations is more likely.

As explained above, Fama selects each month the bill with maturity closest to six months. An alternative set of bills is formed here by instead selecting each month the bill that matures immediately before the original bill selected by Fama. In most cases, the alternative bill has one week less until maturity than the original bill. As in the original data set, the bill selected is used in subsequent months to provide prices for successively lower maturities. When last used, the bill's maturity is approximately three weeks. The alternative set of bills generated by this procedure is used to compute forward rates for maturities from one to six months (less one week in each case); forward premiums for maturities two through six are computed as the forward rates minus the three-week rate.[12] These alternative forward premiums are hereafter referred to as those with nonmatching maturities, as opposed to the original set with matching maturities, in which the maturity of each forward premium matches the maturity of a bill used to compute excess returns.

---

[12]As in Fama's original data, all rates are standardized by multiplying the continuously compounded daily rates by 30.4.

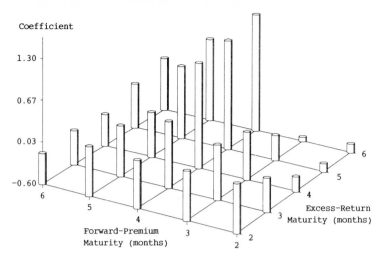

Fig. 2. Plot of coefficients estimated in regressions of excess returns on nonmatched-maturity forward premiums of Treasury bills with maturities of two to six months, March 1959 to November 1985.

Panel B of table 1 contains the estimated correlations between the excess returns and the set of nonmatching forward premiums. Unlike what we observe with the original data in panel A, the diagonal elements in panel B show little if any tendency to be the largest in a given row. Although many of the correlations in panel B are slightly lower than their counterparts in panel A, the differences are largest for the diagonal elements.

Panel B of table 2 reports results of regression (19) using the nonmatching forward premiums. The same decrease in the importance of the diagonal elements is evident in the regression coefficients. Fig. 2 plots the regression coefficients for the overall period, and the contrast with fig. 1 is clear. The forward premium whose maturity is closest to that of the excess return does not, in general, appear to play a special role in predicting the excess return. In fact, the coefficient on the forward premium for four months (less one week) tends to be large in all of the regressions.

The differences between the results in tables 2 and 3 are somewhat inconsistent with the first explanation offered above, wherein a large number of autocorrelated state variables enter as in (6). In that scenario, one might expect the close-maturity (one-week difference) forward premium to be a reasonably good substitute for the matched-maturity forward premium, so that the close-maturity forward premium would still make the dominant contribution in the multiple regression. On the other hand, the difference in the results produced by the two data sets is consistent with the presence of measurement error that is uncorrelated across different bills. If the measurement error in

Table 3

Chi-square statistic for tests of the number of latent variables in expected excess returns of Treasury bills with maturities up to six months, March 1959 to November 1985. The tests use the generalized method of moments with excess returns for monthly maturities $2, 3, \ldots, 6$ as dependent variables and with forward premiums for maturities $2, 3, \ldots, 6$ as instruments (in addition to a constant). Heteroskedasticity is allowed, but the disturbances are assumed serially uncorrelated. The chi-square statistic tests the overidentifying restrictions implied by the latent-variable specification. The $p$-value (in parentheses) is the probability under the null hypothesis that the test statistic would exceed the reported value.

| Dates | Latent variables (degrees of freedom) | | | |
|---|---|---|---|---|
| | 1 (16) | 2 (9) | 3 (4) | 4 (1) |
| *Panel A.* Forward premiums with matching maturities as instruments | | | | |
| 3/1959–11/1985 | 66.28 (0.000) | 53.69 (0.000) | 31.22 (0.000) | 8.73 (0.003) |
| 3/1959–7/1972 | 53.62 (0.000) | 33.37 (0.001) | 24.36 (0.000) | 10.59 (0.001) |
| 8/1972–11/1985 | 38.70 (0.001) | 29.62 (0.001) | 17.57 (0.001) | 5.01 (0.025) |
| 3/1959–8/1979 | 67.38 (0.000) | 53.31 (0.000) | 34.77 (0.000) | 10.65 (0.001) |
| *Panel B.* Forward premiums with nonmatching maturities as instruments | | | | |
| 3/1959–11/1985 | 47.66 (0.000) | 23.55 (0.005) | 6.41 (0.171) | 1.06 (0.303) |
| 3/1959–7/1972 | 37.35 (0.002) | 20.99 (0.013) | 9.52 (0.049) | 2.16 (0.142) |
| 8/1972–11/1985 | 31.89 (0.010) | 17.54 (0.041) | 2.55 (0.636) | 0.08 (0.782) |
| 3/1959–8/1979 | 49.42 (0.000) | 27.60 (0.001) | 15.17 (0.004) | 6.51 (0.011) |
| *Panel C.* Lagged forward premiums as instruments | | | | |
| 4/1959–11/1985 | 38.02 (0.002) | 18.57 (0.029) | 7.38 (0.117) | 2.62 (0.105) |
| 4/1959–7/1972 | 26.33 (0.050) | 9.49 (0.394) | 3.87 (0.424) | 0.00 (0.975) |
| 8/1972–11/1985 | 21.77 (0.151) | 8.44 (0.491) | 3.43 (0.488) | 0.26 (0.611) |
| 4/1959–8/1979 | 22.45 (0.129) | 12.74 (0.692) | 1.70 (0.790) | 0.18 (0.676) |

$p(\tau, t)$ [cf. (8) and (9)] is uncorrelated with errors in prices of other bills, then the errors in the nonmatched forward premiums are uncorrelated with the errors in the excess returns. In that case, the close-maturity forward premium need not play a unique role in a model with, for example, one state variable, whereas the matched-maturity premium would appear to make a unique contribution because of the correlation between its measurement error and the measurement error in the excess return. The latent-variable tests presented below in section 4.3 produce different inferences depending on the set of forward premiums used as instruments to predict excess returns. Whether measurement errors of plausible magnitudes can account for these differences is discussed in section 4.4.

Another approach to the measurement error problem is to use lagged values of the forward premiums, so that the prices used to compute the forward premiums are observed before any of the prices used to compute the excess returns. The linearity of the conditional means in (7) also holds for lagged values. That is, $E\{x(t+1)|x(t-s)\}$ is linear in $x(t-s)$ for $s > 0$. Therefore, the linearity of (13) and the accompanying rank restriction on the coefficient matrix $\boldsymbol{B}_2$ also obtain with $\boldsymbol{f}(t-s)$ in place of $\boldsymbol{f}(t)$ (although the values of the coefficients will in general be different). Panel C of table 2 reports the results of regressions using the excess returns and forward premiums from the original set of bills but with the forward premiums lagged one month. In general, these regressions explain less variance than in the previous cases. Nevertheless, for each equation the hypothesis that the coefficients on the forward premiums jointly equal zero can be rejected at conventional significance levels. The patterns of the estimated coefficients do not suggest the strong linear independence that is evident in the results with the nonlagged forward premiums in panel A. This set of lagged forward premiums, as well as the two sets of nonlagged forward premiums, is used below in formal tests of this linear independence.

### 4.3. Tests of the number of latent variables in expected returns

As shown earlier, the pricing models discussed in section 2 imply that the $N \times M$ coefficient matrix $\boldsymbol{B}_2$ in (16) has rank $K$, where $N$ is the number of assets and $K$ is the number of state variables in the pricing relation. Assume that the first $K$ rows of $\boldsymbol{B}_2$ are linearly independent. That is, the first $K$ equations relate expected excess returns on a set of $K$ 'reference assets' to $\boldsymbol{f}(t)$, the vector of forward premiums.[13] Then the matrix $\boldsymbol{B}_2$, given that it has rank $K$, can be written as

$$\boldsymbol{B}_2 = \begin{bmatrix} \boldsymbol{L} \\ \boldsymbol{QL} \end{bmatrix}, \tag{20}$$

where $\boldsymbol{L}$ is a $K \times M$ matrix of rank $K$ and $\boldsymbol{Q}$ is $(N-K) \times K$. In other words, the last $N-K$ rows of $\boldsymbol{B}_2$ are linear combinations of the first $K$ rows.

---

[13] In this application, the reference assets are chosen to have nonadjacent maturities.

The restriction in (20) is tested using the generalized method of moments [Hansen (1982)], which exploits the condition that the disturbance vector $u(t+1)$ in (16) must be orthogonal to a vector of instruments. The instruments are the variables used to form conditional expectations at time $t$. Given the representation of conditional expectations in (13), the instruments in this case consist of a constant plus the $M$ forward premiums, thus yielding $N \cdot (M+1)$ orthogonality conditions. Hansen (1982) provides a test statistic that is distributed in large samples as $\chi^2$ if a set of overidentifying restrictions holds. The degrees of freedom equal the number of orthogonality conditions minus the number of parameters estimated, and for the restrictions in (20) the degrees of freedom equal $(N-K) \cdot (M-K)$. With five assets ($N=5$) and five forward premiums ($M=5$), the degrees of freedom equal $(5-K)^2$.

Given the processes assumed for the state variables [(1) and (4)], the disturbance vector $u(t+1)$ is nonnormal and heteroskedastic. As applied here, the GMM approach allows such behavior, although the disturbances are assumed to be serially uncorrelated. Campbell (1987) applies this same test to different data, and Hansen and Hodrick (1983) use the GMM approach to test a similar restriction assuming serially correlated but homoskedastic disturbances. Gibbons and Ferson (1985) test a similar restriction using a likelihood ratio test, where the disturbances are assumed to obey the conditions of the standard normal regression model. The null hypotheses tested in the latter two studies include restrictions in addition to those represented in (20). Hansen and Hodrick test whether the rank of $[b_1 \ B_2]$ equals $K$, where $K=1$ in their case.[14] Gibbons and Ferson test whether

$$[b_1 \ B_2] = \begin{bmatrix} L^* \\ Q^*L^* \end{bmatrix} \quad \text{and} \quad Q^*1_{(K+1)} = 1_{N-(K+1)}, \tag{21}$$

where $L^*$ is a $(K+1) \times M$ matrix of rank $K+1$, $1_p$ denotes a $p$-vector of ones, and the dependent variables are raw returns rather than excess returns. These additional restrictions involving the intercept vector $b_1$ arise from assuming that a pricing relation with $K$ betas holds for expected discrete-period returns. The models of the term structure considered here restrict the rank of $B_2$, but the intercept restrictions included in (21) are not implied for discrete-period returns.[15]

Tests are conducted for the overall period from March 1959 through November 1985 as well as for three subperiods. The first two subperiods are simply the first and second halves of the overall period, and the remaining

---

[14]Campbell reports results both with and without this additional restriction.

[15]These restrictions would be appropriate, however, for expected instantaneous rates of return.

subperiod runs from March 1959 through August 1979.[16] This last subperiod is chosen to exclude the period beginning in October 1979, when the Federal Reserve announced a change in operating procedure. Some researchers argue that the interest-rate process experienced structural shifts associated with this event.[17]

Panel A of table 3 reports the chi-square statistics and the associated *p*-values for tests of one, two, three, and four latent variables in expected returns, where the original forward premiums with matching maturities are used as instruments. The first three hypotheses ($K = 1, 2, 3$) are rejected strongly, with *p*-values of 0.001 or less in the overall period and in both subperiods. The hypothesis $K = 4$, which restricts only one parameter, also produces *p*-values of 0.003 or less in all but the August 1972 to November 1985 subperiod, where the *p*-value is 0.025. In general, these results suggest that the number of latent variables required to describe expected excess returns is no less than the number of assets considered (five). In other words, these tests indicate that the five rows of $B_2$, whose estimated values are plotted in fig. 1, are linearly independent.

Panel B of table 3 reports the same tests as conducted in table 2, except that the alternative nonmatched-maturity forward premiums are used as instruments. The hypotheses $K = 3$ and $K = 4$ generally are not rejected at conventional significance levels. Exceptions occur in the March 1959 to August 1979 subperiod, where the *p* values are 0.004 and 0.011 for tests of $K = 3$ and $K = 4$. The hypothesis $K = 2$ produces *p*-values of 0.013 and 0.041 in the two equal-length subperiods, but the *p*-values are 0.005 and 0.001 in the overall period and the March 1959 to August 1979 subperiod. Whether one views these results as supporting $K = 2$ may depend in part on how strongly one maintains the assumption that the parameters underlying the maturity-dependent coefficients in the pricing relations [e.g., (2) and (5)] remain constant over the longer sample periods. It seems reasonable to conclude that evidence against $K = 2$ is, at best, mixed. The evidence against $K = 1$ remains strong, although the *p*-value in the second subperiod is 0.010.

Panel C of table 3 reports results of the same tests using forward premiums lagged one month. For a given hypothesis, the *p*-value in panel C generally exceeds the *p*-value in panel B. The hypotheses $K = 1$ and $K = 2$ produce *p*-values of 0.002 and 0.029 in the overall period, but all other *p*-values exceed conventional significance levels. In considering these results, however, the reader should bear in mind that the $R^2$s are also typically smaller in the regressions of excess returns on lagged forward premiums (cf. panel C of table

---

[16]Recall that, in the notation used here, the observation for $t = 8/79$ corresponds to the excess return during 9/79 [cf. eq. (16)].

[17]See, for example, Huizinga and Mishkin (1984) and Huizinga and Leiderman (1985).

2). Thus, the power to reject higher values of $K$ might be less than in the previous cases.

Inferences about the number of latent variables in expected excess returns differ sharply depending on whether the maturities of the forward premiums used as instruments match the maturities of the excess returns. With the first set of matching-maturity forward premiums, the tests reject the hypothesis that the number of latent variables required is less than five, the number of assets considered. Using the nonmatching set, the tests suggest that the number of latent variables required to describe expected returns on bills with maturities up to six months equals two, possibly three. These differences in the results for the latent-variable tests confirm the differences in the patterns of the regression coefficients observed in the previous section. Again, the greater number of latent variables apparently required with the matching-maturity forward premiums could reflect asset-specific measurement errors.

### 4.4. A closer look at the effects of measurement error

An obvious question raised by the previous discussion is whether measurement errors with plausible characteristics can account for the differences in results. Although it is difficult to specify the precise nature of the measurement errors, a rough feel for reasonable magnitudes might be gained by examining bid–ask spreads. The pricing models discussed earlier pertain to a single equilibrium price and do not include a framework in which to handle separate bid and ask prices. The price data used here are constructed by averaging bid and ask quotations. Suppose that the equilibrium price that is appropriate for the pricing model lies somewhere within the quoted bid–ask range but is not necessarily the average. It would be useful to know whether such measurement errors would be sufficient to affect inferences about the number of latent variables.

Let $P(\tau, t)$ denote the average of the bid and ask prices, which is used here as the observed price (with $\tau$ and $t$ as defined earlier). Let $P^*(\tau, t)$ denote the true equilibrium price, and let $P^b(\tau, t)$ and $P^a(\tau, t)$ denote the bid and ask prices. As before, lower case letters denote logs of these prices. Define the relative pricing error and the relative bid–ask spread:

$$\eta(\tau, t) \equiv p(\tau, t) - p^*(\tau, t), \tag{22}$$

$$s(\tau, t) \equiv p^a(\tau, t) + p^b(\tau, t). \tag{23}$$

For each of maturities two through six, $s(\tau, t)$ was computed each month using the reported bid and ask prices of the bills in the original (Fama's) data set. For maturities two through six, the average values of $s(\tau, t)$ are 0.00027, 0.00023, 0.00041, 0.00047, and 0.00041. Given these magnitudes, the arithmetic average of the bid and ask prices is very close to the geometric average. That is, $p(\tau, t)$ is well approximated by

$$p(\tau, t) = p^b(\tau, t) + 0.5s(\tau, t). \tag{24}$$

Assume that the true price is given by

$$p^*(\tau, t) = p^b(\tau, t) + \nu(\tau, t)s(\tau, t), \tag{25}$$

where $\nu(\tau, t)$ is distributed uniformly on the interval $[0, 1]$ and independently across $\tau$ and $t$. This essentially amounts to an assumption that the true price is distributed uniformly over the bid–ask interval and that measurement errors are independent across bills. Combining (22), (24), and (25) gives

$$\eta(\tau, t) = [0.5 - \nu(\tau, t)]s(\tau, t). \tag{26}$$

Note that the excess return on the $\tau$-maturity bill, $h(\tau, t + 1)$, and the forward premium with the matched maturity, $f(\tau, t + 1)$, both contain the error $\eta(\tau, t)$ [cf. eqs. (8) and (9)].[18] It is easily verified that

$$\operatorname{var}\{\eta(\tau, t)\} = \tfrac{1}{12}\mathrm{E}\{[s(\tau, t)]^2\}. \tag{27}$$

Based on sample means of $s(\tau, t)^2$, the values of (27) for maturities two through six (times $10^7$) are 0.103, 0.075, 0.196, 0.278, and 0.253. The variances of the monthly excess returns for the same maturities (times $10^7$) are 5.19, 14.42, 30.85, 53.38, and 79.62. The variances of the forward premiums (times $10^7$) are 3.35, 3.60, 3.47, 6.34, and 6.85. Thus, the variances of the errors are 6% or less of the variances of the forward premiums and much less than the variances of the excess returns.

To investigate whether errors of this nature could affect the latent-variable tests in the manner suggested earlier, the following experiment was performed. For each month and maturity, the relative spread $s(\tau, t)$ was combined with a uniform random number $\nu(\tau, t)$, using (26), to produce an error $\eta(\tau, t)$. These errors were then added to the excess returns for maturities two through six and to the corresponding forward premiums constructed from the alternative (nonmatching) set of bills. Latent-variable tests of $K = 3$ and $K = 4$ were then conducted for the overall 1959–1985 period using these new excess returns and forward premiums.

The above procedure was repeated ten times. For the tests of $K = 3$, the $p$-values range from 0.008 to 0.040 and average 0.019 across the ten trials.

---

[18]In addition, the excess return contains $\eta(\tau - 1, t + 1)$ and the forward premium contains $\eta(\tau, t)$. Both quantities also contain $\eta(1, t)$, but this same error is present in forward premiums for all maturities and therefore should not induce a maturity-specific contribution.

Recall that, without the additional generated errors, the same data produce a $p$-value of 0.171 for the hypothesis $K = 3$ (table 4, panel B). The tests of $K = 4$ produce $p$-values that range from 0.007 to 0.066 and average 0.039 across the ten trials with the additional generated errors. Again, recall that a test of $K = 4$ using the same data, but without the added errors, produces a $p$-value of 0.303.

The above experiments suggest that errors induced by fluctuations of true prices within the bid–ask range are sufficient to produce rejections of hypotheses that would otherwise not be rejected. Indeed, it appears that one would be led to the same inference obtained with the original set of matched-maturity data – that there are as many latent variables as maturities. The errors modeled include no errors in the bid and ask quotations themselves, and thus seem to represent a fairly conservative specification of the magnitudes of possible measurement errors.[19]

### 4.5. Results for bills with longer maturities

This section extends the previous analysis of expected excess returns on bills with maturities up to six months to bills with maturities from seven to twelve months. Returns and forward rates for the longer-maturity bills are taken from a data set constructed by Fama (1984b) and updated by CRSP. The file is constructed like the data set described in section 4.1. Each month the bill with maturity closest to twelve months is selected; this bill provides the prices for maturities eleven through seven in subsequent months. The data cover the period December 1963 through November 1985.[20]

The longer maturities are analyzed separately here because the data available for maturities seven through twelve differ from the data for the shorter maturities in an important way. Since one-year bills are issued only once a month, the longer-maturity data set already uses all outstanding bills with maturities greater than six months. Thus, unlike for the shorter maturities, an alternative set of forward premiums with nonmatching maturities cannot be constructed for maturities seven through twelve.

Regressions of excess returns on forward premiums for maturities seven through twelve produce patterns similar to those reported earlier for the matching-maturity forward premiums with the shorter maturities: the coeffi-

---

[19] The experiments reported probably understate somewhat the effect of errors limited to the kind specified in (26). In the above framework, the excess returns and forward premiums to which the generated errors are added already contain (uncorrelated) errors of similar magnitudes. Thus, the relative increases in explanatory power produced by adding the matching errors would be less than if the other errors were absent.

[20] There are 14 months during this period in which data for one or more of the longer maturities are unavailable. These months are omitted in the subsequent tests.

cient on the forward premium whose maturity matches that of the excess return tends to be large. Given the strong possibility that measurement error is the source of these patterns, forward premiums for the longer maturities are not attractive instruments for the latent-variable tests. Nevertheless, the excess returns on these longer maturities can be used with the previous set of instruments to investigate the number of latent variables necessary to describe expected excess returns on a wider array of maturities.

Panel A of table 4 reports results of the latent-variables tests using excess returns for maturities two through twelve. The instruments used are the nonmatching-maturity forward premiums for maturities two through six, the same instruments used in panel B of table 3. In general, the *p*-value for a given hypothesis is larger for the eleven-asset case (table 4, panel A) than for the five-asset case (table 3, panel B). Indeed, even the *p*-values for a model with two latent variables are 0.11 or more, whereas they ranged from 0.001 to 0.041 in panel B of table 3. Thus, if a hypothesis is not rejected at a given significance level using excess returns on five maturities, that hypothesis is not rejected using eleven maturities.

The increases in *p*-values obtained with the larger set of maturities should probably not lead one to accept hypotheses that would have been rejected using fewer maturities. The tests using the larger set of maturities use a somewhat smaller sample, in both total number of time-series observations and the number of observations per estimated parameter. Differences in finite-sample behavior of the test statistic could account for the larger *p*-values. For example, the Monte Carlo results of Tauchen (1985) suggest, in a different application, that the GMM chi-square test of overidentifying restrictions shows a slight tendency to accept the null hypothesis too often in smaller samples. It seems reasonable to conclude that increasing the number of maturities considered does not increase the number of latent variables that are required to describe expected excess returns.

As discussed above, the forward premiums for the longer maturities are less attractive as instruments because of the potential problems arising from common measurement errors in matching-maturity forward premiums and excess returns. The longer-maturity forward premiums, however, may contain true information about expected excess returns that is not captured by shorter-maturity forward premiums. As a partial check of the latter possibility, part B of table 4 reports latent-variable tests where the nine-month forward premium is added to the set of instruments and the nine-month excess return is excluded (to eliminate the matching-maturity problem). In multiple regressions of the longer-maturity excess returns on the longer-maturity forward premiums, the nine-month forward premium appears to contain significant explanatory power for all maturities, whereas the other forward premiums tend to contribute reliably only in predicting the matched-maturity excess return. Thus, the nine-month forward premium is selected on the basis of its

Table 4

Chi-square statistic for tests of the number of latent variables in expected excess returns of Treasury bills with maturities up to twelve months, December 1963 to November 1985. The tests are conducted using the generalized method of moments with monthly excess returns as dependent variables and with forward premiums as instruments (in addition to a constant). Heteroskedasticity is allowed, but the disturbances are assumed serially uncorrelated. The chi-square statistic tests the overidentifying restrictions implied by the latent-variable specification. The $p$-value (in parentheses) is the probability under the null hypothesis that the test statistic would exceed the reported value.

| Dates | Latent variables | | | |
|-------|------|------|------|------|
|       | 1 | 2 | 3 | 4 |

Panel A.  Excess returns for eleven maturities (2–12); five forward premiums as instruments (maturities 2–6)

| Dates | 1 | 2 | 3 | 4 |
|-------|------|------|------|------|
| 12/1963–11/1985 | 64.80 (0.008) | 31.05 (0.269) | 14.37 (0.571) | 2.99 (0.886) |
| 12/1963–11/1974 | 55.95 (0.048) | 35.78 (0.120) | 19.40 (0.248) | 9.08 (0.247) |
| 12/1974–11/1985 | 50.46 (0.124) | 26.47 (0.493) | 10.24 (0.854) | 2.26 (0.944) |
| 12/1963–8/1979 | 65.56 (0.007) | 36.19 (0.111) | 21.04 (0.177) | 10.32 (0.171) |
| Degrees of freedom | 40 | 27 | 16 | 7 |

Panel B.  Excess returns for ten maturities (2–8, 10–12); six forward premiums as instruments (maturities 2–6, 9)

| Dates | 1 | 2 | 3 | 4 |
|-------|------|------|------|------|
| 12/1963–11/1985 | 79.50 (0.001) | 45.93 (0.053) | 22.12 (0.392) | 7.55 (0.819) |
| 12/1963–11/1974 | 61.73 (0.049) | 46.65 (0.046) | 28.16 (0.136) | 17.67 (0.126) |
| 12/1974–11/1985 | 49.73 (0.291) | 30.77 (0.529) | 18.51 (0.617) | 7.28 (0.839) |
| 12/1963–8/1979 | 69.24 (0.012) | 49.28 (0.026) | 30.40 (0.084) | 18.13 (0.112) |
| Degrees of freedom | 45 | 32 | 21 | 12 |

Panel C.  Excess returns for eleven maturities (2–12); eleven lagged forward premiums as instruments (maturities 2–12)

| Dates | 1 | 2 | 3 | 4 |
|-------|------|------|------|------|
| 1/1964–11/1985 | 126.39 (0.038) | 93.56 (0.161) | 78.96 (0.099) | 52.18 (0.351) |
| 1/1964–8/1979 | 114.47 (0.153) | 100.33 (0.072) | 79.82 (0.088) | 64.91 (0.063 |
| Degrees of freedom | 100 | 81 | 64 | 49 |

in-sample ability to predict excess returns on various maturities. In spite of this preselection method, inferences about the number of latent variables are similar to those obtained previously. The overall-period $p$-values are 0.053 for $K = 2$ and 0.392 for $K = 3$. Thus, it still appears that two or three latent variables are sufficient to describe expected excess returns on bills with maturities of two through twelve months.

Table 5

Comparisons of within-sample and one-step-ahead forecasts of excess returns on Treasury bills with maturities up to twelve months, December 1963 to November 1985.

| Maturity | Two latent variables[a] | | Two adjacent maturities[b] | | Maturities 2–6[c] | |
|---|---|---|---|---|---|---|
| | Mean square error[d] | Percent explained[e] | Mean square error[d] | Percent explained[e] | Mean square error[d] | Percent explained[e] |
| Panel A. Within-sample forecasts, 12/1963–11/1985 | | | | | | |
| 2 | 0.060 | 4.64 | — | — | 0.056 | 10.01 |
| 3 | 0.156 | 9.10 | 0.156 | 8.62 | 0.154 | 9.87 |
| 4 | 0.338 | 8.86 | 0.353 | 4.91 | 0.335 | 9.66 |
| 5 | 0.578 | 11.10 | 0.600 | 7.73 | 0.578 | 11.22 |
| 6 | 0.862 | 10.94 | 0.891 | 7.94 | 0.861 | 11.08 |
| 7 | 1.035 | 10.09 | 1.107 | 3.79 | 1.034 | 10.17 |
| 8 | 1.413 | 9.43 | 1.482 | 5.01 | 1.413 | 9.45 |
| 9 | 1.962 | 10.37 | 2.093 | 4.35 | 1.960 | 10.44 |
| 10 | 2.491 | 10.56 | 2.634 | 5.40 | 2.489 | 10.63 |
| 11 | 2.964 | 10.18 | 3.163 | 4.14 | 2.963 | 10.21 |
| 12 | 3.481 | 10.64 | — | — | 3.480 | 10.65 |
| Panel B. One-step-ahead forecasts, 12/1974–11/1985 | | | | | | |
| 2 | 0.120 | − 29 33 | — | — | 0.122 | − 31.32 |
| 3 | 0.280 | − 8.30 | 0.256 | 1.21 | 0.286 | − 10.33 |
| 4 | 0.607 | − 5.95 | 0.575 | − 0.04 | 0.606 | − 5.85 |
| 5 | 1.015 | 0.96 | 0.992 | 3.16 | 1.035 | − 0.97 |
| 6 | 1.531 | 2.79 | 1.550 | 1.56 | 1.577 | − 0.02 |
| 7 | 1.752 | 1.90 | 1.757 | 1.61 | 1.773 | 0.74 |
| 8 | 2.456 | 0.80 | 2.497 | − 0.09 | 2.499 | − 0.95 |
| 9 | 3.448 | 0.80 | 3.393 | 2.36 | 3.503 | − 0.80 |
| 10 | 4.327 | 0.45 | 4.199 | 3.37 | 4.339 | 0.17 |
| 11 | 5.192 | 2.06 | 5.153 | 2.79 | 5.243 | 1.11 |
| 12 | 6.056 | 2.47 | — | — | 6.115 | 1.51 |

[a] The results labeled 'Two latent variables' are obtained using the generalized method of moments, with excess returns for maturities 2–12 as dependent variables and forward premiums for maturities 2–6 (in addition to a constant) as instruments.

[b] The results labeled 'Two adjacent maturities' are obtained from ordinary least-squares regression of the excess return for each maturity $\tau$ on two forward premiums, one for maturity $\tau - 1$ and one for maturity $\tau + 1$.

[c] The results labeled 'Maturities 2–6' are obtained from ordinary least-squares regression of the excess return for each maturity on the set of nonmatching forward premiums for maturities 2–6.

[d] The numbers in this column are multiplied by 100,000.

[e] $(VAR-MSE)/VAR \times 100$, where $VAR$ is the total variance of the excess return and $MSE$ is the mean square error.

Panel C of table 4 reports results using lagged forward premiums. In this case it is possible to use forward premiums for all eleven maturities as instruments. That is, since the forward premiums are lagged, it is not necessary to have an alternative set of bills for the longer maturities to avoid the measurement-error problem discussed earlier. The test of $K = 1$ produces a $p$-value of 0.038 in the overall period, but all other $p$-values are 0.063 or higher. Again, the inclusion of longer maturities does not lead to the rejection of hypotheses that are not rejected by the shorter-maturity tests.

Table 5 provides additional descriptive evidence on the relative explanatory power of the model with two latent variables. Panel A compares the within-sample fit for the overall period with two alternatives. In the first alternative, the excess return for maturity $\tau$ is regressed on the forward premiums for maturities $\tau - 1$ and $\tau + 1$. (Recall that the own-maturity forward premium would introduce possible spurious explanatory power as a result of measurement error.) This alternative allows more maturity-specific information to enter the conditional expected excess return. The second alternative uses the same instruments as the two-latent-variable model – forward premiums with maturities of two through six months – but no latent-variable restriction is imposed. In other words, the excess return for a given maturity is simply regressed on the five forward premiums for maturities two through six. Panel B of table 5 presents results for the same three cases, except the models are estimated using data only up to the month preceding the forecast month. The first subperiod is used as the base period for the initial forecast, so the one-step-ahead monthly forecasts cover the second subperiod, December 1974 through November 1985. Both panels (A and B) report, for each model and maturity, the mean squared forecast error (MSE) and the percentage difference between the total excess return variance and the MSE.[21] The two-latent-variable model outperforms the adjacent-maturity specification for all maturities within the sample but only three maturities (6, 7, and 8) in the one-step-ahead forecasts. The latent-variable model performs marginally worse than the unrestricted model within the sample (as it must) but outperforms it for all but one maturity (four months) in the one-step-ahead forecasts.

## 5. Changes in the term structure of expected excess returns

### 5.1. Business cycles and the slope of the term structure

As Fama (1984b) observes, average bill returns over the sample period of this study increase with maturity up to about nine months and then decline with maturity, and this same humped term structure is present in average

---

[21] The negative numbers in table 5 represent cases in which the variance of the forecast error exceeds the variance of the excess return.

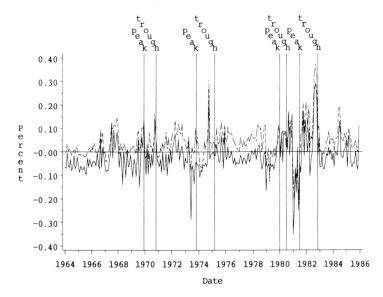

Fig. 3. Differences in expected monthly percent returns on Treasury bills with maturities of two, six, and twelve months estimated in a model with two latent variables. The solid line plots the difference for twelve months minus six months, and the dashed line plots the difference for six months minus two months. Vertical lines indicate business-cycle peaks and troughs.

forward premiums. In a subsequent paper, Fama (1986) observes that, although the structure of forward premiums is humped on average, the shape of that structure shifts over time. Forward premiums tend to be upward sloping during periods of economic expansion and humped or downward sloping around recessions. Since Fama argues that forward premiums are approximately equal to expected excess returns, the same behavior is attributed to the term structure of expected excess returns.

If a model with, say, two latent variables is to be an adequate description of expected excess returns on bills of all maturities, then such a model should produce similar shifts in the shape of the term structure. Although a two-variable model can produce shifts in the shape of the term structure (indeed, so can a one-variable model), it remains to be investigated here whether the model estimated in the previous section does so.

Shifts in the shape of the estimated term structure can be seen fig. 3, which plots differences in the fitted expected returns between twelve-month and six-month bills (solid line) and between six-month and two-month bills (dashed line). The fitted values are obtained from the two-latent-variable model with forward premiums for maturities two through six as instruments (the model used for $K = 2$ in panel A of table 4). As shown in the figure, the two-latent-variable model produces rich variation in the term structure of expected excess returns. Although the term structure is humped on average (the average fitted values essentially reproduce the sample average excess returns), periods of both upward- and downward-sloping structures are common. When the dashed line plots above zero and the solid line plots below zero, the term structure is humped. When both lines plot above (below) zero, the term structure slopes upward (downward).

The plots in fig. 3 suggest that changes in the shape of the term structure of expected returns are related to business cycles. Vertical rules on the graph indicate business-cycle peaks and troughs, as reported by the National Bureau of Economic Research [see Moore and Zarnowitz (1984)]. Periods in which the solid line (twelve months minus six months) is most prominently negative precede business-cycle peaks, especially the peaks beginning the most severe recessions, in 1973–1975 and 1982–1983. In other words, the term structure of expected returns is often downward sloping, at least for the longer maturities, as the economy heads into recessions.

The largest positive values of the solid line (twelve months minus six months) precede the troughs ending the two most severe recessions, and relatively large positive slopes also surround the trough in 1980. That is, the term structure of expected returns slopes upward as the economy heads into recoveries. Thus, although the term structure is somewhat humped on average over the sample period, the sharpest departures from this average pattern appear to accompany turning points in economic activity.

The estimates of expected returns in fig. 3 are functions of two latent variables extracted from forward premiums with maturities *up to only six months*. That is, in addition to restricting the vector of expected returns to lie in two dimensions, the model uses only information in prices of bills with maturities of six months or less to estimate expected monthly returns on bills with longer maturities. It is noteworthy that this model produces shifts in the term structure of expected returns similar to those Fama (1986) observes based on forward premiums for the entire range of maturities.

## 5.2. A variance-based interpretation

One framework in which to analyze the above shifts in the pattern of expected returns is a model developed by Breeden (1986) using the time–state preference approach. This discrete-period framework has a close analogue in the continuous-time framework of Cox, Ingersoll, and Ross. As Breeden (1986, pp. 21–22) observes, however, the discrete-period framework relates yields on finite-maturity instruments to the conditional distribution of consumption at specific future dates, whereas the continuous-time framework provides a relation between the instantaneous rate of interest and the instantaneous mean and variance of consumption. This characteristic of the discrete-period model provides a convenient framework in which to analyze the business-cycle-related shifts in the term structure described above.

Breeden (1986) shows that the price of a $\tau$-period discount instrument can be approximated by a 'mean–variance' formulation involving the mean and variance of aggregate consumption,

$$p(\tau, t) = -\tau\rho - \gamma\left[E_t\{c_{t+\tau}\} - c_t\right] + \frac{\gamma^2}{2}\operatorname{var}_t\{c_{t+\tau}\},\qquad(28)$$

where $p(\tau, t)$ is the (log) price of a $\tau$-period bill, $c_t$ is the natural log of aggregate consumption at time $t$, $\rho$ is the rate of pure time preference, $\gamma$ is the coefficient of relative risk aversion, and $E_t$ and $\operatorname{var}_t$ denote the mean and the variance conditioned on information available at time $t$. As Breeden notes, obtaining (28) as an exact representation requires stronger assumptions, such as constant relative risk aversion and lognormally distributed consumption [Rubinstein (1974)], but the equation may also provide a useful approximation in more general models.

The above model is used here to analyze the differences between expected holding-period returns on bills of different maturities. Substituting (28) into the expression for the holding-period return $H(\tau, t + 1)$ $[= p(\tau - 1, t + 1) - p(\tau, t)]$ and taking the expectation conditional on information at time $t$ gives

$$E_t\{H(\tau, t + 1)\} = \rho + \gamma\left[E_t\{c_{t+1}\} - c_t\right]$$

$$+ \frac{\gamma^2}{2}\left[E_t\{\operatorname{var}_{t+1}\{c_{c+\tau}\}\} - \operatorname{var}_t\{c_{t+\tau}\}\right]$$

$$= \rho + \gamma\left[E_t\{c_{t+1}\} - c_t\right]$$

$$- \frac{\gamma^2}{2}\operatorname{var}_t\{E_{t+1}\{c_{t+\tau}\}\}.\qquad(29)$$

Eq. (29) then implies that the difference between expected holding-period returns on bills with different maturities, say $\tau$ and $s$, can be written

$$E_t\{H(\tau, t + 1) - H(s, t + 1)\}$$

$$= \frac{\gamma^2}{2}\left[\operatorname{var}_t\{E_{t+1}\{c_{t+s}\}\} - \operatorname{var}_t\{E_{t+1}\{c_{t+\tau}\}\}\right].\qquad(30)$$

That is, the difference between expected returns on bills of different maturities is the difference between variances of expected consumption for two different times in the future.

Assume that $\tau > s$ in eq. (30). When the expected return on the shorter-maturity bill exceeds that of the longer-maturity bill, then future expected consumption for time $t + \tau$ has greater variance than future expected consumption for time $t + s$. This situation would correspond to a downward-sloping structure of expected returns, and recall from fig. 3 that such behavior typically occurs during the year preceding a business-cycle peak. In other words, expected consumption for the more distant month is more variable entering a recession. The reverse occurs with upward-sloping structures. In that case, expected consumption for the closer month is more variable. Recall again from fig. 3 that such behavior of expected returns typically precedes recoveries. Together, both cases suggest that the variance of expected consumption is greater for months during a recession. Although this exercise is very preliminary, the implied behavior of variability of expected consumption in relation to the business cycle seems plausible.

## 6. Conclusions

Models of the term structure developed by Cox, Ingersoll, and Ross (1985) – CIR – imply that expected excess returns are linear functions of forward premiums, where the number of latent variables captured by the forward premiums equals the number of state variables in the pricing relation. Restrictions on the number of latent variables can be tested using the generalized method of moments, which allows for the heteroskedasticity and nonnormality of the unexpected excess returns implied by the CIR models.

Forward premiums are used to predict excess returns in the latent-variable tests. When the maturities of the forward premiums match those of the excess returns, the number of state variables required to describe expected excess returns can appear to be large because of measurement errors. An alternative set of forward premiums with nonmatching maturities is likely to reduce the problems arising from measurement error.

Based on forward premiums with nonmatching maturities, the generalized method-of-moments latent-variable tests reject a CIR single-variable specification of the term structure for nominally default-free bonds, but two or three latent variables appear to be sufficient to describe expected excess returns on bills with maturities from two to twelve months. A two-latent-variable model is consistent with a two-factor CIR model that incorporates inflation uncertainty.

The term structure of expected excess returns fitted from a two-latent-variable model appears to shift over time in relation to turning points in business cycles. Downward-sloping structures tend to precede recessions, and upward-sloping structures tend to precede recoveries. Such behavior is consistent with an explanation in which the variance of expected consumption is greater for months during recessions. This behavior of expected returns for bills with maturities of up to twelve months is produced using information in prices of bills with maturities of six months or less. Business-cycle-related shifts in the shape of the term structures of expected returns are also observed by Fama (1986) based on forward rates for the full range of maturities.

By examining expected returns conditional on forward premiums, this study focuses on the number of relevant state variables in the term structure of Treasury bills, but the identity of the state variables is not investigated. An interesting direction for future research would be to investigate whether similar behavior in expected returns can be explained by models in which identities for the state variables are imposed. An investigation of the number of latent variables in expected returns on discount bonds of longer maturities would also be useful (although prices on such bonds would have to be estimated from prices of coupon bonds). It is possible that some state variables may have little impact on short-maturity instruments but could affect longer-maturity prices significantly.

# References

Breeden, Douglas T., 1986, Consumption, production, inflation, and interest rates: A synthesis, Journal of Financial Economics 16, 3–39.

Brennan, Michael J. and Eduardo S. Schwartz, 1980, Conditional predictions of bond prices and returns, Journal of Finance 35, 405–419.

Brennan, Michael J. and Eduardo S. Schwartz, 1982, An equilibrium model of bond pricing and a test of market efficiency, Journal of Financial and Quantitative Analysis 17, 301–329.

Brown, Stephen J. and Philip H. Dybvig, 1986, The empirical implications of the Cox, Ingersoll, Ross theory of the term structure of interest rates, Journal of Finance 41, 617–630.

Campbell, John Y., 1987, Stock returns and the term structure, Journal of Financial Economics 18, 373–399.

Cox, John C., Jonathan E. Ingersoll, and Stephen A. Ross, 1985, A theory of the term structure of interest rates, Econometrica 53, 385–407.

Fama, Eugene F., 1976, Forward rates as predictors of future spot rates, Journal of Financial Economics 3, 361–377.

Fama, Eugene F., 1984a, The information in the term structure, Journal of Financial Economics 13, 509–528.

Fama, Eugene F., 1984b, Term premiums in bond returns, Journal of Financial Economics 13, 529–546.

Fama, Eugene F., 1986, Term premiums and default premiums in money markets, Journal of Financial Economics, 17, 175–196.

Fama, Eugene F. and Kenneth R. French, 1988, Permanent and temporary components of stock prices, Journal of Political Economy, forthcoming.

Fama, Eugene F. and G. William Schwert, 1977, Asset returns and inflation, Journal of Financial Economics 5, 115–146.

Ferson, Wayne E., Shmuel Kandel, and Robert F. Stambaugh, 1987, Tests of asset pricing with time-varying expected risk premiums and market betas, Journal of Finance 42, 201–220.

French, Kenneth R., G. William Schwert, and Robert F. Stambaugh, 1987, Expected stock returns and volatility, Journal of Financial Economics 19, 3–29.

Gibbons, Michael R. and Wayne Ferson, 1985, Testing asset pricing models with changing expectations and an unobservable market portfolio, Journal of Financial Economics 14, 217–236.

Gibbons, Michael R. and Krishna Ramaswamy, 1986, The term structure of interest rates: Empirical evidence, Working paper (Stanford University, Stanford, CA).

Hall, Robert E., 1981, Intertemporal substitution in consumption, Working paper (Stanford University, Stanford, CA).

Hansen, Lars Peter, 1982, Large sample properties of the generalized method of moments estimators, Econometrica 50, 1029–1054.

Hansen, Lars Peter and Robert J. Hodrick, 1983, Risk averse speculation in the forward foreign exchange market: An econometric analysis of linear models, in Jacob A. Frenkel, ed., Exchange rates and international macroeconomics (University of Chicago Press, Chicago, IL).

Hansen, Lars Peter and Kenneth J. Singleton, 1982, Generalized instrumental variables estimation of nonlinear rational expectation models, Econometrica 50, 1269–1286.

Hansen, Lars Peter and Kenneth J. Singleton, 1983, Stochastic consumption, risk aversion, and the temporal behavior of asset returns, Journal of Political Economy 91, 249–265.

Hsieh, David A., 1983, A heteroscedasticity-consistent covariance matrix estimator for time series regressions, Journal of Econometrics 22, 281–290.

Huizinga, John and Leonardo Leiderman, 1985, Interest rates, money supply announcements and monetary base announcements, Working paper (University of Chicago, Chicago, IL and Tel Aviv University, Tel Aviv).

Huizinga, John and Frederick S. Mishkin, 1984, Inflation and real interest rates on assets with different risk characteristics, Journal of Finance 39, 699–712.

Johnson, Norman L. and Samuel Kotz, 1972, Distributions in statistics: Continuous multivariate distributions (Wiley, New York).

Keim, Donald B. and Robert F. Stambaugh, 1986, Predicting returns in the stock and bond markets, Journal of Financial Economics 17, 357–390.

Marsh, Terry A. and Eric R. Rosenfeld, 1983, Stochastic processes for interest rates and equilibrium bond prices, Journal of Finance 38, 635–646.

Moore, Geoffrey H. and Victor Zarnowitz, 1984, The development and role of the National Bureau's business cycle chronologies, Working paper no. 1394 (National Bureau of Economic Research, Cambridge, MA)

Oldfield, George S. and Richard J. Rogalski, 1987, Stationary properties of Treasury bill term structure movements, Journal of Monetary Economics 19, 229–254.

Richard, Scott F., 1978, An arbitrage model of the term structure of interest rates, Journal of Financial Economics 6, 33–57.

Rubinstein, Mark, 1974, An aggregation theorem for securities markets, Journal of Financial Economics 1, 225–244.

Startz, Richard, 1982, Do forecast errors or term premia really make the difference between long and short rates?, Journal of Financial Economics 10, 323–329.

Tauchen, George, 1985, Statistical properties of generalized method of moments estimates of structural parameters using financial market data, Working paper (Duke University, Durham, NC).

Vasicek, Oldrich, 1977, An equilibrium characterization of the term structure, Journal of Financial Economics 5, 177–188.

White, Halbert, 1980, A heteroskedasticity-consistent covariance matrix estimator and a direct test for heteroskedasticity, Econometrica 48, 817–838.

# BUSINESS CONDITIONS AND EXPECTED RETURNS ON STOCKS AND BONDS*

Eugene F. FAMA

*University of Chicago, Chicago, IL 60637, USA*

Kenneth R. FRENCH

*NBER and University of Chicago, Chicago, IL 60637, USA*

Received January 1989, final version received August 1989

Expected returns on common stocks and long-term bonds contain a term or maturity premium that has a clear business-cycle pattern (low near peaks, high near troughs). Expected returns also contain a risk premium that is related to longer-term aspects of business conditions. The variation through time in this premium is stronger for low-grade bonds than for high-grade bonds and stronger for stocks than for bonds. The general message is that expected returns are lower when economic conditions are strong and higher when conditions are weak.

## 1. Introduction

There is mounting evidence that stock and bond returns are predictable. Some argue that predictability implies market inefficiency. Others contend that it is a result of rational variation in expected returns. We offer evidence on this issue. The evidence centers on whether there is a coherent story that relates the variation through time of expected returns on bonds and stocks to business conditions. The specific questions we address include:

(1) Do the expected returns on bonds and stocks move together? In particular, do the same variables forecast bond and stock returns?

(2) Is the variation in expected bond and stock returns related to business conditions? Are the relations consistent with intuition, theory, and existing evidence on the exposure of different assets to changes in business conditions?

*The comments of John Cochrane, Bradford Cornell, Kevin Murphy, Richard Roll, G. William Schwert (the editor), and John Campbell (the referee) are gratefully acknowledged. This research is supported by the National Science Foundation (Fama) and the Center for Research in Security Prices (French).

Journal of Financial Economics 25 (1989) 23–49. North-Holland

Our tests indicate that expected excess returns (returns net of the one-month Treasury bill rate) on corporate bonds and stocks move together. Dividend yields, commonly used to forecast stock returns, also forecast bond returns. Predictable variation in stock returns is, in turn, tracked by variables commonly used to measure default and term (or maturity) premiums in bond returns. The default-premium variable (the default spread) is the difference between the yield on a market portfolio of corporate bonds and the yield on Aaa bonds. The term- or maturity-premium variable (the term spread) is the difference between the Aaa yield and the one-month bill rate.

The dividend yield and the default spread capture similar variation in expected bond and stock returns. The major movements in these variables, and in the expected return components they track, seem to be related to long-term business episodes that span several measured business cycles. The dividend yield and the default spread forecast high returns when business conditions are persistently weak and low returns when conditions are strong.

The term spread is more closely related to the shorter-term business cycles identified by the National Bureau of Economic Research (NBER). In particular, the term spread – and the component of expected returns it tracks – are low around measured business-cycle peaks and high near troughs.

There are clear patterns across assets in the slopes from regressions of returns on the forecasting variables. The slopes for the term spread are positive and similar in magnitude for all the stock portfolios and (long-term) bond portfolios we examine. This suggests that the spread tracks a term or maturity premium in expected returns that is similar for all long-term assets. A reasonable and old hypothesis is that the premium compensates for exposure to discount-rate shocks that affect all long-term securities (stocks and bonds) in roughly the same way.

In contrast to the slopes for the term spread, the slopes for the default spread and the dividend yield increase from high-grade to low-grade bonds and from bonds to stocks. This pattern corresponds to intuition about the business risks of the assets, that is, the sensitivity of their returns to unexpected changes in business conditions. The slopes suggest that the default spread and the dividend yield track components of expected returns that vary with the level or price of some business-conditions risk.

Does the expected-return variation we document reflect rational pricing in an efficient market? On the plus side, it is comforting that three forecasting variables, all related to business conditions, track common variation in the expected returns on bonds and stocks. It is appealing that the term spread, known to track a maturity premium in bond returns, identifies a similar premium in stock returns. It is also appealing that a measure of business conditions like the default spread captures expected-return variation that increases from high-grade bonds to stocks in a way that corresponds to intuition about the business-conditions risks of assets. Finally, it is comforting that variation in the dividend yield, which might otherwise be interpreted as the result of 'bubbles' in stock prices, forecasts bond returns as well as stock returns, and captures much the same variation in expected bond and stock returns as the default spread.

What one takes as comforting evidence for market rationality is, however, somewhat a matter of predilection. As always, the ultimate judgment must be left to the reader.

## 2. Data

### 2.1. Common stocks

We use the value- and equal-weighted portfolios of New York Stock Exchange (NYSE) stocks, from the Center for Research in Security Prices (CRSP), to represent the behavior of stock returns. The value-weighted portfolio is weighted toward large stocks; equal-weighted returns are affected more by small stocks. The two portfolios thus provide a convenient way to examine the behavior of stock returns as a function of firm size, a dimension known to be important in describing the cross-section of expected stock returns [Banz (1981)] and the variation through time of expected returns [Keim and Stambaugh (1986), Fama and French (1988a)].

### 2.2. Corporate bonds

To study corporate bond returns, we use a sample maintained by Ibbotson Associates (obtained for us by Dimensional Fund Advisors). This database has monthly returns and yields for 1926–1987. The sample includes 100 bonds, chosen to approximate a value-weighted market portfolio of corporate bonds with maturities longer than one year. The sample starts in 1926 with 100 randomly chosen bonds, with probability of selection proportional to face value outstanding. Random selection based on face value is used at the start of each following year to add and delete bonds to maintain a 100-bond sample that approximates a value-weighted market portfolio. We use the portfolio of all 100 bonds (called All), and portfolios of bonds rated Aaa, Aa, A, Baa, and below Baa (LG, low-grade). Portfolio returns and yields are price-weighted averages of individual bond returns and yields. The average maturity of bonds in these portfolios is almost always more than ten years.

### 2.3. Explanatory variables for excess returns

The tests attempt to measure and interpret variation in expected excess returns for return horizons $T$ of one month, one quarter, and one to four years. A one-month excess return is the difference between the continuously compounded one-month return on a bond or stock portfolio and the continuously compounded one-month Treasury bill return (from Ibbotson Associates). Excess returns for quarterly and one- to four-year holding periods are obtained by cumulating monthly excess returns. The monthly, quarterly, and annual excess returns are nonoverlapping. The two- to four-year returns are overlapping annual (end-of-year) observations. Henceforth, the word return, used alone, implies excess return.

The tests center on regressions of future stock and bond returns, $r(t, t + T)$, on a common set of variables, $X(t)$, known at $t$,

$$r(t, t + T) = \alpha(T) + \beta(T) X(t) + \varepsilon(t, t + T).\qquad(1)$$

One of the explanatory variables is the dividend yield, $D(t)/P(t)$, on the value-weighted NYSE portfolio, computed by summing monthly dividends on the portfolio for the year preceding time $t$ and dividing by the value of the portfolio at $t$. [See Fama and French (1988b).] We use yields based on annual dividends to avoid seasonals in dividends. These annual yields are used to forecast the returns, $r(t, t + T)$, for all horizons.

The hypothesis that dividend yields forecast stock returns is old [see, for example, Dow (1920) and Ball (1978)]. The intuition of the efficient-markets version of the hypothesis is that stock prices are low in relation to dividends when discount rates and expected returns are high (and vice versa), so $D/P$ varies with expected returns. There is a similar prediction, however, if variation in dividend yields is due to irrational bubbles in stock prices. In this case, dividend yields and expected returns are high when prices are temporarily irrationally low (and vice versa). Evidence that dividend yields forecast stock returns is in Rozeff (1984), Shiller (1984), Flood, Hodrick, and Kaplan (1986), Campbell and Shiller (1988), and Fama and French (1988b). The novel result here is that $D/P$ also forecasts bond returns.

Expected returns on long-term corporate bonds can vary through time for at least two reasons: (a) variation in default premiums (differences between the expected returns on low- and high-grade bonds with similar maturities) and (b) variation in term or maturity premiums (differences between the expected returns on long- and short-term bonds).

To identify variation in term or maturity premiums, we use the term spread, $TERM(t)$, the difference between the time $t$ yield on the Aaa bond portfolio and the one-month bill rate. This choice is consistent with evidence that spreads of long- over short-term interest rates forecast differences between long- and short-term bond returns [see, for example, Fama (1976, 1984, 1986, 1988), Shiller, Campbell, and Schoenholtz (1983), Keim and Stambaugh (1986), and Fama and Bliss (1987)]. Our novel result is that *TERM* tracks a time-varying term premium in stock returns similar to that in long-term bond returns.

To track default premiums, we use the default spread, $DEF(t)$, the difference between the time $t$ yield on the portfolio of (All) 100 corporate bonds and the Aaa yield. This choice is in line with evidence in Fama (1986) and Keim and Stambaugh (1986) that spreads of low- over high-grade interest rates forecast spreads of low- over high-grade bond returns.

The regression results are robust to changes in the definitions of the variables used to forecast returns. The dividend yield on the equal-weighted NYSE portfolio forecasts returns about as well as the yield on the value-weighted portfolio. Substituting a low-grade (Baa or below) bond yield for the market-portfolio bond yield in the default spread has little effect on the results. We use a market-portfolio bond yield because it is less subject to changes through time in the meaning of bond ratings. Substituting a long-term Treasury bond yield for the Aaa yield in the default and term spreads also has little effect on the results. We choose the Aaa yield to avoid potential problems caused by the change in the tax status of Treasury bonds (from nontaxable to taxable) in the early 1940s.

## 3. Business conditions and the behavior of the forecasting variables

### 3.1. Autocorrelations

The autocorrelations of the variables used to forecast returns are information about the behavior of expected returns. For the 1927–1987 and 1941–1987 periods used in the regressions, the autocorrelations of the dividend yield, the default spread, and the term spread (table 1) are large at the first-order (annual) lag, but tend to decay for longer lags. This suggests that $D/P$, $DEF$, and $TERM$ track components of expected returns that are autocorrelated but show some tendency toward mean reversion.

The autocorrelations of $TERM$ for 1941–1987 are smaller than those of $D/P$ and $DEF$. Beyond the first (one-year) lag, the autocorrelations of $TERM$ for 1941–1987 are close to 0. Thus for the last 47 years of the sample, the component of expected returns tracked by $TERM$ is much less persistent than those tracked by $D/P$ and $DEF$. This result is in line with our story that $TERM$ tracks variation in expected returns in response to short-term variation in business conditions, whereas $DEF$ and $D/P$ track expected-return variation that relates to more persistent aspects of business conditions. The business-conditions part of this story comes next.

### 3.2. Plots of the forecasting variables

Since we measure the variation of expected returns with linear regressions of returns on the forecasting variables, plots of the forecasting variables picture the components of expected returns they capture.

Table 1

Summary statistics for annual observations on one-year excess returns on the bond and stock portfolios, and the dividend yield ($D/P$), default spread ($DEF$), and term spread ($TERM$).[a]

| | Mean | S.D. | Autocorrelations | | | | | | | |
|---|---|---|---|---|---|---|---|---|---|---|
| | | | 1 | 2 | 3 | 4 | 5 | 6 | 7 | 8 |
| | | | | 1927–1987 | | | | | | |
| Aaa | 0.74 | 6.69 | 0.21 | 0.05 | −0.06 | −0.10 | −0.16 | 0.05 | −0.03 | −0.04 |
| Aa | 0.67 | 6.82 | 0.20 | −0.05 | −0.13 | −0.15 | −0.13 | 0.03 | −0.02 | −0.10 |
| A | 0.87 | 8.38 | 0.25 | −0.15 | −0.24 | −0.13 | −0.02 | 0.12 | −0.05 | −0.13 |
| Baa | 1.45 | 8.65 | 0.24 | −0.13 | −0.24 | −0.14 | −0.01 | 0.15 | −0.01 | −0.07 |
| LG | 2.25 | 12.36 | 0.32 | −0.03 | −0.21 | −0.21 | −0.05 | 0.13 | 0.05 | 0.11 |
| VW | 5.70 | 20.81 | 0.10 | −0.19 | −0.06 | −0.13 | −0.01 | −0.02 | 0.15 | 0.07 |
| EW | 8.80 | 28.26 | 0.13 | −0.18 | −0.12 | −0.22 | −0.10 | −0.11 | 0.11 | 0.05 |
| $D/P$ | 4.49 | 1.36 | 0.62 | 0.29 | 0.20 | 0.20 | 0.28 | 0.32 | 0.24 | 0.17 |
| $DEF$ | 0.96 | 0.68 | 0.83 | 0.70 | 0.57 | 0.51 | 0.49 | 0.54 | 0.52 | 0.51 |
| $TERM$ | 1.99 | 1.25 | 0.54 | 0.36 | 0.21 | 0.22 | 0.26 | 0.14 | 0.18 | 0.05 |
| | | | | 1941–1987 | | | | | | |
| Aaa | −0.01 | 7.05 | 0.21 | −0.03 | −0.13 | −0.16 | −0.25 | −0.03 | −0.11 | −0.11 |
| Aa | 0.08 | 7.02 | 0.23 | −0.14 | −0.12 | −0.21 | −0.17 | −0.06 | −0.05 | −0.14 |
| A | 0.55 | 7.29 | 0.26 | −0.13 | −0.19 | −0.15 | −0.02 | −0.02 | −0.07 | −0.18 |
| Baa | 1.38 | 7.36 | 0.26 | −0.20 | −0.17 | −0.11 | 0.01 | 0.05 | −0.01 | −0.15 |
| LG | 2.71 | 9.88 | 0.30 | −0.01 | −0.13 | −0.03 | 0.17 | 0.16 | 0.06 | −0.02 |
| VW | 6.97 | 16.25 | −0.03 | −0.27 | 0.08 | 0.30 | 0.13 | −0.13 | 0.18 | 0.05 |
| EW | 9.84 | 21.58 | 0.06 | −0.27 | −0.03 | 0.18 | −0.01 | −0.22 | 0.12 | −0.03 |
| $D/P$ | 4.33 | 1.20 | 0.79 | 0.62 | 0.52 | 0.43 | 0.36 | 0.35 | 0.37 | 0.30 |
| $DEF$ | 0.74 | 0.45 | 0.74 | 0.61 | 0.34 | 0.38 | 0.42 | 0.51 | 0.46 | 0.43 |
| $TERM$ | 1.76 | 1.23 | 0.46 | 0.24 | 0.04 | 0.13 | 0.20 | 0.01 | 0.06 | −0.13 |

[a] One-year excess returns are sums of one-month excess returns (the difference between the continuously compounded one-month return on a portfolio and the one-month bill rate). Aaa,...,LG are bond portfolios formed according to Moody's rating groups. VW and EW are the value- and equal-weighted NYSE stock portfolios. $D/P$ is the ratio of dividends on the VW portfolio for year $t$ to the value of the portfolio at the end of the year. $DEF$ is the difference between the end-of-year yield on All (the portfolio of the 100 corporate bonds in the sample) and the Aaa yield. $TERM$ is the difference between the end-of-year Aaa yield and the one-month bill rate. The yields and the bill rate in $DEF$ and $TERM$ are annualized. As in the later regressions, the periods for $D/P$, $DEF$, and $TERM$ are one year prior to those for returns, e.g., 1926–1986 rather than 1927–1987.

If bonds are priced rationally, the default spread, a spread of lower- over high-grade bond yields, is a measure of business conditions. Fig. 1 shows that $DEF$ indeed takes its highest values during the depression of the 1930s, and there are upward blips during the less severe recessions after World War II – for example, 1957–1958, 1974–1975, and 1980–1982. Although $DEF$ shows some business-cycle variation, its major swings seem to go beyond the business cycles measured by the NBER. $DEF$ is high during the 1930s and the early years of World War II, a period of general economic uncertainty [Officer

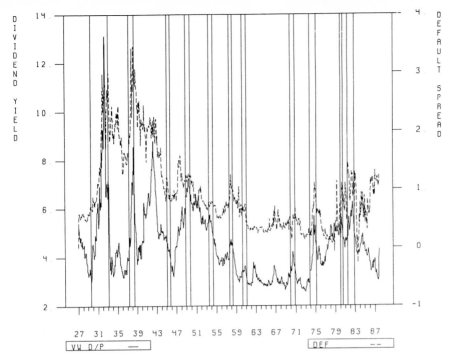

Fig. 1. Beginning-of-month values of the value-weighted dividend yield, *D/P*, and the default spread, *DEF*, in percent.

Vertical grid lines are NBER business-cycle peaks (P) and trough (T). The dates are:

| | | | | | | | |
|---|---|---|---|---|---|---|---|
| 8/29(P) | 3/33(T) | 11/48(P) | 10/49(T) | 4/60(P) | 2/61(T) | 1/80(P) | 7/80(T) |
| 5/37(P) | 6/38(T) | 7/53(P) | 5/54(T) | 12/69(P) | 11/70(T) | 7/81(P) | 11/82(P) |
| 2/45(P) | 10/45(T) | 8/57(P) | 4/58(T) | 11/73(P) | 3/75(T) | | |

(1973) and Schwert (1988)]. It is consistently lower during the 1953–1973 period of stronger and more stable economic conditions, which nevertheless includes four measured recessions.

Similar comments apply to the dividend yield. Indeed, the correlation between *D/P* and *DEF* (0.61 for 1927–1987 and 0.75 for 1941–1987) is apparent in fig. 1. We interpret the figure as saying that the forecast power of the dividend yield and the default spread reflects time variation in expected bond and stock returns in response to aspects of business conditions that tend to persist beyond measured business cycles. This interpretation is buttressed by the high and persistent autocorrelation of *D/P* and *DEF* observed in table 1.

In contrast, fig 2 shows that, except for the 1933–1951 period, the variation of the term spread is more closely related to measured business cycles. *TERM*

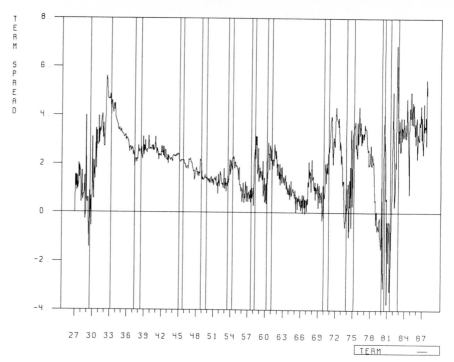

Fig. 2. Beginning-of-month values of the term spread, *TERM*, in percent.

Vertical grid lines are NBER business-cycle peaks (P) and troughs (T). The dates are:

| | | | | | | | |
|---|---|---|---|---|---|---|---|
| 8/29(P) | 3/33(T) | 11/48(P) | 10/49(T) | 4/60(P) | 2/61(T) | 1/80(P) | 7/80(T) |
| 5/37(P) | 6/38(T) | 7/53(P) | 5/54(T) | 12/69(P) | 11/70(T) | 7/81(P) | 11/82(P) |
| 2/45(P) | 10/45(T) | 8/57(P) | 4/58(T) | 11/73(P) | 3/75(T) | | |

tends to be low near business-cycle peaks and high near troughs. The details of the story are in fig. 3 which shows the components of *TERM*, the Aaa yield and the one-month bill rate.

From 1933 to 1951, the bill rate is stable and close to 0. This period includes much of the Great Depression and then the period during and after World War II, when the Federal Reserve fixed bill rates. For the rest of the sample, the bill rate always rises during expansions and falls during contractions. Indeed, fig. 3 suggests that, outside of the 1933–1951 period, the bill rate comes close to defining the business peaks and troughs identified by the NBER. (The NBER says that interest rates are not used to date business cycles.)

Fama (1988) argues that the business-cycle variation in short-term interest rates is a mean-reverting tendency, which implies that the variation in long-term rates is less extreme. This is confirmed by the behavior of the Aaa yield in

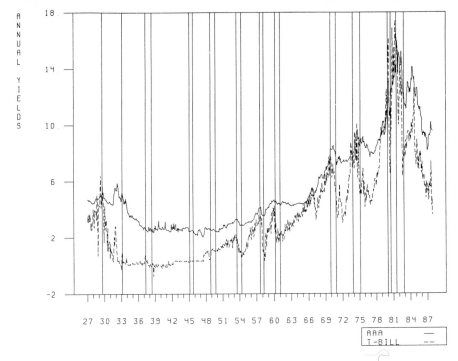

Fig. 3. Beginning-of-month values of the Aaa bond yield and the (annualized) one-month Treasury bill rate, in percent.

Vertical grid lines are NBER business-cycle peaks (P) and troughs (T). The dates are:

| | | | | | | |
|---|---|---|---|---|---|---|
| 8/29(P) | 3/33(T) | 11/48(P) | 10/49(T) | 4/60(P) | 2/61(T) | 1/80(P) | 7/80(T) |
| 5/37(P) | 6/38(T) | 7/53(P) | 5/54(T) | 12/69(P) | 11/70(T) | 7/81(P) | 11/82(P) |
| 2/45(P) | 10/45(T) | 8/57(P) | 4/58(T) | 11/73(P) | 3/75(T) | | |

fig. 3. The Aaa yield rises less than the bill rate during expansions and falls less during contractions. As a result, the term spread – the Aaa yield minus the bill rate – has a clear business-cycle pattern. For all business cycles after 1951, *TERM* is higher at the trough than at the preceding or following peak.[1,2]

[1] Kessel (1965) documents that yields on long-term Treasury bonds rise less during business expansions and fall less during contractions than yields on short-term bills. Thus spreads of long-term over short-term Treasury yields have a clear countercyclical pattern. Figs. 2 and 3 show that the cyclical behavior of interest rates documented by Kessel extends to the 1963–1987 period not included in his sample.

[2] The business-cycle behavior of the one-month bill rate suggests that the 'anomalous' negative relations between stock returns $r(t, t + T)$ and the time $t$ bill rate [documented by Fama and Schwert (1977) and others] just reflects countercyclical variation in expected returns like that captured by *TERM*. Chen (1989) finds that the bill rate and *TERM* indeed have similar roles in stock-return regressions. He also finds that the negative relations between stock returns and the bill rate are typically weaker than the positive relations between stock returns and *TERM*.

Table 2

Slopes, t-statistics, and $R^2$ from multiple regressions of excess returns on the term spread (TERM) and the value-weighted dividend yield (D/P) or the default spread (DEF); 1927–1987.[a]

$$r(t, t+T) = a + bD(t)/P(t) + cTERM(t) + e(t, t+T)$$

Portfolios

| T | Aaa | Aa | A | Baa | LG | VW | EW |
|---|---|---|---|---|---|---|---|
| **Slopes for D/P** | | | | | | | |
| M | 0.04 | 0.01 | −0.05 | −0.03 | 0.07 | 0.21 | 0.43 |
| Q | 0.20 | 0.14 | 0.03 | 0.14 | 0.48 | 1.09 | 2.05 |
| 1 | 0.30 | −0.21 | −0.64 | −0.49 | 0.39 | 2.79 | 5.75 |
| 2 | 1.09 | 0.25 | 0.99 | 0.91 | 3.92 | 8.89 | 15.66 |
| 3 | 1.83 | 1.17 | 2.91 | 2.87 | 7.83 | 12.20 | 20.21 |
| 4 | 2.72 | 2.16 | 4.14 | 4.47 | 10.54 | 15.37 | 23.29 |
| **Slopes for TERM** | | | | | | | |
| M | 0.23 | 0.24 | 0.26 | 0.26 | 0.26 | 0.31 | 0.47 |
| Q | 0.57 | 0.52 | 0.59 | 0.55 | 0.60 | 0.65 | 0.96 |
| 1 | 3.36 | 3.30 | 3.92 | 3.36 | 3.61 | 1.56 | 2.69 |
| 2 | 4.23 | 4.22 | 4.46 | 4.15 | 4.41 | −1.27 | −0.38 |
| 3 | 5.01 | 4.62 | 4.86 | 4.63 | 4.66 | −1.54 | −0.17 |
| 4 | 5.09 | 4.61 | 5.50 | 5.22 | 6.06 | 0.32 | 4.07 |
| **Regression $R^2$** | | | | | | | |
| M | 0.04 | 0.04 | 0.03 | 0.02 | 0.01 | 0.01 | 0.01 |
| Q | 0.06 | 0.04 | 0.03 | 0.02 | 0.02 | 0.02 | 0.04 |
| 1 | 0.39 | 0.33 | 0.30 | 0.20 | 0.11 | 0.02 | 0.07 |
| 2 | 0.28 | 0.22 | 0.17 | 0.13 | 0.15 | 0.12 | 0.22 |
| 3 | 0.26 | 0.19 | 0.21 | 0.18 | 0.24 | 0.18 | 0.27 |
| 4 | 0.24 | 0.19 | 0.28 | 0.26 | 0.36 | 0.25 | 0.34 |

| T | Aaa | Aa | A | Baa | LG | VW | EW |
|---|---|---|---|---|---|---|---|
| **t-statistics for D/P slopes** | | | | | | | |
| M | 0.96 | 0.21 | −0.55 | −0.23 | 0.43 | 0.78 | 1.26 |
| Q | 1.07 | 0.69 | 0.09 | 0.31 | 0.79 | 1.09 | 1.58 |
| 1 | 0.65 | −0.45 | −0.87 | −0.68 | 0.30 | 1.31 | 2.31 |
| 2 | 1.38 | 0.31 | 0.95 | 0.62 | 1.62 | 3.13 | 4.98 |
| 3 | 2.24 | 1.66 | 6.49 | 2.62 | 3.21 | 3.77 | 4.91 |
| 4 | 3.91 | 2.76 | 5.20 | 6.22 | 5.94 | 5.08 | 4.74 |
| **t-statistics for TERM slopes** | | | | | | | |
| M | 3.12 | 3.57 | 3.23 | 3.19 | 2.27 | 1.68 | 1.93 |
| Q | 1.75 | 1.63 | 1.83 | 1.74 | 1.37 | 1.03 | 1.10 |
| 1 | 5.44 | 5.25 | 5.81 | 4.88 | 3.78 | 0.82 | 1.01 |
| 2 | 3.98 | 3.83 | 2.83 | 2.80 | 1.85 | −0.38 | −0.07 |
| 3 | 3.52 | 3.27 | 2.56 | 2.47 | 1.70 | −0.36 | −0.03 |
| 4 | 2.39 | 2.15 | 2.36 | 2.66 | 2.95 | 0.09 | 0.73 |

$$r(t, t+T) = a + bDEF(t) + cTERM(t) + e(t, t+T)$$

Portfolios

| T | Aaa | Aa | A | Baa | LG | VW | EW |
|---|---|---|---|---|---|---|---|
| **Slopes for DEF** | | | | | | | |
| M | 0.07 | 0.07 | 0.07 | 0.05 | 0.27 | 0.04 | 0.41 |
| Q | 0.31 | 0.34 | 0.47 | 0.54 | 1.30 | 0.99 | 2.78 |
| 1 | 0.76 | 0.41 | 0.76 | 1.49 | 4.12 | 4.38 | 11.59 |
| 2 | 4.18 | 3.51 | 6.41 | 6.70 | 13.49 | 14.62 | 29.22 |
| 3 | 7.21 | 7.14 | 11.12 | 11.83 | 22.25 | 19.96 | 37.61 |
| 4 | 10.11 | 9.66 | 13.62 | 15.29 | 27.07 | 24.56 | 41.41 |
| **Slopes for TERM** | | | | | | | |
| M | 0.22 | 0.23 | 0.24 | 0.24 | 0.22 | 0.34 | 0.47 |
| Q | 0.55 | 0.48 | 0.49 | 0.47 | 0.42 | 0.70 | 0.83 |
| 1 | 3.25 | 3.15 | 3.58 | 2.89 | 2.73 | 1.20 | 1.35 |
| 2 | 3.48 | 3.41 | 3.13 | 2.73 | 2.10 | -2.53 | -3.47 |
| 3 | 3.63 | 3.06 | 2.75 | 2.32 | 1.02 | -3.30 | -4.29 |
| 4 | 3.09 | 2.56 | 2.94 | 2.29 | 1.68 | -1.89 | -0.45 |
| **Regression $R^2$** | | | | | | | |
| M | 0.04 | 0.04 | 0.03 | 0.02 | 0.01 | 0.00 | 0.01 |
| Q | 0.05 | 0.04 | 0.03 | 0.03 | 0.03 | 0.01 | 0.02 |
| 1 | 0.39 | 0.33 | 0.29 | 0.20 | 0.15 | 0.00 | 0.07 |
| 2 | 0.32 | 0.26 | 0.25 | 0.22 | 0.25 | 0.05 | 0.16 |
| 3 | 0.34 | 0.29 | 0.33 | 0.31 | 0.36 | 0.09 | 0.20 |
| 4 | 0.34 | 0.31 | 0.40 | 0.41 | 0.45 | 0.13 | 0.23 |
| **t-statistics for DEF slopes** | | | | | | | |
| M | 0.78 | 0.74 | 0.50 | 0.30 | 0.99 | 0.09 | 0.67 |
| Q | 0.85 | 0.91 | 0.84 | 0.85 | 1.30 | 0.56 | 1.12 |
| 1 | 0.79 | 0.46 | 0.57 | 1.12 | 1.62 | 1.15 | 2.38 |
| 2 | 1.96 | 1.75 | 2.86 | 2.47 | 3.04 | 2.18 | 2.73 |
| 3 | 2.01 | 2.14 | 3.21 | 5.51 | 4.61 | 2.25 | 2.52 |
| 4 | 2.11 | 2.07 | 3.20 | 4.46 | 4.64 | 2.42 | 2.80 |
| **t-statistics for TERM slopes** | | | | | | | |
| M | 2.81 | 3.21 | 3.02 | 3.04 | 1.99 | 1.83 | 2.00 |
| Q | 1.51 | 1.36 | 1.48 | 1.41 | 0.97 | 1.01 | 0.92 |
| 1 | 4.41 | 4.49 | 4.89 | 3.96 | 3.08 | 0.60 | 0.52 |
| 2 | 2.89 | 3.07 | 2.04 | 1.97 | 1.19 | -0.74 | -0.81 |
| 3 | 1.80 | 1.74 | 1.26 | 1.24 | 0.50 | -0.84 | -0.80 |
| 4 | 0.98 | 0.88 | 1.03 | 0.99 | 0.76 | -0.51 | -0.12 |

[a] The regressions for $T$ = one month (M), one quarter (Q), and one year use overlapping returns. The regressions for two- to four-year returns use overlapping annual observations. The numbers of observations in the regressions are (M) 732, (Q) 244, (1 yr) 61, (2 yr) 60, (3 yr) 59, and (4 yr) 58. The standard errors in the t-statistics for the slopes are adjusted for heteroscedasticity and (for two- to four-year returns) the sample autocorrelation of overlapping residuals with the method of Hansen (1982) and White (1980). See note to table 1 for definition of portfolios.

Table 3

Slopes, $t$-statistics, and $R^2$ from multiple regressions of excess returns on the term spread ($TERM$) and the value-weighted dividend yield ($D/P$) or the default spread ($DEF$); 1941–1987.[a]

$$r(t, t+T) = a + bD(t)/P(t) + cTERM(t) + e(t, t+T)$$

**Portfolios**

| $T$ | Aaa | Aa | A | Baa | LG | VW | EW |
|---|---|---|---|---|---|---|---|
| | | | | *Slopes for D/P* | | | |
| M | 0.13 | 0.11 | 0.11 | 0.13 | 0.30 | 0.40 | 0.53 |
| Q | 0.36 | 0.34 | 0.36 | 0.42 | 0.94 | 1.31 | 1.78 |
| 1 | 0.40 | 0.27 | 0.74 | 1.23 | 3.33 | 5.49 | 7.96 |
| 2 | 1.00 | 0.62 | 2.05 | 3.15 | 7.67 | 11.84 | 16.70 |
| 3 | 1.41 | 0.91 | 2.93 | 4.34 | 10.88 | 15.65 | 21.22 |
| 4 | 2.41 | 1.76 | 3.87 | 5.29 | 12.66 | 18.48 | 23.43 |
| | | | | *Slopes for TERM* | | | |
| M | 0.25 | 0.28 | 0.31 | 0.32 | 0.31 | 0.48 | 0.51 |
| Q | 0.62 | 0.60 | 0.73 | 0.75 | 0.77 | 1.13 | 1.17 |
| 1 | 3.64 | 3.56 | 3.87 | 3.57 | 3.27 | 1.64 | 1.33 |
| 2 | 4.29 | 4.18 | 4.25 | 4.16 | 3.71 | -1.34 | -2.90 |
| 3 | 4.41 | 3.81 | 3.83 | 3.62 | 2.71 | -3.95 | -6.35 |
| 4 | 3.73 | 3.07 | 3.27 | 3.51 | 3.27 | -2.40 | -2.67 |
| | | | | *Regression $R^2$* | | | |
| M | 0.04 | 0.06 | 0.08 | 0.08 | 0.05 | 0.03 | 0.03 |
| Q | 0.06 | 0.05 | 0.08 | 0.10 | 0.10 | 0.06 | 0.06 |
| 1 | 0.39 | 0.37 | 0.44 | 0.41 | 0.35 | 0.16 | 0.18 |
| 2 | 0.21 | 0.18 | 0.24 | 0.30 | 0.44 | 0.36 | 0.37 |
| 3 | 0.13 | 0.08 | 0.15 | 0.24 | 0.46 | 0.53 | 0.48 |
| 4 | 0.09 | 0.04 | 0.13 | 0.25 | 0.51 | 0.60 | 0.50 |

| $T$ | Aaa | Aa | A | Baa | LG | VW | EW |
|---|---|---|---|---|---|---|---|
| | | | | *t-statistics for D/P slopes* | | | |
| M | 2.75 | 2.58 | 2.54 | 2.81 | 3.82 | 2.88 | 2.99 |
| Q | 1.91 | 1.89 | 1.97 | 2.42 | 3.28 | 2.93 | 3.03 |
| 1 | 0.75 | 0.47 | 1.31 | 2.14 | 3.91 | 3.45 | 3.67 |
| 2 | 0.87 | 0.49 | 1.58 | 2.56 | 3.97 | 4.18 | 3.87 |
| 3 | 1.37 | 0.78 | 2.27 | 3.11 | 3.65 | 4.94 | 3.31 |
| 4 | 3.78 | 1.94 | 3.65 | 3.83 | 4.21 | 5.26 | 3.18 |
| | | | | *t-statistics for TERM slopes* | | | |
| M | 2.77 | 3.55 | 4.35 | 4.81 | 3.32 | 3.29 | 2.97 |
| Q | 1.51 | 1.52 | 2.07 | 2.43 | 1.89 | 2.17 | 1.82 |
| 1 | 4.74 | 5.07 | 5.68 | 5.57 | 4.10 | 0.94 | 0.66 |
| 2 | 3.25 | 3.48 | 3.64 | 4.06 | 3.04 | -0.63 | -0.89 |
| 3 | 2.13 | 2.09 | 1.95 | 2.31 | 2.01 | -1.23 | -1.27 |
| 4 | 1.11 | 0.97 | 1.02 | 1.40 | 1.45 | -0.75 | -0.64 |

Portfolios

$$r(t, t+T) = a + bDEF(t) + cTERM(t) + e(t, t+T)$$

Slopes for DEF

| T | Aaa | Aa | A | Baa | LG | VW | EW |
|---|---|---|---|---|---|---|---|
| M | 0.23 | 0.27 | 0.30 | 0.36 | 0.84 | 0.52 | 0.91 |
| Q | 0.57 | 0.68 | 0.80 | 1.09 | 2.72 | 2.18 | 3.70 |
| 1 | 1.42 | 1.11 | 2.87 | 4.51 | 11.15 | 10.98 | 18.62 |
| 2 | 6.25 | 5.13 | 9.01 | 11.73 | 24.48 | 24.83 | 39.56 |
| 3 | 10.01 | 8.66 | 13.83 | 17.45 | 36.15 | 36.07 | 54.33 |
| 4 | 13.35 | 11.16 | 16.32 | 19.90 | 40.18 | 41.99 | 57.36 |

Slopes for TERM

| T | Aaa | Aa | A | Baa | LG | VW | EW |
|---|---|---|---|---|---|---|---|
| M | 0.25 | 0.27 | 0.30 | 0.31 | 0.29 | 0.46 | 0.48 |
| Q | 0.61 | 0.58 | 0.71 | 0.71 | 0.68 | 1.09 | 1.08 |
| 1 | 3.60 | 3.53 | 3.79 | 3.46 | 3.03 | 1.75 | 1.31 |
| 2 | 4.05 | 3.95 | 4.01 | 3.94 | 3.44 | -0.89 | -2.57 |
| 3 | 3.94 | 3.33 | 3.38 | 3.18 | 2.19 | -3.47 | -6.12 |
| 4 | 3.22 | 2.59 | 2.85 | 3.12 | 2.92 | -1.60 | -1.97 |

Regression $R^2$

| T | Aaa | Aa | A | Baa | LG | VW | EW |
|---|---|---|---|---|---|---|---|
| M | 0.04 | 0.06 | 0.08 | 0.08 | 0.06 | 0.02 | 0.02 |
| Q | 0.05 | 0.05 | 0.08 | 0.10 | 0.11 | 0.04 | 0.04 |
| 1 | 0.40 | 0.38 | 0.46 | 0.45 | 0.45 | 0.09 | 0.13 |
| 2 | 0.27 | 0.22 | 0.32 | 0.41 | 0.59 | 0.21 | 0.29 |
| 3 | 0.23 | 0.16 | 0.29 | 0.42 | 0.70 | 0.39 | 0.44 |
| 4 | 0.21 | 0.14 | 0.27 | 0.43 | 0.71 | 0.43 | 0.42 |

t-statistics for DEF slopes

| T | Aaa | Aa | A | Baa | LG | VW | EW |
|---|---|---|---|---|---|---|---|
| M | 1.87 | 2.35 | 2.93 | 3.08 | 3.89 | 1.43 | 1.77 |
| Q | 1.22 | 1.49 | 1.80 | 2.31 | 3.25 | 1.61 | 1.84 |
| 1 | 1.08 | 0.73 | 1.90 | 2.79 | 4.37 | 2.12 | 2.79 |
| 2 | 1.62 | 1.20 | 2.24 | 3.74 | 5.79 | 3.01 | 3.82 |
| 3 | 1.65 | 1.31 | 2.49 | 5.00 | 9.42 | 4.17 | 4.04 |
| 4 | 1.85 | 1.44 | 2.56 | 4.26 | 11.52 | 3.94 | 3.78 |

t-statistics for TERM slopes

| T | Aaa | Aa | A | Baa | LG | VW | EW |
|---|---|---|---|---|---|---|---|
| M | 2.64 | 3.39 | 4.13 | 4.52 | 2.99 | 3.21 | 2.83 |
| Q | 1.44 | 1.44 | 1.96 | 2.25 | 1.64 | 2.03 | 1.62 |
| 1 | 4.59 | 4.97 | 5.61 | 5.55 | 4.41 | 0.99 | 0.61 |
| 2 | 3.26 | 3.61 | 3.86 | 4.89 | 4.82 | -0.38 | -0.70 |
| 3 | 1.74 | 1.69 | 1.51 | 1.74 | 1.28 | -0.96 | -1.16 |
| 4 | 0.87 | 0.75 | 0.81 | 1.12 | 1.05 | -0.40 | -0.49 |

[a]The regressions for $T$ = one month (M), one quarter (Q), and one year use nonoverlapping returns. The regressions for two- to four-year returns use overlapping annual observations. The numbers of observations in the regressions are (M) 564, (Q) 188, (1 yr) 47, (2 yr) 46, (3 yr) 45, and (4 yr) 44. The standard errors in the t-statistics for the slopes are adjusted for heteroscedasticity and (for two- to four-year returns) the sample autocorrelation of overlapping residuals with the method of Hansen (1982) and White (1980). See note to table 1 for definition of portfolios.

The term spread is not highly correlated with the dividend yield or the default spread. (Over the 1941–1987 period, *TERM* has a correlation of 0.16 with $D/P$ and 0.18 with *DEF*.) Yet all three variables are related to business conditions. Since the regressions, presented next, show that $D/P$, *DEF*, and *TERM* forecast returns on bonds and stocks, we infer that the variation of expected returns has a rich mix of components that relate to long- and short-term aspects of business conditions.

## 4. The regressions

Tables 2 and 3 show results for 1927–1987 and 1941–1987 from multiple regressions of bond and stock returns on the term spread and the dividend yield or the default spread. Slopes and *t*-statistics (not shown) for 1946–1987 and 1957–1987 are similar to those for 1941–1987. Thus the results for 1941–1987 are a good view of expected-return variation for the 47-year period after the Great Depression.

We argue that the regressions for 1927–1987 and 1941–1987 tell a similar story about the expected-return variation tracked by $D/P$, *DEF*, and *TERM*. The regression $R^2$ and the *t*-statistics for the regression slopes in tables 2 and 3 nevertheless illustrate that the forecast power of the three variables is stronger and more consistently reliable across different portfolios and return horizons for periods after the Great Depression. (See also table 5 below.)

### 4.1. Business conditions and common variation in expected returns

Tables 2 and 3 show that our forecasting variables have information about expected returns on stocks and bonds. All the regression slopes for the default spread and almost all the slopes for the dividend yield and the term spread are positive. Many of the slopes, especially for 1941–1987, are more than 2 standard errors from 0. The dividend yield, a variable from the stock market that is known to forecast stock returns, also forecasts corporate bond returns. The default and term spreads, variables from the bond market that are known to forecast bond returns, also forecast stock returns. In short, the three forecasting variables track components of expected returns that are common across assets.

The relatively high correlation between *DEF* and $D/P$ (0.61 for 1927–1987 and 0.75 for 1941–1987) implies that the default spread and the dividend yield track similar predictable components of returns. Given the relation between long-term business conditions and these two forecasting variables (fig. 1), we infer that *DEF* and $D/P$ track components of expected returns that are high during periods like the Great Depression, when business is persistently poor and low during periods like 1953–1973, when business is persistently strong. Fig. 1 and the regression slopes also imply that there are upward blips in the expected-return variation signaled by *DEF* and *D/P* during post-World War II recessions, especially the two major recessions of 1974–1975 and 1980–1982.

Fig. 2 says that the term spread is related to the shorter-term business cycles identified by the NBER. The component of expected returns captured by *TERM* is low around business-cycle peaks and high around troughs. This *TERM* component of expected returns is less persistent than the expected-return variation captured by *D/P* and *DEF*. Nevertheless, a general message from the regressions is that all three forecasting variables signal that expected returns are low when times are good and higher when they are poor.

## 4.2. Business conditions and cross-sectional patterns in expected returns

As indicated earlier, the slopes from regressions of returns on the default spread are in line with intuition about the business risks of bonds and stocks. The *DEF* slopes tend to be larger for lower-grade than for higher-grade bonds, larger for stocks than for bonds, and larger for the equal-weighted stock portfolio than for the value-weighted portfolio. The slopes for the dividend yield, especially for 1941–1987, also tend to increase from higher- to lower-grade bonds, from bonds to stocks, and from big stocks to small stocks.

The pattern in the slopes for *D/P* and *DEF* implies that the two variables track variation in expected returns that is largest for stocks and smallest for high-grade bonds. Thus, like the general level of expected returns, the differences between the expected returns on stocks and bonds vary with *D/P* and *DEF*. The spreads of the expected returns of stocks over bonds, and of low-grade over high-grade bonds, are high when the economy is weak, but they narrow when business conditions are strong.

Unlike the slopes for the default spread and the dividend yield, the slopes for the term spread in tables 2 and 3 are quite similar for different (long-term) bond portfolios. For example, in the monthly regressions for 1927–1987, the *TERM* slopes for the bond portfolios are between 0.22 and 0.24. The *TERM* slopes for the stock portfolios are in turn similar to those for bonds, at least for monthly, quarterly, and annual returns, where the slopes are estimated more precisely. The results suggest that *TERM* captures a term premium in expected returns that is largely a function of maturity and so is similar for all long-term securities. This inference is supported by the evidence in Keim and Stambaugh (1986) and Fama (1988) that variables like *TERM* (spreads of long-term over short-term bond yields) capture variation in the expected returns on Treasury bonds that increases with maturity.

What risk is associated with the term premium? The major difference between short- and long-maturity securities of the same quality is the higher sensitivity of long-maturity prices to general shifts in the level of discount rates. An old hypothesis [for example, Hicks (1947) and Kessel (1965)], easily accommodated in modern multifactor asset-pricing models, is that the term premium compensates for this discount-rate risk. The compensation is low around business-cycle peaks and high around troughs.

## 4.3. Cross-sectional patterns in expected returns: Formal tests

Table 4 shows *F*-tests of the hypothesis that the slopes for *D/P*, *DEF*, or *TERM* are equal across portfolios. *F*-tests are shown for nonoverlapping monthly, quarterly, and annual returns, where larger sample sizes imply that the tests are likely to have power. The *F*-tests are largely consistent with our inferences about the patterns in the regression slopes in tables 2 and 3.

The *F*-tests always reject the hypothesis that the slopes for *DEF* or *D/P* are the same for the seven stock and bond portfolios. The tests, especially for 1941–1987, also reject the equal-slope hypothesis for the five bond portfolios. Thus the pattern in the slopes for *DEF* or *D/P* (increasing from high-grade to low-grade bonds, from bonds to stocks, and from big stocks to small stocks) apparently reflects reliable differences across assets in the variation through time of expected returns.

The *F*-tests of the hypothesis that *TERM* tracks a maturity premium that is the same for all long-term securities are less clearcut. When only bonds are considered, the *F*-tests are all consistent with the hypothesis that the *TERM* slopes are the same for the five portfolios. When stocks are included, however, the tests for 1941–1987 and the tests on the monthly slopes for 1927–1987 tend to reject the hypothesis that the *TERM* slopes are the same for the seven stock and bond portfolios. We infer that *TERM* tracks what is essentially, but perhaps not entirely, a maturity premium in expected returns.

## 4.4. Explanatory power and the return horizon

The regression $R^2$ in tables 2 and 3 tend to increase with the holding period for both stock and bond returns. The $R^2$ are typically less than 0.1 for monthly and quarterly returns, but are often greater than 0.3 for one- to four-year returns. This pattern of stronger explanatory power for longer return horizons has a simple and interesting explanation that is linked to our business-conditions story for the variation in expected returns.

The dividend yield and the default spread are largely measures of long-term business conditions. Their autocorrelations decay slowly across longer lags (table 1). Thus the information in *D/P* and *DEF* about future one-period expected returns also decays slowly; that is, the current values of *D/P* and *DEF* contain information about distant one-period expected returns. Since the slopes for long-horizon returns cumulate the information in the independent variables, the slopes for *D/P* and *DEF* in tables 2 and 3 almost always increase with the return horizon.

Table 4

F-tests that regression slopes are equal across portfolios.[a]

| $T$ | Obs. | 5 bond & 2 stock portfolios | | 5 bond portfolios | |
|---|---|---|---|---|---|

Part A: $R(t, t+T) = a + bD(t)/P(t) + cTERM(t) + e(t, t+T)$

| $T$ | Obs. | D/P | TERM | D/P | TERM |
|---|---|---|---|---|---|
| | | 1927–1987 | | | |
| M | 732 | 9.97 (0.000) | 1.84 (0.075) | 3.72 (0.005) | 0.40 (0.807) |
| Q | 244 | 13.21 (0.000) | 0.43 (0.887) | 2.11 (0.077) | 0.11 (0.978) |
| 1 | 61 | 9.77 (0.000) | 1.53 (0.154) | 2.13 (0.077) | 0.65 (0.627) |
| | | 1941–1987 | | | |
| M | 564 | 14.42 (0.000) | 5.27 (0.000) | 5.94 (0.000) | 1.51 (0.196) |
| Q | 188 | 13.60 (0.000) | 2.34 (0.022) | 5.01 (0.001) | 0.71 (0.586) |
| 1 | 47 | 24.55 (0.000) | 2.67 (0.010) | 9.61 (0.000) | 0.36 (0.839) |

Part B: $R(t, t+T) = a + bDEF(t) + cTERM(t) + e(t, t+T)$

| $T$ | Obs. | DEF | TERM | DEF | TERM |
|---|---|---|---|---|---|
| | | 1927–1987 | | | |
| M | 732 | 2.23 (0.029) | 1.88 (0.068) | 1.37 (0.243) | 0.10 (0.982) |
| Q | 244 | 5.03 (0.000) | 0.49 (0.844) | 2.44 (0.046) | 0.21 (0.932) |
| 1 | 61 | 7.11 (0.000) | 1.72 (0.103) | 2.66 (0.033) | 0.62 (0.652) |
| | | 1941–1987 | | | |
| M | 564 | 10.17 (0.000) | 4.66 (0.000) | 8.57 (0.000) | 1.17 (0.324) |
| Q | 188 | 11.78 (0.000) | 1.81 (0.081) | 8.60 (0.000) | 0.44 (0.782) |
| 1 | 47 | 23.45 (0.000) | 2.44 (0.019) | 16.65 (0.000) | 0.62 (0.652) |

[a] The $F$-statistics test the hypothesis that the slopes (tables 2 and 3) from regressions of monthly (M), quarterly (Q), or annual (1) returns on the term spread (TERM) and the default spread (DEF) or the dividend yield (D/P) are equal for the five bond portfolios or for the five bond portfolios and the two stock portfolios. [See Theil (1971, p. 314).] P-values are in parentheses.

Table 5

Slopes, *t*-statistics, and $R^2$ from multiple regressions of real returns on the term spread (*TERM*) and the value-weighted dividend yield (*D/P*) or the default spread (*DEF*); 1953–1987.[a]

$$r(t, t+T) = a + bD(t)/P(t) + cTERM(t) + e(t, t+T)$$

| T | Aaa | Aa | A | Baa | LG | VW | EW | Aaa | Aa | A | Baa | LG | VW | EW |
|---|---|---|---|---|---|---|---|---|---|---|---|---|---|---|
| | Slopes for *D/P* | | | | | | | *t*-statistics for *D/P* slopes | | | | | | |
| M | 0.27 | 0.24 | 0.23 | 0.25 | 0.28 | 0.57 | 0.76 | 1.88 | 1.84 | 1.87 | 2.07 | 2.02 | 2.31 | 2.50 |
| Q | 0.76 | 0.73 | 0.77 | 0.81 | 0.88 | 2.01 | 2.65 | 1.38 | 1.40 | 1.54 | 1.73 | 1.72 | 2.87 | 2.72 |
| 1 | 0.32 | 0.32 | 1.10 | 1.58 | 1.83 | 7.80 | 11.28 | 0.24 | 0.23 | 0.85 | 1.31 | 1.29 | 2.69 | 3.01 |
| 2 | 2.09 | 2.01 | 3.97 | 4.74 | 5.82 | 16.76 | 22.67 | 0.55 | 0.51 | 1.02 | 1.28 | 1.48 | 2.93 | 3.20 |
| 3 | 3.50 | 3.37 | 5.98 | 6.41 | 8.30 | 18.64 | 24.02 | 0.80 | 0.76 | 1.33 | 1.52 | 1.75 | 2.60 | 2.71 |
| 4 | 5.66 | 5.34 | 7.85 | 8.08 | 9.32 | 19.18 | 23.35 | 1.23 | 1.21 | 1.63 | 2.03 | 1.98 | 2.75 | 2.44 |
| | Slopes for *TERM* | | | | | | | *t*-statistics for *TERM* slopes | | | | | | |
| M | 0.27 | 0.31 | 0.34 | 0.35 | 0.33 | 0.54 | 0.54 | 2.87 | 3.71 | 4.45 | 4.93 | 3.31 | 3.61 | 3.04 |
| Q | 0.74 | 0.73 | 0.85 | 0.86 | 0.84 | 1.36 | 1.30 | 1.75 | 1.80 | 2.36 | 2.73 | 1.99 | 2.58 | 1.99 |
| 1 | 4.40 | 4.38 | 4.64 | 4.28 | 4.00 | 2.47 | 1.58 | 4.45 | 4.70 | 5.15 | 5.11 | 4.15 | 1.32 | 0.75 |
| 2 | 4.99 | 4.98 | 4.93 | 4.75 | 4.19 | -0.94 | -3.83 | 2.53 | 2.72 | 2.79 | 3.03 | 2.65 | -0.39 | -1.13 |
| 3 | 4.53 | 4.07 | 3.85 | 3.45 | 2.18 | -4.08 | -8.39 | 1.54 | 1.58 | 1.45 | 1.50 | 0.92 | -1.01 | -1.53 |
| 4 | 3.05 | 2.55 | 2.53 | 2.48 | 1.44 | -3.00 | -5.53 | 0.64 | 0.57 | 0.57 | 0.65 | 0.37 | -0.69 | -1.18 |
| | Regression $R^2$ | | | | | | | | | | | | | |
| M | 0.05 | 0.07 | 0.09 | 0.09 | 0.06 | 0.04 | 0.03 | | | | | | | |
| Q | 0.07 | 0.07 | 0.10 | 0.12 | 0.08 | 0.08 | 0.07 | | | | | | | |
| 1 | 0.39 | 0.40 | 0.46 | 0.44 | 0.33 | 0.17 | 0.18 | | | | | | | |
| 2 | 0.17 | 0.17 | 0.21 | 0.25 | 0.23 | 0.33 | 0.38 | | | | | | | |
| 3 | 0.08 | 0.06 | 0.10 | 0.13 | 0.14 | 0.38 | 0.44 | | | | | | | |
| 4 | 0.03 | 0.02 | 0.07 | 0.11 | 0.12 | 0.35 | 0.33 | | | | | | | |

Portfolios

$$r(t, t+T) = a + bDEF(t) + cTERM(t) + e(t, t+T)$$

Portfolios

Slopes for DEF

| $T$ | Aaa | Aa | A | Baa | LG | VW | EW |
|---|---|---|---|---|---|---|---|
| M | 0.68 | 0.99 | 0.97 | 0.91 | 1.08 | 1.04 | 1.29 |
| Q | 1.87 | 2.65 | 2.72 | 2.77 | 3.60 | 4.78 | 5.85 |
| 1 | 5.79 | 7.29 | 9.49 | 10.51 | 12.75 | 23.33 | 30.27 |
| 2 | 24.22 | 24.98 | 29.73 | 29.25 | 30.91 | 43.43 | 52.31 |
| 3 | 35.21 | 36.54 | 41.55 | 38.99 | 42.02 | 46.14 | 49.56 |
| 4 | 44.16 | 43.67 | 48.24 | 44.49 | 45.21 | 53.55 | 49.21 |

Slopes for TERM

| $T$ | Aaa | Aa | A | Baa | LG | VW | EW |
|---|---|---|---|---|---|---|---|
| M | 0.26 | 0.29 | 0.32 | 0.33 | 0.31 | 0.53 | 0.52 |
| Q | 0.72 | 0.70 | 0.82 | 0.83 | 0.80 | 1.32 | 1.25 |
| 1 | 4.31 | 4.25 | 4.55 | 4.22 | 3.91 | 2.83 | 2.17 |
| 2 | 4.95 | 4.92 | 5.05 | 4.96 | 4.52 | 0.56 | -1.73 |
| 3 | 4.55 | 4.05 | 4.12 | 3.81 | 2.75 | -2.18 | -5.82 |
| 4 | 3.80 | 3.26 | 3.54 | 3.52 | 2.63 | -0.64 | -2.68 |

Regression $R^2$

| $T$ | Aaa | Aa | A | Baa | LG | VW | EW |
|---|---|---|---|---|---|---|---|
| M | 0.05 | 0.09 | 0.10 | 0.10 | 0.07 | 0.04 | 0.03 |
| Q | 0.06 | 0.08 | 0.11 | 0.13 | 0.11 | 0.07 | 0.04 |
| 1 | 0.43 | 0.45 | 0.54 | 0.53 | 0.45 | 0.17 | 0.14 |
| 2 | 0.38 | 0.39 | 0.47 | 0.50 | 0.46 | 0.22 | 0.20 |
| 3 | 0.34 | 0.36 | 0.42 | 0.44 | 0.42 | 0.24 | 0.20 |
| 4 | 0.32 | 0.33 | 0.38 | 0.41 | 0.37 | 0.28 | 0.12 |

t-statistics for DEF slopes

| $T$ | Aaa | Aa | A | Baa | LG | VW | EW |
|---|---|---|---|---|---|---|---|
| M | 1.73 | 2.91 | 3.20 | 2.79 | 3.01 | 1.43 | 1.43 |
| Q | 1.24 | 1.98 | 2.12 | 2.09 | 2.56 | 1.97 | 1.80 |
| 1 | 1.56 | 2.11 | 2.61 | 3.16 | 2.99 | 2.27 | 2.52 |
| 2 | 2.95 | 3.06 | 3.68 | 4.04 | 3.22 | 2.42 | 2.43 |
| 3 | 3.45 | 3.61 | 4.77 | 5.04 | 4.50 | 2.70 | 2.20 |
| 4 | 3.67 | 3.67 | 4.75 | 4.24 | 5.72 | 3.22 | 2.14 |

t-statistics for TERM slopes

| $T$ | Aaa | Aa | A | Baa | LG | VW | EW |
|---|---|---|---|---|---|---|---|
| M | 2.68 | 3.47 | 4.22 | 4.62 | 3.12 | 3.55 | 2.97 |
| Q | 1.65 | 1.70 | 2.24 | 2.56 | 1.89 | 2.43 | 1.85 |
| 1 | 4.54 | 4.96 | 5.67 | 5.68 | 4.99 | 1.52 | 0.97 |
| 2 | 3.30 | 3.83 | 4.47 | 5.40 | 4.51 | 0.24 | -0.46 |
| 3 | 1.49 | 1.51 | 1.43 | 1.48 | 1.02 | -0.54 | -0.99 |
| 4 | 0.75 | 0.69 | 0.75 | 0.85 | 0.61 | -0.15 | -0.61 |

[a] The regressions for $T$ = one month (M), one quarter (Q), and one year use nonoverlapping returns. The regressions for two- to four-year returns use overlapping annual observations. The numbers of observations in the regressions are (M) 420 (Q) 140, (1 yr) 35, (2 yr) 34, (3 yr) 33, and (4 yr) 32. The standard errors in the t-statistics for the slopes are adjusted for heteroscedasticity and (for two- to four-year returns) the sample autocorrelation of overlapping residuals with the method of Hansen (1982) and White (1980). See note to table 1 for definition of portfolios.

The term spread is more closely related to shorter-term measured business cycles. The first-order autocorrelations of annual observations on *TERM* are large for both 1927–1987 and 1941–1987 (table 1), but the higher-order autocorrelations for 1941–1987 are close to 0. Consistent with this pattern, the 1941–1987 *TERM* slopes in table 3 tend to increase with the return horizon out to one or two years, and then flatten or decline.

Since the variances of the regression fitted values grow like the squares of the slopes, slopes that increase with the return horizon can explain, in large part, why the regression $R^2$ tends to increase with the return horizon. In economic terms, $D/P$, *DEF*, and, to a lesser extent, *TERM* track autocorrelated components of expected returns, generated by persistence in business conditions, that become larger fractions of return variation for longer return horizons. In this view, the explanatory power (high $R^2$) of regressions for long-horizon returns is a simple consequence of persistence in short-horizon expected returns. [Fama and French (1988b) discuss this in more detail.]

## 5. Interpretation

### 5.1. Consumption smoothing

Consumption smoothing is a common feature of intertemporal asset-pricing models [see, for example, Merton (1973), Lucas (1978), and Breeden (1979)]. Like the permanent-income model of Modigliani and Brumberg (1955) and Friedman (1957), the asset-pricing models predict that consumption depends on wealth rather than current income. When income is high in relation to wealth, investors want to smooth consumption into the future by saving more. If the supply of capital-investment opportunities is not also unusually large, higher desired savings lead to lower expected security returns. Conversely, investors want to save less when income is temporarily low. Again, without an offsetting reduction in capital-investment opportunities, lower desired savings tend to push expected returns up. Thus variation in expected returns opposite to business conditions is consistent with modern asset-pricing models.

We find that expected *excess* returns (returns net of the one-month bill rate) are inversely related to business conditions. Some versions of the consumption-smoothing story – for example, Abel (1988) as interpreted by Chen (1989) – do predict that expected excess returns vary opposite to current business conditions. More typically, however, consumption-smoothing models predict that expected *real* returns vary opposite to business conditions. See, for example, Hansen and Singleton (1983) and Breeden (1986). It is thus interesting to check whether our forecasting variables also track expected real returns.

Table 5 replicates the regressions using real returns on the bond and stock portfolios for 1953–1987. We choose 1953–1987 to show some results for a period that is free of any unusual effects of the Great Depression, World War II, the Korean War, and the pegging of Treasury-bill interest rates preceding the 1951 accord between the Treasury and the Federal Reserve. (The potential effects of these episodes on the results for 1927–1987 and 1941–1987 seem to concern many readers.) The timeliness and reliability of inflation rates estimated from the U.S. Consumer Price Index also improve in 1953 [Fama (1975)].

The 1953–1987 results for real returns are similar to the 1941–1987 results for excess returns. In short, given that $D/P$, $DEF$, and $TERM$ move opposite to business conditions, the regressions for real returns show that, like expected excess returns, expected real returns move opposite to business conditions.

## 5.2. Other explanations

We do not mean to suggest that consumption smoothing is the whole story for the variation in expected returns. Another reasonable hypothesis is that the risks for which $D/P$, $DEF$, and $TERM$ are proxies are higher when times are poor and lower when times are good. [Schwert (1988) provides suggestive evidence.]

It also seems likely that variation in capital-investment opportunities (the 'productivity shocks' of the business-cycles literature) generates some of the variation in expected returns. For example, there is suggestive evidence that investment opportunities play a role in the expected-return variation tracked by the term spread. Thus Chen (1989) formally documents the clear impression from fig. 2 that $TERM$ is positively related to future real activity. Since $TERM$ is low near business-cycle peaks and high near troughs, Chen's results suggest that poor prospects for future real activity (and thus investments) near business peaks may help explain low expected returns around peaks. Likewise, good prospects for future activity and investment after business troughs may contribute to high expected returns around troughs.

Our evidence documents variation in expected returns related to business conditions, but the evidence does not distinguish among the many potential explanations. Fleshing out the theoretical and empirical details of a story for the apparently rich variation in expected returns on bonds and stocks in response to business conditions is an exciting challenge.

## 6. Comparisons

### 6.1. Keim and Stambaugh (1986)

The paper closest to ours is Keim and Stambaugh (1986). They also test for common variation in expected returns on bonds and stocks. At least for bonds, they also find strong evidence that expected returns vary through time. Their tests are limited to monthly returns, however, so they miss the increase in forecast power for longer return horizons observed here. Moreover, they do not attempt to relate expected returns to business conditions.

Keim and Stambaugh's evidence for stock returns is rather weak. They find strong evidence of time-varying expected returns only for the month of January. In their (table 2) regressions for all months of the 1928–1978 sample period, six of nine regression slopes for stock returns are within 2 standard errors of 0. When they split the data into subperiods (1928–1952 and 1953–1978), even this weak evidence of forecast power disappears.

To some extent, our stronger evidence on the predictability of stock returns comes from looking at return horizons longer than a month. Like those of Keim and Stambaugh, our results for monthly 1927–1987 returns are not strong. On the other hand, there is nothing in their subperiod tests that corresponds to our strong evidence on the predictability of stock returns for 1941–1987 (table 3), 1953–1987 (table 5), and 1967–1986 (table 6, below). We think these differences in results are due more to the choice of forecasting variables.

Their yield variable is the spread between the yield on bonds rated under Baa and the one-month bill rate. In our terms, their yield spread is like the sum of the default spread and the term spread. Since *DEF* and *TERM* track different components of expected returns, the sum can give an attenuated picture of the variation in expected returns. The sum also smears the differences in the patterns of the slopes for *DEF* and *TERM* that are among our more interesting and novel results.

The other two variables Keim and Stambaugh use to forecast returns are (1) minus the log of the ratio of the value of the Standard and Poor's 500 index to its average value over the preceding 45 years, and (2) minus the log of the average price of the shares of firms in the smallest quintile of NYSE stocks. Our tests indicate that these variables have less power to forecast stock returns than the dividend yield, the default spread, and the term spread, especially for periods after the Great Depression.

Our purpose is not to criticize Keim and Stambaugh. Their paper is painstaking and pathbreaking. A reasonable view of our work is that it (1) refines their choice of forecasting variables, (2) extends their tests on monthly returns to longer return horizons, (3) explains why expected (bond and stock) returns account for more return variation for longer return horizons, and, most important, (4) begins to tell a story that relates the common variation in expected bond and stock returns to business conditions.

### 6.2. Chen, Roll, and Ross (1986)

Our time-series evidence on the expected-return variation tracked by the default and term spreads complements the cross-section evidence of Chen, Roll, and Ross (1986). They argue (as we do) that the default spread is a measure of business conditions. Thus covariances of asset returns with shocks to *DEF* are likely to help explain differences in expected returns in the multifactor asset-pricing models of Merton (1973) and Ross (1976). Their cross-section tests on stock returns support this hypothesis. They find that business risks (measured by the covariances of returns with shocks to *DEF*) and expected returns are larger for the stocks of smaller firms.

We find complementary evidence in our time-series tests. The variation in expected returns tracked by the default spread increases from high-grade to low-grade bonds, from bonds to stocks, and from big stocks to small stocks. Thus our results support and enrich their default-spread story.

Chen, Roll, and Ross also argue that the term spread is a measure of business conditions. In their tests, however, covariances with shocks to *TERM* show little power to explain the cross-section of expected stock returns. Again, this is consistent with our evidence. Our time-series tests suggest that all long-term securities (stocks and bonds) will have similar covariances with shocks to *TERM*. As a result, *TERM* will have power in cross-section tests only when securities with a range of maturities are included.

## 7. Out-of-sample forecasts

### 7.1. A statistical issue

In models like (1) that regress future returns on current yields, it is reasonable to assume that the residual, $\varepsilon(t, t + T)$, is uncorrelated with the independent variable, $X(t)$, and with past values of $X$. Stambaugh (1986) argues, however, that the residual is often correlated with future values of $X$. For example, in regressions of nominal bond returns on bond yields, the unexpected return from $t - T$ to $t$, $\varepsilon(t - T, t)$, and the yield shock between $t - T$ and $t$ will be negatively correlated because shocks to yields produce opposite shocks to returns. In this case, Stambaugh shows that if the yield, $X(t)$, is positively autocorrelated, the ordinary least-squares (OLS) slope in (1) is upward biased; the estimated slope overstates forecast power.

When we apply Stambaugh's bias-adjustment procedure to our excess-return regressions, the estimates suggest that OLS slopes for $D/P$ and *DEF* are slightly upward biased, but the slopes for *TERM* are downward biased. The bias-adjusted slopes do not change the inferences about explanatory power drawn above. Since the bias-adjusted slopes are based on strong assumptions [$X(t)$ is a first-order autoregression, and $\varepsilon(t - T, t)$ and shocks to $X(t)$ are only contemporaneously correlated], we do not show them. Instead, we examine the robustness of the OLS results with out-of-sample forecasts.

### 7.2. Construction of the forecasts

We forecast returns for horizons from one month to four years. Since the effective samples for the longer horizons are small, we would like a long period to estimate the regressions and a long period to examine their out-of-sample forecasts. As tables 2 and 3 illustrate, however, the precision of the regression slopes falls if much of the volatile 1926–1940 period is used in the estimates. As a compromise, we forecast returns for the 21-year period 1967–1987 using rolling 30-year regression estimates that start in 1937.

Each forecast is from a regression estimated with returns that begin and end in the preceding 30-year period. For example, to forecast the first one-year return (1967), we use coefficients estimated with the 30 returns for 1937–1966. To forecast the first four-year return (1967–1970), we use coefficients estimated with the 27 overlapping annual observations on four-year returns that begin and end in the 1937–1966 period. For monthly and quarterly returns, the 30-year estimation period rolls forward in monthly or quarterly steps. For one- to four-year returns, the estimation period rolls forward in annual increments.

Although $D/P$ and $DEF$ capture similar components of expected returns, the results in tables 2 and 3 ($t$-statistics and regression $R^2$) suggest that $D/P$ makes better forecasts of stock returns, while $DEF$ is more informative for bond returns. Thus for the out-of-sample forecasts for bonds we use regressions of returns on $DEF$ and $TERM$. For stocks, regressions of returns on $D/P$ and $TERM$ are used to forecast monthly and quarterly returns. Since tables 2 and 3 say that $TERM$ does not have explanatory power for horizons beyond a quarter, only $D/P$ is used to forecast longer-horizon stock returns.

## 7.3. Forecast results

Table 6 compares the out-of-sample forecasts for 1967–1987 with the in-sample $R^2$ from regressions estimated on the 1967–1987 period. To simplify the comparisons, out-of-sample forecast power is also measured in terms of $R^2$. The out-of-sample $R^2$ is $1 - (MSE_R/MSE_N)$, where $MSE_R$ is the mean-squared-error of the out-of-sample regression forecasts for 1967–1987 and $MSE_N$ is the mean-squared-error of naive forecasts. Each naive forecast is just the average return during the 30-year period preceding the out-of-sample forecast (the same 30-year period used to obtain the slopes for the out-of-sample regression forecast). For example, the naive one-year return forecast for 1967 is the average annual return for 1937–1966. The naive four-year return forecast for 1967–1970 is four times the average annual return for 1937–1966.

The out-of-sample $R^2$ in table 6 tend to be smaller than the in-sample $R^2$ for 1967–1987, but the differences between in-sample and out-of-sample forecast power also tend to be small. Overall the results suggest that our OLS regressions have a bit of the Stambaugh (1986) bias problem; that is, the regression slopes and $R^2$ are slightly overstated.

The important result in table 6, however, is that the out-of-sample $R^2$ behave much like the in-sample $R^2$. Thus for higher-grade bonds (Aaa, Aa, A,

Table 6

$R^2$ for out-of-sample forecasts and for in-sample regressions for the 1967–1987 period.[a]

|   | Out | In | Out | In | Out | In | Out | In | Out | In |
|---|-----|----|-----|----|-----|----|-----|----|-----|----|
|   | Aaa | | Aa | | A | | Baa | | LG | |
| M | 0.03 | 0.04 | 0.06 | 0.08 | 0.08 | 0.09 | 0.08 | 0.09 | 0.06 | 0.06 |
| Q | −0.00 | 0.05 | 0.02 | 0.06 | 0.05 | 0.09 | 0.05 | 0.09 | 0.06 | 0.09 |
| 1 | 0.41 | 0.51 | 0.44 | 0.52 | 0.48 | 0.60 | 0.40 | 0.50 | 0.47 | 0.57 |
| 2 | 0.33 | 0.34 | 0.34 | 0.34 | 0.39 | 0.42 | 0.37 | 0.40 | 0.52 | 0.52 |
| 3 | 0.26 | 0.28 | 0.29 | 0.29 | 0.37 | 0.38 | 0.37 | 0.34 | 0.58 | 0.52 |
| 4 | 0.10 | 0.23 | 0.12 | 0.22 | 0.23 | 0.31 | 0.22 | 0.30 | 0.41 | 0.41 |
|   | VW | | EW | | | | | | | |
| M | 0.04 | 0.05 | 0.03 | 0.04 | | | | | | |
| Q | 0.07 | 0.10 | 0.05 | 0.08 | | | | | | |
| 1 | 0.18 | 0.15 | 0.19 | 0.23 | | | | | | |
| 2 | 0.33 | 0.39 | 0.35 | 0.45 | | | | | | |
| 3 | 0.40 | 0.53 | 0.45 | 0.53 | | | | | | |
| 4 | 0.38 | 0.59 | 0.46 | 0.50 | | | | | | |

[a] Each out-of-sample forecast is from regression coefficients estimated on the returns that begin and end in the preceding 30-year period. The bond return forecasts use *DEF* and *TERM*. The monthly (M) and quarterly (Q) stock return forecasts use $D/P$ and *TERM*; longer-horizon stock return forecasts use only $D/P$. See note to table 1 for definitions of portfolios and variables. For monthly and quarterly returns, the 30-year estimation period and the subsequent forecast period roll forward in monthly or quarterly steps. For one- to four-year returns, the estimation and forecast periods roll forward in annual increments.

The out-of-sample $R^2$ (Out) is $1 - (MSE_R / MSE_N)$, where $MSE_R$ is the mean-squared-error of the out-of-sample regression forecasts for 1967–1987 and $MSE_N$ is the mean-squared-error of naive forecasts. Each naive forecast is just the average return during the 30-year period preceding the out-of-sample forecast (the same 30-year period used to obtain the slopes for the out-of-sample regression forecast). The in-sample $R^2$ (In) are from regressions for 1967–1987.

The out-of-sample $R^2$ for two-, three-, and four-year stock returns are substantially larger than those in Fama and French (1988b). The higher values here reflect the use of $MSE_N$ as the benchmark (the denominator in $R^2$) against which the out-of-sample $MSE_R$ are compared. Fama and French (1988b) use the variance of the out-of-sample realized returns as the denominator for the out-of-sample $R^2$. For the overlapping two- to four-year returns, the out-of-sample variance and the resulting $R^2$ are biased downward.

and Baa), the shorter-term forecast power of *TERM* is more important than the longer-term forecast power of *DEF*. As a result, for these portfolios, both in- and out-of-sample $R^2$ increase from 0.09 or less for monthly and quarterly returns to an impressive 0.40 or more for annual returns, and then decay some for two-, three-, and four-year returns. In contrast, the longer-term forecast power of *DEF* and $D/P$ is relatively more important for low-grade bonds and the two stock portfolios. For these portfolios, the in- and out-of-sample $R^2$ increase from 0.10 or less for monthly returns to an impressive 0.40 or more in three- and four-year returns. In short, since the out-of-sample $R^2$ reproduce the interesting patterns in the in-sample $R^2$, the out-of-sample tests support our basic inferences about the variation in expected returns.

## 8. Conclusions

The default spread is a business-conditions variable, high during periods like the Great Depression when business is persistently poor and low during periods like 1953–1973 when the economy is persistently strong. The dividend yield is correlated with the default spread and moves in a similar way with long-term business conditions. For most of the 1927–1987 period, the term spread is related to shorter-term measured business cycles. It is low near business-cycle peaks and high near troughs. The fact that the three variables forecast stock and bond returns then suggests that the implied variation in expected returns is largely common across securities, and is negatively related to long- and short-term variation in business conditions.

One story for these results is that when business conditions are poor, income is low and expected returns on bonds and stocks must be high to induce substitution from consumption to investment. When times are good and income is high, the market clears at lower levels of expected returns. It is also possible, however, that variation in expected returns with business conditions is due to variation in the risks of bonds and stocks. Our regressions allow us to identify variation in expected returns. To decide how this variation splits between changes in the levels of different risks and their prices, other approaches will be needed.

What economic forces drive the economy between long- and short-term good and bad times? Invention? Changes in tastes for current versus uncertain future consumption? Government monetary and fiscal policies? These are, of course, the central and largely unanswered questions of macroeconomics. Answers to such questions are probably necessary, however, to explain our evidence that long- and short-term economic conditions produce a rich mix of variation in expected asset returns.

## References

Abel, Andrew, 1988, Stock prices under time varying dividend risk – An exact solution in an infinite horizon general equilibrium model, Journal of Monetary Economics 22, 375–393.

Ball, Ray, 1978, Anomalies in relationships between securities' yields and yield-surrogates, Journal of Financial Economics 6, 103–126.

Banz, Rolf W., 1981, The relationship between return and market value of common stocks, Journal of Financial Economics 9, 3–18.

Breeden, Douglas T., 1979, An intertemporal asset pricing model with stochastic consumption and investment opportunities, Journal of Financial Economics 7, 265–296.

Breeden, Douglas T., 1986, Consumption, production, inflation, and interest rates: A synthesis, Journal of Financial Economics 16, 3–39.

Campbell, John Y. and Robert Shiller, 1988, The dividend–price ratio and expectations of future dividends and discount factors, Review of Financial Studies 1, 195–228.

Chen, Nai-fu, 1989, Financial investment opportunities and the real economy, Working paper no. 266 (Center for Research in Security Prices, University of Chicago, Chicago, IL).

Chen, Nai-fu, Richard Roll, and Stephen A. Ross, 1986, Economic forces and the stock market, Journal of Business 56, 383–403.

Dow, Charles H., 1920, Scientific stock speculation, The Magazine of Wall Street (New York).

Fama, Eugene F., 1975, Short-term interest rates as predictors of inflation, American Economic Review 653, 269–282.

Fama, Eugene F., 1976, Forward rates as predictors of future spot rates, Journal of Financial Economics 3, 361–377.

Fama, Eugene F., 1984, The information in the term structure, Journal of Financial Economics 13, 509–528.

Fama, Eugene F., 1986, Term premiums and default premiums in money markets, Journal of Financial Economics 17, 175–196.

Fama, Eugene F., 1988, Term-structure forecasts of interest rates, inflation, and real returns, Working paper no. 233 (Center for Research in Security Prices, University of Chicago, Chicago, IL).

Fama, Eugene F. and Robert R. Bliss, 1987, The information in long-maturity forward rates, American Economic Review 77, 680–692.

Fama, Eugene F. and Kenneth R. French, 1988a, Permanent and temporary components of stock prices, Journal of Political Economy 96, 246–273.

Fama, Eugene F. and Kenneth R. French, 1988b, Dividend yields and expected stock returns, Journal of Financial Economics 22, 3–25.

Fama, Eugene F. and G. William Schwert, 1977, Asset returns and inflation, Journal of Financial Economics 5, 115–146.

Flood, Robert P., Robert J. Hodrick, and Paul Kaplan, 1986, An evaluation of recent evidence on stock market bubbles, Unpublished manuscript (National Bureau of Economic Research, Cambridge, MA).

Friedman, Milton, 1957, A theory of the consumption function (Princeton University Press, Princeton, NJ).

Hansen, Lars P., 1982, Large sample properties of generalized method of moments estimators, Econometrica 50, 1029–1054.

Hansen, Lars P. and Kenneth J. Singleton, 1983, Stochastic consumption, risk aversion, and the temporal behavior of asset returns, Journal of Political Economy 91, 249–265.

Hicks, John R., 1946, Value and capital, 2nd ed. (Oxford University Press, London).

Keim, Donald B. and Robert F. Stambaugh, 1986, Predicting returns in the stock and bond markets, Journal of Financial Economics 17, 357–390.

Kessel, Reuben A., 1965, The cyclical behavior of the term structure of interest rates, Occasional paper no. 91 (National Bureau of Economic Research, Cambridge, MA).

Lucas, Robert E., 1978, Asset prices in an exchange economy, Econometrica 46, 1429–1445.

Merton, Robert C., 1973, An intertemporal capital asset pricing model, Econometrica 41, 867–887.

Modigliani, Franco and Richard Brumberg, 1955, Utility analysis and the consumption function, in: K. Kurihara, ed., Post Keynesian economics (G. Allen, London).

Officer, R.R., 1973, The variability of the market factor of the New York Stock Exchange, Journal of Business 46, 434–453.

Ross, Stephen A., 1976, The arbitrage theory of capital asset pricing, Journal of Economic Theory 13, 341–360.

Rozeff, Michael, 1984, Dividend yields are equity risk premiums, Journal of Portfolio Management, 68–75.

Schwert, G. William, 1988, Why does stock market volatility change over time?, Unpublished manuscript (University of Rochester, Rochester, NY).

Shiller, Robert J., 1984, Stock prices and social dynamics, Brookings Papers on Economic Activity 2, 457–498.

Shiller, Robert J., John Y. Campbell, and Kermit L. Schoenholtz, 1983, Forward rates and future policy: Interpreting the term structure of interest rates, Brookings Papers on Economic Activity 1, 173–217.

Stambaugh, Robert F., 1986, Bias in regressions with lagged stochastic regressors, Working paper no. 156 (Center for Research in Security Prices, University of Chicago, Chicago, IL).

Theil, Henri, 1971, Principles of econometrics (Wiley, New York, NY).

White, Halbert, 1980, A heteroskedasticity-consistent covariance matrix estimator and direct test for heteroskedasticity, Econometrica 48, 817–838.

# V

# TAXES

**1** Litzenberger, R. H., and K. Ramaswamy, "The Effects of Dividends on Common Stock Prices: Tax Effects or Information Effects?" *Journal of Finance,* 37 (May 1982), pp. 429-443.
**2** Constantinides, G. M., and J. E. Ingersoll, "Optimal Bond Trading with Personal Taxes," *Journal of Financial Economics*, 10 (September 1984), pp. 229-336.

Much of the capital markets literature deals with models of frictionless markets. This is a useful abstraction for many purposes, but it can give misleading results when real market frictions affect securities differentially. An obvious example is the effect that taxes have on the pricing of securities. Anyone reading the *Wall Street Journal* can easily see that the yields on tax-exempt municipal bonds are lower than the taxable yields on U.S. Treasury securities.

Because the tax code has changed often in the past, and probably will change often in the future, we feel it is important to include papers that contain methodological insights into the study of tax effects. Since the Tax Reform Act of 1986, realized capital gains and dividend payments on common stocks have been taxed at the same marginal rates (although a small differential occurs again in 1991), so many detailed predictions of **Litzenberger and Ramaswamy (1982)** and **Constantinides and Ingersoll (1984)** are no longer valid. Nevertheless, these papers provide good examples of how to analyze problems of differential taxation. Extending their analysis to new forms of the tax code should help interested students to keep up with the effects of taxation as it changes in the future.

**Litzenberger and Ramaswamy (1982)** emplasize the effects that differential taxation of capital gains and dividends has on the pricing of common stocks. Until 1986, realized capital gains were taxed at a fraction, often one-half, of the rate on dividends and other income. Because gains are only taxed when they are realized, investors can reduce the effective tax rate. In the extreme, stocks that are passed through an estate are exempt from the capital gains tax, although estate taxes may be due. Since investors are interested in after-tax disposable income to fund their consumption, stocks that have more of their total return as capital gains would be preferred. Thus, the price of high-dividend-yield stocks would be lower, making the before-tax return higher, to offset the higher effective tax rate on dividend returns.

A competing hypothesis is that some taxpayers, such as pension funds, are tax-exempt, so they are indifferent to the form of return. Corporations pay a lower tax rate on dividends from other corporations' stock than they do on capital gains. Thus, there are important clienteles that do not have the aversion to dividend income that is implied by the tax code for individuals.

**Litzenberger and Ramaswamy (1982)** use a variety of tests to study the returns to stocks with different levels of dividend yields. As suggested by the title of the paper, they are particularly interested in controlling for the good news that would be associated with an announcement that a firm has increased its dividend payment (and the bad news that it has cut its payment). They conclude there is evidence that firms with higher dividend yields sell for lower prices. That is, they have higher before-tax risk-adjusted expected returns.

**Constantinides and Ingersoll (1984)** ask whether the passive "buy-and-hold" strategy is optimal in a world with different taxes on capital gains and dividends. They note there are several valuable options created by the tax code. Before 1986, the tax rate on capital gains depended on the length of time an investment had been held. Short-term gains and losses, less than 6 to 12 months, were taxed as ordinary income, while long-term gains and losses were taxed at lower rates. Thus, it paid to realize short-term losses just before they became long-term, and it paid to postpone gains until they became long-term. Also, **Constantinides and Ingersoll (1984)** argue that it pays to realize long-term gains to set up a new basis so the opportunity for future short-term losses is available. Finally, even if long-term gains are not taxed at favorably lower rates, establishing capital losses early, though equivalent gains will be established later, reduces the present value of tax liabilities. This tax-timing option is most valuable when interest rate volatility is high. Thus, a dynamic strategy based on annual taxation is better than a passive "buy-and-hold" strategy, even when investors have no special knowledge about the future behavior of bond prices.

# The Effects of Dividends on Common Stock Prices
# Tax Effects or Information Effects?

ROBERT H. LITZENBERGER and KRISHNA RAMASWAMY*

## I. Introduction

THERE HAS BEEN considerable controversy concerning the effect of dividend yields on common stock returns. The controversy centers on whether or not the positive association between common stock returns and dividend yields reported in a number of empirical studies can be attributed entirely to information effects. The purpose of this paper is to provide a brief critique of the theory and of the available empirical evidence (Section II), and to present some new empirical results (Section III). It is shown that there is a positive and non-linear relationship between common stock returns and expected dividend yield. The prediction rule for expected dividends is based solely on information that would have been available to the investor *ex-ante*. These results cannot, therefore, be attributed to the favorable or unfavorable information that would be present in a proxy for expected dividend yield that anticipates the occurrence (or lack thereof) of a dividend.

## II.1 Review of Theory

Brennan (1970) was the first to develop an After-tax Capital Asset Pricing Model. The model was derived under the assumptions of unlimited borrowing and lending at the risk free rate of interest and unrestricted short sales. The dollar dividends paid by corporations were assumed to be certain and known to investors. The equilibrium relationship derived is given by

$$E(\tilde{R}_i - r_f) = b_0\beta_i + c_0(d_i - r_f) \tag{1}$$

where $\tilde{R}_i$ is the before tax total rate of return on asset $i$, $\beta_i$ and $d_i$ are the systematic risk and the dividend yield on asset $i$ respectively, and $r_f$ is the risk free rate of interest. Note that the structural parameters $b_0$ and $c_0$ in this pricing relationship are not dependent on the level of the dividend yield. The parameter $c_0$ is a weighted average of the marginal tax rates of investors, with the weights being proportional to the individuals' global risk tolerances at the optimum. Thus $c_0 > 0$, and since by assumption individuals are risk averse, $b_0 > 0$.

Litzenberger and Ramaswamy (1979) extended the Brennan (1970) model to allow for margin constraints and for income related constraints on borrowing. The latter constraint serves to limit the interest deductions individuals can utilize to the amount of dividend income their portfolios generate. Those individuals for

---

* Stanford University and Columbia University.

THE JOURNAL OF FINANCE • VOL. XXXVII, NO. 2 • MAY 1982

whom this constraint is binding would find increased dividends desirable in that such increases serve to effectively relax the constraint. The equilibrium relationship so derived is given by

$$E(\tilde{R}_i - r_f) = a_1 + b_1\beta_i + c_1(d_i - r_f) \tag{2}$$

where $a_1 > 0$ is the risk premium on a zero beta portfolio that has a dividend yield equal to the riskless rate, and reflects the presence of the margin constraint. The model implies that $c_1$ is positive or negative, depending on whether the income related borrowing constraint is non binding or binding[1] for all individuals (see Litzenberger and Ramaswamy (1979, pp. 171–172). Note that in this model, as in Brennan's model, the parameter $c_1$ is independent of the level of the dividend yield $d_i$.

Miller and Scholes (1978) argue that the tax code permits strategies that enable one to escape the income tax on dividends altogether. Sufficient leverage of an equity portfolio can create interest expenses that can be used to offset the dividend income entirely. They argue that any unwanted risk in this levered position can be removed by the purchase of whole life insurance which contains a tax deferred investment component. In this model, a distinction is made between *accumulators* who are assumed to hold all the risky assets and employ the above strategy, and *non accumulators* who do not hold risky assets at all. The implication is that the effective marginal tax rate applicable to dividend income is zero and therefore the coefficient of dividend yield is zero. For a non accumulator not to hold equities at all, it must be the case that for each equity the after tax expected rate of return on the equity is less than the after tax rate of interest. This follows from the first order conditions for the standard portfolio problem of an investor evaluated at the point where all the wealth is invested in the riskless asset:

$$E[\tilde{r}_i - \tau d_i - r_f(1 - \tau)]u'(w_0 r_f(1 - \tau)) \le 0 \; \forall i \tag{3}$$

where $\tilde{r}_i$ is the before tax rate of return on security $i$, $\tau$ is the marginal tax rate applicable to the nonaccumulator's income, $w_0$ his initial wealth, and $u(\cdot)$ his monotone increasing and concave von Neumann-Morgenstern utility function. If this condition does not hold for each asset, it would be optimal for the investor to hold some equities. Thus even if accumulators were able to costlessly defer the tax on the interest on their money market investments, the marginal tax bracket of non accumulators would enter any equilibrium relationship.

Ross (1977) and Bhattacharya (1979) have argued that dividend policy could be employed as a signalling mechanism, whereby firms with profitable projects are able and willing to pay higher dividends in order to segregate themselves from firms with less profitable projects. They provide a rationale for value maximizing firms paying positive dividends when the risk premiums per unit of dividend yield is positive in equilibrium. Stern (1979) has argued that such information signalling via dividends is excessively costly.

A model of asset prices in the presence of short selling restrictions, together

[1] The assertion of value maximizing behavior by firms in this context does not have a strong theoretical basis: see Litzenberger and Ramaswamy (1979), fn 2.

with a much simplified taxation scheme with individuals in diverse but constant marginal tax brackets, was derived in Litzenberger and Ramaswamy (1980). The implication of the model is that the differences in tax brackets in the presence of short selling restrictions would induce dividend clienteles, with the tendency of low (high) tax bracket individuals to hold high (low) dividend yield stocks: covariances among individual securities as well as the levels of yields determine the clientele that holds a given security. For the proper subset of all stocks that are held by a given clientele, the equilibrium relationship indicates that the before-tax risk premium on a stock is linearly related to its beta (measured relative to the clientele's optimal risk asset portfolio) and to the dividend yield. However, across groups the coefficient on dividend yield is a decreasing function of yield. Thus the existence of short selling restrictions tends to mitigate the tax effects of dividend changes since a corporation that attempts a sizable dividend cut would affect the clientele that holds the stock, and the associated coefficient on dividend yield would increase.

## II.2 Review of Empirical Evidence and Relationship to the Present Study

In a pioneering empirical test of the effects of dividend yields on common stock returns Black and Scholes (1974) concluded that

> it is not possible to demonstrate that the expected returns of high yield stocks differ from the expected returns on low yield stocks either before *or after taxes*. (emphasis added)

In spite of the ambiguous implication for the after-tax CAPM, the Black and Scholes study has frequently been cited as providing evidence against the existence of tax effects (see, for example, Miller and Scholes (1978)). Rosenberg and Marathé (1978) attribute the ambiguity of the conclusion in Black and Scholes (1974) to (a) the loss of efficiency which arises from grouping stocks into portfolios and (b) the inefficiency of their estimation procedures, which are identical to ordinary least-squares. Using a two stage generalized least-squares procedure that accounts for the problem of errors in variables, and using a more complete specification of the covariance matrix of the disturbance terms, Rosenberg and Marathé find a positive and significant relationship between dividend yields and common stock returns. The difference between these results and those of Black and Scholes cannot be attributed to the use of different dividend yield variables. Both studies use an average dividend yield over the prior twelve month period as a surrogate for the expected dividend yield.

Neither the Black-Scholes study nor the Rosenberg-Marathé study distinguishes between ex-dividend and non ex-dividend months in developing their proxies for the expected dividend yield. Presumably the rationale for ignoring the distinction is that in a world of transactions costs the effect of dividend yields on required return may occur in more than a single month. The recent work by Green (1980) provides some theoretical support for the position that dividend yield effects would be spread over time. Litzenberger and Ramaswamy (1979) used yield variables that distinguished between ex-dividend months and non ex-dividend months and found significant positive coefficients in both ex-months and non ex-months. However, the coefficient in ex-months was more than twice as large as the coefficient in non ex-months. Litzenberger and Ramaswamy (1979, fn 8) note that

> It might be argued that the persistent dividend effect is due to the fact that the dividend variable used incorporates knowledge of the ex-dividend month, which the investor may not have.

They then introduce a dividend yield variable that does not incorporate knowledge of the ex-dividend month except when the announcement occurred in a prior month. The test using this variable implicitly assumes that the effect of dividend yields on common stock returns is distributed uniformly throughout the quarter, and is therefore similar in spirit to the Rosenberg-Marathé and the Black-Scholes tests. The coefficient of the dividend yield variable in this test was positive and statistically significant.

Recently, Miller and Scholes (1981) have argued that the observed relationship between common stock returns and dividend yields is attributable to the favorable information contained in the knowledge that a firm will actually declare any dividend. They note that there is a group of

> zero dividend paying firms consisting of those unfortunates who would have paid a dividend in month $t$ on their regular quarterly schedule, but whose directors voted to omit the dividend. As the old story goes, there may be an important clue in the fact that a dog does not bark! Although these firms have declared and paid a dividend within the same month, they have declared a dividend of zero and hence are not recorded on the CRSP tapes as having declared a dividend. They are placed for test purposes in the complementary zero-dividend group where their adverse information effect serves to pull down the mean excess return of the zero-dividend firms. An upward twist is thereby imparted to the slope coefficient relating realized returns to dividend yields. (p. 13)

There are nine post Black and Scholes studies cited in Miller and Scholes which examine the relationship between returns on NYSE common stocks and dividend yields. The eight we were able to obtain all reported a significant and average relationship between returns and dividend yields. These results[2] are summarized in Table 1. It should be noted that only three studies, namely Litzenberger and Ramaswamy (1979, 1980) and Hess (1979), use a dividend yield variable that depends on prior knowledge of ex-dividend months: the same three studies also report that the effect of yields is non-linear. Thus, the Miller-Scholes explanation cannot be invoked for the remaining studies. While some of the authors cited in Table 1 do not attribute the significant yield effects to taxes, with the possible exception of Bradford and Gordon (1980), these results cannot be attributed to an information effect. Both Bradford and Gordon and Morgan (1981) employ

---

[2] Note that there was no test of an average linear relationship in Litzenberger and Ramaswamy (1980), where a test of the Tax induced CAPM was presented: therefore, there is no entry in Table 1. There is also no test reported by Hess (1979) which conforms to a test of the type reported in Table 1. We thank Professor Stone for providing us with the updated numbers reported here.

**Table 1**

Summary of Results of Tests of Average Relationship between
Common Stock Returns and Dividend Yields

| Author(s) | Test Period and Interval | Estimated Coefficient on Yield |
|---|---|---|
| Blume (1980), p. 571 | 1936–76, quarterly | 0.52 (2.07) |
| Bradford and Gordon (1980), p. 127 | 1926–78, monthly | 0.1762 (8.51) |
| Litzenberger and Ramaswamy (1979) | 1936–77, monthly | 0.236 (8.62) |
| Morgan (1980) | 1936–77, monthly | 0.209 (11.0) |
| Rosenberg and Marathé (1979), pp. 203–206 | 1931–66, monthly | 0.395 (1.88) |
| Stone and Bartter (1979) | 1947–70, monthly | 0.56 (2.00) |

*Note. t*-values are in parentheses under each coefficient.

sophisticated prediction rules to develop an expected yield variable. The Bradford and Gordon prediction rule is based on a pooled time series and cross-section regression of dividend yields on recent past dividends, market returns and yield, the recent capital gain on the stock, the riskless rate of interest and a constant. However, in estimating the parameters of this rule they use data from the entire sample period: thus the estimated relationship between returns and yields is based on data that would not have been available to the investor *ex-ante*. The Morgan prediction rule is based on a Box-Jenkins time series model fitted to grouped data and only uses data that would have been available to the investor *ex-ante*. Neither Bradford and Gordon nor Morgan examine the linearity of the relationship between returns and predicted yields.

Recently Miller and Scholes (1981) have examined the relative coefficients on predicted dividend yield (conditional on it being an ex-month) for stocks that announced their dividends prior to the ex-month versus stocks that announced their dividend during the ex-month. They found that the coefficient for stocks that announced prior to the ex-month was substantially smaller than the coefficient for stocks that announced during the ex-month. They interpret this evidence as supporting their thesis that the dividend yield effects are attributable entirely to the information effect. This fails to recognize that the average number of days from the beginning of an ex-month to the ex-date is greater for stocks that announce within the ex-month than for stocks that announce prior to the ex-month. From the work of Green (1980) it follows that the effect of yield on common stock returns would not just occur on the ex-day. If it is hypothesized that the tax effect occurs uniformly over a two week period, the effect would *ceteris paribus*, be less for a stock that goes ex-dividend on the second day of the month than for a stock that goes ex-dividend in the third or fourth week of the month. Thus, when examining the relative impact of dividend yield between those stocks that announced prior to the month and those that announced and went ex-dividend within the same month, it would be important to account for the number of days in the month until the ex-date, expressed as a fraction of the two week period.

## III. Empirical Tests

In this section the econometric procedures are described briefly: a more complete description is available in Litzenberger and Ramaswamy (1979, 1980). Then the development[3] of the dividend yield variables follows, and the results of tests with these variables are presented. Consistent with the Litzenberger and Ramaswamy (1980) study,[4] the empirical tests presented here assume that individuals fall into five tax clienteles and that each clientele holds one-fifth of the market value of all New York Stock Exchange (NYSE) stocks. The portfolios of the clienteles are assumed to correspond to the optimum portfolios in market equilibrium under certainty: that is, having ranked available stocks in a given year by their (past) annual dividend yield, five portfolios are formed by proceeding down this ranking until a fifth of the market value of stocks is reached, and then until two-fifths is reached, and so on. The first (group) portfolio is then a value weighted portfolio of the lowest dividend yield stocks, comprising a fifth of the market value of all stocks. The next portfolio (a fifth of the market value) contains the next lowest dividend yield stocks, and so on. This procedure ignores the influence of covariances on the tax related clientele and should only be viewed as an approximation to the true optimal portfolios. The underlying tax related clientele model is

$$E(\tilde{R}_i) - r_f = b_g \beta_{ig} + T_g(d_i - r_f), \qquad \forall i \in g, \qquad g = 1, 2, \cdots 5 \qquad (4)$$

where $\beta_{ig}$ is the beta of the $i^{\text{th}}$ security with respect to the optimal portfolio of group $g$ and $T_g$ the marginal tax bracket of group $g$. Following the earlier work in Litzenberger and Ramaswamy (1980), and justified under a condition described there, the beta used in the tests is the standard beta with respect to the return on the market portfolio. Thus the structural model estimated is

$$\tilde{R}_{it} - r_{ft} = \gamma_{0g} + \gamma_{1g}\beta_{it} + \gamma_{2g}(d_{it} - r_{ft}) + \tilde{\varepsilon}_{it}, \qquad \forall i \in g, \qquad g = 1, 2, \cdots 5. \qquad (5)$$

This is the basic model estimated and presented below. The econometric techniques are described in Litzenberger and Ramaswamy (1979). The Maximum Likelihood Estimator (MLE) developed there is used in each cross-section to arrive at estimates $\{\hat{\gamma}_{0gt}, \hat{\gamma}_{1gt}, \hat{\gamma}_{2gt}\}$ in month $t$.

The computational procedure employed took the standard steps. First,

---

[3] Common stock return data were obtained from the monthly returns tape file provided by the Center for Research in Security Prices (CRSP) at the University of Chicago. The data on dividend distributions, the announcement dates and ex-dates, together with other relevant data are also provided on the master file by CRSP. The same service also provides the return series on a value-weighted index of all NYSE stocks. This series was used as a proxy for the returns on the 'market' portfolio ($\tilde{R}_m$). The riskless return series ($r_{ft}$) was constructed from the returns on prime commercial paper and the returns on U.S. Treasury bills.

[4] In Litzenberger and Ramaswamy (1980), stocks were ranked by yield at the beginning of the calendar year, so that the composition of the groups did not change for a year. In this study we have ranked and formed the groups every month. Aside from this, there are no differences in the estimating procedures.

estimating the betas (and their standard errors) of all available securities using 60 months of data prior to month $t$. Second, running a cross sectional regression in month $t$ using the MLE procedure. Third, finding the time series average of the estimated coefficients $\{\hat{\gamma}_{0gt}, \hat{\gamma}_{1gt}, \hat{\gamma}_{2gt}, t = 1, 2, \cdots T\}$ from the $T$ cross sections.

The measurement errors in the betas are correlated over time because 58 months of overlapping data are used to estimate security betas employed in successive cross-section regressions. This induces autocorrelation in the time series of estimated coefficients. The $t$-values reported in the tables are computed under the assumption that these coefficients follow a first order auto regressive process. The magnitude of the first order autocorrelation coefficient is generally small, so higher order schemes are ignored.[5]

## III.2 Results for the Tax-Clientele CAPM: Dividend Variable $d_1$

The first procedure employed to estimate the expected dividend yield $d_{1it}$ (subscript 1 refers to the *first* procedure) is identical to the yield variable used in the earlier studies (Litzenberger and Ramaswamy (1979, 1980)). This provides a basis for comparison with subsequent tests.

$$d_{1it} = \begin{cases} 0 \text{ if month } t \text{ was not an ex-dividend month for security } i; \text{ or if it was,} \\ \text{it was not a regular dividend announced prior to } t. \\ D_{it}/P_{it-1} \text{ if month } t \text{ was an ex-dividend month with } D_{it} \text{ the dollar} \\ \text{dividend per share announced prior to the month.} \\ \hat{D}_{it}/P_{it-1} \text{ if the security went ex in the month and this was a recurring} \\ \text{dividend.} \end{cases}$$

Here $\hat{D}_{it}$ is the previous (going back at most 12 months) recurring, taxable dividend per share adjusted for any changes in the number of shares outstanding in the interim, and $P_{it-1}$ is the price at the end of month $t - 1$. The use of this variable assumes that the investor had prior knowledge of the ex-dividend months, though the surrogate for the dividend is based on information that would have been available to the investor *ex-ante*. The results using this variable are presented in Table 2. These results are consistent with the predictions of the Tax-clientele CAPM and indicate a pronounced non-linear effect of yields on common stock returns.

Because the dividend yield variable $d_1$ employed in these tests incorporates knowledge of the ex-dividend months, the results may suffer from the biases discussed at length in Miller and Scholes (1981). Thus the observed positive but non-linear association between common stock returns and yields could arise from this "information" effect. There are two simple procedures for purging the coefficient of potential information effects. The first is to construct an expected dividend yield variable based on information the investor has prior to the test

---

[5] In each table below, the mean ad the associated $t$-value are

$$\tilde{\gamma}_j = \sum_{t=1}^{T} \hat{\gamma}_{jt}/T, \quad \text{and} \quad t(\hat{\gamma}_j) = \hat{\gamma}_j/(\hat{\sigma}_u/N(1-\rho))[N - 2\rho/(1 - \rho^2)]^{1/2},$$

where $\rho$ is the estimated first order autocorrelation coefficient and $\hat{\sigma}_u$ is the standard error of the regression of $\hat{\gamma}_{jt}$ on $\hat{\gamma}_{jt-1}$.

**Table 2**

**Pooled Time Series and Cross Section Test of Tax Clientele CAPM, 1940–80**

| 5 groups: dividend variable $d_1$ used | | | |
| --- | --- | --- | --- |
| $E(\tilde{R}_i) - r_f = \gamma_0 + \gamma_1\beta_i + \gamma_2(d_{1i} - r_f),\ \forall i \in g, g = 1, 2, \cdots 5$ | | | |
| Group | $\hat{\gamma}_0$ | $\hat{\gamma}_1$ | $\hat{\gamma}_2$ |
| I (Low yield) | 0.00478 | 0.00518 | 0.665 |
|  | (2.26) | (2.12) | (3.91) |
| II | 0.00217 | 0.00459 | 0.516 |
|  | (1.07) | (1.94) | (4.83) |
| III | 0.00338 | 0.00422 | 0.415 |
|  | (1.70) | (1.77) | (7.05) |
| IV | 0.00159 | 0.00663 | 0.274 |
|  | (0.88) | (2.68) | (7.04) |
| V (High Yield) | 0.00327 | 0.00631 | 0.125 |
|  | (1.74) | (2.66) | (3.98) |

month, and the second is to use a sample of stocks known not to incorporate unavailable information for the cross-sectional regressions.

## Expected Dividend Yield Variable Based on Prediction Rule ($d_2$)

In assessing the cash return in the future from purchasing a common stock, an investor would incorporate information regarding the periodicity of past payments as well as their (possibly changing) magnitude over time. Past studies (see for example Lintner (1956) and Fama and Babiak (1968)) have examined the payout behavior of U.S firms but these studies have ignored the within year timing of payouts and so are not immediately applicable here. While the majority of NYSE firms pays dividends on a quarterly schedule, there are several that pay dividends semi-annually or annually, and at least one that has paid regular monthly dividends. It is clear then that a prediction rule for expected dividend yield for a given firm based solely on past payments data for that firm would be free of these differences in payment schedules. For reasons of computational ease, however, this study uses a prediction rule that is based on the payment data of all firms for five years prior to the cross-sectional test period. Thus the expected yield so constructed reflects the payment behavior of the average firm, and is not the most efficient construct, though it is expedient computationally. The forecast dividend yield, labeled $d_{2it}^e$ for stock $i$ in period $t$, is constructed as follows. Using data from 60 months prior to month $t$, a pooled time series-cross section regression is used to estimate the parameters of the following model:

$$\tilde{D}_{i\tau}/P_{i\tau-1} = \alpha_{0t} + \sum \alpha_{jt}\delta_{ij}(D_{i\tau-}/P_{i\tau-1}) + \tilde{u}_{i\tau} \quad (j = 3, 4, 6, 7, 12, 13)$$

$$\tau = t - 1, t - 2, \cdots t - 60 \qquad i = 1, 2, \cdots N \quad (8)$$

where

$D_{i\tau}$ = regular dividend to security $i$ in period $\tau$, if any.

$D_{i\tau-}$ = the most recent regular dividend to security $i$ prior to period $\tau$, if any in last 12 months adjusted for changes in number of shares outstanding in the interim.

$\delta_{ij}$ = 1 if period $\tau - j$ was a regular ex-dividend month. and 0 if otherwise.

$P_{i\tau-1}$ = the closing price in month $\tau - 1$.

Note that the dividend $D_{i\tau-}$ on the right hand side of the equation is the most recent regular dividend: thus the RHS variable $D_{i\tau-}/P_{i\tau-1}$ corresponds to the naive yield explanatory variable based on the most recent dividend, going back at most 12 months. The lags $\{j = 3, 4, 6, 7, 12, 13\}$ were chosen because although firms may slip forward or backward in their payment schedule, it is firms that are late in the announcement (these had a regular dividend 4 or 7 or 13 months ago) that are likely to announce and go ex-dividend within the same month, and it is precisely these firms that can cause unanticipated surprises and disappointments.[6] The forecast dividend yield $\hat{d}_{2it}^e$ was then found as

$$\hat{d}_{2it}^e = \hat{a}_{0t} + \sum \hat{\alpha}_{jt}\delta_{ij}(D_{it-}/P_{it-1}), \qquad (j = 3, 4, 6, 7, 12, 13) \qquad (9)$$

and the variable that was used in the cross-sectional regression in month $t$ is $d_{2it}$, defined as either $D_{it}/P_{it-1}$ if taxable dividend $D_{it}$ was announced prior to month $t$, or $\hat{d}_{2it}^e$ otherwise. Thus the expected dividend yield variable $d_{2it}$ incorporates only information the investor would possess at the end of month $t - 1$.

Table 3 presents results from a test of the Tax-Clientele CAPM based on the expected yield variable $d_{2it}$. The coefficients on the dividend yield variables are positive and significant for all the groups except the last (highest yield) group. Furthermore these coefficients decline with the level of yield as predicted by the model.[7] In comparison with the coefficients obtained in Table 2, which used the yield variable $d_{1it}$, the coefficients on yield in Table 3 are approximately 8 basis points lower. One explanation for this is that there is information contained in the prior knowledge of the ex-dividend month which biases the slopes ($\hat{\gamma}_2$) in Table 2 upward. Another explanation is that the prediction rule employed is not the most efficient in which case the coefficients in Table 3 would be biased downward.

In Panel A of Table 4, the Tax-clientele CAPM is estimated with the coefficient on beta constrained to be the same across the five groups: this corresponds to the

---

[6] Clearly alternative rules are possible, with lags at $j = 2, 5$ and 11: we have tried only this structure.

[7] The MLE estimating procedure produces linear estimators: for example, the estimate of $\hat{\gamma}_2$ in a monthly cross-sectional regression for a given group is a weighted combination of the monthly rates of return of the stocks in that group. Since the weights sum to zero, this estimator is the rate of return on a self-financing portfolio. The MLE procedures is designed to produce an estimator of $\hat{\gamma}_2$ that, asymptotically, has a zero beta—a requirement for the estimator to be asymptotically unbiased (see Litzenberger and Ramaswamy (1979), pp. 173–81). To test for possible misspecification, the betas of the monthly estimates $\hat{\gamma}_2$ for each group were computed, and these were negative for 4 of the 5 groups. Using a procedure suggested by Sharpe (1981) the coefficients in Table 3 were then adjusted. The resulting adjusted estimators for $\hat{\gamma}_2$ changed only slightly: these are 0.599, 0.481, 0.365, 0.236, and 0.045.

**Table 3**

As in Table 2 above: dividend variable based on prediction rule $d_2$ used

| Group | $\hat{\gamma}_0$ | $\hat{\gamma}_1$ | $\hat{\gamma}_2$ |
|---|---|---|---|
| I (Low Yield) | 0.00477 | 0.00502 | 0.555 |
| | (2.22) | (2.06) | (2.83) |
| II | 0.00206 | 0.00468 | 0.486 |
| | (1.01) | (1.97) | (4.18) |
| III | 0.00339 | 0.00427 | 0.339 |
| | (1.69) | (1.78) | (5.32) |
| IV | 0.00176 | 0.00665 | 0.212 |
| | (0.98) | (2.70) | (4.74) |
| V (High Yield) | 0.00365 | 0.00622 | 0.022 |
| | (1.94) | (2.62) | (0.65) |

*Note: t* values are in parentheses under each coefficient.

**Table 4**

*PANEL A* Pooled Time Series Cross-Section Test of Tax Clientele CAPM, Five Groups, 1940–80. Slope on Beta Constrained to be same across groups. Dividend Yield Variable used: $d_{2i}$

$$E(\tilde{R}_i) - r_f = \gamma_0 + \gamma_1\beta_i + \sum_{g=1}^{5} \gamma_{2g}\delta_{ig}(d_{2i} - r_f), \forall i$$

| $\hat{\gamma}_0$ | $\hat{\gamma}_1$ | $\hat{\gamma}_{21}$ | $\hat{\gamma}_{22}$ | $\hat{\gamma}_{23}$ | $\hat{\gamma}_{24}$ | $\hat{\gamma}_{25}$ |
|---|---|---|---|---|---|---|
| 0.00346 | 0.00491 | 0.155 | 0.488 | 0.366 | 0.267 | 0.058 |
| (2.05) | (2.22) | (1.18) | (3.55) | (5.29) | (5.63) | (1.45) |

*PANEL B* Same as Panel A, but with dummy variable $\delta_{i0}$ added. $\delta_{i0} = 1$ if stock $i$ paid zero dividend in the previous year

$$E(\tilde{R}_i) - r_f = \gamma_0 + \gamma_1\beta_i + \sum_{g=1}^{5} \gamma_{2g}\delta_{ig}(d_{2i} - r_f) + \gamma_3\delta_{i0}, \forall i$$

| $\hat{\gamma}_0$ | $\hat{\gamma}_1$ | $\hat{\gamma}_{21}$ | $\hat{\gamma}_{22}$ | $\hat{\gamma}_{23}$ | $\hat{\gamma}_{24}$ | $\hat{\gamma}_{25}$ | $\hat{\gamma}_3$ |
|---|---|---|---|---|---|---|---|
| 0.00367 | 0.00466 | 0.231 | 0.482 | 0.362 | 0.268 | 0.059 | 0.00181 |
| (1.60) | (2.34) | (1.54) | (2.95) | (5.58) | (6.42) | (2.18) | (0.88) |

*Note: t*-values are in parentheses under each coefficient.

cross-sectional regression

$$\tilde{R}_{it} - r_{ft} = \gamma_0 + \gamma_1\beta_{it} + \sum_{g=1}^{5} \gamma_{2g}\delta_{ig}(d_{2it} - r_{ft}) + \tilde{\epsilon}_{it} \qquad i = 1, 2, \cdots N_t \quad (10)$$

where $\delta_{ig} = 1$ if security $i$ is in group $g$ and zero otherwise. The results indicate that, except for the coefficient $\gamma_1$ of the lowest yield group,[8] the coefficients are positive and declining in the predicted manner. It should be noted that the non dividend paying stocks are all in Group I, and for these stocks the predicted

---

[8] Since Group I contains a large number of nondividend paying stocks, there is reason to suspect the distributional properties of $\hat{\gamma}_{21}$ relative to the others ($\hat{\gamma}_{32}$ to $\hat{\gamma}_{25}$). We are currently exploring this issue.

dividend yield $d_{2it}$ would always be equal to $\hat{\alpha}_0$: this is clearly an inefficient and biased predictor.[9] To test for a separate influence first noticed by Blume (1980) of non dividend paying stocks, relation (10) is estimated with a dummy variable:

$$\tilde{R}_{it} - r_{ft} = \gamma_0 + \gamma_1\beta_{it} + \sum_{g=1}^{5} \gamma_{2g}\delta_{ig}(d_{2it} - r_{ft}) + \gamma_3\delta_{i0} + \tilde{\varepsilon}_{it}, \qquad \forall i \qquad (11)$$

where $\delta_{i0} = 1$ if the stock has no dividend in the past 12 months and 0 otherwise. The results of this test are in Panel B: they indicate that the pattern of the coefficients is as in Panel A, and that the coefficient $\gamma_{21}$ increases. The coefficient on the dummy variable $\delta_{i0}$ indicates that the before-tax risk premium to non-dividend paying stocks is approximately 2.16%. This is lower than estimates reported by Blume (1980) and Litzenberger and Ramaswamy (1980), and unlike these studies, it is insignificant.

### Estimation of Tax-Clientele CAPM with a Subsample of Stocks ($d_3$)

An alternative procedure which purges the coefficient on yield of potential information effects is to restrict the sample of stocks used to estimate the parameters of the Tax-clientele CAPM. There are several ways to restrict the sample: one is to use only those stocks that have announced a dividend prior to the ex-month. This suffers from the immediate criticism that the cross-sectional variation in dividend yields is greatly reduced and hence the test is inefficient. Another possibility is to use the whole sample but set the dividend yield for those that have no announcement prior to the test month to zero. This biases the coefficient downward, because it eliminates the correlation between expected yield and realized return for those stocks that announced and went ex-dividend in the same month. The subsample chosen here is based on the conjecture that if a firm paid a regular dividend in the previous month, it is not likely to pay a regular dividend in the current month. Thus the restricted sample consists of those stocks that have announced prior to the test month, in which case the anticipated yield $D_{it}/P_{it-1}$ was used, and those stocks that went ex-dividend in the previous month, in which case the dividend yield was set to zero. This yield variable is written $d_{3it}$. This subsample is free of any potential information effects. In Table 5, the results of the Tax-clientele CAPM with this subsample are presented. Because there were some groups (notably the low yield groups) which had very few stocks, or even no stocks that paid a dividend in the early months, not all the cross-sectional regressions could be conducted. A cross-sectional regression (across firms in a given group) was conducted in a given month only if there were at least 5 stocks that had announced a dividend prior to the month, and if there were at least 20 stocks that were candidates for the subsample. The results indicate that there is a positive association between returns and yields within each group subsample. As before, the coefficient of yield in the highest yield group is not significant.

The problem with every subsample is that it throws away information, and thus reduces the efficiency of the estimator. The results in tables 3 and 4 indicate, however, that these alternative approaches to avoiding undesired 'information'

---

[9] The average value of $\hat{\alpha}_0$, computed from 1936–1980, was 0.000996. In no case was $\hat{\alpha}_0$ negative.

**Table 5**

**Pooled Time Series and Cross-Section Test of Tax
Clientele CAPM, Five Groups, 1940–80**
(Subsample of Stocks that have announced prior to
ex-month, and those that have just gone ex-dividend
in the previous month)
Dividend Yield Variable Used: $d_{3i}$

$$E(\tilde{R}_i) - r_f = \gamma_0 + \gamma_1\beta_i + \gamma_2(d_{3i} - r_f), \quad \forall i \in g,$$
$$g = 1, 2, \cdots 5$$

| Group | $\hat{\gamma}_0$ | $\hat{\gamma}_1$ | $\hat{\gamma}_2$ | |
|---|---|---|---|---|
| I (Low Yield) | 0.00715 | 0.00216 | 0.629 | Obs* = 450 |
| | (2.07) | (0.66) | (2.56) | |
| II | 0.00008 | 0.00610 | 0.380 | Obs = 463 |
| | (0.23) | (1.60) | (2.72) | |
| III | 0.00359 | 0.00306 | 0.331 | Obs = 477 |
| | (1.57) | (1.15) | (4.25) | |
| IV | −0.00207 | 0.00866 | 0.135 | Obs = 487 |
| | (−1.01) | (3.32) | (2.65) | |
| V (High Yield) | −0.00029 | 0.00755 | 0.049 | Obs = 489 |
| | (−0.16) | (3.14) | (1.38) | |

*Obs is the number of cross-sectional months over which these
estimates have been computed. There are 492 months in total
possible.

*Note:* $t$-values are in parentheses under each coefficient.

effects provide reasonably close estimates of the effect of yield on common stock returns. These results also indicate that in light of the observed non-linear association between yields and common stock returns, the emphasis on an average linear effect in the literature is misplaced. Nevertheless, in the interest of providing a comparison to prior studies and of exploring the possible information effect in tests of the After-tax CAPM, the next section examines the results of tests of a linear relationship.

## III.3 Results of Tests of After Tax CAPM

In this section the results of the After Tax CAPM which predicts a linear relationship between expected returns and yield are presented. The results in Panels A, B, C of Table 6 correspond to the results in Table 2, Table 3, and Table 5 respectively. Panel A reports results that extend those in Litzenberger and Ramaswamy (1979) through 1980: the dividend yield variable $d_{1it}$ is employed here. Panel B reports results with the predicted yield $d_{2it}$: the average coefficient $\hat{\gamma}_2$ is 0.151 and statistically significant at the 0.05 level. The drop in the coefficient on yield between Panels A and B is approximatetly 8 basis points. Panel C reports results with the subsample of securities that have either announced a dividend prior to the ex-month, or have just paid a regular dividend. The coefficient $\hat{\gamma}_3$ here is 0.135 and this is statistically significant as well.

The drop in the coefficient on yield in Panel B from its value in Panel A could be due to information effects. Alternatively, decline could be attributed to the tax effect occurring over a period prior to the ex-date, as suggested by Green (1980).

**Table 6**

**Pooled Time Series and Cross Section Test of After Tax CAPM, 1940–80**

$$E(\tilde{R}_i) - r_f = \gamma_0 + \gamma_1\beta_i + \gamma_2(d_i - r_f), \forall i$$

|  | $\hat{\gamma}_0$ | $\hat{\gamma}_1$ | $\hat{\gamma}_2$ |
|---|---|---|---|
| **PANEL A** | | | |
| Dividend variable $d_{1i}$ used | 0.00313 | 0.00484 | 0.233 |
| | (1.81) | (2.15) | (8.79) |
| **PANEL B** | | | |
| Dividend variable $d_{2i}$ based on prediction rule, used | 0.00337 | 0.00470 | 0.151 |
| | (1.95) | (2.08) | (5.39) |
| **PANEL C** | | | |
| Subsample dividend variable $d_{3i}$ used | 0.00097 | 0.00527 | 0.135 |
| | (0.52) | (2.33) | (4.38) |

*Note:* $t$-values are in parentheses under each coefficient.

**Table 7**

**Pooled Time Series and Cross-Section Test of After Tax CAPM, 1940–80 With Scaled Yield Variables**

$$E(\tilde{R}_i) - r_f = \gamma_0 + \gamma_1\beta_i + \gamma_2(s_i \cdot d_i - r_f), \forall i$$

|  | $\hat{\gamma}_0$ | $\hat{\gamma}_1$ | $\hat{\gamma}_2$ |
|---|---|---|---|
| **PANEL A** | | | |
| Dividend yield variable $d_{1i}$ used | 0.00318 | 0.00499 | 0.401 |
| | (1.85) | (2.21) | (14.29) |
| **PANEL B** | | | |
| Subsample dividend yield variable $d_{3i}$ used | 0.00107 | 0.00529 | 0.297 |
| | (0.57) | (2.34) | (7.19) |

The time from the beginning of the month to the ex-date is frequently less than 2 weeks for stocks that announce prior to the ex-month. Assuming the tax effect occurs uniformly over the two week period prior to the ex-date, the dividend variable for stocks that went ex-dividend within the first two weeks of the month may be scaled by the ratio of the number of days until the ex-date to two weeks. If this explanation of the decline in the coefficient is valid, the coefficients of the scaled variables for the subsample and for the total sample should be of the same magnitude.

Let $ND_i$ be the number of days from the beginning of the month to the ex-date for the $i^{\text{th}}$ stock. Then the scale factor that was employed is given by $s_i = \text{Min}\{ND_i/15., 1.\}$. Panels A and B of Table 7 report results of tests identical to those in Panels A and C of Table 6 respectively; except that the yield variables $d_{1it}$ in Table 5 and $d_{3it}$ in Table 7 have both been scaled by $s_i$. As is evident, the coefficients are not of the same order of magnitude, lending little support to the hypothesis that the tax effect is spread over a two week period prior to the ex-date. It is possible, of course that the scale factor applied is incorrect.

The lack of significance of the dividend yield coefficient in the Black-Scholes study has been subject to alternative interpretations. Rosenberg and Marathé (1979) have attributed this to the inefficiency of the OLS estimating procedure

**Table 8**

Pooled Time Series and Cross Section
Test of After Tax CAPM, 1936–78
Twenty-five Portfolios* in Cross
Sections

$$E(\tilde{R}_p) - r_f = \gamma_0 + \gamma_1\beta_p + \gamma_2(d_{1p} - r_f),$$
$$p = 1, 2, \cdots 25$$

| $\hat{\gamma}_0$ | $\hat{\gamma}_1$ | $\hat{\gamma}_2$ |
|---|---|---|
| 0.00466 | 0.00592 | 0.125 |
| (2.73) | (1.98) | (0.21) |

*Portfolios ranked first by annual yield, last 12 months and within 5 portfolios so formed, ranked by beta to construct 5 portfolios. Equal numbers of stocks in each portfolio.

*Note:* $t$-values in parentheses under each coefficient; $t$ values in Table 8 are not corrected for first order autocorrelation in coefficients.

and to the loss in efficiency which arises from grouping stocks into portfolios. Miller and Scholes (1981) argue that the Black-Scholes study points up the absence of a long-run dividend yield effect by virtue of its use of an expected annual yield variable from past data, and that the use of a short-run variable (such as $d_{1it}$) is beset with potential information effects. The power of the Black-Scholes procedure was examined by replicating the Black-Scholes study, but using the dividend yield variable, $d_{1it}$. If the procedure is sufficiently powerful this should result in a statistically significant yield coefficient, since the dividend yield variable which impounds knowledge of the ex-dividend months is used.

There are some differences in the replication which must be noted. Twenty-five portfolios of stocks, with equal numbers of stocks in each group, were formed by ranking *every month* first by yield (defined as the sum of all dividends, adjusted for splits, etc., divided by the end of the previous month price), forming five portfolios, and then ranking stocks in each of the five portfolios by beta. Thus the composition of the portfolios varies from month to month. For $n_t$ stocks in *each* of the twenty-five portfolios in month $t$, the dividend yield of the portfolio is computed as:

$$d_{1pt} = \sum_{i=1}^{n_t} d_{1it}/n_t. \tag{13}$$

The value weighted index $\tilde{R}_m$ is used to compute betas. In addition, the yield variable employed on the RHS of the cross sectional regression is $(d_{1pt} - r_{ft})$, and not $(d_{1pt} - d_{mt})/d_{mt}$ as used by Black and Scholes.

The results are reported in Table 8. The coefficient on dividend yield is insignificant, implying that the Black-Scholes procedure as replicated here is not sufficiently powerful to pick up potential information effects.

## IV. Conclusion

This study has presented empirical evidence consistent with the Tax-Clientele CAPM: the data indicate that there is a positive but non-linear association between common stock returns and dividend yields. The prediction rule for the expected dividend yield is based solely on information that would have been available to the investor *ex-ante*, and hence is free from potential information effects that are contained in dividend yield variables that anticipate the occurrence (or lack thereof) of a dividend. Nevertheless, the results here are similar to those obtained earlier.

Whether the effect of dividend yields on common stock returns (as indicated by the data) can be attributed to taxes or is due to some omitted variable(s) remains an open question. The conclusion of the present study is that these significant yield effects cannot be pinned to the information content in the prior knowledge that the firm will declare a dividend of unknown magnitude.

## REFERENCES

Bhattacharya, S., 1979, Imperfect information, dividend policy and the bird-in-the-hand fallacy, *The Bell Journal of Economics*, 10, 259–270.

Black, F. and M. Scholes, 1974, The effects of dividend yield and dividend policy on common stock prices and returns, *Journal of Financial Economics*, 1, 1–22.

Blume, M. E., 1980, Stock returns and dividend yields: some more evidence, *Review of Economics and Statistics*, 62, 567–577.

Bradford, D. F. and R. H. Gordon, 1980, Taxation and the stock market valuation of capital gains and dividends, *Journal of Public Economics*, 14, 109–136.

Brennan, M. J., 1970, Investor taxes, market equilibrium and corporation finance, Unpublished Ph.D. Dissertation (Massachusetts Institute of Technology, Cambridge, Mass.).

Charest, G., 1978, Dividend information, stock returns and market efficiency—II, *Journal of Financial Economics*, 5.

Elton, E. and M. Gruber, 1970, Marginal stockholder tax rates and the clientele effect, *Review of Economics and Statistics*, 52, 68–74.

Fama, E. and H. Babiak, 1968, Dividend policy: an empirical analysis, *Journal of the American Statistical Association*, 63, 1132–61.

Green, J., 1980, Taxation and the ex-dividend day behavior of common stock prices, *National Bureau of Economic Research*, W. P. 496, Cambridge, Mass.

Hess, P., 1979, The empirical relationship between dividend yields and stock returns: tax effects or non-stationarities in expected returns, mimeo, The Ohio State University, Columbus, Ohio.

Lintner, J., 1956, Distribution of incomes of corporations among dividends, retained earnings and taxes, *American Economic Review*, 46, 97–113.

Litzenberger, R. H. and K. Ramaswamy, 1979, The effects of personal taxes and dividends on capital asset prices: theory and empirical evidence, *Journal of Financial Economics*, 7, 163–195.

Litzenberger, R. H. and K. Ramaswamy, 1980, Dividends, short-selling restrictions, tax-induced investor clienteles and market equilibrium, *Journal of Finance*, 35, 469–482.

Miller, M. and M. Scholes, 1978, Dividends and taxes, *Journal of Financial Economics*, 6, 333–364.

Miller, M. and M. Scholes, 1981, Dividends and taxes: some empirical evidence, W. P. 55, Center for Research in Security Prices, Graduate School of Business, University of Chicago, Chicago, Illinois.

Morgan, I. G., 1980, Dividends and capital asset prices, (Unpublished mimeo, School of Business, Queens University, Kingston, Ontario).

Rosenberg, B. and V. Marathé, 1979, Tests of capital asset pricing hypotheses, *Research in Finance*, 1, 115–223.

Ross, S. A., 1977, The determination of financial structure: the incentive signalling approach. *The Bell Journal of Economics*, 8, 23–40.

Sharpe, W. F., 1981, Some factors in New York Stock Exchange security returns, 1931–1979, Unpublished mimeo (August 1981), Graduate School of Business, Stanford University, Stanford, California.

Stern, J., The dividend question, Opinion Column, *Wall Street Journal*, July 15, 1979.

Stone, B. K. and B. J. Bartter, 1979, The effect of dividend yield on stock returns: empirical evidence on the relevance of dividends, W. P. E-76-8, Georgia Institute of Technology, Atlanta, Georgia.

# OPTIMAL BOND TRADING WITH PERSONAL TAXES*

George M. CONSTANTINIDES

*University of Chicago, Chicago, IL 60637, USA*

Jonathan E. INGERSOLL, Jr.

*Yale University, New Haven, CT 06520, USA*

Received May 1982, final version received April 1984

Tax considerations governing bondholders' optimal trading include: capital loss realization; capital gain deferment; change of the long-term holding period status to short-term by sale of the bond and repurchase, to realize future losses short-term; raising the basis above par by sale of the bond and repurchase, to deduct the amortized premium from ordinary income. The optimal policy which incorporates transactions costs and conforms to the IRS code substantially differs from the buy-and-hold and continuous-realization policies. Failure to account for optimal trading may seriously bias econometric estimation of the yield curve and the tax bracket of the marginal bondholders.

## 1. Introduction

The yield curve implied by the prices of Treasury notes and bonds and corporate bonds is of interest to economists and practitioners alike: it reflects the investors' beliefs about the future course of the short-term interest rate. In calculating the yield curve, the tax bracket of the marginal bondholder is either taken to be some given number or is estimated simultaneously with the yield curve. The implied tax bracket of the marginal investor is of independent interest. It provides a direct (but incomplete) test of Miller's (1977) theory on the optimal capital structure of firms. It may also be useful for determining fair prices for other assets.

There are two major problems in estimating pure discount rates (the yield curve of zero coupon bonds) and the implied marginal tax rate. The first

*Earlier versions of the paper were presented at the annual AFA meeting in Washington, DC, and at workshops at the Universities of Chicago, Michigan, and Rochester, Massachusetts Institute of Technology, Yale University and New York University. We would like to thank Mark Wolfson, Steve Schaefer (the referee), Rene Stulz, and the participants at the above meeting and workshops for helpful comments. Part of this research was conducted during the academic year 1981–82 when the second author was a Batterymarch Fellow. Additional support was provided by the Sloan Foundation.

Journal of Financial Economics 13 (1984) 299–335. North-Holland

problem is that of differing clienteles, studied in detail by Schaefer (1981, 1982a). For a given investor some bonds of particular maturities and coupon rates may be dominated by combinations of other bonds. In this case tax clienteles naturally arise. If there is no one clientele for which every bond remains undominated, then the concept of the 'marginal taxable investor' who 'sets' all prices may well be meaningless.

The second problem is that of the assumed investment horizon. This is the focus of the present paper. By necessity we ignore the problem of tax clienteles. Extant estimation procedures assume either that the bond is held to maturity, without intermediate realization of capital gains and losses (the buy-and-hold policy), or that capital gains and losses are realized every period as they occur (the continuous realization policy). Both the buy-and-hold and the continuous realization policy lead to relatively simple bond pricing formulae. This facilitates the estimation of the yield curve and the implied tax bracket of the marginal investor.

The assumption that bondholders follow either a buy-and-hold or a continuous realization policy, rather than the optimal trading policy, is at variance with reality and, as we demonstrate, may seriously bias the estimation of the yield curve and the implied tax bracket of the marginal investor. Perusal of the *Wall Street Journal* provides convincing evidence that investment advisors – and presumably their clients – are aware of the optimal trading policies which frequently differ sharply from a buy-and-hold or continuous realization policy. By definition, the marginal bondholder is an economic agent (or group of agents) of sufficient stature to set bond prices at the margin. It is questionable then to assert that the marginal investor follows a suboptimal trading policy through ignorance.

The present paper unifies two recent strands of research, the pricing of bonds with stochastically varying interest rates and investment opportunity set and the pricing of stocks in the presence of personal taxes. Cox, Ingersoll and Ross (1981, 1983) present an equilibrium theory of bond pricing and the term structure of interest rates, in particular explaining the valuation of a deterministic stream of cash flows but with a stochastically varying interest rate and investment opportunity set. Constantinides (1983, 1984) and Constantinides and Scholes (1980) discuss the optimal trading of stocks and options in the presence of personal taxes and present an equilibrium theory of stock pricing, in particular explaining the effect of optimal realization of capital gains and losses on the pricing of stocks.

Tax considerations which govern a bondholder's optimal trading policy include the following: realization of capital losses, short-term if possible; deferment of the realization of capital gains, especially if they are short-term; changing the holding period status from long- to short-term by sale of the bond and repurchase, so that future capital losses may be realized short-term; and raising the basis through sale of the bond and repurchase in order to deduct from ordinary income the amortized premium. Because of the interaction of these factors, no simple characterization of the optimal trading policy is possible. We can say, however, that it differs substantially from the buy-and-hold irrespective of whether the bondholder is a bank, a bond dealer, or an individual. We obtain these strong results even when we allow for transactions costs and explicitly consider numerous IRS regulations designed to curtail tax avoidance.

The paper is organized as follows. In section 2 we outline the tax provisions in four representative tax scenarios which may apply to the elusive marginal bondholder. The formal model is presented in section 3. Closed-form solutions for the prices of consol bonds and the value of the timing option are presented in section 4 for a special case. In section 5 we derive the optimal trading policies under more general conditions, and in section 6 we illustrate the effect of taxes on the prices of bonds and on the value of the timing option. The estimation of the yield curve and the tax bracket of the marginal investor is grossly biased if the value of the timing option is ignored. This point is illustrated in section 7. In section 8 we discuss municipal bonds. Concluding remarks are offered in section 9.

## 2. The tax environment

To avoid a profusion of details in our discussion we abstract from many of the nuances of the regulations governing the taxation of income, as defined by the tax code and its interpretation by the Internal Revenue Service and the courts. We do emphasize, however, certain important aspects of the code, which, though largely ignored in finance, may materially affect bond prices and the estimation of the yield curve and the marginal tax rate. We also provide some historical perspective to familiarize the reader with major changes in the tax code which may be reflected in a time series of bond yields.

At least four broad classes of potential marginal investors warrant examination: individuals, banks and bond dealers, corporations, and tax-exempt institutions. Consider first the tax rules applicable to individual investors.

Coupon income (net of interest expense) is taxed at the individual's marginal tax rate on ordinary income, the maximum rate being currently 50%. Between 1970 and 1980, coupon income was classified as 'unearned income' and was taxed at a maximum rate of 72%. Prior to the seventies, the top marginal tax rate varied from a low of 7% in 1913 to a high of 95% in 1945. In our calculations we assume that the marginal tax rate on coupon income for an individual is $\tau_c = 0.5$.[1]

---

[1] Miller (1977) shows that, under simple tax rules, the marginal bondholder is in the corporate tax bracket, providing partial justification for our choice of the tax rate. In any case, our qualitative results are insensitive to the assumed rate.

The taxation of capital gains is complex. Unrealized gains and losses remain untaxed. Gains and losses are taxed in the year that they are realized. A realized gain or loss is the difference between the sales price (less cost of sale) and the basis. For most assets the basis is just the purchase price (plus cost of purchase), but for some bonds the purchase price is subject to adjustment.

We consider only original issue par bonds, defined as such by the IRS if the original issue discount does not exceed $\frac{1}{4}$ of 1 percent multiplied by the number of full years to maturity. For these bonds, if the purchase price in the secondary market is below par, no adjustment is made and the basis is just the purchase price. If the purchase price is above par, this difference is amortized linearly to the maturity date.[2] The amount amortized in a tax year is allowed as a deduction against ordinary income and the bond's basis is correspondingly reduced. There is no specific limitation on this deduction. In our calculations the amortized amount is (negatively) taxed at the rate $\tau_c = 0.5$.

Realized capital gains and losses are either short-term or long-term. The required holding period for long-term treatment is currently one year. This has varied many times since capital gains were first differentiated from ordinary income in 1922. In the years 1942–1977 the holding period was six months. Prior to that time there were three or more categories of long-term capital gains with required holding periods as long as ten years.

Net short-term capital gains are taxed as ordinary income. Net long-term capital gains are currently taxed at 40% of the investor's marginal tax rate on ordinary income. This treatment has also been changed. The tax rate on long-term gains has varied from 20% to 80% of the tax rate on ordinary income. In addition there have been periods in which alternate treatment could be elected (or, was required for large capital gains).

Net short-term capital losses and 50% of net long-term capital losses are deducted from ordinary income and may jointly reduce the taxable ordinary income by a maximum of $3,000 (until 1976, $1,000). Unused losses are carried forward indefinitely. Short-term losses and long-term gains, incurred in the same year, offset each other dollar for dollar, instead of being taxed at their respective rates.

We define $\tau_s$ to be the *marginal* tax rate on short-term capital gains and losses. This rate is not necessarily equal to the marginal tax rate on ordinary income: if the investor has net short-term losses and the deduction limit is binding, $\tau_s = 0$; if the investor has net short-term losses but larger long-term gains, $\tau_s$ is 40% of the marginal tax rate on ordinary income. Likewise, we define $\tau_L$ to be the *marginal* tax rate on long-term capital gains and losses.

---

[2]Amortization is optional for Treasury and corporate bonds. Since for practically all individuals the marginal tax rate on ordinary income is no less than the capital gains tax rate, amortization of the basis dominates foregoing this option. The amortization method need not be straight line, but may be that customarily used by the individual, if it is deemed to be reasonable. If the bond is callable, the basis is amortized to the call price at the call date or to par at maturity, whichever yields the smaller amortization. If there are alternate call dates the rule is complex.

If an asset is sold at a loss within thirty days before or after the acquisition of 'substantially identical' property, the IRS can disallow the loss deduction under the 'wash sale' rule. An investor has a high probability of circumventing this rule by purchasing instead another bond with a slightly different coupon or maturity. In any case, this rule is not applicable to dealers or individual taxpayers who are in the business of trading bonds. Consequently we ignore the wash sale rule throughout this paper.

We consider three representative tax scenarios for an individual bondholder and one scenario for banks or bond dealers, as defined by the marginal rates $\tau_c$, $\tau_s$, and $\tau_L$.

(I)   *The marginal investor is an individual. Coupon income is taxed at the rate $\tau_c = 0.5$. Realized short-term and long-term gains and losses are taxed at the rate $\tau_s = \tau_L = 0.25$. The deduction limit is not binding.*

This scenario is plausible if the individual is periodically forced to sell some of his portfolio assets by factors beyond his control (or, of more importance than the tax consequences) and, on average, realizes large long-term gains. Then the deduction limit is not binding. Since short-term losses must be used to offset the long-term gains, the marginal tax rate is the long-term gains rate.[3] We take the long-term gains rate to be half of the investor's marginal tax rate on ordinary income, as it was between 1942 and 1979. We also assume that the investor can always defer the realization of short-term gains until the holding period exceeds one year and then realize the gains long-term.

(II)  *The marginal investor is an individual. Coupon income is taxed at the rate $\tau_c = 0.5$. Realized short-term gains and losses are taxed at the rate $\tau_s = 0.5$. Realized long-term gains and losses are taxed at the rate $\tau_L = 0.25$. The deduction limit is not binding.*

Scenario II is the least plausible one because it ignores both the deduction limit and the (unfavorable to the taxpayer) offsetting of long-term gains with short-term losses.[4] Since investors have a tax incentive to realize losses and defer gains (at least, short-term gains), the assumption that the deduction limit is not binding may be tenuous and is relaxed in the next scenario.

---

[3]Similarly the right to deduct half of the long-term losses from income, even under the current 40% rule for long-term capital gains, could not be used. Losses could only be deducted from other capital gains. Thus, the effective tax rate on both long-term gains and losses is the same.

[4]The individual may mitigate this offset provision of the tax law by realizing long-term gains and short- and long-term losses in alternate tax years; however, we do not explicitly model this. See Constantinides (1984). This procedure may also help to avoid the unfavorable long-term gain and loss offset.

(III) *The marginal investor is an individual. Coupon income is taxed at the rate $\tau_c = 0.5$. Short- and long-term gains and losses remain untaxed, i.e., $\tau_s = \tau_L = 0$.*

One justification for this scenario is to assume that the individual realizes losses and defers gains. At the margin losses can only be carried forward as the deduction limit is binding. The only tax 'game' permitted under this scenario is to realize a gain on a bond in order to raise its basis above par and start deducting the premium amortization against ordinary income. As we shall see, this policy is profitable.

Although corporations are taxed differently from individuals, the tax regulations on non-bank corporations that hold bonds for reasons not directly related to their business operations are sufficiently similar to those applying to individuals that the previous scenarios remain at least qualitatively correct. The primary distinction is that a net capital loss (short- and long-term combined) cannot be deducted in any amount from ordinary income, but may be carried back for three years and forward for five as a short-term loss to offset gains. Banks and (corporate or individual) bond dealers are taxed differently, however.

For banks and dealers, bond coupons and all realized capital gains and losses are treated as ordinary income or loss without explicit limitation. Net operating losses of banks are carried back for ten years and forward for five years. In the following scenario we effectively assume that the bank has positive net earnings in every ten-year period so that loss benefits are earned immediately. Corporate earnings and losses are taxed at the corporate rate of 50%. (The current corporate tax rate is 46% on earnings in excess of $100,000. In the past it has been as high as 54%.) The same scenario applies to a bond dealer with marginal personal or corporate tax rate on ordinary income equal to 50%.

(IV) *The marginal holder is a bank or bond dealer. Coupon income and all capital gains and losses are taxed at the rate $\tau_c = \tau_s = \tau_L = 0.5$. There is no deduction limit.*

In each of the scenarios, I–IV, the tax rates $\tau_c$, $\tau_s$ and $\tau_L$ are assumed to remain constant over time because we wish to focus on the long-run effect of taxes on bond prices. Certain trading policies not examined here would become optimal at the time that tax provisions were about to change. For example, when the effective maximum rate on long-term capital gains was changed from 28% to 20% by the 1978 Tax Revenue Act, individuals paying the 28% rate should have deferred realizing their capital gains, ceteris paribus. Similarly if an investor's income were to change sufficiently to place him in a different tax bracket, the optimal trading policy might be affected.

We also examine bond prices in each of the four tax scenarios under the assumption that the bondholder is (artificially) constrained to follow a buy-and-hold policy and compare the bond prices, tax timing option, and yields to the case when the investor follows optimal policies. The buy-and-hold economy is taken as our primary benchmark in which there are no price effects induced by tax trading.

We do not explicitly examine a scenario in which the marginal bondholder is exempt from all taxes. This might be considered a serious omission because tax-exempt intermediaries currently hold more than one-third of all the outstanding government and corporate bonds and account for an even greater proportion of the trading volume. Furthermore, liberalized tax-deferred retirement plans provide growing opportunities for taxable individuals to defer the tax on coupons, dividends and capital gains until retirement. If the marginal investor is tax-exempt, then there are obviously no tax-induced 'biases' in bond prices.[5] However, since the no-trading policy is not dominated by any other for a tax-exempt investor (in a perfect market), we may assume the buy-and-hold policy. Consequently bond prices should equal the benchmark values, and standard estimation techniques, such as McCulloch's (1975), should verify that the marginal tax bracket is zero.

### 3. The model

Our goal is to find the price of a default-free bond with par value one, continuous coupon rate $c$, and maturity date $T$. The bond is perfectly divisible and may be bought or sold with zero transactions costs.[6] The bond price is a function of the state vector $Y$ (defined below) and time $t$, i.e., $P = P(Y, t; c, T)$.

We price the coupon bond relative to short-term (instantaneous) lending via a riskless, 'single-period' bond with maturity $dt$ and before-tax yield $r(Y, t)$. The single-period bond is perfectly divisible and may be bought or sold with zero transactions costs. Effectively there is unlimited riskless lending over the time interval $dt$ at the before-tax interest rate $r$. If an investor's tax rate on ordinary income is $\tau_c$, his after-tax interest rate is $(1 - \tau_c)r$.

We assume that, throughout the term to this coupon bond's maturity, some investor with marginal tax rates $\tau_c$, $\tau_s$, and $\tau_L$ (on coupon income, short-term capital gains and losses, and long-term capital gains and losses, respectively) is indifferent between buying the coupon bond or investing in the single-period

---

[5]Even in this case, however, when taxes do not affect bond prices, taxed investors will still benefit from following trading policies different from the buy-and-hold. The value of trading optimally will of course depend upon what taxes they must pay. Thus, the timing option will have the same qualitative properties it does in one of the examined scenarios.

[6]Transactions costs on bonds are small and are of the order of magnitude of the bid–asked spread. In section 6 (table 6) we introduce transactions costs and show that the pricing implications and the value of the timing option remain largely unaffected.

bond. That there exists some tax bracket $(\tau_c, \tau_s, \tau_L)$ with the property that an investor in this tax bracket is indifferent between the two investments over a time interval d$t$, is a weak assumption. The strong part of our assumption is that *investors in the same tax bracket are at the margin throughout the bond's term to maturity.* In a richer model (beyond our present scope) one might allow for the possibility that the bond is passed from one tax clientele to another as it approaches maturity or as it becomes a premium or discount bond due to shifts in interest rates. Since we wish to focus on the already complex problem of the optimal realization of capital gains and losses, we abstract from issues related to changing tax clienteles.[7]

At each point of time and for each coupon bond there is a reservation purchase price defined to be such that a (marginal) investor in the given tax bracket $(\tau_c, \tau_s, \tau_L)$ is indifferent between purchasing the coupon bond now or investing in the single-period bond over the time interval d$t$. This equilibrium condition is formalized below as the after-tax version of the local expectations hypothesis. After purchasing the coupon bond, the investor follows the derived optimal trading policy as opposed to a continuous realization or a buy-and-hold policy.

Each bondholder also has a reservation sale price which depends on his cost basis and the length of time for which he has held the bond. In general the prevailing reservation purchase and sale prices differ. We assume that the government supplies all maturity and coupon bonds with infinite elasticity at the reservation purchase price of the (marginal) investor and that all trades take place at this price, denoted $P$.[8] When the reservation sale price exceeds the reservation purchase price, only the government supplies the bond. When the reservation purchase price exceeds the reservation sale price, the seller earns a 'producer's' surplus which we attribute to his tax timing option.

The value of the bond to an investor, $V(Y, t; c, T; \hat{P}, \hat{\imath})$, is defined as the present value of the stream of cash flows associated with the bond, assuming that the optimal policy in realizing capital gains and losses is followed. The symbols $\hat{P}$ and $\hat{\imath}$ denote the current cost basis and the time at which the bond

---

[7]Tax clienteles for bonds is an important issue extensively discussed by Schaefer (1981, 1982a, 1982b) under the assumption that bonds are held to maturity. As we demonstrate below, under tax laws similar to those in the U.S., a buy-and-hold policy is inferior to trading schemes which involve (among other things) early realization of capital losses. Under British regulations, which imposed no long-term capital gains tax on 'gilt' securities prior to 1962 or after 1969, such trading schemes have no direct benefits, so a buy-and-hold policy is not necessarily inferior. Neither need it be correct, however. Even in Schaefer's world, *future* changes in interest rates or the introduction of new bonds may cause an existing bond to become dominated for its current clientele. The anticipation of such events should be reflected in the bond's current price, and this may mask some clientele effects.

[8]Alternatively, we could assume that bonds are fixed in supply and some investors are occasionally forced to trade for reasons unrelated to optimal tax trading. 'Liquidity purchasers' will never pay above their reservation price because the discount bond is available. 'Liquidity sellers', however, may not be able to hold out for their reservation price.

was purchased. Because of amortization of the basis, $\hat{P}$ may differ from the price at which the bond was purchased.

At those 'stopping times' at which the investor either by choice or by force sells the bond and realizes a capital gain or loss, the value to the investor is simply the after-tax proceeds from its immediate sale. The bond's maturity date is an obvious stopping time for all investors. At maturity, the capital gain or loss is unavoidably realized, hence

$$V(Y, T; c, T; \hat{P}, \hat{t}) = 1 - \tau(t, \hat{t})(1 - \hat{P}), \tag{1}$$

where $\tau(t, \hat{t})$ is the short- or long-term tax rate depending on the bond's status.

A similar result is true at any stopping time prior to maturity when the investor sells his bonds. For the sequence of (possibly random) stopping times, $t = t_1, t_2, \ldots$, at which the investor realizes a capital gain or loss,

$$V(Y, t; c, T, \hat{P}, \hat{t}) = P - \tau(t, \hat{t})(P - \hat{P}) \quad \text{at} \quad t = t_1, t_2, \ldots . \tag{2}$$

Stopping times may differ across investors. At the stopping times chosen by the investor the 'smooth-pasting' (or 'high contact') condition also must hold,[9]

$$\frac{\partial V}{\partial Y_n} = [1 - \tau(t, \hat{t})] \frac{\partial P}{\partial Y_n} \quad \text{for} \quad n = 1, 2, \ldots, N, \quad \text{at} \quad t_1^\circ, t_2^\circ, \ldots . \tag{3}$$

The smooth-pasting condition is not imposed at those stopping times where a realization is forced. Forced realizations are assumed to be caused by events exogenous to the model, e.g., an unanticipated and unavoidable need for consumption or portfolio revision. Forced realizations are formally modelled as Poisson arrivals with constant force $\lambda$. The Poisson process is independent of the process which generates the movements of the state variables.

For a marginal investor the time of purchase is also an optimal stopping time since, by definition, he is indifferent to the purchase. Thus,

$$V(Y, t; c, T; P, t) = P, \tag{4a}$$

$$\frac{\partial V}{\partial Y_n} = (1 - \tau_s) \frac{\partial P}{\partial Y_n}, \qquad n = 1, \ldots, N. \tag{4b}$$

This condition provides the link between the value of the bond and its market price. It may also be interpreted as an alternative description of the marginal investor. Eq. (4a) need not hold for non-marginal investors who either receive a

---

[9] Merton (1973) demonstrates that this condition is the result of optimizing behavior in the context of option pricing. It is formally derived in Grigelionis and Shiryaev (1966).

surplus by purchasing the bond at the prevailing price or find buying the bond to be dominated by lending at the short-term rate.

At all other times, the investor's value of the bond exceeds the after-tax proceeds from immediate sale. and the investor optimally defers the realization of a capital gain or loss. The set of states and times $\{Y, t\}$ at which this occurs is referred to as the continuation region, i.e., in the continuation region

$$V(Y, t; c, T; \hat{P}, \hat{t}) > P - \tau(t, \hat{t})(P - \hat{P}).\tag{5}$$

In the continuation region, the investor's after-tax rate of return on his bond is

$$\{dV + (1 - \tau_c)c\,dt + \max[0, (\hat{P} - 1)\tau_c\,dt/(T - t)]\}/V.\tag{6}$$

The term $(\hat{P} - 1)\tau_c\,dt/(T - t)$ is the tax benefit of the linearly amortized premium when the basis is above par.

We assume the after-tax version of the local expectations hypothesis:[10] The after-tax expected rate of return on the coupon bond (measured via the value function) equals the after-tax single-period rate of interest over the period $\{t, t + dt\}$, i.e.,

$$E\big[\{dV + (1 - \tau_c)c\,dt + \max[0, (\hat{P} - 1)\tau_c\,dt/(T - t)]\}/V\big]$$

$$= (1 - \tau_c)r\,dt,\tag{7}$$

for all $Y$, $t$, $\hat{P}$, and $\hat{t}$.

We assume that the state of the economy at time $t$ is summarized by a vector $\{Y_n(t)\}_{N \times 1}$. This vector also summarizes the history of the economy, $Y(\tau)$, $\tau < t$, to the extent that it is of current economic relevance. The state variables are jointly Markov with movements determined by the system of stochastic differential equations

$$dY_n(t) = \mu_n(Y, t)\,dt + \sigma_n'(Y, t)\,dw(t), \qquad n = 1, 2, \ldots, N,\tag{8}$$

where $\mu_n$ is a scalar, $\sigma_n$ is a $K$-dimensional vector, $K \leq N$, and $dw(t)$ is the increment of the Wiener process $w(t)$ in $R^K$. The variance–covariance matrix $\{\sigma_n'\sigma_m\}$ is positive semidefinite and of rank $K$ (positive definite, if $K = N$).

---

[10]See Cox, Ingersoll and Ross (1981) for a discussion of the different forms of the expectations hypothesis. In another paper (1983) they show how this assumption may be weakened by incorporating a risk premium into the drift terms for the state variables. As discussed there, the absence of arbitrage opportunities is insufficient to close the model as it is in option pricing. The difference here is that the state variables need not be prices.

If $\{Y, t\}$ lies in the continuation region, the expected value of $dV$ due to the movement of the state variables $Y, t$, is given by Ito's Lemma, as the first three terms of eq. (9) below. The expected value of $dV$ due to a stochastic forced realization is $[P - \tau(t, \hat{\imath})(P - \hat{P}) - V]\lambda dt$. The term in the brackets multiplying $\lambda$ is the loss incurred when the investor is forced to deviate from his optimal policy. The term $\lambda dt$ is the probability of a forced realization over $[t, t + dt]$. Also, the expected value of $dV$ due to the amortization of the premium is $-(\partial V/\partial \hat{P})\max[0, (\hat{P} - 1) dt/(T - t)]$. Then eq. (7) becomes

$$\frac{1}{2} \sum_{n=1}^{N} \sum_{m=1}^{N} \frac{\partial^2 V}{\partial Y_n \partial Y_m} \sigma_n' \sigma_m + \sum_{n=1}^{N} \frac{\partial V}{\partial Y_n} \mu_n + \frac{\partial V}{\partial t}$$

$$+ [P - \tau(t, \hat{\imath})(P - \hat{P}) - V]\lambda + (1 - \tau_c)c$$

$$+ \left(\tau_c - \frac{\partial V}{\partial \hat{P}}\right)\max[0, (\hat{P} - 1)/(T - t)] - (1 - \tau_c)rV = 0. \tag{9}$$

The solution to this differential equation, subject to the boundary conditions (1) through (5), provides the bond price, $P$, the value of a bond to the investor, $V$, and the optimal policy for the realization of capital gains and losses.[11]

For general functions $\sigma_n(Y, t)$ and $\mu_n(Y, t)$, a closed-form solution does not typically exist. In section 4 we illustrate the solution procedure in a simplified version of this problem and discuss the economic implications. In section 5 we provide numerical solutions to the general problem.

## 4. An example

In this section we begin to examine the value of the timing option regarding the realization of capital gains and losses on bonds and to analyze the effect of the capital gains tax on their pricing. To discuss these issues in the simplest possible setting and through closed-form solutions, we make a number of simplifying assumptions.

We assume that there is only one state variable, the short-term rate of interest, $r$, with movements determined by the stochastic differential equation

$$dr = \alpha r^2 dt + sr^{\frac{3}{2}} dw(t), \tag{10}$$

---

[11] The now-familiar American put pricing problem provides a useful analogy. Let $G(S, K, T)$ denote the value of a put with striking price $K$ and time to maturity $T$ on a stock with price $S$. Eq. (2) is analogous to the condition at exercise, $G(S^*, K, T) = K - S^*$. The 'smooth-pasting' condition analogous to (3) is $G_S(S^*, K, T) = -1$. Together these relations are sufficient to derive both the pricing function $G$ and the optimal exercise policy $S^*(T)$. Similarly here we derive both the value function and the optimal realization policy $Y^*$ conditional on the bond price function. Eq. (4) then provides the closure finally giving all three.

where $dw(t)$ is the increment of the scalar Wiener process $w(t)$.[12] The price, $P(r; c)$, of an infinite maturity coupon bond is then a function of the short-term interest rate, $r$, but is independent of the current time, $t$, because the process generating interest rate movements is stationary.

We also assume that the tax rates on all capital gains and losses are equal, i.e., $\tau_s = \tau_L \equiv \tau$. Thus the length of time over which the bond has been held is irrelevant, and the consol's value to an investor, $V(r; c; \hat{P})$, is also independent of the current time, $t$. Finally, we assume away forced realizations, i.e., $\lambda = 0$.

It is easy to prove that any investor's optimal policy is to realize capital losses immediately and defer capital gains indefinitely.[13] Given the basis, $\hat{P}$, the continuation region is defined by the range of interest rates such that $P(r; c) > \hat{P}$. In the continuation region the differential equation (9) becomes

$$\frac{1}{2} s^2 r^3 \frac{\partial^2 V}{\partial r^2} + \alpha r^2 \frac{\partial V}{\partial r} - (1 - \tau_c) r V + (1 - \tau_c) c = 0, \qquad P(r; c) > \hat{P}.$$

(11)

The boundary condition (4a) becomes

$$V(r; c; \hat{P}) = \hat{P} \quad \text{at} \quad P(r; c) = \hat{P}, \tag{12}$$

and the 'smooth-pasting' conditions (3) and (4b) become

$$\frac{\partial V(r; c; \hat{P})}{\partial r} = (1 - \tau) \frac{\partial P(r, c)}{\partial r} \quad \text{at} \quad P(r; c) = \hat{P}. \tag{13}$$

The bond price $P(r; c)$ is a function of the interest rate, $r$, and of the parameters $c$, $\alpha$, $s$, $\tau$, and $\tau_c$. Inspection of eq. (10) indicates that the parameters $\alpha$ and $s$ are dimensionless as are the parameters $\tau$ and $\tau_c$. The units of the coupon yield $c$ are dollars per unit of time, and the unit of the interest rate is the inverse of the time unit. The bond price must be proportional to the coupon rate, and since it is invariant to changes in the unit of time, it must also

[12] We may alternatively consider (10) as the risk-adjusted interest rate dynamics with $\alpha = \mu + \pi$, where $\mu$ measures the expected change in the short rate and $\pi$ captures the risk premium due on interest-rate-sensitive securities. Cox, Ingersoll and Ross (1980) discuss this interpretation for the stochastic process in (10).

[13] This statement is formally proved in Constantinides (1983). If the tax rates $\tau_s$ and $\tau_L$ are unequal the optimal policy is a great deal more complex. Under these circumstances, the optimal policy for trading stocks is discussed in Constantinides (1984) and the optimal policy for trading bonds is discussed in section 5 of this paper.

be inversely proportional to $r$. Hence

$$P(r; c) = Hc/r,\tag{14}$$

where $H$ is a function of only the parameters $\alpha$, $s$, $\tau$, and $\tau_c$.

Since we have determined the functional form of $P$, we can simplify (11) with the aid of eq. (14) to eliminate $r$ and its derivatives, obtaining

$$\frac{s^2}{2}P^2 V_{PP} + (s^2 - \alpha) P V_P - (1 - \tau_c) V + \frac{(1 - \tau_c) P}{H} = 0, \qquad P > \hat{P}.\tag{15}$$

The general solution to eq. (15) is given below:[14]

$$V = \frac{(1 - \tau_c) P}{(1 - \tau_c + \alpha - s^2) H} + A \hat{P}^{1-\eta} P^{\eta} + A' \hat{P}^{1-\eta'} P^{\eta'}, \qquad P > \hat{P},\tag{16}$$

where $A$, $A'$ are arbitrary constants to be determined, and $\eta$, $\eta'$ ($\eta < 0 < \eta'$) are the roots of the quadratic equation

$$\frac{s^2}{2}\eta(\eta - 1) + (s^2 - \alpha)\eta - (1 - \tau_c) = 0.\tag{17}$$

By homogeneity, the coefficients of $P^{\eta}$ and $P^{\eta'}$ must be proportional to the parameters $\hat{P}^{1-\eta}$ and $\hat{P}^{1-\eta'}$, respectively. Thus, $A$ and $A'$ depend only on the parameters $\alpha$, $s$, $\tau$, and $\tau_c$.

The following argument determines $A'$. Since the optimal trading policy involves no sales at any price above the basis, $\hat{P}$ must have a negligible effect on the value function whenever $P \gg \hat{P}$. Formally

$$\lim_{P/\hat{P} \to \infty} (\partial V / \partial \hat{P}) = 0.\tag{18}$$

This condition is satisfied only if $A' = 0$. The remaining two constants can be determined using (12) and (13). Substituting (16) into (12) and setting $A' = 0$, we obtain

$$\frac{(1 - \tau_c) P}{(1 - \tau_c + \alpha - s^2) H} + AP = P.\tag{19}$$

---

[14]For a meaningful solution the parameters of the interest rate process must satisfy $s^2 - \alpha < 1 - \tau_c$. From (22) and (23) the expected rate of price appreciation and the limit (as $r$ goes to zero) of the expected rate of appreciation of the value function are both $(s^2 - \alpha)r$. Thus, if the stated condition is violated the expected rates of return including coupons must exceed the after-tax rate of interest $(1 - \tau_c)r$ and the expectations hypothesis cannot obtain as was assumed. Furthermore, given that the dynamics may be interpreted in a risk-adjusted sense, as discussed in footnote 12, no other equilibrium is possible either.

Similarly, substituting (16) into (13) and setting $A' = 0$, we obtain

$$\frac{1 - \tau_c}{\left(1 - \tau_c + \alpha - s^2\right)H} + A\eta = 1 - \tau. \tag{20}$$

We solve for $H$ and $A$ and obtain

$$P(r; c) = \frac{(1 - \tau_c)c}{\left(1 - \tau_c + \alpha - s^2\right)\{1 - \tau/(1 - \eta)\}r}, \tag{21}$$

and

$$V(r; c; \hat{P}) = (1 - \tau)P + \tau\hat{P}, \qquad\qquad P \leq \hat{P},$$

$$= \left(1 - \frac{\tau}{1 - \eta}\right)P + \left(\frac{\tau}{1 - \eta}\right)P^\eta\hat{P}^{1-\eta}, \qquad P > \hat{P}, \tag{22}$$

where

$$\eta \equiv -\left[s^2/2 - \alpha + \left\{\left(s^2/2 - \alpha\right)^2 + 2s^2(1 - \tau_c)\right\}^{\frac{1}{2}}\right]/s^2$$

is the negative root of (17).

Eq. (21) shows that the price of a consol bond is increasing in the capital gains tax rate of the marginal investor. A high capital gains rate does not hurt the investor because he is never forced to realize gains and his optimal policy is to defer indefinitely the realization of capital gains. In fact a high capital gains rate is a benefit because it enables him to obtain larger tax rebates by realizing a capital loss whenever such a loss occurs. Provided that forced realizations are not too frequent, the same conclusion also applies to a finite maturity par bond, as indeed is demonstrated in the numerical solutions of section 6. If the bond currently sells at par, the investor can be neutral to the capital gains tax by following the naive policy of deferring both gains and losses. The intelligent policy of deferring gains and realizing losses can only turn the taxation to his advantage, and he therefore benefits by a high capital gains tax rate.

Using Ito's Lemma and eqs. (10) and (11), we find the consol dynamics to be

$$dP/P = (s^2 - \alpha)r\,dt - s\sqrt{r}\ dw \equiv \gamma r\,dt - s\sqrt{r}\ dw. \tag{23}$$

The expected capital gains rate, $\gamma r$, can be either positive or negative. We write the bond price in terms of $\gamma$ and obtain

$$P(r; c) = \frac{c/r}{\{1 - \gamma/(1 - \tau_c)\}\{1 - \tau/(1 - \eta)\}}. \tag{21'}$$

We observe that the bond price is increasing (decreasing) in the ordinary income tax rate, if capital gains (losses) are expected. This indeterminancy is due to the light taxation of capital gains relative to interest and coupon income in this model. If capital gains are expected, the consol's current coupon yield is less than the interest rate, and an increase in $\tau_c$ represents a greater loss for potential holdings in the instantaneous bond than in the consol.

We use two benchmarks to measure the value of the tax timing option. The first is the price of the consol, $P_H$, in an economy where the marginal investor follows a buy-and-hold policy. This benchmark is also the consol's price in an economy with zero capital gains tax.[15] Hence, we write

$$P_H = \frac{(1 - \tau_c)c}{(1 - \tau_c - \gamma)r}.$$ (24)

The second benchmark is the consol price, $P_C$, in an economy where the marginal bondholder realizes all gains and losses continuously. Proceeding as before, we find that this consol price satisfies the equation

$$(1 - \tau)\left\{\frac{s^2}{2}r^3 P_C'' + \alpha r^2 P_C'\right\} - (1 - \tau_c)rP_C + (1 - \tau_c)c = 0,$$ (25)

with solution

$$P_C = \frac{(1 - \tau_c)c}{\{1 - \tau_c - \gamma(1 - \tau)\}r}.$$ (26)

Note that $P_C \gtrless P_H$ as $\gamma \lessgtr 0$: A continuous realization policy dominates the buy-and-hold policy whenever capital losses are expected.

The tax effect on the consol's price is expressed relative to the two benchmarks as follows:

$$\frac{P - P_H}{P} = \frac{\tau}{1 - \eta},$$ (27a)

$$\frac{P - P_C}{P} = \frac{\tau}{1 - \eta}\left[1 + \frac{\gamma(1 - \eta - \tau)}{1 - \tau_c - \gamma(1 - \tau)}\right].$$ (27b)

When the buy-and-hold benchmark is used, the timing option's value derives from the right to realize capital losses early. When the continuous-realization

---

[15] The buy-and-hold price is unaffected by the capital gains tax rate of the marginal investor for the simple reason that no capital gains tax is ever paid. This result differs from that reported in Constantinides (1983) for stocks. Although the tax liability is also postponed indefinitely for equities, the expected rate of growth in price, adjusted for risk, equals the discount rate so the present value of the tax liability is not negligible. In our problem, the expected rate of growth in price, $\gamma r$, must be smaller than the discount rate $(1 - \tau_c)r$. See footnote 14.

Table 1

The value of the timing option as a percentage of the consol price.[a]

|  | s = 0.604 | | | s = 0.172 | | |
|---|---|---|---|---|---|---|
|  | $\alpha = 0$ | $\alpha = s^2$ | $\alpha = 0.44$ | $\alpha = 0$ | $\alpha = s^2$ | $\alpha = 0.44$ |
| Buy-and-hold benchmark | 7.7 | 11.2 | 11.9 | 3.4 | 3.9 | 11.7 |
| Continuous realization benchmark | 44.9 | 11.2 | 9.0 | 4.9 | 3.9 | 0.5 |

[a]Computed for infinitely lived investors. Interest rate follows the risk-adjusted stochastic process $dr = \alpha r^2 dt + sr^{\frac{3}{2}} dw$. Marginal bondholder's tax rates are $\tau_c = 0.5$ on coupon income and $\tau = 0.25$ on all capital gains.

benchmark is used, the timing option measures the value of deferring capital gains.

To measure the magnitude of the timing option we require estimates of the parameters $\alpha$ and $s$ and the marginal tax bracket. Using the Ibbotson and Sinquefield (1982) data the annualized standard deviation of changes in the short rate over the period 1926–1981 is 2.2%. Using eq. (10) and $r = 0.11$ we set $s = (0.022)(0.11)^{-\frac{3}{2}} = 0.604$. In the same study the reported standard deviation of annualized returns on long-term U.S. Treasury bonds is 5.7%. If we take this number as an estimate of the standard deviation of returns on a consol, then using (23) and $r = 0.11$ we obtain $s = (0.057)/\sqrt{0.11} = 0.172$.[16]

Ibbotson and Sinquefield do not report the average change in the interest rate, so somewhat arbitrarily we examine the two cases $\alpha = 0$ and $\alpha = s^2$ which correspond to zero expected change in the interest rate and in the consol price, respectively. If we choose to interpret $\alpha$ as a risk premium measure, then under the assumption of no drift in the interest rate, the expected rate of return on a consol is $r(1 + \alpha)$. Ibbotson and Sinquefield estimate that investors expected on average a premium of 131 basis points on twenty-year bonds. This gives an estimate for $\alpha$ of 0.44 based on the average interest rate.

Table 1 displays the value of the timing option as a percentage of price [eqs. (27a) and (27b)]. For the higher variance process the timing option contributes a significant portion of the bond's value as measured against either benchmark. For the lower variance process the timing option remains important except in the case when large capital losses are expected and the continuous realization

[16]The Ibbotson and Sinquefield estimate based on a portfolio of long-term bonds may be a downwardly biased estimate of the standard deviation of a consol's rate of return for two reasons:
(a) They considered a portfolio of bonds with an average maturity of 20 years (not infinite).
(b) The variability of a portfolio of bonds generally underestimates the return variability of each bond. For example, a shock in the economy which raises the price of ten-year bonds and lowers the price of thirty-year bonds may leave the portfolio's price essentially unchanged and contribute little to the variability of the portfolio's return. The same shock, however, may have a significant impact on the consol's return.
Both of our estimates of $s$, particularly the first, may also be negatively biased because the interest rate was substantially less than 11% for most of this period.

benchmark is employed. We conclude that the potential effect of tax trading on bond prices cannot be safely ignored in practice.

## 5. Optimal bond trading: The general case

We examine a discrete-time version of the model outlined in section 3, focusing on the distinction between short- and long-term gains and losses, the effect of the amortization deduction and transactions costs. Since our primary concern is on how optimal trading affects the bond prices, we confine our attention to the marginal bondholder.

We assume that the trading interval is one year.[17] If an asset is sold one year after purchase, we assume that the holding period is short-term or long-term at the investor's discretion. Since the cutoff point is one year after purchase, the investor can make the holding period long- or short-term, by delaying or advancing the bond sale by only one day. By a simple dominance argument, all capital gains are realized long-term. Similarly, whenever the investor realizes a capital loss one year after purchasing the bond, he does so short-term.

We maintain our assumption that there are no forced realizations. On each trading date the investor either holds his bond, deferring the realization of a capital gain or loss, or sells his bond and immediately repurchases its, thereby realizing a capital gain or loss and re-establishing a short-term status. The following set of factors determines whether the investor holds his bond or executes a wash sale:

(a) If the bond price is below the basis, the investor would like to sell the bond and receive the tax deduction immediately. The reason becomes more compelling if the bond was purchased one year earlier, so that this is the only chance to realize the capital loss short-term.

(b) If the bond price is above the basis, the investor would like to defer the realization of the capital gain and thereby defer the tax liability. As stated previously, he never realizes a short-term gain because he can wait one more day. Nevertheless, he may wish to realize a long-term gain as explained in (c) and (d).

(c) A short-term holding status is beneficial to the investor. This status helps when he realizes a capital loss, because he realizes it short-term, and it never hurts, even when the investor realizes a capital gain, because he can always wait one more day and convert to the long-term status. The short-term status turns out to be a very important factor governing the optimal liquidation policy. Under certain realistic conditions, an investor may realize a capital gain solely to convert to the beneficial short-term status.

---

[17]The choice of one year is primarily a matter of convenience, coinciding with both the minimum holding period for long-term gains and the length of the tax year. If the holding period were shorter, as it was until recently, and the offset provision were to be considered, then an additional complication would arise. The value of short-term losses in the first part of the year could not be determined until it was known if there were later offsetting long-term capital gains.

(d) The peculiar amortization rules on bonds introduce another twist to this already complex problem. If the bond's basis is above par, this difference is linearly amortized over its remaining term to maturity with the 'loss' applied against the investor's ordinary income. The present value of this tax deduction is high for short maturity bonds, but decreases with longer maturity, because of the linearity of the amortization rule. For short maturity bonds the benefit in establishing a basis above par may be sufficiently large to make it optimal to realize a capital gain.

We assume that the short-term rate of interest, $r$, is the only state variable and that it follows a driftless binomial random walk with two reflecting barriers. We consider two specifications for the interest rate process. In the low-variance process, the interest rate takes on the twenty-one values, $0.04, 0.05, 0.06, \ldots, 0.24$. At each point in time the interest rate either increases or decreases by 0.01, each with probability one half, unless it is currently at one of the reflecting barriers, 0.04 or 0.24. If the interest rate is equal to one of the reflecting barriers, then at the next date it remains unchanged or takes on the value 0.05 or 0.23, respectively, with probability one half. The reader may verify that the unconditional distribution of $r$ is uniform over the twenty-one points. The standard deviation of changes in the interest rate is $\sigma_r \equiv \mathrm{std}(r(t + 1)|r(t)) = 0.01$ per year, independent of the state (except in the end-point states).

In the high-variance process, the interest rate takes one of the eleven values, $0.04, 0.06, \ldots, 0.24$. The probabilities of increase or decrease by 0.02 are as in the low-variance process with the same reflecting barriers at 0.04 and 0.24. The standard deviation of the changes in the interest rate in the high-variance process is $\sigma_r = 0.02$ per year. From the Ibbotson and Sinquefield (1982) study, the annualized standard deviation of the short-term rate is 0.022. The low-variance process then underestimates the interest rate variability, while the high-variance process reflects the average variability in the period 1926–1981.

As we shall see, the low-variance process implies, on average, that the standard deviation of the annual rate of return of twenty-year Treasury bonds is 5.66%, if priced under the buy-and-hold policy, and 5.82% if priced under the optimal policy with $\tau_s = \tau_L = 0.25$ (scenario I). For the high-variance process, the corresponding numbers are 9.47% and 8.73%. From the Ibbotson and Sinquefield (1982) study this standard deviation is 5.7% for long-term Treasury bonds over the 1926–1981 period. Therefore the low-variance process reflects the actual *initial* variability of long-term bonds over that period.[18] The high-variance process, however, may be more representative of recent history.

In discrete time, the differential equation (9) becomes a difference equation which we may solve numerically subject to the boundary conditions. Equiva-

---

[18]See, however, the second caveat in footnote 16. In addition, when the low-variance process is used, the simulated volatility of a twenty-year bond over its life will be lower than the historic average because the low-variance process understates the variance of the short-term rate and hence the variance of short-term bonds.

lently and more directly we obtain the bond price and the value of a bond to the marginal investor by dynamic programming, at dates $T, T-1, T-2, \ldots,$ etc.

Eqs. (28) and (29) establish the bond price and value of a bond to the investor at maturity, i.e., at $t = T$. At maturity the ex-coupon bond is priced at par which we take to be unity,

$$P(r, T; c, T) = 1. \tag{28}$$

The value of the bond to an investor is the after-tax sale proceeds. By the maturity date, the bond basis cannot exceed one, because the excess will have been completely amortized by then. Thus only a gain can be realized at maturity, and the appropriate capital gains tax rate is the long-term rate. Thus,

$$V(r, T; c, T; \hat{P}, \hat{\imath}) = 1 - \tau_L + \tau_L \hat{P}. \tag{29}$$

With the terminal values established, the bond's price and its value to a given investor at points in time prior to maturity can now be obtained through dynamic programming. We distinguish between the cases in which amortization is and is not utilized.

The bond price is what a marginal investor is willing to pay for it. His alternative is investing in the short-term asset over the next year in which case his investment increases at the prevailing after-tax interest rate. He is indifferent to buying the bond, therefore, only if the after-tax coupon and amortization benefit plus the expectation of the value function next period is greater than the current bond price by exactly the after-tax foregone interest. If the bond is selling today for less than par, then its price is the appropriate basis in the value function. If the bond is priced above par, then $(P-1)/(T-t)$ will be amortized in the next year, and the basis in the value function next year is less than the prevailing price by this amount. Thus at time $t$,

$$P = \left[1 + (1 - \tau_c)r\right]^{-1}\{(1 - \tau_c)c$$
$$+ \mathrm{E}_t\left[V(\tilde{r}(t+1), t+1; c, T; P, t]\right]\} \quad \text{if} \quad P \le 1, \tag{30}$$

and

$$P = \left[1 + (1 - \tau_c)r\right]^{-1}\{(1 - \tau_c)c + (P-1)\tau_c/(T-t)$$
$$+ \mathrm{E}_t\left[V(\tilde{r}(t+1), t+1; c, T; P - (P-1)/(T-t), t]\right]\} \quad \text{if} \quad P > 1. \tag{31}$$

The bond price, $P$, is the solution to (30) and (31).[19]

---

[19] The right-hand side of (30) is positive at $P = 0$ since the first term is, and the right-hand side of (31) is less than $P$ for large values [since the maximum benefit of future tax losses is $\tau_c(P-1)$]. These expressions are continuous at $P = 1$. Therefore a solution to (30) and (31) exists. For the dynamics assumed, the solution is also unique.

The value of a long position in the bond is the greater of the after-tax proceeds from immediate sale and the discounted value of the benefits if the bond is retained. The after-tax proceeds from immediate sale are

$$P - \tau(t, \hat{\imath})(P - \hat{P}). \tag{32}$$

If the bond is retained, the discounted benefits are

$$
\left[1 + (1 - \tau_c)r\right]^{-1}\left\{(1 - \tau_c)c\right.
$$
$$
\left. + \mathrm{E}_t\left[V(\tilde{r}(t+1), t+1; c, T; \hat{P}, t)\right]\right\} \quad \text{if} \quad \hat{P} \le 1, \tag{33}
$$

and

$$
\left[1 + (1 - \tau_c)r\right]^{-1}\left\{(1 - \tau_c)c + (\hat{P} - 1)\tau_c/(T - t)\right.
$$
$$
\left. + \mathrm{E}_t\left[V(\tilde{r}(t+1), t+1; c, T; \hat{P} - (\hat{P} - 1)/(T - t), \hat{\imath})\right]\right\} \quad \text{if} \quad \hat{P} > 1. \tag{34}
$$

In comparing eqs. (30) and (33) we note that $P = V(r, t; c, T; P, t)$ so the relation in (4a) is satisfied.

We illustrate the optimal trading policies for a bond with a 14 percent stated coupon payable annually, in the four tax scenarios.

(I)   *Treasury bond held by a high-tax-bracket individual, with $\tau_c = 0.5$, $\tau_s = \tau_L = 0.25$.*

Table 2 reports the bond prices and values, $V$, for the high variance interest rate process, for a range of interest rates and bases, and for maturities 1, 5 and 20 years.[20] If both the basis and the bond price are less than one, the amortization feature is not in effect and the simple trading rule is to realize a loss and defer a gain as indicated by daggers. If either the basis or the bond price exceeds one, the amortization feature becomes relevant and complicates the rule. Asterisks and daggers mark the states in which a wash sale is optimal. In these states the value function is equal to the after-tax proceeds from an immediate sale as stated in (32). Asterisks indicate the realization of capital gains establishing a new or higher amortizable basis. Daggers denote the realization of a capital loss. In unmarked states the value of holding exceeds

---

[20] Some of the entries in this table as well as those in table 3 give the value function for states which could never arise along the optimal path. For example, since losses are always realized when the basis is below par, the basis can never be substantially in excess of the current price in this situation. These entries, therefore, give the value of changing to the optimal policy from a suboptimal position.

Table 2

Treasury bond prices and values of a long position under tax scenario I.[a]

| Interest rate | Bond price | Basis | | | | | | |
|---|---|---|---|---|---|---|---|---|
| | | 0.7 | 0.8 | 0.9 | 1.0 | 1.1 | 1.2 | 1.3 |
| | | *Maturity = 1 year* | | | | | | |
| 0.06 | 1.0755 | *0.98 | *1.01 | *1.03 | *1.06 | 1.09 | 1.14 | 1.18 |
| 0.10 | 1.0364 | *0.95 | *0.98 | *1.00 | *1.03 | 1.07 | 1.11 | 1.16 |
| 0.14 | 1.0000 | 0.93 | 0.95 | 0.98 | *1.00 | 1.05 | 1.09 | 1.14 |
| 0.18 | 0.9762 | 0.91 | 0.94 | 0.96 | †0.98 | 1.03 | 1.07 | 1.12 |
| 0.22 | 0.9535 | 0.90 | 0.92 | 0.94 | †0.97 | 1.01 | 1.05 | 1.10 |
| | | *Maturity = 5 years* | | | | | | |
| 0.06 | 1.3363 | *1.18 | *1.20 | *1.23 | *1.25 | *1.28 | *1.30 | *1.33 |
| 0.10 | 1.1771 | *1.06 | *1.08 | *1.11 | *1.13 | *1.16 | 1.18 | 1.22 |
| 0.14 | 1.0197 | 0.95 | 0.97 | 0.99 | *1.01 | 1.05 | 1.08 | 1.12 |
| 0.18 | 0.9110 | 0.88 | 0.89 | 0.91 | †0.93 | 0.96 | 1.00 | 1.04 |
| 0.22 | 0.8354 | 0.81 | 0.83 | †0.85 | †0.88 | †0.90 | 0.93 | 0.97 |
| | | *Maturity = 20 years* | | | | | | |
| 0.06 | 1.7358 | 1.48 | *1.50 | *1.53 | *1.55 | *1.58 | *1.60 | *1.63 |
| 0.10 | 1.4187 | 1.26 | 1.27 | 1.29 | 1.31 | 1.34 | 1.36 | *1.39 |
| 0.14 | 1.1044 | 1.03 | 1.04 | 1.06 | 1.08 | 1.10 | †1.13 | †1.15 |
| 0.18 | 0.8793 | 0.85 | 0.86 | †0.88 | †0.91 | †0.93 | †0.96 | †0.98 |
| 0.22 | 0.7429 | 0.74 | †0.76 | †0.78 | †0.81 | †0.83 | †0.86 | †0.88 |

[a] Tax scenario I is characterized by a tax rate on coupon income of $\tau_c = 0.5$ and a tax rate on short-and long-term capital gains of $\tau_s = \tau_L = 0.25$ corresponding to a situation in which the offset rule is binding but the deduction limit is not. Coupon rate on bond is 0.14 paid annually. Interest rate follows high-variance process with standard deviation of 0.02 per year. The solid line divides the states with capital gains, realized or not, from those with capital losses. Asterisks and daggers mark the states in which the optimal policy is to perform a wash sale. Asterisks indicate the realization of a long term capital gain establishing a new or higher amortizable basis. Daggers denote the realization of a long-term capital loss.

the after-tax proceeds from a sale and no sale is executed. For example, when the interest rate is 14% a five-year bond sells for 1.0197. With a basis of 1.3 a tax rebate of 0.07 could be earned by realizing a capital loss; however, the total value of the wash sale, $1.02 + 0.07 = 1.09$, is less than that of holding the bond, 1.12, and continuing to amortize the higher basis.

For one-year bonds, if the bond sells at a premium, $P > 1$, and the basis is below the bond price, $\hat{P} < P$, the investor realizes a capital gain in order to establish a higher basis and benefit from the amortization of the basis, Conversely, if the bond price drops below the basis, $P < \hat{P}$, the investor defers realization of the loss to continue amortizing the original premium. For five-year bonds the amortization benefit is reduced and large capital gains may be deferred, or capital losses may be realized even at the expense of foregoing future amortization benefits. For example, if the bond price rises to 1.1097 from a basis of 1.0, the investor realizes a capital gain; but if $\hat{P} < 1.0$, the investor defers the capital gain. The amortization benefit becomes negligible for twenty-year bonds. For example, if $P = 1.42$ and $\hat{P} \leq 1.3$, the investor optimally defers the realization of a capital gain and thereby foregoes the amortization benefit of increasing the basis to 1.42. In fact, if $P = 0.88$ and $\hat{P} = 1.1$, 1.2, or 1.3, the investor foregoes the amortization benefit and realizes the capital loss.

(II)   *Treasury bond held by a high-tax-bracket individual with* $\tau_c = 0.5$, $\tau_s = 0.5$, $\tau_L = 0.25$.

Table 3 reports the bond price and values, $V$, for the high variance interest rate process, for a range of interest rates and bases, and for maturities 1, 5, and 20 years. Asterisks, daggers and double daggers mark the states where the optimal policy is to perform a wash sale. Panel A reports results when the bond has been held for longer than one year, $t - \hat{t} > 1$, while panel B reports results when the bond has been held for just one year, $t - \hat{t} = 1$. Note that the value function in the two panels can differ only when a wash sale is executed and a capital loss is realized. When a gain is realized, it is presumed to be long-term so the taxes paid are the same. When no wash sale occurs, the ensuing status must be long-term regardless of the current status.

These tables indicate that the investor performs a wash sale of long-term bonds practically every year in order to revert to the short-term status. This is emphasized by the double daggers which mark states in which a wash sale is executed to this end alone. The desirability of the short-term status seems to dominate all other considerations.

(III)   *Treasury bond held by a high-tax-bracket individual with* $\tau_c = 0.5$, $\tau_s = \tau_L = 0$.

The optimal trading policy is quite simple and need not be illustrated in a table. Whenever the bond price is above par and the basis, the investor makes a wash sale to establish a higher basis and deduct from future ordinary income the premium amortization. The investor has no tax incentives to perform any other trades.

(IV)   *Treasury bond held by a bank or bond dealer with* $\tau_c = \tau_s = \tau_L = 0.5$.

Again the optimal policy can be described without a table. The investor optimally realizes all capital losses and defers the realization of capital gains. He never realizes a capital gain in order to establish a higher basis with the benefit of the amortization deduction. The tax rate on ordinary income is the same as that on capital gains so amortization 'losses' at best exactly offset the capital gain and occur later. Neither does he defer the realization of a capital loss in order to maintain the benefit of the amortization deduction.

Table 3

Treasury bond prices and values of a long position under tax scenario II.[a]

| Interest rate | Bond price | Basis | | | | | | |
|---|---|---|---|---|---|---|---|---|
| | | 0.7 | 0.8 | 0.9 | 1.0 | 1.1 | 1.2 | 1.3 |

Panel A: Long-Term Status

*Maturity = 1 year*

| 0.06 | 1.0755 | *0.98 | *1.01 | *1.03 | *1.06 | 1.09 | 1.14 | 1.18 |
| 0.10 | 1.0364 | *0.95 | *0.98 | *1.00 | *1.03 | 1.07 | 1.11 | 1.16 |
| 0.14 | 1.0000 | 0.93 | 0.95 | 0.98 | ‡1.00 | 1.05 | 1.09 | 1.14 |
| 0.18 | 0.9762 | 0.91 | 0.94 | 0.96 | †0.98 | 1.03 | 1.07 | 1.12 |
| 0.22 | 0.9535 | 0.90 | 0.92 | 0.94 | †0.97 | 1.01 | 1.05 | 1.10 |

*Maturity = 5 years*

| 0.06 | 1.3476 | *1.19 | *1.21 | *1.24 | *1.26 | *1.29 | *1.31 | *1.34 |
| 0.10 | 1.1919 | *1.07 | *1.09 | *1.12 | *1.14 | *1.17 | †1.19 | 1.22 |
| 0.14 | 1.0368 | 0.95 | *0.98 | *1.00 | *1.03 | †1.05 | 1.08 | 1.12 |
| 0.18 | 0.9177 | 0.88 | 0.89 | ‡0.91 | †0.94 | †0.96 | 1.00 | 1.04 |
| 0.22 | 0.8357 | 0.81 | 0.83 | †0.85 | †0.88 | †0.90 | 0.93 | 0.97 |

*Maturity = 20 years*

| 0.06 | 1.9200 | *1.62 | *1.64 | *1.67 | *1.69 | *1.72 | *1.74 | *1.77 |
| 0.10 | 1.6138 | *1.39 | *1.41 | *1.44 | *1.46 | *1.49 | *1.51 | *1.54 |
| 0.14 | 1.2672 | *1.13 | *1.15 | *1.18 | *1.20 | *1.23 | *1.25 | †1.28 |
| 0.18 | 0.9791 | ‡0.91 | ‡0.93 | ‡0.96 | †0.98 | †1.01 | †1.03 | †1.06 |
| 0.22 | 0.7856 | ‡0.76 | †0.79 | †0.81 | †0.84 | †0.86 | †0.89 | †0.91 |

Panel B: Short-Term Status

*Maturity = 1 year*

| 0.06 | 1.0755 | *0.98 | *1.01 | *1.03 | *1.06 | †1.09 | †1.14 | †1.19 |
| 0.10 | 1.0364 | *0.95 | *0.98 | *1.00 | *1.03 | †1.07 | †1.12 | †1.17 |
| 0.14 | 1.0000 | 0.93 | 0.95 | 0.98 | ‡1.00 | †1.05 | †1.10 | †1.15 |
| 0.18 | 0.9762 | 0.91 | 0.94 | 0.96 | †0.99 | †1.04 | †1.09 | †1.14 |
| 0.22 | 0.9535 | 0.90 | 0.92 | 0.94 | †0.98 | †1.03 | †1.08 | †1.13 |

*Maturity = 5 years*

| 0.06 | 1.3476 | *1.19 | *1.21 | *1.24 | *1.26 | *1.29 | *1.31 | *1.34 |
| 0.10 | 1.1919 | *1.07 | *1.09 | *1.12 | *1.14 | *1.17 | †1.20 | †1.25 |
| 0.14 | 1.0368 | 0.95 | *0.98 | *1.00 | *1.03 | †1.07 | †1.12 | †1.17 |
| 0.18 | 0.9177 | 0.88 | 0.89 | ‡0.91 | †0.96 | †1.01 | †1.06 | †1.11 |
| 0.22 | 0.8375 | 0.81 | 0.83 | †0.87 | †0.92 | †0.97 | †1.02 | †1.07 |

*Maturity = 20 years*

| 0.06 | 1.9200 | *1.62 | *1.64 | *1.67 | *1.69 | *1.72 | *1.74 | *1.77 |
| 0.10 | 1.6138 | *1.39 | *1.41 | *1.44 | *1.46 | *1.49 | *1.51 | *1.54 |
| 0.14 | 1.2672 | *1.13 | *1.15 | *1.18 | *1.20 | *1.23 | *1.25 | †1.28 |
| 0.18 | 0.9791 | ‡0.91 | ‡0.93 | ‡0.96 | †0.99 | †1.04 | †1.09 | †1.14 |
| 0.22 | 0.7856 | ‡0.76 | †0.79 | †0.84 | †0.89 | †0.94 | †0.99 | †1.04 |

[a] Tax scenario II is characterized by a tax rate on coupon income and short-term capital gains of $\tau_c = \tau_s = 0.5$ and a tax rate on long-term capital gains of $\tau_L = 0.25$ corresponding to a situation in which neither the offset rule nor the deduction limit is binding. Coupon rate on bond is $c = 0.14$, paid annually. Interest rate follows the high-variance process with standard deviation of 0.02 per year. The solid line divides the states with capital gains, realized or not, from those with capital losses. Asterisks, daggers, and double daggers mark the states in which the optimal policy is to perform a wash sale. In each case, one of the benefits is re-establishing a short-term holding status. Asterisks and double daggers indicate the realization of a long-term capital gain. The former also denote the establishing of a new or higher amortizable basis. Double daggers also indicate the realization of a long-term capital gain; however, in these cases the only benefit is the re-establishing of a short-term holding period. Daggers indicate the realization of a long- or short-term capital loss in panels A and B, respectively.

## 6. Bond prices and the tax timing option

Table 4 displays simulated Treasury bond prices that would be established by the marginal investor following the optimal trading policy under each of the four tax scenarios. We assume that the current value of the short-term interest rate is 14%. For comparison, the 14% coupon bond would be priced just above par if the marginal investor followed a buy-and-hold policy. The exact buy-

Table 4

Treasury bond prices established by optimal trading policies; tax scenarios I–IV.[a,b]

| Maturity | High-variance process $\sigma_r = 0.02$ per year | | | | Low-variance process $\sigma_r = 0.01$ per year | | | |
|---|---|---|---|---|---|---|---|---|
| | I | II | III | IV | I | II | III | IV |
| *Coupon rate c = 0.06* | | | | | | | | |
| 5 | 0.802 | 0.803 | 0.837 | 0.748 | 0.801 | 0.801 | 0.836 | 0.746 |
| 10 | 0.690 | 0.706 | 0.728 | 0.642 | 0.681 | 0.683 | 0.721 | 0.628 |
| 15 | 0.624 | 0.664 | 0.655 | 0.592 | 0.607 | 0.613 | 0.641 | 0.568 |
| 20 | 0.584 | 0.644 | 0.605 | 0.566 | 0.561 | 0.578 | 0.586 | 0.535 |
| 25 | 0.558 | 0.633 | 0.570 | 0.551 | 0.531 | 0.560 | 0.548 | 0.516 |
| 30 | 0.540 | 0.627 | 0.545 | 0.542 | 0.512 | 0.553 | 0.523 | 0.505 |
| *Coupon rate c = 0.10* | | | | | | | | |
| 5 | 0.904 | 0.912 | 0.923 | 0.878 | 0.901 | 0.901 | 0.918 | 0.874 |
| 10 | 0.861 | 0.903 | 0.889 | 0.840 | 0.844 | 0.855 | 0.864 | 0.821 |
| 15 | 0.841 | 0.923 | 0.874 | 0.833 | 0.812 | 0.842 | 0.831 | 0.800 |
| 20 | 0.832 | 0.947 | 0.865 | 0.836 | 0.796 | 0.846 | 0.812 | 0.792 |
| 25 | 0.828 | 0.969 | 0.859 | 0.841 | 0.787 | 0.857 | 0.801 | 0.791 |
| 30 | 0.825 | 0.986 | 0.853 | 0.847 | 0.783 | 0.869 | 0.796 | 0.792 |
| *Coupon rate c = 0.14* | | | | | | | | |
| 5 | 1.020 | 1.037 | 1.039 | 1.010 | 1.009 | 1.017 | 1.018 | 1.004 |
| 10 | 1.054 | 1.118 | 1.103 | 1.043 | 1.023 | 1.054 | 1.048 | 1.019 |
| 15 | 1.082 | 1.199 | 1.153 | 1.080 | 1.035 | 1.096 | 1.075 | 1.037 |
| 20 | 1.104 | 1.267 | 1.188 | 1.113 | 1.047 | 1.137 | 1.097 | 1.055 |
| 25 | 1.120 | 1.320 | 1.209 | 1.139 | 1.057 | 1.172 | 1.114 | 1.071 |
| 30 | 1.132 | 1.359 | 1.221 | 1.159 | 1.067 | 1.201 | 1.127 | 1.085 |
| *Coupon rate c = 0.18* | | | | | | | | |
| 5 | 1.161 | 1.176 | 1.184 | 1.147 | 1.150 | 1.157 | 1.163 | 1.142 |
| 10 | 1.276 | 1.344 | 1.342 | 1.255 | 1.244 | 1.275 | 1.282 | 1.231 |
| 15 | 1.350 | 1.484 | 1.453 | 1.339 | 1.301 | 1.367 | 1.365 | 1.292 |
| 20 | 1.401 | 1.593 | 1.527 | 1.402 | 1.337 | 1.440 | 1.422 | 1.337 |
| 25 | 1.436 | 1.676 | 1.574 | 1.450 | 1.363 | 1.496 | 1.460 | 1.370 |
| 30 | 1.460 | 1.746 | 1.601 | 1.485 | 1.382 | 1.536 | 1.484 | 1.396 |

[a] Computed at the midpoint of the interest rate range, $r = 0.14$. For each process $\sigma_r$ is the annual standard deviation of changes in the short-term rate of interest.

[b] Tax scenarios are described by their capital gains tax rates, $\tau_s$ short-term and $\tau_L$ long-term. If the investor is an individual, these depend on whether the short-term loss/long-term gain offset rule and the $3,000 deduction limit are binding. For banks and dealers these rules are not applicable. In each case the ordinary tax rate is $\tau_c = 0.5$.

(I)   Offset rule binding, deduction limit not binding, $\tau_s = \tau_L = 0.25$.
(II)  Neither rule binding, $\tau_s = 0.5$, $\tau_L = 0.25$.
(III) Deduction limit binding, offset rule irrelevant, $\tau_s = \tau_L = 0$.
(IV)  Bank or dealer at margin, $\tau_s = \tau_L = 0.5$.

and-hold prices range from 1.002 to 1.071 for the high-variance process and from 1.001 to 1.030 for the low-variance process.[21]

The prices which prevail under tax scenario II are uniformly higher than those under scenario I since investors are not subject to the restrictive offset provision of the tax code but can exploit in full their short-term losses. Furthermore, except for the bonds of five-year maturity, tax scenario II typically results in the highest price. We would expect the second scenario to yield high prices because short-term losses provide valuable rebates and a short-term holding period is relatively cheap to establish. This advantage is least valuable for short maturity bonds because they are the least volatile. Consequently all of the five-year bonds and a few of the other short maturity bonds are priced highest under tax scenario III. There are two distinct reasons.

First, for discount bonds the buy-and-hold price is highest under tax scenario III since the guaranteed capital gain escapes all taxation. Second, with a zero capital gains tax rate, it is costless to establish an above-par amortizable basis. For sufficiently short maturities these two effects dominate.

A comparison of the pricing under scenarios I, III, and IV is also of interest. While their interpretation is radically different, they actually differ in only one respect. The capital gain tax rates, both long- and short-term, are 0.25, 0, and 0.5, respectively. All other taxes are the same. Scenario III with the lowest tax rate has prices which are uniformly highest; nevertheless, the high tax rate in scenario IV does not always induce the lowest price. Again there is a tradeoff between the value of capital losses and the cost of capital gains. The former is more important for the volatile longer maturity bonds. The latter is more important for the shorter maturity bonds, particularly those selling below par.

Litzenberger and Rolfo (1984b) note that, under the buy-and-hold policy, the price of a discount bond is linearly increasing in the coupon rate: in comparing three discount bonds with the same maturity, prices $P_1, P_2, P_3$, and coupon rates $c_1, c_2, c_3$, where $c_1 < c_2 < c_3$, the after-tax cash flows of the bond $P_2$ are replicated by a portfolio of bonds $P_1$ and $P_3$ with weights $\alpha$ and $1 - \alpha$, where $c_2 = \alpha c_1 + (1 - \alpha)c_3$. A similar argument also applied to premium bonds, but the rate at which the bond price increases in the coupon rate is higher for premium than for discount bonds, reflecting the tax-advantageous amortization of the premium. Considering discount and premium bonds together, under the buy-and-hold policy the bond price is piece-wise linear, increasing, and convex in the coupon rate.

Examination of table 4 reveals that the price–coupon relation is also convex for the bond prices under the various optimal policies. However, now the

---

[21] Buy-and-hold prices are computed with the formula (35) below. Even though the interest rate is not expected to increase or decrease from 14%, the yield curve is slightly downward sloping due to Jensen's inequality, and prices are above par. For these and other premium bonds the buy-and-hold policy assumes that the excess above par is amortized and deducted year by year. Thus no capital losses (or gains) are earned on premium bonds under the buy-and-hold policy. Therefore this benchmark price is the same for all scenarios.

Table 5

Value of the timing option on Treasury bonds measured as the percentage difference between the prices under the optimal and buy-and-hold policies; tax scenarios I–IV.[a,b]

| Maturity | High-variance process $\sigma_r = 0.02$ per year | | | | Low-variance process $\sigma_r = 0.01$ per year | | | |
|---|---|---|---|---|---|---|---|---|
| | I | II | III | IV | I | II | III | IV |
| | *Coupon rate c = 0.06* | | | | | | | |
| 5 | 0.0% | 0.1 | 0.0 | 0.1 | 0.0 | 0.0 | 0.0 | 0.0 |
| 10 | 0.5 | 2.8 | 0.2 | 1.6 | 0.1 | 0.3 | 0.0 | 0.4 |
| 15 | 1.3 | 7.2 | 0.4 | 3.4 | 0.4 | 1.4 | 0.0 | 1.3 |
| 20 | 2.0 | 11.1 | 0.5 | 5.1 | 0.9 | 3.7 | 0.1 | 2.4 |
| 25 | 2.6 | 14.2 | 0.4 | 6.3 | 1.3 | 6.5 | 0.2 | 3.4 |
| 30 | 3.0 | 16.4 | 0.4 | 7.1 | 1.8 | 8.9 | 0.3 | 4.2 |
| | *Coupon rate c = 0.10* | | | | | | | |
| 5 | 0.2 | 1.1 | 0.4 | 0.4 | 0.0 | 0.1 | 0.0 | 0.1 |
| 10 | 1.5 | 6.1 | 2.5 | 2.2 | 0.3 | 1.6 | 0.2 | 0.9 |
| 15 | 2.6 | 11.2 | 4.3 | 4.2 | 0.8 | 4.4 | 0.9 | 2.0 |
| 20 | 3.4 | 15.1 | 5.5 | 5.8 | 1.4 | 7.4 | 1.6 | 3.1 |
| 25 | 3.9 | 17.9 | 6.9 | 6.9 | 2.0 | 10.0 | 2.4 | 4.0 |
| 30 | 4.1 | 19.7 | 6.2 | 7.7 | 2.4 | 12.1 | 3.0 | 4.7 |
| | *Coupon rate c = 0.14* | | | | | | | |
| 5 | 1.7 | 3.3 | 3.5 | 0.8 | 0.8 | 1.6 | 1.7 | 0.4 |
| 10 | 3.9 | 9.4 | 8.1 | 2.8 | 1.9 | 4.8 | 4.2 | 1.5 |
| 15 | 5.0 | 14.2 | 10.8 | 4.7 | 2.6 | 8.0 | 6.1 | 2.7 |
| 20 | 5.4 | 17.6 | 12.0 | 6.1 | 3.0 | 10.7 | 7.4 | 3.7 |
| 25 | 5.5 | 19.8 | 12.4 | 7.0 | 3.3 | 12.7 | 8.2 | 4.5 |
| 30 | 5.4 | 21.2 | 12.2 | 7.6 | 3.4 | 14.3 | 8.6 | 5.0 |
| | *Coupon rate c = 0.18* | | | | | | | |
| 5 | 1.7 | 2.9 | 3.6 | 0.5 | 0.9 | 1.5 | 2.0 | 0.2 |
| 10 | 3.5 | 8.4 | 8.3 | 2.0 | 1.9 | 4.3 | 4.8 | 0.8 |
| 15 | 4.2 | 12.8 | 11.0 | 3.4 | 2.3 | 7.0 | 6.9 | 1.6 |
| 20 | 4.4 | 15.9 | 12.3 | 4.5 | 2.3 | 9.3 | 8.2 | 2.3 |
| 25 | 4.4 | 18.1 | 12.8 | 5.3 | 2.4 | 11.1 | 8.9 | 2.9 |
| 30 | 4.3 | 20.0 | 12.7 | 5.9 | 2.5 | 12.2 | 9.2 | 3.4 |

[a] Computed at the midpoint of the interest rate range, $r = 0.14$. For each process $\sigma_r$ is the annual standard deviation of changes in the short-term rate of interest.

[b] Tax scenarios are described by their capital gains tax rates $\tau_s$ short-term and $\tau_l$ long-term. If the investor is an individual, these depend on whether the short-term loss/long-term gain offset rule and the $3000 deduction limit are binding. For banks and dealers these rules are not applicable. In each case the ordinary tax rate is $\tau_c = 0.5$.

(I)  Offset rule binding, deduction limit not binding, $\tau_s = \tau_L = 0.25$.
(II)  Neither rule binding, $\tau_s = 0.5$, $\tau_L = 0.25$.
(III)  Deduction limit binding, offset rule irrelevant, $\tau_s = \tau_L = 0$.
(IV)  Bank or dealer at margin, $\tau_s = \tau_L = 0.5$.

relation is strictly convex throughout for both premium and discount bonds.[22] The different buy-and-hold linear relations contribute to this, but the strict convexity is due to the tax timing effect. The basic intuition for this convexity comes from Merton's (1973) study of stock purchase options. The right to realize capital gains and losses optimally and the right to amortize (even under

[22] The strict convexity cannot be illustrated in table 4 because at least three premium and three discount bonds would be required.

a buy-and-hold policy) convey a valuable option to the bondholder. If we compare a single bond to a portfolio of bonds with the same total coupons and face value, the latter must be at least as valuable since its 'options' can be exercised singly. The convexity is empirically tested in Litzenberger and Rolfo (1984b).

With different tax clientelles each following a buy-and-hold policy, the linear price–coupon relation may become convex or concave. Thus, the tax timing effect discussed in this paper and the buy-and-hold clientele effect may reinforce or cancel one another and it is difficult to distinguish them empirically. Previous evidence in support of clientele effects could be due, at least in part, to tax trading within a single tax bracket.

It is frequently asserted that discount bond prices are higher than what is justified by the term structure of interest rates, reflecting the fact that a portion of the return is realized as a lightly taxed capital gain. Our discussion of table 4 demonstrates that this is just one of several tax effects on bond prices. The direction and magnitude of the tax effect depends critically on the tax scenario applicable to the marginal investor and on whether the marginal investor follows a passive or optimal trading policy.

We now turn our attention to the tax timing option, defined as the difference between the bond prices under the optimal and buy-and-hold policies.[23,24] Table 5 reports the value of the timing option as a percentage of the bond price under the optimal policy. In each case the buy-and-hold price is calculated using the corresponding long-term capital gains tax rate $(0.25, 0.25, 0, 0.5)$. If this price is above par, the amortization is deducted every year. Thus no capital losses (or gains) are earned under the buy-and-hold policy for premium bonds, and the benchmark price is the same for all scenarios. For discount bonds the buy-and-hold prices vary across the scenarios and are inversely related to the long-term capital gains tax rate. The timing option varies widely for different coupon rates, maturities, and tax scenarios, but in most cases it represents a substantial fraction of the bond price just as the example in section 4 illustrates.

The one exception is deep discount bonds under tax scenario III. Here the timing option is worth little since there is only a small probability of ever amortizing a premium and no other tax trading benefit is possible. For bonds selling near or above par, however, the timing option is more important under tax scenario III than under scenarios I or IV. The binding deduction limit under scenario III is a mixed blessing. On the one hand the individual may not

---

[23]An alternative definition of the timing option is the difference between the bond prices under the optimal and continuous realization policies. The assumption of a buy-and-hold policy is by far the more common in previous research. The two definitions are compared in the example of section 4.

[24]Since the interest rate dynamics employed here are without drift, the results are most similar to the case $\alpha = 0$ in the continuous time model. The buy-and-hold benchmark resulted in smaller timing options in that case so our choice is conservative.

obtain tax rebates from the government by realizing capital losses. On the other hand he can costlessly realize capital gains in order to raise the basis and take advantage of the amortization deduction.

For tax scenario III the timing option's relative value is increasing in the coupon rate. The only tax trading benefit comes from the establishment of an amortizable basis. For deep discount bonds the probability of ever doing so is low and the timing option has little value. For bonds with higher coupon rates, and therefore higher prices, the timing option is increasingly valuable. For premium bonds, however, the rate of increase of the timing option slackens since the expected capital gains component of the bond's return is negative and there is a decreasing chance of future price rises to create the opportunity for further amortization deductions.

For the other three tax scenarios the option–coupon relation has an inverted U-shape. Low coupon, deep discount bonds have large expected capital gains and therefore little chance of future deductible losses. Near par bonds can benefit from either a deductible decrease in price or an increase in price which is later amortizable. As under scenario III premium bonds have reduced changes for future increases in amortization. While they do have the largest expected decreases in price, these are deductible only to the extent that they exceed the amortization and only if future amortization is foregone.

The reported values show that the tax timing option is typically increasing in maturity. This is due to both the increased value of standard options when their maturities are lengthened and the greater volatility of the longer maturity bonds underlying these options. This feature explains why the 25- and 30-year 10% coupon bonds are more expensive than those with 10- to 20-year maturities even though the interest rate is above the coupon rate at 14% and the yield curve is essentially flat.

Although longer maturity bonds generally have more valuable timing options, it does not follow that a larger tax subsidy flow is available on long bonds. For example, holding two 15-year bonds in succession may provide greater total tax benefit than a single 30-year bond provides. One way to compare the benefits of different maturity bonds is to express the timing option on an annualized basis. The maturity of bonds with the largest annualized benefits would then represent the natural 'habitat' of investors particularly concerned with tax benefits. The annualized tax subsidy on a $T$-year bond is approximately $r(1 - \tau_c)/[1 - \exp(-r(1 - \tau_c)T)]$ per dollar value of the timing option. Using this approximation we establish that the lowest annual subsidy is on short maturity bonds. On bonds with ten or more years to maturity the benefits are fairly constant, regardless of the tax scenario.

Annualizing the timing option also permits us to normalize the tax benefits relative to the rate of return earned on the bond. For example, under the four scenarios tax benefits provide on average 7, 32, 18 and 10%, respectively, of the total return expected on the 25-year, 14% coupon bond.

The tax timing effect on bond prices also provides a possible explanation of why discounts are so prevalent in the seasoned bond market. Since Treasury bonds are issued at par and are not callable (except occasionally during their last five years before maturity), we should, in the absence of tax timing effects, expect an equal probability of observing seasoned bonds at a premium or discount under a random walk assumption and in the absence of any risk or term premiums. If long-term bonds are riskier and command higher expected returns, then bonds issued at par should later sell at premium prices, at least on average, when these high-term premiums are no longer justified by their reduced risk. Only if interest rates rise dramatically should discounts be observed.

The value added to a long-term bond by its tax timing option lets it be issued at par with a coupon rate below what would otherwise be required. For example (see table 4) under scenario II and no term premiums, a thirty-year bond could be issued at par with a coupon rate just above 10%, even though the interest rate was 14% and rates were not expected to change. The other prices in this section of table 4 show the expected path of this bond's price over its life. With no change in the interest rate, the expected outcome is that the bond would fall in price about ten points over a period of twenty years before recovering in value.

We have so far ignored transactions costs. A bid–ask spread or other costs of trading will reduce the value of the timing option since the optimal policies involve substantially more trading than the buy-and-hold policy. Constantinides has examined the optimal tax trading policy on stocks in the presense of proportional transactions costs.[25] In a simple continuous-time lognormal model he found that investors should not realize losses immediately, but should wait until the price falls to a specific fraction of the basis. A similar rule applies to our model in section 4. The modifications to the optimal trading policies of the models here are more complicated, but the basic idea remains the same: Trades are deferred until capital gains and losses are larger than in the absence of transactions costs.

Table 6 displays the value of the timing option when trading is costly. The round-trip transaction cost is represented by a bid–ask spread of 0.2, 0.5 or 1.0 percent of par.[26] The timing option retains a large fraction of its value even with sizeable transactions costs. Bonds of ten or more years to maturity retain at least half of the original timing option even with one percent transactions costs. The reduction may not be as large as we might have expected because transactions costs are not entirely a dead weight loss. The cost of purchase is

---

[25] In an earlier version of Constantinides (1983).

[26] U.S. Treasury bonds are typically quoted with spreads of one-quarter to one-half of a point in the *Wall Street Journal*. A few have spreads of one-eighth of one point. Treasury note spreads are usually one-eighth to one-quarter of a point.

Table 6

Effects of transactions costs on the timing option; tax scenarios I–IV.[a,b]

| Maturity | Value of timing option (%) for $k =$ | | | | Value of timing option (%) for $k =$ | | | |
|---|---|---|---|---|---|---|---|---|
| | 0.0 | 0.2 | 0.5 | 1.0 | 0.0 | 0.2 | 0.5 | 1.0 |
| | *Tax scenario I* | | | | *Tax scenario II* | | | |
| 5 | 1.7% | 1.4 | 1.0 | 0.5 | 3.3 | 2.8 | 2.0 | 1.2 |
| 10 | 3.9 | 3.3 | 2.7 | 2.0 | 9.4 | 8.4 | 7.0 | 5.0 |
| 15 | 5.0 | 4.4 | 3.8 | 3.0 | 14.2 | 13.1 | 11.4 | 8.7 |
| 20 | 5.4 | 4.8 | 4.2 | 3.5 | 17.6 | 16.3 | 14.4 | 11.4 |
| 25 | 5.5 | 4.9 | 4.3 | 3.7 | 19.8 | 18.4 | 16.5 | 13.2 |
| 30 | 5.4 | 4.8 | 4.2 | 3.6 | 21.2 | . 19.9 | 17.8 | 14.4 |
| | *Tax scenario III* | | | | *Tax scenario IV* | | | |
| 5 | 3.5 | 3.2 | 2.7 | 1.9 | 0.8 | 0.6 | 0.4 | 0.2 |
| 10 | 8.1 | 7.6 | 6.9 | 5.9 | 2.8 | 2.6 | 2.3 | 1.9 |
| 15 | 10.8 | 10.1 | 9.3 | 8.2 | 4.7 | 4.5 | 4.2 | 3.7 |
| 20 | 12.0 | 11.3 | 10.4 | 9.2 | 6.1 | 5.8 | 5.5 | 5.0 |
| 25 | 12.4 | 11.6 | 10.7 | 9.4 | 7.0 | 6.7 | 6.4 | 5.9 |
| 30 | 12.2 | 11.4 | 10.5 | 9.2 | 7.6 | 7.4 | 7.0 | 6.6 |

[a]Computed at midpoint of interest rate range, $r = 0.14$. Interest rate follows high-variance process with standard deviation of 0.02 per year. Coupon rate on bond is $c = 0.14$. $k$ measures the transactions costs (bid–ask spread) as a percent of par.

[b]Tax scenarios are described by their capital gains tax rates $\tau_s$ short-term and $\tau_L$ long-term. If the investor is an individual, these depend on whether the short-term loss/long term gain offset rule and the $3,000 deduction limit are binding. For banks and dealers these rules are not applicable. In each case the ordinary tax rate is $\tau_c = 0.5$.

(I)   Offset rule binding, $\tau_s = \tau_L = 0.25$.
(II)  Neither rule binding, $\tau_s = 0.5$, $\tau_L = 0.25$.
(III) Deduction limit binding, offset rule irrelevant, $\tau_s = \tau_L = 0$.
(IV)  Bank or dealer at margin, $\tau_s = \tau_L = 0.5$.

added to the basis while the cost of sale is deducted from the sales proceeds. Effectively, the taxing authority subsidizes the costs of trading.

Transactions costs decrease the value of the timing option on short maturity bonds more than they do on long maturity bonds. With one point bid-ask spread, the five-year bond losses 71, 64, 46 or 75 percent of its timing option under the four tax scenarios while bonds of at least fifteen years to maturity never give up more than 40 percent. At thirty-year maturities the examined bonds always retain at least two-thirds of the value of their timing option.

## 7. The tax-adjusted yield curve and implied tax rates

We have demonstrated that bond prices set by the marginal investor following the optimal trading policy are markedly different from those set under a buy-and-hold or continuous-realization policy. In this section we explore the implications of these differences when interest rate and tax bracket estimates are inferred from market prices.

Previous authors typically have assumed that a particular marginal investor holds the bond to maturity. Under this assumption the price at time zero of a bond with maturity date $T$, coupon rate $c$, and par value one is the solution to

$$P = (1 - \tau_c) c \sum_{t=1}^{T} \pi_t + (1 - \tau_L + \tau_L P) \pi_T, \qquad P \leq 1, \qquad (35a)$$

or

$$P = [(1 - \tau_c) c + \tau_c (P - 1)/T] \sum_{t=1}^{T} \pi_t + \pi_T, \qquad P > 1, \qquad (35b)$$

where $\pi_t$ is the price at time zero of one dollar after tax at time $t$. Given a set of bond prices, the resulting set of eqs. (35) can be inverted to solve for the discount factors and the tax rates.[27]

Robichek and Niebuhr (1970) do this by imposing the additional assumptions, $\tau_L = 0.5\tau_c$, and a flat term structure, $\pi_t = (1 + y)^{-t}$. They then solve for the remaining unknowns, $\tau_c$ and $y$, using just two bonds. Their estimates of the marginal tax bracket for the year 1968 range from 37.5% to 50%, depending on the pair of bonds used (and disregarding the cheapest flower bond).

McCulloch (1975) also assumes $\tau_L = 0.5\tau_c$. He does not require a flat term structure but estimates the tax bracket and a cubic spline for the discount function to minimize a weighted sum of the squared deviations between actual and modeled prices. Using data from 1963–1966 he concludes that 'the effective tax rate that best explains the prices of U.S. Treasury securities lies somewhere in the range 0.22 to 0.33'. For later data from 1973 the best estimate of the tax rate is only 0.19.

Litzenberger and Rolfo (1984a) estimate tax brackets under a variety of assumptions about the capital gains tax rate. When they set $\tau_L = 0.5\tau_c$ ($\tau_L = 0.4\tau_c$ after October 1978), they confirm McCulloch's estimates. For the period 1973 to 1980 their yearly U.S. tax bracket estimates range from 12% in 1979 to 45% in 1976. The average is 28%.

Pye (1969) estimates the tax bracket of the marginal bondholder using various combinations of discount and par, taxable and exempt bonds. The analysis closest to ours compares par and moderately discounted taxable bonds. Pye concludes that the effective tax rate at the margin varies between 10% and 36% over the period 1967–1968.

Our analysis provides a possible explanation of these findings which is nevertheless consistent with the true marginal tax bracket being substantially higher as suggested by Miller (1977). If bond prices are set by investors who

---

[27]McCulloch (1975) and Litzenberger and Rolfo (1984a) explicitly and Caks (1977) implicitly use equations identical to (35a). Only McCulloch and Litzenberger and Rolfo recognize the premium amortization embodied in (35b). See also Pye (1969), Robichek and Niebuhr (1970), and Schaefer (1981).

follow an optimal trading policy, estimates of the yield curve and the marginal tax bracket obtained under the assumption of a naive buy-and-hold policy may be biased. To test for bias, we generate a sample of simulated bond prices under the assumption of optimal trading policies with known tax rates and yield curves. We then estimate the yield curve and tax rate from this sample by a procedure which is in the spirit of the methods discussed.

Since our 'data' is simulated and, therefore, not subject to measurement error, there is no statistical advantage in using many prices. Thus, like Robichek and Niebuhr, we use an exact 'estimation' requiring only a few bonds. We eliminate the need of assuming a flat term structure, however, by using four rather than two bonds. In fact with four bonds no smoothness requirement for the yield curve even of the weak type assumed by McCulloch is required.

For each estimation we use two different coupon bonds from each of two adjacent maturities. Under an assumed buy-and-hold policy, the two longer bonds with maturity $T + 1$ are priced according to

$$P' = (1 - \tau_c)c \sum_{t=1}^{T} \pi_t + \left[1 - \tau_L + \tau_L P' + (1 - \tau_c)c\right]\pi_{T+1}, \qquad P' \le 1,$$

(36a)

or

$$P' = \left[(1 - \tau_c)c + \tau_c(P' - 1)/(T + 1)\right]\sum_{t=1}^{T} \pi_t$$

$$+ \left[(1 - \tau_c)c + \tau_c(P' - 1)/(T + 1) + 1\right]\pi_{T+1}, \qquad P' > 1, \quad (36b)$$

while the shorter maturity bonds are priced by (35).

Substituting the four bond prices into (35) and (36) gives four equations in the five unknowns, $\sum \pi_t$, $\pi_T$, $\pi_{T+1}$, $\tau_c$, and $\tau_L$. If we assume $\tau_L = \tau_c/2$, the system of equations is now fully specified. We eliminate $\pi_T$, $\pi_{T+1}$, $\tau_c$, and $\tau_L$ to obtain a quadratic equation in the variable $\sum \pi_t$. Solving for this unknown and then the others yields two solution sets. Only one of these satisfies the constraints $0 \le \pi_{T+1} \le \pi_T \le 1$ and $\tau_c \le 100\%$, and this is the one chosen.[28]

Tables 7 and 8 report the errors in the estimated forward rates and the estimated tax brackets on coupon income (correct tax bracket $\tau_c = 50\%$ in each case) for different maturities, tax scenarios, coupon rates and interest rate variances.[29] The errors are usually opposite in sign since an increase in the tax

---

[28] In some cases the estimated tax rates are negative.

[29] The error in the estimated forward rate is the deviation between the estimate and the true forward rate calculated from the binomial model. The true forward rate is not equal to the future expected spot rate, 14% in this case, due to Jensen's inequality.

Table 7

Errors (basis points) in estimated forward rates under the buy-and-hold assumption with $\tau_L = 0.5\tau_c$; tax scenarios I–IV.[a,b]

| Forecast period | Std. dev.[c] | High-variance process $\sigma_r = 0.02$ per year | | | | Std. dev.[c] | Low-variance process $\sigma_r = 0.01$ per year | | | |
|---|---|---|---|---|---|---|---|---|---|---|
| | | I | II | III | IV | | I | II | III | IV |
| *Coupon rates c = 0.08, 0.10* | | | | | | | | | | |
| 5 | 400 | 39 | 203 | −136 | 466 | 200 | 5 | 27 | −201 | 470 |
| 10 | 549 | 85 | 266 | 22 | 357 | 300 | 17 | 201 | −134 | 350 |
| 15 | 595 | 98 | 255 | 126 | 287 | 403 | 33 | 243 | −64 | 284 |
| 20 | 620 | 105 | 283 | 243 | 238 | 426 | 42 | 271 | 10 | 246 |
| 25 | 625 | 98 | 296 | 391 | 198 | 468 | 50 | 292 | 87 | 212 |
| 30 | 631 | 82 | 338 | 657 | 179 | 497 | 57 | 318 | 175 | 192 |
| *Coupon rates c = 0.04, 0.06* | | | | | | | | | | |
| 5 | 400 | 5 | 30 | −200 | 467 | 200 | 0 | 0 | −201 | 420 |
| 10 | 549 | 7 | 129 | −146 | 328 | 300 | 13 | 45 | −167 | 338 |
| 15 | 595 | 6 | 112 | −125 | 260 | 403 | 6 | 65 | −138 | 262 |
| 20 | 620 | 4 | 97 | −105 | 211 | 426 | 7 | 141 | −114 | 222 |
| 25 | 625 | 0 | 67 | −97 | 151 | 468 | 7 | 149 | −94 | 188 |
| 30 | 631 | −23 | 47 | −83 | 94 | 497 | 0 | 127 | −79 | 138 |

[a] Computed at midpoint of interest rate range $r = 0.14$. Errors reported in basis points. For each process $\sigma_r$ is the annual standard deviation of changes in the short-term rate of interest.

[b] Tax scenarios are described by their capital gains tax rates $\tau_s$ short-term and $\tau_L$ long-term. If the investor is an individual, these depend on whether the short-term loss/long-term gain offset rule and the $3,000 deduction limit are binding. For banks and dealers these rules are not applicable. In each case the ordinary tax rate is $\tau_c = 0.5$.

(I)    Offset rule binding, deduction limit not binding, $\tau_s = \tau_L = 0.25$.
(II)   Neither rule binding, $\tau_s = 0.5$, $\tau_L = 0.25$.
(III)  Deduction limit binding, offset rule irrelevant, $\tau_s = \tau_L = 0$.
(IV)   Bank or dealer at margin, $\tau_s = \tau_L = 0.5$.

[c] Standard deviation of single-period interest rate being forecasted.

rate decreases the effective discount rate and errors of opposite signs have partially offsetting effects. In most cases the interest rate is overestimated while the tax bracket is underestimated. In the extreme, the tax rate is estimated to be negative.

The errors are usually smaller for the low-variance process, as we would expect, since the timing option then has less value and buy-and-hold prices are more accurate. For the same reason, errors are smaller when the deep discount bonds are used in the estimation.

The estimates are generally most accurate under tax scenario I. Again this corresponds to the case when the timing option has the least value. Tax scenario II yields very poor results as does scenario III when near par bonds are used. Tax scenario IV is interesting because the implied tax bracket is about the same for all maturities. It ranges between 20% to 30%, disturbingly reminiscent of the tax rate estimated by McCulloch. (By construction, the actual tax rates in this case are all 50%.)

While the errors in the forward rates are often large, the computed numbers are almost invariably within one standard deviation of both the true forward

Table 8

Estimated tax brackets under the buy-and-hold assumption with $\tau_L = 0.5\tau_c$; tax scenarios I–IV.[a,b]

| Maturity | High-variance process $\sigma_r = 0.02$ per year | | | | Low-variance process $\sigma_r = 0.01$ per year | | | |
|---|---|---|---|---|---|---|---|---|
| | I | II | III | IV | I | II | III | IV |
| *Coupon rates $c = 0.08, 0.10$* | | | | | | | | |
| 5 | 44% | 17 | 52 | 20 | 49 | 45 | 63 | 18 |
| 10 | 36 | 17 | 28 | 23 | 47 | 11 | 53 | 27 |
| 15 | 35 | 0 | 14 | 25 | 44 | 7 | 42 | 31 |
| 20 | 35 | −17 | −6 | 26 | 42 | −2 | 30 | 31 |
| 25 | 38 | −26 | −36 | 29 | 40 | −15 | 16 | 31 |
| 30 | 44 | −48 | −108 | 27 | 38 | −33 | −4 | 30 |
| *Coupon rates $c = 0.04, 0.06$* | | | | | | | | |
| 5 | 49 | 44 | 63 | 18 | 50 | 50 | 63 | 26 |
| 10 | 48 | 20 | 55 | 27 | 47 | 39 | 59 | 28 |
| 15 | 47 | 20 | 56 | 29 | 48 | 30 | 56 | 32 |
| 20 | 47 | 18 | 54 | 30 | 47 | 8 | 54 | 32 |
| 25 | 48 | 24 | 56 | 39 | 47 | 5 | 52 | 33 |
| 30 | 55 | 27 | 55 | 50 | 49 | 11 | 51 | 43 |

[a] Computed at the midpoint of interest rate range, $r = 0.14$. For each process $\sigma_r$ is the annual standard deviation of changes in the short-term rate of interest.

[b] Tax scenarios are described by their capital gains tax rates $\tau_s$ short-term and $\tau_L$ long-term. If the investor is an individual, these depend on whether the short-term loss/long-term gain offset rule and the $3,000 deduction limit are binding. For banks and dealers these rules are not applicable. In each case the ordinary tax rate is $\tau_c = 0.5$.

(I)   Offset rule binding, deduction limit not binding, $\tau_s = \tau_L = 0.25$.
(II)  Neither rule binding, $\tau_s = 0.5$, $\tau_L = 0.25$.
(III) Deduction limit binding, offset rule irrelevant, $\tau_s = \tau_L = 0$.
(IV)  Bank or dealer at margin, $\tau_s = \tau_L = 0.5$.

rate and the single-period rate expected to prevail at the forecast time. Consequently, verifying the induced tax trading bias in the forward rates would require a large sample of data. Furthermore, even with large amounts of data available, the errors probably could not be distinguished from liquidity or other term premia. It is interesting to note that the positive errors are at least qualitatively consistent with the usually claimed upward bias in the yield curve.

We also tried estimation under the buy-and-hold assumption with $\tau_L = 0$ and $\tau_L = \tau_c$. These rates are correct for tax scenarios III and IV, respectively, but the estimates are not noticeably improved, probably because the buy-and-hold policy is 'too far' from optimal.

## 8. Municipal bonds

The tax treatment of municipal bonds differs from the tax treatment of Treasury and corporate bonds in two important respects. First, coupon income on municipal bonds is exempt from Federal tax. Second, if the purchase price

Table 9

Value of the timing option on municipal bonds measured as the percentage difference between the prices under the optimal and buy-and-hold policies; tax scenarios I, II and IV.[a,b]

| Maturity | High-variance process $\sigma_r = 0.02$ per year | | | Low-variance process $\sigma_r = 0.01$ per year | | |
|---|---|---|---|---|---|---|
| | I | II | IV | I | II | IV |
| *Coupon rate c = 0.03* | | | | | | |
| 5 | 0.0% | 0.1 | 0.1 | 0.0 | 0.0 | 0.0 |
| 10 | 0.5 | 2.6 | 1.6 | 0.1 | 0.3 | 0.4 |
| 15 | 1.2 | 6.6 | 3.4 | 0.4 | 1.0 | 1.3 |
| 20 | 1.9 | 10.5 | 5.1 | 0.7 | 1.9 | 2.4 |
| 25 | 2.5 | 13.6 | 6.3 | 1.0 | 3.0 | 3.4 |
| 30 | 3.0 | 15.9 | 7.1 | 1.2 | 4.1 | 4.2 |
| *Coupon rate c = 0.05* | | | | | | |
| 5 | 0.1 | 0.8 | 0.4 | 0.0 | 0.1 | 0.1 |
| 10 | 0.7 | 3.8 | 2.2 | 0.2 | 1.2 | 0.9 |
| 15 | 1.5 | 7.2 | 4.2 | 0.6 | 2.9 | 2.0 |
| 20 | 2.2 | 10.0 | 5.8 | 1.0 | 4.5 | 3.1 |
| 25 | 2.8 | 12.2 | 6.1 | 1.3 | 5.8 | 4.0 |
| 30 | 3.2 | 13.8 | 7.7 | 1.5 | 6.8 | 4.7 |
| *Coupon rate c = 0.07* | | | | | | |
| 5 | 0.2 | 1.0 | 0.8 | 0.1 | 0.5 | 0.4 |
| 10 | 0.9 | 3.3 | 2.8 | 0.5 | 1.7 | 1.5 |
| 15 | 1.8 | 5.7 | 4.7 | 0.9 | 2.9 | 2.7 |
| 20 | 2.4 | 7.9 | 6.1 | 1.2 | 3.9 | 3.7 |
| 25 | 3.0 | 9.6 | 7.0 | 1.5 | 4.8 | 4.5 |
| 30 | 3.4 | 11.1 | 7.6 | 1.7 | 5.4 | 5.0 |
| *Coupon rate c = 0.09* | | | | | | |
| 5 | 0.6 | 1.2 | 0.5 | 0.3 | 0.6 | 0.2 |
| 10 | 1.4 | 3.1 | 2.0 | 0.7 | 1.5 | 0.8 |
| 15 | 2.1 | 4.9 | 3.4 | 1.0 | 2.2 | 1.6 |
| 20 | 2.6 | 6.6 | 4.5 | 1.3 | 2.7 | 2.3 |
| 25 | 2.9 | 8.1 | 5.3 | 1.4 | 3.2 | 2.9 |
| 30 | 3.2 | 9.4 | 5.9 | 1.5 | 3.7 | 3.4 |

[a]Computed at the midpoint of the interest rate range $r = 0.14$. For each process $\sigma_r$ is the annual standard deviation of changes in the short-term rate of interest.

[b]Tax scenarios are described by their capital gains tax rates. If the investor is an individual, these depend on whether the short-term loss/long-term gain offset rule and the $3,000 deduction limit are binding. For banks and dealers these rules are not applicable. In each case the ordinary tax rate is $\tau_c = 0.5$.
(I)   Offset rule binding, deduction limit not binding, $\tau_s = \tau_L = 0.25$.
(II)   Neither rule binding, $\tau_s = 0.5$, $\tau_L = 0.25$.
(IV)   Bank or dealer at margin, $\tau_s = \tau_L = 0.5$.
Timing option is always zero under tax scenario III.

in the secondary market is above par the difference must be amortized but the amortized amount is not allowed as a deduction, even though the bond's tax basis is correspondingly reduced. In effect the taxation of bond coupons and of premium amortization are symmetric: for Treasury bonds, the coupons and premium amortization are taxed at the individual's marginal tax rate on ordinary income; for municipal bonds the coupons and premium amortization remain untaxed.

Coupon income on municipal bonds may be subject to state tax, but in our calculations we ignore state taxes. We consider this a good first approximation for two reasons. Many states exempt from state tax the coupons on bonds issued by municipalities within the state so the marginal holders of such bonds may well be exempt from taxes. Also, while state tax rates vary widely across states, they are generally very low relative to the Federal tax rates of investors who would consider holding municipal bonds.[30]

The main difference between the optimal trading policies for municipal and taxable bonds is that no trades are ever made at a price above par since there is no advantage in establishing an amortizeable basis. Since this is the only trading advantage of taxable bonds under tax scenario III, the value of the timing option on municipal bonds is zero in this scenario. At the opposite extreme is tax scenario IV. In this case it is never optimal to establish an above par basis on a taxable bond, so the right to amortize such a basis contributes nothing to the value of the timing option. Thus under scenario IV, the value of the timing option on a municipal bond is equal to that on a taxable bond with the same after-tax coupons. Under tax scenarios I and II the timing option on municipal bonds is less valuable than the option on coupon-equivalent taxable bonds.

Table 9 presents the value of the timing option on municipal bonds. When municipals are deep discount, the timing option under scenarios I and II is nearly as valuable as on coupon-equivalent taxable bonds. The same is true on short-maturity municipals even if the discount is small. These, of course, are the cases when the right to amortize the basis in the future has negligible value. On premium municipal bonds the timing option is substantially smaller than on coupon equivalent taxables, especially if the comparison is made between short-maturity bonds. For example, under tax scenario II the timing option on short-maturity municipals is one-third as large as the timing option on short-term taxables; the timing option on long-term municipals is one-half as large as the timing option on long-term taxables.

## 9. Concluding remarks

This paper extended the work of Cox, Ingersoll and Ross (1981, 1983) on valuing bonds and combined it with the work of Constantinides (1983, 1984) and Constantinides and Scholes (1980) on optimal trading policies. We determined that the tax timing option is an important fraction of the bond price.

We also discussed how the price distortion affects standard estimation techniques for extracting interest rates and marginal tax brackets from observed bond prices. We found the implied errors to be substantial.

---

[30]As of 1980 seven states had no individual income tax on interest. More than half the states had maximum marginal tax rates at or below 7%. In only three states was the maximum tax rate above 11%. The highest rate was Minnesota's 16%.

Our paper only examined the case when the tax bracket of the marginal bondholder remains unchanged. That is, an investor may buy and sell the bond in the course of the optimal trading policy, but the bond remains in the hands of investors in the same tax bracket throughout its term to maturity. The next step should be to recognize the existence of tax clienteles as in Schaefer (1981); but unlike Schaefer, to explore the implications of the bondholders' following optimal trading policies and of the bond being passed from one tax bracket investor to another as its maturity shortens or as it changes from a discount to a premium bond.

# References

Caks, J., 1977, The coupon effect on yield to maturity, Journal of Finance 32, 103–115.

Constantinides, G.M., 1984, Optimal stock trading with personal taxes: Implications for prices and the abnormal January returns, Journal of Financial Economics 13, 65–89.

Constantinides, G.M., 1983, Capital market equilibrium with personal tax, Econometrica 51, 611–636.

Constantinides, G.M. and M.S. Scholes, 1980, Optimal liquidation of assets in the presence of personal taxes: Implications for asset pricing, Journal of Finance 35, 439–449.

Cox, J.C., J.E. Ingersoll, Jr. and S.A. Ross, 1980, An analysis of variable rate loan contracts, Journal of Finance 35, 389–403.

Cox, J.C., J.E. Ingersoll, Jr. and S. A. Ross, 1981, A re-examination of traditional hypotheses about the term structure of interest rates, Journal of Finance 36, 769–799.

Cox, J.C., J.E. Ingersoll, Jr. and S.A. Ross, 1983, A theory of the term structure of interest rates, Econometrica, forthcoming.

Grigelionis, B.I. and A.N. Shiryaev, 1966, On Stefan's problem and optimal stopping rules for Markov processes, Theory of Probability and Its Applications 11, 541–558.

Ibbotson, R.G. and R.A. Sinquefield, 1982, Stocks, bonds, bills and inflation: The past and the future (Financial Analysts Research Foundation, University of Virginia, Charlottesville, VA).

Litzenberger, R.H. and J. Rolfo, 1984a, An international study of tax effects on government bonds, Journal of Finance 39, 1–22.

Litzenberger, R.H. and J. Rolfo, 1984b, Arbitrage pricing, transaction costs and taxation of capital gains: A study of government bonds with the same maturity date, Journal of Financial Economics, this issue.

McCulloch, J.H., 1975, The tax-adjusted yield curve, Journal of Finance 30, 811–830.

Merton, R.C., 1973, Theory of rational option pricing, Bell Journal of Economics and Management Science 4, 141–183.

Miller, M.H., 1977, Debt and Taxes, Journal of Finance 32, 261–275.

Miller, M.H. and M.S. Scholes, 1978, Dividends and taxes, Journal of Financial Economics 6, 333–364.

Pye, G., 1969, On the tax structure of interest rates, Quarterly Journal of Economics 83, 562–579.

Robichek, A. A. and W. D. Niebuhr, 1970, Tax-induced bias in reported treasury yields, Journal of Finance 25, 1081–1090.

Schaefer, S.M., 1981, Measuring a tax-specific term structure of interest rates in the market for British government securities, Economic Journal 91, 415–438.

Schaefer, S.M., 1982a, Tax induced clientele effects in the market for British government securities: Placing bounds on security values in an incomplete market, Journal of Financial Economics 10, 121–159.

Schaefer, S.M., 1982b, Taxes and security market equilibrium, in: W.F. Sharpe and C.M. Cootner, eds., Financial economics: Essays in honor of Paul H. Cootner (Prentice-Hall, Englewood Cliffs, NJ), 159–178.

# VI

# PORTFOLIO EVALUATION AND MANAGEMENT

**1** Black, F., "The Investment Policy Spectrum: Individuals, Endowment Funds, and Pension Funds," *Financial Analysts Journal*, 32 (January 1976), pp. 23-31.
**2** Mayers, D., and E. M. Rice, "Measuring Portfolio Performance and the Empirical Content of Asset Pricing Models," *Journal of Financial Economics*, 7 (March 1979), pp. 3-28.
**3** Henrikkson, R. D., "Market Timing and Mutual Fund Performance: An Empirical Investigation," *Journal of Business*, 57 (January 1984), pp. 73-96.

Jensen (1968, 1969) provided an early application of portfolio theory, the Capital Asset Pricing Model, and the efficient markets hypothesis by studying the performance of managed mutual fund portfolios. From the perspective of efficient markets, the question is whether the active trading activities of money managers improve the returns realized by investors. From the perspective of the CAPM, the question is whether the beta coefficient adequately measures the differences in risk among different types of mutual fund portfolios.

**Black (1976)** addresses the question of portfolio diversification by arguing that individuals should hold diversified portfolios, including their direct investments, their pension investments, and their future human capital. The implication of this analysis is that pension fund managers and endowment fund managers should not seek diversification by itself, since the beneficiaries of these accounts can diversify their individual wealth through other forms of savings.

**Mayers and Rice (1979)** study the measure of risk-adjusted abnormal returns developed by Jensen (1968) to see whether it correctly identifies money managers that have superior information. They are particularly concerned with the benchmark problems raised by **Roll (1977)**.

**Henrikkson (1984)** applies a test developed by Henrikkson and Merton (1981) to study market-timing ability by mutual fund managers. If managers had superior information about periods when stock returns were likely to be lower than Treasury bill rates, they would want to reduce their market risk exposure at those times. Thus, **Henrikkson** studies whether the returns to mutual funds are more sensitive to market movements when stock prices increase than when they decrease. Consistent with prior studies, he finds little evidence that mutual fund managers have market-timing ability.

# The Investment Policy Spectrum:
## Individuals, Endowment Funds and Pension Funds

by Fischer Black

Assuming that a fund manager is primarily concerned with the welfare
of those who ultimately receive the gains or losses, how should he decide
on the fund's risk level? On its division among broad asset classes such as
common stocks and bonds? On the proper degree of diversification? Answers to these questions based on casual intuition are giving way to
answers based on modern capital theory.

Investment policy, as I use the term, means such things as the choice of a risk level for an investor's portfolio, the division of the portfolio among broad classes of investments such as common stocks and bonds, the policy of taking capital losses whenever possible and letting gains go unrealized, or the reverse policy of taking capital gains and letting losses go unrealized. It means such things as the decision on how widely diversified a portfolio is to be or, conversely, how much it is to be concentrated in particular investments considered especially attractive.

I will assume, in this article, that the stock and bond markets are extremely efficient, so that the expected gains from trading stocks and bonds or from attempting to outguess movements in the market as a whole are exceeded by the total costs of doing the required analysis and executing the resulting transactions. This assumption is consistent with most of the empirical evidence on the performance of professionally managed portfolios. Only a very few portfolios give evidence of consistently superior performance.[1]

If an investor feels that buying and selling individual bonds and stocks based on his opinions of their relative attractiveness is worthwhile, then he may wish to use some of the concepts developed by Treynor and Black.[2] Those concepts are broadly

---

1. Footnotes appear at end of article.

---

*Fischer Black is Professor of Finance, Sloan School of Management, Massachusetts Institute of Technology. This article was written while he was at the Graduate School of Business, University of Chicago. Dr. Black is grateful to Jacques Dreze, Richard Ennis, Merton Miller, Dennis Tito and Peter Williamson for comments on earlier versions of the article.*

consistent with the ideas in this article.

I will assume also that markets are efficient in the sense that the value of a company's stock reflects everything that is known (to at least a few investors) about the company.[3] For example, I will assume that the effects of a company's pension fund policy on the company's current and future earnings are fully discounted in the price of its stock. This means that when the value of the pension fund assets declines, the value of the company's stock will tend to decline too, because the contributions that the company has to make to the pension fund will have increased. This will be particularly true in a company whose pension fund assets have a value equal to a substantial fraction of the value of the company's other assets.

The article is written from the point of view of an individual investor who has a relatively clear idea of the risks he is taking in all his investments, who thinks of the risk of his total portfolio as the standard deviation (or variance) of the portfolio return over a short future interval, and who wants to maximize his expected return at a chosen level of risk. It is written primarily from the point of view of a pension fund or endowment fund manager who is concerned with the welfare of those who ultimately receive the gains or losses in the fund, rather than from the point of view of a fund manager who is concerned with the welfare of corporate managers or endowment fund trustees. In practice, however, the welfare of the managers and trustees is often an important consideration, so some attention is given to their interests.

## INDIVIDUALS

For an individual, the main investment policy decision is how much risk to take in his portfolio. Given what we know about the ability of investment managers to select stocks that will do better than other stocks, the individual will normally want to buy and hold a highly diversified portfolio of stocks, mixed with some form of borrowing or lending.[4] He will not be doing any trading on information about stocks. In principle it will be better for the individual to hold mutual fund shares. If there are no funds available that come close to meeting his investment objectives, however, then he may be forced to hold his stocks directly.

The stock portion of his portfolio may be close to the market portfolio. For example, he may be able to find a mutual fund that holds a portfolio like the Standard & Poor's 500 stock portfolio, with each stock weighted by the total dollar amount of that stock outstanding.

There is some evidence that low beta stocks tend to be underpriced relative to high beta stocks, and therefore give higher returns than one would expect given their betas.[5] If the investor believes this evidence, then he may want to put more emphasis on low beta stocks than the Standard & Poor's 500 provides.

Some major classes of assets—such as residential real estate and foreign assets—are not included in the Standard & Poor's 500. The investor may also want to put more emphasis on these assets than the Standard & Poor's 500 provides. One asset that deserves special attention is the investor's "human capital," the present value of his lifetime income from sources other than his financial assets. Since his human capital may form a major part of the investor's portfolio of risky assets, and since he can't sell any substantial portion of his human capital, he may want to eliminate financial assets the values of which correlate highly with the value of his human capital. For example, an investor may want to avoid holding his employer's common stock, unless he gets special inducements from the employer to hold it.

The investor's tax bracket will affect his portfolio in several ways. If he holds bonds and is in a very high tax bracket, he will often choose tax-exempt bonds over taxable bonds. And so long as interest rates are substantially higher than dividend rates on stocks, the high tax bracket investor is more likely to borrow than the low tax bracket investor: The higher his tax bracket, the lower the after-tax interest rate is relative to the expected after-tax return on stocks.

Investors in high tax brackets will try to realize losses and to avoid realizing gains. They may use put and call options, commodities futures, real estate, and other "tax shelters" to convert income into capital gains, or to transfer income from one year to the next, or to eliminate taxable income or capital gains altogether.

There is even a form of investment company that makes it possible for an investor to avoid both taxes on realized capital gains and taxes on dividend income.[6] The investment company does not pay out its dividend income, so it is not eligible to be taxed as an investment company. But any corporation, including an investment company, has an exclusion for tax purposes equal to 85 per cent of its dividend income. If the expenses of the investment company amount to 15 per cent of its dividend income, and if it avoids realizing capital gains, then it won't have any taxes to pay.

To avoid realizing capital gains, the company can have a policy of not selling stock unless forced to do so by redemptions. If it is a closed end investment company, there are no redemptions, and it doesn't have even this problem. When it does have to sell for any reason, it will sell whatever stocks are below cost. If markets are efficient, this method for choosing stocks to sell will not hurt performance of the portfolio. Most funds find that, when there are no redemptions, there are usually many stocks selling below cost. Only when all the remaining stocks are selling above cost and there is no tax loss carryforward will this strategy give any taxable realized capital gains.

If the shareholders of such an investment company don't sell their shares, neither the company nor its shareholders will pay any taxes on the dividend income or capital gains from its portfolio. The shareholders will be able to reduce or eliminate their tax liabilities.

Thus an individual's stock portfolio should be close to a market portfolio, with possible extra holdings of assets not well represented in the market portfolio, and minus holdings of assets closely related in value to his human capital. It should be managed insofar as possible to avoid giving him taxable distributions.[7] The remaining policy decision that the individual has to make is how much of this portfolio to hold—in other words, how much risk to take. Higher risk is undesirable in itself, but higher risk in a well diversified portfolio generally means higher expected return. The investor must decide how much to increase both his expected return and his risk by increasing the amount of money he keeps in risky assets. He can invest part of his wealth in bonds or savings accounts or the like, and part in stocks; or he can invest all of it in stocks; or he can borrow to invest more than his wealth in stocks.

Actually, he has many such decisions to make. He must decide at each point in his lifetime how much risk to take, and thus how much of his wealth to hold in stocks. He has to decide how to shift his holdings as the value of his portfolio fluctuates. When his portfolio goes up because the market goes up, does he sell off some of his stocks? Or buy more stocks? Or leave his holdings of stocks unchanged? How does he revise his portfolio when he learns of an unexpected inheritance?

It turns out that how he revises his portfolio over his lifetime can make a big difference. For example, suppose an individual switches back and forth between the market and a savings account every year at the start of the year. If he is in the market,

he gets out; and if he is out, he gets in. This is a variant of what he might be doing if he were trying to forecast the market. Half the time, he will have all his money in the market, and half the time, he will have all his money in a savings account.

An alternative strategy would be to keep half his money in the market every year, and the rest in a savings account. (Note that this means selling some of his stocks after every rise in the market, and buying more stocks after every fall.) If we think of the expected return on the market as being con-

Drawing by Whitney Darrow, Jr.;
©1964 The New Yorker Magazine, Inc.

*"What do you recommend for the short haul?"*

stant over time, then this strategy will have the same expected return as the strategy of switching back and forth between the market and a savings account. But it would have much lower risk. In fact, if we measure risk by the variance of the return on the whole portfolio over a two-year period, this strategy would have half the risk of the first strategy.

The reason why the second strategy has lower risk than the first is that it involves a form of diversification to have money in the market in two successive years. The investor may gain in the first year and lose in the second, or he may lose in the first year and gain in the second. It is the same sort of diversification that he gets when he puts money into two different stocks. His losses on one may be offset by gains on the other. This kind of diversification I call "time diversification."[8] Diversification across time reduces risk just like diversification across stocks.

One way for an investor to get good time diversification is to keep a constant fraction of his wealth invested in stocks. Suppose for example, that he intends to keep half his wealth invested in stocks at all times. If his stocks go up in value by $1000 over some short period of time, he will sell stocks worth $500 and put the proceeds in his savings account. Similarly, if the value of his stocks goes down by $1000, he will take $500 out of his savings account and invest it in stocks. Following the conservative strategy of keeping half in the market and half in a savings account means selling after the market goes up and buying after the market goes down.

On the other hand, an investor may choose an aggressive strategy. Consider, for example, an investor who borrows to keep one and a half times his wealth in the market at all times. Then if his stocks go up in value by $1000, he is going to borrow an additional $500 to invest in stocks. And if his stocks go down by $1000, he will sell stocks worth $500 and use the proceeds to reduce his loan. Following this aggressive strategy means buying after the market goes up and selling after the market goes down. If there is no serial correlation in market returns, then an increase in the market is no more likely to be followed by another increase than a decrease, so neither of these strategies is better than buy-and-hold so far as market timing is concerned. Both strategies give time diversification: The choice between them is simply a matter of how much risk the individual wants to take.

An individual will lose very little by limiting himself to one of the family of strategies that entails keeping a constant fraction of his wealth in stocks. If he chooses a strategy from this family, then the only major policy decision he has to make is what that fraction will be. He can ignore, at least as a first approximation, all the other elements that might influence the amount of risk he wants to take, like his age and his wealth.

## ENDOWMENT FUNDS

In talking about endowment funds, I will refer most often to college and university endowment funds, but many of the points I make will be applicable in slightly modified form to other kinds of endowment funds.

For part of an endowment fund, the investment policy may be limited by the terms of the gift that created the endowment. For example, the donor may have given stock with the understanding that it will not be sold for a period of time. Or the terms of the gift may be interpreted as specifying that only the dividend and interest income may be spent, and this may have some influence on investment policy. But in most universities there is also a part of the endowment fund that is unrestricted in both its investment and the rate at which it may be spent. If this is a large enough part of the fund, we can treat the fund as a whole as if its investment policy and the rate at which it may be spent were unrestricted.

It is important to see the endowment fund as just one of the university's sources of income. In most universities, the endowment fund provides a relatively small fraction of the budget. The other sources of income include tuition, alumni contributions, government grants and foundation grants. For the university, and for anyone interested in the university, with the possible exception of those responsible for managing the endowment fund, the relevant risk is the risk of all these sources of income taken together, not just the risk of the endowment fund itself.

All the sources of income include "market risk" that cannot be diversified away. When the economy does well, contributions to universities rise, tuition payments are easier to make, and the government gets more taxes, which makes it more apt to give money to universities. So it is not only the endowment fund that is able to provide more to a university when times are good.

The non-market risk in the endowment fund, the part of the risk that can be diversified away, is in fact pretty well diversified away when it is mixed with the risk in the other sources of income for the university. The endowment fund is in effect only a small part of the university portfolio, thinking of these other sources of income as the remainder of the portfolio. This means that an endowment fund needs to be much less concerned about diversification than an individual. Normally, no great harm will be done if the endowment fund contains just four stocks, for example. However, the rules governing the behavior of endowment fund trustees and the interests of the trustees as well generally lead them to choose relatively well diversified portfolios. If a poorly diversified portfolio happens to do very badly, the trustees are likely to suffer. The conflict between the interests of the trustees and the interests of the ultimate beneficiaries of the fund suggests that the rules governing trustees may be in need of revision.

In setting the level of market risk in the endowment fund, the market risk in the university's other sources of income should be taken into account at the same time. If the endowment fund provides only ten per cent of the university's income, then a ten per cent change in the market risk of the endowment fund means only a one per cent change in the market risk of the university's income as a whole.

In other words, when setting the objectives of an endowment fund, it should really be treated as a small part of a portfolio, not as a total portfolio.

Not only is the endowment fund a small part of the university portfolio, the university portfolio may be a small part of the portfolios of the individuals who have a financial interest in the university. But who are those individuals? If the university were a privately owned corporation, we could say that the individuals with the primary financial interest in the university, who bear most of the risk in the university portfolio, are the individuals who own shares in the university.

But most universities are not privately owned. The typical university is a non-profit institution, like the typical hospital or savings and loan association or mutual insurance company. A non-profit institution has just as much risk as a privately owned institution of the same type, but the risk is borne by different people. For example, much of the risk in a mutual insurance company is borne by the policyholders, while the risk in a stock insurance company is borne primarily by the shareholders. (The managers may bear a substantial amount of risk in both mutual and stock insurance companies.)

The equity interest in a university is spread among all the people associated with the university. The people who benefit if the university gets more income are the faculty, the administration, the staff, the trustees and the students. Future students and faculty members also bear some of the university risk. So do those who would be students or faculty members if the university's income were high enough. Because none of these people can buy or sell their equity interests in the university, they have an interest only during (and to some extent, before) their association with the university.

So there is a large group of people who are actually or potentially affiliated with the university who have an equity interest in it. The income that each such person gets from the university is part of his total income. And the risk that he gets from the risk in the university's income is part of his total risk. He will have other risky assets such as common stock or real estate, and he will have other risky sources of income. The endowment fund risk is a small part of the university's income risk, and the university's income risk will be a small part of the total risk of most individuals associated with the university. The endowment fund risk will be a very small part of the typical individual's total risk.

This means that the degree of diversification in the endowment fund portfolio is particularly unimportant when viewed in the light of its effect on the diversification of the total portfolios of most of those who bear the endowment fund risk. It means that the level of market risk in the endowment fund is not very important either. It is very easy for the typical individual to make changes in his portfolio to offset any changes in risk in the endowment fund. If the endowment fund goes from a beta of 1.0 to a beta of 2.0, that will change the typical individual's risk who has an interest in it very slightly, and he could offset it by decreasing the beta of another part of his portfolio.

This does not mean that the endowment fund can simply aim at maximizing its expected return and ignore the risk it incurs in doing so. It means that so long as the expected return of the fund is related to its beta in the way that the capital asset pricing model suggests, both the risk and the expected return of the fund are unimportant to the individual.[9] So long as the fund gets an expected return commensurate with its market risk, the typical individual doesn't care how much risk it takes, because it is only a small part of his portfolio.

The people for whom the endowment fund is most important are those who are with the university for the longest period of time and who get a large part of their income from the university. For these people, the level of market risk in the fund and the extent to which the fund is diversified may not be a matter of indifference. This includes the faculty, especially the tenured faculty, the administration, and some of the staff. So it is their utility functions and preferences that should be taken into account in setting objectives for the endowment fund, if we say that it makes a difference what objectives are set for the endowment fund. But even if we say this, it's not likely to be clear what they would like to have done.

Some, who have income primarily from the university, might be conservative and prefer a conservative investment policy that minimizes fluctuations in their income or the risks of being fired. Others wanting to take a lot of risk without any convenient way to do so in their personal portfolios at reasonable cost, might prefer an aggressive investment policy in their endowment fund.

One possible way to resolve this conflict of interest would be for those affiliated with the university on a long-term basis to vote on the investment policy of the endowment fund. This would represent such a break with tradition that it is probably not possible. And if the endowment fund really makes up only a small part of each of their portfolios, then the investment policy of the endowment fund is probably not important enough to justify the expense of setting up a voting procedure and informing those who are to vote.

Moreover, in practice there is usually a relatively small group of individuals who control a university and who could not get positions of equivalent power with other organizations. These individuals are usually able to control the policies of the endowment fund, and tend to have more interest in its success than other individuals. If the university suffers a decline in income, many of the faculty and most of the students can switch jobs or schools. Those who cannot, because of their positions of power within the university, are the ones who suffer most.

It is sometimes claimed that because the endowment fund is going to be around for a long time, it can afford to take a lot of risk. I have been unable to find any sense in which this seems correct. The risk in the endowment fund must be borne ultimately by individuals. Most of the risk will be borne by individuals who are currently affiliated with the university. To some extent, the risk can be transferred from those currently associated with the university to their successors. It may even be transferred in part to individuals who have not yet been born. But it must be attributed to individuals, and the extent to which it can be passed on to future generations is limited. If a decline in the value of the endowment fund is not met by a decline in the rate of spending from the endowment fund in a short time, the expected future value of the endowment fund will be greatly reduced.

Let us look for a moment at the endowment funds of all the universities in the country as a group. At one time it was claimed that the performance of university endowment funds was inferior to the performance of other funds, and that our educational system faced a crisis unless endowment fund performance was improved. We now know that there is no evidence that the risk-adjusted performance of endowment funds has been worse than that of other funds, so the only meaning that this statement might have is that endowment funds have been taking too little risk. Indeed, in recent years, endowment funds have been increasing their risk levels, partly by switching from bonds to stocks. But it is not clear that this makes much sense, if we take a broad enough point of view.

If society wants to increase the amount it spends on education, there are much more direct ways of doing it. The most obvious is an increase in tuition levels. An increase in the risk taken by endowment funds will tend to increase the fraction of its income that society spends on education only when economic conditions are exceptionally good. When economic conditions are exceptionally bad, a high level of risk in endowment funds will tend to mean a reduction in the fraction of income spent on education.

## PENSION FUNDS

For a non-insured corporate pension fund, the individuals with the most interest in the gains and losses of the fund are the corporation's shareholders.[10] The pension benefits are fixed by contract. So long as the pension plan is not changed, and so long as the corporation does not go out of business, the pension benefits are independent of the gains and losses in the fund.

The corporation promises certain pension benefits to its employees, and then makes contributions to a fund out of which the benefits are to be paid. But the corporation has a responsibility for paying the benefits regardless of the level of funding of the pension fund. In other words, the corporation could conceivably not make any contributions to the pension fund, and it would still have to pay the benefits when they come due, if it is able.[11]

In that situation, any gains or losses in the pension fund portfolio accrue primarily to the corporation, and thus to its shareholders. Gains in the pension fund benefit the pension beneficiaries to some extent, because a larger pension fund seems to make it easier for employees to extract higher pension benefits from their employer, and because a larger pension fund makes it less likely that the corporation will be unable to pay the promised benefits.

If the pension fund does well, then future contributions by the corporation to the pension fund will be reduced. If the pension fund does poorly, then future corporate contributions will be increased. Assuming that stock prices accurately reflect future earnings prospects, an increase in the value of the pension fund will mean an increase in the value of the company's stock, and a decrease in the value of the pension fund will mean a decrease in the value of the company's stock. This is how the gains and losses in a corporation's pension fund are transmitted to its shareholders.

Thus we have a situation very much like that of the endowment fund: The pension fund is a corporate asset, and is normally a relatively small part of the total value of the corporation. The corporate shares are themselves held by individuals who hold other assets in their portfolios as well. So the pension fund represents a small part of the portfolio of assets held by the typical corporate shareholder.

We can conclude again that, from the point of view of those with the major financial interest in the pension fund, diversification is not very important. An individual wants his total portfolio to be well diversified, but he does not care about the diversification of a particular small part of the portfolio. The major exceptions to this statement are the pension fund trustees, who are legally responsible for the management of the fund, and who may derive considerable economic power from managing the fund. They will generally have an interest in diversifying the portfolio, and will be in a position to make sure it is diversified. The potential liability of a trustee when a poorly diversified fund does badly will often be large compared with the value of his entire portfolio of risky assets.

Similarly, it is not very important to anyone but the trustees how much market risk the pension fund portfolio has. The corporate shareholders will simply take whatever risk they find into account in adjusting the risk of their total portfolios. If the pension fund goes from a beta of 1.0 to a beta of 2.0, the shareholders can offset this by reducing the betas of other assets they hold, or by changing the amount of borrowing or lending they do.

When there is a significant risk that the corporation will go out of business and leave a pension fund portfolio that is not large enough to pay the promised benefits, however, the level of risk in the pension fund can make a difference. It may make a difference to the corporate shareholders, to the pension beneficiaries, and to the government, where the government is insuring payments to the beneficiaries. When there is a significant risk that the corporation will go out of business, an increase in the risk of the pension fund—either because of an increase in beta or because of a reduced level of

diversification—will cause an increase in the probability that neither the pension fund assets nor the corporate assets will be sufficient to pay the promised benefits. Such an increase in risk will reduce the value of the claim that the pension beneficiaries have on the corporation, and will increase the value of the claim they have on the insuring agency of the government.

The extreme case of a pension fund portfolio that increases the risk that the pension beneficiaries will not be paid by the corporation is where the pension fund holds only shares in the corporation of which it is a part. Then the circumstances under which the corporation would go bankrupt and lose its value in satisfying pension beneficiaries are exactly the same as the circumstances under which the pension fund would go to zero value. Under these circumstances, the beneficiaries would collect only from the government. So that particular policy can be quite risky for the government.

Tax considerations are important in determining the yield objective for the pension fund and in deciding when to realize gains and losses. If the pension fund can trade off yield for unrealized capital appreciation, or if it can trade off realized capital gains for unrealized gains, then the corporation will be able to make larger deductible contributions to the fund, and will thus be able to postpone some of its tax liabilities. A corporation that defers tax payments saves an amount equal to the interest on those tax payments.

If a corporation takes the opposite approach, and tries to maximize the yield and realized gains in its pension fund, then it will reduce its current contributions to the pension fund. This will increase current reported earnings, but at the expense of increasing taxes and reducing the rate of growth of earnings. The rate of growth of earnings will be reduced for two reasons: because the reduction in current pension fund contributions means higher contributions will have to be made later on, and because the present value of the company's tax liability is increased. If the market takes all this into account in pricing the company's stock, the policy of maximizing yield and realized gains at the expense of unrealized gains will result in a lower stock price than the opposite policy. The increase in the company's current reported earnings will be more than offset by a fall in its price-earnings ratio.

Thus the pension fund should be managed as if its income and capital gains were taxable. The effective taxes that the corporation has to pay on the pension fund income and capital gains are quite different than the taxes an individual would have to pay, however. Municipal bonds do not have tax advantages for the pension fund. Realized capital gains are effectively taxed at the full corporate income tax rate, to the extent that they are brought into pension fund income. But they are brought into income only over a period of years, which reduces the effective tax rate. Even unrealized gains must eventually be brought into income, so it is not possibile for the pension fund to delay realizing gains indefinitely, as an individual can.

If the stock market takes into account such things as the value of a company's pension fund and the magnitude of its potential tax liabilities in valuing its stock, if there is very little chance that the company will go out of business, and if a fully funded pension fund will not induce the employees to demand much higher pensions, then the company should try to *maximize* its tax deductible contributions to the pension fund. It should try to keep the fund "overfunded," rather than underfunded, so long as the IRS allows contributions to the pension fund to be deducted from income for tax purposes. It should do this in spite of the fact that higher contributions to the pension fund may mean lower current reported earnings per share. It should do this even if it has to borrow money or sell stock to make its pension fund contributions.

It is not a question of whether investments in the pension fund are more or less profitable than other investments the company makes. The investments in the pension fund are profitable in themselves, and should be made regardless of what other investments the company has to make. If the company needs additional funds to make other profitable investments, the efficient U. S. capital markets will supply them readily.

Having a low realized return on the pension fund may even help the company influence the actuarial rate of return used in calculating the required payments to the pension fund (and the payments that the IRS will allow the company to deduct). The actuaries have some latitude in choosing an assumed rate of return. The usual practice is for the company to encourage the actuaries to choose a high return, so the company can minimize its contributions and increase its current reported earnings per share. But if the company is trying to maximize its deductible contributions, it will want to encourage the actuaries to choose a low return.

If we look at the company's cash flows, rather than at its earnings, and if we combine pension fund operations with the company's other operations, it's especially easy to see the advantages of maximizing the deductible contributions to the pension fund. Assuming that the probability of bankruptcy is zero, and that the pension plan will not be changed, the payment from the corporation to the pension fund is really just a transfer within the corporation. It doesn't count as a cash inflow or outflow. So if the corporation is able to increase its deductible contributions to the pension fund, the only effect on the company's cash flows is the reduction in its tax payments. There is no evidence that a policy that increases a company's cash flows, both present and future, while reducing its reported earnings, will have a negative effect on its stock price. More likely, this policy will increase the price of the stock. However, these effects may well be dominated by the effects of the level of funding on future changes in the terms of the plan. A more fully funded plan is more likely to be liberalized, which will help the beneficiaries at the expense of the corporation and its shareholders. A less fully funded plan is more likely to be restricted, partly because the corporation will have more to gain by restricting it. So, in the end, a corporation may do well to resist higher contributions to the pension fund, not because of the impact of the level of contributions on reported earnings, but rather because of the impact of the level of contributions on the terms of the plan. ∎

### Footnotes

1. For evidence of this, see Michael C. Jensen, "The Performance of Mutual Funds in the Period 1945-1964," *Journal of Finance* (May 1968), pp. 389-419.
2. See Jack L. Treynor and Fischer Black, "How to Use Security Analysis to Improve Portfolio Selection," *Journal of Business* (January 1973), pp. 66-86.
3. See Eugene F. Fama, "Efficient Capital Markets: A Review of Theory and Empirical Evidence," *Journal of Finance* (May 1970), pp. 383-417.
4. See J. Peter Williamson, "Measuring and Forecasting of Mutual Fund Performance: Choosing an Investment Strategy," *Financial Analysts Journal* (November/December 1972), pp. 78ff.
5. See Fischer Black, Michael C. Jensen, and Myron Scholes, "The Capital Asset Pricing Model: Some Empirical Tests," *Studies in the Theory of Capital Markets,* Michael C. Jensen, ed. (New York: Praeger, 1972), pp. 79-121.
6. Since this was written, I have discovered that such an investment company exists. It is called American Birthright Trust, 210 Royal Palm Way, Palm Beach, Florida. Standard Shares, a closed-end investment company, also uses these methods.
7. This does not mean that a taxable investor should avoid high yield stocks. See Fischer Black and Myron Scholes, "The Effects of Dividend Yield and Dividend Policy on Common Stock Prices and Returns," *Journal of Financial Economics* (May 1974), pp. 1-22.
8. This concept was originated by James Tobin, in

"The Theory of Portfolio Selection," *The Theory of Interest Rates,* F. H. Hahn and F. P. R. Brechling, eds. (London: Macmillan, 1965), pp. 3-51.

9. For a description of the capital asset pricing model, see Michael C. Jensen, "Capital Markets: Theory and Evidence," *Bell Journal of Economics and Management Science* (Autumn 1972), pp. 357-398.

10. For a discussion of pension fund strategy under somewhat different assumptions, see Irwin Tepper, "Optimal Financial Strategies for Trusteed Pension Plans," *Journal of Financial and Quantitative Analysis* (June 1974), pp. 357-376.

11. Actually, corporations also have the ability to change the terms of a pension plan, and thereby reduce their obligations. For an enlightening discussion of the risks borne by pension beneficiaries and corporate shareholders, see Walter Bagehot, "Risk and Reward in Corporate Pension Funds," *Financial Analysts Journal* (January/February 1972), pp. 80-84.

# MEASURING PORTFOLIO PERFORMANCE AND THE EMPIRICAL CONTENT OF ASSET PRICING MODELS

David MAYERS*

*University of California, Los Angeles, CA 90024, USA*

Edward M. RICE*

*University of Illinois, Urbana-Champaign, IL 61801, USA*

Received June 1978, revised version received November 1978

Recent work by Richard Roll has challenged the worth of portfolio performance measures based on the capital asset pricing model. This paper demonstrates that Roll's conclusions are due to his focusing on a 'truly' ex-ante efficient index. Using a choice and information theoretic framework, we show that an appropriate index is efficient relative to the probabilities assessed by the 'market'. Residual analyses and portfolio performance tests, using such an index, yield meaningful results for a wide class of information structures. Roll's primary criticisms, however, relate to tests of the asset pricing model itself. We argue that these criticisms are vastly overstated.

## 1. Introduction

Richard Roll's (1977) criticism of the capital asset pricing model presents an exciting intellectual challenge. We have found especially challenging his conclusions concerning the use of the security market line as a benchmark for asset or portfolio performance and for residual analysis. These conclusions do not depend on the asset pricing model being invalid. Nor for the main part do they depend on the market portfolio identification problem. Roll's conclusion (10) summarizes his objections on these points:

> Deviations from the return/beta linearity relation are frequently linked with some other phenomenon. The validity of such linkages is criticised using the Jensen measure of portfolio performance as an example. If the 'market' proxy used in the calculations is exactly (not significantly different from) ex-post efficient, *all* of the individual Jensen performance measures gross of expenses will be identically (not significantly different

*We have benefitted greatly from the thoughtful comments and suggestions of L. Dann, M. Jensen, C.F. Lee, J. Long, R. Roll, C. Smith, R. Verrecchia and the referee, G.W. Schwert. Responsibility for the content of the paper, of course, is ours.

Journal of Financial Economics 7 (1979) 3–28. © North-Holland Publishing Company

from) zero. They can be (significantly) non-zero only if the proxy market portfolio is (significantly) not efficient. But if the proxy market portfolio is not efficient, what is the justification for using it as a benchmark in performance evaluation?[1]

This statement is explicitly critical of the use of the security market line as a benchmark for asset or portfolio performance. If one agrees with the point being made in the rhetorical question, that the benchmark portfolio should be efficient, then the statement is strongly critical. It effectively eliminates the usefulness of the security market line as a benchmark. In a companion piece Roll (1978) criticizes in detail the accepted methodology of portfolio evaluation.

Our discussion has focused on Roll's (1977) conclusion (10). This is justifiable because (a) most of what we have to say concerns this conclusion and because (b) this conclusion is the most damning. It is the most damning because it implies that the theory has little operational usefulness, even if the theory is valid.

Empirically validating any economic theory is a difficult task. And it is in this area that Roll's (1977) contribution must be considered as paramount. His analysis is primarily concerned with problems associated with the testability of the theory. His conclusions based squarely on the mathematics of the efficient set are unassailable. However, his conclusion (4) we consider severe:

> The theory is not testable unless the exact composition of the true market portfolio is known and used in the tests. This implies that the theory is not testable unless *all* individual assets are included in the sample.[2]

The importance of Roll's criticism should be self-evident. Few economic theories have attained the level of operational elegance achieved by the Sharpe (1964), Lintner (1965) and Black (1972) models of capital asset pricing. The theory has been directly applied in a large number and variety of empirical studies. Tests of capital market efficiency, the effects of information events on share prices, the performance of mutual fund managers and the efficiency of other markets (e.g., merger studies) are a sample of the variety of such studies. In addition, there has been a plethora of related studies, for example, studies concerned with the problems of measuring the asset pricing model's implied measure of risk. One merely has to skim the title pages of the finance journals over the past decade to become impressed by the central position assumed by this model in the field of finance.

[1]Roll (1977, p. 132).
[2]Roll (1977, p. 130).

Our analysis is primarily concerned with the appropriateness of using the security market line for the purpose of evaluating portfolio performance. Our approach is choice and information theoretic within the framework of a general equilibrium capital asset pricing model. Our analysis is unique in this respect. We define an individual as superior with respect to the information he holds. We then query whether a Security Market Line (SML) analysis will correctly designate him as superior. This is opposed to earlier analyses that define superiority with respect to a given benchmark.[3] In other words we try to answer the question concerning the appropriateness of the benchmark.

Section 2 that follows contains a synthesis and discussion of Roll's analysis. Our discussion introduces our primary objection – that Roll does not allow for the possibility of superior performance. Section 3 contains our choice and information theoretic analysis. We demonstrate that the security market line can be a useful tool for detecting superior performance. In section 4 we examine residual analysis and conclude that residual analysis is useful. In section 5 we offer some thoughts with regard to the problems associated with joint hypotheses and proxies in asset pricing theory tests. We see little reason to either reject the theory of asset pricing or the information provided by tests of the theory solely on the basis of the existence of these problems. Section 6 concludes our study.

## 2. A synthesis and discussion of Roll's analysis

Roll's (1977) conclusion (10) is based on several statements derived from the mathematics of the efficient set. To help understand Roll's conclusion and our analysis, the following selected statements from Roll (1978) are repeated:[4]

S3: If the selected index is mean/variance efficient, then the betas of all assets are related to their mean returns by the same linear function.

S4: If, for some selected index, the betas of all assets are related to their mean returns by the same linear function, then that index is mean variance efficient.

S6: For every ranking of performance obtained with a mean/variance non-efficient index, there exists another non-efficient index which reverses the ranking.

These three statements are sufficient for an understanding of the analysis leading to Roll's conclusion (10). The statements are true for ex ante probability assessments as well as for ex post sample statistics. Thus, for

---

[3]An exception is Jensen (1972).

[4]These statements are derived from the efficient set mathematics as outlined in Roll (1977). The derived statements in Roll (1978), however, relate more directly to the issue at hand.

example, if the selected index happens to be ex post mean/variance efficient,[5] all individual assets and portfolios would plot exactly on the security market line derived from the selected index (S3).[6] No portfolio or asset could indicate either superior or inferior performance using the securities market line criterion. If the selected index happens to be ex ante efficient, there could be deviations from the ex post security market line, but they would be statistically insignificant and would tend to disappear in repeated sampling over many intervals (S3).[7] Statements S4 and S6 tell us that if we do find significant deviations from the security market line, the selected index is not mean/variance efficient and the deviations can tell us nothing about the relative performance of portfolios or assets. These results are true whether the portfolios under evaluation are constant composition portfolios or portfolios of changing composition across time. That is, as long as the selected index is ex ante mean/variance efficient for all time intervals under consideration S3 will rule whether the portfolios are of constant or changing composition.

The above would appear to leave little room for positive statements to be made concerning portfolio or asset performance; this is the point of Roll's (1977) conclusion (10). For example, if in a securities market line analysis one discovers significant deviations from the empirical line, what can be said? One can say (for sure) that the index was not mean/variance efficient (from S3), and S6 implies that any statements about performance are questionable. On the other hand, a finding of no significant deviations in an analysis is consistent with the index having been mean/variance efficient in which case no portfolio manager or investment advisor could have consistently picked winners relative to the benchmark. This finding would be consistent with the simultaneous hypotheses of capital market efficiency and the index being mean/variance efficient,[8] but no positive statement about performance can be made.

Thus, Roll's conclusion (10) concerning portfolio performance appears sustained. Roll (1978, p. 1060) amplifies this conclusion by stating:

> Individual *differences* in portfolio selection ability cannot be measured by the securities market line criterion. This was the general thrust of the preceding argument. If the index is ex ante mean/variance efficient, the

[5]An index is ex post mean/variance efficient if it lies on the sample efficient frontier derived from the realized average return vector and sample covariance matrix. Why anybody would ever want to use such an index is not obvious. The concept of ex post efficiency is without economic content and the probability of an ex ante efficient portfolio ever being ex post efficient most certainly would be small (what statisticians refer to as a set of measure zero).

[6]This assumes that portfolio returns are measured gross of any expenses generated by the portfolio manager.

[7]Footnote 6 applies here as well.

[8]Capital market efficiency refers to efficiency in an information sense as opposed to a mean/variance sense.

criterion will be unable to discriminate between winners and losers. If the index is not ex ante efficient, the criterion will designate winners and losers; but another index could cause the criterion to designate different winners and losers and there is no objective way to ascertain which index is correct.[9]

We claim the contrary; that individual differences in portfolio selection ability can be measured by the securities market line criterion. However, in order to be able to detect superior performance, the possibility of such must be allowed. When assuming that the selected index is mean/variance efficient, with respect to the correctly assessed efficient frontier, Roll assumes away the possibility of superior performance.[10] He is certainly right that, when such an index is used as a benchmark, superior performance will be undetected. Under this assumption, superior performance is impossible. This benchmark is efficient with respect to all that is knowable – all probability distributions are correctly assessed – and consequently there can be no superior performance relative to this benchmark.

An interpretation of mean/variance efficiency that allows superior performance is as follows. We posit that the benchmark index is mean/variance efficient relative to the joint probability density function of returns assessed by the 'market'. We use the term 'market' metaphorically as in Fama (1976, p. 168):

> Thus, in deriving testable implications of the hypothesis that the capital market is efficient, we structure the world in terms of a 'market' that assesses probability distributions on future prices then sets current prices on the basis of these assessed distributions. Strictly speaking, this implies that investors have monolithic opinions about available information and act single-mindedly to ensure that their assessments are properly reflected in current prices. What we really have in mind, however, is a market where there is indeed disagreement among investors but where the force of common judgments is sufficient to produce an orderly adjustment of prices to new information.

If the capital market is inefficient in processing information, the joint probability density function of returns assessed by the market may differ from the correct joint probability density function and significant deviations

---

[9]By individual differences, we presume Roll means simply whether an individual is designated as a winner or a loser. We do not address the issue of whether meaningful comparisons between winners, for example, can be made. There may be a problem associated with comparing performance between managers of portfolios with different risk.

[10]Roll (1978, p. 1061) briefly discusses a concept of 'perfect ability', but this is neither necessary nor sufficient for superior performance. The correctly assessed efficient frontier is derived using the probability density functions of nature's irreducible stochastic elements, and therefore correctly captures all information that is knowable.

from the empirical security market line may be observed. Of course, if this is the case our index is not mean/variance efficient with respect to the correctly assessed efficient frontier. However, with this interpretation relative to the index we can designate winners in the sense that those managers or advisers who plot deviations significantly above the line are superior relative to the 'market'. Of course, if we find no significant deviations, the simultaneous hypotheses of the capital market being efficient in information processing and the mean/variance efficiency of the index relative to market beliefs are sustained.[11]

Another issue raised in the Roll (1978, p. 1060) quote above is concerned with the sensitivity of ranking to the choice of index. This issue follows directly from statement 6. It is true that choosing an index that is inefficient relative to the market's assessed efficient frontier can yield incorrect performance evaluations and that another similarly inefficient index could reverse the rankings. The task of choosing an index that is mean/variance efficient relative to the appropriate set of beliefs is an important task. The capital asset pricing model suggests that the value – weighted market portfolio should be such an index. We postpone until section 5 our discussion of problems associated with obtaining a good measure of the returns on the market portfolio.

## 3. Portfolio performance

In this section we formalize our discussion and demonstrate that the security market line can be a useful tool in detecting superior portfolio performance. To do this, we presume an individual with better information than the market about some aspect of security returns and show he will, on average, plot above the ex post Security Market Line (SML). We are unable to show this superior designation under completely general information, thus the logical possibility of incorrect designation by the SML remains. The conditions needed for proving correct designation are relatively weak, however.

Previous analyses have assumed that a superior portfolio manager plots above the security market line. In fact superiority has been defined, '... as a portfolio whose returns are consistently greater than those implied by its level of systematic risk'.[12] Roll's analysis calls into question the assumption that superior performance implies and is implied by plotting above the security market line. We define superiority in an information sense. One individual is superior if he has better information than others. The question

---

[11]'This is the rub in tests of market efficiency. Any test is simultaneously a test of efficiency and of assumptions about the characteristics of market equilibrium.' [Fama (1976, p. 137)].

[12]Jensen (1969, p. 192).

we then address is whether an individual who meets our definition of superiority will be so designated in an SML analysis.

A one-to-one correspondence in winner/loser designations between information superiority and SML superiority would, of course, validate the SML criterion. Less than a one-to-one correspondence does *not* imply we should reject the criterion, however. That is, if the SML is useful in showing superior performance under a wide variety of, but not all conditions, the criterion can still be useful unless a better criterion can be shown to exist.

At this point some discussion on the philosophy of the analysis to follow is in order. We would like to have a completely general equilibrium framework for analysis. The capital asset pricing model, for example, is a general equilibrium model, but this framework assumes homogeneous beliefs among market participants. Thus, we have a problem if we assume a capital asset pricing model general equilibrium and we allow an individual to have better information than that implied by the homogeneous beliefs that establish the equilibrium. One way around this problem is to assume a general equilibrium as used by Hirshleifer (1975). He assumes an economy that is dominated by agents who share homogeneous beliefs and an individual with deviant beliefs. The deviant belief individual is assumed to have essentially 'zero weight' in the economy. In reality, of course, if one performs an SML analysis and detects superior performance, the assumed general equilibrium model (CAPM) cannot literally hold. However, by attributing very little weight to the deviant individual, it can hold approximately.[13]

The remainder of this section is divided into two parts, each considering a different level of information a portfolio manager might have. Roll (1978) identifies two types of relevant information: (1) privileged information about specific securities, or (2) information on general market conditions. In the following part of this section we consider information of type (1). In the second part we consider the general case, where the portfolio manager has information about both individual securities and the market return.

## 3.1. A model with informed and uninformed individuals: Security specific information

Our model assumes an individual with better assessments than the market

---

[13]Another way around the homogeneous belief problem is through the concept of 'consensus beliefs'. This alternative scenario allows for widely diverse, heterogeneous beliefs on the part of asset traders. While the beliefs are heterogeneous, the arrived-at prices represent some sort of consensus of the market participants. That is, there is some probability belief, which, if held by all traders, would result in the same prices as those currently existing. This no-price-difference probability belief can serve as the market assessment, if this probability distribution is multivariate normal or if all investors have quadratic utility (more important in the finite states of the world model), prices are those arrived at in the CAPM with homogeneous probability beliefs. The existence of a 'consensus belief' has been formally demonstrated by Verrecchia (1978).

about specific securities. We assume *all* individuals assess the mean and variance of the market return identically. In particular, our informed individual has access to an 'information service' which gives him one of $L$ messages each period. After receiving any particular message $j=1,...,L$, we represent the informed individual's beliefs as a vector,

$$\pi^{Ij} = (\pi_1^{Ij},...,\pi_N^{Ij}), \qquad \sum_{s=1}^{N} \pi_s^{Ij} = 1,$$

which represents the probabilities he assigns to the $N$ possible states of the world. We represent the market probability assessments (uninformed) as[14,15]

$$\pi^{U} = (\pi_1^{U},...,\pi_N^{U}), \qquad \sum_{s=1}^{N} \pi_s^{U} = 1.$$

We can thus define any message $j$ by its vector

$$\eta^{j} = \pi^{Ij} - \pi^{U}, \qquad \sum_{s=1}^{N} \eta_s^{j} = 0,$$

which represents the changes in probability assessments associated with message $j$.

For our informed individual, there is also a probability distribution for receipt of the various messages.[16] We represent this as the vector

$$q = (q_1,...,q_L), \qquad \sum_{j=1}^{L} q_j = 1,$$

where $q_j$ is the probability of receiving message $j$. We further assume that given any $j$,

$$\eta^{j} \neq 0 \quad \text{but} \quad E^{Ij}(R_M) = E^{U}(R_M),$$

where $E^{Ij}$ is the expectations operator on probability beliefs $\pi^{Ij}$, $E^{U}$ is the same operator on $\pi^{U}$, and $R_M$ is the market rate of return. This assumption rules out the possibility of no information while maintaining our assumption of security information only (no market information).[17]

---

[14]We are here assuming that the market ($\pi^U$) assessment remains stationary over time. This is similar to the assumptions of most of the econometric work on the CAPM.

[15]The informed individual is our 'zero weight' deviant, thus prices are as if the uninformed beliefs are homogeneous.

[16]We assume, as in footnote 14, that this distribution is stationary over time.

[17]This is somewhat stronger than the assumption we need here, which is that $\eta^{j} \neq 0$ for some $j$ where $q_j > 0$. We make this assumption for analytical and expository convenience.

We also assume that the informed and the uninformed have rational expectations. This rational expectations assumption is clear in the context of this model. That is, since the market never receives message $j$, each period it maintains the prior probability assessment $\pi^U$. Given message $j$, the informed individual has probability assessment $\pi^{Ij} \neq \pi^U$. Yet both expectations can be rational, given the information available to each agent if and only if

$$\sum_{j=1}^{L} q_j \eta_S^j = 0 \quad \text{for every } S. \tag{A}$$

For if the informed expectations were 'fulfilled', the unconditional (on $j$) probability distribution would have to be

$$\sum_{j=1}^{L} q_j \pi^{Ij} = \sum_{j=1}^{L} q_j(\pi^U + \eta^j)$$

$$= \sum_{j=1}^{L} q_j \pi^U + \sum_{j=1}^{L} q_j \eta^j$$

$$= \pi^U + \sum_{j=1}^{L} q_j \eta^j. \tag{B}$$

From (B), it is clear that if (A) does not hold, $\pi^U$ will not be the observed unconditional distribution. Similarly from (B), if (A) holds, $\pi^U$ will be the observed unconditional distribution. Thus, we assume (A) holds and the informed expectations are fulfilled. People all have rational, but possibly different expectations.

We suppose that the market prices assets according to the capital asset pricing model (CAPM) of Sharp (1964), Lintner (1965), and Mossin (1966) in a complete market. We assume that investors have quadratic utility (consistent with the CAPM) so that they select mean/variance efficient portfolios relative to their probability beliefs.[18]

In a complete market, any portfolio $K$ can be represented as a vector,

$$Y_K = (Y_{K1}, \ldots, Y_{KN}),$$

where $Y_{Ks}$ represents the units of consumption received by holding portfolio $K$ if state $s$ occurs. For any individual $i$, we let $U_{is}$ represent his utility conditional on state $s$ occurring and $U_i$ represent his unconditional utility function. We assume that utility is separable such that

---

[18]The quadratic utility assumption is used in the proof that follows in that it insures that any individual with beliefs $\pi^U$ will optimally hold some combination of the market portfolio and the risk-free asset.

$$U_i(C_i, Y_i) = U_i(C_i) + \sum_{s=1}^{N} \pi_s^i U_{is}(Y_{is}).$$

Here $C_i$ measures $i$'s current consumption and $Y_i$ is the portfolio held by individual $i$.

Also in a complete market, the following conditions must hold:

(a)     $\displaystyle V_r = \sum_s \omega_s X_{rs}$     for all securities $r$,

(b)     $\displaystyle \omega_s = \frac{\partial U_i(C_i, Y_i)}{\partial Y_{is}} \bigg/ \frac{\partial U_i(C_i, Y_i)}{\partial C_i}$

$$= \pi_s^i \frac{\partial U_{is}(Y_{is})}{\partial Y_{is}} \bigg/ \frac{\partial U_i(C_i)}{\partial C_i} \qquad \text{for all individuals } i.$$

Condition (a) states that the value of the $r$th security, $V_r$, is the sum of the priced payoffs, where $\omega_s$ is the price of a contingent claim on a unit of consumption in state $s$ and $X_{rs}$ is the total payoff (in units of consumption) of security $r$ in state $s$. Condition (b) notes that in equilibrium all individuals equate their marginal rates of substitution of future expected consumption for current consumption to the relevant state contingent claim prices.

Having completed our choice and information theoretic framework we now proceed with the analysis. Our concern is with the following theorem:

*Theorem.   If investor $I$'s probability beliefs are correct, he will on average plot above the security market line as drawn by the uninformed investors. An equivalent way of stating this would be that investor $I$ expects to plot above the security market line drawn by the uninformed investors. Symbolically, the statement of the theorem is*

$$E^I(R_I) > R_F + [E^U(R_M) - R_F]\beta_I^U,$$

*where $E^I(R_I)$ is the informed investor's unconditional expected return from his portfolio, $R_F$ is the risk-free rate, $E^U(R_M)$ is the uninformed's expectation of the return on the market portfolio and $\beta_I^U$ is $\mathrm{cov}(R_I, R_M)/\mathrm{var}(R_M)$ as assessed by the uninformed.*

*Proof.*   We first wish to show that given any message $j$,

$$E^{Ij}(R_I) > R_F + [E^U(R_M) - R_F]\beta_{Ij}^U, \tag{1}$$

where the $Ij$ superscript indicates the expectation is with respect to the probability assessment $\pi^{Ij}$. The $U$ superscripts likewise indicate expectations with probability assessments $\pi^U$. This condition has an obvious relationship to the security market line.

The formal proof of condition (1) is in the appendix. The condition is established by constructing a hypothetical uninformed individual-with the same utility function and current consumption choice as our informed individual. We show the informed individual buys more future consumption than does the uninformed in states where his probability assessments are larger than are the uninformed's $(\eta_s^j = \pi_s^{Ij} - \pi_s^U > 0)$. Likewise he buys less than the uninformed in states where his probability assessment is less. We then show that the informed individual, because his probabilities are correct, earns a higher average return than the uninformed expects him to. Since the uninformed individual expects him to plot directly on the security market line, using the uninformed estimate of beta, the informed individual will beat the security market line.

Condition (1) is a conditional expectation and the theorem is concerned with the unconditional expectation. The unconditional expected return of the informed's portfolio, $E^I(R_I)$, is obtained by averaging condition (1) over messages,

$$E^I(R_I) = \sum_{j=1}^{L} q_j E^{Ij}(R_I)$$

$$> R_F + [E^U(R_M) - R_F] \sum_{j=1}^{L} q_j \beta_{Ij}^U. \tag{2}$$

This proves the theorem if the uninformed investors estimate the portfolio beta of the informed individual as the average of his single period portfolio betas.

*The time series estimation problem.* In fact, however, the uninformed investor is likely to use the time series of realized portfolio returns to directly measure the informed-individual's beta with least-squares estimation techniques. We now proceed to prove the theorem if this econometrically estimated ex post beta, $\beta_I^E$, is used by the uninformed investor. The econometrically estimated beta is

$$\beta_I^E = \frac{\text{cov}(R_I, R_M)}{\sigma^2(R_M)}$$

$$= \sum_j \frac{q_j [E^{Ij}(R_{Ij} R_M) - E^{Ij}(R_{Ij}) E^U(R_M)]}{\sigma_U^2(R_M)}, \tag{3}$$

using the rational expectations assumption, where $\sigma_U^2(R_M)$ is the variance of the market return assessed with the uninformed beliefs. Since the informed individual has no information about the market, his expectation of the market return and the variance of the return assessed with his beliefs will be the same as the uninformed mean and variance. This reduces eq. (3) to

$$\beta_I^E = \sum_j q_j \beta_{Ij}^I. \tag{4}$$

A necessary assumption for the proof is that

$$\sum_{j=1}^{L} q_j \beta_{Ij}^U = \sum_{j=1}^{L} q_j \beta_{Ij}^I.$$

Here, $\beta_{Ij}^U$ is the covariance of the informed individual's portfolio return with the market return divided by the variance of the market return, assessed with the (uninformed) $\pi^U$ distribution. $\beta_{Ij}^I$ is the same ratio assessed with the (informed) $\pi^{Ij}$ expectations. This assumption is then that the average beta of the informed individual's portfolio is the same whether assessed with the informed or uninformed expectations. The assumption will hold when information is in some sense 'symmetric' with respect to market returns; i.e., there is as much information ($\eta_s$ deviation) about high market return states as about low market return states. We will discuss the effects of relaxing this assumption later in this section.

Thus, we assume that the average beta using the informed's expectations will be equal to the average beta using uninformed expectations. This, combined with eq. (4), establishes that

$$\beta_I^E = \sum_j q_j \beta_{Ij}^U,$$

and thus

$$E^I(R_I) > R_F + [E^U(R_M) - R_F]\beta_I^E, \tag{5}$$

from (2). This proves the theorem in the case where the uninformed investors use standard time series regression techniques to estimate the informed investor's portfolio beta.

We can now discuss the effects of relaxing the assumption that the average $\beta_{Ij}^U$ must equal the average $\beta_{Ij}^I$. Without this condition, the above proof will not go through and we can not generally support the standard security market line analysis using an econometric beta.[19] However, a modification of

[19]The condition will not hold for all information possibilities. In particular, consider a situation where the information in message $j$ is only about favorable states of the world; that is, $\eta_s^j \neq 0$ only when $X_s > E^U(X_s)$. Here, the informed individual's expectation of his return will be greater than the market's expectation of his return only when the market return is greater than average. This must result in $\beta_{Ij}^I$ being greater than $\beta_{Ij}^U$. If this condition holds for all messages, then the average $\beta_{Ij}^I$ must be greater than the average $\beta_{Ij}^U$ for this individual.

the econometric technique can still be used to make unambiguous statements about portfolio performance.

That is, instead of estimating the beta of the *portfolio* of the informed individual through time series analysis, we can use the betas of the *individual securities* composing his portfolio by weighting these individual security betas by the informed individual's portfolio weights. In a particular period, we arrive at an estimate of $\beta_{Ij}^U$ for that period. Averaging these single period estimates over time, we arrive at an estimate of $\sum_j q_j \beta_{Ij}^U$. From eq. (2), we know that if we use this average $\beta_{Ij}^U$ in our portfolio performance test, we are able to detect superior performance for the case of security specific information. Thus, using individual security betas and averaging as described above, we can obtain a beta that validates the security market line criterion.

## 3.2. General information

Thus, with security-specific information the informed investor will be correctly designated in a security market line analysis. We now discuss the problem in the context of general information. Hence, we remove the restriction that $E^{Ij}(R_M) = E^U(R_M)$. As stated at the beginning of this section, with completely general information the possibility of incorrect designation by the SML remains. In the remainder of this section we derive a sufficient condition for an informed individual, with general information, to be correctly designated in an SML analysis. We also relate our analysis to a similar analysis done by Jensen (1972). Jensen's analysis refers directly to a potential econometric problem that arises in the framework of our analysis.

As shown in the appendix, if the informed individual's consumption and wealth are constant across messages, condition (2) will hold:[20]

$$E^I(R_I) = \sum_{j=1}^L q_j E^{Ij}(R_I) > R_F + [E^U(R_M) - R_F] \sum_{j=1}^L q_j \beta_{Ij}^U.$$

This proves the theorem if the uninformed investors estimate the portfolio beta of the informed individual as the average of his single period betas. Thus, the sufficient condition for validating the security market line benchmark, if the beta of the portfolio is measured as the average single period uninformed beta, is that the portfolio manager with constant wealth selects the same consumption regardless of the message.

*The time series estimation problem.*  In this general case, however, we have a

---

[20]In our scenario messages are received across time. Consequently, we are assuming the informed's consumption and wealth are time independent as well as message constant. The reader should keep in mind that the assumptions are sufficient but not necessary for condition (2) to hold.

very difficult time extending this proof to include the SML drawn with the beta estimated using the time series of realized portfolio returns. Where information was security specific we were able to demonstrate the plausibility of a correspondence between the econometrically estimated beta, $\beta_I^E$, and the average of the single period uninformed betas. With general information this correspondence is less plausible. For example, eq. (3),

$$\beta_I^E = \sum_j \frac{q_j[E^{Ij}(R_{Ij}R_M) - E^{Ij}(R_{Ij})E^U(R_M)]}{\sigma_U^2(R_M)},$$

can no longer be interpreted as a weighted average of any one individual's assessments.[21]

However, Jensen's (1972) analysis indicates this econometric problem is of little empirical relevance. Jensen's analysis of the time series estimation problem associated with assessing performance focuses initially on the situation where the informed investor has information about expected market conditions only. Under his assumptions, the optimal adjustment of a portfolio manager to information about the market return involves setting

$$\beta_{It} = \beta_I + \theta_I \pi_t',$$

where $\theta_I(>0)$ is a parameter that depends on the risk aversion of the informed individual and his confidence in his prediction of the market return, and $\pi_t'$ is the difference between his expectation of the market return in period $t$ and the uninformed expectation.[22] Since $E(\pi_t')$ is zero, $\beta_I$ is the average beta of the informed investor's portfolio.

Jensen goes on to show that this optimal adjustment will normally result in an econometric overestimate of $\beta_I$. That is,[23]

$$\text{Plim } \hat{\beta}_I = \beta_I + \theta_I \rho^2 E^U(R_M - R_F),$$

where $\rho$ is the correlation between $E^I(R_M)$ and the observed $R_M$ (across time). Thus, if the informed individual has any predictive ability ($\rho > 0$), his

---

[21]With $E^{Ij}(R_M) = E^U(R_M)$ the numerator of the right-hand side of eq. (3) is a weighted average of $\text{cov}^{Ij}(R_{Ij}, R_M)$, but with the general information assumption the right-hand side includes uninformed expectations as well as informed.

[22]We have simplified Jensen's analysis for the purposes of our paper. In particular, we have assumed $\pi_t^* = \pi_t'$ in his terminology (or that the informed forecasts are 'optimal') and have translated his terminology and symbols into our framework where possible. Also, note that $\theta_I$ is assumed independent of $t$ in this formulation. It is at this point that Jensen implicitly introduced the same assumptions that we do; i.e., those constraining the informed individual's wealth and consumption to be the same across time.

[23]We assume here and in what follows that $E(\pi')^3 = 0$, or that the forecasts are 'symmetric' about $E(R_M)$. This makes the exposition and results much simpler.

beta estimate will be biased upward; only where he has no ability whatsoever ($\rho = 0$) will the econometric estimate of beta be unbiased.

This problem of bias in the beta coefficient has consequences for portfolio performance evaluation. Again, Jensen shows that the manager's ability to predict will result in an econometric estimate of his distance above the security market line as

$$\text{Plim } \hat{\delta} = \delta_I + \theta_I \rho^2 \sigma^2(R_M) - \theta_I \rho^2 [E^U(R_M - R_F)]^2,$$

where $\delta_I$ is a measure of the superior performance due to the informed individual's ability to predict returns on specific securities. Jensen goes on to show that the second term, $\theta_I \rho^2 \sigma^2(R_M)$, is the correct measurement of the excess return the portfolio manager receives for his ability to forecast the market. Thus, the informed manager's estimated performance will be biased downward by the last term and any superiority will be understated. In fact, if $\sigma(R_M) < E^U(R_M - R_F)$, the portfolio manager would show up econometrically as having worse performance than if he could not predict the market return at all! However, from an empirical standpoint this possibility is uninteresting.[24]

What then have we been able to show? For a broad classification of information, security specific, we have shown a one-to-one correspondence between information superiority and SML designation. This one-to-one correspondence can obtain using standard time series estimation procedures. We have also shown sufficient conditions for correct designation in the general information case. Jensen's analysis indicates that, despite a downward bias, standard time series estimation procedures yield the correct designation here as well. The possibility of incorrect designation in the general information case remains. However, the sufficient conditions for correct designation are *not* so strong as to reject the SML criterion or its usefulness for the general information case. Our analysis does not indicate that inferior managers will be incorrectly designated;[25] only that a possibility of incorrectly designating a superior manager exists.

## 4. On residual analysis

As mentioned in the introduction, Roll's (1977) conclusion (10) can be easily interpreted as being critical of the empirical methodology known as residual analysis. In this section we address the issue of the usefulness of

---

[24]Fisher and Lorie (1970) report the post World War II (1945–1965) standard deviation of annual rates of return on the arithmetic index of NYSE stocks as 0.197. They also reported the average annual rate of return on this index over the same period as 0.138. If the average riskless rate was about 0.04 over this period then an estimate is that $\sigma(R_M) \cong 2E^U(R_M - R_F)$.

[25]An inferior manager would be one with no information advantage who generates expenses, or one whose information advantage is outweighed by the generated expenses.

residual analysis as an empirical tool. We find, first, that only a very special, inappropriate index would be unable, as Roll suggests, to pick up deviations from the security market line. Second, we show that residuals computed against the market index will be appropriate if assets are priced according to the capital asset pricing model.

Residual analysis is an empirical methodology designed to measure the effects of information events on security prices. The effects are measured by comparing a security's return when the information event occurs to the ex ante expected return. As such, the problem of residual analysis differs from the problem of portfolio evaluation in an important way. Portfolios of securities selected by investment managers are selected ex ante. Presumably the managers have expectations of superior future performance. Contrarily, residual analysis involves an ex post selection rule. That is, a security is picked for a residual analysis 'portfolio' because some event specific to that security has occurred and the desire is to determine the effect of the event on the price of the security. Thus, even if the index used were mean-variance efficient with respect to all information available at the beginning of the period, positive and negative deviations would be detected by a security market line type residual analysis. It appears that only if the index were ex post efficient in a very special way, as we shall explain below, would these deviations be undetected.

Looking at the specifics of residual analysis should help clarify this point. Let us examine, then, the two factor market model type of residual analysis as performed by Mandelker (1974), Jaffe (1974) and others. This methodology requires the estimation of the security market line for each date residuals are desired. Historically, this estimation has been accomplished by regressing a portfolio return vector on a vector of the associated portfolio betas for each date.[26] The estimated regression coefficients are used as the parameters of the security market lines. To perform the residual analysis, betas are calculated for each security in the residual analysis portfolio. Then residuals are estimated using the calculated betas, the securities' returns and the regression coefficients. If $\hat{\gamma}_{0t}$ and $\hat{\gamma}_{1t}$ are the estimated regression coefficients for a particular date, a residual, $\hat{e}_{rt}$, is estimated for a security $r$ in the portfolio as

$$\hat{e}_{rt} = R_{rt} - \hat{\gamma}_{0t} - \hat{\gamma}_{1t}\hat{\beta}_r,$$

where $R_{rt}$ is the realized return of security $r$ in period $t$ and $\hat{\beta}_r$ is the estimated beta from the previous period.

Roll's mathematics tells us that all deviations from the security market line

[26]See Fama and MacBeth (1973) for the details. The portfolio return vectors are from the dates of interest, and the vectors of portfolio betas are always estimated from sample periods prior to the dates of interest.

are zero if an efficient portfolio is used as the index. The required index need be efficient relative to the observed expected return vector and the same variance–covariance matrix used in computing beta. In residual analysis, returns for *specific* time periods are used and betas are not calculated over these same time periods. Thus, to apply mathematical identities to get zero residuals in the analysis described above, one must employ an index that is mean/variance efficient

(1) treating the realized return vector for period $t$ as the relevant average return vector; and

(2) treating the sample covariance matrix of the previous period (on which betas are measured) as the relevant covariance matrix.[27]

Such an index would thus involve a special form of ex post efficiency.

Why one would advocate the use of this index is unclear. As stated earlier, the security market line is used in residual analysis to compute the *ex ante* expected return on a security (before an information event). Using any type of *ex post* efficient index will be inappropriate for yielding this *ex ante* expected return.

Having established our first conclusion of this section we now proceed to show that residual analysis, using the market portfolio as the index, is valid. This, of course, is contrary to the criticism implied by Roll's conclusion (10).[28]

Our model is essentially that of the last section. We assume that all individuals in the economy are initially uninformed. We assume further that the market prices assets according to the capital asset pricing model and efficiently processes all information available at the beginning of the period. The expected return-risk relationship is thus

$$E^U(R_r) = \sum_s \pi_s^U X_{rs} \Big/ \sum_s \omega_s X_{rs} - 1$$
$$= R_F + [E^U(R_M) - R_F]\beta_r^U,$$

where $R_r$ is the return on security $r$, $X_{rs}$ is the payoff of security $r$ in state $s$, and $\beta_r^U$ is the market's assessment of the beta of security $r$. With this scenario the market portfolio is truly ex ante efficient. During the period, an information event occurs that changes the correct probability distribution to

---

[27]Furthermore, this same covariance matrix must be used in calculation of the betas that are put into the cross sectional regression yielding $\hat{\gamma}_{0t}$ and $\hat{\gamma}_{it}$.

[28]Roll's most recent paper (1978) does recognize that residual analysis is valid under certain conditions.

$\pi_S^I$. Residual analysis is concerned with firm specific information, hence we retain the assumptions that $E^I(R_M) = E^U(R_M)$ and that $\sigma_I^2(R_M) = \sigma_U^2(R_M)$.

Let us now examine the residuals we should expect in this model using the market portfolio as the index. By arguing as in section 3.1, the expected residual, $e_{rt}$, will be[29]

$$E^I(e_{rt}) = E^I(R_{rt}) - R_F - [E^U(R_M) - R_F]\beta_r^U$$

$$= \left(\sum_s (\pi_s^I - \pi_s^U)X_{rs}\right)\Big/ V_r,$$

where $V_r$ is the value of security $r$. This equation seems to give us exactly what we desire in a residual, the difference between the expected return given the information event $\{(\sum_s \pi_s^I X_{rs})/V_r\}$ and the ex ante expected return $\{(\sum_s \pi_s^U X_{rs})/V_r\}$.

Additional intuition about the residual can be gained by rewriting our last equation as

$$E^I(e_{rt}) = \frac{1}{V_r}\text{cov*}(\eta_s, X_{rs}),$$

where cov* indicates a sample covariance and $\eta_s$ represents, as in section 3, the change in probability of state $s$ due to the information event. This residual will then be expected to be positive or negative as this sample covariance is positive or negative.

Notice now that the covariance will be positive for favorable information and negative for unfavorable information. That is, favorable information should show increases in the probabilities (high $\eta_s$) of high payoff states for the security (high $X_{rs}$); it should also show decreases in the probabilities (low $\eta_s$) of low payoff states (low $X_{rs}$). This should clearly result in a positive covariance in the above equation, if the information is favorable. One can show, analogously, that unfavorable information will result in a negative covariance.

Thus, if assets are priced as in the capital asset pricing model, residual analysis will measure the effects desired. A favorable information event for security $r$ will generally be associated with positive residuals for that security; an unfavorable information event will generally be associated with negative residuals. Furthermore, the expected residual for a period with an information event will be the change in the expected return caused by the new information.

---

[29]See the proof in the appendix to section 3.1 for the development of the formula.

## 5. On tests of the asset pricing model

At this point in the paper we have accomplished our primary intentions, and we now turn to Roll's (1977) conclusion (4) which we consider severe. Roll preludes his (1977) study by citing Pirsig (1974):

> If the horn honks and the mechanic concludes that the whole electrical system is working, he is in deep trouble....

As a prelude to this section we offer the conjecture that the honking horn does provide *some* information and that if the mechanic is prohibited from further tests, he ought not ignore the information provided by the proxy.

Roll (1977) identifies three problems with tests of the capital asset pricing model:[30]

(a) The *only* testable implication of the model is that the true market portfolio is mean/variance efficient.
(b) The return of the *true* market portfolio is not used in any of the empirical tests to date and is virtually impossible to measure. The theory is not testable unless the *exact* value-weighted market portfolio of all assets is used.
(c) All tests of the model involve joint hypotheses, one of which is that the market portfolio is correctly measured. Since we know the market portfolio is not correctly measured, the rejection of the joint hypothesis tells us very little.

We sympathize with all 3 problems and believe they are all of some importance. Criticism (a), especially, seems to have cleared up some of the confusion involved in earlier tests. However, criticisms (b) and (c) impose extremely severe criteria on empirical work that few, if any, econometric studies can meet.

Criticism (b) seems to say that no proxy for the market return will suffice for testing the theory. Roll correctly suggests that the use of a proxy variable increases the risk of type I and type II error in testing. Yet, it is almost impossible to find the 'true' measure of any variable in economics. Proxies must be used constantly to test all types of economic theories. Are we to abandon studies of inflation because the change in the Consumer Price Index (CPI) is merely a proxy for the inflation rate? Are we to abandon concentration studies because the 4-firm concentration ratio is merely a proxy for the concentration of an industry? Are we to abandon all empirical studies?

Clearly, Roll finds something especially worrisome about proxies for the

---

[30]This is *our* summary of his criticisms, which he states somewhat differently.

return on the market portfolio. But the only 'special' problem he discusses[31] is that highly correlated proxies can yield different conclusions about the validity of the CAPM. This problem is again, however, not unique to CAPM tests. Consider, for example, the testing of a theory which explains some variable $Y$ as a function of inflation. Suppose the following regression is run over $N$ periods:

$$Y_t = a + b(\Delta CPI_t) + u_t,$$

where $\Delta CPI$ is used as a proxy for inflation. Suppose further that the results offer some support for the theory, with a significant $t$-statistic on $b$ and $R^2 = 0.25$. Now, by the geometry of the situation, there must be some other proxy for inflation, correlated 0.866 with $\Delta CPI$, which shows no relationship at all to $Y$ ($R^2 = 0.00$).[32] This proxy can also be constructed simply by assigning different weights to the price series that compose the $CPI$, if we have $N$ linearly independent price change vectors for individual goods.[33] It seems that this proxy and the many others like it have exactly the same problem that Roll finds so worrisome in the market proxy.

Problem (c) is also a common one in economic research. That is, virtually all tests of economic models involve joint hypotheses. The simple supply–demand model, for example, is not independently testable; it must be tested in conjunction with some hypothesis about how one of the curves has shifted. Other models are tested jointly with, if nothing else, the hypothesis that the data and variables used correspond to the theory presented. In fact, linking the CAPM with this last hypothesis is the joint hypothesis Roll finds so troublesome.

What we have done so far is to argue that the problems Roll sees in the CAPM tests are also found in other econometric studies. Unfortunately, this is not sufficient to refute, or even really minimize, his criticisms. In fact, he is certainly correct in that a *definitive* test of the theory cannot be made without solving these problems. It is also unfortunately true, however, that definitive tests are nearly always impossible.

We disagree with Roll in his almost total condemnation of all empirical studies to date, implying that they provide virtually *no* information at all. We believe there is some information in these tests, even with imperfect proxies

---

[31]Roll also discusses an econometric aggregation problem in the portfolio grouping technique, but this is not a proxy problem. The aggregation problem is again a familiar one to econometricians.

[32]Since $R = 0.5$ is the cosine of the angle between the $Y$ vector and the $\Delta CPI$ vector in $N$-space, the angle between these two must be $60°$. Thus, there is some vector, $X$, in the same plane as $Y$ and $\Delta CPI$ that is $30°$ from $\Delta CPI$ and $90°$ from $Y$. The correlation between $X$ and $\Delta CPI$ will be $\cos 30° = 0.866$; the correlation between $X$ and $Y$ will be $\cos 90° = 0$.

[33]It may be that some goods would have to be given negative weights, but this is the same problem Roll mentions in his criticism of Black, Jensen, and Scholes (1972).

testing joint hypotheses. More importantly, this information is the *best* available. It does no good to ignore this information without providing some better information in its place.[34] In an ideal world, these problems would not exist – and we would certainly support the creation of such a world, were it costless – but this provides little justification for rejecting (ignoring) studies done in the world in which we now live.

## 6. Summary and concluding thoughts

Our examination has been concerned with the empirical relevance of the capital asset pricing model. In particular, we have explored the worth of (1) tests of portfolio performance using the security market line benchmark, (2) tests of the effects of information events through residual analyses, and (3) tests of the CAPM itself. We conclude that, although there are potential problems with all three types of tests, they are valid tests.

Superior portfolio managers are reasonably detectable in a properly performed security market line analysis. Favorable and unfavorable information events will be similarly, on average, identified with positive and negative residuals. Thus, Roll's rhetorical question on the use of an index that is not 'truly' efficient is answered. The appropriate index is one that is efficient relative to the 'market' ex ante beliefs. If the market is not processing information efficiently, the appropriate index should not be truly efficient. Furthermore, the capital asset pricing model tells us that the value-weighted market portfolio is efficient relative to the market beliefs.

We sympathize with the criticisms offered by Roll concerning tests of the CAPM itself. However, we argue that these criticisms can be leveled at virtually any econometric study. We conclude that the tests provide some information about the validity of the model and should not be dismissed out-of-hand.

Finally, Roll's criticism should not be interpreted as a rejection of the capital asset pricing model itself. One must replace this theory with an alternative theory that predicts better and/or is more useful in order to invalidate the CAPM. Even evidence itself is not enough to invalidate the theory. As Stigler (1966) puts it:

> The answer is that it takes a theory to beat a theory; If there is a theory that is right 51 percent of the time, it will be used until a better one comes along.

In the case of the CAPM, it is far from clear what the suggested alternative is.

---

[34]In fairness to Roll, he is moving in this direction in Part II of his paper.

## Appendix

*Proof of condition (1).* We restate here condition (1),[35]

$$E^{Ij}(R_I) > R_F + [E^U(R_M) - R_F]\beta^U_{Ij},$$

and conditions (a) and (b),

$$V_r = \sum_s \omega_s X_{rs}, \qquad\qquad \text{for all securities } r,$$

$$\omega_s = \frac{\partial U_i(C_i, Y_i)}{\partial Y_{is}} \bigg/ \frac{\partial U_i(C_i, Y_i)}{\partial C_i}$$

$$= \pi^i_s \frac{\partial U_{is}(Y_{is})}{\partial Y_{is}} \bigg/ \frac{\partial U_i(C_i)}{\partial C_i}, \qquad \text{for all individuals } i.$$

We represent $I$'s optimal portfolio and current consumption, given message $j$, as $(Y^j_{I1},\ldots, Y^j_{IN})$ and $C^j_I$, respectively. Condition (b) means that

$$\frac{\partial U_I(C^j_I)}{\partial C_I} = \frac{\pi^{Ij}_s}{\omega_s} \cdot \frac{\partial U_{Is}(Y^j_{Is})}{\partial Y_{Is}}, \qquad (\forall s).$$

Now, let us construct a hypothetical individual $U$ who holds beliefs $\pi^U$ and has the same utility function as $I$. In general, for the same wealth as $I$, $U$ will not select $C^j_U = C^j_I$. However, we select wealth for $U$ such that $C^j_U = C^j_I$.
For individual $U$ also,

$$\frac{\partial U_U(C^j_U)}{\partial C_U} = \frac{\pi^U_s}{\omega_s} \cdot \frac{\partial U_{Us}(Y^j_{Us})}{\partial Y_{Us}}, \qquad (\forall s).$$

However, with our assumptions of identical utility functions and $C^j_U = C^j_I$,

$$\frac{\partial U_I(C^j_I)}{\partial C_I} = \frac{\pi^U_s}{\omega_s} \cdot \frac{\partial U_{Is}(Y^j_{Us})}{\partial Y_{Us}} = \frac{\pi^{Ij}_s}{\omega_s} \cdot \frac{\partial U_{Is}(Y^j_{Is})}{\partial Y_{Is}}.$$

Using the last equality and rearranging yields

$$\frac{\partial U_{Is}(Y^j_{Is})/\partial Y_{Is}}{\partial U_{Is}(Y^j_{Us})/\partial Y_{Us}} = \frac{\pi^U_s}{\pi^{Ij}_s}.$$

This result yields the following implications for quadratic utility (since it is

---

[35]All notation is as defined in the text. To shorten this appendix we refer to the informed individual as $I$ and the uninformed as $U$.

concave):

$$\pi_s^U > \pi_s^{Ij} \rightarrow Y_{Us}^j > Y_{Is}^j,$$
$$\pi_s^U = \pi_s^{Ij} \rightarrow Y_{Us}^j = Y_{Is}^j,$$
$$\pi_s^U < \pi_s^{Ij} \rightarrow Y_{Us}^j < Y_{Is}^j. \tag{A.1}$$

This gives us the condition

$$(\pi_s^{Ij} - \pi_s^U)(Y_{Is}^j - Y_{Us}^j) \gtreqless 0, \quad (\forall s). \tag{A.2}$$

And if $\pi_s^{Ij} \neq \pi_s^U$,

$$(\pi_s^{Ij} - \pi_s^U)(Y_{Is}^j - Y_{Us}^j) > 0.$$

Individual $I$'s expectation of his portfolio return is

$$E^{Ij}(R_I) = \sum_s \pi_s^{Ij} Y_{Is}^j \bigg/ \sum_s \omega_s Y_{Is}^j - 1$$

$$= \sum_s (\pi_s^{Ij} - \pi_s^U) Y_{Is}^j \bigg/ \sum_s \omega_s Y_{Is}^j + \sum_s \pi_s^U Y_{Is}^j \bigg/ \sum_s \omega_s Y_{Is}^j - 1. \tag{A.3}$$

Using the CAPM which we have assumed,

$$E^U(R_I) = \sum_s \pi_s^U Y_{Is}^j \bigg/ \sum_s \omega_s Y_{Is}^j - 1$$

$$= R_F + [E^U(R_M) - R_F] \beta_{Ij}^U. \tag{A.4}$$

From eqs. (A.3) and (A.4),

$$E^{Ij}(R_I) - (R_F + [E^U(R_M) - R_F] \beta_{Ij}^U) = \sum_s (\pi_s^{Ij} - \pi_s^U) Y_{Is}^j \bigg/ \sum_s \omega_s Y_{Is}^j$$

$$= \sum_s (\pi_s^{Ij} - \pi_s^U)(Y_{Is}^j - Y_{Us}^j) \bigg/ \sum_s \omega_s Y_{Is}^j$$

$$+ \sum_s (\pi_s^{Ij} - \pi_s^U) Y_{Us}^j \bigg/ \sum_s \omega_s Y_{Is}^j. \tag{A.5}$$

We want to determine the sign of the right-hand side. From CAPM theory, because $U$'s expectations are equal to those of the market, $U$'s portfolio must be a linear combination of the risk-free rate of return and the market portfolio, i.e., there exist $\alpha_1$ and $\alpha_2$ such that $Y^j_{Us} = \alpha^j_1 + \alpha^j_2 X_s$, ($\forall s$), where $X_s = \sum_r X_{rs}$ is the total consumption available in state $s$.

Hence,

$$\sum_s (\pi^{Ij}_s - \pi^U_s) Y^j_{Us} = \sum_s (\pi^{Ij}_s - \pi^U_s)(\alpha^j_1 + \alpha^j_2 X_s)$$

$$= \alpha^j_1 \sum_s (\pi^{Ij}_s - \pi^U_s) + \alpha^j_2 \sum_s (\pi^{Ij}_s - \pi^U_s) X_s.$$

Since $\sum_s \pi^{Ij}_s = 1 = \sum_s \pi^U_s$,

$$\sum_s (\pi^{Ij}_s - \pi^U_s) Y^j_{Us} = \alpha^j_2 \sum_s \pi^{Ij}_s X_s - \alpha^j_2 \sum_s \pi^U_s X_s$$

$$= \alpha^j_2 \left( \sum_s \omega_s X_s \right)(E^{Ij}(R_M) + 1) - \alpha^j_2 \left( \sum_s \omega_s X_s \right)(E^U(R_M) + 1)$$

$$= 0,$$

since $E^{Ij}(R_M) = E^U(R_M)$ which we assumed.

Hence, from eq. (A.5),

$$E^{Ij}(R_I) - (R_F + [E^U(R_M) - R_F]\beta^U_{Ij}) = \sum_s \frac{(\pi^{Ij}_s - \pi^U_s)(Y^j_{Is} - Y^j_{Us})}{\sum_s \omega_s Y^j_{Is}} \qquad \text{(A.6)}$$

But, by condition (A.2) if $\pi^{Ij}_s \neq \pi^U_s$ for some $s$, the right-hand side of (A.6) is greater than zero. Hence,

$$E^{Ij}(R_I) - (R_F + [E^U(R_M) - R_F]\beta^U_{Ij}) > 0,$$

which establishes condition (1).

*Demonstration of condition (2) with general information.* Our assumptions are that the informed individual's consumption and wealth are constant across messages. Formally these assumptions imply

$$C^j_I = C^*_I,$$

and

$$\sum_s \omega_s Y^j_{Is} = K = W - C^*_I.$$

Condition (2) is established by showing that

$$E^I(R_I) = \sum_{j=1}^{L} q_j E^{Ij}(R_I)$$

$$> R_F + [E^U(R_M) - R_F] \sum_{j=1}^{L} q_j \beta_{Ij}^U. \qquad (2)$$

The right-hand side of eq. (A.5) above indicates this will be established if

$$\sum_{j=1}^{L} q_j \left( \sum_s (\pi_s^{Ij} - \pi_s^U) Y_{Us}^j \Big/ \sum_s \omega_s Y_{Is}^j \right) \geq 0,$$

since the first term on the right-hand side of eq. (A.5) will be positive when weighted and summed over $q_j$ by condition (A.2). By assumption $\sum_s \omega_s Y_{Is}^j = k$ and $Y_{Us}^j$ is constant across $j$. Consequently, the numerator of (A.7) is important,

$$\sum_j q_j \sum_s (\pi_s^{Ij} - \pi^U) Y_{Us}^j = \sum_j q_j \sum_s (\pi_s^{Ij} - \pi_s^U)(\alpha_1 + \alpha_2 X_s).$$

$\alpha_1$ disappears as before and

$$\sum_j q_j \sum_s (\pi_s^{Ij} - \pi_s^U) Y_{Us}^j = \alpha_2 \sum_s \omega_s X_s \left[ \sum_j q_j E^{Ij}(R_M) - E^U(R_M) \right].$$

Now, $\sum_j q_j E^{Ij}(R_M) = E^U(R_M)$ i.e., the unconditional probabilities of $I$ and $U$ are the same. Thus, condition (2) for this case is established.

### References

Black, F., M.C. Jensen and M. Scholes, 1972, The capital asset pricing model: Some empirical tests, in: M.C. Jensen, ed., Studies in the theory of capital markets (Praeger, New York).

Black, F., 1972, Capital market equilibrium with restricted borrowing, Journal of Business 45, 444–454.

Blume, M.E. and I. Friend, 1973, A new look at the capital asset pricing model, Journal of Finance 28, 551–566.

Fama, E.F., 1976, Foundations of finance (Basic Books, New York).

Fama, E.F. and J.D. MacBeth, 1973, Risk, return and equilibrium: Empirical tests, Journal of Political Economy 71, 607–636.

Fisher, L. and J.H. Lorie, 1970, Some studies of variability of returns on investments in common stocks, Journal of Business 43, 99–134.

Hirshleifer, J., 1975, Speculation and equilibrium: Information, risk, and markets, Quarterly Journal of Economics 89, 519–542.

Jaffe, J.F., 1974, Special information and insider trading, Journal of Business 47, 410–428.

Jensen, M.C., 1968, The performance of mutual funds in the period 1945–1964, Journal of Finance 23, 389–416.

Jensen, M.C., 1969, Risk, the pricing of capital assets, and the evaluation of investment portfolios, Journal of Business 42, 167–247.

Jensen, M.C., 1972, Optimal utilization of market forecasts and the evaluation of investment performance, in: G.P. Szegö and K. Shell. eds.. Mathematical methods in investment and finance (North-Holland, Amsterdam).

Lintner, J., 1965, The valuation of risk assets and the selection of risky investments in stock portfolios and capital budgets, Review of Economics and Statistics 47, 13–37.

Mandelker, G., 1974, Risk and return: The case of merging firms, Journal of Financial Economics 1, 303–335.

Mossin, J., 1966, Equilibrium in a capital asset market, Econometrica 34, 768–783.

Roll, R., 1973, Evidence on the 'growth-optimum' model, Journal of Finance 28, 551–566.

Roll, R., 1977, A critique of the asset pricing theory's tests; Part I: On past and potential testability of the theory, Journal of Financial Economics 4, 129–176.

Roll, R., 1978, Ambiguity when performance is measured by the securities market line, Journal of Finance 33, 1051–1069.

Sharpe, W.F., 1964, Capital asset prices: A theory of market equilibrium under conditions of risk, Journal of Finance 19, 425–442.

Stigler, G.J., 1966, The theory of price, 3rd ed. (Macmillan, New York).

Verrecchia, R.E., 1978, A proof of the existence of 'consensus beliefs', University of Illinois working paper.

**Roy D. Henriksson**

*University of California, Berkeley*

# Market Timing and Mutual Fund Performance: An Empirical Investigation

## I. Introduction

The evaluation of investment performance is of importance for allocating investment funds efficiently and setting appropriate management fees. Because actively managed mutual funds are an important form of investment in the United States, a valid question is whether the active management has achieved a sufficient increase in returns to offset the associated costs of information and transactions, as well as the management fees charged. As a corollary, the ability to earn superior returns based on superior forecasting ability would be a violation of the efficient markets hypothesis[1] and would have far-reaching implications for the theory of finance.[2]

Henriksson and Merton (1981) present statistical techniques for testing forecasting ability with a particular emphasis on the market-timing ability of investment managers. The tests are derived from the basic model of market timing developed by Merton (1981), where the forecaster predicts when stocks will outperform riskless securities and when riskless securities will outperform stocks but does not predict the magnitude of the relative returns.

The evaluation of the performance of investment managers is a topic of considerable interest to practitioners and academics alike. Using both the parametric and nonparametric tests for the evaluation of forecasting ability presented by Henriksson and Merton, the market-timing ability of 116 open-end mutual funds is evaluated for the period 1968–80. The empirical results do not support the hypothesis that mutual fund managers are able to follow an investment strategy that successfully times the return on the market portfolio.

1. For an excellent discussion of the theory of market efficiency, see Fama (1970).

2. For a description of some of the previous work on the evaluation of investment performance, see Henriksson and Merton (1981).

(*Journal of Business*, 1984, vol. 57, no. 1, pt. 1)

Henriksson and Merton present both parametric and nonparametric tests of market-timing ability. The parametric tests require the assumption of either the capital asset pricing model (CAPM)[3] or a multifactor return structure. Based strictly on observable returns, the tests permit the identification of the separate contributions from market-timing ability and micro forecasting. The nonparametric tests do not require any specific structure of returns but do require knowledge of the actual forecasts or a good proxy for them.

This paper evaluates the market-timing performance of 116 open-end mutual funds using the parametric and nonparametric techniques presented by Henriksson and Merton (1981). In Section II, the statistical techniques developed by Henriksson and Merton are presented. The results of the parametric tests are presented in Section III and the results of the nonparametric tests, based on proxies for the forecasts, are presented in Section IV. In both cases, no evidence of market-timing ability is found.

## II. Techniques for Testing Market-timing Ability

Merton (1981) developed a framework for evaluating market-timing ability that does not require knowledge of the distribution of returns on the market or any particular model of security valuation. It takes the simple form that the investment manager forecasts either that the stock market will provide a greater return than riskless securities—that is, $Z_M(t) > R(t)$—or that riskless securities will provide a greater return than stocks—that is, $R(t) > Z_M(t)$, where $Z_M(t)$ is the one-period return per dollar on the market portfolio and $R(t)$ is the one-period return per dollar on riskless securities. The forecaster does not attempt, or is not able, to predict by how much stocks will perform better or worse than riskless securities. Based on his forecast, the investment manager will adjust the relative proportions of the market portfolio and riskless securities that are held in the fund.

The model can be formally described in terms of the probabilities of a correct forecast, conditional on $Z_M(t) - R(t)$. Let $\gamma(t)$ be the manager's forecast variable where $\gamma(t) = 1$ if the forecast, made at time $t - 1$ for the period $t$, is that $Z_M(t) > R(t)$ and $\gamma(t) = 0$ if the forecast is that $Z_M(t) \leq R(t)$. The probabilities for $\gamma(t)$ conditional on the realized return on the market are

$$p_1(t) = \text{prob}[\gamma(t) = 0 \quad Z_M(t) \leq R(t)]$$
$$1 - p_1(t) = \text{prob}[\gamma(t) = 1 \quad Z_M(t) \leq R(t)]$$

(1a)

---

3. Jensen (1972a) provides a comprehensive review of the CAPM.

and

$$p_2(t) = \text{prob}[\gamma(t) = 1 \quad Z_M(t) > R(t)]$$
$$1 - p_2(t) = \text{prob}[\gamma(t) = 0 \quad Z_M(t) > R(t)]. \tag{1b}$$

Therefore, $p_1(t)$ is the conditional probability of a correct forecast, given that $Z_M(t) \leq R(t)$, and $p_2(t)$ is the conditional probability of a correct forecast, given that $Z_M(t) > R(t)$. Neither $p_1(t)$ nor $p_2(t)$ depends on the level or distribution of the return of the market. The probability of a correct forecast depends only on whether or not $Z_M(t) > R(t)$.

Merton showed that a necessary and sufficient condition for a forecaster's predictions to have no value is that $p_1(t) + p_2(t) = 1$. Under this condition, knowledge of the forecast would not cause an investor to change his prior estimate of the distribution of returns on the market portfolio and, therefore, would not pay anything for the information. The existence of forecasting ability will result in $p_1(t) + p_2(t) > 1$.[4]

## A.   A Nonparametric Test of Market Timing

Henriksson and Merton's (1981) nonparametric tests take advantage of the fact that the conditional probabilities of a correct forecast can be used to measure forecasting ability and yet they do not depend on the distribution of returns on the market or any particular model for security valuation. The tests examine the null hypothesis that the market timer has no forecasting ability; that is, $H_0 : p_1(t) + p_2(t) = 1$, where the conditional probabilities of a correct forecast, $p_1(t)$ and $p_2(t)$, are not known. We want to determine the probability, $P$, that a given outcome from our sample came from a population that satisfies our null hypothesis.

Henriksson and Merton show that the null hypothesis is defined by the hypergeometric distribution:

$$P(n_1 | N_1, N, n) = \frac{\dbinom{N_1}{n_1} \dbinom{N_2}{n - n_1}}{\dbinom{N}{n}}, \tag{2}$$

---

4. For a more thorough presentation of this framework for evaluation, see Merton (1981) and Henriksson and Merton (1981). These papers also discuss the potential problems of using the unconditional probability of a correct forecast to evaluate forecasting ability. The use of the unconditional probability of a correct forecast requires additional information regarding the frequency distribution of the returns, whereas this information is not required to evaluate forecasting ability based on the conditional probabilities of a correct forecast.

where $n_1 \equiv$ number of correct forecasts, given $Z_M \leq R$; $n \equiv$ number of times forecast that $Z_M \leq R$; $N_1 \equiv$ number of observations where $Z_M \leq R$; $N_2 \equiv$ number of observations where $Z_M > R$; and $N \equiv N_1 + N_2 =$ total number of observations. The distribution is independent of both $p_1$ and $p_2$; thus, to test the null hypothesis it is unnecessary to estimate either of the conditional probabilities. So, provided that the forecasts are known, all the variables necessary for the test are directly observable. Given $N_1$, $N_2$, and $n$ the distribution of $n_1$ is determined by (2) for the null hypothesis, where the feasible range for $n_1$ is given by

$$n_1 \equiv \max(0, n - N_2) \leq n_1 \leq \min(N_1, n) \equiv \bar{n}_1. \qquad (3)$$

Equations (2) and (3) can be used to establish confidence intervals for testing the hypothesis of no market-timing ability. For a standard two-tail test[5] with a confidence level of $c$, one could reject the null hypothesis if $n_1 \geq \bar{x}(c)$ or if $n_1 \leq \underline{x}(c)$ where $\bar{x}$ and $\underline{x}$ are determined from the solutions of[6]

$$\sum_{n_1 = \bar{x}}^{\bar{n}_1} \binom{N_1}{n_1} \binom{N_2}{n - n_1} \bigg/ \binom{N}{n} = \frac{(1 - c)}{2} \qquad (4a)$$

$$\sum_{n_1 = n_1}^{\underline{x}} \binom{N_1}{n_1} \binom{N_2}{n - n_1} \bigg/ \binom{N}{n} = \frac{(1 - c)}{2}. \qquad (4b)$$

## B. A Parametric Test of Market Timing

To use the nonparametric tests to evaluate forecasting ability, the predictions of the forecaster must be obtainable. However, such information is rarely available for mutual funds. Thus it is necessary either to use a proxy for the forecasts or to make additional assumptions with respect to the generating process of security returns. Henriksson and Merton present a parametric test of market-timing ability requiring only observable returns data based on the additional assumption that securities are priced according to the CAPM, although the tests are easily adaptable to a multifactor framework.

In pathfinding papers, Jensen (1968, 1969) used a CAPM framework to evaluate the performance of open-end mutual funds over the period

---

5. If the forecasts are known, Henriksson and Merton argue that if forecasters behave rationally, then a one-tail test is more appropriate, as it should never be the case that $p_1(t) + p_2(t) < 1$. In this paper, however, the forecasts are not known. As the proxy that is used will be affected by management fees and transaction costs, it is possible that $p_1(t) + p_2(t) < 1$. Therefore, a two-tail test is more appropriate.

6. Because the hypergeometric distribution is discrete, the strict equalities of (4a) and (4b) will not usually be obtainable. Therefore, in (4a), $\bar{x}$ should be interpreted as the lowest value of $x$ for which the summation does not exceed $(1 - c)/2$. In (4b), $\underline{x}$ should be interpreted as the highest value of $x$ for which the summation does not exceed $(1 - c)/2$.

1945–64. He found no evidence that mutual funds were able to generate superior returns. However, Jensen did not allow for the possibility that the mutual funds were undertaking market-timing strategies.

Henriksson and Merton allow for the possibility of market-timing ability. They assume that the investment manager chooses among discretely different systematic risk levels for the fund, dependent on his forecast. In our analysis we assume that the fund has two target risk levels, one for when the forecaster predicts $Z_M > R$ and one for when he predicts $Z_M \leqq R$. The technique can be extended to multiple target risk levels, and this possibility will be discussed in Section III.

The per period return on the investment manager's fund is assumed to be of the form

$$Z_P(t) = R(t) + [b + \theta(t)]x(t) + \lambda + \epsilon_p(t) \qquad (5)$$

where $b$ is the unconditional (on the forecast) expected value of $\beta(t)$; $\theta(t)$ is the unanticipated (dependent on the forecast) component of $\beta(t)$; $x(t) \equiv Z_M(t) - R(t)$; $\lambda$ is the expected excess return from microforecasting; and $\epsilon_p(t)$ has the following characteristics:

$$E[\epsilon_p(t)] = 0$$

$$E[\epsilon_p(t)|x(t)] = 0 \qquad (6)$$

$$E[\epsilon_p(t)|\epsilon_p(t - i)] = 0 \quad i = 1, 2, 3, \ldots ,$$

In this form, $\eta_1(t) = b + \theta(t)$ is the target level of systematic risk when the forecaster predicts $Z_M(t) \leqq R(t)$ and $\eta_2(t) = b + \theta(t)$ is the target level of systematic risk corresponding to a forecast of $Z_M(t) > R(t)$.

Using the returns process described in (5), least squares regression analysis can be used to estimate the separate contributions from security analysis and market timing. This regression specification is of the form

$$Z_p(t) - R(t) = \alpha_p + \beta_1 x(t) + \beta_2 y(t) + \epsilon(t) \qquad (7)$$

where $y(t) \equiv \max[0, R(t) - Z_M(t)] = \max[0, -x(t)]$.

This specification comes from the analysis of the value of market-timing ability in Merton (1981). He showed that up to an additive noise term, the returns per dollar from a portfolio involved in market timing as described here are identical to those of a partial "protective put" option investment strategy,[7] where for each dollar of investment, $[p_n\eta_2 + (1 - p_2)\eta_1]$ dollars are invested in the market portfolio; $(p_1 + p_2 - 1)(\eta_2 - \eta_1)$ put options on the market portfolio are purchased with an exercise price (per dollar of the market portfolio) of $R(t)$; and the balance is invested in riskless securities. The value of the market tim-

---

7. For a description of the "protective put" option investment strategy, see Merton, Scholes, and Gladstein (1982).

ing is reflected in the fact that the put options are obtained for free. The variable $y(t)$ in (7) represents the return on one such option.

Henriksson and Merton show that the large sample least squares estimates of $\beta_1$, $\beta_2$, and $\alpha_p$ can be written as

$$\text{plim } \hat{\beta}_1 = p_2\eta_2 + (1 - p_2)\eta_1 \tag{8}$$

$$\text{plim } \hat{\beta}_2 = (p_1 + p_2 - 1)(\eta_2 - \eta_1) \tag{9}$$

$$\text{plim } \hat{\alpha}_p = \lambda. \tag{10}$$

From (8), plim $\hat{\beta}_1 = E[\beta(t)|x(t) > 0]$. The market-timing ability of the forecaster is measured by $\beta_2$, which will equal zero if either the forecaster has no ability ($p_1(t) + p_2(t) = 1$) or does not act on his forecast ($\eta_1 = \eta_2$).

In addition, (7) has the characteristic that

$$\lim_{N \to \infty} \left[ \frac{\Sigma \epsilon_p(t)}{N} \right] = 0. \tag{11}$$

Thus, the coefficients from least squares estimation of (7) provide consistent estimates of the parameters of portfolio performance. However, ordinary least squares estimation is inefficient because $\beta(t)$ is not stationary. As Henriksson and Merton show, this causes the standard deviation of $\epsilon_p$ to be an increasing function of $|x(t)|$. Thus, it is necessary to correct for heteroscedasticity to improve the efficiency of the estimates.

While this parametric procedure separates the contributions of micro forecasting and macro forecasting, the analysis is dependent on the specified return-generating process. Empirical tests of the CAPM by Black, Jensen, and Scholes (1972), Blume and Friend (1973), and Fama and MacBeth (1973) seem to show that the security market line (SML) relationship

$$Z_i(t) = R(t) + \beta_i x(t) + \epsilon \tag{12}$$

does not hold for individual securities. In particular, they found evidence of a "zero-beta" effect, where the return on low-beta securities tended to be greater than predicted by (12) and the return on high-beta securities tended to be lower than predicted by (12). If this deviation from the model is the result of a second factor that is uncorrelated with the return on the market portfolio, it will affect the estimates of $\alpha_p$ in (7) but will not affect the estimates of $\beta_2$. As the primary focus of this study is on market-timing ability, the existence of a zero-beta factor should not affect the results. While not done here, Henriksson and Merton's methodology can easily be adapted to take this second factor into account.

However, Roll (1977) has questioned the validity of the tests of the CAPM mentioned above because they are not based on the true market portfolio. He shows how misspecification of the market portfolio can cause these results. However, Stambaugh (1982) shows that the empirical results of the tests of the CAPM do not seem to be very sensitive to the composition of the "market" portfolio.

In addition, Roll (1977, 1978) attacks the use of the SML for portfolio evaluation. Roll argues that if the market portfolio is ex post mean-variance efficient, then all securities will lie exactly on the SML, as well as any portfolio where the securities are held for the entire sample period. Mayers and Rice (1979), however, show that this will not be the case if the investment manager is allowed to change the composition of his fund.

Roll also questions the meaning of the estimates of $\alpha_p$ when the true market portfolio is not known. This issue is not addressed here, as the focus of this paper is on the market-timing ability of mutual funds, and the measures of forecasting ability used are not dependent on $\alpha_p$. As long as the portfolio used as a proxy for the true market portfolio is highly correlated with the true market portfolio,[8] then $\hat{\beta}_2$ will be a reasonable measure of timing ability with respect to the true market.[9] Intuitively, this is because small errors in the proxy for the realized return on the market portfolio will usually not change the correctness of a forecast as the forecaster is assumed to predict only direction and not magnitude.

In addition, investment managers may not be attempting to forecast the returns on the true market portfolio. Instead, they may attempt timing with respect to the universe of securities that they tend to invest

---

8. The correlation will almost certainly be high, as the stocks of companies traded on the NYSE must account for a substantial portion of the total market, considering the magnitude of the dollar value of the stocks.

9. By combining the riskless asset with the true market portfolio, it is possible to form a portfolio that is perfectly correlated with the market portfolio and has the same expected return as the market proxy. The excess return on the market proxy will be $bx(t) + \epsilon(t)$ where $x(t)$ is the excess return on the true market portfolio, $b$ is the proportion of the new portfolio that is made up of the market portfolio, and $\epsilon(t)$ is a variable with the characteristics that $E[\epsilon(t)] = 0$, $E[\epsilon(t)|x(t)] = 0$, and $E[\epsilon(t)^2] = \sigma^2$. As modeled, the correlation between the true market portfolio and the market proxy will be a decreasing function of $\sigma$. To consider the effect of misspecification, we will examine the large sample least squares estimate of $\beta_2$ which can be written as

$$\text{plim } \hat{\beta}_2 = (\rho_{py} - \rho_{px}\rho_{xy})\sigma_p/(1 - \rho_{xy}^2)\sigma_y. \tag{F1}$$

If our investment manager is only interested in forecasting with respect to the market portfolio, then the difference in the expected estimate of $\beta_2$ because a proxy is used instead of the true market portfolio will only be a function of $\sigma^2$ as the variables in (F1) will differ only by a function of $\sigma^2$. If $\sigma^2$ is small (relative to $\sigma_x^2$), then the estimation error will be small. If the investment manager also attempts to forecast with respect to $\epsilon(t)$, then $\beta_2$, as estimated, will be a combined measure of forecasting ability with respect to both $x(t)$ and $\epsilon(t)$. Of course, if it were possible to determine the values of $\epsilon(t)$, then it could be treated as a second factor and evaluated separately. In either case, if the manager is attempting to forecast $\epsilon(t)$, then this forecasting should be taken into account in the evaluation.

in. Inspection of the holdings of the mutual funds in the sample show that in most cases, this is a trade-off between equities and high-grade fixed income securities. Predominately, the equities were those traded on the New York Stock Exchange (NYSE): thus the NYSE Composite seems to be a reasonable proxy for the market portfolio. Precisely. in this paper timing is tested with respect to a portfolio replicating the securities traded on the NYSE.

## III. Empirical Results: Parametric Tests

As it was not possible to obtain the actual market-timing forecasts of the mutual fund managers, it was necessary either to use a proxy for the forecast or to assume a specific return-generating process. In this section, the parametric tests described in Section II are run on the assumption that the CAPM holds.

Both the parametric and nonparametric tests examined the performance of 116 open-end mutual funds using monthly data from February 1968 to June 1980. The returns data include all dividends paid by the fund and are net of all management costs and fees. The returns data were obtained from Standard & Poor's *Over-the-Counter Daily Stock Price Record* and Wiesenberger Investment Companies Service (1975, 1980). A list of the funds in the sample, including the objective of the individual funds, is presented in the Appendix.

Monthly returns (including dividends on the NYSE Index) are used for the returns on the market portfolio. This index is a value-weighted portfolio of all stocks traded on the NYSE. The returns on Treasury bills are used for the riskless asset and are obtained from Ibbotson and Sinquefield (1979).[10] The Treasury-bill return used is the 1-month holding period return on the shortest maturity bill with at least a 30-day maturity.

Using the returns process described in (5), weighted least squares regression analysis, with a correction for heteroscedasticity, is used to obtain the separate contributions from micro forecasting and market timing. The regression specification is as shown in (7)

$$Z_p(t) - R(t) = \alpha_p + \beta_1 x(t) + \beta_2 y(t) + \epsilon(t). \tag{7}$$

The correction for heteroscedasticity in the parametric tests is of the following form. Least squares estimation is run for each fund using the regression specification found in (7). Then the absolute value of the residuals from this estimation, $|\epsilon(t)|$, are used as the dependent variable in the regression of

$$|\epsilon_i(t)| = \phi_i + \Omega_{1i} x_1(t) + \Omega_{2i} x_2(t) + \xi_i. \tag{13}$$

---

10. Treasury bill returns for 1979 and 1980 were calculated using data from the *Wall Street Journal*.

**TABLE 1**  Parametric Tests: $Z_p(t) - R(t) = \hat{\alpha}_p + \hat{\beta}_1 x(t) + \hat{\beta}_2 y(t)$; 116 Open-End Mutual Funds, Sample Split by Time

| Sample | 1968:2–1980:6 | 1968:2–1974:4 | 1974:5–1980:6 |
|---|---|---|---|
| Mean (SD): | | | |
| $\hat{\alpha}$ $(\sigma_\alpha)$ | .0007 (.0041) | −.0010 (.0053) | .0022 (.0057) |
| $\hat{\beta}_1(\sigma_{\beta_1})$ | .92 (.21) | 1.01 (.27) | .86 (.20) |
| $\hat{\beta}_2(\sigma_{\beta_2})$ | −.07 (.15) | −.02 (.21) | −.08 (.18) |
| Number of funds: | | | |
| Reject $\hat{\alpha} = 0$ at 5%* | 11+ 8− | 6+ 13− | 21+ 5− |
| Reject $\hat{\alpha} = 0$ at 1% | 6+ 4− | 4+ 4− | 10+ 1− |
| Reject $\hat{\beta}_2 = 0$ at 5% | 3+ 9− | 1+ 4− | 2+ 3− |
| Reject $\hat{\beta}_2 = 0$ at 1% | 1+ 1− | 0+ 1− | 1+ 1− |
| $\hat{\alpha} > 0$ | 59 | 32 | 67 |
| $\hat{\beta}_2 > 0$ | 44 | 64 | 46 |

NOTE.—Only one fund had a significantly positive $\hat{\alpha}$ in both periods. Only one fund had a significantly positive $\hat{\beta}_2$ in both periods. No funds had significantly negative $\hat{\alpha}$ or $\hat{\beta}_2$ in both periods. $F$-test: number of funds that reject hypothesis that coefficients are equal in both periods are 45 at 5%, 26 at 1%.

\* + Denotes number of funds with significantly positive estimates.

− Denotes number of funds with significantly negative estimates.

where $x_1 \equiv \min[0, x(t)]$ and $x_2 \equiv \max[0, x(t)]$, to estimate the degree of heteroscedasticity with respect to the realized excess return on the market. The variables in (7), including the constant, are then divided by $[\hat{\phi}_i + \hat{\Omega}_{1i}x_1(t) + \hat{\Omega}_{2i}x_2(t)]$ and the coefficients for $\alpha_p$, $\beta_1$, and $\beta_2$ are reestimated.[11]

The tests are run for the entire period, February 1968–June 1980, as well as for the subperiods February 1968–April 1974 and May 1974–June 1980. The results are summarized in table 1.[12]

The results show little evidence of market-timing ability. In fact, 62% of the funds had negative estimates of market timing, as shown by $\hat{\beta}_2$. Using the assumption that the returns from the mutual funds and the market portfolio follow a joint-normal distribution, only three of the funds exhibited positive estimates for $\beta_2$ with 95% confidence.[13]

11. The specification of the heteroscedasticity correction directly follows from the specification of each period's estimation error, as shown in (26) in Henriksson and Merton (1981). While it would be technically more correct to run a number of iterations of the correction described above, there was virtually no change in the results when this was done for a number of the funds. In fact, there was little difference in the results from using ordinary least squares, without the heteroscedasticity correction, and the results from using the weighted least squares estimation described above.

12. The results for the individual funds for all of the tests run are available from the author on request.

13. The confidence interval mentioned is that which would be used to evaluate each fund in isolation. It does not take into account the fact that there are 116 funds in my sample, which are certainly not independent of one another. To test for the market-timing ability for the sample as a whole, the "seemingly unrelated regression model" of Zellner (1962) can be used to test the significance of the timing variable with respect to the entire sample. However, since the explanatory variables are the same for all of the individual funds in the sample, the point estimates of the individual coefficients will not change. It is therefore virtually certain that the results from this technique would not show significantly positive market-timing ability.

TABLE 2   Parametric Tests: $Z_p(t) - R(t) = \hat{\alpha}_p + \hat{\beta}_1 x(t)$; Results Assuming No
Market-timing Activity

| Sample | 1968:2–1980:6 | 1968:2–1974:4 | 1974:5–1980:6 |
|---|---|---|---|
| Mean (SD): | | | |
| $\hat{\alpha}$ $(\sigma_\alpha)$ | $-.0002$ (.0027) | $-.0013$ (.0036) | .0011 (.0038) |
| $\hat{\beta}_1 (\sigma_{B_1})$ | .96  (.23) | 1.02  (.25) | .90  (.21) |
| Number of funds: | | | |
| Reject $\hat{\alpha} = 0$ at 5% | 5+ 13− | 4+ 18− | 20+ 6− |
| Reject $\hat{\alpha} = 0$ at 1% | 2+ 8− | 1+ 12− | 7+ 2− |
| $\hat{\alpha} > 0$ | 52 | 38 | 68 |

NOTE.—Only one fund had a significantly positive $\hat{\alpha}$ in both periods. Only two funds had a
significantly negative $\hat{\alpha}$ in both periods. $F$-test: number of funds that reject hypothesis that
coefficients are equal in both periods: 50 at 5%; 33 at 1%.

And only one of the three exhibited significantly positive estimates of
$\beta_2$ in both subperiods.

While there were many more significantly positive estimates of $\alpha$ for
the overall period and the two subperiods, again only one of the funds
exhibited significantly positive estimates in both periods. None of the
funds had significantly negative estimates of $\alpha$ or $\beta_2$ in both periods.

For the funds in the sample, the correlation between the estimate of
$\alpha$ in the first period and the second period was .15. For $\hat{\beta}_2$, the correlation between the two periods was .34. In fact, using a $2 \times 2$ test of
independence, it is not possible to reject the hypothesis that the estimates of $\alpha$ for each fund are independent for the two periods or the
hypothesis that the estimates of $\beta_2$ for each fund are independent for
the two periods.

Further evidence of the instability of the parameters can be found in
the results of tests of the hypothesis that the coefficients in (7) are equal
in both subperiods. Using an $F$-test,[14] 45 of the funds reject the hypothesis with 95% probability and 26 reject with 99% probability.

These results are similar to those from the regression specification
used by Jensen (1968, 1969):

$$Z_p(t) - R(t) = \alpha_p + \beta_p[Z_M(t) - R(t)] + \epsilon_p(t), \qquad (14)$$

where possible market-timing activity is ignored. This is as would be
expected, since there does not appear to be any evidence of market-
timing ability.

The results from regressions using the specification in (14) are summarized in table 2. Estimates of $\alpha$ tend to be slightly lower when
market-timing activity is ignored, reflecting the fact that the coefficient
for the omitted variable, $\hat{\beta}_2$, was on average slightly negative for the
sample when the regression specification as shown in (7) was used.

14. For a description of the $F$-test run, see Fisher (1970).

**TABLE 3**    **Parametric Tests: $Z_p(t) - R(t) = \hat{\alpha}_p + \hat{\beta}_1 x(t) + \hat{\beta}_2 y(t)$; without Heteroscedasticity Correction**

| Sample | 1968:2–1980:6 | 1968:2–1974:4 | 1974:5–1980:6 |
|---|---|---|---|
| Mean (SD): | | | |
| $\hat{\alpha}\ (\sigma_\alpha)$ | .0008 (.0044) | −.0010 (.0054) | .0023 (.0062) |
| $\hat{\beta}_1(\sigma_{\beta_1})$ | .90    (.19) | 1.00    (.25) | .85    (.19) |
| $\hat{\beta}_2(\sigma_{\beta_2})$ | −.07    (.18) | −.02    (.23) | −.08    (.21) |
| Number of funds: | | | |
| Reject $\hat{\alpha} = 0$ at 5% | 8+  5− | 5+ 10− | 18+  6− |
| Reject $\hat{\alpha} = 0$ at 1% | 5+  2− | 2+  2− | 8+  2− |
| Reject $\hat{\beta}_2 = 0$ at 5% | 3+ 13− | 3+  6− | 3+ 13− |
| Reject $\hat{\beta}_2 = 0$ at 1% | 1+  8− | 0+  1− | 1+  7− |
| $\hat{\alpha} > 0$ | 55 | 31 | 65 |
| $\hat{\beta}_2 > 0$ | 47 | 64 | 54 |

NOTE.—Only one fund had a significantly positive $\hat{\alpha}$ in both periods. Only one fund had a significantly negative $\hat{\alpha}$ in both periods. Only one fund had a significantly positive $\hat{\beta}_2$ in both periods. Only two funds had significantly negative $\hat{\beta}_2 s$ in both periods.

When market-timing activity is ignored, only one fund exhibited significantly positive estimates of $\alpha$ in both subperiods. This was the same fund that had significantly positive estimates of $\alpha$ in both subperiods when market-timing activity was taken into account. In addition, two funds had significantly negative estimates of $\alpha$ in both subperiods.

Tests of the hypothesis that the coefficients in (14) are equal in both subperiods again provides evidence that the parameters are not stationary. When an *F*-test is used, 50 of the funds reject the hypothesis with 95% probability and 33 reject with 99% probability.

The results for regressions as specified in (7), but without the heteroscedasticity correction, are summarized in table 3. As can be seen, the results are not qualitatively different than those with the correction, as shown in table 1. The major difference is that when heteroscedasticity is not taken into account, a greater number of "significant" negative estimates of $\beta_2$ were found and fewer "significant" estimates of $\alpha$ were found.

While the possible existence of heteroscedasticity did not seem to have much effect on the results, strong evidence was found that it indeed does exist. Examining the regressions run using (13) in the correction for heteroscedasticity shows that 73 funds had significantly negative estimates of $\Omega_1$ and 57 funds had significantly positive estimates of $\Omega_2$ at the 95% probability level. Of these, 55 of the negative estimates of $\Omega_1$ were significant with 99% probability, as were 45 of the positive estimates of $\Omega_2$.

As the values of $x_1(t)$ will always be either zero or negative and the values of $x_2(t)$ will always be either zero or positive, these results imply that the absolute size of the residuals is increasing with the absolute

**TABLE 4**  **Parametric Tests:** $Z_p(t) - R(t) = \hat{\alpha}_p + \hat{\beta}_1 x(t)\ \hat{\beta}_2 y(t)$; **Sample Split by Magnitude of** $|x(t)|$, **1968:2–1980:6**

| Sample | Small Magnitudes | Large Magnitudes |
|---|---|---|
| Mean (SD) | | |
| $\hat{\alpha}\ (\sigma_\alpha)$ | .0017 (.0057) | .0034 (.0075) |
| $\hat{\beta}_1(\sigma_{\beta_1})$ | .91  (.45) | .87  (.20) |
| $\hat{\beta}_2(\sigma_{\beta_2})$ | −.23  (.54) | −.14  (.26) |
| Number of funds: | | |
| Reject $\hat{\alpha} = 0$ at 5% | 9+ 5− | 4+ 2− |
| Reject $\hat{\alpha} = 0$ at 1% | 3+ 2− | 1+ 1− |
| Reject $\hat{\beta}_2 = 0$ at 5% | 2+ 8− | 3+ 2− |
| Reject $\hat{\beta}_2 = 0$ at 1% | 0+ 2− | 1+ 1− |
| $\hat{\alpha} > 0$ | 73 | 78 |
| $\hat{\beta}_2 > 0$ | 35 | 39 |

NOTE.—Two funds had significantly positive $\hat{\alpha}$'s for both groups. $F$-Test: number of funds that reject hypothesis that coefficients are equal for both groups are 10 at 5%; one at 1%.

magnitude of the market return. Henriksson and Merton show that these results can be caused by imperfect market-timing activity.

The tests of market-timing ability depend on the assumption that the conditional probabilities of correct forecasts are uniform over the entire range of outcomes where $Z_M > R$ and $Z_M \leqq R$. This assumption will be violated if the forecaster is able to predict periods of extreme market movement better than other periods. To test for this, the sample data was split in half by the magnitude of the excess market return, $|x(t)|$. Periods where the absolute value of $x(t)$ are greater than the sample median are split from those below the median. For the sample period, the median value of $|x(t)|$ is 3.1% per month.

A summary of the results for the 116 funds, with the sample split by the magnitude of $|x(t)|$, is shown in table 4. Only two of the funds (including the only fund when the sample was split by time) had significantly positive estimates of $\alpha$ in both samples. None of the funds had significantly positive estimates of $\beta_2$ in both samples or significantly negative estimates of $\alpha$ or $\beta_2$ in both samples.

The evidence does not support the hypothesis that investment managers are able to forecast large changes in the market or that it is necessary to model more than two levels of systematic risk. While three funds (out of 116) had significantly positive estimates of market-timing ability in the sample of large magnitude returns, all three had large negative (significant in two of the cases) estimates of $\alpha$ that more than offset the gains from market timing.

Ten of the funds did reject (at the 5% level) the hypothesis that the coefficients are equal for both the high-magnitude and low-magnitude samples. Those 10, however, did not exhibit any market-timing ability. In fact, the 10 appeared to do quite poorly with regard to market timing. By segmenting the sample by magnitude, estimates of the level of systematic risk are obtained for four different ranges of market returns. It is possible to compare the ranking of the level of systematic risk (from low to high) for each range of returns with the ranking of the market return for each range. For the 10 funds that reject the hypothesis that the coefficients are equal for both high-magnitude returns and low-magnitude returns, the correlation between the ranking of the level of systematic risk and the ranking of the market return for each range was $-.55$. The 10 funds seemed to be moving in the wrong direction in their market-timing activities.

Further examination of the estimates for the individual funds, using (7) with the heteroscedasticity correction, shows the existence of a strong negative correlation between $\hat{\alpha}$ and $\hat{\beta}_2$. For the total period, 49 of 59 funds with positive estimates of $\alpha$ had negative estimates of $\beta_2$. Of the 57 funds with negative estimates of $\alpha$, 34 had positive estimates of $\beta_2$. In all but two of the cases where either $\hat{\alpha}$ or $\hat{\beta}_2$ are significantly different from zero, the two coefficients have different signs. In the two exceptions, in both cases, the estimate of $\alpha$ is significantly negative and the estimate of $\beta_2$ is also negative but small and not significant. While this negative correlation can be partially explained by measurement error in the estimates, as the covariance around the *true* values of $\alpha$ and $\beta_2$ will be negative, the results are so strong that this is not likely to be the entire explanation.[15]

The negative correlation was strong in both subperiods as well. As the market portfolio performed worse than riskless securities in the first period and performed better than riskless securities in the second period, the negative correlation between $\alpha$ and $\beta_2$ does not seem to depend on the market return for the period being examined.[16]

The negative correlation between estimates of $\alpha$ and $\beta_2$ seems to imply that funds that earn superior returns from stock selection also seem to have negative market-timing ability and performance. This is quite disturbing, as Treynor and Black (1973) showed that investment managers can effectively separate their stock-selection activities from their decision regarding the market risk of their fund. As this result has also been found in two previous studies using completely different

15. As the measurement error is relative to the true values of $\alpha$ and $\beta_2$ for the sample period, the results seem to imply that the true values of $\alpha$ and $\beta_2$ must either be opposite in sign or very close to zero in most cases. For the sample period, many of the funds had returns that exceeded the returns from the market portfolio and from riskless securities. As the average excess return on the market portfolio was approximately zero, the superior return must show up in the estimates of $\alpha$ or $\beta_2$ or both. Yet the negative correlation was the strongest for the funds that had the highest returns.

16. The negative correlation also existed when the tests were run without the heteroscedasticity correction and in both samples when the data were split by the magnitude of the market return. There were no qualitative changes in the results when investment periods longer than a month were used. In fact, the negative correlation was found even when the tests were run using random portfolios.

methodologies over different sample periods,[17] the possibility of misspecification of the return-generating process must be considered.

One potential source of error is misspecification of the market portfolio. This results from the fact that the proxy used for the market portfolio, the NYSE Index, does not include all risky assets. While it seems unlikely that the universe of investment opportunities relevant to the mutual funds in the sample has sufficiently different characteristics from the assets of the NYSE Index to cause the negative correlation of $\hat{\alpha}$ and $\hat{\beta}_2$, it is possible, especially for a particular sample period.

Another potential source of error is omission of relevant factors in addition to the return on the market portfolio from the return-generating process. If the omitted factor can be identified, then the return-generating process can be modified to take into account the omitted factor, and a multifactor version of the parametric test presented by Henriksson and Merton can be used. However, as the identity of the omitted variable, if it exists, is not known, a different procedure is used to focus on the potential biases.

To take into account the influence of these potential sources of error on the returns of mutual funds, the excess return on an equally weighted portfolio of all 116 funds in the sample, net of the influence of the return on the market portfolio, is added to (7) as a second factor. Formally, this factor is defined as

$$w(t) \equiv Z_{EW}(t) - R(t) - \beta_{EW}x(t), \tag{15}$$

where $Z_{EW}(t)$ is the return, in period $t$, from the equally weighted portfolio of all 116 funds, and $\beta_{EW}$ is the least squares regression coefficient using the following specification:

$$Z_{EW}(t) - R(t) = \alpha_{EW} + \beta_{EW}x(t) + \epsilon(t). \tag{16}$$

For the total sample period, 1968:2–1980:6, the estimate of $\beta_{EW} = .942$ with a standard error of .013 and the estimate of $\alpha_{EW} = -.0002$ (i.e., $-.02\%$ per month) with a standard error of .0006.

As defined, $w(t)$ serves as a proxy for both assets omitted from the market proxy and relevant factors omitted from the returns-generating process as specified in (5).

The expanded regression specification for portfolio returns, taking into account the mutual fund factor, $w(t)$, is

$$Z_p(t) - R(t) = \alpha_p + \beta_1 x(t) + \beta_2 y(t) + \delta_1 w(t) + \delta_2 v(t) + \epsilon(t), \tag{17}$$

17. In an unpublished paper, Rex Thompson (1973) used a quadratic term as described in Jensen (1972b) to test for market timing using data for the period 1960–69. Stanley Kon (1981) used the switching regression methodology to test for timing during the period 1960–76.

**TABLE 5**  Parametric Tests: $Z_p(t) - R(t) = \hat{\alpha}_p + \hat{\beta}_1 x(t) + \hat{\beta}_2 y(t) + \hat{\delta}_1 w(t) + \hat{\delta}_2 v(t)$; with Mutual Fund Factor, 1968:2–1980:6

| Sample | Mean | SD |
|---|---|---|
| $\hat{\alpha}$ | $-.0004$ | .0037 |
| $\hat{\beta}_1$ | .94 | .22 |
| $\hat{\beta}_2$ | .00 | .15 |
| $\hat{\delta}_1$ | .98 | .96 |
| $\hat{\delta}_2$ | .05 | .69 |
| Number of funds: | | |
| Reject at $\hat{\alpha} = 0$ at 5% | 3+ 10− | |
| Reject at $\hat{\alpha} = 0$ at 1% | 1+ 2− | |
| Reject at $\hat{\beta}_2 = 0$ at 5% | 3+ 6− | |
| Reject at $\hat{\beta}_2 = 0$ at 1% | 1+ 1− | |
| Reject at $\hat{\delta}_1 = 0$ at 5% | 63+ 1− | |
| Reject at $\hat{\delta}_1 = 0$ at 1% | 44+ 1− | |
| Reject at $\hat{\delta}_2 = 0$ at 5% | 1+ 1− | |
| Reject at $\hat{\delta}_2 = 0$ at 1% | 0+ 0− | |
| $\hat{\alpha} > 0$ | 44 | |
| $\hat{\beta}_2 > 0$ | 70 | |
| $\hat{\delta}_1 > 0$ | 110 | |
| $\hat{\delta}_2 > 0$ | 58 | |

where $v(t) \equiv \max[0, -w(t)]$. This specification allows for possible timing of the mutual fund factor as well as the market portfolio.

The results from (17) are summarized in table 5. For the sample period, the mutual fund factor is predominately positively correlated with the performance of the mutual funds and appears to play an important role in explaining the behavior of returns for many of the funds. For the sample, 64 funds have estimates of $\delta_1$ significantly different from zero at the 95% confidence level. For all but one of the 64 funds, the estimate of $\delta_1$ is positive. At the 99% confidence level, 44 of the funds have estimates of $\delta_1$ significantly different from zero, with only one having a significantly negative estimate. For the entire sample of 116 funds, only six had negative point estimates of $\delta_1$.[18]

The funds did not demonstrate any significant timing ability with respect to the mutual fund factor, as only one fund had a significantly positive estimate of $\delta_2$ and one fund had an estimate of $\delta_2$ that was significantly negative. In both cases, the point estimates were significantly different from zero at the 95% confidence level but not at the 99% confidence level.

The inclusion of the mutual fund factor did change the estimates of the other coefficients, as the number of funds with positive estimates of

18. After running this test, I discovered that in an unpublished paper Black, Farrell, and Scholes (1972) used a similar approach to test for a mutual fund factor. They also found that this factor's coefficient was significantly positive for many of the funds in their sample. Their estimation period was 1960–69.

α fell from 59 to 44 while the number of funds with positive estimates of market-timing ability increased from 44 to 70. It did not change the number of significant positive estimates of market-timing ability, and the only fund to have a positive estimate of market-timing ability with 99% confidence was also the only fund to have an estimate of $\beta_2$ significant at that level for the entire sample period in table 1. In fact, it was also the only fund to exhibit significant market-timing ability in both time subperiods examined.

The mutual fund factor did not explain the negative correlation between $\hat{\alpha}$ and $\hat{\beta}_2$. For the 45 funds with positive estimates of $\alpha$, 28 also had negative estimates of $\hat{\beta}_2$, while 54 of the 71 funds with negative estimates of $\alpha$ had positive estimates of $\beta_2$.

While the number of funds with significant coefficients for the mutual fund factor is consistent with either the misspecification of the market portfolio or the omission of other relevant factors in (5), the results are also consistent with the hypothesis that mutual funds tend to follow similar investment strategies. This is sometimes referred to as the "herd" effect.

## IV.  Nonparametric Tests

Because of the negative correlation between $\alpha$ and $\beta_2$, the specification used for the parametric tests must be questioned. The nonparametric test described in Section II does not require a specified model of returns and therefore avoids this problem. However, the nonparametric test requires that the forecaster's predictions are known or that a proxy for the forecasts can be found. As the market-timing forecasts of mutual funds are not available, it is necessary to use a proxy for the forecasts.

Henriksson (1980) used changes in the proportion of equities held in the portfolios of mutual funds as a proxy for the market-timing forecasts. Using quarterly data from 1973–80 for 186 mutual funds, he found no evidence of market-timing ability. However, his proxy will be measured with error if the fund manager's forecast intervals do not correspond to the quarterly periods for which data are available or if the funds follow an adjustment process for the level of market-related risk more complex than those modeled by Henriksson. Such measurement error will bias the results against detecting superior forecasting, even if the forecaster does have market-timing ability. Also, the limited availability of the data makes it difficult to find significant forecasting ability.

To avoid measurement errors in the proxy, the actual returns of the mutual funds are used as the measure of performance and compared with the performance of a feasible passive strategy. The returns of the mutual funds and the passive strategy are compared using the $2 \times 2$

**TABLE 6**      Nonparametric Tests: 116 Open-End Funds, Return on Fund versus Passive Strategy Reflecting Fund, Null Hypothesis: $p_1 + p_2 = 1$

|  | 1968:2–1980:6 | 1968:2–1974:4 | 1974:5–1980:6 |
|---|---|---|---|
| Average estimated $(p_1 + p_2)$ | .984 | .947 | 1.021 |
| Standard deviation | .115 | .148 | .168 |
| Number of funds: |  |  |  |
|   Reject null at 5% | 4+ | 4+ | 7+ |
|   Reject null at 1% | 1+ | 2+ | 3+ |
|   Estimate $(p_1 + p_2) > 1$ | 54 | 39 | 65 |

NOTE.—Correlation (period 1, period 2) = .05. Only one fund exhibited positive forecasting ability in both periods.

test of independence described in Section II. The returns of the passive strategy are segmented around $R(t)$ and the null hypothesis, $H_0: p_1(t) + p_2(t) = 1$, reflects the probabilities of the mutual fund's outperforming the passive strategy, conditional on whether or not the return on the passive strategy exceeds the return on riskless securities. In this form, the test examines the total performance of the fund and not just the market-timing ability. It examines whether or not active portfolio management can generate returns in excess of those earned by a feasible passive strategy.

The passive strategy used is a portfolio consisting of the market portfolio and Treasury bills with the proportion of the portfolio invested in the market portfolio equal to the β of the fund where β is measured using

$$Z_p(t) - R(t) = \alpha + \beta x(t) + \epsilon(t). \tag{18}$$

The tests did not seem to be sensitive to the passive strategy chosen, as others were also used with little change in the results.

The results of the nonparametric test for the individual funds are summarized in table 6 and figure 1. On average, the funds appear to do slightly worse than the passive strategy, which is consistent with the hypothesis of no forecasting ability and the use of returns that are net of management costs and fees.

Four funds were able to reject the null hypothesis of no forecasting ability at the 95% confidence level for the entire sample. However, only one fund was able to reject the null hypothesis in both subperiods, the same fund that also had significantly positive estimates for α for both subperiods in the parametric tests. In fact, in every case where the null hypothesis is rejected, both for the total period and the two subperiods, the same fund had a positive estimate of α and a negative estimate of $\beta_2$ in the parametric test for the same period. All but two of these funds had estimates of α that were significantly different from zero. In every case where a fund had a significantly positive estimate of market-timing ability in the parametric tests, that same fund had a

1968:2 - 1980:6

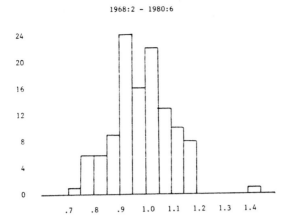

1968:2 - 1974:4

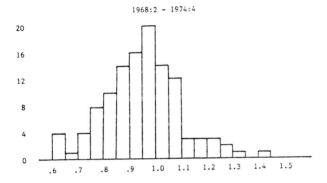

1974:5 - 1980:6

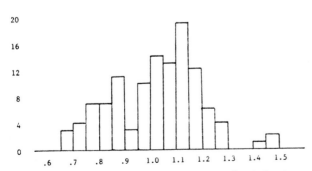

FIG. 1.—Mutual fund results. Nonparametric test fund: fund return versus passive strategy, $E(p_1 + p_2)$.

TABLE 7     **Nonparametric Tests: Return on Fund versus Passive Strategy, Sample Split by Magnitude of $|x(t)|$, 1968:2–1980:6\***

| Magnitude | Less than Median | Greater than Median |
|---|---|---|
| Averaged estimated $(p_1 + p_2)$ | .986 | .990 |
| Standard deviation | .161 | .123 |
| Number of funds: | | |
|   Reject null at 5% | 8 | 1 |
|   Reject null at 1% | 2 | 1 |
|   Estimated $(p_1 + p_2) > 1$ | 55 | 52 |

NOTE.—None of the funds exhibited positive forecasting ability for both samples.
\* Median $|x(t)| = .0308$.

negative estimate of overall performance in the nonparametric tests, that is, est$(p_1 + p_2) < 1$.

As in the parametric tests, there appeared to be very little relationship between the performance of the first subperiod and the second subperiod for the individual funds. The correlation between the estimates of $p_1 + p_2$ for the same fund in the two subperiods was .05. Overall, the funds tended to do better in the second subperiod than the first.

The sample is also split by the magnitude of the absolute value of the excess return on the passive strategy to examine the assumption that the forecaster is no better at predicting large magnitude changes than small ones. The results for the individual funds are summarized in table 7. None of the funds exhibited significantly superior performance in both samples, and the results provide no evidence that the forecasters are better able to forecast large magnitude changes than small. For the sample of 116 funds, 56 had a higher estimate of $p_1 + p_2$ for the sample of large-magnitude returns than for the sample of small-magnitude returns.

## V.  Mutual Fund Returns

As a final comparison, the actual sample period returns from the investment of $1.00 at the beginning of the period for each of the 116 mutual funds are examined and compared with the results of the parametric and nonparametric tests. The returns for the individual funds are summarized in table 8 and figure 2.

Even though the average level of systematic risk for the mutual funds was less than that of the market portfolio, the funds on average did worse than the market portfolio in the first subperiod where the excess return on the market portfolio was negative, and the funds performed better than the market portfolio in the second subperiod when the excess return on the market was positive.

Of the eight funds that finished the total period with over $3.00

TABLE 8      Total Returns: 116 Open-End Mutual Funds, Return on Initial
Investment of $1.00

| | 1968:2–1980:6 | 1968:2–1974:4 | 1974:5–1980:6 |
|---|---|---|---|
| Average for 116 funds | $2.09 | $1.07 | $1.95 |
| Standard deviation | .96 | .31 | .56 |
| Market portfolio | $2.09 | $1.14 | $1.84 |
| Riskless securities | $2.19 | $1.41 | $1.55 |
| Number of funds: | | | |
|   Return greater than market portfolio | 45 | 45 | 55 |
|   Return greater than riskless securities | 42 | 8 | 95 |

(starting with the $1.00 investment), all had positive estimates of $\alpha$ in the parametric tests and only one had a positive estimate of $\beta_2$. The only fund to reject the null hypothesis for both subperiods in the non-parametric tests and to have a significantly positive estimate of $\alpha$ in both subperiods in the parametric tests also had the greatest return over the sample period.[19] The fund earned over $3.00 in both sub-periods and earned $9.58 overall, exceeding the next highest fund by $4.40.

The four funds that rejected the null hypothesis for the total period in the nonparametric tests all had a return greater than the average for the 116 funds, with two of them ranking first and second in total returns. The four funds had returns of $9.58, $5.18, $2.65, and $2.43. The returns for the three funds that had significantly positive estimates of $\beta_2$ in the parametric tests were $1.94, $1.95, and $2.21, with the fund that had significant estimates in both periods earning $1.94.

## VI.   Conclusion

The empirical results obtained using techniques developed by Henriksson and Merton (1981) do not support the hypothesis that mutual fund managers are able to follow an investment strategy that successfully times the return on the market portfolio. This is observed in both the parametric and nonparametric tests. Only three funds had significantly positive estimates of market-timing ability in the parametric tests for the period from 1968:2 to 1980:6, and only one fund had significant estimates in both subperiods when the sample was split in half. All three had negative overall estimates of performance in the non-parametric tests and total returns for the period very close to the average of all funds in the sample.

Of the four funds that exhibited superior performance in the non-

19. This fund was Templeton Growth.

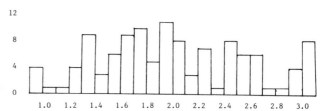

FIG. 2.—Mutual fund returns: return on initial investment of $1.00, 1968:2–1980:6 distribution of funds ($).

parametric tests, only one did so in both subperiods, and all four had positive estimates of $\alpha$ and negative estimates of $\beta_2$ in the parametric tests.

Strong evidence of nonstationarity in the performance parameters was found in both the parametric and nonparametric tests. In addition, no evidence was found that forecasters are more successful in their market-timing activity with respect to predicting large changes in the value of the market portfolio relative to smaller changes. The absolute magnitude of the returns on the market portfolio did not seem to have an influence on the measures of performance evaluation.

The specification used in the parametric tests must be questioned because of the persistence of a negative correlation between $\hat{\alpha}$ and $\hat{\beta}_2$, which raises new questions regarding the validity of using the CAPM to evaluate portfolio performance when the possibility of market timing is allowed for. Although it does not explain the negative correlation, a mutual fund factor was added to the specification used and was found to be significant for 64 of the 116 funds in the sample. One possible explanation of this result is the existence of a factor omitted in the return-generating process modeled.

## Appendix

### Mutual Fund Sample

| Fund No. | Fund Name | Objective* |
|---|---|---|
| 1 | Axe-Houghton Stock | G |
| 2 | Boston Foundation Fund | S-G-I |
| 3 | Broad Street Investment Corp. | G-I |
| 4 | Bullock Fund | G-I |
| 5 | Canadien Fund | G |
| 6 | Century Shares Trust | G |
| 7 | Chase Fund of Boston | MCG |
| 8 | Chemical Fund | G |
| 9 | Colonial Fund | G-I |

| 10 | Colonial Growth Shares | G |
| 11 | Commerce Income Shares | G-I |
| 12 | Composite Fund | G-I-S |
| 13 | Composite Bond & Stock Fund | I-S-G |
| 14 | Common Stock Fund of Stage Bond & Mortgage Co. | G |
| 15 | Corporate Leaders Trust B | G-I |
| 16 | Decatur Income Fund | I |
| 17 | Delaware Fund | G-I-S |
| 18 | DeVegh Mutual Fund | G |
| 19 | Dividend Shares | G-I |
| 20 | Dreyfus Fund | G |
| 21 | Eaton & Howard Balance Fund | I-G-S |
| 22 | Eaton & Howard Stock Fund | G-I |
| 23 | Energy Fund | G |
| 24 | Fairfield Fund | MCG |
| 25 | Fidelity Fund | G-I |
| 26 | Fidelity Trend Fund | G |
| 27 | Financial Dynamics Fund | MCG |
| 28 | Financial Industrial Fund | G-I |
| 29 | First Investors Fund | I |
| 30 | Fund of America | MCG |
| 31 | Founders Growth Fund | MCG |
| 32 | Founders Mutual Fund | G-I |
| 33 | Franklin Custodian Fund—Income Series | I |
| 34 | Fundamental Investors | G-I |
| 35 | Guardian Mutual Fund | G-I |
| 36 | Investment Co. of America | G-I |
| 37 | Investors Mutual | I-S-G |
| 38 | Investors Stock Fund | G-I |
| 39 | Investors Variable Payment Fund | G |
| 40 | Istel Fund | G-I |
| 41 | Investment Trust of Boston | G-I |
| 42 | Ivest Fund | MCG |
| 43 | Johnston Capital Appreciation Fund | G |
| 44 | Keystone Income Fund (K1) | I |
| 45 | Keystone Growth Fund (K2) | G |
| 46 | Keystone High-Grade Common Stock Fund (S1) | G-I |
| 47 | Keystone Growth Common Stock Fund (S3) | G |
| 48 | Keystone Speculative Common Stock Fund (S4) | MCG |
| 49 | Lexington Research Fund | G |
| 50 | Life Insurance Investors Fund | G |
| 51 | Loomis-Sayles Capital Development Fund | G |
| 52 | Loomis-Sayles Mutual Fund | G-I-S |
| 53 | Manhattan Fund | G |
| 54 | Massachusetts Fund | S-I-G |
| 55 | Midamerica Mutual Fund | G |
| 56 | Mutual Investing Foundation—MIF Fund | I |
| 57 | Mutual Investing Foundation—MIF Growth Fund | G |
| 58 | Massachusetts Investors Growth Stock Fund | G |
| 59 | Massachusetts Investors Trust | G-I |
| 60 | Mutual Shares Corp. | MCG |
| 61 | National Investors Corp. | G |
| 62 | Nation-Wide Securities | I-S-G |
| 63 | New World Fund | G-I |
| 64 | Northeast Investors Trust | I |
| 65 | National Dividend Fund | I |
| 66 | National Stock Fund | G-I |

| 67  | One William Street Fund                            | G-I    |
|-----|----------------------------------------------------|--------|
| 68  | Oppenheimer Fund                                   | MCG    |
| 69  | Penn Square Mutual Fund                            | G      |
| 70  | Philadelphia Fund                                  | G-I    |
| 71  | Pilgrim Fund                                       | G      |
| 72  | Pilot Fund                                         | MCG    |
| 73  | Pine Street Fund                                   | G-I    |
| 74  | Provident Fund for Income                          | I      |
| 75  | Puritan Fund                                       | I      |
| 76  | Putnam Fund of Boston                              | S-I-G  |
| 77  | Putnam International Equities Fund                 | MCG    |
| 78  | Putnam Growth Fund                                 | G      |
| 79  | Putnam Income Fund                                 | I      |
| 80  | Putnam Investors Fund                              | G      |
| 81  | Research Equity Fund                               | MCG    |
| 82  | Revere Fund                                        | MCG    |
| 83  | SAFECO Equity Fund                                 | G-I    |
| 84  | Salem Fund                                         | G      |
| 85  | Scudder Common Stock Fund                          | G      |
| 86  | Scudder Income Fund                                | I-S    |
| 87  | Scudder International Fund                         | G      |
| 88  | Scudder Special Fund                               | MCG    |
| 89  | Security Equity Fund                               | G      |
| 90  | Security Investment Fund                           | I      |
| 91  | Selected American Shares                           | G-I    |
| 92  | Sentinel Balanced Fund                             | I-G-S  |
| 93  | Sentinel Common Stock Fund                         | G-I    |
| 94  | Shareholders' Trust of Boston                      | S-I-G  |
| 95  | Kemper Growth Fund                                 | MCG    |
| 96  | Stein, Roe & Farnham Capital Opportunities Fund    | G      |
| 97  | Stein, Roe & Farnham Stock Fund                    | G      |
| 98  | St. Paul Capital Fund                              | G-I    |
| 99  | St. Paul Growth Fund                               | G      |
| 100 | Technology Fund                                    | G-I    |
| 101 | Templeton Growth Fund                              | G      |
| 102 | Twentieth Century Growth Investors                 | MCG    |
| 103 | Union Income Fund                                  | I      |
| 104 | United Accumulative Fund                           | G      |
| 105 | United Income Fund                                 | I      |
| 106 | United Science and Energy Fund                     | G      |
| 107 | Value Line Income Fund                             | I      |
| 108 | Value Line Fund                                    | G      |
| 109 | Value Line Special Situations Fund                 | MCG    |
| 110 | Varied Industry Plan                               | G-I    |
| 111 | Vance Sanders Common Stock Fund                    | G      |
| 112 | Vance Sanders Investors Fund                       | G-I-S  |
| 113 | Wall Street Fund                                   | G-I-S  |
| 114 | Washington Mutual Investors Fund                   | G-I    |
| 115 | Wellington Fund                                    | S-I-G  |
| 116 | Windsor Fund                                       | G      |

* Primary objective according to Wiesenberger (1980): G ≡ growth; I ≡ income; MCG ≡ maximum capital gain; and S ≡ stability.

# References

Black, F.; Farrell, J. L.; and Scholes, M. 1972. Common factors in mutual fund performance and their influence on performance evaluation. Working Paper. Chicago: University of Chicago, Graduate School of Business.

Black, F.; Jensen, M. C.; and Scholes, M. 1972. The capital asset pricing model: Some empirical tests. In M. C. Jensen (ed.), *Studies in the Theory of Capital Markets*. New York: Praeger.

Blume, M. E., and Friend, I. 1973. A new look at the capital asset pricing model. *Journal of Finance* 28 (March): 19–34.

Fama, E. 1970. Efficient capital markets: A review of theory and empirical work. *Journal of Finance* 25 (May): 383–417.

Fama, E., and MacBeth, J. D. 1973. Risk, return, and equilibrium: Empirical tests. *Journal of Political Economy* 81:607–36.

Fisher, F. M. 1970. Tests of equality between sets of coefficients in two linear regressions: An expository note. *Econometrica* 38 (March): 361–66.

Henriksson, R. D. 1980. Tests of market timing and mutual fund performance. Working Paper no. 1136-80. Cambridge, Mass.: MIT, Sloan School of Management.

Henriksson, R. D., and Merton, R. C. 1981. On market timing and investment performance. II. Statistical procedures for evaluating forecasting skills. *Journal of Business* 54 (October): 513–33.

Ibbotson, R., and Sinquefield, R. 1979. *Stocks, Bonds, Bills and Inflation: Historical Returns (1965–1978)*. Charlottesville, Va.: Financial Analysts Research Foundation.

Jensen, M. C. 1968. The performance of mutual funds in the period 1945–1964. *Journal of Finance* 23 (May): 389–416.

Jensen, M. C. 1969. Risk, the pricing of capital assets, and the evaluation of investment portfolios. *Journal of Business* 42 (April): 167–247.

Jensen, M. C. 1972a. Capital markets: Theory and evidence. *Bell Journal of Economics and Management Science* 3 (Fall): 357–98.

Jensen, M. C. 1972b. Optimal utilization of market forecasts and the evaluation of investment performance. In G. P. Szego and K. Shell (eds.), *Mathematical Methods of Investment and Finance*. Amsterdam: North Holland.

Kon, S. J. 1981. The market timing performance of mutual fund managers. Working paper. New York: New York University.

Mayers, D., and Rice, E. M. 1979. Measuring portfolio performance and the empirical content of asset pricing models. *Journal of Financial Economics* 7 (March): 3–28.

Merton, R. C. 1981. On market timing and investment performance. I. An equilibrium theory of value for market forecasts. *Journal of Business* 54 (July): 363–406.

Merton, R. C.; Scholes, M.; and Gladstein, M. L. 1982. The returns and risks of alternative put-option portfolio investment strategies. *Journal of Business* 55 (January): 1–55.

Roll, R. 1977. A critique of the asset pricing theory's tests. Part I. On past and potential testability of the theory. *Journal of Financial Economics* 4 (March): 129–76.

Roll, R. 1978. Ambiguity when performance is measured by the securities market line. *Journal of Finance* 33 (September): 1051–69.

Stambaugh, R. F. 1982. On the exclusion of assets from tests of the two-parameter model: A sensitivity analysis. *Journal of Financial Economics* 10 (November): 237–68.

Thompson, R. 1973. The effects of the optimal utilization of market forecasts on mutual fund performance in the period 1960–1969. Working Paper. Rochester, N.Y.: University of Rochester, Graduate School of Business.

Treynor, J., and Black, F. 1973. How to use security analysis to improve portfolio selection. *Journal of Business* 46 (January): 66–86.

Wiesenberger Investment Companies Service. Various years. *Investment Companies*. New York: Warren, Gorham & Lamont.

Zellner, A. 1962. An efficient method for estimating seemingly unrelated regressions and tests for aggregation bias. *Journal of the American Statistical Association* 57 (June): 348–68.

# VII

# THE PRICING OF OPTIONS AND OTHER DERIVED ASSETS

**1** Whaley, R. E., "Valuation of American Call Options on Dividend-Paying Stocks: Empirical Tests," *Journal of Financial Economics*, 10 (March 1982), pp. 29-59.
**2** Phillips, S. M., and C. W. Smith, "Trading Costs for Listed Options: The Implications for Market Efficiency," *Journal of Financial Economics*, 8 (June 1980), pp. 179-201.
**3** French, K. R., "A Comparison of Futures and Forward Prices," *Journal of Financial Economics*, 12 (November 1983), pp. 311-342.

Contingent claims, where the payoff to investors is a function of the behavior of another security's price, have become an important growth area in both academic research and real financial markets. Since 1973, the growth of organized options markets like the Chicago Board Options Exchange (CBOE) and the growth of financial futures markets have been phenomenal. There has been a parallel development in financial theory in the Black and Scholes (1973) option pricing model and its extensions. The dynamic hedging methods pioneered by Black and Scholes have provided a powerful set of pricing tools to modern financial economics. [See Smith (1976) and Cox, Ross, and Rubinstein (1979) for a review of this literature.]

**Whaley (1982)** provides a comprehensive test of option pricing models using daily data from the CBOE. He extends the Black and Scholes model to reflect the effects of dividend payments that occur before the maturity date of the contract. Using a variety of tests, he finds that his modified model for option prices does well at explaining the prices of CBOE-listed options.

**Phillips and Smith (1980)** analyze the effects of transaction costs on tests of option pricing models. In particular, they show that many violations of arbitrage (boundary) conditions found in early tests using CBOE data were probably due to bid-ask spreads. Thus, the number of profit opportunities available to option traders was much smaller than these early tests suggested.

**French (1983)** develops models for futures and forward prices. The daily settling-up process in futures markets distinguishes futures contracts from forward contracts, where settlement occurs at the maturity date. Using daily data on silver and copper prices from 1968 to 1980, he finds there are differences between the behavior of futures and forward prices but the predictions of the theory cannot explain these differences.

# VALUATION OF AMERICAN CALL OPTIONS ON DIVIDEND-PAYING STOCKS

## Empirical Tests

### Robert E. WHALEY*

*Vanderbilt University, Nashville, TN 37203, USA*

Received March 1981, final version received June 1981

This paper examines the pricing performance of the valuation equation for American call options on stocks with known dividends and compares it with two suggested approximation methods. The approximation obtained by substituting the stock price net of the present value of the escrowed dividends into the Black–Scholes model is shown to induce spurious correlation between prediction error and (1) the standard deviation of stock return, (2) the degree to which the option is in-the-money or out-of-the-money, (3) the probability of early exercise, (4) the time to expiration of the option, and (5) the dividend yield of the stock. A new method of examining option market efficiency is developed and tested.

## 1. Introduction

Perhaps the most significant development in the financial economics literature of the last decade is the option valuation work of Black and Scholes (1973). Under a somewhat stringent set of assumptions they derive the first closed form solution to the call option pricing problem. Their most exacting assumption disallows income distributions on the underlying security. It is somewhat disconcerting when, for example, less than five percent of the options listed on the Chicago Board Options Exchange are written on non-dividend-paying stocks.

In this paper a model for pricing American call options on dividend-paying stocks is presented and compared with prior approximate solutions to the problem. Section 3 reviews prior empirical work on option pricing models. That work is concerned with three issues: (1) estimating the standard deviation of stock return, (2) testing alternative option pricing models, and (3) testing the efficiency of options markets. After a description of the data, these issues are addressed in turn. A new method of estimating stock volatility is presented in section 5. Using the standard deviation estimates, model option value is

*Comments and suggestions by Kenneth M. Gaver, Hans R. Stoll, and the referee, Clifford W. Smith, and editorial assistance by Michael C. Jensen are gratefully acknowledged. This research was supported by the Vanderbilt University Research Council.

JFE—B

calculated and compared with approximations previously used. In section 7 the profitability of a riskless hedging strategy of buying options undervalued by the model and selling options overvalued by the model is examined. Finally, the paper is summarized and conclusions are drawn.

## 2. Theory of option valuation

The general equilibrium pricing solution to the call option pricing problem derived by Black and Scholes (1973) incorporates the following assumptions:

(A.1)  All individuals can borrow or lend without restriction at the instantaneous riskless rate of interest, $r$, and that rate is constant through the life of option, $T$.

(A.2)  Stock price movement through time is described by the stochastic differential equation

$$dP/P = \mu \, dt + \sigma \, dz,$$

where $\mu$ is the instantaneous expected rate of return on the stock, $\sigma$ is the instantaneous standard deviation of stock return (assumed to be constant over the life of the option), the $dz$ is a standard unit normally distributed variable.

(A.3)  The capital market is free from transaction costs (e.g., brokerage fees, transfer taxes, short selling and indivisibility constraints) and tax differentials between dividend and capital gain income.

(A.4)  The stock pays no dividends during the option's time to expiration.

The value of a European call,[1] denoted $c(P, T, X)$, provided by Black and Scholes is

$$c(P, T, X) = PN_1(d_1) - X e^{-rT} N_1(d_2),  \tag{1}$$

where

$$d_1 = \{\ln(P/X) + (r + 0.5\sigma^2)T\}/\sigma\sqrt{T}, \qquad d_2 = d_1 - \sigma\sqrt{T},$$

$X$ is the option's contracted exercise price, and $N_1(d)$ is the univariate cumulative normal density function with upper integral limit $d$.

The assumed absence of income distributions on the underlying security causes the Black–Scholes formula to overstate the value of an American call option on a

---

[1]Assuming the common stock underlying the call option has no income distributions to shareholders, the value of the American call is equal to the value of the European call. See Merton (1973, p. 144) or Smith (1976, pp. 8–11).

stock with dividend payments during the option's time to expiration. A dividend paid during the option's life reduces the stock price at the ex-dividend instant, and thereby reduces the probability that the stock price will exceed the exercise price at the option's expiration.

In order to introduce a discrete dividend payment into the option pricing problem it is usually assumed that:

(A.4′) The stock pays a certain dividend, $D$, at the ex-dividend instant, $t$ ($t < T$), and the stock price simultaneously falls by a known amount, $\alpha D$.

With the amount and timing of the dividend payment known, a simple approximation for the value of the American call is the value of a European call, $c(S, T, X)$, where $S$ is the stock price net of the present value of the escrowed dividend payment, $S_\tau = P_\tau - \alpha D e^{-r(t-\tau)}$ for $\tau < t$ and $S_\tau = P_\tau$ for $t \leq \tau \leq T$. Note that by using the lower stock price the model's price is adjusted downward to allow for the stock price decline at the ex-dividend date.

Unfortunately, this approximation ignores a second dividend-induced effect in that it presumes that the call will not be exercised prior to expiration. Smith (1976, pp. 13–14) demonstrates that the American option holder may benefit from exercising early, just prior to the ex-dividend instant. To compensate for this possibility Black (1975, pp. 41, 61) recommends an approximate value equal to the higher of the values of a European call where the stock price net of the present value of the escrowed dividend is substituted for the stock price and a European call where the time to ex-dividend is substituted for the time to expiration, that is,

$$\max\left[c(S, T, X), c(P, t, X)\right]. \tag{2}$$

The first option within the maximum value operator assumes the probability of early exercise is zero, while the second option assumes it is one.

The American call option on a stock with a known dividend, however, may be characterized by an early exercise probability between zero and one. For some time, this option pricing problem was thought to be insoluble.[2] If the stock price follows a lognormal diffusion process, there exists some non-zero probability that the dividend cannot be paid. Roll (1977) and Geske (1979) resolve the problem by assuming that the stock price net of the present value of the escrowed

---

[2]Schwartz (1977) provides a numerical method by which the value of an American call on a stock with known dividends can be approximated.

dividend follows the lognormal process. That is, if Assumption (A.2) is amended such that:

(A.2') Stock price movement through time is described by the stochastic differential equation

$$dS/S = \mu\, dt + \sigma\, dz,$$

where $S$ represents the stock price net of the present value of the escrowed dividend,

the solution to American call option pricing problem, as provided by Whaley (1981), is

$$C(S, T, X) = S[N_1(b_1) + N_2(a_1, -b_1; -\sqrt{t/T})]$$

$$- X\, e^{-rT}[N_1(b_2)\, e^{r(T-t)} + N_2(a_2, -b_2; -\sqrt{t/T})]$$

$$+ \alpha D\, e^{-rt} N_1(b_2), \tag{3}$$

where

$$a_1 = \{\ln(S/X) + (r + 0.5\sigma^2)T\}/\sigma\sqrt{T}, \qquad a_2 = a_1 - \sigma\sqrt{T},$$

$$b_1 = \{\ln(S/S_t^*) + (r + 0.5\sigma^2)t\}/\sigma\sqrt{t}, \qquad b_2 = b_1 - \sigma\sqrt{t},$$

and $N_2(a, b; \rho)$ is the bivariate cumulative normal density function with upper integral limits $a$ and $b$, and correlation coefficient $\rho$. $S_t^*$ is the ex-dividend stock price determined by

$$c(S_t^*, T-t, X) = S_t^* + \alpha D - X, \tag{4}$$

above which the option will be exercised just prior to the ex-dividend instant.

Note that if the American call is neither a dominant nor a dominated security its value is bounded from below by the Black approximation. The first term within the maximum value operator of expression (2) represents the price of the call if there were no chance of early exercise. Since the right to early exercise has a non-negative value, $C(S, T, X) \geq c(S, T, X)$. The second term represents the price of a call with maturity $t$. At $t$, its payoffs are 0, if $S_t + \alpha D < X$, and $S_t + \alpha D - X$, if $S_t + \alpha D \geq X$. At $t$, however, the American call is worth $c(S_t, T-t, X)$, if $S_t + \alpha D < X$, and $\max[c(S_t, T-t, X), S_t + \alpha D - X]$, if $S_t + \alpha D \geq X$. In the absence of dominance, therefore, $C(S, T, X) \geq c(P, t, X)$, and, if the arguments are combined, $C(S, T, X) \geq \max[c(S, T, X), c(P, t, X)]$.

## 3. Review of option pricing tests

Previous empirical analyses of option pricing models have been concerned to varying degrees with three issues — volatility estimation, model specification and market efficiency. While a detailed description of each study is beyond the scope of this paper, a brief overview of the salient features relating to these issues is warranted.

### 3.1. Volatility estimation

Of the determinants in the call option pricing formulas, all but one are known or can be estimated with little difficulty. The exercise price and the time to expiration are terms written into the option contract; the stock price and the riskless rate are easily accessible market-determined values. The dividend information, if it is required, can be fairly accurately estimated by casual inspection of the stock's historical dividend series. The problem parameter is the expected volatility of the stock return.

An obvious candidate to proxy for the volatility expectation is an historical estimate obtained from the stock's realized return series. Black and Scholes (1972), as well as Galai (1977) and Finnerty (1978), use this estimate in valuing calls using the Black–Scholes option pricing model. Black and Scholes, however, recognize that a substantial amount of the observed deviation of the model's price from the market price may be attributable to an 'errors-in-the-variables' problem. In fact, they note that there is a tendency of the model to overprice options with high standard deviation estimates and to underprice options with low standard deviation estimates.

Latane and Rendleman (1976) investigate the predictive ability of a weighted implied standard deviation vis-à-vis the historical estimate. If there are $n$ options on a stock at a particular point in time, $n$ implied standard deviations, $\hat{\sigma}_j$, $j = 1, \ldots, n$, may be obtained by setting the option's market price equal to the model price,

$$C_j = C_j(\sigma_j),$$

and solving for $\sigma_j$, where all of the remaining arguments of $C(\cdot)$ are assumed to be known. If these estimates are then weighted and averaged,

$$\hat{\sigma} = \sum_{j=1}^{n} \omega_j \hat{\sigma}_j \Big/ \sum_{j=1}^{n} \omega_j,$$

where $\omega_j$ is the weight applied to the $j$th estimate, a weighted implied standard deviation is realized.

Previous researchers employ various weighting schemes. Schmalensee and

Trippi (1978) and Patell and Wolfson (1979), for example, use an equal weighted average, $\omega_j = 1/n, j = 1, \ldots, n$. Latane and Rendleman, on the other hand, weight according to the partial derivative of the call price with respect to the standard deviation of stock return, that is, $\omega_j = \partial C_j / \partial \hat{\sigma}_j, \ j = 1, \ldots, n$. In doing so, the standard deviation estimates of options which are theoretically more sensitive to the value of $\sigma$ are weighted more heavily than those which are not. Chiras and Manaster (1978) follow a similar logic in using the elasticity of the call price with respect to standard deviation, $\omega_j = (\partial C_j / \partial \hat{\sigma}_j)(\hat{\sigma}_j / C_j), j = 1, \ldots, n$.

Regardless of the weighting scheme, however, there appears to be strong empirical support in favor of an implied volatility measure. Latane and Rendleman and Chiras and Manaster correlate the historical and the implied measures on the actual standard deviation of return[3] and conclude that the implied estimate is a markedly superior predictor. The market apparently uses more information than merely an historical estimate in assessing the stock's volatility expectation.

## 3.2. Model specification

The valuation equation most commonly employed in past research has been either the Black–Scholes relation $c(P, T, X)$ or the approximation $c(S, T, X)$. Black and Scholes, for example, examine Over-the-Counter (OTC) option prices during the period May 1966 through July 1969. They apply their model directly with no dividend adjustment since the OTC options are protected. For protected options the exercise price is reduced by the amount of the dividend on the ex-dividend date. For unprotected options this is tantamount to reducing the stock price by the present value of the escrowed dividends. Galai compares the Black–Scholes price with and without the dividend adjustment by using unprotected Chicago Board Options Exchange (CBOE) pricing data and concludes that the latter model provides a more adequate description of the observed structure of call option prices. Studies by Merton, Scholes and Galdstein (1978) and MacBeth and Merville (1979) employ the approximation $c(S, T, X)$.

Chiras and Manaster account for dividends by transforming the payments into a constant, continuous dividend yield and applying the Merton (1973a) model. While this method uses dividend information in valuing the option, the transformation of discretely-timed dividend payments to a continuous dividend yield effectively assumes away the American option holder's early exercise dilemma.

Schmalensee and Trippi apply the Black–Scholes model without dividend adjustment to CBOE options to compute implied standard deviations, but try to minimize the dividend problem by concentrating on options whose underlying

---

[3]While Latane and Rendleman (1976) and Chiras and Manaster (1978) refer to the standard deviation computed with stock returns generated during the option's life as the 'actual standard deviation of return', it is only an estimate of the realized volatility.

stocks have low dividend yields. Latane and Rendleman and Finnerty use the Black–Scholes formula directly, with no consideration of the effects of the dividend payments.

Of the tested option pricing models, it appears that the Black–Scholes formula with the stock price net of the present value of the escrowed dividends provides the best explanation of the observed structure call option prices to date. Galai demonstrates a substantial increase in trading profits by employing this approximation instead of the Black–Scholes model with the stock price cum dividend. Black and Scholes, Black, and MacBeth and Merville, however, report certain systematic biases in the application of the model that are worth investigating in the present study. For instance, the degree of under- and over-pricing appears to be related to the standard deviation of the stock return — options on high-risk stocks tend to be overpriced and the options on low-risk stocks tend to be underpriced. Further, the degree of under- and over-pricing appears to be related to the difference between the stock price and the exercise price (i.e., how far in-the-money or out-of-the-money the option is), and the time to expiration of the option.

### 3.3. Market efficiency

The tests of option market efficiency usually involve an option trading strategy that is designed to create a riskless portfolio, which should, in an efficient capital market, yield the riskless rate of interest. The key insight into the Black–Scholes development is, in fact, the premise that risk substitutes have the same equilibrium rate of return. By taking a long (short) position in one call option and a short (long) position of $\partial C/\partial P$ shares of the stock, a riskless hedge is created, which, if continuously rebalanced through time, leads to a partial differential equation whose solution, subject to the terminal date boundary conditions, is the Black–Scholes call option pricing model.

From the standpoint of empirical investigation, continuous rebalancing is not possible, and discrete readjustment of the portfolio position is substituted. Undervalued (overvalued) options are identified, and are bought (sold) and hedged against a short (long) position of $\partial C/\partial P$ shares of the stock. All of the hedge positions are aggregated and the excess dollar returns [i.e., dollar returns on the hedge portfolio less the investment cost times (one plus the riskless rate of interest)] computed. The process is repeated on each trading date so that a time series of excess dollar returns is generated. A regression of the portfolio returns on a stock market index is usually included to verify that the hedge position is riskless, and, if so, the intercept term and its corresponding standard error provide a means of testing whether significantly positive (negative) returns are earned.

Latane and Rendleman use this procedure in testing option market efficiency, however, they aggregate separately the undervalued and the overvalued positions. The problem with this approach is that the returns on each portfolio have downward bias since the call options have a predictable decrease in value over the trading interval $\Delta t$, all other things remaining constant. For a detailed discussion on this point, see Boyle and Emanuel (1980).

Black and Scholes, Galai, and Finnerty combine the undervalued and the overvalued positions into one portfolio, long in the former group and short in the latter. If the characteristics of the long options (i.e., the stock prices, exercise prices, times to expiration and standard deviations of stock return) are nearly the same as those of the short options, the portfolio will be approximately riskless over the interval $\Delta t$.

Chiras and Manaster choose to hedge each undervalued option against an overvalued option on the same stock, thereby eliminating the need for investment in the stock. Unfortunately the requisite of being able to identify both an undervalued and an overvalued option on the same stock unduly restricts the number of options that may be included in the sample. In fact, the technique is so restrictive that Chiras and Manaster are left with an average of less than 12 options in each of their 23 cross-sections.[4]

## 4. Data

The data employed in this study consisted of weekly closing price observations for all Chicago Board Options Exchange (CBOE) call options written on 91 dividend-paying stocks during the 160 week period January 17, 1975 through February 3, 1978. The prices of the stocks, options and Treasury Bills were compiled from various issues of the *Wall Street Journal*. Wherever necessary, adjustments were made for stock splits and stock dividends. The riskless rate appropriate to each option was estimated by interpolating the effective yields of the two Treasury Bills whose maturities most closely preceeded and exceeded the option's time to expiration.[5] The dividend information was gleaned from *Standard and Poor's Stock Reports*, and the weekly stock return data were generated from the *Center for Research in Security Prices* (CRSP) daily return file. The market index was the value-weighted portfolio of NYSE and AMEX securities provided on the CRSP return file.

Three exclusion criteria were imposed on the option pricing information. First, the option's underlying stock had to have *exactly* one dividend paid during the option's remaining life. Without a dividend paid, the American call option formula would have reduced to the simple Black–Scholes model, and, since the focus of study is on investigating the effects of the dividend payment on the observed structure of call option prices, options with expiration dates before the

---

[4]See Chiras and Manaster (1978, p. 230).
[5]The rate of interest for a particular Treasury Bill was assumed to be the annualized, arithmetic average of the rates implied by the bid and ask prices.

stock's next ex-dividend date were eliminated. With more than one dividend paid before expiration, the structure of the valuation equation would have become more complex, requiring, among other things, the evaluation of an approximation for a trivariate or higher-order multivariate cumulative normal density function. Since the computational cost of such an integral approximation is high,[6] options with times to expiration including more than one ex-dividend date were, likewise, excluded.

The second restriction eliminated options whose premia were below fifty cents. CBOE regulation generally prohibits traders from establishing new positions in these options so that the reported prices may not accurately reflect transacting prices.

The remaining constraint was imposed to facilitate the market efficiency test design. For each cross-section $t$, all options employed were required to have three consecutive weekly prices. The first week's price, $C_{t-1}$, was required to compute the implied standard deviation of stock return.[7] This estimate was, in turn, employed in the valuation process of $C_t$ at $t$ in order to establish whether the option was under- or over-priced. The price, $C_{t+1}$, was used to compute the holding period return of the option over the trading interval $t$ to $t+1$.

Descriptive statistics of the remaining sample data are included in table 1. The means, standard deviations, mean absolute deviations and percentile ranges of the 15,582 sets of option pricing information are reported. On average, the samp options are on-the-money, with the mean stock price only slightly exceeding the mean exercise price. The riskless rate standard deviation is low during the sample period, indicating that interest rate uncertainty is not a potential problem.

Certain limitations of the data should be noted. All of the option pricing formulas require that the stock price be known at the exact instant the option is priced. However, the stock price is the 3:00 p.m. EST Friday closing in New York,[8] while the option price is the 3:00 p.m. CST Friday closing in Chicago. Further, the closing price is the price for the last transaction, which may have occurred before the market closing and which may be either a bid or an ask price. To the extent that the closing quotations may not accurately reflect the prices at which the securities may be transacted, random noise in the empirical results should be expected.

In all applications of the American call option formula and the two approximation techniques to follow, the coefficient $\alpha$ preceding the dividend variable was assumed to be equal to one. There are several reasons why the

---

[6]For further discussion, see Milton (1972).

[7]The motivation for using the previous week's implied standard deviation in the option valuation process is discussed in the next section.

[8]During the sample period, all options, with exception of those written on Houston Oil and Minerals Corporation, were written on stocks listed on the New York Stock Exchange. Houston Oil was listed on the American Stock Exchange.

Table 1

Distributions of the prices and the parameters of the sample's 15,582 CBOE call options (with a single dividend to be paid during the option's life and a price of at least $0.50 per option) during the period January 17, 1975 through February 3, 1978.

| | Call price $C$ | Stock price $P$ | Exercise price $X$ | Years to expiration $T$ | Annualized riskless rate $r$ | Amount of escrowed dividend $D$ | Years to ex-dividend $t$ |
|---|---|---|---|---|---|---|---|
| Mean | $4.139 | $48.838 | $48.288 | 0.3178 | 0.0569 | $0.3756 | 0.1645 |
| Standard deviation | 5.240 | 39.547 | 38.735 | 0.1246 | 0.0067 | 0.3696 | 0.1133 |
| Mean absolute deviation | 2.856 | 22.521 | 22.516 | 0.0930 | 0.0057 | 0.2172 | 0.0788 |
| Deciles 0.10 | 1.000 | 20.500 | 20.000 | 0.1753 | 0.0485 | 0.1100 | 0.0521 |
| 0.20 | 1.313 | 27.125 | 25.000 | 0.2192 | 0.0507 | 0.1500 | 0.0740 |
| 0.30 | 1.750 | 31.500 | 30.000 | 0.2521 | 0.0525 | 0.2000 | 0.0986 |
| 0.40 | 2.155 | 35.250 | 35.000 | 0.2712 | 0.0541 | 0.2500 | 0.1233 |
| 0.50 | 2.750 | 39.250 | 40.000 | 0.2959 | 0.0555 | 0.2750 | 0.1452 |
| 0.60 | 3.375 | 44.375 | 45.000 | 0.3288 | 0.0576 | 0.3313 | 0.1671 |
| 0.70 | 4.250 | 49.750 | 50.000 | 0.3534 | 0.0607 | 0.4000 | 0.1890 |
| 0.80 | 5.625 | 58.875 | 60.000 | 0.3863 | 0.0641 | 0.5000 | 0.2110 |
| 0.90 | 8.250 | 76.875 | 80.000 | 0.4822 | 0.0666 | 0.6500 | 0.2904 |

coefficient may be less than one, however. Differential income tax rates between dividends and capital gains, transaction costs, and the time interval between the ex-dividend and dividend payment dates may cause the stock price decline at the ex-dividend instant to be an amount less than the dividend. Since there was no manageable way of handling these institutional restrictions,[9] they were ignored.

## 5. Implied standard deviation estimation

### 5.1. Procedure

The methodology implemented to impute the estimate of the future volatility of the stock return differs from the previous studies in three important ways. First, rather than explicitly weighting the implied standard deviations of a particular stock where the weights are assigned in an ad hoc fashion, the call prices are allowed to provide an implicit weighting scheme that yields an estimate of standard deviation which has as little prediction error as is possible.[10] At a point in time options written on the same stock may be represented as

$$C_j = C_j(\sigma) + \varepsilon_j, \tag{5}$$

where $C_j$ is the market price of the option, $C_j(\sigma)$ is the model's price (where all argument values are known, with exception of $\sigma$), and $\varepsilon_j$ is a random disturbance term. The estimate of $\sigma$ is then determined by minimizing the sum of squared residuals,

$$\min_{\{\hat{\sigma}\}} \sum_{j=1}^{n} e_j^2, \tag{6}$$

where $e_j$ is the observed residual and $\hat{\sigma}$ is the estimated parameter.

The nonlinear estimation procedure applied to minimize the sum of squared residuals is the first order linearization process described by Eisner and Pindyck (1973, pp. 30–34).[11] As adapted to the present problem, the iterative technique begins with an expansion of $C_j$ into a Taylor series around some initialization value $\sigma_0$, that is,

$$C_j = C_j(\sigma_0) + \frac{\partial C_j}{\partial \sigma}\bigg|_{\sigma_0} (\sigma - \sigma_0) + \dots \text{higher-order terms} \dots + \varepsilon_j. \tag{7}$$

---

[9]Actually, the time lapse between the ex-dividend and dividend payment dates may be handled quite easily. During the sample period the average riskless rate was 5.69% per year and the average time between the ex-dividend and dividend payment dates was 26 days or 0.071 years. The value of $\alpha$ is therefore approximately $e^{-0.0569(0.071)} = 0.996$.

[10]Implied standard deviations are accurate only insofar as the call option model is correctly specified. In general, the implied volatility will not be the 'best' estimator of the stock's future standard deviation of return.

[11]For a review of nonlinear estimation techniques, see Spang (1962) or, more recently, Goldfeld and Quandt (1972).

Ignoring the higher-order terms and gathering known values on the left-hand side of the equation,

$$C_j - C_j(\sigma_0) + \sigma_0 \frac{\partial C_j}{\partial \sigma}\bigg|_{\sigma_0} = \sigma \frac{\partial C_j}{\partial \sigma}\bigg|_{\sigma_0} + \varepsilon_j. \tag{8}$$

Applying ordinary least squares (OLS) to (8) yields an estimate of $\sigma$. If that estimate satisfies an acceptable tolerance,

$$|(\hat{\sigma}_1 - \sigma_0)/\sigma_0| < \kappa, \tag{9}$$

where $\kappa$ is a small positive constant, $\hat{\sigma}_1$ is the estimate of $\sigma$. If, the tolerance test fails, eq. (5) is linearized around the realized parameter estimate $\hat{\sigma}_1$, and OLS is reapplied. The process is repeated for $\hat{\sigma}_i$, $i = 2, \ldots$, until the tolerance criterion is satisfied.

The second difference between the implied volatility estimation procedure is with respect to the timing of the estimation. It has apparently become an accepted practice to compute the implied standard deviation at the same instant at which the option is priced.[12] Conceptually, this procedure is difficult to understand in that, at an instant in time, the valuation equation is assumed to price options correctly (when the implied volatility is computed), and, yet, simultaneously, is assumed to price options incorrectly (when the model is used to identify whether the option is under- or over-priced). As an empirical matter, this procedure eliminates from study all single options written on a stock at a particular instant. With only one option, the model will exactly price the option since the volatility estimate at $t$ is that standard deviation which equates the observed call price to the model's price. Moreover, even if two or more options are available, Phillips and Smith (1980, pp. 189–192) point out that contemporaneous estimation of volatility and valuation of options leads to a selection bias which systematically identifies bid prices as undervalued options and ask prices as overvalued options. To circumvent these problems, the implied volatility is computed at $t-1$. The conceptual problem is alleviated, at least in part, a larger sample size is retained, and a potential source of selection bias is eliminated.

Finally, unlike the previous empirical studies which compute a single volatility estimate on the basis of all of the options written on a stock at a particular point in time, the present study uses only those options which share a common maturity. Patell and Wolfson (1979, pp. 119–123) argue and demonstrate empirically that the standard deviation implied by the price of a longer-lived option written on a stock is greater than the standard deviation implied by the price

---

[12]Latane and Rendleman (1976), Chiras and Manaster (1978) and MacBeth and Merville (1979), among others, use this approach.

of a shorter-lived option if there is an anticipated information event between the expirations of the two options. Given that the difference between option lives is typically three months for CBOE call options, an information release, such as, for example, an earnings announcement, may be expected, and, hence, maturity-specific implied stock volatilities, rather than a single implied volatility common to all maturities, are most appropriate.

## 5.2. Results

For each stock, implied standard deviations were computed weekly using the previous period's call prices and a tolerance criterion of $\kappa = 0.0001$.[13] The numbers of options included in each computation are summarized in table 2. The 15,582 sets of call price information yielded 9,318 implied standard deviations, each computation including an average of 1.67 options of common maturity. Of the 9,318 computations, 936 were estimates for a second option maturity, or, equivalently, 1.11 estimates of the stock's volatility were obtained each week.

Descriptive statistics for the implied standard deviations computed on the basis of the valuation equation $C(S, T, X)$ are reported in table 3. On average, $\hat{\sigma}$ was 0.3004 on an annualized basis. The percentile ranges indicate that the distribution of volatilities is skewed to the left, with the lowest value being 0.0493 and the highest being 1.0379. Implied volatility estimates were also computed on the basis of the approximation models $c(S, T, X)$ and $\max[c(S, T, X), c(P, t, X)]$, and the results were nearly identical to those of $C(S, T, X)$.

Table 2

The number of options of common maturity included in each implied standard deviation computation.

| Number of maturities of options written on a stock | Number of options of common maturity written on a stock | | | | | | Number of implied standard deviation estimates |
|---|---|---|---|---|---|---|---|
| | 1 | 2 | 3 | 4 | 5 | 6 | |
| 1 | 4,056 | 3,202 | 880 | 219 | 22 | 3 | 8,382 |
| 2 | 455 | 432 | 43 | 2 | 2 | 2 | 936 |
| Total number of implied standard deviation estimates | | | | | | | 9,318 |
| Total number of call prices used | | | | | | | 15,582 |

[13]With the maximum absolute relative error ($\kappa$) set at 1 one-hundredth of 1 percent, an average of slightly more than 4 iterations were required for convergence.

Table 3

Distribution of the 9,318 implied standard deviations computed using the 15,582 sample call option prices and the valuation equation for an American call option on a stock with a known dividend.

|  | | Implied standard deviation of stock return $\hat{\sigma}$ |
| --- | --- | --- |
| Mean | | 0.3004 |
| Standard deviation | | 0.1082 |
| Mean absolute deviation | | 0.0855 |
| Deciles | 0.10 | 0.1801 |
| | 0.20 | 0.2104 |
| | 0.30 | 0.2340 |
| | 0.40 | 0.2577 |
| | 0.50 | 0.2826 |
| | 0.60 | 0.3092 |
| | 0.70 | 0.3423 |
| | 0.80 | 0.3865 |
| | 0.90 | 0.4529 |

## 6. Tests of option valuation

### 6.1. Procedure

Using the implied standard deviation estimates developed according to the procedure outlined in the preceding section, options were valued according to: (1) the American call option valuation equation, $C(S, T, X)$, (2) the Black approximation, $\max[c(S, T, X), c(P, t, X)]$, and (3) the Black–Scholes formula applied to the stock price net of the present value of the escrowed dividend, $c(S, T, X)$.[14] For each model the following cross-sectional regressions, designed to examine the difference between actual ($C$) and model ($\hat{C}$) option values, were estimated:

Test 1:   $C_j = \alpha_0 + \alpha_1 \hat{C}_1 + \mu_j,$

Test 2:   $\dfrac{C_j - \hat{C}_j}{\hat{C}_j} = \alpha_0 + \alpha_1 \hat{\sigma}_j + \mu_j,$

[14]Using the previous week's implied standard deviation may have introduced an 'errors-in-the-variables' problem in the tests of this section. Patell and Wolfson (1979) document that the implied standard deviation of common stock return is 'high' near earnings announcements dates, and, to the extent that such an information release may have occurred between volatility estimation at week $t-1$ and option valuation at week $t$, there will be inaccuracy in the test results.

Test 3: $\quad \dfrac{C_j - \hat{C}_j}{\hat{C}_j} = \alpha_0 + \alpha_1 \left( \dfrac{S_j - X_j e^{-r_j T_j}}{X_j e^{-r_j T_j}} \right) + \mu_j,$

Test 4: $\quad \dfrac{C_j - \hat{C}_j}{\hat{C}_j} = \alpha_0 + \alpha_1 p_j + \mu_j,$

Test 5: $\quad \dfrac{C_j - \hat{C}_j}{\hat{C}_j} = \alpha_0 + \alpha_1 T_j + \mu_j,$

Test 6: $\quad \dfrac{C_j - \hat{C}_j}{\hat{C}_j} = \alpha_0 + \alpha_1 d_j + \mu_j,$

where $p_j$ denotes the probability of early exercise, $d_j$ denotes the dividend yield, $\mu_j$ is a disturbance term, and all other notation is as it was previously defined.

## 6.2. Results

To begin, all observations were pooled, and the grand means and standard deviations of the option prices were computed. The results were as follows:

| Value | Mean | Standard deviation |
|---|---|---|
| Observed | $4.1388 | $5.2400 |
| $C(S, T, X)$ | 4.1291 | 5.1025 |
| $\max\left[c(S, T, X), c(P, t, X)\right]$ | 4.1198 | 5.1025 |
| $c(S, T, X)$ | 4.1071 | 5.1036 |

While the American call formula provided prices which are closer to the observed prices, all of the formulas yielded prices which are, on average, within three and a half cents of the observed market price.

The simple linear regression of market price on the model value is in the spirit of Theil's (1966) 'line of perfect forecast'. With perfect prediction the values of the coefficients $\alpha_0$ and $\alpha_1$ in the regression

$$C_j = \alpha_0 + \alpha_1 \hat{C}_j + \mu_j, \tag{10}$$

should be indistinguishable from zero and one, respectively. The estimate of $\alpha_0$ and its corresponding standard error provide a means of testing the degree of bias in the valuation equation; the estimate of $\alpha_1$ and its standard error provide a means of testing the degree of inefficiency.[15] The coefficient of determination from the regression reflects the degree to which the valuation equation is able to explain the variation in the observed call prices.

Observed market prices were regressed on each model's prices in each of the 160 cross-sections, where the number of observations included in the regressions averaged 97.3875 and ranged from 30 to 157. The average values of the weekly parameter estimates, $\bar{\alpha}_0$ and $\bar{\alpha}$, the Student $t$ ratios testing the hypotheses that the average value of the intercept term is equal to zero, $t(\bar{\alpha}_0)$,[16] and that the average value of the slope term is equal to one, $t(\bar{\alpha}_1)$, and the two-tailed probability levels that the $t$-values will be exceeded in absolute magnitude by a random variable following a Student $t$ distribution $p[t(\bar{\alpha}_0)]$ and $p[t(\bar{\alpha}_1)]$, are reported as Test 1 of table 4. The first-order serial correlation of the parameter estimates, $\rho(\hat{\alpha}_0)$ and $\rho(\hat{\alpha}_1)$, and the average of the coefficients of determination, $\bar{R}^2$, are also included.

All of the models seem to perform extremely well, with the explained variation being greater than 98 percent in all cases. Although there do not appear to be perceptible differences between the models, it is likely as a result of prediction error being small in relation to the magnitude of call price. In fact, when call price was regressed on the boundary condition max $[0, S - X \, e^{-rT}]$ in each of the 160 cross-sections, the average coefficient of determination was 87 percent. In subsequent tests the focus will be on relative prediction error so that the attenuating influence of heteroscedasticity will be reduced. Before leaving the results of Test 1, however, it is interesting to note that all models demonstrate a slight tendency to overprice low-priced options and to underprice high-priced options (i.e., $\bar{\alpha}_1 > 1$).

The remaining tests focused on identifying systematic behavior in the relative prediction error [i.e., $(C - \hat{C})/\hat{C}$] of the valuation models. As a preliminary investigation, the relative prediction errors of all cross-sections were, again, pooled, and the grand means and standard deviations computed. The results were as follows:

| Model | Mean | Standard deviation |
|---|---|---|
| $C(S, T, X)$ | 0.0108 | 0.2382 |
| $\max [c(S, T, X), c(P, t, X)]$ | 0.0148 | 0.2396 |
| $c(S, T, X)$ | 0.0215 | 0.2524 |

[15] When the forecast model underestimates high (low) values and overestimates low (high) values (i.e., $\hat{\alpha}_1 \neq 1$), it is said to be inefficient.

[16] The Student $t$ ratio for the intercept term, for example, was computed as $t(\bar{\alpha}_0) = \sqrt{160} \bar{\alpha}_0 / s(\hat{\alpha}_0)$. This methodology is not unlike that employed by Fama and MacBeth (1973, pp. 619–624).

The American call formula more clearly dominates when these figures are considered: both the mean and the standard deviation of the relative prediction error are lower than they are for either of the suggested approximations.

Test 2 addressed the underpricing of low-risk and overpricing of high-risk options issue. Both Black and Scholes and MacBeth and Merville document this phenomenon, but both authors' models exclude the premium for early exercise. If the probability of early exercise is correlated with the standard deviation of stock return, the American call formula should reduce the systematic pricing discrepancy.

The results reported for Test 2 in table 4 indicate that there exists a significantly positive relationship between prediction error and stock volatility for all models. The American call serves to reduce the magnitude of the slope coefficient and the coefficient of determination, but the hypothesis that there is no relationship between the variables is soundly rejected. All models appear to overprice options on high-risk stocks and to underprice options on low-risk stocks.

Test 3 attempted to uncover systematic underpricing and overpricing of in-the-money and out-of-the-money options — again, a result that has been the cause of consternation. The findings indicate that the relationship is not as strong as one may have been led to believe. The null hypothesis of a zero slope coefficient cannot be rejected at the 5 percent level for any of the valuation models. Again, the American call formula did better than the alternative models, with its slope coefficient being lower and less significant.

The fourth regression examined whether pricing inaccuracy was related to the probability of early exercise. In this test the independent variable $p$ was computed as

$$\int_{S_t^*}^{\infty} L(S_t) \, dS_t,$$ [17]

where $S_t^*$ represents the ex-dividend stock price above which the American option holder will exercise just prior to the ex-dividend instant and $L(\cdot)$ is a log-normal density function. Since the simple approximation does not account for the prospect of early exercise and since the Black approximation does so only in an ad hoc fashion, the results should range from a strong relationship for the simple model to no relationship for the American call formula.

---

[17]When a riskless hedge can be formed between the call option and its underlying stock, the value of the American call on a stock with a known dividend is the sum of the discounted conditional expected value of the option's worth if exercised just prior to the ex-dividend instant, $e^{-rt}[E(S_t \mid S_t > S_t^*) - X + \alpha D] \, \mathrm{prob}(S_t > S_t^*)$, and the discounted conditional expected value of the option's worth if exercised at expiration, $e^{-rT}[E(S_T \mid S_T > X \text{ and } S_t \leq S_t^*) - X] \, \mathrm{prob}(S_T > X \text{ and } S_t \leq S_t^*)$. In the American call option formula (3), $N_1(b_2)$ represents $\mathrm{prob}(S_t > S_t^*)$ and $N_2(a_2, -b_2; -\sqrt{t/T})$ represents $\mathrm{prob}(S_T > X \text{ and } S_t \leq S_t^*)$. For the present purpose of measuring the probability of early exercise, therefore, $N_1(b_2)$ was used.

Table 4

Average values of parameter estimates of the 160 weekly cross-sectional regressions testing for systematic relation between call option model relative prediction error and call option model determinants over the period January 17, 1975 through February 3, 1978.[a]

| Test[b] | Model[c] for $\hat{C}$ | $\bar{\alpha}_0$ | $t(\bar{\alpha}_0)$ | $p[t(\bar{\alpha}_0)]$ | $\rho(\bar{\alpha}_0)$ | $\bar{\alpha}_1$ | $t(\bar{\alpha}_1)$ | $p[t(\bar{\alpha}_1)]$ | $\rho(\bar{\alpha}_1) \cdot \bar{R}^2$ | |
|---|---|---|---|---|---|---|---|---|---|---|
| 1. $C = \alpha_0 + \alpha_1 \hat{C}$ | $C(S,T,X)$ | −0.0508 | −3.92[d] | 0.00 | 0.51 | 1.0088 | 2.61[d] | 0.01 | 0.28 | 0.98 |
| | max $[c(S,T,X), c(P,t,X)]$ | −0.0425 | −3.30 | 0.00 | 0.50 | 1.0092 | 2.74 | 0.01 | 0.28 | 0.98 |
| | $c(S,T,X)$ | −0.0300 | −2.27 | 0.02 | 0.53 | 1.0091 | 2.70 | 0.01 | 0.29 | 0.98 |
| 2: $\dfrac{C-\hat{C}}{\hat{C}} = \alpha_0 + \alpha_1 \hat{\sigma}$ | $C(S,T,X)$ | 0.1413 | 13.70 | 0.00 | −0.09 | −0.4326 | −14.54 | 0.00 | 0.02 | 0.06 |
| | max $[c(S,T,X), c(P,t,X)]$ | 0.1541 | 14.78 | 0.00 | −0.08 | −0.4628 | −15.32 | 0.00 | 0.04 | 0.07 |
| | $c(S,T,X)$ | 0.1831 | 14.94 | 0.00 | −0.03 | −0.5467 | −14.49 | 0.00 | 0.10 | 0.08 |
| 3: $\dfrac{C-\hat{C}}{\hat{C}} = \alpha_0 + \alpha_1 \left( \dfrac{S - X e^{-rT}}{X e^{-rT}} \right)$ | $C(S,T,X)$ | 0.0103 | 2.24 | 0.03 | 0.12 | −0.0780 | −1.76 | 0.08 | 0.14 | 0.05 |
| | max $[c(S,T,X), c(P,t,X)]$ | 0.0144 | 3.11 | 0.00 | 0.12 | −0.0802 | −1.80 | 0.07 | 0.14 | 0.05 |
| | $c(S,T,X)$ | 0.0209 | 4.31 | 0.00 | 0.15 | −0.0818 | −1.83 | 0.07 | 0.14 | 0.05 |
| 4: $\dfrac{C-\hat{C}}{\hat{C}} = \alpha_0 + \alpha_1 p$ | $C(S,T,X)$ | 0.0095 | 2.03 | 0.04 | 0.07 | 0.0117 | 1.19 | 0.23 | 0.07 | 0.01 |
| | max $[c(S,T,X), c(P,t,X)]$ | 0.0111 | 2.36 | 0.02 | 0.07 | 0.0347 | 3.54 | 0.00 | 0.09 | 0.02 |
| | $c(S,T,X)$ | 0.0101 | 2.14 | 0.03 | 0.07 | 0.0963 | 7.03 | 0.00 | 0.13 | 0.03 |
| 5: $\dfrac{C-\hat{C}}{\hat{C}} = \alpha_0 + \alpha_1 T$ | $C(S,T,X)$ | 0.0199 | 1.82 | 0.07 | −0.10 | −0.0389 | −1.19 | 0.24 | −0.08 | 0.02 |
| | max $[c(S,T,X), c(P,t,X)]$ | 0.0308 | 2.68 | 0.01 | −0.08 | −0.0628 | −1.77 | 0.08 | −0.05 | 0.02 |
| | $c(S,T,X)$ | 0.0611 | 3.43 | 0.00 | 0.00 | −0.1475 | −2.42 | 0.02 | 0.16 | 0.02 |
| 6: $\dfrac{C-\hat{C}}{\hat{C}} = \alpha_0 + \alpha_1 d$ | $C(S,T,X)$ | 0.0060 | 1.17 | 0.24 | 0.06 | 0.4612 | 0.96 | 0.34 | 0.09 | 0.02 |
| | max $[c(S,T,X), c(P,t,X)]$ | 0.0019 | 0.37 | 0.71 | 0.08 | 1.4309 | 2.91 | 0.00 | 0.11 | 0.02 |
| | $c(S,T,X)$ | −0.0067 | −1.29 | 0.20 | 0.09 | 3.1658 | 5.73 | 0.00 | 0.17 | 0.02 |

[a]Test specification notation:
$\hat{\sigma}$ = implied deviation of stock return.
$S$ = stock price net of the present value of the escrowed dividend.
$X$ = exercise price,
$r$ = annualized riskless rate of return,
$T$ = years to expiration,
$p$ = probability of early exercise,
$d$ = $D/P$ = quarterly dividend divided by stock price.

Column heading notation:
$\bar{\alpha}_i$ = average value of parameter estimate,
$t(\bar{\alpha}_i)$ = Student $t$ value testing the hypothesis that the average value of the parameter estimate, $\bar{\alpha}_i$, is equal to zero,
$p[t(\bar{\alpha}_i)]$ = two-tailed probability that $t(\bar{\alpha}_i)$ will be exceeded in absolute magnitude by a random variable following a Student $t$ distribution,
$\rho(\bar{\alpha}_i)$ = first-order serial correlation of the weekly parameter estimate $\bar{\alpha}_i$,
$\bar{R}^2$ = average value of the coefficient of determination from the 160 regressions.

[b]For convenience the subscript $j$ and the disturbance term $\mu_j$ are omitted from the test specifications.

[c]The models are $c(S, T, X)$, the value for an American call option on a stock with a known dividend; max $[c(S, T, X), c(P, t, X)]$, the approximate call option value using the higher of the values of a European call, where the stock price net of the present value of the escrowed dividend is substituted for the stock price variable, and a European call, where the time to ex-dividend is substituted for the time to expiration variable; and $c(S, T, X)$, the approximate call option value using the value of a European call, where the stock price net of the present value of the escrowed dividend is substituted for the stock price variable.

[d]All $t$-ratios except those of Test 1 are computed on the basis of a null hypothesis that $\bar{\alpha}_i = 0$. Those of Test 1 are computed on the basis of $\bar{\alpha}_0 = 0$ and $\bar{\alpha}_1 = 1$.

The results of Test 4 reflect the expected behavior. The relationship between the prediction error of the approximation $c(S, T, X)$ and the early exercise probability is strongly significant, with the $t$-value of the slope coefficient exceeding 7. The Black approximation apparently improves matters, but the relationship remains significant. The American call formula almost completely eliminates the association.

The fifth regression was included to test for the previously reported relationship between pricing error and the time to expiration of the option. The results show that while there exists a significantly negative relationship for the commonly applied approximation $c(S, T, X)$ (i.e., it underprices short-lived options and overprices long-lived options) it virtually disappears when the American call formula is used.

The final regression tested for systematic relationship between prediction error and the dividend yield on the stock.[18] Here there should be a significant relationship using the approximation methods, but none with the American call formula. The magnitude of the early exercise premium is importantly influenced by the amount of the dividend payment, and, since neither of the approximations account for the premium adequately, prediction error should be found.

The results of Test 6 are consistent with expectations. With the approximation methods the relationship between prediction error and dividend yield is strongly significant, and with the American call formula it is virtually non-existent.

As a precautionary measure, the prediction errors of the three models were regressed on various combinations of the independent variables in Tests 2 through 6. The aforementioned results seemed to be robust in that whenever standard deviation was included as an explanatory variable, it appeared in a significantly negative fashion, with its coefficient being of the same order of magnitude as that in Test 2. None of the remaining variables had a significant impact on the prediction error of $C(S, T, X)$, independent of what other variables were included in the regression.

Finally, it should be noted that Tests 1 through 6, along with the multiple regressions, were performed on each cross-section as well as on the pooled observations, although only the former results are reported. Chow (1960) tests of the joint hypothesis that $\alpha_{0\tau} = \alpha_0$ and $\alpha_{1\tau} = \alpha_1$, $\tau = 1, \ldots, 160$, were computed for each of the tests, and at the 0.0001 percent significance level all values of $F(318,15262)$ were in excess of the critical value.

In summary, of the models tested, the American call option pricing formula provides the best description of the observed structure of call option prices. For options whose prices exceeded \$0.50 and whose remaining lives included exactly one ex-dividend date, the relative prediction error of $C(S, T, X)$ was markedly lower than those of the alternative models, and was not systematically related to:

---

[18]The dividend yield variable was computed by dividing the escrowed quarterly dividend by the stock price.

(1) the degree to which the option was in-the-money or out-of-the-money, (2) the probability of early exercise, (3) the option's remaining time to expiration, or (4) the stock's dividend yield. The American call formula did not, however, eliminate, although it did reduce, the association between prediction error and the standard deviation of stock return. Further research into this relationship is clearly warranted.

The simple approximation $c(S, T, X)$ had results which were, for the most part, consistent with previous findings. Its prediction errors were related to the stock's volatility, to the option's time to expiration, and to all but one of the other variables considered. The degree to which the options is in-the-money or out-of-the-money apparently does not significantly affect the model's prediction error, contrary to previous evidence.

The Black approximation yielded results very much similar to those of the simple approximation, although its mean and standard deviation of relative prediction error were lower. The early exercise premium is apparently an integral component in pricing the American call option.

## 7. Test of market efficiency

### 7.1. Procedure

The empirical evidence shows that the correspondence between observed and model prices is closest for $C(S, T, X)$. Nevertheless sufficient deviation could exist to permit trading profits. In an efficient options market, no costless arbitrage opportunities can exist. If a portfolio is formed by buying 'undervalued' and selling 'overvalued' options in proportions such that no wealth is used and no risk is assumed, its expected return is equal to zero.[19,20]

Underlying the weighting scheme employed to form the costless arbitrage position is the premise that asset prices are determined by security market relation[21]

$$E(\tilde{r}_i) = r + \beta_i[E(\tilde{r}_m) - r], \tag{11}$$

where $E(\tilde{r}_i)$ and $E(\tilde{r}_m)$ are the instantaneous expected returns on asset $i$ and the market, respectively, $r$ is the riskless rate of interest, and $\beta_i \equiv \text{cov}(\tilde{r}_i, \tilde{r}_m)/\text{var}(\tilde{r}_m)$ is

---

[19]The null hypothesis of a zero expected return on the costless arbitrage portfolio jointly tests the propositions that: (1) the American call option model is correctly specified, (2) the implied volatility of common stock return is an accurate reflection of the expected volatility, and (3) the options market is efficient.

[20]Costless arbitrage portfolio test methodology has been used in previous tests of capital asset pricing. See, for example, Black and Scholes (1974) and Watts (1978).

[21]The continuous time version of the capital asset pricing model was derived by Merton (1973b).

asset $i$'s instantaneous relative systematic risk. For portfolios the relation is

$$E(\tilde{r}_p)=r+\beta_p[E(\tilde{r}_m)-r], \tag{12}$$

where $E(\tilde{r}_p)=\sum \omega_i E(\tilde{r}_i)$, $\beta_p=\sum \omega_i \beta_i$ and $\sum \omega_i=1$, and $\omega_i$ denotes the proportional investment in security $i$.

The riskless hedge position consists of two portfolios: the first containing undervalued options (denoted by the subscript $u$), and the second containing overvalued options ($o$). Applying eq. (12), the expected returns on these portfolios are

$$E(\tilde{r}_u)=r+\beta_u[E(\tilde{r}_m)-r], \tag{13}$$

and

$$E(\tilde{r}_o)=r+\beta_o[E(\tilde{r}_m)-r], \tag{14}$$

respectively. If the undervalued securities are bought and the overvalued sold, the expected return on the hedge position ($h$) is

$$E(\tilde{r}_h)=E(\tilde{r}_u)-E(\tilde{r}_o)\doteq(\beta_u-\beta_o)[E(\tilde{r}_m)-r]. \tag{15}$$

If the constraint $\beta_u=\beta_o$ is additionally imposed, the expected return of this zero-investment, zero-risk hedge portfolio becomes

$$E(\tilde{r}_h)=0\cdot[E(\tilde{r}_m)-r]=0. \tag{16}$$

On first appearance the practical matter of creating a riskless arbitrage portfolio may seem as simple as investing equally in the options of the under-valued and the overvalued portfolios, and then hedging one portfolio against the other. Unfortunately this scheme does not ensure a perfect risk hedge, that is, $\beta_u=\beta_o$. To circumvent this problem a modest adjustment is made in the equal-weighted averaging procedure. First, the options in the undervalued (overvalued) portfolio are ranked in descending order of systematic risk. Two portfolios are then formed: the first by equal-weighted investment of one dollar in the high-risk options, and the second by equal-weighted investment of one dollar in the low-risk options. Where the number of options in the undervalued option portfolio is odd, the low-risk portfolio contains the extra option. Wealth is then allocated between the two portfolios such that

$$\omega_u^H \beta_u^H + \omega_u^L \beta_u^L = \beta^*, \tag{17a}$$

$$\omega_u^H + \omega_u^L = 1, \tag{17b}$$

$$\omega_u^H, \omega_u^L > 0, \tag{17c}$$

where $\omega_u^H$ is the proportion of wealth invested in the high-risk, undervalued option portfolio and $\omega_u^L$ is the proportion in the low-risk, undervalued option portfolio. $\beta^*$ is an arbitrary value of $\beta$, as is to be described subsequently. Applying a similar procedure to the overvalued options,

$$\omega_o^H \beta_o^H + \omega_o^L \beta_o^L = \beta^*, \tag{18a}$$

$$\omega_o^H + \omega_o^L = 1, \tag{18b}$$

$$\omega_o^H, \omega_o^L > 0. \tag{18c}$$

Going long one dollar in the dollar in the undervalued option portfolio and short one dollar in the overvalued option portfolio, the net investment position is

$$(\omega_u^H + \omega_u^L) - (\omega_o^H + \omega_o^L) = 1 - 1 = 0, \tag{19}$$

and the net risk position is

$$(\omega_u^H \beta_u^H + \omega_u^L \beta_u^L) - (\omega_o^H \beta_o^H + \omega_o^L \beta_o^L) = \beta^* - \beta^* = 0, \tag{20}$$

exactly the desired costless arbitrage result.

The selection of an appropriate value of $\beta^*$ is somewhat arbitrary, although it should be chosen such that the allocation among the undervalued and the overvalued options is as even as possible. To accomplish this result $\beta^*$ is set equal to the arithmetic average of the systematic risk coefficients of the options contained in the sample in week $t$. In this way there is reasonable assurance that the distribution of wealth among securities is fairly even, and the constraints (17c) and (18c) are satisfied.

Implementing the concept of systematic risk coefficients for call options presents interrelated problems. Since the stock return generating process is stationary through time [Assumption (A.2)], the call option return process is non-stationary — the mean and the standard deviation decrease as the option approaches maturity. With respect to the test methodology, this non-stationarity poses two problems: (1) how to estimate the option's beta, and (2) how to compensate for the systematic risk change in the 'riskless' hedge position.

The estimation problem is resolved by employing an estimate of the stock beta and an estimate of the elasticity of the call price with respect to the stock price. Each week the most recent 100 weeks of historical stock returns $(R_{P\tau})$ are regressed on the historical observed returns of a market index $(R_{m\tau})$,[22] that is,

$$R_{P\tau} = \alpha_P + \beta_P R_{m\tau} + v_{P\tau}, \qquad \tau = t - 99, \ldots, t. \tag{21}$$

[22]The log-linear investment relative form of the market model regression may have been more appropriate in this instance since the theoretical arguments were expressed in terms of instantaneous rates of return. Weekly returns, however, were used so as to provide a consistency in units with the weekly option portfolio rebalancing activity.

to estimate the stock's systematic risk coefficient. The estimate, $\hat{\beta}_P$, is then multiplied by the elasticity of call price with respect to stock price to obtain an estimate of the call option's systematic risk, that is,

$$\hat{\beta}_C = \eta \cdot \hat{\beta}_P,^{23} \tag{22}$$

where $\eta (\equiv (\partial C/\partial P)(P/C))$ denotes the elasticity.

The remaining concern about non-stationarity has to do with the discretely-adjusted option trading activity. Since an option's risk decreases deterministically as it approaches maturity, all other things remaining constant, the risks of the undervalued and the overvalued portfolios decrease over the investment interval $\Delta t$. However, if the overvalued options are shorted, the decrease in the risk of the undervalued option position should be approximately offset by the increase in the risk of the overvalued option position, as long as the composite characteristics of the two option portfolios are nearly the same. In other words, although non-stationarity is a problem when one considers only a long or only a short position in an option or a portfolio of options, hedging long options against short options should compensate for its effect.

### 7.2. Results

Descriptive summary statistics of the stock betas, elasticities and call option betas are reported in table 5. On average, the stock beta was close to one, with the

Table 5

Distribution of the 15,582 call option systematic risk estimates based upon the market model regressions of stock returns and the elasticities of the call option price with respect to stock price.

|  | Stock's systematic risk estimate $\hat{\beta}_P$ | Elasticity of call price with respect to stock price $\eta$ | Call option's systematic risk estimate $\hat{\beta}_C$ |
|---|---|---|---|
| Mean | 1.18 | 8.66 | 10.03 |
| Standard deviation | 0.35 | 4.06 | 5.00 |
| Mean absolute deviation | 0.27 | 3.04 | 3.85 |
| Deciles     0.10 | 0.80 | 4.44 | 4.58 |
| 0.20 | 0.91 | 5.40 | 5.90 |
| 0.30 | 1.00 | 6.19 | 7.04 |
| 0.40 | 1.10 | 6.99 | 8.10 |
| 0.50 | 1.17 | 7.86 | 9.22 |
| 0.60 | 1.27 | 8.77 | 10.47 |
| 0.70 | 1.36 | 9.92 | 11.85 |
| 0.80 | 1.45 | 11.39 | 13.74 |
| 0.90 | 1.62 | 13.48 | 16.58 |

[23] By definition $\beta_C \equiv \mathrm{cov}(\tilde{r}_C, \tilde{r}_m)/\mathrm{var}(\tilde{r}_m)$. If the call option and stock instantaneous rates of return are perfectly correlated, that is, $\tilde{r}_C = \eta \tilde{r}_P$, $\beta_C = \mathrm{cov}(\eta \tilde{r}_P, \tilde{r}_m)/\mathrm{var}(\tilde{r}_m) = \eta \beta_P$.

distribution appearing slightly skewed to the left. The average elasticity was about 8.66, indicating that option prices are very sensitive to shifts in the stock price. The options were extremely risky, with their average beta exceeding 10.

The portfolio formation procedure involved creating two equal-weighted portfolios of undervalued and of overvalued options. The two undervalued option portfolios were weighted such that constraints (17a) and (17b) were satisfied, and the two overvalued option portfolios were weighted such that constraints (18a) and (18b) were satisfied. Portfolio rebalancing occurred weekly so that 160 sets of weights were created. A summary of the portfolio compositions using the American call option valuation equation to identify undervalued and overvalued options is included in table 6.[24] The technique worked well, with

Table 6

Distributions of the allocations among the high-risk and low-risk undervalued and high-risk and low-risk overvalued option portfolios used in forming the costless arbitrage position in each of the 160 weeks during the period January 17, 1975 through February 3, 1978.

| | | | Undervalued | | | Overvalued | | |
|---|---|---|---|---|---|---|---|---|
| | | Portfolio[a] risk $\beta^*$ | Number of options $n_u$ | High-[b] risk portfolio weight $\omega_u^H$ | Low-[b] risk portfolio weight $\omega_u^L$ | Number of options $n_o$ | High-[b] risk portfolio weight $\omega_o^H$ | Low-[b] risk portfolio weight $\omega_o^L$ |
| Mean | | 9.9939 | 48.78 | 0.6192 | 0.3808 | 48.61 | 0.3198 | 0.6802 |
| Standard deviation | | 2.4274 | 18.27 | 0.0959 | 0.0959 | 19.14 | 0.1478 | 0.1478 |
| Mean absolute deviation | | 2.0261 | 14.51 | 0.0745 | 0.0745 | 15.47 | 0.1148 | 0.1148 |
| Deciles | 0.10 | 6.5801 | 28.00 | 0.4993 | 0.2572 | 24.00 | 0.1384 | 0.5123 |
| | 0.20 | 7.7246 | 35.00 | 0.5467 | 0.3008 | 32.00 | 0.2176 | 0.5536 |
| | 0.30 | 8.4664 | 38.00 | 0.5748 | 0.3363 | 38.00 | 0.2619 | 0.5958 |
| | 0.40 | 9.2773 | 41.00 | 0.6030 | 0.3598 | 42.00 | 0.2995 | 0.6304 |
| | 0.50 | 9.9085 | 47.00 | 0.6247 | 0.3761 | 46.00 | 0.3280 | 0.6730 |
| | 0.60 | 10.8531 | 52.00 | 0.6403 | 0.3985 | 52.00 | 0.3749 | 0.7010 |
| | 0.70 | 11.6174 | 56.00 | 0.6669 | 0.4270 | 57.00 | 0.4115 | 0.7459 |
| | 0.80 | 12.2248 | 63.00 | 0.7037 | 0.4553 | 66.00 | 0.4483 | 0.7860 |
| | 0.90 | 13.1151 | 75.00 | 0.7459 | 0.5021 | 75.00 | 0.5003 | 0.8621 |

[a]The value of $\beta^*$ is the arithmetic average of the systematic risk coefficients of all options contained in the sample in each week.

[b]To form the costless arbitrage position each week, four portfolios are initially created by equal-weighted investments in high-risk and low-risk undervalued and high-risk and low-risk overvalued options. The four weights listed in these columns are the weights applied to the equal-weighted portfolios in order to match the systematic risk characteristics of the undervalued and overvalued option positions at $\beta^*$. By going long one dollar in the undervalued option position and short one dollar in the overvalued option position, a costless (i.e., $\$1 - 1 = 0$), riskless (i.e., $\beta^* - \beta^* = 0$) arbitrage portfolio is formed.

[24]The 'picking of outliers' using the American call formula may systematically identify bid prices as undervalued options and ask prices as overvalued options, and, hence, the rate of return on the hedge portfolio may be slightly overstated. For an explanation of this selection bias, see Phillips and Smith (1980, pp. 186–187).

more than 80 percent of the allocations falling within the 0.2–0.8 range and with the constraints (17c) and (18c) satisfied in all of the cross-sections. Not surprisingly, the significantly negative relationship between prediction error and standard deviation of stock return influenced the structure of the costless arbitrage portfolio. The high-risk undervalued position and the low-risk overvalued portfolio were, in general, weighted more heavily in matching the systematic risks of the undervalued and the overvalued positions.

With the weekly portfolio compositions computed, generating the hedge portfolio return series became a matter of weighting and averaging the weekly option returns. To test whether the hedge portfolio had zero systematic risk during the sample period, the hedge returns were regressed on the market returns $(\tau = 1, \ldots, 160)$. The OLS regression results were

$$R_{h\tau} = 0.0258 - 0.4469 R_{m\tau} + e_{h\tau}, \qquad R^2 = 0.0128, \quad \hat{\rho} = -0.007,$$
$$\quad (4.59) \quad\;\; (-1.43)$$

$$s(R_h)/s(R_m) = 2.95,$$

where the values in parentheses are $t$-ratios, $\hat{\rho}$ is the estimated first-order serial correlation in the disturbance term and $s(\cdot)$ denotes the estimated standard deviation.[25] Although the absolute magnitude of the slope coefficient appears large, its size relative to the average option risk level reported in table 6, 9.9939, is small, and at the 15 percent significance level the null hypothesis that the portfolio has zero systematic risk cannot be rejected.

The null hypothesis of a zero expected return on the costless arbitrage portfolio was tested under two distributional assumptions. First, assuming the hedge returns were drawn from a normal distribution, a Student $t$ test,

$$t = \sqrt{n}\,\bar{x}/s,$$

was performed. The mean $(\bar{x})$ and the standard deviation $(s)$ of the 160 sample returns were 0.0246 and 0.0707, respectively, so that the Student $t$ ratio was 4.41. If expected returns were, on average, realized during the sample period, the null hypothesis is rejected at the 0.0019 percent significance level.

If the hedging of the undervalued option portfolio against the overvalued portfolio did not adequately control for the nonstationarity of the option return process, the hedge portfolio's return distribution might be asymmetric, with the direction of the asymmetry contingent upon whether the deterministic decrease in the value of the undervalued options outweighed the deterministic increase in

---

[25]Using the CRSP equal-weighted market index the regression results were:
$$R_{h\tau} = 0.0280 - 0.4851 R_{m\tau} + e_{h\tau}, \quad \text{with a coefficient of determination of 0.0180.}$$
$$\quad (4.75) \;\; (-1.70)$$

the value of the overvalued options or vice versa. Assuming that the hedge returns were drawn from a non-normal distribution, a Johnson (1978) modified $t$ test,

$$t_{\text{JOHN}} = \sqrt{n} [\bar{x} + \hat{\mu}_3/6s^2 n + \hat{\mu}_3 \bar{x}^2/3s^4]/s,$$

was performed, where $\hat{\mu}_3$ denotes the third central sample moment. The Johnson $t$ ratio was 4.08, and, at the 0.0115 percent significance level, the null hypothesis was rejected. The difference between the Student $t$ and the Johnson $t$ ratios, however, indicates that the hedge return distribution was slightly negatively skewed.

With the null hypothesis of a zero hedge return rejected, the question arose whether investors could realize positive trading profits after transaction costs by enacting the costless arbitrage trading strategy. To answer this question, the effect of a proportional transaction cost rate, $F$, was simulated. At the beginning of each week each dollar of after-transaction-cost proceeds from the overvalued option portfolio sold short, $\$1(1-F)$, was assumed to be invested in the undervalued option portfolio, $\$1(1-F)/(1+F)$. At the end of the week, the long position was closed yielding proceeds $\$(1-F)(1-F)(1+r_u)/(1+F)$, and the short position was covered costing $\$1(1+F)(1+r_o)$. The after-transaction-cost return on the hedge portfolio $(r_h^t)$ was, therefore,

$$r_h^t = (1-F)(1-F)(1+r_u)/(1+F) - (1+F)(1+r_o).$$

The mean after-transaction-cost hedge return was assumed to be equal to zero, the mean realized returns of the undervalued and the overvalued option portfolios, 1.2515 percent and $-1.2137$ percent, were substituted for $r_u$ and $r_o$, respectively, and the value of $F^*$ was computed.[26] A proportional transaction cost rate of 0.616 percent was sufficient to eliminate all of the trading profits that could be realized by implementing the costless arbitrage activity.

In Phillips and Smith (1980, p. 184) the average bid–ask spread for CBOE call options priced at more than \$0.50 was reported as 4.5 percent of the average of the bid and ask prices. Assuming that the option prices used in the present test are halfway between the bid and ask prices,[27] the value of $F^*$, 0.616 percent, can be thought of as one-half of the bid–ask spread as a percentage of price, and can be compared with one-half of the value of the Phillips and Smith estimate, 2.25 percent. In sum, option market efficiency is soundly supported. The profits from

---

[26]The solution for the maximum transaction cost rate was computed using the formula, $F^* = (1 + k - 2\sqrt{k})/(1-k)$, where $k = (1 + \bar{R}_o)/(1 + \bar{R}_u)$ and $\bar{R}_u$ and $\bar{R}_o$ are the realized returns on the undervalued and overvalued portfolios. The remaining root of the quadratic equation did not yield a solution for $F^*$ between 0 and 1.

[27]Again, it should be reminded that there may be a selection bias in the beginning of week prices since the model may have systematically picked out bid and ask prices as undervalued and overvalued options, respectively. See footnote 23.

buying undervalued options and selling overvalued options are insufficient to cover the market makers spread, let alone the remaining trading costs such as commissions and transfer fees.

## 8. Summary and conclusions

This study examines the pricing performance of three methods for valuing American call options on dividend-paying stocks. The methods include: (1) the simple approximation obtained by substituting the stock price net of the present value of the escrowed dividend into the Black–Scholes formula, (2) the Black approximation obtained by taking the higher of the Black–Scholes formula value using stock price net of the present value of the escrowed dividend and the Black–Scholes formula value using the time to ex-dividend as the time to expiration variable, and (3) the correctly specified equation for the American call option on a stock with a known dividend. Previous empirical investigations have focused on the simple approximation method, and have found several disturbing relationships between the degree of under- and over-pricing and the determinants of call value, for example, the standard deviation of stock return, the degree to which the option is in-the-money or out-of-the-money, and the option's time to expiration. This study shows that these correlations are, for the most part, spurious in nature, induced by the approximation's failure to account for the American call option holder's early exercise privilege.

The American call formula is shown to alleviate all of the dependencies except the relationship between prediction error and the standard deviation of stock return. Even when the American call formula is used, there remains a tendency of the model to underprice options on low-risk stocks and to overprice options on high-risk stocks. This phenomenon may be attributable to several sources: (1) non-stationarity of stock return standard deviation parameter, (2) the assumption of a known dividend, and (3) the assumption of zero tax rate differential between dividend and capital gain income.

The American call formula also better describes the observed structure of call option prices than either of the approximations. Both the mean and the standard deviation of the relative prediction errors are lower. Since the cost of implementing the correct pricing equation is only slightly higher than the approximations, it should be used for pricing American calls and for computing implied standard deviations. If an approximation is desired, however, the results of this study indicate that the Black approximation is more accurate than the simpler method.

Previous studies have also documented that weighted implied standard deviations are better predictors of future return volatility than historical estimates. In this study standard deviations based upon minimizing the sum of squared deviations of the observed call prices from the model's prices are used. In a preliminary investigation the minimum sum of squares estimates were compared with three weighted implied standard deviation measures, where the weights were: (1) equal, (2) the partial derivative of the model price with respect to stock return standard deviation, and (3) the elasticity of model price with respect to stock return standard deviation. The test results, not reported here, indicate that the minimum sum of squares method yields more accurate estimates of subsequent realized volatility than the weighted average methods.

The volatility estimation methodology employed here also differs from previous studies in two other respects. First, contemporaneous volatility estimation and option valuation is avoided. The standard deviation parameter used in option valuation process is obtained by computing the implied standard deviation from the option prices in the previous week. In this way, the presumption that the model prices and, yet, does not price options correctly at a given instant is unnecessary, and single options written on a stock in a given week are retained in the sample. Second, an implied standard deviation is computed for each option maturity. Aggregating all options written on a stock presupposes that the market's assessment of a stock's volatility is independent of the length of time into the future for which it is estimated. Available empirical evidence suggests otherwise.

This study also investigates Chicago Board Options Exchange efficiency using the American call option formula and a costless arbitrage hedging strategy. At the beginning of each week during the sample period January 17, 1975 through February 3, 1978, underpriced and overpriced options are hedged against one another in proportions such that a zero-risk, zero-investment option portfolio is formed. At the end of each week the position is closed, and the gain or loss is realized. The average weekly return using this trading strategy is 2.63 percent, and the null hypothesis of a zero expected return on the hedge portfolio is rejected. A proportional transaction cost rate of less than 1 percent, however, is sufficient to eliminate the trading profits, and the Chicago Board Options Exchange must be deemed to be an efficient market.

## References

Black, F., 1975, Fact and fantasy in the use of options, Financial Analysts Journal 31, 36–41, 61–72.
Black, F. and M. Scholes, 1972, The valuation of option contracts and a test of market efficiency, Journal of Finance 27, 399–418.
Black, F. and M. Scholes, 1973, The pricing of options and corporate liabilities, Journal of Political Economy 81, 637–659.
Black, F. and M. Scholes, 1974, The effects of dividend yield and dividend policy on common stock prices and returns, Journal of Financial Economics 1, 1–22.
Boyle, P. P. and D. Emanuel, 1980, Discretely adjusted option hedges, Journal of Financial Economics 8, 259–282.
Chiras, D.P. and S. Manaster, 1978, The informational content of option prices and a test of market efficiency, Journal of Financial Economics 6, 213–234.
Chow, G.C., 1960, Tests of equality between sets of coefficients in two linear regressions, Econometrica 28, 591–605.

Eisner, M. and R.S. Pindyck, 1973, A generalized approach to estimation as implemented in the TROLL/1 system, Annals of Economic and Social Measurement 2/1, 29–51.

Fama, E.F. and J.D. MacBeth, 1973, Risk, return, and equilibrium: Empirical tests, Journal of Political Economy 81, 607–636.

Finnerty, J.E., 1978, The Chicago Board Options Exchange and market efficiency, Journal of Financial and Quantitative Analysis 13, 29–38.

Galai, D., 1977, Tests of option market efficiency of the Chicago Boards Options Exchange, Journal of Business 50, 167–197.

Geske, R., 1979, A note on an analytical valuation formula for unprotected American call options on stocks with known dividends, Journal of Financial Economics 7, 375–380.

Goldfeld, S.M. and R.E. Quandt, 1972, Nonlinear methods in econometrics (North-Holland, Amsterdam).

Johnson, N.J., 1978, Modified *t*-tests and confidence intervals for asymetrical populations, Journal of the American Statistical Association 73, 536–544.

Latane, H. and R.J. Rendleman, 1976, Standard deviation of stock price ratios implied by option premia, Journal of Finance 31, 369–382.

MacBeth, J.D. and L.J. Merville, 1979, An empirical examination of the Black–Scholes call option pricing model, Journal of Finance 34, 1173–1186.

Merton, R.C., 1973a, The theory of rational option pricing, Bell Journal of Economics and Management Science 4, 141–183.

Merton, R.C., 1973b, An intertemporal capital asset pricing model, Econometrica 41, 867–888.

Merton, R.C., M.S. Scholes and M.L. Galdstein, 1978, The returns and risk of alternative call option portfolio investment strategies, Journal of Business 51, 183–242.

Milton, R.C., 1972, Computer evaluation of the multivariate normal integral, Technometrics 14, 881–889.

Patell, J.M. and M.A. Wolfson, 1979, Anticipated information releases reflected in call option prices, Journal of Accounting and Economics 1, 117–140.

Phillips, S.M. and C.W. Smith, 1980, Trading costs for listed options: The implications for market efficiency, Journal of Financial Economics 8, 179–201.

Roll, R., 1977, An analytical valuation formula for unprotected American call options on stocks with known dividends, Journal of Financial Economics 5, 251–258.

Schmalensee, R. and R.R. Trippi, 1978, Common stock volatility expectations implied by option premia, Journal of Finance 33, 129–147.

Schwartz, E.S., 1977, The valuation of warrants: Implementing a new approach, Journal of Financial Economics 4, 79–93.

Smith, C.W., 1976, Option pricing: A review, Journal of Financial Economics 3, 3–51.

Spang, H.A., 1962, A review of minimization techniques for nonlinear functions, SIAM Review 4, 343–365.

Watts, R., 1978, Systematic 'abnormal' returns after quarterly earnings announcements, Journal of Financial Economics 6, 127–150.

Whaley, R.E., 1981, On the valuation of American call options on stocks with known dividends, Journal of Financial Economics 9, 207–211.

# TRADING COSTS FOR LISTED OPTIONS

## The Implications for Market Efficiency*

### Susan M. PHILLIPS

*The University of Iowa, Iowa City, IA 52240, USA*

### Clifford W. SMITH, Jr.

*University of Rochester, Rochester, NY 14627, USA*

Received October 1979, final version received March 1980

This paper reexamines the anomalous evidence concerning the efficiency of the listed options exchanges. We focus on the structure of trading costs in that market, and note several costs which generally have been ignored, the largest of which is the bid–ask spread. When we adjust the published trading rules for our estimates of these trading costs, the reported abnormal returns are eliminated.

## 1. Introduction and summary

The efficiency of organized options exchanges is questioned in recent studies by Galai (1977, 1978), Trippi (1977), Chiras/Manaster (1978) and Klemkosky/Resnick (1979a, b). Although these authors all conclude their evidence is inconsistent with market efficiency, none of their studies carefully examines trading costs. As Jensen (1978) indicates, market efficiency implies that economic profits from trading are zero, where economic profits are risk-adjusted returns *net of all costs*. In this paper we analyze the structure of costs facing traders in the options markets. We examine the costs for traders who have a comparative advantage in arbitrage to determine whether trading costs are sufficiently large to eliminate the reported abnormal returns; if they are, market efficiency cannot be rejected and the inefficiency conclusion is unjustified.

*Overview of the paper*: In section 2, after summarizing the out-of-pocket costs of trading, we examine and estimate the transaction cost implicit in the

*This research was partially supported by the Managerial Economics Research Center, Graduate School of Management, University of Rochester. We thank M. Jensen, W. Schwert, L. Wakeman, J. Warner, R. Watts, and J. Zimmerman and the referee, M. Rubinstein for their comments and criticisms of this paper.

bid–ask spread for both the options markets and the stock market. We detail the sources and implications of information costs in establishing the positions required for tests of option market efficiency. Following Galai, we distinguish between ex post and ex ante trading profits, recognizing that the prices which signal ex post profit opportunities will not necessarily generate economic profits when a trading rule is implemented. In section 3, we indicate how the inclusion of the costs modifies the return to the Galai, Trippi, Chiras/Manaster, and Klemkosky/Resnick trading rules. Since much of the previous evidence on options market efficiency concludes that only seatholders on the exchange can earn abnormal returns, in section 4 we examine the expenditures necessary to become a seatholder and the implications of the opportunity cost of that investment for conclusions of options market inefficiency. In section 5 we present our conclusions.

## 2. Costs in options trading

Pricing of transactions services on most security exchanges involves two components: commissions and other explicit fees, plus the bid–ask spread. Although the costs of floor trading and clearing fees are well documented, most examinations of market efficiency of security exchanges ignore the bid–ask spread. The bid–ask spread reflects the charge by market makers for assuming the trader's undesired inventory position. Additionally, information costs are implicit in the specification of various trading rules. Both the explicit costs of commissions and the implicit costs of the bid–ask spread and information are relevant to questions of market efficiency since each must be incurred in implementing a trading rule.

### 2.1. Summary of explicit costs in trading listed options

We examine three groups — (1) options market makers, (2) arbitrageurs, and (3) non-member individual traders — as low cost traders effecting transactions in the options markets.[1] A market maker is a member of the exchange who contractually agrees to stand ready to buy and sell put and call options. Arbitrageurs are generally employees of a special trading division of one of the larger retail brokerage firms. Through the firm's exchange memberships, arbitrageurs have direct access to the trading floors of both options and stock exchanges. Since individual non-member traders do not have direct access to exchange floors, they contract with exchange members to provide that access.

The cost structures facing these investors directly reflect the institutional,

---

[1]Stock exchange specialists are not considered because they are prohibited by the exchanges from trading in options on stocks for which they make a market.

regulatory, and contractual arrangements under which they trade. The different classes of traders generally have cost advantages in varying areas; the costs of stock and option executions and the financing and capital requirements of each type of trader are quite different. Arbitrageurs generally effect their own stock transactions, so their out-of-pocket cost of trading equity claims is generally lower than for options market makers. The reverse is true for options market makers: they execute their own options transactions but contract out their stock executions. Individual traders contract all executions. These differences in structure and regulation lead to different costs in various hedging activities.

In addition to commissions, other costs face all traders. These are SEC transactions fees, net capital charges, the New York State transfer tax, and the cost of margin regulations. These costs are detailed in the appendix and their magnitudes are summarized in table 1.[2]

## 2.2. The bid–ask spread

The bid–ask spread is the difference between the highest quote to buy and the lowest offer to sell registered in the market. These recorded offers come from two sources: (1) quotes from market makers/specialists, and (2) customer's limit orders recorded on the exchange's limit order book. A market maker who performs the passive function of providing liquidity on the exchange continually quotes a higher price at which he is willing to sell than buy. Thus he expects to make a fraction of a point on each trade, and protect himself from customers who have additional information.[3] The size of the spread depends on a number of variables specific to the security including price, trading activity, etc.[4]

Any trader who actively seeks to establish a hedge must deal with other market participants, and thus must incur the expense of the bid–ask spread. Clearly, an individual or arbitrageur incurs the expense of the spread, but (perhaps not so clearly) a market maker also does. Market makers obviously

---

[2]In the appendix, we also examine regulatory constraints which affect the ability of traders to engage effectively in certain arbitrage activities. These provisions include exchange-imposed limitations on aggregate position size, constraints on the timing of the exercise of options positions, trading restrictions on out-of-the-money options, requirements to separate traders' transactions from transactions in which the trader acts as an agent of a customer, the short sale rule, and the so called 'zone requirements' and 'affirmative and negative obligation requirements' which limit market makers' activities.

[3]See Bagehot (1971).

[4]The original derivation and estimation of the supply function for market-making services was completed by Demsetz (1968) using NYSE securities. Tinic (1972), Tinic/West (1972, 1974), Benston/Hagerman (1974), Hamilton (1976, 1978), and Stoll (1978) have since extended and further tested the Demsetz model using various segments of the securities markets. In general, all of these authors found that price, some measure of trading activity, and competition were significant influences on the price charged by market makers for liquidity services.

Table 1

Summary of transactions costs for options market makers, arbitrageurs, and individuals in the options markets.

| | Options market maker | Arbitrageur | Individual |
|---|---|---|---|
| Floor trading and clearing | | | |
| Options | $0.50–1.00/contract | $1.50–1.70/contract ' | $10.00–65.00/contract |
| Stock | 5.00–12.50/round lot | 1.00–4.00/round lot | 5.70–48.70/round lot |
| New York State transfer tax | 0.00–6.25/round lot | 0.00–6.25/round lot | 0.00–6.25/round lot |
| SEC transactions fee | 0.00003 of sale | 0.00003 of sale | —[a] |
| Margin requirements | Regulation T | Regulation T & U | Regulation T & U |
| Net capital charges | 3/4 point above NY call rate | NY call rate | —[a] |

[a]Not a separate charge (should be reflected in the commission).

have the expense for trades on other exchanges; but to actively establish a position in his own security he must deal with the limit order book or, if on the CBOE, a competing market maker.[5]

Although we believe the bid–ask spread is an important trading cost in the options market, estimation of the appropriate magnitude of this cost is no simple matter. The average bid–ask spread overstates the cost for three reasons. First, trades occur inside the spread. In Phillips/Roberts (1979), analysis of the quotations and transactions occurring in selected dually traded options classes on the AMEX and CBOE in March and April 1977 indicates that on average 57 to 62 percent of the transactions occur at the bid or ask, with approximately 40 percent inside the spread. Second, of the 60 percent, presumably a number of the trades reflect new information and, although coincident with the bid or ask, are close to the true price. And third, if observed spreads are weighted by volume to complete the average spread, the weighted average would be lower than the simple average because securities with high volume tend to have lower spreads. However, the average bid–ask spread understates the cost if trading rules systematically pick out transactions for which the bid–ask spread is large and if the bid–ask spread differs across transactions.

The problem of estimation of the appropriate transactions cost associated with the bid–ask spread apparently is not easily solved. Data on prices alone would not allow one to infer which trades were initiated by buy or sell orders. Even if the data were augmented with reported bid–ask quotes, trades inside the spread are direct evidence that the quotes do not represent the effective supply and demand prices.[6] Apparently convincing establishment of the appropriate magnitude would require execution of the rule. Operationally, in this paper we employ the average bid–ask spread to adjust the reported returns to trading rules for trading costs.

To estimate the spread for stocks and options, we collected bid and ask quotations for options and underlying stocks. We then computed average daily spreads as a percentage of price and on an absolute dollar basis. For stocks, the spreads (ask minus bid) were calculated from the bid and ask quotations which were in effect at 1:00 am and 2:00 pm (EST) as reported in the July 1977 NYSE Transaction Journal. In addition, average percentage spreads were calculated by dividing the spread by the average of bid and ask prices, i.e., ((ask − bid)/(ask + bid)/2). Since there are five options exchanges which trade put options and each was allowed to trade put options on five

[5]Alternatively, if the market maker chooses to engage in arbitrage, he must expect to earn at least as much as if he continued to provide liquidity services. See section 4, below.

[6]Even if available, the use of bid and ask quotations would provide an underestimate of the returns to operating a trading rule. Given the direction of the bias, if abnormal returns were documented, market efficiency could be rejected.

stocks, our sample consisted of 1000 stock spread observations for the twenty trading days in July (two per stock per day).

In order to estimate the cost of liquidity to effect options transactions, the dollar and percentage spreads for the options classes in which both puts and calls are available also were calculated from the observed 11:00 am and 2:00 pm (EST) bid and ask quotations in effect on the CBOE for the weeks of June 27, 1977; September 19, 1977; December 5, 1977 and February 13, 1978.[7]

Table 2 contains the frequency distributions of the dollar and percentage spreads for the options traded on the CBOE and for stocks with listed options trading on organized exchanges. The options data are presented separately for puts and calls and for options whose prices are greater than $0.50.[8] The percentage spreads for stocks are generally lower than for options — the average spread for stocks is less than 1 percent, while the average spread for call options is 30 percent and for puts 15 percent. For options priced at more than $0.50, the spread drops to 4.5 percent for calls and 5.9 percent for puts. The dollar spreads for stocks and options are closer, between $16.00 and $20.00.[9]

## 2.3. Information costs: Ex ante versus ex post profits

To demonstrate market inefficiency, an implementable trading rule (which generates economic profits) must be specified. Galai (1975, 1977, 1978) points out that many of the tests of market efficiency, especially in the options markets, do not specify a trading strategy which a trader could have duplicated. Observing a set of prices which, ex post, would have allowed one to establish a position that generates abnormal returns does not imply market inefficiency. He argues that it must be further demonstrated that a trader observing those prices could have executed trades which yield profits. Thus Galai distinguishes between ex post and ex ante trading rules: an ex post rule assumes that trades can be instituted at the same prices which

---

[7]Four weeks were randomly selected for the examination of absolute and relative options premium spreads. Since put options were only opened for trading in July 1977, use of data for that month would not have allowed an examination of options spreads over several strike prices. That is, the put options trading in July 1977 all would have been at or near the money (i.e., the stock price would be approximately equal to the exercise price of the option).

[8]There are restrictions on trading in options whose closing price on the previous day was less than or equal to $0.50. See the appendix.

[9]Care should be employed in the interpretation of the data presented in table 2. While competing market makers on the CBOE provide strong incentives to keep the bid–ask quotes updated on a timely basis this is not the case for the specialists on the NYSE, AMEX, or PHLX. Thus, the reported bid–ask spreads for exchanges which use specialists are expected to be less accurate than those with competing market makers.

Table 2

Frequency distribution of average percentage and absolute dollar spreads (per 100 shares or per contract) between bid and ask prices of NYSE optioned stocks and CBOE options for which both puts and calls are traded. The distributions of spreads for options are reported both including and excluding options whose prices are less than $0.50.

| Percentage spreads | NYSE | CBOE calls | | CBOE puts | |
|---|---|---|---|---|---|
| | | All | $C \geqq \$0.50$ | All | $P > \$0.50$ |
| 0.0–0.2 | 59 | 7 | 5 | 7 | 5 |
| 0.2–0.4 | 213 | 0 | 0 | 0 | 0 |
| 0.4–0.6 | 275 | 7 | 7 | 3 | 3 |
| 0.6–0.8 | 176 | 6 | 6 | 0 | 0 |
| 0.8–1.0 | 170 | 16 | 16 | 3 | 3 |
| 1.0–1.2 | 38 | 13 | 13 | 6 | 6 |
| 1.2–1.5 | 45 | 50 | 50 | 6 | 6 |
| 1.5–2.0 | 23 | 49 | 49 | 19 | 15 |
| 2.0–3.0 | 1 | 166 | 163 | 109 | 105 |
| 3.0–5.0 | 0 | 188 | 181 | 181 | 161 |
| 5.0–8.0 | 0 | 116 | 112 | 132 | 127 |
| 8.0–12.0 | 0 | 55 | 49 | 70 | 66 |
| 12.0–20.0 | 0 | 35 | 13 | 44 | 23 |
| 20.0–30.0 | 0 | 17 | 1 | 11 | 3 |
| 30.0–50.0 | 0 | 32 | 3 | 9 | 0 |
| 50.0–100.0 | 0 | 21 | 2 | 6 | 3 |
| 100.0–200.0 | 0 | 98 | 0 | 26 | 0 |
| $n$ | 1000 | 876 | 670 | 632 | 526 |
| Mean (%) | 0.62 | 29.85 | 4.51 | 15.00 | 5.77 |
| Median (%) | 0.56 | 4.23 | 3.39 | 4.76 | 4.44 |

| Dollar spreads | NYSE | CBOE calls | | CBOE puts | |
|---|---|---|---|---|---|
| | | All | $C > \$0.50$ | All | $P > \$0.50$ |
| 0.000–6.250 | 0 | 311 | 145 | 169 | 145 |
| 6.250–12.500 | 421 | 252 | 225 | 220 | 196 |
| 12.500–25.000 | 421 | 215 | 213 | 143 | 136 |
| 25.000–50.000 | 156 | 90 | 79 | 83 | 59 |
| > 50.000 | 2 | 8 | 8 | 17 | 17 |
| $n$ | 1000 | 876 | 670 | 632 | 526 |
| Mean ($) | 20.46 | 16.05 | 18.23 | 18.84 | 19.10 |
| Medium ($) | 25.00 | 12.50 | 12.50 | 12.50 | 12.50 |

generate the profit signal, an ex ante rule implements the trades employing a subsequent set of prices.[10]

To implement a trading rule after observing the signal the arbitrageur (or market maker) frequently must place simultaneous orders in at least two but perhaps three or four different markets. If market orders are placed, a price change in any of the markets can eliminate the arbitrage opportunity.[11] Thus, as long as price changes can occur prior to execution of the orders, the trading rule is not riskless. If limit orders (rather than market orders) are placed, there is a positive probability that only part of a hedge will be executed (e.g., he may get the stock, but not the call). Thus, his position is not hedged.[12]

*The bid–ask spread and selection bias.* Given the evidence presented in table 2 of a substantial bid–ask spread in the options market, the use of transactions prices in ex post trading rules leads to a subtle form of selection bias; the use of ex ante tests reduces this. Most trading rules employed in the options literature involve a process of 'looking for outliers'. If a trading rule attempts to pick out undervalued calls for purchase, and it is assumed that the call could be purchased at observed prices (i.e., an ex post test) then the trading rule will systematically pick out, as undervalued, call prices from transactions initiated by orders to sell. In such a case, the trading rule is simulated using prices to initiate the position which systematically deviate from the prices at which the trades could have been made; the rule systematically use prices from the wrong side of the bid–ask spread. If the

---

[10]Ex post tests which employ closing prices both to generate the signal of profit opportunities and to establish the initial position in the securities from which returns are measured raise the possibility of measured abnormal returns because of noncontemporaneous data. For example, if a stock price changes at 2:00 pm but the last trade in an option on that stock was earlier, a trading rule which looks for mispriced options is more likely to identify that option as mispriced. If the trading rule is simulated using the same closing prices to establish positions in the securities, abnormal returns are likely to be measured. These results are spurious because this test does not represent an implementable trading rule. This source of bias can be controlled either by employing an ex ante test or by using intra-day data to ensure that observed prices are contemporaneous.

If the trading rule only employs closing prices from the CBOE, this problem is probably not major. Prior to February 28, 1979, reported prices on the CBOE were determined by a closing rotation so they should have reflected the information at the close of business. However, the closing prices on the CBOE after February 1979 and the American Options Exchange, as well as the stock exchanges are simply the last trade.

[11]When an apparent profit opportunity is indicated, that signal can be based on incomplete or inaccurate prior information. For example, to check the market price of the stock, market makers and arbitrageurs generally must rely on the last-sale information from the consolidated transaction tape. This information is subject to transmission delays and errors by the employees of the exchange.

[12]Traders typically refer to simultaneous transactions in two options on the same stock (e.g., which differ in expiration date or exercise price) as a spread rather than a hedge. However, even if the trading rule can be executed by placing all orders on one exchange, unless the various parts can be negotiated simultaneously the same problems occur.

position is mechanically closed at a later date, that closing price will on average be at the midpoint of the bid–ask spread. Thus, in addition to the cost of the full bid–ask spread, ex post trading rules which look for outliers are subject to a selection bias which should average half the bid–ask spread.

The selection bias can be avoided by employing an ex ante test, or reduced by using bid–ask quotes as signals for the trading rule. But if observations on quotes (rather than prices) are to be used as a signal to implement the trading rule, it should be noted that the exchanges only require that the quote information be valid for 100 shares. Quote information 'in size' (i.e., for multiple contracts) is not necessarily available.

## 3. Adjusting previous studies for estimated transactions costs

### 3.1. Galai's hedge and spread tests

Galai (1977) examines the pricing of listed call options on the Chicago Board Options Exchange and bases his tests of these prices on the Black/Scholes (1973) call pricing model. He replicates the Black/Scholes (1972) hedging strategy, in which a position in an option is matched with a position in the underlying stock to eliminate the risk of the aggregate position. Specifically, Galai compares the observed call price, $C$, with the Black/Scholes model value, $C_{BS}$,

$$C_{BS} = S N \left\{ \frac{\ln(S/X) + (r + \sigma^2/2)T}{\sigma\sqrt{T}} \right\} - X e^{-rT} N \left\{ \frac{\ln(S/X) + (r - \sigma^2/2)T}{\sigma\sqrt{T}} \right\}$$

(1)

where

$C_{BS}$ = Black/Scholes model value of the call,
$S$ = market price of the stock,
$X$ = exercise price of the call,
$T$ = time to expiration of the call,
$\sigma^2$ = variance rate on the stock,
$r$ = riskless rate,
$N\{\cdot\}$ = cumulative standard normal distribution function.

Galai then classifies options as overvalued or undervalued, compared with the Black/Scholes model.

In his ex post hedging test, Galai uses data from April, 1973 to November, 1973. He simulates the purchase of undervalued options (i.e., $C < C_{BS}$) while selling short the appropriate amount of stock and lending, and the writing of overvalued options while purchasing stock and borrowing. Galai finds that by adjusting this hedge daily, he can make abnormal returns of $10 per hedge per day. In his ex ante hedging test Galai establishes the hedge at closing prices from the next day's trading.[13] Again by adjusting prices daily, Galai's ex ante hedging test generates an abnormal return of $5.00 per hedge per day before transactions costs.

A return of $5.00 per hedge per day is insufficient to generate economic profits from trading. Galai's hedge requires purchasing one call contract while selling a fraction, $\partial C/\partial S (<1)$, of a round lot of stock. As we reported in section 2, the average bid–ask spread for a call contract is $16.00 and for a round lot of stock is $20.00; thus our estimated bid–ask spread for the call alone more than eliminates Galai's $5.00 average profit.[14]

Galai also considers a spreading strategy, where call options which differ only in expiration dates are simultaneously bought and sold by buying undervalued and writing overvalued calls.[15] With daily data, Galai finds that the ex post spreading strategy yields approximately $8.20 per spread per day before transactions costs. The returns to his ex ante test are lower, approximately $4.00 per spread per day. Again he concludes that the market does not seem perfectly efficient to market makers.

Employing this strategy requires daily round-trip transactions in two call option series.[16] But our estimated bid–ask spread of $16.00 for one call is sufficient to offset Galai's $4.00 average profit.

### 3.2. Galai's boundary conditions tests

Galai's (1978) tests of CBOE call prices are based on Merton's (1973) dominance conditions. Merton establishes that in a perfect market the call price must be greater than the stock price minus the discounted exercise price minus the sum of the discounted dividend payments,

$$C \gtreqless S - e^{-rT} X - \sum_{\tau < T} e^{-r\tau} D_\tau, \tag{2}$$

where $D_\tau$ is the dividend to be paid in $\tau$ periods ($\tau < T$).

---

[13]Galai (1977, 1978) is careful to indicate the potential data problems from using closing prices. Galai (1977, p. 172) warns: 'In analyzing the results, one should keep in mind the following problems: (1) The closing prices for options are not necessarily transactions prices. (2) Closing prices are sometimes artificial. (3) Closing prices do not always reflect a synchronization of the transactions on the CBOE and NYSE.'

[14]While the bid–ask spread eliminates Galai's reported average profit. the question of his largest reported profits remains an open question. We cannot tell whether abnormal returns would be available if, instead of using as a signal all over or underpriced options, the signal were required to exceed $20, for example. To test this, different signal levels could be examined to find an 'optimum' which could then be tested on a hold out sample of prices.

[15]Specifically, comparing two calls, $i$ and $j$, if $i$ is undervalued Galai buys (writes) one call $i$ and writes (buys) a quantity $(\partial C_i/\partial S)/(\partial C_i/\partial S)$ of call $j$. This procedure eliminates the systematic risk of the spread.

[16]Note that since the spread ratio can be different from 1; Galai's spread tests can involve purchases or sales of multiple contracts.

If eq. (2) is violated then by buying the call, selling the stock and lending, profits are assured, ignoring trading costs. Galai finds that of the 16,327 observations on calls and stock, 482 violations were observed. The average profit before transactions costs associated with the ex post test of dominance violations was $36.30. In his ex ante test, Galai repeats the trading rule, but establishes the position using closing prices from the next day's trading. He finds an average profit of $12.00.

To exploit the apparent profit opportunities from violations of Merton's lower boundary condition, round-trip transactions in both call and stock must be undertaken. From table 2, the average transaction cost for Galai's strategy implicit in the bid–ask spread is between $35 and $40. Again, this would appear to eliminate the $12.00 reported average profit.

### 3.3. Trippi's trading rule

Trippi (1977) devises a trading rule based on deviations in implied variance rates across call series written on the same stock. Following Latané/Rendleman (1976), Trippi notes that if the observed call price is employed on the left-hand side of eq. (1), an implicit function for the implied variance rate, $\hat{\sigma}^2$, results

$$\hat{\sigma}^2 = f(C, S, X, T, r). \tag{3}$$

Although a closed form solution for eq. (3) has not been derived, Trippi uses numerical techniques to solve eq. (1) for $\hat{\sigma}^2$. He then uses the average implied variance rate from different call options on a stock to calculate an expected market value for each option.

Trippi's trading strategy consists of the following steps: (1) Compute the average implied variance rate over different calls for each stock each week. (2) Using the average implied variance rate compute the implied value of the call, $\hat{C}$, using eq. (1). (3) Purchase options where the market price, $C$, is less than the implied market value, $\hat{C}$, by more than fifteen percent (i.e., $C < \hat{C}/1.15$); and write options where $C > 1.15\hat{C}$.

Trippi uses weekly closing stock and option prices from August 30, 1974, through March 14, 1975. He excludes options where: (1) the call price is less than $1.00; (2) time to expiration is less than three weeks; or (3) call prices are less than 1.3 times the stock price minus the exercise price. Application of his trading rule selects 403 options, 201 short and 202 long positions. On average, Trippi earns 11.4 percent per option per week.

This trading rule requires weekly round-trip transactions in calls. Moreover, Trippi's reported return is likely to be overstated because of selection bias. Since Trippi's ex post test uses the same prices to identify over- and under-priced calls in establishing his position, he will systematically have to purchase calls when the observed price resulted from a sell order and sell calls when the observed price resulted from a buy order. However, in closing the position at the next week's price, he will on average be at the midpoint of the bid–ask spread. The transactions cost associated with the spread can be as high as 1.5 times the bid–ask spread. As reported in table 1, the bid–ask spread for calls selling at prices greater than $0.50 is 4.5 percent. Thus, this trading cost will be approximately 6.75 percent. The addition of commissions would appear to eliminate average abnormal returns to non-exchange-member traders; however the average abnormal returns to market makers and arbitrageurs still appear positive.[17]

### 3.4. Chiras/Manaster's trading rule

Chiras/Manaster (1978) employ Merton's (1973) adjustment for dividend payments to the Black/Scholes call pricing model,

$$C_M = S e^{-\delta T} N \left\{ \frac{\ln (S/X) + (r - \delta + \sigma^2/2)T}{\sigma \sqrt{T}} \right\}$$

$$- X e^{-rT} N \left\{ \frac{\ln (S/X) + (r - \delta - \sigma^2/2)T}{\sigma \sqrt{T}} \right\} \tag{4}$$

where

$C_M$ = Merton dividend adjusted model value of the call,
$\delta$ = (assumed constant and continuously paid) dividend yield.

Like Trippi, they use numerical solution techniques to find the implied standard deviation (ISD) which makes the right-hand side of eq. (4) equal to the observed market price of the call, $C$. Since many options are traded on each stock, Chiras/Manaster have an average of 6.3 implied standard deviations for each stock on each month. They calculate a weighted average of the implied standard deviations (WISD) for each stock. Their trading strategy is:

(1) An 'implied market value' (IMV) is calculated for each option by using the value of its associated WISD in the evaluation equation.
(2) The observed option price is compared to the IMV.

[17]Trippi's methods are not explained in great detail, and thus his results should be interpreted with some care. For example, although his inclusion criteria are quite specific, he does not report how many alternative criteria were examined prior to that set which generated returns in excess of 11 percent. Since he reports no results from a hold-out sample, his results could be attributed to selection bias associated with searching for a trading strategy. This possibility is made more plausible because of the similarity between the Chiras/Manaster and Trippi tests and the differences in reported magnitudes. Finally, Trippi only reports raw returns, he makes no adjustment for risk.

(3) Options whose price exceeds the IMV by at least 10 percent are selected as 'eligible short positions' (ESPs). Options for which the IMV exceeds the price by 10 percent or more are selected as 'eligible long positions' (ELPs).

(4) A risk-free hedge is created between an ESP and an ELP for each stock having at least one of each type of option. For stocks having several ESPs or ELPs the two options with the maximum percentage difference from their IMVs are selected for the hedge.

(5) The amount of each option included in the hedged position is determined by the value of its hedge ratio (derivation shown below) so that each pair of options will produce offsetting gains and losses from an in-stantaneous movement in the underlying stock price.

(6) All option positions are closed one month later.

The hedge ratio is the reciprocal of the derivative of (4) with respect to the stock price, $(\partial C/\partial S)^{-1}$,

$$(\partial C/\partial S)^{-1} = e^{\delta T}/N \left\{ \frac{\ln(S/X) + (r - \delta + \sigma^2/2)T}{\sigma\sqrt{T}} \right\} > 1. \tag{5}$$

The hedge ratio, $(\partial C/\partial S)^{-1}$, gives the number of options that must be sold in order to offset the instantaneous unexpected change in the stock price and thus establish a riskless hedge. Using monthly data from June, 1973, to April, 1975, the Chiras/Manaster procedure generates an average return of 9.7 percent per hedge per month.

The Chiras/Manaster trading rule requires monthly opening and closing of both long and short positions in selected call options; moreover, it requires purchasing and writing multiple contracts to establish each hedge, since each hedge ratio is greater than one. Specifically, Chiras/Manaster calculated the return to their hedge as

$$R = [Q_L(C'_L - C_L) - Q_S(C'_S - C_S)] / [Q_L C_L + Q_S C_S], \tag{6}$$

where the subscripts L and S refer to the quantities ($Q$) and prices ($C$) of the long (undervalued) and short (overvalued) calls. Primes ($'$) indicate prices one month later. Chiras/Manaster report abnormal returns as a percentage of the total dollar value of the hedge (i.e., they assume a 100 percent margin requirement in writing calls). With positive trading costs, the prices Chiras/Manaster used are biased; the purchase prices, $C_L$ and $C'_S$, are too low, and the sale prices, $C'_L$ and $C_S$, are too high. Furthermore, their trading rule suffers from the same selection bias problem as Trippi's procedure, since they calculate implied variance rates, look for overvalued and undervalued options, and then trade on the same set of prices. Because their test is for ex post profit opportunities the appropriate adjustment can be as high as 1.5 times the bid–ask spread. These adjustments appear to eliminate Chiras/Manaster's reported average profits.[18]

### 3.5. Klemkosky/Resnick's trading rule

Klemkosky/Resnick (1979a, b) adjust the Gould/Galai (1974) put–call parity model for dividend payments. They check whether

$$(C - P - S)e^{rT} + X + \sum_{\tau < T} D_\tau e^{-r(T-\tau)} \leq 0, \tag{7}$$

where

$P$ = value of the put,
$D_\tau$ = dividend payment $\tau$ periods in the future $(\tau < T)$.

They also check the Merton (1973) and Roll (1977) sufficient condition for no premature exercise of a call on a dividend paying stock,

$$\sum_{\tau < T} D_\tau e^{-r\tau} \leq X(1 - e^{-rT}). \tag{8}$$

Using intraday prices from the options and stock exchanges for twelve trading days between July 1977 and June 1978, Klemkosky/Resnick (1979a) require that the observed prices occur within one minute of each other. They find 147 instances where the left-hand side of (7) was positive and greater than $20 (their estimate of transactions costs). The average appears to be approximately $35. In their ex ante test, Klemkosky/Resnick (1979b) use violations of the put–call parity restriction in (7) as a signal to institute a trade. The trade is established at market prices after imposing both 5 and 15 minute lags. By only acting on signals for which the indicated ex post profit would exceed $40, the trading rule earns an average of $58 per hedge.

Simultaneous transactions in put, call and stock markets are necessary to exploit the apparent abnormalities found by Klemkosky/Resnick; to implement their procedure, one must write a call, buy a put, and buy stock. Thus

---

[18]Using data provided by Chiras/Manaster, we modified the returns to their trading rule for estimated average costs reported in table 2. The dollar return per hedge fell from a profit of $133 to a loss of $68 per hedge when we used the $18.23 per contract cost and adjusted for selection bias. We also calculated the return to their trading rule using the 4.51 percent estimated spread; the dollar return fell from $133 to $51 per hedge. The difference in the estimated returns between the adjustments reflects the fact that options selected by the Chiras/Manaster trading rule tend to have prices below the mean for all listed options. If there are economies of scale in trading costs, the dollar adjustment will tend to overestimate, while the percentage adjustment will tend to underestimate, the costs for options priced below the mean.

the sum of bid–ask spreads for each type of security must be included. Using averages, this exceeds $50 per hedge.[19]

## 4. The market for exchange seats and market efficiency

When examining the evidence on options market efficiency, Galai, Trippi, Chiras/Manaster, and Klemkosky/Resnick conclude that exchange members could earn abnormal returns employing their trading rules. We have indicated that when the bid–ask spread is explicitly included as a cost of trading, the profits are generally eliminated; however even if the profits remained, we believe there is a logical problem with their argument.

If the market for exchange seats is efficient,[20] the price of a seat reflects the capitalized value of the expected future net cash flows to the marginal seatholder.[21] Thus, the investment in the exchange seat establishes an opportunity cost. Without accounting for that opportunity cost one would expect to observe 'abnormal' returns to seatholders; alternatively, only if the returns exceed that opportunity cost are security markets inefficient.

There are still a number of unanswered questions about the specific nature of the opportunity cost reflected in the seat price. First, the available evidence on arbitrage opportunities for market makers only documents the magnitudes of the anomalous price relationships; the frequency with which they occur, especially intraday, has yet to be examined. Both dimensions of the distribution are important. Second, we do not understand the nature of the trade-offs between engaging in arbitrage activities and the provision of liquidity services. The extant work on the market making function by Garman (1976) and Amihud/Mendelson (1980) restricts the analysis to liquidity motivated trades; the impact of the investment in information either by traders or market makers and its implications for the market making function has not been examined.

## 5. Conclusions

Jensen (1978, p. 95) points out that:

We seem to be entering a stage where widely scattered and as yet incohesive evidence is arising which seems to be inconsistent with the

---

[19]Since their (1979 a) test is for ex post profit opportunities and is subject to selection bias, the appropriate transactions cost is 1.5 times the bid–ask spread. However by employing intraday data, Klemkosky/Resnick avoid the selection bias problems associated with the use of closing prices.

[20]See Schwert (1977a, b) for evidence on the efficiency of the market for seats on the NYSE and AMEX from 1926–1972.

[21]Dann/Mayers/Rabb (1977, p. 19, fn. 28) point out to the extent that cash flows from arbitrage ever exceed those from the provision of liquidity services (either from acting as agent for non-seatholders and accomplishing their trades, or from acting as a market maker) the seat price will be higher to reflect the capitalized incremental cash flows.

theory. As better data become available and as our econometric sophistication increases we are beginning to find inconsistencies that our cruder data and tests missed in the past.

In attempting to resolve some of these inconsistencies, we have examined the structure of transactions costs facing traders in the organized options markets. Our major conclusions are: (1) There are several sources of direct and indirect costs associated with trading which have been generally ignored in previous studies of trading rules/market efficiency; the largest of these is the bid–ask spread. (2) When trading rules involving options markets are employed, a subtle form of selection bias arises from looking for outliers. With positive bid–ask spreads, the trading rule tends to pick security prices generated by orders from 'the wrong side of the market'. (3) To decide if abnormal returns are available to a seatholder, the opportunity cost associated with the use of the seat must be computed. However, if markets for exchange seats are efficient, then the capitalized rents available from the ability to trade at lower cost will be reflected in the price of the seat.

We believe these conclusions go far in explaining the reported inconsistencies with the efficient markets hypothesis.

## Appendix: Costs in trading options

In addition to the direct incremental transactions costs facing efficient traders, there are indirect transactions costs generated by SEC and self-regulatory organization rules which constrain the trading activities of market participants. Only if the regulatory constraints are completely ineffective do they not impose costs. On the other hand, if market participants must find alternative means of effecting transactions to reduce the impact of the regulations, search costs are incurred — fixed, not incremental, per trade. The full cost of regulatory constraints is composed of loss of income atributable to the inability to effect transactions as desired and/or search costs incurred in avoidance activities. Finally there are fixed costs associated with exchange membership which must be covered in order to earn a normal return to the investment in a seat. In this appendix we identify these sources of direct and indirect costs to traders.

### A.1. Floor trading and clearing fees: Option exchanges

On May 1, 1975, the commission structure in the securities industry became negotiated. Prior to that time, commissions were fixed by the exchange on which the security was traded. Table A.1 gives the basic commission schedules which were in force on the Chicago Board Options Exchange prior to deregulation. Although discounts are sometimes available, this schedule provides a benchmark for the commissions which individuals can expect.

When the options exchanges were first permitted by the Securities and Exchange Commission (SEC) to begin the trading of standardized options, the Options Clearing Corporation (OCC) was formed. The OCC is directly regulated by the SEC and all transactions in options must be cleared through the OCC. Since the capital requirements for membership in the OCC are fairly stringent, many potential members of the options exchanges have elected to clear through a few OCC members.[22] Over a period of time, the institutional and contractual arrangements have developed so that now options market makers are able to contract with the clearing firms for services involving clearing, bookkeeping, regulatory compliance and provision of financial and pricing information.

Floor trading and clearing fees are paid by market makers to their clearing firms for these services. Depending on individual contractual arrangements between the clearing firm and the market maker, floor trading and clearing fees range from $0.50 to $1.00 per contract. These fees are negotiable and generally lower for market makers who have high trading volumes, establish low-risk portfolio positions, and are well capitalized.

Although retail brokerage firms, for whom arbitrageurs work, could elect to belong to the OCC and therefore clear for themselves, most arbitrageurs contract their options transactions to OCC member firms by having market makers execute their options orders. Therefore, their fees for this service are somewhat higher than those incurred by market makers. Arbitrageurs' floor trading fees generally range from $1.50 to $1.70 per contract.[23]

## A.2. Floor trading and clearing fees: Stock exchanges

Table A.1 also contains the basic commission schedules which were in force on the New York Stock Exchange prior to deregulation on May 1, 1975. The SEC (1978) reports that for individuals the average discount from these commissions was 18.3% in December 1977; average commissions per share ranged from 5.7 cents for trades greater than ten thousand shares to 48.7 cents for trades less than two hundred shares.

Options market makers generally are not members of any stock exchanges, so must act as customers to effect transactions.[24] Usually the clearing firms

[22]For example, one clearing firm, First Options Corp., clears for over one third of the market makers on the CBOE.

[23]Since these fees are negotiable, it is possible that a few arbitrage arrangements result in lower fees. However, fees must be high enough to allow market makers a normal return for the services they provide.

[24]Some CBOE members are beginning to purchase seats on the Midwest Stock Exchange to lower the cost of stock executions, but with the advent of negotiated floor commissions many market makers believe that the cost of a nonmember NYSE execution does not justify the purchase of a stock exchange seat.

Table A.1

Minimum commission schedules fixed by the New York Stock Exchange (NYSE) and the Chicago Board Options Exchange (CBOE) prior to May 1, 1975.

| Type of order | Money involved in the order ($) | | Minimum commission schedule | |
|---|---|---|---|---|
| | At least | But less than | Stocks (NYSE)[a] | Options (CBOE) |
| Single trading unit orders (shares and options priced at $1 and above) | 0 | 800 | 2.0% of money + $ 6.40 | 1.3% of money + $12.00 |
| | 800 | 2,500 | 1.3% of money + $12.00 | 1.3% of money + $12.00 |
| | 2,500 and above | | 0.9% of money + $22.00 | 0.9% of money + $22.00 |
| | | | *Note:* The commission on a single trading unit order shall not exceed $65.00. *Note:* Odd lots. $2 less. | *Note:* The commission on a single trading unit order shall not exceed $65.00 nor be less than $25.00. |
| Multiple trading unit orders (shares and options priced at $1 and above) | 0 | 2,500 | 1.3% of money + $ 12.00 | 1.3% of money + $12.00 |
| | 2,500 | 20,000 | 0.9% of money + $ 22.00 | 0.9% of money + $22.00 |
| | 20,000 | 30,000 | 0.6% of money + $ 82.00 | 0.6% of money + $82.00 |
| | 30,000 | 300,000 | 0.4% of money + $142.00 | As mutually agreed |
| | 300,000 and above | | As mutually agreed | As mutually agreed |
| | | | *Add:* $6.00 per trading unit for 1st to 10th trading unit, $4.00 per trading unit for 11th trading unit and above. *Note:* In no case shall the commission per trading unit on a multiple trading unit order exceed the commission for a single trading unit order. | |
| Single and multiple trading unit orders (shares and options priced below $1) | 0 | 1,000 | 8.4% of money | As mutually agreed. Source applies stock schedule in box to the left. |
| | 1,000 | 10,000 | 5.0% of money + $ 34.00 | |
| | 10,000 and above | | 4.0% of money + $134.00 | |

[a]For all stock orders $5,000 and below in value: *Add* 10% to commission calculated above. For all stock orders above $5,000 in value: *Add* 24.2% to commission calculated above.

effect the stock transactions for their market makers as members of stock exchanges or through correspondent arrangements. The cost to market makers for executing stock transactions ranges from \$5.00–\$12.50 per round lot. Since floor commissions are negotiable, the cost of the execution is usually a function of the size of the transaction and the frequency of orders placed by the clearing firm.

The arbitrageurs, as employees of firms which generally are NYSE members, have direct access to the floors of the stock exchanges and can execute their stock transactions directly through their floor representatives. Floor commission rates for the NYSE range from \$1.00–\$4.00 per round lot. The average appears to be \$2.00 per round lot.

### A.3. Position and exercise limits

The exchanges all have specified limitations on the sizes of positions that members (and their customers) can take and on the number of contracts that can be exercised within a specified time period. The maximum position limit restriction in effect for all options exchanges is 1000 contracts (long or short) of the put and call class on the same side of the market covering the same underlying security. Depending on existing portfolio composition, traders can be prohibited from acting on profit signals which are based on the put–call parity or other dominance restrictions. In addition, traders are prohibited from exercising more than 1000 option contracts of a particular class within five consecutive business days.

### A.4. Trading restrictions on out-of-the-money options

A number of restrictions limit trading activity when options are more than \$5 out-of-the-money, based on the previous day's closing price in the primary market, or when the previous day's closing price of the option was less than \$0.50 per unit of trading.[25] These restrictions on out-of-the-money options constrain entry. Consequently, option arbitrage hedging based on the put-call parity relationship is restricted to at-the-money put and call options series. If the put (call) is deep in the money then a corresponding call (put) with the same exercise price is likely to be subject to the exchange restrictions governing out-of-the-money options.

### A.5. Short sale rule

Both arbitrageurs and options market makers are subject to the SEC's short sale rule: short sales may only be executed on an uptick. This

---

[25]Allowed trades include: (1) transactions to close existing positions; (2) writing covered options (i.e., the writer owns the underlying stock), (3) one-for-one spreads (i.e., the writer simultaneously purchases and writes calls on the same stock), and (4) options written by market makers.

provision increases the cost of executing short sales. Both market makers and arbitrageurs experience delays in executing short sale orders and before the order is executed the price of the stock can change. The arbitrage hedge position then is at risk both because of the price change and the delay.

### A.6. Market maker trading restrictions

Market makers are subject to various exchange-specific rules which serve to inhibit their trading activity. First, defined proportions of market makers' transactions must be effected in certain physical exchange locations called 'trading zones'. Market makers are assigned to these zones by the exchange which nominally wishes to assure continuous quotations for all options traded on that exchange.[26] Furthermore, zone requirements provide one basis for granting market makers exemptions from the usual customer margin requirements.

A second series of restrictions on options market makers' activities can be collectively called 'affirmative and negative obligations'. Affirmative obligations imply that when a market maker is in a crowd where a particular security is traded, he must respond to a request from another member for a quote on that security. Further, that quote must be close to the last sale based on an exchange-specified formula. Negative obligations generally imply that the market maker cannot displace customer orders: that is, customer orders must be filled before those of a market maker.

A final group of restrictions limiting market makers' trading activities center around the traditional separation of principal and agency transactions. These transactions are separated because of the alleged conflict of interest which is believed to exist if a trader acting in a fiduciary capacity on behalf of a public customer executes that customer's order from his own account. For market makers, the separation of agency and principal transactions is accomplished by exchange regulations. Some exchanges have different classes of members while other exchanges require that a member cannot act as broker and a dealer on the same day. In the latter case, an exchange member acting as a broker on any one day cannot effect arbitrage hedges or spreads for his own account when a signalled profit opportunity is observed.

In addition to the exchange rules, arbitrageurs have developed their own procedures to assure separation of agency and principal transactions. If the security is listed on two or more exchanges, the retail firms generally direct customer orders to one exchange and principal orders to another. If the security is not dually listed, arbitrage firms generally do not execute their own transactions on the exchange floor, but rather execute through other

---

[26]All options written on a specific stock trade at a particular post or pit. A zone frequently encompasses more than one post.

market makers (or specialists). This contracting arrangement has been developed particularly in the options area because crossing an arbitrageur's order with a firm customer's order creates a potential liability to the firm (breach of fiduciary responsibility) greater than the cost of contracting out the execution.

## A.7. Margin requirements

Option market makers, arbitrageurs, and individuals are all subject to margin requirements. This legislation specifies maximum percentages of assets value which can be financed with debt. The real cost of the margin requirements is related to the degree to which the constraint on the choice of financing is binding. If margin requirements are nonbinding constraints, and if less debt than the maximum allowable would be chosen, then the cost of the margin regulation is zero.

Options market makers are exempt from the Federal Reserve Board's margin requirements for options transactions, but not for their stock positions. Any position in a specialty security taken by a specialist or a market maker is exempt from the margin requirements. Traditionally, the FRB has allowed this exemption, arguing that specialists and market makers as part of their market making obligations are likely to assume undesired inventory positions; if they must stand ready to buy and sell securities, they should not be hampered by financing restrictions. Regulation T governs the extension of credit by broker–dealers for the purpose of purchasing and carrying securities and the extension of credit by the clearing corporations for effecting stock transactions. Although some margin relief for stock positions is allowed market makers who acquire certain hedge positions, the inventory carrying cost of stock positions is higher than for options positions. The interest rate on the load for stock positions is the N.Y. call rate (the cost to the clearing firm) plus 3/4 point.

Arbitrageurs generally are subject to the margin requirements under Regulation U, governing the extension of credit for financing and carrying securities by banks. Depending on the composition and commitment of the assets of the retail firm, the arbitrageur has access to unused customer debit balances to execute stock–option hedges. Arbitrageurs are subject to the same uniform margin requirements for options positions as customers under either Regulation T or U. The brokerage firms can typically borrow at the N.Y. call rate.

## A.8. Exchange seats

Exchange members or seatholders own the assets of the exchange; thus seats are equity claims in the exchange. The markets for seats on various stock and options exchanges are essentially similar in form. Each exchange maintains an anonymous auction market. Whenever a new bid or ask price is brought to the market all interested participants are informed. (In general, seats can only be purchased by individuals, not partnerships or corporations.) Generally, there are no direct out-of-pocket trading costs in the market for seats beyond the costs. of applying for exchange membership. Although reported bid–ask spreads for seats are large, trades regularly occur within the spread. Thus trading costs associated with the scale of seats appear to be relatively small. Table A.2 summarizes the cost associated with seats for various exchanges.

Table A.2

Prices of seats on the stock and options exchanges, March 1979.

| Exchange | Seat price ($) | Exchange dues ($) |
|---|---|---|
| New York Stock Exchange (NYSE) | 125,000 | 1,500/year |
| Chicago Board Options Exchange (CBOE) | 115,000 | 800/year |
| American Stock Exchange (AMEX) | 62,500 | 800/year |
| Philadelphia Stock Exchange (PHLX) | | |
|     Stock | 500 | 1,000/year |
|     Options | 5,000 | 1,000/year |
| Midwest Stock Exchange (MSE) | | |
|     Stock & options | 6,900 | 2,200/year |
|     Options | 6,900 | 1,000/year |
| Pacific Stock Exchange (PSE) | 4,300 | |

[a]Exchange dues on the Pacific Stock Exchange depend on the value of the transactions per month:

| $ 0M–10M | $0.1325/thousand |
|---|---|
| $10M–15M | $0.0880/thousand |
| $50M– | $0.0660/thousand |

## References

Amihud, Y. and H. Mendelson, 1980, Dealership market: Market making with inventory, Journal of Financial Economics, forthcoming.

Bagehot, W. 1971, The only game in town, Financial Analysts Journal 27, 12–22.

Benston, G.J. and R. Hagerman, 1974, Determinants of bid–ask spreads in the over-the-counter market, Journal of Financial Economics 1, 353–364.

Black, F. and M. Scholes, 1972, The valuation of option contracts and a test of market efficiency, Journal of Finance 27, 399–417.

Black, F. and M. Scholes, 1973, The pricing of options and corporate liabilities, Journal of Political Economy 81, 637–659.

Chiras, D. and S. Manaster, 1978, The information content of option prices and a test of market efficiency, Journal of Financial Economics 6, 213–234.

Dann, L., D. Mayers and R.J. Raab, Jr., 1977, Trading rules, large blocks and the speed of price adjustment, Journal of Financial Economics 4, 3–22.

Demsetz, H., 1968, The cost of transacting, Quarterly Journal of Economics 82, 33–53.

Fama, E.F., 1970, Efficient capital markets: a review of theory and empirical work, Journal of Finance 25, 38–417.

Fama, E.F., 1976, Foundations of finance (Basic Books, New York).

Fama, E.F. and M.E. Blume, 1966, Filter rules and stock market trading, Journal of Business 39, 226–241.

Fama, E.F. and G.W. Schwert, 1977, Asset returns and inflation, Journal of Financial Economics 5, 115–146.

Galai, D., 1975, Pricing of options and the efficiency of the Chicago Board Options Exchange, Unpublished Ph.D. dissertation (University of Chicago, Chicago, IL).

Galai, D., 1977, Tests of market efficiency and the Chicago Board Options Exchange, Journal of Business 50, 167–197.

Galai, D., 1978, Empirical tests of boundary conditions for CBOE options, Journal of Financial Economics 6, 187–211.

Garman, M.B., 1976, Market microstructure, Journal of Financial Economics 3, 257–275.

Gould, J.P. and D. Galai, 1974, Transactions costs and the relationship between put and call prices, Journal of Financial Economics 1, 105–129.

Hamilton, J.L., 1976, Competition, scale economies, and transactions cost in the stock market, Journal of Financial and Quantitative Analysis 11, 779–802.

Hamilton, J.L., 1978, Marketplace organization and marketability: NASDAQ, the stock exchange, and the national market system, Journal of Finance 33, 487–503.

Ibbotson, R.G. and R.A. Sinquefield, 1976, Stocks bonds, bills and inflation: Year-by-year historical returns (1926–1974), Journal of Business 49, 11–43.

Jensen, M.C., 1978, Some anomalous evidence regarding market efficiency, Journal of Financial Economics 6, 95–101.

Klemkosky, R.C. and B.G. Resnick, 1979a, Put-call parity and market efficiency, Journal of Finance 34, 1141–1155.

Klemkosky, R.C. and B.G. Resnick, 1979b, An ex ante test of options market efficiency, Unpublished manuscript (University of Indiana, Bloomington, IN).

Latané, H.A. and R.J. Rendleman, 1976, Standard deviation of stock price ratios implied by options prices, Journal of Finance 31, 369–381.

Merton, R.C., 1978, Theory of rational option pricing, Bell Journal of Economics and Management Science 4, 141–183.

Phillips, S.M. and D. Roberts, 1979, Analysis of dually listed options, Unpublished manuscript (University of Iowa, Iowa City, IA).

Schwert, G.W., 1977a, Stock exchange seats as capital assets, Journal of Financial Economics 4, 51–78.

Schwert, G.W., 1977b, Public regulation of national securities exchanges: A test of the capture hypothesis, The Bell Journal of Economics 8, 128–150.

Securities and Exchange Commission, 1978, The securities industry in 1977 (S.E.C., Washington, DC).

Smith, C.W., 1976, Option pricing: A review, Journal of Financial Economics 3, 3–51.

Stoll, H., 1978, The pricing of security dealer services: An empirical study of NASDAQ stocks, Journal of Finance 33, 1153–1172.

Tinic, S.M. 1972, The economics of liquidity services, Quarterly Journal of Economics 86, 79–93.

Tinic, S.M. and R. West, 1972, Competition and the pricing of dealer services in the over-the-counter market, Journal of Financial and Quantitative Analysis 7, 1707–1727.

Tinic, S.M. and R. West, 1974, Marketability of common stocks in Canada and the USA: A comparison of agent versus dealer dominated markets, Journal of Finance 29, 729–746.

Trippi, R., 1977, A test of option market efficiency using a random-walk valuation model, Journal of Economics and Business 29, 93–98.

# A COMPARISON OF FUTURES AND FORWARD PRICES*

## Kenneth R. FRENCH

*University of Chicago, Chicago, IL 60637, USA*

Received September 1982, final version received May 1983

This paper uses the pricing models of Cox, Ingersoll and Ross (1981), Richard and Sundaresan (1981), and French (1982) to examine the relation between futures and forward prices for copper and silver. There are significant differences between these prices. The average differences are generally consistent with the predictions of the futures and forward price models. However, these models are not helpful in describing intra-sample variations in the futures–forward price differences. This failure is apparently caused by measurement errors in both the price differences and in the explanatory variables.

## 1. Introduction

Futures and forward contracts are very similar; both contracts represent an agreement to trade an asset at a specific time in the future. Because of this similarity, these contracts are often treated as though they are identical. However, futures and forward contracts are not identical; the daily gain or loss from holding a futures contract is transferred between the traders at the end of each day, while the profits or losses from holding a forward contract accumulate until the contract matures. A number of recent papers have examined the theoretical implications of this difference for the relation between futures and forward prices. For example, Margrabe (1976), Cox, Ingersoll and Ross (1977), and Jarrow and Oldfield (1981) demonstrate that these prices will not be equal unless interest rates are non-stochastic. Cox, Ingersoll and Ross (1981), Richard and Sundaresan (1981), and French (1982) build models of futures and forward prices which allow them to make more specific predictions about the relation between these prices. This paper examines the accuracy of many of these predictions for silver and copper contracts.

*This paper is based on my doctoral thesis at the University of Rochester. I am very grateful to my dissertation committee, G. William Schwert (Chairman), Michael Jensen, John Long, and Charles Plosser, for their guidance. I have also received helpful comments from Robert Jarrow, Scott Richard, Richard Roll, Richard Ruback, Dennis Sheehan, René Stulz, Lee Wakeman, Jerold Zimmerman and the referee, Douglas Breeden. Financial support was generously provided by the Managerial Economics Research Center, Graduate School of Management, University of Rochester; the Center for the Study of Futures Markets, Graduate School of Business, Columbia University; the Foundation for Research in Economics and Education; and the Richard D. Irwin Foundation. I would also like to thank Christopher Snyder of Data Resources, Inc., and Richard Brealey for providing data. This work was completed while I was a post-doctoral fellow at the University of California, Los Angeles.

A forward contract is simply a sales agreement in which delivery and payment are deferred. All of the terms of the sale, such as the asset to be delivered, the time of delivery, and the purchase price (called the forward price), are specified when the contract is written. No payments are made until the contract matures. At that time the seller delivers the asset and the buyer pays the forward price. Since the asset can be purchased just before delivery and re-sold immediately afterward, a forward contract can be viewed as a bet about the maturity price of the commodity. The payoff on this bet is equal to the difference between the forward price and the maturity spot price.

A futures contract can also be viewed as a bet about the maturity price of the asset, but the parties to this bet settle-up daily.[1] At the end of each day's trading, the current futures price is compared with the closing price from the previous day. If the futures price has fallen, the investor who is long in the contract (committing himself to purchase the commodity) must pay the short investor the amount of the decrease. If the futures price has risen, the long investor receives the amount of the increase from the short investor. When the contract matures, the long investor purchases the commodity at the previous day's closing, or settlement, price. Since the commodity can be re-sold immediately at the prevailing spot price, the sum of the cashflows between the two futures traders is equal to the difference between the original futures price and the maturity spot price. This is very similar to the cashflow from the forward contract 'bet'. However, with a forward contract the profits are transferred at maturity, while the profits from a futures contract are transferred at the end of each day.[2]

Despite the differences between these contracts, most commodity traders treat futures contracts as though they are forward contracts. For example, by implicitly modelling futures contracts as forward contracts, futures traders have developed several 'arbitrage' conditions relating futures prices, spot prices, and storage costs. Many economists seem to agree that the daily settling-up has a negligible effect on futures prices. In developing their models of futures prices, Dusak (1973), Grauer (1977), and Grauer and Litzenberger (1979) abstract from the settling-up provisions of these contracts entirely. Other authors, such as Black (1976), explicitly recognize the daily settling-up, but they still conclude that futures and forward prices will be the same.

In light of this consensus about the similarity between futures and forward prices, the empirical evidence in this paper may be surprising. There are significant differences between these prices for both copper and silver contracts. For example, during the 1974–1980 sample period, the average futures–forward price differences are about 0.1%, 0.4%, and 0.8% for 3, 6, and 12 month silver contracts, respectively.

[1]This settling-up is often called 'marking-to-market'.
[2]Strictly speaking, each futures contract is a bet about the next day's futures price.

The next section of this paper outlines the pricing models of Cox, Ingersoll and Ross (1981), Richard and Sundaresan (1981), and French (1982). These models imply that futures and forward prices will differ in predictable ways. For example, the models predict that the price for a forward contract is related to the interest rate on a long-term bond that matures at the same time as the contract, while the futures price is related to the return from rolling over one-day bonds until the contract matures. These prices will be identically equal only if interest rates are non-stochastic.

Section 3 compares futures and forward prices for copper and silver and tests many of the predictions of the pricing models outlined in section 2. In general, the average price differences are consistent with the predictions. However, the models are not helpful in describing intra-sample variations in the futures–forward price differences. This failure is apparently caused by measurement errors in both the price differences and in the explanatory variables.

Section 4 contains a brief summary and some conclusions.

## 2. Models of futures and forward prices

This section uses models developed by Cox, Ingersoll and Ross (1981), Richard and Sundaresan (1981), and French (1982) to examine the theoretical differences between futures and forward prices. All of these models assume that there are no taxes or transaction costs and that individuals can borrow and lend at the same nominal interest rate.[3]

### 2.1. Arbitrage models

Futures and forward contracts provide a wide variety of intertemporal exchange opportunities. For example, by initiating a long forward contract and purchasing risk-free bonds, an individual can buy an asset today that will be delivered in the future. To see the mechanics of this transaction, define $f(t, T)$ as the forward price on day $t$ for a contract that matures on day $T$ and define $R(t, T)$ as the yield to maturity on a riskless discount bond that pays one dollar on day $T$. The current price of this bond is

$$B(t, T) \equiv \exp[-(T-t)R(t, T)]. \tag{1}$$

A trader can make a delayed purchase by initiating one forward contract and investing $f(t, T)B(t, T)$ dollars in riskless bonds. When the contract matures, he receives $f(t, T)$ dollars from the bonds and exchanges this for one unit of the commodity. In effect, an investment of $f(t, T)B(t, T)$ today

---

[3]The models also assume that investors will not default on any contract. This implies that there is a finite upper bound on the daily price changes and on the daily interest rates.

yields one unit of the commodity on day $T$. Alternatively, the trader could reverse the strategy and obtain $f(t, T)B(t, T)$ dollars today in exchange for the asset at time $T$.

Because this intertemporal exchange is available, investors must be marginally indifferent between $f(t, T)B(t, T)$ dollars today and one unit of the commodity on day $T$. By defining $\tilde{P}(T)$ as the (unknown) price of the commodity at time $T$, this indifference can be expressed in purely dollar terms; $f(t, T)B(t, T)$ must be the value on day $t$ of $\tilde{P}(T)$ dollars on day $T$. Equivalently, the forward price must equal the present value of the maturity spot price times the gross return from a long-term bond,

$$f(t, T) = \exp[(T-t)R(t, T)]PV_{t, T}[\tilde{P}(T)]. \tag{2}$$

In eq. (2), $PV_{t, T}(\cdot)$ denotes the present value at time $t$ of a payment received at time $T$.

For example, consider a forward contract on a stock that pays no dividends. Since the current stock price must be the present value of the future stock price, the forward price is equal to

$$f(t, T) = \exp[(T-t)R(t, T)]P(t). \tag{3}$$

This result is intuitively appealing. Using a forward contract to purchase the stock on day $T$ is equivalent to purchasing the stock today, except the forward contract allows the payment to be deferred. Therefore, the forward price is equal to the deferred value of the current stock price.

The present value of the maturity spot price is not observable for most commodities; a more complete model must be introduced to evaluate the payment in (2) and to determine the forward price. However, eq. (2) is useful for highlighting the differences between futures and forward prices.

Cox, Ingersoll and Ross (1981) and French (1982) develop a similar expression for futures prices. They demonstrate that the futures price must equal the present value of the product of the maturity spot price and the gross return from rolling over one-day bonds,

$$F(t, T) = PV_{t, T}\left\{\exp\left[\sum_{\tau=t}^{T-1} \tilde{R}(\tau, \tau+1)\right]\tilde{P}(T)\right\}. \tag{4}$$

In this equation, $F(t, T)$ is the futures price on day $t$ for a contract that matures on day $T$ and $R(\tau, \tau+1)$ is the continuously compounded interest rate on a one-day bond from day $\tau$ to day $\tau+1$.

Eqs. (2) and (4) indicate that the difference between forward and futures prices is related to the difference between holding a long-term bond and rolling over a series of one-day bonds. The only cashflow that is relevant to the forward trader is agreed on today and paid on the maturity date. Therefore, the relevant interest rate in determining the forward price is the known yield on a multi-period bond. On the other hand, while the futures trader knows the total payments he will have to make, the timing of these cashflows is only determined as the contract matures. Because of this uncertainty, the futures price is a function of the unknown one-day interest rates that are expected to arise over the life of contract. In general, the futures price will not equal the forward price unless these interest rates are non-stochastic.

Cox, Ingersoll and Ross use the arbitrage models in eqs. (2) and (4) to develop several propositions about the relation between forward and futures prices. In a continuous-time, continuous-state economy, they find that the difference between these prices is equal to

$$F(t, T) - f(t, T) = -PV_{t, T}\left\{\int_t^T \tilde{F}(w, T)\mathrm{cov}[\tilde{F}(w, T), \tilde{B}(w, T)]\,\mathrm{d}w\right\}/B(t, T). \quad (5)$$

In this equation, $\mathrm{cov}[\tilde{F}(w, T), \tilde{B}(w, T)]$ is defined as the local covariance at time $w$ between the percentage change in the futures price and the percentage change in the bond price. This result has several implications. For example, the local covariance between the futures and bond prices is almost certainly positive for financial assets, such as treasury bills. Therefore, the forward price should be above the futures price for these assets. On the other hand, one would expect the futures price to be above the forward price for most real commodities. Unexpected inflation and changes in expected inflation probably play a major role in determining the covariance between bond prices and commodity prices. Since unexpected inflation moves bond prices and commodity prices in opposite directions, the covariance should be negative and the futures–forward price difference should be positive.[4]

Eq. (5) also implies that the difference between the futures and forward prices will be related to the variance of both the futures prices and the bond prices. Specifically, if the correlation between the futures and bond prices is constant, the absolute value of the price difference will be an increasing function of the market's expectation of both the futures and bond price variances.

Cox, Ingersoll and Ross also use the arbitrage models to show that the

---

[4]The local covariance between the futures price and the bond price may be positive for some commodities. For example, if a commodity is used in the production of a durable good, an increase in the expected real interest rate will reduce the demand for the commodity. Therefore, changes in the expected real interest rate will tend to make the commodity and bond prices move together. However, since the inflation rate is much more volatile than the expected real interest rate, the covariance is still expected to be negative for most commodities.

difference between the futures and forward prices can be expressed as

$$F(t, T) - f(t, T) = PV_{t, T}\left\{\exp\left[\int_t^T \tilde{r}(w)\, dw\right]\int_t^T [\tilde{P}(w)/\tilde{B}(w, T)]\right.$$

$$\left. \times \{\mathrm{var}[\tilde{B}(w, T)] - \mathrm{cov}[\tilde{P}(w), \tilde{B}(w, T)]\}\, dw\right\}, \qquad (6)$$

if the commodity is stored costlessly over the contract period. In this equation, $\tilde{r}(w)$ is the instantaneous interest rate at time $w$, $\mathrm{var}[\tilde{B}(w, T)]$ is the local variance of the percentage change in the bond price, and $\mathrm{cov}[\tilde{P}(w), \tilde{B}(w, T)]$ is the local covariance between the percentage change in the spot price and the percentage change in the bond price. This result implies that the futures–forward price difference will be a decreasing function of the market's expectation of the spot price variance if the price difference is negative and if the local correlation between the spot and bond prices is constant.

## 2.2. Utility based models

The relation between futures and forward prices can be explored further by assuming that markets are complete and that there is some rational individual who acts to maximize a time-additive expected utility function of the form

$$J = E_t\left\{\sum_{\tau=t}^{\infty} \exp[-\rho(\tau - t)]\, U[\tilde{C}(\tau)]\right\}. \qquad (7)$$

In eq. (7), $\tilde{C}(\tau)$ is a vector indicating the (non-negative) quantity of each good consumed on day $\tau$, and $\rho$ is a utility discount factor. Further, $U(\cdot)$ is a single period, von Neumann–Morgenstern utility function that is increasing, strictly quasi-concave, and differentiable. Finally, define $\tilde{\lambda}(\tau)$ as the marginal value of a dollar that is received at time $\tau$. For notational convenience, this marginal value is discounted back to day $t$. In other words, $\tilde{\lambda}(\tau)$ is the discounted marginal utility of money on day $\tau$,

$$\tilde{\lambda}(\tau) = \exp[-\rho(\tau - t)]\, \tilde{u}(i, \tau)/\tilde{P}(i, \tau). \qquad (8)$$

In this expression, $\tilde{P}(i, \tau)$ is the price of any commodity that is consumed on day $\tau$ and $\tilde{u}(i, \tau)$ is the marginal utility of this commodity on day $\tau$. Notice that, unlike $\tilde{\lambda}(\tau)$, $\tilde{u}(i, \tau)$ is not discounted back to day $t$.

The discussion in the previous section shows that investors must be marginally indifferent between $f(t, T)$ dollars today and $\exp[(T - t)R(t, T)]\tilde{P}(T)$

dollars on day $T$. For an individual with the time-additive utility function in (7), this indifference can be expressed as

$$f(t, T)\lambda(t) = \exp[(T - t)R(t, T)] E_t[\tilde{P}(T)\tilde{\lambda}(T)]; \tag{9}$$

the marginal utility of $f(t, T)$ dollars today must equal the expected marginal utility of $\exp[(T - t)R(t, T)]\tilde{P}(T)$ dollars at time $T$. Equivalently, the forward price must equal

$$f(t, T) = \exp[(T - t)R(t, T)] E_t[\tilde{P}(T)\tilde{\lambda}(T)/\lambda(t)]. \tag{10}$$

If this condition were not satisfied, the individual could increase his life-time expected utility by using a portfolio of forward contracts and bonds to transfer money between day $t$ and day $T$.[5]

The time-additive utility function can also be used to characterize futures prices. Eq. (4) implies that, in equilibrium,[6] investors are indifferent between $F(t, T)$ dollars today and $\exp[\sum_{\tau=t}^{T-1} \tilde{R}(\tau, \tau+1)] \tilde{P}(T)$ dollars at time $T$. This indifference can be expressed as

$$F(t, T)\lambda(t) = E_t\left\{\exp\left[\sum_{\tau=t}^{T-1} \tilde{R}(\tau, \tau+1)\right]\tilde{P}(T)\tilde{\lambda}(T)\right\}, \tag{11}$$

or

$$F(t, T) = E_t\left\{\exp\left[\sum_{\tau=t}^{T-1} \tilde{R}(\tau, \tau+1)\right]\tilde{P}(T)\tilde{\lambda}(T)/\lambda(t)\right\}. \tag{12}$$

Eqs. (10) and (12) reemphasize that the forward price is a function of the gross return from holding a long-term bond while the futures price is a function of the gross return from rolling over one-day bonds.[7]

## 3. A comparison of futures and forward prices

As the discussion in section 1 indicates, the similarity between futures and forward prices often leads people to view them as identical contracts. The models of futures and forward prices described in the previous section highlight the theoretical differences between these contracts. This section examines the empirical effects of these differences and tests several predictions of the models.

---

[5]Eq. (10) and eq. (12) below actually follow directly from eqs. (2) and (4) using the relation $PV_{t,T}(\tilde{Y}) = E_t[\tilde{Y}\tilde{\lambda}(T)/\lambda(t)]$.

[6]In equilibrium, no investor wants to make additional trades at the existing prices.

[7]The models in eqs. (10) and (12) are developed by Richard and Sundaresan (1981) and French (1982). In addition, the forward price model in (10) is similar to the futures price models in Grauer (1977) and Grauer and Litzenberger (1979).

## 3.1. Matching futures and forward prices

The tests in this section compare futures and forward prices for silver and copper from 1968 through 1980. Most of the organized forward activity during this period occurred on the London Metal Exchange (LME).[8] Members of this exchange trade spot and forward contracts on silver, copper, and several other metals. Although other contracts are available, the standard silver contracts have maturities of 3, 6, and 12 months and the standard copper contract has a 3-month maturity. A new set of contracts is written each day. For example, the 3-month silver contract initiated on February 10, 1977, matured on May 10, while the contract written on February 11 matured on May 11.

The futures prices reflect trading on two exchanges in the United States — the Commodity Exchange (Comex) in New York and the Chicago Board of Trade (CBT).[9] The contract maturities used in these markets follow a different convention than that used in forward markets. While forward traders write contracts with a specific time until maturity, such as 3 months, futures traders write contracts for specific maturity months. Further, futures contracts are traded continually for up to 2 years. For example, an investor could initiate a December 1978 silver contract any time from January 1977 until it matured two years later.

In comparing futures and forward prices one would like to simultaneously observe futures and forward contracts for the same commodity and the same maturity. The different maturity structures used in the futures and forward markets make this difficult. The discussion in the first two sections assumes that futures and forward contracts have precise maturity dates. While this is true for forward contracts, it is not true for most futures contracts, including those examined here. Instead, a short futures trader may choose to make delivery any time during the maturity month. The exchange's clearinghouse then assigns the shipment to the long trader with the 'oldest' contract. The tests reported in this section assume that futures contracts mature in the first week of the delivery month.[10]

The futures and forward prices have several other characteristics that make comparisons between them difficult. For example, both Comex and the CBT impose limits on the daily price movement of any futures contract that is not

---

[8]Silver contracts began trading on the LME in February 1968. The London Bullion Market prices for silver spot and forward contracts are used before 1973.

[9]The commodity price data are obtained from several sources: the Commodity Services, Inc., data bank, provided by the Center for the Study of Futures Markets at Columbia University; the Data Resources, Inc., commodities data bank; the *Wall Street Journal*; and the *Journal of Commerce*.

[10]Specifically, the tests use prices observed on Fridays. The relevant Friday for each futures contract is chosen so that the matching forward contract matures during the first week of the futures delivery month. All of the tests have been replicated using four other maturity periods: the second, third, and fourth week of the maturity month and the first business day of that month. The results are not substantially different for the different maturity assumptions.

in its delivery month. These limits constrain the futures price to lie within a range determined by the previous day's settlement price. If a limit is reached, the day's trading is effectively stopped unless the equilibrium price moves back within the limits. In other words, when a limit move occurs the reported price may be significantly different from the unobserved market-clearing price. To reduce the effect of this measurement error, any futures price that reflects a limit move is not included in the tests.

Perhaps the biggest problems encountered in trying to match futures and forward prices arise because the forward contracts are traded in Great Britain while the futures contracts are traded in the United States.[11] Ideally, the futures and forward prices should be observed simultaneously. In fact, prices from the London exchanges are recorded several hours before the American prices are observed. This difference introduces measurement error between the futures and forward prices.

Two other complications are potentially more serious. First, American futures prices are denominated in dollars while London forward contracts are denominated in pounds sterling. Before these prices can be compared, they must be converted into the same currency. Second, silver or copper in London is not exactly the same commodity as it is in New York or Chicago because of transportation costs and international trade restrictions.

One way to deal with these problems is to assume that the expected difference between the exchange-adjusted spot prices is a constant fraction of the expected spot prices,

$$E_t[\tilde{P}(T,\$)] = (1+b)E_t[\tilde{P}(T,\pounds)\tilde{X}(T,T)]. \tag{13}$$

In this expression, $\tilde{P}(T,\$)$ is the spot price at time $T$ denominated in dollars, $\tilde{P}(T,\pounds)$ is the spot price in pounds, and $\tilde{X}(T,T)$ is the spot exchange rate between dollars and pounds at time $T$. Although the expected basis differential, $b$, is assumed to be constant through time, it may vary across commodities. For example, since the cost of transporting silver between London and the United States is small relative to the value of the commodity, one expects that the absolute value of the basis differential for

---

[11]The price controls imposed in the United States from August 15, 1971, through April 30, 1974, could cause more problems. Both the spot prices and the futures prices for copper and silver were subject to these controls. For example, during the first 90 days of the control period none of the futures contracts was allowed to trade above its May 25, 1970, price or the average of the prices for the 30 days preceding August 15, 1971, whichever was higher. Because of the potential distortions caused by the price controls, all of the tests have been duplicated using three separate subperiods: a pre-control period, from January 1, 1968, through August 14, 1971; a price control period from August 15, 1971, through April 30, 1974; and a post-control period from May 1, 1974, through December 31, 1980. Surprisingly, the price controls do not affect the results of these tests. For a more complete description of the price controls imposed on the copper and silver markets and some tests of the effect of these controls, see Levich and White (1981).

silver is small. On the other hand, the basis differential for copper may be higher because the relative transportation costs are higher.

Under this constant-expected-basis-differential model, the American forward price can be estimated by the product of the London forward price, the forward exchange rate, and the basis adjustment,[12]

$$f(t, T, \$) = (1 + b)f(t, T, \pounds)X(t, T). \tag{14}$$

Table 1 presents estimates of the basis differential for silver and copper as a percentage of the spot price.[13] The British spot prices used in these estimates are measured by prices from the London Metal Exchange. Explicit spot prices for copper and silver are not available from the American futures exchanges. Instead, the price for the deliverable futures contract — called the cash price — is used. For example, the December silver futures price is used to estimate the American spot price during December.

The estimates of the basis differential for silver in table 1 are very small. For example, the average differential over the full 1968–1980 sample period is less than 0.1%, with a $t$-statistic of 0.53.[14] This is consistent with the relatively small transportation costs for silver. The estimates for copper are much larger; the average basis differential for the full sample period is −0.34% and the average for the first subperiod, from 1968 through 1973, is −1.87%.

The forward prices that are converted from pounds to dollars in the tests below all have maturities of 3 months or more. Therefore, it is only necessary to assume that the expected basis differential is constant for forecast horizons of at least 3 months. This is weaker than assuming that the basis differential always equals $b$,

$$P(t, \$) = (1 + b)P(t, \pounds)X(t, t). \tag{15}$$

---

[12]This conversion also assumes that, conditional on the information available at time $t$, the covariance of the marginal utility of a dollar with the difference between the basis-adjusted maturity spot prices is zero; $\text{cov}_t[\lambda(T, \$), (1 + b)\tilde{P}(T, \pounds)\tilde{X}(T, T) - \tilde{P}(T, \$)] = 0$.

French (1982) demonstrates that eq. (14) holds under the assumption that this covariance is zero and that the expected basis differential, $b$, is zero. Extending this result to the general case of any constant expected basis differential is straightforward.

[13]Although the model in eq. (13) is specified in terms of the levels of the spot prices, these estimates and all of the tests below use the logarithms of the prices. This eliminates some heteroskedasticity.

The exchange rates used in table 1 and in the tests below are obtained from the *Bank of England Quarterly Bulletin*, the Federal Reserve Bank of New York, and Data Resources, Inc. Although daily data are available during most of the period, only the exchange rates for Friday are available from 1968 through 1970. This does not cause problems for most of the tests because they only use futures and forward prices that are observed on Friday. However, for tests involving daily data, the Friday exchange rate is used for the next four days during this period.

[14]The $t$-statistics in table 1 are adjusted for autocorrelation at lags one and two since these are allowed under the constant-expected-basis-differential model.

## Table 1

Estimates of the basis differentials and tests of the constant-expected-basis-differential model.[a]

| | Number | Mean | Std. dev. | t-stat. | $S(r_3)$ | $r_1$ | $r_2$ | $r_3$ | $r_4$ | $r_5$ | $r_6$ |
|---|---|---|---|---|---|---|---|---|---|---|---|
| Silver | | | | | | | | | | | |
| 1/68–12/80 | 146 | 0.080 | 1.863 | 0.526 | 0.086 | 0.025 | −0.044 | −0.011 | 0.249 | 0.053 | 0.018 |
| 1/68–12/73 | 66 | −0.015 | 1.533 | 0.056 | 0.160 | 0.446 | 0.179 | −0.002 | 0.182 | 0.269 | 0.259 |
| 1/74–12/80 | 80 | 0.158 | 2.104 | 1.000 | 0.120 | −0.149 | −0.143 | −0.019 | 0.283 | 0.011 | −0.065 |
| Copper | | | | | | | | | | | |
| 1/68–12/80 | 112 | −0.349 | 3.558 | 0.605 | 0.178 | 0.795 | 0.520 | 0.576 | 0.428 | 0.376 | 0.400 |
| 1/68–12/73 | 37 | −1.868 | 3.955 | 2.236 | 0.395 | 0.897 | 0.146 | 0.682 | 0.409 | 0.366 | 0.716 |
| 1/74–12/80 | 75 | 0.400 | 3.107 | 0.578 | 0.218 | 0.839 | 0.665 | 0.580 | 0.411 | 0.288 | 0.219 |

[a]The percentage basis differential is estimated by $\log[P(t,\$)/P(t,£)X(t,t)] \cdot 100$. Under the constant-expected-basis-differential model, the autocorrelations after lag 2 should not be significantly different from zero. The autocorrelation at lag $i$ is denoted by $r_i$ and $S(r_3)$ is the standard error for the autocorrelation at lag 3, estimated using Bartlett's (1946) approximation. Copper has fewer observations than silver during the first sample period because fewer copper contracts were traded during this period.

The expectational model does not rule out differences between the basis-adjusted spot prices. However, since the conditional expected value of these differences is zero, differences that are at least 3 months apart must be independent. The autocorrelations reported in table 1 provide a test of this implication.

The estimates for silver support the constant-expected-basis-differential model. Since these estimates use monthly observations, the autocorrelations should be approximately zero after the second lag. In fact, almost all of the autocorrelations for the silver price differences are close to zero. For example, only the autocorrelation at lag 4 is significant during the 1968–1980 period.[15] The results for copper are less consistent with the model. For example, all of the estimates for the 1968–1980 sample period are significantly positive. Because of these large autocorrelations, the futures and forward price comparisons involving converted copper prices should be interpreted cautiously.[16]

## 3.2. A preliminary look at the data

Before comparing individual futures and forward prices, it is helpful to examine the general properties of the cash, spot, futures, and forward prices that are used in the tests below. Tables 2 and 3 summarize the daily percentage changes in the prices for silver and copper contracts. These changes are equal to the daily logarithmic price relatives. For example, the daily percentage change in the spot price for London silver is equal to $\log[P(t, £)/P(t-1, £)] * 100$.

Most of the tests in this paper use copper and silver prices from 1968 through 1980. However, metal prices were unusually volatile during the last two years of this sample period. For example, the cash price for silver rose from $5.98 per ounce on January 2, 1979, to $52.25 on January 21, 1980. By the end of 1980, the cash price had fallen back down to $16.58. Because of this unusual behavior during 1979 and 1980, tables 2 and 3 summarize the daily price changes when these two years are included in the sample and when they are not.

Comparisons of the behavior of futures and forward prices are complicated by the price limits in the futures markets. Although limit moves are not included in the futures price series (nor in any of the tests below), the price

---

[15]The standard errors for the autocorrelations beyond the second lag are estimated using Bartlett's (1946) approximation. Under the hypothesis that the differences are uncorrelated after lag 2, these standard errors are equal to $S(r_3) = \{N^{-1}[1 + 2r_1{}^2 + 2r_2{}^2]\}^{\frac{1}{2}}$.

[16]All of the tests below were also performed using a second conversion technique. This technique assumes that the market uses the current basis differential as its forecast of the future differential, so the American forward price is estimated as $f(t, T, \$) = f(t, T, £) X(t, T) \{P(t, \$)/P(t, £) X(t, t)\}$. The results using this conversion technique are very similar to the results reported below.

limits reduce the apparent volatility of the futures prices because they make it impossible to observe large price changes. Because of this problem, tables 2 and 3 report estimates for two different sets of converted forward prices. The first set includes all of the forward prices that are available during the sample period. The second set is more restrictive; it only includes a forward price if a matching futures price is also available. In other words, a forward price is not included if the matching futures contract was not traded or if its price reflects a limit move.

The standard deviations for silver in table 2 indicate that the price limits do have a noticeable effect. For example, the estimated standard deviation for the daily change in the 3-month futures prices over the full 1968–1980 sample period is 1.5%, while the London forward prices and the first set of converted forward prices have standard deviations of approximately 2.7%. If the converted forward price series is restricted to days when non-limit futures prices are available, the estimate falls to 1.6%. However, the evidence still suggests that unconstrained American prices would be less volatile than the London or converted prices. First, the standard deviations for the restricted forward prices remain higher than the standard deviations for the futures prices. While this difference may still be caused by the price limits,[17] the second piece of evidence is not affected by this bias. Since silver (and copper) futures prices are not constrained by price limits during a contract's delivery month, the standard deviations for the cash prices are not artificially reduced. Therefore, direct comparisons between the cash and spot prices are appropriate. These comparisons indicate that the standard deviations for the American cash prices are consistently lower than the standard deviations for the London or converted spot prices.

Because of the price limits, the standard deviations for the futures prices are fairly constant through time. However, the estimates for the cash, spot and forward prices indicate that the silver price volatility increased dramatically over the sample period. For example, even if the very turbulent 1979–1980 period is excluded, the standard deviations for the spot and forward prices increased by more than 50% from the first to the second subperiod. It is also interesting that the estimated standard deviations for the forward prices do not appear to be related to the maturity of the contracts.

The summary statistics for the daily changes in the copper prices are presented in table 3. These results are slightly different from the results in

---

[17]Selection bias can still occur because the futures and forward prices are not perfectly correlated. A large change in the forward price can be included in the sample if it is associated with a smaller change in the futures price. However, large changes in the futures price are never included.

It may appear that the difference between the closing times of the London and American markets can also contribute to the selection bias problem. For example, if a limit move is caused by information that arrives after the London market closes on day $t$, this information will lead to a large change in the forward price on day $t + 1$. However, a limit move on day $t$ eliminates the price changes for both day $t$ and day $t + 1$.

**Table 2**

Means, standard deviations, and t-statistics of the daily percentage changes in the futures and forward prices for silver.[a]

**Left panel**

| Contract | Statistic | American prices | London prices | Converted prices | Restricted converted[b] prices |
|---|---|---|---|---|---|
| **1/68–12/80** | | | | | |
| Cash or spot contracts | Mean | 0.085 | 0.060 | 0.054 | 0.034 |
| | Std. dev. | 2.372 | 2.849 | 2.880 | 2.923 |
| | t-stat. | 1.805 | 1.190 | 1.046 | 0.574 |
| | Number | 2563 | 3145 | 3145 | 2441 |
| 3-month contracts | Mean | 0.060 | 0.059 | 0.058 | 0.017 |
| | Std. dev. | 1.479 | 2.719 | 2.772 | 1.623 |
| | t-stat. | 1.941 | 1.225 | 1.164 | 0.480 |
| | Number | 2266 | 3143 | 3070 | 2167 |
| **1/68–12/73** | | | | | |
| Cash or spot contracts | Mean | 0.022 | 0.045 | 0.042 | 0.025 |
| | Std. dev. | 1.549 | 1.586 | 1.610 | 1.645 |
| | t-stat. | 0.488 | 1.092 | 0.983 | 0.510 |
| | Number | 1166 | 1456 | 1456 | 1124 |
| 3-month contracts | Mean | 0.040 | 0.046 | 0.041 | 0.036 |
| | Std. dev. | 1.431 | 1.586 | 1.630 | 1.466 |
| | t-stat. | 0.909 | 1.119 | 0.934 | 0.795 |
| | Number | 1456 | 1456 | 1405 | 1026 |
| **1/74–12/80** | | | | | |
| Cash or spot contracts | Mean | 0.137 | 0.074 | 0.064 | 0.042 |
| | Std. dev. | 2.883 | 3.599 | 3.635 | 3.679 |
| | t-stat. | 1.771 | 0.839 | 0.726 | 0.410 |
| | Number | 1397 | 1689 | 1689 | 1317 |
| 3-month contracts | Mean | 0.079 | 0.017 | 0.073 | -0.001 |
| | Std. dev. | 1.522 | 3.406 | 3.454 | 1.753 |
| | t-stat. | 1.792 | 0.851 | 0.864 | 0.018 |
| | Number | 1187 | 1687 | 1665 | 1141 |
| 6-month contracts | Mean | 0.020 | 0.086 | 0.089 | -0.003 |
| | Std. dev. | 1.470 | 3.852 | 3.887 | 2.150 |
| | t-stat. | 0.460 | 0.876 | 0.899 | 0.037 |
| | Number | 1159 | 1551 | 1525 | 1024 |
| 12-month contracts | Mean | 0.076 | 0.074 | 0.074 | 0.007 |
| | Std. dev. | 1.623 | 3.487 | 3.538 | 2.219 |
| | t-stat. | 1.590 | 0.839 | 0.817 | 0.104 |
| | Number | 1167 | 1545 | 1515 | 1021 |

**Right panel**

| Contract | Statistic | American prices | London prices | Converted prices | Restricted converted[b] prices |
|---|---|---|---|---|---|
| **1/68–12/78** | | | | | |
| Cash or spot contracts | Mean | 0.059 | 0.047 | 0.037 | 0.034 |
| | Std. dev. | 1.831 | 2.223 | 2.223 | 2.332 |
| | t-stat. | 1.502 | 1.092 | 0.855 | 0.657 |
| | Number | 2166 | 2662 | 2662 | 2064 |
| 3-month contracts | Mean | 0.053 | 0.047 | 0.044 | 0.017 |
| | Std. dev. | 1.451 | 2.019 | 2.047 | 1.518 |
| | t-stat. | 1.662 | 1.199 | 1.101 | 0.491 |
| | Number | 2044 | 2662 | 2599 | 1955 |
| **1/74–12/78** | | | | | |
| Cash or spot contracts | Mean | 0.102 | 0.050 | 0.032 | 0.044 |
| | Std. dev. | 2.113 | 2.180 | 2.809 | 2.952 |
| | t-stat. | 1.530 | 0.614 | 0.391 | 0.459 |
| | Number | 1000 | 1206 | 1206 | 940 |
| 3-month contracts | Mean | 0.069 | 0.047 | 0.048 | -0.005 |
| | Std. dev. | 1.472 | 2.442 | 2.449 | 1.573 |
| | t-stat. | 1.449 | 0.674 | 0.683 | 0.091 |
| | Number | 965 | 1206 | 1194 | 929 |
| 6-month contracts | Mean | 0.014 | 0.052 | 0.056 | -0.021 |
| | Std. dev. | 1.463 | 3.189 | 3.183 | 2.154 |
| | t-stat. | 0.288 | 0.567 | 0.608 | 0.288 |
| | Number | 951 | 1191 | 1175 | 886 |
| 12-month contracts | Mean | 0.081 | 0.049 | 0.049 | 0.083 |
| | Std. dev. | 1.635 | 2.653 | 2.672 | 2.274 |
| | t-stat. | 1.531 | 0.635 | 0.623 | 0.109 |
| | Number | 957 | 1191 | 1171 | 881 |

[a]The percentage price change is defined as log($P_t/P_{t-1}$)·100. The American prices are cash and futures prices. The London prices are spot and forward prices, denominated in pounds sterling. The converted prices are London spot and forward prices converted to dollars. The estimates for the unrestricted series use all of the available converted prices, while the restricted estimates only use prices if the matching American prices are also available.

Table 3

Means, standard deviations, and t-statistics of the daily percentage changes in the futures and forward prices for copper.[a]

| | | American prices | London prices | Converted prices | Restricted converted prices | American prices | London prices | Converted prices | Restricted converted prices |
|---|---|---|---|---|---|---|---|---|---|
| | | **1/68–12/80** | | | | **1/68 12/78** | | | |
| Cash or spot Contracts | Mean | -0.011 | 0.010 | 0.006 | -0.021 | -0.023 | 0.012 | 0.004 | -0.037 |
| | Std. dev. | 1.793 | 1.904 | 1.926 | 1.895 | 1.553 | 1.717 | 1.726 | 1.466 |
| | t-stat. | -0.272 | 0.303 | 0.164 | 0.473 | -0.574 | 0.372 | 0.112 | 0.939 |
| | Number | 1793 | 3216 | 3216 | 1751 | 1440 | 2728 | 2728 | 1413 |
| 3-month contracts | Mean | -0.013 | 0.009 | 0.005 | -0.419 | -0.018 | 0.011 | 0.003 | -0.042 |
| | Std. dev. | 1.540 | 1.879 | 1.924 | 1.371 | 1.445 | 1.343 | 1.373 | 1.267 |
| | t-stat. | -0.322 | 0.273 | 0.138 | 1.176 | -0.457 | 0.427 | 0.117 | 1.187 |
| | Number | 1542 | 3215 | 3136 | 1483 | 1333 | 2727 | 2660 | 1283 |
| | | **1/68–12/73** | | | | | | | |
| Cash or spot contracts | Mean | 0.032 | 0.038 | 0.036 | -0.038 | | | | |
| | Std. dev. | 1.500 | 1.863 | 1.869 | 1.594 | | | | |
| | t-stat. | 0.484 | 0.781 | 0.733 | 0.542 | | | | |
| | Number | 519 | 1481 | 1481 | 512 | | | | |
| 3-month contracts | Mean | -0.013 | 0.035 | 0.029 | -0.022 | | | | |
| | Std. dev. | 1.298 | 1.271 | 1.312 | 1.180 | | | | |
| | t-stat. | 0.266 | 1.051 | 0.823 | 0.501 | | | | |
| | Number | 745 | 1482 | 1427 | 713 | | | | |
| | | **1/74–12/80** | | | | **1/74–12/78** | | | |
| Cash or spot contracts | Mean | -0.029 | -0.013 | -0.020 | -0.014 | -0.055 | -0.018 | -0.034 | -0.036 |
| | Std. dev. | 1.899 | 1.939 | 1.974 | 2.006 | 1.582 | 1.525 | 1.539 | 1.389 |
| | t-stat. | 0.548 | 0.288 | 0.423 | 0.254 | 1.049 | 0.419 | 0.748 | 0.773 |
| | Number | 1274 | 1735 | 1735 | 1239 | 921 | 1247 | 1247 | 901 |
| 3-month contracts | Mean | -0.013 | -0.013 | -0.015 | -0.060 | -0.025 | -0.017 | -0.026 | -0.067 |
| | Std. dev. | 1.736 | 2.274 | 2.314 | 1.527 | 1.634 | 1.424 | 1.441 | 1.369 |
| | t-stat. | 0.205 | 0.236 | 0.271 | 1.093 | 0.375 | 0.428 | 0.643 | 1.165 |
| | Number | 797 | 1733 | 1709 | 770 | 588 | 1245 | 1233 | 570 |

[a]The percentage price change is defined as $\log(P_t/P_{t-1}) \cdot 100$. The American prices are cash and futures prices. The London prices are spot and forward prices, denominated in pounds sterling. The converted prices are London spot and forward prices converted to dollars. The estimates for the unrestricted series use all of the available converted prices, while the restricted estimates only use prices if the matching American prices are also available.

table 2. For example, the standard deviations for the futures prices are approximately equal to the standard deviations for both the restricted and the unrestricted forward price series during both the 1968–1973 subperiod and the 1974–1978 subperiod. The effect of the future price limits is only noticeable when the more volatile 1979 and 1980 prices are included in the sample.[18]

The behavior of the copper price variances through time is also slightly different from the behavior for silver. The standard deviations for the copper and silver price changes are all about 1.5% during the first subperiod. However, the estimates for copper are much lower than the estimates for silver from 1974 through 1980; while silver's variance increases from the first to the second subperiod, copper's variance remains fairly constant. In fact, the standard deviations for copper do not increase unless 1979 and 1980 are added to the sample period.

Autocorrelations for the daily copper and silver price changes are presented in table 4. The autocorrelations for the spot, cash, and 3-month price series are estimated using data from 1968 through 1980, while the autocorrelations for the 6- and 12-month series are estimated from 1974 through 1980. The most striking result in table 4 is that almost all of the first-order autocorrelations are negative and relatively large. Only five of these autocorrelations are within four standard errors of zero. This serial correlation would seem to suggest a profitable trading opportunity; buy on the day after a price drop and sell after a rise. However, it is more likely that the correlation is caused by measurement error than by market inefficiency. For example, suppose the measurement error in today's reported spot price for silver is positive. This introduces a positive bias in today's price change and a negative bias in tomorrow's price change. This pattern would cause a negative first-order autocorrelation in the observed price changes. If the measurement error is negative, the pattern is reversed but the final result is the same. In view of this measurement error hypothesis, it is interesting to note that four of the five smallest first-order autocorrelations are for cash and futures prices.

To summarize the results from tables 2 through 4, there are some noticeable differences between the behavior of the futures prices and the behavior of the forward prices. For example, the evidence in tables 2 and 3 indicates that, because of the futures price limits, the variance of the observed futures prices is generally lower than the variance of the forward prices. In addition, the first-order autocorrelations in table 4 suggest that the London spot and forward prices contain more measurement error than the American cash and futures prices. The data also indicate that the variability of the daily price changes increases from 1968 to 1980. The silver price volatility

---

[18]In fact, only 3% of the 3-month copper futures prices observed from 1968 through 1978 reflect limit moves, while 9% of the prices for 1979 and 1980 are limit moves.

Table 4

Autocorrelations of the daily percent changes in the cash, spot, futures and forward prices for copper and silver.[a]

| | Number | $S(r_1)$ | $r_1$ | $r_2$ | $r_3$ | $r_4$ | $r_5$ | $r_6$ |
|---|---|---|---|---|---|---|---|---|
| | | | *Silver* | | | | | |
| Cash prices | 2364 | 0.021 | 0.050 | 0.008 | −0.026 | 0.018 | −0.057 | 0.036 |
| London spot prices | 3054 | 0.018 | −0.172 | −0.025 | 0.052 | 0.020 | −0.054 | −0.035 |
| Converted spot prices | 3054 | 0.018 | −0.170 | −0.029 | 0.048 | 0.016 | −0.052 | −0.034 |
| Restricted spot prices | 2213 | 0.021 | −0.216 | 0.006 | 0.025 | 0.037 | −0.015 | 0.013 |
| 3-month contracts | | | | | | | | |
| Futures prices | 2081 | 0.022 | −0.111 | 0.010 | −0.044 | 0.081 | −0.083 | 0.034 |
| London forward prices | 3051 | 0.018 | −0.131 | −0.023 | 0.045 | 0.026 | −0.051 | −0.045 |
| Converted forward prices | 2947 | 0.018 | −0.133 | −0.028 | 0.041 | 0.022 | −0.048 | −0.037 |
| Restricted forward prices | 1954 | 0.023 | −0.203 | −0.021 | 0.012 | 0.020 | −0.012 | 0.036 |
| 6-month contracts | | | | | | | | |
| Futures prices | 1037 | 0.031 | −0.148 | 0.020 | −0.015 | 0.028 | −0.062 | 0.005 |
| London forward prices | 1505 | 0.026 | −0.195 | −0.045 | 0.038 | 0.018 | −0.054 | −0.043 |
| Converted forward prices | 1467 | 0.026 | −0.195 | −0.042 | 0.026 | 0.026 | −0.059 | −0.045 |
| Restricted forward prices | 905 | 0.033 | −0.244 | 0.007 | −0.038 | 0.078 | −0.028 | −0.019 |
| 12-month contracts | | | | | | | | |
| Futures prices | 1057 | 0.031 | −0.018 | 0.038 | −0.015 | 0.017 | −0.043 | 0.019 |
| London forward prices | 1496 | 0.026 | −0.150 | −0.028 | 0.038 | 0.034 | −0.075 | −0.064 |
| Converted forward prices | 1452 | 0.026 | −0.150 | −0.028 | 0.022 | 0.039 | −0.079 | −0.058 |
| Restricted forward prices | 906 | 0.033 | −0.141 | −0.035 | 0.038 | 0.035 | −0.017 | −0.018 |
| | | | *Copper* | | | | | |
| Cash prices | 1636 | 0.025 | −0.023 | −0.039 | 0.042 | 0.027 | 0.069 | −0.060 |
| London spot prices | 3160 | 0.018 | −0.106 | −0.050 | 0.058 | 0.015 | 0.015 | 0.003 |
| Converted spot prices | 3160 | 0.018 | −0.093 | −0.048 | 0.052 | 0.015 | 0.016 | 0.008 |
| Restricted spot prices | 1585 | 0.025 | −0.137 | −0.062 | 0.054 | 0.036 | 0.056 | −0.003 |
| 3-month contracts | | | | | | | | |
| Futures prices | 1407 | 0.027 | −0.064 | −0.039 | 0.007 | 0.001 | 0.081 | −0.058 |
| London forward prices | 3158 | 0.018 | −0.192 | −0.020 | −0.013 | 0.064 | 0.005 | 0.018 |
| Converted forward prices | 3043 | 0.018 | −0.188 | −0.024 | −0.020 | 0.056 | 0.009 | 0.019 |
| Restricted forward prices | 1329 | 0.027 | −0.053 | −0.057 | 0.048 | 0.064 | 0.061 | −0.056 |

[a]$r_\tau$ is the autocorrelation at lag $\tau$; $S(r_1)$ is the standard error of the first-order autocorrelation. The cash, spot, and 3-month autocorrelations are estimated from 1/68 to 12/80. The 6- and 12-month autocorrelations are estimated from 1/74 to 12/80. The converted prices are London spot and forward prices converted to dollars. The estimates for the unrestricted series use all of the available converted prices, while the restricted estimates only use the converted prices if the matching American prices are also available.

appears to grow over the whole sample period. Although the variance of the copper prices is fairly constant from 1968 through 1978, the variances for both commodities increase significantly during the 1979–1980 period.

### 3.3. The differences between futures and forward prices and tests of the Cox–Ingersoll–Ross propositions

The simplest way to examine whether there is an empirically relevant difference between futures and forward prices is to compare them individually. Table 5 summarizes the percentage differences between matching futures and forward prices, defined as $\log[F(t, T)/f(t, T)] * 100$, for both copper and silver. These differences are measured at 3 months to maturity for the copper contracts and at 3, 6, and 12 months to maturity for the silver contracts. Since the futures contracts mature at monthly intervals, this process generates monthly observations.[19] For example, the January price difference for the 3-month silver series reflects futures and forward contracts that mature in April, while the February difference involves contracts that mature in May. The forward prices in table 5 (and in the tests below) are converted from pounds sterling to dollars using three different estimates of the basis differential for each commodity. The forward prices in the 1968–1980 comparisons are converted using the full-period estimates of the basis differential. The conversions for the subperiod tests use the basis differential estimated over the matching subperiod.

The futures–forward price differences for silver in table 5 indicate that, on average, the futures prices are larger than the forward prices. Four of the five estimates are significantly positive at the 5% level. Moreover, the difference between the futures and forward prices increases with the maturity of the contract; the average differences from 1974 through 1980 are about 0.1%, 0.4%, and 0.8% for the 3-, 6- and 12-month contracts, respectively.

The relation between the futures and forward prices for copper is less clearcut. It appears that the futures prices are lower than the forward prices during the first subperiod and higher than the forward prices during the second subperiod; the average price differences are $-0.9\%$ and $0.1\%$, respectively. However, the $t$-statistics for these estimates are only 1.55 and 0.21.[20]

Table 5 also contains some evidence about two of the propositions developed by Cox, Ingersoll and Ross (1981). They hypothesize that the futures–forward price difference is equal to

$$F(t, T) - f(t, T) = -PV_{t, T} \left\{ \int_{t}^{T} \tilde{F}(w, T) \text{cov}[\tilde{F}(w, T), \tilde{B}(w, T)] dw \right\} / B(t, T), \quad (16)$$

where $\text{cov}[\tilde{F}(w, T), \tilde{B}(w, T)]$ is the local covariance at time $w$ between the percentage change in the futures price and the percentage change in the bond price. This instantaneous covariance may be changing stochastically as the futures contract and the bond contract move toward maturity at time $T$.

---

[19]Futures contracts do not mature every month so some months will not be represented in these series.

[20]It is interesting that, although the average price difference for the second subperiod is positive, the $t$-statistic for the average difference of the full period, $-1.68$, is more negative than the $t$-statistic for the first subperiod, $-1.55$. This happens because different estimates of the basis differential are used for the full sample period and for each subperiod.

However, if the covariance is always positive during the contract period, the integral in (16) will be positive and the forward price should be higher than the futures price. On the other hand, if the local covariance is always negative, the futures price should be above the forward price.

Cox, Ingersoll and Ross also show that the futures–forward price difference can be expressed as

$$F(t, T) - f(t, T) = PV_{t, T} \left\{ \exp\left[ \int_t^T \tilde{r}(w)\,\mathrm{d}w \right] \int_t^T [\tilde{P}(w)/\tilde{B}(w, T)] \right.$$

$$\left. \times \{ \mathrm{var}[\tilde{B}(w, T)] - \mathrm{cov}[\tilde{P}(w), \tilde{B}(w, T)] \}\,\mathrm{d}w \right\}, \qquad (17)$$

if the commodity is stored costlessly over the contract period. This leads to the prediction that, if the local variance of the bond price is always larger than the local covariance between the spot price and the bond price, the futures price will be above the forward price. If the variance is smaller than the covariance, the futures price should be below the forward price.

The simplest way to test these hypotheses is to assume that the local variances and covariances are constant and the same for all contracts.[21] Under this assumption the local covariance in eq. (16) is measured in two steps. First, the covariance between the daily percentage change in the futures price and the daily percentage change in the bond price is estimated for each pair of futures and forward contracts. These covariances are then averaged across contracts. The local variances and covariances in eq. (17) are estimated in the same way. The results of this process are reported in the second and third columns of table 5.[22]

Under the first CIR proposition, if the covariance between the bond prices and the futures prices is positive the futures–forward price difference should be negative. The results in table 5 provide some support for this hypothesis.

[21]This assumption cannot be strictly true since the local variances and covariances must converge to zero as the contracts approach maturity and the bond prices converge to one. However, estimates of the variances and covariances measured over the full contract period can be used to predict whether the relevant integrals are positive or negative. For example if the futures price is roughly constant, the average covariance between the futures price and the bond price is approximately proportional to the integral in eq. (16).

[22]All of the variances and covariances in table 5 have been multiplied by $10^6$. The bond prices used to estimate these variables are measured by the 3-, 6- and 12-month treasury bill prices provided by the Federal Reserve Bank of New York and Data Resources, Inc. For example, when a futures contract has 12, 11, or 10 months to maturity, its daily price changes are compared with the price changes for treasury bills that will mature in approximately 12 months. When the futures contract has between 9 and 5 months to maturity, the 6-month treasury bill series is used. The 3-month bills are used during the last four months of the contract period. A 1-month treasury bill series is also available, but its bid/ask spread is very large. For example, the average daily spread from 1973 through 1980 is 0.32%. The average daily bid/ask spread for the 3-month series over this period is 0.025%.

## Table 5
Futures–forward price differences and tests of the Cox–Ingersoll–Ross propositions.[a]

| | | log(fut/for) • 100 | cov(F, B) | var(B) − cov(P, B) |
|---|---|---|---|---|
| | | **1968–1980** | | |
| 3-month silver | Mean | 0.297 | 0.231 | 0.803 |
| | Std. dev. | 1.325 | 1.917 | 4.203 |
| | t-stat. | 2.372 | 0.889 | 1.319 |
| | Number | 112 | 140 | 154 |
| 3-month copper | Mean | −0.701 | 0.371 | 0.158 |
| | Std. dev. | 3.744 | 1.442 | 0.843 |
| | t-stat. | 1.685 | 2.556 | 1.506 |
| | Number | 81 | 127 | 154 |
| | | **1968–1973** | | |
| 3-month silver | Mean | 0.485 | 0.139 | 0.110 |
| | Std. dev. | 1.332 | 0.530 | 0.795 |
| | t-stat. | 2.651 | 1.193 | 0.653 |
| | Number | 53 | 68 | 70 |
| 3-month copper | Mean | −0.861 | 0.189 | 0.008 |
| | Std. dev. | 3.464 | 0.734 | 0.310 |
| | t-stat. | 1.552 | 1.195 | 0.150 |
| | Number | 39 | 56 | 70 |
| | | **1974–1980** | | |
| 3-month silver | Mean | 0.136 | 0.318 | 1.380 |
| | Std. dev. | 1.325 | 2.630 | 5.595 |
| | t-stat. | 0.788 | 0.648 | 1.267 |
| | Number | 59 | 72 | 84 |
| 6-month silver | Mean | 0.444 | 0.019 | 1.543 |
| | Std. dev. | 1.489 | 2.338 | 4.985 |
| | t-stat. | 2.251 | 0.041 | 1.369 |
| | Number | 57 | 63 | 84 |
| 12-month silver | Mean | 0.846 | −1.945 | 2.187 |
| | Std. dev. | 1.678 | 5.240 | 4.038 |
| | t-stat. | 3.670 | 1.533 | 2.294 |
| | Number | 53 | 72 | 79 |
| 3-month copper | Mean | 0.109 | 0.515 | 0.283 |
| | Std. dev. | 3.325 | 1.808 | 1.094 |
| | t-stat. | 0.212 | 2.347 | 1.556 |
| | Number | 42 | 71 | 84 |

[a]Under the first CIR proposition, if the covariance between the daily percentage change in the futures price and the daily percentage change in the bond price is positive, the futures–forward price difference should be negative. If the covariance is negative, the price difference difference should be positive. Under the second CIR proposition, if the bond price variance is larger than its covariance with the spot price, the futures–forward price difference should be positive. If the variance-covariance difference is negative, the price difference should also be negative. The t-statistics for the covariances and the variance-covariance differences are adjusted for serial correlation.

For example, the average covariance for copper from 1968 through 1980 is 0.37, with a $t$-statistic of 2.56.[23] Using the CIR model, this implies that the futures prices will be below the forward prices. The average price difference of $-0.7\%$ is consistent with this prediction. The results for 12-month silver contracts also support the CIR hypothesis; the average covariance from 1974 through 1980 is $-1.9$ and, as the model predicts, the average futures–forward price difference is significantly positive. Unfortunately, the other comparisons do not provide much evidence. All but one of the other average covariances are approximately zero. The estimated covariance for 3-month copper contracts from 1974 through 1980 is significantly positive. However, since the $t$-statistic for the average futures–forward price difference for these contracts is only 0.21, one cannot reject the hypothesis that the true difference is negative, as the model predicts.

The results in table 5 provide more support for the second CIR proposition. Under this hypothesis, a positive difference between the variance of the bond prices and the covariance of the bond and spot prices should be associated with a positive difference between the futures and forward prices. The estimates for silver are all consistent with this model. For example, the average variance–covariance difference for 12 month silver contracts is 2.2, with a $t$-statistic of 2.29, and, as the model predicts, the price difference is significantly positive. Only the negative price differences for copper do not support the model.

The evidence in table 5 indicates that the average differences between the observed futures and forward prices are consistent with the CIR propositions. These propositions may also help to explain variations among the futures–forward price differences. For example, if the covariance between futures prices and bond prices in eq. (16) is not constant across contracts, changes in this covariance should be related to changes in the price differences. To examine this hypothesis, the covariance is estimated over each 3-, 6- and 12-month contract period. Then the futures contracts (and the matching forward contracts) are divided into two groups. Those contracts with negative estimated covariances are assigned to one group, while those with positive estimates are assigned to the other. Under the null hypothesis, the futures prices for the first group should be larger than the matching forward prices. In the second group, the futures prices should be below the forward prices.

The first half of table 6 describes the results of this segmentation. The 3-month contracts in this table are compared over the full 1968–1980 sample period, while the 6- and 12-month contracts are compared from 1974

---

[23]The $t$-statistics for the covariances and the variance–covariance differences are adjusted to reflect the serial correlation caused by the overlapping estimation periods.

Table 6

Futures–forward price differences sorted by covariances and variance-covariance differences.[a]

| | | cov(F, B) < 0 | cov(F, B) > 0 | Diff. | var(B) > cov(P, B) | var(B) < cov(P, B) | Diff. |
|---|---|---|---|---|---|---|---|
| 3-month silver | Mean | 0.328 | 0.270 | 0.058 | 0.363 | 0.236 | 0.127 |
| | Std. dev. | 1.097 | 1.522 | 0.260 | 1.119 | 1.499 | 0.251 |
| | t-stat. | 2.071 | 1.374 | 0.225 | 2.384 | 1.199 | 0.508 |
| | Number | 48 | 60 | 108 | 54 | 58 | 112 |
| 6-month silver | Mean | 0.380 | 0.496 | -0.116 | 0.459 | 0.434 | 0.025 |
| | Std. dev. | 1.114 | 2.041 | 0.430 | 1.348 | 1.589 | 0.405 |
| | t-stat. | 1.930 | 1.114 | -0.270 | 1.597 | 1.616 | 0.062 |
| | Number | 32 | 21 | 53 | 22 | 35 | 57 |
| 12-month silver | Mean | 0.662 | 1.255 | -0.594 | 0.605 | 0.925 | -0.319 |
| | Std. dev. | 1.226 | 2.405 | 0.508 | 1.579 | 1.721 | 0.536 |
| | t-stat. | 3.149 | 2.152 | -1.169 | 1.381 | 3.399 | -0.596 |
| | Number | 34 | 17 | 51 | 13 | 40 | 53 |
| 3-month copper | Mean | -0.591 | -0.775 | 0.185 | -0.661 | -0.729 | 0.068 |
| | Std. dev. | 4.358 | 3.364 | 0.863 | 3.881 | 3.688 | 0.847 |
| | t-stat. | -0.779 | -1.563 | 0.214 | -0.978 | -1.369 | 0.080 |
| | Number | 33 | 46 | 79 | 33 | 48 | 81 |

[a]Under the first CIR proposition, the futures–forward price difference should be positive if the covariance between the bond prices and the futures prices is negative and it should be negative if the covariance is positive. The difference between the two groups should be positive.

Under the second CIR proposition, if the variance of the bond price changes is larger than the covariance between the bond price changes and the spot price changes, the futures–forward price differences should be positive. If the variance is less than the covariance, the price difference should be negative. The difference between the two groups should be positive.

through 1980.[24] In general, the covariances are not useful in discriminating among the price differences. The comparisons between the two groups are randomly distributed about zero. For example, three of the four *t*-statistics comparing the two groups are between −0.3 and 0.3 and none is larger than 1.2.[25]

The second CIR proposition can be tested in the same way. First, the variance of the percentage change in the bond price and the covariance between the percentage change in the bond price and the percentage change in the spot price are estimated over the life of each pair of futures and forward contracts. Then the contracts are sorted into two groups. If the bond price variance is larger than the covariance between the bond and spot prices, the futures and forward contracts are assigned to the first group. If this difference is negative, the contracts are assigned to the second group. Using the CIR model, the futures–forward price differences should be positive in the first group and negative in the second.

The results of this stratification process are summarized in the second half of table 6. Again, the 3-month contracts are compared over the full 1968–1980 sample period, while the 6- and 12-month contracts are compared from 1974 through 1980. The results in table 6 do not provide any support for the second CIR hypothesis. For example, although the model predicts that the price difference should be negative when the variance is smaller than the covariance, three of the four differences for the second group are positive. Moreover, although the average difference for the first group should be larger than the average for the second group, the comparisons between the groups are distributed randomly about zero.[26]

Although the results in table 6 do not support the CIR propositions, they are not as inconsistent with the models as they seem. First, the tests involving the 3-, 6- and 12-month silver contracts are not independent. For example, the variance–covariance difference for the 6-month contract that matures in June is estimated with bond and spot prices from January through June, while the estimate of the difference for the 3-month June

---

[24]To be included in the sample, each pair of contracts must have a futures price and a converted forward price available on the contracting date described in footnote 10. In addition, there must be at least 10 days of futures and bond price data available during each month of the contracts' life.

[25]Two other methods for stratifying the sample were also tried. One approach assigns contracts to the two groups only if the correlation between the bond and futures prices is significantly different from zero. The second method only assigns those contracts whose monthly covariances are either all positive or all negative. The results using these stratification techniques are similar to those reported.

[26]A second stratification technique was also tried. If the difference between the variance and the covariance is positive in each month during the estimation period the contract pair is assigned to the first group. If this difference is negative during each month, the contracts are assigned to the second group. All other futures–forward pairs are dropped from the sample. There is no discernible difference between the futures–forward prices differences for these two groups.

contracts uses the same data during April, May, and June. A more important problem arises because the models imply that the futures–forward price differences are related to the market's expectations of the relevant variances and covariances; these expectations are unobservable. The tests in table 6 use estimates of the realized variances and covariances as proxies for the market's expectations. Since these proxies contain measurement error, many of the price pairs may be assigned to the wrong group in table 6. This could mask the true relation between the price differences and the expected variances and covariances.

The Cox, Ingersoll, and Ross models make several other predictions that may be less sensitive to these measurement error problems. For example, if the local correlation between futures price changes and bond price changes is constant, the first CIR proposition implies that the absolute value of the futures–forward price difference is an increasing function of the market's expectation of both the futures price variance and the bond price variance. Analogously, the second proposition implies that the price difference is a decreasing function of the spot price variance if the price difference is negative and if the local correlation between the spot and bond prices is constant.

As Cox, Ingersoll and Ross demonstrate, their second proposition can be re-expressed as

$$F(t, T) - f(t, T) = - PV_t \left\{ \exp \left[ \int_t^T \tilde{r}(w) \, dw \right] \int_t^T \tilde{f}(w, T) \right.$$

$$\left. \times \text{cov}[\tilde{f}(w, T), \tilde{B}(w, T)] \, dw \right\}. \tag{18}$$

This leads to one more prediction; if the local correlation between the forward price and the bond price is constant, the absolute value of the futures–forward price difference is an increasing function of the market's expectation of the forward price variance.

To test these predictions, the variances of the relevant variables are regressed against the futures–forward price differences. These variances are estimated over the life of the matching contracts.[27] For example, each futures price variance is computed using the daily price changes for an individual futures contract as it approaches maturity. The bond price variances are measured in two different ways. Under the first approach, which is also used for the forward prices, the variances for the 3-, 6- and 12-month regressions are estimated using the matching 3-, 6- and 12-month price series. Under the second approach, the bond price variances are estimated by the variance of

---

[27]These tests have been replicated using variances estimated over the period immediately before the contract date. The results from the two sets of variances are very similar.

the percentage changes in the daily federal funds return during each contract period.[28]

Table 7 presents regressions of these variances against the futures–forward price differences.[29] The 3-month regressions in this table are estimated over the full 1968–1980 sample period. The 6- and 12-month regressions are estimated from 1974 through 1980.

The results in table 7 are similar to the results in table 6; although they are consistent with the CIR propositions, they do not provide much support for these propositions. For example, the models imply that the absolute value of the price differences will increase with the variance of the futures, forward, and bond prices. Since the futures price is generally above the forward price for silver, this means that the slope coefficient in the silver regressions involving these variances should be positive. On the other hand, the price differences for copper are usually negative. Therefore, the slope coefficients for all of the copper regressions — including the spot price regression — should be negative. In fact, the estimates appear to be randomly distributed about zero.[30] These results are particularly ambiguous because only two of the twenty estimates are significantly different from zero. The results in table 7 neither support nor refute the CIR propositions.[31]

It appears that the Cox, Ingersoll and Ross propositions are useful in describing the average differences between futures and forward prices. However, without better estimates of the market's expectations of the relevant variances and covariances, neither hypothesis is able to discriminate among the individual differences.

### 3.4. Futures–forward price differences and interest rate differences

The models in section 2 imply that the difference between futures and forward prices should be related to the difference between short- and long-term interest rates. In fact, if the marginal utility of the commodity,

---

[28]The federal funds returns are provided by the Federal Reserve Bank of New York.

[29]The regressions in table 7 suffer from at least two econometric problems. First, the error terms are serially correlated and, second, each futures–forward price difference may be correlated with the previous error terms. Generalized least squares is usually used to solve the first problem. However, as Hansen and Hodrick (1980) demonstrate, GLS would lead to inconsistent estimates in this case. Fortunately, the ordinary least squares estimators in table 7 are consistent and asymptotically normal [see Hansen (1980)]. The usual estimated covariance matrix for the OLS coefficients, appropriately modified to reflect the serial correlation in the error terms, provides a consistent estimate of the covariance matrix of the asymptotic distribution; writing the regressions in table 7 in matrix notation, $Y = X\gamma + e$, the estimated covariance matrix for the OLS coefficients is $\hat{\Sigma} = (X'X)^{-1}X'\hat{\Omega}X(X'X)^{-1}$, where $\hat{\Omega}$ is the estimated covariance matrix for the error terms. The standard errors in table 7 are based on this estimated covariance matrix.

[30]These regressions have also been estimated using the absolute value of the futures–forward price differences. The coefficients in these regressions are very similar to the estimates reported in table 7.

[31]Part of this ambiguity may be caused by measurement errors in the observed futures–forward price differences. The effect of these measurement errors is discussed in the next section.

### Table 7
Regressions of variances against futures–forward price differences.[a]

|  | Number | Intercept | Slope | $R^2$ | Number | Intercept | Slope | $R^2$ |
|---|---|---|---|---|---|---|---|---|
|  |  | *Treasury bill prices* |  |  |  | *Federal funds returns* |  |  |
| 3-month silver | 112 | 0.007 (3.893) | 0.018 (0.176) | 0.00 | 112 | 0.744 (5.440) | −17.733 (2.535) | 0.07 |
| 6-month silver | 57 | 0.026 (2.544) | 0.139 (0.459) | 0.00 | 57 | 0.339 (2.312) | 2.587 (0.746) | 0.01 |
| 12-month silver | 51 | 0.102 (1.923) | −0.150 (0.087) | 0.00 | 51 | 0.250 (1.961) | 5.517 (1.430) | 0.04 |
| 3-month copper | 81 | 0.011 (3.598) | 0.051 (0.653) | 0.01 | 81 | 0.621 (4.712) | −11.520 (3.522) | 0.21 |
|  |  | *Futures prices* |  |  |  | *Converted forward prices* |  |  |
| 3-month silver | 86 | 0.036 (5.348) | 0.335 (0.814) | 0.01 | 90 | 0.270 (1.325) | −0.712 (0.062) | 0.00 |
| 6-month silver | 55 | 0.037 (2.990) | 0.361 (1.006) | 0.01 | 56 | 0.132 (2.527) | −0.373 (0.269) | 0.00 |
| 12-month silver | 54 | 0.042 (1.996) | 0.826 (0.981) | 0.10 | 51 | 0.118 (2.407) | −1.943 (1.187) | 0.02 |
| 3-month copper | 73 | 0.031 (6.953) | −0.110 (0.977) | 0.02 | 63 | 0.618 (1.043) | 11.655 (0.731) | 0.01 |
|  |  | *Converted spot prices* |  |  |  |  |  |  |
| 3-month silver | 111 | 0.266 (1.604) | 0.368 (0.040) | 0.00 |  |  |  |  |
| 6-month silver | 57 | 0.440 (1.298) | 0.800 (0.084) | 0.00 |  |  |  |  |
| 12-month silver | 51 | 0.445 (1.440) | −6.554 (0.663) | 0.01 |  |  |  |  |
| 3-month copper | 80 | 0.031 (3.840) | −0.275 (1.424) | 0.04 |  |  |  |  |

[a]The dependent variable in these regressions is the variance of the indicated variable, estimated over the contract period. The independent variable is the percentage difference between the futures price and the converted forward price. The *t*-statistics, adjusted for the serial correlation caused by the overlapping estimation periods, are in parentheses.

$\bar{P}(T)\bar{\lambda}(T)$, is assumed to be independent of the nominal interest rate,[32] eqs. (8) and (10) can be used to write the ratio of the futures and forward prices as

$$F(t, T)/f(t, T) = E_t\left\{\exp\left[\sum_{\tau=t}^{T-1} \bar{R}(\tau, \tau+1)\right]\right\}\Big/\exp[(T-t)R(t, T)]. \quad (19)$$

[32]The following set of conditions is sufficient for this assumption to hold:
(1) The price of some commodity (commodity $N$) is independent of the marginal utility of all commodities.
(2) The expected value of the continuously compounded real rate of return on nominal bonds is constant. This real rate is defined in terms of commodity $N$.

The ratio of the futures price and the forward price should equal the ratio of the expected gross return from rolling over one-day bonds and the gross return from investing in a $(T-t)$ day bond.

Since the expected return from rolling over one-day bonds is unobservable, the prediction in eq. (19) cannot be tested directly. One alternative is to use the actual return, which is observed at time $T$,

$$\frac{F(t, T)}{f(t, T)} = \exp\left[\sum_{\tau=t}^{T-1} R(\tau, \tau+1) - \varepsilon(t, T)\right]\bigg/ \exp[(T-t)R(t, T)]. \qquad (20)$$

In this expression, $\varepsilon(t, T)$ is equal to the market's error in forecasting the cumulated one-day returns. Eq. (20) can be tested by estimating the regression

$$\sum_{\tau=t}^{T-1} R(\tau, \tau+1) - (T-t)R(t, T) = \alpha + \beta\log[F(t, T)/f(t, T)] + \varepsilon(t, T). \qquad (21)$$

Table 8 presents ordinary least squares estimates of this regression for copper and silver.[33] Under the null hypothesis, the intercept should equal zero and the slope should equal one. This hypothesis can be rejected for all of the regressions summarized in table 8. Although most of the estimates of $\alpha$ are not significantly different from' zero, all of the estimates of $\beta$ are quite significantly different from one. For example, the largest slope coefficient is estimated for the 3-month silver price regression from 1974 through 1980. The value of this coefficient is 0.058 and it has a standard error of 0.029. In other words, the largest estimate of $\beta$ is more than 30 standard errors below one. The values of $F$-statistics testing the joint hypothesis that $\alpha$ equals zero and $\beta$ equals one are over 50 for all of the regressions.

The evidence in table 8 indicates that the observed differences between the short- and long-term interest rates are not useful in explaining the observed differences between the futures and forward prices. However, these results do not necessarily imply that the underlying model is wrong. Instead, they may be caused by measurement errors in the observed price differences. For example, each day's forward prices are recorded in London about five hours before the futures prices are recorded in America. Many of the largest positive and negative price differences are probably caused by information that arrives after the London market closes but before the American markets do. These measurement errors in the price differences bias the slope

---

[33]The regressions in table 8 suffer from the same econometric problems as the regressions in table 7. These problems are discussed in footnote 29.

The one-day bond returns used to estimate the regressions in table 8 are measured by the overnight federal funds rate. The long-term interest rates, with maturities of 3, 6 and 12 months, are measured by the return on American treasury bills.

Table 8

Regressions of interest rate differences on futures–forward price differences.[a]

| | Number | Intercept | Slope | $R^2$ |
|---|---|---|---|---|
| *3-month silver* | | | | |
| 1/68–12/80 | 110 | 0.031 (0.045) | 0.035 (0.022) | 0.03 |
| 1/68–12/73 | 53 | 0.109 (0.063) | 0.002 (0.029) | 0.00 |
| 1/74–12/80 | 57 | −0.033 (0.057) | 0.058 (0.029) | 0.09 |
| *6-month silver* | | | | |
| 1/74–12/80 | 57 | −0.128 (0.133) | 0.006 (0.048) | 0.00 |
| *12-month silver* | | | | |
| 1/74–12/80 | 53 | −0.034 (0.167) | 0.001 (0.055) | 0.00 |
| *3-month copper* | | | | |
| 1/68–12/80 | 79 | 0.050 (0.047) | −0.028 (0.011) | 0.12 |
| 1/68–12/73 | 39 | −0.019 (0.067) | −0.043 (0.015) | 0.27 |
| 1/74–12/80 | 40 | 0.077 (0.073) | −0.022 (0.019) | 0.05 |

[a]The dependent variable in this regression is the cumulated one-day federal funds interest rate minus the treasury bill interest rate over the contract period. The independent variable is the percentage difference between the futures price and the converted forward price. Under the null hypothesis, the intercept should be zero and the slope coefficient should be one. The asymptotic standard errors are in parentheses.

coefficients in table 8 toward zero. This problem is particularly troublesome because, under the null hypothesis, the variation in the true, unobserved, price differences is probably small relative to the variance of the measurement errors.[34]

---

[34]Ignoring the econometric problems discussed in footnote 29, the probability limit of the estimated slope coefficient is equal to plim $\hat{\beta} = \beta/[1 + \sigma_w^2/\sigma_x^2]$, where $\sigma_w^2$ is the variance of the measurement errors and $\sigma_x^2$ is the variance of the true price differences. Therefore, the bias in the slope coefficient increases as the relative variance of the measurement errors increases.

## 4. Summary and conclusions

This paper uses the pricing models of Cox, Ingersoll and Ross (1981), Richard and Sundaresan (1981), and French (1982) to examine the relation between futures and forward prices for copper and silver. There are significant differences between these prices. The average differences are generally consistent with the predictions of both arbitrage and utility-based models. However, these models are not helpful in explaining intra-sample variations in the futures–forward price differences.

There are several possible reasons why the futures and forward price models do not help in discriminating among the price differences. The most obvious explanation is that the models are incomplete. For example, the models abstract from market imperfections like taxes and transactions costs. If these factors play an important role in determining the futures and forward prices, one may observe differences in these prices that are unrelated to the factors examined here.

An alternative interpretation of the evidence in this paper says that the theoretical models do describe the underlying price differences, but, because of measurement errors, the models are not useful in discriminating among the observed differences. Under this hypothesis, the models fail to capture movements in the observed price differences because measurement errors mask the variations in the true price differences. However, the models correctly predict the average observed price differences because aggregating across contracts reduces the effect of the measurement errors.

These measurement errors take two forms. First, the futures–forward price differences are measured with error. For example, the individual prices are only recorded in discrete steps, such as eighths of a dollar or tenths of a pound. Also, the prices in each pair are not matched precisely. This problem is especially acute because the forward prices are observed in London and the futures prices are observed approximately five hours later in New York and Chicago. These errors in measuring the futures–forward price differences can have a particularly large effect if the variation in the true price differences is small.

A second type of measurement error arises because all of the predictions involve variables that must be estimated. The tests involving the Cox, Ingersoll and Ross predictions provide good examples of this problem. The CIR propositions indicate that the futures–forward price differences should be related to the market's expectation of local variances and covariances. However, neither these expectations nor the realized values of the variables are observable. Although several approaches are used to estimate the variances and covariances, none of them is powerful enough to discriminate among the various price differences.

Earlier studies of the empirical relation between futures and forward prices do not provide much help in determining if the results reported here are caused by problems with the theoretical models or by problems with the data. Several papers have been written comparing the prices for treasury bill futures contracts with the forward prices implied by the interest rates on treasury bills traded in the spot market.[35] The evidence in these papers indicates that, on average, the futures prices for contracts with approximately four or more months to maturity are significantly lower than the matching forward prices. As the contracts approach maturity, this relation is reversed; the implied forward prices tend to be lower than the matching futures prices. Cornell and Reinganum (1981) compare futures and forward prices for foreign exchange contracts. Although they observe differences between individual prices, they find that the average difference is not significantly different from zero. Unfortunately, none of these papers examines the relation between the observed price differences and the theoretical models studied here. More tests are needed to support or reject these models.

The results in this paper have important implications for other research. Most commodity exchanges in the United States trade futures contracts. However, since forward contracts are easier to analyze, many economists treat the observed prices as though they were forward prices. This simplification can be misleading. The studies comparing the futures prices and implied forward prices for treasury bills provide a good example of the problems this may cause. The authors of many of these studies claim that the futures prices should equal the forward prices implied in the spot market. When they observe differences between these prices, they interpret this as evidence of market inefficiency. The results in this paper suggest that these price differences may actually be caused by differences between futures and forward contracts.

[35]See, for example, Puglisi (1978), Capozza and Cornell (1979), Rendleman and Carabini (1979), and Vignola and Dale (1980).

# References

Bartlett, M.S., 1946, On the theoretical specification of sampling properties of autocorrelated time series, Journal of the Royal Statistical Society (Suppl.) 8, 27–41.

Black, F., 1976, The pricing of commodity contracts, Journal of Financial Economics 3, Jan./March, 167–179.

Capozza, D. and B. Cornell, 1979, Treasury bill pricing in the spot and futures markets, Review of Economics and Statistics 61, Nov., 513–520.

Cornell, B. and M. Reinganum, 1981, Forward and futures prices: Evidence from the foreign exchange markets, Journal of Finance 36, Dec., 1035–1045.

Cox, J., J. Ingersoll and S. Ross, 1977, A theory of the term structure of interest rates and the valuation of interest-dependent claims, Working paper (Graduate School of Business, Stanford University, Stanford, CA).

Cox, J., J. Ingersoll and S. Ross, 1981, The relation between forward prices and futures prices, Journal of Financial Economics 9, Dec., 321–346.

Dusak, K., 1973, Futures trading and investor returns: An investigation of commodity market risk premiums, Journal of Political Economy 81, Nov./Dec., 1387–1406.

French, K.R., 1982, The pricing of futures and forward contracts, Ph.D. dissertation (University of Rochester, Rochester, NY).

Grauer, F., 1977, Equilibrium in commodity futures markets: Theory and tests, Ph.D. dissertation (Stanford University, Stanford, CA).

Grauer, F. and R. Litzenberger, 1979, The pricing of commodity futures contracts, nominal bonds and other risky assets under commodity price uncertainty, Journal of Finance 34, March, 69–83.

Hansen, L., 1980, Large sample properties of generalized method of moments estimators, Working paper (Graduate School of Industrial Administration, Carnegie-Mellon University, Pittsburgh, PA).

Hansen, L. and R. Hodrick, 1980, Forward exchange rates as optimal predictors of future spot rates: An econometric analysis, Journal of Political Economy 88, Oct., 829–853.

Jarrow, R. and G. Oldfield, 1981, Forward contracts and futures contracts, Journal of Financial Economics 9, Dec., 373–382.

Levich, R. and L. White, 1981, Price controls and futures contracts: an examination of the markets for copper and silver during 1971–1974, Working paper (Center for the Study of Futures Markets, Columbia Business School, New York).

Margrabe, W., 1976, A theory of forward and futures prices, Working paper (The Wharton School, University of Pennsylvania, Philadelphia, PA).

Puglisi, D., 1978, Is the futures market for treasury bills efficient?, Journal of Portfolio Management 4, Winter, 64–67.

Rendleman, R. and C. Carabini, 1979, The efficiency of the treasury bill futures market, Journal of Finance 39, Sept., 895–914.

Richard, S.F. and M. Sundaresan, 1981, A continuous time equilibrium model of forward prices and futures prices in a multigood economy, Journal of Financial Economics 9, 347–372.

Vignola, A. and C. Dale, 1980, The efficiency of the treasury bill futures market: An analysis of alternative specifications, Journal of Financial Research 3, Fall, 169–188.

# REFERENCES

Amihud, Y., and H. Mendelson, "Asset Pricing and the Bid-Ask Spread", *Journal of Financial Economics*, 17 (December 1986), pp. 223-249.

Black, F., "The Investment Policy Spectrum: Individuals, Endowment Funds, and Pension Funds," *Financial Analysts Journal*, 32 (January 1976), pp. 23-31.

Black, F., and M. Scholes, "The Pricing of Options and Corporate Liabilities," *Journal of Political Economy*, 81 (1983), pp. 637-654.

Bloomfield, T., R. Leftwich, and J. B. Long, "Portfolio Strategies and Performance," *Journal of Financial Economics*, 5 (November 1977), pp. 201-218.

Bradley, M., A. Desai, and E. H. Kim, "Synergistic Gains from Corporate Acquisitions and Their Division between the Stockholders of Target and Acquiring Firms," *Journal of Financial Economics*, 21 (May 1988), pp. 3-40.

Breeden, D. T., "An Intertemporal Asset Pricing Model with Stochastic Consumption and Investment Opportunities," *Journal of Financial Economics*, 7 (1979), pp. 265-296.

Breeden, D. T., M. R. Gibbons, and R. H. Litzenberger, "Empirical Tests of the Consumption-Oriented CAPM," *Journal of Finance*, 44 (June 1989), pp. 231-262.

Brown, R. A., and L. B. Siegel, "Introduction to International Bonds," in B. R. Bruce (ed.), *Quantitative International Investing: A Handbook of Analytical and Modeling Techniques and Strategies,* Chicago: Probus Publishing Co., 1990, chap. 8, pp. 91-107.

Brown, S. J., and J. B. Warner, "Measuring Security Price Performance," *Journal of Financial Economics*, 8 (September 1980), pp. 205-258.

Brown, S. J., and J. B. Warner, "Using Daily Stock Returns: The Case of Event Studies," *Journal of Financial Economics*, 14 (March 1985), pp. 3-31.

Campbell, J. Y., "Stock Returns and the Term Structure," *Journal of Financial Economics*, 18 (1987), pp. 373-399.

Constantinides, G. M., and J. E. Ingersoll, "Optimal Bond Trading with Personal Taxes," *Journal of Financial Economics*, 10 (September 1984), pp. 299-336.

Cox, J. C., J. E. Ingersoll, and S. A. Ross, "Theory of the Term Structure of Interest Rates," *Econometrica*, 53 (1985), pp. 385-407.

Cox, John C., Stephen A. Ross, and Mark Rubinstein, "Option Pricing: A Simplified Approach," *Journal of Financial Economics*, 7 (September 1979), pp. 229-263.

Fama, E. F., "Efficient Capital Markets: A Review of Theory and Empirical Work," *Journal of Finance*, 25 (May 1970), pp. 383-417.

Fama, E. F., "A Note on the Market Model and the Two-Parameter Model," *Journal of Finance*, 28 (December 1973), pp. 1181-1185.

Fama, E. F., "Stock Returns, Real Activity, Inflation, and Money," *American Economic Review*, 71 (1981), pp. 545-565.

Fama, E. F., "The Information in the Term Structure," *Journal of Financial Economics*, 13 (1984), pp. 509-528.

Fama, E. F., "Term Premiums and Default Premiums in Money Markets," *Journal of Financial Economics*, 17 (1986), pp. 175-196.

Fama, E. F., "Efficient Capital Markets II," *Journal of Finance*, 46 (June 1991).

Fama, E. F., and K. R. French, "Permanent and Transitory Components of Stock Prices," *Journal of Political Economy*, 96 (April 1988a), pp. 246-273.

Fama, E. F., and K. R. French, "Dividend Yields and Expected Stock Returns," *Journal of Financial Economics*, 22 (October 1988b), pp. 3-25.

Fama, E. F., and K. R. French, "Business Conditions and Expected Returns on Stocks and Bonds," *Journal of Financial Economics*, 25 (November 1989), pp. 23-49.

Fama, E. F., and G. W. Schwert, "Asset Returns and Inflation," *Journal of Financial Economics*, 5 (November 1977), pp. 115-146.

French, K. R., "Stock Returns and the Weekend Effect," *Journal of Financial Economics*, 8 (March 1980), pp. 55-69.

French, K. R., "A Comparison of Futures and Forward Prices," *Journal of Financial Economics*, 12 (November 1983), pp. 311-342.

French, K. R., and R. Roll, "Stock Return Variances: The Arrival of Information and the Reaction of Traders," *Journal of Financial Economics*, 17 (September 1986), pp. 5-26.

Gibbons, M. R., "Multivariate Tests of Financial Models: A New Approach," *Journal of Financial Economics*, 10 (1982), pp. 3-28.

Gibbons, M. R., S. A. Ross, and J. Shanken, "A Test of the Efficiency of a Given Portfolio," *Econometrica*, 57 (September 1989), pp. 1121-1152.

Henrikkson, R. D., "Market Timing and Mutual Fund Performance: An Empirical Investigation," *Journal of Business*, 57 (January 1984), pp. 73-96.

Henrikkson, R. D., and R. C. Merton, "On Market Timing and Investment Performance; II: Statistical Procedures for Evaluating Forecasting Skills," *Journal of Business*, 54 (October 1981), pp. 513-533.

Ibbotson Associates, *Stocks, Bonds, Bills, and Inflation: 1989 Yearbook*, Chicago: Ibbotson Associates, 1989.

Ibbotson, R. G., R. C. Carr, and A. W. Robinson, "International Equity and Bond Returns," *Financial Analysts Journal* (July 1982), pp. 61-83.

Ibbotson, R. G., L. B. Siegel, and M. B. Waring, "Introduction to International Equities," in B. R. Bruce (ed.), *Quantitative International Investing: A Handbook of Analytical and Modeling Techniques and Strategies*, Chicago: Probus Publishing Co., 1990, chap. 2, pp. 5-21.

Jensen, M. C., and G. A. Bennington, "Random Walks and Technical Theories: Some Additional Evidence," *Journal of Finance*, 25 (May 1970), pp. 469-482.

Jensen, M. C., "The Performance of Mutual Funds in the Period 1945–1964," *Journal of Finance*, 23 (1968), pp. 389-416.

Jensen, M. C., "Risk, the Pricing of Capital Assets, and the Evaluation of Investment Portfolios," *Journal of Business*, 42 (April 1969), pp. 167-247.

Jensen, M. C., "Some Anomalous Evidence regarding Market Efficiency," *Journal of Financial Economics*, 6 (June 1978), pp. 95-101.

Keim, D. B., "Size-Related Anomalies and Stock Return Seasonality: Further Empirical Evidence," *Journal of Financial Economics*, 12 (June 1983), pp. 13-32.

Keim, D. B., and R. F. Stambaugh, "A Further Investigation of the Weekend Effect in Stock Returns," *Journal of Finance*, 39 (July 1984), pp. 819-835.

Keim, D. B., and R. F. Stambaugh, "Predicting Returns in the Stock and Bond Markets," *Journal of Financial Economics*, 17 (1986), pp. 357-390.

Litzenberger, R. H., and K. Ramaswamy, "The Effects of Dividends on Common Stock Prices: Tax Effects or Information Effects?" *Journal of Finance*, 37 (May 1982), pp. 429-443.

Lloyd-Davies, P., and M. Canes, "Stock Prices and the Publication of Second-Hand Information," *Journal of Business*, 51 (January 1978), pp. 43-56.

Markowitz, H., *Portfolio Selection: Efficient Diversification of Investments*, New York: Wiley, 1959.

Mayers, D., and E. M. Rice, "Measuring Portfolio Performance and the Empirical Content of Asset Pricing Models," *Journal of Financial Economics*, 7 (March 1979), pp. 3-28.

Mikkelson, W. H., and M. M. Partch, "Stock Price Effects and Costs of Secondary Distributions," *Journal of Financial Economics*, 14 (June 1985), pp. 165-194.

Officer, R. R., "The Variability of the Market Factor of New York Stock Exchange," *Journal of Business*, 46 (1973), pp. 434-453.

Patell, J. M., and M. A. Wolfson, "The Intraday Speed of Adjustment of Stock Prices to Earnings and Dividend Announcements," *Journal of Financial Economics*, 13 (June 1984), pp. 232-252.

Phillips, S. M. and C. W. Smith, "Trading Costs for Listed Options: The Implications for Market Efficiency," *Journal of Financial Economics*, 8 (June 1980), pp. 179-201.

Roberts, H., "Stock Market 'Patterns' and Financial Analysis: Methodological Suggestions," *Journal of Finance*, 14 (March 1959), pp. 1-10.

Roll, R., "A Critique of the Asset Pricing Theory's Tests; Part I: On Past and Potential Testability of the Theory," *Journal of Financial Economics*, 4 (March 1977), pp. 129-176.

Ross, S. A., "The Arbitrage Theory of Capital Asset Pricing," *Journal of Economic Theory*, 13 (1976), pp. 341-360.

Schwert, G. W., "Using Financial Data to Measure Effects of Regulation," *Journal of Law and Economics*, 24 (April 1981), pp. 121-158.

Schwert, G. W., "Size and Stock Returns, and Other Empirical Regularities," *Journal of Financial Economics*, 12 (June 1983), pp. 3-12.

Schwert, G. W., "Why Does Stock Market Volatility Change over Time?" *Journal of Finance*, 44 (December 1989a), pp. 1115-1153.

Schwert, G. W., "Business Cycles, Financial Crises, and Stock Volatility," *Carnegie-Rochester Conference Series on Public Policy*, 31 (Autumn 1989b), pp. 83-125.

Schwert, G. W., "Stock Volatility and the Crash of '87," *Review of Financial Studies*, 3 (1990a), pp. 77-102.

Schwert, G. W., "Stock Market Volatility," *Financial Analysts Journal*, 46 (May-June 1990b), pp. 23-34.

Schwert, G. W., "Indexes of United States Stock Prices from 1802 to 1987," *Journal of Business*, 63 (July 1990c), pp. 399-426.

Seyhun, H. N., "Insiders' Profits, Cost of Trading, and Market Efficiency," *Journal of Financial Economics*, 16 (June 1986), pp. 189-212.

Shanken, J., "The Arbitrage Pricing Theory: Is It Testable?" *Journal of Finance*, 37 (December 1982), pp. 1129-1140.

Shanken, J., "Multivariate Tests of the Zero-Beta CAPM," *Journal of Financial Economics*, 14 (September 1985), pp. 327-348.

Sharpe, W. F., "Capital Asset Prices: A Theory of Market Equilibrium under Conditions of Risk," *Journal of Finance*, 19 (1964), pp. 425-442.

Smith, C. W., "Option Pricing: A Review," *Journal of Financial Economics*, 3 (January 1976), pp. 3-51.

Stambaugh, R. F., "On the Exclusion of Assets from Tests of the Two-Parameter Model: A Sensitivity Analysis," *Journal of Financial Economics*, 10 (1982), pp. 237-268.

Stambaugh, R. F., "The Information in Forward Rates: Implications for Models of the Term Structure," *Journal of Financial Economics*, 21 (May 1988), pp. 41-70.

Whaley, R. E., "Valuation of American Call Options on Dividend-Paying Stocks: Empirical Tests," *Journal of Financial Economics*, 10 (March 1982), pp. 29-59.

Wilson, J. W., and C. P. Jones, "A Comparison of Annual Common Stock Returns: 1871-1925 with 1926-1985," *Journal of Business*, 60 (April 1987), pp. 239-258.

Zellner, A., *An Introduction to Bayesian Inference in Econometrics*, New York: Wiley, 1971.